Lecture Notes in Computer Science 12827

More information about this subseries at http://www.springer.com/series/7410

Tal Malkin · Chris Peikert (Eds.)

Advances in Cryptology – CRYPTO 2021

41st Annual International Cryptology Conference, CRYPTO 2021
Virtual Event, August 16–20, 2021
Proceedings, Part III

 Springer

Editors
Tal Malkin
Columbia University
New York City, NY, USA

Chris Peikert
University of Michigan
Ann Arbor, MI, USA

ISSN 0302-9743   ISSN 1611-3349   (electronic)
Lecture Notes in Computer Science
ISBN 978-3-030-84251-2   ISBN 978-3-030-84252-9   (eBook)
https://doi.org/10.1007/978-3-030-84252-9

LNCS Sublibrary: SL4 – Security and Cryptology

This Springer imprint is published by the registered company Springer Nature Switzerland AG
The registered company address is: Gewerbestrasse 11, 6330 Cham, Switzerland

Preface

The 41st International Cryptology Conference (Crypto 2021), sponsored by the International Association of Cryptologic Research (IACR), was held during August 16–20, 2021. Due to the ongoing COVID-19 pandemic, and for the second consecutive year, Crypto was held as an online-only virtual conference, instead of at its usual venue of the University of California, Santa Barbara. In addition, six affiliated workshop events took place during the days immediately prior to the conference.

The Crypto conference continues its substantial growth pattern: this year's offering received a record-high 430 submissions for consideration, of which 103 (also a record) were accepted to appear in the program. The two program chairs were not allowed to submit a paper, and Program Committee (PC) members were limited to two submissions each. Review and extensive discussion occurred from late February through mid-May, in a double-blind, two-stage process that included an author rebuttal phase (following the initial reviews) and extensive discussion by reviewers. We thank the 58-person PC and the 390 external reviewers for their efforts to ensure that, during the continuing COVID-19 pandemic and unusual work and life circumstances, we nevertheless were able to perform a high-quality review process.

The PC selected four papers to receive recognition via awards, along with invitations to the Journal of Cryptology, via a voting-based process that took into account conflicts of interest (the program chairs did not vote).

- The Best Paper Award went to "On the Possibility of Basing Cryptography on EXP $\neq$ BPP" by Yanyi Liu and Rafael Pass.
- The Best Paper by Early Career Researchers Award, along with an Honorable Mention for Best Paper, went to "Linear Cryptanalysis of FF3-1 and FEA" by Tim Beyne.
- Honorable Mentions for Best Paper also went to "Efficient Key Recovery for all HFE Signature Variants" by Chengdong Tao, Albrecht Petzoldt, and Jintai Ding; and "Three Halves Make a Whole? Beating the Half-Gates Lower Bound for Garbled Circuits" by Mike Rosulek and Lawrence Roy.

In addition to the regular program, Crypto 2021 included two invited talks, by Vanessa Teague on "Which e-voting problems do we need to solve?" and Jens Groth on "A world of SNARKs." The conference also carried forward the long-standing tradition of having a rump session, organized in a virtual format.

The chairs would also like to thank the many other people whose hard work helped ensure that Crypto 2021 was a success:

- Vladimir Kolesnikov (Georgia Institute of Technology)—Crypto 2021 general chair.
- Daniele Micciancio (University of California, San Diego), Thomas Ristenpart (Cornell Tech), Yevgeniy Dodis (New York University), and Thomas Shrimpton (University of Florida)—Crypto 2021 Advisory Committee.

- Carmit Hazay (Bar Ilan University)—Crypto 2021 workshop chair.
- Bertram Poettering and Antigoni Polychroniadou—Crypto 2021 rump session chairs.
- Kevin McCurley, for his critical assistance in setting up and managing the HotCRP paper submission and review system, conference website, and other technology.
- Kevin McCurley, Kay McKelly, and members of the IACR's emergency pandemic team for their work in designing and running the virtual format.
- Anna Kramer and her colleagues at Springer.

July 2021

Tal Malkin
Chris Peikert

Organization

General Chair

Vladimir Kolesnikov   Georgia Institute of Technology, USA

Program Committee Chairs

Tal Malkin   Columbia University, USA
Chris Peikert   University of Michigan and Algorand, Inc., USA

Program Committee

Abhi Shelat   Northeastern University, USA
Andrej Bogdanov   Chinese University of Hong Kong, Hong Kong
Antigoni Polychroniadou   JP Morgan AI Research, USA
Brice Minaud   Inria and École Normale Supérieure, France
Chaya Ganesh   Indian Institute of Science, India
Chris Peikert   University of Michigan and Algorand, Inc., USA
Claudio Orlandi   Aarhus University, Denmark
Daniele Venturi   Sapienza University of Rome, Italy
David Cash   University of Chicago, USA
David Wu   University of Virginia, USA
Dennis Hofheinz   ETH Zurich, Switzerland
Divesh Aggarwal   National University of Singapore, Singapore
Dominique Unruh   University of Tartu, Estonia
Elena Andreeva   Technical University of Vienna, Austria
Elena Kirshanova   Immanuel Kant Baltic Federal University, Russia
Fabrice Benhamouda   Algorand Foundation, USA
Fang Song   Portland State University, USA
Frederik Vercauteren   KU Leuven, Belgium
Ghada Almashaqbeh   University of Connecticut, USA
Itai Dinur   Ben-Gurion University, Israel
Jean-Pierre Tillich   Inria, France
Jeremiah Blocki   Purdue University, USA
John Schanck   University of Waterloo, Canada
Jonathan Bootle   IBM Research, Switzerland
Joseph Jaeger   University of Washington, USA
Junqing Gong   East China Normal University, China
Lisa Kohl   CWI Amsterdam, The Netherlands
Manoj Prabhakaran   IIT Bombay, India
Marcel Keller   CSIRO's Data61, Australia
Mariana Raykova   Google, USA

Mike Rosulek	Oregon State University, USA
Mor Weiss	Bar-Ilan University, Israel
Muthuramakrishnan Venkitasubramaniam	University of Rochester, USA
Ni Trieu	Arizona State University, USA
Nir Bitansky	Tel Aviv University, Israel
Nuttapong Attrapadung	AIST, Japan
Omer Paneth	Tel Aviv University, Israel
Paul Grubbs	NYU, Cornell Tech and University of Michigan, USA
Peihan Miao	University of Illinois at Chicago, USA
Peter Schwabe	Max Planck Institute for Security and Privacy, Germany, and Radboud University, The Netherlands
Ran Canetti	BU, USA, and Tel Aviv University, Israel
Romain Gay	IBM Research, Switzerland
Ron Steinfeld	Monash University, Australia
Rosario Gennaro	City University of New York, USA
Ryo Nishimaki	NTT Secure Platform Laboratories, Japan
Sandro Coretti	IOHK, Switzerland
Sikhar Patranabis	Visa Research, USA
Sina Shiehian	UC Berkeley and Stony Brook University, USA
Siyao Guo	NYU Shanghai, China
Stanislaw Jarecki	University of California, Irvine, USA
Tal Malkin	Columbia University, USA
Tarik Moataz	Aroki Systems, USA
Thomas Peters	UC Louvain, Belgium
Thomas Peyrin	Nanyang Technological University, Singapore
Tianren Liu	University of Washington, USA
Viet Tung Hoang	Florida State University, USA
Xavier Bonnetain	University of Waterloo, Canada
Yu Yu	Shanghai Jiao Tong University, China

Additional Reviewers

Aaram Yun	Akshayaram Srinivasan
Aarushi Goel	Akshima
Aayush Jain	Alain Passelègue
Abhishek Jain	Alex Bienstock
Adrien Benamira	Alex Lombardi
Agnes Kiss	Alexander Golovnev
Aishwarya Thiruvengadam	Alexander Hoover
Ajith Suresh	Alexander May
Akin Ünal	Alexandre Wallet
Akinori Kawachi	Alexandru Cojocaru
Akira Takahashi	Alice Pellet-Mary
Akshay Degwekar	Alin Tomescu

Amin Sakzad
Amit Singh Bhati
Amitabh Trehan
Amos Beimel
Anat Paskin-Cherniavsky
Anca Nitulescu
André Chailloux
Andre Esser
André Schrottenloher
Andrea Coladangelo
Andreas Hülsing
Antonin Leroux
Antonio Florez-Gutierrez
Archita Agarwal
Ariel Hamlin
Arka Rai Choudhuri
Arnab Roy
Ashrujit Ghoshal
Ashutosh Kumar
Ashwin Jha
Atsushi Takayasu
Aurore Guillevic
Avijit Dutta
Avishay Yanay
Baiyu Li
Balazs Udvarhelyi
Balthazar Bauer
Bart Mennink
Ben Smith
Benjamin Diamond
Benjamin Fuller
Benny Applebaum
Benoît Cogliati
Benoit Libert
Bertram Poettering
Binyi Chen
Bo-Yin Yang
Bogdan Ursu
Bruno Freitas dos Santos
Bryan Parno
Byeonghak Lee
Carl Bootland
Carles Padro
Carmit Hazay
Carsten Baum
Cecilia Boschini

Chan Nam Ngo
Charles Momin
Charlotte Bonte
Chen Qian
Chen-Da Liu-Zhang
Chenkai Weng
Chethan Kamath
Chris Brzuska
Christian Badertscher
Christian Janson
Christian Majenz
Christian Matt
Christina Boura
Christof Paar
Christoph Egger
Cody Freitag
Dahmun Goudarzi
Dakshita Khurana
Damian Vizar
Damiano Abram
Damien Stehlé
Damien Vergnaud
Daniel Escudero
Daniel Jost
Daniel Masny
Daniel Tschudi
Daniel Wichs
Dario Catalano
Dario Fiore
David Gerault
David Heath
Debbie Leung
Dean Doron
Debapriya Basu Roy
Dima Kogan
Dimitrios Papadopoulos
Divya Gupta
Divya Ravi
Dominique Schröder
Eduardo Soria-Vazquez
Eldon Chung
Emmanuela Orsini
Eran Lambooij
Eran Omri
Eshan Chattopadhyay
Estuardo Alpirez Bock

Evgenios Kornaropoulos
Eysa Lee
Fabio Banfi
Felix Engelmann
Felix Günther
Ferdinand Sibleyras
Fermi Ma
Fernando Virdia
Francesco Berti
François-Xavier Standaert
Fuyuki Kitagawa
Gaëtan Cassiers
Gaëtan Leurent
Gayathri Annapurna Garimella
Geoffroy Couteau
Georg Fuchsbauer
Ghous Amjad
Gildas Avoine
Giorgos Panagiotakos
Giorgos Zirdelis
Giulio Malavolta
Guy Rothblum
Hamidreza Khoshakhlagh
Hamza Abusalah
Hanjun Li
Hannah Davis
Haoyang Wang
Hart Montgomery
Henry Corrigan-Gibbs
Hila Dahari
Huijia Lin
Ian McQuoid
Ignacio Cascudo
Igors Stepanovs
Ilan Komargodski
Ilia Iliashenko
Ingrid Verbauwhede
Itamar Levi
Ittai Abraham
Ivan Damgård
Jack Doerner
Jacob Schuldt
James Bartusek
Jan Czajkowski
Jan-Pieter D'Anvers
Jaspal Singh

Jean Paul Degabriele
Jesper Buus Nielsen
Jesús-Javier Chi-Domínguez
Ji Luo
Jian Guo
Jiaxin Pan
Jiayu Xu
Joanne Adams-Woodage
João Ribeiro
Joël Alwen
Julia Hesse
Julia Len
Julian Loss
Junichi Tomida
Justin Holmgren
Justin Thaler
Kai-Min Chung
Katerina Sotiraki
Katharina Boudgoust
Kathrin Hövelmanns
Katsuyuki Takashima
Kazuhiko Minematsu
Keita Xagawa
Kevin Yeo
Kewen Wu
Khoa Nguyen
Koji Nuida
Kristina Hostáková
Laasya Bangalore
Lars Knudsen
Lawrence Roy
Lejla Batina
Lennart Braun
Léo Colisson
Leo de Castro
Léo Ducas
Léo Perrin
Lin Lyu
Ling Song
Luca De Feo
Luca Nizzardo
Lucjan Hanzlik
Luisa Siniscalchi
Łukasz Chmielewski
Maciej Obremski
Madalina Bolboceanu

Mahimna Kelkar
Maria Eichlseder
María Naya-Plasencia
Marilyn George
Marios Georgiou
Mark Abspoel
Mark Simkin
Mark Zhandry
Markulf Kohlweiss
Marshall Ball
Marta Mularczyk
Martin Albrecht
Martin Hirt
Mary Wooters
Masayuki Abe
Matteo Campanelli
Matthias Fitzi
Mia Filic
Michael Reichle
Michael Rosenberg
Michael Walter
Michele Orru
Miguel Ambrona
Mingyuan Wang
Miran Kim
Miruna Rosca
Miyako Ohkubo
Mohammad Hajiabadi
Mohammad Hossein Faghihi Sereshgi
Monosij Maitra
Morgan Shirley
Mridul Nandi
Muhammed F. Esgin
Mustafa Khairallah
Naomi Ephraim
Nathan Manohar
Naty Peter
Navid Alamati
Ngoc Khanh Nguyen
Nicholas Spooner
Nicholas-Philip Brandt
Nico Döttling
Nicolas Resch
Nicolas Sendrier
Nikolaos Makriyannis
Nikolas Melissaris

Nils Fleischhacker
Nina Bindel
Nirvan Tyagi
Niv Gilboa
Noah Stephens-Davidowitz
Olivier Blazy
Olivier Bronchain
Omri Shmueli
Orfeas Stefanos Thyfronitis Litos
Orr Dunkelman
Oxana Poburinnaya
Patrick Derbez
Patrick Longa
Patrick Towa
Paul Rösler
Paul Zimmermann
Peter Gazi
Peter Rindal
Philippe Langevin
Pierre Briaud
Pierre Meyer
Pierrick Gaudry
Pierrick Mèaux
Po-Chu Hsu
Prabhanjan Ananth
Prashant Vasudeval
Pratik Sarkar
Pratik Soni
Pratyay Mukherjee
Pratyush Mishra
Qian Li
Qiang Tang
Qipeng Liu
Quan Quan Tan
Rachit Garg
Radu Titiu
Rajeev Raghunath
Rajendra Kumar
Ran Cohen
Raymond K. Zhao
Riad Wahby
Rishab Goyal
Rishabh Bhadauria
Rishiraj Bhattacharyya
Ritam Bhaumik
Robi Pedersen

Rohit Chatterjee
Rolando La Placa
Roman Langrehr
Rongmao Chen
Rupeng Yang
Ruth Ng
Saba Eskandarian
Sabine Oechsner
Sahar Mazloom
Saikrishna Badrinarayanan
Sam Kim
Samir Hodzic
Sanjam Garg
Sayandeep Saha
Schuyler Rosefield
Semyon Novoselov
Serge Fehr
Shai Halevi
Shashank Agrawal
Sherman S. M. Chow
Shi Bai
Shifeng Sun
Shivam Bhasin
Shota Yamada
Shuai Han
Shuichi Katsumata
Siang Meng Sim
Somitra Sanadhya
Sonia Belaïd
Sophia Yakoubov
Srinivas Vivek
Srinivasan Raghuraman
Sruthi Sekar
Stefano Tessaro
Steve Lu
Steven Galbraith
Stjepan Picek
Sumegha Garg
Susumu Kiyoshima
Sven Maier
Takahiro Matsuda
Takashi Yamakawa
Tal Moran
Tamer Mour
Thom Wiggers

Thomas Agrikola
Thomas Attema
Thomas Debris-Alazard
Thomas Decru
Tiancheng Xie
Tim Beyne
Titouan Tanguy
Tommaso Gagliardoni
Varun Maram
Vassilis Zikas
Venkata Koppula
Vincent Zucca
Virginie Lallemand
Ward Beullens
Wei Dai
Willy Quach
Wouter Castryck
Xiao Liang
Xiao Wang
Xiong Fan
Yael Kalai
Yan Bo Ti
Yann Rotella
Yannick Seurin
Yaobin Shen
Yashvanth Kondi
Yfke Dulek
Yiannis Tselekounis
Yifan Song
Yilei Chen
Yixin Shen
Yongsoo Song
Yu Long Chen
Yu Sa
Yue Guo
Yuncong Hu
Yupeng Zhang
Yuriy Polyakov
Yuval Ishai
Zahra Jafargholi
Zeyong Li
Zhengfeng Ji
Zichen Gui
Zuoxia Yu
Zvika Brakerski

Contents – Part III

Models

A Rational Protocol Treatment of 51% Attacks. 3
 Christian Badertscher, Yun Lu, and Vassilis Zikas

MoSS: Modular Security Specifications Framework. 33
 Amir Herzberg, Hemi Leibowitz, Ewa Syta, and Sara Wrótniak

Tight State-Restoration Soundness in the Algebraic Group Model. 64
 Ashrujit Ghoshal and Stefano Tessaro

Separating Adaptive Streaming from Oblivious Streaming Using
the Bounded Storage Model. 94
 Haim Kaplan, Yishay Mansour, Kobbi Nissim, and Uri Stemmer

Applied Cryptography and Side Channels

Provable Security Analysis of FIDO2 125
 Manuel Barbosa, Alexandra Boldyreva, Shan Chen,
 and Bogdan Warinschi

SSE and SSD: Page-Efficient Searchable Symmetric Encryption 157
 Angèle Bossuat, Raphael Bost, Pierre-Alain Fouque, Brice Minaud,
 and Michael Reichle

Towards Tight Random Probing Security. 185
 Gaëtan Cassiers, Sebastian Faust, Maximilian Orlt,
 and François-Xavier Standaert

Secure Wire Shuffling in the Probing Model 215
 Jean-Sébastien Coron and Lorenzo Spignoli

Cryptanalysis

Differential-Linear Cryptanalysis from an Algebraic Perspective 247
 Meicheng Liu, Xiaojuan Lu, and Dongdai Lin

Meet-in-the-Middle Attacks Revisited: Key-Recovery, Collision,
and Preimage Attacks 278
 Xiaoyang Dong, Jialiang Hua, Siwei Sun, Zheng Li, Xiaoyun Wang,
 and Lei Hu

Revisiting the Security of DbHtS MACs: Beyond-Birthday-Bound
in the Multi-user Setting   309
  Yaobin Shen, Lei Wang, Dawu Gu, and Jian Weng

Thinking Outside the Superbox.   337
  Nicolas Bordes, Joan Daemen, Daniël Kuijsters, and Gilles Van Assche

Cryptanalysis of Full LowMC and LowMC-M with Algebraic Techniques. . . .   368
  Fukang Liu, Takanori Isobe, and Willi Meier

The Cost to Break SIKE: A Comparative Hardware-Based Analysis
with AES and SHA-3   402
  Patrick Longa, Wen Wang, and Jakub Szefer

Improved Torsion-Point Attacks on SIDH Variants   432
  *Victoria de Quehen, Péter Kutas, Chris Leonardi, Chloe Martindale,
  Lorenz Panny, Christophe Petit, and Katherine E. Stange*

Codes and Extractors

Smoothing Out Binary Linear Codes and Worst-Case Sub-exponential
Hardness for LPN.   473
  Yu Yu and Jiang Zhang

Silver: Silent VOLE and Oblivious Transfer from Hardness of Decoding
Structured LDPC Codes.   502
  Geoffroy Couteau, Peter Rindal, and Srinivasan Raghuraman

Non-malleable Codes for Bounded Parallel-Time Tampering   535
  Dana Dachman-Soled, Ilan Komargodski, and Rafael Pass

Improved Computational Extractors and Their Applications   566
  Dakshita Khurana and Akshayaram Srinivasan

Adaptive Extractors and Their Application to Leakage Resilient
Secret Sharing   595
  *Nishanth Chandran, Bhavana Kanukurthi,
  Sai Lakshmi Bhavana Obbattu, and Sruthi Sekar*

Secret Sharing

Upslices, Downslices, and Secret-Sharing with Complexity of 1.5^n   627
  Benny Applebaum and Oded Nir

Asymptotically-Good Arithmetic Secret Sharing over $\mathbb{Z}/p^\ell\mathbb{Z}$ with Strong
Multiplication and Its Applications to Efficient MPC.   656
  Ronald Cramer, Matthieu Rambaud, and Chaoping Xing

Large Message Homomorphic Secret Sharing from DCR and Applications. . .   687
  Lawrence Roy and Jaspal Singh

Traceable Secret Sharing and Applications   718
  Vipul Goyal, Yifan Song, and Akshayaram Srinivasan

Quadratic Secret Sharing and Conditional Disclosure of Secrets   748
  Amos Beimel, Hussien Othman, and Naty Peter

Constructing Locally Leakage-Resilient Linear Secret-Sharing Schemes   779
  Hemanta K. Maji, Anat Paskin-Cherniavsky, Tom Suad,
  and Mingyuan Wang

Author Index   809

Models

A Rational Protocol Treatment of 51% Attacks

Christian Badertscher[1] , Yun Lu[2(✉)] , and Vassilis Zikas[3]

[1] IOHK, Zurich, Switzerland
christian.badertscher@iohk.io
[2] University of Edinburgh, Edinburgh, UK
Y.Lu-59@sms.ed.ac.uk
[3] Purdue University, West Lafayette, USA
vzikas@cs.purdue.edu

Abstract. Game-theoretic analyses of cryptocurrencies and—more generally—blockchain-based decentralized ledgers offer insight on their economic robustness and behavior when even their underpinning cryptographic assumptions fail. In this work we utilize the recently proposed blockchain adaptation of the rational protocol design (RPD) framework [EUROCRYPT '18] to analyze 51% double-spending attacks against Nakamoto-style proof-of-work based cryptocurrencies. We first observe a property of the originally proposed utility class that yields an unnatural conclusion against such attacks, and show how to devise a utility that avoids this pitfall and makes predictions that match the observable behavior—i.e., that renders attacking a dominant strategy in settings where an attack was indeed observed in reality. We then propose a generic remedy to the underlying protocol parameters that provably deter adversaries controlling a majority of the system's resources from attacks on blockchain consistency, including the 51% double-spending attack. This can be used as guidance to patch systems that have suffered such attacks, e.g., Ethereum Classic and Bitcoin Cash, and serves as a demonstration of the power of game-theoretic analyses.

1 Introduction

The classical cryptographic analysis of blockchain ledgers establishes worst-case guarantees on their security either by proving central security properties [GKL15, PSs17], such as *consistency/common-prefix*—the stable parts of the chains held by honest parties are prefixes of one-another—*liveness*—new blocks with recent transactions keep being added–or by proving that the protocol realizes an ideal ledger functionality [BMTZ17]. Typically such analyses rely on an assumed limitation on the adversary's influence/presence in the system. In particular, the majority of an underlying resource—e.g., hashing power for proof-of-work (PoW)-based protocols such as Bitcoin [Nak08] and Ethereum [But13]

We refer to our full version [BLZ21] for the complete formal proofs and definitions.

© International Association for Cryptologic Research 2021
T. Malkin and C. Peikert (Eds.): CRYPTO 2021, LNCS 12827, pp. 3–32, 2021.
https://doi.org/10.1007/978-3-030-84252-9_1

(before version 2.0), or stake in Proof-of-Stake (PoS)-based protocols such as Algorand, Ouroboros, and Snow White [KRDO17, BGK+18, CM19, DPS19]—is owned/contributed by parties who honestly run the protocol.

Although such an analysis is instrumental for understanding the properties and limitations of the analyzed ledgers and gaining confidence in their security, it does not take into account a fundamental property of such systems, namely that the ledger's state is often associated with some monetary value and therefore the protocol's security might rely on how profitable an attack might be. Thus, in addition to the classical cryptographic analysis of such systems, it is useful to analyze their so-called *economic robustness*, namely their level of protection or susceptibility to attacks by an incentive-driven (also called rational) attacker. Such an analysis can fortify the security of these systems by proving a fallback rational assumption, e.g., assuming an incentives model of the attacker, security is maintained even when certain cryptographic assumptions fail, or indicate that the proven security is fragile by pointing out natural incentives that lead to violating the security assumptions. Additionally, it can offer a higher resolution picture of the systems guarantees—e.g., its tendency to decentralize [BKKS20]—and/or more realistic estimates of the parameters associated with its security properties—e.g., relation between the density of honest blocks (that is, the chain-quality parameter [GKL15]) and the properties of the communication network [ES14, NKMS16]. Perhaps, even more interesting, it can offer insight on the system's behavior when the main (cryptographic) assumption fails, e.g., when the attacker controls a 51% fraction of the underlying resource of the blockchain protocol.

Motivated by the recent (repeated) 51% double-spending attacks that have drained millions of dollars from popular blockchain-based cryptocurrencies, we devise a game-theoretic analysis of such attacks for Nakamoto-style systems, e.g., Bitcoin, Bitcoin Cash/Gold, Ethereum (Classic), etc. We use the adaptation of the rational protocol design (RPD) framework by Garay *et al.* [GKM+13] to blockchains, which was recently proposed by Badertscher *et al.* [BGM+18], to analyze the utility of an attacker against these systems as a function of their basic parameters.

A central question to the relevance for practice of any game-theoretic analysis is to what extent the model and assumed utilities capture the incentives of real world attacks. Indeed, if the utilities are disconnected from reality, they can lead to counter-intuitive statements. We demonstrate an instance of such an artifact in [BGM+18] and propose a different class of utilities which is both natural and avoids this artifact. We validate our utility against a range of security parameters matching those of Ethereum Classic, a PoW-based system that fell victim to 51% double-spending attacks. We observe that when the payoff for double-spending is high, attacking is indeed a dominating strategy. That is, predictions of our utility choice match reality. We then use our framework to devise a generic tuning of one of the core parameters of such blockchains—namely, the number cutOff of most-recent blocks needed to be dropped to achieve the so-called common-prefix property with parameter cutOff (cf. [BMTZ17, BGM+18, GKL15])—to deter any attacks on consistency by a rational attacker with our utility. Stated differently, we show how an incentive model can serve, possibly in addition to cryptographic assumptions, to find a robust protocol parameterization. This thereby demonstrates how our model and analysis can be used to improve the economic robustness of such blockchains, and offers a guide to how to "patch" such protocols to avoid future occurrences.

1.1   Related Literature

A number of works have focused on a rational analysis of decentralized ledgers and cryptocurrencies (e.g., [Ros11, CKWN16, ES14, Eyal5, SBBR16, SSZ16, LTKS15, TJS16, NKMS16, PS17, GKW+16] to mention some). Typically, these works abstract away the computational aspects of cryptographic tools (signatures, hash-functions, etc.) and provide a game which captures certain aspects of the execution that are relevant for the rational analysis. In contrast, RPD uses a cryptographic simulation-based framework to incorporate these computational considerations into the analyzed game, ensuring that predictions about attacker behavior hold for the actual protocol and not only for an idealized version (unless the idealization is obtained via a cryptographic composition argument such as UC). Incorporating such computational considerations within a rational treatment is highly non-trivial (see [GKM+13, CCWrao20] for a discussion). We discuss the RPD framework in more detail in the following section.

The term *51% (double-spending) attack* is defined in [Inv] as an attack where the adversary gains any majority (not necessarily just 51%) of mining power and reverses transactions in order to double-spend its coins, often by creating a deep fork in the chain. The site CoinDesk keeps track of news of 51% attacks [Coia], of which there are quite many: most recently, Verge suffered an attack with 200 days worth of transactions erased in Feb, 2021. Also recently, Ethereum Classic suffered three 51% attacks in the same month of August, 2020, prompting a solution called MESS to mitigate such attacks which still may not provide robust security [Coib]. Other recent victims of such attacks include well-known coins such as Bitcoin Gold (Jan 2020), and Bitcoin Cash (May 2019). A major avenue of 51% double-spending attacks is the use of rented hash power [For]. The site https://www.crypto51.app/ gives rough estimates on the vulnerability of different coins, based on whether 51% of hashing power can be rented via a service called Nicehash. In some cases, e.g. Bitcoin Gold, it is estimated to only cost a few hundred dollars to have 51% of hashing power for 1 h.

Previous works have considered the ability of blockchain protocols to recover from 51% attacks. In [AKWW19], conditioned on honest majority being satisfied on expectation, Bitcoin was proven to be resilient against a (temporary) dishonest majority. In [BGK+20], no such condition is assumed and the authors give concrete recovery bounds as a function of the actual power of the adversary (captured as a budget to go over majority hashing power). We use the latter work for our analysis of the blockchain's security against incentive-driven attackers.

The profitability of 51% double-spending attacks have also been analyzed in previous works. The work of [Bud18] explores these attacks through an economics perspective, and leaving the cost of the attack as a parameter that is computed via simulations. The work of [JL20] computes probability of attack by modeling attacks as random walk of two independent Poisson counting processes (PCPs). In comparison, our rational analyses are done in the Rational Protocol Design (RPD) framework, where a fork is formally defined as a command in a UC ledger functionality. Another technique proposed is the Markov Decision Process (MDP) model, which is used by both [GKW+16] and [HSY+21]. In this model, the adversary takes a series of actions relevant to double-spending: adopting or overriding the honest party's chain, waiting, or stopping. Solving the MDP allows these works to reason about the optimal double-spending adversary. While we do not analyze an optimal double-spending adversary, our model is more general. We do not restrict the actions of the adversary, which allows us to analyze conditions under which the protocol is secure against attacks on consistency by *any* incentive-driven adversary. Moreover, since standard MDP solvers cannot solve infinite state MDPs, the MDP is restricted to only consider situations where the chain length is less than some length c [GKW+16].

1.2   Our Results

We start by devising a utility in RPD which naturally captures the incentives of an attacker to provoke a double-spending attack. To this direction, we observe that the utility considered in [BGM+18] does not capture such an incentive. Intuitively, the reason is that the utility in [BGM+18] essentially only considers incentives related to the consensus layer of the protocol. This means that an attacker is rewarded when successfully mining a block, but is not rewarded depending on the block contents—i.e. what kinds of transactions are in the block. Their extension to a utility function to include transaction fees does not apply to double-spending attacks. In this case, the (only) reason to attack the blockchain stems from the existence of a super-polynomial transaction fee, and assuming a moderate range of fees, no incentive to attack is present. We discuss why super-polynomial quantities are generally problematic in Sect. 4. It follows from [BGM+18] that the attacker with these utility functions (and assuming moderate transaction fees) has no incentive to fork over mining honestly. Yet, looking at real-life double-spending attacks, this is clearly not the case. To capture double-spending, we introduce a special payoff that the attacker receives when successfully creating a deep-enough fork (i.e., orphans a sufficiently long valid chain). Intuitively, this payoff corresponds to the utility that the attacker receives when it double-spends by replacing the orphaned chain with his own.

Perhaps counter-intuitively, when analyzing Bitcoin[1] with this extended utility function, the attacker is still indifferent between forking and honest mining. We demonstrate this artifact and pinpoint the reason for it: Intuitively, the utility function from [BGM+18] (with or without the extra payoff for forking) rewards

---

[1] Our analysis uses Bitcoin as a representative example of Nakamoto-style blockchain ledgers, but similarly any blockchain protocol which realizes the ledger from [BMTZ17, BGK+18] could be analyzed.

the attacker by the same amount in all rounds in which it creates (mines) a block. This means that given any adversary that provokes a fork, there is always an honest-mining adversary who achieves more utility without forking by simply accumulating block rewards over a longer period of time. We distill the source of this issue in a property which we call *unbounded incentives*, and demonstrate that any utility which satisfies this property will make any deviation from passive mining a weakly *dominated* strategy.

We then devise a revision of this utility class which allows us to avoid the above counter-intuitive artifact. This utility, which satisfies a property we term *limited horizons*—a strong negation of unbounded incentives—has the property that the (actual) rewards of an adversary mining a block diminish with time. This is a natural way to avoid reasoning about extremely "long-lived" adversaries, i.e., that take decisions based on payoffs too far in the future, and captures features which are well-known in utility theory [Ber54]—intuitively, earning $10 today is more attractive than $1 million in 100 years, an example of the "St. Petersburg Paradox". We next turn in analyzing the profitability of 51% double-spending attacks, by showing how our revised utility can actually capture them. We provide a range of payoffs for double-spending which would incentivize an attack. Then we visualize our result using concrete parameters estimated from those of Ethereum Classic, for which performing the attack is indeed a dominant strategy. This demonstrates that the above result can explain, in a game-theoretic framework, how recent victims of 51% attacks are vulnerable.

Finally, we discuss whether and how the blockchain protocol can be tuned so that such 51% double-spending attacks are deterred. In fact, we provide a much stronger tuning, which deters attacks on consistency by any incentive-driven adversary. The tuning depends on the costs (e.g. electricity or cost to rent hashing power), positive payoffs (e.g. block rewards and payoff for causing a fork, from double-spending or otherwise), and protocol parameters (e.g. the difficulty of creating a block). Intuitively, for any combination of these parameters, we show how the window size of the underlying blockchain protocol can be adjusted so that it is not rational for the attacker to perform this attack. At the core of this results is a lemma that relates the incentive model to an attack pattern, which coupled with the self-healing properties of Nakamoto-style PoW, leads to the desired estimate of a safe parameter. We view this as a demonstration that game theory can aid us in fortifying blockchains even when assumptions made by the cryptographic analyses fail.

2   Preliminaries

2.1   The Bitcoin Backbone Protocol

The abstraction of the Bitcoin protocol that is used in the cryptographic literature is known as the *Bitcoin backbone protocol* [GKL15, PSs17, BMTZ17] which we denote by $\Pi^{\mathcal{B}}$. In this abstraction, Bitcoin is modeled as a round-based protocol, where a number of participants (the miners) are connected via a multicast network with bounded delay Δ (unknown to the protocol). In every round, each party adopts the longest chain $\mathcal{C} = B_0||\ldots||B_k$ of block B_i (connected by hash-pointers) it has received so far, where B_0 is the unique genesis block of the system. Each party tries to extend this longest chain an by additional block, via running the PoW-lottery: an extension of chain $\mathcal{C}$ by a new block B_{k+1} can only be valid, if its hash $H(B_{k+1})$ belongs to a dedicated small portion of the output domain of the function (typically, the hash must have a lot of leading zeros). In such analyses, the hash function is modeled using a random-oracle functionality $\mathcal{F}_{\mathrm{RO}}$ that returns uniform values upon each query. Therefore, when extending the chain, each party makes a certain number of *mining queries* per round (that is, RO-queries with candidate blocks B_{k+1} containing a random nonce to obtain the hash) and we call a mining query *successful*, if the output is below the threshold. In the setting with fixed PoW difficulty, we can assign a success probability p to each such mining query. Finally, if a miner is successful, it will send the new chain over the multicast network to all other miners.

Cryptographic Security. The main security guarantee[2] proven for the Bitcoin protocol is eventual *consistency*: every block that is deep enough can be considered immutable and only the most recent, `cutOff` number of blocks might be transient. This `cutOff`-consistency (where the cutoff parameter is often left implicit if clear from context) guarantee states that at any point in time, the prefix of $\mathcal{C}$ consisting of $|\mathcal{C}| - $ `cutOff` blocks is common to all honest miners:

Definition 1 (Consistency). *Let $\mathcal{C}_1 \preccurlyeq \mathcal{C}_2$ denote the prefix-of relation, then the consistency guarantee (with parameter* `cutOff`*) states that at any two points in time $a \leq b$ in an execution, where party P at round a holds chain $\mathcal{C}_1$ and party P' at round b holds chain $\mathcal{C}_2$, we have that $\mathcal{C}_1|_{\mathtt{cutOff}} \preccurlyeq \mathcal{C}_2$, where the notation $\mathcal{C}|_k$ denotes the prefix of $\mathcal{C}$ obtained by removing the most recent k blocks (and if k exceeds the length of $\mathcal{C}$, it is defined to correspond to the genesis block).*

In the cryptographic setting (without incentives), such a guarantee only holds if we restrict the adversary to have a minority of mining power. That is, given $n_a^{(r)}$ and $n_h^{(r)}$ denote the numbers of adversarial and honest mining queries in round r, respectively, then the protocol $\Pi^{\mathcal{B}}$ is secure if in any round r the inequality $n_a^{(r)} < \theta_{pow} \cdot n_h^{(r)}$ holds, with $\theta_{pow} := (1-p)^{(2\Delta+1)\mathsf{T}_{ub}}$ being the well-established security threshold for Bitcoin (often stated in its linear approximation $1 - 2(\Delta + 1)p\mathsf{T}_{ub}$) [GKL15,PSs17,BMTZ17], where the quantity T_{ub} denotes the upper bound on the number of mining queries per round. Throughout this work, we work in the so-called *flat model* of Bitcoin for notational simplicity [GKL15,BGM+18], where each miner gets one mining query per round (and the adversary's power is the number of corrupted miners). We note that sometimes it is convenient to assume a lower bound T_{lb} on the number of mining queries (a.k.a. participation) per round, in particular when arguing about the

---

[2] While other security guarantees exist, such as *chain quality*, our focus in this paper is consistency.

guaranteed growth of the blockchain over time in combination with the security threshold. Finally, we point out that even if there are no adversarial players, an upper bound T_{ub} on the number of queries is necessary for security in the fixed difficulty setting, when aiming for a common prefix guarantee for some target parameter cutOff. As the failure probability of Bitcoin becomes negligible as a function of cutOff (more precisely, the relevant factor is of the order $2^{-\Omega(\text{cutOff})}$), we often treat it as a (of course polynomial-bounded) function $\text{cutOff}(\kappa)$ of a security parameter κ, and (in symbolic notation) $\text{cutOff} = \omega(\log(\kappa))$ is at least required to obtain a negligible probability of a failure.

Bitcoin Backbone and UC. The RPD framework is based on the UC framework. As such, the above Bitcoin backbone protocol $\Pi^{\mathcal{B}}$ is seen as a UC protocol as in [BMTZ17], where it is proven to UC-realize a strong transaction ledger functionality $\mathcal{G}_{\text{LEDGER}}$ under the honest majority assumption. We give here just the explanation of how the ideal consistency guarantee looks like: the functionality $\mathcal{G}_{\text{LEDGER}}$ ensures that at any point in time, there is only one unique ledger state (sequences of transactions packed in blocks), where the state is append-only (that is, whatever appears as a block in the state is immutable). Furthermore, different honest parties see different prefixes of this state, with the guarantee that these *views* are increasing and within a window of windowSize (a ledger parameter) blocks from the tip of the state. Note that the cut-off parameter of Bitcoin corresponds exactly to the size of that window in the realized ledger $\mathcal{G}_{\text{LEDGER}}$. More precisely, whenever Bitcoin satisfies Definition 1, then the above mentioned correspondence holds and the ledger state is a single chain of blocks [BMTZ17].

In UC, the protocol $\Pi^{\mathcal{B}}$ assumes a couple of hybrid functionalities. First, the round-based structure is achieved using UC-synchronous tools (assuming a clock functionality), a network, and a random oracle, where restrictions on the mining queries can be captured by functionality wrappers restricting the number of RO evaluations, e.g. [BMTZ17, GKO+20]. One extremely helpful aspect of UC in the context of RPD is the compatibility with the composition theorem [GKM+13]. In this work this is leveraged as follows. The Bitcoin backbone $\Pi^{\mathcal{B}}$ admits a modular structure that isolates the lottery aspect as a submodule of the system. Technically, the proofs in [BMTZ17, PSs17] show that whenever the PoW-lottery UC-realizes the *state exchange* functionality $\mathcal{F}_{\text{STX}}$ (in [PSs17] the related concept is called $\mathcal{F}_{\text{tree}}$), the Nakamoto-style longest chain rule protocol (under the above honest-majority security threshold) realizes the ledger. This intermediate step is important due to two things: first, it models an idealized mining process where each mining query is an independent Bernoulli trial with success probability p (and hence abstracts away those real-life negligible probability events that would destroy independence), and second it abstracts away the low-level details of the chain structure (where e.g., "hash collisions" could cause disruptions). It is proven in [BMTZ17] that the proof-of-work layer of Bitcoin (in the random oracle model) UC-realizes $\mathcal{F}_{\text{STX}}$. Moreover, since it only abstracts the lottery part of the system, this realization does not depend on any security threshold. We can therefore leverage composition when analyzing the utilities of Bitcoin and work with the idealized lottery directly.

2.2 Rational Protocol Design

The Rational Protocol Design framework (RPD) allows us to analyze the security of the blockchain without assuming honest majority. Although consistency and other security properties are lost if an attacker can arbitrarily break honest majority, assuming attackers are *rational* offers an alternate method of limiting his actions. That is, although the attacker is free to act in any way (e.g. corrupt more than majority hashing power), he will only do so if it is profitable. Building on [BGM+18], our analysis is based on the Rational Protocol Design (RPD) framework introduced in [GKM+13]. RPD analyzes the security of protocols, such as Bitcoin, with respect to an incentive-driven adversary. In this model, a protocol designer D plays an *attack game* $\mathcal{G}$ with an attacker A. First, the designer D comes up with a protocol Π. Then, the attacker A—who is informed about Π—comes up with an adversarial strategy $\mathcal{A}$ to attack Π. The utility of the attacker (resp. designer) is then defined on the *strategy profile* $(\Pi, \mathcal{A})$, and is denoted $u_A(\Pi, \mathcal{A})$ (resp. $u_D(\Pi, \mathcal{A})$). In this work, we focus on the attacker's utility $u_A(\Pi, \mathcal{A})$.

The game $\mathcal{G}$ is defined with respect to an attack model $\mathcal{M} = (\mathcal{F}, \langle\mathcal{F}\rangle, v_A, v_D)$. $\mathcal{F}$ is the functionality which the designer would like to implement such as a ledger that provides certain ideal guarantees as described above. However, when certain assumptions, e.g. honest majority for Bitcoin, are not met (which as stated above we explicitly do not want to demand *a priori*), we cannot hope to get $\mathcal{F}$. Instead, the designer D's protocol Π (in our case, the Bitcoin protocol $\Pi^{\tilde{B}}$) only implements a weaker functionality. This weaker functionality that Bitcoin implements when lifting the honest majority assumption is proven to be $\mathcal{G}^{\tilde{B}}_{\text{WEAK-LEDGER}}$ in [BGM+18] and provided in our full version [BLZ21] for completeness. Intuitively, the weak ledger is derived from the stronger version [BMTZ17] by introducing a few weaknesses. For example, it allows the adversary to fork the ledger state and hence allows it to break consistency (this event corresponds to a deep reorganization of the blockchain in the real world). This is allowed by the FORK command in $\mathcal{G}^{\tilde{B}}_{\text{WEAK-LEDGER}}$. Given the views of the simulator and environment in an ideal world execution, the value functions v_A and v_D assign payoffs to the attacker and designer respectively, when certain events happen in the views, such as when the simulator forks the blockchain via $\mathcal{G}^{\tilde{B}}_{\text{WEAK-LEDGER}}$. Finally, utilities u_A and u_D are functions of payoffs (defined with v_A and v_D) of simulators that can simulate $\mathcal{A}$ in Π in the environment $\mathcal{Z}$. Looking ahead, the goal of RPD is to find conditions under which a rational attacker would not invoke the weaknesses of $\mathcal{G}^{\tilde{B}}_{\text{WEAK-LEDGER}}$ (e.g., it is too costly to perform an attack). For example, if under a class of utilities, no rational attacker invokes the FORK command, then we essentially obtain a stronger ledger (i.e., the same except that this command is absent and hence the ledger state remains a unique chain) against attackers incentivized by this class of utilities.

2.3 Utility of the Attacker From [BGM+18]

We detail the attacker's utility in [BGM+18], which in the RPD framework captures the expected payoff of a particular adversarial strategy $\mathcal{A}$ in a given protocol Π (in our case $\Pi = \Pi^{\mathcal{B}}$). This payoff is calculated based on different *events* that occur in the real execution and the corresponding ideal experiment where a black-box simulator is attempting to simulate this adversarial strategy.

Specifically, the work of [BGM+18] considers the following events:

1. Event $W^{\mathsf{A}}_{q,r}$, for each pair $(q, r) \in \mathbb{N}^2$: The simulator simulates q mining queries by the adversary in round r of the simulated execution.
2. Event $I^{\mathsf{A}}_{b,r}$, for each pair $(b, r) \in \mathbb{N}^2$: The simulator inserts b blocks into the state of the ledger in round r, such that all these blocks were previously queries to the (simulated) random oracle by the adversary. Informally, this event occurs when an honest party views these blocks as "confirmed" (part of his own ledger state).

A different payoff is associated with each event. In order to make q mining queries and invoke event $W^{\mathsf{A}}_{q,r}$, the attacker must pay $q \cdot \mathtt{mcost}$, where $\mathtt{mcost}$ is the cost of making a mining query (e.g. electricity cost per hash query). When b blocks made by the adversary are inserted into the ledger and event $I^{\mathsf{A}}_{b,r}$ occurs, the attacker receives payoff $b \cdot \mathtt{breward} \cdot \mathtt{CR}$. Here $\mathtt{breward}$ is the reward for making a block in the currency of the blockchain (e.g. Bitcoins), and $\mathtt{CR}$ is an exchange rate to the same currency used for $\mathtt{mcost}$ (e.g. USD).

Then, [BGM+18] defines the following attacker's utility for a strategy profile $(\Pi, \mathcal{A})$. Let $\mathcal{C}_{\mathcal{A}}$ denote the set of simulators that can emulate an adversary $\mathcal{A}$ in the ideal world with access to the weaker ledger functionality $\mathcal{G}^{\mathcal{B}}_{\text{WEAK-LEDGER}}$, and $\mathcal{Z}$ denote an environment. The *real payoff* of an adversary $\mathcal{A}$ attacking the protocol is defined as the minimum payoff over all simulators in $\mathcal{C}_{\mathcal{A}}$. If $\mathcal{C}_{\mathcal{A}} = \emptyset$ (there are no simulators that can simulate $\mathcal{A}$) then $u_{\mathsf{A}}(\Pi, \mathcal{A}) = \infty$ by definition. Then, the utility $u_{\mathsf{A}}(\Pi, \mathcal{A})$ is the real payoff, maximized over all possible environments $\mathcal{Z}$ (we assume for simplicity that environments are closed and run in polynomial time in the security parameter [Can01]).

$$u_{\mathsf{A}}(\Pi, \mathcal{A}) := \sup_{\mathcal{Z} \in \text{ITM}} \left\{ \inf_{\mathcal{S}^{\mathcal{A}} \in \mathcal{C}_{\mathcal{A}}} \left\{ \sum_{(b,r) \in \mathbb{N}^2} (b \cdot \mathtt{breward} \cdot \mathtt{CR} \cdot \Pr[I^{\mathsf{A}}_{b,r}]) \right. \right. \tag{1}$$
$$\left. \left. - \sum_{(q,r) \in \mathbb{N}^2} q \cdot \mathtt{mcost} \cdot \Pr[W^{\mathsf{A}}_{q,r}] \right\} \right\}.$$

The work of [GKM+13] introduces the following notion of security against incentive-driven adversaries: No matter the utility achieved by an adversary $\mathcal{A}$ running the protocol Π in the real world, there exists an adversary $\mathcal{A}'$ running the dummy protocol with access to the ideal functionality $\mathcal{F}$ that achieves the same or better utility. In other words, even the best adversary attacking Π, cannot achieve better utility than one who does not invoke any of the "bad events" in $\langle \mathcal{F} \rangle$. Note that here $\mathcal{F}$ can be any strengthening of its weaker version. For example, the weak ledger without the option to break consistency would be a strengthening of $\mathcal{G}_{\text{WEAK-LEDGER}}^{\text{B}}$ in which case attack-payoff security implies that there is no incentive (even for a majority-controlling adversary) to create a fork (that is, a deep reorganization) even though he technically could be able to.

Strictly speaking, the utilities are also functions in the security parameter κ (the environment obtains the parameter as input in UC) but we omit it for notational simplicity. We note that as functions in the security parameter κ, the asymptotic behavior of the involved functions is the relevant aspect.

Definition 2 (Attack payoff security [GKM+13]). *Let* $\mathcal{M} = (\mathcal{F}, \langle \mathcal{F} \rangle, v_\text{A}, v_\text{D})$ *be an attack model inducing utility* u_A, *and let* $\Phi^{\mathcal{F}}$ *be the dummy* $\mathcal{F}$-*hybrid protocol. A protocol* Π *is* attack-payoff secure *for* $\mathcal{M}$ *if for all* $\mathcal{A}$, *there is an* $\mathcal{A}'$ *such that* $u_\text{A}(\Pi, \mathcal{A}) \leq u_\text{A}(\Phi^{\mathcal{F}}, \mathcal{A}') + \mathsf{negl}(\kappa)$

This notion of attack-payoff security does not necessarily mean an incentive-driven adversary will honestly follow the protocol—there is no restriction on the honestly of the actions of $\mathcal{A}'$ in the above definition. To capture this stronger requirement in the context of Bitcoin, we also consider a stronger notion introduced by [BGM+18]: the attacker is incentivized to always choose a *front-running, passive-mining* adversary over any (potentially malicious) strategy. Informally, this passive adversary behaves exactly like an honest party (mining with all his hashing power and releasing a block he has found immediately), except the adversary's messages are always delivered before the honest parties' (front-running). Front-running gives the adversary an advantage since if an adversary's block is concurrently competing with an honest party's block to be appended to the longest chain, the adversary always wins.

Definition 3 (Front-running, passive-mining adversary [BGM+18]). *The front-running adversarial strategy* $\mathcal{A} \in \mathbb{A}_{fr}$ *is specified as follows: Upon activation in round* $r > 0$, $\mathcal{A}$ *activates in a round-robin fashion all its (passively) corrupted parties, say* $p_1, \ldots, p_t$. *When corrupt party* p_i *generates some new message to be sent through the network,* $\mathcal{A}$ *immediately delivers it to all its recipients. In addition, upon any activation, any message submitted to the network* $\mathcal{F}_{\text{N-MC}}$ *by an honest party is maximally delayed.*

Π^{B} was proved to be strongly attack-payoff in [BGM+18] for the utility in Eq. 1. Informally, a protocol is strongly attack-payoff secure if there is always a passive adversarial strategy that is at least as good as any malicious strategy. In this work, we are also interested in the case where security does not hold: we say an adversary $\mathcal{A}$ *breaks* strong attack-payoff security if $u_\text{A}(\Pi, \mathcal{A})$ exceeds $u_\text{A}(\Pi, \mathcal{A}')$ for any $\mathcal{A}' \in \mathbb{A}_{fr}$, by a non-negligible amount.

Definition 4 (Strongly attack-payoff secure [BGM+18]). *A protocol* Π *is* strongly attack-payoff secure *for attack model* $\mathcal{M}$ *if there is a* $\mathcal{A}' \in \mathbb{A}_{fr}$ *such that for all* $\mathcal{A}$, $u_\text{A}(\Pi, \mathcal{A}) \leq u_\text{A}(\Pi, \mathcal{A}') + \mathsf{negl}(\kappa)$

In our work, we will follow the approach from [BGM+18] that simplifies the proofs when analyzing the utilities from mining in the protocol $\Pi^{\mathcal{B}}$ by utilizing the composition theorem of RPD. As explained above, instead of analyzing the probabilities of payoff-inducing events for $\Pi^{\mathcal{B}}$ which uses the random oracle as the lottery, one can analyze probabilities for the *modular* ledger protocol w.r.t. an idealized lottery that makes use of the state exchange functionality $\mathcal{F}_{\text{STX}}$ (for completeness, defined in full version [BLZ21]). In more detail: when a party (or the adversary in the name of a corrupted party) wishes to extend a chain, they would invoke $\mathcal{F}_{\text{STX}}$ with a SUBMIT-NEW command, which performs a coin toss and informs him whether he is successful. If the party is successful, the functionality includes this new chain into a tree data structure and allows the party to multicast this new chain with a SEND command; this multicasting is done automatically for honest parties. Due to the correspondence of RO queries in the Bitcoin protocol and the SUBMIT-NEW-commands in the modularized Bitcoin protocol [BMTZ17], the events defined for $u_{\text{A}}^{\mathcal{B}}(\Pi, \mathcal{A})$ (for the full Bitcoin protocol) above remain valid and meaningful also in this hybrid world, because the black-box simulator for the overall Bitcoin protocol simulates one RO-query (as a reaction to an input by a corrupted party) whenever the (black-box) simulator for the modular ledger protocol simulates one SUBMIT-NEW-command, as a reaction to the corresponding input by the same party [BGM+18].

3   Artifacts of Unbounded Incentives

In this section, we discuss an artifact of the utility function Eq. 1, which we will eliminate in the next section. Concretely, we prove that this RPD utility is inappropriate to capture the most realistic situation of attackers that attack the system, e.g., attempt a fork to profit from double-spending. To do so, we prove Lemma 1 and 2, which roughly show this surprising fact: if running the protocol (semi-)honestly is profitable in expectation, then there is no incentive for an adversary to fork. The intuitive reason for this is clear: Any fixed payoff for forking incurred by the adversary can be offset by an adversary who runs slightly longer (and still polynomially long) but does not fork. This, however, is an artifact of the asymptotic definition and does not reflect real-world incentive-driven attack scenarios, where mining is anticipated to be profitable—otherwise no one would mine—but attackers still perform forking attacks (in particular, in order to double-spend coins). We distill a property of the utility from [BGM+18] that is the reason this artifact, which we call *unbounded incentives*, and prove that any utility satisfying this property will suffer from the same artifact. Looking ahead to the following section, we will propose a natural adaptation of this utility function that does not suffer from the above artifact (and where in particular the duration of an attack actually starts to matter).

3.1   Demonstrating the Artifact

Let us first consider the straightforward adaptation of the utility from Eq. 1 to model the payoff (e.g. double-spending) an adversary gains by forking the ledger.

Define the event K as: There is a round r where the simulator uses the FORK command of the weak ledger functionality $\mathcal{G}^{\mathcal{B}}_{\text{WEAK-LEDGER}}$ (see [BLZ21] for formal definition) that allows the simulator to invoke a fork. Let fpayoff be the payoff for invoking the fork. Then, the utility $u_{\mathtt{f}}$ becomes:

$$u_{\mathtt{f}}(\Pi, \mathcal{A}) := \sup_{\mathcal{Z} \in \text{ITM}} \left\{ \inf_{\mathcal{S}^{\mathcal{A}} \in \mathcal{C}_{\mathcal{A}}} \left\{ \sum_{(b,r) \in \mathbb{N}^2} b \cdot \mathtt{breward} \cdot \mathtt{CR} \cdot \Pr[I^{\mathtt{A}}_{b,r}] \right. \right.$$

$$\left. \left. - \sum_{(q,r) \in \mathbb{N}^2} q \cdot \mathtt{mcost} \cdot \Pr[W^{\mathtt{A}}_{q,r}] + \mathtt{fpayoff} \cdot \Pr[K] \right\} \right\}. \quad (2)$$

Below, we show that for the utility function $u_{\mathtt{f}}$ above, the Bitcoin protocol $\Pi^{\mathcal{B}}$ is strongly attack-payoff secure as long as mining is profitable. Our proof takes advantage of the artifact of unbounded incentives: informally, first we show that the payoff of any polynomial-run-time adversary $\mathcal{A}$ is bounded by a polynomial $p(\kappa)$ of the security parameter; then, we show that there is a passive, front-running adversary whose run-time is also polynomial (albeit bigger than that of $\mathcal{A}$), and who achieves at least $p(\kappa)$ utility.[3]

Lemma 1 (Attack payoff security with forking). *Let $T_{\text{ub}} > 0$ be the upper bound on total number of mining queries per round, $p \in (0,1)$ be the probability of success of each mining query, and $\mathtt{cutOff} = \omega(\log(\kappa))$ be the consistency parameter. Let $\mathcal{M}$ be a model whose induced utility $u_{\mathtt{f}}$ has parameters $\mathtt{fpayoff}, \mathtt{breward}, \mathtt{CR}, \mathtt{mcost} \geq 0$. The Bitcoin protocol $\Pi^{\mathcal{B}}$ is strongly attack-payoff secure in $\mathcal{M}$ if $p \cdot \mathtt{breward} \cdot \mathtt{CR} - \mathtt{mcost} > 0$.*

3.2   A First Attempt to Eliminate the Artifact

Although we proved that Bitcoin is strongly attack payoff secure even with a payoff for forking, this is actually not a good sign, as this result does not reflect reality. In reality, attackers do fork blockchains to gain profit via e.g. double-spending transactions. Thus, the fact that we can prove Lemma 1 means that there must be a problem with our assumptions.

Why were we able to prove Lemma 1? It turns out the utility function we used has the weakness that it considers an attacker who does not care about the ephemeral payoff for forking—he can simply obtain more utility via block rewards if he just put in a bit more hashing power for mining. Thus, somewhat counter-intuitively, to model incentives for forking attacks, we must consider utilities that limit the amount of mining an attacker can do.

A first natural instinct may be to incorporate in the utility the (often substantial) initial investment (e.g. cost of buying mining rigs) an attacker must

---

[3] We note that for the simple utility function presented in [BGM+18] other proof techniques could conclude attack-payoff security without the runtime-extension argument. The main point here is to demonstrate the importance of considering the attack duration in the utility function.

make before being able to participate in the blockchain protocol. This turns out to be not only a natural extension, but also a very simple one. Concretely, we capture this investment as *cost of party corruption*: in order to use party for mining, the adversary needs to corrupt him, which corresponds to acquiring its mining equipment. Formally, for each $g \in \mathbb{N}$ define C_g^A as follows: The maximum number of corrupted parties at any round is g. Let $\mathtt{ccost}(g)$ be the cost of event C_g^A, i.e. corrupting g parties. Then we define the utility function:

$$
\begin{aligned}
u_{\mathtt{f,c}}(\Pi, \mathcal{A}) := \sup_{\mathcal{Z} \in \mathrm{ITM}} \Bigg\{ \inf_{\mathcal{S}^{\mathcal{A}} \in \mathcal{C}_{\mathcal{A}}} \Bigg\{ & \sum_{(b,r) \in \mathbb{N}^2} b \cdot \mathtt{breward} \cdot \mathrm{CR} \cdot \Pr[I_{b,r}^A] \\
& - \sum_{(q,r) \in \mathbb{N}^2} q \cdot \mathtt{mcost} \cdot \Pr[W_{q,r}^A] \\
& + \mathtt{fpayoff} \cdot \Pr[K] \\
& - \sum_{g \in \mathbb{N}} \mathtt{ccost}(g) \cdot \Pr[C_g^A] \Bigg\} \Bigg\}.
\end{aligned}
\tag{3}
$$

Interestingly, as we see below, this natural extension is still insufficient to align the model with the reality that forking attacks occur. Indeed, even with this additional cost, we can still prove a result similar Lemma 1. Concretely, the following lemma shows that for $u_{\mathtt{f,c}}$ above, we can prove the statement as the one in Lemma 1 about $\Pi^{\mathcal{B}}$ being attack-payoff secure by again exploiting the artifact of unbounded incentives.

Lemma 2 (Attack payoff security with forking, with cost of corruption). *Let $T_{\mathrm{ub}} > 0$ be the upper bound on total number of mining queries per round, $p \in (0,1)$ be the probability of success of each mining query, and $\mathtt{cutOff} = \omega(\log(\kappa))$ be the consistency parameter. Let $\mathcal{M}$ be the model whose induced utility $u_{\mathtt{f,c}}$ has parameters $\mathtt{fpayoff}, \mathtt{breward}, \mathrm{CR}, \mathtt{mcost} \geq 0$, $\mathtt{ccost}(\cdot) : \mathbb{N} \to \mathbb{R}^+$. The Bitcoin protocol is strongly attack-payoff secure in $\mathcal{M}$ if $p \cdot \mathtt{breward} \cdot \mathrm{CR} - \mathtt{mcost} > 0$.*

3.3 The Source of the Artifact: Unbounded Incentives

Distilling the issue in above lemmas, we observe that that as long as the adversary keeps accumulating rewards as rounds are added to the protocol—i.e., mining remains profitable—he does not care about the payoff for forking: there always exists a polynomial-time, passively mining strategy that simply gains the same amount of utility by mining a bit more. However, not only do real-life attackers in fact profit from forks, even the assumption on the profitability of mining forever is unrealistic: any attacker is at least limited in time by e.g. the anticipated age of the universe, and cannot, in practice, keep accumulating utility in perpetuity.

Thus, to make accurate prediction about the attackability of a blockchain protocol the utility function must exclude the eternal profitability of passive mining. We generalize this intuition, by defining the notion of *unbounded incentives*:

a utility function has *unbounded incentives* if there is an adversarial strategy $\mathcal{A} \in \mathbb{A}_{\mathbf{fr}}$ such that for any polynomial $h(\kappa)$, $\mathcal{A}$ can gain better payoff than $h(\kappa)$. (Conversely, we will say that a utility has bounded incentives if there is no such passive adversary.).

It is straighforward to verify that the utilities we have seen so far have unbounded incentives, which explains the effect of the artifact exploited in the above lemmas. In fact, in the following there is a simple argument for a generic statement about the strong attack-payoff security of utility functions that have unbounded incentives.

Lemma 3. *Let $\mathcal{M}$ be a model inducing a utility function u_A. Assume for any adversary $\mathcal{A}$, in any real execution of the protocol his payoff is polynomially-bounded.[4] If u_A has unbounded incentives for a protocol Π, then Π is strongly attack-payoff secure for $\mathcal{M}$.*

4   An RPD Analysis of Forks

In this section, we will tune our utility function to avoid the issue of *unbounded incentives* isolated in the previous section. A straw man approach would be to make `fpayoff` a super-polynomial function of the security parameter. But this would imply a very unnatural assumption, which, intuitively, corresponds to ensuring that the polynomially-bounded adversaries are *always* incentivized to fork. This would have the opposite effect and introduce a different artifact: it would make attack-payoff security impossible, and making a 51% attack always a dominant strategy no matter the systems parameters, contradicting the observable fact that many blockchains have not fallen to 51% attacks.

Instead, we make `breward` a function of time, which captures e.g., inflation, or simply that the adversary only plans to stay in the system for a limited amount of time. We refer to this adaptation of $u_{\mathrm{f,c}}$ as u_{buy}:

$$u_{\mathrm{buy}}(\Pi, \mathcal{A}) := \sup_{\mathcal{Z} \in \mathrm{ITM}} \left\{ \inf_{\mathcal{S}^{\mathcal{A}} \in \mathcal{C}_{\mathcal{A}}} \left\{ \sum_{(b,r) \in \mathbb{N}^2} b \cdot \mathtt{breward}(r) \cdot \mathrm{CR} \cdot \Pr[I^{\mathtt{A}}_{b,r}] \right.\right.$$

$$- \sum_{(q,r) \in \mathbb{N}^2} q \cdot \mathtt{mcost} \cdot \Pr[W^{\mathtt{A}}_{q,r}]$$

$$+ \mathtt{fpayoff} \cdot \Pr[K]$$

$$\left.\left. - \sum_{g \in \mathbb{N}} \mathtt{ccost}(g) \cdot \Pr[C^{\mathtt{A}}_g] \right\} \right\}. \quad (4)$$

We also define a version of this utility u_{rent} (formally defined in full version [BLZ21]), which models the attacker renting hashing queries by replacing

---

[4] This is true for the utility function $u^{\mathcal{B}}_A$ in Eq. 1 (as well as the utility functions we will consider)—no adversary can get payoff that is superpolynomial in the run time of the execution.

mcost with parameter rcost (rent cost) and setting ccost$(\cdot) = 0$. Renting especially has been observed in real attacks, such as the August 2020 attacks on Ethereum Classic [For].

Note that while breward is a function of time, we let the cost of a mining query, that is mcost/rcost, remain constant. We do so to model the attacker's anticipated monetary budget to launch and maintain an attack, such as the costs for renting a certain amount of hashing power (which are generally paid upfront), or cost of electricity (which realistically appears to be relatively stable). Further, the parameter fpayoff should be seen as an abstract excess payoff for the attacker arising from forking that is able to capture various use-cases. In the prototypical (double-spend) example where the attacker sells some coins for fiat currency and later tries to regain the coins with a successful attack, it corresponds to this extra fiat inflow gained prior to attacking the blockchain. We note that the utility functions could be tweaked to allow for all parameters to be time-dependent without changing the results qualitatively as long as the relations among the parameters required by the definitions and theorems (which are time-dependent in our treatment already) still hold.

To capture realistic utilities, we restrict to instances of our utility function which satisfy what we call *limited horizons* (Definition 5). Roughly, limited horizons constrains utilities by requiring that passive mining eventually becomes unprofitable. Recall that in light of the St. Petersburg Paradox discussed in the introduction, rational parties become increasingly reluctant to invest some monetary budget for potential rewards gained only later in a randomized process (e.g. due to uncertainty about the future or other specific utility-relevant considerations like relative inflation between several quantities). We cast this general idea as a rather simple condition based on our utility function.

After defining limited horizons, in Sect. 4.1, we will first address a technical challenge imposed when payoff-parameters in the utility functions are non-constant. Then, in Sect. 4.2 we show that limited horizons implies bounded incentives (i.e., the opposite of unbounded incentives) through Lemma 5. More precisely, limited horizon is a strong negation[5] of unbounded incentives. Looking ahead, we will prove that when utilities have limited horizons, there is always a large enough payoff for forking such that (strong) attack-payoff security is broken. Informally, a utility function u_{buy} (resp. u_{rent}) has limited horizons if there is a time limit after which passive mining becomes unprofitable.

Definition 5 (Limited Horizons). *We say u_{buy} in Eq. 4 (resp. u_{rent}, formally defined in our full version), parameterized by* breward$(\cdot) : \mathbb{N} \to \mathbb{R}_{\geq 0}$, mcost, fpayoff ≥ 0, *and non-decreasing function* ccost$(\cdot) : \mathbb{N} \to \mathbb{R}_{\geq 0}$ *(resp.* breward$(\cdot) : \mathbb{N} \to \mathbb{R}_{\geq 0}$, rcost, fpayoff ≥ 0*) satisfies* limited horizons *(resp.* limited horizons with renting*) if* breward$(\cdot)$ *is a non-increasing function such that* $\exists x \in \mathbb{N} : p \cdot \mathsf{CR} \cdot \mathsf{breward}(x) < \mathsf{mcost}$.

---

[5] Note that the *strong negation* of an assertion A is one which implies $\neg A$, but is not necessarily implied by $\neg A$.

Remark. Technically, u_{rent} is a special case of the case of u_{buy} (since the utilities are the same if we set $\mathtt{mcost} = \mathtt{rcost}$ and set $\mathtt{ccost}(\cdot) = 0$); however semantically they are different: $\mathtt{rcost}$ represents the cost of renting a hashing query, which usually is much higher than $\mathtt{mcost}$ which represents the cost (e.g. electricity) of an adversary mining with his own equipment. Nevertheless, to reduce redundancies in the technical sections, we will analyze the utility u_{buy} in Eq. 4 (with a general $\mathtt{ccost}(\cdot)$, including when $\mathtt{ccost}(\cdot) = 0$), and state the results for the renting case as corollaries.

4.1 Addressing Technical Issue of Non-constant Payoff for Block Rewards

In this section, we address a technical issue with considering a non-constant $\mathtt{breward}$—recall that in limited horizons, $\mathtt{breward}$ is a non-increasing function of time/round number. By our definition (which follows that of [BGM+18]), the event $I_{b,r}^{\mathtt{A}}$ happens when b blocks are placed into the ledger of some honest party. This is intuitive—the block reward should be given only when the block is "confirmed" to be in the ledger. However, there is a delay between when a block is broadcasted, and when it makes it into the common prefix of an honest chain. This delay is a random variable which depends on the amount of (honest and corrupt) hashing power in the protocol, the network delay, and the adversary's strategy. Fortunately, we can lower and upper bound such a delay (which we denote by t_{lb}, t_{ub} respectively), as we show in the following lemma. This will in turn allow us to avoid the complication of analyzing when blocks enter the ledger state and instead analyze when locks broadcasted by the adversary to honest parties (whose events are easier to analyze). Note that we choose to analyze time-of-block-broadcast, instead of time-of-block-creation, since the adversary may choose to withhold successfully-mined blocks instead of broadcasting them immediately, making time-of-broadcast more suitable for incorporating such adversarial strategies.

We first define a useful quantity $t_{\delta}^{\Delta}(q)$. As we will see, this quantity, which is derived from the *chain growth* property of Nakamoto-style blockchains, is the maximum time for honest chains to grow by $\mathtt{cutOff}$ blocks, given that in each round there are at least q honest mining queries.

Definition 6 (Maximum time to grow $\mathtt{cutOff}$ blocks). *For network delay* Δ, *and* $p, \delta \in (0,1)$, *we denote* $t_{\delta}^{\Delta}(q) := \frac{\mathtt{cutOff}}{(1-\delta)\gamma}$, *where* $\gamma := \frac{h}{1+h\Delta}$ *and* $h := 1 - (1-p)^q$.

Let $t_{lb} := 0$ and $t_{ub} := t_{\delta}^{\Delta}(\mathrm{T}_{\mathrm{ub}})$. Let $B_{b,r}^{\mathtt{A}}$ denote the event: At round r, the adversary broadcasts b blocks made by parties that are corrupted at the time of the blocks' creation, and which are part of the longest chain at round r. Let u_{buy}^{h} be u_{buy} except $\sum_{(b,r)\in\mathbb{N}^2} b \cdot \mathtt{breward}(r) \cdot \mathrm{CR} \cdot \Pr[I_{b,r}^{\mathtt{A}}]$ (which considers time of block confirmation) is replaced with $\sum_{(b,r)\in\mathbb{N}^2} b \cdot \mathtt{breward}(r + t_{lb}) \cdot \mathrm{CR} \cdot \Pr[B_{b,r}^{\mathtt{A}}]$ $= \sum_{(b,r)\in\mathbb{N}^2} b \cdot \mathtt{breward}(r) \cdot \mathrm{CR} \cdot \Pr[B_{b,r}^{\mathtt{A}}]$ (which considers time of block broadcast).

Similarly, let u^l_{buy} replace the same term in u_{buy} with $\sum_{(b,r)\in\mathbb{N}^2} b \cdot \text{breward}(r + t_{ub}) \cdot \text{CR} \cdot \Pr[B^A_{b,r}]$. (See full version [BLZ21] for formal definitions.)

The following lemma tells us that instead of analyzing the utility function defined on when a block is confirmed in the ledger we can instead approximate by only analyzing when a block is broadcasted. This will be helpful in our proof of Lemma 5 on the utility of the optimal front-running, passive adversary.

Lemma 4 (Translating time-of-block-confirmation to time-of-block-broadcast: u^h_{buy} and u^l_{buy}). *For any utility function satisfying limited horizons (in fact, we only require that $\text{breward}(\cdot)$ is a non-increasing function), satisfies the following: For all adversaries $\mathcal{A}$, and front-running, passive $\mathcal{A}'$,*

$$u_{\text{buy}}(\Pi^{\mathcal{B}}, \mathcal{A}) \leq u^h_{\text{buy}}(\Pi^{\mathcal{B}}, \mathcal{A}) + \text{negl}(\kappa) \quad and$$

$$u_{\text{buy}}(\Pi^{\mathcal{B}}, \mathcal{A}') + \text{negl}(\kappa) \geq u^l_{\text{buy}}(\Pi^{\mathcal{B}}, \mathcal{A}').$$

Proof. The first inequality is obvious: By limited horizons, giving block rewards using time-of-block-broadcast (i.e., u^h_{buy}) gives the attacker a higher payoff.

The second inequality: Let the environment be one which maintains T_{ub} parties in each round after r. The bound follows then from the chain-growth lower bound which states the minimum chain length increase during a time period, depending on the honest parties' hashing power and the network delay (cf. [BMTZ17,PSs17]). This concludes the proof. $\qquad\square$

4.2 Optimal Utility of Front-Running, Passive Adversaries

We show in this section if a utility satisfies limited horizons, then it also satisfies bounded incentives. We do so by proving the following optimal utility of a passive, front-running adversary. We define u^h_{honest} and u^l_{honest} which, as we will see in Lemma 5 below, are the upper and lower bounds on the optimal utility obtained by a front running, passive adversary in $\Pi^{\mathcal{B}}$.

Definition 7 (Bounds u^h_{honest} and u^l_{honest} for optimal front-running, passive adversary). *We define the quantity*

$$u^h_{\text{honest}}(\text{breward}, \text{CR}, \text{mcost}, \text{ccost})$$

$$:= g \cdot p \cdot \text{CR} \cdot \sum_{x=1}^{t} [\text{breward}(x + t_{lb}) - \text{mcost}] - \text{ccost}(g)$$

with

$$t := \arg\max_{x\in\mathbb{N}}(p \cdot \text{CR} \cdot \text{breward}(x + t_{lb}) \geq \text{mcost}),$$

$$g := \arg\max_{g\in[0,\mathsf{T}_{ub}]}(mg - \text{ccost}(g)),$$

$$for\ m := \sum_{x=1}^{t}(p \cdot \text{CR} \cdot \text{breward}(x + t_{lb}) - \text{mcost}),$$

and the quantity

$$u_{\text{honest}}^{\text{l}}(\text{breward}, \text{CR}, \text{mcost}, \text{ccost})$$

$$:= g \cdot p \cdot \text{CR} \cdot \sum_{x=1}^{t} [\text{breward}(x + t_{ub}) - \text{mcost}] - \text{ccost}(g)$$

with

$$t := \arg\max_{x \in \mathbb{N}} (p \cdot \text{CR} \cdot \text{breward}(x + t_{ub}) \geq \text{mcost}),$$

$$g := \arg\max_{g \in [0, T_{ub}]} (mg - \text{ccost}(g)),$$

$$\text{for } m := \sum_{x=1}^{t} (p \cdot \text{CR} \cdot \text{breward}(x + t_{ub}) - \text{mcost}).$$

We simplify the above upper and lower bounds on the optimal front-running, passive adversaries as $u_{\text{honest}}^{\text{h}}$ and $u_{\text{honest}}^{\text{l}}$, when the parameters to the utility function are clear from context. As discussed before, although we prove the optimal passive adversary for u_{buy}, the renting case for utility u_{rent} is a direct corollary by setting $\text{ccost}(\cdot) = 0$ and $\text{mcost} = \text{rcost}$.

Intuitively, the following lemma is established by proving that (1) due to limited horizons, there is a fixed time t after which an optimal passive adversary will not mine, and (2) it is optimal for a passive adversary to corrupt parties statically. Then, we can re-write the utility of a front-running, passive adversary as a function of his running time t, and the number of parties he corrupts g. Optimizing for t and g gives us the optimal utility of this passive adversary.

Lemma 5 (Optimal utility of a front-running passive adversary, for incentives with limited horizons). *Let $T_{ub} > 0$ be the upper bound on total number of mining queries per round, $p \in (0,1)$ be the probability of success of each mining query, and $\text{cutOff} = \omega(\log(\kappa))$ be the consistency parameter. Given parameters such that u_{buy} satisfies limited horizons and protocol $\Pi^{\mathcal{B}}$, for $\mathcal{A}$ the optimal adversary in $\mathbb{A}_{fr}$, $u_{\text{buy}}(\Pi^{\mathcal{B}}, \mathcal{A}) \leq u_{\text{honest}}^{\text{h}} + \text{negl}(\kappa)$ and $u_{\text{buy}}(\Pi^{\mathcal{B}}, \mathcal{A}) + \text{negl}(\kappa) \geq u_{\text{honest}}^{\text{l}}$*

This lemma directly implies that any utility with limited horizons also has bounded incentives.

5   Analyzing 51% Attacks

We can now utilize our above framework to analyze one of the most common types of forking attacks, known as 51% *double-spending* attack [Inv]. We analyze a range of parameters for utility functions with limited horizons, for which a 51% double-spending adversary breaks the strong attack-payoff security of protocol $\Pi^{\mathcal{B}}$ (formalized by Theorem 1). In more detail, first we will show a general lemma relating the number of honest/adversarial hashes per round, to the time it takes to fork with a 51% double-spending attack (Lemma 6). Then, in Theorem 1 we will show that if the payoff for a successful attack (fpayoff) satisfies certain conditions, then an adversary performing a 51% double-spending attack achieves better utility than any passive-mining strategy. This fpayoff is quantified as a function of the parameters of the protocol and the utility function.

We call the following strategy a *51% double-spending attack*: The adversary obtains any majority fraction ("51%" is just a colloquial name) of the hashing power, and uses it to secretly mine an extension of the currently longest chain (i.e., keeping successful blocks private to himself), and which he will release after some time. We say that a 51% double-spending attack is *successful* if, when released, the adversary's secret chain is at least as long as the honest chain, and causes the ledger state of some honest party to fork (which in reality corresponds to a roll-back of more than cutOff blocks, in order to adopt the released attack chain). If this happens, some transactions on the reversed blockchain ledger state may become orphaned (no longer part of the ledger state), thus allowing the attacker to double-spend his coins.

5.1   Time to Fork

We start by showing a general lemma that relates the amount of honest and adversarial hashing power in a system, to the time to cause a fork via a 51% double-spending attack. That is, how long it takes for an adversary with majority hashing power to secretly create a chain that, when released, would cause an honest party to roll back, or discard, more than cutOff blocks of his own chain in order to adopt the new one.

Definition 8. *We say that an adversary $\mathcal{A}$ causes a fork in a protocol Π if, except with negligible probability in κ, all simulators $\mathcal{S}^{\mathcal{A}} \in \mathcal{C}_{\mathcal{A}}$ (i.e. those which in fact simulate $\mathcal{A}$ according to UC emulation) use the FORK command[6].*

The FORK command, which allows forking the confirmed ledger state (and hence corresponds to rolling back more than cutOff blocks in the real world), is necessary and sufficient to simulate an adversary who succeeds in a 51% double-spending attack. We compute the (upper bound) time for a 51% double-spending adversary to fork, which is obtained by the time for honest parties to grow their chain by cutOff blocks (for which we can use guaranteed chain-growth of Nakamoto-style blockchains. Since the adversary has more hashing power (and thus more random oracle queries that can be issued sequentially) than the honest party, and since we assume cutOff $= \omega(\log(\kappa))$ and that the adversary does not interfere with the honest parties' mining, this implies that the adversary's secretly-mined chain will be longer than the honest parties' chain, and be the only source for a large rollback, with overwhelming probability in κ.

---

[6] If $\mathcal{C}_{\mathcal{A}} = \emptyset$, then in any case by definition the utility of $\mathcal{A}$ is infinite.

Lemma 6 (Time to Fork with 51% Attack). *Let* cutOff $= \omega(\log(\kappa))$, $[r, r+ t]$ *be any time interval (starting from some round $r \geq 0$) of $t \geq 1$ rounds, $\Delta \geq 1$ be the network delay, $p \in (0,1)$ the success probability of one mining query.*

Then for all $\delta, \delta' \in (0,1)$, $\alpha \geq \frac{1+\delta}{1-\delta}$, and $q \geq 1$ such that $t \geq t_{\delta'}^{\Delta}(q)$ (Definition 6) the following holds. Suppose in time interval $[r, r + t]$, (1) the honest parties make at least q mining queries per round, and (2) in total they make at most q_t queries. Then, the adversary $\mathcal{A}$ who performs a 51% double-spending attack for at least αq_t queries during the time interval and then releases his secretly-mined chain, causes a fork in the protocol $\Pi^{\mathcal{B}}$.[7]

A visualization. In Fig. 1, the (upper-bound) time to fork with exactly 51% corruption, is graphed against the total number of rigs in the system. The graph uses the formula from Lemma 6. We use current parameters for Ethereum Classic as the source of the concrete parameters for this figure, and refer the reader to our full version for more details.

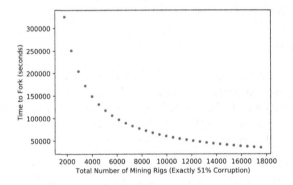

Fig. 1. Time to create a fork via 51% attack, versus the total number of mining rigs. Here the adversary corrupts exactly 51%.

5.2   Payoff of 51% Double-Spending Attacks

In this section, we prove Theorem 1 and its corollary Theorem 2, which quantify the size of the payoff for double-spending, under which a 51% double-spending attack can break strong attack-payoff security. That is, the attacker achieves better utility than *any* passive mining strategy. While one may think that it is always profitable to attack if there is no assumption on the honest majority of hashing power, there are a few things that may deter an attacker. For example, the costs of buying or renting mining equipment for the attack may become too high compared to the diminished block rewards as time goes on. Our statement below quantifies an amount of payoff for forking (e.g. how much an attacker

---

[7] More concretely, he succeeds except with probability at most $\exp\left(-\frac{\delta^2 \alpha \mu}{2+\delta}\right) + \exp\left(-\frac{\delta^2 \mu}{2}\right) + \exp\left(-\frac{\delta'^2 t\gamma}{2+\delta}\right)$.

can double-spend) to incentivize a 51% double-spending attack. Intuitively, the result below says that as long as the payoff for forking (`fpayoff`) is larger than the loss of utility from withholding blocks and corrupting a large number of parties to perform the attack, then there is a 51% attack strategy that is more profitable than *any* front-running, passive adversary.

Theorem 1 (51% Double-Spending Attacks that Break (Strong) Attack-Payoff Security (u_{buy})). *Let $T_{\mathsf{ub}} > 2$ be the upper bound on total number of mining queries per round, $p \in (0,1)$ be the probability of success of each mining query, and `cutOff` $= \omega(\log(\kappa))$ be the consistency parameter. Then, the protocol $\Pi^{\mathcal{B}}$ is not attack-payoff secure/strongly attack-payoff secure in any attack model $\mathcal{M}$ whose induced utility function u_{buy} satisfies limited horizons, if for some $\delta \in (0,1)$, $\alpha > 1$ and $g = \frac{T_{\mathsf{ub}}}{1+\alpha}$ the following holds:*

$$\texttt{fpayoff} > u_{\mathrm{honest}}^{\mathrm{h}} - \alpha \cdot g \cdot t_\delta^\Delta(g) \left(p \cdot \texttt{CR} \cdot \texttt{breward}(t_\delta^\Delta(g) + t_{ub}) - \texttt{mcost} \right) - \texttt{ccost}(\alpha g).$$

We state the case where the adversary mines with rented equipment (and uses utility function u_{rent}), as a direct corollary to Theorem 1.

Theorem 2 (51% Double-Spending Attacks that Break (Strong) Attack-Payoff Security (u_{rent})). *Let $T_{\mathsf{ub}} > 2$ be the upper bound on total number of mining queries per round, $p \in (0,1)$ be the probability of success of each mining query, and `cutOff` $= \omega(\log(\kappa))$ be the consistency parameter. Then, the protocol $\Pi^{\mathcal{B}}$ is not attack-payoff secure/strongly attack-payoff secure in any attack model $\mathcal{M}$ whose induced utility function u_{rent} satisfies limited horizons, if for any $\delta \in (0,1)$, $\alpha > 1$ and $g = \frac{T_{\mathsf{ub}}}{1+\alpha}$ the following holds:*

$$\texttt{fpayoff} > u_{\mathrm{honest}}^{\mathrm{h}} - \alpha \cdot g \cdot t_\delta^\Delta(g) \left(p \cdot \texttt{CR} \cdot \texttt{breward}(t_\delta^\Delta(g) + t_{ub}) - \texttt{mcost} \right).$$

5.3 Visualizations with Concrete Values

We will visualize Theorems 1 and 2 through Figs. 2 and 3. We consider two utility functions, one where the adversary buys mining equipment, and one where the adversary rents. We then graph the utilities of passive/non-passive adversaries, against the maximum fraction of corrupted parties. The concrete parameters are based on current (as of writing, Feb. 2021) parameters for Ethereum Classic. The outline is given in our full version.

In Fig. 2, we consider the incentives of a 51% attacker who rents his hashing power, using the price for renting of 1.96 BTC/TH/day (Bitcoin per terahash per day), at $50,000$/BTC. In this case, it is in fact not profitable to mine passively (and thus the optimal passive strategy is to not mine at all). However, when the adversary corrupts more than majority of hashing power, it may become profitable to mine in order to create a fork. It is less profitable for the adversary to corrupt a larger fraction of the parties, as cost of renting becomes too high. We remark that even when it is not profitable to mine (passively) using rented rigs, this does not exclude incentivizing honest parties from mining with e.g., bought equipment.

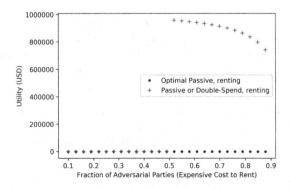

Fig. 2. Utility of the passive/51% double-spending attacker who rents hashing power, versus the fraction of adversarial parties. Here we consider an expensive cost to rent hashing power (1.96 BTC/TH/day, at $50,000/BTC).

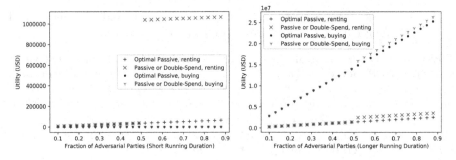

Fig. 3. Utility of the passive/51% double-spending attacker versus the fraction of adversarial parties. We consider an attacker who runs for a short duration (1 week) and a long duration (40 weeks).

In the next two examples in Fig. 3, we compare the utility of the attacker who mines with purchased rigs, and one who mines with rented rigs. For the attack who buys hashing power, each rig costs $3000, and mining (electricity) costs $0.000047/s. For the attacker who rents, for more interesting comparisons we consider a cheaper cost to rent hashing power (1.96 BTC/TH/day, at a cheaper $22,000/BTC). We consider two scenarios: the attacker either (1) only plans to mine for a short duration of one week, or (2) plans to mine for a longer duration of 40 weeks (time is expressed in seconds in the code). For the purposes of the graphs, we account for the possible variance of Bitcoin-USD exchange rates by using an average exchange rate over the relevant period of time. In either case, to more closely model reality, we restrict the duration of the attack, where the adversary may obtain a majority of hashing power, to 3 days (which, in the code, simply means we do not show attacks that last longer than 3 days).

We see a big difference between the two scenarios. In the short duration case, it is much more profitable to mine or attack with rented rigs. In fact, it is not even profitable to fork using purchased rigs, as the cost of purchase is higher than the payoff for double-spending. The long duration case is the opposite. Although it may be profitable to mine in both cases, it is vastly more profitable to mine and attack with purchased rigs than rented rigs. This agrees with our intuition and reality: the high initial investment of buying mining equipment is offset in the long run by the lower cost of mining. Moreover, an attacker who is only interested in mining in order to perform a 51% attack for a short time is incentivized to use hash renting services.

6 Mitigating 51% Attacks

In previous sections, we studied utility functions with limited horizons, in which an attacker is incentivized to perform a 51% double-spending attack and break (strong) attack-payoff security. In this section, we turn to analyzing how to *defend* against 51% attacks. Specifically, given an attacker's utility function with limited horizons, and a cut-off parameter cutOff that achieves security in the honest majority setting, we show a way to amplify cutOff to obtain security against a rational (and possibly dishonest majority) attacker.

To show attack payoff security, one must show that for *any* adversarial strategy attacking the protocol, there is another adversary who attacks the dummy protocol with access to the ideal ledger functionality $\mathcal{G}_{\text{LEDGER}}$[8], which achieves the same or better utility.

Even more difficult, we place very few restrictions on the adversary: he may corrupt any fraction of parties (e.g. more than majority) and perform any currently known (e.g. block withholding) or unknown strategy. The only restriction we place on the attacker is that he is incentive-driven. Fortunately, a rational attacker is limited by his utility function. As we show, given a utility function satisfying limited horizon, we are able to bound the amount of mining an incentive-driven adversary will do, even in presence of a payoff for forking. Then, by choosing a large enough consistency parameter cutOff, we ensure that attackers are disincentivized from creating a fork.

More specifically: We first present in Sect. 6.1 a result that shows that if an adversary's hasing resources are limited by a budget B, then there is a bound on the interval of rounds where the blockchain is at risk of a consistency failure (Lemma 7). For this, we apply a result from [BGK+20] that, roughly, shows how fast a blockchain's consistency can recover after an attack by an adversary with a given budget (the self-healing property of Bitcoin). Based on this fundamental property, we present in Sect. 6.2, the main result of the section: Given a utility function with limited horizons, we show a condition on the parameter cutOff, depending only on the utility function and protocol parameters, such that $\Pi^{\mathcal{B}}$ is attack-payoff secure. To do so, we show that an adversary who spends too much budget will begin to lose utility (Lemma 8), and then combine this result with that of Sect. 6.1.

---

[8] Recall this is the ledger functionality that has consistency and liveness (following from the liveness results in [BGK+20]), but since we will amplify the cut-off parameter cutOff, we achieve less good parameters.

6.1   Budget to Vulnerability Period

Assume an instance of the Bitcoin backbone protocol with cut-off parameter ℓ. We distinguish here between ℓ and `cutOff` for clarity, since we will eventually amplify ℓ to obtain our final cut-off parameter `cutOff`.

Under the honest majority condition, we know that a consistency failure (expressed as the probability that blocks which are ℓ deep in an honest parties adopted chain can be reverted) appears with probability negligible in ℓ (and consequently also in any security parameter κ as long as $\ell = \omega(\log(\kappa))$). We now recall (and state a simple corollary from) the result from [BGK+20], which defines a relationship between an adversary's violation of honest-majority (measured as a so-called budget B by which it can violate the honest-majority condition) and the time until Bitcoin (and more generally, Nakamoto-style PoW chains) self-heals after the adversary returns to below 50% hashing power. That is, until Bitcoin can again guarantee consistency for the part of the chain that is at least ℓ blocks deep in a longest chain held by an honest party. The self-healing time depends on the budget and the parameter ℓ. Recall that θ_{pow} is the usual security threshold for Bitcoin as explained in Sect. 2.1.

Definition 9 $((\theta_{pow}, \epsilon, \mathsf{T_{lb}}, \mathsf{T_{ub}}, B)$-**adversary** *[BGK+20]).* Let $\theta_{pow}, \epsilon \in (0,1)$, $\mathsf{T_{lb}}, \mathsf{T_{ub}}, B \in \mathbb{N}$. A $(\theta_{pow}, \epsilon, \mathsf{T_{lb}}, \mathsf{T_{ub}}, B)$-*adversary*[9] *satisfying the following: At every round i, let n_a^i and n_h^i be the mining queries made by corrupt and honest parties in this round. Then, (1) For all i, $\mathsf{T_{lb}} \le n_a^i + n_h^i \le \mathsf{T_{ub}}$, and (2) For all i, $n_a^i \le (1 - \epsilon) \cdot \theta_{pow} \cdot n_h^i + B_i$, where $B_i \ge 0$ and $\sum_i B_i = B$.*

We say the adversary attacks between rounds $a < b$ if $B_i = 0$ for any $i < a$ or $i > b$ (i.e. he spends all his budget between rounds a and b).

We say an adversary spends budget B over t rounds, if the adversary has budget B, and only spends it in rounds $r_1 < r_2 < \cdots < r_t$, such that $\sum_i B_{r_i} = B$.

The behavior of a blockchain protocol under an attack by an $(\theta_{pow}, \epsilon, \mathsf{T_{lb}}, \mathsf{T_{ub}}, B)$-adversary is described by a *vulnerability period*. The vulnerability period is an upper bound on number of rounds before and after an adversary performs the attack, such that protocol is still at risk of a (non-negligible) consistency failure.

Definition 10 (Consistency self-healing property and vulnerability period *[BGK+20]).* *A protocol is self-healing with vulnerability period (τ_l, τ_h) with respect to consistency, and against a $(\theta_{pow}, \epsilon, \mathsf{T_{lb}}, \mathsf{T_{ub}}, B)$-adversary who attacks between rounds (a, b), if the consistency failure event $\mathsf{ConsFail}_\ell(r)$ occurs except with at most negligible probability unless $r \in [\rho_\alpha - \tau_l, \rho_\beta + \tau_h]$. $\mathsf{ConsFail}_\ell(r)$ is defined as the event that ℓ-consistency is violated in an execution for rounds (r, r'), w.r.t. some round $r' > r$, and any two pairs of honest parties.*

In other words, outside of these "dangerous" rounds $[a - \tau_l, b + \tau_h]$, chains adopted by honest parties are guaranteed to diverge by at the most recent ℓ blocks. Below, [BGK+20] gives a characterization of the vulnerability period in terms of the budget B.

---

[9] Here the environment is also included in this statement.

Theorem 3 (*[BGK+20]*). *A Nakamoto-style PoW blockchain with an upper bound T_{ub} of hashing queries per round, maximum network delay Δ, success probability p, and cut-off parameter ℓ satisfies the consistency self-healing property with vulnerability period $(\tau_l, \tau_h) = (O(B), O(B) + O(\ell))$ against any $(\theta_{pow}, \epsilon, T_{lb}, T_{ub}, B)$-adversary, for any $\epsilon, T_{lb} > 0$.*

The vulnerability period only bounds the number of "bad" rounds before the attack, and after *all* the budget is spent. For our treatment, we consider a more applicable version of the vulnerability period. In Lemma 7, we show the maximum number of consecutive rounds where ConsFail may occur, by applying the above theorem in a piece-wise fashion. For example, if the adversary spends his budget over a long period of time (e.g., spend a bit of the budget, wait for 2 years, then spend more of his budget), the theorem is not directly suitable for our needs, but it is possible to isolate those "spending" rounds and applying the theorem to each such region. Then, since the total hashing power in the system is bounded, we can use this maximum consecutive "bad" rounds to bound the maximum number of blocks that can be rolled back at any given round.

Lemma 7 (Max consecutive consistency failure rounds and associated number of blocks and rollback). *In the same setting as above in Theorem 3, except with negligible probability the following holds: for any adversary with budget B, spent over t rounds (that is, for t different rounds i it holds that $B_i > 0$), there is a maximum number $R(B, t, \ell) = O(B) + O(\ell t)$ of consecutive rounds r_j where $\mathrm{ConsFail}_\ell(r_j)$ occurs, during which at most $W(B, t, \ell) = 2T_{ub}p \cdot R(B, t, \ell)$ blocks are created.*

Looking ahead, this means that at any point in time, prefixes of honest parties' chains must agree (except with negligible probability) when dropping the most recent $W(B, t, \ell) + \ell$ blocks. Here, we omit the dependency on p because we treat it as a constant parameter of the protocol.

6.2   Attack-Payoff Security

In this section we will show the following: For any utility function with limited horizons, we give a characterization of how to adjust the consistency parameter (depending on the protocol parameters and those of the utility function) such that $\Pi^{\mathcal{B}}$ is attack payoff secure. To do so, we will first upper bound the utility of adversaries who spends a total budget B over some time t, given a utility function u_{buy} with limited horizons (Lemma 8, and Corollary 1 for utility function u_{rent}). In Theorem 4, we then combine this lemma with the result of the previous subsection, and present our characterization of parameters for which $\Pi^{\mathcal{B}}$ is attack-payoff secure—i.e. for which forks are disincentivized.

Below, we quantify an upper bound $u_{buy}^{ub}(B, t)$ on the utility of *any* adversary spending budget of at least B over exactly t rounds, assuming the utility function satisfies limited horizons. Why are we interested in this quantity? Recall $W(B, t)$—which informally represents an interval of blocks where consistency might fail—increases with B and t. Looking ahead, we will find a large enough $W(B, t)$ that disincentivizes attacks (i.e., $u_{\text{buy}}^{\text{ub}}(B, t) < 0$). To show that the upper-bound $u_{\text{buy}}^{\text{ub}}(B, t)$ is useful, later we will show that it is possible use it to derive a maximum B, t, which we denote by $\bar{B}, \bar{t}$.

Lemma 8 (Upper bound utility of adversary spending budget at least B, over time t).

Suppose $u_{\text{buy}}(\Pi^{\mathcal{B}}, \mathcal{A})$ satisfies limited horizons. Then an adversary $\mathcal{A}$ with budget at least $B > 0$, and who spends it over exactly $t \geq \frac{B}{T_{\text{ub}} - \bar{n}_a}$ rounds, achieves utility at most $u_{\text{buy}}(\Pi^{\mathcal{B}}, \mathcal{A}) \leq u_{\text{buy}}^{\text{ub}}(B, t)$ where

$$u_{\text{buy}}^{\text{ub}}(B, t) := \sum_{x=1}^{t_h} T_{\text{ub}} \cdot (p \cdot \text{CR} \cdot \text{breward}(x) - \text{mcost})$$

$$+ \sum_{x=t_h+1}^{t} (\bar{n}_a + 1) \cdot (p \cdot \text{CR} \cdot \text{breward}(x) - \text{mcost})$$

$$- \text{ccost}\left(\bar{n}_a + \frac{B}{t}\right) + \text{fpayoff}$$

and where $t_h := \arg\max_{x \in \mathbb{N}}(p \cdot \text{CR} \cdot \text{breward}(x) \geq \text{mcost})$, $\bar{n}_a := \frac{(1-\epsilon) \cdot \theta_{pow} \cdot T_{\text{lb}}}{1+(1-\epsilon) \cdot \theta_{pow}}$.

If $t < \frac{B}{T_{\text{ub}} - \bar{n}_a}$ (in this case it is not possible to spend budget B over t rounds) or $B \leq 0$, then $u_{\text{buy}}^{\text{ub}}(B, t)$ is undefined.

As a corollary, by setting $\text{ccost}(\cdot) = 0$ and $\text{mcost} = \text{rcost}$, we obtain an upper bound on the utility of any adversary who spends at least budget B, assuming the utility function satisfies limited horizons with renting.

Corollary 1. *Suppose $u_{\text{rent}}(\Pi^{\mathcal{B}}, \mathcal{A})$ satisfies limited horizons with renting. Then an adversary $\mathcal{A}$ who spends budget of at least $B > 0$ over exactly $t \geq \frac{B}{T_{\text{ub}} - \bar{n}_a}$ rounds, achieves utility at most $u_{\text{rent}}(\Pi^{\mathcal{B}}, \mathcal{A}) \leq u_{\text{rent}}^{\text{ub}}(B, t)$ where*

$$u_{\text{rent}}^{\text{ub}}(B, t) := \sum_{x=1}^{t_h} T_{\text{ub}} \cdot (p \cdot \text{CR} \cdot \text{breward}(x) - \text{rcost})$$

$$+ \sum_{x=t_h+1}^{t} (\bar{n}_a + 1) \cdot (p \cdot \text{CR} \cdot \text{breward}(x) - \text{rcost}) + \text{fpayoff}$$

and where $t_h := \arg\max_{x \in \mathbb{N}}(p \cdot \text{CR} \cdot \text{breward}(x) \geq \text{rcost})$, $\bar{n}_a := \frac{(1-\epsilon) \cdot \theta_{pow} \cdot T_{\text{lb}}}{1+(1-\epsilon) \cdot \theta_{pow}}$.

A natural question is whether the upper bound $u_{\text{buy}}^{\text{ub}}(B, t)$ and $u_{\text{rent}}^{\text{ub}}(B, t)$ will be useful for bounding B, t. We remark that it is not even trivially clear whether they bounded, as the budget does not limit how many rounds (when honest majority is satisfied) the adversary can mine. Below, we show that there indeed exist a maximum B, t for which $u_{\mathsf{buy}}^{\mathsf{ub}}(B, t) \geq 0$ (resp. $u_{\mathsf{rent}}^{\mathsf{ub}}(B, t) \geq 0$, which we denote by $\bar{B}, \bar{t}$. In our full version, we give examples of $\bar{B}, \bar{t}$ using numbers from Ethereum Classic, Feb. 2021 (same as our other graphs).

Lemma 9. $\bar{B} := \arg\max_{B>0} \left(u_{\mathsf{buy}}^{\mathsf{ub}}(B, \cdot) \geq 0 \right)$ and $\bar{t} := \arg\max_{t>0} \left(u_{\mathsf{buy}}^{\mathsf{ub}}(\cdot, t) \geq 0 \right)$ exist, or $\forall t > 0, u_{\mathsf{buy}}^{\mathsf{ub}}(\cdot, t) < 0$. The same is true when replacing $u_{\mathsf{buy}}^{\mathsf{ub}}$ with $u_{\mathsf{rent}}^{\mathsf{ub}}$ in the statement.

Finally, we can make a general statement about the attack payoff security of protocol $\Pi^{\bar{B}}$ for any utility function satisfying limited horizons. Informally: our utility function limits how much budget B (spent over how many rounds t) any incentive-driven attacker could reasonably have. Then, if the window size is large enough to accommodate the largest of such budgets, the protocol is attack-payoff secure. In the following, $u_{\mathsf{buy}}^{\mathsf{ub}}(B, t)$, $u_{\mathsf{honest}}^{\mathsf{l}}$, and $W(B, t)$ are from Lemma 8, Lemma 5, and Lemma 7 respectively. The equivalent statement for utility function u_{rent} can be obtained by using the corollaries of the results above for the case of renting.

Theorem 4. Let $T_{\mathsf{ub}}, T_{\mathsf{lb}} > 0$ be the upper and lower bounds on total number of mining queries per round and $p \in (0, 1)$ be the probability of success of each mining query and let $\ell = \omega(\log(\kappa))$. Then, $\Pi^{\bar{B}}$ with consistency parameter $\mathtt{cutOff}$ is attack-payoff secure in any model $\mathcal{M}$, whose induced utility u_{buy} satisfies limited horizons, whenever the condition holds that

$$\mathtt{cutOff} \quad > \quad \ell + \max_{(B,t):u_{\mathsf{buy}}^{\mathsf{ub}}(B,t) > u_{\mathsf{honest}}^{\mathsf{l}}} W(B, t, \ell).$$

The same statement is true replacing u_{buy} with u_{rent} and $u_{\mathsf{buy}}^{\mathsf{ub}}$ with $u_{\mathsf{rent}}^{\mathsf{ub}}$.

We remark the protocol is not *strong* attack-payoff secure: Recall a front-running adversary always maximally delays honest parties' messages. Intuitively, this reduces the mining power in the system, which delays the time between a block is broadcasted, and when it becomes part of the ledger. In effect, this reduces the payoff for block rewards for utilities with limited horizons.

Acknowledgment. Yun Lu and Vassilis Zikas acknowledge support from Sunday Group Inc.

References

[AKWW19] Avarikioti, G., Käppeli, L., Wang, Y., Wattenhofer, R.: Bitcoin security under temporary dishonest majority. In: Goldberg, I., Moore, T. (eds.) FC 2019. LNCS, vol. 11598, pp. 466–483. Springer, Cham (2019). https://doi.org/10.1007/978-3-030-32101-7_28

[Ber54] Bernoulli, D.: Exposition of a new theory on the measurement of risk. Econometrica **22**(1), 23–36 (1954)

[BGK+18] Badertscher, C., Gazi, P., Kiayias, A., Russell, A., Zikas, V.: Ouroboros genesis: composable proof-of-stake blockchains with dynamic availability. In: Lie, D., Mannan, M., Backes, M., Wang, X. (eds.) ACM CCS 2018, pp. 913–930. ACM Press, October 2018

[BGK+20] Badertscher, C., Gazi, P., Kiayias, A., Russell, A., Zikas, V.: Consensus redux: distributed ledgers in the face of adversarial supremacy. Cryptology ePrint Archive, Report 2020/1021 (2020). https://eprint.iacr.org/2020/1021

[BGM+18] Badertscher, C., Garay, J., Maurer, U., Tschudi, D., Zikas, V.: But why does it work? A rational protocol design treatment of Bitcoin. In: Nielsen, J.B., Rijmen, V. (eds.) EUROCRYPT 2018. LNCS, vol. 10821, pp. 34–65. Springer, Cham (2018). https://doi.org/10.1007/978-3-319-78375-8_2

[BKKS20] Brünjes, L., Kiayias, A., Koutsoupias, E., Stouka, A.-P.: Reward sharing schemes for stake pools. In: IEEE European Symposium on Security and Privacy, EuroS&P 2020, Genoa, Italy, 7–11 September 2020, pp. 256–275. IEEE (2020)

[BLZ21] Badertscher, C., Lu, Y., Zikas, V.: A rational protocol treatment of 51% attacks. Cryptology ePrint Archive, Report 2021/897 (2021). https://eprint.iacr.org/2021/897

[BMTZ17] Badertscher, C., Maurer, U., Tschudi, D., Zikas, V.: Bitcoin as a transaction ledger: a composable treatment. In: Katz, J., Shacham, H. (eds.) CRYPTO 2017. LNCS, vol. 10401, pp. 324–356. Springer, Cham (2017). https://doi.org/10.1007/978-3-319-63688-7_11

[Bud18] Budish, E.: The economic limits of Bitcoin and the Blockchain. Technical report, National Bureau of Economic Research (2018)

[But13] Buterin, V.: A next-generation smart contract and decentralized application platform (2013). https://github.com/ethereum/wiki/wiki/White-Paper

[Can01] Canetti, R.: Universally composable security: a new paradigm for cryptographic protocols. In: 42nd FOCS, pp. 136–145. IEEE Computer Society Press, October 2001

[CCWrao20] Chung, K.-M., Hubert Chan, T.-H., Wen, T., Shi, E. (random author ordering): Game-theoretically fair leader election in o(log log n) rounds under majority coalitions. Cryptology ePrint Archive, Report 2020/1591 (2020). https://eprint.iacr.org/2020/1591

[CKWN16] Carlsten, M., Kalodner, H.A., Matthew Weinberg, S., Narayanan, A.: On the instability of Bitcoin without the block reward. In: Weippl, E.R., Katzenbeisser, S., Kruegel, C., Myers, A.C., Halevi, S. (eds.) ACM CCS 2016, pp. 154–167. ACM Press, October 2016

[CM19] Chen, J., Micali, S.: Algorand: a secure and efficient distributed ledger. Theor. Comput. Sci. **777**, 155–183 (2019)

[Coia] 51% attacks archives. https://www.coindesk.com/tag/51-attack. publisher=CoinDesk

[Coib] Ethereum classic's mess solution won't provide 'robust' security against 51% attacks: Report. https://www.coindesk.com/ethereum-classic-mess-security-51-attacks-report. publisher=CoinDesk

[DPS19] Daian, P., Pass, R., Shi, E.: Snow White: robustly reconfigurable consensus and applications to provably secure proof of stake. In: Goldberg, I., Moore, T. (eds.) FC 2019. LNCS, vol. 11598, pp. 23–41. Springer, Cham (2019). https://doi.org/10.1007/978-3-030-32101-7_2

[ES14]   Eyal, I., Sirer, E.G.: Majority is not enough: Bitcoin mining is vulnera-
          ble. In: Christin, N., Safavi-Naini, R. (eds.) FC 2014. LNCS, vol. 8437,
          pp. 436–454. Springer, Heidelberg (2014). https://doi.org/10.1007/978-
          3-662-45472-5_28
[Eya15]   Eyal, I.: The miner's dilemma. In: 2015 IEEE Symposium on Security
          and Privacy, pp. 89–103. IEEE Computer Society Press, May 2015
[For]   Rented hash power for 51% attacks is a 'huge vulnerability' for proof-
          of-work blockchains, says etc labs ceo. https://forkast.news/hash-
          power-51-attack-rent-huge-vulnerability-proof-of-work-blockchain/.
          publisher=Forkast
[GKL15]   Garay, J., Kiayias, A., Leonardos, N.: The Bitcoin backbone protocol:
          analysis and applications. In: Oswald, E., Fischlin, M. (eds.) EURO-
          CRYPT 2015. LNCS, vol. 9057, pp. 281–310. Springer, Heidelberg (2015).
          https://doi.org/10.1007/978-3-662-46803-6_10
[GKM+13] Garay, J.A., Katz, J., Maurer, U., Tackmann, B., Zikas, V.: Rational
          protocol design: cryptography against incentive-driven adversaries. In:
          54th FOCS, pp. 648–657. IEEE Computer Society Press, October 2013
[GKO+20] Garay, J., Kiayias, A., Ostrovsky, R.M., Panagiotakos, G., Zikas, V.:
          Resource-restricted cryptography: revisiting MPC bounds in the proof-
          of-work era. In: Canteaut, A., Ishai, Y. (eds.) EUROCRYPT 2020. LNCS,
          vol. 12106, pp. 129–158. Springer, Cham (2020). https://doi.org/10.1007/
          978-3-030-45724-2_5
[GKW+16] Gervais, A., Karame, G.O., Wüst, K., Glykantzis, V., Ritzdorf, H., Cap-
          kun, S.: On the security and performance of proof of work blockchains.
          In: Weippl, E.R., Katzenbeisser, S., Kruegel, C., Myers, A.C., Halevi, S.
          (eds.) ACM CCS 2016, pp. 3–16. ACM Press, October 2016
[HSY+21] Han, R., Sui, Z., Yu, J., Liu, J., Chen, S.: Fact and fiction: challenging the
          honest majority assumption of permissionless blockchains. In: Proceed-
          ings of the 2021 ACM Asia Conference on Computer and Communica-
          tions Security, ASIA CCS 2021, pp. 817–831. Association for Computing
          Machinery, New York (2021)
[Inv]   51% attack. https://www.investopedia.com/terms/1/51-attack.asp. pub-
          lisher=Investopedia
[JL20]   Jang, J., Lee, H.-N.: Profitable double-spending attacks. Appl. Sci.
          10(23), 8477 (2020)
[KRDO17] Kiayias, A., Russell, A., David, B., Oliynykov, R.: Ouroboros: a provably
          secure proof-of-stake blockchain protocol. In: Katz, J., Shacham, H. (eds.)
          CRYPTO 2017. LNCS, vol. 10401, pp. 357–388. Springer, Cham (2017).
          https://doi.org/10.1007/978-3-319-63688-7_12
[LTKS15] Luu, L., Teutsch, J., Kulkarni, R., Saxena, P.: Demystifying incentives in
          the consensus computer. In: Ray, I., Li, N., Kruegel, C. (eds.) ACM CCS
          2015, pp. 706–719. ACM Press, October 2015
[Nak08]   Satoshi Nakamoto. Bitcoin: A peer-to-peer electronic cash system (2008).
          http://bitcoin.org/bitcoin.pdf
[NKMS16] Nayak, K., Kumar, S., Miller, A., Shi, E.: Stubborn mining: generalizing
          selfish mining and combining with an eclipse attack. In: S&P (2016)
[PS17]   Pass, R., Shi, E.. FruitChains: a fair blockchain. In: Michael Schiller, E.,
          Schwarzmann, A.A. (eds.) 36th ACM PODC, pp. 315–324. ACM, July
          2017

[PSs17] Pass, R., Seeman, L., Shelat, A.: Analysis of the blockchain protocol in asynchronous networks. In: Coron, J.-S., Nielsen, J.B. (eds.) EUROCRYPT 2017. LNCS, vol. 10211, pp. 643–673. Springer, Cham (2017). https://doi.org/10.1007/978-3-319-56614-6_22

[Ros11] Rosenfeld, M.: Analysis of bitcoin pooled mining reward systems. CoRR (2011)

[SBBR16] Schrijvers, O., Bonneau, J., Boneh, D., Roughgarden, T.: Incentive compatibility of Bitcoin mining pool reward functions. In: Grossklags, J., Preneel, B. (eds.) FC 2016. LNCS, vol. 9603, pp. 477–498. Springer, Heidelberg (2017). https://doi.org/10.1007/978-3-662-54970-4_28

[SSZ16] Sapirshtein, A., Sompolinsky, Y., Zohar, A.: Optimal selfish mining strategies in Bitcoin. In: Grossklags, J., Preneel, B. (eds.) FC 2016. LNCS, vol. 9603, pp. 515–532. Springer, Heidelberg (2017). https://doi.org/10.1007/978-3-662-54970-4_30

[TJS16] Teutsch, J., Jain, S., Saxena, P.: When cryptocurrencies mine their own business. In: Grossklags, J., Preneel, B. (eds.) FC 2016. LNCS, vol. 9603, pp. 499–514. Springer, Heidelberg (2017). https://doi.org/10.1007/978-3-662-54970-4_29

MoSS: Modular Security Specifications Framework

Amir Herzberg[1(✉)], Hemi Leibowitz[2], Ewa Syta[3],
and Sara Wrótniak[1]

[1] Department of Computer Science and Engineering, University of Connecticut,
Storrs, CT, USA
[2] Department of Computer Science, Bar-Ilan University, Ramat Gan, Israel
[3] Department of Computer Science, Trinity College, Hartford, CT, USA

Abstract. Applied cryptographic protocols have to meet a rich set of
security requirements under diverse environments and against diverse
adversaries. However, currently used security specifications, based on
either simulation [11,27] (e.g., 'ideal functionality' in UC) or games [8,
29], are *monolithic*, combining together different aspects of protocol
requirements, environment and assumptions. Such security specifications
are complex, error-prone, and foil reusability, modular analysis and incre-
mental design.

We present the *Modular Security Specifications (MoSS) framework*,
which cleanly separates the *security requirements* (goals) which a protocol should achieve, from the *models* (assumptions) under which each
requirement should be ensured. This modularity allows us to reuse individual models and requirements across different protocols and tasks, and
to compare protocols for the same task, either under different assumptions or satisfying different sets of requirements. MoSS is flexible and
extendable, e.g., it can support both *asymptotic* and *concrete* definitions
for security.

So far, we confirmed the applicability of MoSS to two applications:
secure broadcast protocols and PKI schemes.

1 Introduction

Precise and correct models, requirements and proofs are the best way to ensure
security. Unfortunately, it is hard to write them, and easy-to-make subtle errors
often result in vulnerabilities and exploits; this happens even to the best cryptographers, with the notable exception of the reader. Furthermore, 'the devil
is in the details'; minor details of the models and requirements can be very
significant, and any inaccuracies or small changes may invalidate proofs.

Provable security has its roots in the seminal works rigorously proving security for constructions of cryptographic primitives, such as signature schemes [18],
encryption schemes [17] and pseudorandom functions [16]. Provable security
under well-defined assumptions is expected from any work presenting a new
design or a new cryptographic primitive. With time, the expectation of a

T. Malkin and C. Peikert (Eds.): CRYPTO 2021, LNCS 12827, pp. 33–63, 2021.
https://doi.org/10.1007/978-3-030-84252-9_2

provably-secure design has also extended to applied cryptographic protocols, with seminal works such as [4,7]. After repeated discoveries of serious vulnerabilities in 'intuitively designed' protocols [15], proofs of security are expected, necessary and appreciated by practitioners. However, provable security is notoriously challenging and error-prone for applied cryptographic protocols, which often aim to achieve complex goals under diverse assumptions intended to reflect real-world deployment scenarios. In response, we present the MoSS framework.

MoSS: Modular Security Specifications. In MoSS, a *security specification* includes a set of *models* (assumptions) and specific *requirements* (goals); models and requirements are defined using *predicates* and probability functions. By defining each model and requirement separately, we allow modularity, standardization and reuse. This modularity is particularly beneficial for applied protocols, due to their high number of requirements and models; see Fig. 1.

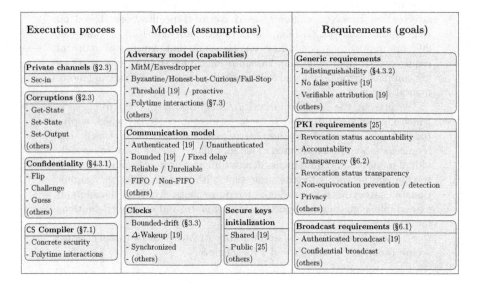

Fig. 1. The MoSS framework allows security to be specified *modularly*, i.e., 'à la carte', with respect to a set of individually-defined models (assumptions), requirements (properties/goals) and even operations of the execution process. Models, requirements and operations defined in this paper or in [19,25] are marked accordingly. Many models, and some ('generic') requirements, are applicable to different types of protocols.

MoSS also includes a well-defined *execution process* (Fig. 2 and Algorithm 1), as necessary for provable security. For simplicity, the 'core' execution process is simple, and supports modular extensions, allowing support for some specific features which are not always needed. Let us now discuss each of these three components of MoSS in more detail.

Models are used to reflect different assumptions made for a protocol, such as the adversary capabilities, communication (e.g., delays and reliability), synchronization, initialization and more. For each 'category' of assumptions, there are multiple options available: e.g., MitM or eavesdropper for the adversary model; threshold for the corruption model; asynchronous, synchronous, or bounded delay for the communication delays model; or asynchronous, synchronous, syntonized, or bounded drift for the clock synchronization model. Often, a model can be reused in many works, since, in MoSS, each model is defined independently of other models and of requirements, as one or more pairs of a small predicate ('program') and a probability function. This approach facilitates the reuse of models and also makes it easier to write, read and compare different works. For example, many protocols, for different tasks, use the same clock and communication models, e.g., synchronous communication and clocks. At the same time, protocols for the same task may use different models, e.g., bounded delay communication and bounded drift clocks.

Requirements refer to properties or goals which a protocol aims for. Protocols for the same problem may achieve different requirements, which may be comparable (e.g., equivocation detection vs. equivocation prevention) or not (e.g., accountability vs. transparency). While many requirements are task specific, some *generic* requirements are applicable across different tasks; e.g., a *no false positive* requirement to ensure that an honest entity should never be considered 'malicious' by another honest entity.

Execution Process. MoSS has a well-defined execution process (see Fig. 2 and Algorithm 1) which takes as input a protocol to execute, an adversary, parameters and a set of *execution operations*. The execution operations allow customized extensions of the execution process, i.e., they enhance the basic execution process with operations which may not always be required. We use these additional operations to define specifications such as indistinguishability, shared-key initialization and entity corruptions.

Related Work. A significant amount of work in applied cryptography is informally specified, with specifications presented as a textual list of assumptions (models) and goals (requirements). Obviously, this informal approach does not facilitate provable security. For provable security, there are two main approaches for defining security specifications: simulation-based and game-based.

The *simulation-based approach*, most notably Universal Composability (UC) [11,12], typically defines security as indistinguishability between executions of the given protocol with the adversary, and executions of an 'ideal functionality', which blends together the model and requirements, with a *simulator*. There are multiple extensions and alternatives to UC, such as iUC, GNUC, IITM and simplified-UC [10,21,23,30], and other simulation-based frameworks such as constructive cryptography (CC) [26,27] and reactive systems [1]. Each of these variants defines a specific, fixed execution model. An important reason for the popularity of the simulation-based approach is its support for *secure composition* of protocols; another reason is the fact that some important tasks, e.g., zero-knowledge (ZK), seem to require simulation-based definitions. However, for many tasks, especially applied tasks, game-based definitions are more natural and easier to work with.

Table 1. A comparison of different approaches to security specifications. An execution process defines executions (runs). A protocol aims to satisfy certain *requirements* assuming certain *models*. Simulation-based specifications, such as UC [12], ensure *provably-secure composition* of protocols but do not allow one protocol to meet multiple separately-defined specifications. Some tasks, e.g. zero-knowledge, may only have simulation-based specifications.

Approach	Specifications			Multiple	Prov.-secure
	Exec Process	Models	Requirements	specifications	composition
Informal	-	List	List	Yes	No
Game-based	Game per goal; models are part of game			Yes	No
Simulation-based	Fixed		Indistinguishable from Ideal Functionality	No	Yes
MoSS	Extensible	List	List	Yes	No

The *game-based approach* [8,20,29] is also widely adopted, especially among practitioners, due to its simpler, more intuitive definitions and proofs of security. In this approach, each requirement is defined as a *game* between the adversary and the protocol. The game incorporates the models, the execution process, and the specific requirement (e.g., indistinguishability). However, the game-based approach does have limitations, most notably, there is no composition theorem for game-based specifications and it may be inapplicable to tasks such as zero-knowledge proofs and multi-party computation.

Both 'game-based' and 'simulation-based' security specifications are *monolithic*: an ideal functionality or a game, combining security requirements with different aspects of the model and the execution process. Even though different requirements and models are individually presented in their informal descriptions, the designers and readers have to validate directly that the formal, monolithic specifications correctly reflect the informal descriptions.

Such monolithic specifications are not a good fit for analysis of applied protocols, which have complex requirements and models, and it stands in sharp contrast to the standard engineering approach, where specifications are gradually developed and carefully verified at each step, often using automated tools. While there exist powerful tools to validate security of cryptographic protocols [2], there are no such tools to validate the *specifications*.

We began this work after trying to write simulation-based as well as game-based specifications for PKI schemes, which turned out to be impractical given the complexity of realistic modeling aspects; this motivated us to develop modular security specification, i.e., MoSS.

In Table 1, we compare MoSS to game-based and simulation-based security specifications. The advantage of MoSS is its *modularity*; a security specification consists of one or more *models*, one or more *requirements* and, optionally, some execution process operations. Each model and requirement is defined independently, as one or more pairs of a small *predicate* (which is, typically, a simple program) and a probability function. Models are often applicable to different tasks, and some requirements are generic and apply to multiple tasks. This modular approach allows to reuse models and requirements, which makes it easier to write, understand and compare specifications. For example, in the full version [19], we present a simplified instance of an authenticated-broadcast protocol assuming (well-defined) bounded delay and bounded clock drift models. The *same* models are used for PKI schemes in [25].

The use of separate, focused models and requirements also allows a *gradual protocol development and analysis*. To illustrate, we first analyze the authenticated-broadcast protocol assuming only a secure shared-key initialization model, which suffices to ensure authenticity but not freshness. We then show that the protocol also achieves freshness when we also assume bounded clock drift. Lastly, we show that by additionally assuming bounded-delay communication, we can ensure a bounded delay for the broadcast protocol. This gradual approach makes the analysis easier to perform and understand (and to identify any design flaws early on), especially when compared to proving such properties using monolithic security specifications (all at once). Using MoSS is a bit like playing Lego with models and requirements!

Concrete security [5] is especially important for protocols used in practice as it allows to more precisely define security of a given protocol and to properly select security parameters, in contrast to asymptotic security. Due to its modularity, MoSS also supports concrete security in a way we consider simple and even elegant; see Sect. 7.2.

Ensuring Polytime Interactions. As pointed out in [11,22], the 'classical' notion of PPT algorithms is not sufficient for analysis of interactive systems, where the same protocol (and adversary) can be invoked many times. This issue is addressed by later versions of UC and in some other recent frameworks, e.g., GNUC [21]. The extendability of MoSS allows it to handle these aspects relatively simply; see Sect. 7.3.

Modularity Lemmas. In Sect. 5, we present several *asymptotic security modularity lemmas*, which allow combining 'simple' models and requirements into composite models and requirements, taking advantage of MoSS's modularity. We provide proofs and corresponding Concrete security modularity lemmas in [19].

Limitations of MoSS. Currently, MoSS has two significant limitations: the lack of *computer-aided tools*, available for both game-based and simulation-based approaches [2,3,9,28], and the lack of *composability*, an important property proven for most simulation-based frameworks, most notably UC [11].

We believe that MoSS is amenable to computer-aided tools. For example, a tool may transform the modular MoSS security specifications into a monolithic game or an ideal functionality, allowing to use the existing computer-aided tools. However, development of such tools is clearly a challenge yet to be met. Another open challenge is to prove a composability property directly for MoSS security specifications, or to provide (MoSS-like) modular specifications for UC and other simulation-based frameworks.

It is our hope that MoSS may help to bridge the gap between the theory and practice in cryptography, and to facilitate *meaningful, provable security* for practical cryptographic protocols and systems.

Real-world Application of MoSS: PKI. Public Key Infrastructure (PKI) schemes, a critical component of applied cryptography, amply illustrate the challenges of applying provable security in practice and serve as a good example of how MoSS might benefit practical protocols. Current PKI systems are mostly based on the X.509 standard [14], but there are many other proposals, most notably, Certificate Transparency (CT) [24], which add significant goals and cryptographic mechanisms. Realistic PKI systems have non-trivial requirements; in particular, synchronization is highly relevant and needed to deal with even such basic aspects as revocation.

Recently, we presented the first rigorous study [25] of practical[1] PKI schemes by using MoSS. Specifically, we defined model and requirement predicates for practical PKI schemes and proved security of the X.509 PKI scheme. The analysis uses the bounded-delay and bounded-drift model predicates; similarly, follow-up work is expected to reuse these models and requirement predicates to prove security for additional PKI schemes, e.g., Certificate Transparency.

Organization. Section 2 introduces **Exec**, the adversary-driven execution process. Section 3 and Sect. 4 present models and requirements, respectively. Section 5 presents modularity lemmas. Section 6 shows how to apply MoSS to two different applications, a simplified authenticated broadcast protocol and PKI schemes. Section 7 describes extensions of the framework to achieve concrete security and to ensure polytime interactions. We conclude and discuss future work in Sect. 8.

2   Execution Process

A key aspect of MoSS is the separation of the execution process from the model $\mathcal{M}$ under which a protocol $\mathcal{P}$ is analyzed, and the requirements $\mathcal{R}$ that define $\mathcal{P}$'s goals. This separation allows different model assumptions using the same execution process, simplifying the analysis and allowing reusability of definitions and results. In this section, we present MoSS's execution process, which defines the execution of a given protocol $\mathcal{P}$ 'controlled' by a given adversary $\mathcal{A}$. We say that it is 'adversary-driven' since the adversary controls all inputs and invocations of the entities running the protocol.

2.1 $\text{Exec}_{\mathcal{A},\mathcal{P}}$: An Adversary-Driven Execution Process

The execution process $\text{Exec}_{\mathcal{A},\mathcal{P}}(params)$, as defined by the pseudo-code in Algorithm 1, specifies the details of running a given protocol $\mathcal{P}$ with a given adversary $\mathcal{A}$, both modeled as efficient (PPT) functions, given parameters $params$. Note that the model $\mathcal{M}$ is not an input to the execution process; it is only applied to the transcript T of the protocol run produced by $\text{Exec}_{\mathcal{A},\mathcal{P}}$, to decide if the adversary adhered to the model, in effect restricting the adversary's capabilities. $\text{Exec}_{\mathcal{A},\mathcal{P}}$ allows the adversary to have an *extensive control* over the execution; the adversary decides, at any point, which entity is invoked next, with what operation and with what inputs.

---

[1] Grossly-simplified PKI ideal functionalities were studied, e.g., in [21], but without considering even basic aspects such as revocation and expiration.

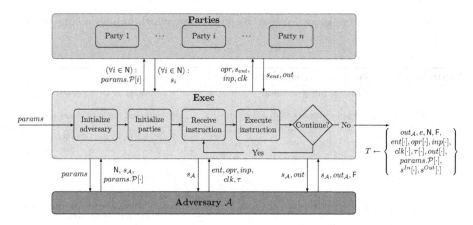

Fig. 2. A high level overview of MoSS's execution process showing the interactions between the parties to the protocol and the adversary in $\mathbf{Exec}_{\mathcal{A},\mathcal{P}}$. (Note: e, in the final execution transcript T, is the total number of iterations of the loop.)

Notation. To allow the execution process to apply to protocols with multiple functions and operations, we define the entire protocol $\mathcal{P}$ as a *single* PPT algorithm and use parameters to specify the exact operations and their inputs. Specifically, to invoke an operation defined by $\mathcal{P}$ over some entity i, we use the following notation: $\mathcal{P}[opr](s, inp, clk)$, where opr identifies the specific 'operation' or 'function' to be invoked, s is the *local state* of entity i, inp is the set of inputs to opr, and clk is the value of the local clock of entity i. The output of such execution is a tuple (s', out), where s' is the state of entity i *after* the operation is executed and out is the output of the executed operation, which is made available to the adversary. We refer to $\mathcal{P}$ as an 'algorithm' (in PPT) although we do not consider the operation as part of the input, i.e., formally, $\mathcal{P}$ maps from the operations (given as strings) to algorithms; this can be interpreted as $\mathcal{P}$ accepting the 'label' as additional input and calling the appropriate 'subroutine', making it essentially a single PPT algorithm.

Algorithm 1 uses the standard *index notation* to refer to cells of arrays. For example, $out[e]$ refers to the value of the eth entry of the array out. Specifically, e represents the index (counter) of execution events. Note that e is *never* given to the protocol; every individual entity has a separate state, and may count the events that *it* is involved in, but if there is more than one entity, an entity cannot know the current value of e - it is *not* a clock. Even the adversary does not control e, although, the adversary can keep track of it in its state, since it is invoked (twice) in every round. Clocks and time are handled differently, as we now explain.

In every invocation of the protocol, one of the inputs set by the adversary is referred to as the *local clock* and denoted clk. In addition, in every event, the adversary defines a value τ which we refer to as the *real time clock*. Thus, to refer to the local clock value and the real time clock value of event e, the execution process uses $clk[e]$ and $\tau[e]$, respectively. Both clk and τ are included in the transcript T; this allows a model predicate to enforce different *synchro-*

nization models/assumptions - or not to enforce any, which implies a completely asynchronous model.

Algorithm 1. Adversary-Driven Execution Process $\mathrm{Exec}_{\mathcal{A},\mathcal{P}}(params)$

1: $(s_{\mathcal{A}}, \mathsf{N}, params.\mathcal{P}[\cdot]) \leftarrow \mathcal{A}['\mathrm{Init}'](params)$ ▷ *Initialize $\mathcal{A}$ with params*

2: $\forall i \in \mathsf{N} :\ s_i \leftarrow \mathcal{P}['\mathrm{Init}'] \, (\bot, params.\mathcal{P}[i], \bot)$ ▷ *Initialize entities' local states*

3: $e \leftarrow 0$ ▷ *Initialize loop's counter*

4: **repeat**

5:     $e \leftarrow e + 1$ ▷ *Advance the loop counter*

6:     $(ent[e], opr[e], inp[e], clk[e], \tau[e]) \leftarrow \mathcal{A}(s_{\mathcal{A}})$ ▷ *$\mathcal{A}$ selects entity $ent[e]$, operation $opr[e]$, input $inp[e]$, clock $clk[e]$, and real time $\tau[e]$ for event e*

7:     $s^{In}[e] \leftarrow s_{ent[e]}$ ▷ *Save input state*

8:     $(s_{ent[e]}, out[e]) \leftarrow \mathcal{P}\,[opr[e]]\,(s_{ent[e]}, inp[e], clk[e])$

9:     $s^{Out}[e] \leftarrow s_{ent[e]}$ ▷ *Save output state*

10:    $(s_{\mathcal{A}}, out_{\mathcal{A}}, \mathsf{F}) \leftarrow \mathcal{A}\,(s_{\mathcal{A}}, out[e])$ ▷ *$\mathcal{A}$ decides when to terminate the loop ($out_{\mathcal{A}} \neq \bot$), based on $out[e]$*

11: **until** $out_{\mathcal{A}} \neq \bot$

12: $T \leftarrow \left(out_{\mathcal{A}}, e, \mathsf{N}, \mathsf{F}, ent[\cdot], opr[\cdot], inp[\cdot], clk[\cdot], \tau[\cdot], out[\cdot], params.\mathcal{P}[\cdot], s^{In}[\cdot], s^{Out}[\cdot]\right)$

13: Return T ▷ *Output transcript of run*

Construction. The execution process (Algorithm 1) consists of three main components: the initialization, main execution loop and termination.

Initialization (lines 1-3). In line 1, we allow the adversary to set their state $s_{\mathcal{A}}$, to choose the set of entities N, and to choose parameters $params.\mathcal{P}[i]$ for protocol initialization for each entity $i \in \mathsf{N}$. The values of $params.\mathcal{P}[\cdot]$ can be restricted using *models* (see Sect. 3). In line 2, we set the initial state s_i for each entity i by invoking the protocol-specific 'Init' operation with input $params.\mathcal{P}[i]$; note that this implies a convention where protocols are initialized by this operation - all other operations are up to the specific protocol. The reasoning behind such convention is that initialization is an extremely common operation in many protocols; that said, protocols without initialization can use an empty 'Init' operation and protocols with a complex initialization process can use other operations defined in $\mathcal{P}$ in the main execution loop (lines 4-11), to implement an initialization process which cannot be performed via a single 'Init' call. In line 3, we initialize e, which we use to index the events of the execution, i.e., e is incremented by one (line 5) each time we complete one 'execution loop' (lines 4-11).

Main Execution Loop (lines 4-11). The execution process affords the adversary $\mathcal{A}$ extensive control over the execution. Specifically, in each event e, $\mathcal{A}$ determines (line 6) an operation $opr[e]$, along with its inputs, to be invoked by an entity $ent[e] \in \mathsf{N}$. The adversary also selects $\tau[e]$, the global, real time clock value.

Afterwards, the event is executed (line 8). The entity's input and output states are saved in $s^{In}[e]$ and $s^{Out}[e]$, respectively (lines 7 and 9), which allows models to place restrictions on the states of entities.

In line 10, the adversary processes the output $out[e]$ of the operation $opr[e]$. The adversary may modify its state $s_\mathcal{A}$, and outputs a value $out_\mathcal{A}$; when $out_\mathcal{A} \neq \bot$, the execution moves to the termination phase; otherwise the loop continues.

Termination (lines 12-13). Upon termination, the process returns the *execution transcript* T (line 13), containing the relevant values from the execution. Namely, T contains the adversary's output $out_\mathcal{A}$, the index of the last event e, the set of entities N, and the set of faulty entities F (produced in line 10), the values of $ent[\cdot], opr[\cdot], inp[\cdot], clk[\cdot], \tau[\cdot]$ and $out[\cdot]$ for all invoked events, the protocol initialization parameters $params.\mathcal{P}[\cdot]$ for all entities in N, and the entity's input state $s^{In}[\cdot]$ and output state $s^{Out}[\cdot]$ for each event. We allow $\mathcal{A}$ to output F to accommodate different fault modes, i.e., an adversary model can specify which entities are included in F (considered 'faulty') which then can be validated using an appropriate model.

2.2   The Extendable Execution Process

In Sect. 2.1, we described the design of the generic $\mathbf{Exec}_{\mathcal{A},\mathcal{P}}$ execution process, which imposes only some basic limitations. We now describe the *extendable* execution process $\mathbf{Exec}^{\mathcal{X}}_{\mathcal{A},\mathcal{P}}$, an extension of $\mathbf{Exec}_{\mathcal{A},\mathcal{P}}$, which provides additional flexibility with only few changes to $\mathbf{Exec}_{\mathcal{A},\mathcal{P}}$. The extendable execution process $\mathbf{Exec}^{\mathcal{X}}_{\mathcal{A},\mathcal{P}}$ allows MoSS to (1) handle different kinds of entity-corruptions (described next) and (2) define certain other models/requirements, e.g., indistinguishability requirements (Sect. 4.3); other applications may be found.

The $\mathbf{Exec}^{\mathcal{X}}_{\mathcal{A},\mathcal{P}}$ execution process, as defined by the pseudo-code in Algorithm 1, specifies the details of running a given protocol $\mathcal{P}$ with a given adversary $\mathcal{A}$, both modeled as efficient (PPT) functions, given *a specific set of execution operations* $\mathcal{X}$ and parameters $params$. The set[2] $\mathcal{X}$ is a specific *set of extra operations* through which the execution process provides built-in yet flexible support for various adversarial capabilities. For example, the set $\mathcal{X}$ can contain functions which allow the adversary to perform specific functionality on an entity, functionality which the adversary cannot achieve via the execution of $\mathcal{P}$. We detail and provide concrete examples of such functionalities in Sect. 2.3.

Changes to the $\mathbf{Exec}_{\mathcal{A},\mathcal{P}}$ Execution Process. In addition to the extensive control the adversary had over the execution, the adversary now can decide not only which entity is invoked next, but also whether the operation is from the set $\mathcal{X}$ of execution operations, or from the set of operations supported by $\mathcal{P}$; while we did not explicitly write it, some default values are returned if the adversary specifies an operation which does not exist in the corresponding set.

---

[2] We use the term 'set', but note that $\mathcal{X}$ is defined as a single PPT algorithm, similarly to how $\mathcal{P}$ is defined.

To invoke an operation defined by $\mathcal{P}$ over some entity i, we use the same notation as before, but the output of such execution contains an additional output value *sec-out*, where *sec-out*$[e][\cdot]$ is a 'secure output' - namely, it contains values that are shared only with the execution process itself, and *not shared with the adversary*; e.g., such values may be used, if there is an appropriate operation in $\mathcal{X}$, to establish a 'secure channel' between parties, which is not visible to $\mathcal{A}$. In *sec-out*, the first parameter denotes the specific event e in which the secure output was set; the second one is optional, e.g., may specify the 'destination' of the secure output. Similarly, $\mathcal{X}$ is also defined as a single PPT algorithm and we use a similar notation to invoke its operations: $\mathcal{X}[opr](s_{\mathcal{X}}, s, inp, clk, ent)$, where opr, s, inp, clk are as before, and $s_{\mathcal{X}}$ is the execution process's state and ent is an entity identifier.

Algorithm 2. Extendible Adversary-Driven Execution Process $\mathrm{Exec}^{\mathcal{X}}_{\mathcal{A},\mathcal{P}}(params)$

1: $(s_{\mathcal{A}}, \mathsf{N}, params.\mathcal{P}[\cdot]) \leftarrow \mathcal{A}[\text{`Init'}](params)$ ▷ *Initialize $\mathcal{A}$ with params*

2: $\forall i \in \mathsf{N} : s_i \leftarrow \mathcal{P}[\text{`Init'}](\bot, params.\mathcal{P}[i], \bot)$ ▷ *Initialize entities' local states*

3: $s_{\mathcal{X}} \leftarrow \mathcal{X}[\text{`Init'}](params, params.\mathcal{P}[\cdot])$ ▷ *Initial exec state*

4: $e \leftarrow 0$ ▷ *Initialize loop's counter*

5: **repeat**

6:      $e \leftarrow e + 1$ ▷ *Advance the loop counter*

7:      $(ent[e], opr[e], \textbf{type}[e], inp[e], clk[e], \tau[e]) \leftarrow \mathcal{A}(s_{\mathcal{A}})$ ▷ *$\mathcal{A}$ selects entity $ent[e]$, operation $opr[e]$, input $inp[e]$, clock $clk[e]$, and real time $\tau[e]$ for event e*

8:      $s^{In}[e] \leftarrow s_{ent[e]}$ ▷ *Save input state*

9:      **if** $type[e] = \text{`}\mathcal{X}\text{'}$ **then**   ▷ *If $\mathcal{A}$ chose to invoke an operation from $\mathcal{X}$.*

10:          $(s_{\mathcal{X}}, s_{ent[e]}, out[e], sec\text{-}out[e][\cdot]) \leftarrow \mathcal{X}[opr[e]](s_{\mathcal{X}}, s_{ent[e]}, inp[e], clk[e], ent[e])$

11:      **else**   ▷ *$\mathcal{A}$ chose to invoke an operation from $\mathcal{P}$.*

12:          $(s_{ent[e]}, out[e], sec\text{-}out[e][\cdot]) \leftarrow \mathcal{P}[opr[e]](s_{ent[e]}, inp[e], clk[e])$

13:      **end if**

14:      $s^{Out}[e] \leftarrow s_{ent[e]}$ ▷ *Save output state*

15:      $(s_{\mathcal{A}}, out_{\mathcal{A}}, \mathsf{F}) \leftarrow \mathcal{A}(s_{\mathcal{A}}, out[e])$ ▷ *$\mathcal{A}$ decides when to terminate the loop ($out_{\mathcal{A}} \neq \bot$), based on $out[e]$*

16: **until** $out_{\mathcal{A}} \neq \bot$

17: $T \leftarrow \left(out_{\mathcal{A}}, e, \mathsf{N}, \mathsf{F}, ent[\cdot], opr[\cdot], type[\cdot], inp[\cdot], clk[\cdot], \tau[\cdot], out[\cdot], params.\mathcal{P}[\cdot], s^{In}[\cdot], s^{Out}[\cdot], sec\text{-}out[\cdot][\cdot]\right)$

18: Return T ▷ *Output transcript of run*

Construction. The extended execution process (Algorithm 2) consists of the following modifications. The initialization phase (lines 1-4) has one additional line (line 3), where we initialize the 'execution operations state' $s_{\mathcal{X}}$; this state is used by execution operations (in $\mathcal{X}$), allowing them to be defined as (stateless) functions. Note that any set of execution operations $\mathcal{X}$ is assumed to contain an 'Init' operation, and we may omit the 'Init' operation from the notation when specifying $\mathcal{X}$; if it is omitted, the 'default' 'Init' operation is assumed, which simply outputs $(params, params.\mathcal{P}[\cdot])$. The rest of the initialization lines are the same.

The main execution loop (lines 5-16) is as before, but with one difference, where the adversary $\mathcal{A}$ determines in line 7 the type of operation $type[e]$ to be invoked by an entity $ent[e] \in \mathbb{N}$. The operation type $type[e] \in \{`\mathcal{X}', `\mathcal{P}'\}$ indicates if the operation $opr[e]$ is protocol-specific (defined in $\mathcal{P}$) or is it one of the execution process operations (defined in $\mathcal{X}$). (If $type[e] \notin \{`\mathcal{X}', `\mathcal{P}'\}$, then the execution process assumes that the operation is protocol-specific.) Afterwards, the event is executed (lines 9-12) through the appropriate algorithm, based on the operation type, either $\mathcal{X}$, if $type[e] = `\mathcal{X}'$, or $\mathcal{P}$ otherwise.

The termination phase (lines 17-18) is the same as before, but also includes in the transcript the $type[\cdot]$ values and the $sec\text{-}out[\cdot][\cdot]$ for all invoked events. Private values, such as entities' private keys, are not part of the execution transcript unless they were explicitly included in the output due to an invocation of an operation from $\mathcal{X}$ that would allow it.

Note: We assume that $\mathcal{X}$ operations are always defined such that whenever $\mathcal{X}$ is invoked, it does not run $\mathcal{A}$ and only runs $\mathcal{P}$ at most once (per invocation of $\mathcal{X}$). Also, in lines 7 and 15, the operation to $\mathcal{A}$ is not explicitly written in the pseudo-code. We assume that in fact nothing is given to $\mathcal{A}$ for the operation (length 0) - this implies that $\mathcal{A}$ will not be re-initialized during the execution process.

2.3   Using $\mathcal{X}$ to Define Specification and Entity-Faults Operations

The 'default' execution process is defined by an empty $\mathcal{X}$ set. This provides the adversary $\mathcal{A}$ with *Man-in-the-Middle (MitM)* capabilities, and even beyond: $\mathcal{A}$ receives all outputs, including messages sent, and controls all inputs, including messages received; furthermore, $\mathcal{A}$ controls the values of the local clocks. A non-empty set $\mathcal{X}$ can be used to define *specification operations* and *entity-fault operations*; let us discuss each of these two types of execution process operations.

Specification Operations. Some model and requirement specifications require a special execution process operation, possibly involving some information which must be kept private from the adversary. One example are *indistinguishability* requirements, which are defined in Sect. 4.3.1 using three operations in $\mathcal{X}$: 'Flip', 'Challenge' and 'Guess', whose meaning most readers can guess (and confirm the guess in Sect. 4.3.1).

The 'Sec-in' $\mathcal{X}$-Operation. As a simple example of a useful specification operation, we now define the *'Sec-in'* operation, which allows the execution process to provide a secure input from one entity to another, *bypassing* the adversary's MitM capabilities. This operation can be used for different purposes, such as to assume secure shared-key initialization - for example, see [19]. We define the 'Sec-in' operation in Eq. 1.[3]

$$\mathcal{X}[\text{'Sec-in'}](s_{\mathcal{X}}, s, e', clk, ent) \equiv [s_{\mathcal{X}} \| \mathcal{P}[\text{'Sec-in'}](s, sec\text{-}out[e'][ent], clk)] \quad (1)$$

As can be seen, invocation of the 'Sec-in' operation returns the state $s_{\mathcal{X}}$ unchanged (and unused); the other outputs are simply defined by invoking the 'Sec-in' operation of the protocol $\mathcal{P}$, with input *sec-out*[e'][ent] - the *sec-out* output of the event e' intended for entity *ent*.

Entity-fault Operations. It is quite easy to define $\mathcal{X}$-operations that facilitate different types of entity-fault models, such as *honest-but-curious, byzantine (malicious), adaptive, proactive, self-stabilizing, fail-stop* and others. Let us give informal examples of three fault operations:

'Get-state': provides $\mathcal{A}$ with the entire state of the entity. Assuming no other entity-fault operation, this is the 'honest-but-curious' adversary; note that the adversary may invoke 'Get-state' after each time it invokes the entity, to know its state all the time.

'Set-output': allows $\mathcal{A}$ to force the entity to output specific values. A 'Byzantine' adversary would use this operation whenever it wants the entity to produce specific output.

'Set-state': allows $\mathcal{A}$ to set any state to an entity. For example, the 'self-stabilization' model amounts to an adversary that may perform a 'Set-state' for every entity (once, at the beginning of the execution).

See discussion in [19], and an example: use of these 'fault operations' to define the *threshold security* model $\mathcal{M}^{|F| \leq f}$, assumed by many protocols.

Comments. Defining these aspects of the execution in $\mathcal{X}$, rather than having a particular choice enforced as part of the execution process, provides significant flexibility and makes for a simpler execution process.

Note that even when the set $\mathcal{X}$ is non-empty, i.e., contains some non-default operations, the adversary's *use* of these operations may yet be restricted for the adversary to satisfy a relevant *model*. We present model specifications in Sect. 3.

The operations in $\mathcal{X}$ are defined as (stateless) *functions*. However, the execution process provides state $s_{\mathcal{X}}$ that these operations may use to store values across invocations; the same state variable may be used by different operations. For example, the 'Flip', 'Challenge' and 'Guess' $\mathcal{X}$-operations, used to define *indistinguishability* requirements in Sect. 4.3.1, use $s_{\mathcal{X}}$ to share the value of the bit flipped (by the 'Flip' operation).

---

[3] We use $\equiv$ to mean 'is defined as'.

3   Models

The execution process, described in Sect. 2, specifies the details of running a protocol $\mathcal{P}$ against an adversary $\mathcal{A}$ which has an extensive control over the execution. In this section, we present two important concepts of MoSS: a *model* $\mathcal{M}$, used to define assumptions about the adversary and the execution, and *specifications* (π, β). We use specifications[4] to define both models (in this section) and requirements (in Sect. 4).

A MoSS (model/requirement) specification is a pair of functions (π, β), where $\pi(T, params)$ is called the *predicate* (and returns $\top$ or $\bot$) and $\beta(params)$ is the *base (probability) function* (and evaluates to values from 0 to 1). The predicate π is applied to the execution-transcript T and defines whether the adversary 'won' or 'lost'. The base function β is the 'inherent' probability of the adversary 'winning'; it is often simply zero ($\beta(x) = 0$), e.g., for forgery in a signature scheme, but sometimes a constant such as half (for indistinguishability specifications) or a function such as 2^{-l} (e.g., for l-bit MAC) of the parameters *params*.

A MoSS model is defined as a set of (one or more) specifications, i.e., $\mathcal{M} = \{(\pi_1, \beta_1), \ldots\}$. When the model contains only one specification, we may abuse notation and write $\mathcal{M} = (\pi, \beta)$ for convenience.

For example, consider a model $\mathcal{M} = (\pi, 0)$. Intuitively, adversary $\mathcal{A}$ *satisfies model* $(\pi, 0)$, if for (almost) all execution-transcripts T of $\mathcal{A}$, predicate π holds, i.e.: $\pi(T, params) = \top$, where *params* are the parameters used in the execution process (Sect. 3.1). One may say that the model ensures that *the (great) power that the adversary holds over the execution is used 'with great responsibility'*.

The separation between the execution process and the model allows to use the same - relatively simple - execution process for the analysis of many different protocols, under different models (of the environment and adversary capabilities). Furthermore, it allows to define multiple simple models, each focusing on a different assumption or restriction, and require that the adversary satisfy all of them.

As depicted in Fig. 1, the model captures all of the assumptions regarding the environment and the capabilities of the adversary, including aspects typically covered by the (often informal) *communication model, synchronization model* and *adversary model*:

Adversary model: The adversary capabilities such as MitM vs. eavesdropper, entity corruption capabilities (e.g., threshold or proactive security), computational capabilities and more.

Communication model: The properties of the underlying communication mechanism, such as reliable or unreliable communication, FIFO or non-FIFO, authenticated or not, bounded delay, fixed delay or asynchronous, and so on.

---

[4] We use the term 'specification' to refer to a *component* of a model (or of a requirement - see Sect. 4). This is not to be confused with 'security specification', which we use to mean a model, requirement, and specific execution process.

Synchronization model: The availability and properties of per-entity clocks.
Common models include purely asynchronous clocks (no synchronization),
bounded-drift clocks, and synchronized or syntonized clocks.

The definitions of models and their predicates are often simple to write and
understand - and yet, reusable across works.

In Sect. 3.1, we define the concept of a specification. In Sect. 3.2, we define the
notion of a *model-satisfying adversary*. Finally, in Sect. 3.3, we give an example
of a model. For additional examples of models, see [19].

3.1   Specifications

We next define the *specification*, used to define both *models* and *requirements*.

A specification is a pair (π, β), where π is the *specification predicate* and β
is the *base function*. A *specification predicate* is a predicate whose inputs are
execution transcript T and parameters *params*. When $\pi(T, params) = \top$, we
say that execution satisfies the predicate π for the given value of *params*. The
base function gives the 'base' probability of success for an adversary. For integrity
specifications, e.g. forgery, the base function is often either zero or 2^{-l}, where
l is the output block size; and for indistinguishability-based specifications (see
Sect. 4.3), the base function is often $\frac{1}{2}$.

We next define the *advantage*[5] of adversary $\mathcal{A}$ against protocol $\mathcal{P}$ for specification predicate π using execution operations $\mathcal{X}$, as a function of the parameters
params. This is the probability that $\pi(T, params) = \bot$, for the transcript T of
a random execution: $T \leftarrow \mathbf{Exec}^{\mathcal{X}}_{\mathcal{A},\mathcal{P}}(params)$.

**Definition 1 (Advantage of adversary $\mathcal{A}$ against protocol $\mathcal{P}$ for speci-
fication predicate π using execution operations $\mathcal{X}$).** *Let $\mathcal{A}, \mathcal{P}, \mathcal{X}$ be algorithms and let π be a specification predicate. The advantage of adversary $\mathcal{A}$
against protocol $\mathcal{P}$ for specification predicate π using execution operations $\mathcal{X}$ is
defined as:*

$$\epsilon^{\pi}_{\mathcal{A},\mathcal{P},\mathcal{X}}(params) \stackrel{def}{=} \Pr \begin{bmatrix} \pi\,(T, params) = \bot, \ where \\ T \leftarrow \mathbf{Exec}^{\mathcal{X}}_{\mathcal{A},\mathcal{P}}(params) \end{bmatrix} \tag{2}$$

3.2   Model-Satisfying Adversary

Models are sets of specifications, used to restrict the capabilities of the adversary
and the events in the execution process. This includes limiting of the possible
faults, defining initialization assumptions, and defining the communication and
synchronization models. We check whether a given adversary $\mathcal{A}$ followed the
restrictions of a given model $\mathcal{M}$ in a given execution by examining whether a
random transcript T of the execution satisfies each of the model's specification
predicates. Next, we define what it means for adversary $\mathcal{A}$ to *poly-satisfy model
$\mathcal{M}$ using execution operations $\mathcal{X}$.*

---

[5] Note that the advantage of $\mathcal{A}$ is the *total* probability of $\mathcal{A}$ winning, i.e., it does not
depend on a base function.

Definition 2 (Adversary $\mathcal{A}$ poly-satisfies model $\mathcal{M}$ using execution operations $\mathcal{X}$). *Let $\mathcal{A}, \mathcal{X} \in PPT$, and let $\mathcal{M}$ be a set of specifications, i.e., $\mathcal{M} = \{(\pi_1, \beta_1), \ldots\}$. We say that adversary $\mathcal{A}$ poly-satisfies model $\mathcal{M}$ using execution operations $\mathcal{X}$, denoted $\mathcal{A} \models_{poly}^{\mathcal{X}} \mathcal{M}$, if for every protocol $\mathcal{P} \in PPT$, params $\in \{0,1\}^*$, and specification $(\pi, \beta) \in \mathcal{M}$, the advantage of $\mathcal{A}$ against $\mathcal{P}$ for π using $\mathcal{X}$ is at most negligibly greater than $\beta(params)$, i.e.:*

$$\mathcal{A} \models_{poly}^{\mathcal{X}} \mathcal{M} \overset{def}{=} \left[\begin{array}{l} (\forall \, \mathcal{P} \in PPT, params \in \{0,1\}^*, (\pi, \beta) \in \mathcal{M}) : \\ \epsilon_{\mathcal{A}, \mathcal{P}, \mathcal{X}}^{\pi}(params) \leq \beta(params) + Negl(|params|) \end{array} \right] \tag{3}$$

3.3   Example: The Bounded-Clock-Drift Model $\mathcal{M}_{\Delta_{clk}}^{\text{Drift}}$

To demonstrate a definition of a model, we present the $\mathcal{M}_{\Delta_{clk}}^{\text{Drift}}$ model, defined as $\mathcal{M}_{\Delta_{clk}}^{\text{Drift}} = (\pi_{\Delta_{clk}}^{\text{Drift}}, 0)$. The predicate $\pi_{\Delta_{clk}}^{\text{Drift}}$ bounds the clock drift, by enforcing two restrictions on the execution: (1) each local-clock value ($clk[\hat{e}]$) must be within Δ_{clk} drift from the real time $\tau[\hat{e}]$, and (2) the real time values should be monotonically increasing. As a special case, when $\Delta_{clk} = 0$, this predicate corresponds to a model where the local clocks are fully synchronized, i.e., there is no difference between entities' clocks. See Algorithm 3.

Algorithm 3. The $\pi_{\Delta_{clk}}^{\text{Drift}}$ $(T, params)$ predicate, used by the $\mathcal{M}_{\Delta_{clk}}^{\text{Drift}} \equiv (\pi_{\Delta_{clk}}^{\text{Drift}}, 0)$ model

---

1: **return** (
2:   $\forall \hat{e} \in \{1, \ldots, T.e\}$:   ▷ *For each event*
3:     $|T.clk[\hat{e}] - T.\tau[\hat{e}]| \leq \Delta_{clk}$ ▷ *Local clock is within Δ_{clk} drift from real time*
4:     **and if** $\hat{e} \geq 2$ **then** $T.\tau[\hat{e}] \geq T.\tau[\hat{e}-1]$ ▷ *In each consecutive event, the real time difference is monotonically increasing*
)

---

4   Requirements

In this section we define and discuss *requirements*. Like a model, a *requirement* is a set of specifications $\mathcal{R} = \{(\pi_1, \beta_1), \ldots\}$. When the requirement contains only one specification, we may abuse notation and write $\mathcal{R} = (\pi, \beta)$ for convenience. Each requirement specification $(\pi, \beta) \in \mathcal{R}$ includes a predicate (π) and a base function (β). A requirement defines one or more properties that a protocol aims to achieve, e.g., security, correctness or liveness requirements. By separating between models and requirements, MoSS obtains modularity and reuse; different protocols may satisfy the same requirements but use different models, and the same models can be reused for different protocols, designed to satisfy different requirements.

The separation between the definition of the model and of the requirements also allows definition of *generic requirement predicates.*, which are applicable to protocols designed for different tasks, which share some basic goals. We identify several generic requirement predicates that appear relevant to many security protocols. These requirement predicates focus on attributes of messages, i.e., non-repudiation, and on detection of misbehaving entities (see [19]).

4.1   Model-Secure Requirements

We next define what it means for a protocol to satisfy a requirement under some model. First, consider a requirement $\mathcal{R} = (\pi, \beta)$, which contains just one specification, and let b be the outcome of π applied to $(T, params)$, where T is a transcript of the execution process $(T = \mathbf{Exec}_{\mathcal{A}, \mathcal{P}}^{\mathcal{X}}(params))$ and $params$ are the parameters, i.e., $b \leftarrow \pi(T, params)$; if $b = \bot$ then we say that $requirement$ $predicate$ π was not $satisfied$ in the execution of $\mathcal{P}$, or that the $adversary$ won in this execution. If $b = \top$, then we say that $requirement$ $predicate$ π was $satisfied$ in this execution, or that the $adversary$ $lost$.

We now define what it means for $\mathcal{P}$ to $poly\text{-}satisfy$ $\mathcal{R}$ under model $\mathcal{M}$ using execution operations $\mathcal{X}$.

Definition 3 (Protocol $\mathcal{P}$ poly-satisfies requirement $\mathcal{R}$ under model $\mathcal{M}$ using execution operations $\mathcal{X}$). *Let $\mathcal{P}, \mathcal{X} \in PPT$, and let $\mathcal{R}$ be a set of specifications, i.e., $\mathcal{R} = \{(\pi_1, \beta_1), \ldots\}$. We say that protocol $\mathcal{P}$ poly-satisfies requirement $\mathcal{R}$ under model $\mathcal{M}$ using execution operations $\mathcal{X}$, denoted $\mathcal{P} \models_{poly}^{\mathcal{M}, \mathcal{X}} \mathcal{R}$, if for every PPT adversary $\mathcal{A}$ that poly-satisfies $\mathcal{M}$ using execution operations $\mathcal{X}$, every parameters $params \in \{0,1\}^*$, and every specification $(\pi, \beta) \in \mathcal{R}$, the advantage of $\mathcal{A}$ against $\mathcal{P}$ for π using $\mathcal{X}$ is at most negligibly greater than $\beta(params)$, i.e.:*

$$\mathcal{P} \models_{poly}^{\mathcal{M}, \mathcal{X}} \mathcal{R} \overset{def}{=} \left[\begin{array}{c} (\forall\ \mathcal{A} \in PPT\ s.t.\ \mathcal{A} \models_{poly}^{\mathcal{X}} \mathcal{M},\ params \in \{0,1\}^*,\ (\pi, \beta) \in \mathcal{R}) : \\ \epsilon_{\mathcal{A}, \mathcal{P}, \mathcal{X}}^{\pi}(params) \leq \beta(params) + Negl(|params|) \end{array} \right]$$

$$(4)$$

4.2   Example: The No False Accusations Requirement $\mathcal{R}_{\mathsf{NFA}}$

Intuitively, the *No False Accusations (NFA)* requirement $\mathcal{R}_{\mathsf{NFA}}$ states that a non-faulty entity $a \notin \mathsf{F}$ would *never (falsely) accuse* of a fault another non-faulty entity, $b \notin \mathsf{F}$. It is defined as $\mathcal{R}_{\mathsf{NFA}} = (\pi_{\mathsf{NFA}}, 0)$. To properly define the π_{NFA} requirement predicate, we first define a convention for one party, say $a \in \mathsf{N}$, to output an Indicator of Accusation, i.e., 'accuse' another party, say $i_{\mathsf{M}} \in \mathsf{N}$, of a fault. Specifically, we say that at event $\hat{e}_A$ of the the execution, entity $ent[\hat{e}_A]$ accuses entity i_{M}, if $out[\hat{e}_A]$ is a triplet of the form (IA, i_{M}, x). The last value in this triplet, x, should contain the clock value at the *first* time that $ent[\hat{e}_A]$ accused i_{M}; we discuss this in [19] as the value x is not relevant for the requirement predicate, and is just used as a convenient convention for some protocols.

The No False Accusations (NFA) predicate π_{NFA} checks whether the adversary was able to cause one honest entity, say Alice, to accuse another honest entity, say Bob (i.e., both Alice and Bob are in $\mathsf{N} - \mathsf{F}$). Namely, $\pi_{\mathsf{NFA}}(T, params)$ returns $\bot$ only if $T.out[e] = (\mathsf{IA}, j, x)$, for some $j \in T.\mathsf{N}$, and both j and $T.ent[e]$ are honest (i.e., $j, T.ent[e] \in T.\mathsf{N} - T.\mathsf{F}$).

Algorithm 4. No False Accusations Predicate $\pi_{\mathsf{NFA}}(T, params)$

1: **return** $\neg($
2:   $T.ent[T.e] \in T.\mathsf{N} - T.\mathsf{F}$ $\triangleright\, T.ent[T.e]$ *is an honest entity*
3:   **and** $\exists j \in T.\mathsf{N} - T.\mathsf{F}, x$ **s.t.** $(\mathsf{IA}, j, x) \in T.out[T.e]$ $\triangleright\, T.ent[T.e]$ *accused an honest entity*
    $)$

4.3   Supporting Confidentiality and Indistinguishability

The MoSS framework supports specifications for diverse goals and scenarios. We demonstrate this by showing how to define 'indistinguishability game'-based definitions, i.e., confidentiality-related specifications.

4.3.1   Defining Confidentiality-Related Operations

To support confidentiality, we define the set $\mathcal{X}$ to include the following three operations: 'Flip', 'Challenge', 'Guess'.

- 'Flip': selects a uniformly random bit $s_{\mathcal{X}}.b$ via coin flip, i.e., $s_{\mathcal{X}}.b \xleftarrow{\mathsf{R}} \{0, 1\}$.
- 'Challenge': executes a desired operation with *one out of two possible inputs*, according to the value of $s_{\mathcal{X}}.b$. Namely, when $\mathcal{A}$ outputs $opr[e] =$ 'Challenge', the execution process invokes:

$$\mathcal{P}[inp[e].opr]\left(s_{ent[e]}, inp[e].inp[s_{\mathcal{X}}.b], clk[e]\right)$$

  where $inp[e].opr \in \mathcal{P}$ (one of the operations in $\mathcal{P}$) and $inp[e].inp$ is an 'array' with two possible inputs, of which only one is randomly chosen via $s_{\mathcal{X}}.b$, hence, the $inp[e].inp[s_{\mathcal{X}}.b]$ notation.
- 'Guess': checks if a 'guess bit', which is provided by the adversary as input, is equal to $s_{\mathcal{X}}.b$, and returns the result in $sec\text{-}out[e]$. The result is put in $sec\text{-}out$ to prevent the adversary from accessing it.

   These three operations are used as follows. The 'Flip' operation provides **Exec** with access to a random bit $s_{\mathcal{X}}.b$ that is not controlled or visible to $\mathcal{A}$. Once the 'Flip' operation is invoked, the adversary can choose the 'Challenge' operation, i.e., $type[e] = \mathcal{X}$ and $opr[e] =$ 'Challenge', and can specify any operation of $\mathcal{P}$ it wants to invoke ($inp[e].opr$) and any two inputs it desires ($inp[e].inp$). However, **Exec** will invoke $\mathcal{P}[inp[e].opr]$ with only one of the inputs, according to the value of the random bit $s_{\mathcal{X}}.b$, i.e., $inp[e].inp[s_{\mathcal{X}}.b]$; again, since $\mathcal{A}$ has no access to $s_{\mathcal{X}}.b$, $\mathcal{A}$ neither has any knowledge about which input is selected nor can influence this selection. (As usual, further assumptions about the inputs can be specified using a model.) Then, $\mathcal{A}$ can choose the 'Guess' operation and provide its guess of the value of $s_{\mathcal{X}}.b$ (0 or 1) as input.

4.3.2   The Generic Indistinguishability Requirement $\mathcal{R}^{\pi}_{\text{IND}}$ and the Message Confidentiality Requirement $\mathcal{R}^{\pi_{\text{MsgConf}}}_{\text{IND}}$

To illustrate how the aforementioned operations can be used in practice, we define the indistinguishability requirement $\mathcal{R}^{\pi}_{\text{IND}}$ as $\mathcal{R}^{\pi}_{\text{IND}} = (\text{IND}^{\pi}, \frac{1}{2})$, where the IND^{π} predicate is shown in Algorithm 5. IND^{π} checks that the adversary invoked the 'Guess' operation during the last event of the execution and examines whether the 'Guess' operation outputted $\top$ in its secure output and whether the π model was satisfied. The adversary 'wins' against this predicate when it guesses correctly during the 'Guess' event. Since an output of $\bot$ by a predicate corresponds to the adversary 'winning' (see, e.g., Definition 1), the IND^{π} predicate returns the *negation* of whether the adversary guessed correctly during the last event of the execution. The base function of the $\mathcal{R}^{\pi}_{\text{IND}}$ requirement is $\frac{1}{2}$, because the probability that the adversary guesses correctly should not be significantly more than $\frac{1}{2}$.

Algorithm 5. $\text{IND}^{\pi}(T, params)$ Predicate

1: **return** $\neg($

2:     $T.type[T.e] = `\mathcal{X}$'

3:     **and** $T.opr[T.e] = $ 'Guess' **and** $T.sec\text{-}out[T.e] = \top$ ▷ *The last event is a 'Guess' event and $\mathcal{A}$ guessed correctly*

4:     **and** $\pi(T, params)$ ▷ *The model predicate π was met*

    $)$

We can use IND^{π} to define more specific requirements; for example, we use the π_{MsgConf} predicate (Algorithm 6) to define $\mathcal{R}^{\pi_{\text{MsgConf}}}_{\text{IND}} = (\text{IND}^{\pi_{\text{MsgConf}}}, \frac{1}{2})$, which defines message confidentiality for an encrypted communication protocol. Namely, assume $\mathcal{P}$ is an encrypted communication protocol, which includes the following two operations: (1) a 'Send' operation which takes as input a message m and entity i_R and outputs an encryption of m for i_R, and (2) a 'Receive' operation, which takes as input an encrypted message and decrypts it.

The π_{MsgConf} specification predicate (Algorithm 6) ensures that:
- $\mathcal{A}$ only asks for 'Send' challenges (since we are only concerned with whether or not $\mathcal{A}$ can distinguish outputs of 'Send').
- During each 'Send' challenge, $\mathcal{A}$ specifies two messages of equal length and the same recipient in the two possible inputs. This ensures that $\mathcal{A}$ does not distinguish the messages based on their lengths.
- $\mathcal{A}$ does not use the 'Receive' operation at the challenge receiver receiving from the challenge sender to decrypt any output of a 'Send' challenge.

5   Modularity Lemmas

MoSS models and requirements are defined as sets of specifications, so they can easily be combined by simply taking the union of sets. There are some

---

Algorithm 6. $\pi_{\mathsf{MsgConf}}\,(T,\,params)$ Predicate

---

1: **return** (

2:    $\forall \hat{e} \in \{1, \ldots, T.e\}$ **s.t.** $T.type[\hat{e}] = `\mathcal{X}`$ **and** $T.opr[\hat{e}] = $ 'Challenge':

3:      $T.inp[\hat{e}].opr = $ 'Send'   ▷ *Every 'Challenge' event is for 'Send' operation*

4:      **and** $|T.inp[\hat{e}].inp[0].m| = |T.inp[\hat{e}].inp[1].m|$ ▷ *Messages have equal length*

5:      **and** $\exists\ i_S, i_R \in T.N$ **s.t.**   ▷ *There is one specific sender i_S and one specific receiver i_R*

6:        $T.inp[\hat{e}].inp[0].i_R = T.inp[\hat{e}].inp[1].i_R = i_R$ ▷ *i_R is the recipient for both messages*

7:      **and** $T.ent[\hat{e}] = i_S$ ▷ *i_S is the sender*

8:      **and** $\nexists\ \hat{e}'$ **s.t.** $T.opr[\hat{e}'] = $ 'Receive'   ▷ *There is no 'Receive' event $\hat{e}'$*

      and $T.inp[\hat{e}'].c = T.out[\hat{e}].c$

9:      **and** $T.ent[\hat{e}'] = i_R$ ▷ *Where $\mathcal{A}$ uses decrypts the output of the challenge*

      and $T.inp[\hat{e}'].i_S = i_S$

)

---

intuitive properties one expects to hold for such modular combinations of models or requirements. In this section we present the model and requirement *modularity* lemmas, which essentially formalize these intuitive properties. The lemmas can be used in analysis of applied protocols, e.g., to allow a proof of a requirement under a weak model to be used as part of a proof of a more complex requirement which holds only under a stronger model. We believe that they may be helpful when applying formal methods, e.g., for automated verification and generation of proofs.

In this section, we present the asymptotic security lemmas; the (straightforward) proofs of the asymptotic security lemmas are in [19]. The concrete security lemmas and their proofs are in [19].

In the following lemmas, we describe model $\widehat{\mathcal{M}}$ as *stronger* than a model $\mathcal{M}$ (and $\mathcal{M}$ as *weaker* than $\widehat{\mathcal{M}}$) if $\widehat{\mathcal{M}}$ includes all the specifications of $\mathcal{M}$, i.e., $\mathcal{M} \subseteq \widehat{\mathcal{M}}$. Similarly, we say that a requirement $\widehat{\mathcal{R}}$ is *stronger* than a requirement $\mathcal{R}$ (and $\mathcal{R}$ is *weaker* than $\widehat{\mathcal{R}}$) if $\widehat{\mathcal{R}}$ includes all the specifications of $\mathcal{R}$, i.e., $\mathcal{R} \subseteq \widehat{\mathcal{R}}$. Basically, stronger models enforce more (or equal) constraints on the adversary or other assumptions, compared to weaker ones, while stronger requirements represent more (or equal) properties achieved by a protocol or scheme, compared to weaker ones.

5.1   Asymptotic Security Model Modularity Lemmas

The model modularity lemmas give the relationships between stronger and weaker models. They allow us to shrink stronger models (assumptions) into weaker ones and to expand weaker models (assumptions) into stronger ones as needed - and as intuitively expected to be possible.

The first lemma is the *model monotonicity lemma (asymptotic security)*. It shows that if an adversary $\mathcal{A}$ satisfies a stronger model $\widehat{\mathcal{M}}$, then $\mathcal{A}$ also satisfies any model that is weaker than $\widehat{\mathcal{M}}$.

Lemma 1 (Model monotonicity lemma (asymptotic security)).

For any set $\mathcal{X}$ of execution process operations, for any models $\mathcal{M}$ and $\widehat{\mathcal{M}}$ such that $\mathcal{M} \subseteq \widehat{\mathcal{M}}$, if an adversary $\mathcal{A}$ poly-satisfies $\widehat{\mathcal{M}}$ using $\mathcal{X}$, then $\mathcal{A}$ poly-satisfies $\mathcal{M}$ using $\mathcal{X}$, namely:

$$\mathcal{A} \models_{poly}^{\mathcal{X}} \widehat{\mathcal{M}} \Rightarrow \mathcal{A} \models_{poly}^{\mathcal{X}} \mathcal{M} \tag{5}$$

We next show the *models union lemma (asymptotic security)*, which shows that if an adversary satisfies two models $\mathcal{M}$ and $\mathcal{M}'$, then $\mathcal{A}$ also satisfies the stronger model that is obtained by taking the union of $\mathcal{M}$ and $\mathcal{M}'$.

Lemma 2 (Models union lemma (asymptotic security)).

For any set $\mathcal{X}$ of execution process operations and any two models $\mathcal{M}, \mathcal{M}'$, if an adversary $\mathcal{A}$ poly-satisfies both $\mathcal{M}$ and $\mathcal{M}'$ using $\mathcal{X}$, then $\mathcal{A}$ poly-satisfies the 'stronger' model $\widehat{\mathcal{M}} \equiv \mathcal{M} \cup \mathcal{M}'$ using $\mathcal{X}$, namely:

$$\left(\mathcal{A} \models_{poly}^{\mathcal{X}} \mathcal{M} \wedge \mathcal{A} \models_{poly}^{\mathcal{X}} \mathcal{M}' \right) \Rightarrow \mathcal{A} \models_{poly}^{\mathcal{X}} \widehat{\mathcal{M}} \tag{6}$$

We next show the *requirement-model monotonicity lemma (asymptotic security)*, which shows that if a protocol satisfies a requirement under a weaker model, then it satisfies the same requirement under a stronger model (using the same operations set $\mathcal{X}$). This is true, because if we are assuming everything that is included in the stronger model, then we are assuming everything in the weaker model (by Lemma 1), which implies that the protocol satisfies the requirement for such adversaries.

Lemma 3 (Requirement-model monotonicity lemma (asymptotic security)).

For any models $\mathcal{M}$ and $\widehat{\mathcal{M}}$ such that $\mathcal{M} \subseteq \widehat{\mathcal{M}}$, if a protocol $\mathcal{P}$ poly-satisfies requirement $\mathcal{R}$ under $\mathcal{M}$ using the execution process operations set $\mathcal{X}$, then $\mathcal{P}$ poly-satisfies $\mathcal{R}$ under $\widehat{\mathcal{M}}$ using $\mathcal{X}$, namely:

$$\mathcal{P} \models_{poly}^{\mathcal{M}, \mathcal{X}} \mathcal{R} \Rightarrow \mathcal{P} \models_{poly}^{\widehat{\mathcal{M}}, \mathcal{X}} \mathcal{R} \tag{7}$$

5.2   Asymptotic Security Requirement Modularity Lemmas

The requirement modularity lemmas prove relationships between stronger and weaker *requirements*, assuming the same model $\mathcal{M}$ and operations set $\mathcal{X}$. They allow us to infer that a protocol satisfies a particular weaker requirement given that it satisfies a stronger one, or that a protocol satisfies a particular stronger requirement given that it satisfies its (weaker) 'sub-requirements'.

The *requirement monotonicity lemma (asymptotic security)* shows that if a protocol satisfies a stronger requirement $\widehat{\mathcal{R}}$, then it satisfies any requirement that is weaker than $\widehat{\mathcal{R}}$ (under the same model $\mathcal{M}$ and using the same operations set $\mathcal{X}$).

Lemma 4 (Requirement monotonicity lemma (asymptotic security)).

For any set $\mathcal{X}$ of execution process operations, any model $\mathcal{M}$, and any requirements $\mathcal{R}$ and $\widehat{\mathcal{R}}$ such that $\mathcal{R} \subseteq \widehat{\mathcal{R}}$, if a protocol $\mathcal{P}$ poly-satisfies the (stronger) requirement $\widehat{\mathcal{R}}$ under $\mathcal{M}$ using $\mathcal{X}$, then $\mathcal{P}$ poly-satisfies $\mathcal{R}$ under $\mathcal{M}$ using $\mathcal{X}$, namely:

$$\mathcal{P} \models_{poly}^{\mathcal{M}, \mathcal{X}} \widehat{\mathcal{R}} \Rightarrow \mathcal{P} \models_{poly}^{\mathcal{M}, \mathcal{X}} \mathcal{R} \tag{8}$$

Finally, the *requirements union lemma (asymptotic security)* shows that if a protocol satisfies two requirements $\mathcal{R}$ and $\mathcal{R}'$, then it satisfies the stronger requirement that is obtained by taking the union of $\mathcal{R}$ and $\mathcal{R}'$ (under the same model $\mathcal{M}$ and operations set $\mathcal{X}$).

Lemma 5 (Requirements union lemma (asymptotic security)).

For any set $\mathcal{X}$ of execution process operations, any models $\mathcal{M}$ and $\mathcal{M}'$, and any two requirements $\mathcal{R}$ and $\mathcal{R}'$, if a protocol $\mathcal{P}$ poly-satisfies $\mathcal{R}$ under $\mathcal{M}$ using $\mathcal{X}$ and poly-satisfies $\mathcal{R}'$ under $\mathcal{M}'$ using $\mathcal{X}$, then $\mathcal{P}$ poly-satisfies the 'combined' (stronger) requirement $\widehat{\mathcal{R}} \equiv \mathcal{R} \cup \mathcal{R}'$ under model $\widehat{\mathcal{M}} \equiv \mathcal{M} \cup \mathcal{M}'$ using $\mathcal{X}$, namely:

$$\left(\mathcal{P} \models_{poly}^{\mathcal{M}, \mathcal{X}} \mathcal{R} \wedge \mathcal{P} \models_{poly}^{\mathcal{M}', \mathcal{X}} \mathcal{R}' \right) \Rightarrow \mathcal{P} \models_{poly}^{\widehat{\mathcal{M}}, \mathcal{X}} \widehat{\mathcal{R}} \tag{9}$$

6   Using MoSS for Applied Specifications

In this section, we give a taste of how MoSS can be used to define applied security specifications, with realistic, non-trivial models and requirements. In Sect. 6.1, we discuss AuthBroadcast, a simple authenticated broadcasting protocol, which we use to demonstrate the use of MoSS's modularity lemmas. In Sect. 6.2 we discuss PKI schemes, which underlie the security of countless real-world applications, and show how MoSS enables rigorous requirements and models for PKI schemes. The definitions we show are only examples from [25], which present full specification and analysis of PKI schemes. The AuthBroadcast protocol is also not a contribution; we present it as an example.

6.1   AuthBroadcast: Authenticated Broadcast Protocol

In [19], we present the AuthBroadcast protocol, a simple authenticated broadcast protocol that we developed and analyzed to help us fine-tune the MoSS definitions. AuthBroadcast enables a set of entities N to broadcast authenticated messages to each other, i.e., to validate that a received message was indeed sent by a member of N. The protocol uses a standard deterministic message authentication scheme MAC which takes as input a tag length, key, and message and outputs a tag. In this subsection, we present a few details as examples of the use of MoSS; in particular, AuthBroadcast addresses shared-key initialization, an aspect which does not exist in PKI schemes. We define $\mathcal{M}_{\mathcal{X}[\text{'Sec-in'}]}^{\text{KeyShare}}$ and $\mathcal{M}_{\mathcal{P}[\text{'Sec-in'}]}^{\text{Exclude}}$, two simple models for shared-key initialization. These models can be reused for specifications of many other tasks.

The MoSS framework allows the analysis of the same protocol under different models, as we demonstrate here. Specifically, we present the analysis of AuthBroadcast in several steps, where in each step, we prove that AuthBroadcast satisfies a requirement - assuming increasingly stronger models:

1. We first show that AuthBroadcast ensures *authentication* of received messages assuming that a key is shared securely once among all entities and valid n and 1^κ parameters are given to the protocol. Namely, we show that AuthBroadcast poly-satisfies $\mathcal{R}_{\text{Auth}_\infty}^{\text{Broadcast}}$ under $\mathcal{M}_{\text{SecKeyInit}}$ using $\mathcal{X}$-operations {'Sec-in'}.

2. We then show that AuthBroadcast ensures *authentication and freshness* of received messages under a stronger model that also assumes a weak-level of clock synchronization (bounded clock drift). Namely, we show that AuthBroadcast poly-satisfies $\mathcal{R}_{\text{Auth}_{f(\Delta)}}^{\text{Broadcast}}$ under $\mathcal{M}_{\text{Drift}_{\Delta_{clk}}}^{\text{SecKeyInit}}$ using $\mathcal{X}$-operations {'Sec-in'} for $f(\Delta) = \Delta + 2\Delta_{clk}$, where Δ_{clk} is the assumed maximal clock drift.

3. Finally, we show that AuthBroadcast ensures *correct bounded-delay delivery/receipt* of broadcast messages (which implies authenticity and freshness as well) under an even stronger model which also assumes a bounded delay of communication and a sufficiently large freshness interval given to the protocol. Specifically, we show that AuthBroadcast poly-satisfies $\mathcal{R}_{\text{Receive}_{\Delta_{com}}}^{\text{Broadcast}}$ under $\mathcal{M}_{\text{Drift}_{\Delta_{clk}},\text{Delay}_{\Delta_{com}}}^{\text{SecKeyInit}}$ using $\mathcal{X}$-operations {'Sec-in'}, where Δ_{clk} is the assumed maximal clock drift and Δ_{com} is the assumed maximal communication delay.

6.2 Specifications for PKI Scheme

PKI schemes are an essential building block for protocols utilizing public key cryptography. Unfortunately, there have been multiple incidents and vulnerabilities involving PKI, resulting in extensive research on improving security of PKI. Provably-secure PKI schemes were presented in [13], however, these specifications did not cover aspects critical in practice, such as timely revocation or transparency. We next briefly discuss one of the PKI security specifications defined using MoSS.

Sample Model: $\mathcal{M}_{\Delta_{clk}}^{\text{Drift}}$. [25] defines several models covering assumptions regarding the adversary capabilities, the environment (communication and synchronization) and the initialization, assumed by different PKI protocols. The bounded clock drift model $\mathcal{M}_{\Delta_{clk}}^{\text{Drift}}$ (presented in Sect. 3.3) is an example of a *generic model* which is common to many applied protocols and can be reused among different works and tasks.

Sample Requirement: ΔTRA. PKI schemes have multiple security requirements, from simple requirements such as accountability to more complex requirements such as equivocation detection and prevention as well as transparency. Intuitively, the Δ-transparency (ΔTRA) requirement specifies that a certificate attested as Δ-transparent must be available to all 'interested' parties, i.e., *monitors*, within Δ time of its transparency attestation being issued by a proper authority, typically referred to as a *logger*. This requirement is defined as the pair $(\pi_{\Delta TRA}, 0)$, where the $\pi_{\Delta TRA}$ predicate is defined in Algorithm 7, as a conjunction of the simple sub-predicates, defined in [25].

Algorithm 7. The Δ-transparency (ΔTRA) predicate $\pi_{\Delta TRA}$

$$\pi_{\Delta TRA}(T, params) \equiv \left\{ \begin{array}{l} (\psi, \rho, pk, \iota, \iota_M) \leftarrow T.out_A; \\[4pt] \text{return } \neg \left[\begin{array}{l} \text{HONESTENTITY}(T, params, \iota) \wedge \\ \text{CORRECTPUBLICKEY}(T, params, \iota, pk, \rho.\iota) \wedge \\ \text{VALIDCERTIFICATEATTESTATION}(T, params, \{\Delta TRA\}, \psi, pk, \rho) \wedge \\ \text{HONESTENTITY}(T, params, \iota_M) \wedge \\ \text{ISMONITOR}(T, params, \iota_M, \rho.\iota) \wedge \\ \text{HONESTMONITORUNAWAREOFCERTIFICATE}(T, params, \psi, \rho) \wedge \\ \text{WASNOTACCUSED}(params, \iota_M, \rho.\iota) \end{array} \right] \end{array} \right\} ;$$

Let us explain the operation of $\pi_{\Delta TRA}$. This predicate ensures that for a certificate ψ and Δ-transparency attestation ρ as attested by an entity $\rho.\iota$, there is an honest entity $\iota \in N$ (HONESTENTITY), and ι confirmed that $\rho.\iota$'s public key is pk (CORRECTPUBLICKEY). Then, it verifies that ψ is a valid certificate attested as Δ-transparent using ρ (VALIDCERTIFICATEATTESTATION). *However*, there exists another *honest* entity $\iota_M \in N$ (HONESTENTITY) which monitors $\rho.\iota$ (ISMONITOR) but is unaware of ψ (HONESTMONITORUNAWARE OFCERTIFICATE) - although it should, and yet, there was no accusation of misbehavior issued[6] (WASNOTACCUSED).

This design for a predicate as a conjuncture of sub-predicate is typical and rather intuitive, and it illustrates another aspect of modularity: the sub-predicates are easy to understand and validate, and are also reusable; for example, a predicate to validate an entity's public key (VALIDCERTIFICATEATTESTATION) or that an entity is honest (HONESTENTITY) can be useful for other, unrelated to PKI protocols.

7 Concrete Security and Ensuring Polytime Interactions

In this section, we present the CS *compiler* (Sect. 7.1), which transforms the adversary into an 'equivalent' algorithm, which provides three additional outputs: the total runtime of the adversary, the number of bit flips by the adversary, and the initial size of the adversary's state. We then use the CS compiler for two applications. First, in Sect. 7.2, we extend MoSS to support *concrete security*.

---

[6] Notice that ι, ι_M are honest, but $\rho.\iota$ is not necessarily honest, and therefore, WASNOTACCUSED is needed, because $\rho.\iota$ might not cooperate in order for ι_M to not be aware of ψ.

Finally, in Sect. 7.3, we show how the CS compiler allows to ensure *polytime interactions*, and in particular, limit the adversary so that its runtime is polynomial in the security parameter.

7.1   The CS Compiler

The extension that will allow us to give concrete security definitions (Sect. 7.2) and to enforce polytime interactions (Sect. 7.3), is a *compiler*, denoted CS (which stands for both '*CtrSteps*' and 'Concrete Security').

The input to CS is an (adversary) algorithm $\mathcal{A}$, and the output, $CS(\mathcal{A})$, is an algorithm which outputs the same output as $\mathcal{A}$ would produce, and three additional values, added to the final $out_{\mathcal{A}}$ output of $\mathcal{A}$: $out_{\mathcal{A}}.CtrSteps$, the number of steps of $\mathcal{A}$ throughout the execution; $out_{\mathcal{A}}.CtrBitFlips$, the number of bit-flip operations performed by $\mathcal{A}$; and $out_{\mathcal{A}}.LenInitState$, the size of the initial state output by $\mathcal{A}$.

Now, instead of running the execution process directly over input adversary $\mathcal{A}$, we run $\mathbf{Exec}^{\mathcal{X}}_{CS(\mathcal{A}),\mathcal{P}}(params)$, i.e., we run the 'instrumented' adversary $CS(\mathcal{A})$. This way, in the execution transcript, we receive these three measured values ($out_{\mathcal{A}}.CtrSteps$, $out_{\mathcal{A}}.CtrBitFlips$ and $out_{\mathcal{A}}.LenInitState$). It remains to describe the operation of CS.

Note that CS maintains its own state, which contains, as part of it, the state of the adversary $\mathcal{A}$. This creates a somewhat confusing situation, which may be familiar to the reader from constructions in the theory of complexity, or, esp. to practitioners, from the relation between a virtual machine and the program it is running. Namely, the execution process received the algorithm $CS(\mathcal{A})$ as the adversary, while $CS(\mathcal{A})$ is running the 'real' adversary $\mathcal{A}$. Thus, the state maintained by the execution process is now of $CS(\mathcal{A})$; hence, we refer to this state as $s_{CS(\mathcal{A})}$.

The state $s_{CS(\mathcal{A})}$ consists of four variables. The first variable contains the state of the original adversary $\mathcal{A}$. We denote this variable by $s_{CS(\mathcal{A})}.s_{\mathcal{A}}$; this unwieldy notation is trying to express the fact that from the point of view of the 'real' adversary $\mathcal{A}$, this is its (entire) state, while it is only part of the state $s_{CS(\mathcal{A})}$ of the $CS(\mathcal{A})$ algorithm (run as the adversary by the execution process).

The other three variables in the state $s_{CS(\mathcal{A})}$ are invisible to $\mathcal{A}$, since they are not part of $s_{CS(\mathcal{A})}.s_{\mathcal{A}}$. These are: $s_{CS(\mathcal{A})}.CtrSteps$, a counter which the algorithm $CS(\mathcal{A})$ uses to sum up the total runtime (steps) of $\mathcal{A}$; $s_{CS(\mathcal{A})}.CtrBitFlips$, a counter which $CS(\mathcal{A})$ uses to sum up the number of random bits flipped by $\mathcal{A}$; and, finally, $s_{CS(\mathcal{A})}.LenInitState$, which stores the size of the initial state output by $\mathcal{A}$.

Whenever the execution process invokes $CS(\mathcal{A})$, then $CS(\mathcal{A})$ 'runs' $\mathcal{A}$ on the provided inputs, measuring the time (number of steps) until $\mathcal{A}$ returns its response, as well as the number of random bits (coin flips) used by $\mathcal{A}$. When $\mathcal{A}$ returns a response, $CS(\mathcal{A})$ increments the $s_{CS(\mathcal{A})}.CtrSteps$ counter by the run-time of $\mathcal{A}$ in this specific invocation and increments the $s_{CS(\mathcal{A})}.CtrBitFlips$ counter by the number of bit flips of $\mathcal{A}$ in this invocation. When $\mathcal{A}$ returns a response $(s_{\mathcal{A}}, N, params.\mathcal{P}[\cdot])$ after being invoked by $CS(\mathcal{A})[\text{'Init'}](params)$

in line 1, then $\mathsf{CS}(\mathcal{A})$ additionally sets $s_{\mathsf{CS}(\mathcal{A})}.LenInitState \leftarrow |s_{\mathcal{A}}|$. Finally, $\mathsf{CS}(\mathcal{A})$ checks if $\mathcal{A}$ signaled termination of the execution process. When $\mathcal{A}$ signals termination (by returning $out_{\mathcal{A}} \neq \bot$), then the $\mathsf{CS}(\mathcal{A})$ algorithm sets $out_{\mathcal{A}}.CtrSteps$, $out_{\mathcal{A}}.CtrBitFlips$, and $out_{\mathcal{A}}.LenInitState$ to $s_{\mathsf{CS}(\mathcal{A})}.CtrSteps$, $s_{\mathsf{CS}(\mathcal{A})}.CtrBitFlips$, and $s_{\mathsf{CS}(\mathcal{A})}.LenInitState$, respectively, i.e., adds to $out_{\mathcal{A}}$ the computed total runtime of $\mathcal{A}$ during this execution, the number of bit flips of $\mathcal{A}$ during this execution, and the size of the initial state output by $\mathcal{A}$[7]; of course, we still have $out_{\mathcal{A}} \neq \bot$ and therefore the execution process terminates - returning as part of $out_{\mathcal{A}}$ the total runtime of $\mathcal{A}$ and the size of the initial state output by $\mathcal{A}$. Although these values are carried in $out_{\mathcal{A}}$, the adversary cannot modify or view them.

7.2   Concrete Security

We new describe how we can use CS to support *concrete security* [6] in MoSS. In concrete security, the adversary's advantage is a function of the 'adversary resources', which may include different types of resources such as the runtime (in a specific computational model), length (of inputs, keys, etc.), and the number of different operations that the adversary invokes (e.g., 'oracle calls'). Notice that since we explicitly bound the adversary's runtime, we do not need to require the adversary to be a PPT algorithm.

  To be more specific, we provide *bounds* on adversary resources, including runtime and number of coin-flips (random bits), as *parameters* in *params*; this allows the adversary to limit its use of resources accordingly. We (next) define the *Concrete Security model* $\mathcal{M}^{\mathrm{CS}}$, which validates that the adversary, indeed, does not exceed the bounds specified in *params*. To validate the bounds on the adversary's runtime and number of coin-flips (random bits), $\mathcal{M}^{\mathrm{CS}}$ uses $out_{\mathcal{A}}.CtrSteps$ and $out_{\mathcal{A}}.CtrBitFlips$, hence, this model should be applied to the transcript $T \leftarrow \mathbf{Exec}^{\mathcal{X}}_{\mathsf{CS}(\mathcal{A}),\mathcal{P}}(params)$, produced by running the 'instrumented adversary' $\mathsf{CS}(\mathcal{A})$.

7.2.1   The Concrete Security Model $\mathcal{M}^{\mathrm{CS}}$ and Resource Bounds
Concrete security defines the adversary's advantage as a function of the *bounds* on adversary resources, specified in *params*. Specifically, we adopt the following conventions for the adversary resource parameters. First, *params* includes an array *params.bounds.maxCalls*, where each entry *params.bounds.maxCalls[type][opr]* contains the maximum number of calls that $\mathcal{A}$ is allowed to make to operation *opr* of type *type*. Second, *params* includes the field *params.bounds.maxSteps*, which is the maximum number of steps that the adversary is allowed to take, and the field *params.bounds.maxBitFlips*, which is the maximum number of bit flips that the adversary is allowed to use.

---

[7] Note this would override any values that $\mathcal{A}$ may write on $out_{\mathcal{A}}.CtrSteps$, $out_{\mathcal{A}}.CtrBitFlips$, and $out_{\mathcal{A}}.LenInitState$, i.e., we essentially forbid the use of $out_{\mathcal{A}}.CtrSteps$, $out_{\mathcal{A}}.CtrBitFlips$, and $out_{\mathcal{A}}.LenInitState$ by $\mathcal{A}$.

Algorithm 8. $\pi^{\mathrm{CS}}(T, params)$ Predicate

1: **return** (

2:    $\forall\ type \in params.bounds.maxCalls$:

3:    $\forall\ opr \in params.bounds.maxCalls[type]$:   ▷ Maximum number of calls to each operation with bounds is not exceeded

4:    $\left| \left\{ \hat{e} \;\middle|\; \begin{array}{l} \hat{e} \in \{1, \ldots, T.e\} \text{ and} \\ T.type[\hat{e}] = type \text{ and} \\ T.opr[\hat{e}] = opr \end{array} \right\} \right| \leq params.bounds.maxCalls[type][opr]$

  and $T.out_{\mathcal{A}}.CtrSteps \leq params.bounds.maxSteps$ ▷ Maximum number of steps taken by $\mathcal{A}$ is not exceeded

  and $T.out_{\mathcal{A}}.CtrBitFlips \leq params.bounds.maxBitFlips$ ▷ Maximum number of bit flips used by $\mathcal{A}$ is not exceeded

)

The Concrete Security model $\mathcal{M}^{\mathrm{CS}}$ validates that the adversary never exceeds these bounds; it is defined as $\mathcal{M}^{\mathrm{CS}} = \{(\pi^{\mathrm{CS}}, 0)\}$, i.e., we expect the adversary to *always* limit itself to the bounds specified in $params.bounds$.

The π^{CS} predicate (Algorithm 8) ensures that: (1) $\mathcal{A}$ does not exceed the bounds in $params.bounds.maxCalls$ on the number of calls to each operation, (2) $\mathcal{A}$ does not exceed the bound $params.bounds.maxSteps$ on the number of steps it takes, and (3) $\mathcal{A}$ does not exceed the bound $params.bounds.maxBitFlips$ on the number of bit flips it uses.

7.2.2   Satisfaction of Concrete-Security Models and Requirements

When using MoSS for concrete security analysis, for a specification (π, β), the function $\beta(params)$ is a *bound* on the probability of the adversary winning. Namely, there is no additional 'negligible' probability for the adversary to win, as we allowed in the asymptotic definitions. When $\mathcal{A}$ satisfies $\mathcal{M}$, for every specification in $\mathcal{M}$, the probability of $\mathcal{A}$ winning is *bounded* by the base function β. Similarly, when $\mathcal{P}$ satisfies $\mathcal{R}$ under some model $\mathcal{M}$, for every $\mathcal{A}$ that satisfies $\mathcal{M}$ and every specification in $\mathcal{R}$, the probability of $\mathcal{A}$ winning is *bounded* by the base function β.

This implies that the base function is likely to differ when using MoSS for asymptotic analysis versus concrete security analysis; e.g., in asymptotic analysis, a specification $(\pi, 0)$ may be used, but in concrete security analysis, (π, β) may be used instead, where β is a function that returns values in $[0, 1]$, which depend on the resources available to the adversary, e.g., maximal runtime (steps). This difference should be familiar to readers familiar with concrete-security definitions and results, e.g., [5]. However, often we can use the same predicate π in both types of analysis.

We now give the concrete definition of a model-satisfying adversary. Note that the base function $\beta(params)$ is a function of the parameters ($params$), including the bounds on the adversary resources ($params.bounds$). To make these bounds meaningful, a model-satisfying adversary *always* has to satisfy $\mathcal{M}^{CS}$ (see Sect. 7.2.1).

Definition 4. (Adversary $\mathcal{A}$ CS-satisfies model $\mathcal{M}$ using execution operations $\mathcal{X}$). *Let $\mathcal{A}, \mathcal{X}$ be algorithms and let $\mathcal{M}$ be a set of specifications, i.e., $\mathcal{M} = \{(\pi_1, \beta_1), \ldots\}$. We say that adversary $\mathcal{A}$ CS-satisfies model $\mathcal{M}$ using execution operations $\mathcal{X}$, denoted $\mathcal{A} \models_{\mathsf{CS}}^{\mathcal{X}} \mathcal{M}$, if for every protocol $\mathcal{P}$, $params \in \{0,1\}^*$, and specification $(\pi, \beta) \in \mathcal{M} \cup \mathcal{M}^{CS}$, the advantage of $\mathsf{CS}(\mathcal{A})$ against $\mathcal{P}$ for π using $\mathcal{X}$ is bounded by $\beta(params)$, i.e.:*

$$\mathcal{A} \models_{\mathsf{CS}}^{\mathcal{X}} \mathcal{M} \stackrel{def}{=} \left[\begin{array}{c} (\forall\ \mathcal{P}, params \in \{0,1\}^*, (\pi, \beta) \in \mathcal{M} \cup \mathcal{M}^{CS}) : \\[2mm] \epsilon_{\mathsf{CS}(\mathcal{A}),\mathcal{P},\mathcal{X}}^{\pi}(params) \leq \beta(params) \end{array} \right] \qquad (10)$$

We also give the concrete definition of requirement-satisfying protocol.

Definition 5 (Protocol $\mathcal{P}$ CS-satisfies requirement $\mathcal{R}$ under model $\mathcal{M}$ using execution operations $\mathcal{X}$). *Let $\mathcal{P}, \mathcal{X}$ be algorithms, and let $\mathcal{R}$ be a set of specifications, i.e., $\mathcal{R} = \{(\pi_1, \beta_1), \ldots\}$. We say that protocol $\mathcal{P}$ CS-satisfies requirement $\mathcal{R}$ under model $\mathcal{M}$ using execution operations $\mathcal{X}$, denoted $\mathcal{P} \models_{\mathsf{CS}}^{\mathcal{M}, \mathcal{X}} \mathcal{R}$, if for every adversary $\mathcal{A}$ that CS-satisfies $\mathcal{M}$ using execution operations $\mathcal{X}$, every parameters $params \in \{0,1\}^*$, and every specification $(\pi, \beta) \in \mathcal{R}$, the advantage of $\mathsf{CS}(\mathcal{A})$ against $\mathcal{P}$ for π using $\mathcal{X}$ is bounded by $\beta(params)$, i.e.:*

$$\mathcal{P} \models_{\mathsf{CS}}^{\mathcal{M}, \mathcal{X}} \mathcal{R} \stackrel{def}{=} \left[\begin{array}{c} (\forall\ \mathcal{A}\ s.t.\ \mathcal{A} \models_{\mathsf{CS}}^{\mathcal{X}} \mathcal{M},\ params \in \{0,1\}^*,\ (\pi, \beta) \in \mathcal{R}) : \\[2mm] \epsilon_{\mathsf{CS}(\mathcal{A}),\mathcal{P},\mathcal{X}}^{\pi}(params) \leq \beta(params) \end{array} \right] \qquad (11)$$

Note that if adversary $\mathcal{A}$ CS-satisfies $\mathcal{M}$ using $\mathcal{X}$ for a model $\mathcal{M} = \{(\pi_1, \beta_1), \ldots\}$ where every base function is a positive negligible function in the security parameter (i.e., $|params|$), then $\mathcal{A}$ poly-satisfies $\mathcal{M}'$ using $\mathcal{X}$ for $\mathcal{M}' = \{(\pi_1, 0), \ldots\}$ - i.e., $\mathcal{A}$ satisfies a model with the same predicates as $\mathcal{M}$ but with all zero-constant base functions in the asymptotic sense. Similarly, if protocol $\mathcal{P}$ CS-satisfies $\mathcal{R}$ under $\mathcal{M}$ using $\mathcal{X}$ for a requirement $\mathcal{R} = \{(\pi_1, \beta_1), \ldots\}$ where every base function is a positive negligible function in $|params|$, then $\mathcal{P}$ poly-satisfies $\mathcal{R}'$ under $\mathcal{M}$ using $\mathcal{X}$ for $\mathcal{R}' = \{(\pi_1, 0), \ldots\}$.

7.3   Ensuring Polytime Interactions

We next discuss a very different application of the CS Compiler (Subsect. 7.1): ensuring polytime interactions. Let us first explain the polytime interaction challenge. In most of this work, as in most works in cryptography, we focus on PPT algorithms and asymptotically polynomial specifications. For instance, consider Definition 2, where we require $\mathcal{A}, \mathcal{X}, \mathcal{P} \in PPT$ and bound the advantage by the base function plus a negligible function - i.e., a function which is smaller than any positive polynomial in the length of the inputs, for sufficiently large inputs.

However, when analyzing interacting systems as facilitated by MoSS, there is a concern: each of the algorithms might be in PPT, yet the *total* runtime can be *exponential* in the size of the *original input*. For example, consider an adversary $\mathcal{A}$, that, in every call, outputs a state which is twice the size of its input state. Namely, if the size of the adversary's state in the beginning was l, then after e calls to the adversary algorithm $\mathcal{A}$, the size of $s_{\mathcal{A}}$ would be $2^e \cdot l$, i.e., exponential in the number of steps e.

For asymptotic analysis, we may want to ensure *polytime interactions*, i.e., to limit the total running time of $\mathcal{A}$ and $\mathcal{P}$ during the execution to be polynomial. Let us first focus on the adversary's runtime. To limit the adversary's total runtime by a polynomial in the length of its initial input, i.e., length of *params*, we use the CS Compiler, i.e., consider the execution transcript of $\mathbf{Exec}_{\mathsf{CS}(\mathcal{A}),\mathcal{P}}^{\mathcal{X}}(params)$. Specifically, we use the fact that the transcript T includes the size of the initial state output by $\mathcal{A}$ in $T.s_{\mathcal{A}}.LenInitState$, as well as the total number of steps taken by $\mathcal{A}$ in $T.s_{\mathcal{A}}.CtrSteps$.

Define the model $\mathcal{M}_{\mathrm{polyAdv}}$ as $\mathcal{M}_{\mathrm{polyAdv}} = (\pi_{\mathrm{polyAdv}}, 0)$, where the π_{polyAdv} predicate, shown in Algorithm 9, verifies that $T.s_{\mathcal{A}}.CtrSteps$ is bounded by $2 \cdot T.s_{\mathcal{A}}.LenInitState$. When T is a transcript returned by $\mathbf{Exec}_{\mathsf{CS}(\mathcal{A}),\mathcal{P}}^{\mathcal{X}}(params)$, this means that the number of steps taken by $\mathcal{A}$ over the whole execution does not exceed twice[8] the size of the initial state output by $\mathcal{A}$, which is bounded by a polynomial in $|params|$. Hence, model $\mathcal{M}_{\mathrm{polyAdv}}$ ensures that the total runtime of the adversary, over the entire execution, is polynomial in the size of the input parameters.

Algorithm 9. The π_{polyAdv} $(T, params)$ Predicate

1: **return** $\left(T.out_{\mathcal{A}}.CtrSteps \leq 2 \cdot T.out_{\mathcal{A}}.LenInitState\right)$

The $\mathcal{M}_{\mathrm{polyAdv}}$ model ensures polynomial runtime of the adversary, and hence also a polynomial number of invocations of the protocol. In some situations it is also important to similarly restrict the *protocols*, e.g., when proving an impossibility or lower-bound on protocols. Note that for most 'real' protocols, such restrictions hold immediately from assuming the protocol is a PPT algorithm, since such protocols use bounded-size state and messages (outputs); and total runtime is polynomial even if we allow linear growth in state and outputs. We can focus on such 'reasonable' protocols by including an appropriate requirement in the specifications. See the full version [19] for more on this topic.

8   Conclusions and Future Work

The MoSS framework enables modular security specifications for applied cryptographic protocols, combining different models and requirements, each defined

---

[8] We allow the total runtime to be *twice* the length of the adversary's initial state, to give the adversary additional time so it can also output this initial state, and is left with enough time for the execution.

separately. As a result, MoSS allows comparison of protocols based on the requirements they satisfy and the models they assume. Definitions of models, and even some generic requirements, may be reused across different works. While, obviously, it takes some effort to learn MoSS, we found that the rewards of modularity and reusability justify the effort.

Future work includes the important challenges of (1) developing computer-aided mechanisms that support MoSS, e.g., 'translating' the modular MoSS specifications into a form supported by computer-aided proof tools, or developing computer-aided proof tools for MoSS specifically, possibly using the modularity lemmas of Sect. 5, (2) extending the MoSS framework to support secure composition, and (3) exploring the ability to support MoSS-like modular specifications in simulation-based frameworks such as UC, and the ability to support simulation-based specifications in MoSS. Finally, we hope that MoSS will prove useful in specification and analysis of applied protocols, and the identification and reuse of standard and generic models and requirements.

Acknowledgments. We thank the anonymous reviewers for their insightful and constructive feedback; among other things, it helped us improve the definitions of models and requirements. We also thank Yuval Ishay, Sergio Rajsbaum, Juan Garay and Iftach Haitner for their comments and suggestions on earlier drafts of the paper. Special thanks to Oded Goldreich for his encouragement and for suggesting a simplified way to ensure total polynomial time, which was the basis for our current 'interactive polytime adversary' (Sect. 7.3). Part of the work was done while Ewa Syta had a visiting position at University of Connecticut. This work was partially supported by the Comcast Corporation. The opinions expressed are of the authors and not of their university or funding sources.

References

1. Backes, M., Pfitzmann, B., Waidner, M.: A general composition theorem for secure reactive systems. In: Theory of Cryptography Conference. Springer (2004)
2. Barbosa, M., et al.: Sok: computer-aided cryptography. In: IEEE Symposium on Security and Privacy (2021)
3. Barthe, G., Grégoire, B., Heraud, S., Béguelin, S.Z.: Computer-aided security proofs for the working cryptographer. In: Annual Cryptology Conference (2011)
4. Bellare, M., Canetti, R., Krawczyk, H.: A modular approach to the design and analysis of authentication and key exchange protocols. IACR Cryptol. ePrint Arch **1998**, 9 (1998). http://eprint.iacr.org/1998/009
5. Bellare, M., Desai, A., Jokipii, E., Rogaway, P.: A concrete security treatment of symmetric encryption. In: FOCS, pp. 394–403 (1997)
6. Bellare, M., Kilian, J., Rogaway, P.: The security of the cipher block chaining message authentication code. J. Comput. Syst. Sci. 61(3), 362–399 (2000)
7. Bellare, M., Rogaway, P.: Entity authentication and key distribution. In: Stinson, D.R. (ed.) Advances in Cryptology–CRYPTO '93. Lecture Notes in Computer Science, vol. 773, pp. 232–249. Springer-Verlag (22–26 Aug 1993)

8. Bellare, M., Rogaway, P.: The security of triple encryption and a framework for code-based game-playing proofs. In: EUROCRYPT (2006)
9. Blanchet, B.: A computationally sound mechanized prover for security protocols. IEEE Trans. Depend. Secure Comput. (2008)
10. Camenisch, J., Krenn, S., Küsters, R., Rausch, D.: iUC: Flexible universal composability made simple. In: EUROCRYPT (2019)
11. Canetti, R.: Universally composable security: a new paradigm for cryptographic protocols. In: IEEE Symposium on Foundations of Computer Science (2001)
12. Canetti, R.: Universally composable security. Journal of the ACM (JACM) **67**(5), 1–94 (2020)
13. Canetti, R., Shahaf, D., Vald, M.: Universally Composable Authentication and Key-exchange with Global PKI. Cryptology ePrint Archive, Report 2014/432 (2014). https://eprint.iacr.org/2014/432
14. CCITT, B.B.: Recommendations X. 509 and ISO 9594-8. Information Processing Systems-OSI-The Directory Authentication Framework (Geneva: CCITT) (1988)
15. Degabriele, J.P., Paterson, K., Watson, G.: Provable security in the real world. IEEE Security & Privacy **9**(3), 33–41 (2010)
16. Goldreich, O., Goldwasser, S., Micali, S.: How to construct random functions. Journal of the ACM **33**(4), 792–807 (1986)
17. Goldwasser, S., Micali, S.: Probabilistic Encryption. Journal of Computer and System Sciences **28**(2), 270–299 (1984)
18. Goldwasser, S., Micali, S., Rivest, R.L.: A digital signature scheme secure against adaptive chosen-message attacks. SIAM J. Comput. (1988)
19. Herzberg, A., Leibowitz, H., Syta, E., Wrótniak, S.: Moss: modular security specifications framework - full version. Cryptology ePrint Archive, Report 2020/1040 (2020). https://eprint.iacr.org/2020/1040
20. Herzberg, A., Yoffe, I.: The layered games framework for specifications and analysis of security protocols. IJACT **1**(2), 144–159 (2008). https://www.researchgate.net/publication/220571819_The_layered_games_framework_for_specifications_and_analysis_of_security_protocols
21. Hofheinz, D., Shoup, V.: GNUC: A new universal composability framework. Journal of Cryptology **28**(3), 423–508 (2015)
22. Hofheinz, D., Unruh, D., Müller-Quade, J.: Polynomial runtime and composability. Journal of Cryptology **26**(3), 375–441 (2013)
23. Küsters, R., Tuengerthal, M., Rausch, D.: The IITM model: a simple and expressive model for universal composability. J. Cryptol., 1–124 (2020)
24. Laurie, B., Langley, A., Kasper, E.: Certificate Transparency. RFC 6962 (2013). https://doi.org/10.17487/RFC6962
25. Leibowitz, H., Herzberg, A., Syta, E.: Provable security for PKI schemes. Cryptology ePrint Archive, Report 2019/807 (2019). https://eprint.iacr.org/2019/807
26. Lochbihler, A., Sefidgar, S.R., Basin, D., Maurer, U.: Formalizing constructive cryptography using crypthol. In: Computer Security Foundations (2019)
27. Maurer, U.: Constructive cryptography-a new paradigm for security definitions and proofs. In: Workshop on Theory of Security and Applications (2011)
28. Meier, S., Schmidt, B., Cremers, C., Basin, D.: The TAMARIN prover for the symbolic analysis of security protocols. In: Computer Aided Verification (2013)

29. Shoup, V.: Sequences of games: a tool for taming complexity in security proofs. Cryptology ePrint Archive, Report 2004/332 (2004)
30. Wikström, Douglas: Simplified l. In: Kushilevitz, Eyal, Malkin, Tal (eds.) TCC 2016. LNCS, vol. 9562, pp. 566–595. Springer, Heidelberg (2016). https://doi.org/10.1007/978-3-662-49096-9_24

Tight State-Restoration Soundness in the Algebraic Group Model

Ashrujit Ghoshal$^{(\boxtimes)}$ and Stefano Tessaro

Paul G. Allen School of Computer Science & Engineering,
University of Washington, Seattle, USA
{ashrujit,tessaro}@cs.washington.edu

Abstract. Most efficient zero-knowledge arguments lack a concrete security analysis, making parameter choices and efficiency comparisons challenging. This is even more true for non-interactive versions of these systems obtained via the Fiat-Shamir transform, for which the security guarantees generically derived from the interactive protocol are often too weak, even when assuming a random oracle.

This paper initiates the study of *state-restoration soundness* in the algebraic group model (AGM) of Fuchsbauer, Kiltz, and Loss (CRYPTO '18). This is a stronger notion of soundness for an interactive proof or argument which allows the prover to rewind the verifier, and which is tightly connected with the concrete soundness of the non-interactive argument obtained via the Fiat-Shamir transform.

We propose a general methodology to prove tight bounds on state-restoration soundness, and apply it to variants of Bulletproofs (Bootle et al., S&P '18) and Sonic (Maller et al., CCS '19). To the best of our knowledge, our analysis of Bulletproofs gives the *first* non-trivial concrete security analysis for a non-constant round argument combined with the Fiat-Shamir transform.

Keywords: Zero-knowledge proof systems · Concrete security · Fiat-Shamir transform · Algebraic group model · State-restoration soundness

1 Introduction

The last decade has seen zero-knowledge proof systems [1] gain enormous popularity in the design of efficient privacy-preserving systems. Their concrete efficiency is directly affected by the choice of a security parameter, yet *concrete security* analyses are rare and, as we explain below, hit upon technical barriers, even in ideal models (such as the random-oracle [2] or the generic-group models [3,4]). This has led to parameter choices not backed by proofs, and to efficiency comparisons across protocols with possibly incomparable levels of security. This paper addresses the question of narrowing this gap for protocols whose security can be analyzed in the Algebraic Group Model [5].

© International Association for Cryptologic Research 2021
T. Malkin and C. Peikert (Eds.): CRYPTO 2021, LNCS 12827, pp. 64–93, 2021.
https://doi.org/10.1007/978-3-030-84252-9_3

A CONCRETE EXAMPLE. It is convenient to start with an example to illustrate the challenges encountered in proving concrete security of proof systems. We focus on Bulletproofs [6], which are argument systems with applications across the cryptocurrencies[1] and in verifiably deterministic signatures [9], which in turn optimize prior work [10]. The soundness[2] analysis (of their interactive version) is asymptotic, based on the hardness of the *discrete logarithm problem* (DLP). Even when instantiated from 256-bit elliptic curves, due to the absence of a tight, concrete, reduction, we have no formal guarantee on concrete security. Indeed, recent work [11] gives concrete soundness bounds in the generic-group model with somewhat unfavorable dependence on the size of the statement being proved, and no better analysis is known.

Even more importantly, existing bounds are for the *interactive* version of the protocol, but Bulletproofs are meant to be used *non-interactively* via the Fiat-Shamir (FS) transform [12]. However, the (folklore) analysis of the FS transform gives no useful guarantees: Namely, for a soundness bound ε on the *interactive* ZK proof system, the resulting NIZK has soundness $q^r \varepsilon$, where q is the number of random-oracle queries, and r is the number of challenges sent by the verifier. For Bulletproofs, we have $\varepsilon \geq 2^{-256}$ (this is the probability of merely *guessing* the discrete log), and if (say) $r = \Theta(\log(n)) \geq 16$, we only get security for (at best) $q \leq 2^{16}$ queries, which is clearly insufficient.

OVERVIEW OF THIS PAPER. This paper studies the concrete security of succinct proof systems in the *algebraic group model* (AGM) [5], with the goal of developing (near-)exact security bounds. The AGM considers in particular *algebraic* provers that provide representations of group elements to the reduction (or to the extractor), and has been successful to study security in a variety of contexts. More specifically, this work is the first to look at *multi*-round *public-coin* protocols *and* their non-interactive version obtained via the Fiat-Shamir transform. For the latter, we aim for bounds with *linear* degradation in the number of random oracle queries q even for a large number of rounds r, as opposed to the q^r degradation obtained from naïve analyses. Prior work [5] has focused on the simpler case of linear-PCP based SNARKs [13], which are built from two-move interactive proofs and without the FS transform.

The soundness of non-interactive systems resulting from the FS transform is tightly related to the *state-restoration soundness* [14,15] of the underlying interactive protocol, where the cheating prover can *rewind* the verifier as it pleases, until it manages to complete a full accepting interaction with the verifier. No non-trivial bounds on state-restoration soundness are currently known on any non-constant round *argument*.

We propose a general framework to quantitatively study state-restoration version of *witness-extended emulation* (wee) [16,17] (which implies both state-restoration soundness and a proof-of-knowledge property) in the AGM. We then

---

[1] In particular, Bulletproofs have been deployed in Monero [7] and Signal's upcoming MobileCoin [8].

[2] In this introduction, security is with respect to soundness – usually the analysis of zero-knowledge security is much more straightforward.

and apply it to three case studies, which include two variants of Bulletproofs, as well as Sonic [18]. These protocols have previously been analyzed only with respect to plain soundness in the interactive setting. The analysis of Bulletproofs relies in particular on the Forking Lemma of Bootle *et al.* [10], which was only very recently made concrete [11]. We believe that our framework can be applied to a number of other protocols, such as Hyrax [19], Dory [20] or pairing-based instantiations of IOPs [21,22], and leave their analysis for future work.

Remark 1. We stress that our approach differs formally from prior and concurrent works (e.g., [18,22]) which use the AGM to give a heuristic validation of the security of a *component* of a protocol, which is then however assumed to satisfy extractability properties compatible with a standard-model proof (i.e., an AGM extractor is used as a standard-model extractor.) Here, we aim for full analyses in the AGM, and as we point out in our technical overview below, these approaches actually do not give a full-fledged proof in the AGM (beyond not giving a proof in the standard model either).

BULLETPROOFS. We apply our framework to two instantiations of Bulletproofs – the first is for *range proofs*, and the other is for general satisfiability of arithmetic circuits. For example, in the former, a prover shows in $O(\log n)$ rounds that for a given Pedersen commitment $C = g^v h^r$ in a cyclic group $\mathbb{G}$ of prime order p we have $v \in [0, 2^n)$. (Here, clearly, $2^n \leq p$.)

For the final non-interactive protocol obtained via the FS transform, our result implies that an (algebraic) t-time prover making q random-oracle queries can break security as a Proof of Knowledge (when properly formalized) with advantage roughly

$$\varepsilon(t, q) \leq O(qn/p) + \mathsf{Adv}_{\mathbb{G}}^{\mathsf{dl}}(t) , \qquad (1)$$

where $\mathsf{Adv}_{\mathbb{G}}^{\mathsf{dl}}(t)$ is the advantage of breaking the DLP within time t. In the generic group model, this is roughly $O(t^2/p)$, and this bound justifies the instantiation of Bulletproofs from a 256-bit curve. For arithmetic circuit satisfiability, we obtain a similar bound.

TIGHTNESS AND DISCUSSION. Assuming $\mathsf{Adv}_{\mathbb{G}}^{\mathsf{dl}}(t) \sim t^2/p$ (which is true in the generic group model), the above bound implies in particular that for most values of n,[3] the term $O(qn/p)$ is not leading. Still, we show that the dependence on n is necessary – in particular, we show that there exist n, p for which we can construct a cheating prover that can break soundness with probability $\Omega(qn/p)$, meaning that this part of the bound is tight. (Our argument can be extended to all bounds claimed in the paper.) Also, the term $\mathsf{Adv}_{\mathbb{G}}^{\mathsf{dl}}(t)$ is clearly necessary, given that breaking the DLP would directly give us an attack. This makes our bound essentially exact (up to small constants).

AGM AND COMPOSITION. A challenging aspect of our analysis is the difficulty of dealing with composition. The core of the Bulletproofs is indeed its $O(\log(n))$-round *inner-product argument*. In the standard model, and in the interactive

---

[3] For the circuit satisfiability version of our result, one should think of $n = 2^{20}$ and $p = 2^{256}$ as representative values.

case, it is not hard to reduce the security (as a proof of knowledge) of the full-fledged system using Bulletproofs to the analysis of the underlying inner-product argument, but it is not that clear how to do this generically in the AGM. In particular, in the AGM, the adversary provides representations of group elements to the reduction (or the extractor), and these are as a function of all priorly given group elements. The problem is that when analyzing a protocol in *isolation* (such as the inner-product argument) the bases to which elements are described are not necessarily the same as those that would be available to a cheating algebraic prover against the *full* protocol. This makes it hard to use an extractor for the inner-product argument in isolation as a sub-routine to obtain an extractor for a protocol using it. Also, because we consider state-restoration soundness, a sub-protocol can be initiated by a cheating prover several times, with several choices of these basis elements.

The downside of this is that our analyses are not modular, at least not at a level which considers sub-protocols are isolated building blocks – we give two different analyses for two different instantiations of Bulletproofs, and the shared modularity is at the algebraic level.

We discuss this further at the end of our technical overview below.

SONIC. As a second application, we study Sonic [18]. This is a constant-round protocol, and in particular with $3M + 2$ challenges for some constant $M \geqslant 1$. In this case, the folklore analysis of the FS transform can be used to obtain a non-trivial bound, incurring a multiplicative loss of q^{3M+2} from the soundness of the interactive version. Here, we want to show that this loss is not necessary and also obtain a bound which degrades linearly in q. Moreover, no concrete bound on the concrete soundness of Sonic was given in the interactive setting.

We ignore the stronger requirement of updatable witness-extended emulation because our pedagogical point here is that our framework can improve soundness even for constant-round protocols.

We also note that Sonic's proof already uses the AGM to justify security of the underlying polynomial commitment scheme, but follows a (heuristic) pattern described above where the resulting extractor is expected to behave as a standard-model one, and is used within a standard-model proof.

ADAPTIVE VS NON-ADAPTIVE SOUNDNESS. It is important to understand that one can consider both *adaptive* and *non-adaptive* provers, where the former also chooses the *input* for which it attempts to provide a proof. Clearly, one expects adaptive provers to be harder to handle, but this is not necessarily true for *algebraic* provers – in particular, *if* the input contains group elements, the extractor can obtain useful information (and, possibly, directly extract) from their group representation. While this does not render the proof trivial at all, it turns out that for non-adaptive security, the proof is *even harder*. In this paper, we deal mostly with adaptive provers, but for the case of range proofs (where the inputs are commitments in a group), we also give a proof for non-adaptive security – the resulting bound is increased to the square root of the adaptive bound, due to our limited use of rewinding.

RELATED WORK: PROOFS VS ARGUMENTS. We clarify that state-restoration soundness has been studied for several forms of interactive *proofs* [14,15,23,24], also in its equivalent form of "round-by-round" soundness. Some proof systems satisfy it directly (such as those based on the sumcheck protocol [25]), whereas any proof with non-trivial (plain) soundness can be amplified into one with sufficient stare-restoration soundness (e.g., with parallel repetition). This is because (similar to our statement about the Fiat-Shamir transform above) one can naïvely infer that a concrete soundness bound ε implies a state-restoration soundness bound $q^r \varepsilon$, where r is the number of challenges, and thus ε needs to be smaller than q^{-r}.

However, we do not know of any non-trivial bounds on state-restoration soundness for multi-round arguments based on computational assumptions (as opposed to, say, arguments in the ROM), and moreover, soundness amplification (e.g., [26–29]) does not reduce soundness beyond the largest negligible function, and this is insufficient to absorb the q^r loss.

BEYOND THE AGM. Our results are inherently based on online extraction, which is only meaningful in ideal models or using knowledge assumptions. One scenario where ideal models are inherently used is in the compilation of IOPs into NIZKs in the ROM via the BCS transform [14] – it is unclear whether our technique can be used to give tight state-restoration soundness bounds for systems such as Aurora [30] and STARK [31].

CONCURRENT WORK. In a recently updated version of [32], Bünz *et al.* analyse the soundness of the non-interactive inner-product argument of Bulletproofs in the AGM. We provide a brief comparison with their result in the full version [34], but note here that their analysis is asymptotic, and gives weaker concrete security (insufficient for instantiations on 256-bit curves) when made concrete.

1.1   Overview of Our Techniques

We give a general framework to derive tight bounds on state-restoration soundness in the AGM. In fact, we will target the stronger notion of *witness-extended emulation* [16,17], which we adapt to state-restoration provers. Recall first that the main characteristic of the AGM is that it allows the reduction, or in our case the extractor, to access representations of group elements. A contribution of independent interest is to set up a formal framework to define extraction in the AGM.

PREFACE: ONLINE EXTRACTION IN THE AGM. In the AGM, the reduction (or an extractor) obtains *representations* of each group element in terms of all previously seen group elements. A useful feature of the AGM is that it often (but not always) allows us to achieve *online witness extraction*, as already observed in [5,33]. In other words, by looking at the representation of the group elements provided by the prover *in a single interaction*, the extractor is able to extract a witness, without the need of rewinding.

Online extraction however immediately appears to be very useful to tame the complexity of state-restoration provers. Indeed, one can visualize an interaction of an adversarial state-restoration prover $\mathcal{P}^*$ with the verifier V as defining an *execution tree*. In particular, $\mathcal{P}^*$ wins if it manages to create a path in the execution tree associated with an accepting (simple) transcript $\tau = (a_1, c_1, a_2, \ldots, c_r, a_{r+1})$, where $a_1, a_2, \ldots, a_{r+1}$ are $\mathcal{P}^*$'s messages, and $c_1, \ldots, c_r$ are the verifier's challenges. (We focus on public-coin protocols here.) Online extraction from a single transcript τ *directly* implies extraction here, because a witness can directly be extracted *locally* from the path τ (and the corresponding representations of group elements), disregarding what happened in the rest of the execution tree. In particular, the probability that $\mathcal{P}^*$ succeeds equals the probability that a witness is extracted. Without online extraction, we would have to use rewinding – but current techniques [10,11] do not seem to easily extend to state-restoration provers.

However, this only holds for *perfect* online extraction – in general, we may be able to generate transcripts which are accepting, but for which no witness can be extracted. This is typically because of two reasons:

- **Bad Challenges.** A bad choice of challenges may prevent witness extraction.
- **Violating an assumption.** A transcript is accepting, but the resulting interaction corresponds to a violation of some underlying assumption (i.e., one can extract a non-trivial discrete logarithm relation).

Our framework will exactly follow this pattern. For an r-challenge public-coin protocol, we identify bad challenges, i.e., for each $i \in [r]$, input x, and partial transcript $\tau' = (a_1, c_1, \ldots, a_{i-1}, c_{i-1}, a_i)$, we define a set of bad challenges c_i which would make extraction impossible. Crucially, these sets are defined according to a *simple interaction transcript* (i.e., not a state-restoration one) and can be defined according to the representation of group elements in the transcript so far. Then, given a transcript τ with no bad challenges, we show that:

- We can either extract a witness for x from τ (and the representations of the group elements in τ).
- We can use τ (and the representation of the group elements in terms of the public parameters) to break some underlying assumption.

To illustrate this, we give a non-trivial example next, which considers a simplified instance of the inner product argument at the core of Bulletproofs, but which already captures all subtleties of the model.

INNER-PRODUCT ARGUMENT OF BULLETPROOFS. In the inner product argument the prover proves that a group element $P \in \mathbb{G}$ is a well-formed commitment to vectors $\mathbf{a}, \mathbf{b} \in \mathbb{Z}_p^n$ and their inner-product $\langle \mathbf{a}, \mathbf{b} \rangle$.[4] More precisely, the prover wants to prove to the verifier that $P = \mathbf{g}^{\mathbf{a}} \mathbf{h}^{\mathbf{b}} u^{\langle \mathbf{a}, \mathbf{b} \rangle}$ where $\mathbf{g} \in \mathbb{G}^n$, $\mathbf{h} \in \mathbb{G}^n$, $u \in \mathbb{G}$ are independent generators of $\mathbb{G}$.

---

[4] We use boldface to denote vectors. For two vectors $\mathbf{a} = (a_1, \ldots, a_n), \mathbf{g} = (g_1, \ldots, g_n)$, we use $\mathbf{g}^{\mathbf{a}}$ to denote $\prod_{i=1}^{n} g_i^{a_i}$.

Here, we shall focus on the special case $n = 2$ first, and below discuss challenges in scaling our analysis up to any n. The prover first sends to the verifier group elements L, R where

$$L = g_2^{a_1} h_1^{b_2} u^{a_1 b_2} \ , \quad R = g_1^{a_2} h_2^{b_1} u^{a_2 b_1} \ .$$

The verifier samples x uniformly at random from $\mathbb{Z}_p^*$ and sends it to the prover. We then define

$$P' = L^{x^2} P R^{x^{-2}} \ , \quad g' = g_1^{x^{-1}} g_2^x \ , \quad h' = h_1^x h_2^{x^{-1}} \ .$$

The prover sends $a' = a_1 x + a_2 x^{-1}$ and $b' = b_1 x^{-1} + b_2 x$ to the verifier, which in turns accepts if and only if

$$P' = (g')^{a'} (h')^{b'} u^{a'b'} \ .$$

EXTRACTION FOR $n = 2$. For this discussion, we focus in particular on the notion of *adaptive* soundness – i.e., the prover provides P along with its representation, i.e., we get $\mathbf{a}' = (p_{g_1}, p_{g_2})$, $\mathbf{b}' = (p_{h_1}, p_{h_2})$ and p_u such that $P = \mathbf{g}^{\mathbf{a}'} \mathbf{h}^{\mathbf{b}'} u^{p_u}$. At first, it looks like we are done – after all, we can just check whether $\langle \mathbf{a}', \mathbf{b}' \rangle = p_u$, and if so, output $(\mathbf{a}', \mathbf{b}')$ as our witness. Unfortunately, things are not *that* simple – we need to ensure that no accepting transcript $\tau = ((L, R), x, (a', b'))$, i.e., such that $P' = (g')^{a'} (h')^{b'} u^{a'b'}$, is ever produced if $\langle \mathbf{a}', \mathbf{b}' \rangle \neq p_u$, for otherwise our naïve extraction would fail.

To this end, we will prove that if the cheating prover can produce an accepting interaction such while $\langle \mathbf{a}', \mathbf{b}' \rangle \neq p_u$, then we can solve the discrete logarithm problem in the group $\mathbb{G}$. We construct an adversary $\mathcal{A}$ that takes as inputs g_1, g_2, h_1, h_2, u and attempts to return a non-trivial discrete logarithm relation between them. (Breaking this is *tightly* equivalent to breaking the discrete logarithm problem.) Concretely, the adversary $\mathcal{A}$ gives g_1, g_2, h_1, h_2, u as input to the cheating prover $\mathcal{P}$, which first returns an adaptively chosen input $P \in \mathbb{G}$, along with is algebraic representation

$$P = g_1^{p_{g_1}} g_2^{p_{g_2}} h_1^{p_{h_1}} h_2^{p_{h_2}} u^{p_u} \ .$$

The adversary then simulates the execution of $\mathcal{P}$ with a honest verifier further, and assumes it generates an accepting transcript $\tau = ((L, R), x, (a', b'))$ – this transcript contains the representations of L, R such that $L = g_1^{l_{g_1}} g_2^{l_{g_2}} h_1^{l_{h_1}} h_2^{l_{h_2}} u^{l_u}$ and $R = g_1^{r_{g_1}} g_2^{r_{g_2}} h_1^{r_{h_1}} h_2^{r_{h_2}} u^{r_u}$ and since it is an accepting transcript we have

$$L^{x^2} P R^{x^{-2}} = g_1^{x^{-1} a'} g_2^{x^1 a'} h_1^{x^1 b'} h_2^{x^{-1} b'} u^{a'b'} \ .$$

We can plug in the representations of L, R into the equality and obtain values $e_{g_1}, e_{g_2}, e_{h_1}, e_{h_2}, e_u$ such that

$$g_1^{e_{g_1}} g_2^{e_{g_2}} h_1^{e_{h_1}} h_2^{e_{h_2}} u^{e_u} = 1 \ . \tag{2}$$

For example $e_{g_1} = x^{-1} a' - l_{g_1} x^2 - r_{g_1} x^{-2} - p_{g_1}$ and $e_u = a'b' - l_u x^2 - r_u x^{-2} - p_u$.

The adversary $\mathcal{A}$ then simply outputs $(e_{g_1}, e_{g_2}, e_{h_1}, e_{h_2}, e_u)$ – it has found a non-trivial discrete logarithm relation if $(e_{g_1}, e_{g_2}, e_{h_1}, e_{h_2}, e_u) \neq (0, 0, 0, 0, 0)$, which we next show happens with very high probability if $p_u \neq p_{g_1}p_{h_1} + p_{g_2}p_{h_2}$.

Suppose $(e_{g_1}, e_{g_2}, e_{h_1}, e_{h_2}, e_u) = (0, 0, 0, 0, 0)$. From $e_{g_1} = 0$, we have that $x^{-1}a' - l_{g_1}x^2 - r_{g_1}x^{-2} - p_{g_1} = 0$. Since $x \neq 0$, we get that $a' = l_{g_1}x^3 + r_{g_1}x^{-1} + p_{g_1}x$. Similarly from $e_{g_2} = 0$, we would get $a' = l_{g_2}x + p_{g_2}x^{-1} + r_{g_2}x^{-3}$. With high probability over the choice of x's, by the Schwartz-Zippel Lemma, we can infer by equating both right-hand sides that

$$a' = xp_{g_1} + x^{-1}p_{g_2} .$$

Similarly, from $e_{h_1} = 0$ and $e_{h_2} = 0$, we obtain that

$$b' = x^{-1}p_{h_1} + xp_{h_2}$$

for most x's. Finally, from $e_u = 0$, we similarly learn that

$$a'b' = x^2 l_u + p_u + x^{-2}r_u .$$

Hence from the above

$$x^2 l_u + p_u + x^{-2}r_u = p_{g_1}p_{h_1} + p_{g_2}p_{h_2} + p_{g_1}p_{h_2}x^2 + p_{g_2}p_{h_1}x^{-2} .$$

Since we have that $p_{g_1}p_{h_1} + p_{g_2}p_{h_2} \neq p_u$, the above equality holds with very small probability over the choice of x's.

Hence we have shown that $(e_{g_1}, e_{g_2}, e_{h_1}, e_{h_2}, e_u) = (0, 0, 0, 0, 0)$ with very small probability. Therefore $\mathcal{A}$ succeeds with high probability.

NON-ADAPTIVE SECURITY. The above proof exploits the fact that the prover *provides* a representation of P – this corresponds to the case of an *adaptive* prover. But there are scenarios where the prover may be non-adaptive and not be able to do that – for example, the input P has been generated by *another* party, and the prover tries to prove knowledge with respect to this P. It turns out that in this case, one needs a different proof. In fact, one *could* give an extraction strategy which does not require knowing an initial representation for P, but it is then hard to give a reduction to the discrete logarithm problem to show correctness.

We stress that non-adaptive provers and adaptive provers are equivalent in many applications – they only differ when the input includes group elements. We give a formalization and a case study (for Bulletproofs range proofs) in the full version [34]. There, we can actually give a reduction to the discrete logarithm problem (to bound the probability of failing to extract), but this requires rewinding *once* – this allows us to prove a bound which is the square root of the bound for adaptive provers.

THE RECURSIVE PROTOCOL FOR $n = 4$. Scaling the protocol to an arbitrary n proceeds via recursion. For concreteness, let us focus on the case $n = 4$. The prover first sends to the verifier group elements L, R where

$$L = g_3^{a_1} g_4^{a_2} h_1^{b_3} h_2^{b_4} u^{a_1 b_3 + a_2 b_4} , \quad R = g_1^{a_3} g_2^{a_4} h_3^{b_1} h_4^{b_2} u^{a_3 b_1 + a_4 b_2} .$$

The verifier samples x uniformly at random from $\mathbb{Z}_p^*$ and sends it to the prover. The prover and the verifier both compute

$$P' = L^{x^2} P R^{x^{-2}} \, , \; g_1' = g_1^{x^{-1}} g_3^x \, , \; g_2' = g_2^{x^{-1}} g_4^x \, , \; h_1' = h_1^x h_3^{x^{-1}} \, , \; h_2' = h_2^x h_4^{x^{-1}} \, .$$

The prover also computes $a_1' = a_1 x + a_3 x^{-1}$, $a_2' = a_2 x + a_4 x^{-1}$, $b_1' = b_1 x^{-1} + b_3 x$ and $b_2' = b_2 x^{-1} + b_4 x$. Observe that $P' = (g_1')^{a_1'} (g_2')^{a_2'} (h_1')^{b_1'} (h_3')^{b_2'} u^{a_1' b_1' + a_2' b_2'}$. Now, the prover and the verifier engage, recursively, in the protocol for $n = 2$ with inputs $(g_1', g_2'), (h_1', h_2'), u, P', (a_1', a_2'), (b_1', b_2')$. The difficulty in analyzing this is that we would like our proof strategy to be recursive, i.e., given we analyzed the protocol for n secure, we can now infer that the one for $2n$ also is secure. This will not be so direct, unfortunately. One major technical issue is for example that the recursive call uses different generators than the ones used for the calling protocol – in our case, here, $(g_1', g_2'), (h_1', h_2')$ – however, when looking at the combined protocol in the AGM, all element representations would be with respect to the generators $g_1, \ldots, g_4, h_1, \ldots, h_4$, and this makes it difficult to directly recycle the above analysis.

THE CHALLENGES WITH COMPOSITION. The inability to leverage recursion to simplify the approach from the previous paragraph is not an isolated incident. We note that a non-trivial aspect of our analyses is due to the lack of easy composition properties in the AGM. In particular, we encounter the following problem – if we have a protocol Π' (e.g., the inner-product argument) which is used as a sub-protocol for Π (a Bulletproofs range proof), and we prove extractability for Π', it is not clear we can infer extractability for Π in a modular way by just calling the extractor for Π'. This is because a stand-alone analysis of Π' may assume group elements output by a malicious prover $\mathcal{P}'$ are represented with respect to some set of basis elements – say, the generators $g_1, \ldots, g_n, h_1, \ldots, h_n, u$ in the concrete example of inner-product argument described above. However, when Π' is used within Π, the generators of the inner-product argument are functions of *different group* elements. When studying a prover $\mathcal{P}$ attacking Π, then, representations of group elements are with respect to this different set of group elements, and this makes it hard to use an extractor for Π' directly, as it assumes different representations.

This is a problem we encounter in our analyses, and which prevents us from abstracting a theorem for the inner-product argument which we could use, in a plug-and-play way, to imply security of higher-level protocols using it. The flip side is that this lack of composability also comes to our advantage – our extractors will in fact not even need to extract anything from the transcript of an accepting execution of the inner-product argument, but only use the fact that it is accepting to infer correctness of the extracted value.

THE ISSUE WITH PRIOR AGM ANALYSES. Composition issues seemingly affect existing analyses of proof systems in the literature (e.g., [18, 22]), whenever some components are analyzed in the AGM (typically, a polynomial commitment scheme), but the overall proof is expressed in the standard model. As far as we can tell, unlike this work, one cannot directly extract a full AGM analysis from these works – let us elaborate on this.

Obviously, from a purely formal perspective, the standard model and the algebraic group model cannot be quite mixed, as in particular the AGM extractor for the component cannot be used in the standard model – the only formally correct way to interpret the analysis is as *fully* in the AGM, but part of the analysis does not leverage the full power of the model, and is effectively a standard-model reduction. Yet, in order for composition to be meaningful, it is important to verify that the basis elements assumed in the AGM analysis of the components are the same available to a prover attacking the complete protocol. While we cannot claim any issues (in fact, we give an analysis of Sonic in this paper with a concrete bound), it does appear that all existing works do not attempt to provide a formal composition – they use the existence of an AGM extractor as a heuristic validation for the existence of a standard-model extractor, rather than making formally correct use as an AGM extractor within an AGM proof. Making this composition sound is potentially non-trivial. Having said this, for pairing-based polynomial commitment schemes, the basis elements are generally the same, and thus this can likely be made rigorous fairly easily (unlike the case of inner-product arguments).

2 Preliminaries

Let $\mathbb{N} = \{0, 1, 2, \ldots\}$ represent the set of all natural numbers and let $\mathbb{N}^+ = \mathbb{N} \backslash \{0\}$. For $N \in \mathbb{N}^+$, let $[N] = \{1, \ldots, N\}$. We use $\Pr[\mathsf{G}]$ to denote the probability that the game G returns true. Let $\mathbb{G}$ be a cyclic group of prime order p with identity 1 and let $\mathbb{G}^* = \mathbb{G} \backslash \{1\}$ be the set of its generators. We use boldface to denote a vector, e.g., $\mathbf{g} \in \mathbb{G}^n$ is a vector of n group elements with its ith element being g_i, i.e., $\mathbf{g} = (g_1, \ldots, g_n)$. For two vectors $\mathbf{a} = (a_1, \ldots, a_n), \mathbf{g} = (g_1, \ldots, g_n)$, we use $\mathbf{g}^{\mathbf{a}}$ to denote $\prod_{i=1}^n g_i^{a_i}$. We use python notation to denote slices of vectors:

$$\mathbf{g}_{[:l]} = (g_1, \ldots, g_l) \in \mathbb{G}^l \ , \ \mathbf{g}_{[l:]} = (g_{l+1}, \ldots, g_n) \in \mathbb{G}^{n-l} \ .$$

For $z \in \mathbb{Z}_p^*$, we use $\mathbf{z}^n$ to denote the vector $(1, z, z^2, \ldots, z^{n-1})$. Similarly, we use $\mathbf{z}^{-n}$ to denote the vector $(1, z^{-1}, z^{-2}, \ldots, z^{-n+1})$. If Z is a variable, $\mathbf{Z}^n$ represents the vector $(1, Z, Z^2, \ldots, Z^{n-1})$. Our vectors are indexed starting from 1, so $\mathbf{z}_{[1:]}^{n+1}$ is the vector $(z, z^2, \ldots, z^n)$. The operator $\circ$ denotes the Hadamard product of two vectors, i.e., $\mathbf{a} = (a_1, \ldots, a_n), \mathbf{b} = (b_1, \ldots, b_n), \mathbf{a} \circ \mathbf{b} = (a_1 b_1, \ldots, a_n b_n)$. We use capitalized boldface letters to denote matrices, e.g., $\mathbf{W} \in \mathbb{Z}_p^{n \times m}$ is a matrix with n rows and m columns.

We denote the inner product of two vectors $\mathbf{a}, \mathbf{b} \in \mathbb{Z}_p^n$ using $\langle \mathbf{a}, \mathbf{b} \rangle$. We also define vector polynomials, e.g., $f(X) = \sum_{i=0}^d \mathbf{f}_i X^i$, where each coefficient $\mathbf{f}_i$ is a vector in $\mathbb{Z}_p^n$.

The function $\mathsf{bit}(k, i, t)$ returns the bit k_i where $(k_1, \ldots, k_t)$ is the t-bit representation of k.

SCHWARTZ-ZIPPEL LEMMA. The polynomial ring in variables $X_1, \ldots, X_n$ over the field $\mathbb{F}$ is denoted by $\mathbb{F}[X_1, \ldots, X_n]$.

Game $G_\mathbb{G}^{\mathsf{dl}}(\mathcal{A}, \lambda)$:	**Game $G_{\mathbb{G},n}^{\mathsf{dl\text{-}rel}}(\mathcal{A}, \lambda)$:**	**Game $G_\mathbb{G}^{q\text{-}\mathsf{dl}}(\mathcal{A}, \lambda)$:**
$g \leftarrow_\$ \mathbb{G}_\lambda{}^*; \; h \leftarrow_\$ \mathbb{G}_\lambda$	$g_1, \ldots, g_n \leftarrow_\$ \mathbb{G}_\lambda$	$g \leftarrow_\$ \mathbb{G}_\lambda{}^*$
$a \leftarrow_\$ \mathcal{A}_\lambda(g, h)$	$(a_1, \ldots, a_n) \leftarrow_\$ \mathcal{A}_\lambda(g_1, \ldots, g_n)$	$x \leftarrow_\$ \mathbb{Z}_{p(\lambda)}$
Return $(g^a = h)$	Return $(\prod_{i=1}^n g_i^{a_i} = 1 \wedge (a_1, \ldots, a_n) \neq \mathbf{0}^n)$	$x' \leftarrow_\$ \mathcal{A}_\lambda(\{g^{x^d}\}_{d=-q}^q)$
		Return $(x = x')$

Fig. 1. The games used to define the advantage of a non-uniform adversary $\mathcal{A} = \{\mathcal{A}_\lambda\}_{\lambda \in \mathbb{N}^+}$ against the discrete logarithm problem, the discrete logarithm relation problem and the q-DLOG problem in a family of cyclic groups $\mathbb{G} = \{\mathbb{G}_\lambda\}_{\lambda \in \mathbb{N}^+}$ with prime order $p = p(\lambda)$. The set $\mathbb{G}_\lambda{}^*$ is the set of generators of $\mathbb{G}_\lambda$.

Lemma 1 (Schwartz-Zippel Lemma). *Let $\mathbb{F}$ be a finite field and let $f \in \mathbb{F}[X_1, \ldots, X_n]$ be a non-zero n variate polynomial with maximum degree d. Let S be a subset of $\mathbb{F}$. Then $\Pr[f(x_1, \ldots, x_n) = 0] \leqslant d/|S|$, where the probability is over the choice of $x_1, \ldots, x_n$ according to $x_i \leftarrow_\$ S$.*

In particular if p is a prime and $f \in \mathbb{Z}_p[X]$ is a polynomial of degree d and x is sampled uniformly at random from $\mathbb{Z}_p^*$, then $\Pr[f(x) = 0] \leqslant d/(p-1)$. Further this implies that if $g(X) = f(X)/X^i$ for $i \in \mathbb{N}$ and x is sampled uniformly at random from $\mathbb{Z}_p^*$, then $\Pr[g(x) = 0] = \Pr[f(x) = 0] \leqslant d/(p-1)$.

THE DISCRETE LOGARITHM PROBLEM. The game $G_\mathbb{G}^{\mathsf{dl}}$ in Fig. 1 is used for is used for defining the advantage of a non-uniform adversary $\mathcal{A} = \{\mathcal{A}_\lambda\}_{\lambda \in \mathbb{N}^+}$ against the discrete logarithm problem in a family of cyclic groups $\mathbb{G} = \{\mathbb{G}_\lambda\}_{\lambda \in \mathbb{N}^+}$ of prime order $p = p(\lambda)$ with identity 1 and set of generators $\mathbb{G}^* = \{\mathbb{G}_\lambda^*\}_{\lambda \in \mathbb{N}^+} = \{\mathbb{G}_\lambda \backslash \{1\}\}_{\lambda \in \mathbb{N}^+}$. We define $\mathsf{Adv}_\mathbb{G}^{\mathsf{dl}}(\mathcal{A}, \lambda) = \Pr\left[G_\mathbb{G}^{\mathsf{dl}}(\mathcal{A}, \lambda)\right]$.

THE DISCRETE LOGARITHM RELATION PROBLEM. The game $G_{\mathbb{G},n}^{\mathsf{dl\text{-}rel}}$ in Fig. 1 is used for defining the advantage of a non-uniform adversary $\mathcal{A} = \{\mathcal{A}_\lambda\}_{\lambda \in \mathbb{N}^+}$ against the discrete logarithm relation problem in a family of cyclic groups $\mathbb{G} = \{\mathbb{G}_\lambda\}_{\lambda \in \mathbb{N}^+}$. We define $\mathcal{A} = \{\mathcal{A}_\lambda\}_{\lambda \in \mathbb{N}^+}$ as $\mathsf{Adv}_{\mathbb{G},n}^{\mathsf{dl\text{-}rel}}(\mathcal{A}, \lambda) = \Pr\left[G_{\mathbb{G},n}^{\mathsf{dl\text{-}rel}}(\mathcal{A}, \lambda)\right]$. The following lemma shows that hardness of the discrete logarithm relation problem in $\mathbb{G}$ is tightly implied by the hardness of discrete logarithm problem in a family of cyclic groups $\mathbb{G} = \{\mathbb{G}_\lambda\}_{\lambda \in \mathbb{N}^+}$.

Lemma 2. *Let $n \in \mathbb{N}^+$. Let $\mathbb{G} = \{\mathbb{G}_\lambda\}_{\lambda \in \mathbb{N}^+}$ be a family of cyclic groups with order $p = p(\lambda)$. For every non-uniform adversary $\mathcal{A} = \{\mathcal{A}_\lambda\}_{\lambda \in \mathbb{N}^+}$ there exists a non-uniform adversary $\mathcal{B} = \{\mathcal{B}_\lambda\}_{\lambda \in \mathbb{N}^+}$ such that for all $\lambda \in \mathbb{N}^+$, $\mathsf{Adv}_{\mathbb{G},n}^{\mathsf{dl\text{-}rel}}(\mathcal{A}, \lambda) \leqslant \mathsf{Adv}_\mathbb{G}^{\mathsf{dl}}(\mathcal{B}, \lambda) + 1/p$. Moreover, $\mathcal{B}$ is nearly as efficient as $\mathcal{A}$.*

We refer the reader to [11] for a proof of this lemma.

THE q-DLOG PROBLEM. The game $G_\mathbb{G}^{q\text{-}\mathsf{dl}}$ in Fig. 1 is used for defining the advantage of a non-uniform adversary $\mathcal{A} = \{\mathcal{A}_\lambda\}_{\lambda \in \mathbb{N}^+}$ against the q-DLOG problem in a family of groups $\mathbb{G} = \{\mathbb{G}_\lambda\}_{\lambda \in \mathbb{N}^+}$. We define $\mathsf{Adv}_\mathbb{G}^{q\text{-}\mathsf{dl}}(\mathcal{A}, \lambda) = \Pr\left[G_\mathbb{G}^{q\text{-}\mathsf{dl}}(\mathcal{A}, \lambda)\right]$.

Game $\mathsf{SRS}_{\mathsf{IP}}^{\mathcal{P}}(\lambda)$:	**Oracle** $\mathbf{O}_{\mathrm{ext}}(\tau = (a_1, c_1, \ldots, a_{i-1}, c_{i-1}), a_i)$:
win ← false; tr ← ε	If $\tau \in$ tr then
pp ←$\$$ IP.Setup(1^λ)	If $i \leqslant r$ then
$(x, \mathsf{st}_{\mathcal{P}})$ ←$\$$ $\mathcal{P}_\lambda$(pp)	c_i ←$\$$ Ch_i; tr ← tr $\|$ (τ, a_i, c_i); Return c_i
Run $\mathcal{P}_\lambda^{\mathbf{O}_{\mathrm{ext}}}(\mathsf{st}_{\mathcal{P}})$	Else if $i = r + 1$ then
Return win	$d \leftarrow$ IP.V(pp, x, (τ, a_i)); tr ← tr $\|$ (τ, a_i)
	If $d = 1$ then win ← true
	Return d
	Return $\perp$

Fig. 2. Definition of state-restoration soundness. The game SRS defines state-restoration soundness for a non-uniform prover $\mathcal{P}$ and a public-coin interactive proof IP. Here, IP has $r = r(\lambda)$ challenges and the i-th challenge is sampled from Ch_i.

We note that there are other problems known as q-DLOG which are not equivalent to the one we use here. We use the version stated above because it was the version used in the analysis of Sonic [18] which we analyse in this paper.

3 Interactive Proofs and State-Restoration Soundness

We introduce our formalism for handling interactive proofs and arguments, which is particularly geared towards understanding their concrete state-restoration soundness.

INTERACTIVE PROOFS. An *interactive proof* [1] IP is a triple of algorithms: (1) the *setup algorithm* IP.Setup which generates the public parameters pp, (2) the *prover* IP.P and (3) the *verifier* IP.V. In particular, the prover and the verifier are interactive machines which define a two-party protocol, where the prover does not produce any output, and the verifier outputs a decision bit $d \in \{0, 1\}$. We let $\langle$IP.P(x), IP.V(y)$\rangle$ denote the algorithm which runs an execution of the prover and the verifier on inputs x and y, respectively, and outputs the verifier's decision bit. We say that IP is *public coin* if all messages sent from IP.V to IP.P are fresh random values from some understood set (which we refer to as *challenges*).

COMPLETENESS. A *relation* R is (without loss of generality) a subset of $\{0, 1\}^* \times \{0, 1\}^* \times \{0, 1\}^*$. We denote a relation R that uses specified public parameters pp, instance x and witness w as $\{(\mathsf{pp}, x, w) : f_R(\mathsf{pp}, x, w)\}$ where $f_R(\mathsf{pp}, x, w)$ is a function that returns true if $(\mathsf{pp}, x, w) \in R$ and false otherwise. For every $\lambda \in \mathbb{N}^+$ and every $\mathcal{A}$, define the following experiment:

$$\mathsf{pp} \leftarrow\$ \mathsf{IP.Setup}(1^\lambda) \, , \quad (x, w) \leftarrow\$ \mathcal{A}(\mathsf{pp}) \, , \quad d \leftarrow\$ \langle \mathsf{IP.P}(\mathsf{pp}, x, w), \mathsf{IP.V}(\mathsf{pp}, x) \rangle \, .$$

Then, we say that IP is an interactive proof for the relation R if for all $\mathcal{A}$ and all $\lambda \in \mathbb{N}^+$, in the above experiment the event $(d = 1) \vee ((\mathsf{pp}, x, w) \notin R)$ holds with probability one.

STATE-RESTORATION SOUNDNESS. We target a stronger notion of soundness – *state-restoration soundness* (SRS) [14, 15] – which (as we show below) tightly reduces to the soundness of the non-interactive proof obtained via the Fiat-Shamir transform. The SRS security game allows the cheating prover to *rewind* the verifier as it pleases, and wins if and only if it manages to produce *some* accepting interaction. We only consider an $r(\lambda)$-challenge *public-coin* interactive proof IP, and consider the case where challenges are drawn uniformly from some sets $\mathsf{Ch}_1, \ldots, \mathsf{Ch}_r$. We also assume that the verifier is described by an algorithm which given pp, x, and a *transcript* $\tau = (a_1, c_1, \ldots, a_r, c_r, a_{r+1})$, outputs a decision bit $d \in \{0, 1\}$. We overload notation and write IP.V(pp, x, τ) for this output.

Our definition considers a game $\mathsf{SRS}_{\mathsf{IP}}^{\mathcal{P}}(\lambda)$ (which is formalized in Fig. 2) that involves a non-uniform cheating prover $\mathcal{P} = \{\mathcal{P}_\lambda\}_{\lambda \in \mathbb{N}}$. (Henceforth, whenever we have any non-uniform adversary $\mathcal{A}$, it is understood $\mathcal{A} = \{\mathcal{A}_\lambda\}_{\lambda \in \mathbb{N}}$ – we shall not specify this explicitly). The prover is initially responsible for generating the input x on which it attempts to convince the verifier on *some* execution. Its rewinding access to the verifier is ensured by an oracle $\mathbf{O}_{\mathsf{ext}}$, to which it has access. Roughly speaking, the oracle allows the prover to build an *execution tree*, which is extended with each query to it by the prover. This execution tree can be inferred from tr, which sequentially logs all (valid) queries to $\mathbf{O}_{\mathsf{ext}}$ by the prover. For a partial transcript τ', we write $\tau' \in$ tr to mean that a partial execution corresponding to τ' can be inferred from tr.

We then associate the probability of winning the game with the srs *advantage metric*, $\mathsf{Adv}_{\mathsf{IP}}^{\mathsf{srs}}(\mathcal{P}, \lambda) = \Pr\left[\mathsf{SRS}_{\mathcal{P}}^{\mathsf{IP}}(\lambda)\right]$. For notational convenience, we do not restrict the input x not to have a witness. Therefore, if IP is an interactive proof for a relation R, we cannot hope to show that $\mathsf{Adv}_{\mathsf{IP}}^{\mathsf{srs}}(\mathcal{P}, \lambda)$ is small *for all* $\mathcal{P}$. Clearly, if $\mathcal{P}$ outputs (x, a) such that $(\mathsf{pp}, x, a) \in R$, then a is a witness and $\mathcal{P}$ can simply (honestly) convince the verifier. The classical notion of state-restoration soundness is recovered by only considering $\mathcal{P}$'s which output x such that $(\mathsf{pp}, x, w) \notin R$ for any w.

4   Proofs of Knowledge in the AGM

THE ALGEBRAIC GROUP MODEL. We start here with a brief review of the AGM [5]. For an understood group $\mathbb{G}$ with prime order p, an *algebraic* algorithm $\mathcal{A}_{\mathsf{alg}}$ is an interactive algorithm whose inputs and outputs are made of distinct group elements and strings. Furthermore, each (encoding) of a group element X output by $\mathcal{A}_{\mathsf{alg}}$ is accompanied by a *representation* $(x_{A_1}, x_{A_2}, \ldots, x_{A_k}) \in \mathbb{Z}_p^k$ such that $X = \prod_{i=1}^{k} A_i^{x_{A_i}}$, where $A_1, \ldots, A_k$ are all group elements previously input *and* output by $\mathcal{A}_{\mathsf{alg}}$. Generally, we write $[X]$ for a group element X *enhanced* with its representation, e.g., $[X] = (X, x_{A_1}, x_{A_2}, \ldots, x_{A_k})$. In particular, when we use a group element X output by $\mathcal{A}_{\mathsf{alg}}$, e.g. it is *input* to a reduction or used in a cryptographic game, we write $[X]$ to make explicit that the representation is available, whereas write X only when the representation is omitted. The notation extends to a mix of group elements and strings $a - [a]$ enhances each group element with its representation.

Game $\text{WEE-1}_{\text{IP}}^{\mathcal{P}_{\text{alg}},\mathcal{D}}(\lambda)$:	Oracle $\mathbf{O}_{\text{ext}}^1(\tau = (a_1, c_1, \ldots, a_{i-1}, c_{i-1}), a_i)$:
$\text{tr} \leftarrow \varepsilon$	If $\tau \in \text{tr}$ then
$\text{pp} \leftarrow_{\$} \text{IP.Setup}(1^\lambda)$	$\quad$ If $i \leqslant r$ then
$([x], \text{st}_{\mathcal{P}}) \leftarrow_{\$} \mathcal{P}_{\text{alg},\lambda}(\text{pp})$	$\quad\quad c_i \leftarrow_{\$} \text{Ch}_i; \text{tr} \leftarrow \text{tr} \, \| \, (\tau, a_i, c_i); \text{return } c_i$
Run $\mathcal{P}_{\text{alg},\lambda}^{\mathbf{O}_{\text{ext}}^1}(\text{st}_{\mathcal{P}})$	$\quad$ Else if $i = r + 1$ then
$b \leftarrow_{\$} \mathcal{D}(\text{tr})$	$\quad\quad d \leftarrow \text{IP.V}(\text{pp}, x, \tau \, \| \, a_i)$
Return $(b = 1)$	$\quad\quad$ Return d
	Return $\perp$
Game $\text{WEE-0}_{\text{IP},R}^{\mathcal{E},\mathcal{P}_{\text{alg}},\mathcal{D}}(\lambda)$:	Oracle $\mathbf{O}_{\text{ext}}^0(\tau = (a_1, c_1, \ldots, a_{i-1}, c_{i-1}), a_i)$:
$\text{tr} \leftarrow \varepsilon$	If $\tau \in \text{tr}$ then
$\text{pp} \leftarrow_{\$} \text{IP.Setup}(1^\lambda)$	$\quad$ If $i \leqslant r$ then
$([x], \text{st}_{\mathcal{P}}) \leftarrow_{\$} \mathcal{P}_{\text{alg},\lambda}(\text{pp})$	$\quad\quad (\text{resp}, \text{st}_{\mathcal{E}}) \leftarrow_{\$} \mathcal{E}(\text{st}_{\mathcal{E}}, [(\tau, a_i)])$
$\text{st}_{\mathcal{E}} \leftarrow (1^\lambda, \text{pp}, [x])$	$\quad\quad \text{tr} \leftarrow \text{tr} \, \| \, (\tau, a_i, \text{resp})$
Run $\mathcal{P}_{\text{alg},\lambda}^{\mathbf{O}_{\text{ext}}^0}(\text{st}_{\mathcal{P}})$	$\quad\quad$ Return resp
$w \leftarrow_{\$} \mathcal{E}(\text{st}_{\mathcal{E}}, \perp)$	$\quad$ Else if $i = r + 1$ then
$b \leftarrow_{\$} \mathcal{D}(\text{tr})$	$\quad\quad d \leftarrow \text{IP.V}(\text{pp}, x, \tau \, \| \, a_i)$
Return $(b = 1) \wedge$	$\quad\quad$ Return d
$\quad (\text{Acc}(\text{tr}) \Rightarrow (\text{pp}, x, w) \in R)$	Return $\perp$

Fig. 3. Definition of online srs-wee security in the AGM. The games WEE-1, WEE-0 define online srs-wee security in the AGM for a non-uniform algebraic prover $\mathcal{P}_{\text{alg}}$, a distinguisher $\mathcal{D}$, an extractor $\mathcal{E}$ and a public-coin interactive proof IP. We assume here that IP has $r = r(\lambda)$ challenges and the i-th challenge is sampled from Ch_i.

DEFINING AGM EXTRACTION. We formalize a notion of proof-of-knowledge (PoK) security in the AGM, following the lines of witness-extended emulation [16,17], which we extend to provers that can rewind the verifier.

We will be interested in cases where the AGM allows for online extraction, i.e., the additional group representations will allow for extraction without rewinding the prover. We target an adaptive notion of security, where the input is generated by the adversarial prover *itself*, depending on the public parameters pp, and can contain group elements.

ONLINE SRS-WEE SECURITY. The definition consists of two games – denoted $\text{WEE-1}_{\text{IP}}^{\mathcal{P}_{\text{alg}},\mathcal{D}}$ and $\text{WEE-0}_{\text{IP},R}^{\mathcal{E},\mathcal{P}_{\text{alg}},\mathcal{D}}$, and described in Fig. 3. The former captures the real game, lets our prover $\mathcal{P} = \{\mathcal{P}_\lambda\}_{\lambda \in \mathbb{N}}$ interact with an oracle $\mathbf{O}_{\text{ext}}^1$ as in the state-restoration soundness game defined above, which additionally stores a transcript tr. The latter is finally given to a *distinguisher* $\mathcal{D}$ which outputs a decision bit. In contrast, the *ideal* game delegates the role of answering $\mathcal{P}$'s oracle queries to a (stateful) extractor $\mathcal{E}$. The extractor, at the end of the execution, also outputs a witness candidate for w. The extractor in particular exploits here the fact that $\mathcal{P}$ is algebraic by learning the representation of every input to the oracle $\mathbf{O}_{\text{ext}}^0$. (This representation can be thought, without loss of generality, as being in terms of all group elements contained in pp.) Here, the final output of the game is not merely $\mathcal{D}$'s decision bit – should the latter output 1, the output of the game is true only if additionally the extracted witness is correct assuming the interaction with $\mathbf{O}_{ext}^0$ resulted in an accepting execution – a condition we capture via the predicate $\mathsf{Acc(tr)}$.

For an interactive proof IP and an associated relation R, non-uniform algebraic prover $\mathcal{P}_{alg}$, a distinguisher $\mathcal{D}$, and an extractor $\mathcal{E}$, we define

$$\mathsf{Adv}_{\mathsf{IP},R}^{\mathsf{sr-wee}}(\mathcal{P}_{alg}, \mathcal{D}, \mathcal{E}, \lambda) = \Pr\left[\mathsf{WEE}\text{-}1_{\mathsf{IP}}^{\mathcal{P}_{alg}, \mathcal{D}}(\lambda)\right] - \Pr\left[\mathsf{WEE}\text{-}0_{\mathsf{IP},R}^{\mathcal{E},\mathcal{P}_{alg}, \mathcal{D}}(\lambda)\right] . \quad (3)$$

One can consider also scenarios where the prover may be non-adaptive – for example, the input has been generated by *another* party, and the prover tries to prove knowledge with respect to this input. For this reason, introduce the notion of non-adaptive srs-wee in the full version [34].

4.1   The Basic Framework

We develop a general framework that we will use, via Theorem 1, to derive concrete AGM bounds on srs-wee security. Our goal, in particular, is to give conditions on *single* path executions – i.e., executions not involving any rewinding of the verifier by the prover, which could be seen as root-to-leaf paths in an execution tree generated by the interaction of a state-restoration prover.

TRANSCRIPTS. From now on, let us fix an interactive *public-coin* proof IP = (IP.Setup, IP.P, IP.V) for a relation R. Assume further this protocol has exactly r rounds of challenges. Then, we represent a (potential) *single-execution* transcript generated by an algebraic prover in different forms, depending on whether we include the representations of group elements or not. Specifically, we let the (plain) transcript be $\tau = (\mathsf{pp}, x, a_1, c_1, a_2, c_2, \ldots, a_r, c_r, a_{r+1})$, where pp are the generated parameters, x is the input produced by $\mathcal{P}_{alg}$, $c_i \in \mathsf{Ch}_i$ for all $i \in \{1, \ldots, r\}$ are the challenges, and $a_1, \ldots, a_{r+1}$ are the prover's messages. The corresponding *extended transcript* with representations is denoted as $[\tau] = (\mathsf{pp}, [x], [a_1], c_1, [a_2], c_2, \ldots, [a_r], c_r, [a_{r+1}])$.

In particular, the representation of each group element contained in a_i is with respect to all elements contained in $\mathsf{pp}, x, a_1, \ldots, a_{i-1}$. We let $\mathcal{T}^{\mathsf{IP}}$ be the set of all possible extended transcripts $[\tau]$. We also let $\mathcal{T}_{\mathsf{Acc}}^{\mathsf{IP}} \subseteq \mathcal{T}^{\mathsf{IP}}$ be the set of *accepting* transcripts $[\tau]$, i.e., $\mathsf{IP.V}(\tau) = 1$.

PATH EXTRACTION. We now would like to define a function e which extracts a witness from any accepting transcript $[\tau] \in \mathcal{T}_{\mathsf{Acc}}^{\mathsf{IP}}$. For a particular function e we now define the set of extended transcripts on which it succeeds in extracting a valid witness, i.e.,

$$\mathcal{T}_{\mathsf{correct}}^{\mathsf{IP},\mathsf{e},R} = \left\{[\tau] = (\mathsf{pp}, [x], \ldots) \in \mathcal{T}_{\mathsf{Acc}}^{\mathsf{IP}} : w \leftarrow \mathsf{e}([\tau]), (\mathsf{pp}, x, w) \in R\right\} .$$

Therefore, a natural extractor $\mathcal{E}$ just answers challenges honestly, and applies e to a path in the execution tree which defines an accepting transcript, and returns the corresponding witness w. The probability of this extractor failing can be upper bounded naïvely by the probability that the prover generates, in its execution tree, a path corresponding to an extended transcript $[\tau] \in \mathcal{T}_{\mathsf{Acc}}^{\mathsf{IP}} \setminus \mathcal{T}_{\mathsf{correct}}^{\mathsf{IP,e},R}$. This is however not directly helpful, as the main challenge is to actually estimate this probability.

BAD CHALLENGES. In all of our examples, the analysis of the probability of generating a transcript in $\mathcal{T}_{\mathsf{Acc}}^{\mathsf{IP}} \setminus \mathcal{T}_{\mathsf{correct}}^{\mathsf{IP,e},R}$ will generally consist of an *information-theoretic* and a *computational part*.

The information-theoretic part will account to choosing some *bad challenges*. We capture such choices of bad challenges by defining, for any partial extended transcript $[\tau'] = (\mathsf{pp}, [x], [a_1], c_1, \ldots, [a_i])$, a set $\mathsf{BadCh}(\tau') \subseteq \mathsf{Ch}_i$ of such bad challenges. (Crucially, whether a challenge is bad or not only depends on the extended transcript so far.) We now denote as $\mathcal{T}_{\mathsf{BadCh}}^{\mathsf{IP}}$ the set of all extended transcripts which contain at least one bad challenge. It turns out that the probability of generating such a bad challenge is easily bounded by $q \cdot \varepsilon$ for a prover making q oracle queries, assuming $|\mathsf{BadCh}(\tau')| / |\mathsf{Ch}_i| \leq \varepsilon$.

The only case that the extractor can now fail is if the execution tree contains an extended transcript $[\tau]$ in the set $\mathcal{T}_{\mathsf{fail}}^{\mathsf{IP,e},R} = \mathcal{T}_{\mathsf{Acc}}^{\mathsf{IP}} \setminus (\mathcal{T}_{\mathsf{correct}}^{\mathsf{IP,e},R} \cup \mathcal{T}_{\mathsf{BadCh}}^{\mathsf{IP}})$. We denote the probability that this happens in $\mathsf{SRS}_{\mathsf{IP}}^{\mathcal{P}_{\mathsf{alg}}}(\lambda)$ as $p_{\mathsf{fail}}(\mathsf{IP}, \mathcal{P}_{\mathsf{alg}}, \mathsf{e}, R, \lambda)$. Generally, in all of our applications, upper bounding this probability for a suitably defined extractor will constitute the computational core of the proof – i.e., we will prove (generally tight) reductions to breaking some underlying assumption.

THE MASTER THEOREM. We are now ready to state our master theorem, which assumes the formal set up.

Theorem 1 (Master Theorem). *Let* IP *be an* $r = r(\lambda)$*-challenge public coin interactive proof for a relation* R*. Assume there exist functions* BadCh *and* e *for* IP *as described above, and let* p_{fail} *be as defined above. Let* τ' *be a partial transcript such that the challenge that comes right after is sampled from* Ch_i*. Assume that for all* $i \in \{1, \ldots, r\}$*, we have* $|\mathsf{BadCh}(\tau')| / |\mathsf{Ch}_i| \leq \varepsilon$*, for some* $\varepsilon \in [0, 1]$*. Then, there exists an extractor* $\mathcal{E}$ *that uses* e *such that for any non-uniform algebraic prover* $\mathcal{P}_{\mathsf{alg}}$ *making at most* $q = q(\lambda)$ *queries to its oracle, and any (computationally unbounded) distinguisher* $\mathcal{D}$*, for all* $\lambda \in \mathbb{N}^+$*,*

$$\mathsf{Adv}_{\mathsf{IP},R}^{\mathsf{sr-wee}}(\mathcal{P}_{\mathsf{alg}}, \mathcal{D}, \mathcal{E}, \lambda) \leq q\varepsilon + p_{\mathsf{fail}}(\mathsf{IP}, \mathcal{P}_{\mathsf{alg}}, \mathsf{e}, R, \lambda) \ .$$

The time complexity of the extractor $\mathcal{E}$ *is* $O(q \cdot t_V + t_{\mathsf{e}})$ *where* t_V *is the time required to run* $\mathsf{IP.V}$ *and* t_{e} *is the time required to run* e*.*

The proof of this theorem is straightforward has been deferred to the full version [34].

4.2 The Fiat-Shamir Transform

The Fiat-Shamir transform uses a family of hash functions $\mathcal{H}$ to convert a r-challenge public coin interactive protocol (proof or argument) IP to a non-interactive argument $\mathsf{FS}[\mathsf{IP}, \mathcal{H}]$. When $\mathcal{H}$ is modelled as a random oracle, we denote the non-interactive argument using $\mathsf{FS}^{\mathbf{RO}}[\mathsf{IP}]$. In $\mathsf{FS}[\mathsf{IP}, \mathcal{H}]$,

---

Game $\mathsf{FS\text{-}EXT\text{-}1}_{\mathsf{IP},R}^{\mathcal{P}_{\mathsf{alg}},\mathcal{E}}(\lambda)$:

$\mathsf{pp} \leftarrow_{\$} \mathsf{IP.Setup}(1^{\lambda}); ([x],\mathsf{st}_{\mathcal{P}}) \leftarrow_{\$} \mathcal{P}_{\mathsf{alg},\lambda}(\mathsf{pp}); H \leftarrow_{\$} \Omega_{\mathsf{hLen}(\lambda)}$
$[\pi] \leftarrow_{\$} \mathcal{P}_{\mathsf{alg},\lambda}^{H}(\mathsf{st}_{\mathcal{P}}); (a_1,c_1,\ldots,a_r,c_r,a_{r+1}) \leftarrow \pi$
$\mathsf{accept} \leftarrow (\mathsf{IP.V}(\mathsf{pp},x,\pi) = 1) \wedge (\forall i \in [r] : c_i = H(\mathsf{pp},x,a_1,c_1,\ldots,a_i)[: \mathsf{cLen}_i])$
$w \leftarrow_{\$} \mathcal{E}(1^{\lambda},\mathsf{pp},[x],[\pi]); \mathrm{Return}\ (\mathsf{accept} \wedge (\mathsf{pp},x,w) \notin R)$

Fig. 4. Definition of fs-ext-1 security in the AGM. The game FS-EXT-1 defines fs-ext-1 security in the AGM for a non-uniform algebraic prover $\mathcal{P}_{\mathsf{alg}}$, an extractor $\mathcal{E}$ and a non-interactive argument obtained by applying the Fiat-Shamir transform to an interactive protocol IP. Here, IP has $r = r(\lambda)$ challenges where the ith challenge is of length $\mathsf{cLen}_i = \mathsf{cLen}_i(\lambda)$ such that $\mathsf{sLen}(\lambda) \leqslant \mathsf{cLen}_i(\lambda) \leqslant \mathsf{hLen}(\lambda)$. The set $\Omega_{\mathsf{hLen}(\lambda)}$ contains all functions mapping $\{0,1\}^*$ to $\{0,1\}^{\mathsf{hLen}(\lambda)}$.

a hash function H is first sampled from $\mathcal{H}$. A proof on public parameters pp and input x is $\pi = (a_1,c_1,a_2,c_2,\ldots,a_r,c_r,a_{r+1})$, such that $c_i = H(\mathsf{pp},x,a_1,c_1,\ldots,a_{i-1},c_{i-1},a_i)[: \mathsf{cLen}_i]$ for $i \in \{1,\ldots,r\}$, and IP.V returns 1 on input (pp,x,π).

FS-EXT-1 SECURITY. We formalize a notion of proof-of-knowledge (PoK) security in the AGM for non-interactive arguments obtained by applying the Fiat-Shamir transform to an interactive protocol IP. For simplicity, this notion just captures extractability instead of witness-extended emulation. We define a notion of soundness called fs-ext-1 that captures the setting where the prover has to commit to the instance beforehand. It is formally defined using the game FS-EXT-1 in Fig. 4.

For an interactive proof IP and an associated relation R, algebraic prover $\mathcal{P}_{\mathsf{alg}}$, and an extractor $\mathcal{E}$, we define $\mathsf{Adv}_{\mathsf{FS}^{\mathsf{RO}}[\mathsf{IP}],R}^{\mathsf{fs\text{-}ext\text{-}1}}(\mathcal{P}_{\mathsf{alg}},\mathcal{E},\lambda) = \mathrm{Pr}\left[\mathsf{FS\text{-}EXT\text{-}1}_{\mathsf{IP},R}^{\mathcal{P}_{\mathsf{alg}},\mathcal{E}}(\lambda)\right]$.

The following theorem connects the online srs-wee security of a public-coin protocol IP and the fs-ext-1 soundness of non-interactive protocol $\mathsf{FS}^{\mathsf{RO}}[\mathsf{IP}]$, obtained by applying the Fiat-Shamir transform using a random oracle.

Theorem 2. *Let R be a relation. Let IP be a $r = r(\lambda)$-challenge public coin interactive protocol for the relation R where the length of the ith challenge is $\mathsf{cLen}_i(\lambda)$ such that $\mathsf{sLen}(\lambda) \leqslant \mathsf{cLen}_i(\lambda) \leqslant \mathsf{hLen}(\lambda)$ for $i \in \{1,\ldots,r\}$. Let $\mathcal{E}$ be an extractor for IP. We can construct an extractor $\mathcal{E}^*$ for $\mathsf{FS}^{\mathsf{RO}}[\mathsf{IP}]$ such that for every non-uniform algebraic prover $\mathcal{P}_{\mathsf{alg}}^*$ against $\mathsf{FS}^{\mathsf{RO}}[\mathsf{IP}]$ that makes $q = q(\lambda)$ random oracle queries, there exists a non-uniform algebraic prover $\mathcal{P}_{\mathsf{alg}}$ and $\mathcal{D}$ such that for all $\lambda \in \mathbb{N}^+$,*

$$\mathsf{Adv}_{\mathsf{FS}^{\mathsf{RO}}[\mathsf{IP}],R}^{\mathsf{fs\text{-}ext\text{-}1}}(\mathcal{P}_{\mathsf{alg}}^*,\mathcal{E}^*,\lambda) \leqslant \mathsf{Adv}_{\mathsf{IP},R}^{\mathsf{sr\text{-}wee}}(\mathcal{P}_{\mathsf{alg}},\mathcal{D},\mathcal{E},\lambda) + (q+1)/2^{\mathsf{sLen}(\lambda)}.$$

Moreover, $\mathcal{P}_{\mathsf{alg}}$ makes at most q queries to its oracle and is nearly as efficient as $\mathcal{P}_{\mathsf{alg}}^*$. The extractor $\mathcal{E}^*$ is nearly as efficient as $\mathcal{E}$.

This proof of this theorem is deferred to the full version [34].

In the above theorem we considered challenges in IP to be bitstrings – however, this can be adapted to protocols where the challenges are from sets that

---

Game FS-EXT-2$_{\mathsf{IP},R}^{\mathcal{P}_{\mathsf{alg}},\mathcal{E}}(\lambda)$:

$\mathsf{pp} \leftarrow\!\!{}_\$ \, \mathsf{IP.Setup}(1^\lambda); \ H \leftarrow\!\!{}_\$ \, \Omega_{\mathsf{hLen}(\lambda)}; \ ([x],[\pi]) \leftarrow\!\!{}_\$ \, \mathcal{P}_{\mathsf{alg},\lambda}^H(\mathsf{pp})$

$(a_1, c_1, \ldots, a_r, c_r, a_{r+1}) \leftarrow \pi$

$\mathsf{accept} \leftarrow (\mathsf{IP.V}(\mathsf{pp}, x, \pi) = 1) \wedge (\forall i \in [r] : c_i = H(\mathsf{pp}, x, a_1, c_1, \ldots, a_i)[: \mathsf{cLen}_i])$

$w \leftarrow\!\!{}_\$ \, \mathcal{E}(1^\lambda, \mathsf{pp}, [x], [\pi]); \ \mathrm{Return} \ (\mathsf{accept} \wedge (\mathsf{pp}, x, w) \notin R)$

Fig. 5. Definition of fs-ext-2 security in the AGM. The game FS-EXT-2 defines fs-ext-2 security in the AGM for a non-uniform algebraic prover $\mathcal{P}_{\mathsf{alg}}$, an extractor $\mathcal{E}$ and a non-interactive argument obtained by applying the Fiat-Shamir transform to an interactive protocol IP. Here, IP has $r = r(\lambda)$ challenges where the ith challenge is of length $\mathsf{cLen}_i = \mathsf{cLen}_i(\lambda)$ such that $\mathsf{sLen}(\lambda) \leqslant \mathsf{cLen}_i(\lambda) \leqslant \mathsf{hLen}(\lambda)$. The set $\Omega_{\mathsf{hLen}(\lambda)}$ contains all functions mapping $\{0,1\}^*$ to $\{0,1\}^{\mathsf{hLen}(\lambda)}$.

are not bitstrings. The denominator of the fraction of the bound would become the size of smallest set from which the challenges are sampled, e.g., if the challenges in the a protocol were all from the set $\mathbb{Z}_p^*$, the fraction would become $(q+1)/(p-1)$.

We can also consider an adaptive notion of soundness where the prover can output the instance and proof together – we call this notion fs-ext-2. It is formally defined using the game FS-EXT-2 in Fig. 5. Unlike fs-ext-1, here the prover need not commit to the instance beforehand and can output the instance and proof together. For an interactive proof IP and an associated relation R, algebraic prover $\mathcal{P}_{\mathsf{alg}}$, and an extractor $\mathcal{E}$, we define $\mathsf{Adv}_{\mathsf{FS}^{\mathbf{RO}}[\mathsf{IP}],R}^{\mathsf{fs\text{-}ext\text{-}2}}(\mathcal{P}_{\mathsf{alg}}, \mathcal{E}, \lambda) =$

$\Pr\left[\mathsf{FS\text{-}EXT\text{-}2}_{\mathsf{IP},R}^{\mathcal{P}_{\mathsf{alg}},\mathcal{E}}(\lambda)\right]$.

We assume that IP has BadCh, e functions as described previously. Further, we assume $\mathcal{T}_{\mathsf{BadCh}}^{\mathsf{IP}}$ is defined as above. We use $p_{\mathsf{fail},\mathsf{FS}}(\mathsf{FS}^{\mathbf{RO}}[\mathsf{IP}], \mathcal{P}_{\mathsf{alg}}, \mathsf{e}, R, \lambda)$ to denote the probability that in FS-EXT-2$_{\mathsf{IP},R}^{\mathcal{P}_{\mathsf{alg}},\mathcal{E}}$, $\mathcal{P}_{\mathsf{alg}}$ outputs $([x],[\pi])$, accept is true, $\pi \notin \mathcal{T}_{\mathsf{BadCh}}^{\mathsf{IP}}$ but e on input $([x],[\pi])$ fails to produce a valid witness. The following theorem upper bounds the fs-ext-2 soundness of non-interactive protocol $\mathsf{FS}^{\mathbf{RO}}[\mathsf{IP}]$.

Theorem 3. *Let* IP *be an* $r = r(\lambda)$-*challenge public coin interactive proof for a relation* R *where the length of the* i^{th} *challenge is* $\mathsf{cLen}_i(\lambda)$ *such that* $\mathsf{sLen}(\lambda) \leqslant \mathsf{cLen}_i(\lambda) \leqslant \mathsf{hLen}(\lambda)$ *for* $i \in \{1, \ldots, r\}$. *Assume there exist functions* BadCh *and* e *as described previously and let* $p_{\mathsf{fail},\mathsf{FS}}$ *be as described above. Let* τ' *be a partial transcript such that the challenge that comes right after is sampled from* Ch_i. *Assume that for all* $i \in \{1, \ldots, r\}$, *we have that* $|\mathsf{BadCh}(\tau')| / |\mathsf{Ch}_i| \leqslant \varepsilon$ *for some* $\varepsilon \in [0,1]$. *Then, there exists an extractor* $\mathcal{E}^*$ *that uses* e *such that for any non-uniform algebraic prover* $\mathcal{P}_{\mathsf{alg}}^*$ *for* $\mathsf{FS}^{\mathbf{RO}}[\mathsf{IP}]$ *making at most* $q = q(\lambda)$ *queries to its random oracle, for all* $\lambda \in \mathbb{N}^+$,

$$\mathsf{Adv}_{\mathsf{FS}^{\mathbf{RO}}[\mathsf{IP}],R}^{\mathsf{fs\text{-}ext\text{-}2}}(\mathcal{P}_{\mathsf{alg}}^*, \mathcal{E}^*, \lambda) \leqslant q\varepsilon + p_{\mathsf{fail},\mathsf{FS}}(\mathsf{FS}^{\mathbf{RO}}[\mathsf{IP}], \mathcal{P}_{\mathsf{alg}}^*, \mathsf{e}, R, \lambda) .$$

The time complexity of the extractor $\mathcal{E}^*$ *is* $O(q \cdot t_V + t_{\mathsf{e}})$ *where* t_V *is the time required to run* IP.V *and* t_{e} *is the time required to run* e.

$\mathsf{InPrd.P}(((n, \mathbf{g}, \mathbf{h}, u), P), (\mathbf{a}, \mathbf{b}))$

$\mathbf{g}^{(0)} \leftarrow \mathbf{g}; \mathbf{h}^{(0)} \leftarrow \mathbf{h}$

$n_0 \leftarrow n; P^{(0)} \leftarrow P; \mathbf{a}^{(0)} \leftarrow \mathbf{a}; \mathbf{b}^{(0)} \leftarrow \mathbf{b}$

For $i = 1, \dots, \log n$

$\quad n_i \leftarrow n_{i-1}/2$

$\quad c_L \leftarrow \langle \mathbf{a}^{(i)}[: n_i], \mathbf{b}^{(i)}[n_i :] \rangle$

$\quad c_R \leftarrow \langle \mathbf{a}^{(i)}[n_i :], \mathbf{b}^{(i)}[: n_i] \rangle$

$\quad L_i \leftarrow \left(\mathbf{g}_{[n_i:]}^{(i-1)} \right)^{\mathbf{a}^{(i)}[:n_i]} \left(\mathbf{h}_{[:n_i]}^{(i-1)} \right)^{\mathbf{b}^{(i)}[n_i:]} u^{c_L}$

$\quad R_i \leftarrow \left(\mathbf{g}_{[:n_i]}^{(i-1)} \right)^{\mathbf{a}^{(i)}[n_i:]} \left(\mathbf{h}_{[n_i:]}^{(i-1)} \right)^{\mathbf{b}^{(i)}[:n_i]} u^{c_R}$

$\xrightarrow{\quad L_i, R_i \quad}$

$\xleftarrow{\quad x_i \quad}$

$\mathbf{g}^{(i)} \leftarrow \left(\mathbf{g}_{[:n_i]}^{(i-1)} \right)^{x_i^{-1}} \circ \left(\mathbf{g}_{[n_i:]}^{(i-1)} \right)^{x_i}$

$\mathbf{h}^{(i)} \leftarrow \left(\mathbf{h}_{[:n_i]}^{(i-1)} \right)^{x_i} \circ \left(\mathbf{h}_{[n_i:]}^{(i-1)} \right)^{x_i^{-1}}$

$P^{(i)} \leftarrow L_i^{x_i^2} P^{(i-1)} R_i^{x_i^{-2}}$

$\mathbf{a}^{(i)} \leftarrow \mathbf{a}^{(i-1)}[: n_i] x^{-1} + \mathbf{a}^{(i)}[n_i :] x$

$\mathbf{b}^{(i)} \leftarrow \mathbf{b}^{(i-1)}[: n_i] x + \mathbf{b}^{(i)}[n_i :] x^{-1}$

$g \leftarrow \mathbf{g}^{(\log n)}; h \leftarrow \mathbf{h}^{(\log n)}$

$a \leftarrow \mathbf{a}^{(\log n)}; b \leftarrow \mathbf{b}^{(\log n)}$

$\xrightarrow{\quad a, b \quad}$

$\mathsf{InPrd.V}((n, \mathbf{g}, \mathbf{h}, u), P)$

$\mathbf{g}^{(0)} \leftarrow \mathbf{g}; \mathbf{h}^{(0)} \leftarrow \mathbf{h}$

$n_0 \leftarrow n; P^{(0)} \leftarrow P$

For $i = 1, \dots, \log n$

$\quad n_i \leftarrow n_{i-1}/2$

$x_i \leftarrow_\$ \mathbb{Z}_p^*$

$\mathbf{g}^{(i)} \leftarrow \left(\mathbf{g}_{[:n_i]}^{(i-1)} \right)^{x_i^{-1}} \circ \left(\mathbf{g}_{[n_i:]}^{(i-1)} \right)^{x_i}$

$\mathbf{h}^{(i)} \leftarrow \left(\mathbf{h}_{[:n_i]}^{(i-1)} \right)^{x_i} \circ \left(\mathbf{h}_{[n_i:]}^{(i-1)} \right)^{x_i^{-1}}$

$P^{(i)} \leftarrow L_i^{x_i^2} P^{(i-1)} R_i^{x_i^{-2}}$

$g \leftarrow \mathbf{g}^{(\log n)}; h \leftarrow \mathbf{h}^{(\log n)}$

Return $(P^{(\log n)} = g^a h^b u^{ab})$

Fig. 6. Bulletproofs inner-product argument InPrd.

The proof of this theorem is similar to Theorem 1 and has been omitted.

5   Online srs-wee Security of Bulletproofs

In this section, we shall apply our framework to prove online srs-wee security in the AGM for two instantiations of Bulletproofs- range proofs (RngPf) and proofs for arithmetic circuit satisfiability (ACSPf). We first introduce the Bulletproofs inner product argument (InPrd) in Sect. 5.1 which forms the core of both RngPf and ACSPf. Then, in Sects. 5.2 and 5.3 we introduce and analyze online srs-wee security of RngPf and ACSPf respectively.

5.1   Inner Product Argument InPrd

We shall assume that $\mathsf{InPrd} = \mathsf{InPrd}[\mathbb{G}]$ is instantiated on an understood family of groups $\mathbb{G} = \{\mathbb{G}_\lambda\}_{\lambda \in \mathbb{N}^+}$ of order $p = p(\lambda)$. Using InPrd, a prover can convince a verifier that $P \in \mathbb{G}$ is a well-formed commitment to vectors $\mathbf{a}, \mathbf{b} \in \mathbb{Z}_p^n$ and their inner-product $\langle \mathbf{a}, \mathbf{b} \rangle$. More precisely, the prover wants to prove to the verifier that $P = \mathbf{g}^{\mathbf{a}} \mathbf{h}^{\mathbf{b}} u^{\langle \mathbf{a}, \mathbf{b} \rangle}$ where $\mathbf{g} \in \mathbb{G}^n, \mathbf{h} \in \mathbb{G}^n, u \in \mathbb{G}$ are independent generators of $\mathbb{G}$. We assume that n is a power of 2 without loss of generality since if needed, one can pad the input appropriately to ensure that this holds. The prover and the verifier for InPrd is formally defined in Fig. 6.

$\mathsf{RngPf.P}(((n, \mathbf{g}, \mathbf{h}, g, h, u), V), (v, \gamma))$	$\mathsf{RngPf.V}((n, \mathbf{g}, \mathbf{h}, g, h, u), V)$
$\mathbf{a}_L \leftarrow \mathsf{BinRep}(v, n); \mathbf{a}_R \leftarrow \mathbf{a}_L - \mathbf{1}^n$	
$\alpha \leftarrow\!\!\text{\$}\; \mathbb{Z}_p; A \leftarrow h^\alpha \mathbf{g}^{\mathbf{a}_L} \mathbf{h}^{\mathbf{a}_R}$	
$\mathbf{s}_L \leftarrow\!\!\text{\$}\; \mathbb{Z}_p^n; \mathbf{s}_R \leftarrow\!\!\text{\$}\; \mathbb{Z}_p^n$	
$\rho \leftarrow\!\!\text{\$}\; \mathbb{Z}_p; S \leftarrow h^\rho \mathbf{g}^{\mathbf{s}_L} \mathbf{h}^{\mathbf{s}_R}$ $\xrightarrow{\;A, S\;}$	
$\xleftarrow{\;y, z\;}$	$y, z \leftarrow\!\!\text{\$}\; \mathbb{Z}_p^*$
$l(X) \leftarrow (\mathbf{a}_L - z \cdot \mathbf{1}^n) + \mathbf{s}_L \cdot X$	$\delta(y, z) \leftarrow (z - z^2) \cdot \langle \mathbf{1}^n, \mathbf{y}^n \rangle$
$r(X) \leftarrow \mathbf{y}^n \circ (\mathbf{a}_R + z \cdot \mathbf{1}^n + \mathbf{s}_R \cdot X)$	$\quad - z^3 \cdot \langle \mathbf{1}^n, \mathbf{2}^n \rangle$
$\quad + z^2 \cdot \mathbf{2}^n$	
$t(X) \leftarrow \langle l(X), r(X) \rangle = t_0 + t_1 X + t_2 X^2$	
$\beta_1, \beta_2 \leftarrow\!\!\text{\$}\; \mathbb{Z}_p$	
$T_i \leftarrow g^{t_i} h^{\beta_i} \text{ for } i \in \{1, 2\}$ $\xrightarrow{\;T_1, T_2\;}$	
$\xleftarrow{\;x\;}$	$x \leftarrow\!\!\text{\$}\; \mathbb{Z}_p^*$
$\mathbf{l} \leftarrow l(x); \mathbf{r} \leftarrow r(x); \hat{t} \leftarrow \langle \mathbf{l}, \mathbf{r} \rangle$	
$\beta_x \leftarrow \beta_2 \cdot x^2 + \beta_1 \cdot x + z^2 \gamma; \mu \leftarrow \alpha + \rho \cdot x$ $\xrightarrow{\;\beta_x, \mu, \hat{t}\;}$	
$\xleftarrow{\;w\;}$	$w \leftarrow\!\!\text{\$}\; \mathbb{Z}_p^*$
$\mathbf{h}' \leftarrow \mathbf{h}^{\mathbf{y}^{-n}}; u' \leftarrow u^w$	$\mathbf{h}' \leftarrow \mathbf{h}^{\mathbf{y}^{-n}}; u' \leftarrow u^w$
$P \leftarrow A S^x \mathbf{g}^{-z \cdot \mathbf{1}^n} \mathbf{h}'^{z \cdot \mathbf{y}^n + z^2 \cdot \mathbf{2}^n}$	$P \leftarrow A S^x \mathbf{g}^{-z \cdot \mathbf{1}^n} \mathbf{h}'^{z \cdot \mathbf{y}^n + z^2 \cdot \mathbf{2}^n}$
$P' \leftarrow h^{-\mu} P(u')^{\hat{t}}$	$P' \leftarrow h^{-\mu} P(u')^{\hat{t}}$
$\mathsf{InPrd.P}((\mathbf{g}, \mathbf{h}', u', P'), (\mathbf{l}, \mathbf{r})) \;\Longleftrightarrow\;$	$\mathsf{InPrd.V}(\mathbf{g}, \mathbf{h}', u', P') \rightarrow b$
	$R \leftarrow V^{z^2} g^{\delta(y, z)} T_1^x T_2^{x^2}$
	If $b = 1 \wedge g^{\hat{t}} h^{\beta_x} = R$ then
	$\quad$ Return 1
	Return 0

Fig. 7. Prover and Verifier for RngPf. The function $\mathsf{BinRep}(v, n)$ outputs the n-bit representation of v. The symbol $\Longleftrightarrow$ denotes the interaction between InPrd.P and InPrd.V with the output of the InPrd.V being b.

5.2   Online srs-wee Security of RngPf

We shall assume that $\mathsf{RngPf} = \mathsf{RngPf}[\mathbb{G}]$ is instantiated on an understood family of groups $\mathbb{G} = \{\mathbb{G}_\lambda\}_{\lambda \in \mathbb{N}^+}$ of order $p = p(\lambda)$. The argument RngPf is an argument of knowledge for the relation

$$R = \left\{ \left((n \in \mathbb{N}, g, h \in \mathbb{G}), V \in \mathbb{G}, (v, \gamma \in \mathbb{Z}_p) \right) : g^v h^\gamma = V \wedge v \in [0, 2^n - 1] \right\}. \quad (4)$$

Description of RngPf. $\mathsf{RngPf.Setup}$ returns $\mathbf{g} \in \mathbb{G}^n, \mathbf{h} \in \mathbb{G}^n, g, h, u \in \mathbb{G}$ where $\mathbf{g}, \mathbf{h}$ are vectors of independent generators and g, h, u are other independent generators of the group $\mathbb{G}$. The prover and verifier for RngPf are defined in Fig. 7.

In Theorem 4, we analyze the online srs-wee security for RngPf. Since RngPf has a group element V in its input, the analysis of non-adaptive srs-wee security would differ from the online srs-wee analysis. In the full version [34], we analyse the non-adaptive srs-wee security of RngPf – it turns out that the proof is even harder for this case because the function e does not have the representation of V. The resulting bound is increased to the square root of the adaptive bound, due to our limited use of rewinding.

Theorem 4. *Let* $\mathbb{G} = \{\mathbb{G}_\lambda\}_{\lambda \in \mathbb{N}^+}$ *be a family of groups of order* $p = p(\lambda)$. *Let* $\mathsf{RngPf} = \mathsf{RngPf}[\mathbb{G}]$ *be the interactive argument as defined in Fig. 7, for the relation R in (4). We can construct an extractor $\mathcal{E}$ such that for any non-uniform algebraic prover $\mathcal{P}_{\mathsf{alg}}$ making at most $q = q(\lambda)$ queries to its oracle, there exists a non-uniform adversary $\mathcal{F}$ with the property that for any (computationally unbounded) distinguisher $\mathcal{D}$, for all $\lambda \in \mathbb{N}^+$,*

$$\mathsf{Adv}^{\mathsf{sr-wee}}_{\mathsf{RngPf}, R}(\mathcal{P}_{\mathsf{alg}}, \mathcal{D}, \mathcal{E}, \lambda) \leqslant (14n + 8)q/(p - 1) + \mathsf{Adv}^{\mathsf{dl}}_{\mathbb{G}}(\mathcal{F}, \lambda) + 1/p .$$

Moreover, the time complexity of the extractor $\mathcal{E}$ is $O(q \cdot n)$ and that of adversary $\mathcal{F}$ is $O(q \cdot n)$.

We show that the bound above is tight in Theorem 5. Using Theorem 2, we get the following corollary.

Corollary 1. *Let* $\mathbb{G} = \{\mathbb{G}_\lambda\}_{\lambda \in \mathbb{N}^+}$ *be a family of groups of order* $p = p(\lambda)$. *Let* $\mathsf{RngPf} = \mathsf{RngPf}[\mathbb{G}]$ *be the interactive argument as defined in Fig. 7, for the relation R in 4. Let $\mathsf{FS}^{\mathsf{RO}}[\mathsf{RngPf}]$ be the non-interactive argument obtained by applying the Fiat-Shamir transform to RngPf using a random oracle. We can construct an extractor $\mathcal{E}$ such that for any non-uniform algebraic prover $\mathcal{P}_{\mathsf{alg}}$ making at most $q = q(\lambda)$ queries to the random oracle there exists a non-uniform adversary $\mathcal{F}$ with the property that for all $\lambda \in \mathbb{N}^+$,*

$$\mathsf{Adv}^{\mathsf{fs-ext-1}}_{\mathsf{FS}^{\mathsf{RO}}[\mathsf{RngPf}], R}(\mathcal{P}_{\mathsf{alg}}, \mathcal{E}, \lambda) \leqslant ((14n + 9)q + 1)/(p - 1) + \mathsf{Adv}^{\mathsf{dl}}_{\mathbb{G}}(\mathcal{F}, \lambda) + 1/p .$$

Moreover, the time complexity of the extractor $\mathcal{E}$ is $O(q \cdot n)$ and that of adversary $\mathcal{F}$ is $O(q \cdot n)$.

In order to prove Theorem 4, we invoke Theorem 1 by defining BadCh and e and showing that $\varepsilon \leqslant (14n + 8)/(p - 1)$ and there exists an adversary $\mathcal{F}$ such that $p_{\mathsf{fail}}(\mathsf{RngPf}, \mathcal{P}_{\mathsf{alg}}, \mathsf{e}, R, \lambda) \leqslant \mathsf{Adv}^{\mathsf{dl}}_{\mathbb{G}}(\mathcal{F}) + 1/p$. In more detail, we construct a function h such that for an accepting transcript $\tau \notin \mathcal{T}^{\mathsf{RngPf}}_{\mathsf{BadCh}}$ if $\mathsf{e}([\tau])$ fails to produce a valid witness, then $\mathsf{h}([\tau])$ returns a non-trivial discrete logarithm relation with respect to the generators. This h is used to construct an adversary $\mathcal{H}$ against the discrete logarithm relation problem and we invoke Lemma 2 to transform into adversary $\mathcal{F}$ against the discrete logarithm problem, thus upper bounding $p_{\mathsf{fail}}(\mathsf{RngPf}, \mathcal{P}_{\mathsf{alg}}, \mathsf{e}, R, \lambda)$ using $\mathsf{Adv}^{\mathsf{dl}}_{\mathbb{G}}(\mathcal{F})$.

Proof (Theorem 4). We extend the notation for representation of group elements introduced in Sect. 4 for representation with respect to vector of group elements like $\mathbf{g}$. The representation of a group element $A = \mathbf{g}^{a_{\mathbf{g}}} g^{a_g}$ with respect to $(\mathbf{g}, g)$ is $[A] = (A, a_{\mathbf{g}}, a_g)$ where $a_{\mathbf{g}} = (a_{g_1}, \cdots, a_{g_n})$.

DEFINING BadCh AND UPPER BOUNDING ε. To start off, we define $\mathsf{BadCh}(\tau')$ for all partial transcripts τ'. Let Ch be the set from which the challenge that just follows τ' is sampled. We use a helper function CheckBad to define $\mathsf{BadCh}(\tau')$. The function CheckBad takes as input a partial extended transcript $[\tau']$ and a challenge $c \in \mathsf{Ch}$ and returns true if and only if $c \in \mathsf{BadCh}(\tau')$. For each verifier challenge in RngPf, there is a definition of CheckBad in Fig. 8. Every CheckBad function defines several bad conditions that depend on τ' – most of these bad conditions are checked using the predicate SZ. This predicate takes as input a vector of polynomials and a corresponding vector of points to evaluate the polynomial on and returns true iff any of the polynomials is non-zero but its evaluation at the corresponding point is zero. One can safely ignore the details of the definitions of CheckBad functions for now – the rationale behind their definitions shall become apparent later on.

The following lemma establishes an upper bound of $(14n + 8)/(p - 1)$ on $|\mathsf{BadCh}(\tau')|/|\mathsf{Ch}|$.

Lemma 3. *Let τ' be a partial transcript for* RngPf. *Let* Ch *be the set from which the challenge that comes right after τ' is sampled. Then,* $|\mathsf{BadCh}(\tau')|/|\mathsf{Ch}| \leqslant (14n + 8)/(p - 1)$.

The proof of this lemma has been deferred to the full version [34].

DEFINING e. Let τ be a transcript of RngPf as defined below.

$$\tau = \big((n, \mathbf{g}, \mathbf{h}, u, g, h), V; (A, S), (y, z), (T_1, T_2), x, (\beta_x, \mu, \hat{t}), w, (L_1, R_1), x_1, \quad (5)$$
$$(L_2, R_2), x_2, \ldots, (L_{\log n}, R_{\log n}), x_{\log n}, (a, b)\big) .$$

Let us represent using $\tau|_c$ the prefix of τ just before the challenge c. For example $\tau|_{(y,z)} = \big((n, \mathbf{g}, \mathbf{h}, u, g, h), V, (A, S)\big)$. The function e simply returns (v_g, v_h) (Fig. 9). However, its output is a valid witness only if $v_{\mathbf{g}} = v_{\mathbf{h}} = \mathbf{0}^n, v_u = 0$ and $v_g \in [0, 2^n - 1]$.

PROVING AN UPPER BOUND ON $p_{\mathsf{fail}}(\mathsf{RngPf}, \mathcal{P}_{\mathsf{alg}}, \mathsf{e}, R, \lambda)$. We construct an adversary $\mathcal{H}$ against the discrete logarithm relation problem that takes as input independent generators $\mathbf{g}, \mathbf{h}, g, h, u$ of the group $\mathbb{G}$ and works as follows. It simulates the game $\mathsf{SRS}_{\mathsf{RngPf}}$ to $\mathcal{P}_{\mathsf{alg}}$ using public parameters $n, \mathbf{g}, \mathbf{h}, g, h, u$. If $\mathcal{P}_{\mathsf{alg}}$ manages to produce an accepting transcript τ, $\mathcal{H}$ calls a helper function h on input $[\tau]$ and outputs whatever h outputs. We shall define h in such a way that for $\tau \notin \mathcal{T}_{\mathsf{BadCh}}^{\mathsf{RngPf}}$ if $\mathsf{e}([\tau])$ does not return a valid witness, then $\mathsf{h}([\tau])$ returns a non-trivial discrete logarithm relation. In other words, we have that whenever $\mathsf{e}([\tau])$ fails to extract a valid witness for an accepting transcript $\tau \notin \mathcal{T}_{\mathsf{BadCh}}^{\mathsf{RngPf}}$, $\mathcal{H}$ succeeds. So we have that $p_{\mathsf{fail}}(\mathsf{RngPf}, \mathcal{P}_{\mathsf{alg}}, \mathsf{e}, R, \lambda) \leqslant \mathsf{Adv}_{\mathbb{G}, 2n+3}^{\mathsf{dl\text{-}rel}}(\mathcal{H})$. Using Lemma 2 we would have that there exists an adversary $\mathcal{F}$ such that $p_{\mathsf{fail}}(\mathsf{RngPf}, \mathcal{P}_{\mathsf{alg}}, \mathsf{e}, R, \lambda) \leqslant \mathsf{Adv}_{\mathbb{G}}^{\mathsf{dl}}(\mathcal{F}) + 1/p$. We also have that $\mathcal{F}$ is nearly as efficient as $\mathcal{H}$.

DEFINING h. We next describe the h function. Let τ, as defined in 5, be an accepting transcript. $V^{z^2} g^{\delta(y,z)} T_1^x T_2^{x^2} = g^{\hat{t}} h^{\beta_x}$. must hold since τ is an accepting transcript.

Procedure CheckBad($[\tau']$, (y, z)):

$//[\tau'] = ((n, \mathbf{g}, \mathbf{h}, u, g, h), [V], ([A], [S]))$
$f(Y, Z) \leftarrow Z^2(v_g - \langle a_\mathbf{g}, \mathbf{2}^n \rangle) - Z\langle a_\mathbf{g} - a_\mathbf{h} - \mathbf{1}^n, \mathbf{Y}^n \rangle - \langle a_\mathbf{g} \circ a_\mathbf{h}, \mathbf{Y}^n \rangle$
Return $\mathsf{SZ}(f(Y, Z), (y, z))$

Procedure CheckBad($[\tau']$, x):

$//[\tau'] = ((n, \mathbf{g}, \mathbf{h}, u, g, h), [V], ([A], [S]), (y, z), ([T_1], [T_2]))$
$f_1(X) \leftarrow v_g z^2 + t_{1g} X + t_{2g} X^2; \quad f_2(X) \leftarrow v_h z^2 + t_{1h} X + t_{2h} X^2$
$f_3(X) \leftarrow v_u z^2 + t_{1u} X + t_{2u} X^2; \quad \delta(y, z) \leftarrow (z - z^2)\langle \mathbf{1}^n, \mathbf{y}^n \rangle - z^3 \langle \mathbf{1}^n, \mathbf{2}^n \rangle$
$l(X) \leftarrow (a_\mathbf{g} - z \cdot \mathbf{1}^n) + s_\mathbf{g} \cdot X; \quad r(X) \leftarrow \mathbf{y}^n \circ (a_\mathbf{h} + z \cdot \mathbf{1}^n + s_\mathbf{h} \cdot X) + z^2 \cdot \mathbf{2}^n$
$f_4(X) \leftarrow v_g z^2 + \delta(y, z) + t_{1g} X + t_{2g} X^2 - \langle l(X), r(X) \rangle$
Return $\mathsf{SZ}(f_1(X), x) \vee \mathsf{SZ}(f_2(X), x) \vee \mathsf{SZ}(f_3(X), x) \vee \mathsf{SZ}(f_4(X), x)$

Procedure CheckBad($[\tau']$, w):

$//[\tau'] = ((n, \mathbf{g}, \mathbf{h}, u, g, h), [V], ([A], [S]), (y, z), ([T_1], [T_2]), x, (\beta_x, \mu, \hat{t}))$
$\mathbf{l} \leftarrow (a_\mathbf{g} - z \cdot \mathbf{1}^n) + s_\mathbf{g} \cdot x; \quad \mathbf{r} \leftarrow (a_\mathbf{h} + x s_\mathbf{h} + z \mathbf{1}^n) \circ \mathbf{y}^n + z^2 \mathbf{2}^n; \quad f(W) \leftarrow W \hat{t} - W \langle \mathbf{l}, \mathbf{r} \rangle$
Return $\mathsf{SZ}(f(W), w)$

Procedure CheckBad($[\tau']$, x_m):

$//[\tau'] = ((n, \mathbf{g}, \mathbf{h}, u, g, h), [V], ([A], [S]), (y, z), ([T_1], [T_2]), x, (\beta_x, \mu, \hat{t}), w,$
$\qquad ([L_1], [R_1]), x_1, \ldots, ([L_m], [R_m]))$
$p'_\mathbf{g} \leftarrow a_\mathbf{g} + x s_\mathbf{g} - z \mathbf{1}^n; \quad p'_\mathbf{h} \leftarrow a_\mathbf{h} + x s_\mathbf{h} + \mathbf{y}^{-n} \circ (z \mathbf{y}^n + z^2 \mathbf{2}^n); \quad p'_u \leftarrow a_u + x s_u + w \hat{t}$
For $j = 0, \ldots, n-1$ do
$\qquad f^\mathbf{g}_{m,j}(X) \leftarrow l_{mg_{1+j}} + X^2 + r_{mg_{1+j}} X^{-2} + p'_{g_{1+j}} + \sum_{i=1}^{m-1} (l_{ig_{1+j}} x_i^2 + r_{ig_{1+j}} x_i^{-2})$
$\qquad f^\mathbf{h}_{m,j}(X) \leftarrow l_{mh_{1+j}} X^2 + r_{mh_{1+j}} X^{-2} + p'_{h_{1+j}} + \sum_{i=1}^{m-1} (l_{ih_{1+j}} x_i^2 + r_{ih_{1+j}} x_i^{-2})$
$f^u_m(X) \leftarrow l_{mu} X^2 + r_{mu} X^{-2} + p'_u + \sum_{i=1}^{m-1} (l_{iu} x_i^2 + r_{iu} x_i^{-2})$
flag $\leftarrow$ false
For $t = 1, \ldots, m-1$ do for $j = 0, \ldots, n/2^t - 1$ do
$\qquad$ flag $\leftarrow$ flag $\vee \mathsf{SZ}(f^\mathbf{g}_{m,j}(X) \cdot x_t^2 - f^\mathbf{g}_{m,j+n/2^t}(X), x_m) \vee \mathsf{SZ}(f^\mathbf{h}_{m,j}(X) - f^\mathbf{h}_{m,j+n/2^t}(X) \cdot x_t^2, x_m)$
For $j = 0, \ldots, n/2^m - 1$ do
$\qquad$ flag $\leftarrow$ flag $\vee \mathsf{SZ}(f^\mathbf{g}_{m,j}(X) \cdot X^2 - f^\mathbf{g}_{m,j+n/2^m}(X), x_m) \vee \mathsf{SZ}(f^\mathbf{h}_{m,j}(X) - f^\mathbf{h}_{m,j+n/2^m}(X) \cdot$
$X^2, x_m)$
flag $\leftarrow$ flag $\vee \mathsf{SZ}\left(f^u_m(X) - w \cdot \sum_{j=0}^{n/2^m-1} f^\mathbf{g}_{m,j}(X) \cdot f^\mathbf{h}_{m,j}(X) \cdot y^j, x_m\right)$
Return flag

Fig. 8. The functions CheckBad function for the RngPf.

Procedure e($[\tau]$):

$//[\tau] = ((n, \mathbf{g}, \mathbf{h}, u, g, h), [V]; ([A], [S]), (y, z), ([T_1], [T_2]), x, (\beta_x, \mu, \hat{t}), w,$
$\qquad ([L_1], [R_1]), x_1, \ldots, ([L_{\log n}], [R_{\log n}]), x_{\log n}, (a, b))$
$v^* \leftarrow v_g; \quad \gamma^* \leftarrow v_h;$ Return (v^*, γ^*)

Fig. 9. The function e for RngPf.

Procedure $\mathsf{h}([\tau])$:

$//[\tau] = ((n, \mathbf{g}, \mathbf{h}, u, g, h), [V]; ([A], [S]), (y, z), ([T_1], [T_2]), x, (\beta_x, \mu, \hat{t}), w,$
$\qquad ([L_1], [R_1]), x_1, \ldots, ([L_{\log n}], [R_{\log n}]), x_{\log n}, (a, b))$

$\delta(y, z) \leftarrow (z - z^2)\langle \mathbf{1}^n, \mathbf{y}^n \rangle - z^3 \langle \mathbf{1}^n, \mathbf{2}^n \rangle$

$e_{\mathbf{g}}^{(1)} \leftarrow v_{\mathbf{g}} z^2 + t_{1\mathbf{g}} x + t_{2\mathbf{g}} x^2;\ e_{\mathbf{h}}^{(1)} \leftarrow v_{\mathbf{h}} z^2 + t_{1\mathbf{h}} x + t_{2\mathbf{h}} x^2;\ e_u^{(1)} \leftarrow v_u z^2 + t_{1u} x + t_{2u} x^2$

$e_g^{(1)} \leftarrow v_g z^2 + \delta(y, z) + t_{1g} x + t_{2g} x^2 - \hat{t};\ e_h^{(1)} \leftarrow v_h z^2 + t_{1h} x + t_{2h} x^2 - \beta_x$

If $(e_{\mathbf{g}}^{(1)}, e_{\mathbf{h}}^{(1)}, e_u^{(1)}, e_g^{(1)}, e_h^{(1)}) \neq (\mathbf{0}^n, \mathbf{0}^n, 0, 0, 0)$ then return $(e_{\mathbf{g}}^{(1)}, e_{\mathbf{h}}^{(1)}, e_u^{(1)}, e_g^{(1)}, e_h^{(1)})$

$p_{\mathbf{g}}' \leftarrow (a_{\mathbf{g}}) + x s_{\mathbf{g}} - z\mathbf{1}^n;\ p_{\mathbf{h}}' \leftarrow a_{\mathbf{h}} + x s_{\mathbf{h}} + \mathbf{y}^{-n} \circ (zy^n + z^2 \mathbf{2}^n)$

$p_g' \leftarrow a_g + x s_g;\ p_h' \leftarrow a_h + x s_h - \mu;\ p_u' \leftarrow a_u + x s_u + w\hat{t}$

For $k = 0$ to $n - 1$ do

$\qquad e_{g_{k+1}}^{(2)} \leftarrow p_{g_{1+k}}' + \sum_{i=1}^{\log n} l_{ig_{1+k}} x_i^2 + r_{ig_{1+k}} x_i^{-2} - a \cdot \prod_{i=1}^{\log n} x_i^{(-1)^{1 - \mathrm{bit}(k, i, \log n)}}$

$\qquad e_{h_{k+1}}^{(2)} \leftarrow p_{h_{1+k}}' + \sum_{i=1}^{\log n} l_{ih_{1+k}} x_i^2 + r_{ih_{1+k}} + x_i^{-2} - by^{(-(k))} \cdot \prod_{i=1}^{\log n} x_i^{(-1)^{\mathrm{bit}(k, i, \log n)}}$

$e_{\mathbf{g}}^{(2)} \leftarrow (e_{g_1}^{(2)}, \ldots, e_{g_n}^{(2)});\ e_{\mathbf{h}}^{(2)} \leftarrow (e_{h_1}^{(2)}, \ldots, e_{h_n}^{(2)});\ e_u^{(2)} \leftarrow p_u' + \sum_{i=1}^{\log n} l_{iu} x_i^2 + r_{iu} x_i^{-2} - w \cdot ab$

$e_g^{(2)} \leftarrow \sum_{i=1}^{\log n} l_{ig} x_i^2 + r_{ig} x_i^{-2} + p_g';\ e_h^{(2)} \leftarrow \sum_{i=1}^{\log n} l_{ih} x_i^2 + r_{ih} x_i^{-2} + p_h'$

Return $(e_{\mathbf{g}}^{(2)}, e_{\mathbf{h}}^{(2)}, e_u^{(2)}, e_g^{(2)}, e_h^{(2)})$

Fig. 10. The function h for RngPf.

The function h can plug in the representations of T_1, T_2, V into the above equation and compute $e_{\mathbf{g}}^{(1)}, e_{\mathbf{h}}^{(1)}, e_g^{(1)}, e_h^{(1)}, e_u^{(1)}$ such that $\mathbf{g}^{e_{\mathbf{g}}^{(1)}} \mathbf{h}^{e_{\mathbf{h}}^{(1)}} g^{e_g^{(1)}} h^{e_h^{(1)}} u^{e_u^{(1)}} = 1$. If not all of these are zero, h returns $e_{\mathbf{g}}^{(1)}, e_{\mathbf{h}}^{(1)}, e_g^{(1)}, e_h^{(1)}, e_u^{(1)}$.

Again since τ is an accepting transcript, $\mathsf{InPrd.V}$ must have returned 1 and hence $P^{(\log n)} = (\mathbf{g}^{(\log n)})^a (\mathbf{h}^{(\log n)})^b u^{ab}$ must hold. All the terms in the above equality can be expressed in terms of $\mathbf{g}, \mathbf{h}, g, h, u$ and one can compute $e_{\mathbf{g}}^{(2)}, e_{\mathbf{h}}^{(2)}, e_g^{(2)}, e_h^{(2)}, e_u^{(2)}$ such that $\mathbf{g}^{e_{\mathbf{g}}^{(2)}} \mathbf{h}^{e_{\mathbf{h}}^{(2)}} g^{e_g^{(2)}} h^{e_h^{(2)}} u^{e_u^{(2)}} = 1$. The function h computes and returns $e_{\mathbf{g}}^{(2)}, e_{\mathbf{h}}^{(2)}, e_g^{(2)}, e_h^{(2)}, e_u^{(2)}$. We define the function h formally in Fig. 10. It follows from the description of h that it runs in time $O(n)$. The running time of $\mathcal{H}$ consists of the time required to answers q queries, run $\mathsf{RngPf.V}$ in at most q paths in the execution tree and the time required to run h. Hence its time complexity is $O(q \cdot n)$. Using Lemma 2, time complexity of $\mathcal{F}$ is $O(q \cdot n)$.

RELATING h, e. In order to complete the proof of Theorem 4, in the following lemma we show that – for an accepting transcript τ such that $\tau \notin \mathcal{T}_{\mathsf{BadCh}}^{\mathsf{RngPf}}$ if $\mathsf{e}([\tau])$ does not return a valid witness, then $\mathsf{h}([\tau])$ returns a non-trivial discrete logarithm relation. Proving this lemma would conclude the proof of Theorem 4.

Lemma 4. *Let τ, as defined in 5, be an accepting transcript of* RngPf *such that* $\tau \notin \mathcal{T}_{\mathsf{BadCh}}^{\mathsf{RngPf}}$. *If* $\mathsf{e}([\tau])$ *returns* (v^*, γ^*) *such that at least one of the following hold:* $g^{v^*} h^{\gamma^*} \neq V$ *or* $v^* \notin [0, 2^n - 1]$, *then* $\mathsf{h}([\tau])$ *returns a non-trivial discrete logarithm relation.*

Proof (Lemma 4). For simplicity, we shall prove the contrapositive of the statement, i.e., assuming $h([\tau])$ returns a trivial discrete logarithm relation, then $g^{v^*} h^{\gamma^*} = V$ and $v^* \in [0, 2^n - 1]$.

In order to prove $g^{v^*} h^{\gamma^*} = V$ and $v^* \in [0, 2^n - 1]$, it suffices to show that $v_{\mathbf{g}} = v_{\mathbf{h}} = \mathbf{0}^n$, $v_u = 0$ and $v_g \in [0, 2^n - 1]$. Let us denote using $\tau|_c$ the partial transcript that is the prefix of τ just before the challenge c. For example $\tau|_{(y,z)} = ((n, \mathbf{g}, \mathbf{h}, u, g, h), V, (A, S))$. Since we assumed that $h([\tau])$ returns $(\mathbf{0}^n, \mathbf{0}^n, 0, 0, 0)$, we have that for $i = 1, 2$, $(e_{\mathbf{g}}^{(i)}, e_{\mathbf{h}}^{(i)}, e_g^{(i)}, e_h^{(i)}, e_u^{(i)}) = (\mathbf{0}^n, \mathbf{0}^n, 0, 0, 0)$.

Writing out the expression for $e_{\mathbf{g}}^{(1)}$ we get $v_{\mathbf{g}} z^2 + t_{1\mathbf{g}} x + t_{2\mathbf{g}} x^2 = \mathbf{0}^n$. Since $\tau \notin T_{\mathsf{BadCh}}^{\mathsf{RngPf}}$, we have that $x \notin \mathsf{BadCh}(\tau|_x)$. Therefore, $\mathsf{SZ}(f_1(X), x)$ is $\mathtt{false}$ where f_1 is as defined in $\mathsf{CheckBad}(\tau', x)$. Since we have here that $f_1(x) = 0$, the polynomial $f_1(X)$ is the zero vector polynomial. Since $z \neq 0$ it follows that $v_{\mathbf{g}} = \mathbf{0}^n$. Similarly using $e_{\mathbf{h}}^{(1)} = \mathbf{0}^n$ and $e_u^{(1)} = 0$ we can show that $v_{\mathbf{h}} = \mathbf{0}^n$ and $v_u = 0$ respectively. Writing out the expression for $e_g^{(1)}$ we have $v_g z^2 + \delta(y, z) + t_{1g} x + t_{2g} x^2 - \hat{t} = 0$. Hence,

$$\hat{t} = v_g z^2 + \delta(y, z) + t_{1g} x + t_{2g} x^2 . \tag{6}$$

Using $e_{\mathbf{g}}^{(2)} = \mathbf{0}^n$ we get for all $k \in \{0, \dots, n-1\}$

$$p'_{g_{1+k}} + \sum_{i=1}^{\log n} (l_{ig_{1+k}} x_i^2 + r_{ig_{1+k}} x_i^{-2}) - a \cdot \prod_{i=1}^{\log n} x_i^{(-1)^{1-\mathsf{bit}(k,i,\log n)}} = 0 . \tag{7}$$

Using $e_{\mathbf{h}}^{(2)} = \mathbf{0}^n$ we get for all $k \in \{0, \dots, n-1\}$

$$p'_{h_{1+k}} + \sum_{i=1}^{\log n} (l_{ih_{1+k}} x_i^2 + r_{ih_{1+k}} x_i^{-2}) - by^{(-(k))} \cdot \prod_{i=1}^{\log n} x_i^{(-1)^{\mathsf{bit}(k,i,\log n)}} = 0 . \tag{8}$$

Using $e_u^{(2)} = 0$ we get that

$$p'_u + \sum_{i=1}^{\log n} (l_{iu} x_i^2 + r_{iu} x_i^{-2}) - w \cdot ab = 0 . \tag{9}$$

We shall next use the following lemma which essentially says that if all of $e_{\mathbf{g}}^{(2)}, e_{\mathbf{h}}^{(2)}, e_u^{(2)}, e_g^{(2)}, e_h^{(2)}$ are zero and $\tau \notin T_{\mathsf{BadCh}}^{\mathsf{RngPf}}$, then $w \cdot \langle p'_{\mathbf{g}}, p'_{\mathbf{h}} \circ \mathbf{y}^n \rangle = p'_u$.

Lemma 5. *Let τ, as shown in (5), be an accepting transcript of RngPf such that $\tau \notin T_{\mathsf{BadCh}}^{\mathsf{RngPf}}$. Let*

$$p'_{\mathbf{g}} = a_{\mathbf{g}} + x s_{\mathbf{g}} - z \mathbf{1}^n , p'_{\mathbf{h}} = a_{\mathbf{h}} + x s_{\mathbf{h}} + \mathbf{y}^{-n} \circ (z \mathbf{y}^n + z^2 \mathbf{2}^n) , p'_u = a_u + x s_u + w \hat{t} .$$

Suppose, the for all $k \in \{0, \dots, n-1\}$

$$\left(\sum_{i=1}^{\log n} (l_{ig_{1+k}} x_i^2 + r_{ig_{1+k}} x_i^{-2}) + p'_{g_{1+k}} \right) - a \cdot \left(\prod_{i=1}^{\log n} x_i^{(-1)^{1-\mathsf{bit}(k,i,\log n)}} \right) = 0 ,$$

$$\left(\sum_{i=1}^{\log n} (l_{ih_{1+k}} x_i^2 + r_{ih_{1+k}} x_i^{-2}) + p'_{h_{1+k}} \right) - by^{(-(k))} \cdot \left(\prod_{i=1}^{\log n} x_i^{(-1)^{\mathrm{bit}(k,i,\log n)}} \right) = 0 .$$

Also, $\left(\sum_{i=1}^{\log n} (l_{iu} x_i^2 + r_{iu} x_i^{-2}) \right) + p'_u - w \cdot ab = 0.$ Then $w \cdot \langle p'_{\mathbf{g}}, p'_{\mathbf{h}} \circ \mathbf{y}^n \rangle = p'_u.$

The proof of this lemma is a generalization of the proof that we gave for the inner product argument for $n = 2$ in the technical overview. We defer the proof of Lemma 5 to the full version [34].

Since τ is an accepting transcript of RngPf and $\tau \notin T_{\mathsf{BadCh}}^{\mathsf{RngPf}}$ and (7) to (9) hold, using Lemma 5, we get $w\langle p'_{\mathbf{g}}, p'_{\mathbf{h}} \circ \mathbf{y}^n \rangle = p'_u$. Plugging in the values of $p'_{\mathbf{g}}, p'_{\mathbf{h}}, p'_u$ we get

$$w \cdot \langle a_{\mathbf{g}} + x s_{\mathbf{g}} - z\mathbf{1}^n, (a_{\mathbf{h}} + x s_{\mathbf{h}} + z\mathbf{1}^n) \circ \mathbf{y}^n + z^2 \mathbf{2}^n \rangle = a_u + x s_u + w\hat{t} .$$

Since $\tau \notin T_{\mathsf{BadCh}}^{\mathsf{RngPf}}$, we have that $w \notin \mathsf{BadCh}(\tau|_w)$. Therefore, $\mathsf{SZ}(f(W), w)$ is $\mathtt{false}$ where f is as defined in $\mathsf{CheckBad}(\tau', w)$. Since we have here that $f(w) = 0$, the polynomial $f(W)$ must be the zero polynomial. In particular its W term must be zero, i.e., $\langle a_{\mathbf{g}} + x s_{\mathbf{g}} - z\mathbf{1}^n, (a_{\mathbf{h}} + x s_{\mathbf{h}} + z\mathbf{1}^n) \circ \mathbf{y}^n + z^2 \mathbf{2}^n \rangle = \hat{t}$. Plugging in the value of $\hat{t}$ obtained in (6) and using $x \notin \mathsf{BadCh}(\tau|_x)$, we have that

$$v_g z^2 + \delta(y, z) - \langle a_{\mathbf{g}} - z\mathbf{1}^n, (a_{\mathbf{h}} + z\mathbf{1}^n) \circ \mathbf{y}^n + z^2 \mathbf{2}^n \rangle = 0 .$$

Plugging in the value of $\delta(y, z)$, rearranging and simplifying we get

$$z^2 (v_g - \langle a_{\mathbf{g}}, \mathbf{2}^n \rangle) - z\langle a_{\mathbf{g}} - a_{\mathbf{h}} - \mathbf{1}^n, \mathbf{y}^n \rangle - \langle a_{\mathbf{g}} \circ a_{\mathbf{h}}, \mathbf{y}^n \rangle = 0 .$$

Using $(y, z) \notin \mathsf{BadCh}(\tau|_{(y,z)})$, we get that $v_g - \langle a_{\mathbf{g}}, \mathbf{2}^n \rangle = 0$, $a_{\mathbf{g}} - a_{\mathbf{h}} - \mathbf{1}^n = \mathbf{0}^n$, $a_{\mathbf{g}} \circ a_{\mathbf{h}} = \mathbf{0}^n$. Note that $a_{\mathbf{g}} - a_{\mathbf{h}} - \mathbf{1}^n = \mathbf{0}^n$ and $a_{\mathbf{g}} \circ a_{\mathbf{h}} = \mathbf{0}^n$ imply that $a_{\mathbf{g}} \in \{0,1\}^n$. Further $v_g - \langle a_{\mathbf{g}}, \mathbf{2}^n \rangle = 0$, i.e., $v_g = \langle a_{\mathbf{g}}, \mathbf{2}^n \rangle$. So, $v_g \in [0, 2^n - 1]$. Therefore, v^*, γ^* output by $\mathsf{e}([\tau])$ satisfy $V = g^{v^*} h^{\gamma^*}$ and $v^* \in [0, 2^n - 1]$. This concludes the proof of Lemma 4 and Theorem 4. □

Further for a prover $\mathcal{P}_{\mathsf{alg}}$ for $\mathsf{FS}^{\mathsf{RO}}[\mathsf{RngPf}]$, and the e we define in the proof of Theorem 4, we can upper bound $p_{\mathsf{fail},\mathsf{FS}}(\mathsf{FS}^{\mathsf{RO}}[\mathsf{RngPf}], \mathcal{P}_{\mathsf{alg}}, \mathsf{e}, R, \lambda)$ using techniques very similar to those used in the proof of Theorem 4. This is because we can prove that if the prover outputs an instance and an accepting proof and e fails to produce a valid witness, then we can compute a non-trivial discrete logarithm relation from the representation of the transcript and instance unless one of the challenges in the transcript are bad which we can show happens with small probability. Then using Theorem 3 we obtain a bound for the fs-ext-2 security of $\mathsf{FS}^{\mathsf{RO}}[\mathsf{RngPf}]$ similar to the one we obtained for fs-ext-1 security in Corollary 1.

TIGHTNESS OF THEOREM 4. We next argue that the factor $O(nq/(p-1))$ in Theorem 4 is tight. We first note that the protocol RngPf can be used for the following relation

$$R' = \left\{ (n \in \mathbb{N}, g, V \in \mathbb{G}, v \in \mathbb{Z}_p) : g^v = V \wedge v \in [0, 2^n - 1] \right\} , \tag{10}$$

by fixing γ to 0.

We shall construct a cheating prover $\mathcal{P}$ (that makes $O(q)$ queries to $\mathbf{O}_{\mathrm{ext}}$) for the relation R' that outputs an instance $V = g^v$ such that $v \notin [0, 2^n - 1]$ but can still convince the RngPf verifier with probability $\Omega(nq/(p-1))$ if n divides $p-1$. This would imply that the bound in Theorem 4 is tight up to constant factors.

Theorem 5. *Let* $\mathbb{G} = \{\mathbb{G}_\lambda\}_{\lambda \in \mathbb{N}^+}$ *be a family of groups of prime order* $p = p(\lambda)$. *Let* RngPf $=$ RngPf$[\mathbb{G}]$ *be the interactive argument for the relation* R' *in (10) obtained by setting* $\gamma = 0$ *in the protocol defined in Fig. 7. If* n *divides* $p - 1$, *we can construct a non-uniform prover* $\mathcal{P}$ *making at most* $q + \log n + 1$ *queries to its oracle, such that for all* $\lambda \in \mathbb{N}^+$, $\mathsf{Adv}^{\mathsf{srs}}_{\mathsf{RngPf}}(\mathcal{P}, \lambda) = (n-1)q/(p-1)$.

The proof of this theorem has been deferred to the full version [34].

5.3 Online srs-wee Security for ACSPf

In this section, we introduce ACSPf and apply our framework to prove online srs-wee security. As shown in [10], any arithmetic circuit with n multiplication gates can be represented using a constraint system that has three vectors $\mathbf{a}_L, \mathbf{a}_R, \mathbf{a}_O \in \mathbb{Z}_p^n$ representing the left inputs, right inputs, and outputs of multiplication gates respectively, so that $\mathbf{a}_L \circ \mathbf{a}_R = \mathbf{a}_O$, with additional $Q \leqslant 2n$ linear constraints. The linear constraints can be represented as $\mathbf{a}_L \cdot \mathbf{W}_L + \mathbf{a}_R \cdot \mathbf{W}_R + \mathbf{a}_O \cdot \mathbf{W}_O = \mathbf{c}$, where $\mathbf{W}_L, \mathbf{W}_R, \mathbf{W}_O \in \mathbb{Z}_p^{Q \times n}$.

We shall assume that ACSPf $=$ ACSPf$[\mathbb{G}]$ is instantiated on an understood family of groups $\mathbb{G} = \{\mathbb{G}_\lambda\}_{\lambda \in \mathbb{N}^+}$ of order $p = p(\lambda)$. The argument ACSPf is an argument of knowledge for the relation

$$R = \Big\{ \big((n, Q \in \mathbb{N}), (\mathbf{W}_L, \mathbf{W}_R, \mathbf{W}_O \in \mathbb{Z}_p^{Q \times n}, \mathbf{c} \in \mathbb{Z}_p^Q), (\mathbf{a}_L, \mathbf{a}_R, \mathbf{a}_O \in \mathbb{Z}_p^n) \big) :$$

$$\mathbf{a}_L \circ \mathbf{a}_R = \mathbf{a}_O \wedge \mathbf{W}_L \cdot \mathbf{a}_L + \mathbf{W}_R \cdot \mathbf{a}_R + \mathbf{W}_O \cdot \mathbf{a}_O = \mathbf{c} \Big\}. \tag{11}$$

The description of ACSPf is deferred to the full version [34]. We prove the following theorem that gives an upper bound on the advantage against online srs-wee security of ACSPf.

Theorem 6. *Let* $\mathbb{G} = \{\mathbb{G}_\lambda\}_{\lambda \in \mathbb{N}^+}$ *be a family of groups of order* $p = p(\lambda)$. *Let* ACSPf $=$ ACSPf$[\mathbb{G}]$ *be the Bulletproofs interactive argument system for arithmetic circuit satisfiability for the relation* R *in (11). We can construct an extractor* $\mathcal{E}$ *such that for any non-uniform algebraic prover* $\mathcal{P}_{\mathsf{alg}}$ *making at most* $q = q(\lambda)$ *queries to its oracle, there exists a non-uniform adversary* $\mathcal{F}$ *with the property that for any (computationally unbounded) distinguisher* $\mathcal{D}$, *for all* $\lambda \in \mathbb{N}^+$, $\mathsf{Adv}^{\mathsf{sr\text{-}wee}}_{\mathsf{ACSPf}, R}(\mathcal{P}_{\mathsf{alg}}, \mathcal{D}, \mathcal{E}, \lambda) \leqslant ((14n + 8)q)/p - 1 + \mathsf{Adv}^{\mathsf{dl}}_{\mathbb{G}}(\mathcal{F}, \lambda) + 1/p$.

Moreover, the time complexity of the extractor $\mathcal{E}$ *is* $O(q \cdot n)$ *and that of adversary* $\mathcal{F}$ *is* $O(q \cdot n)$.

We can show that the bound in Theorem 6 is tight by constructing a cheating prover like we did in Theorem 5. Using Theorem 2, we can get a corollary about fs-ext-1 security of $\mathsf{FS}^{\mathbf{RO}}[\mathsf{ACSPf}]$ which we include in the full version [34]. Additionally, using techniques similar to those in the proof of Theorem 6, we can prove a similar bound for fs-ext-2 security of $\mathsf{FS}^{\mathbf{RO}}[\mathsf{ACSPf}]$. The proof of Theorem 6 is similar to the proof of Theorem 4 and has been deferred to the full version [34].

6   Online srs-wee Security of Sonic

We apply our framework to prove srs-wee security of Sonic [18] which is an inter-active argument for arithmetic circuit satisfiability based on pairings (we refer to this argument as SnACSPf). The argument SnACSPf is again an argument of knowledge for the relation 11. The description of SnACSPf has been deferred to the full version [34]. We prove the following theorem that establishes an upper bound on the advantage against online srs-wee security of SnACSPf.

Theorem 7. *Let* $\mathbb{G} = \{\mathbb{G}_\lambda\}_{\lambda \in \mathbb{N}^+}$ *be a family of groups with order* $p = p(\lambda)$. *Let* $\mathbb{G}_T = \{\mathbb{G}_{T,\lambda}\}_{\lambda \in \mathbb{N}^+}$ *be a family of groups such that there exists a bilinear map* $e : \mathbb{G} \times \mathbb{G} \to \mathbb{G}_T$. *Let* SnACSPf $=$ SnACSPf$[\mathbb{G}, \mathbb{G}_T, e]$ *be the Sonic interactive argument system for the relation* R *in (11). We can construct an extractor* $\mathcal{E}$ *such that for any non-uniform algebraic prover* $\mathcal{P}_{\mathsf{alg}}$ *making at most* $q = q(\lambda)$ *queries to its oracle, there exist non-uniform adversaries* $\mathcal{F}_1, \mathcal{F}_2, \mathcal{F}_3$ *with the property that for any (computationally unbounded) distinguisher* $\mathcal{D}$, *for all* $\lambda \in \mathbb{N}^+$,

$$\mathsf{Adv}^{\mathsf{sr\text{-}wee}}_{\mathsf{SnACSPf}, R}(\mathcal{P}_{\mathsf{alg}}, \mathcal{D}, \mathcal{E}, \lambda) \leqslant \frac{18nq}{p-1} + \mathsf{Adv}^{4n\text{-}\mathsf{dl}}_{\mathbb{G}}(\mathcal{F}_1, \lambda) + \mathsf{Adv}^{\mathsf{dl}}_{\mathbb{G}}(\mathcal{F}_2, \lambda) + \mathsf{Adv}^{\mathsf{dl}}_{\mathbb{G}}(\mathcal{F}_3, \lambda).$$

Moreover, the time complexities of the extractor $\mathcal{E}$ *and adversaries* $\mathcal{F}_1, \mathcal{F}_2, \mathcal{F}_3$ *are all* $O(q \cdot n)$.

We can show that the bound in Theorem 7 is tight by constructing a cheating prover like we did in Theorem 5. Using Theorem 2, we can get a corollary about fs-ext-1 security of $\mathsf{FS}^{\mathbf{RO}}[\mathsf{SnACSPf}]$ which we state in the full version [34]. Additionally, using techniques similar to those in the proof of Theorem 7, we can prove a similar bound for fs-ext-2 security of $\mathsf{FS}^{\mathbf{RO}}[\mathsf{SnACSPf}]$. The proof of Theorem 7 has been deferred to the full version [34].

Acknowledgements. We thank Joseph Jaeger for extensive discussions and his involvement in the earlier stages of this work. We thank the anonymous reviewers for helpful comments. This work was partially supported by NSF grants CNS-1930117 (CAREER), CNS-1926324, CNS-2026774, a Sloan Research Fellowship, and a JP Morgan Faculty Award.

References

1. Goldwasser, S., Micali, S., Rackoff, C.: The knowledge complexity of interactive proof-systems (extended abstract). In: 17th ACM STOC, pp. 291–304. ACM Press (May 1985)
2. Bellare, M., Rogaway, P.: Random oracles are practical: a paradigm for designing efficient protocols. In: Denning, D.E., Pyle, R., Ganesan, R., Sandhu, R.S., Ashby, V. (eds.) ACM CCS 1993, pp. 62–73. ACM Press (Nov 1993)
3. Shoup, V.: Lower bounds for discrete logarithms and related problems. In: Fumy, W. (ed.) EUROCRYPT 1997. LNCS, vol. 1233, pp. 256–266. Springer, Heidelberg (1997). https://doi.org/10.1007/3-540-69053-0_18

4. Maurer, U.: Abstract models of computation in cryptography. In: Smart, N.P. (ed.) Cryptography and Coding 2005. LNCS, vol. 3796, pp. 1–12. Springer, Heidelberg (2005). https://doi.org/10.1007/11586821_1

5. Fuchsbauer, G., Kiltz, E., Loss, J.: The algebraic group model and its applications. In: Shacham, H., Boldyreva, A. (eds.) CRYPTO 2018, Part II. LNCS, vol. 10992, pp. 33–62. Springer, Cham (2018). https://doi.org/10.1007/978-3-319-96881-0_2

6. Bünz, B., Bootle, J., Boneh, D., Poelstra, A., Wuille, P., Maxwell, G.: Bulletproofs: short proofs for confidential transactions and more. In: 2018 IEEE Symposium on Security and Privacy, pp. 315–334. IEEE Computer Society Press (May 2018)

7. Monero to become first billion-dollar crypto to implement 'bulletproofs' tech. https://www.coindesk.com/monero-to-become-first-billion-dollar-crypto-to-implement-bulletproofs-tech

8. Signal adds a payments feature—with a privacy-focused cryptocurrency. https://www.wired.com/story/signal-mobilecoin-payments-messaging-cryptocurrency/

9. Nick, J., Ruffing, T., Seurin, Y., Wuille, P.: MuSig-DN: Schnorr multi-signatures with verifiably deterministic nonces. Cryptology ePrint Archive, Report 2020/1057 (2020). https://eprint.iacr.org/2020/1057

10. Bootle, J., Cerulli, A., Chaidos, P., Groth, J., Petit, C.: Efficient zero-knowledge arguments for arithmetic circuits in the discrete log setting. In: Fischlin, M., Coron, J.-S. (eds.) EUROCRYPT 2016, Part II. LNCS, vol. 9666, pp. 327–357. Springer, Heidelberg (2016). https://doi.org/10.1007/978-3-662-49896-5_12

11. Jaeger, J., Tessaro, S.: Expected-time cryptography: generic techniques and applications to concrete soundness. In: Pass, R., Pietrzak, K. (eds.) TCC 2020, Part III. LNCS, vol. 12552, pp. 414–443. Springer, Cham (2020). https://doi.org/10.1007/978-3-030-64381-2_15

12. Fiat, A., Shamir, A.: How to prove yourself: practical solutions to identification and signature problems. In: Odlyzko, A.M. (ed.) CRYPTO 1986. LNCS, vol. 263, pp. 186–194. Springer, Heidelberg (1987). https://doi.org/10.1007/3-540-47721-7_12

13. Groth, J.: On the size of pairing-based non-interactive arguments. In: Fischlin, M., Coron, J.-S. (eds.) EUROCRYPT 2016, Part II. LNCS, vol. 9666, pp. 305–326. Springer, Heidelberg (2016). https://doi.org/10.1007/978-3-662-49896-5_11

14. Ben-Sasson, E., Chiesa, A., Spooner, N.: Interactive oracle proofs. In: Hirt, M., Smith, A. (eds.) TCC 2016, Part II. LNCS, vol. 9986, pp. 31–60. Springer, Heidelberg (2016). https://doi.org/10.1007/978-3-662-53644-5_2

15. Holmgren, J.: On round-by-round soundness and state restoration attacks. Cryptology ePrint Archive, Report 2019/1261 (2019). https://eprint.iacr.org/2019/1261

16. Lindell, Y.: Parallel coin-tossing and constant-round secure two-party computation. In: Kilian, J. (ed.) CRYPTO 2001. LNCS, vol. 2139, pp. 171–189. Springer, Heidelberg (2001). https://doi.org/10.1007/3-540-44647-8_10

17. Groth, J., Ishai, Y.: Sub-linear zero-knowledge argument for correctness of a shuffle. In: Smart, N. (ed.) EUROCRYPT 2008. LNCS, vol. 4965, pp. 379–396. Springer, Heidelberg (2008). https://doi.org/10.1007/978-3-540-78967-3_22

18. Maller, M., Bowe, S., Kohlweiss, M., Meiklejohn, S.: Sonic: zero-knowledge SNARKs from linear-size universal and updatable structured reference strings. In: Cavallaro, L., Kinder, J., Wang, X., Katz, J. (eds.) ACM CCS 2019, pp. 2111–2128. ACM Press (Nov 2019)

19. Wahby, R.S., Tzialla, I., Shelat, A., Thaler, J., Walfish, M.: Doubly-efficient zkSNARKs without trusted setup. In: 2018 IEEE Symposium on Security and Privacy, pp. 926–943. IEEE Computer Society Press (May 2018)

20. Lee, J.: Dory: efficient, transparent arguments for generalised inner products and polynomial commitments. Cryptology ePrint Archive: 2020/1274 (2020)

21. Bünz, B., Fisch, B., Szepieniec, A.: Transparent SNARKs from DARK compilers. In: Canteaut, A., Ishai, Y. (eds.) EUROCRYPT 2020, Part I. LNCS, vol. 12105, pp. 677–706. Springer, Cham (2020). https://doi.org/10.1007/978-3-030-45721-1_24

22. Chiesa, A., Hu, Y., Maller, M., Mishra, P., Vesely, N., Ward, N.: Marlin: preprocessing zkSNARKs with universal and updatable SRS. In: Canteaut, A., Ishai, Y. (eds.) EUROCRYPT 2020, Part I. LNCS, vol. 12105, pp. 738–768. Springer, Cham (2020). https://doi.org/10.1007/978-3-030-45721-1_26

23. Canetti, R., Chen, Y., Holmgren, J., Lombardi, A., Rothblum, G.N., Rothblum, R.D.: Fiat-Shamir from simpler assumptions. Cryptology ePrint Archive, Report 2018/1004 (2018). https://eprint.iacr.org/2018/1004

24. Canetti, R., et al.: Fiat-Shamir: from practice to theory. In: Charikar, M., Cohen, E. (eds.) 51st ACM STOC, pp. 1082–1090. ACM Press (Jun 2019)

25. Lund, C., Fortnow, L., Karloff, H.J., Nisan, N.: Algebraic methods for interactive proof systems. In: 31st FOCS, pp. 2–10. IEEE Computer Society Press (Oct 1990)

26. Haitner, I.: A parallel repetition theorem for any interactive argument. In: 50th FOCS, pp. 241–250. IEEE Computer Society Press (Oct 2009)

27. Håstad, J., Pass, R., Wikström, D., Pietrzak, K.: An efficient parallel repetition theorem. In: Micciancio, D. (ed.) TCC 2010. LNCS, vol. 5978, pp. 1–18. Springer, Heidelberg (2010). https://doi.org/10.1007/978-3-642-11799-2_1

28. Chung, K.-M., Liu, F.-H.: Parallel repetition theorems for interactive arguments. In: Micciancio, D. (ed.) TCC 2010. LNCS, vol. 5978, pp. 19–36. Springer, Heidelberg (2010). https://doi.org/10.1007/978-3-642-11799-2_2

29. Berman, I., Haitner, I., Tsfadia, E.: A tight parallel repetition theorem for partially simulatable interactive arguments via smooth KL-divergence. In: Micciancio, D., Ristenpart, T. (eds.) CRYPTO 2020, Part III. LNCS, vol. 12172, pp. 544–573. Springer, Cham (2020). https://doi.org/10.1007/978-3-030-56877-1_19

30. Ben-Sasson, E., Chiesa, A., Riabzev, M., Spooner, N., Virza, M., Ward, N.P.: Aurora: transparent succinct arguments for R1CS. In: Ishai, Y., Rijmen, V. (eds.) EUROCRYPT 2019, Part I. LNCS, vol. 11476, pp. 103–128. Springer, Cham (2019). https://doi.org/10.1007/978-3-030-17653-2_4

31. Ben-Sasson, E., Bentov, I., Horesh, Y., Riabzev, M.: Scalable zero knowledge with no trusted setup. In: Boldyreva, A., Micciancio, D. (eds.) CRYPTO 2019, Part III. LNCS, vol. 11694, pp. 701–732. Springer, Cham (2019). https://doi.org/10.1007/978-3-030-26954-8_23

32. Bünz, B., Maller, M., Mishra, P., Tyagi, N., Vesely, P.: Proofs for inner pairing products and applications. Cryptology ePrint Archive: 2019/1177 (2020)

33. Fuchsbauer, G., Plouviez, A., Seurin, Y.: Blind Schnorr signatures and signed ElGamal encryption in the algebraic group model. In: Canteaut, A., Ishai, Y. (eds.) EUROCRYPT 2020, Part II. LNCS, vol. 12106, pp. 63–95. Springer, Cham (2020). https://doi.org/10.1007/978-3-030-45724-2_3

34. Ghoshal, A., Tessaro, S.: Tight state-restoration soundness in the algebraic group model. Cryptology ePrint Archive, Report 2020/1351 (2020). https://eprint.iacr.org/2020/1351

Separating Adaptive Streaming
from Oblivious Streaming Using
the Bounded Storage Model

Haim Kaplan[1,2], Yishay Mansour[1,2], Kobbi Nissim[3], and Uri Stemmer[2,4(✉)]

[1] Tel Aviv University, Tel Aviv, Israel
haimk@tau.ac.il, mansour.yishay@gmail.com
[2] Google Research, Tel Aviv, Israel
[3] Georgetown University, Washington D.C., USA
kobbi.nissim@georgetown.edu
[4] Ben-Gurion University of the Negev, Be'er-Sheva, Israel
stemmer@post.bgu.ac.il

Abstract. Streaming algorithms are algorithms for processing large data streams, using only a limited amount of memory. Classical streaming algorithms typically work under the assumption that the input stream is chosen independently from the internal state of the algorithm. Algorithms that utilize this assumption are called *oblivious* algorithms. Recently, there is a growing interest in studying streaming algorithms that maintain utility also when the input stream is chosen by an *adaptive adversary*, possibly as a function of previous estimates given by the streaming algorithm. Such streaming algorithms are said to be *adversarially-robust*.

By combining techniques from *learning theory* with cryptographic tools from the *bounded storage model*, we separate the oblivious streaming model from the adversarially-robust streaming model. Specifically, we present a streaming problem for which every adversarially-robust streaming algorithm must use polynomial space, while there exists a classical (oblivious) streaming algorithm that uses only polylogarithmic space. This is the first general separation between the capabilities of these two models, resolving one of the central open questions in adversarial robust streaming.

H. Kaplan—Partially supported by the Israel Science Foundation (grant 1595/19), the German-Israeli Foundation (grant 1367/2017), and by the Blavatnik Family Foundation.

Y. Mansour—This project has received funding from the European Research Council (ERC) under the European Union's Horizon 2020 research and innovation program (grant agreement No. 882396), by the Israel Science Foundation (grant number 993/17) and the Yandex Initiative for Machine Learning at Tel Aviv University.

K. Nissim—Supported by NSF grant No. 1565387 TWC: Large: Collaborative: Computing Over Distributed Sensitive Data and by a gift to Georgetown University, the Data Co-Ops project.

U. Stemmer—Partially Supported by the Israel Science Foundation (grant 1871/19) and by the Cyber Security Research Center at Ben-Gurion University of the Negev.

© International Association for Cryptologic Research 2021
T. Malkin and C. Peikert (Eds.): CRYPTO 2021, LNCS 12827, pp. 94–121, 2021.
https://doi.org/10.1007/978-3-030-84252-9_4

Keywords: Adversarially-robust streaming · Bounded storage model ·
Separation from oblivious streaming

1   Introduction

Consider a scenario in which data items are being generated one by one, e.g., IP traffic monitoring or web searches. Generally speaking, streaming algorithms aim to process such data streams while using only a limited amount of memory, significantly smaller than what is needed to store the entire data stream. Streaming algorithms have become a central and crucial tool for the analysis of massive datasets.

A typical assumption when designing and analyzing streaming algorithms is that the entire stream is *fixed* in advance (and is just provided to the streaming algorithm one item at a time), or at least that the choice of the items in the stream is *independent* of the internal state (and coin tosses) of the streaming algorithm. We refer to this setting as the *oblivious* setting. Recently, there has been a growing interest in streaming algorithms that maintain utility even when the choice of stream items depends on previous answers given by the streaming algorithm, and can hence depend on the internal state of the algorithm [1,2,6,7,13,14,16,18,21, 26]. Such streaming algorithms are said to be *adversarially robust*.

Hardt and Woodruff [16] presented a negative result showing that, generally speaking, *linear* streaming algorithms cannot be adversarially robust.[1] This result does not rule out non-linear algorithms. Indeed, strong positive results were shown by [6,18,26] who constructed (non-linear) adversarially robust algorithms for many problems of interest, with small overhead compared to the oblivious setting. This includes problems such as estimating frequency moments, counting the number of distinct elements in the stream, identifying heavy-hitters in the stream, estimating the median of the stream, entropy estimation, and more. The strong positive results of [6,18,26] raise the possibility that adversarial robustness can come "for free" in terms of the additional costs to memory, compared to what is needed in the oblivious setting.

Question 1.1. *Does adversarial streaming require more space than oblivious streaming?*

We provide a positive answer to this question. Specifically, we present a streaming problem for which every adversarially-robust streaming algorithm must use polynomial space, while there exists an oblivious streaming algorithm that uses only polylogarithmic space.

1.1   Streaming Against Adaptive Adversaries

Before describing our new results, we define our setting more precisely. A stream of length m over a domain X consists of a sequence of updates $x_1, \ldots, x_m \in X$. For $i \in [m]$ we write $\vec{x}_i = (x_1, \ldots, x_i)$ to denote the first i updates of the stream.

---

[1] A streaming algorithm is *linear* if for some (possibly randomized) matrix A, its output depends only on A and Af, where f is the *frequency vector* of the stream.

Let $g : X^* \to \mathbb{R}$ be a function (for example, g might count the number of distinct elements in the stream). At every time step i, after obtaining the next element in the stream x_i, our goal is to output an approximation for $g(\vec{x}_i)$. Throughout the paper we use α for the approximation parameter and β for the confidence parameter.

The adversarial streaming model, in various forms, was considered by [1,2, 6,7,13,14,16,18,21,26]. We give here the formulation presented by Ben-Eliezer et al. [6]. The adversarial setting is modeled by a two-player game between a (randomized) StreamingAlgorithm and an Adversary. At the beginning, we fix a function g. Then the game proceeds in rounds, where in the ith round:

1. The Adversary chooses an update $x_i \in X$ for the stream, which can depend, in particular, on all previous stream updates and outputs of StreamingAlgorithm.
2. The StreamingAlgorithm processes the new update x_i and outputs its current response z_i.

The goal of the Adversary is to make the StreamingAlgorithm output an incorrect response z_i at some point i in the stream, that is $z_i \notin (1 \pm \alpha) \cdot g(\vec{x}_i)$. For example, in the distinct elements problem, the adversary's goal is that at some step i, the estimate z_i will fail to be a $(1 + \alpha)$-approximation of the true current number of distinct elements.

1.2 Our Results

Loosely speaking, we show a reduction from a problem in learning theory, called *adaptive data analysis (ADA)*, to the problem of adversarial streaming. Our results then follow from known impossibility results for the adaptive data analysis problem. In the ADA problem, given a sample S containing n independent samples from some unknown distribution $\mathcal{D}$ over a domain X, the goal is to provide answers to a sequence of adaptively chosen queries w.r.t. $\mathcal{D}$. Importantly, the answers must be accurate w.r.t. the (unknown) underlying distribution $\mathcal{D}$; not just w.r.t. the empirical sample S. In more detail, in the ADA problem, on every time step i we get a query $q_i : X \to \{0, 1\}$, and we need to respond with an answer a_i that approximates $q_i(\mathcal{D}) \triangleq \mathbb{E}_{x \sim \mathcal{D}}[q_i(x)]$. Observe that if all of the queries were fixed before the sample S is drawn, then we could simply answer each query q_i with its empirical average $q_i(S) \triangleq \frac{1}{n}\sum_{x \in S} q_i(x)$. Indeed, by the Hoeffding bound, in such a case these answers provide good approximations to the true answers $q_i(\mathcal{D})$. Furthermore, the number of queries ℓ that we can support can be exponential in the sample size n. However, this argument breaks completely when the queries are chosen adaptively based on previous answers given by the mechanism, and the problem becomes much more complex. While, information-theoretically, it is still possible to answer an exponential number of queries (see [5,11]), it is known that every *computationally efficient* mechanism cannot answer more than n^2 adaptive queries using a sample of size n.

We show that the ADA problem can be phrased as a streaming problem, where the first n elements in the stream are interpreted as "data points" and later elements in the stream are interpreted as "queries". In order to apply existing impossibility results for the ADA problem, we must overcome the following two main challenges.

Challenge 1 and its Resolution. The difficulty in the ADA problem is to maintain accuracy w.r.t. the unknown underlying distribution (and not just w.r.t. the given input sample, which is easy). In the streaming setting, however, there is no underlying distribution, and we cannot require a streaming algorithm to be accurate w.r.t. such a distribution. Instead, we require the streaming algorithm to give accurate answers only w.r.t. the input sample (i.e., w.r.t. the dataset defined by the first n elements in the stream). We then show that if these n elements are sampled i.i.d. from some underlying distribution, then we can use *compression arguments* to show that if the streaming algorithm has small space complexity, and if its answers are accurate w.r.t. the empirical sample, then its answers must in fact be accurate also w.r.t. this underlying distribution. In other words, even though we only require the streaming algorithm to give accurate answers w.r.t. the empirical sample, we show that if it uses small space complexity then its answers must *generalize* to the underlying distribution. This allows us to formulate a link to the ADA problem. We remark that, in the actual construction, we need to introduce several technical modifications in order to make sure that the resulting streaming problem can be solved with small space complexity in the oblivious setting.

Challenge 2 and its Resolution. The impossibility results we mentioned for the ADA problem only hold for *computationally efficient* mechanisms.[2] In contrast, we aim for an information-theoretic separation. We therefore cannot apply existing negative results for the ADA problem to our setting as is. Informally, the reason that the negative results for the ADA problem only hold for computationally efficient mechanisms is that their constructions rely on the existence of an efficient *encryption scheme* whose security holds under computational assumptions. We replace this encryption scheme with a different scheme with information-theoretic security against adversaries with *bounded storage* capabilities. Indeed, in our setting, the "adversary" for this encryption scheme will be the streaming algorithm, whose storage capabilities are bounded.

We obtain the following theorem.

Theorem 1.2. *For every w, there exists a streaming problem over domain of size $\mathrm{poly}(w)$ and stream length $O(w^5)$ that requires at least w space to be solved in the adversarial setting to within (small enough) constant accuracy, but can be solved in the oblivious setting using space $O(\log^2(w))$.*

1.2.1   Optimality of Our Results in Terms of the Flip-Number

The previous works of [6,18,26] stated their positive results in terms of the following definition.

---

[2] While there exist information theoretic impossibility results for the ADA problem, they are too weak to give a meaningful result in our context.

Definition 1.3 (Flip number [6]**).** *Let g be a function defining a streaming problem. The (α, m)-flip number of g, denoted as λ, is the maximal number of times that the value of g can change (increase or decrease) by a factor of at least $(1 + \alpha)$ during a stream of length m.*

The works of [6, 18, 26] presented general frameworks for transforming an oblivious streaming algorithm $\mathcal{A}$ into an adversarially robust streaming algorithm $\mathcal{B}$ with space complexity (roughly) $\sqrt{\lambda} \cdot \text{Space}(\mathcal{A})$. That is, the results of [6, 18, 26] showed that, generally, adversarial robustness requires space blowup at most (roughly) $\sqrt{\lambda}$ compared to the oblivious setting. For the streaming problem we present (see Theorem 1.2) it holds that the flip-number is $O(w^2)$. That is, for every w, we present a streaming problem with flip-number $\lambda = O(w^2)$, that requires at least $w = \Omega(\sqrt{\lambda})$ space to be solved in the adversarial setting to within (small enough) constant accuracy, but can be solved in the oblivious setting using space $O(\log^2(w))$. This means that, in terms of the dependency of the space complexity in the flip-number, our results are nearly tight. In particular, in terms of λ, our results show that a blowup of $\tilde{\Omega}(\sqrt{\lambda})$ to the space complexity is generally unavoidable in the adversarial setting.

1.2.2   A Reduction from Adaptive Data Analysis

Informally, we consider the following streaming problem, which we call the Streaming Adaptive Data Analysis (SADA) problem. On every time step $i \in [m]$ we get an update $x_i \in X$. We interpret the first n updates in the stream $x_1, \ldots, x_n$ as "data points", defining a multiset $S = \{x_1, \ldots, x_n\}$. This multiset does not change after time n.

The next updates in the stream (starting from time $i = n+1$) define "queries" $q : X \to \{0, 1\}$ that should be evaluated by the streaming algorithm on the multiset S. That is, for every such query q, the streaming algorithm should respond with an approximation of $q(S) = \frac{1}{n}\sum_{x \in S} q(x)$. A technical issue here is that every such query is described using $|X|$ bits (represented using its truth table), and hence, cannot be specified using a single update in the stream (which only consists of $\log |X|$ bits). Therefore, every query is specified using $|X|$ updates in the stream. Specifically, starting from time $i = n+1$, every bulk of $|X|$ updates defines a query $q : X \to \{0, 1\}$. At the end of every such bulk, the goal of the streaming algorithm is to output (an approximation for) the average of q on the multiset S. On other time steps, the streaming algorithm should output 0.

As we mentioned, we use *compression arguments* to show that if the streaming algorithm is capable of accurately approximating the average of every such query on the multiset S, and if it uses small space, then when the "data points" (i.e., the elements in the first n updates) are sampled i.i.d. from some distribution $\mathcal{D}$ on X, then the answers given by the streaming algorithm must in fact be accurate also w.r.t. the expectation of these queries on $\mathcal{D}$. This means that the existence of a streaming algorithm for the SADA problem implies the existence of an algorithm for the adaptive data analysis (ADA) problem, with related parameters. Applying known impossibility results for the ADA problem, this results in a contradiction. However, as we mentioned, the impossibility results we need for the ADA problem only hold for *computationally efficient* mechanisms. Therefore, the construction outlined here only rules out *computationally efficient* adversarially-robust streaming algorithms for the SADA problem. To get an information-theoretic separation, we modify the definition of the SADA problem and rely on cryptographic techniques from the *bounded storage* model.

Remark 1.4. *In Sect. 6 we outline a variant of the SADA problem, which is more "natural" in the sense that the function to estimate is symmetric. That is, it does not depend on the order of elements in the stream. For this variant, we show a computational separation (assuming the existence of a sub-exponentially secure private-key encryption scheme).*

2 Preliminaries

Our results rely on tools and techniques from learning theory (in particular *adaptive data analysis* and *compression arguments*), and cryptography (in particular *pseudorandom generators* and *encryption schemes*). We now introduce the needed preliminaries.

2.1 Adaptive Data Analysis

A *statistical query* over a domain X is specified by a predicate $q : X \rightarrow \{0,1\}$. The value of a query q on a distribution $\mathcal{D}$ over X is $q(\mathcal{D}) = \mathbb{E}_{x \sim \mathcal{D}}[q(x)]$. Given a database $S \in X^n$ and a query q, we denote the empirical average of q on S as $q(S) = \frac{1}{n} \sum_{x \in S} q(x)$.

In the adaptive data analysis (ADA) problem, the goal is to design a *mechanism* $\mathcal{M}$ that answers queries w.r.t. an unknown distribution $\mathcal{D}$ using only i.i.d. samples from it. Our focus is the case where the queries are chosen adaptively and adversarially. Specifically, $\mathcal{M}$ is a stateful algorithm that holds a collection of samples $(x_1, \ldots, x_n)$, takes a statistical query q as input, and returns an answer z. We require that when $x_1, \ldots, x_n$ are independent samples from $\mathcal{D}$, then the answer z is close to $q(\mathcal{D})$. Moreover we require that this condition holds for every query in an adaptively chosen sequence $q_1, \ldots, q_\ell$. Formally, we define an accuracy game $\mathsf{Acc}_{n,\ell,\mathcal{M},\mathbb{A}}$ between a mechanism $\mathcal{M}$ and a stateful *adversary* $\mathbb{A}$ (see Algorithm 1).

Definition 2.1 ([11]). *A mechanism $\mathcal{M}$ is (α, β)-statistically-accurate for ℓ adaptively chosen statistical queries given n samples if for every adversary $\mathbb{A}$ and every distribution $\mathcal{D}$,*

$$\Pr_{\substack{S \sim \mathcal{D}^n \\ \mathsf{Acc}_{n,\ell,\mathcal{M},\mathbb{A}}(S)}} \left[\max_{i \in [\ell]} |q_i(\mathcal{D}) - z_i| \leq \alpha \right] \geq 1 - \beta. \tag{1}$$

Remark 2.2. *Without loss of generality, in order to show that a mechanism $\mathcal{M}$ is (α, β)-statistically-accurate (as per Definition 2.1), it suffices to consider only deterministic adversaries $\mathbb{A}$. Indeed, given a randomized adversary $\mathbb{A}$, if requirement (1) holds for every fixture of its random coins, then it also holds when the coins are random.*

Algorithm 1. The Accuracy Game $\mathsf{Acc}_{n,\ell,\mathcal{M},\mathbb{A}}$.

Input: A database $S \in X^n$.

1. The database S is given to $\mathcal{M}$.
2. For $i = 1$ to ℓ,
   (a) The adversary $\mathbb{A}$ chooses a statistical query q_i.
   (b) The mechanism $\mathcal{M}$ gets q_i and outputs an answer z_i.
   (c) The adversary $\mathbb{A}$ gets z_i.
3. Output the transcript $(q_1, z_1, \ldots, q_\ell, z_\ell)$.

We use a similar definition for empirical accuracy:

Definition 2.3 ([11]). *A mechanism $\mathcal{M}$ is (α, β)-empirically accurate for ℓ adaptively chosen statistical queries given a database of size n if for every adversary $\mathbb{A}$ and every database S of size n,*

$$\Pr_{\mathsf{Acc}_{n,\ell,\mathcal{M},\mathbb{A}}(S)} \left[\max_{i \in [\ell]} |q_i(S) - z_i| \leq \alpha \right] \geq 1 - \beta.$$

2.2 Transcript Compressibility

An important notion that allows us to argue about the utility guarantees of an algorithm that answers adaptively chosen queries is *transcript compressibility*, defined as follows.

Definition 2.4 ([10]). *A mechanism $\mathcal{M}$ is* transcript compressible to $b(n, \ell)$ *bits if for every deterministic adversary $\mathbb{A}$ there is a set of transcripts $H_\mathbb{A}$ of size $|H_\mathbb{A}| \leq 2^{b(n,\ell)}$ such that for every dataset $S \in X^n$ we have*

$$\Pr\left[\mathsf{Acc}_{n,\ell,\mathcal{M},\mathbb{A}}(S) \in H_\mathbb{A}\right] = 1.$$

The following theorem shows that, with high probability, for every query generated throughout the interaction with a transcript compressible mechanism it holds that its empirical average is close to its expectation.

Theorem 2.5 ([10]). *Let $\mathcal{M}$ be transcript compressible to $b(n, \ell)$ bits, and let $\beta > 0$. Then, for every adversary $\mathbb{A}$ and for every distribution $\mathcal{D}$ it holds that*

$$\Pr_{\substack{S \sim \mathcal{D}^n \\ \mathsf{Acc}_{n,\ell,\mathcal{M},\mathbb{A}}(S)}} \left[\exists i \text{ such that } |q_i(S) - q_i(\mathcal{D})| > \alpha\right] \leq \beta,$$

where

$$\alpha = O\left(\sqrt{\frac{b(n, \ell) + \ln(\ell/\beta)}{n}}\right).$$

2.3   Pseudorandom Generators in the Bounded Storage Model

Our results rely on the existence of pseudorandom generators providing information theoretic security against adversaries with bounded storage capabilities. This security requirement is called the *bounded storage model*. This model was introduced by Maurer [20], and has generated many interesting results, e.g., [3,4,8,9,12,17,19,20]. We give here the formulation presented by Vadhan [24].

The bounded storage model utilizes a short seed $K \in \{0,1\}^b$ (unknown to the adversary) and a long stream of public random bits $X_1, X_2, \ldots$ (known to all parties). A *bounded storage model (BSM) pseudorandom generator* is a function $\mathrm{PRG} : \{0,1\}^a \times \{0,1\}^b \to \{0,1\}^c$, typically with $b, c \ll a$. Such a scheme is to be used as follows. Initially, two (honest) parties share a seed $K \in \{0,1\}^b$ (unknown to the adversary). At time $t \in [T]$, the next a bits of the public stream $(X_{(t-1)a}, \ldots, X_{ta})$ are broadcast. The adversary is allowed to listen to this stream, however, it cannot store all of it as it has bounded storage capabilities. The honest parties apply $\mathrm{PRG}(\cdot, K)$ to this stream obtain c pseudorandom bits, denoted as $Y_t \in \{0,1\}^c$.

We now formally define security for a BSM pseudorandom generator. Let ρa be the bound on the storage of the adversary $\mathcal{A}$ (we refer to ρ as the *storage rate* of the adversary). We write $S_t \in \{0,1\}^{\rho a}$ to denote the state of the adversary at time t. We consider the adversary's ability to distinguish two experiments—the "real" one, in which the pseudorandom generator is used, and an "ideal" one, in which truly random bits are used. Let $\mathcal{A}$ be an arbitrary function representing the way the adversary updates its storage and attempts to distinguish the two experiments at the end.

Real Experiment:

- Let $X = (X_1, X_2, \ldots, X_{Ta})$ be a sequence of uniformly random bits, let $K \leftarrow \{0,1\}^b$ be the key, and let the adversary's initial state by $S_0 = 0^{\rho a}$.
- For $t = 1, \ldots, T$:
    - Let $Y_t = \mathrm{PRG}\left(X_{(t-1)a+1}, \ldots, X_{ta}, K\right) \in \{0,1\}^c$ be the pseudorandom bits.
    - Let $S_t = \mathcal{A}\left(Y_1, \ldots, Y_{t-1}, S_{t-1}, X_{(t-1)a+1}, \ldots, X_{ta}\right) \in \{0,1\}^{\rho a}$ be the adversary's new state.
- Output $\mathcal{A}\left(Y_1, \ldots, Y_T, S_T, K\right)$

Ideal Experiment:

- Let $X = (X_1, X_2, \ldots, X_{Ta})$ be a sequence of uniformly random bits, let $K \leftarrow \{0,1\}^b$ be the key, and let the adversary's initial state by $S_0 = 0^{\rho a}$.
- For $t = 1, \ldots, T$:
    - Let $Y_t \leftarrow \{0,1\}^c$ be truly random bits.
    - Let $S_t = \mathcal{A}\left(Y_1, \ldots, Y_{t-1}, S_{t-1}, X_{(t-1)a+1}, \ldots, X_{ta}\right) \in \{0,1\}^{\rho a}$ be the adversary's new state.
- Output $\mathcal{A}\left(Y_1, \ldots, Y_T, S_T, K\right) \in \{0,1\}$.

Note that at each time step we give the adversary access to all the past Y_i's "for free" (i.e. with no cost in the storage bound), and in the last time step, we give the adversary the adversary the key K.

Definition 2.6 ([24])**.** *We call* PRG $: \{0,1\}^a \times \{0,1\}^b \to \{0,1\}^c$ *an ε-secure BSM pseudorandom generator for storage rate ρ if for every adversary $\mathcal{A}$ with storage bound ρa, and every $T \in \mathbb{N}$, the adversary $\mathcal{A}$ distinguishes between the real and ideal experiments with advantage at most $T\varepsilon$. That is,*

$$\left| \Pr_{\text{real}} [\mathcal{A}(Y_1, \dots, Y_T, S_T, K) = 1] - \Pr_{\text{ideal}} [\mathcal{A}(Y_1, \dots, Y_T, S_T, K) = 1] \right| \le T \cdot \varepsilon$$

Remark 2.7. *No constraint is put on the computational power of the adversary except for the storage bound of ρa (as captured by $S_t \in \{0,1\}^{\rho a}$). This means that the distributions of $(Y_1, \dots, Y_T, S_T, K)$ in the real and ideal experiments are actually close in a statistical sense – they must have statistical difference at most $T \cdot \varepsilon$.*

We will use the following result of Vadhan [24]. We remark that this is only a special case of the results of Vadhan, and refer the reader to [24] for a more detailed account.

Theorem 2.8 ([24])**.** *For every $a \in \mathbb{N}$, every $\varepsilon > \exp\left(-a/2^{O(\log^* a)}\right)$, and every $c \le a/4$, there is a BSM pseudorandom generator* PRG $: \{0,1\}^a \times \{0,1\}^b \to \{0,1\}^c$ *such that*

1. PRG *is ε-secure for storage rate $\rho \le 1/2$.*
2. PRG *has key length $b = O(\log(a/\varepsilon))$.*
3. *For every key K,* PRG$(\cdot, K)$ *reads at most $h = O(c + \log(1/\varepsilon))$ bits from the public stream (nonadaptively).*
4. PRG *is computable in time $\mathrm{poly}(h, b)$ and uses workspace $\mathrm{poly}(\log h, \log b)$ in addition to the h bits read from the public stream and the key of length b.*

3   The Streaming Adaptive Data Analysis (SADA) Problem

In this section we introduce a streaming problem, which we call the Streaming Adaptive Data Analysis (SADA) problem, for which we show a strong positive result in the oblivious setting and a strong negative result in the adversarial setting.

Let $X = \{0,1\}^d \times \{0,1\}^b$ be a data domain, let $\gamma \geq 0$ be a fixed constant, and let PRG : $\{0,1\}^a \times \{0,1\}^b \to \{0,1\}^c$ be a BSM pseudorandom generator, where $c = 1$. We consider the following streaming problem. On every time step $i \in [m]$ we get an update $x_i = (p_i, k_i) \in X$. We interpret the first n updates in the stream $x_1, \ldots, x_n$ as pairs of "data points" and their corresponding "keys". Formally, we denote by S the multiset containing the pairs $x_1, \ldots, x_n$. For technical reasons,[3] the multiset S also contains $\frac{\gamma n}{1-\gamma}$ copies of some arbitrary element $\perp$. This multiset does not change after time n.

Starting from time $j = n + 1$, each bulk of $(a + 1) \cdot 2^d$ updates re-defines a "function" (or a "query") that should be evaluated by the streaming algorithm on the multiset S. This function is defined as follows.

1. For $p \in \{0,1\}^d$ (in lexicographic order) do
   (a) Let $x^{p,1}, \ldots, x^{p,a} \in X$ denote the next a updates, and let $\Gamma^p \in \{0,1\}^a$ be the bitstring containing the first bit of every such update.
   (b) Let $x^{p,a+1}$ denote the next update, and let σ^p denote its first bit.
   (c) For every $k \in \{0,1\}^b$, let $Y_k^p = \mathrm{PRG}(\Gamma^p, k)$ and define $f(p,k) = \sigma^p \oplus Y_k^p$.
2. Also set $f(\perp) = 1$.

This defines a function $f : \left(\{0,1\}^d \times \{0,1\}^b\right) \cup \{\perp\} \to \{0,1\}$.

Definition 3.1 (The (a, b, d, m, n, γ)-SADA Problem). *At the end of every such bulk, defining a function f, the goal of the streaming algorithm is to output (an approximation for) the average of f on the multiset S. On other time steps, the streaming algorithm should output 0.*

Remark 3.2. *In the definition above, m is the total number of updates (i.e., the length of the stream), n is the number of updates that we consider as "date points", γ is a small constant, and a, b, d are the parameters defining the domain and the PRG.*

4   An Oblivious Algorithm for the SADA Problem

In the oblivious setting, we can easily construct a streaming algorithm for the SADA problem using *sampling*. Specifically, throughout the first phase of the execution (during the first n time steps) we maintain a small representative sample from the "data items" (and their corresponding "keys") from the stream. In the second phase of the execution we use this sample in order to answer the given queries. Consider Algorithm ObliviousSADA, specified in Algorithm 2. We now analyze its utility guarantees. We will assume that ObliviousSADA is executed with a sampling algorithm SAMP that returns a uniformly random sample. This can be achieved, e.g., using Reservoir Sampling [25].

---

[3] Specifically, recall that the error in the ADA problem is additive while the error in the streaming setting is multiplicative. We add a (relatively small) number of $\perp$'s to S in order to bridge this technical gap.

Algorithm 2. ObliviousSADA

Setting: On every time step we obtain the next update, which is an element of $X = \{0,1\}^d \times \{0,1\}^b$.

Algorithm used: A sampling algorithm SAMP that operates on a stream of elements from the domain X and maintains a representative sample.

1. Instantiate algorithm SAMP.
2. REPEAT n times
   (a) Obtain the next update in the stream $x = (p, k)$.
   (b) Output 0.
   (c) Feed the update x to SAMP.
3. Feed (one by one) $\frac{\gamma n}{1-\gamma}$ copies of $\perp$ to SAMP.
4. Let D denote the sample produced by algorithm SAMP.
5. REPEAT (each iteration of this loop spans over $2^d(a+1)$ updates that define a query)
   (a) Let v denote the multiplicity of $\perp$ in D, and set $F = \frac{v}{|D|}$.
   (b) For every $p \in \{0,1\}^d$ in lexicographic order do
       i. Denote $K_p = \{k : (p, k) \in D\}$. That is, K_p is the set of all keys k such that (p, k) appears in the sample D.
       ii. REPEAT a times
           – Obtain the next update x
           – For every $k \in K_p$, feed the first bit of x to PRG$(\cdot, k)$.
           – Output 0.
       iii. For every $k \in K_p$, obtain a bit Y_k from PRG$(\cdot, k)$.
       iv. Obtain the next update and let σ be its first bit (and output 0).
       v. For every $k \in K_p$ such that $\sigma \oplus Y_k = 1$: Let $v_{(p,k)}$ denote the multiplicity of (p, k) in D, and set $F \leftarrow F + \frac{v_{(p,k)}}{|D|}$.
   (c) Output F.

Theorem 4.1. *Algorithm* ObliviousSADA *is* (α, β)-*accurate for the SADA problem in the oblivious setting.*

Proof. Fix the stream $\vec{x}_m = (x_1, \ldots, x_m)$. We assume that ObliviousSADA is executed with a sampling algorithm SAMP that returns a sample D containing $|D|$ elements, sampled uniformly and independently from $S = (x_1, \ldots, x_n, \perp, \ldots, \perp)$. This can be achieved, e.g., using Reservoir Sampling [25]. As the stream is fixed (and it is of length m), there are at most m different queries that are specified throughout the execution. By the Chernoff bound, assuming that $|D| \geq \Omega\left(\frac{1}{\alpha^2 \gamma} \ln(\frac{m}{\beta})\right)$, with probability at least $1 - \beta$, for every query f throughout the execution we have that $f(D) \in (1 \pm \alpha) \cdot f(S)$. The theorem now follows by observing that the answers given by algorithm ObliviousSADA are exactly the empirical average of the corresponding queries on D. $\square$

Observation 4.2. *For constant* α, β, γ, *using the pseudorandom generator from Theorem 2.8, algorithm* ObliviousSADA *uses space* $O\left(\left(\log(\frac{1}{\varepsilon}) + b + d\right) \cdot \log(m)\right)$.

Algorithm 3. AnswerQueries

Input: A database $P \in (\{0,1\}^d)^n$ containing n elements from $\{0,1\}^d$.
Setting: On every time step we get a query $q : \{0,1\}^d \to \{0,1\}$.
Algorithm used: An adversarially robust streaming algorithm $\mathcal{A}$ for the SADA problem with (α, β)-accuracy for streams of length m. We abstract the coin tosses of $\mathcal{A}$ using *two* random strings, r_1 and r_2, of possibly unbounded length. Initially, we execute $\mathcal{A}$ with access to r_1, meaning that every time it tosses a coin it gets the next bit in r_1. At some point, we switch the random string to r_2, and henceforth $\mathcal{A}$ gets its coin tosses from r_2.
Algorithm used: BSM pseudorandom generator PRG : $\{0,1\}^a \times \{0,1\}^b \to \{0,1\}$, as in the definition of the SADA problem.

1. For every $p \in \{0,1\}^d$ sample $k_p \in \{0,1\}^b$ uniformly.
2. Sample $r_1 \in \{0,1\}^\nu$ uniformly, and instantiate algorithm $\mathcal{A}$ with read-once access to bits of r_1. Here ν bounds the number of coin flips made by $\mathcal{A}$.
3. For every $p \in P$, feed the update (p, k_p) to $\mathcal{A}$.
4. Sample $r_2 \in \{0,1\}^\nu$ uniformly, and switch the read-once access of $\mathcal{A}$ to r_2. (The switch from r_1 to r_2 is done for convenience, so that after Step 3 we do not need to "remember" the position for the next coin from r_1.)
5. REPEAT $\ell \triangleq \frac{m-n}{(a+1)\cdot 2^d}$ times
   (a) Obtain the next query $q : \{0,1\}^d \to \{0,1\}$.
   (b) For every $p \in \{0,1\}^d$ do
       i. Sample $\Gamma \in \{0,1\}^a$ uniformly.
       ii. Feed a updates (one by one) to $\mathcal{A}$ s.t. the concatenation of their first bits is Γ.
       iii. Let $Y = \text{PRG}(\Gamma, k_p)$.
       iv. Feed to $\mathcal{A}$ an update whose first bit is $Y \oplus q(p)$.
   (c) Obtain an answer z from $\mathcal{A}$.
   (d) Output z.

Proof. The algorithm maintains a sample D containing $O(\log m)$ elements, where each element is represented using $b + d$ bits. In addition, the pseudorandom generator uses $O(\log(\frac{1}{\varepsilon}))$ bits of memory, and the algorithm instantiates at most $|D| = O(\log m)$ copies of it. $\qquad\square$

5   An Impossibility Result for Adaptive Streaming

Suppose that there is an adversarially robust streaming algorithm $\mathcal{A}$ for the SADA problem. We use $\mathcal{A}$ to construct an algorithm that gets a sample P containing n points in $\{0,1\}^d$, and answers adaptively chosen queries $q : \{0,1\}^d \to \{0,1\}$. Consider Algorithm AnswerQueries, specified in Algorithm 3.

By construction, assuming that $\mathcal{A}$ is accurate for the SADA problem, we get that AnswerQueries is empirically-accurate (w.r.t. its input database P). Formally,

Claim 5.1. *If $\mathcal{A}$ is (α, β)-accurate for the SADA problem, then* `AnswerQueries` *is $\left(\frac{\alpha}{1-\gamma}, \beta\right)$-empirically-accurate for $\frac{m-n}{(a+1)\cdot 2^d}$ adaptively chosen statistical queries given a database of size n. Here γ is a fixed constant (mentioned above).*

Proof Sketch. Let q denote the query given at some iteration, and let f denote the corresponding function specified to algorithm $\mathcal{A}$ during this iteration. The claim follows from the fact that, by construction, for every (p, k) we have that $f(p, k) = q(p)$. Specifically, w.h.p., the answers given by $\mathcal{A}$ are α-accurate w.r.t. $P \cup \{\bot, \ldots, \bot\}$, and hence, $\frac{\alpha}{1-\gamma}$-accurate w.r.t. P.   □

We now show that algorithm `AnswerQueries` is transcript-compressible. To that end, for every choice of $\vec{\Gamma}, \vec{k}, r_1, r_2$ for the strings Γ, the keys k, and the random bitstrings r_1, r_2 used throughout the execution, let us denote by `AnswerQueries`$_{\vec{\Gamma}, \vec{k}, r_1, r_2}$ algorithm `AnswerQueries` after fixing these elements.

Claim 5.2. *If algorithm $\mathcal{A}$ uses space at most w, then, for every $\vec{\Gamma}, \vec{k}, r_1, r_2$, we have that algorithm* `AnswerQueries`$_{\vec{\Gamma}, \vec{k}, r_1, r_2}$ *is transcript-compressible to w bits.*

Proof Sketch. Assuming that the adversary who generates the queries q is deterministic (which is without loss of generality) we get that the entire transcript is determined by the state of algorithm $\mathcal{A}$ at the end of Step 3.   □

Remark 5.3. *The "switch" from r_1 to r_2 is convenient in the proof of Claim 5.2. Otherwise, in order to describe the state of the algorithm after Step 3 we need to specify both the internal state of $\mathcal{A}$ and the position for the next coin from r_1.*

Combining Claims 5.1 (empirical accuracy), and 5.2 (transcript-compression), we get the following lemma.

Lemma 5.4. *Suppose that $\mathcal{A}$ is (α, β)-accurate for the SADA problem for streams of length m using memory w. Then for every $\beta' > 0$, algorithm* `AnswerQueries` *is $\left(\frac{\alpha}{1-\gamma} + \alpha', \beta + \beta'\right)$-statistically-accurate for $\ell = \frac{m-n}{(a+1)\cdot 2^d}$ queries, where*

$$\alpha' = O\left(\sqrt{\frac{w + \ln(\frac{\ell}{\beta'})}{n}}\right).$$

Proof. Fix a distribution $\mathcal{D}$ over $\{0, 1\}^d$ and fix an adversary $\mathbb{A}$ that generates the queries q_i. Consider the execution of the accuracy game Acc (given in Algorithm 1). By Claim 5.1,

$$\Pr_{\substack{S \sim \mathcal{D}^n \\ \mathsf{Acc}_{n, \ell, \texttt{AnswerQueries}, \mathbb{A}}(S)}} \left[\exists i \text{ such that } |q_i(S) - z_i| > \frac{\alpha}{1 - \gamma}\right] \leq \beta,$$

where the z_i's denote the answers given by the algorithm. In addition, by Claim 5.2 and Theorem 2.5, for every fixing of $\vec{\Gamma}, \vec{k}, r_1, r_2$ we have that

$$\Pr_{\substack{S \sim \mathcal{D}^n \\ \mathsf{Acc}_{n, \ell, \texttt{AnswerQueries}, \mathbb{A}}(S)}} \left[\exists i \text{ such that } |q_i(S) - q_i(\mathcal{D})| > \alpha' \,\Big|\, \vec{\Gamma}, \vec{k}, r_1, r_2\right] \leq \beta', \quad (2)$$

where

$$\alpha' = O\left(\sqrt{\frac{w + \ln(\ell/\beta')}{n}}\right).$$

Since Inequality (2) holds for *every* fixing of $\vec{\Gamma}, \vec{k}, r_1, r_2$, it also holds when sampling them. Therefore, by the triangle inequality and the union bound,

$$\Pr_{\substack{S \sim \mathcal{D}^n \\ \mathrm{Acc}_{n,\ell,\mathtt{AnswerQueries},\mathbb{A}}(S)}} \left[\exists i \text{ such that } |z_i - q_i(\mathcal{D})| > \frac{\alpha}{1-\gamma} + \alpha'\right]$$

$$\leq \Pr_{\substack{S \sim \mathcal{D}^n \\ \mathrm{Acc}_{n,\ell,\mathtt{AnswerQueries},\mathbb{A}}(S)}} \left[\exists i \text{ such that } |q_i(S) - z_i| > \frac{\alpha}{1-\gamma} \text{ or } |q_i(S) - q_i(\mathcal{D})| > \alpha'\right]$$

$$\leq \beta + \beta'.$$

$\square$

To obtain a contradiction, we rely on the following impossibility result for the ADA problem. Consider an algorithm $\mathcal{M}$ for the ADA problem that gets an input sample $P = (p_1, \dots, p_n)$ and answers (adaptively chosen) queries q. The impossibility result we use states that if $\mathcal{M}$ computes the answer to every given query q only as a function of the value of q on points from P (i.e., only as a function of $q(p_1), \dots, q(p_n)$), then, in general, $\mathcal{M}$ cannot answer more than n^2 adaptively chosen queries. An algorithm $\mathcal{M}$ satisfying this restriction is called a *natural* mechanism. Formally,

Definition 5.5 ([15]). *An algorithm that takes a sample P and answers queries q is natural if for every input sample P and every two queries q and q' such that $q(p) = q'(p)$ for all $p \in P$, the answers z and z' that the algorithm gives on queries q and q', respectively, are identical if the algorithm is deterministic and identically distributed if the algorithm is randomized. If the algorithm is stateful, then this condition should hold when the algorithm is in any of its possible states.*

We will use the following negative result of Steinke and Ullman [23] (see also [15, 22]).

Theorem 5.6 ([23]). *There exists a constant $c > 0$ such that there is no natural algorithm that is (c, c)-statistically-accurate for $O(n^2)$ adaptively chosen queries given n samples over a domain of size $\Omega(n)$.*

We have already established (in Lemma 5.4) that algorithm `AnswerQueries` is statistically-accurate for $\ell = \frac{m-n}{(a+1) \cdot 2^d}$ adaptively chosen queries, where ℓ can easily be made bigger then n^2 (by taking m to be big enough). We now want to apply Theorem 5.6 to our setting in order to get a contradiction. However, algorithm `AnswerQueries` is not exactly a natural algorithm (though, as we next explain, it is very close to being natural). The issue is that the answers produced by the streaming algorithm $\mathcal{A}$ can (supposedly) depend on the value

---

Algorithm 4. `AnswerQueriesOTP`

Input: A database $P \in (\{0,1\}^d)^n$ containing n elements from $\{0,1\}^d$.

Setting: On every time step we get a query $q : \{0,1\}^d \to \{0,1\}$.

Algorithm used: An adversarially robust streaming algorithm $\mathcal{A}$ for the SADA problem with (α, β)-accuracy for streams of length m. We abstract the coin tosses of $\mathcal{A}$ using *two* random strings, r_1 and r_2, of possibly unbounded length. Initially, we execute $\mathcal{A}$ with access to r_1, meaning that every time it tosses a coin it gets the next bit in r_1. At some point, we switch the random string to r_2, and henceforth $\mathcal{A}$ gets its coin tosses from r_2.

Algorithm used: BSM pseudorandom generator $\text{PRG} : \{0,1\}^a \times \{0,1\}^b \to \{0,1\}$, as in the definition of the SADA problem.

1. For every $p \in \{0,1\}^d$ sample $k_p \in \{0,1\}^b$ uniformly.
2. Sample $r_1 \in \{0,1\}^\nu$ uniformly, and instantiate algorithm $\mathcal{A}$ with read-once access to bits of r_1. Here ν bounds the number of coin flips made by $\mathcal{A}$.
3. For every $p \in P$, feed the update (p, k_p) to $\mathcal{A}$.
4. Sample $r_2 \in \{0,1\}^\nu$ uniformly, and switch the read-once access of $\mathcal{A}$ to r_2. (The switch from r_1 to r_2 is done for convenience, so that after Step 3 we do not need to "remember" the position for the next coin from r_1.)
5. REPEAT $\ell \triangleq \frac{m-n}{(a+1) \cdot 2^d}$ times
   (a) Obtain the next query $q : \{0,1\}^d \to \{0,1\}$.
   (b) For every $p \in \{0,1\}^d$ do
      i. Sample $\Gamma \in \{0,1\}^a$ uniformly.
      ii. Feed a updates (one by one) to $\mathcal{A}$ s.t. the concatenation of their first bits is Γ.
      iii. If $p \in P$ then let $Y = \text{PRG}(\Gamma, k_p)$. Otherwise sample $Y \in \{0,1\}$ uniformly.
      iv. Feed to $\mathcal{A}$ an update whose first bit is $Y \oplus q(p)$.
   (c) Obtain an answer z from $\mathcal{A}$.
   (d) Output z.

---

of the given queries outside of the input sample. Therefore, we now tweak algorithm `AnswerQueries` such that it becomes a natural algorithm. The modified construction is given in Algorithm `AnswerQueriesOTP`, where we marked the modifications in red. Consider Algorithm `AnswerQueriesOTP`, specified in Algorithm 4.

Lemma 5.7. *Algorithm* `AnswerQueriesOTP` *is natural.*

Proof Sketch. This follows from the fact that the value of the given queries outside of the input sample P are completely "hidden" from algorithm $\mathcal{A}$ (namely, by the classic "one-time pad" encryption scheme), and by observing that the answer z given by algorithm `AnswerQueriesOTP` on a query q is determined by the state of algorithm $\mathcal{A}$ at the end of the corresponding iteration of Step 5. □

We now argue that the modification we introduced (from `AnswerQueries` to `AnswerQueriesOTP`) has basically no effect on the execution, and hence, algorithm `AnswerQueriesOTP` is both natural and statistically-accurate. This will lead to a contradiction.

Lemma 5.8. *Suppose that $\mathcal{A}$ has space complexity w. Denote $\ell = \frac{m-n}{(a+1)\cdot 2^d}$. If* PRG *is an ε-secure BSM pseudorandom generator against adversaries with storage $O(w+\ell+b\cdot 2^d)$, then for every input database P and every adversary $\mathbb{A}$, the outcome distributions of $\mathsf{Acc}_{n,\ell,\texttt{AnswerQueries},\mathbb{A}}(P)$ and $\mathsf{Acc}_{n,\ell,\texttt{AnswerQueriesOTP},\mathbb{A}}(P)$ are within statistical distance $2^d m \varepsilon$.*

Proof. Recall that the outcome of $\mathsf{Acc}_{n,\ell,\texttt{AnswerQueries},\mathbb{A}}(P)$ is the transcript of the interaction $(q_1, z_1, \ldots, q_\ell, z_\ell)$, where q_i are the queries given by $\mathbb{A}$, and where z_i are the answers given by `AnswerQueries`. We need to show that the distributions of $(q_1, z_1, \ldots, q_\ell, z_\ell)$ during the executions with `AnswerQueries` and `AnswerQueriesOTP` are close. Without loss of generality, we assume that $\mathbb{A}$ is deterministic (indeed, if the lemma holds for every deterministic $\mathbb{A}$ then it also holds for every randomized $\mathbb{A}$). Hence, the transcript $(q_1, z_1, \ldots, q_\ell, z_\ell)$ is completely determined by the answers given by the mechanism. So we only need to show that $(z_1, \ldots, z_\ell)$ is distributed similarly during the two cases. Note that, as we are aiming for constant accuracy, we may assume that each answer z_i is specified using a constant number of bits (otherwise we can alter algorithm $\mathcal{A}$ to make this true while essentially maintaining its utility guarantees).

Now, for every $g \in \{0, 1, 2, \ldots, 2^d\}$, let `AnswerQueries`$_g$ denote an algorithm similar to algorithm `AnswerQueries`, except that in Step 5(b)iii, we set $Y = \mathrm{PRG}(\Gamma, k_p)$ if $p \in P$ or if $p \geq g$, and otherwise we sample $Y \in \{0, 1\}$ uniformly. Observe that `AnswerQueries`$_0 \equiv$ `AnswerQueries` and that `AnswerQueries`$_{2^d} \equiv$ `AnswerQueriesOTP`. We now show that for every g it hods that the statistical distance between $\mathsf{Acc}_{n,\ell,\texttt{AnswerQueries}_g,\mathbb{A}}(P)$ and $\mathsf{Acc}_{n,\ell,\texttt{AnswerQueries}_{g+1},\mathbb{A}}(P)$ is at most εm, which proves the lemma (by the triangle inequality).

Fix an index $g \in \{0, 1, \ldots, 2^d - 1\}$. Let Acc_g^* be an algorithm that simulates the interaction between $\mathbb{A}$ and `AnswerQueries`$_g$ on the database P, except that during an iteration of Step 5b with $p = g$, algorithm Acc_g^* gets Γ and Y as input, where Γ is sampled uniformly and where Y is either sampled uniformly from $\{0, 1\}$ or computed as $Y = \mathrm{PRG}(\Gamma, k)$ for some key k sampled uniformly from $\{0, 1\}^b$ (unknown to `AnswerQueries`$_g$). These two cases correspond to $\mathsf{Acc}_{n,\ell,\texttt{AnswerQueries}_{g+1},\mathbb{A}}(P)$ and $\mathsf{Acc}_{n,\ell,\texttt{AnswerQueries}_g,\mathbb{A}}(P)$, respectively.

Observe that Acc_g^* can be implemented with storage space at most $\hat{W} = O(w + \ell + b \cdot 2^d)$, specifically, for storing the internal state of algorithm $\mathcal{A}$ (which is w bits), storing all previous answers $z_1, z_2, \ldots, z_i$ (which is $O(\ell)$ bits), and storing all the keys k_p for $p \neq g$ (which takes at most $b \cdot 2^d$ bits). Note that, as we assume that $\mathbb{A}$ is deterministic, on every step we can compute the next query from the previously given answers.

Now, when Acc_g^* is given truly random bits Y, then it can be viewed as an adversary acting in the ideal experiment for PRG (see Sect. 2.3), and when Acc_g^* is given pseudorandom bits then it can be viewed as an adversary acting in the real experiment. By Theorem 2.8, assuming that PRG is ε-secure against adversaries with storage $\hat{W}$, then the distribution on the storage of Acc_g^* in the two cases is close up to statistical distance εm. The lemma now follows from the fact that the sequence of answers $(z_1, \ldots, z_\ell)$ is included in the storage of Acc_g^*. □

Combining Lemma 5.4 (stating that $\mathsf{AnswerQueries}$ is statistically-accurate) with Lemma 5.8 (stating that $\mathsf{AnswerQueries}$ and $\mathsf{AnswerQueriesOTP}$ are close) we get that $\mathsf{AnswerQueriesOTP}$ must also be statistically-accurate. Formally,

Lemma 5.9. *Suppose that* $\mathcal{A}$ *is* (α, β)-*accurate for the SADA problem for streams of length* m *using memory* w, *and suppose that* PRG *is an* ε-*secure BSM pseudorandom generator against adversaries with storage* $O(w + \ell + b \cdot 2^d)$, *where* $\ell = \frac{m-n}{(a+1) \cdot 2^d}$. *Then for every* $\beta', \varepsilon > 0$, *we have that algorithm* $\mathsf{AnswerQueriesOTP}$ *is* $\left(\frac{\alpha}{1-\gamma} + \alpha', \beta + \beta' + 2^d m \varepsilon\right)$-*statistically-accurate for* ℓ *queries where*

$$\alpha' = O\left(\sqrt{\frac{w + \ln(\frac{\ell}{\beta'})}{n}}\right).$$

So, Lemmas 5.7 and 5.9 state that algorithm $\mathsf{AnswerQueriesOTP}$ is both natural and statistically-accurate. To obtain a contradiction to Theorem 5.6, we instantiate Lemma 5.9 with the pseudorandom generator from Theorem 2.8. We obtain the following result.

Theorem 5.10. *For every* w, *there exists a streaming problem over domain of size* $\mathrm{poly}(w)$ *and stream length* $O(w^5)$ *that requires at least* w *space to be solved in the adversarial setting to within (small enough) constant accuracy, but can be solved in the oblivious setting using space* $O(\log^2(w))$.

Proof. To contradict Theorem 5.6, we want the (natural) algorithm $\mathsf{AnswerQueriesOTP}$ to answer more than n^2 queries over a domain of size $\Omega(n)$. So we set $\ell = \frac{m-n}{(a+1) \cdot 2^d} = \Omega(n^2)$ and $d = O(1) + \log n$. Note that with these settings we have $m = \Theta(n^3 \cdot a)$.

By Lemma 5.9, in order to ensure that $\mathsf{AnswerQueriesOTP}$'s answers are accurate (to within some small constant), we set $n = \Theta(w + \log(m))$ (large enough). We assume without loss of generality that $w \geq \log(m)$, as we can always increase the space complexity of $\mathcal{A}$. So $n = \Theta(w)$, and $m = \Theta(w^3 \cdot a)$.

In addition, to apply Lemma 5.9, we need to ensure that the conditions on the security of PRG hold. For a small constant $\tau > 0$, we use the pseudorandom generator from Theorem 2.8 with $\varepsilon = \frac{\tau}{m \cdot 2^d} = O(\frac{1}{mn}) = O(\frac{1}{mw})$. To get security against adversaries with storage $O(w + \ell + b \cdot 2^d) = O(w^2 + bw)$, we need to ensure

$$a = \Omega\left(w^2 + bw\right) \qquad \text{and} \qquad b = \Omega\left(\log\left(\frac{a}{\varepsilon}\right)\right) = \Theta(\log(am)).$$

It suffices to take $a = \Theta(w^2)$ and $b = \Theta(\log(wm)) = \Theta(\log(w))$. Putting everything together, with these parameters, by Lemma 5.9, we get that algorithm

`AnswerQueriesOTP` answers $\ell = \Omega(n^2)$ adaptive queries over domain of size $\Omega(n)$, which contradicts Theorem 5.6. This means that an algorithm with space complexity w cannot solve the (a, b, d, m, n, γ)-SADA problem to within (small enough) constant accuracy, where $a = \Theta(w^2)$, and $b = d = O(\log(w))$, and $m = \Theta(w^5)$, and $n = \Theta(w)$.

In contrast, by Observation 4.2, for constant α, β, γ, the oblivious algorithm `ObliviousSADA` uses space $O(\log^2(w))$ in this settings. $\square$

Remark 5.11. *A natural requirement from a function g, defining a streaming problem, is that the desired outcome does not change significantly from one update to the next (such a function is said to be "insensitive"). In the SADA problem, however, this is not the case. Nevertheless, our separation result can be shown to hold also for such an insensitive function. For example, for a parameter $k \in \mathbb{N}$, we could modify the definition of the SADA problem to ask for the average of the last k given functions, instead of only the last function. This would limit the changes to at most $1/k$. Our separation continues to hold because in the reduction from the ADA problem we could simply ask every query k times.*

6   A Computational Separation

In the previous sections we presented a streaming problem that can be solved in the oblivious setting using small space complexity, but requires large space complexity to be solved in the adversarial setting. Even though this provides a strong separation between adversarial streaming and oblivious streaming, a downside of our result is that the streaming problem we present (the SADA problem) is somewhat unnatural.

Question 6.1. *Is there a "natural" streaming problem for which a similar separation holds?*

In particular, one of the "unnatural" aspects of the SADA problem is that the target function depends on the *order* of the elements in the stream (i.e., it is an asymmetric function). Asymmetric functions can sometimes be considered "natural" in the streaming context (e.g., counting the number of inversions in a stream or finding the longest increasing subsequence). However, the majority of the "classical" streaming problems are defined by symmetric functions (e.g., counting the number of distinct elements in the stream or the number of heavy hitters).

Question 6.2. *Is there a symmetric streaming problem that can be solved using polylogarithmic space (in the domain size and the stream length) in the oblivious setting, but requires polynomial space in the adversarial setting?*

In this section we provide a positive answer to this question for *computationally efficient* streaming algorithms. That is, unlike our separation from the previous sections (for the SADA problem) which is information theoretic, the separation we present in this section (for a symmetric target function) is computational. We consider Question 6.2 (its information theoretic variant) to be an important question for future work.

6.1   The SADA2 Problem

Let $\kappa \in \mathbb{N}$ be a security parameter, let $m \in \mathbb{N}$ denote the length of the stream, and let $d \in \mathbb{N}$ and $\gamma \in (0, 1)$ be additional parameters. Let (Gen, Enc, Dec) be a semantically secure private-key encryption scheme, with key length κ and ciphertext length $\psi = \text{poly}(\kappa)$ for encrypting a message in $\{0, 1\}$. We consider a streaming problem over a domain $X = \{0, 1\}^{1+d+\log(m)+\psi}$, where an update $x \in X$ has two possible types (the type is determined by the first bit of x):

Data update: $x = (0, p, k) \in \{0, 1\} \times \{0, 1\}^d \times \{0, 1\}^\kappa$,
Query update: $x = (1, p, j, c) \in \{0, 1\} \times \{0, 1\}^d \times \{0, 1\}^{\log m} \times \{0, 1\}^\psi$.

We define a function $g : X^* \to [0, 1]$ as follows. Let $\vec{x} = \{x_1, \dots, x_i\}$ be a sequence of updates. For $p \in \{0, 1\}^d$, let $x_{i_1} = (0, p, k_{i_1}), \dots, x_{i_\ell} = (0, p, k_{i_\ell})$ denote all the "data updates" in $\vec{x}$ with the point p, and let $k_{i_1}, \dots, k_{i_\ell}$ denote their corresponding keys (some of which may be identical). Now let $k_p = k_{i_1} \wedge \cdots \wedge k_{i_\ell}$. That is, k_p is the bit-by-bit AND of all of the keys that correspond to "data updates" with the point p. Now let S be the set that contains the pair (p, k_p) for every p such that there exists a "data update" in $\vec{x}$ with the point p. Importantly, S is a *set* rather than a multiset. Similarly to the previous sections, we also add special symbols, $\perp_1, \dots, \perp_{\gamma 2^d}$, to S. Formally, S is constructed as follows.

---

1. Initiate $S = \{\perp_1, \dots, \perp_{\gamma 2^d}\}$.
2. For every $p \in \{0, 1\}^d$:
   (a) Let $x_{i_1} = (0, p, k_{i_1}), \dots, x_{i_\ell} = (0, p, k_{i_\ell})$ denote all the "data updates" in $\vec{x}$ (i.e., updates beginning with 0) that contain the point p.
   (b) If $\ell > 0$ then let $k_p = k_{i_1} \wedge \cdots \wedge k_{i_\ell}$ and add (p, k_p) to S.

We now define the query q that corresponds to $\vec{x}$. First, $q(\perp_1) = \cdots = q(\perp_{\gamma 2^d}) = 1$. Now, for $p \in \{0, 1\}^d$, let

$$j_p^{\max} = \max \left\{ j : \exists c \in \{0, 1\}^\psi \text{ such that } (1, p, j, c) \in \vec{x} \right\}.$$

That is, $j_p^{\max}$ denotes the maximal index such that $(1, p, j_p^{\max}, c)$ appears in $\vec{x}$ for some $c \in \{0, 1\}^\psi$. Furthermore, let $x_{i_1} = (1, p, j_p^{\max}, c_{i_1}), \dots, x_{i_\ell} = (1, p, j_p^{\max}, c_{i_\ell})$ denote the "query updates" with p and $j_p^{\max}$. Now let $c_p = c_{i_1} \wedge \cdots \wedge c_{i_\ell}$. That is, c_p is the bit-by-bit AND of all of the ciphertexts that correspond to "query updates" with p and $j_p^{\max}$. If the point p does not appear in any "query update" then we set $c_p = \vec{1}$ by default. The query $q : (\{0, 1\}^d \times \{0, 1\}^\kappa) \to \{0, 1\}$ is defined as $q(p, k) = \text{Dec}(c_p, k)$.

Algorithm 5. ObliviousSADA2

Setting: On every time step we obtain the next update, which is an element of $X = \{0,1\}^{1+d+\log(m)+\psi}$.

1. Let D be a sample (multiset) containing $O(\frac{1}{\alpha^2\gamma^2}\ln(\frac{m}{\beta}))$ i.i.d. elements chosen uniformly from $\{0,1\}^d \cup \{\bot_1,\ldots,\bot_{\gamma 2^d}\}$, and let $D_\bot \leftarrow D \cap \{\bot_1,\ldots,\bot_{\gamma 2^d}\}$, and let $D_X \leftarrow D \setminus D_\bot$.
2. For every $p \in D_X$, let $\text{inS}_p \leftarrow 0$, let $k_p \leftarrow \vec{1}$, let $j_p \leftarrow 0$, and let $c_p \leftarrow \vec{1}$.
3. REPEAT
   (a) Obtain the next update in the stream x.
   (b) If the first bit of x is 0 then
      i. Denote $x = (0,p,k)$.
      ii. If $p \in D_X$ then let $\text{inS}_p \leftarrow 1$ and let $k_p \leftarrow k_p \wedge k$.
   (c) If the first bit of x is 1 then
      i. Denote $x = (1,p,j,c)$.
      ii. If $p \in D_X$ and $j = j_p$ then set $c_p \leftarrow c_p \wedge c$.
      iii. If $p \in D_X$ and $j > j_p$ then set $c_p \leftarrow c$ and $j_p \leftarrow j$.
   (d) Let $v \leftarrow |\{p \in D_X : \text{inS}_p = 1\}| + |D_\bot|$ and let $z \leftarrow \frac{|D_\bot|}{v}$.
   (e) For every $p \in D_X$ such that $\text{inS}_p = 1$ set $z \leftarrow z + \frac{\text{Dec}(c_p,k_p)}{v}$.
   (f) Output z.

Finally, the value of the function g on the stream $\vec{x}$ is defined to be

$$g(\vec{x}) = q(S) = \frac{1}{|S|}\left[\gamma 2^d + \sum_{(p,k_p)\in S} q(p,k_p)\right].$$

That is, $g(\vec{x})$ returns the average of q on S. Observe that g is a symmetric function.

Definition 6.3 (The (d,m,κ,γ)-SADA2 Problem). *At every time step $i \in [m]$, after obtaining the next update $x_i \in X$, the goal is to approximate $g(x_1,\ldots,x_i)$.*

6.2   An Oblivious Algorithm for the SADA2 Problem

In this section we present an oblivious streaming algorithm for the SADA2 problem. The algorithm begins by sampling a multiset D containing a small number of random elements from the domain $\{0,1\}^d \cup \{\bot_1,\ldots,\bot_{\gamma 2^d}\}$. The algorithm then proceeds by maintaining the set S and the query q (which are determined by the input stream; as in the definition of the SADA2 problem) only w.r.t. elements that appear in the sample D. As we next explain, in the oblivious setting, this suffices in order to accurately solve the SADA2 problem. Consider algorithm ObliviousSADA2, given in Algorithm 5.

Theorem 6.4. *Assume that $2^d = \Omega(\frac{1}{\gamma}\ln(\frac{m}{\beta}))$ and $|D| \geq \Omega(\frac{1}{\alpha^2\gamma^2}\ln(\frac{m}{\beta}))$. Then* `ObliviousSADA2` *is (α,β)-accurate for the SADA2 problem in the oblivious setting.*

Proof. Fix the stream $\vec{x}_m = (x_1,\ldots,x_m)$. Fix a time step $i \in [m]$, and consider the prefix $\vec{x}_i = (x_1,\ldots,x_i)$. Let $S_i = S_i(\vec{x}_i)$ be the *set* and let $q_i = q_i(\vec{x}_i)$ be the *query* defined by $\vec{x}_i$, as in the definition of the SADA2 problem. Consider the multiset $T = \{(p,k_p) : p \in D_X \text{ and } \texttt{inS}_p = 1\} \cup D_\perp$. Let z_i be the answer returned in Step 3f after precessing the update x_i. Observe that z_i is exactly the average of q_i on the multiset T, that is, $z_i = q_i(T)$.

Recall that $|S_i| \geq \gamma 2^d$, and recall that every element in D is sampled uniformly from $\{0,1\}^d \cup \{\perp_1,\ldots,\perp_{\gamma 2^d}\}$. Therefore, $\mathbb{E}_D[|D \cap S_i|] \geq |D| \cdot \frac{\gamma 2^d}{2^d + \gamma 2^d} = |D| \cdot \frac{\gamma}{1+\gamma}$. By the Chernoff bound, assuming that $2^d = \Omega(\frac{1}{\gamma}\ln(\frac{m}{\beta}))$, then with probability at least $1 - \frac{\beta}{m}$ we have that $|D \cap S_i| \geq \frac{\gamma}{2}|D|$. We proceed with the analysis assuming that this is the case.

Now, for every $t \geq \frac{\gamma}{2}|D|$, when conditioning on $|D \cap S_i| = t$ we have that T is a sample containing t i.i.d. elements from S_i. In that case, again using the Chernoff bound, with probability at least $1 - \frac{\beta}{m}$ we have that $z_i = q_i(T) \in (1 \pm \alpha) \cdot q_i(S_i)$, assuming that $t \geq \Omega(\frac{1}{\alpha^2\gamma}\ln(\frac{m}{\beta}))$. This assumption holds when $|D| \geq \Omega(\frac{1}{\alpha^2\gamma^2}\ln(\frac{m}{\beta}))$.

So, for every fixed i, with probability at least $1 - O(\frac{\beta}{m})$ we have that $z_i \in (1 \pm \alpha) \cdot q_i(S_i)$. By a union bound, this holds for every time step i with probability at least $1 - O(\beta)$. $\qquad\square$

Observation 6.5. *For constant α,β,γ, algorithm* `ObliviousSADA2` *uses space $\tilde{O}(\log(m) \cdot \log|X|)$, in addition to the space required by* Dec.

6.3   A Negative Result for the SADA2 Problem

We now show that the SADA2 problem cannot be solved efficiently in the adversarial setting. To that end, suppose we have an adversarially robust streaming algorithm $\mathcal{A}$ for the SADA2 problem, and consider algorithm `AnswerQueries2` that uses $\mathcal{A}$ in order to solve the ADA problem. Recall that in the SADA2 problem the collection of "data updates" is treated as a *set*, while the input to an algorithm for the ADA problem is a *multiset*. In the following claim we show that `AnswerQueries2` is empirically-accurate w.r.t. its input (when treated as a set).

Claim 6.6. *Let $P \in (\{0,1\}^d)^*$ be an input multiset, let $\tilde{P}$ be the set containing every point that appears in P, and assume that $|\tilde{P}| = n$. If $\mathcal{A}$ is (α,β)-accurate for the SADA2 problem, then* `AnswerQueries2`(P) *is $\left(\alpha + \frac{\gamma \cdot 2^d}{n},\beta\right)$-empirically-accurate for $\frac{m-n}{2^d}$ adaptively chosen statistical queries w.r.t. the set $\tilde{P}$.*

Proof Sketch. Let q denote the query given at some iteration, and let $q_{\vec{x}}$ and $S_{\vec{x}}$ denote the query and the dataset specified by the updates given to algorithm $\mathcal{A}$.

Algorithm 6. AnswerQueries2

Input: A database P containing n elements from $\{0,1\}^d$.

Setting: On every time step we get a query $q : \{0,1\}^d \to \{0,1\}$.

Algorithm used: An adversarially robust streaming algorithm $\mathcal{A}$ for the (d, m, κ, γ)-SADA2 problem with (α, β)-accuracy for streams of length m. We abstract the coin tosses of $\mathcal{A}$ using *two* random strings, r_1 and r_2, of possibly unbounded length. Initially, we execute $\mathcal{A}$ with access to r_1, meaning that every time it tosses a coin it gets the next bit in r_1. At some point, we switch the random string to r_2, and henceforth $\mathcal{A}$ gets its coin tosses from r_2.

Algorithm used: Encryption scheme $(\mathsf{Gen}, \mathsf{Enc}, \mathsf{Dec})$, as in the definition of the SADA2 problem.

1. For every $p \in \{0,1\}^d$ sample $k_p \leftarrow \mathsf{Gen}(1^\kappa)$ independently.
2. Sample $r_1 \in \{0,1\}^\nu$ uniformly, and instantiate algorithm $\mathcal{A}$ with read-once access to bits of r_1. Here ν bounds the number of coin flips made by $\mathcal{A}$.
3. For every $p \in P$, feed the update $(0, p, k_p)$ to $\mathcal{A}$.
4. Sample $r_2 \in \{0,1\}^\nu$ uniformly, and switch the read-once access of $\mathcal{A}$ to r_2. (The switch from r_1 to r_2 is done for convenience, so that after Step 3 we do not need to "remember" the position for the next coin from r_1.)
5. For $j = 1$ to $\ell \triangleq \frac{m-n}{2^d}$ do
   (a) Obtain the next query $q_j : \{0,1\}^d \to \{0,1\}$.
   (b) For every $p \in \{0,1\}^d$ do
      i. Let $c_p = \mathsf{Enc}(q_j(p), k_p)$.
      ii. Feed the update $(1, p, j, c_p)$ to $\mathcal{A}$.
   (c) Obtain an answer z from $\mathcal{A}$.
   (d) Output z.

The claim follows from the fact that, by construction, for every $p \in \tilde{P}$ we have that $q(p) = q_{\vec{x}}(p, k_p)$. Therefore,

$$
q_{\vec{x}}(S_{\vec{x}}) = \frac{1}{|S_{\vec{x}}|} \left[\gamma \cdot 2^d + \sum_{p \in \tilde{P}} q(p) \right] = \frac{1}{n + \gamma 2^d} \left[\gamma \cdot 2^d + \sum_{p \in \tilde{P}} q(p) \right]
$$

$$
= \frac{\frac{\gamma \cdot 2^d}{n}}{1 + \frac{\gamma \cdot 2^d}{n}} + \frac{1}{n + \gamma 2^d} \sum_{p \in \tilde{P}} q(p).
$$

Therefore, $q_{\vec{x}}(S_{\vec{x}}) \le \frac{\gamma \cdot 2^d}{n} + q(\tilde{P})$, and also $q_{\vec{x}}(S_{\vec{x}}) \ge \frac{1}{n + \gamma 2^d} \sum_{p \in \tilde{P}} q(p)$ which means that $q(\tilde{P}) \le \frac{n + \gamma 2^d}{n} \cdot q_{\vec{x}}(S_{\vec{x}}) \le q_{\vec{x}}(S_{\vec{x}}) + \frac{\gamma 2^d}{n}$. So, whenever the answers given by $\mathcal{A}$ are α-accurate w.r.t. $q_{\vec{x}}(S_{\vec{x}})$, they are also $\left(\alpha + \frac{\gamma 2^d}{n} \right)$-accurate w.r.t. $\tilde{P}$. $\square$

We now show that algorithm AnswerQueries2 is transcript-compressible. To that end, for every choice of $\vec{k}, r_1, r_2, \vec{r}_{\mathsf{Enc}}$ for the keys k, the random bitstrings r_1, r_2, and the randomness used by Enc at its different executions, let us denote by `AnswerQueries2`$_{\vec{k},r_1,r_2,\vec{r}_{\mathrm{Enc}}}$ algorithm `AnswerQueries2` after fixing these elements.

Claim 6.7. *If algorithm $\mathcal{A}$ uses space at most w, then, for every $\vec{k}, r_1, r_2$, we have that algorithm* `AnswerQueries2`$_{\vec{k},r_1,r_2,\vec{r}_{\mathrm{Enc}}}$ *is transcript-compressible to w bits.*

Proof Sketch. Assuming that the adversary who generates the queries q is deterministic (which is without loss of generality) we get that the entire transcript is determined by the state of algorithm $\mathcal{A}$ at the end of Step 3.   □

Similarly to our arguments from Sect. 5, since algorithm `AnswerQueries2` is both empirically-accurate and transcript-compressible, we get that it is also statistically-accurate. Since we only argued empirical-accuracy when treating the input multiset as a set, we will only argue for statistical-accuracy w.r.t. the uniform distribution, where we have that the difference between a random set and a random multiset is small. Formally,

Lemma 6.8. *Suppose that $\mathcal{A}$ is (α, β)-accurate for the SADA2 problem for streams of length m using memory w. Then for every $\beta' > 0$, algorithm* `AnswerQueries2` *is $\left(\tilde{\alpha}, \tilde{\beta}\right)$-statistically-accurate for $\ell = \frac{m-n}{2^d}$ queries w.r.t. the uniform distribution over $\{0,1\}^d$, where $\tilde{\beta} = O\left(\beta + \beta' + \exp\left(-\frac{n^2}{3 \cdot 2^d}\right)\right)$ and*

$$
\tilde{\alpha} = O\left(\alpha + \frac{\gamma \cdot 2^d}{n} + \frac{n}{2^d} + \sqrt{\frac{w + \ln(\frac{\ell}{\beta'})}{n}}\right).
$$

Proof Sketch. The proof is analogous to the proof of Lemma 5.4, with the following addition. Let P be a multiset containing n i.i.d. uniform samples from $\{0,1\}^d$, and let $\tilde{P}$ be the set containing every element of P. As we are considering the uniform distribution on $\{0,1\}^d$, then by the Chernoff bound, with probability at least $1 - \exp(-\frac{n^2}{3 \cdot 2^d})$, it holds that the set $\tilde{P}$ and the multiset P differ by at most $\frac{n^2}{2 \cdot 2^d}$ points, i.e., by at most an $\frac{n}{2 \cdot 2^d}$-fraction of the points. In that case, for every query q we have that $|q(P) - q(\tilde{P})| \le \frac{n}{2 \cdot 2^d}$.   □

So algorithm `AnswerQueries2` is statistically-accurate. To obtain a contradiction, we modify the algorithm such that it becomes natural. Consider algorithm `AnswerQueries2Natural`. As before, the modifications are marked in red.

Observation 6.9. *Algorithm* `AnswerQueries2Natural` *is natural.*

Proof Sketch. This follows from the fact that the value of the given queries outside of the input sample P are ignored, and are replaced with (encryptions of) zero.   □

The following lemma follows from the assumed security of the encryption scheme.

Algorithm 7. AnswerQueries2Natural

Input: A database P containing n elements from $\{0,1\}^d$.

Setting: On every time step we get a query $q : \{0,1\}^d \to \{0,1\}$.

Algorithm used: An adversarially robust streaming algorithm $\mathcal{A}$ for the (d, m, κ, γ)-SADA2 problem with (α, β)-accuracy for streams of length m. We abstract the coin tosses of $\mathcal{A}$ using *two* random strings, r_1 and r_2, of possibly unbounded length. Initially, we execute $\mathcal{A}$ with access to r_1, meaning that every time it tosses a coin it gets the next bit in r_1. At some point, we switch the random string to r_2, and henceforth $\mathcal{A}$ gets its coin tosses from r_2.

Algorithm used: Encryption scheme $(\mathrm{Gen}, \mathrm{Enc}, \mathrm{Dec})$, as in the definition of the SADA2 problem.

1. For every $p \in \{0,1\}^d$ sample $k_p \leftarrow \mathrm{Gen}(1^\kappa)$ independently.
2. Sample $r_1 \in \{0,1\}^\nu$ uniformly, and instantiate algorithm $\mathcal{A}$ with read-once access to bits of r_1. Here ν bounds the number of coin flips made by $\mathcal{A}$.
3. For every $p \in P$, feed the update $(0, p, k_p)$ to $\mathcal{A}$.
4. Sample $r_2 \in \{0,1\}^\nu$ uniformly, and switch the read-once access of $\mathcal{A}$ to r_2. (The switch from r_1 to r_2 is done for convenience, so that after Step 3 we do not need to "remember" the position for the next coin from r_1.)
5. For $j = 1$ to $\ell \triangleq \frac{m-n}{2^d}$ do
   (a) Obtain the next query $q_j : \{0,1\}^d \to \{0,1\}$.
   (b) For every $p \in \{0,1\}^d$ do
       i. If $p \in P$ then let $c_p = \mathrm{Enc}(q_j(p), k_p)$. Otherwise let $c_p = \mathrm{Enc}(0, k_p)$.
       ii. Feed the update $(1, p, j, c_p)$ to $\mathcal{A}$.
   (c) Obtain an answer z from $\mathcal{A}$.
   (d) Output z.

Lemma 6.10. *Suppose that* $(\mathrm{Gen}, \mathrm{Enc}, \mathrm{Dec})$ *is semantically secure private-key encryption scheme with key length* $\kappa = \kappa(m)$ *against adversaries with time* $\mathrm{poly}(m)$. *Fix* $\alpha \in (0,1)$. *Let* $\mathbb{A}$ *be a data analyst with running time* $\mathrm{poly}(m)$. *For a mechanism* $\mathcal{M}$ *that answers queries, consider the interaction between* $\mathcal{M}$ *and* $\mathbb{A}$, *and let* E *denote the event that* $\mathcal{M}$ *failed to be* α-*statistically accurate at some point during the interaction. Then, for an input database* P *sampled uniformly from* $\{0,1\}^d$ *it holds that*

$$\left| \Pr_{P, \mathbb{A}, \textit{AnswerQueries2}(P)} [E] - \Pr_{P, \mathbb{A}, \textit{AnswerQueries2Natural}(P)} [E] \right| \leq \mathrm{negl}(\kappa).$$

The proof of Lemma 6.10 is straightforward from the definition of security. We give here the details for completeness. To that end, let us recall the formal definition of security of an encryption scheme. Consider a pair of oracles $\mathcal{E}_0$ and $\mathcal{E}_1$, where $\mathcal{E}_1(k_1, \ldots, k_N, \cdot)$ takes as input an index of a key $i \in [N]$ and a message M and returns $\mathrm{Enc}(M, k_i)$, and where $\mathcal{E}_0(k_1, \ldots, k_N, \cdot)$ takes the same input but returns $\mathrm{Enc}(0, k_i)$. An encryption scheme $(\mathrm{Gen}, \mathrm{Enc}, \mathrm{Dec})$ is *secure* if no computationally efficient adversary can tell whether it is interacting with $\mathcal{E}_0$ or with $\mathcal{E}_1$. Formally,

Algorithm 8. An adversary $\mathcal{B}$ for the encryption scheme

Algorithm used: An adversarially robust streaming algorithm $\mathcal{A}$ for the (d, m, κ, γ)-SADA2 problem with (α, β)-accuracy for streams of length m.

Algorithm used: A data analyst $\mathbb{A}$ that outputs queries and obtains answers.

Algorithm used: Encryption scheme (Gen, Enc, Dec).

Oracle access: $\mathcal{E}_b(k_1, \ldots, k_N, \cdot)$ where $b \in \{0, 1\}$ and where $N = 2^d$ and $k_1, \ldots, k_N \leftarrow \text{Gen}(1^\kappa)$.

1. Let P be a multiset containing n uniform samples from $\{0, 1\}^d$.
2. For every $p \in P$ sample $\bar{k}_p \leftarrow \text{Gen}(1^\kappa)$ independently.
3. Instantiate algorithm $\mathcal{A}$.
4. For every $p \in P$, feed the update $(0, p, \bar{k}_p)$ to $\mathcal{A}$.
5. Instantiate the data analyst $\mathbb{A}$.
6. For $j = 1$ to $\ell \triangleq \frac{m-n}{2^d}$ do
   (a) Obtain the next query $q_j : \{0, 1\}^d \to \{0, 1\}$ from the data analyst $\mathbb{A}$.
   (b) For every $p \in \{0, 1\}^d$ do
       i. If $p \in P$ then let $c_p = \text{Enc}(q_j(p), \bar{k}_p)$. Otherwise let $c_p \leftarrow \mathcal{E}_b(p, q_j(p))$.
       ii. Feed the update $(1, p, j, c_p)$ to $\mathcal{A}$.
   (c) Obtain an answer z from $\mathcal{A}$, and give z to $\mathbb{A}$.
7. Output 1 if and only if event E occurs.

Definition 6.11. *Let* $m : \mathbb{R} \to \mathbb{R}$ *be a function. An encryption scheme* (Gen, Enc, Dec) *is* m-secure *if for every* $N = \text{poly}(m(\kappa))$, *and every* $\text{poly}(m(\kappa))$-*time adversary* $\mathcal{B}$, *the following holds.*

$$
\left| \Pr_{\substack{k_1, \ldots, k_N \\ \mathcal{B}, \text{Enc}}} \left[\mathcal{B}^{\mathcal{E}_0(k_1, \ldots, k_N, \cdot)} = 1 \right] - \Pr_{\substack{k_1, \ldots, k_N \\ \mathcal{B}, \text{Enc}}} \left[\mathcal{B}^{\mathcal{E}_1(k_1, \ldots, k_N, \cdot)} = 1 \right] \right| = \text{negl}(\kappa),
$$

where the probabilities are over sampling $k_1, \ldots, k_N \leftarrow \text{Gen}(1^\kappa)$ *and over the randomness of* $\mathcal{B}$ *and* Enc.

Remark 6.12. *When* m *is the identity function we simply say that* (Gen, Enc, Dec) *is* secure. *Note that in this case, security holds against all adversaries with runtime polynomial in the security parameter* κ. *We will further assume the existence of a* sub-exponentially secure *encryption scheme. By that we mean that there exist a constant* $\tau > 0$ *such that* (Gen, Enc, Dec) *is* m-secure *for* $m(\kappa) = 2^{\kappa^\tau}$. *That is, we assume the existence of an encryption scheme in which security holds agains all adversaries with runtime polynomial in* 2^{κ^τ}.

To prove Lemma 6.10 we construct an adversary $\mathcal{B}$ for (Gen, Enc, Dec) such that its advantage in breaking the security of this scheme is exactly the difference in the probability of event E between the execution with `AnswerQueries2` or with `AnswerQueries2Natural`. This implies that the difference between these two probabilities is negligible.

Proof of Lemma 6.10. Let $\mathbb{A}$ be a data analyst with running time poly(m), and consider algorithm $\mathcal{B}$. First observe that if $\mathcal{A}$ and $\mathbb{A}$ are computationally efficient (run in time poly(m)) then so is algorithm $\mathcal{B}$.

Now observe that when the oracle is $\mathcal{E}_1$ and when $k_1, \ldots, k_N$ are chosen randomly from Gen(1^κ) then $\mathcal{B}^{\mathcal{E}_1(k_1,\ldots,k_N,\cdot)}$ simulates the interaction between $\mathbb{A}$ and AnswerQueries2 on a uniformly sampled database P. Similarly, when the oracle is $\mathcal{E}_0$ and when $k_1, \ldots, k_N$ are chosen randomly from Gen(1^κ) then $\mathcal{B}^{\mathcal{E}_0(k_1,\ldots,k_N,\cdot)}$ simulates the interaction between $\mathbb{A}$ and AnswerQueries2Natural on a uniformly sampled database P. Thus,

$$\left| \Pr_{P,\mathbb{A},\text{AnswerQueries2}(P)}[E] - \Pr_{P,\mathbb{A},\text{AnswerQueries2Natural}(P)}[E] \right|$$

$$= \left| \Pr_{\substack{k_1,\ldots,k_N \\ \mathcal{B},\text{Enc}}}\left[\mathcal{B}^{\mathcal{E}_1(k_1,\ldots,k_N,\cdot)} = 1\right] - \Pr_{\substack{k_1,\ldots,k_N \\ \mathcal{B},\text{Enc}}}\left[\mathcal{B}^{\mathcal{E}_0(k_1,\ldots,k_N,\cdot)} = 1\right] \right| = \text{negl}(\kappa).$$

□

So, algorithm AnswerQueries2Natural is natural, and when $\mathcal{A}$ and $\mathbb{A}$ are computationally efficient, then the probability that AnswerQueries2Natural fails to be statistically-accurate is similar to the probability that AnswerQueries2 fails, which is small. We therefore get the following lemma.

Lemma 6.13. *Algorithm* AnswerQueries2Natural *is natural. In addition, if* (Gen, Enc, Dec) *is an m-secure private-key encryption scheme with key length* $\kappa = \kappa(m)$, *and if $\mathcal{A}$ is an adversarially robust streaming algorithm for the* (d, m, κ, γ)-*SADA2 problem with space w and runtime* poly(m), *then algorithm* AnswerQueries2Natural *is* $\left(\tilde{\alpha}, \tilde{\beta}\right)$-*statistically-accurate for* $\ell = \frac{m-n}{2^d}$ *queries w.r.t. the uniform distribution over* $\{0,1\}^d$, *and w.r.t. a data analyst $\mathbb{A}$ with running time* poly(m), *where* $\tilde{\beta} = O\left(\beta + \beta' + \exp\left(-\frac{n^2}{3 \cdot 2^d}\right) + \text{negl}(\kappa)\right)$ *and*

$$\tilde{\alpha} = O\left(\alpha + \frac{\gamma \cdot 2^d}{n} + \frac{n}{2^d} + \sqrt{\frac{w + \ln(\frac{\ell}{\beta'})}{n}}\right).$$

We now restate Theorem 5.6, in which we simplified the results of Steinke and Ullman. In this section we use the stronger formulation of their results, given as follows.

Theorem 6.14 ([23]). *There exists a constant $c > 0$ such that no natural algorithm is* (c, c)-*statistically-accurate for* $O(n^2)$ *adaptively chosen queries given n samples over a domain of size* $\Omega(n)$. *Furthermore, this holds even when assuming that the data analyst is computationally efficient (runs in time* poly(n^2)) *and even when the underlying distribution is the uniform distribution.*

Combining Lemma 6.13 with Theorem 6.14 we obtain the following result.

Theorem 6.15. *Assume the existence of a sub-exponentially secure private-key encryption scheme. Then, the* $(d = \Theta(\log m), m, \kappa = \text{polylog}(m), \gamma = \Theta(1))$-*SADA2 problem can be solved in the oblivious setting to within constant accuracy using space* $\text{polylog}(m)$ *and using* $\text{polylog}(m)$ *runtime (per update). In contrast, every adversarially robust algorithm for this problem with* $\text{poly}(m)$ *runtime per update must use space* $\text{poly}(m)$.*

References

1. Ahn, K.J., Guha, S., McGregor, A.: Analyzing graph structure via linear measurements. In: Rabani, Y. (ed.) Proceedings of the 23rd Annual ACM-SIAM Symposium on Discrete Algorithms, SODA 2012, Kyoto, Japan, 17–19 January 2012, pp. 459–467. SIAM (2012)
2. Ahn, K.J., Guha, S., McGregor, A.: Graph sketches: sparsification, spanners, and subgraphs. In: Benedikt, M., Krötzsch, M., Lenzerini, M. (eds.) Proceedings of the 31st ACM SIGMOD-SIGACT-SIGART Symposium on Principles of Database Systems, PODS 2012, Scottsdale, AZ, USA, 20–24 May 2012, pp. 5–14. ACM (2012)
3. Aumann, Y., Ding, Y.Z., Rabin, M.O.: Everlasting security in the bounded storage model. IEEE Trans. Inf. Theory **48**(6), 1668–1680 (2002)
4. Aumann, Y., Rabin, M.O.: Information theoretically secure communication in the limited storage space model. In: Wiener, M. (ed.) CRYPTO 1999. LNCS, vol. 1666, pp. 65–79. Springer, Heidelberg (1999). https://doi.org/10.1007/3-540-48405-1_5
5. Bassily, R., Nissim, K., Smith, A.D., Steinke, T., Stemmer, U., Ullman, J.: Algorithmic stability for adaptive data analysis. In: Wichs, D., Mansour, Y. (eds.) Proceedings of the 48th Annual ACM SIGACT Symposium on Theory of Computing, STOC 2016, Cambridge, MA, USA, 18–21 June 2016, pp. 1046–1059. ACM (2016)
6. Ben-Eliezer, O., Jayaram, R., Woodruff, D.P., Yogev, E.: A framework for adversarially robust streaming algorithms. CoRR, abs/2003.14265 (2020)
7. Ben-Eliezer, O., Yogev, E.: The adversarial robustness of sampling. CoRR, abs/1906.11327 (2019)
8. Cachin, C., Maurer, U.: Unconditional security against memory-bounded adversaries. In: Kaliski, B.S. (ed.) CRYPTO 1997. LNCS, vol. 1294, pp. 292–306. Springer, Heidelberg (1997). https://doi.org/10.1007/BFb0052243
9. Ding, Y.Z., Rabin, M.O.: Hyper-encryption and everlasting security. In: Alt, H., Ferreira, A. (eds.) STACS 2002. LNCS, vol. 2285, pp. 1–26. Springer, Heidelberg (2002). https://doi.org/10.1007/3-540-45841-7_1
10. Dwork, C., Feldman, V., Hardt, M., Pitassi, T., Reingold, O., Roth, A.: Generalization in adaptive data analysis and holdout reuse. In: Advances in Neural Information Processing Systems (NIPS), Montreal, December 2015 (2015)
11. Dwork, C., Feldman, V., Hardt, M., Pitassi, T., Reingold, O., Roth, A.: Preserving statistical validity in adaptive data analysis. In: ACM Symposium on the Theory of Computing (STOC), June 2015. ACM (2015)
12. Dziembowski, S., Maurer, U.: Optimal randomizer efficiency in the bounded-storage model. J. Cryptol. **17**(1), 5–26 (2004)
13. Gilbert, A.C., Hemenway, B., Rudra, A., Strauss, M.J., Wootters, M.: Recovering simple signals. In: 2012 Information Theory and Applications Workshop, pp. 382–391 (2012)

14. Gilbert, A.C., Hemenway, B., Strauss, M.J., Woodruff, D.P., Wootters, M.: Reusable low-error compressive sampling schemes through privacy. In: 2012 IEEE Statistical Signal Processing Workshop (SSP), pp. 536–539 (2012)
15. Hardt, M., Ullman, J.: Preventing false discovery in interactive data analysis is hard. In: FOCS, 19–21 October 2014. IEEE (2014)
16. Hardt, M., Woodruff, D.P.: How robust are linear sketches to adaptive inputs? In STOC, 1–4 June 2013, pp. 121–130. ACM (2013)
17. Harnik, D., Naor, M.: On everlasting security in the *hybrid* bounded storage model. In: Bugliesi, M., Preneel, B., Sassone, V., Wegener, I. (eds.) ICALP 2006. LNCS, vol. 4052, pp. 192–203. Springer, Heidelberg (2006). https://doi.org/10.1007/11787006_17
18. Hassidim, A., Kaplan, H., Mansour, Y., Matias, Y., Stemmer, U.: Adversarially robust streaming algorithms via differential privacy. In: Larochelle, H., Ranzato, M., Hadsell, R., Balcan, M., Lin, H. (eds.) Advances in Neural Information Processing Systems 33: Annual Conference on Neural Information Processing Systems 2020, NeurIPS 2020, 6–12 December 2020, virtual (2020)
19. Lu, C.-J.: Encryption against storage-bounded adversaries from on-line strong extractors. J. Cryptol. **17**(1), 27–42 (2004)
20. Maurer, U.M.: Conditionally-perfect secrecy and a provably-secure randomized cipher. J. Cryptol. **5**(1), 53–66 (1992)
21. Mironov, I., Naor, M., Segev, G.: Sketching in adversarial environments. SIAM J. Comput. **40**(6), 1845–1870 (2011)
22. Nissim, K., Smith, A.D., Steinke, T., Stemmer, U., Ullman, J.: The limits of post-selection generalization. In: Bengio, S., Wallach, H.M., Larochelle, H., Grauman, K., Cesa-Bianchi, N., Garnett, R. (eds.) Advances in Neural Information Processing Systems 31: Annual Conference on Neural Information Processing Systems 2018, NeurIPS 2018, Canada, Montréal, 3–8 December 2018, pp. 6402–6411 (2018)
23. Steinke, T., Ullman, J.: Interactive fingerprinting codes and the hardness of preventing false discovery. In: COLT, pp. 1588–1628 (2015)
24. Vadhan, S.P.: Constructing locally computable extractors and cryptosystems in the bounded-storage model. J. Cryptol. **17**(1), 43–77 (2004)
25. Vitter, J.S.: Random sampling with a reservoir. ACM Trans. Math. Softw. **11**(1), 37–57 (1985)
26. Woodruff, D.P., Zhou, S.:. Tight bounds for adversarially robust streams and sliding windows via difference estimators. CoRR, abs/2011.07471 (2020)

Applied Cryptography and Side Channels

Provable Security Analysis of FIDO2

Manuel Barbosa[1], Alexandra Boldyreva[2], Shan Chen[3(✉)],
and Bogdan Warinschi[4,5]

[1] University of Porto (FCUP) and INESC TEC, Porto, Portugal
mbb@fc.up.pt
[2] Georgia Institute of Technology, Atlanta, USA
sasha@gatech.edu
[3] Technische Universität Darmstadt, Darmstadt, Germany
shan.chen@tu-darmstadt.de
[4] University of Bristol, Bristol, UK
csxbw@bristol.ac.uk
[5] Dfinity, Zug, Switzerland

Abstract. We carry out the first provable security analysis of the new
FIDO2 protocols, the promising FIDO Alliance's proposal for a standard
for *passwordless* user authentication. Our analysis covers the core components of FIDO2: the W3C's Web Authentication (WebAuthn) specification and the new Client-to-Authenticator Protocol (CTAP2).

Our analysis is *modular*. For WebAuthn and CTAP2, in turn, we
propose appropriate security models that aim to capture their intended
security goals and use the models to analyze their security. First, our
proof confirms the authentication security of WebAuthn. Then, we show
CTAP2 can only be proved secure in a weak sense; meanwhile, we identify a series of its design flaws and provide suggestions for improvement.
To withstand stronger yet realistic adversaries, we propose a generic protocol called sPACA and prove its strong security; with proper instantiations, sPACA is also more efficient than CTAP2. Finally, we analyze the
overall security guarantees provided by FIDO2 and WebAuthn+sPACA
based on the security of their components.

We expect that our models and provable security results will help
clarify the security guarantees of the FIDO2 protocols. In addition, we
advocate the adoption of our sPACA protocol as a substitute for CTAP2
for both stronger security and better performance.

1 Introduction

Motivation. Passwords are pervasive yet insecure. According to some studies, the
average consumer of McAfee has 23 online accounts that require a password [17],
and the average employee using LastPass has to manage 191 passwords [22]. Not
only are the passwords difficult to keep track of, but it is well-known that achieving strong security while relying on passwords is quite difficult (if not impossible). According to the Verizon Data Breach Investigations Report [34], 81% of

---

S. Chen—Did most of his work while at Georgia Institute of Technology.

© International Association for Cryptologic Research 2021
T. Malkin and C. Peikert (Eds.): CRYPTO 2021, LNCS 12827, pp. 125–156, 2021.
https://doi.org/10.1007/978-3-030-84252-9_5

hacking-related breaches relied on either stolen and/or weak passwords. What some users may consider an acceptable password, may not withstand sophisticated and powerful modern password cracking tools. Moreover, even strong passwords may fall prey to phishing attacks and identity fraud. According to Symantec, in 2017, phishing emails were the most widely used means of infection, employed by 71% of the groups that staged cyber attacks [31].

An ambitious project which tackles the above problem is spearheaded by the Fast Identity Online (FIDO) Alliance. A truly international effort, the alliance has working groups in the US, China, Europe, Japan, Korea and India and has brought together many companies and types of vendors, including Amazon, Google, Microsoft, Apple, RSA, Intel, Yubico, Visa, Samsung, major banks, etc.

The goal is to enable user-friendly passwordless authentication secure against phishing and identity fraud. The core idea is to rely on security devices (controlled via biometrics and/or PINs) which can then be used to register and later seamlessly authenticate to online services. The various standards defined by FIDO formalize several protocols, most notably Universal Authentication Framework (UAF), the Universal Second Factor (U2F) protocols and the new FIDO2 protocols: W3C's Web Authentication (WebAuthn) and FIDO Alliance's Client-to-Authenticator Protocol v2.0 (CTAP2[1]).

FIDO2 is moving towards wide deployment and standardization with great success. Major web browsers including Google Chrome and Mozilla Firefox have implemented WebAuthn. In 2018, Client-to-Authenticator Protocol (CTAP)[2] was recognized as international standards by the International Telecommunication Union's Telecommunication Standardization Sector (ITU-T). In 2019, WebAuthn became an official web standard. Also, Android and Windows Hello earned FIDO2 Certification. Although the above deployment is backed-up by highly detailed description of the security goals and a variety of possible attacks and countermeasures, these are informal [21].

Our Focus. We provide the first provable security analysis of the FIDO2 protocols. Our focus is to clarify the formal trust model assumed by the protocols, to define and prove their exact security guarantees, and to identify and fix potential design flaws and security vulnerabilities that hinder their widespread use. Our analysis covers the actions of human users authorizing the use of credentials via *gestures* and shows that, depending on the capabilities of security devices, such gestures enhance the security of FIDO2 protocols in different ways. We concentrate on the FIDO2 authentication properties and leave the study of its arguably less central anonymity goals for future work.

Related Work. Some initial work in this direction already exists. Hu and Zhang [25] analyzed the security of FIDO UAF 1.0 and identified several vulnerabilities in different attack scenarios. Later, Panos *et al.* [32] analyzed FIDO UAF 1.1 and explored some potential attack vectors and vulnerabilities. However, both works were informal. FIDO U2F and WebAuthn were analyzed using the applied pi-calculus and ProVerif tool [23,27,33]. Regarding an older version

---

[1] The older version is called CTAP1/U2F.
[2] CTAP refers to both versions: CTAP1/U2F and CTAP2.

of FIDO U2F, Pereira *et al.* [33] presented a server-in-the-middle attack and Jacomme and Kremer [27] further analyzed it with a structured and fine-grained threat model for malware. Guirat and Halpin [23] confirmed the authentication security provided by WebAuthn while pointed out that the claimed privacy properties (i.e., account unlinkability) failed to hold due to the same attestation key pair used for different servers.

However, *none* of the existing work employs the cryptographic provable security approach to the FIDO2 protocols in the course of deployment. In particular, there is no analysis of CTAP2, and the results for WebAuthn [27] are limited in scope: as noted by the authors themselves, their model "makes a number of simplifications and so much work is needed to formally model the complete protocol as given in the W3C specification". The analysis in [27] further uses the *symbolic* model (often called the Dolev-Yao model [18]), which captures weaker adversarial capabilities than those in computational models (e.g., the Bellare-Rogaway model [10]) employed by the provable security approach we adopt here.

The works on two-factor authentication (e.g., [16,29]) are related to our work, but the user in such protocols has to use the password *and* the two-factor device during each authentication/login. With FIDO2, *there is no password* during user registration or authentication. The PIN used in FIDO2 is meant to authorize a client (e.g., a browser) access to an authenticator device (e.g., an authentication token); the server does not use passwords at all.[3] Some two-factor protocols can also generate a binding cookie after the first login to avoid using the two-factor device or even the password for future logins. However, this requires trusting the client, e.g., a malicious browser can log in as the user without having the two-factor device (or the password). FIDO2 uses the PIN to prevent an attacker with a stolen device from authenticating to a server from a new client.

Our work is not directly applicable to federated authentication protocols such as Kerberos, OAuth, or OpenID. FIDO2 allows the user to keep a single hardware token that it can use to authenticate to multiple servers without having to use a federated identity. The only trust anchor is an attestation key pair for the token. To the best of our knowledge, there are no complete and formal security models for federated authentication in the literature, but such models would differ significantly from the ones we consider here. It is interesting to see how FIDO2 and federated authentication can be used securely together; we leave this as an interesting direction for future work. Our work could, however, be adapted to analyze some second-factor authentication protocols like Google 2-step [2].

FIDO2 Overview. FIDO2 consists of two core components (see Fig. 1 for the communication channels and Fig. 2 for the simplified FIDO2 flow).

WebAuthn is a web API that can be built into browsers to enable web applications to integrate user authentication. At its heart, WebAuthn is a *password-less* "challenge-response" scheme between a server and a user. The user relies on a trusted authenticator device (e.g., a security token or a smartphone) and a possibly untrusted client (e.g., a browser or an operating system installed on

---

[3] Some form of prior user authentication method is required for registration of a new credential, but this is a set-up assumption for the protocol.

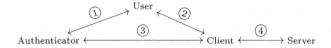

Fig. 1. Communication channels

Fig. 2. FIDO2 flow (simplified): double arrow = CTAP2 authorized message.

the user's laptop). Such a device-assisted "challenge-response" scheme works as follows (details in Sect. 5). First, in the registration phase, the server sends a random challenge to the security device through the client. In this phase, the device signs the challenge using its long-term embedded attestation secret key, along with a new public key credential to use in future interactions; the credential is included in the response to the server. In the subsequent interactions, which correspond to user authentication, the challenge sent by the server is signed by the device using the secret key corresponding to the credential. In both cases, the signature is verified by the server.

The other FIDO2 component, CTAP2, specifies the communication between an authenticator device and the client (usually a browser). Its goal is to guarantee that the client can only use the authenticator with the user's permission, which the user gives by 1) entering a PIN when the authenticator powers up and 2) directly using the authenticator interface (e.g., a simple push-button) to authorize registration and authentication operations. CTAP2 specifies how to configure an authenticator with a user's PIN. Roughly speaking, its security goal is to "bind" a trusted client to the set-up authenticator by requiring the user to provide the correct PIN, such that the authenticator accepts only messages sent from a "bound" client. We remark that, surprisingly, CTAP2 relies on the (unauthenticated) Diffie-Hellman key exchange. The details are in Sect. 7.

Our Contributions. We perform the first thorough cryptographic analysis of the authentication properties guaranteed by FIDO2 using the provable security approach. Our analysis is conducted in a *modular* way. That is, we first analyze WebAuthn and CTAP2 components separately and then derive the overall security of a typical use of FIDO2. We note that our models, although quite different, follow the Bellare-Rogaway model [10] that was proposed to analyze key exchange protocols, which defines oracle queries to closely simulate the real-world adversarial abilities. Its extensions (like ours) have been widely used to analyze real-world protocols such as TLS 1.3 [13,19], Signal [14], etc.

Provable Security of WebAuthn. We start our analysis with the simpler base protocol, WebAuthn. We define the class of *passwordless authentication (PlA)* protocols that capture the syntax of WebAuthn. Our PlA model considers an authenticator and a server (often referred to as a relying party) communicating through a client, which consists of two phases. The server is assumed to know the attestation public key that uniquely identifies the authenticator. In the *registration* phase the authenticator and the server communicate with the intention to establish some joint state corresponding to this registration session: this joint state fixes a credential, which is bound to the authenticator's attestation public key vk and a server identity id_S (e.g., a server domain name). The server gets the guarantee that the joint state is stored in a specific authenticator, which is assumed to be tamper-proof. The joint state can then be used in the *authentication* phase. Here, the authenticator and the server engage in a message exchange where the goal of the server is to verify that it is interacting with the same authenticator that registered the credential bound to (vk, id_S).

Roughly speaking, a PlA protocol is secure if, whenever an authentication/registration session completes on the server side, there is a unique partnered registration/authentication session which completed successfully on the authenticator side. For authentication sessions, we further impose that there is a unique associated registration session on both sides, and that these registration sessions are also uniquely partnered. This guarantees that registration contexts (i.e., the credentials) are *isolated* from one another; moreover, if a server session completes an authentication session with an authenticator, then the authenticator must have completed a registration session with the server earlier. We use the model thus developed to prove the security of WebAuthn under the assumption that the underlying hash function is collision-resistant and the signature scheme is unforgeable. Full details can be found in Sect. 5.

Provable Security of CTAP2. Next we study the more complex CTAP2 protocol. We define the class of *PIN-based access control for authenticators (PACA)* protocols to formalize the general syntax of CTAP2. Although CTAP2 by its name may suggest a two-party protocol, our PACA model involves the user as an additional participant and therefore captures human interactions with the client and the authenticator (e.g., the user typing its PIN into the browser window or rebooting the authenticator). A PACA protocol runs in three phases as follows. First, in the authenticator setup phase, the user "embeds" its PIN into the authenticator via a client and, as a result, the authenticator stores a PIN-related long-term state. Then, in the binding phase, the user authorizes the client to "bind" itself to the authenticator (using the same PIN). At the end of this phase, the client and the authenticator end up with a (perhaps different) binding state. Finally, in the access channel phase, the client is able to send any authorized message (computed using its binding state) to the authenticator, which verifies it using its own binding state. Note that the final established access channel is *unidirectional*, i.e., it only guarantees authorized access from the client to the authenticator but not the other way.

Our model captures the security of the access channels between clients and authenticators. The particular implementation of CTAP2 operates as follows. In the binding phase, the authenticator privately sends its associated secret called pinToken (generated upon power-up) to the trusted client and the pinToken is then stored on the client as the binding state. Later, in the access channel phase, that binding state is used by the bound client to authenticate messages sent to the authenticator. We note that, by the CTAP2 design, each authenticator is associated with a *single* pinToken per power-up, so multiple clients establish multiple access channels with the same authenticator using the *same* pinToken. This limits the security of CTAP2 access channels: for a particular channel from a client to an authenticator to be secure (i.e., no attacker can forge messages sent over that channel), *none* of the clients bound to the same authenticator during the same power-up can be compromised.

Motivated by the above discussion, we distinguish between unforgeability (UF) and strong unforgeability (SUF) for PACA protocols. The former corresponds to the weak level of security discussed above. The latter, captures *strong* fine-grained security where the attacker can compromise any clients except those involved in the access channels for which we claim security. As we explain later (Sect. 6), SUF also covers certain *forward secrecy* guarantees for authentication. For both notions, we consider a powerful attacker that can manipulate the communication between parties, compromise clients (that are not bound to the target authenticator) to reveal the binding states, and corrupt users (that did not set up the target authenticator) to learn their secret PINs.

Even with the stronger trust assumption (made in UF) on the bound clients, we are unable to prove that CTAP2 realizes the expected security model: we describe an attack that exploits the fact that CTAP2 uses unauthenticated Diffie-Hellman. Since it is important to understand the limits of the protocol, we consider a further refinement of the security models which makes stronger trust assumptions on the binding phase of the protocol. Specifically, in the *trusted binding* setting the attacker cannot launch active attacks against the client during the binding phase, but it may try to do so against the authenticator, i.e., it cannot launch man-in-the-middle (MITM) attacks but it may try to impersonate the client to the authenticator. We write UF-t and SUF-t for the security levels which consider trusted binding and the distinct security goals outlined above. In summary we propose four notions: by definition SUF is the strongest security notion and UF-t is the weakest one. Interestingly, UF and SUF-t are *incomparable* as established by our separation result discussed in Sect. 7 and Sect. 8. Based on our security model, we prove that CTAP2 achieves the weakest UF-t security and show that it is not secure regarding the three stronger notions. Finally, we identify a series of design flaws of CTAP2 and provide suggestions for improvement.

Improving CTAP2 Security. CTAP2 cannot achieve UF security because in the binding phase it uses unauthenticated Diffie-Hellman key exchange which is vulnerable to MITM attacks. This observation suggests a change to the protocol which leads to stronger security. Specifically, we propose a generic sPACA protocol (for strong PACA), which replaces the use of unauthenticated Diffie-Hellman in the binding phase with a *password-authenticated key exchange (PAKE)* protocol. Recall that PAKE takes as input a common password and outputs the same random session key for both parties. The key observation is that the client and the authenticator share a value (derived from the user PIN) which can be viewed as a password. By running PAKE with this password as input, the client and the authenticator obtain a strong key which can be used as the binding state to build the access channel. Since each execution of the PAKE (with different clients) results in a fresh independent key, we can prove that sPACA is a SUF-secure PACA protocol. Furthermore, we compare the performance of CTAP2 and sPACA (with proper PAKE instantiations). The results show that our sPACA protocol is also more efficient, so it should be considered for adoption.

Composed Security of CTAP2 and WebAuthn. Finally, towards our main goal of the analysis of full FIDO2 (by full FIDO2 we mean the envisioned usage of the two protocols), we study the composition of PlA and PACA protocols (cf. Sect. 9). The composed protocol, which we simply call PlA+PACA, is defined naturally for an authenticator, user, client, and server. The composition, and the intuition that underlies its security, is as follows. Using PACA, the user (via a client) sets a PIN for the authenticator. This means that only clients that obtain the PIN from the user can "bind" to the authenticator and issue commands that it will accept. In other words, PACA establishes the access channel from the bound client to the authenticator. Then, the challenge-response protocols of PlA run between the server and the authenticator, via a PACA-bound client. The server-side guarantees of PlA are preserved, but now the authenticator can control client access to its credentials using PACA; this composition result is intuitive and easy to prove given our modular formalization.

Interestingly, we formalize an even stronger property that shows that FIDO2 gives end-to-end mutual authentication guarantees between the server and the authenticator when clients and servers are connected by an authenticated server-to-client channel (e.g., a TLS connection). The mutual authentication guarantees extend the PlA guarantees: authenticator, client, and server must all be using the same registration context for authentication to succeed. We note that Transport Layer Security (TLS) provides a server-to-client authenticated channel, and hence this guarantee applies to the typical usage of FIDO2 over TLS. Our results apply to WebAuthn+CTAP2 (under a UF-t adversarial model) and WebAuthn+sPACA (under a SUF adversarial model).

We conclude with an analysis of the role of user gestures in FIDO2. We first show that SUF security offered by sPACA allows the user, equipped with an authenticator that can display a simple session identifier, to detect and prevent attacks from malware that may compromise the states of PACA clients previously bound to the authenticator. (This is not possible for the current version of CTAP2.) We also show how simple gestures can allow a human user to keep track of which server identity is being used in PlA sessions.

Summary. Our analyses clarify the security guarantees FIDO2 should provide for the various parties involved in the most common usage scenario where: 1) the user owns a simple hardware token that is capable of accepting push-button gestures and, optionally, to display a session identifier code (akin to bluetooth pairing codes); 2) the user configures the token with a PIN using a trusted machine; 3) the user connects/disconnects the token on multiple machines, some trusted, some untrusted, and uses it to authenticated to multiple servers.

In all these interactions, the server is assured that during authentication it can recognize if the same token was used to register a key, and that this token was bound to the client it is talking to since the last power-up (this implies entering the correct PIN *recently*). This guarantee assumes that the client is not corrupted (i.e., the browser window where the user entered the PIN is isolated from malicious code and can run the CTAP2 protocol correctly) and that an active attack against the client via the CTAP2 API to guess the user entered PIN is detected (we know this is the case on the token side, as CTAP2 defines a blocking countermeasure).

Assuming a server-to-client authenticated channel, the user is assured that while it is in possession of the PIN, no one can authenticate on her behalf, except if she provides the PIN to a corrupted browser window. Moreover, the scope of this possible attack is limited to the current power-up period. If we assume that registration was conducted via an honest client, then we know that all authentication sessions with honest clients are placed to the correct server. Finally, if the token is stolen, the attacker still needs to guess the PIN (without locking the token) in order to impersonate the user.

With our proposed modifications, FIDO2 will meet this level of security. Without them, these guarantees will only hold assuming weaker client corruption capabilities and more importantly, the attacker cannot perform active man-in-the-middle attacks during all binding sessions, which may be unrealistic.

2   Preliminaries

In the full version of this paper [6], we recall the definitions of pseudorandom functions (PRFs), collision-resistant hash function families, message authentication codes (MACs), signature schemes, the computational Diffie-Hellman (CDH) problem and strong CDH (sCDH) problem, as well as the corresponding advantage measures $\mathbf{Adv}^{\mathsf{prf}}$, $\mathbf{Adv}^{\mathsf{coll}}$, $\mathbf{Adv}^{\mathsf{euf\text{-}cma}}$, $\mathbf{Adv}^{\mathsf{euf\text{-}cma}}$, $\mathbf{Adv}^{\mathsf{cdh}}$, $\mathbf{Adv}^{\mathsf{scdh}}$. There we also recall the syntax for PAKE and its security of perfect forward secrecy and explicit authentication.

3   Execution Model

The protocols we consider involve four disjoint sets of parties. Formally, the set of parties $\mathcal{P}$ is partitioned into four disjoint sets of users $\mathcal{U}$, authenticators (or tokens for short) $\mathcal{T}$, clients $\mathcal{C}$, and servers $\mathcal{S}$. Each party has a well-defined and non-ambiguous identifier, which one can think of as being represented as an integer; we typically use P, U, T, C, S for identifiers bound to a party in a security experiment and id for the case where an identifier is provided as an input in the protocol syntax.

For simplicity, we do not consider certificates or certificate checks but assume the public key associated with a party is supported by a *public key infrastructure*

(PKI) and hence certified and bound to the party's identity. This issue arises explicitly only for attestation public keys bound to authenticators in Sect. 4.

The possible communication channels are represented as double-headed arrows in Fig. 1. In FIDO2, the client is a browser and the user-client channel is the browser window, which keeps no long-term state. The authenticator is a hardware token or mobile phone that is connected to the browser via an untrusted link that includes the operating system, some authenticator-specific middleware, and a physical communication channel that connects the authenticator to the machine hosting the browser. The authenticator exposes a simple interface to the user that allows it to perform a "gesture", confirming some action; ideally the authenticator should also be able to display information to the user (this is natural when using a mobile phone as an authenticator but not so common in USB tokens or smartcards). Following the intuitive definitions of *human-compatible communications* by Boldyreva *et al.* [12], we require that messages sent to the user be *human-readable* and those sent by the user be *human-writable.*[4] The user PIN needs to be *human-memorizable*.

We assume authenticators have a good source of random bits and keep volatile and static (or long-term) storage. Volatile storage is erased every time the device goes through a power-down/power-up cycle, which we call a *reboot*. Static storage is assumed to be initialized using a procedure carried out under special setup trust assumptions; in the case of this paper we will consider the setup procedures to generate an attestation key pair for the authenticator and to configure a user PIN, i.e., to "embed" the PIN in the authenticator.

Trust Model. For each of the protocols we analyze in the paper we specify a trust model, which justifies our proposed security models. Here we state the trust assumptions that are always made throughout the paper. First, human communications (①②) are authenticated and private. This in practice captures the direct human-machine interaction between the human user and the authenticator device or the client terminal, which involves physical senses and contact that we assume cannot be eavesdropped or interrupted by an attacker. Second, client-authenticator communications (③) are not protected, i.e., neither authenticated nor private. Finally, authenticators are assumed to be tamper-proof, so our models will not consider corruption of their internal state.

Modeling Users and Their Gestures. We do not include in our protocol syntaxes and security models explicit state keeping and message passing for human users, i.e., there are no *session oracles* for users in the security experiments. We shortly explain why this is the case. The role of the user in these protocols is to a) first check that the client is operating on correct inputs, e.g., by looking at the browser window to see if the correct server identity is being used; b) possibly (if the token has the capability to display information) check that the token and client are operating on consistent inputs; and c) finally confirm to the token that this is the case. Therefore, the user itself plays the role of an out-of-band secure

---

[4] We regard understandable information displayed on a machine as human-readable and typing in a PIN or rebooting an authenticator as human-writable.

channel via which the consistency of information exchanged between the client and the token can be validated.

We model this with a public gesture predicate G that captures the semantics of the user's decision. Intuitively, the user decision $d \in \{0, 1\}$ is given by $d = G(x, y)$, where x and y respectively represent the information conveyed to the user by the client and the token in step b) above. Note that x, y may not be input by the user. Tokens with different user interface capabilities give rise to different classes of gesture predicates. For example, if a user can observe a server domain name id on the token display before pressing a button, then we can define the gesture of checking that the token displayed an identifier id that matches the one displayed by the client id* as $G(\text{id}^*, \text{id}) = (\text{id}^* \stackrel{?}{=} \text{id})$.

User actions are hardwired into the security experiments as direct inputs to either a client or a token, which is justified by our assumption that users interact with these entities via fully secure channels. We stress that here G is a modeling tool, which captures the sequence of interactions a), b), c) above. Providing a gesture means physical possession of the token, so an attacker controlling only some part of the client machine (e.g., malware) is *not* able to provide a gesture. Moreover, requiring a gesture from the user implies that the user can detect when some action is requested from the token.

4   Passwordless Authentication

We start our analysis with the simpler FIDO2 component protocol, WebAuthn. In order to analyze the authentication security of WebAuthn we first define the syntax and security model for *passwordless authentication (PlA)* protocols.

4.1   Protocol Syntax

A PlA protocol is an interactive protocol among three parties: a token (representing a user), a client, and a server. The token is associated with an attestation public key that is pre-registered to the server. The protocol defines two types of interactions: registration and authentication. In registration the server requests the token to register some initial authentication parameters. If this succeeds, the server can later recognize the same token using a challenge-response protocol.

The possible communication channels are as shown in Fig. 1, but we do not include the user. Servers are accessible to clients via a communication channel that models Internet communications.

The state of token T, denoted by st_T, is partitioned into the following (static) components: i) an attestation key pair (vk_T, ak_T) and ii) a set of registration contexts $\text{st}_T.\text{rct}$. A server S also keeps its registration contexts $\text{st}_S.\text{rcs}$. Clients do not keep long-term state.[5] All states are initialized to the empty string ε.

A PlA protocol consists of the following algorithms and subprotocols:

---

[5] Some two-factor protocols may have a "trust this computer" feature that requires the client to store some long-term states. This is not included in our model as to the best of our knowledge FIDO2 does not have that feature.

Key Generation: This algorithm, denoted by Kg, is executed *at most once* for each authenticator; it generates an attestation key pair (vk, ak).

Register: This subprotocol is executed among a token, a client, and a server. The token inputs its attestation secret key ak_T; the client inputs an intended server identity $\hat{\mathsf{id}}_S$; and the server inputs its identity id_S (e.g., a server domain name) and the token's attestation public key vk_T. At the end of the subprotocol, each party that successfully terminates obtains a new registration context, and sets its *session identifier* that can be used to uniquely name a (registration or authentication) session. Note that the token may successfully complete the subprotocol while the server may fail to, in the same run.

Authenticate: This subprotocol is executed between a token, a client, and a server. The token inputs its registration contexts; the client inputs an intended server identity $\hat{\mathsf{id}}_S$; and the server inputs its identity id_S and registration contexts. At the end of the subprotocol, the server *accepts* or *rejects*. Each party on success sets its session identifier and updates the registration contexts.

Restricted class of protocols. For both Register and Authenticate, we focus on 2-pass challenge-response protocols with the following structure:

- Server-side computation is split into four procedures: rchallenge and rcheck for registration, achallenge and acheck for authentication. The challenge algorithms are probabilistic, which take the server's input to the Register or Authenticate subprotocol and return a challenge. The check algorithms get the same input, the challenge, and a response. rcheck outputs the updated registration contexts rcs that are later input by acheck; acheck outputs a bit b (1 for accept and 0 for reject) and updates rcs.
- Client-side computation is modeled as two deterministic functions rcommand and acommand that capture possible checks and translations performed by the client before sending the challenges to the token. These algorithms output commands denoted by M_r, M_a respectively, which they generate from the input intended server identity and the challenge. The client may append some information about the challenge to the token's response before sending it to the server, which is an easy step that we do not model explicitly.
- Token-side computation is modeled as two probabilistic algorithms rresponse and aresponse that, on input a command and the token's input to the Register or Authenticate subprotocol, generate a response and update the registration contexts rct. In particular, rresponse outputs the updated registration contexts rct that are later input by aresponse; aresponse may also update rct.

Correctness. Correctness imposes that for any server identities $\mathsf{id}_S, \hat{\mathsf{id}}_S, \bar{\mathsf{id}}_S$ the following probability is 1:

$$\Pr\left[\;b = ((\mathsf{id}_S \overset{?}{=} \hat{\mathsf{id}}_S) \wedge (\mathsf{id}_S \overset{?}{=} \bar{\mathsf{id}}_S))\;\middle|\; \begin{aligned} &(ak, vk) \overset{\$}{\leftarrow} \mathsf{Kg}(\,)\\ &c_r \overset{\$}{\leftarrow} \mathsf{rchallenge}(\mathsf{id}_S, vk)\\ &M_r \leftarrow \mathsf{rcommand}(\hat{\mathsf{id}}_S, c_r)\\ &(R_r, \mathsf{rct}) \overset{\$}{\leftarrow} \mathsf{rresponse}(ak, M_r)\\ &\mathsf{rcs} \leftarrow \mathsf{rcheck}(\mathsf{id}_S, vk, c_r, R_r)\\ &c_a \overset{\$}{\leftarrow} \mathsf{achallenge}(\mathsf{id}_S, \mathsf{rcs})\\ &M_a \leftarrow \mathsf{acommand}(\bar{\mathsf{id}}_S, c_a)\\ &(R_a, \mathsf{rct}) \overset{\$}{\leftarrow} \mathsf{aresponse}(\mathsf{rct}, M_a)\\ &(b, \mathsf{rcs}) \leftarrow \mathsf{acheck}(\mathsf{id}_S, \mathsf{rcs}, c_a, R_a) \end{aligned}\right]$$

Intuitively, correctness requires that the server always accepts an authentication that is consistent with a prior registration, if and only if the client's input intended server identities match the server identity received from the server. Note that the latter check is performed by the client rather than the human user. It helps to prevent a so-called server-in-the-middle attack identified in [33].

4.2   Security Model

Trust Model. Before defining security we clarify that there are no security assumptions on the communication channels shown in Fig. 1. Again, authenticators are assumed to be tamper-proof, so the model will not consider corruption of their internal state. (Note that clients and servers keep *no* secret state.) We assume the key generation stage, where the attestation key pair is created and installed in the token, is either carried out within the token itself, or performed in a trusted context that leaks nothing about the attestation secret key.

Session Oracles. As with the Bellare-Rogaway model [10], to capture multiple sequential and parallel PlA executions (or instances), we associate each party $P \in \mathcal{T} \cup \mathcal{S}$ with a set of session oracles $\{\pi_P^{i,j}\}_{i,j}$, which models two types of PlA instances corresponding to registration and authentication. We omit session oracles for clients, since all they do can be performed by the adversary. For servers and tokens, session oracles are structured as follows: $\pi_P^{i,0}$ refers to the i-th registration instance of P, whereas $\pi_P^{i,j}$ for $j \geq 1$ refers to the j-th authentication instance of P associated with $\pi_P^{i,0}$ after this registration completed. A party's static storage is maintained by the security experiment and shared among all of its session oracles.

Security Experiment. The security experiment is run between a challenger and an adversary $\mathcal{A}$. At the beginning of the experiment, the challenger runs $(ak_T, vk_T) \overset{\$}{\leftarrow} \mathsf{Kg}(\,)$ for all $T \in \mathcal{T}$ to generate their attestation key pairs and assign unique identities $\{\mathsf{id}_S\}_{S \in \mathcal{S}}$ to all servers. The challenger also manages the attestation public keys $\{vk_T\}_{T \in \mathcal{T}}$ and provides them to the server oracles as needed. The adversary $\mathcal{A}$ is given all attestation public keys and server identities and then allowed to interact with session oracles via the following queries:

- Start($\pi_S^{i,j}$). The challenger instructs a specified server oracle $\pi_S^{i,j}$ to execute rchallenge (if $j = 0$) or achallenge (if $j > 0$) to start the Register or Authenticate subprotocol and generate a challenge c, which is given to $\mathcal{A}$.
- Challenge($\pi_T^{i,j}, M$). The challenger delivers a specified command M to a specified token oracle $\pi_T^{i,j}$, which processes the command using rresponse (if $j = 0$) or aresponse (if $j > 0$) and returns the response to $\mathcal{A}$.
- Complete($\pi_S^{i,j}, T, R$). The challenger delivers a specified token response R to a specified server oracle $\pi_S^{i,j}$, which processes the response using rcheck and vk_T (if $j = 0$) or acheck (if $j > 0$) and returns the result to $\mathcal{A}$.

We assume without loss of generality that each query is only called once for each instance and allow the adversary to get the full state of the server via Start and Complete queries.

Partners. We follow the seminal work by Bellare *et al.* [9] to define partnership via *session identifiers*. A server registration oracle $\pi_S^{i,0}$ and a token registration oracle $\pi_T^{k,0}$ are each other's *partner* if they agree on the same session identifier, which indicates a "shared view" that must be defined by the analyzed protocol and must be the same for both parties, usually as a function of the communication trace. A server authentication oracle $\pi_S^{i,j}$ ($j > 0$) and a token authentication oracle $\pi_T^{k,l}$ ($l > 0$) are each other's *partner* if: i) they agree on the session identifier and ii) $\pi_S^{i,0}$ and $\pi_T^{k,0}$ are each other's partner.

We note that a crucial aspect of this definition is that the authentication session partnership holds only if the token and the server are also partnered for the associated registration sessions: a credential registered in a server should not be used to authenticate a token using another credential.

Advantage Measure. Let Π be a PlA protocol. We define the passwordless authentication advantage $\mathbf{Adv}_\Pi^{\mathsf{pla}}(\mathcal{A})$ as the probability that a server oracle accepts but it is not uniquely partnered with a token oracle. In other words, a secure PlA protocol guarantees that, if a server oracle accepts, then there exists a unique token oracle that has derived the same session identifier, and no other server oracle has derived the same session identifier.

5   The W3C Web Authentication Protocol

In this section, we present the cryptographic core of W3C's Web Authentication (WebAuthn) protocol [15] of FIDO2 and analyze its security.

Protocol Description. We show the core cryptographic operations of WebAuthn in Fig. 3 in accordance with PlA syntax.[6] For WebAuthn, a server identity is an effective domain (e.g., a hostname) of the server URL. The attestation key pair is generated by the key generation algorithm Kg of a signature scheme Sig = (Kg, Sign, Ver). (Note that WebAuthn supports the RSASSA-PKCS1-v1_5 and RSASSA-PSS signature schemes [30].) In Fig. 3, we use H to denote the

---

[6] We do not include the WebAuthn explicit reference to user interaction/gestures at this point, as this will be later handled by our PACA protocol.

Authenticator T (ak_T, vk_T)		Client C (id$_S$)		Server S (id$_S$, vk_T)
Register:				
				rchallenge:
				$rs \xleftarrow{\$} \{0,1\}^{\geq \lambda}$, $uid \xleftarrow{\$} \{0,1\}^{4\lambda}$
		rcommand:	$\xleftarrow{\quad cc \quad}$	$cc \leftarrow (\text{id}_S, uid, rs)$
		$(\text{id}, uid, r) \leftarrow cc$		
rresponse:	$\xleftarrow{\quad M_r \quad}$	if id $\neq$ id$_S$: halt		
$(\text{id}_S, uid, h_r) \leftarrow M_r$		$M_r \leftarrow (\text{id}_S, uid, \mathsf{H}(r))$		
$(pk, sk) \xleftarrow{\$} \mathsf{Sig.Kg}()$				
$n \leftarrow 0, cid \xleftarrow{\$} \{0,1\}^{\geq \lambda}$				
$ad \leftarrow (\mathsf{H}(\text{id}_S), n, cid, pk)$		$R_r = (ad, \sigma, r)$		rcheck:
$\sigma \leftarrow \mathsf{Sig.Sign}(ak_T, (ad, h_r))$		$\xrightarrow{\hspace{3cm}}$		$(h, n, cid, pk) \leftarrow ad$
				halt if $r \neq rs$ or $h \neq \mathsf{H}(\text{id}_S)$ or $n \neq 0$
				or $\mathsf{Sig.Ver}(vk_T, (ad, \mathsf{H}(r)), \sigma) = 0$
rct.insert$((\text{id}_S, uid, cid, sk, n))$				rcs.insert$((uid, cid, pk, n))$
Authenticate:				
				achallenge:
				$rs \xleftarrow{\$} \{0,1\}^{\geq \lambda}$
		acommand:	$\xleftarrow{\quad cr \quad}$	$cr \leftarrow (\text{id}_S, rs)$
		$(\text{id}, r) \leftarrow cr$		
aresponse:	$\xleftarrow{\quad M_a \quad}$	if id $\neq$ id$_S$: halt		
$(\text{id}_S, h_r) \leftarrow M_a$		$M_a \leftarrow (\text{id}_S, \mathsf{H}(r))$		
$(uid, cid, sk, n) \leftarrow$ rct.get(id$_S$)				
$n \leftarrow n + 1, ad \leftarrow (\mathsf{H}(\text{id}_S), n)$		$R_a = (cid, ad, \sigma, uid, r)$		acheck:
$\sigma \xleftarrow{\$} \mathsf{Sig.Sign}(sk, (ad, h_r))$		$\xrightarrow{\hspace{3cm}}$		$(uid', pk, n) \leftarrow$ rcs.get(cid)
				$(h, n_t) \leftarrow ad$
				reject if $uid \neq uid'$ or $r \neq rs$
				or $h \neq \mathsf{H}(\text{id}_S)$ or $n_t \leq n$
				or $\mathsf{Sig.Ver}(pk, (ad, \mathsf{H}(r)), \sigma) = 0$
rct.insert$((\text{id}_S, uid, cid, sk, n))$				accept; rcs.insert$((uid, cid, pk, n_t))$

Fig. 3. The WebAuthn protocol

SHA-256 hash function and λ to denote the default parameter 128 (in order to accommodate potential parameter changes). WebAuthn supports two types of operations: Registeration and Authentication (cf. Figure 1 and Fig. 2 in [15]), respectively corresponding to the PlA Register and Authenticate subprotocols. In the following description, we assume each token is registered at most once for a server; this is without loss of generality since otherwise one can treat the one token as several tokens sharing the same attestation key pair.

- In registration, the server generates a random string rs of length at least $\lambda = 128$ bits and a random 512-bit user id uid, forms a challenge cc with rs, uid and its identity id$_S$, and then sends it to the client. Then, the client checks if the received server identity matches its input (i.e., the intended server), then passes the received challenge (where the random string is hashed) to the token. The token generates a key pair (pk, sk) with Sig.Kg, sets the signature counter n to 0,[7] and samples a credential id cid of length at least $\lambda = 128$ bits; it then computes an attestation signature (on $\mathsf{H}(\text{id}_S), n, cid, pk$ and the random string hash h_r) and sends the signed (public) credential and signature to the client as a response; the token also inserts the generated credential into its registration contexts. Upon receiving the response, the server checks

---

[7] The signature counter is mainly used to detect cloned tokens, but it also helps in preventing replay attacks (if such attacks are possible).

the validity of the attestation signature and inserts the credential into its registration contexts.

- In authentication, the server also generates a random string rs, but no uid is sampled; it then forms a challenge cr with rs and its identity id_S, and sends it to the client. Then, the client checks if the received id_S matches its input and passes the challenge (where the random string is hashed) to the token. The token retrieves the credential associated with the authenticating server id_S from its registration contexts, increments the signature counter n, computes an authentication signature (on $\mathsf{H}(\mathsf{id}_S), n$ and the random string hash h_r), and sends it to the client together with $\mathsf{H}(\mathsf{id}_S), n$ and the retrieved credential id cid and user id uid; the token also updates the credential with the new signature counter. Upon receiving the response, the server retrieves the credential associated with the credential id cid and checks the validity of the signature counter and the signature; if all checks pass, it accepts and updates the credential with the new signature counter.

It is straightforward to check that WebAuthn is a correct PlA protocol.

WebAuthn Analysis. The following theorem (proved in the full version [6]) assesses PlA security of WebAuthn uses $(ad, \mathsf{H}(r))$ as the session identifier.

Theorem 1. *For any efficient adversary $\mathcal{A}$ that makes at most q_S queries to* Start *and q_C queries to* Challenge, *there exist efficient adversaries $\mathcal{B}, \mathcal{C}$ such that (recall $\lambda = 128$):*

$$\mathbf{Adv}^{\mathsf{pla}}_{\mathrm{WebAuthn}}(\mathcal{A}) \leq \mathbf{Adv}^{\mathsf{coll}}_{\mathsf{H}}(\mathcal{B}) + q_S \mathbf{Adv}^{\mathsf{euf\text{-}cma}}_{\mathsf{Sig}}(\mathcal{C}) + (q_S^2 + q_C^2) \cdot 2^{-\lambda}.$$

The security guarantees for the WebAuthn instantiations follow from the results proving RSASSA-PKCS1-v1_5 and RSASSA-PSS to be EUF-CMA in the random oracle model under the RSA assumption [11,28] and the assumption that SHA-256 is collision-resistant.

6   PIN-Based Access Control for Authenticators

In this section, we define the syntax and security model for *PIN-based access control for authenticators* (PACA) protocols. The goal of the protocol is to ensure that after PIN setup and possibly an arbitrary number of authenticator reboots, the user can employ the client to issue PIN-authorized commands to the token, which the token can use for access control, e.g., to unlock built-in functionalities that answer client commands.

6.1   Protocol Syntax

A PACA protocol is an interactive protocol involving a human user, an authenticator (or token for short), and a client. The state of token T, denoted by st_T, consists of static storage $\mathsf{st}_T.\mathsf{ss}$ that remains intact across reboots and volatile storage $st_T.vs$ that gets reset after each reboot. $st_T.ss$ is comprised of: i) a private secret $st_T.s$ and ii) a public retries counter $st_T.n$, where the latter is used to limit the maximum number of consecutive failed active attacks (e.g., PIN guessing attempts) against the token. $st_T.vs$ consists of: i) power-up state $st_T.ps$ and ii) binding states $st_T.bs_i$ (together denoted by $st_T.bs$). A client C may also keep binding states, denoted by $bs_{C,j}$. All states are initialized to the empty string ε.

A PACA protocol is associated with an arbitrary public gesture predicate G and consists of the following algorithms and subprotocols, all of which can be executed a number of times, except if stated otherwise:

Reboot: This algorithm represents a power-down/power-up cycle and it is executed by the authenticator *with mandatory user interaction*. We use $st_T.vs \xleftarrow{\$} reboot(st_T.ss)$ to denote the execution of this algorithm, which inputs its static storage and resets all *volatile* storage. Note that one should always run this algorithm to power up the token at the beginning of PACA execution.

Setup: This subprotocol is executed *at most once* for each authenticator. The user inputs a PIN through the client and the token inputs its volatile storage. In the end, the token sets up its *static* storage and the client (and through it the user) gets an indication of whether the subprotocol completed successfully.

Bind: This subprotocol is executed by the three parties to establish an access channel over which commands can be issued. The user inputs its PIN through the client, whereas the token inputs its static storage and power-up state. At the end of the subprotocol, each of the token and client that successfully terminates gets a (volatile) binding state and sets the session identifier. In either case (success or not), the token may update its static retries counter.[8] We assume the client always initiates this subprotocol once it gets the PIN from the user.

Authorize: This algorithm allows a client to generate authorized commands for the token. The client inputs a binding state $bs_{C,j}$ and a command M. We denote $(M, t) \xleftarrow{\$} authorize(bs_{C,j}, M)$ as the generation of an authorized command.

Validate: This algorithm allows a token to verify authorized commands sent by a client with respect to a user decision (where the human user inputs the public gesture predicate G). The token inputs a binding state $st_T.bs_i$, an authorized command (M, t), and a user decision $d = G(x, y)$. We denote $b \leftarrow validate(st_T.bs_i, (M, t), d)$ as the validation performed by the token to obtain an accept or reject indication.

Correctness. For an arbitrary public predicate G, we consider any token T and any sequence of PACA subprotocol executions that includes the following (which may not be consecutive): i) a Reboot of T; ii) a successful Setup using PIN

---

[8] When such an update is possible, the natural assumption often made in cryptography requires that incoming messages are processed in an atomic way by the token, which avoids concurrency issues. Note that Bind executions could still be concurrent.

fixing $\mathsf{st}_T.\mathsf{ss}$ via some client; iii) a Bind with PIN creating token-side binding state $\mathsf{st}_T.\mathsf{bs}_i$ and client-side binding state $\mathsf{bs}_{C,j}$ at a client C; iv) authorization of command M by C as $(M,t) \xleftarrow{\$} \mathsf{authorize}(\mathsf{bs}_{C,j}, M)$; and v) validation by T as $b \leftarrow \mathsf{validate}(\mathsf{st}_T.\mathsf{bs}_i, (M,t), d)$. If no Reboot of T is executed after iii), then correctness requires that $b = 1$ if and only if $\mathsf{G}(x,y) = 1$ (i.e., $d = 1$) holds.

Remark. The above PACA syntax may seem overly complex but it is actually difficult (if not impossible) to decompose. First, Setup and Bind share the same power-up state generated by Reboot so cannot be separated into two independent procedures. Then, although Authorize and Validate together can independently model an access channel, detaching them from PACA makes it difficult to define security in a general way: Bind may not establish random symmetric keys; it could, for instance, output asymmetric key pairs.

6.2   Security Model

Trust Model. Before defining our security model, we first state the assumed security properties for the involved communication channels, as shown in Fig. 1 excluding the client-server channel. We assume that Setup is carried out over an authenticated channel where the adversary can only eavesdrop communications between the client and authenticator; this is a necessary assumption, as there are no pre-established authentication parameters between the parties.

Session Oracles. To capture multiple sequential and parallel PACA executions, each party $P \in \mathcal{T} \cup \mathcal{C}$ is associated with a set of session oracles $\{\pi_P^i\}_i$, where π_P^i models the i-th PACA instance of P. For clients, session oracles are totally independent from each other and they are assumed to be available throughout the protocol execution. For tokens, the static storage and power-up state are maintained by the security experiment and shared by all oracles of the same token. Token oracles keep only binding states (if any). If a token is rebooted, its binding states got reset and hence become *invalid*, i.e., those states will be no longer accessible to anyone including the adversary.

Security Experiment. The security experiment is executed between a challenger and an adversary $\mathcal{A}$. At the beginning of the experiment, the challenger fixes an arbitrary distribution $\mathscr{D}$ over a PIN dictionary $\mathcal{PIN}$ associated with PACA; it then samples independent user PINs according to $\mathscr{D}$, denoted by $\langle\mathsf{pin}_U \xleftarrow{\mathscr{D}} \mathcal{PIN}\rangle_{U \in \mathcal{U}}$. Without loss of generality, we assume each user holds only one PIN. The challenger also initializes states of all oracles to the empty string. Then, $\mathcal{A}$ is allowed to interact with the challenger via the following queries:

- Reboot(T). The challenger runs Reboot for token T, marking all previously used instances π_T^i (if any) as *invalid*[9] and setting $\mathsf{st}_T.\mathsf{vs} \xleftarrow{\$} \mathsf{reboot}(\mathsf{st}_T.\mathsf{ss})$.
- Setup(π_T^i, π_C^j, U). The challenger inputs pin_U through π_C^j and runs Setup between π_T^i and π_C^j; it returns the trace of communications to $\mathcal{A}$. After this

---

[9] All queries are ignored if they refer to an oracle π_P^i marked as invalid.

query, T is *set up*, i.e., $\mathsf{st}_T.\mathsf{ss}$ is set and available, for the rest of the experiment. Oracles created in this query, i.e., π_T^i and π_C^j, must never have been used before and are always marked *invalid* after Setup completion.[10]

- Execute(π_T^i, π_C^j). The challenger runs Bind between π_T^i and π_C^j using the same pin_U that set up T; it returns the trace of communications to $\mathcal{A}$. This query allows the adversary to access honest Bind executions in which it can only take passive actions, i.e., eavesdropping. The resulting binding states on both sides are kept as $\mathsf{st}_T.\mathsf{bs}_i$ and $\mathsf{bs}_{C,j}$ respectively.

- Connect(T, π_C^j). The challenger asks π_C^j to initiate the Bind subprotocol with T using the same pin_U that set up T; it returns the first message sent by π_C^j to $\mathcal{A}$. Note that no client oracles can be created for active attacks if Connect queries are disallowed, since we assume the client is the initiator of Bind. This query allows the adversary to launch an active attack against a client oracle.

- Send(π_P^i, m). The challenger delivers m to π_P^i and returns its response (if any) to $\mathcal{A}$. If π_P^i completes the Bind subprotocol, then the binding state is kept as $\mathsf{st}_T.\mathsf{bs}_i$ for a token oracle and as $\mathsf{bs}_{C,i}$ for a client oracle. This query allows the adversary to launch an active attack against a token oracle or completing an active attack against a client oracle.

- Authorize(π_C^j, M). The challenger asks π_C^j to authorize command M; it returns the authorized command $(M, t) \xleftarrow{\$} \mathsf{authorize}(\mathsf{bs}_{C,j}, M)$.

- Validate($\pi_T^i, (M, t)$). The challenger asks π_T^i (that received a user decision d) to validate (M, t); it returns the validation result $b \leftarrow \mathsf{validate}(\mathsf{st}_T.\mathsf{bs}_i, (M, t), d)$.

- Compromise(π_C^j). The challenger returns $\mathsf{bs}_{C,j}$ and marks π_C^i as *compromised*.

- Corrupt(U). The challenger returns pin_U and marks pin_U as *corrupted*.

Partners. We say a token oracle π_T^i and a client oracle π_C^j in binding sessions are each other's *partner* if they have both completed their Bind executions and agree on the same session identifier. As with our PlA model, session identifiers must be properly defined by the analyzed protocol. Moreover, we also say π_C^j is T's *partner* (and hence T may have multiple partners). Note that, as mentioned before, if a token is rebooted then all of its existing session oracles (if any) are invalidated. A *valid* partner refers to a valid session oracle.

Security Goals. We define 4 levels of security for a PACA protocol Π. All advantage measures define PAKE-like security: the adversary's winning probability should be negligibly larger than that of the trivial attack of guessing the user PIN (known as *online dictionary attacks* with more details in the full version [6]).

Unforgeability (UF). We define $\mathbf{Adv}_\Pi^{\mathsf{uf}}(\mathcal{A})$ as the probability that there exists a token oracle π_T^i that accepts an authorized command (M, t) for gesture G and at least one of the following conditions does *not* hold:

---

[10] Session oracles used for Setup are separated since they may cause ambiguity in defining session identifiers for binding sessions.

1) G approves M, i.e., $\mathsf{G}(x,y) = 1$;
2) (M,t) was output by one of T's valid partners π_C^j.

The adversary must be able to trigger this event without: i) corrupting pin_U that was used to set up T, before π_T^i accepted (M,t); or ii) compromising any of T's partners created after T's last reboot and before π_T^i accepted (M,t).

The above captures the attacks where the attacker successfully makes a token accept a forged command, without corrupting the user PIN used to set up the token or compromising any of the token's partners. In other words, a UF-secure PACA protocol protects the token from unauthorized access even if it is stolen and possessed by an attacker. Nevertheless, UF considers only weak security for access channels, i.e., compromising one channel could result in compromising all channels (with respect to the same token after its last reboot).

Unforgeability with Trusted Binding (UF-t). We define $\mathbf{Adv}_{\Pi}^{\mathsf{uf\text{-}t}}(\mathcal{A})$ the same as $\mathbf{Adv}_{\Pi}^{\mathsf{uf}}(\mathcal{A})$ except that the adversary is *not* allowed to make Connect queries.

As mentioned before, the attacker is now forbidden to launch active attacks against clients (that input user PINs) during binding; it can still, however, perform active attacks against tokens. This restriction captures the minimum requirement for proving the security of CTAP2 (using our model), which is the main reason we define UF-t. Clearly, UF security implies UF-t security.

Strong Unforgeability (SUF). We define $\mathbf{Adv}_{\Pi}^{\mathsf{suf}}(\mathcal{A})$ as the UF advantage, with one more condition captured:

3) π_T^i and π_C^j are each other's unique valid partner.

More importantly, the adversary considered in this strong notion is allowed to compromise T's partners, provided that it has not compromised π_C^j. It is also allowed to corrupt pin_U used to set up T even before the command is accepted, *as long as π_T^i has set its binding state.*

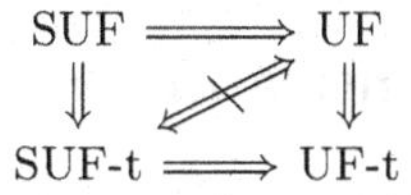

$$\begin{array}{ccc} \text{SUF} & \Longrightarrow & \text{UF} \\ \Downarrow & \diagup\!\!\!\!\!\nearrow & \Downarrow \\ \text{SUF-t} & \Longrightarrow & \text{UF-t} \end{array}$$

Fig. 4. Relations between PACA security notions.

The above captures similar attacks considered in UF but in a strong sense, where the attacker is allowed to compromise the token's partners. This means SUF considers strong security for access channels, i.e., compromising any channel does not affect other channels. It hence guarantees a unique binding between an accepted command and an access channel (created by uniquely partnered token and client oracles running Bind), which explains condition 3). Finally, the attacker is further allowed to corrupt the user PIN *immediately* after the access channel establishment. This guarantees *forward secrecy* for access channels, i.e., once the channel is created its security will no longer be affected by later PIN corruption. Note that SUF security obviously implies UF security.

Strong Unforgeability with Trusted Binding (SUF-t). For completeness we can also define $\mathbf{Adv}_{\Pi}^{\mathsf{suf\text{-}t}}(\mathcal{A})$, where the adversary is *not* allowed to make Connect queries. Again, it is easy to see that SUF security implies SUF-t security.

Relations Between PACA Security Notions. Figure 4 shows the implication relations among our four defined notions. Note that UF and SUF-t do not imply each other, for which we will give separation examples in Sects. 7 and 8.

Improving (S)UF-t Security with User Confirmation. Trusted binding excludes active attacks against the client (during binding), but online dictionary attacks are still possible against the token. Such attacks can be mitigated by requiring user confirmation (e.g., pressing a button) for Bind execution, such that only honest Bind executions will be approved when the token is possessed by an honest user. We argue that the confirmation overhead is quite small for CTAP2-like protocols since the user has to type its PIN into the client anyway; the security gain is meaningful as now *no* online dictionary attacks (that introduce non-negligible adversarial advantage) can happen to unstolen tokens.

A Practical Implication of SUF Security. We note that SUF security has a practical meaning: an accepted command can be traced back to a unique access channel. This means that an authenticator that allows a human user to confirm a session identifier (that determines the channel) for a command can allow a human user to detect rogue commands issued by an adversary (e.g., malware) that compromised one of the token's partners (e.g., browsers).

PACA Security Bounds. In our theorems for PACA security shown later, we fix q_S (i.e., the number of Setup queries) as one adversarial parameter to bound the adversary's success probability of online dictionary attacks (e.g., the first bound term in Theorem 2 and the PAKE advantage term in Theorem 3), while for PAKE security the number of SEND queries q_s is used (see [9] or the full version [6] for example). This is because PACA has a token-side retries counter to limit the total number of failed PIN guessing attempts (across reboots).

7 The Client to Authenticator Protocol V2.0

In this section, we present the cryptographic core of the FIDO Alliance's CTAP2, analyze its security using PACA model, and make suggestions for improvement. Protocol Description. CTAP2's cryptographic core lies in its authenticator API [11] which we show in Fig. 5 in accordance with PACA syntax. One can also refer to its specification (Fig. 1, [1]) for a command-based description.[12] The

---

[11] The rest of CTAP2 does not focus on security but specifies transport-related behaviors like message encoding and transport-specific bindings.

[12] There the command used for accessing the retries counter $\mathsf{st}_T.\mathsf{n}$ is omitted because PACA models it as public state. Commands for PIN resets are also omitted and left for future work, but capturing those is not hard by extending our analysis since CTAP2 changes PIN by simply running the first part of Bind (to establish the encryption key and verify the old PIN) followed by the last part of Setup (to set a new PIN). Without PIN resets, our analysis still captures CTAP2's core security aspects and our PACA model becomes more succinct.

Authenticator T		Client C (pin_U)
Reboot:		
$(a, aG) \stackrel{\$}{\leftarrow} \text{ECKG}_{\mathbb{G},G}(\,)$, $pt \stackrel{\$}{\leftarrow} \{0,1\}^{k\lambda}$, $m \leftarrow 3$		
$\text{st}_T.\text{ps} \leftarrow (a, aG, pt, m)$, $\text{st}_T.\text{bs} \leftarrow \varepsilon$		

Setup:

$$\xleftarrow{\quad \text{cmd} = 2 \quad}$$
$$\xrightarrow{\quad aG \quad} \quad (b, bG) \stackrel{\$}{\leftarrow} \text{ECKG}_{\mathbb{G},G}(\,), \ K \leftarrow \text{H}(baG.x)$$
$$\xleftarrow{\quad \text{cmd} = 3 \quad} \quad c_p \leftarrow \text{CBC}_0.\text{E}(K, \text{pin}_U)$$
$$K \leftarrow \text{H}(abG.x) \qquad \xleftarrow{\quad bG, c_p, \boxed{t_p} \quad} \quad \boxed{t_p \leftarrow \text{HMAC}'(K, c_p)}$$
$\boxed{\text{if } t_p \neq \text{HMAC}'(K, c_p)\text{: halts}}$
$\text{pin}_U \leftarrow \text{CBC}_0.\text{D}(K, c_p)$
if $\text{pin}_U \notin \mathcal{PIN}$: halt
$\text{st}_T.\text{s} \leftarrow \text{H}'(\text{pin}_U)$, $\text{st}_T.\text{n} \leftarrow 8 \qquad \xrightarrow{\quad \text{ok} \quad}$

Bind:

$$\xleftarrow{\quad \text{cmd} = 2 \quad}$$
if $\text{st}_T.\text{n} = 0$: blocks access $\qquad \xrightarrow{\quad aG \quad} \quad (b, bG) \stackrel{\$}{\leftarrow} \text{ECKG}_{\mathbb{G},G}(\,), \ K \leftarrow \text{H}(baG.x)$
$$\xleftarrow{\quad \text{cmd} = 5 \quad} \quad c_{ph} \leftarrow \text{CBC}_0.\text{E}(K, \text{H}'(\text{pin}_U))$$
$K \leftarrow \text{H}(abG.x)$, $\text{st}_T.\text{n} \leftarrow \text{st}_T.\text{n} - 1 \qquad \xleftarrow{\quad bG, c_{ph} \quad}$
if $\text{st}_T.\text{s} \neq \text{CBC}_0.\text{D}(K, c_{ph})$:
$\qquad m \leftarrow m - 1$, $(a, aG) \stackrel{\$}{\leftarrow} \text{ECKG}_{\mathbb{G},G}(\,)$
$\qquad$ halt (if $m = 0$: reboot)
$m \leftarrow 3$, $\text{st}_T.\text{n} \leftarrow 8$
$c_{pt} \leftarrow \text{CBC}_0.\text{E}(K, pt) \qquad \xrightarrow{\quad c_{pt} \quad}$
$\text{st}_T.\text{bs}_i \leftarrow pt \qquad\qquad\qquad\qquad\qquad\qquad\qquad \text{bs}_{C,j} \leftarrow \text{CBC}_0.\text{D}(K, c_{pt})$

Validate: | | **Authorize:**
if $t \neq \text{HMAC}'(\text{st}_T.\text{bs}_i, M)$: $\qquad \xleftarrow{\quad M, t \quad} \qquad t \leftarrow \text{HMAC}'(\text{bs}_{C,j}, M)$
$\qquad m \leftarrow m - 1$, reject
$\qquad$ if $m = 0$: reboot
$m \leftarrow 3$, collects user decision d
accept if $d = 1 \qquad\qquad\qquad \xrightarrow{\quad \text{uv} = 1 \quad}$

Fig. 5. The CTAP2 protocol (and CTAP2* that excludes the boxed contents).

PIN dictionary $\mathcal{PIN}$ of CTAP2 consists of 4~63-byte strings.[13] In Fig. 5, the client inputs an arbitrary user PIN $\text{pin}_U \in \mathcal{PIN}$. We use $\text{ECKG}_{\mathbb{G},G}$ to denote the key generation algorithm of the NIST P-256 elliptic-curve Diffie-Hellman (ECDH) [26], which samples an elliptic-curve secret and public key pair (a, aG), where G is an elliptic-curve point that generates a cyclic group $\mathbb{G}$ of prime order $|\mathbb{G}|$ and a is chosen at random from the integer set $\{1, \ldots, |\mathbb{G}| - 1\}$. Let H denote the SHA-256 hash function and H' denote SHA-256 with output truncated to the first $\lambda = 128$ bits; $\text{CBC}_0 = (\mathcal{K}, \text{E}, \text{D})$ denotes the (deterministic) encryption scheme AES-256-CBC [20] with fixed $\text{IV} = 0$; HMAC' denotes the MAC HMAC-SHA-256 [8] with output truncated to the first $\lambda = 128$ bits. Note that we use the symbol λ to denote the block size in order to accommodate parameter changes in future versions of CTAP2.

---

[13] PINs memorized by users are at least 4 Unicode characters and of length at most 63 bytes in UTF-8 representation.

- Reboot generates $st_T.ps$ by running $ECKG_{\mathbb{G},G}$, sampling a $k\lambda$-bit pinToken pt (where $k \in \mathbb{N}_+$ can be any fixed parameter, e.g., $k = 2$ for a 256-bit pt), and resetting the mismatch counter $m \leftarrow 3$ that limits the maximum number of consecutive mismatches. It also erases the binding state $st_T.bs$ (if any).
- Setup is essentially an unauthenticated ECDH followed by the client transmitting the (encrypted) user PIN to the token. The shared encryption key is derived from hashing the x-coordinate of the ECDH result. A $HMAC'$ tag of the encrypted PIN is also attached for authentication; but as we will show this is actually useless. The token checks if the tag is correct and if the decrypted PIN pin_U is valid; if so, it sets the static secret $st_T.s$ to the PIN hash and sets the retries counter $st_T.n$ to the default value 8.
- Bind also involves an unauthenticated ECDH but followed by the transmission of the encrypted PIN hash. First, if $st_T.n = 0$, the token blocks further access unless being reset to factory default state, i.e., erasing all static and volatile state. Otherwise, the token decrements $st_T.n$ and checks if the decrypted PIN hash matches its stored static secret. If the check fails, it decrements the mismatch counter m, generates a new key pair, then halts; if $m = 0$, it further requires a reboot to enforce user interaction (and hence user detectability). If the check passes, it resets the retries counter, sends back the encrypted pinToken, and uses its pinToken as the binding state $st_T.bs_i$; the client then uses the decrypted pinToken as its binding state $bs_{C,j}$.
- Authorize generates an authorized command by attaching a $HMAC'$ tag.
- Validate accepts the command if and only if the tag is correct and the user gesture approves the command. The default CTAP2 gesture predicate G_1 always returns true, since only physical user presence is required. The mismatch counter is also updated to trigger user interaction.

It is straightforward to check that CTAP2 is a correct PACA protocol.

CTAP2 Analysis. The session identifier of CTAP2 is defined as the full communication trace of the Bind execution.

Insecurity of CTAP2. It is not hard to see that CTAP2 is not UF-secure (and hence not SUF-secure). An attacker can query Connect to initiate the Bind execution of a client oracle that inputs the user PIN, then impersonate the token to get the PIN hash, and finally use it to get the secret binding state pt from the token. CTAP2 is not SUF-t-secure either because compromising any partner of the token reveals the common binding state pt used to access all token oracles.

UF-t Security of CTAP2. The following theorem (proved in the full version [6]) confirms CTAP2's UF-t security, by modeling the hash function H (with fixed 256-bit input) and truncated HMAC $HMAC'$ as random oracles $\mathcal{H}_1, \mathcal{H}_2$.

Theorem 2. *Let $\mathscr{D}$ be an arbitrary distribution over $\mathcal{PIN}$ with min-entropy $h_{\mathscr{D}}$. For any efficient adversary $\mathcal{A}$ making at most q_S, q_E, q_R, q_V queries respectively to Setup, Execute, Reboot, Validate, and $q_{\mathcal{H}}$ random oracle queries to $\mathcal{H}_2$,* *there exist efficient adversaries $\mathcal{B}, \mathcal{C}, \mathcal{D}$ such that (recall $\lambda = 128$):*

$$\mathbf{Adv}^{\mathsf{uf\text{-}t}}_{\mathrm{CTAP2}}(\mathcal{A}) \leq 8q_{\mathsf{S}} \cdot 2^{-h_{\mathscr{D}}} + (q_{\mathsf{S}} + q_{\mathsf{E}})\mathbf{Adv}^{\mathsf{scdh}}_{\mathbb{G}, G}(\mathcal{B}) + \mathbf{Adv}^{\mathsf{coll}}_{\mathsf{H}'}(\mathcal{C})$$
$$+ 2(q_{\mathsf{S}} + q_{\mathsf{E}})\mathbf{Adv}^{\mathsf{prf}}_{\mathrm{AES\text{-}256}}(\mathcal{D}) + q_{\mathsf{V}} \cdot 2^{-k\lambda} + q_{\mathsf{S}}q_{\mathcal{H}} \cdot 2^{-2\lambda}$$
$$+ (12q_{\mathsf{S}} + 2|\mathcal{U}|q_{\mathsf{R}}q_{\mathsf{E}} + q_{\mathsf{R}}^2 q_{\mathsf{E}} + (k+1)^2 q_{\mathsf{E}} + q_{\mathsf{V}}) \cdot 2^{-\lambda}.$$

We remark that for conciseness the above theorem does not show what security should be achieved by CBC_0 for CTAP2's UF-t security to hold, but directly reduces to the PRF security of the underlying AES-256 cipher. Actually, the proof of the above theorem also shows that it is sufficient for CBC_0 to achieve a novel security notion that we call *indistinguishability under one-time chosen and then random plaintext attack (IND-1$PA)*, which (defined in the full version [6]) we think would be of independent interest. We prove in the full version [6] that the IND-1$PA security of CBC_0 can be reduced to the PRF security of AES-256.

SUF-t $\not\Rightarrow$ UF. Note that we can modify CTAP2 to achieve SUF-t security by using independent pinTokens for each Bind execution, but this is not UF-secure due to unauthenticated ECDH. This shows that SUF-t does not imply UF.

CTAP2 Improvement. Here we make suggestions for improving CTAP2 per se, but we advocate the adoption of our proposed efficient PACA protocol with stronger SUF security in Sect. 8.

Setup Simplification. First, we notice that the Setup authentication procedures (boxed in Fig. 5) are useless, since there are no pre-established authentication parameters between the token and client. In particular, a MITM attacker can pick its own aG to compute the shared key K and generate the authentication tag. More importantly, CTAP2 uses the same key K for both encryption and authentication, which is considered bad practice and the resulting security guarantee is elusive; this is why we have to model HMAC' as a random oracle. Therefore, we suggest removing those redundant authentication procedures (or using checksums), then the resulting protocol, denoted by CTAP2*, is also UF-t-secure, with the proof in the full version [6] where HMAC' is treated as an EUF-CMA-secure MAC.[14] Furthermore, one can use a simple one-time pad (with appropriate key expansion) instead of CBC_0 to achieve the same UF-t security. This is because only one encryption is used in Setup and hence one-time security provided by a one-time pad is sufficient.

Unnecessary Reboots. In order to prevent attacks that block the token without user interaction, CTAP2 requires a token reboot after 3 consecutive failed binding attempts. Such reboots do not enhance security as the stored PIN hash is not updated, but they could cause usability issues since reboots invalidate all established access channels by erasing the existing binding states. We therefore suggest replacing reboots with tests of user presence (e.g., pressing a button) that do not affect existing bindings. Note that reboots are also introduced for

---

[14] Note that HMAC-SHA-256 has been proved to be a PRF (and hence EUF-CMA) assuming SHA-256's compression function is a PRF [7].

Authenticator T		Client C (pin$_U$)
Reboot:		
$(a, aG) \xleftarrow{\$} \mathsf{ECKG}_{\mathbb{G}, G}(\,)$, $m \leftarrow 3$		
st$_T$.ps $\leftarrow (a, aG, m)$, st$_T$.bs $\leftarrow \varepsilon$		
Setup:	$\xleftarrow{\quad bG \quad}$	
		$(b, bG) \xleftarrow{\$} \mathsf{ECKG}_{\mathbb{G}, G}(\,)$
$K \leftarrow \mathsf{H}(abG.x)$	$\xrightarrow{\quad aG \quad}$	$K \leftarrow \mathsf{H}(baG.x)$
pin$_U \leftarrow \mathsf{CBC}_0.\mathsf{D}(K, c_p)$	$\xleftarrow{\quad c_p \quad}$	$c_p \leftarrow \mathsf{CBC}_0.\mathsf{E}(K, \mathsf{pin}_U)$
if pin$_U \notin \mathcal{PIN}$: halts		
st$_T$.s $\leftarrow \mathsf{H}'(\mathsf{pin}_U)$, st$_T$.n $\leftarrow 8$	$\xrightarrow{\quad ok \quad}$	
Bind:		
if st$_T$.n $= 0$: blocks access	$\mathsf{PAKE}(\mathsf{H}'(\mathsf{pin}_U))$	
st$_T$.n $\leftarrow$ st$_T$.n $- 1$	$\xLeftrightarrow{\qquad\qquad}$	
if PAKE outputs $sk_T \in \{0,1\}^\kappa$:		if PAKE outputs $sk_C \in \{0,1\}^\kappa$:
$\quad m \leftarrow 3$, st$_T$.n $\leftarrow 8$		
$\quad$ st$_T$.bs$_i \leftarrow sk_T$		$\mathsf{bs}_{C,j} \leftarrow sk_C$
otherwise:		
$\quad m \leftarrow m - 1$, halts		
$\quad$ (if $m = 0$: tests user presence)		
Validate:	$\xleftarrow{\quad M, t \quad}$	**Authorize:**
reject if $t \neq \mathsf{HMAC}'(\mathsf{st}_T.\mathsf{bs}_i, M)$		$t \leftarrow \mathsf{HMAC}'(\mathsf{bs}_{C,j}, M)$
collects user decision d		
accept if $d = 1$	$\xrightarrow{\quad uv = 1 \quad}$	

Fig. 6. The sPACA protocol

user interaction in Validate executions; this however is completely useless when CTAP2 already requires a test of user presence before accepting each command.

User Confirmation for Binding. As discussed at the end of Sect. 6, we suggest CTAP2 require user confirmation for Bind executions to improve security. Note that here user confirmation is used to detect and prevent malicious Bind executions rather than confirming honest ones.

8   The Secure PACA Protocol

In this section, we propose a generic PACA protocol that we call sPACA for *secure PACA*, prove its SUF security, and compare its performance with CTAP2 when instantiating the underlying PAKE of sPACA with CPace [24].

Protocol Description. We purposely design our sPACA protocol following CTAP2 such that the required modification is minimized if sPACA is adopted. As shown in Fig. 6, sPACA employs the same PIN dictionary $\mathcal{PIN}$ and cryptographic primitives as CTAP2 and additionally relies on a PAKE protocol PAKE initiated by the client. Compared to CTAP2, sPACA does not have pinTokens, but instead establishes independent random binding states in Bind executions by running PAKE between the token and the client (that inputs the user PIN) on the shared PIN hash; it also excludes unnecessary reboots. We also note that the length of session keys $sk_T, sk_C \in \{0,1\}^\kappa$ established by PAKE is determined by the concrete PAKE instantiation; typically $\kappa \in \{224, 256, 384, 512\}$ when the keys are derived with a SHA-2 hash function.

sPACA Analysis. The session identifier of sPACA is simply that of PAKE.

SUF Security of sPACA. The following theorem (proved in the full version [6]) confirms SUF security of sPACA by modeling H as a random oracle.

Theorem 3. *Let* PAKE *be a 3-pass protocol where the client is the initiator and let $\mathscr{D}$ be an arbitrary distribution over $\mathcal{PIN}$ with min-entropy $h_{\mathscr{D}}$. For any efficient adversary $\mathcal{A}$ making at most q_S, q_C, q_E queries respectively to* Setup, Connect, Execute, *there exist efficient adversaries $\mathcal{B}, \mathcal{C}, \mathcal{D}, \mathcal{E}, \mathcal{F}$ such that:*

$$\mathbf{Adv}^{\mathsf{suf}}_{\mathsf{sPACA}}(\mathcal{A}) \leq q_S \mathbf{Adv}^{\mathsf{cdh}}_{\mathbb{G}, G}(\mathcal{B}) + \mathbf{Adv}^{\mathsf{coll}}_{\mathsf{H}'}(\mathcal{C}) + 2q_S \mathbf{Adv}^{\mathsf{prf}}_{\mathsf{AEStext}-256}(\mathcal{D})$$
$$+ \mathbf{Adv}_{\mathsf{PAKE}}(\mathcal{E}, 16q_S + 2q_C, h_{\mathscr{D}}) + (q_C + q_E)\mathbf{Adv}^{\mathsf{euf\text{-}cma}}_{\mathsf{HMAC}'}(\mathcal{F}) + 12q_S \cdot 2^{-\lambda}.$$

Note that it is crucial for PAKE to guarantee *explicit* authentication, otherwise, the token might not be able to detect wrong PIN guesses and then decrement its retries counter to prevent exhaustive PIN guesses.[15] Also note that the PAKE advantage bound may itself include calls to an independent random oracle. PAKE can be instantiated with variants of CPace [24] or SPAKE2 [3,5] that include explicit authentication. Both protocols were recently considered by the IETF for standardization and CPace was selected in the end.[16] They both meet the required security property, as they have been proved secure in the UC setting which implies the game-based security notion we use [4,24].

UF $\not\Rightarrow$ SUF-t. Note that one can easily transform sPACA into a protocol that is still UF secure, but not SUF-t secure: similar to CTAP2, let the authenticator generate a global pinToken used as binding states for all its partners and send it (encrypted with the session key output by PAKE) to its partners at the end of Bind executions. This shows that UF does not imply SUF-t.

Performance Comparison of CTAP2 and sPACA. It is straightforward to see from Fig. 5 and Fig. 6 that CTAP2 and sPACA differ mainly in their Bind executions, while sPACA has slightly better performance than CTAP2 in other subprotocols. We therefore compare their performance for binding (where sPACA is instantiated with CPace) in terms of message flows, computations (for group exponentiations, hashes, AES) on both sides, and communication complexity. Among these three factors, the number of flows reflects the network latency cost that usually dominates the performance. Therefore, one can observe that sPACA (with CPace) is more efficient than CTAP2 from the results summarized in Table 1, which we explain as follows.

---

[15] One does not actually need explicit token-to-client authentication in the proof, as clients do not have long-term secret to protect. This would allow removing the server-side authentication component from the PAKE instantiation for further efficiency. We do not propose to do this and choose to rely on the standard *mutual* explicit authentication property to enable direct instantiation of a standardized protocol.

[16] https://mailarchive.ietf.org/arch/msg/cfrg/j88r8N819bw88xCOyntuw_Ych-I.

Table 1. Performance comparison of CTAP2 and sPACA for binding.

Protocol	Flow	Token			Client			Communication
		Exp	Hash	AES	Exp	Hash	AES	$(\lambda = 128)$
CTAP2	4	2	1	$2k$	2	2	$2k$	$4\lambda + 2k\lambda$ (e.g., $k = 2$)
sPACA[CPace]	3	2	4	0	2	5	0	$4\lambda + 2\kappa$ (e.g., $\kappa = 256$)

First, CPace needs 3 flows when explicit authentication is required and hence so does sPACA, while CTAP2 needs 4. Besides, if Bind is executed when the client already has a command to issue, the last CPace message can be piggy-backed with the authorized command, leading to a very efficient 2-flow binding.[17] As shown in Fig. 5, CTAP2 requires two Diffie-Hellman group exponentiations and $2k$ AES computations (for pt of k-block length) on both sides; the token computes one hash while the client computes two (one for hashing PIN). For sPACA, CPace requires two Diffie-Hellman group exponentiations and four hashes on both sides; the client also needs to compute the PIN hash beforehand. In short, sPACA incurs 3 more hashes while CTAP2 involves $2k$ more AES computations. Note that the most expensive computations are group exponentiations, for which both protocols have two. Regarding communication complexity, both protocols exchange two group elements and two messages of the same length as the binding states, so they are equal if, say, $\kappa = k\lambda = 256$. Overall, sPACA (with CPace) is more efficient than CTAP2 due to less flows.

Finally, we note that the cryptographic primitives in sPACA could be instantiated with more efficient ones compared to those in CTAP2 without compromising security. For instance, as mentioned before, one can use a very efficient one-time pad (with appropriate key expansion) instead of CBC_0 in Setup.

9   Composed Security of PlA and PACA

In this section we discuss the composed security of PlA and PACA and the implications of this composition for FIDO2 and WebAuthn+sPACA. The composed protocol, which we simply refer to as PlA+PACA, is defined in the natural way, and it includes all the parties that appear in Fig. 1. We give a typical flow for registration in Fig. 7, where we assume PACA Setup and Bind have been correctly executed. The server's role is purely that of a PlA server. The client receives the server challenge via an authenticated channel (i.e., it knows the true server identity id_S when it gets a challenge from the server). It then authorizes the challenge using the PACA protocol and sends it to the authenticator. The authenticator first validates the PACA command (possibly using a user gesture) and, if successful, it produces a PlA response that is conveyed to the server.

---

[17] This piggy backing has the extra advantage of associating the end of the binding state with a user gesture by default, which helps detect online dictionary attacks against the token as stated in Sect. 6.

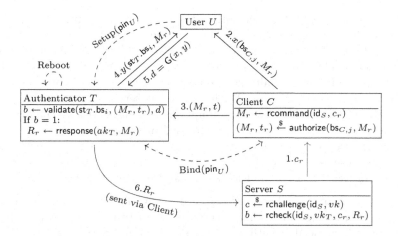

Fig. 7. Full PlA+PACA registration flow: black = PACA, blue = PlA, red = authenticated (e.g., TLS), dashed = PACA algorithms/subprotocols. (Color figure online)

The flow for authentication looks exactly the same, apart from the fact that the appropriate PlA authentication algorithms are used instead. The requirement on the token is that it supports the combined functionalities of PlA and PACA protocols and that it is able to validate the correct authorization of two types of commands, (M_r, t_r) and (M_a, t_a), that correspond to PlA registration and authentication. These commands are used to control access to the PlA registration and authentication functionalities. In the full version of this paper [6] we formally give a syntax for such composed protocols.

A crucial aspect of our security results is that we convey the *two-sided* authentication guarantees offered by PlA+PACA, and not only the server-side guarantees. In fact, the server-side guarantees given by the composed protocol are almost those offered by PlA, as the server is simply a PlA server: if a token was used to register a key, then the server can recognize the same token in authentication; furthermore, PACA security requires that the authentication must have been carried by a PACA-bound client. But how do the client and user know which server they are registering at? What guarantees does a user have such that registered credentials cannot be used in a different server? What does a user know about how client security affects the effectiveness of access control for the token? We answer these questions next.

Security Model. We give a very short description of the security model here (the details are in the full version [6]). We define a security property called *user authentication (UA)* for the composed protocol. We analyze the PlA+PACA composition in a trust model as with our PACA model but we further require a server-to-client explicit authentication guarantee. This captures a basic guarantee given by TLS, whereby the client knows the true identity of the server that generates the challenge and is ensured the integrity of the received challenge; it

allows formalizing explicit server authentication guarantees given to the token
and user by the composed protocol. We allow the adversary to create arbitrary
bindings between clients and tokens, used to deliver arbitrary commands to those
created token oracles. We model server-to-token interactions via a unified query:
the adversary can request challenges from server S, via client C aimed at a specific client-token PACA binding. We hardwire the server's true identity to the
challenges, which is justified by our assumption of an authenticated channel from
server to client. The token oracles are modeled in the obvious way: if a PACA
command is accepted, then it is interpreted as in the PlA security experiment
and the response is given to the adversary. Compromise of binding states and
corruption of user PINs are modeled as in the PACA security experiment.

Security Guarantees. The security goal we define for the composed protocol
requires that a server oracle that accepts is uniquely partnered with a token
oracle, which is associated with a unique PACA-bound client oracle (that has
established an access channel), and these oracles agree on the exchanged messages in all passes of the challenge-response authentication session; this also holds
for the associated registration session. We show that such server-side security for
the composed protocol follows from security of its PlA and PACA components.
Then, it is not hard to see that PlA correctness guarantees the above token and
client oracles agree on the accepting server's identity and that PlA correctness
and server-to-client explicit authentication (e.g., offered by TLS) guarantees that
user approval (i.e., $d = 1$) via an uncompromised access channel implies that only
the intended server can be authenticated to.

We now give a brief intuition on how the server-side result can be proved
assuming the underlying PlA and PACA components are secure. Suppose a
server authentication oracle $\pi_S^{i,j}$ ($j > 0$) accepts and its associated server registration oracle $\pi_S^{i,0}$ took as input the attestation public key of token T:

- PlA security guarantees a unique partner oracle in T, which determines two
  partner token oracles: $\pi_T^{k,0}$ for registration and $\pi_T^{k,l}$ ($l > 0$) for authentication.
- Token oracles are, by construction, created on acceptance of PACA com-
  mands. Therefore, token T must have accepted PACA commands to create
  the above PlA partner token oracles.
- PACA security binds a PACA command accepted by the token to a unique
  PACA partner client oracle (in the SUF/SUF-t corruption model) or to a set
  of PACA partner client oracles (in the UF/UF-t corruption model).
- PlA security also guarantees unique server-side partnered oracles $\pi_S^{i,0}$ and $\pi_S^{i,j}$
  (which generated a challenge that is consistent with the token's view); this
  implies that the two accepted PACA commands are produced respectively by
  unique PACA partner client oracles π_C^m and π_C^n (in either corruption model),
  i.e., π_C^m has a consistent view with $\pi_S^{i,0}$ and $\pi_T^{k,0}$ in registration and so does
  π_C^n with $\pi_S^{i,j}$ and $\pi_T^{k,l}$ in authentication.

The above argument guarantees that *unique* server, token and client oracles are
bound to the execution of PlA+PACA registration and authentication, as we
claimed before. If this does not hold, then either the PlA protocol or the PACA

protocol can be broken (reduction to the PACA protocol security can be done by considering the same corruption model as in PlA+PACA).

The details are in the full version of this paper [6].

Implications for FIDO2. The above result implies that FIDO2 components WebAuthn and CTAP2 securely compose to achieve the UA security guarantees under a weak corruption model UF-t: the protocol is broken if the adversary can corrupt *any* client that has access to the target token since the last power-up, or if the adversary can launch an *active* attack against an uncorrupted client (that the target user inputs its PIN into) via the CTAP2 API (i.e., the user thinks it is embedding the PIN into the token but it is actually giving it to the adversary). Such attacks are excluded by the trust model assumed for the client platform.

Security in the SUF Model. The above result also implies that WebAuthn composes with our sPACA protocol from Sect. 8 to give UA security in the strongest corruption model we considered. Intuitively, no active attacks against the Bind subprotocol can help the attacker beyond simply guessing the user PIN. The corruption of clients (e.g., browsers) that have previously been bound to the token may be detected with the help of the user.

User Gestures Can Upgrade Security. UA gives strong guarantees to the server and client. However, it is not very clear what guarantees it gives to the human user. Apparently, there is a guarantee that an attacker that does not control the token cannot force an authentication, as it will be unable to provide a gesture. Furthermore, an attacker that steals the token must still guess the PIN in a small number of tries to succeed in impersonating the user.

One very important aspect of user awareness is to deal with malware attacks that may corrupt clients that have been bound to the token. Here, assuming SUF security has been established, the user can help prevent attackers from abusing the binding, provided that the token supports gestures that permit identifying the client-to-token access channel that is transmitting each command. In the weaker UF model there is no way to prevent this kind of abuse, as corrupting one access channel implies corrupting all access channels to the same token.

Gestures can also be used to give explicit guarantees to the user that the server identity used in a PlA session is the intended one. For example, there could be ambiguity with multiple (honest and malicious) client browser windows issuing concurrent commands from multiple servers. Suppose gesture G permits confirming which client session is issuing the registration and authentication commands.[18] In this case we get a strong guarantee that the token registered a credential or authenticated via an honest client in the server with identifier $id_S^\star$, where $id_S^\star$ was explicitly confirmed by the user on the client interface, provided that the honest client session issued only one command to the token. Alternatively, G can be defined to directly confirm the specific $id_S^\star$ value that can be displayed by the authenticator itself and we get the same guarantee.

---

[18] Confirming a client session means that the client browser and token somehow display a human-readable identifier that the user can crosscheck and confirm.

If the gesture cannot confirm consistency between client and token, then the user will not be able to distinguish which access channel is transmitting the PIA command and know for sure which id_S the command it is approving refers to. However, our composition result does show that trivial gestures are sufficient if the user establishes only one access channel with the token per power-up, as then there is no ambiguity as to which access channel is used and only a single client is provided with the intended server identity as input.

10 Conclusion

We performed the first provable security analysis of the new FIDO2 protocols for a standard of passwordless user authentication. We identified several shortcomings and proposed stronger protocols. We hope our results will help clarify the security guarantees of the FIDO2 protocols and help the design and deployment of more secure and efficient passwordless user authentication protocols.

Acknowledgments. We thank the anonymous reviewers for their valuable comments. We thank Alexei Czeskis for help with FIDO2 details. A. Boldyreva and S. Chen were partially supported by the National Science Foundation under Grant No. 1946919. M. Barbosa was funded by National Funds through the Portuguese Foundation for Science and Technology in project PTDC/CCI-INF/31698/2017.

References

1. FIDO Alliance. Client to authenticator protocol (CTAP) - proposed standard (2019). https://fidoalliance.org/specs/fido-v2.0-ps-20190130/fido-client-to-authenticator-protocol-v2.0-ps-20190130.html
2. Google 2-step verification (2020). https://www.google.com/landing/2step/
3. Abdalla, M., Barbosa, M.: Perfect forward security of SPAKE2. Cryptology ePrint Archive, Report 2019/1194 (2019). https://eprint.iacr.org/2019/1194
4. Abdalla, M., Barbosa, M., Bradley, T., Jarecki, S., Katz, J., Xu, J.: Universally composable relaxed password authenticated key exchange. Cryptology ePrint Archive, Report 2020/320 (2020). https://eprint.iacr.org/2020/320
5. Abdalla, M., Pointcheval, D.: Simple password-based encrypted key exchange protocols. In: Menezes, A. (ed.) CT-RSA 2005. LNCS, vol. 3376, pp. 191–208. Springer, Heidelberg (2005). https://doi.org/10.1007/978-3-540-30574-3_14
6. Barbosa, M., Boldyreva, A., Chen, S., Warinschi, B.: Provable security analysis of FIDO2. Cryptology ePrint Archive, Report 2020/756 (2020). https://eprint.iacr.org/2020/756
7. Bellare, M.: New proofs for NMAC and HMAC: security without collision-resistance. In: Dwork, C. (ed.) CRYPTO 2006. LNCS, vol. 4117, pp. 602–619. Springer, Heidelberg (2006). https://doi.org/10.1007/11818175_36
8. Bellare, M., Canetti, R., Krawczyk, H.: Keying hash functions for message authentication. In: Koblitz, N. (ed.) CRYPTO 1996. LNCS, vol. 1109, pp. 1–15. Springer, Heidelberg (1996). https://doi.org/10.1007/3-540-68697-5_1

9. Bellare, M., Pointcheval, D., Rogaway, P.: Authenticated key exchange secure against dictionary attacks. In: Preneel, B. (ed.) EUROCRYPT 2000. LNCS, vol. 1807, pp. 139–155. Springer, Heidelberg (2000). https://doi.org/10.1007/3-540-45539-6_11

10. Bellare, M., Rogaway, P.: Entity authentication and key distribution. In: Stinson, D.R. (ed.) CRYPTO 1993. LNCS, vol. 773, pp. 232–249. Springer, Heidelberg (1994). https://doi.org/10.1007/3-540-48329-2_21

11. Bellare, M., Rogaway, P.: The exact security of digital signatures-how to sign with RSA and rabin. In: Maurer, U. (ed.) EUROCRYPT 1996. LNCS, vol. 1070, pp. 399–416. Springer, Heidelberg (1996). https://doi.org/10.1007/3-540-68339-9_34

12. Boldyreva, A., Chen, S., Dupont, P.A., Pointcheval, D.: Human computing for handling strong corruptions in authenticated key exchange. In: CSF 2017, pp. 159–175. IEEE (2017)

13. Chen, S., Jero, S., Jagielski, M., Boldyreva, A., Nita-Rotaru, C.: Secure communication channel establishment: TLS 1.3 (over TCP fast open) versus QUIC. J. Cryptol. **34**(3), 1–41 (2021)

14. Cohn-Gordon, K., Cremers, C., Dowling, B., Garratt, L., Stebila, D.: A formal security analysis of the Signal messaging protocol. J. Cryptol. **33**(4), 1914–1983 (2020)

15. Consortium, W.W.W., et al.: Web authentication: an API for accessing public key credentials level 1–W3C recommendation (2019). https://www.w3.org/TR/webauthn

16. Czeskis, A., Dietz, M., Kohno, T., Wallach, D., Balfanz, D.: Strengthening user authentication through opportunistic cryptographic identity assertions. CCS **2012**, 404–414 (2012)

17. Davis, G.: The past, present, and future of password security (2018)

18. Dolev, D., Yao, A.: On the security of public key protocols. IEEE Trans. Inf. Theory **29**(2), 198–208 (1983)

19. Dowling, B., Fischlin, M., Günther, F., Stebila, D.: A cryptographic analysis of the TLS 1.3 handshake protocol. Cryptology ePrint Archive, Report 2020/1044 (2020). https://eprint.iacr.org/2020/1044

20. Dworkin, M.: Recommendation for block cipher modes of operation. methods and techniques. Technical report, National Inst of Standards and Technology Gaithersburg MD Computer security Div (2001)

21. FIDO: Specifications overview. https://fidoalliance.org/specifications/

22. Gott, A.: LastPass reveals 8 truths about passwords in the new Password Exposé (2017)

23. Guirat, I.B., Halpin, H.: Formal verification of the W3C web authentication protocol. In: 5th Annual Symposium and Bootcamp on Hot Topics in the Science of Security, p. 6. ACM (2018)

24. Haase, B., Labrique, B.: AuCPace: efficient verifier-based PAKE protocol tailored for the IIoT. IACR Transactions on Cryptographic Hardware and Embedded Systems, pp. 1–48 (2019)

25. Hu, K., Zhang, Z.: Security analysis of an attractive online authentication standard: FIDO UAF protocol. China Commun. **13**(12), 189–198 (2016)

26. Igoe, K., McGrew, D., Salter, M.: Fundamental elliptic-curve Cryptography Algorithms. RFC 6090 (2011). https://doi.org/10.17487/RFC6090

27. Jacomme, C., Kremer, S.: An extensive formal analysis of multi-factor authentication protocols. In: CSF 2018, pp. 1–15. IEEE (2018)

28. Jager, T., Kakvi, S.A., May, A.: On the security of the PKCS# 1 v1. 5 signature scheme. In: CCS 2018, pp. 1195–1208 (2018)

29. Jarecki, S., Krawczyk, H., Shirvanian, M., Saxena, N.: Two-factor authentication with end-to-end password security. In: Abdalla, M., Dahab, R. (eds.) PKC 2018. LNCS, vol. 10770, pp. 431–461. Springer, Cham (2018). https://doi.org/10.1007/978-3-319-76581-5_15

30. Moriarty, K., Kaliski, B., Jonsson, J., Rusch, A.: PKCS #1: RSA Cryptography Specifications Version 2.2. RFC 8017 (2016). https://doi.org/10.17487/RFC8017

31. Nahorney, B.: Email threats 2017. Symantec, Internet Security Threat Report (2017)

32. Panos, C., Malliaros, S., Ntantogian, C., Panou, A., Xenakis, C.: A security evaluation of FIDO's UAF protocol in mobile and embedded devices. In: Piva, A., Tinnirello, I., Morosi, S. (eds.) TIWDC 2017. CCIS, vol. 766, pp. 127–142. Springer, Cham (2017). https://doi.org/10.1007/978-3-319-67639-5_11

33. Pereira, O., Rochet, F., Wiedling, C.: Formal analysis of the FIDO 1.x protocol. In: Imine, A., Fernandez, J.M., Marion, J.-Y., Logrippo, L., Garcia-Alfaro, J. (eds.) FPS 2017. LNCS, vol. 10723, pp. 68–82. Springer, Cham (2018). https://doi.org/10.1007/978-3-319-75650-9_5

34. Verizon: 2017 data breach investigations report (2017). https://enterprise.verizon.com/resources/reports/2017_dbir.pdf

SSE and SSD: Page-Efficient Searchable Symmetric Encryption

Angèle Bossuat[1]([⊠]), Raphael Bost[2], Pierre-Alain Fouque[5], Brice Minaud[3,4], and Michael Reichle[3,4]

[1] Quarkslab and Université de Rennes 1, Rennes, France
[2] Direction Générale de l'Armement, Paris, France
[3] Inria, Paris, France
[4] École Normale Supérieure, CNRS, PSL University, Paris, France
[5] Université de Rennes 1, Rennes, France

Abstract. Searchable Symmetric Encryption (SSE) enables a client to outsource a database to an untrusted server, while retaining the ability to securely search the data. The performance bottleneck of classic SSE schemes typically does not come from their fast, symmetric cryptographic operations, but rather from the cost of memory accesses. To address this issue, many works in the literature have considered the notion of locality, a simple design criterion that helps capture the cost of memory accesses in traditional storage media, such as Hard Disk Drives. A common thread among many SSE schemes aiming to improve locality is that they are built on top of new memory allocation schemes, which form the technical core of the constructions.

The starting observation of this work is that for newer storage media such as Solid State Drives (SSDs), which have become increasingly common, locality is not a good predictor of practical performance. Instead, SSD performance mainly depends on *page efficiency*, that is, reading as few pages as possible. We define this notion, and identify a simple memory allocation problem, *Data-Independent Packing* (DIP), that captures the main technical challenge required to build page-efficient SSE. As our main result, we build a page-efficient and storage-efficient data-independent packing scheme, and deduce the Tethys SSE scheme, the first SSE scheme to achieve at once $\mathcal{O}(1)$ page efficiency and $\mathcal{O}(1)$ storage efficiency. The technical core of the result is a new generalization of cuckoo hashing to items of variable size. Practical experiments show that this new approach achieves excellent performance.

1 Introduction

In Searchable Symmetric Encryption (SSE), a client holds a collection of documents, and wishes to store them on an untrusted cloud server. The client also wishes to be able to issue search queries to the server, and retrieve all documents

R. Bost—The views and conclusions contained herein are those of the author and should not be interpreted as necessarily representing the official policies or endorsements, either expressed or implied, of the DGA or the French Government.

T. Malkin and C. Peikert (Eds.): CRYPTO 2021, LNCS 12827, pp. 157–184, 2021.
https://doi.org/10.1007/978-3-030-84252-9_6

matching the query. Meanwhile, the honest-but-curious server should learn as little information as possible about the client's data and queries. Searchable Encryption is an important goal in the area of cloud storage, since the ability to search over an outsourced database is often a critical feature. The goal of SSE is to enable that functionality, while offering precise guarantees regarding the privacy of the client's data and queries with respect to the host server.

Compared to other settings related to computation over encrypted data, such as Fully Homomorphic Encryption, a specificity of SSE literature is the focus on high-performance solutions, suitable for deployment on large real-world datasets. To achieve this performance, SSE schemes accept the leakage of some information on the plaintext dataset, captured in security proofs by a leakage function. The leakage function is composed of setup leakage and query leakage. The setup leakage is the total leakage prior to query execution, and typically reveals the size of the index, and possibly the number of searchable keywords. For a static scheme, the query leakage usually reveals the repetition of queries, and the set of document indices matching the query. Informally, the security model guarantees that the adversary does not learn any information about the client's data and queries, other than the previous leakages.

In particular, the allowed leakage typically reveals nothing about keywords that have *not yet* been queried. Although this requirement may seem natural and innocuous, it has deep implications about the storage and memory accesses of SSE schemes. At Eurocrypt 2014, Cash and Tessaro [CT14] proved an impossibility result that may be roughly summarized as follows. If an SSE scheme reveals nothing about the number of documents matching *unqueried* keywords, then it cannot satisfy the following three efficiency properties simultaneously: (1) constant storage efficiency: the size of the encrypted database is at most linear in the size of the plaintext data; (2) constant read efficiency: the amount of data read by the server to answer a query is at most linear in the size of the plaintext answer; (3) constant locality: the memory accesses made by the server to answer a query consist of a constant number of contiguous accesses. Thus, a secure SSE scheme with constant storage efficiency and read efficiency cannot be *local*: it must perform a superconstant number of disjoint memory accesses.

In practice, many SSE schemes (*e.g.* [CGKO06, CJJ+13, Bos16]) make one random memory access per entry matching the search query. As explained in [CJJ+14, MM17], making many small random accesses hampers performance: hard disks drives (HDD) were designed for large sequential accesses, and solid state drives (SSD) use a leveled design that does not accommodate small reads well. As discussed *e.g.* in [BMO17], this results in the fact that in many settings, the performance bottleneck for SSE is not the cost of cryptographic operations (which rely on fast, symmetric primitives), but the cost of memory accesses.

As a consequence, SSE scheme designers have tried to reduce the number of disk accesses needed to process a search query, *e.g.* by grouping entries corresponding to the same keywords in blocks [CJJ+14, MM17], or by using more complex allocation mechanisms [ANSS16, ASS18, DPP18]. However, no optimal solution is possible, due to the previously mentioned impossibility result of Cash and Tessaro. In the static case, the first construction by Asharov *et al.* from STOC 2016 achieves linear server storage and constant locality, at the cost of logarithmic read efficiency (the amount of data read by the server to answer a query is bounded by the size of the plaintext answer times $\mathcal{O}(\log N)$, where N is the size of the plaintext database) [ANSS16]. The logarithmic factor was reduced to $\log^\gamma N$ for $\gamma < 1$ by Demertzis *et al.* at Crypto 2018 [DPP18].

An interesting side-effect of this line of research is that it has highlighted the connection between Searchable Encryption and memory allocation schemes with certain security properties. The construction from [ANSS16] relies on a two-dimensional variant of the classic balls-and-bins allocation problem. Likewise, the construction from [DPP18] uses several memory allocation schemes tailored to different input sizes.

1.1 Overview of Contributions

As discussed above, memory accesses are a critical bottleneck for SSE performance. This has led to the notion of locality, and the construction of many SSE schemes aiming to improve locality, such as [CT14, ANSS16, MM17, DP17, DPP18]. The motivation behind the notion of locality is that it is a simple criterion that captures the performance of traditional storage media such as HDDs. In recent years, other storage media, and especially SSDs, have become more and more prevalent. To illustrate that point, the number of SSDs shipped worldwide is projected to overtake HDD shipments in 2021 [Sta21].

However, locality as a design target, was proposed assuming an implementation on a HDD. The starting point of our work is that for SSDs, locality is no longer a good predictor of practical performance. This raises two questions: first, is there a simple SSE design criterion to capture SSD performance, similar to locality for HDDs? And can we design SSE schemes that fulfill that criterion?

The answer to the first question is straightforward: for SSDs, performance is mainly determined by the number of memory pages that are accessed, regardless of whether they are contiguous. This leads us to introduce the notion of page efficiency. The page efficiency of an SSE scheme is simply the number of pages that the server must access to process a query, divided by the number of pages of the plaintext answer to the query. Page efficiency is an excellent predictor of SSD performance. This is supported by experiments in Sect. 5. Some of the technical reasons behind that behavior are also discussed in the full version.

The main contribution of this work is to give a positive answer to the second question, by building a page-efficiency SSE scheme, called Tethys. Tethys achieves page efficiency $\mathcal{O}(1)$ and storage efficiency $\mathcal{O}(1)$, with minimal leakage. Here, $\mathcal{O}(1)$ denotes an absolute constant, independent of not only the database size, but also the page size. We also construct two additional variants, Pluto and Nilus$_t$, that offer practical trade-offs between server storage and page efficiency. An overview of these schemes is presented on Table 1, together with a comparison with some relevant schemes from the literature.

Similar to local SSE schemes such as [ANSS16] and its follow-ups, the core technique underpinning our results is a new memory allocation scheme. In order

Table 1. Trade-offs between SSE schemes. Here, p is the number elements per page, k is the number of keywords, and λ is the security parameter (assuming $k \geq \lambda$). *Page cost $aX + b$ means that in order to process a query whose plaintext answer is at most X pages long, the server needs to access at most $aX + b$ memory pages. Page efficiency is page cost divided by X in the worst case. Client storage is the size of client storage, where the unit is the storage of one element or address. Storage efficiency is the number of pages needed to store the encrypted database, divided by the number of pages of the plaintext database.*

Schemes	Client st.	Page cost	Page eff.	Storage eff.	Source
Π_{bas}	$\mathcal{O}(1)$	$\mathcal{O}(Xp)$	$\mathcal{O}(p)$	$\mathcal{O}(1)$	[CJJ+14]
$\Pi_{\text{pack}}, \Pi_{\text{2lev}}$	$\mathcal{O}(1)$	$\mathcal{O}(X)$	$\mathcal{O}(1)$	$\mathcal{O}(p)$	[CJJ+14]
1-Choice	$\mathcal{O}(1)$	$\widetilde{\mathcal{O}}(\log N)\,X$	$\widetilde{\mathcal{O}}(\log N)$	$\mathcal{O}(1)$	[ANSS16]
2-Choice	$\mathcal{O}(1)$	$\widetilde{\mathcal{O}}(\log\log N)\,X$	$\widetilde{\mathcal{O}}(\log\log N)$	$\mathcal{O}(1)$	[ANSS16]
Tethys	$\mathcal{O}(p\log\lambda)$	$2X + 1$	3	$3 + \varepsilon$	Sect. 4
Pluto	$\mathcal{O}(p\log\lambda)$	$X + 2$	3	$3 + \varepsilon$	Full version
Nilus$_t$	$\mathcal{O}(p\log\lambda)$	$2tX + 1$	$2t + 1$	$1 + (2/e)^{t-1}$	Full version

to build Tethys, we identify and extract an underlying combinatorial problem, which we call *Data-Independent Packing* (DIP). We show that a secure SSE scheme can be obtained generically from any DIP scheme, and build Tethys in that manner.

Similar to standard bin packing, the problem faced by a DIP scheme is to pack items of variable size into buckets of fixed size, in such a way that not too much space is wasted. At the same time, data independence requires that a given item can be retrieved by inspecting a few buckets whose location is independent of the sizes of other items. That may seem almost contradictory at first: we want to pack items closely together, in a way that does not depend on item sizes. The solution we propose is inspired by a generalization of cuckoo hashing, discussed in the technical overview below.

We note that the DIP scheme we build in this way has other applications beyond the scope of this article. One side result is that it can also be used to reduce the leakage of the SSE scheme with tunable locality from [DP17]. Also, we sketch a construction for a length-hiding static ORAM scheme that only has constant storage overhead.

Finally, we have implemented Tethys to analyze its practical performance. The source code is publicly available (link in Sect. 5). The experiments show two things. First, experimental observations match the behavior predicted by the theory. Second, when benchmarked against various existing static SSE schemes, Tethys achieves, to our knowledge, unprecedented performance on SSDs: without having to rely on a very large ciphertext expansion factor (less than 3 in our experiments), we are able to stream encrypted entries and decrypt them from a medium-end SSD at around half the raw throughput of that SSD.

1.2 Technical Overview

In single-keyword SSE schemes, the encrypted database is realized as an inverted index. The index maps each keyword to the (encrypted) list of matching document indices. The central question is how to efficiently store these lists, so that accessing some lists reveals no information about the lengths of other lists.

Page efficiency asks that in order to retrieve a given list, we should have to visit as few pages as possible. The simplest solution for that purpose is to pad all lists to the next multiple of one page, then store each one-page chunk separately using a standard hashing scheme. That padding approach is used in some classic SSE constructions, such as [CJJ+14]. While the approach is page-efficient, it is not storage-efficient, since all lists need to be padded to the next multiple of p.

In practice, with a standard page size of 4096 bytes, and assuming 64-bit document indices, we have $p = 512$. Regardless of the size of the database, if it is the case that most keywords match few documents, say, less than 10 documents, then server storage would blow up by a factor 50. More generally, whenever the dataset contains a large ratio of small lists, padding becomes quite costly, up to a factor $p = 512$ in storage in the worst case. Instead, we would like to upper-bound the storage blowup by a small constant, independent of both the input dataset, and the page size.

Another natural approach is to adapt SSE schemes that target locality. It is not difficult to show that an SSE scheme with locality L and read efficiency R has page efficiency $\mathcal{O}(L + R)$ (Theorem 2.1). However, due to Cash and Tessaro's impossibility result, it is not possible for any scheme with constant storage efficiency and locality $\mathcal{O}(1)$ (such as [ANSS16] and its follow-ups) to have read efficiency $\mathcal{O}(1)$; and all such schemes result in superconstant page efficiency.

Ultimately, a new approach is needed. To that end, we first introduce the notion of *data-independent packing* (DIP). A DIP scheme is a purely combinatorial allocation mechanism, which assigns lists of variable size into buckets of fixed size p. (Our definition also allows to store a few extra items in a stash.) The key property of a DIP scheme is data independence: each list can be retrieved by visiting a few buckets, whose locations are independent of the sizes of other lists.

We show that a secure SSE scheme SSE(D) can be built generically from any DIP scheme D. The page efficiency and storage efficiency of the SSE scheme SSE(D) can be derived directly from similar efficiency measures for the underlying DIP scheme D. All SSE schemes in this paper are built in that manner.

We then turn to the question of building an efficient DIP scheme. Combinatorially, what we want is a DIP scheme with constant page efficiency (the number of buckets it visits to retrieve a list is bounded linearly by the number of buckets required to read the list), and constant storage efficiency (the total number of buckets it uses is bounded linearly by the number of buckets required to store all input data contiguously). The solution we propose, TethysDIP, is inspired by cuckoo hashing. For ease of exposition, we focus on lists of size at most one page. Each list is assigned two uniformly random buckets as possible destinations. It is required that the full list can be recovered by reading the two buckets, plus a stash. To ensure data independence, all three locations are accessed, regardless of where list elements are actually stored. Since the two buckets for each list are drawn independently and uniformly at random, data independence is immediate.

Once each list is assigned its two possible buckets, we are faced with two problems. The first problem is algorithmic: how should each list be split between its two destination buckets and the stash, so that the stash is as small as possible, subject to the constraint that the assignment is correct (all list elements are stored, no bucket receives more than p elements)? We prove that a simple max flow computation yields an optimal solution to this optimization problem. To see this, view buckets as nodes in a graph, with lists corresponding to edges between their two destination buckets, weighted by the size of the list. Intuitively, if we start from an arbitrary assignment of items to buckets, we want to find as many disjoint paths as possible going from overfull buckets to underfull buckets, so that we can "push" items along those paths. This is precisely what a max flow algorithm provides.

The second (and harder) problem we face is analytic: can we prove that a valid assignment exists with overwhelming probability, using only $\mathcal{O}(n/p)$ buckets (for constant storage efficiency), and a stash size independent of the database size? Note that a negligible probability of failure is critical for security, because the probability of failure depends on the list length distribution, which we wish to hide. Having a small stash size, that does not grow with the database size, is also important, because in the final SSE scheme, we will ultimately store the stash on the client side.

In the case of cuckoo hashing, results along those lines are known, see for example [ADW14]. However, our situation is substantially different. Cuckoo hashing with buckets of capacity $p > 1$ has been analyzed in the literature [DW05], including in the presence of a stash [KMW10]. Such results go through the analysis of the *cuckoo graph* associated with the problem: similar to the graph discussed earlier, vertices are buckets, and each item gives rise to one edge connecting the two buckets where it can be assigned. A crucial difference in our setting compared to regular cuckoo hashing with buckets of capacity p is that edges are not uniformly distributed. Instead, each list of length x generates x edges between the same two buckets.

Thus, we need an upper bound that holds for a family of non-uniform edge distributions (those that arise from an arbitrary number of lists with an arbitrary number of elements each, subject only to the total number of elements being equal to the database size n). Moreover, we want an upper bound that holds simultaneously for all members of that family, since we want to hide the length distribution. What we show is that the probability of failure for any such distribution can be upper-bounded by the case where all lists have the maximum size p, up to a polynomial factor. Roughly speaking, this follows from a convexity argument, combined with a majorization argument, although the details are intricate. We are then able to adapt existing analyses for the standard cuckoo graph.

In the end, TethysDIP has the following features: every item can be retrieved by visiting 2 data-independent table locations (and the stash), the storage efficiency is $2 + \varepsilon$, and the stash size is $p\omega(\log \lambda)$. All those quantities are the same as regular cuckoo hashing, up to a scaling factor p in the stash size, which is unavoidable (see full version for more details). Since regular cuckoo hashing is a special case of our setting, the result is tight.

In the full version, we present two other DIP schemes, PlutoDIP and NilusDIP$_t$. Both are variants of the main TethysDIP construction, and offer trade-offs of practical interest between storage efficiency and page efficiency. In particular, NilusDIP rests on the observation that our main analytical results, regarding the optimality and stash size bound of TethysDIP, can be generalized to buckets of size tp rather than p, for an arbitrary integer t. This extension yields a storage efficiency $1 + (2/e)^{t-1}$, which tends exponentially fast towards the information theoretical minimum of 1. The price to pay is that page efficiency is $2t$, because we need to visit two buckets, each containing t pages, to retrieve a list.

1.3   Related Work

Our work mainly relates to two areas: SSE and cuckoo hashing. We discuss each in turn.

In [ANSS16], Asharov et al. were the first to explicitly view SSE schemes as an allocation problem. That view allows for very efficient schemes, and is coherent with the fact that the main bottleneck is the IO and not the cryptographic overhead, as observed by Cash et al. [CJJ+13]. Our work uses the same approach, and builds an SSE scheme on top of an allocation scheme.

As proved by Cash and Tessaro [CT14], no SSE scheme can be optimal simultaneously in locality, read efficiency, and storage efficiency (see also [ASS18]). Since then, many papers have constructed schemes with constant locality and storage efficiency, while progressively improving read efficiency: starting from $\mathcal{O}(\log N \log \log N)$ in [ANSS16] to $\mathcal{O}(\log^\gamma N)$ in [DPP18] for any fixed $\gamma > 2/3$, and finally $\mathcal{O}(\log \log N \log^2 \log \log N)$ when all lists have at most $N^{1-1/\log \log N}$ entries [ANSS16], or $\mathcal{O}(\log \log \log N)$ when they have at most $N^{1-1/o(\log \log \log N)}$ entries [ASS18]. On the other hand, some constructions achieve optimal read efficiency, and sublinear locality, at the cost of increased storage, such as the family of schemes by Papamanthou and Demertzis [DP17].

Contrary to the previous line of work, we aim to optimize page efficiency and not locality. At a high level, there is a connection between the two: both aim to store the data matching a query in close proximity. A concrete connection is given in Theorem 2.1. Nevertheless, to our knowledge, no previous SSE scheme with linear storage has achieved page efficiency $\mathcal{O}(1)$. The Π_{pack} scheme from [CJJ+14] achieves page efficiency $\mathcal{O}(1)$ by padding all lists to a multiple of the page size, and storing lists by chunks of one page. However, this approach has storage efficiency p in the worst case. The Π_{2lev} variant from [CJJ+14] incurs the same cost, because it handles short lists in the same way as Π_{pack}. In practice, such schemes will perform well for long lists, but will incur a factor up to p when there are many small lists, which can be prohibitive, as a typical value of p is $p = 512$ (*cf.* Sect. 1.2). On the other hand, Π_{pack} and its variants are dynamic schemes, whereas Tethys is static.

TethysDIP is related to one of the allocation schemes from [DPP18], which uses results by Sanders *et al.* [SEK03]. That allocation scheme can be generalized to handle the same problem as TethysDIP, but we see no way of doing so that would achieve storage and page efficiency $\mathcal{O}(1)$. Another notable difference is that we allow for a stash, which makes it possible to achieve a negligible probability of failure (the associated analysis being the most technically challenging part of this work). An interesting relationship between our algorithm in the algorithm from [SEK03] is discussed in Sect. 4.1.

As Data-Independent Packing scheme, TethysDIP is naturally viewed as a packing algorithm with oblivious lookups. The connection between SSE and oblivious algorithms is well-known, and recent works have studied SSE with fully oblivious accesses [MPC+18, KMO18].

We now turn to cuckoo hashing [PR04]. As noted earlier, TethysDIP (resp. $\mathsf{NilusDIP}_t$) includes standard cuckoo hashing with a stash (resp. with buckets of size $t > 1$) as a special case, and naturally extends those settings to items of variable size. Moreover, our proof strategy essentially reduces the probability of failure of TethysDIP (resp. $\mathsf{NilusDIP}_t$) to their respective cuckoo hashing special cases. As such, our work relies on the cuckoo hashing literature, especially works on bounding stash sizes [KMW10, ADW14]. While TethysDIP generalizes some of these results to items of variable size, we only consider the static setting. Extending TethysDIP to the dynamic setting is an interesting open problem.

Finally, some aspects of TethysDIP relate to graph orientability. Graph orientability studies how the edges of an undirected graph may be oriented in order to achieve certain properties, typically related either to the in- or outdegree sequence of the resulting graph, or to k-connectivity. This is relevant to our TethysDIP algorithm, insofar as its analysis is best formulated as a problem of deleting the minimum number of edges in a certain graph, so that every vertex has outdegree less than a given capacity p (cf. Sect. 4). As such, it relates to deletion orientability problems, such as have been studied in [HKL+18]. Many variants of this problem are NP-hard, such as minimizing the number of *vertices* that must be deleted to achieve the same property, and most of the literature is devoted to a more fine-grained classification of their complexity. In that respect, it seems we are "lucky" that our particular optimization target (minimizing the so-called overflow of the graph) can be achieved in only quadratic time. We did not find mention of this fact in the orientability literature.

Organization of the Paper. Section 2 provides the necessary background and notation, and introduces definitions of storage and page efficiency. Section 3 introduces the notion of data-independent packing (DIP), and presents a generic construction of SSE from a DIP scheme. Section 4 gives an efficient construction of DIP. Section 5 concludes with practical experiments.

2   Background

2.1   Notation

Let $\lambda \in \mathbb{N}$ be the security parameter. For a distribution probability X, we denote by $x \leftarrow X$ the process of sampling a value x from the distribution. If $\mathcal{X}$ is a set, $x \leftarrow \mathcal{X}$ denotes the process of sampling x uniformly at random from $\mathcal{X}$. Logarithm in base 2 is denoted by $\log(\cdot)$. A function $f(\lambda)$ is *negligible* in λ if it is $\mathcal{O}(\lambda^{-c})$ for every $c \in \mathbb{N}$. If so, we write $f = \mathsf{negl}(\lambda)$.

Let $\mathsf{W} = \{w_1, \ldots, w_k\}$ be the set of keywords, where each keyword w_i is represented by a machine word, each of $\mathcal{O}(\lambda)$ bits, in the unit-cost RAM model, as in [ANSS16]. The plaintext database is regarded as an inverted index. To each keyword w_i is associated a list $\mathsf{DB}(w_i) = (\mathsf{ind}_1, \ldots, \mathsf{ind}_{\ell_i})$ of document identifiers matching the keyword, each of length $\mathcal{O}(\lambda)$ bits. The plaintext database is $\mathsf{DB} = (\mathsf{DB}(w_1), \ldots, \mathsf{DB}(w_k))$. Uppercase N denotes the total number of keyword-document pairs in DB, $N = |\mathsf{DB}| = \sum_{i=1}^{k} \ell_i$, as is usual in SSE literature.

We now introduce multi-maps. A *multi-map* M consists of k pairs $\{(K_i, \mathsf{vals}_i) : 1 \le i \le k\}$, where $\mathsf{vals}_i = (e_{i,1}, \ldots, e_{i,\ell_i})$ consists of ℓ_i values $e_{i,j}$. (Note that in this context, a *key* is an identification key in a key-value store, and not a cryptographic key.) We assume without loss of generality that the keys K_i are distinct. Throughout, we denote by n the total number of values $n = |\mathsf{M}| := \sum_{i=1}^{k} \ell_i$, following the convention of allocation and hashing literature. For the basic $\mathsf{TethysDIP}$ scheme, $n = N$. We assume (without loss of generality) that values $e_{i,j}$ can be mapped back unambiguously to the key of origin K_i. This will be necessary for our SSE framework, and can be guaranteed by assuming the values contain the associated key. As this comes with additional storage overhead, we discuss some encoding variants in the full version (some of these encodings result in $n > N$).

Throughout the article, the page size p is treated as a variable, independent of the dataset size n. Upper bounds of the form $f(n, p) = \mathcal{O}(g(n, p))$, where the function f under consideration depends on both n and p, mean that there exist constants C, C_n, C_p such that $f(n, p) \le C g(n, p)$ for all $n \ge C_n$, $p \ge C_p$.

2.2   Searchable Symmetric Encryption

At setup, the client generates an encrypted database EDB from the plaintext database DB and a secret key K. The client sends EDB to the server. To issue a search query for keyword w, the client sends a search token τ_w. The server uses the token τ_w and the encrypted database EDB to compute $\mathsf{DB}(w)$. In some cases, the server does not recover $\mathsf{DB}(w)$ directly; instead, the server recovers some data d and sends it to the client. The client then recovers $\mathsf{DB}(w)$ from d.

Formally, a static Searchable Symmetric Encryption (SSE) scheme is a tuple of algorithms ($\mathsf{KeyGen}, \mathsf{Setup}, \mathsf{TokenGen}, \mathsf{Search}, \mathsf{Recover}$).

- $K \leftarrow \mathsf{KeyGen}(1^\lambda)$: the key generation algorithm KeyGen takes as input the security parameter λ in unitary notation and outputs the master key K.

- EDB $\leftarrow$ Setup(K, DB): the setup algorithm takes as input the master key K and a database DB, and outputs an encrypted database EDB.
- $(\tau, \rho) \leftarrow$ TokenGen(K, w): the token generation algorithm takes as input the master key K and a keyword w, and outputs a search token τ (to be sent to the server), and potentially some auxiliary information ρ (to be used by the recovery algorithm).
- $d \leftarrow$ Search(EDB, τ): The search algorithm takes as input the token τ and the encrypted database EDB and outputs some data d.
- $s \leftarrow$ Recover(ρ, d): the recovery algorithm takes as input the output d of the Search algorithm, and potentially some auxiliary information ρ, and outputs the set DB(w) of document identifiers matching the queried keyword w.

The Recover algorithm is used by the client to decrypt the results sent by the server. In many SSE schemes, the server sends the result in plaintext, and Recover is a trivial algorithm that outputs $s = d$.

Security Definition. We use the standard semantic security notion for SSE. A formal definition is given in [CGKO06]. Security is parametrized by a *leakage function* $\mathcal{L}$, composed of the setup leakage $\mathcal{L}_{\mathsf{Setup}}$, and the search leakage $\mathcal{L}_{\mathsf{Search}}$. Define two games, SSEREAL and SSEIDEAL. At setup, the adversary sends a database DB. In SSEREAL, the setup is run normally; in SSEIDEAL, the setup is run by calling a simulator on input $\mathcal{L}_{\mathsf{Setup}}$(DB). The adversary can then adaptively issue search queries for keywords w that are answered honestly in SSEREAL, and simulated by a simulator on input $\mathcal{L}_{\mathsf{Search}}$(DB, w) in SSEIDEAL. The adversary wins if it correctly guesses which game it was playing.

Definition 2.1 (Simulation-Based Security). *Let Π be an SSE scheme, let $\mathcal{L}$ be a leakage function. We say that Π is $\mathcal{L}$-adaptively semantically secure if for all PPT adversary $\mathcal{A}$, there exists a PPT simulator S such that*

$$|\Pr[\mathrm{SSEREAL}_{\Pi,\mathcal{A}}(\lambda) = 1] - \Pr[\mathrm{SSEIDEAL}_{\Pi,S,\mathcal{L},\mathcal{A}}(\lambda) = 1]| = \mathsf{negl}(\lambda).$$

2.3   Locality and Page Efficiency

The notions of locality and read efficiency were introduced by Cash and Tessaro [CT14]. We recall them, followed by our new metrics of page cost and page efficiency. We start with the definition of the *read pattern*. In the following definitions, the quantities EDB, τ are assumed to be computed according to the underlying SSE scheme, *i.e.* given a query for keyword w on the database DB, set $K \leftarrow$ KeyGen(1^λ), EDB $\leftarrow$ EDBSetup(K, DB), $\tau \leftarrow$ TokenGen(K, w).

Definition 2.2 (Read Pattern). *Regard server-side storage as an array of memory locations, containing the encrypted database EDB. When processing the search query Search(EDB, τ) for keyword w, the server accesses memory locations $m_1, \ldots, m_h$. We call these locations the read pattern and denote it with RdPat(τ, EDB).*

Definition 2.3 (Locality). *An SSE scheme has locality L if for any λ, DB, and keyword w, RdPat(τ, EDB) consists of at most L disjoint intervals.*

Definition 2.4 (Read Efficiency). *An SSE scheme has read efficiency R if for any λ, DB, and keyword w, $|\text{RdPat}(\tau, \text{EDB})| \leq R \cdot P$, where P is the number of memory locations needed to store document indices matching keyword w in plaintext (by concatenating indices).*

Definition 2.5 (Storage Efficiency). *An SSE scheme has storage efficiency S if for any λ, DB, $|\text{EDB}| \leq S \cdot |DB|$.*

Optimizing an SSE scheme for locality requires that each read query accesses few non-contiguous memory locations, thus making this operation efficient for HDDs. In the case of SSDs, it is sufficient to optimize for few page accesses (as SSDs efficiently read entire pages of memory). For this reason, we introduce the notions *page cost* and *page efficiency* to measure the efficiency of read queries performed on SSDs. More background is provided in the full version, together with experiments showing that page efficiency is an excellent predictor of SSD read performance (this is also supported by the experiments of Sect. 5).

Definition 2.6 (Page Pattern). *If server-side storage is regarded as an array of pages, when searching for a keyword w, the read pattern RdPat(τ, EDB) induces a number of page accesses $p_1, \ldots, p_{h'}$. We call these pages the page pattern, denoted by PgPat(τ, EDB).*

Definition 2.7 (Page Cost). *An SSE scheme has page cost $aX + b$, where a, b are real numbers, and X is a fixed symbol, if for any λ, DB, and keyword w, $|\text{PgPat}(\tau, \text{EDB})| \leq aX + b$, where X is the number of pages needed to store documents indices matching keyword w in plaintext.*

Definition 2.8 (Page Efficiency). *An SSE scheme has page efficiency P if for any λ, DB, and keyword w, $|\text{PgPat}(\tau, \text{EDB})| \leq P \cdot X$, where X is the number of pages needed to store documents indices matching keyword w in plaintext.*

A scheme with page cost $aX + b$ has page efficiency at most $a + b$. Compared to page efficiency, page cost is a more fine-grained measure that can be helpful when comparing the performance of different SSE schemes. It is clear that page efficiency is a direct counterpart of read efficiency, viewed at the page level, but it is also related to locality: a scheme with good locality and read efficiency immediately yields a scheme with good page efficiency, as formalized in the following theorem.

Theorem 2.1. *Any SSE scheme with read efficiency R and locality L has page efficiency at most $R + 2L$.*

The impossibility result of Cash and Tessaro [CT14] states (with some additional assumptions) that no SSE scheme can have simultaneously storage efficiency, read efficiency and locality $\mathcal{O}(1)$. As a consequence, no scheme with storage efficiency $\mathcal{O}(1)$ can have $R + 2L = \mathcal{O}(1)$. Nevertheless, our Tethys scheme has storage efficiency $\mathcal{O}(1)$ and page efficiency $\mathcal{O}(1)$. This shows that Theorem 2.1, while attractive in terms of genericity and simplicity, is not the best way to build a page-efficient scheme. In the full version, we show that the upper bound from Theorem 2.1 is tight.

Proof of Theorem 2.1. View server-side storage as an array of pages, without modifying the behavior of the scheme in any way. To process keyword w, the scheme makes at most L contiguous memory accesses of lengths $a_1, \ldots, a_L$. We have $\sum a_i \leq Rx$, where x denotes the amount of memory needed to store the plaintext answer (concatenation of document indices matching the query). Each memory access of length a_i covers at most $a_i/p + 2$ pages, where the two extra page accesses account for the fact that the start and end points of the access may not be aligned with server pages. Thus, the number of pages read is at most $\sum(a_i/p + 2) \leq Rx/p + 2L$. It remains to observe that the number of pages needed to store the plaintext answer is at least x/p. Hence, the scheme has page cost (at most) $RX + 2L$, and page efficiency $R + 2L$.   □

3   SSE from Data-Independent Packing

In this section, we define data-independent packing, and based on this notion, provide a framework to construct SSE schemes. In Sect. 4, we will instantiate the framework with an efficient data-independent packing scheme.

3.1   Data-Independent Packing

A data-independent packing (DIP) scheme takes as input an integer m (the number of buckets), and a multi-map M (mapping keys to lists of values). Informally, it will assign the values of the multi-map into m buckets, each containing up to p values, and a stash. It provides a search functionality Lookup that, for a given key, returns the indices of buckets where the associated values are stored. In this section, p denotes the size of a bucket. To ease notation, it is implicitly a parameter of all methods. (In the concrete application to page-efficient SSE, p is the size of a page.)

Definition 3.1 (Data-Independent Packing).
A DIP scheme is a triplet of algorithms (Size, Build, Lookup):

- $m \leftarrow$ Size(n): *Takes as input a number of values n. Returns a number of buckets m.*
- $(B, S) \leftarrow$ Build(M): *Takes as input a multi-map* M $= \{(K_i, (e_{i,1}, \ldots, e_{i,\ell_i})) : 1 \leq i \leq k\}$. *Letting $n = |\mathsf{M}| = \sum_{1 \leq i \leq k} \ell_i$ and $m \leftarrow$ Size(n), returns a pair (B, S), where B is an m-tuple of buckets $(B[1], \ldots, B[m])$, where each bucket $B[i]$ is a set of at most p multi-map values; and the stash S is another set of multi-map values.*
- $\mathcal{I} \leftarrow$ Lookup(m, K, ℓ): *Takes as input the total number of buckets m, a multi-map key K, and a number of items ℓ. Returns a set of bucket indices $I \subseteq [1, m]$.*

Correctness asks that all multi-map values $(e_{i,1}, \ldots, e_{i,\ell_i})$ associated with key K_i are either in the buckets whose indices are returned by $\mathsf{Lookup}(m, K_i, \ell_i)$, or in the stash. Later on, we will sometimes only ask that correctness holds with overwhelming probability over the random coins of Build.

Definition 3.2 (Correctness). *A* DIP *scheme is correct if for all multi-map* $\mathsf{M} = \{(K_i, (e_{i,1}, \ldots, e_{i,\ell_i})) : 1 \leq i \leq k\}$, *the following holds. Letting* $m \leftarrow \mathsf{Size}(|\mathsf{M}|)$, *and* $(B, S) \leftarrow \mathsf{Build}(\mathsf{M})$:

$$\forall i \in [1, k] : \mathsf{M}(K_i) \subseteq S \cup \bigcup_{j \in \mathsf{Lookup}(m, K_i, \ell_i)} B[j].$$

Intuitively, the definition of DIP inherently enforces data independence, in two ways. The first is that the number of buckets $m \leftarrow \mathsf{Size}(n)$ used for storage is solely a function of the number of values n in the multi-map. The second is that Lookup only depends on the queried key, and the number of values associated with that key. Thus, neither Size nor Lookup depend on the multi-map at the input of Build, other than the number of values it contains. It is in that sense that we say those two functions are *data-independent*: they do not depend on the dataset M stored in the buckets, including the sizes of the lists it contains. Looking ahead, when we use a DIP scheme, we will pad all buckets to their maximum size p, and encrypt them, so that the output of Build will also leak nothing more than the number of buckets m.

We supply Lookup with the number of values ℓ associated to the queried key. This is for convenience. If the number of values of the queried key was not supplied as input, it would have to be stored by the DIP scheme. We have found it more convenient to allow that information to be stored in a separate structure in future constructions. Not forcing the DIP scheme to store length information also better isolates the main combinatorial problem a DIP scheme is trying to capture, namely how to compactly store objects of variable size, while being data-independent. How to encode sizes introduces its own separate set of considerations.

Efficiency Measures. Looking ahead to the SSE construction, a bucket will be stored in a single page, and contain some document identifiers of the database. The goal is to keep the total number of buckets m small (quantified by the notion *storage efficiency*), and to ensure that Lookup returns small sets (quantified by the notion *lookup efficiency*). Intuitively, those goals will imply good storage efficiency (with a total storage of m pages, plus some auxiliary data), and good page efficiency (reading from the database requires few page accesses) for the resulting SSE scheme. Finally, the stash will be stored on the client side. Thus, the stash size should be kept small. These efficiency measures are formally defined in the following.

Definition 3.3 (Lookup Efficiency). *A* DIP *scheme has lookup efficiency* L *if for any multi-map* M, *any* $(m, B, S) \leftarrow \mathsf{Build}(\mathsf{M})$ *and any key* K *for which the values* $\mathsf{M}(K)$ *require a minimal number of buckets* x, *we have* $|\mathsf{Lookup}(m, K, \ell)| \leq L \cdot x$.

Definition 3.4 (Storage Efficiency). *A* DIP *scheme has storage efficiency* E *if for any multi-map* M *and any* $(m, B, S) \leftarrow$ Build(M), *it holds that* $m \leq E \cdot (n/p)$.

Definition 3.5 (Stash Size). *A* DIP *scheme has stash size* C *if for any multi-map* M *and any* $(m, B, S) \leftarrow$ Build(M), *it holds that the stash contains at most* C *values.*

It is trivial to build a DIP scheme that disregards one of these properties. For example for good lookup and storage efficiency, we can store all values in the stash. For good storage efficiency and small stash size, it suffices to store all values in $m = \lceil n/p \rceil$ buckets and return all bucket indices $\{1, \cdots, m\}$ in Lookup. Lastly, for good lookup efficiency and stash size, we can pad every list to a multiple of p in size and subsequently split each list into chunks of size p. Each chunk can be stored in a bucket fixed by a hash function. But this scheme has a storage efficiency of p (this last approach is discussed in more detail in Sect. 1.2).

Ensuring good performance with respect to all properties at the same time turns out to be a hard problem. We refer to Sect. 4 for a concrete construction.

SSE *from Data-Independent Packing.* In this section, we give a framework to build an SSE scheme SSE(D) generically from a DIP scheme D with a bucket size p equal to the page size.

We now describe the construction in detail. Let PRF be a secure pseudo-random function mapping to $\{0, 1\}^{2\lambda + \lceil \log(N) \rceil}$. Let Enc be an IND-CPA secure symmetric encryption scheme (assimilated with its encryption algorithm in the notation). We split the output of the PRF into a key of 2λ bits and a mask of $\lceil \log(N) \rceil$ bits. Pseudo-code is provided in Algorithm 1.

Setup. The Setup algorithm takes as input a database DB, and the client's master secret key $K = (K_{\mathsf{PRF}}, K_{\mathsf{Enc}})$. For each keyword w_i, we have a list $\mathsf{DB}(w_i)$ of ℓ_i indices corresponding to the documents that match w_i. First, setup samples $(K_i, m_i) \leftarrow \mathsf{PRF}_{K_{\mathsf{PRF}}}(w_i)$ which will serve as token for w_i later on. To each list is associated the key K_i and the DIP scheme D is then called on the key-list pairs. Recall that D assigns the values to m buckets and a stash. Once that is done, each bucket is padded with dummy values until it contains exactly p values. Then, a table T with N entries is created which stores the length of each list in an encrypted manner. Concretely, T maps K_i to $\ell_i \oplus m_i$ and is filled with random elements until it contains N entries. Note that ℓ_i is encrypted with mask m_i and can be decrypted given m_i. The padded buckets are then encrypted using Enc with key K_{Enc}, and sent to the server in conjunction with the table T. The stash is stored on the client side.

Search. To retrieve all documents matching keyword w_i, the client generates the access token $(K_i, m_i) \leftarrow \mathsf{PRF}_{K_{\mathsf{PRF}}}(w_i)$ and forwards it to the server. The server retrieves $\ell_i \leftarrow T[K_i] \oplus m_i$ and queries D to retrieve the indices $I \leftarrow \mathsf{Lookup}(K_i, \ell_i)$ of the encrypted buckets. The server sends the respective buckets back to the

---

Algorithm 1. SSE(D)

KeyGen(1^λ)

  1: Sample keys K_{PRF}, K_{Enc} for PRF, Enc with security parameter λ

  2: **return** $K = (K_{\mathsf{PRF}}, K_{\mathsf{Enc}})$

Setup(K, DB)

  1: Initialize empty set M, empty table T

  2: $N \leftarrow |\mathsf{DB}|$

  3: **for all** keywords w_i **do**

  4:     $(K_i, m_i) \leftarrow \mathsf{PRF}_{K_{\mathsf{PRF}}}(w_i)$

  5:     $\ell_i \leftarrow |\mathsf{DB}(w_i)|$

  6:     $T[K_i] \leftarrow \ell_i \oplus m_i$

  7: $\mathsf{M} \leftarrow \{K_i, \mathsf{DB}(w_i) : 1 \leq i \leq k\}$

  8: $m, B, S \leftarrow \mathsf{Build}(\mathsf{M})$

  9: Fill T up to size N with random values

 10: Store the stash S on the client

 11: **return** $\mathsf{EDB} = (\mathsf{Enc}_{K_{\mathsf{Enc}}}(B[1]), \ldots, \mathsf{Enc}_{K_{\mathsf{Enc}}}(B[m]), T)$

TokenGen(K, w_i)

  1: $(K_i, m_i) \leftarrow \mathsf{PRF}_{K_{\mathsf{PRF}}}(w_i)$

  2: **return** $\tau_i = (K_i, m_i)$

Search(EDB, τ_i)

  1: Initialize empty set R

  2: Parse τ_i as (K_i, m_i)

  3: Set $\ell_i = T[K_i] \oplus m_i$

  4: $I \leftarrow \mathsf{Lookup}(m, K_i, \ell_i)$

  5: **for all** $j \in I$ **do**

  6:     Add encrypted buckets $B[j]$ to R

  7: **return** R

---

client, who decrypts them to recover the list elements. Finally, the client checks its own stash for any additional elements matching w_i.

Efficiency. The efficiency of SSE(D) heavily relies on the efficiency of D. The server stores the encrypted database EDB consisting of a table of size $N = |\mathsf{DB}|$ and m buckets. The concrete value of m depends on the storage efficiency S of D. By definition, the scheme SSE(D) has storage efficiency $S + 1$. During the search process, SSE(D) accesses one entry of table T and $|I|$ buckets, where I is the set of indices returned by Lookup. As each bucket is stored in a single page, a bucket access requires a single page access. The access to T requires an additional page access. In total, the page efficiency of SSE(D) is $L+1$, where L is the lookup efficiency of D. Note that we assume that Lookup does not make any additional page accesses, as is guaranteed by our construction. Lastly, the client stores the key K and the stash S locally. Thus, the client storage is $C + \mathcal{O}(1)$, where C is the stash size of D.

Security. The leakage profile of the construction is the standard leakage profile of a static SSE scheme. Recall that x_i is the minimal number of pages for the list of documents matching keyword w_i. The leakage during setup is $\mathcal{L}_{\mathsf{Setup}}(\mathsf{DB}) = |\mathsf{DB}| = N$. The leakage during search is $\mathcal{L}_{\mathsf{Search}}(\mathsf{DB}, w_i) = (\ell_i, \mathsf{sp})$, where sp is the *search pattern*, that is, the indices of previous searches for the same keyword (a formal definition is given in [CGKO06]). Let $\mathcal{L} = (\mathcal{L}_{\mathsf{Setup}}, \mathcal{L}_{\mathsf{Search}})$.

Theorem 3.1 (SSE Security). *Let* D *be a* DIP *scheme with storage efficiency* S, *lookup efficiency* L, *and stash size* C. *Assume that* Lookup *does not make any page accesses,* Enc *is an IND-CPA secure encryption scheme and* PRF *is a secure pseudo-random function. Then* $\mathsf{SSE}(\mathsf{D})$ *is a* $\mathcal{L}$-*adaptively semantically secure SSE scheme with storage efficiency* $S + 1$, *page efficiency* $L + 1$, *and client storage* $C + \mathcal{O}(1)$.

The full proof is given in the full version. It is straightforward, and we sketch it here. For Setup, the simulator creates the required number m of buckets, derived from $N = \mathcal{L}_{\mathsf{Setup}}(\mathsf{DB})$, and fills each one with the encryption of arbitrary data using Enc. Similarly, it creates a table T mapping N random values κ to random entries χ. It then creates the simulated database EDB consisting of the buckets and the table. The IND-CPA security of Enc guarantees that the adversary cannot distinguish the simulated buckets from the real ones. Also, the simulated table is indistinguishable from the real table, since the concrete values ℓ_i are masked with a random mask m_i. Thus, the unqueried table entries appear random.

For a (new) search query, the simulator receives from the leakage function the number ℓ_i, and simulates the token $\tau_i = (K_i, \ell_i \oplus T[K_i])$ by choosing K_i uniformly from the unqueried keys κ of table T. The PRF security of PRF guarantees that the adversary cannot distinguish the simulated token from the real one. Note that the adversary recovers the correct value $\ell_i = T[K_i] \oplus (\ell_i \oplus T[K_i])$. This concludes the proof.

While the proof is simple, it relies heavily on the data independence of the DIP scheme. Namely, Lookup does not take the database as input, but only its size. As a consequence, the simulator need not simulate any of the Lookup inputs. Another subtle but important point is that the security argument requires that the correctness of the DIP scheme holds with overwhelming probability over the random coins of Build. Indeed, the probability of a correctness failure may be dependent on the dataset at the input of Build, and thus leak information. Moreover, if a correctness failure occurs, it is not acceptable to run Build again with fresh random coins, as the random coins of Build would then become dependent on the dataset. The same subtlety exists in the proofs of some Oblivious RAM constructions, and has led to flawed proofs when overlooked, as well as concrete distinguishing attacks exploiting this flaw [GM11, Appendix D], [FNO20].

4   Efficient Data-Independent Packing

In this section, we introduce an efficient DIP scheme. As a reminder, a DIP scheme allocates the values of a multi-map into m buckets or a stash. Recall that a multi-map consists of k keys K_i, where each key K_i maps to ℓ_i values

$(e_{i,1}, \ldots, e_{i,\ell_i})$. At first, we restrict ourselves to at most p (one page) values per key for simplicity, *i.e.* $\ell_i \leq p$. The restriction will be removed at the end of the section.

The construction is parametrized by two hash functions H_1, H_2, mapping into the buckets, *i.e.* mapping into $\{1, \ldots, m\}$. H_1 is uniformly random among functions mapping into $\{1, \ldots, m/2\}$, and H_2 is uniformly random among functions mapping into $\{m/2 + 1, \ldots, m\}$. (The distribution of H_1 and H_2, and the fact they have disjoint ranges, is not important for the description of the algorithm; it will only become relevant when bounding the stash size in Theorem 4.3.)

To the i-th key K_i are associated two possible destination buckets for its values, $H_1(K_i)$ and $H_2(K_i)$. Not all values need to be allocated to the same bucket, *i.e.* some values can be allocated to bucket $H_1(K_i)$, and other values to bucket $H_2(K_i)$. If both destination buckets are already full, some values may also be stored in the stash. In the end, for each key K_i, some a values are allocated to bucket $H_1(K_i)$, b values to bucket $H_2(K_i)$, and c values to the stash, with $a + b + c = \ell_i$.

The goal of the TethysDIP algorithm is to determine, for each key, how many values are assigned to each bucket, and how many to the stash, so that no bucket receives more than p values in total, and the stash is as small as possible. We shall see that the algorithm is optimal, in the sense that it minimizes the stash size subject to the previous constraint.

Algorithm Description. Pseudo-code is provided in Algorithm 2. The algorithm takes as input the number of buckets m, and the multi-map $M = \{(K_i, (e_{i,1}, \ldots, e_{i,\ell_i})) : 1 \leq i \leq k\}$. It outputs a dictionary B such that $B[i]$ contains the values $e_{i,j}$ that are stored in bucket number i, for $i \in \{1, \ldots, m\}$, together with a stash S.

The algorithm first creates a graph similar to the cuckoo graph in cuckoo hashing: vertices are the buckets, and for each value $e_{i,j}$, an edge is drawn between its two possible destination buckets $H_1(K_i)$ and $H_2(K_i)$. Note that there may be multiple edges between any two given vertices. Edges are initially oriented in an arbitrary way. Ultimately, each value will be assigned to the bucket at the *origin* of its corresponding edge. This means that the load of a bucket is the outdegree of the associated vertex.

Intuitively, observe that if we have a directed path in the graph, and we flip all edges along this path, then the load of intermediate nodes along the path is unchanged. Meanwhile, the load of the bucket at the origin of the path is decreased by one, and the load of the bucket at the end of the path is increased by one. Hence, in order to decrease the number of values sent to the stash, we want to find as many disjoint paths as possible going from overfull buckets to underfull buckets, and flip all edges along these paths. To find a maximal set of such paths, TethysDIP runs a max flow algorithm (see full version for more details). Then all edges along the paths are flipped. Finally, each value is assigned to the bucket at the origin of its associated edge. If a bucket receives more than p values, excess values are sent to the stash.

Algorithm 2. TethysDIP

Build($m, \mathsf{M} = \{(K_i, (e_{i,1}, \ldots, e_{i,\ell_i})) : 1 \le i \le k\}$)

1: $B \leftarrow m$ empty buckets, $S \leftarrow$ empty stash
2: Create an oriented graph G with m vertices numbered $\{1, \ldots, m\}$
3: **for all** values $e_{i,j}$ **do**
4:    Create an oriented edge $(H_1(K_i), H_2(K_i))$ with label $e_{i,j}$
5: Add separate source vertex s and sink vertex t
6: **for all** vertex v **do**
7:    Compute its outdegree d.
8:    **if** $d > p$ **then**
9:       Add $d - p$ edges from the source s to v
10:    **else if** $d < p$ **then**
11:       Add $p - d$ edges from v to the sink t
12: Compute a max flow from s to t
13: Flip every edge that carries flow
14: **for all** vertex $v \in \{1, \ldots, m\}$ **do**
15:    $B[v] \leftarrow \{e_{i,j} : \text{origin of edge } e_{i,j} \text{ is } v\}$
16: **for all** vertex $v \in \{1, \ldots, m\}$ **do**
17:    **if** $|B[v]| > p$ **then**
18:       $|B[v]| - p$ values are moved from $B[v]$ to S
19: **return** (B, S)

Lookup($m, K, \ell \le p$)

1: returns $\{H_1(K), H_2(K)\}$

Efficiency. We now analyze the efficiency of TethysDIP. Note that each key still maps to at most p values for now. In order to store a given multi-map M, TethysDIP allocates a total number of $m = (2 + \varepsilon)n/p$ buckets. Thus, it has storage efficiency $2 + \varepsilon = \mathcal{O}(1)$. For accessing the values associated to key K, TethysDIP returns the result of the evaluation of the two hash functions at point K. Hence, TethysDIP has lookup efficiency $2 = \mathcal{O}(1)$. The analysis of the stash size is much more involved. In Sect. 4.1, we show that a stash size $p \cdot \omega(\log \lambda)/\log n$ suffices. In particular, the stash size does not grow with the size of the multi-map M.

Handling Lists of Arbitrary Size. The previous description of the algorithm assumes that all lists in the multi-map M are at most one page long, *i.e.* $\ell_i \le p$ for all i. We now remove that restriction. To do so, we are going to preprocess the multi-map M into a new multi-map M' that only contains lists of size at most p.

In more detail, for each key-values pair $(K_i, (e_{i,1}, \ldots, e_{i,\ell_i}))$, we split $(e_{i,1}, \ldots, e_{i,\ell_i})$ into $x_i = \lfloor \ell_i/p \rfloor$ *sublists* $(e_{i,1}, \ldots, e_{i,p}), \ldots, (e_{i,p(x_i-1)+1}, \ldots, e_{i,px_i})$ of size p, plus one sublist of size at most p containing the remaining values $(e_{i,px_i+1}, \ldots, e_{i,\ell_i})$. We associate the j-th sublist to a new key $K_i \| j$ (without loss of generality, assume there is no collision with a previous key). The new multi-map M' consists of all sublists generated in this way, with the j-th sublist of key K_i associated to key $K_i \| j$.

The TethysDIP algorithm is then applied to the multi-map M', which only contains lists of size at most p. In order to retrieve the values associated to key K_i in the original multi-map M, it suffices to query the buckets $H_1(K_i \parallel j)$, $H_2(K_i \parallel j)$ for $j \leq \lceil \ell_i/p \rceil$. Correctness follows trivially. (This approach can be naturally generalized to transform a DIP scheme for lists of size at most p into a general DIP scheme.)

Note that the total number of values in M' is equal to the total number of values n in M, as we only split the lists into sublists. Hence the scheme retains storage efficiency $2 + \varepsilon$ and stash size $p \cdot \omega(\log \lambda)/\log n$. Similarly, for a list of size ℓ, we require at minimum $x = \lceil \ell/p \rceil$ buckets. As we return x evaluations of each hash function, the storage efficiency remains 2.

The Tethys SSE Scheme. We can instantiate the framework given in Sect. 3.1 with TethysDIP. This yields a SSE scheme Tethys := SSE(TethysDIP). As the TethysDIP has constant storage and lookup efficiency, Tethys also has constant storage and page efficiency and the same stash size. This is formalized in the following theorem. Let $\mathcal{L}_{\mathsf{Setup}}(\mathsf{DB}) = |\mathsf{DB}|$ and $\mathcal{L}_{\mathsf{Search}}(\mathsf{DB}, w_i) = (\ell_i, \mathsf{sp})$, where sp is the search pattern. Let $\mathcal{L}(\mathcal{L}_{\mathsf{Setup}}, \mathcal{L}_{\mathsf{Search}})$.

Theorem 4.1. *Assume that* Enc *is an IND-CPA secure encryption scheme,* PRF *is a secure pseudo-random function, and H_1, H_2 are random oracles. Then* Tethys *is an $\mathcal{L}$-adaptively semantically secure SSE scheme with storage efficiency* $\mathcal{O}(1)$, *page efficiency* $\mathcal{O}(1)$, *and client storage* $\mathcal{O}(p \cdot \omega(\log \lambda)/\log n)$.

The TethysDIP scheme inside Tethys requires two hash functions H_1 and H_2. The stash size bound analysis assumes those two functions are uniformly random. In practice, standard hash functions can be used. Formally, to avoid an unnecessary use of the Random Oracle Model, the hash functions can be realized by a PRF, with the client drawing the PRF key and sending it to the server together with the encrypted dataset. By standard arguments, the correctness of TethysDIP still holds with overwhelming probability, assuming the PRF is secure.

4.1   Stash Size Analysis

We now analyze the stash size of TethysDIP. We proceed by first showing that the stash size achieved by TethysDIP is optimal, in the sense given below. We then prove a stash size bound that holds for any optimal algorithm.

Optimality. Given the two hash functions H_1 and H_2, and the multi-map M at the input of TethysDIP, say that an assignment of the multi-map values to buckets is *valid* if every value associated to key K is assigned to one of its two destination buckets $H_1(K)$ or $H_2(K)$, or the stash, and no bucket receives more than p values. TethysDIP is optimal in the sense that the assignment it outputs achieves the minimum possible stash size among all valid assignments. In other words, TethysDIP optimally solves the optimization problem of minimizing the stash size, subject to the constraint that the assignment is valid. This holds true regardless of the choice of hash functions (which need not be random as far as this property is concerned), regardless of the number of buckets m, and regardless of the initial orientation of the graph before the max flow is computed. To formalize this, let us introduce some notation.

The problem solved by TethysDIP is naturally viewed as a graph orientability problem (see related work in Sect. 1). The input of the problem is the graph built in lines 2–4: vertices are buckets $V = \{1, \ldots, m\}$, and each list i gives rise to ℓ_i edges from vertex $H_1(K_i)$ to $H_2(K_i)$. Recall that the outdegree $\mathsf{out}(v)$ of a vertex v is the load of the corresponding bucket. Define the *overflow* of the graph as the quantity $\sum_{v \in V} \max(0, \mathsf{out}(v) - p)$. Observe that this quantity is exactly the number of values that cannot fit into their assigned bucket, hence the number of values that are sent to the stash in line 18. The problem is to orient the edges of the graph so as to minimize that quantity. In the following theorem, TethysDIP is viewed as operating on graphs. Its input is the undirected graph G described just above, and its output is a directed graph D arising from G by orienting its edges according to Algorithm 2.

Theorem 4.2 (Optimality of TethysDIP). *Let G be an undirected graph. Let D be the directed graph output by TethysDIP on input G. Then $\mathsf{overflow}(D)$ is minimal among all directed graphs arising from G.*

The proof of Theorem 4.2 is given in the full version. In short, the proof uses the max-flow min-cut theorem to partition the vertices into two sets S (containing the source) and T (containing the sink), such that after flipping the direction of the flow in line 13, there is no edge going from S to T. Further, it is shown that all overflowing values are in S, and all buckets in S are at capacity or over capacity. Intuitively, the number of overflowing values cannot be decreased, because flipping edges within S can only increase the overflow, and there is no edge going from S to T. We refer to the full version for the full proof.

This shows that TethysDIP finds an optimal solution. Before continuing, we note that the max flow approach of TethysDIP was inspired by a result of Sanders *et al.* [SEK03], which uses a similar algorithm. The relationship between the algorithm by Sanders *et al.* and TethysDIP is worth discussing. The two algorithms have different optimization targets: the goal of the algorithm by Sanders *et al.* is not to minimize the overflow, but to minimize the max load (the load of the most loaded bucket). Another notable difference is that we allow for a stash, which allows us to reach a negligible probability of failure (the associated analysis is the most technically challenging part of this work). Nevertheless, if we disregard the stash, the algorithm from [SEK03] can be reinterpreted in the light of our own algorithm, as follows. Given an algorithm $\mathcal{A}$ that minimizes the overflow, one can build an algorithm $\mathcal{B}$ that minimizes the max load, using a logarithmic number of black-box calls to $\mathcal{A}$. Indeed, $\mathcal{A}$ yields an overflow of zero if and only if the capacity p of buckets is greater than or equal to the smallest attainable max load. Hence, it suffices to proceed by dichotomy until the smallest possible value of the max load is reached. Although it is not presented in this way in [SEK03], the algorithm by Sanders *et al.* can be reinterpreted as being built in that manner, with TethysDIP playing the role of algorithm $\mathcal{A}$. (As a side effect, our proof implies a new proof of Sanders *et al.*'s result.)

Stash Size Bound. The security of Tethys relies on the fact that memory accesses are data-independent. Data independence holds because the two buckets where a given list can be assigned are determined by the two hash functions, independently of the length distribution of other lists. In practice, we want to fix an upper bound on the size of the stash. If the bound were exceeded (so the construction fails), we cannot simply draw new random hash functions and start over. Indeed, from the perspective of the SSE security proof, this would amount to choosing a new underlying DIP scheme when some aspect of the first DIP scheme fails (namely, when the stash is too large). But the choice of DIP scheme would then become data-dependent, invalidating the security argument. It follows that we want to find a bound on the stash size that guarantees a negligible probability of failure in the cryptographic sense, and not simply a low probability of failure. We prove that this can be achieved using only $m = \mathcal{O}(n)$ buckets, and a stash size that does not grow with the size of the multi-map.

Theorem 4.3 (Stash size bound). *Let $\varepsilon > 0$ be an arbitrary constant, and let $p, n \geq p, m \geq (2 + \varepsilon)n/p, s = n^{o(1)}$ be integers. Let L be an arbitrary vector of integers such that $\max L \leq p$ and $\sum L = n$.*

$$\Pr[\mathsf{Fail}_{m,p,s}(L,H)] = \mathcal{O}\left(p \cdot n^{-s/(2p)}\right).$$

In particular, a stash of $\omega(\log \lambda)/\log n$ pages suffices to ensure that TethysDIP succeeds, except with negligible probability.

In that statement, the vector L represents a multi-map with keys mapping to p or less values, H is the pair of hash functions (H_1, H_2), and s is the stash size. $\mathsf{Fail}_{m,p,s}(L,H)$ denotes the probability that it is impossible to orient the edges of the graph G discussed earlier in such a way that the overflow of the resulting orientation is less than s. By Theorem 4.2, as long as such an orientation exists, TethysDIP finds one, so $\mathsf{Fail}_{m,p,s}(L,H)$ is equal to the probability of failure of TethysDIP. The bottom line is that, under mild assumptions about the choice of parameters, a stash of $\omega(\log \lambda)/\log n$ pages suffices to ensure a negligible probability of failure. If $n \geq \lambda$, $\log \lambda$ pages suffice.

Note that the probability of failure *decreases* with n. This behavior is reflected in practical experiments, as shown in Sect. 5. The inverse dependency with n may seem counter-intuitive, but recall that the number of buckets $m > (2 + \varepsilon)n/p$ increases with n. In practice, what matters is that the stash size can be upper-bounded independently of the size n of the database, since it does not increase with n. Ultimately, the stash will be stored on the client side, so this means that client storage does not scale with the size of the database.

The factor $2+\varepsilon$ for storage efficiency matches the cuckoo setting. Our problem includes cuckoo hashing as a special case, so this is optimal (see full version for more details). The constant ε can be arbitrarily small. However, having non-zero

ε has important implications for the structure of the cuckoo graph: there is a phase transition at $\varepsilon = 0$. For instance, if we set $\varepsilon = 0$, the probability that the cuckoo graph contains a component with multiple cycles (causing standard cuckoo hashing to fail) degrades from $\mathcal{O}(1/n)$ to $\sqrt{2/3} + o(1)$ [DK12]. Beyond cuckoo hashing, this phase transition is well-known in the theory of random graphs: asymptotically, if a random graph has m vertices and $n = cm$ edges for some constant c, its largest component has size $\log n$ when $c < 1/2$ a.s., whereas it blows up to $\Omega(n)$ as soon as $c > 1/2$ [Bol01, Chapter 5]. This strongly suggests that a storage overhead factor of $2 + \varepsilon$ is inherent to the approach, and not an artifact of the proofs.

The proof of Theorem 4.3 is given in the full version. In a nutshell, the idea is to use a convexity argument to reduce to results on cuckoo hashing, although the details are intricate. We now provide a high-level overview. The first step is to prove that the expectancy of the stash size for an arbitrary distribution of list lengths is upper-bounded by its expectancy when all lists have length p (while n and m remain almost the same), up to a polynomial factor. The core of that step is a convexity argument: we prove that the minimal stash size, as a function of the underlying graph, is Schur-convex, with respect with the natural order on graphs induced by edge inclusion. The result then follows using some majorization techniques (inspired by the analysis of weighted balls-and-bins problems in [BFHM08]). In short, the first step shows that, for expectancy at least, the case where all lists have length p is in some sense a worst case (up to a polynomial factor). The second step is to show that in that worse case, the problem becomes equivalent to cuckoo hashing with a stash. The third and final step is to slightly extend the original convexity argument, and combine it with some particular features of the problem, to deduce a tail bound on the stash size, as desired. The final step of the proof reduces to stash size bounds for cuckoo hashing. For that purpose, we adapt a result by Wieder [Wie17].

5   Experimental Evaluation

All evaluations and benchmarks have been carried out on a computer with an Intel Core i7 4790K 4.00 GHz CPU with 4 cores (8 logical threads), running Linux Debian 10.2. We used a 250 GiB Samsung 850 EVO SSD and a 4 TiB Seagate IronWolf Pro ST4000NE001 HDD, both connected with SATA, and formatted in ext4. The SSD page size is 4 KiB. The HDD was only used for the benchmarks (see full version), and we use the SSD for the following evaluation.

We chose the setting where document identifiers are encoded on 8 bytes and tags on 16 bytes. This allows us to support databases with up to 2^{64} documents and 2^{48} distinct keywords, with a probability of tag collision at most 2^{-32}. A page fits $p = 512$ entries.

5.1   Stash Size

Although the theory in Sect. 4.1 gives the asymptotic behavior of the size of the stash in TethysDIP, concrete parameters are not provided. We implemented

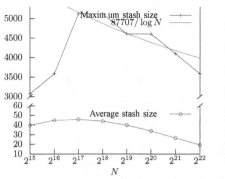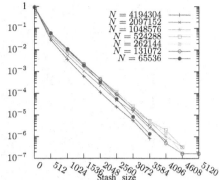

(a) Maximum and average stash size for fixed $\varepsilon = 0.1$.

(b) Experimental probability masses of the stash size for fixed $\varepsilon = 0.1$.

Fig. 1. Experimental evaluation of the stash size made over 6×10^6 worst-case random TethysDIP allocations.

TethysDIP in Rust in order to run a large number of simulations, and evaluate the required stash size in practice. We want an evaluation of the stash size for page size p and an input multi-map with total value count N and bucket count m. A multi-map M_M that maps N/p keys to exactly p values is the worst-case for the stash size (see Sect. 4.1). Thus, we evaluate the stash size of TethysDIP on the input M_M for given p, N, m.

In Fig. 1a, we fix the parameter $\varepsilon = 0.1$ and look at the maximum size of the stash for various values of N. We can see that it fits a $C/\log N$ curve (except for low values of N, where the asymptotic behavior has not kicked in yet), as predicted by the theory. This confirms that the stash size does not increase (and in fact slightly decreases) with N, hence does not scale with the size of the database. In Fig. 1b, for the same experiments, we plot the probability of having a stash of a given size. As was expected from Theorem 4.3, we can see that this probability drops exponentially fast with the size of the stash.

In the full version, we present data that clearly shows the transition phase at $\varepsilon = 0$, also predicted by the theory. The code of these experiments is publicly available [Bos21b].

5.2   Performance

We implemented Tethys in C++, using `libsodium` as the backend for cryptographic operations (HMAC-Blake2 for PRF and ChaCha20 for Enc), and using Linux' `libaio` library for storage accesses. Using `libaio` makes it possible to very efficiently parallelize IOs without having to rely on thread pools: although it does bring a few constraints in the way we access non-volatile storage, it allows for the performance to scale very cheaply, regardless of the host's CPU. As a consequence, our implementation uses only two threads: one for the submission

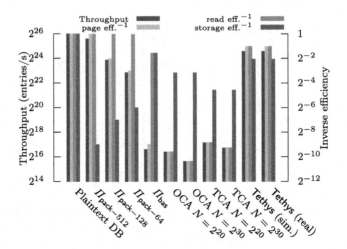

Fig. 2. Throughput, inverse page efficiency, inverse read efficiency, and inverse storage efficiency for various SSE schemes, in log scale. Higher is better. $\Pi_{\mathsf{pack}-n}$ corresponds to Π_{pack} with n entries per block.

of the queries, and the other one to reap the completion queue, decrypt and decode the retrieved buckets.

At setup, the running time of TethysDIP is dominated by a max flow computation on a graph with n edges and $m = (1 + \varepsilon)n/p$ vertices. We use a simple implementation of the Ford-Fulkerson algorithm [FF56], with running time $\mathcal{O}(nf)$, where $f \leq n$ is the max flow. This yields a worst-case bound $\mathcal{O}(n^2)$. Other max flow algorithms, such as [GR98] have running time $\widetilde{\mathcal{O}}\left(n^{3/2}\right)$; because this is a one-time precomputation, we did not optimize this step. We have experimented on the English Wikipedia database, containing about 140 million entries, and 4.6 million keywords. TethysDIP takes about 90 min to perform the full allocation. This is much slower than other SSE schemes, whose setup is practically instant. However, it is only a one-time precomputation. Using Pluto rather than Tethys makes a dramatic difference: most of the database ends up stored in HT (see full version), and TethysDIP completes the allocation in about 4 s.

Regarding online performance, comparing our implementation with available implementations of SSE schemes would be unfair: the comparison would be biased in our favor, because our implementation is optimized down to low-level IO considerations, whereas most available SSE implementations are not. To provide a fair comparison, for each SSE scheme given in the comparison, we analyzed its memory access pattern to deduce its IO workload. We then replayed that workload using the highly optimized fio Flexible I/O Tester (version 3.19) [Axb20]. While doing so, we have systematically advantaged the competition. For example, we have only taken into account the IO cost, not the additional cryptographic operations needed (which can be a significant overhead for some schemes, *e.g.* the One/Two Choice Allocation algorithms). Also, we have completely ignored the overhead induced by the storage data structure: for

Π_{bas} and Π_{pack}, we assume a perfect dictionary, that only makes a single access per block of retrieved entries. Although this is technically possible, it would very costly, as it requires either a Minimal Perfect Hash Function, a very small load factor, or a kind of position map that is small enough to fit into RAM (that last option does not scale). Similarly, for the One-Choice Allocation (OCA) and Two-Choice Allocation (TCA) algorithms, we used the maximum read throughput achieved on our evaluation hardware, and assumed that this throughput was attained when reading consecutive buckets of respective size $\Theta(\log N)$ and $\Theta(\log \log N)$ required by the algorithms. In practice, we fixed the read efficiency of OCA to $3 \log N \log \log N$ and the one of TCA to $8 \log \log N (\log \log \log N)^2$, following [ANSS16]. The code is OpenSource and freely accessible [Bos21a].

We also computed the expected performance of Tethys using the same workload replay technique. The resulting performance measures are very close to our optimized full implementation (less than 0.1% difference on 2^{20} queries over 2^{19} distinct keywords). As that result illustrates, we argue that using simulated IO workloads to compare the performance of SSE schemes is quite accurate. The comparison between Tethys and other SSE schemes is given on Fig. 2, including both the full implementation of Tethys, and its simulated workload.

We observe that Tethys compares very well with previous schemes. It vastly outperforms the One-Choice and Two-Choice allocation algorithms, as well as Π_{bas}, with over 170 times higher throughput. It also competes with all the Π_{pack} variants, its throughput being only exceeded by $\Pi_{\text{pack}-512}$ with a twofold increase, due to the fact that Tethys needs to read two pages for every query. However, Π_{pack} incurs a huge storage cost in the worst case (up to a factor $p = 512$), leaving Tethys as the only scheme that performs well in both metrics. In addition, as explained earlier, our simulation of Π_{pack} does not account for the cost of the hash table implementation it relies on. For example, if we were to choose cuckoo hashing as the underlying hash table in Π_{pack}, the throughputs of $\Pi_{\text{pack}-512}$ and of Tethys would be identical. The Π_{2lev} variant from [CJJ+14] is not included in the comparison, because its worst-case storage efficiency is the same as Π_{pack} (it handles short lists in the same way), and its throughput is slightly lower (due to indirections).

Our experiments show that Tethys is competitive even with insecure, plaintext databases, as the throughput only drops by a factor 2.63, while increasing the storage by a factor $4 + 2\varepsilon$ in the worst case (a database with lists of length 2 only, using the encoding EncodeSeparate from the full version). When sampling lists length uniformly at random between 1 and the page size, the storage efficiency is around 2.25 for $\varepsilon = 0.1$ and a database of size 2^{27}. For the encryption of Wikipedia (4.6 million keywords and 140 million entries), the storage efficiency is 3. (The extra cost beyond $2 + \varepsilon$ is mainly due to using the simpler, but suboptimal EncodeSeparate scheme from the full version.) In the full version, we further present the end-to-end latency of a search query on Tethys.

Finally, we have also plotted inverse read efficiency and inverse page efficiency for each scheme. As is apparent on Fig. 2, inverse page efficiency correlates very strongly with throughput. When computing the correlation between the two across the various experiments in Fig. 2, we get a correlation of 0.98, indicating a near-linear relationship. This further shows the accuracy of page efficiency as a predictor of performance on SSDs.

6   Conclusion

To conclude, we point out some problems for future work. First, like prior work on locality, Tethys only considers the most basic form of SSE: single-keyword queries, on a static database. A generalization to the dynamic setting opens up a number of interesting technical challenges. (A generic conversion from a static to a dynamic scheme may be found in [DP17], but would incur a logarithmic overhead in both storage efficiency and page efficiency.) A second limitation is that the initial setup of our main DIP algorithm, TethysDIP, has quadratic time complexity in the worst case. This is only a one-time precomputation, and practical performance is better than the worst-case bound would suggest, as shown in Sect. 5. Nevertheless, a more efficient algorithm would be welcome. Lastly, when querying a given keyword, Tethys returns entire pages of encrypted indices, some of which might not be associated to the keyword. Using an appropriate encoding, the matching keywords can be identified. While reducing volume leakage, this induces an overhead in communication, unlike other schemes such as Π_{bas} from [CJJ+14], where only matching identifiers are returned. Due to the practical relevance of page efficiency, the intent of this work is that the notion will spur further research.

Acknowledgments. The authors thank Jessie Bertanier for his explanations on the inner workings of SSDs, which motivated our investigation. This work was supported by the ANR JCJC project SaFED and ANR Cyberschool ANR-18-EURE-0004.

References

[ADW14]   Aumüller, M., Dietzfelbinger, M., Woelfel, P.: Explicit and efficient hash families suffice for cuckoo hashing with a stash. Algorithmica **70**(3), 428–456 (2014)

[ANSS16]   Asharov, G., Naor, M., Segev, G., Shahaf, I.: Searchable symmetric encryption: optimal locality in linear space via two-dimensional balanced allocations. In: Wichs, D., Mansour, Y. (eds.) 48th ACM STOC, pp. 1101–1114. ACM Press (June 2016)

[ASS18]   Asharov, G., Segev, G., Shahaf, I.: Tight tradeoffs in searchable symmetric encryption. In: Shacham, H., Boldyreva, A. (eds.) CRYPTO 2018. LNCS, vol. 10991, pp. 407–436. Springer, Cham (2018). https://doi.org/10.1007/978-3-319-96884-1_14

[Axb20]   Axboe, J.: Flexible I/O tester (2020). https://github.com/axboe/fio

[BFHM08]   Berenbrink, P., Friedetzky, T., Hu, Z., Martin, R.: On weighted balls-into-bins games. Theoret. Comput. Sci. **409**(3), 511–520 (2008)

[BMO17]   Bost, R., Minaud, B., Ohrimenko, O.: Forward and backward private searchable encryption from constrained cryptographic primitives. In: Thuraisingham, B.M., Evans, D., Malkin, T., Xu, D. (eds.) ACM CCS 2017, pp. 1465–1482. ACM Press (October/November 2017)

[Bol01] Bollobás, B.: Random Graphs. Cambridge Studies in Advanced Mathematics, 2 edn. Cambridge University Press (2001)

[Bos16] Bost, R.: Σοφος: Forward secure searchable encryption. In: Weippl, E.R., Katzenbeisser, S., Kruegel, C., Myers, A.C., Halevi, S. (eds.) ACM CCS 2016, pp. 1143–1154. ACM Press (October 2016)

[Bos21a] Bost, R.: Implementation of Tethys, and Pluto (2021). https://github.com/OpenSSE/opensse-schemes

[Bos21b] Bost, R.: Supplementary materials (2021). https://github.com/rbost/tethys-sim-rs

[CGKO06] Curtmola, R., Garay, J.A., Kamara, S., Ostrovsky, R. Searchable symmetric encryption: improved definitions and efficient constructions. In: Juels, A., Wright, R.N., De Capitani di Vimercati, S. (eds.) ACM CCS 2006, pp. 79–88. ACM Press (October/November 2006)

[CJJ+13] Cash, D., Jarecki, S., Jutla, C., Krawczyk, H., Roşu, M.-C., Steiner, M.: Highly-scalable searchable symmetric encryption with support for Boolean queries. In: Canetti, R., Garay, J.A. (eds.) CRYPTO 2013. LNCS, vol. 8042, pp. 353–373. Springer, Heidelberg (2013). https://doi.org/10.1007/978-3-642-40041-4_20

[CJJ+14] Cash, D., et al.: Dynamic searchable encryption in very-large databases: data structures and implementation. In: NDSS 2014. The Internet Society (February 2014)

[CT14] Cash, D., Tessaro, S.: The locality of searchable symmetric encryption. In: Nguyen, P.Q., Oswald, E. (eds.) EUROCRYPT 2014. LNCS, vol. 8441, pp. 351–368. Springer, Heidelberg (2014). https://doi.org/10.1007/978-3-642-55220-5_20

[DK12] Drmota, M., Kutzelnigg, R.: A precise analysis of cuckoo hashing. ACM Trans. Algorithms 8, 1–36 (2012)

[DP17] Demertzis, I., Papamanthou, C.: Fast searchable encryption with tunable locality. In: Proceedings of the 2017 ACM International Conference on Management of Data, pp. 1053–1067. ACM (2017)

[DPP18] Demertzis, I., Papadopoulos, D., Papamanthou, C.: Searchable encryption with optimal locality: achieving sublogarithmic read efficiency. In: Shacham, H., Boldyreva, A. (eds.) CRYPTO 2018. LNCS, vol. 10991, pp. 371–406. Springer, Cham (2018). https://doi.org/10.1007/978-3-319-96884-1_13

[DW05] Dietzfelbinger, M., Weidling, C.: Balanced allocation and dictionaries with tightly packed constant size bins. In: Caires, L., Italiano, G.F., Monteiro, L., Palamidessi, C., Yung, M. (eds.) ICALP 2005. LNCS, vol. 3580, pp. 166–178. Springer, Heidelberg (2005). https://doi.org/10.1007/11523468_14

[FF56] Ford, L.R., Fulkerson, D.R.: Maximal flow through a network. Can. J. Math. 8, 399–404 (1956)

[FNO20] Falk, B.H., Noble, D., Ostrovsky, R.: Alibi: a flaw in cuckoo-hashing based hierarchical ORAM schemes and a solution. Cryptology ePrint Archive, Report 2020/997 (2020). https://eprint.iacr.org/2020/997

[GM11] Goodrich, M.T., Mitzenmacher, M.: Privacy-preserving access of outsourced data via oblivious RAM simulation. In: Aceto, L., Henzinger, M., Sgall, J. (eds.) ICALP 2011. LNCS, vol. 6756, pp. 576–587. Springer, Heidelberg (2011). https://doi.org/10.1007/978-3-642-22012-8_46

[GR98] Goldberg, A.V., Rao, S.: Beyond the flow decomposition barrier. J. ACM (JACM) 45(5), 783–797 (1998)

[HKL+18] Hanaka, T., Katsikarelis, I., Lampis, M., Otachi, Y., Sikora, F.: Parameterized orientable deletion. In: SWAT (2018)

[KMO18] Kamara, S., Moataz, T., Ohrimenko, O.: Structured encryption and leakage suppression. In: Shacham, H., Boldyreva, A. (eds.) CRYPTO 2018. LNCS, vol. 10991, pp. 339–370. Springer, Cham (2018). https://doi.org/10.1007/978-3-319-96884-1_12

[KMW10] Kirsch, A., Mitzenmacher, M., Wieder, U.: More robust hashing: Cuckoo hashing with a stash. SIAM J. Comput. **39**(4), 1543–1561 (2010)

[MM17] Miers, I., Mohassel, P.: IO-DSSE: scaling dynamic searchable encryption to millions of indexes by improving locality. In: NDSS 2017. The Internet Society (February/March 2017)

[MPC+18] Mishra, P., Poddar, R., Chen, J., Chiesa, A., Popa, R.A.: Oblix: an efficient oblivious search index. In: 2018 IEEE Symposium on Security and Privacy, pp. 279–296. IEEE Computer Society Press (May 2018)

[PR04] Pagh, R., Rodler, F.F.: Cuckoo hashing. J. Algorithms **51**(2), 122–144 (2004)

[SEK03] Sanders, P., Egner, S., Korst, J.: Fast concurrent access to parallel disks. Algorithmica **35**(1), 21–55 (2003)

[Sta21] Statista: Shipments of hard and solid state disk (HDD/SSD) drives worldwide from 2015 to 2021 (2021). https://www.statista.com/statistics/285474/hdds-and-ssds-in-pcs-global-shipments-2012-2017/

[Wie17] Wieder, U.: Hashing, load balancing and multiple choice. Found. Trends Theor. Comput. Sci. **12**(3–4), 275–379 (2017)

Towards Tight Random Probing Security

Gaëtan Cassiers[1][(✉)], Sebastian Faust[2], Maximilian Orlt[2],
and François-Xavier Standaert[1]

[1] Crypto Group, ICTEAM Institute, UCLouvain, Louvain-la-Neuve, Belgium
{gaetan.cassiers,fstandae}@uclouvain.be
[2] TU Darmstadt, Darmstadt, Germany
{sebastian.faust,maximilian.orlt}@tu-darmstadt.de

Abstract. Proving the security of masked implementations in theoretical models that are relevant to practice and match the best known attacks of the side-channel literature is a notoriously hard problem. The random probing model is a promising candidate to contribute to this challenge, due to its ability to capture the continuous nature of physical leakage (contrary to the threshold probing model), while also being convenient to manipulate in proofs and to automate with verification tools. Yet, despite recent progress in the design of masked circuits with good asymptotic security guarantees in this model, existing results still fall short when it comes to analyze the security of concretely useful circuits under realistic noise levels and with low number of shares. In this paper, we contribute to this issue by introducing a new composability notion, the *Probe Distribution Table (PDT)*, and a new tool (called STRAPS, for the Sampled Testing of the RAndom Probing Security). Their combination allows us to significantly improve the tightness of existing analyses in the most practical (low noise, low number of shares) region of the design space. We illustrate these improvements by quantifying the random probing security of an AES S-box circuit, masked with the popular multiplication gadget of Ishai, Sahai and Wagner from Crypto 2003, with up to six shares.

1 Introduction

Context. Modern cryptography primarily analyzes the security of algorithms or protocols in a black-box model where the adversary has only access to their inputs and outputs. Since the late nineties, it is known that real-world implementations suffer from so-called side-channel leakage, which gives adversaries some information about intermediate computation states that are supposedly hidden. In this work, we focus on an important class of side-channel attacks against embedded devices, which exploits physical leakage such as their power consumption [26] or electro-magnetic radiation [22]. We are in particular concerned with the masking countermeasure [14], which is one of the most investigated solutions to mitigate side-channel attacks. In this context, the main scientific challenge we tackle is to find out security arguments that are at the same time practically relevant and theoretically sound.

© International Association for Cryptologic Research 2021
T. Malkin and C. Peikert (Eds.): CRYPTO 2021, LNCS 12827, pp. 185–214, 2021.
https://doi.org/10.1007/978-3-030-84252-9_7

Two Separated Worlds. In view of the difficulty to model side-channel attacks, their practical and theoretical investigations have first followed quite independent paths. On the practical side, the analysis of masked implementations as currently performed by evaluation laboratories is mostly based on statistical testing. Approaches for this purpose range from detection-based testing, which aims at identifying leakage independently of whether it can be exploited [32], to attack-based testing under various adversarial assumptions, which aims at approximating (if possible bounding) the concrete security level of the implementation with actual (profiled or non-profiled) attacks such as [11, 15] and their numerous follow ups. On the theoretical side, the first model introduced to capture the security of masked implementations is the t-threshold probing model introduced by Ishai, Sahai and Wagner (ISW) [24]. In this model, leaky computation is captured as the evaluation of an arithmetic circuit, and the adversary may choose t wires of the circuit for which she receives the value they carry. The adversary succeeds if she recovers a secret input variable of the circuit.

The pros and cons of both approaches are easy to spot. On the one hand, statistical testing provides quantitative evaluations against concrete adversaries, but the guarantees it offers are inherently heuristic and limited to the specific setting used for the evaluations. On the other hand, theoretical models enable more general conclusions while also having a good potential for automation [5], but they may imperfectly abstract physical leakage. For some imperfections, tweaking the model appeared to be feasible. For example, ISW's threshold probing model initially failed to capture physical defaults such as glitches that can make masking ineffective [27, 28]. Such glitches were then integrated in the model [21] and automated [4, 6, 10]. Yet, it remained that the threshold probing model is inherently unable to capture the continuous nature of physical leakage, and therefore the guarantees it provides can only be qualitative, as reflected by the notion of probing security order (i.e., the number of shares that the adversary can observe without learning any sensitive information). This also implies that so-called horizontal attacks taking advantage of multiple leakage points to reduce the noise of the implementations cannot be captured by this model [7].

An Untight Unifying Approach. As a result of this limitation, the noisy leakage model was introduced by Prouff and Rivain [30]. In this model, each wire in the circuit leaks independently a noisy (i.e., partially randomized) value to the adversary. In an important piece of work, Duc et al. then proved that security in the threshold probing model implies security in the noisy leakage model, for some values of the model parameters [17]. This result created new bridges between the practical and theoretical analyzes of masked implementations. In particular, it made explicit that the security of this countermeasure depends both on a security order (which, under an independence assumption, depends on the number of shares) and on the noise level of the shares' leakage. So conceptually, it implies that it is sound to first evaluate the probing security order of an implementation, next to verify that this security order is maintained in concrete leakages (e.g., using detection-based statistical testing) and finally to assess the noise level. Yet, and as discussed in [18], such an analysis is still not tight: choosing security parameters based on this combination of models and the reductions connecting them would lead to overly expensive implementations compared to a choice based on the best known (profiled) side-channel attacks.

A Tighter Middle-Ground. Incidentally, the reduction of Duc et al. also considered an intermediate level of abstraction denoted as the random probing model. In this model, each wire in the circuit independently leaks its value with probability p (and leaks no information with probability $1 - p$). Technically, it turns out that the aforementioned tightness issue is mostly due to the reduction from the threshold probing model to the random probing model, while there is a closer relationship between the random probing model and the noisy leakage model [19,29]. Since the random probing model remains relatively easy to manipulate (and automate) in circuit-level proofs, it therefore appears as an interesting candidate to analyze masking schemes with tight security guarantees.

Like the noisy leakage model, the random probing model captures the concept of "noise rate", which specifies how the noise level of an implementation must evolve with the number of shares in order to remain secure against horizontal attacks. As a result, different papers focused on the design and analysis of gadgets with good (ideally constant) noise rate [1–3,20,23]. While these papers provide important steps in the direction of asymptotically efficient masking schemes, the actual number of shares they need to guarantee a given security level and/or the noise level they require to be secure remain far from practical. To the best of our knowledge, the most concrete contribution in this direction is the one of Belaïd et al. [8,9], which introduced a compiler that can generate random probing secure circuits from small gadgets satisfying a notion of "random probing expandability", together with a tool (called VRAPS) that quantifies the random probing security of a circuit from its leakage probability. With this tool, they reduce the level of noise required for security to practically acceptable values, but the number of shares required in order to reach a given security level for their (specialized) constructions is still significantly higher than expected from practical security evaluations – we give an example below.

Our Contributions. In this paper, we improve the tightness of masking security proofs in the most practical (low noise, low number of shares) region of the design space, focusing on practical ISW-like multiplication gadgets, integrated in an AES S-box design for illustration purposes. More precisely:

We first introduce STRAPS, a tool for the Sampled Testing of the RAndom Probing Security of small circuits, which uses the Monte-Carlo technique for probability bounding and is released under an open source license.[1]

Since this tool is limited to the analysis of small circuits and/or small security orders due to computational reasons, we next combine it with a new compositional strategy that exploits a new security property for masked gadgets, the Probe Distribution Table (PDT), which gives tighter security bounds for composed circuits and is integrated in the STRAPS tool. This combination of tool and compositional strategy allows us analyzing significantly larger circuits and security orders than an exhaustive approach, while also being able to analyze any circuit (i.e., it does not rely on an expansion strategy [2]).

---

[1] https://github.com/cassiersg/STRAPS.

We finally confirm the practical relevance of our findings by applying them to a masked AES S-box using ISW gadgets. We show how to use them in order to discuss the trade-off between the security order and the noise level (i.e., leakage probability) of concrete masked implementations on formal bases. As an illustration, we use our tools to compare the impact of different refreshing strategies for the AES S-box (e.g., no refresh, simple refreshes or SNI refreshes) in function of the noise level. We can also claim provable security levels for useful circuits that are close to the worst-case attacks discussed in [18] which is in contrast to previous works. Precisely, we are able to prove the same statistical security order (i.e., the highest statistical moment of the leakage distribution that is independent of any sensitive information) as in this reference, for realistic leakage probabilities in the range $[10^{-1}; 10^{-4}]$. For example, our AES S-box with 6 shares and leakage probability of $\approx 10^{-3}$ ensures security against an adversary with up to one billion measurements. Belaïd et al. would need 27 shares to reach the same security.

Open Problems and Related Works. While providing tight results for a masked AES S-box implementation with up to 6 shares, therefore opening the way towards tight random probing security in general, we note that our composition results are not completely tight in certain contexts which (we discuss in the paper and) could pop up in other circuits than the AES S-box. Hence, generalizing our results to be tight for any circuit is an interesting open problem and the same holds for optimizing the complexity of our verification techniques in order to scale with even larger circuits and number of shares.

Besides, we illustrated our results with the popular ISW multiplications in order to show their applicability to non-specialized gadgets, which are concretely relevant for the number of shares and noise levels we consider. Yet, since one of the motivations to use the random probing model is to capture horizontal attacks, it would also be interesting to analyze multiplication algorithms that provide improved guarantees against such attacks thanks to a logarithmic or even constant noise rate and could not be proven so far (e.g., [7,13]).

2   Background

Notations. In this work, we consider Boolean or arithmetic circuits over finite fields $\mathbb{F}_{2^m}$ and refer to the underlying additive and multiplicative operations as $\oplus$ and $\odot$, respectively. For the sake of simplicity we also use these operations for a share-wise composition of vectors $(v_i)_{i \in [n]}$ and $(w_i)_{i \in [n]}$ with $[n] = \{0, 1, \ldots, n-1\}$ such that $(v_i)_{i \in [n]} \odot (w_i)_{i \in [n]} := (v_i \odot w_i)_{i \in [n]}$ and $(v_i)_{i \in [n]} \oplus (w_i)_{i \in [n]} := (v_i \oplus w_i)_{i \in [n]}$. Furthermore, we use the Kronecker product to compose two real matrices $A = (a_{i,j})_{i \in [m], j \in [n]}$, $B = (b_{i,j})_{i \in [k], j \in [l]}$ such that $A \otimes B = (a_{i,j}B)_{i \in [m], j \in [n]}$. We also denote $x \xleftarrow{\$} \mathcal{X}$ as choosing x uniformly at random from the set $\mathcal{X}$, and $\mathcal{X}^{(k)}$ as the set of subsets of $\mathcal{X}$ of size k.

Masking. Masking is a well known countermeasure against side-channel attacks. With an encoding scheme $(\mathsf{Enc}(\cdot), \mathsf{Dec}(\cdot))$, sensitive data x is split into n shares (represented as a vector) $(x_i)_{i \in [n]} \leftarrow \mathsf{Enc}(x)$, and the decoding function takes as input the n shares and recovers the unshared value x, i.e., $x \leftarrow \mathsf{Dec}((x_i)_{i \in [n]})$. For security we require that any subset of $n-1$ shares does not reveal any information about the sensitive data x. In this work, we focus on additive sharing $\mathsf{Dec}((x_i)_{i \in [n]}) = \bigoplus_{i=0}^{n-1} x_i$, which is the most studied scheme.

Circuit Model. As common in masking scheme literature, we model computation as arithmetic circuits operating over a finite field $\mathbb{F}_{2^m}$. The circuit is represented by a directed acyclic graph, where each node is a gate that has a fixed number of input and output wires (incoming and outgoing edges) that carry arithmetic values. We consider the following types of gates in our circuits: addition $\oplus$- and multiplication $\odot$- gates have two input wires and one output wire, and perform the corresponding arithmetic operation. The copy gate $\multimap$ has one input and two outputs, and is used to duplicate a value. Finally, the random gate $\circledR$- has no input and one output, which carries a uniformly distributed value. The constant gate $\circledcirc$- outputs a constant value a.

In a masked circuit the gates are represented by subcircuits called gadgets G. These gadgets operate on encoded inputs and produce encoded outputs. The gadgets contain: (1) A set of gates; (2) The set of wires that connect the inputs and outputs of those gates named internal wires $(\mathcal{W})$; (3) The set of wires only connected with those gates' input named input wires $(\mathcal{I})$; (4) The set of output gates $\hat{\mathcal{O}}$ (which is the subset of its gates that output wires that are not connected to another gate of the gadget). The gadgets, however, contain no output wires, such that each wire in a circuit composed of multiple gadgets belongs to only one of its composing gadgets. For convenience, we also write $\mathcal{O}$ for the set of output wires of the gates in $\hat{\mathcal{O}}$, although these wires are not part of the gadget but are the next gadgets input wires. We denote $\mathcal{A} = \mathcal{W} \cup \mathcal{I}$ the set of all wires in the gadget. The inputs and outputs of a gadget are partitioned in (ordered) sets of n elements named sharings (and each element is a share). A gadget G_f that implements the function $f : \mathbb{F}^l \mapsto \mathbb{F}^k$ with n shares has l input sharings and k output sharings. Let $(y_i^0)_{i \in [n]}, \ldots, (y_i^{k-1})_{i \in [n]}$ be the values of the output sharings when the input sharings have the values $(x_i^0)_{i \in [n]}, \ldots, (x_i^{l-1})_{i \in [n]}$. It must hold that

$$f(\mathsf{Dec}((x_i^0)_{i \in [n]}), \ldots, \mathsf{Dec}((x_i^{l-1})_{i \in [n]})) = (\mathsf{Dec}((y_i^0)_{i \in [n]}), \ldots, \mathsf{Dec}((y_i^{k-1})_{i \in [n]})).$$

In this work, we use various gadgets. First, gadgets that implement linear operations (addition $\mathsf{G}_\oplus$, copy $\mathsf{G}_{\multimap}$, squaring $\mathsf{G}_{.^2}$), which we implement share-wise. Next, we use the ISW multiplication gadget [24]. Finally, we use refresh gadgets $\mathsf{G}_{\circledR}$ which re-randomize a sharing $(x_i)_{i \in [n]}$ to $(y_i)_{i \in [n]}$ such that $\mathsf{Dec}((x_i)_{i \in [n]}) = \mathsf{Dec}((y_i)_{i \in [n]})$. We consider two refresh gadget implementations: the simple refresh and the SNI, randomness-optimized refresh gadgets from [12]. Their algorithmic description is given in the extended version of the paper.

Leakage Model. In this work we consider the p-random probing model as originally introduced by Ishai, Sahai and Wagner [24]. This model defines the following random probing experiment. Let $\mathcal{W}$ be a set of wires in a circuit, $\mathcal{L}_p(\mathcal{W})$

is a random variable with $\mathcal{L}_p(\mathcal{W}) \subseteq \mathcal{W}$, such that each wire $w \in \mathcal{W}$ is in $\mathcal{L}_p(\mathcal{W})$ with probability p (independently for each wire). Following this notation, for a gadget G, we denote by $\mathcal{L}_p(\mathsf{G}) := \mathcal{L}_p(\mathcal{W}, \mathcal{I}) := (\mathcal{L}_p(\mathcal{W}), \mathcal{L}_p(\mathcal{I}))$, where $\mathcal{W}$ and $\mathcal{I}$ are the set of internal and input wires of G, respectively.

For a gadget G, a set of probes is a successful attack for an input sharing $(x_i)_{i \in [n]}$ if the joint distribution of the values carried by the probes depends on $\mathsf{Dec}((x_i)_{i \in [n]})$ (assuming that the other input sharings are public). The security level of G in the p-random probing model (or p-random probing security) with respect to an input sharing $(x_i)_{i \in [n]}$ is the probability (over the randomness in $\mathcal{L}_p$) that a set of probes $\mathcal{L}_p(\mathsf{G})$ is a successful attack. As a result, the security of a gadget in bits is worth $- \log_2(\text{security level})$. We omit to mention the attacked input sharing when the gadget has only one input sharing.

3   Random Probing Security of Small Circuits

In this section, we show how to efficiently compute an upper bound on the random probing security level of relatively small gadgets, and we illustrate the results on well-known masked gadgets. We also describe the high-level ideas that will lead to the STRAPS tool that we describe in Sect. 5.3.

3.1   Derivation of a Random Probing Security Bound

We first derive a way to compute the security level of a gadget for various values of p, using some computationally heavy pre-processing. Next, we explain a way to use statistical confidence intervals to reduce the cost of the pre-processing. Finally, we detail how these techniques are implemented in a practical algorithm.

A Simple Bound. We can obtain the security level of a small circuit by computing first the statistical distribution of $\mathcal{L}_p(\mathsf{G})$ (i.e., $\Pr[\mathcal{L}_p(\mathcal{A}) = \mathcal{A}']$ for each subset $\mathcal{A}' \subset \mathcal{A}$). Then, for each possible set of probes $\mathcal{A}'$, we do a dependency test in order to determine if the set is a successful attack, denoted as $\delta_{\mathcal{A}'} = 1$, while $\delta_{\mathcal{A}'} = 0$ otherwise [8]. There exist various tools that can be used to carry out such a dependency test, such as maskVerif [4] or SILVER [25] (while such tools are designed to prove threshold probing security, they perform dependency tests as a sub-routine). A first naive algorithm to compute the security level ϵ is thus given by the equation

$$\epsilon = \sum_{\substack{\mathcal{A}' \subset \mathcal{A} \\ \text{s.t. } \delta_{\mathcal{A}'} = 1}} \Pr[\mathcal{L}_p(\mathcal{A}) = \mathcal{A}']. \tag{1}$$

The computational cost of iterating over all possible probe sets grows exponentially with $|\mathcal{A}|$: for a circuit with $|\mathcal{A}|$ internal wires, one has to do $2^{|\mathcal{A}|}$ dependency tests, for each value of p (e.g., we have $|\mathcal{A}| = 57$ for the ISW multiplication with three shares). To efficiently cover multiple values of p, we introduce a first improvement to the naive algorithm given by Eq. (1). For each $i \in \{0, \dots, |\mathcal{A}|\}$, we compute the number c_i of sets of probes of size i that are successful attacks $c_i = \left| \{ \mathcal{A}' \in \mathcal{A}^{(i)} \text{ s.t. } \delta_{\mathcal{A}'} = 1 \} \right|$. Then, we can compute

$$\epsilon = \sum_{i=0}^{|\mathcal{A}|} p^i (1-p)^{|\mathcal{A}|-i} c_i, \tag{2}$$

which gives us a more efficient algorithm to compute random probing security, since it re-uses the costly computation of c_i for multiple values of p.

The VRAPS tool [8] computes c_i for small values of i by computing $\delta_{\mathcal{A}'}$ for all $\mathcal{A}' \in \mathcal{A}^{(i)}$. This is however computationally intractable for larger i values, hence they use the bound $c_i \leq \binom{|\mathcal{A}|}{i}$ in such cases.

A Statistical Bound. Let us now show how to improve the bound $c_i \leq \binom{|\mathcal{A}|}{i}$ while keeping a practical computational cost. At a high level, we achieve this by using a Monte-Carlo method whose idea is as follows: instead of computing directly ϵ, we run a randomized computation that gives us information about ϵ (but not its exact value). More precisely, the result of our Monte-Carlo method is a random variable ϵ^U that satisfies $\epsilon^U \geq \epsilon$ with probability at least $1 - \alpha$ (the confidence level), where α is a parameter of the computation. That is, $\Pr_{\mathrm{MC}} \left[\epsilon^U \geq \epsilon \right] \geq 1 - \alpha$, where $\Pr_{\mathrm{MC}}$ means the probability over the randomness used in the Monte-Carlo method.[2] In the rest of this work, we use $\alpha = 10^{-6}$ since we consider that it corresponds to a sufficient confidence level.[3]

Let us now detail the method. First, let $r_i = c_i / |\mathcal{A}^{(i)}|$. We remark that r_i can be interpreted as a probability: $r_i = \Pr_{\mathcal{A}' \xleftarrow{\$} \mathcal{A}^{(i)}} [\delta_{\mathcal{A}'} = 1]$. The Monte-Carlo method actually computes r_i^U such that $r_i^U \geq r_i$ with probability at least $1 - \alpha / (|\mathcal{A}| + 1)$. Once the r_i^U are computed, the result is

$$\epsilon^U = \sum_{i=0}^{|\mathcal{A}|} p^i (1-p)^{|\mathcal{A}|-i} \binom{|\mathcal{A}|}{i} r_i^U, \tag{3}$$

which ensures that $\epsilon^U \geq \epsilon$ for any p with confidence level $1 - \alpha$, thanks to the union bound. Next, r_i^U is computed by running the following experiment: take t_i samples $\mathcal{A}' \xleftarrow{\$} \mathcal{A}^{(i)}$ uniformly at random (this sampling is the random part of the Monte-Carlo method) and compute the number s_i of samples for which $\delta_{\mathcal{A}'} = 1$. By definition, s_i is a random variable that follows a binomial distribution $B(t_i, r_i)$: the total number of samples is t_i and the "success" probability is r_i. We can thus use the bound derived in [33]. If r_i^U satisfies $\mathrm{CDF}_{\mathrm{binom}}(s_i; t_i, r_i^U) = \alpha / (|\mathcal{A}| + 1)$, then $\Pr[r_i^U \geq r_i] = 1 - \alpha / (|\mathcal{A}| + 1)$, which gives

$$r_i^U = \begin{cases} 1 & \text{if } s_i = t_i, \\ x \quad \text{s.t.} \quad I_x(s_i + 1, t_i - s_i) = 1 - \alpha / (|\mathcal{A}| + 1) & \text{otherwise,} \end{cases} \tag{4}$$

---

[2] In other words, $[0, \epsilon^U]$ is a conservative confidence interval for ϵ with nominal coverage probability of $1 - \alpha$.

[3] This parameter is not critical: we can obtain a similar value for ϵ^U with higher confidence level by increasing the amount of computation: requiring $\alpha = 10^{-12}$ would roughly double the computational cost of the Monte-Carlo method.

where $I_x(a, b)$ is the regularized incomplete beta function. We can similarly compute a lower bound ϵ^L such that $\epsilon^L \leq \epsilon$ with confidence coefficient $1 - \alpha$, which we compute by replacing r_i^U with r_i^L in Eq. (3), where:

$$r_i^L = \begin{cases} 0 & \text{if } s_i = 0, \\ x \quad \text{s.t.} \quad I_x(s_i, t_i - s_i + 1) = \alpha/(|\mathcal{A}| + 1) & \text{otherwise.} \end{cases} \tag{5}$$

A Hybrid Algorithm. Our Monte-Carlo method has a main limitation: when $r_i = 0$ the bound r_i^U will not be null (it will be proportional to $1/t_i$). This means that we cannot prove tightly the security of interesting gadgets when p is small. For instance, let us take a fourth-order secure gadget (that is, $r_0 = r_1 = r_2 = r_3 = r_4 = 0$). If $r_1^U \neq 1$, then ϵ^U scales like $r_1^U p$ as p becomes small (other, higher degree, terms become negligible). A solution to this problem would be to set t_i to a large number, such that, in our example, r_1^U would be small enough to guarantee that $r_1^U p \ll r_5 p^5$ for all considered values of p. If we care about $p = 10^{-3}$, this means $r_1^U \ll 10^{-12} \cdot r_5 \leq 10^{-12}$. This is however practically infeasible since the number of samples t_1 is of the order of magnitude $1/r_1^U > 10^{12}$.

There exist another solution, which we call the hybrid algorithm: perform a full exploration of $\mathcal{A}^{(i)}$ (i.e., use the algorithm based on Eq. (2)) when it is not computationally too expensive (i.e., when $|\mathcal{A}^{(i)}|$ is below some limit N_{max}), and otherwise use the Monte-Carlo method. The goal of this hybrid algorithm is to perform a full exploration when $r_i = 0$ (in order to avoid the limitation discussed above), which can be achieved for gadgets with a small number n of shares. Indeed, r_i can be null only for $i < n$ (otherwise there can be probes on all the shares of the considered input sharing), and the number of cases for the full exploration is therefore $|\mathcal{A}^{(i)}| = \binom{|\mathcal{A}|}{i} \leq \binom{|\mathcal{A}|}{n-1}$, which is smaller than N_{max} if n and $|\mathcal{A}|$ are sufficiently small. The latter inequality holds if $|\mathcal{A}| \geq 2(n-1)$, which holds for all non-trivial gadgets.

Algorithm 1 describes how we choose between full enumeration and Monte-Carlo sampling, which is the basis of our STRAPS tool (see Sect. 5.3 for more details). The algorithm adds a refinement on top of the above explanation: if we can cheaply show that r_i is far from zero, we do not perform full exploration even if it would not be too expensive. It accelerates the tool, while keeping a good bound. This optimization is implemented by always starting with a Monte-Carlo sampling loop that takes at most N_{max} samples, with an early stop if s_i goes above the value of a parameter N_t (we typically use parameters such that $N_{max} \gg N_t$). The parameter N_t determines the relative accuracy of the bound we achieve when we do the early stop: in the final sampling, we will have $s_i \approx N_t$, which means that the uncertainty on r_i decreases as N_t increases. The parameter N_{max} has an impact when r_i is small and we do not reach N_t successful attacks: it limits both the maximum size of $\mathcal{A}^{(i)}$ for which full exploration is performed, and the number of samples used for the Monte-Carlo method.

Remark. The Monte-Carlo method is limited to the random probing model and cannot be used to prove security in the threshold probing model since proving

Algorithm 1. Random probing security algorithm: compute r_i^U, r_i^L for a given $\mathcal{A}$ and i. The parameters are N_{max} and N_t.

Require $N_t \leq N_{max}$
$N_{sets} = \binom{|\mathcal{A}|}{i}$
$t_i \leftarrow 1$, $s_i \leftarrow 0$ ▷ t_i: total number of samples, s_i: successful attacks
while $t_i \leq N_{max} \wedge s_i < N_t$ **do**   ▷ First Monte-Carlo sampling loop
      $\mathcal{A}' \xleftarrow{\$} \mathcal{A}^{(i)}$
      if $\delta_{\mathcal{A}'} = 1$ **then**
            $s_i \leftarrow s_i + 1$.
      $t_i \leftarrow t_i + 1$
if $N_{sets} \leq t_i$ **then**   ▷ Enumerate $\mathcal{A}^{(i)}$ if it is cheaper than Monte-Carlo.
      $s_i \leftarrow 0$
      for all $\mathcal{A}' \in \mathcal{A}^{(i)}$ **do**
            if $\delta_{\mathcal{A}'} = 1$ **then**
                  $s_i \leftarrow s_i + 1$
      $r_i^U \leftarrow s_i/N_{sets}$, $r_i^L \leftarrow s_i/N_{sets}$
else   ▷ Re-run Monte-Carlo to avoid bias due to N_t early stopping.
      $s_i \leftarrow 0$
      Repeat t_i **times**
            $\mathcal{A}' \xleftarrow{\$} \mathcal{A}^{(i)}$
            if $\delta_{\mathcal{A}'} = 1$ **then**
                  $s_i \leftarrow s_i + 1$
      Compute r_i^U and r_i^L using Equations (4) and (5).

---

security in this model means proving that $r_i = 0$, which it cannot do. Our hybrid algorithm, however, can prove threshold probing security for the numbers of probes i where it does full enumeration of $\mathcal{A}^{(j)}$ for all $j \in \{0, \ldots, i\}$.

Dependency Test. We use the dependency test algorithm from maskVerif [4], as it offers two important characteristics: (i) it gives the set of input shares on which the probes depend, not only if there is a dependency to the unshared variable (the reason for this appears in Sect. 5.1), and (ii) it is quite efficient. One drawback of the maskVerif dependency test is that in some cases, it wrongly reports that the adversary succeeds, which implies that the statistical lower bound is not anymore a lower bound for the security level, and the statistical upper bound is not completely tight (but it is still an upper bound for the true security level). In this case, we refer to the statistical lower bound as the *stat-only* lower bound. While the stat-only lower bound is not indicative of the security level, it remains useful to quantify the statistical uncertainty and therefore to assess whether one could improve the tightness of the upper bound by increasing the number of samples in the Monte Carlo method.

3.2   Security of Some Simple Gadgets

We now present the results of random probing security evaluations using the previously described tools. First, we discuss the sharewise XOR gadget and the

ISW multiplication gadget with n shares. Next, we discuss the impact of the two parameters of our algorithm (N_{max} and N_t) on the tightness of the results and on the computational complexity (i.e., the execution time) of the tool.

In Fig. 1 (left), we show the security level (with respect to one of the inputs) of the addition gadget for $n = 1, \ldots, 6$ shares. We can see that the security level of the gadget is proportional to p^n, which is expected. Indeed, the graph of this share-wise gadget is made of n connected components (so-called "circuit shares" [12]) such that each share of a given input sharing belongs to a distinct component, and the adversary needs at least one probe in each of them to succeed. This trend can also be linked with the security order in the threshold probing model. Since the gadget is $n - 1$-threshold probing secure, a successful attack contains at least n probes, hence has probability proportional to p^n.

We can observe a similar trend for the ISW multiplication gadget (Fig. 1, right). Since the gadget is $n - 1$-threshold probing secure, the security level scales proportionally to p^n for small values of p. For larger values of p, the security level of this gadget is worse than p^n, which is due to the larger number of wires, and the increased connectivity compared to the addition gadgets. It implies that there are many sets of probes of sizes $n+1$, $n+2$, ... that are successful attacks (which is usually referred to as horizontal attacks in the practical side-channel literature [7]). These sets make up for a large part of the success probability when $p > 0.05$ due to their large number, even though they individually have a lower probability of occurring than a set of size n (for $p < 0.5$).

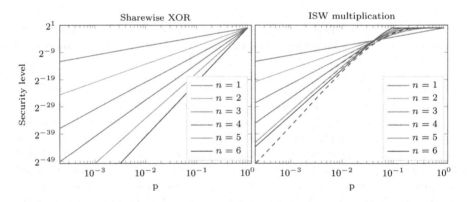

Fig. 1. Security of masked gadgets (with respect to the input sharing x, assuming the input sharing y is public). The continuous line is an upper bound, while the dashed line is the stat-only lower bound. $N_{max} = 10^7$, $N_t = 1000$.

Next, we discuss the impact of parameters N_{max} and N_t in Algorithm 1 on the tightness of the bounds we can compute. We first focus on the impact of N_t, which is shown on Fig. 2. For $N_t = 10$, we have a significant distance between the statistical upper and lower bounds, while the gap becomes small for $N_t = 100$ and $N_t = 1000$. This gap appears as a bounded factor between the upper and lower bounds which, as discussed previously, is related to the accuracy of the estimate of a proportion when we have about N_t positive samples.

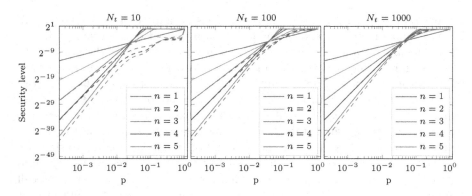

Fig. 2. Impact of the parameter N_t of Algorithm 1 on the security bounds of masked ISW multiplication gadgets (w.r.t. the input sharing x). $N_{max} = 10^7$.

We also look at the impact of N_{max} on Fig. 3. We observe a gap between the bounds for too low N_{max} values, which gets worse as the number of shares increases. Indeed, when N_{max} is too small, we cannot do an enumeration of all the sets of $n - 1$ probes, hence we cannot prove that the security order of the gadget is at least $n - 1$, which means that the upper bound is asymptotically proportional to $p^{n'}$, with $n' < n - 1$.

We finally observed that the computational cost is primarily dependent on N_{max} and the circuit size, while N_t has a lower impact (for the values considered). For instance, the execution time of the tool for the ISW multiplication with $n = 6$, $N_{max} = 10^8$ and $N_t = 100$ is about 33 h on a 24-core computer.

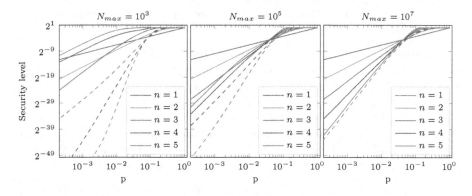

Fig. 3. Impact of the parameter N_{max} of Algorithm 1 on the security bounds of masked ISW multiplication gadgets (w.r.t. the input sharing x). $N_t = 1000$.

4   New Composition Results

In the previous section, it became clear that the tool is limited if it directly computes the security of complex circuits. This leads to the need to investigate composition properties. The existing definitions of random probing composability and random probing expandability in [8] are based on counting probes at the inputs and outputs of gadgets which are needed to simulate the leakage. We have recognized that ignoring the concrete random distribution over the needed input/output wires, and only counting the wires leads to a significant loss of tightness. Therefore we introduce our new security notion, the **PDT**. Before we define the **PDT** in Sect. 4.3 and present the composition results in Sect. 4.4, we recall the idea of simulatability in the leakage setting. Refining the dependency test of Sect. 3, we analyze the information a simulator needs to simulate a gadget's leakage in Sect. 4.2. In contrast to the previous section, we take into account the output gates, which is needed for composition. Further, we recall the definitions of parallel and sequential composition in Sect. 4.1, and present formal definitions adapted for our **PDT**s.

4.1   Definitions

Given two gadgets G_0 and G_1 with n shares, we define in this section the gadgets formed by their sequential composition written $G = G_1 \circ G_0$ or their parallel composition written $G = G_1 || G_0$.

We first introduce notations that allows us to keep track of input wires, output gates and internal wires in gadget compositions. We work with ordered finite sets. That is, given a finite set A (e.g., one of the sets $\mathcal{W}, \mathcal{I}$ or $\hat{\mathcal{O}}$ of a gadget G), we assign to each element of A a unique index in $[|A|] = \{0, 1, \ldots, |A|\}$. Then, given disjoint finite sets A and B, we denote by $C = A||_{(k)}B$ the union of A and B ordered such that a wire with index i in A has index i in C, and a wire with index i in B has index $k + i$ in B. The $||_{(.)}$ operator is right-associative, which means that $A_2||_{(k_1)}A_1||_{(k_0)}A_0 = A_2||_{(k_1)}\left(A_1||_{(k_0)}A_0\right)$.

The sequential composition of gadgets allows implementing compositions of functions and is formally defined next.

Definition 1 (Sequential composition). *Let G_0 and G_1 two gadgets with n shares, input wires $\mathcal{I}_i$, output gates $\hat{\mathcal{O}}_i$, and internal wires $\mathcal{W}_i$, respectively, such that $|\mathcal{I}_1| = |\hat{\mathcal{O}}_0|$. The sequential composition of G_0 and G_1 is the gadget G denoted as $G_1 \circ G_0$ whose set of input wires is $\mathcal{I} = \mathcal{I}_0$ and set of output gates is $\hat{\mathcal{O}} = \hat{\mathcal{O}}_1$. The set of internal wires of G is $\mathcal{W} = \mathcal{W}_1||_{(k_1)}\mathcal{I}_1||_{(k_0)}\mathcal{W}_0$ with $k_1 = |\mathcal{W}_0| + |\mathcal{I}_1|$ and $k_0 = |\mathcal{W}_0|$. The input wires of G_1 are connected to the output gates of G_0 such that for all i the input wire with index i is the output wire of the ith output gate. If G_0 (resp. G_1) implements f_0 (resp. f_1), then G implements $f_1 \circ f_0$.*

The parallel composition of gadgets allows implementing a gadget for the function $f(x, y) = (f_0(x), f_1(y))$, using gadgets implementing f_0 and f_1.

Definition 2 (Parallel composition). *Let G_0 and G_1 two gadgets with n shares, input wires $\mathcal{I}_i$, output gates $\hat{\mathcal{O}}_i$, and internal wires $\mathcal{W}_i$, respectively. The parallel composition of G_0 and G_1 is the gadget G denoted as $G_1 || G_0$ whose set of input wires is $\mathcal{I} = \mathcal{I}_1||_{(|\mathcal{I}_0|)}\mathcal{I}_0$, set of output gates is $\hat{\mathcal{O}} = \hat{\mathcal{O}}_1||_{(|\hat{\mathcal{O}}_0|)}\hat{\mathcal{O}}_0$, and set of internal wires is $\mathcal{W} = \mathcal{W}_1||_{(|\mathcal{W}_0|)}\mathcal{W}_0$.*

Figure 4 illustrates how to renumber the input wires and output gates in the case of gadgets with three inputs wires and three output gates. Figure 4a describes the sequential composition defined in Definition 1 and Fig. 4b describes the parallel composition defined in Definition 2. For example, the input wire set of G' is $\mathcal{I} = \{i_5, i_4, \ldots, i_0\}$ which is the wire union $\mathcal{I} = \mathcal{I}_1 ||_{(|\mathcal{I}_0|)} \mathcal{I}_0$ of the input wires $\mathcal{I}_0 = \{i_2^0, i_1^0, i_0^0\}$ and $\mathcal{I}_1 = \{i_2^1, i_1^1, i_0^1\}$ of the gadgets G_0 and G_1.

We emphasize that both compositions are a basis for dividing a circuit into an arbitrary set of subcircuits. Therefore, if we have a masked gadget implementation of each gate type that appears in a circuit, we can build a masking compiler for that circuit: first decompose the circuit in sequential and parallel compositions down to subcircuits containing a single gate, then replace each gate with the corresponding masked gadget, and finally compose those gadgets according to the initial decomposition. As a case study, we depict a masked AES S-box implementation in Fig. 6. The gadgets G_0-G_{10} are a parallel composition of the basis gadgets and $\mathsf{G}_{\text{S-box}}$ is a sequential composition of the gadgets G_0-G_{10}. The formal description of the S-box composition is given in Table 1.

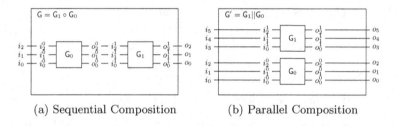

(a) Sequential Composition   (b) Parallel Composition

Fig. 4. Examples of sequential composition (4a) and parallel composition (4b).

4.2 Simulatability

So far, we described how to measure the amount of information leaked by a circuit by analyzing it directly. As observed in previous works, the complexity of such an approach rapidly turns out to be unrealistic. We now formalize simulatability-based definitions following the ideas outlined in [5], which are useful to analyze large circuits thanks to compositional reasoning.

Definition 3 (Simulatability). *A set of wires $\mathcal{W}$ in a gadget G is simulatable by a subset $\mathcal{I}' \subset \mathcal{I}$ of its inputs if there exists a probabilistic simulator function taking as input the values of the inputs $\mathcal{I}'$, and outputs a distribution of values on wires. Conditioned on the values of the wires in $\mathcal{I}$ the distribution output by the simulator is identical to the leakage from wires in $\mathcal{W}$ when the gadget is evaluated (conditioned on $\mathcal{I}$).*

The simulatability of small circuits, and particularly gadgets, is well studied and can be proven with tools such as maskVerif [4] and SILVER [25]. In this work we use the distribution of the smallest set of input wires such that there exists a simulator whose output has the same distribution as the leakage. More precisely, let $\mathcal{W}'$ be a subset of input and internal wires of a gadget G and $\mathcal{O}'$ an arbitrary subset of output wires, then we write $\mathcal{I}' = \mathcal{S}^G(\mathcal{W}', \mathcal{O}')$ to define the smallest subset $\mathcal{I}'$ of input wires of G by which $(\mathcal{W}', \mathcal{O}')$ is perfectly simulatable.

Definition 4 (Simulatability set). *Let* G *be a gadget with input wire, internal wire and output gate sets* $\mathcal{I}$, $\mathcal{W}$, *and* $\hat{\mathcal{O}}$. *Further, let* $\mathcal{O}$ *be the set of output wires of* $\hat{\mathcal{O}}$. *The* simulatability set *of a subset* $\mathcal{W}' \subseteq (\mathcal{W}, \mathcal{I})$ *and* $\mathcal{O}' \subseteq \mathcal{O}$, *denoted* $\mathcal{S}^G(\mathcal{W}', \mathcal{O}')$, *is the smallest subset of* $\mathcal{I}$ *by which* $\mathcal{W}'$ *and* $\mathcal{O}'$ *can be simulated.*

In the random probing model, $\mathcal{W}' = \mathcal{L}_p(G)$ is a random variable, hence the simulatability set $\mathcal{S}^G(\mathcal{L}_p(G), \mathcal{O}')$ is itself a random variable.

We now introduce rules for simulatability of parallel and sequential gadget compositions. Indeed, it is not enough to give a simulator for each gadget, but we also have to ensure that each individual simulator is consistent with the distribution generated by the other simulators, and that each simulator is provided with correct values for the input shares.

Claim 1. *For any parallel gadget composition* $G = G_1 \| G_0$ *with output gates* $\hat{\mathcal{O}} = \hat{\mathcal{O}}_1 \|_{(|\hat{\mathcal{O}}_1|)} \hat{\mathcal{O}}_0$ *an its output wires* $\mathcal{O}$. *It holds that*

$$\mathcal{S}^G(\mathcal{L}_p(G), \mathcal{O}') = \mathcal{S}^{G_1}(\mathcal{L}_p(G_1), \mathcal{O}'_1) \|_{(|\mathcal{I}_0|)} \mathcal{S}^{G_0}(\mathcal{L}_p(G_0), \mathcal{O}'_0)$$

for any subset of output wires $\mathcal{O}' = \mathcal{O}'_1 \|_{(|\mathcal{O}_0|)} \mathcal{O}'_0 \subseteq \mathcal{O}$.

The proof is given in the extended version of the paper.

Claim 2. *For any sequential gadget composition* $G = G_1 \circ G_0$ *with output gates* $\hat{\mathcal{O}}$ *and its output wires* $\mathcal{O}$, *it holds that*

$$\mathcal{S}^G(\mathcal{L}_p(G), \mathcal{O}') \subseteq \mathcal{S}^{G_0}\left(\mathcal{L}_p(G_0), \mathcal{S}^{G_1}(\mathcal{L}_p(G_1), \mathcal{O}')\right)$$

for any subset of output wires $\mathcal{O}' \subseteq \mathcal{O}$.

The proof is given in the extended version of the paper (Fig. 5).

(a) Tight Simulator for Gadget G_i
used in the proof of Claim 1 and 2

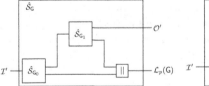

(b) Simulator for a serial gadget compositions. (c) Simulator for a parallel gadget compositions.

Fig. 5. Simulators for the gadgets depicted in Fig. 4 to prove Claims 1 and 2.

4.3   Probe Distributions

In this section, we introduce our new security properties, the **PD** (Probe Distribution) and the **PDT** (Probe Distribution Table). Intuitively, given a set of wires $\mathcal{W}$ and a leakage process $\mathcal{L}$ (hence $\mathcal{L}(\mathcal{W}) \subseteq \mathcal{W}$), the **PD** of $\mathcal{L}(\mathcal{W})$ is a vector of size $2^{|\mathcal{W}|}$ that represents the statistical distribution of $\mathcal{L}(\mathcal{W})$. In more detail, for each subset $\mathcal{W}' \subseteq \mathcal{W}$, there is a corresponding element of the **PD** with value $\Pr[\mathcal{L}(\mathcal{W}) = \mathcal{W}']$. The **PDT** notion extends the idea in a way that makes it useful for analyzing gadget compositions: it links the set of output probes on the gadget to the distribution of the simulatability set of the gadget (i.e., to the inputs needed to simulate the leakage). More precisely, for a gadget G, the **PDT** is a matrix in $[0,1]^{|\mathcal{I}| \times |\mathcal{O}|}$, such that each column is associated to a subset of the outputs $\mathcal{O}' \subseteq \mathcal{O}$. Each column is a **PD** that represents the distribution of $\mathcal{S}^{\mathsf{G}}(\mathcal{L}(\mathsf{G}), \mathcal{O}')$ (viewed as a subset of the set of inputs $\mathcal{I}$). The two main results (Theorems 1 and 2) of the next section relate the **PDT** of a sequential (resp., parallel) gadget composition to the matrix (resp., tensor) product of the **PDT**s of the composing gadgets. We first formalize the mapping between subsets of wires and indices in vectors/matrices.

Definition 5 (Index representation of subsets of wires). *For any set of wires $\mathcal{W}$ of which each element has a unique index in $[|\mathcal{W}|]$, we associate to each subset $\mathcal{W}'$ of $\mathcal{W}$ the index*

$$\tilde{\mathcal{W}}' = \sum_{i \in [|\mathcal{W}|]} b_i 2^i \quad \text{with} \quad \begin{cases} b_i = 1 & \text{if element } i \text{ of } \mathcal{W} \text{ belongs to } \mathcal{W}', \\ b_i = 0 & \text{otherwise.} \end{cases}$$

For example, the wire set $\mathcal{W} = \{\omega_0, \omega_1\}$ has 4 subsets $\mathcal{W}'$, that we represent with their index below:

$$\begin{array}{c|cccc} \mathcal{W}' & \emptyset & \{\omega_0\} & \{\omega_1\} & \{\omega_0, \omega_1\} \\ \hline \tilde{\mathcal{W}}' & 0 & 1 & 2 & 3 \end{array}$$

Let use now give the formal definition of the **PD**.

Definition 6 (Probe Distribution PD). *Let $\mathcal{L}$ be a probabilistic process that outputs subsets of a set of wires $\mathcal{W}$. The probe distribution (**PD**) of $\mathcal{L}$ with respect to $\mathcal{W}$ is $\mathbf{p} \in [0,1]^{2^{|\mathcal{W}|}}$ such that for all $\mathcal{W}' \subset \mathcal{W}$, $\mathbf{p}_{\tilde{\mathcal{W}}'} = Pr[\mathcal{L}(\mathcal{W}) = \mathcal{W}']$.*

The **PD** of $\mathcal{L}_p(\mathcal{W})$ in the previous example is $\mathbf{p} = ((1-p)^2, p(1-p), p(1-p), p^2)$.

We next give the definition of the **PDT**, which can be seen as the **PD**s of $\mathcal{S}^{\mathsf{G}}(\mathcal{L}_p(\mathsf{G}), \mathcal{O}')$ conditioned on the set of output probes $\mathcal{O}'$.

Definition 7 (Probe Distribution Table (PDT)). *Let G be a gadget with input wires $\mathcal{I}$ and output wires $\mathcal{O}$. For any $\mathcal{O}' \subseteq \mathcal{O}$, let $\mathbf{p}_{\tilde{\mathcal{O}}'}$ be the **PD** of $\mathcal{S}^{\mathsf{G}}(\mathcal{L}_p(\mathsf{G}), \mathcal{O}')$. The **PDT** of G (**PDT**$_\mathsf{G}$) is a $[0,1]^{2^{|\mathcal{I}|} \times 2^{|\mathcal{O}|}}$ matrix with all the $\mathbf{p}_{\tilde{\mathcal{O}}'}$ as columns, that is*

$$\boldsymbol{PDT}_\mathsf{G} = (\mathbf{p}_j)_{j \in [2^{|\mathcal{O}|}]},$$

with $j = \tilde{\mathcal{O}}'$ for all subsets $\mathcal{O}' \subseteq \mathcal{O}$. The notation $\boldsymbol{PDT}_\mathsf{G}(\tilde{\mathcal{I}}', \tilde{\mathcal{O}}')$ refers to the element of $\mathbf{p}_{\tilde{\mathcal{O}}'}$ associated to $\mathcal{I}'$.

$\mathbf{PDT_G}(\tilde{\mathcal{I}}', \tilde{\mathcal{O}}') = \Pr\left[\mathcal{S}^G(\mathcal{L}_p(G), \mathcal{O}') = \mathcal{I}'\right]$. Furthermore, the **PDT** of a gadget is independent of its environment (i.e., of the **PD** of its output wires).

A first example of **PDT** is the one of the ⊕- and ⊙- gates (when viewed as gadgets with one share). In the first column, no output has to be simulated, and thus the only leakage comes from the two input wires. For the second column, knowledge of both inputs is needed to simulate the output. This gives:

$$\mathbf{PDT}_{\oplus} = \mathbf{PDT}_{\odot} = \quad
\begin{array}{c|cc}
\textbf{PDT} & \mathcal{O}' = \emptyset & \mathcal{O}' = \{0\} \\
\hline
\mathcal{I}' = \emptyset & (1-p^2) & 0 \\
\mathcal{I}' = \{0\} & p(1-p) & 0 \\
\mathcal{I}' = \{1\} & p(1-p) & 0 \\
\mathcal{I}' = \{0,1\} & p^2 & 1
\end{array}$$

The second example is the simple refresh gadget G_r with two shares where a random value is added to two different wires. The random value leaks three times with probability p (one time in the ⊘ and two times in the ⊕-). Thus the leakage probability of the random value is $q = 1 - (1-p)^3$, and we get:

$$\mathbf{PDT}_{G_r} = \quad
\begin{array}{c|cccc}
\textbf{PDT} & \mathcal{O}' = \emptyset & \mathcal{O}' = \{0\} & \mathcal{O}' = \{1\} & \mathcal{O}' = \{1,0\} \\
\hline
\mathcal{I}' = \emptyset & (1-p)^2 & (1-q)(1-p)^2 & (1-q)(1-p)^2 & 0 \\
\mathcal{I}' = \{0\} & p(1-p) & (q+qp)(1-p) & (1-q)p(1-p) & 0 \\
\mathcal{I}' = \{1\} & p(1-p) & (1-q)p(1-p) & (q+(1-q)p)(1-p) & 0 \\
\mathcal{I}' = \{0,1\} & p^2 & qp+(1-q)p^2 & qp+(1-q)p^2 & 1
\end{array}$$

The **PDT** is related to the security level in the random probing model.

Claim 3. (Security level from PDT). *Let G be a gadget and $\mathbf{PDT_G}$ its Probe Distribution Table. Let s be the the security level of G with respect to an input sharing. If the set of shares of the considered input sharing is $\mathcal{I}'$, then*

$$\mathbf{e}^T \cdot \mathbf{PDT_G} \cdot \mathbf{p}_\emptyset = \sum_{\mathcal{I}'' \supseteq \mathcal{I}'} \mathbf{PDT_G}(\tilde{\mathcal{I}}'', 0) \geq s,$$

*where $\mathbf{p}_\emptyset = (1, 0, \ldots, 0)$ is the **PD** corresponding to no output leakage and $e_i = 1$ for all $i = \tilde{\mathcal{I}}''$ with $\mathcal{I}'' \supseteq \mathcal{I}'$, while $e_i = 0$ otherwise.*

Proof. Let $\mathcal{A}'$ be a set of wires that is an attack, that is, that depends on the considered unshared value which we denote Simulating $\mathcal{A}'$ therefore requires at least all the shares in $\mathcal{I}'$, hence

$$s \leq \Pr_{\mathcal{A}' \leftarrow \mathcal{L}_p(G)}\left[\mathcal{S}^G(\mathcal{A}', \emptyset) \subseteq \mathcal{I}'\right].$$

Then, by definition of $\mathcal{L}_p(G)$ and of the **PDT**,

$$s \leq \Pr\left[\mathcal{S}^G(\mathcal{L}_p(G), \emptyset) \subseteq \mathcal{I}'\right] = \sum_{\mathcal{I}'' \supseteq \mathcal{I}'} \Pr\left[\mathcal{S}^G(\mathcal{L}_p(G), \emptyset) = \mathcal{I}''\right] = \sum_{\mathcal{I}'' \supseteq \mathcal{I}'} \mathbf{PDT_G}(\tilde{\mathcal{I}}'', 0).$$

This proves the inequality. The equality claim holds by construction of $\mathbf{e}$. ☐

We now give a few results that constitute the basis for the composition theorems of the next section. A first result links the **PD** of the input wires needed to simulate the leakage of the gadget and some of its outputs to the **PDT** of the gadget and the **PD** of its outputs. This claim is the foundation for the analysis of sequential gadget composition.

Claim 4. (PDT and PD). *Let* G *be a gadget with output wire set* $\mathcal{O}$ *and input wire set* $\mathcal{I}$. *If a probabilistic process* $\mathcal{L}'(\mathcal{O})$ *has a* **PD** $\mathbf{p}$ *with respect to* $\mathcal{O}$, *then* $\mathbf{PDT_G} \cdot \mathbf{p}$ *is the* **PD** *of* $\mathcal{S}^G(\mathcal{L}_p(G), \mathcal{L}'(\mathcal{O}))$ *with respect to input wires* $\mathcal{I}$.

Proof. The solution can be directly derived from the definitions: Let $(v_i)_{i \in 2^{|\mathcal{I}|}} = \mathbf{PDT_G} \cdot \mathbf{p}$. For any $\mathcal{I}' \subseteq \mathcal{I}$, it holds that

$$v_{\tilde{\mathcal{I}}'} = \sum_{\mathcal{O}' \subseteq \mathcal{O}} \mathbf{PDT_G}(\tilde{\mathcal{I}}', \tilde{\mathcal{O}}') \cdot p_{\tilde{\mathcal{O}}'}$$

$$= \sum_{\mathcal{O}' \subseteq \mathcal{O}} \Pr\left[\mathcal{S}^G(\mathcal{L}_p(G), \mathcal{O}') = \mathcal{I}'\right] \cdot \Pr\left[\mathcal{L}'(\mathcal{O}) = \mathcal{O}'\right]$$

$$= \sum_{\mathcal{O}' \subseteq \mathcal{O}} \Pr\left[\mathcal{S}^G(\mathcal{L}_p(G), \mathcal{O}') = \mathcal{I}', \mathcal{L}'(\mathcal{O}) = \mathcal{O}'\right]$$

$$= \Pr\left[\mathcal{S}^G(\mathcal{L}_p(G), \mathcal{L}'(\mathcal{O})) = \mathcal{I}'\right].$$

The final equation gives the claim since it is exactly the ith entry of the **PD** of $\mathcal{S}^G(\mathcal{L}_p(G), \mathcal{L}'(\mathcal{O}))$ with $i = \tilde{\mathcal{I}}'$. □

We next want to compare two probe distributions $\mathbf{p}, \mathbf{p}'$ to describe a partial order for distributions "$\dot{\leq}$". The high-level idea is that $\mathbf{p}$ is "larger" than $\mathbf{p}'$ (denoted $\mathbf{p} \dot{\geq} \mathbf{p}'$) if $\mathcal{L}$ gives more information than $\mathcal{L}'$. In other words, $\mathbf{p}$ is "larger" than $\mathbf{p}'$ if we can simulate $\mathcal{L}'(\mathcal{W})$ with $\mathcal{L}(\mathcal{W})$, where $\mathcal{L}$ (resp., $\mathcal{L}'$) is the probabilistic process associated to $\mathbf{p}$ (resp., $\mathbf{p}'$).

Definition 8 (Partial order for distributions). *For a set of wires* $\mathcal{W}$, *let* $\mathcal{L}$ *and* $\mathcal{L}'$ *be probabilistic processes with* **PDs** $\mathbf{p}$ *and* $\mathbf{p}'$. *We say that* $\mathbf{p}$ *is larger than* $\mathbf{p}'$ *and write* $\mathbf{p} \dot{\geq} \mathbf{p}'$ *iff the* $\mathcal{L}'$ *is simulatable by* $\mathcal{L}$, *that is, if there exists a probabilistic algorithm* S *that satisfies* $S(\mathcal{X}) \subset \mathcal{X}$ *such that the distribution of* $\mathcal{L}'(\mathcal{W})$ *and* $S(\mathcal{L}(\mathcal{W}))$ *are equal.*

On the one hand, it is clear that the definition is reflexive, antisymmetric, and transitive. Let $\mathbf{p}, \mathbf{p}', \mathbf{p}''$ three **PDs**, it holds:

- $\mathbf{p} \dot{\geq} \mathbf{p}$, since we can always use the identity as simulator.
- If we know $\mathbf{p} \dot{\geq} \mathbf{p}'$ and $\mathbf{p} \dot{\leq} \mathbf{p}'$, both **PDs** describe processes with the same distribution, and we know $\mathbf{p} = \mathbf{p}'$.
- If it holds that $\mathbf{p} \dot{\geq} \mathbf{p}'$ and $\mathbf{p}' \dot{\geq} \mathbf{p}''$, it exists a simulator S' that simulates the process defined by $\mathbf{p}'$ with the process defined by $\mathbf{p}$, and a simulator S'' that does the same for $\mathbf{p}''$ and $\mathbf{p}'$. Hence, $S := S'(S''(\cdot))$ simulates the process defined by $\mathbf{p}''$ with the process of $\mathbf{p}$ and it follows $\mathbf{p} \dot{\geq} \mathbf{p}''$.

On the other hand, the order is only partial since it can happen that we have two probabilistic processes such that for both processes there exist no simulator to simulate the other.

The partial order for **PDs** is respected by linear combinations:

Claim 5. *Let* $(\mathbf{p}_i)_{i \in [k]}$, $(\mathbf{p}'_i)_{i \in [k]}$ *be* **PDs** *such that* $\mathbf{p}_i \dot{\geq} \mathbf{p}'_i$ *for all* i. *let* $(\alpha_i)_{i \in [k]}$ *be such that* $0 \leq \alpha_i \leq 1$ *for all* i *and* $\sum_{i \in [k]} \alpha_i = 1$. *If we denote* $\mathbf{p} = \sum_{i \in [k]} \alpha_i \mathbf{p}_i$ *and* $\mathbf{p}' = \sum_{i \in [k]} \alpha_i \mathbf{p}'_i$, *then* $\mathbf{p}$ *and* $\mathbf{p}'$ *are* **PDs** *and furthermore,* $\mathbf{p} \dot{\geq} \mathbf{p}'$.

Proof. Let $\mathcal{W}$ be a set of wires such that the random processes $(\mathcal{L}_i)_{i\in[k]}$ (resp. $(\mathcal{L}_i')_{i\in[k]}$) have $(\mathbf{p}_i)_{i\in[k]}$ (resp. $(\mathbf{p}_i')_{i\in[k]}$) as **PD**s. Further, let S^i be such that $S^i(\mathcal{L}_i(\mathcal{W}))$ has the same distribution as $\mathcal{L}_i'$. Let $\mathcal{L}$ be such that

$$\Pr\left[\mathcal{L}(\mathcal{W}) = \mathcal{W}'\right] = \sum_{i\in[k]} \alpha_i \Pr\left[\mathcal{L}_i(\mathcal{W}) = \mathcal{W}'\right],$$

and similarly for $\mathcal{L}'$. Firstly, $\mathcal{L}$ and $\mathcal{L}'$ are well-defined: the probabilities given above are non-negative and sum to 1. Next, the **PD** of $\mathcal{L}$ (resp. $\mathcal{L}'$) is $\mathbf{p}$ (resp. $\mathbf{p}'$). Finally, we build the simulator S. Let $\mathcal{L}''$ be a random process that, on input $\mathcal{W}$, selects randomly $i \in [k]$ (such that the probability of taking the value i is α_i), and outputs $S^i(\mathcal{L}_i(\mathcal{W}))$. Then, let S be a random process such that $\Pr[S(\mathcal{W}'') = \mathcal{W}'] = \Pr[\mathcal{L}'' = \mathcal{W}'|\mathcal{L} = \mathcal{W}'']$ for all $\mathcal{W}', \mathcal{W}'' \subseteq \mathcal{W}$. We observe that for all $\mathcal{W}' \subseteq \mathcal{W}$,

$$\Pr[S(\mathcal{L}) = \mathcal{W}'] = \sum_{\mathcal{W}''\subseteq \mathcal{W}} \Pr[S(\mathcal{W}'') = \mathcal{W}'] * \Pr[\mathcal{L} = \mathcal{W}'']$$

$$= \sum_{\mathcal{W}''\subseteq \mathcal{W}} \Pr[\mathcal{L}'' = \mathcal{W}'|\mathcal{L} = \mathcal{W}''] * \Pr[\mathcal{L} = \mathcal{W}'']$$

$$= \Pr[\mathcal{L}'' = \mathcal{W}'].$$

Since $\mathcal{L}''$ has the same distribution as $\mathcal{L}'$, this means that $\Pr[S(\mathcal{L}) = \mathcal{W}'] = \Pr[\mathcal{L}' = \mathcal{W}']$. □

The **PDT** has a partial structure. As described above each column i of the **PDT** is the **PD** of $\mathcal{S}^G(\mathcal{L}_p(G), \mathcal{O}')$ with $\tilde{\mathcal{O}}' = i$. Since we know that the input set required by a leakage simulator can only grow (or stay constant) if it has to simulate additional (output) leakage, we get:

Claim 6. *For any gadget with output wires $\mathcal{O}$, the columns $\mathbf{p}$ of the **PDT** have the following property: $\mathbf{p}_{\tilde{\mathcal{O}}'} \geq \mathbf{p}_{\tilde{\mathcal{O}}''}$ for all $\mathcal{O}'' \subseteq \mathcal{O}' \subseteq \mathcal{O}$.*

Proof. It follows directly from Claim 4. It holds that $\mathcal{S}^G(\mathcal{L}_p(G), \mathcal{O}'') \subseteq \mathcal{S}^G(\mathcal{L}_p(G), \mathcal{O}')$ and thus $\Pr\left[\mathcal{S}^G(\mathcal{L}_p(G), \mathcal{O}'') \subseteq \mathcal{S}^G(\mathcal{L}_p(G), \mathcal{O}')\right] = 1$. The last equation is the claim $p_{\tilde{\mathcal{O}}'} \geq p_{\tilde{\mathcal{O}}''}$. □

Finally, we want to extend the partial order of **PD**s to the whole **PDT**, with the same meaning: if $\mathbf{PDT}_{G_0} \leq \mathbf{PDT}_{G_1}$, the amount of information leaked in G_0 is less than the information leaked in G_1:

Definition 9 (Partial order for PDT's). *Let $\mathbf{A}, \mathbf{B} \in [0,1]^{2^{|\mathcal{I}|} \times 2^{|\mathcal{O}|}}$ be two **PDT**s, we write*

$$\mathbf{A} \overset{.}{\leq} \mathbf{B}$$

*if for any **PD** $\mathbf{p} \in [0,1]^{2^{|\mathcal{O}|}}$ it holds $\mathbf{A} \cdot \mathbf{p} \overset{.}{\leq} \mathbf{B} \cdot \mathbf{p}$.*

As shown in Claim 4, $\mathbf{A} \cdot \mathbf{p}$ and $\mathbf{B} \cdot \mathbf{p}$ are **PD**s, therefore the partial order of **PDT**s is well defined.

Corollary 1 (PDT order is column-wise). *Let PDT and PDT' be PDTs, with columns $(\mathbf{p}_i)_{i\in[|\mathcal{O}|]}$ and $(\mathbf{p}'_i)_{i\in[|\mathcal{O}|]}$ respectively. Then, $PDT \overset{.}{\geq} PDT'$ iff $\mathbf{p}_i \overset{.}{\geq} \mathbf{p}'_i$ for all $i \in [|\mathcal{O}|$.*

Proof. If $\mathbf{PDT} \overset{.}{\geq} \mathbf{PDT}'$, then for any $i \in [|\mathcal{O}|$, let $\mathbf{e}$ be such that $e_j = 1$ if $i = j$ and $e_j = 0$ otherwise. Since $\mathbf{e}$ is a **PD**, we have $\mathbf{p}_i = \mathbf{PDT} \cdot \mathbf{e} \overset{.}{\geq} \mathbf{PDT}' \cdot \mathbf{e} = \mathbf{p}'_i$.

In the other way, let use assume that $\mathbf{p}_i \overset{.}{\geq} \mathbf{p}'_i$, for all i. Then for any **PD** α (whose elements are denoted α_i), $\mathbf{PDT} \cdot \alpha$ is a linear combination of $\mathbf{p}_i$ with coefficients α_i, for which Claim 5 applies. Therefore $\mathbf{PDT} \cdot \alpha \overset{.}{\geq} \mathbf{PDT}' \cdot \alpha$. $\square$

Another useful property is that we can merge the order of **PD**s and **PDT**s:

Claim 7. *Let $\mathbf{A}, \mathbf{B} \in [0,1]^{2^{|\mathcal{I}|} \times 2^{|\mathcal{O}|}}$ be two PDTs, and $\mathbf{p}, \mathbf{p}' \in [0,1]^{2^{|\mathcal{O}|}}$ be two PDs. If $\mathbf{A} \overset{.}{\leq} \mathbf{B}$ and $\mathbf{p} \overset{.}{\leq} \mathbf{p}'$, then $\mathbf{A} \cdot \mathbf{p} \overset{.}{\leq} \mathbf{B} \cdot \mathbf{p}'$.*

Proof. We prove the claim $\mathbf{A} \cdot \mathbf{p} \overset{.}{\leq} \mathbf{B} \cdot \mathbf{p}'$ in two steps. First we show (i) $\mathbf{A} \cdot \mathbf{p} \overset{.}{\leq} \mathbf{A} \cdot \mathbf{p}'$, and then we show (ii) $\mathbf{A} \cdot \mathbf{p}' \overset{.}{\leq} \mathbf{B} \cdot \mathbf{p}'$.

(i) By Definition 8, there exists $\mathcal{W}$, $\mathcal{L}$ and $\mathcal{L}'$ associated to $\mathbf{p}$, $\mathbf{p}'$, respectively, with $\Pr[\mathcal{L}(\mathcal{W}) \subset \mathcal{L}'(\mathcal{W})] = 1$. Further, it holds $\Pr[\mathbf{A}_{\mathcal{L}(\mathcal{W})} \overset{.}{\leq} \mathbf{A}_{\mathcal{L}'(\mathcal{W})}] = 1$ with Claim 6. Hence, $\mathbf{A} \cdot \mathbf{p} \overset{.}{\leq} \mathbf{A} \cdot \mathbf{p}'$.

(ii) $\mathbf{A} \cdot \mathbf{p}' \overset{.}{\leq} \mathbf{B} \cdot \mathbf{p}'$ follows from Definition 9 and $\mathbf{A} \overset{.}{\leq} \mathbf{B}$. $\square$

This leads to the preservation of **PDT** ordering through matrix product.

Corollary 2. *Let $\mathbf{A}$, $\mathbf{B}$, $\mathbf{C}$, $\mathbf{D}$ be PDTs. If $\mathbf{A} \overset{.}{\leq} \mathbf{B}$ and $\mathbf{C} \overset{.}{\leq} \mathbf{D}$, then $\mathbf{A} \cdot \mathbf{C} \overset{.}{\leq} \mathbf{B} \cdot \mathbf{D}$.*

Proof. Let us denote by $\mathbf{X}_{*,i}$ the $(i + 1)$-th column of a matrix $\mathbf{X}$. Then, for all $i \in [|\mathcal{O}|]$, $(\mathbf{A} \cdot \mathbf{C})_{*,i} = \mathbf{A} \cdot \mathbf{C}_{*,i}$ and $(\mathbf{B} \cdot \mathbf{D})_{*,i} = \mathbf{B} \cdot \mathbf{D}_{*,i}$. Hence, by Corollary 1, $\mathbf{A} \cdot \mathbf{C} \overset{.}{\leq} \mathbf{B} \cdot \mathbf{D}$ iff $\mathbf{C}_{*,i} \overset{.}{\leq} \mathbf{D}_{*,i}$ for all i. Using the same Corollary, we have $\mathbf{C}_{*,i} \overset{.}{\leq} \mathbf{D}_{*,i}$. Finally, using Claim 7, we get $\mathbf{A} \cdot \mathbf{C}_{*,i} \overset{.}{\leq} \mathbf{B} \cdot \mathbf{D}_{*,i}$ for all i. $\square$

Finally, we relate the partial order for **PD**s and **PDT**s to the security level.

Claim 8. (Security level bound from PDT bound). *Let s be the security level of a gadget G with respect to a set of input shares $\mathcal{I}'$. Let PDT be the PDT of G and let PDT' be a PDT. If $PDT' \overset{.}{\geq} PDT$, then $\mathbf{e}^T \cdot PDT' \cdot \mathbf{p}_\emptyset \geq s$, where $\mathbf{e}$ is defined as in Claim 3.*

Proof. Using Claim 3, we know that $\mathbf{e}^T \cdot \mathbf{PDT} \cdot \mathbf{p}_\emptyset \geq s$. With Claim 7, we know that $\mathbf{PDT}' \cdot \mathbf{p}_\emptyset \overset{.}{\geq} \mathbf{PDT} \cdot \mathbf{p}_\emptyset$. Let $\mathcal{L}$ (resp. $\mathcal{L}'$) be the random process associated to $\mathbf{PDT}' \cdot \mathbf{p}_\emptyset$ (resp. $\mathbf{PDT} \cdot \mathbf{p}_\emptyset$), and let S be the simulator that simulates $\mathcal{L}$ from $\mathcal{L}'$. We have $S(\mathcal{L}'(\mathcal{I})) \subseteq \mathcal{L}'(\mathcal{I})$, hence $\Pr[\mathcal{I}' \subseteq S(\mathcal{L}'(\mathcal{I}))] \leq \Pr[\mathcal{I}' \subseteq \mathcal{L}'(\mathcal{I})]$. Since S simulates $\mathcal{L}(\mathcal{I})$, $\Pr[\mathcal{I}' \subseteq S(\mathcal{L}'(\mathcal{I}))] = \Pr[\mathcal{I}' \subseteq \mathcal{L}(\mathcal{I})]$, which leads to $\mathbf{e}^T \cdot \mathbf{PDT} \cdot \mathbf{p}_\emptyset = \Pr[\mathcal{I}' \subseteq \mathcal{L}(\mathcal{I})] \leq \Pr[\mathcal{I}' \subseteq \mathcal{L}'(\mathcal{I})] = \mathbf{e}^T \cdot \mathbf{PDT}' \cdot \mathbf{p}_\emptyset$. $\square$

4.4 Composition Rules

In this section, we give the two main composition theorems for the **PDT** of parallel and sequential gadget compositions. Next, we show how the compositions theorems can be used to compute **PDT**s for larger composite gadgets and illustrate our results on the AES S-box example.

Theorem 1 (parallel composition). *Let* G_1 *and* G_2 *be two gadgets with* PDT_{G_0} *and* PDT_{G_1}. *Further let* $G = G_1 || G_0$ *with* PDT_G. *It holds that*

$$PDT_G = PDT_{G_1} \otimes PDT_{G_0}.$$

Proof. Let $\mathcal{I}_0, \mathcal{I}_1, \mathcal{O}_0$, and $\mathcal{O}_1$ the input and output wires of G_0 and G_1, respectively. Hence, $\mathcal{I} = \mathcal{I}_1 ||_{(n)} \mathcal{I}_0$, $\mathcal{O} = \mathcal{O}_1 ||_{(m)} \mathcal{O}_0$ are the input and output wires of G with $n = |\mathcal{I}_0|$ and $m = |\mathcal{O}_0|$. From Definition 2 follows for any $\mathcal{I}' = \mathcal{I}_1' ||_{(n)} \mathcal{I}_0' \subseteq \mathcal{I}$ and $\mathcal{O}' = \mathcal{O}_1' ||_{(m)} \mathcal{O}_0' \subseteq \mathcal{O}$ that $\Pr[\mathcal{S}(\mathcal{L}_p(G) \cup \mathcal{O}') = \mathcal{I}']$ is the matrix entry $(\tilde{\mathcal{I}}', \tilde{\mathcal{O}}')$ of **PDT**$_G$. Considering Claim 1, we get

$$
\begin{aligned}
\mathbf{PDT_G}(\tilde{\mathcal{I}}', \tilde{\mathcal{O}}') &= \Pr\left[\mathcal{S}^G(\mathcal{L}_p(G), \mathcal{O}') = \mathcal{I}'\right] \\
&= \Pr\left[\mathcal{S}^{G_1}\left(\mathcal{L}_p(G_1) \cup \mathcal{O}_1'\right) ||_{(n)} \mathcal{S}^{G_0}\left(\mathcal{L}_p(G_0), \mathcal{O}_0'\right) = \mathcal{I}_1' ||_{(n)} \mathcal{I}_0'\right] \\
&= \Pr\left[\mathcal{S}^{G_1}\left(\mathcal{L}_p(G_0), \mathcal{O}_0'\right) = \mathcal{I}_0', \mathcal{S}^{G_0}\left(\mathcal{L}_p(G_1), \mathcal{O}_1'\right) = \mathcal{I}_1'\right] \\
&= \Pr\left[\mathcal{S}^{G_1}(\mathcal{L}_p(G_0), \mathcal{O}_0') = \mathcal{I}_0'\right] \cdot \Pr\left[\mathcal{S}^{G_0}(\mathcal{L}_p(G_1), \mathcal{O}_1') = \mathcal{I}_1'\right] \\
&= \mathbf{PDT_{G_0}}(\tilde{\mathcal{I}}_0', \tilde{\mathcal{O}}_0') \cdot \mathbf{PDT_{G_1}}(\tilde{\mathcal{I}}_1', \tilde{\mathcal{O}}_1').
\end{aligned}
$$

The last transformation of the formula uses the fact that the set of probes of both gadgets are independent, and the resulting term is exactly the matrix entry $(\tilde{\mathcal{I}}', \tilde{\mathcal{O}}')$ of **PDT**$_{G_1} \otimes$ **PDT**$_{G_0}$. $\square$

Remark. Theorem 1 can be generalized to any parallel composition of sub-circuits, even if those sub-circuits are not gadgets. For instance, a share-wise gadget with n shares is the parallel composition of n identical sub-circuits (a single addition gate for the addition gadget). The **PDT** of the addition gate **PDT**$_\oplus$ is given in Sect. 4.3, therefore **PDT**$_{G_{\oplus,n}}$ can be computed as

$$\mathbf{PDT_{G_{\oplus,n}}} = P\left(\bigotimes_{i=0}^{n-1} \mathbf{PDT_\oplus}\right),$$

where P reorders the index of the input wires from $(x_0^0, x_0^1, x_1^0, x_1^1, \ldots x_{n-1}^0, x_{n-1}^1)$ to $(x_0^0, \ldots, x_{n-1}^0, x_0^1, \ldots, x_{n-1}^1)$ where x_i^0 and x_i^1 are the first and second input wires of the ith addition gate, respectively.

Theorem 2 (sequential composition). *Let* G_0 *and* G_1 *be two gadgets with* PDT_{G_0}, PDT_{G_1}, *and with* n_i *input wires and* m_i *output wires, respectively such that* $m_0 = n_1$. *Further let* $G = G_1 \circ G_0$ *with* PDT_G. *It holds that*

$$PDT_G \dot{\leq} PDT_{G_0} \cdot PDT_{G_1}.$$

Proof. Let $\overline{\mathbf{PDT}} = \mathbf{PDT}_{\mathsf{G}_0} \cdot \mathbf{PDT}_{\mathsf{G}_1}$ and $\mathcal{I}_0, \mathcal{I}_1, \mathcal{O}_0, \mathcal{O}_1$ the input and output wire sets of G_0 and G_1, respectively. It also means that $\mathcal{I}_0$ and $\mathcal{O}_1$ are the input and output wire sets of G. Considering the fact that $\overline{\mathbf{PDT}}$ is the result of a matrix multiplication of $\mathbf{PDT}_{\mathsf{G}_0}$ and $\mathbf{PDT}_{\mathsf{G}_1}$, we get for any $\mathcal{I}' \subseteq \mathcal{I}_0$ and $\mathcal{O}' \subseteq \mathcal{O}_1$

$$\overline{\mathbf{PDT}}(\tilde{\mathcal{I}}'', \tilde{\mathcal{O}}') = \sum_{\mathcal{O}'' \subseteq \mathcal{O}_0} \Pr\left[\mathcal{S}^{\mathsf{G}_0}(\mathcal{L}_p(\mathsf{G}_0), \mathcal{O}'') = \mathcal{I}'\right] \cdot \Pr\left[\mathcal{S}^{\mathsf{G}_1}(\mathcal{L}_p(\mathsf{G}_1), \mathcal{O}') = \mathcal{O}''\right]$$

$$= \sum_{\mathcal{O}'' \subseteq \mathcal{O}_0} \Pr\left[\mathcal{S}^{\mathsf{G}_0}(\mathcal{L}_p(\mathsf{G}_0), \mathcal{O}'') = \mathcal{I}', \mathcal{S}^{\mathsf{G}_1}(\mathcal{L}_p(\mathsf{G}_1), \mathcal{O}') = \mathcal{O}''\right]$$

$$= \Pr\left[\mathcal{S}^{\mathsf{G}_0}\left(\mathcal{L}_p(\mathsf{G}_0), \mathcal{S}^{\mathsf{G}_1}(\mathcal{L}_p(\mathsf{G}_1), \mathcal{O}')\right) = \mathcal{I}'\right].$$

Further, $\mathbf{PDT}_{\mathsf{G}}(\tilde{\mathcal{I}}', \tilde{\mathcal{O}}') = \Pr\left[\mathcal{S}^{\mathsf{G}}(\mathcal{L}_p(\mathsf{G}), \mathcal{O}') = \mathcal{I}'\right]$, and thus for any $\mathcal{O}' \subseteq \mathcal{O}_1$ the columns $\mathbf{PDT}_{\mathsf{G}}(\tilde{\mathcal{O}}')$ and $\overline{\mathbf{PDT}}(\tilde{\mathcal{O}}')$ are the **PD**s of $\mathcal{S}^{\mathsf{G}}(\mathcal{L}_p(\mathsf{G}), \mathcal{O}')$ and of $\mathcal{S}^{\mathsf{G}_0}\left(\mathcal{L}_p(\mathsf{G}_0), \mathcal{S}^{\mathsf{G}_1}(\mathcal{L}_p(\mathsf{G}_1), \mathcal{O}')\right)$, respectively. Because of Claim 2, it holds that

$$\Pr\left[\mathcal{S}^{\mathsf{G}}(\mathcal{L}_p(\mathsf{G}), \mathcal{O}') \subseteq \mathcal{S}^{\mathsf{G}_0}\left(\mathcal{L}_p(\mathsf{G}_0), \mathcal{S}^{\mathsf{G}_1}(\mathcal{L}_p(\mathsf{G}_1), \mathcal{O}')\right)\right] = 1.$$

The last equation proves that it exists a simulator that simulates the simulatability set $\mathcal{S}^{\mathsf{G}}(\mathcal{L}_p(\mathsf{G}), \mathcal{O}')$ with $\mathcal{S}^{\mathsf{G}_0}\left(\mathcal{L}_p(\mathsf{G}_0), \mathcal{S}^{\mathsf{G}_1}(\mathcal{L}_p(\mathsf{G}_1), \mathcal{O}')\right)$. Hence, it holds that $\mathbf{PDT}_{\mathsf{G}}(\tilde{\mathcal{O}}') \dot{\preceq} \overline{\mathbf{PDT}}(\tilde{\mathcal{O}}')$ for any column with $\mathcal{O}' \subseteq \mathcal{O}_1$. Since the inequality holds for any column, the inequality is independent from the distribution of the output wires $\mathcal{O}_1$. It follows that $\mathbf{PDT}_{\mathsf{G}} \mathbf{p} \dot{\preceq} \mathbf{PDT}_{\mathsf{G}_0} \cdot \mathbf{PDT}_{\mathsf{G}_1} \mathbf{p}$ for all **PD**s **p**. This results in the claim of the theorem $\mathbf{PDT}_{\mathsf{G}} \dot{\preceq} \mathbf{PDT}_{\mathsf{G}_0} \cdot \mathbf{PDT}_{\mathsf{G}_1}$. $\qquad\square$

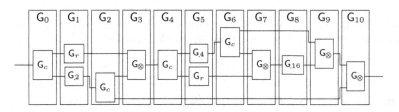

Fig. 6. AES S-box circuit (using the implementation from [31]) as a serial composition of gadgets. The symbols G_c, G_r, $\mathsf{G}_\otimes$ and $\mathsf{G}.x$ are respectively copy, refresh and exponentiation to the power of x gadgets.

Corollary 3. *Let* $(\mathsf{G}_i)_{i \in [k]}$ *be gadgets that can be sequentially composed to form* $\mathsf{G} = \mathsf{G}_{k-1} \circ \cdots \circ \mathsf{G}_0$. *It holds that*

$$PDT_{\mathsf{G}} \dot{\preceq} PDT_{\mathsf{G}_0} \cdot \ldots \cdot PDT_{\mathsf{G}_{k-1}}.$$

Proof. This is a direct consequence of Theorem 2 and Corollary 2. $\qquad\square$

The **PDT** of the AES S-box depicted in Fig. 6 is bounded by $\mathbf{PDT}_{\text{S-box}}$ defined in Table 1. We compute the S-box with the gadgets $\mathsf{G}_{.2}$, $\mathsf{G}_{\otimes}$, G_r, and G_c. In addition, we also use a identity gadget G_{id}^l as a placeholder for composition results (this gadget does not leak and has as many inputs as outputs), whose **PDT** is the identity matrix. As described in Table 1, the gadgets G_0-G_{10} are a parallel composition of the gadgets $\mathsf{G}_{.2}$, $\mathsf{G}_{.4}$, $\mathsf{G}_{.16}$, $\mathsf{G}_{\otimes}$, G_r, G_c, and G_{id}^l (we can compute their **PDT**s using Theorem 1). Thus, $\mathsf{G}_{\text{S-box}}$ is a sequential composition of G_0-G_{10}. We can compute its **PDT** using Corollary 3, as shown in Table 1.

Table 1. Composition of the AES S-box and its approximated **PDT**.

G_0	G_c	$\mathbf{PDT}_{\mathsf{G}_0} = \mathbf{PDT}_{\mathsf{G}_c}$
G_1	$\mathsf{G}_r \| \mathsf{G}_{.2}$	$\mathbf{PDT}_{\mathsf{G}_1} = \mathbf{PDT}_{\mathsf{G}_r} \otimes \mathbf{PDT}_{\mathsf{G}_{.2}}$
G_2	$\mathsf{G}_{id} \| \mathsf{G}_c$	$\mathbf{PDT}_{\mathsf{G}_2} = \mathbf{PDT}_{\mathsf{G}_{id}} \otimes \mathbf{PDT}_{\mathsf{G}_c}$
G_3	$\mathsf{G}_{\otimes} \| \mathsf{G}_{id}$	$\mathbf{PDT}_{\mathsf{G}_3} = \mathbf{PDT}_{\mathsf{G}_{\otimes}} \otimes \mathbf{PDT}_{\mathsf{G}_{id}}$
G_4	$\mathsf{G}_c \| \mathsf{G}_{id}$	$\mathbf{PDT}_{\mathsf{G}_4} = \mathbf{PDT}_{\mathsf{G}_c} \otimes \mathbf{PDT}_{\mathsf{G}_{id}}$
G_5	$\mathsf{G}_{.4} \| \mathsf{G}_r \| \mathsf{G}_{id}$	$\mathbf{PDT}_{\mathsf{G}_5} = \mathbf{PDT}_{\mathsf{G}_{.4}} \otimes \mathbf{PDT}_{\mathsf{G}_r} \otimes \mathbf{PDT}_{\mathsf{G}_{id}}$
G_6	$\mathsf{G}_c \| \mathsf{G}_{id} \| \mathsf{G}_{id}$	$\mathbf{PDT}_{\mathsf{G}_6} = \mathbf{PDT}_{\mathsf{G}_c} \otimes \mathbf{PDT}_{\mathsf{G}_{id}} \otimes \mathbf{PDT}_{\mathsf{G}_{id}}$
G_7	$\mathsf{G}_{id} \| \mathsf{G}_{\otimes} \| \mathsf{G}_{id}$	$\mathbf{PDT}_{\mathsf{G}_7} = \mathbf{PDT}_{\mathsf{G}_{id}} \otimes \mathbf{PDT}_{\mathsf{G}_{\otimes}} \otimes \mathbf{PDT}_{\mathsf{G}_{id}}$
G_8	$\mathsf{G}_{id} \| \mathsf{G}_{.16} \| \mathsf{G}_{id}$	$\mathbf{PDT}_{\mathsf{G}_8} = \mathbf{PDT}_{\mathsf{G}_{id}} \otimes \mathbf{PDT}_{\mathsf{G}_{.16}} \otimes \mathbf{PDT}_{\mathsf{G}_{id}}$
G_9	$\mathsf{G}_{\otimes} \| \mathsf{G}_{id}$	$\mathbf{PDT}_{\mathsf{G}_9} = \mathbf{PDT}_{\mathsf{G}_{\otimes}} \otimes \mathbf{PDT}_{\mathsf{G}_{id}}$
G_{10}	$\mathsf{G}_{\otimes}$	$\mathbf{PDT}_{\mathsf{G}_{10}} = \mathbf{PDT}_{\mathsf{G}_{\otimes}}$
$\mathsf{G}_{\text{S-box}}$	$\mathsf{G}_{10} \circ \mathsf{G}_9 \circ \ldots \circ \mathsf{G}_0$	$\mathbf{PDT}_{\text{S-box}} \dot{\leq} \mathbf{PDT}_{\mathsf{G}_0} \cdot \mathbf{PDT}_{\mathsf{G}_1} \cdot \ldots \cdot \mathbf{PDT}_{\mathsf{G}_{10}}$

We conclude by noting that some well-known matrix product and tensor product distributive and associative properties mirror the properties of the gadget compositions (when the operations are well-defined):

$$(\mathbf{A} \cdot \mathbf{B}) \cdot \mathbf{C} = \mathbf{A} \cdot (\mathbf{B} \cdot \mathbf{C}) \qquad (\mathsf{G}_0 \circ \mathsf{G}_1) \circ \mathsf{G}_2 = \mathsf{G}_0 \circ (\mathsf{G}_1 \circ \mathsf{G}_2)$$
$$(\mathbf{A} \otimes \mathbf{B}) \otimes \mathbf{C} = \mathbf{A} \otimes (\mathbf{B} \otimes \mathbf{C}) \qquad (\mathsf{G}_0 \| \mathsf{G}_1) \| \mathsf{G}_2 = \mathsf{G}_0 \| (\mathsf{G}_1 \| \mathsf{G}_2)$$
$$(\mathbf{A} \cdot \mathbf{B}) \otimes (\mathbf{C} \cdot \mathbf{D}) = (\mathbf{A} \otimes \mathbf{C}) \cdot (\mathbf{B} \otimes \mathbf{D}) \quad (\mathsf{G}_0 \circ \mathsf{G}_1) \| (\mathsf{G}_2 \circ \mathsf{G}_3) = (\mathsf{G}_0 \| \mathsf{G}_2) \circ (\mathsf{G}_1 \| \mathsf{G}_3)$$

This means that our composition theorems give the same result independently of the way we decompose a composite gadget. This gives us freedom to choose, e.g., the most efficient way when we deal with relatively large computations.

5   Practical Security of Composite Circuits

In this section, we adapt the method of Sect. 3 to compute bounds for **PDT**s. We then show how to turn those bounds into gadget security levels using the **PDT** properties and composition theorems. We finally describe the tool that implements our methodology and discuss its result for well-known gadgets.

5.1 Bounding PDTs

We first describe how to adapt the method of Sect. 3 to bound **PDT**s. That is, given a gadget G, we want to generate an upper bound $\mathbf{PDT}^U$ such that $\mathbf{PDT}^U \geq \mathbf{PDT}$ with probability at least $1 - \alpha$ (e.g., $1 - 10^{-6}$), and the $\geq$ operator defined for matrices and vectors as element-wise. We note that $\mathbf{PDT}^U$ is not a **PDT**: the sum of the elements in one of its columns may be ≥ 1.

There are two main differences with the bound of Sect. 3: (1) we have to handle all possible cases for the probes on the output shares of the gadgets (i.e., all the columns of the **PDT**), and (2) we care about the full distribution of the input probes, not only the probability of successful attack.

The upper bound $\mathbf{PDT}^U$ can be computed by grouping probe sets by size (similarly to Eq. (3)):

$$\mathbf{PDT}^U(\tilde{\mathcal{I}}', \tilde{\mathcal{O}}') = \sum_{i=0}^{|\mathcal{W}|} p^i (1-p)^{|\mathcal{W}|-i} \cdot \left|\mathcal{W}^{(i)}\right| \cdot \mathbf{R}_i^U(\tilde{\mathcal{I}}', \tilde{\mathcal{O}}')$$

satisfies $\mathbf{PDT}^U(\tilde{\mathcal{I}}', \tilde{\mathcal{O}}') \geq \mathbf{PDT}(\tilde{\mathcal{I}}', \tilde{\mathcal{O}}')$ if

$$\mathbf{R}_i^U(\tilde{\mathcal{I}}', \tilde{\mathcal{O}}') \geq \frac{\left|\{\mathcal{W}' \subseteq \mathcal{W}^{(i)} \text{ s.t. } \mathcal{S}^{\mathsf{G}}(\mathcal{L}_p(\mathsf{G}), \mathcal{O}') = \mathcal{I}'\}\right|}{\left|\mathcal{W}^{(i)}\right|} \tag{6}$$

for all $i \in \{0, \dots, |\mathcal{W}|\}$. Therefore, if Eq. (6) is satisfied for each $(\mathcal{I}', \mathcal{O}', i)$ tuple with probability at least $1 - \alpha/\left((|\mathcal{W}| + 1) 2^{|\mathcal{I}| \cdot |\mathcal{O}|}\right)$, then $\mathbf{PDT}^U \geq \mathbf{PDT}$ with probability at least $1 - \alpha$ (by the union bound).

The computation of all the elements $P_i^U(\tilde{\mathcal{I}}', \tilde{\mathcal{O}}')$ can be performed identically to the computation of r_i^U in Sect. 3.1, except for changing the criterion for a Monte-Carlo sample $\mathcal{W}'$ to be counted as positive (i.e., be counted in s_i): $\mathcal{S}(\mathcal{W}', \mathcal{O}') = \mathcal{I}'$ (instead of $\delta_{\mathcal{W}'} = 1$). Furthermore, the algorithm can be optimized by running only one sampling for each $(i, \mathcal{O}')$ pair: we take $t_{i,\mathcal{O}'}$ samples, and we classify each sample $\mathcal{W}'$ according to $\mathcal{S}(\mathcal{W}', \mathcal{O}')$. This gives sample counts $s_{i,\mathcal{O}',\mathcal{I}'}$ for all $\mathcal{I}' \subseteq \mathcal{I}$, and from there we can use Eq. (4).[4]

Finally, we use the hybrid strategy of Algorithm 1, with the aforementioned modifications.[5] The computation of a statistical-only lower bound $\mathbf{PDT}^L$ is done in the same way, except that Eq. (5) is used instead of Eq. (4).

5.2 From PDT Bound to Security Level Bound

Let us take positive matrices $A^U \geq A$ and $B^U \geq B$. It always holds that $A^U \otimes B^U \geq A \otimes B$ and $A^U \cdot B^U \geq A \cdot B$. Therefore, if we use **PDT** bounds in

---

[4] The random variables $s_{i,\mathcal{O}',\mathcal{I}'}$ for all $\mathcal{I}' \subseteq \mathcal{I}$ are not mutually independent, hence the derived bounds are not independent from each other, but this is not an issue since the union bound does not require independent variables.

[5] And additionally the change of the condition $s_i < N_t$ by $s_{i,\mathcal{O}'\mathcal{I}} < N_t$. The rationale for this condition is that, intuitively, if we have many "worst-case" samples, then we should have a sufficient knowledge of the distribution $\left(P_i(\tilde{\mathcal{I}}', \tilde{\mathcal{O}}')\right)_{\mathcal{I}' \subseteq \mathcal{I}}$.

composition Theorem 1 (resp., Corollary 3), we get as a result – denoted $\overline{\mathbf{PDT}}^U$ and computed as $A^U \cdot B^U$ (resp., $A^U \otimes B^U$) – a corresponding bound for the composite **PDT** – denoted $\overline{\mathbf{PDT}}$ and computed as $A \cdot B$ (resp., $A \otimes B$): $\overline{\mathbf{PDT}}^U \geq \overline{\mathbf{PDT}} \geq \mathbf{PDT}$. Then, if we use $\overline{\mathbf{PDT}}^U$ in the formula for the computation of the security level (Claim 8) instead of $\overline{\mathbf{PDT}}$, we get

$$s^U = \mathbf{e}^T \cdot \overline{\mathbf{PDT}}^U \cdot \mathbf{p}_\emptyset \geq \mathbf{e}^T \cdot \overline{\mathbf{PDT}} \cdot \mathbf{p}_\emptyset \geq s.$$

We compute the statistical-only lower bound s^L in a similar manner. One should however keep in mind that $s^L \leq s$ does not hold in general, since Claim 8 and the sequential composition theorem only guarantee an upper bound (in addition to the non-tightness coming from the maskVerif algorithm). Again, the statistical-only lower bound is however useful for estimating the uncertainty on the security level that comes from the Monte-Carlo method: if there is a large gap between s^L and s^U, increasing the number of samples in the Monte-Carlo sampling can result in a better s^U (on the other hand, s^L gives a limit on how much we can hope to reduce s^U by increasing the number of samples).

5.3 Tool

We implemented the computation of the above bounds in the open-source tool STRAPS (Sampled Testing of the RAndom Probing Security). This tool contains a few additional algorithmic optimizations that do not change the results but significantly reduce the execution time (e.g., we exploit the fact that, in some circuits, many wires carry the same value, and we avoid to explicitly compute **PDT**s of large composite gadgets to reduce memory usage). Regarding performance, for the computation of the security of the AES S-box (see Fig. 10), almost all of the execution time goes into computing the **PDT** of the ISW multiplication gadgets. Computing the **PDT**s of the other gadgets is much faster as they are smaller, and computing the composition takes a negligible amount of time (less than 1%). The total running time for the AES S-box is less than 5 s for 1, 2 and 3 shares, 30 s for 4 shares, 3 min for 5 shares, and 33 h for 6 shares on a 24-core computer (dual 2.3 GHz Intel(R) Xeon(R) CPU E5-2670 v3).

STRAPS presents a few similarities with VRAPS [8]. While STRAPS mainly computes **PDT** bounds and VRAPS computes random probing expandability bounds, both metrics relate to the random probing security of a gadget, and both tools are based on the maskVerif dependency test algorithm. The main differences between these tools are twofold. First, STRAPS uses a mix of Monte-Carlo sampling and full exploration of the sets of probes, whereas VRAPS does only full exploration. Second, STRAPS computes and uses the simulatability set for a given set of internal and output probes, while VRAPS only stores whether the size of the simulatability set exceeds a given threshold. Thanks to this weaker requirement, VRAPS is able to exploit the set exploration algorithm of maskVerif, which accelerates the full exploration of the sets of probes by avoiding an exhaustive enumeration of all subsets [4].

5.4 Experiments and SOTA Comparison

In this final section, we illustrate how to use our **PDT** bounding tool and the **PDT** composition theorems in order to bound the security of larger circuits, and to extract useful intuitions about the trade-off between the number of shares and level of noise required to reach a given security level. We also compare our results with previous works by Dziembowski et al. [20] and Belaïd et al. [8,9].

We begin by evaluating the impact of using composition theorems instead of a direct security evaluation. In Sect. 3.2, we concluded that directly analyzing the security of even a single multiplication gadget in the random probing model tightly is computationally intensive. On Fig. 7, we show the security of a slightly more complex $ISW(x, SNI\text{-}Ref(x^2))$ gadget evaluated as either the composition of four gadgets (a split gadget, a squaring, an SNI refresh and an ISW multiplication), or as a single gadget (we call it integrated evaluation). We can see that when the gadget becomes large ($n = 5$) and for a similar computational complexity, the results for the **PDT** composition are statistically tighter thanks to the lower size of its sub-gadgets. We also observe that, when upper and lower bounds converge, the security level computed from **PDT** composition is close to the one computed by the integrated evaluation, although the latter one is slightly better. We conclude that the **PDT** composition technique can provide useful results in practically relevant contexts where we build gadget compositions for which the integrated evaluation is not satisfying.

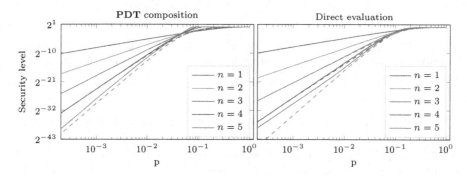

Fig. 7. Security of a cubing gadget $ISW(x, SNI\text{-}Ref(x^2))$. The left plot comes from **PDT** composition while the right plot is a direct security evaluation of the full circuit as a single gadget. The continuous line is an upper bound, while the dashed line is the stat-only lower bound. $N_{max} = 2 \times 10^6$, $N_t = 1000$.

Next, we investigate different refreshing strategies when computing the x^3 operation with an ISW multiplication gadget. Namely, we compare the situation with no refreshing which is known to be insecure in the threshold probing model [16], the simple refreshing with linear randomness complexity which does not offer strong composability guarantees, and an SNI refresh gadget from [12]. The results are illustrated in Fig. 8. In the first case (with no refreshing), we observe the well-known division by two of the statistical security order (reflected by the slope of the security curves in the asymptotic region where the noise is sufficient and curves become linear): the security level is asymptotically proportional to $p^{\lceil (n-1)/2 \rceil}$. On the other side of the spectrum, the composition with an SNI refresh guarantees a statistical security order of $n - 1$. Finally, the most interesting case is the one of the simple refresh gadget, for which we observe a statistical security order reduction for $n \geq 3$, of which the impact may remain small for low noise levels. For instance, we can see that for $p \geq 2 \times 10^{-3}$, the curves for the simple and the SNI refresh gadgets are almost the same, with the security order reduction becoming more and more apparent only for lower values of p. So this analysis provides us with a formal quantitative understanding of a gadget's security level which, for example, suggests that depending on the noise levels, using SNI gadgets may not always be needed.

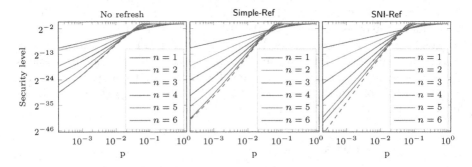

Fig. 8. Security of the cubing $\mathsf{ISW}(x, \mathsf{Ref}(x^2))$, where Ref is identity (no refreshing), Simple-Ref, or SNI-Ref gadget. The continuous line is an upper bound, while the dashed line is the stat-only lower bound. $N_{max} = 10^8$, $N_t = 100$.

We extend this analysis of a simple gadget to the case of a complete AES S-box in Fig. 9. All the previous observations remain valid in this case as well. Furthermore, this figure confirms that our results get close to the ones reported for concrete worst-case attacks in [18]. Namely, already for the (low) number of shares and (practical) levels of noise we consider, we observe a statistical security order of $n - 1$ for a practically relevant (AES S-box) circuit.[6]

Eventually, we compare our bounds with state-of-the-art results for the non-linear part of the AES S-box in Fig. 10, in order to highlight that such tight results were not available with existing solutions. Precisely, we compare our results with the works that provide the best bounds in the low-noise region that we consider: the Simple Refreshing (SR) strategy of Dziembowski et al. [20], and the first (RPE1) [8] and second (RPE2) [9] sets of gadgets from the Random

---

[6] To make the results more easily comparable, one can just assume connect the leakage probability with the mutual information of [18] by just assuming that the mutual information per bit (i.e., when the unit is the field element) equals p.

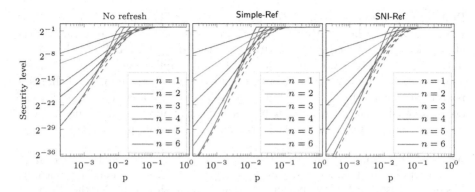

Fig. 9. Security of the non-linear part of an AES S-box in $\mathbb{F}_{256}$, where Ref is either an identity (no refreshing), the Simple-Ref gadget, or the SNI-Ref gadget. The continuous line is an upper bound, while the dashed line is the stat-only lower bound. $N_{max} = 10^8$, $N_t = 100$.

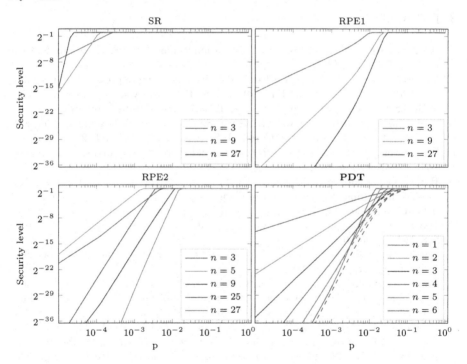

Fig. 10. Security of the non-linear part of an AES S-box in $\mathbb{F}_{256}$, based on the best result of each paper. For the **PDT**, we take use a SNI refresh gadget. All the circuits have a size $\mathcal{O}(n^2)$.

Probing Expansion strategy of Belaïd et al. We see that amongst the previous works we consider here, RPE2 with 27 shares achieves the best maximum tolerated leakage probability and statistical security order. Our **PDT**-based analysis of the SNI-refreshed AES S-box with the ISW multiplication achieves a similar security level with only 6 shares. In this last experiment, the number of shares n is an indicator for the circuit size since all schemes have a circuit size in $\mathcal{O}(n^2)$. So we conclude that our results enable a significant improvement of the provable security claims of practical masked circuits in the random probing model.

Acknowledgments. Gaëtan Cassiers and François-Xavier Standaert are resp. Research Fellow and Senior Associate Researcher of the Belgian Fund for Scientific Research (FNRS-F.R.S.). Maximilan Orlt is founded by the Emmy Noether Program FA 1320/1-1 of the German Research Foundation (DFG). This work has been funded in part by the ERC project 724725 and by Deutsche Forschungsgemeinschaft (DFG, German Research Foundation) - SFB 1119 - 236615297 (Project S7).

References

1. Ajtai, M.: Secure computation with information leaking to an adversary. In: STOC, pp. 715–724. ACM (2011)
2. Ananth, P., Ishai, Y., Sahai, A.: Private circuits: a modular approach. In: Shacham, H., Boldyreva, A. (eds.) CRYPTO 2018, Part III. LNCS, vol. 10993, pp. 427–455. Springer, Cham (2018). https://doi.org/10.1007/978-3-319-96878-0_15
3. Andrychowicz, M., Dziembowski, S., Faust, S.: Circuit compilers with $O(1/\log(n))$ leakage rate. In: Fischlin, M., Coron, J.-S. (eds.) EUROCRYPT 2016, Part II. LNCS, vol. 9666, pp. 586–615. Springer, Heidelberg (2016). https://doi.org/10.1007/978-3-662-49896-5_21
4. Barthe, G., Belaïd, S., Cassiers, G., Fouque, P.-A., Grégoire, B., Standaert, F.-X.: maskVerif: automated verification of higher-order masking in presence of physical defaults. In: Sako, K., Schneider, S., Ryan, P.Y.A. (eds.) ESORICS 2019, Part I. LNCS, vol. 11735, pp. 300–318. Springer, Cham (2019). https://doi.org/10.1007/978-3-030-29959-0_15
5. Barthe, G., et al.: Strong non-interference and type-directed higher-order masking. In: CCS, pp. 116–129. ACM (2016)
6. Barthe, G., Gourjon, M., Grégoire, B., Orlt, M., Paglialonga, C., Porth, L.: Masking in fine-grained leakage models: construction, implementation and verification. IACR Trans. Cryptogr. Hardw. Embed. Syst. **2021**(2), 189–228 (2021)
7. Battistello, A., Coron, J.-S., Prouff, E., Zeitoun, R.: Horizontal side-channel attacks and countermeasures on the ISW masking scheme. In: Gierlichs, B., Poschmann, A.Y. (eds.) CHES 2016. LNCS, vol. 9813, pp. 23–39. Springer, Heidelberg (2016). https://doi.org/10.1007/978-3-662-53140-2_2
8. Belaïd, S., Coron, J.-S., Prouff, E., Rivain, M., Taleb, A.R.: Random probing security: verification, composition, expansion and new constructions. In: Micciancio, D., Ristenpart, T. (eds.) CRYPTO 2020, Part I. LNCS, vol. 12170, pp. 339–368. Springer, Cham (2020). https://doi.org/10.1007/978-3-030-56784-2_12
9. Belaïd, S., Rivain, M., Taleb, A.R.: On the power of expansion: more efficient constructions in the random probing model. IACR Cryptol. ePrint Arch. **2021**, 434 (2021)

10. Bloem, R., Gross, H., Iusupov, R., Könighofer, B., Mangard, S., Winter, J.: Formal verification of masked hardware implementations in the presence of glitches. In: Nielsen, J.B., Rijmen, V. (eds.) EUROCRYPT 2018, Part II. LNCS, vol. 10821, pp. 321–353. Springer, Cham (2018). https://doi.org/10.1007/978-3-319-78375-8_11

11. Brier, E., Clavier, C., Olivier, F.: Correlation power analysis with a leakage model. In: Joye, M., Quisquater, J.-J. (eds.) CHES 2004. LNCS, vol. 3156, pp. 16–29. Springer, Heidelberg (2004). https://doi.org/10.1007/978-3-540-28632-5_2

12. Cassiers, G., Grégoire, B., Levi, I., Standaert, F.X:. Hardware private circuits: From trivial composition to full verification. IEEE Trans. Comput. 1 (2020)

13. Cassiers, G., Standaert, F.: Towards globally optimized masking: from low randomness to low noise rate or probe isolating multiplications with reduced randomness and security against horizontal attacks. IACR Trans. Cryptogr. Hardw. Embed. Syst. **2019**(2), 162–198 (2019)

14. Chari, S., Jutla, C.S., Rao, J.R., Rohatgi, P.: Towards sound approaches to counteract power-analysis attacks. In: Wiener, M. (ed.) CRYPTO 1999. LNCS, vol. 1666, pp. 398–412. Springer, Heidelberg (1999). https://doi.org/10.1007/3-540-48405-1_26

15. Chari, S., Rao, J.R., Rohatgi, P.: Template attacks. In: Kaliski, B.S., Koç, K., Paar, C. (eds.) CHES 2002. LNCS, vol. 2523, pp. 13–28. Springer, Heidelberg (2003). https://doi.org/10.1007/3-540-36400-5_3

16. Coron, J.-S., Prouff, E., Rivain, M., Roche, T.: Higher-order side channel security and mask refreshing. In: Moriai, S. (ed.) FSE 2013. LNCS, vol. 8424, pp. 410–424. Springer, Heidelberg (2014). https://doi.org/10.1007/978-3-662-43933-3_21

17. Duc, A., Dziembowski, S., Faust, S.: Unifying leakage models: from probing attacks to noisy leakage. J. Cryptol. **32**(1), 151–177 (2019)

18. Duc, A., Faust, S., Standaert, F.: Making masking security proofs concrete (or how to evaluate the security of any leaking device), extended version. J. Cryptol. **32**(4), 1263–1297 (2019)

19. Dziembowski, S., Faust, S., Skorski, M.: Noisy leakage revisited. In: Oswald, E., Fischlin, M. (eds.) EUROCRYPT 2015, Part II. LNCS, vol. 9057, pp. 159–188. Springer, Heidelberg (2015). https://doi.org/10.1007/978-3-662-46803-6_6

20. Dziembowski, S., Faust, S., Żebrowski, K.: Simple refreshing in the noisy leakage model. In: Galbraith, S.D., Moriai, S. (eds.) ASIACRYPT 2019, Part III. LNCS, vol. 11923, pp. 315–344. Springer, Cham (2019). https://doi.org/10.1007/978-3-030-34618-8_11

21. Faust, S., Grosso, V., Pozo, S.M.D., Paglialonga, C., Standaert, F.: Composable masking schemes in the presence of physical defaults & the robust probing model. IACR Trans. Cryptogr. Hardw. Embed. Syst. **2018**(3), 89–120 (2018)

22. Gandolfi, K., Mourtel, C., Olivier, F.: Electromagnetic analysis: concrete results. In: Koç, Ç.K., Naccache, D., Paar, C. (eds.) CHES 2001. LNCS, vol. 2162, pp. 251–261. Springer, Heidelberg (2001). https://doi.org/10.1007/3-540-44709-1_21

23. Goudarzi, D., Joux, A., Rivain, M.: How to securely compute with noisy leakage in quasilinear complexity. In: Peyrin, T., Galbraith, S. (eds.) ASIACRYPT 2018, Part II. LNCS, vol. 11273, pp. 547–574. Springer, Cham (2018). https://doi.org/10.1007/978-3-030-03329-3_19

24. Ishai, Y., Sahai, A., Wagner, D.: Private circuits: securing hardware against probing attacks. In: Boneh, D. (ed.) CRYPTO 2003. LNCS, vol. 2729, pp. 463–481. Springer, Heidelberg (2003). https://doi.org/10.1007/978-3-540-45146-4_27

25. Knichel, D., Sasdrich, P., Moradi, A.: SILVER – statistical independence and leakage verification. In: Moriai, S., Wang, H. (eds.) ASIACRYPT 2020. LNCS, vol. 12491, pp. 787–816. Springer, Cham (2020). https://doi.org/10.1007/978-3-030-64837-4_26

26. Kocher, P., Jaffe, J., Jun, B.: Differential power analysis. In: Wiener, M. (ed.) CRYPTO 1999. LNCS, vol. 1666, pp. 388–397. Springer, Heidelberg (1999). https://doi.org/10.1007/3-540-48405-1_25

27. Mangard, S., Popp, T., Gammel, B.M.: Side-channel leakage of masked CMOS gates. In: Menezes, A. (ed.) CT-RSA 2005, Part I. LNCS, vol. 3376, pp. 351–365. Springer, Heidelberg (2005). https://doi.org/10.1007/978-3-540-30574-3_24

28. Nikova, S., Rijmen, V., Schläffer, M.: Secure hardware implementation of nonlinear functions in the presence of glitches. J. Cryptol. **24**(2), 292–321 (2011)

29. Prest, T., Goudarzi, D., Martinelli, A., Passelègue, A.: Unifying leakage models on a Rényi day. In: Boldyreva, A., Micciancio, D. (eds.) CRYPTO 2019, Part I. LNCS, vol. 11692, pp. 683–712. Springer, Cham (2019). https://doi.org/10.1007/978-3-030-26948-7_24

30. Prouff, E., Rivain, M.: Masking against side-channel attacks: a formal security proof. In: Johansson, T., Nguyen, P.Q. (eds.) EUROCRYPT 2013. LNCS, vol. 7881, pp. 142–159. Springer, Heidelberg (2013). https://doi.org/10.1007/978-3-642-38348-9_9

31. Rivain, M., Prouff, E.: Provably secure higher-order masking of AES. In: Mangard, S., Standaert, F.-X. (eds.) CHES 2010. LNCS, vol. 6225, pp. 413–427. Springer, Heidelberg (2010). https://doi.org/10.1007/978-3-642-15031-9_28

32. Schneider, T., Moradi, A.: Leakage assessment methodology - extended version. J. Crypt. Eng. **6**(2), 85–99 (2016)

33. Scholz, F.: Confidence bounds & intervals for parameters relating to the binomial, negative binomial, poisson and hypergeometric distributions with applications to rare events (2008)

Secure Wire Shuffling
in the Probing Model

Jean-Sébastien Coron$^{(\boxtimes)}$ and Lorenzo Spignoli

University of Luxembourg, Esch-sur-Alzette, Luxembourg
{jean-sebastien.coron,lorenzo.spignoli}@uni.lu

Abstract. In this paper we describe the first improvement of the wire shuffling countermeasure against side-channel attacks described by Ishai, Sahai and Wagner at Crypto 2003. More precisely, we show how to get worst case statistical security against t probes with running time $\mathcal{O}(t)$ instead of $\mathcal{O}(t \log t)$; our construction is also much simpler. Recall that the classical masking countermeasure achieves perfect security but with running time $\mathcal{O}(t^2)$. We also describe a practical implementation for AES that outperforms the masking countermeasure for $t \geq 6\,000$.

1 Introduction

The Masking Countermeasure. The study of circuits resistant against probing attacks was initiated by Ishai, Sahai and Wagner in [ISW03]. Their construction is based on the masking countermeasure, where each intermediate variable x is shared into $x = x_1 \oplus \cdots \oplus x_n$, and the shares x_i are processed separately. The ISW construction offers perfect security; this means that an adversary with at most $t < n/2$ probes learns nothing about the secret variables. Rivain and Prouff showed in [RP10] how to adapt the ISW construction to AES, by working in $\mathbb{F}_{2^8}$ instead of $\mathbb{F}_2$; in particular, the non-linear part $S(x) = x^{254}$ of the AES SBox can be efficiently evaluated with only 4 non-linear multiplications over $\mathbb{F}_{2^8}$, and a few linear squarings. In the last few years, numerous variants and improvements of the masking countermeasure have been described: for example, high-order evaluation of any SBOX [CGP+12], high-order table re-computation [Cor14], minimization of randomness usage [FPS17] and efficient implementations of high-order masking [JS17, GJRS18].

The main drawback of the masking countermeasure is that the circuit size is quadratic in the maximum number of probes t in the circuit; namely in the ISW construction and its variants every AND gate gets expanded into a gadget of size $\mathcal{O}(t^2)$; hence the initial circuit C gets expanded into a new circuit of size $\mathcal{O}(|C| \cdot t^2)$. One can divide the new circuit into regions corresponding to each gadget, and by appropriate mask refreshing one can let the adversary put t probes per region, instead of t probes in the full circuit; the maximum number of probes then becomes $|C| \cdot t$ instead of t. But the circuit size remains $\mathcal{O}(|C| \cdot t^2)$, that is quadratic in the maximum number of probes t per region.

© International Association for Cryptologic Research 2021
T. Malkin and C. Peikert (Eds.): CRYPTO 2021, LNCS 12827, pp. 215–244, 2021.
https://doi.org/10.1007/978-3-030-84252-9_8

Statistical Security. To improve the previous complexity, the ISW authors introduced a weaker security model with statistical security only [ISW03]. In this model the adversary can still put t probes wherever he wants in the circuit, but he can now learn a secret variable with some non-zero probability (instead of zero probability as in the perfect security model); this probability should be a negligible function of the security parameter k. The authors described a construction in this model with complexity $\mathcal{O}(|C| \cdot t \log t)$ for at most t probes in the circuit. This is only quasi-linear in the number of probes t, so much better than the classical masking countermeasure. In this asymptotic complexity, a factor $\mathsf{poly}(k)$ is actually hidden in the constant, where k is the security parameter; namely, to achieve $2^{-\Omega(k)}$ statistical security, the size of the protected circuit in [ISW03] is actually $\mathcal{O}(|C| \cdot k^{10} \cdot t \log t)$.

The above result holds in the *stateless model*, in which the adversary must put his t probes in a non-adaptive way, that is before the evaluation of the circuit. The authors also considered the more useful *stateful model*, in which the adversary can move its probes between successive executions of the circuit; however within an execution the model is still non-adaptive. For the stateful model, the authors described a construction with complexity $\mathcal{O}(|C| \cdot t \log t + s \cdot t^3 \log t)$, where s is the number of memory cells in the circuit that must be passed from one execution to the other; for a block-cipher, s would be the number of key bits. Assuming that the circuit size $|C|$ is significantly larger than the key size s, this is again better than the classical masking countermeasure with respect to the number of probes t.

While the masking countermeasure used in the first part of [ISW03] is quite practical and has been widely studied with numerous improvements, the construction in the statistical model, which appears in the second part of [ISW03], has never been investigated up to our knowledge. Our goal in this paper is to describe an improved construction in the statistical model that is better asymptotically and moreover practical, while we argue that the original construction from [ISW03] was essentially unpractical.

The Wire Shuffling Countermeasure from [ISW03]. To achieve the $\mathcal{O}(t \cdot \log t)$ complexity in the statistical model, the ISW paper proceeds in two steps. First, it considers statistical security in the weaker *random probing model*, in which the adversary gets the value of each variable with independent probability p. This is easy to achieve from the classical masking countermeasure. Namely, if we apply the masking countermeasure against $t = k$ probes with $2k + 1$ shares (where k is the security parameter), we get a circuit where each gadget has size at most $c \cdot k^2$ (for some constant c), and secure against k probes per gadget. These k probes per gadget correspond to a fraction $k/(c \cdot k^2) = 1/(c \cdot k)$ of the gadget wires. Hence if we let $p = 1/(10 \cdot c \cdot k)$, then from Chernoff's bound, the probability that in a given gadget the adversary gets more than k probes becomes a negligible function of k; this gives statistical security in the random probing model. Starting from a circuit C, we can therefore obtain an intermediate circuit C' of size $\mathcal{O}(|C| \cdot k^2)$ that is secure in the random probing model with leakage probability $p = \Omega(1/k)$.

In the second step, the ISW paper describes a construction where each wire i of the intermediate circuit C' is expanded into ℓ wires, such that only one of the ℓ wires contains the original signal value v_i from C', while the other wires contain only a dummy value \$; see Fig. 1 for an illustration. We call this construction the wire shuffling countermeasure, as it consists in randomly shuffling the position of the signal among those ℓ wires. More precisely, for each execution the position of the signal v_i in the expanded circuit $\tilde{C}$ is selected randomly and independently among the ℓ wires, for each original wire i of C'.

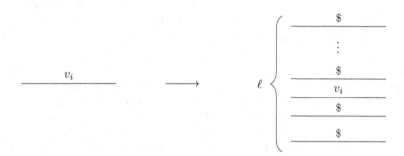

Fig. 1. A wire with signal v_i in C' (left), and the corresponding ℓ wires in $\tilde{C}$ (right); only one of the ℓ wires contain the signal v_i, while the others contain the dummy value \$.

Consider now a gate from the intermediate circuit C'. If the two input wires i and i' from the intermediate circuit C' have their information located at index $j \in [1, \ell]$ and $j' \in [1, \ell]$ in the expanded circuit $\tilde{C}$, one must be able to process the original gate from C' without leaking information on v_i and $v_{i'}$ in the process, except with small probability. One cannot consider all possible index pairs (j, j') as the complexity would be quadratic in ℓ (and eventually quadratic in t). Instead the ISW paper describes a relatively complex construction based on sorting networks with complexity $\mathcal{O}(\ell \log \ell)$; it then proves that with $\ell = \mathcal{O}(t/p^7)$ wires, the probability that each original value v_i is learned by the adversary is at most p. This means that the adversary does not learn more from the worst case probing of the final circuit $\tilde{C}$, than from the p-random probing of the intermediate circuit C'. This implies statistical security for $\tilde{C}$ with circuit size $\mathcal{O}(|C| \cdot t \log t)$, so better than the classical masking countermeasure with complexity $\mathcal{O}(|C| \cdot t^2)$. We stress that for this final circuit $\tilde{C}$, security holds in the worst case probing model as well, where the adversary can freely choose the position of the t probes in the circuit (as opposed to the random probing model where every variable leaks with probability p).

Our Contribution. In this paper we describe a construction that achieves worst-case statistical security against t probes in the stateless model with time complexity $\mathcal{O}(|C| \cdot t)$ instead of $\mathcal{O}(|C| \cdot t \log t)$; our construction is also much simpler. Our technique is as follows. As in [ISW03], we randomly shuffle the position of the signal v_i among the ℓ wires, independently for each original wire i of the intermediate circuit C'. However, we now explicitly compute the index position $j_i \in [1, \ell]$ of each signal v_i among the ℓ wires; whereas in ISW this position was only implicitly determined by the value of the ℓ wires, as one of them would contain the signal v_i while the others would get the dummy value \$ (see Fig. 1).

Consider now two wires i and i' in C', for which the signal is located at positions $j \in [1, \ell]$ and $j' \in [1, \ell]$ in the expanded circuit $\tilde{C}$. Since the positions j and j' of the signal are now explicitly computed, we don't need to use a sorting network as in [ISW03] anymore. Instead, we can simply generate a new random index $j'' \in [1, \ell]$, and cyclically shift the information corresponding to wire i by $\Delta = j'' - j$ positions modulo ℓ, and similarly by $\Delta' = j'' - j'$ positions for wire i'. For both inputs the signal is now located at the common position $j + \Delta = j' + \Delta' = j''$, so now the signal will be processed at this position j''. Such cyclic shift can be computed in time $\mathcal{O}(\ell)$ instead of $\mathcal{O}(\ell \log \ell)$, hence we can get statistical security with time complexity $\mathcal{O}(|C| \cdot t)$ instead of $\mathcal{O}(|C| \cdot t \log t)$. Our construction is also much easier to implement in practice, as we can use a simple table look-up for the cyclic shifts, instead of a complex sorting network.

The main difference between our construction and the original ISW is that the index positions of the signal values are now explicitly computed in the final circuit $\tilde{C}$. This means that those index positions can be probed by the adversary, so we may as well assume that the adversary knows all those index positions. Our proof of security crucially relies on the fact that as in [ISW03], the adversary learns those positions only at the evaluation phase, that is *after* he has committed his probes in the circuit. Therefore when the adversary learns the exact locations it is actually too late: we show that he can only learn the signal values with probability at most p. This means that as previously the adversary does not learn more from the worst case probing of the final circuit $\tilde{C}$, than from the p-random probing of the intermediate circuit C'; this gives worst case statistical security for our final circuit $\tilde{C}$.

For the stateful construction we must add some additional countermeasure, because if the adversary knows the position of the signal v_i at the end of one execution, he can directly probe v_i at the beginning of the next execution; this holds for memory cells that must be transmitted from one execution to the next. In ISW this is achieved by using a t-private encoding of a random cyclic shift for each pack of ℓ wires. Such t-private encoding has complexity $\mathcal{O}(t^2)$, and since for every memory cell this cyclic shift requires a circuit of size $\mathcal{O}(\ell \log \ell)$, the additional complexity is $\mathcal{O}(st^2 \ell \log \ell)$, which gives a complexity $\tilde{\mathcal{O}}(st^3)$ for s memory cells. To get a better complexity we proceed as follows: for each wire i from C' at the end of one execution, we perform a random permutation of the $\ell = \mathcal{O}(t)$ corresponding wires in $\tilde{C}$, but without processing the index location explicitly. For this we use a sequence of $\log_2 \ell$ layers, where in each layer the information in all wires of index j and $j + 2^m$ is randomly swapped, for

$0 \leq m < \log_2 \ell$. The complexity is then $\mathcal{O}(s\ell \log \ell) = \mathcal{O}(st \log t)$, and eventually the circuit complexity is $\mathcal{O}(|C| \cdot t \log t)$. We summarize the time and circuit complexities in Table 1. We see that asymptotically in the stateless model our construction improves the time complexity but not the circuit complexity; in the stateful model we improve both the time and circuit complexities.

Finally, we describe an AES implementation of our shuffling countermeasure, which we compare with an AES implementation of the masking countermeasure. In practice our shuffling construction outperforms the masking countermeasure for $t \geq 6\,000$. We provide the source code in [Cor21].

Table 1. Time and circuit complexity of our new construction vs ISW, where s is the number of memory cells that must be passed from one execution to the other.

		Time complexity (RAM model)	Circuit complexity
Stateless model	ISW, Theorem 3	$\mathcal{O}(|C| \cdot t \log t)$	$\mathcal{O}(|C| \cdot t \log t)$
	Theorem 6	$\mathcal{O}(|C| \cdot t)$	$\mathcal{O}(|C| \cdot t \log t)$
Stateful model	ISW, Theorem 8	$\mathcal{O}(|C| \cdot t \log t + s \cdot t^3 \log t)$	$\mathcal{O}(|C| \cdot t \log t + s \cdot t^3 \log t)$
	Theorem 9	$\mathcal{O}(|C| \cdot t + s \cdot t \log t)$	$\mathcal{O}(|C| \cdot t \log t)$

Software Probing Model. For a software implementation we will work in the RAM model used in algorithmic analysis; see [MS08, Section 2.2]. In this model, each memory access takes unit time, and every memory cell can store an integer whose bit-size is logarithmic in the input size; for a polynomial-time algorithm, this enables to store array indices in a single cell.

Moreover, in the *software probing model*, we assume that during the execution the adversary can only probe the input address and output value of a RAM cell that is read during a table look-up, but not the content of the internal wires of the circuit implementation of the RAM. This software probing model was already used for example in the high-order table look-up countermeasure from [Cor14]. For simplicity we will still describe our construction in terms of an expanded circuit $\tilde{C}$ as in [ISW03]. For a software implementation our circuit $\tilde{C}$ is therefore augmented with a RAM unit, where the adversary can only probe the input address and the input/output value, but not the internal wires of the RAM. For completeness we also provide in the full version of this paper [CS21] a pure circuit description of our countermeasure, with a proof of security in the standard wire probing model.

Related Work. In practice, operation shuffling is often used in addition to the masking countermeasure to improve the resistance against side-channel attacks.

Operation shuffling consists in randomizing the execution order of the cryptographic blocks when the operations are independent; we refer to [VMKS12] for a comprehensive study. For example, for AES one can randomize the evaluation of the 16 Sboxes. In [HOM06], the authors describe an 8-bit implementation of first-order masking of AES, combined with SBOX shuffling with a random starting index; the technique was extended to a 32-bit implementation in [THM07]. In [RPD09], the authors investigate the combination of high-order SBOX masking (but with resistance against first-order attacks only) and shuffling by a random permutation. Namely the shuffling prevents a second-order DPA attack against the SBOX masking countermeasure; the authors can then quantify the efficiency of the main attack paths. The authors of [VMKS12] improve the software implementation of random permutation shuffling, with an efficient permutation generator; see also [VML16, Pap18] for a description of shuffling countermeasures with low randomness usage. The main attack against the shuffling countermeasure is the "integrated DPA" introduced in [CCD00]; it consists in summing the signal over a sliding window. If the signal is spread in t positions, the signal will be reduced by a factor $\sqrt{t}$ only, instead of t without the integration; see [VMKS12] for an improved security analysis.

In summary, operation shuffling has been used in numerous previous work to improve the practical resistance of an implementation against side-channel attacks, but not in provable way against t probes for large t. Conversely, the second part of [ISW03] describes a theoretical construction with complexity $\mathcal{O}(t \log t)$ in the statistical model, but it has never been investigated. In this paper, our goal is to describe an improved construction with provable security in the same model, moreover with complexity $\mathcal{O}(t)$ only, and to compare its performance in practice with the classical masking countermeasure.

2   Preliminaries

In this section we first recall the perfect privacy model and the masking-based construction from the first part of [ISW03]. We then recall the statistical security model and the wire shuffling construction from the second part of [ISW03]. For simplicity we first consider stateless circuits only; we will consider stateful circuits in Sect. 4.

A deterministic circuit C is a directed acyclic graph whose vertices are gates or input/output variables, and whose edges are wires. A randomized circuit is a circuit augmented with gates which have fan-in 0 and output a random bit. The size of a circuit is defined as the number of gates and its depth is the length of the longest path from an input to an output.

2.1   The ISW Model for Perfect Security

In the ISW probing model [ISW03], the adversary is allowed to put at most t probes in the circuit, and must learn nothing from those t probes. For stateless circuits, both inputs and outputs are hidden in every invocation. For this one uses a randomized input *encoder* I and an output *decoder* O; the internal wires of I and O cannot be probed by the adversary.

Definition 1 (Perfect privacy for stateless circuits.). *Let T be an efficiently computable deterministic function mapping a stateless circuit C to a stateless circuit C', and let I, O be as above. We say that (T, I, O) is a t-private stateless transformer if it satisfies:*

1. **Soundness.** *The input-output functionality of $O \circ C' \circ I$ (i.e., the iterated application of I, C', O in that order) is indistinguishable from that of C.*
2. **Privacy.** *We require that the view of any t-limited adversary, which attacks $O \circ C' \circ I$ by probing at most t wires in C', can be simulated from scratch, i.e. without access to any wire in the circuit. The identity of the probed wires has to be chosen in advance by the adversary.*

2.2 The ISW Construction for Perfect Privacy

We recall the classical ISW construction for achieving perfect privacy. We first consider the stateless model; we then explain how the construction can be adapted to the stateful model in Sect. 4. For security against t probes, the construction uses a simple secret-sharing scheme with $n = 2t + 1$ shares. The three algorithms Encode, Decode, and Transform are defined as follow:

- Encode I. Each binary input x is mapped to n binary values. First, $n - 1$ random bits $r_1, \ldots, r_{n-1}$ are independently generated. The encoding of x is composed by these $n-1$ random values together with $r_n = x \oplus r_1 \oplus \ldots \oplus r_{n-1}$. The circuit I computes the encoding of each input bit independently.

- Decode O. The output returned by $T(C)$ has the form $y_1, \ldots, y_n$. The associated output bit of C computed by O is $y_1 \oplus \ldots \oplus y_n$.

- Transform T. Assume without loss of generality that the original circuit C consists of only XOR and AND gates. The transformed circuit C' maintains the invariant that corresponding to each wire in C will be n wires in C' carrying an n-sharing of the value on that wire of C. More precisely, the circuit C' is obtained by transforming the gates of C as follows.
  For a XOR gate with inputs a, b and output c, let in C' be the corresponding wires $a_1, \ldots, a_n$ and $b_1, \ldots, b_n$. From $c = a \oplus b = \bigoplus_{i=1}^{n} a_i \oplus b_i$, we let $c_i = a_i \oplus b_i$ for $1 \leq i \leq n$.
  Consider an AND gate in C with inputs a, b and output c; we have $c = a \wedge b = \bigoplus_{i,j} a_i b_j$. In the transformation of this gate, intermediate values $z_{i,j}$ for $i \neq j$ are computed. For each $1 \leq i < j \leq n$, $z_{i,j}$ is computed uniformly random, while $z_{j,i}$ is set to $(z_{i,j} \oplus a_i b_j) \oplus a_j b_i$. Now, the output bits $c_1, \ldots, c_n$ in C' are defined to be the sequence $c_i = a_i b_i \oplus \bigoplus_{j \neq i} z_{i,j}$; see the full version of this paper [CS21] for an algorithmic description of the AND gadget.

In the transformed circuit $C' = T(C)$, every XOR gate and AND gate in C are therefore expanded to gadgets of size $\mathcal{O}(n)$ and $\mathcal{O}(n^2)$ respectively, and the gadgets in C' are connected in the same way as the gates in C. This completes the description of T.

Theorem 1 (Perfect privacy, stateless model [ISW03]). *The above construction is a perfectly t-private stateless transformer (T, I, O), such that T maps any stateless circuit C of depth d to a randomized stateless circuit of size $\mathcal{O}(|C| \cdot t^2)$ and depth $\mathcal{O}(d \log t)$.*

2.3   The Region Probing Model and t-SNI Security

The above privacy result holds in the worst case probing model, where the adversary can freely chose the position of the t probes in the circuit. Alternatively one can consider the weaker random probing model, where each wire leaks with probability p. To prove security in the random probing model, we first need to consider worst-case privacy in the region probing model, where the adversary can put t probes per region [ADF16], instead of t probes in the full circuit. Recall that a circuit C is a directed acyclic graph whose vertices are gates and whose edges are wires. We partition the set of gates of the circuit into a number of regions, and a wire connecting two gates can therefore meet at most two regions.

The region probing model was already considered in [ISW03], with one region per gadget. The authors claimed that security in this model is achieved thanks to the re-randomization property of the outputs of the AND gadget: for each original output bit, the encoded outputs are $(n - 1)$-wise independent even given the entire n-encoding of the inputs; this would imply security against a stronger type of adversary who may observe at most t' wires in each gadget, where $t' = \Omega(t)$. However we argue that this re-randomization property is actually not enough to achieve security in the region probing model: we exhibit in the full version of this paper [CS21] a simple counterexample, *i.e.* a gadget achieving the re-randomization property but insecure in the region probing model.

The required property for achieving security in the region probing model is actually the t-SNI notion introduced in [BBD+16]. The authors showed that the notion allows for securely composing masked algorithms; i.e. the t-SNI of a full construction can be proven based on the t-SNI of its component gadgets.

Definition 2 (t-SNI security [BBD+16]). *Let G be a gadget taking as input n shares $(a_i)_{1 \leq i \leq n}$ and n shares $(b_i)_{1 \leq i \leq n}$, and outputting n shares $(c_i)_{1 \leq i \leq n}$. The gadget G is said to be t-SNI secure if for any set of t_1 probed intermediate variables and any subset O of output indices, such that $t_1 + |O| \leq t$, there exist two subsets I and J of input indices which satisfy $|I| \leq t_1$ and $|J| \leq t_1$, such that the t_1 intermediate variables and the output variables $c|_O$ can be perfectly simulated from $a|_I$ and $b|_J$.*

To achieve privacy in the region probing model, we consider the ISW construction from Sect. 2.2, in which we additionally perform an $(n - 1)$-SNI mask refreshing algorithm as inputs of each XOR and AND gadgets. Such mask refreshing can be based on the AND gadget, since as showed in [BBD+16], the AND gadget achieves the $(n-1)$-SNI security property (see the full version of this paper [CS21] for a concrete mask refreshing algorithm). We define each region as comprising an AND or XOR gadget, and the mask refreshing of the corresponding output variable, so that each output $z^{(j)}$ is used only once in the next region; see Fig. 2 for an illustration.

Theorem 2 (t-privacy in the region probing model). *Let C be a circuit of fan-out f. Let (I, O, T) be the previous transformer with $n = 2t + 1$ shares, where a $(n-1)$-SNI mask refreshing is applied as input of each XOR and AND gadgets. The transformed circuit is t-private secure where the adversary can put at most t probes per regions, each of size $\mathcal{O}(f \cdot t^2)$.*

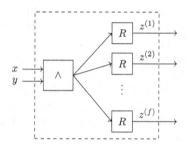

Fig. 2. A region comprises the AND (or XOR) gadget, and the mask refreshing of the output variable.

We provide the proof in the full version of this paper [CS21]. Note that any circuit C can be converted into a circuit of fan-out $f = 2$; therefore we can always obtain regions of size $\mathcal{O}(t^2)$.

2.4   Security in the Random Probing Model

We recall below the privacy definition when the adversary learns each wire with probability p (average-case security), instead of freely choosing the positions of the probes as above (worst-case security); this is the random probing model [ISW03].

Definition 3 (Random probing model [ISW03]). *A circuit transformer $T = T(C, k)$ is said to be (statistically) p-private in the average case if $C' = T(C, k)$ is statistically private against an adversary which corrupts each wire in C' with independent probability p. That is, the joint distribution of the random set of corrupted wires and the values observed by the adversary can be simulated up to a $k^{-\omega(1)}$ statistical distance.*

From Theorem 2, the ISW circuit transformer from Sect. 2.2 with $2k+1$ shares is perfectly private with respect to any adversary corrupting k wires per region. Since each region has size $O(k^2)$, it follows from Chernoff's bound that the view of an adversary corrupting each wire with probability $p = \Omega(1/k)$ can be perfectly simulated, except with negligible failure probability. We provide the proof of Lemma 1 in the full version of this paper [CS21].

Lemma 1 (Random probing security [ISW03]). *There exists a circuit transformer $T(C, k)$ producing a circuit C' of size $\mathcal{O}(|C| \cdot k^2)$, such that T is $\Omega(1/k)$-private in the average case.*

2.5   Worst-Case Statistical Security Model

The masking countermeasure recalled in Sect. 2.2 achieves perfect security against t probes with complexity $\mathcal{O}(t^2)$. To obtain a construction with complexity $\mathcal{O}(t \cdot \log t)$ only, the authors of [ISW03] introduced a relaxation of the security model, in which one tolerates a leakage of the secrets, albeit with a negligible probability; this is called the statistical model of security. We stress that with respect to the probes we are still working in the worst case model, in which the adversary can freely chose the position of the t probes (as opposed to the random probing model above in which every wire leaks with probability p). The definition below is similar to the perfect privacy model, except that now the simulation can fail with negligible probability. For this worst-case statistical model, our main goal in this paper is to improve the wire shuffling countermeasure introduced in [ISW03], with a running time $\mathcal{O}(t)$ instead of $\mathcal{O}(t \cdot \log t)$.

Definition 4 (Statistical privacy for stateless circuits). *Let T be an efficiently computable deterministic function mapping a stateless circuit C to a stateless circuit $\tilde{C}$, and let I, O be as above. We say that (T, I, O) is a statistically t-private stateless transformer if it satisfies:*

1. ***Soundness.*** *The input-output functionality of $O \circ \tilde{C} \circ I$ (i.e., the iterated application of $I, \tilde{C}, O$ in that order) is indistinguishable from that of C.*
2. ***Privacy.*** *We require that the view of any t-limited adversary, which attacks $O \circ \tilde{C} \circ I$ by probing at most t wires in $\tilde{C}$, can be simulated except with negligible probability. The identity of the probed wires has to be chosen in advance by the adversary.*

2.6   The ISW Construction for Statistical Privacy

We now recall the statistically private construction from [ISW03] that achieves complexity $\mathcal{O}(t \cdot \log t)$. For simplicity we first consider the case of stateless circuits; stateful circuits will be considered in Sect. 4. The construction proceeds in two steps. First one applies the classical masking countermeasure, namely the circuit transformer $T(C, k)$ guaranteeing p-privacy in the average case, for $p = \Omega(1/k)$ with security parameter k; see Lemma 1 from Sect. 2.4. Then one transforms its output C' into a larger circuit $\tilde{C}$, where only a fraction of the computation is useful. Namely the circuit $\tilde{C}$ will perform the same computation as C', but only on a small random subset of its wires; the remaining wires of $\tilde{C}$ will contain no useful information for the adversary.

The worst-case probing security of the final circuit $\tilde{C}$ will reduce to the p-random probing security of C' as follows. In the stateless model the adversary must commit its probes before the circuit evaluation. The subset of useful wires in the final circuit $\tilde{C}$ will be only determined during the invocation of $\tilde{C}$, and therefore it will be independent of the set of corrupted wires. This implies the adversary in $\tilde{C}$ will be able to obtain information about the original wires in C' with small probability only; hence the worst-case probing security of $\tilde{C}$ will follow from the p-random probing security of C'.

Thus, the author's construction transforms the circuit $C' = T(C, k)$ to a circuit $\tilde{C}$ as follows. For each wire i of C' one considers ℓ wires of $\tilde{C}$ labeled $(i, 1), \ldots, (i, \ell)$. Every such wires can take a value from the set $\{0, 1, \$\}$. For every wire i in C' carrying a value $v_i \in \{0, 1\}$, the wires $(i, 1), \ldots, (i, \ell)$ in $\tilde{C}$ will carry the value v_i in a random position (independently of other ℓ-tuples), and the value $\$$ in the remaining $\ell - 1$ positions; see Fig. 1 for an illustration.

Formally we define the Encode' and Decode' algorithms for encoding the input wires and decoding the output wires of the intermediate circuit C'. Note that these algorithms must eventually be composed with Encode and Decode from Sect. 2.2.

- Encode'. To encode a value v, first generate at random an index $j \leftarrow_\$ [1, \ell]$ and output an ℓ-tuple in which v will be the j-th element, while the other elements carry a dummy value $\$$. That is, return $(\$, \ldots, \$, v, \$, \ldots, \$)$, where v is at the j-th position.

- Decode'. Given a ℓ-tuple $(\$, \ldots, \$, v, \$, \ldots, \$)$, return v.

We now describe the transformation applied to every gate of the intermediate circuit C'. Suppose that $v_i = v_{i_1} * v_{i_2}$, i.e., the value of wire i in C' is obtained by applying a boolean operation $*$ to the values of wires i_1, i_2 in C'. Such a gate in C' is replaced with a 2ℓ-input, ℓ-output gadget in $\tilde{C}$. The gadget first puts both values v_{i_1} and v_{i_2} in random but adjacent positions, and then combines them to obtain the value $v_{i_1} * v_{i_2}$ in a randomly defined wire out of the ℓ output ones. For this the gadget makes use of *sorting networks* as a building block. A sorting network is a layered circuit from ℓ integer-valued input wires to ℓ integer-valued output wires, that outputs its input sequence in a sorted order[1]. More technically, the gate is processed as follow:

- **Preprocessing.** Compute $\ell + 1$ uniformly and independently random integers $r, r_1, \ldots, r_\ell$ from the range $[0, 2^k]$, where k is the security parameter. For each $1 \le j \le \ell$, use the values $v_{i_1,j}, v_{i_2,j}$ (of wires (i_1, j) and (i_2, j)) to form a pair $(\mathsf{key}_j, \mathsf{val}_j)$ such that:

---

[1] The authors of [ISW03] use the AKS network [AKS83], which achieves the optimal parameters of $\mathcal{O}(\ell \log \ell)$ size and $\mathcal{O}(\log \ell)$ depth.

1. key_j is set to r_j if $v_{i_1,j} = v_{i_2,j} = \$$ and to r otherwise;
2. val_j is set to $\$$ if both $v_{i_1,j}$, $v_{i_2,j}$ are $\$$; to a bit value b if one of $v_{i_1,j}, v_{i_2,j}$ is b and the other is $\$$, and to $b_1 * b_2$ if $v_{i_1,j} = b_1$ and $v_{i_2,j} = b_2$.

- **Sorting.** A sorting network is applied to the above ℓ-tuple of pairs using key as the sorting key. Let $(u_1, \ldots, u_\ell)$ denote the ℓ-tuple of symbols val_j sorted according to the keys key_j.
- **Postprocessing.** The jth output v_j is obtained by looking at u_j, u_{j+1}, u_{j+2}: if u_j, $u_{j+1} \neq \$$ then $v_j = u_j * u_{j+1}$, if $u_j = u_{j+2} = \$$ and $u_{j+1} \neq \$$ then $v_j = u_{j+1}$, and otherwise $v_j = \$$.

This terminates the description of the construction. The above transformation works because if the input signals v_{i_1} and v_{i_2} are initially located at positions j_1 and j_2 for some $j_1 \neq j_2$, then by definition $\text{key}_{j_1} = \text{key}_{j_2} = r$, and therefore after sorting by key_j the signal values v_{i_1} and v_{i_2} will be contiguous; then at the postprocessing phase the output signal $v_{i_1} * v_{i_2}$ will be computed, and located at some random position j_3.[2] This gadget can be implemented by a circuit of size $\mathcal{O}(k \cdot \ell \log \ell)$.

The following lemma proves the worst-case t-private security of the final circuit $\tilde{C}$, from the p-random probing security of the intermediate circuit C'. A minor difference is that we use $\ell = \mathcal{O}(t/p^7)$ instead of $\ell = \mathcal{O}(t/p^4)$ in [ISW03, Lemma 2]. We claim that this is indeed the correct bound, as it comes from the relative size of the maximal matching of a graph of degree 4, which is at most $1/7$ (and not $1/4$ as used in the proof of [ISW03, Lemma 2], see for example [BDD+04]). Note that this technicality does not change the asymptotic behavior with respect to the number of probes t which is still $\mathcal{O}(t \cdot \log t)$, only the dependence with respect to the security parameter k.

Lemma 2. *Suppose that C' is p-private in the average case. Then the circuit $\tilde{C}$, constructed with $\ell = \mathcal{O}(t/p^7)$, is statistically t-private in the worst case.*

The following theorem proves the worst-case statistical t-privacy of the circuit $\tilde{C}$. It is the same as [ISW03, Theorem 3], except that we make the dependence of the circuit size in the security parameter k more explicit; this is to enable a comparison with our new construction, which has an improved complexity not only with respect to the number of probes t but also with respect to k.

Theorem 3. *There exists a statistically t-private stateless transformer $(\tilde{T}, \tilde{I}, \tilde{O})$, such that $\tilde{T}(C, k)$ transforms a circuit C to a circuit $\tilde{C}$ of size $\mathcal{O}(|C| \cdot k^{10} \cdot t \cdot (\log k + \log t))$.*

Proof. The worst-case statistical t-privacy of $\tilde{C}$ follows from Lemma 2. The intermediate circuit $C' = T(C, k)$ has complexity $\mathcal{O}(|C| \cdot k^2)$. Then C' is expanded by a factor $\mathcal{O}(k \cdot \ell \log \ell)$; from Lemma 2 and with $p = \Omega(1/k)$, one can take $\ell = \mathcal{O}(t \cdot k^7)$; the expansion factor is therefore $\mathcal{O}(k \cdot (t \cdot k^7) \log(t \cdot k^7)) = \mathcal{O}(k^8 \cdot t \cdot (\log t + \log k))$. The final complexity is therefore $\mathcal{O}(|C| \cdot k^{10} \cdot t \cdot (\log k + \log t))$. $\square$

---

[2] The same holds if $j_1 = j_2$.

2.7   Random Gate-Probing Model

For proving the security of our new construction, it will be more efficient to work in a slight variant of the random probing model for the intermediate circuit C', in which we assume that every *gate* of the circuit leaks all its information with probability p, instead of every wire. When a gate is leaking, all its input and output wires are leaked (see Fig. 3 for an illustration); we call this variant the *random gate-probing model*. We also assume that the input wires in C' are also leaking with probability p; this is equivalent to considering a "copy gate" applied to each input and also leaking with probability p. Given a circuit C and a set of wires W, we define C_W as the value of the wires in W.

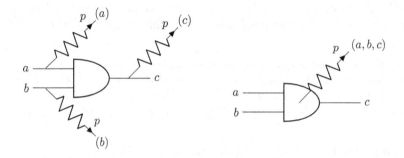

Fig. 3. Random probing model (left) vs random gate-probing model (right).

Definition 5 (Random gate-probing security). *Consider a randomized circuit C' and a random sampling W of its internal wires, where each gate G_i of C' leaks with independent probability p_i. The circuit C' is said (p, ε)-random gate-probing secure if for any $(p_i)_i$ with $p_i \leq p$, there exists a simulator $\mathcal{S}_{C'}$ such that $\mathcal{S}_{C'}(W) \stackrel{id}{=} C'_W(\mathsf{Encode}(\vec{x}))$ for every plain input $\vec{x}$, except with probability at most ε over the sampling of W.*

Note that our above definition is slightly stronger than Definition 3 from [ISW03]. Namely in Definition 3 the simulator produces both the random sampling W and the leaking values, whereas in the above definition the simulator is given W as input and must perfectly simulate the leaking values, except with probability at most ε over the sampling of W. This slightly stronger definition will be more convenient for proving the security of our construction. As in Lemma 1, the masking countermeasure is proven secure in the random gate-probing model via the Chernoff's bound.

Lemma 3. *There exists a circuit transformer $T(C, k)$ producing a circuit C' of size $\mathcal{O}(k^2|C|)$, such that T achieves $(\Omega(1/k), \varepsilon)$-random gate-probing security, where ε is a negligible function of the security parameter k.*

3   Our New Shuffling Countermeasure

In this section we describe our new construction that achieves worst-case probing security with running time $\mathcal{O}(t)$ instead of $\mathcal{O}(t \cdot \log t)$ in [ISW03]. For simplicity we consider stateless circuits only; we will consider stateful circuits in Sect. 4.

3.1   Description

Our construction proceeds in two steps, as in the ISW construction recalled in Sect. 2.6. First we transform the original circuit C into an intermediate circuit $C' = T(C, k)$ with $n = 2k + 1$ shares, using Theorem 2 from Sect. 2.3. Then we transform the circuit C' into a circuit $\tilde{C}$ as follows. The main difference with the original ISW construction recalled in Sect. 2.6 is the usage of a "shuffling index" storing the position of each signal wire from C' in the final circuit $\tilde{C}$.

Wires. For each wire of i of C' we consider ℓ wires of $\tilde{C}$ labeled $(i, 0), \ldots, (i, \ell-1)$ and an index j_i. Let $a_0, \ldots, a_{\ell-1}$ be the value of the ℓ wires. The circuit $\tilde{C}$ will make the invariant that if wire i in C' has value v, then this value appears at position j_i in $\tilde{C}$, that is $a_{j_i} = v$, while the value of the over wires is arbitrary.

Encoding and Decoding. We define the Encode' and Decode' algorithms for encoding the input wires and decoding the output wires of the intermediate circuit C'. As in Sect. 2.6 these algorithms must be composed with Encode and Decode from the masking countermeasure (Sect. 2.2). Note that the index position of the signal is computed explicitly; therefore we don't need the dummy element \$ as in Sect. 2.6 for the $\ell - 1$ other wires, and at the encoding phase we can simply assign them to 0.

- Encode'. To encode a value v, first generate at random an index $j \leftarrow_\$ [0, \ell - 1]$ and output the encoding $(j, (0, \ldots, 0, v, 0, \ldots, 0))$, where v is at the j-th position.

- Decode'. Given $(j, (a_0, \ldots, a_{\ell-1}))$, return a_j.

Algorithm 1. Gate $*$ processing

Input: Encodings $(j, (a_0, a_1, \ldots, a_{\ell-1}))$ and $(j', (b_0, b_1, \ldots, b_{\ell-1}))$
Output: Index j'' and array $(c_0, c_1, \ldots, c_{\ell-1})$ such that $c_{j''} = a_j * b_{j'}$
  1: $j'' \leftarrow_\$ [0, \ell)$
  2: $\Delta = j'' - j,\ \Delta' = j'' - j'$
  3: For all $0 \le i < \ell$, let $a'_i \leftarrow a_{i-\Delta}$ and $b'_i \leftarrow b_{i-\Delta'}$ $\triangleright\ a'_{j''} = a_j,\ b'_{j''} = b_{j'}$.
  4: For all $0 \le i < \ell$, let $c_i \leftarrow a'_i * b'_i$ $\triangleright\ c_{j''} = a_j * b_{j'}$.
  5: **return** $(j'', (c_0, c_1, \ldots, c_{\ell-1}))$

Gates. We consider a gate G in C', taking as input a and b, and outputting $c = a*b$ where $* \in \{\mathsf{XOR}, \mathsf{AND}\}$. We provide a formal description in Algorithm 1 above, where all indices computations are performed modulo ℓ; see also Fig. 4 for an illustration. Let $(a_i)_{0 \leq i < \ell}$ and $(b_i)_{0 \leq i < \ell}$ be the corresponding input wires in $\tilde{C}$, and let j and j' be the corresponding indexes, with $a = a_j$ and $b = b_{j'}$ the signal values in C'. To process the gate in $\tilde{C}$, one generates a random $j'' \leftarrow [0, \ell - 1]$ and then cyclically shifts the ℓ-array (a_i) by $j'' - j$ positions modulo ℓ; similarly the ℓ-array (b_i) is cyclically shifted by $j'' - j'$ positions. The input signals a and b are then located at common position j'', in which the gate G can now be processed; the same gate G is also applied on the other positions that contain arbitrary values; eventually the output signal c is located at position j''.

Finally, a random gate $r \leftarrow \{0, 1\}$ is expanded into a gadget outputting $(j, (r_0, \ldots, r_{\ell-1}))$ with $r_i \leftarrow \{0, 1\}$ for all $0 \leq i < \ell$ and $j \leftarrow [0, \ell)$. This terminates the description of the construction.

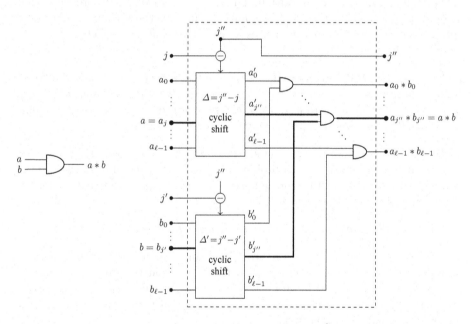

Fig. 4. Original gate in C' (left) and shuffling gadget in $\tilde{C}$ (right). The bold wires contain the original signal value from C'; the other wires contain only dummy values.

Theorem 4. *The transform defined above achieves the soundness property.*

Proof. The intermediate circuit $C' = T(C, k)$ computes the same function as C. Moreover every expanded gate in $\tilde{C}$ computes the same gate as C'. Namely consider the gate $c = a*b$ in C'. In the final circuit $\tilde{C}$ we have $c_{j''} = a'_{j''} * b'_{j''} = a_{j''-\Delta} * b_{j''-\Delta'} = a_j * b_{j'} = a*b = c$ as required. Therefore $\tilde{C} = \tilde{T}(C, k)$ computes the same function as C.   □

Note that Algorithm 1 can be implemented via a table look-up. Namely the ℓ wires can be stored in an array $T[i]$ for $0 \leq i < \ell$, with $T[j] = v$ for the signal index j, and the cyclic shift is performed as in Step 3, that is with the loop $T'[i] \leftarrow T[i - \Delta \bmod \ell]$ for each $0 \leq i < \ell$. The running time of Algorithm 1 is $\mathcal{O}(\ell)$ per gadget.

3.2   Shuffling Security of a Gadget and Composition

As in [ISW03], our goal is to show that the adversary does not learn more from the worst-case probing of the final circuit $\tilde{C}$ than from the p-random probing of the intermediate circuit C'. For this we proceed with a similar compositional approach as in [BBD+16]: 1) we introduce a new security definition for a single gadget in the expanded circuit $\tilde{C}$, 2) we prove that our shuffling gadget from the previous section satisfies this definition, and 3) we show how to get security for the full circuit $\tilde{C}$ by composition. The main benefit of this approach is that 3) only depends on 1), therefore we can later modify the shuffling gadget and still get security for the full circuit, as long as the shuffling gadget satisfies the security definition.

Definition 6 (Shuffling security). *We say that a randomized gadget achieves ℓ-shuffling security if any set of t probes, excluding the input wires of the gadget, can be perfectly simulated from scratch, except with probability at most t/ℓ, where the probability is taken over the randomness used by the gadget.*

In the above definition we exclude the probing of the gadget input wires, because in the composition the probing of the input wires of a gadget can be handled by the probing of the output wires of a previous gadget (except for the input wires of $\tilde{C}$ which we will handle separately).

Lemma 4. *The gadget $\tilde{G}$ as described in Algorithm 1 is ℓ-shuffling secure.*

Proof. We must construct a simulator that can simulate any set of t probes, with failure probability at most t/ℓ. In the simulation the input indices j, j' are fixed, as well as the input arrays $(a_0, \ldots, a_{\ell-1})$ and $(b_0, \ldots, b_{\ell-1})$. From the definition the adversary cannot probe those input arrays; in particular, the adversary cannot probe the signal $a = a_j$ and $b = b_{j'}$.

The proof is based on the fact that the adversary must commit to the position of the probes before the execution of the gadget. Therefore in the simulation the probes have fixed positions while the index j'' is randomly and uniformly distributed in $[0, \ell)$. This implies that for a fixed $i \in [0, \ell)$, the variable a'_i contains the secret value a with probability at most $1/\ell$; the same holds for the variables b'_i and c_i. This implies that the t probes can be perfectly simulated, except with probability at most t/ℓ. $\square$

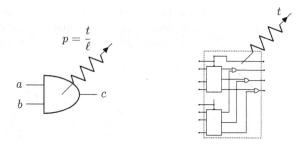

Fig. 5. A set of t probes in a shuffling gadget in $\tilde{C}$ (right) correspond to a gate-leaking probability at most $p = t/\ell$ in C' (left).

Composition. We now prove the worst-case statistical t-privacy of the final circuit $\tilde{C}$, from the p-random probing security of the intermediate circuit C'; see Fig. 5 for an illustration. We provide the proof in the full version of this paper [CS21].

Lemma 5. *Suppose that C' is (p, ε)-random gate probing secure. Then, the circuit $\tilde{C'}$ constructed as described above with $\ell := t/p$ achieves ε-statistical security in the worst case against t probes.*

Eventually our construction has better running time $\mathcal{O}(|C| \cdot t)$ but same circuit complexity $\mathcal{O}(|C| \cdot t \cdot \log t)$ as ISW.

Theorem 5. *There exists a statistically t-private stateless transformer $(\tilde{T}, \tilde{I}, \tilde{O})$, such that $\tilde{T}(C, k)$ transforms a circuit C into a circuit $\tilde{C}$ of running time $\mathcal{O}(|C| \cdot k^3 \cdot t)$ and size $\mathcal{O}(|C| \cdot k^3 \cdot t \cdot (\log k + \log t))$.*

Proof. From Lemma 5, the circuit $\tilde{C}$ achieves statistical privacy in the stateless worst-case model. The intermediate circuit C has size $\mathcal{O}(|C|k^2)$, while the final circuit has running time $\mathcal{O}(|C|k^2\ell)$ and size $\mathcal{O}(|C|k^2\ell \log \ell)$. With $p = t/\ell$ and $p = \Omega(1/k)$ to achieve average-case privacy for C', we get running time $\mathcal{O}(|C| \cdot k^3 \cdot t)$. and size $\mathcal{O}(|C| \cdot k^3 \cdot t \cdot (\log k + \log t))$. $\qquad \square$

3.3 Improved Time Complexity

From the proof of Lemma 5 the previous circuit $\tilde{C}$ is actually secure in the region probing model where the adversary can put t probes per gadget in $\tilde{C}$. We can however further optimize the circuit complexity if we only require security against a total of t probes in the full circuit $\tilde{C}$. Namely in that case we can consider that each gadget of $\tilde{C}$ has t_i probes with the condition $\sum_i t_i \leq t$, instead of $t_i \leq t$ for all i in the proof of Lemma 5. This means that for each corresponding gate in the intermediate circuit C', we can consider a leakage probability $p_i = t_i/\ell$ such that $\sum_i p_i \leq \mu$ over the full circuit C', with $\mu = t/\ell$. Note that this is a much looser condition than in Definition 5, where we required $p_i \leq p = t/\ell$ for all gates. In particular, if we take $t/\ell > 1$, we can tolerate a leakage probability $p_i = 1$ for a fraction of the gates in C', as long as $\sum_i p_i \leq t/\ell$ over all gates of C'; see Fig. 6 for an illustration. To handle this looser condition, we modify the definition of random gate probing security as follows.

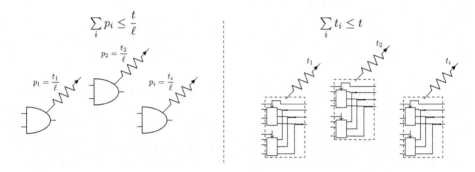

Fig. 6. A total of t probes in the final circuit $\tilde{C}$ (right) corresponds to a total of leaking probabilities at most t/ℓ in the intermediate circuit C' (left).

Definition 7 (Random Σ-gate-probing security). *Consider a randomized circuit C' and a random sampling W of its internal wires, where each gate G_i of C' leaks with independent probability p_i. The circuit C' is said (μ, ε)-random Σ-gate-probing secure if for any $(p_i)_i$ with $\sum_i p_i \leq \mu$, there exists a simulator $S_{C'}$ such that $S_{C'}(W) \overset{id}{=} C'_W(\mathsf{Encode}(\boldsymbol{x}))$ for every plain input $\boldsymbol{x}$, except with probability at most ε over the sampling of W.*

Note that here $\sum_i p_i$ is the average number of leaking gates in the circuit C'. Thanks to the looser condition $\sum_i p_i \leq \mu$, when applying Chernoff's bound on the intermediate circuit $C' = T(C, k)$ secure against k probes, we can prove random Σ-gate-probing security with $\mu = \Omega(k)$ instead of $\Omega(1/k)$. Since we are interested in a practical implementation of our countermeasure (see Sect. 6), we now provide concrete values for $\mu(k)$ and $\varepsilon(k)$ for the intermediate circuit C' based on the masking countermeasure; we provide the proof in the full version of this paper [CS21].

Lemma 6. *There exists a circuit transformer $T(C, k)$ producing a circuit C' of size $\mathcal{O}(k^2|C|)$, such that T achieves (μ, ε)-random Σ-gate-probing security for $\mu = \Omega(k)$ and ε a negligible function of the security parameter k. In particular, one can take $\mu = k/4$ and $\varepsilon = 2^{-k/(12 \log 2)}$.*

Note that the above circuit C' does not need to be secure in the region probing model with k probes per region; namely in the proof of Lemma 6 only the total number of probes matters. Therefore we can use $n = k + 1$ shares with appropriate mask refreshing as in [BBD+16] (instead of $n = 2k + 1$). Eventually, we obtain a statistically t-private stateless transformer with complexity $\mathcal{O}(|C| \cdot k \cdot t)$, instead of $\mathcal{O}(|C| \cdot k^3 \cdot t)$ in Theorem 5; as previously, we proceed by first proving the worst-case security of $\tilde{C}$ from the average-case security of C'.

Lemma 7. *Suppose that C' is (μ, ε)-random Σ-gate-probing secure. Then, the circuit $\tilde{C}$ constructed as described above with $\ell := t/\mu$ achieves ε-statistical security in the worst case against t probes.*

Proof. The proof is essentially the same as the proof of Lemma 5. Instead of having each gadget $\tilde{G}_i$ simulator $\mathcal{S}_i$ fail with probability $p_i \leq p$, the failure probabilities are still independent but with the looser condition $\sum_i p_i \leq \mu = t/\ell$. This gives a sampling W of the gates G_i in C' with the same condition $\sum_i p_i \leq \mu$. Since C' is (μ, ε)-random Σ-gate-probing secure, we obtain that $\tilde{C}$ achieves ε-statistical security in the worst case against t probes. $\qquad\square$

Theorem 6. *There exists a statistically t-private stateless transformer $(\tilde{T}, \tilde{I}, \tilde{O})$, such that $\tilde{T}(C, k)$ transforms a circuit C into a circuit $\tilde{C}$ of running time $\mathcal{O}(|C| \cdot k \cdot t)$.*

Proof. From Lemma 7, the circuit $\tilde{C}$ achieves worst-case statistical t privacy in the stateless model. Its running time is $\mathcal{O}(|C| \cdot k^2 \cdot \ell)$. With $\ell = t/\mu$ and $\mu = k/4$, the running time is $\mathcal{O}(|C| \cdot k \cdot t)$. $\qquad\square$

Note that with running time $\mathcal{O}(|C| \cdot k \cdot t)$ instead of $\mathcal{O}(|C| \cdot k^{10} \cdot t \cdot (\log k + \log t))$ for ISW (see Theorem 3), our construction has an improved complexity also with respect to the security parameter k. In Sect. 6 we describe an implementation for AES that is practical for large t compared to the masking countermeasure, while the original ISW would be completely unpractical.

3.4 Pure Circuit Description

The construction described in Sect. 3.1 can be implemented using table look-ups and is secure in the software probing model, where the adversary can only probe the input address and input/output value of a RAM cell, but not the content of the internal wires of the circuit implementation of the RAM (see Sect. 1). However it is easy to obtain a pure circuit implementation of the construction, using a circuit implementation of a cyclic shift, with complexity $\mathcal{O}(\ell \cdot \log \ell)$. The construction achieves worst-case statistical privacy with complexity $\mathcal{O}(t \log t)$, as the original ISW construction. We refer to the full version of this paper [CS21] for the description and security proof.

4   Statistical Security in the Stateful Model

In this section we consider the more useful stateful model, in which the adversary can move its probes between successive executions of the circuit. We first recall the ISW construction for worst-case statistical security in the stateful model; we will describe our improved construction in Sect. 5.

A *stateful* circuit is a circuit augmented with memory cells. A memory cell is a stateful gate with fan-in 1: on any invocation the gate outputs its previous input, and stores the current input for the next invocation. We denote by $C[s_0]$ the circuit C with memory cells initialized with the initial state s_0. A stateful circuit can also have external input and output wires. For example, for a block-cipher, the secret key is stored in the memory cells, while the input wires receive the plaintext, and the output wires produce the ciphertext.

4.1   Perfect Privacy for Stateful Circuits

We recall the perfect privacy definition from [ISW03]. In the stateful case, we consider the circuit inputs and outputs as public; only the internal state is kept private. The adversary can now access the transformed circuit and invoke it multiple times, choosing freely the new invocation inputs; the adversary may choose the next input based on what it has observed in the previous execution.

Definition 8 (Perfect privacy for stateful circuits.). *Let T be an efficiently computable randomized algorithm mapping a stateful circuit C along with an initial state s_0 to a stateful circuit C' along with an initial state s'_0. We say that T is a t-private stateful transformer if it satisfies:*

1. **Soundness.** *The input-output functionality of C initialized with s_0 is indistinguishable from that of C' initialized with s'_0. This should hold for any sequence of invocations on an arbitrary sequence of inputs. In other words, $C[s_0]$ and $C'[s'_0]$ are indistinguishable to an interactive distinguisher.*
2. **Privacy.** *We require that C' be private against a t-limited interactive adversary. Specifically, the adversary is given access to C' initialized with s'_0 as its internal state. Then, the adversary may invoke C' multiple times, adaptively choosing the inputs based on the observed outputs. Prior to each invocation, the adversary may fix an arbitrary set of t internal wires to which it will gain access in that invocation. To define privacy against such a t-limited adversary, we require the existence of a simulator which can simulate the adversary's view using only a black-box access to C', i.e., without having access to any internal wires.*

The ISW construction for perfect privacy in the stateful model proceeds as follows; see Fig. 7 for an illustration. We use the stateless transformer $T(C, t)$ secure in the region probing model, with t probes per region. Let denote by $E_t(x)$ the encoding used by the stateless transformer, where x is the input being encoded. The initial state s_0 of C is encoded as $s'_0 = E_t(s_0)$.[3] At the i-th invocation, the circuit $C' = T(C, t)$ takes as input an encoded state s'_i and outputs an encoded state s'_{i+1} that is passed to the next circuit execution. Note

---

[3] Here we can use E_t instead of E_{2t} in [ISW03] because we consider a circuit C' already secure in the region probing model.

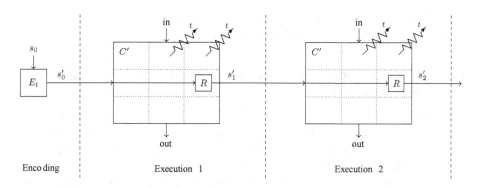

Fig. 7. Illustration of the stateful model. The initial encoding s'_0 used in the first execution gets refreshed into s'_1 before getting passed to the next execution. The adversary can put t probes per region within each execution, where the position of the probes can be changed between executions.

that the encoded state s'_i must be refreshed after each execution; otherwise the adversary could recover the internal state by probing the encoded state t probes at a time; in the circuit C' this is done by using a $(n-1)$-SNI mask refreshing R as output. For a block-cipher, the internal state corresponds to the key whose encoding must be refreshed after each execution. The regular input in of C is unprotected, and need not be encoded before getting fed into C'; for each execution of C', this input is first encoded using E_t and the output out is decoded using the corresponding D_t. This implies that these inputs and outputs are known to the adversary, so that they can be given for free to the simulator.

Perfect privacy in the stateful model follows from perfect privacy in the stateless case, thanks to the region probing model. Namely, a sequence of invocations of the stateful circuit C' can be unwound into a larger stateless circuit C''; in the unwound circuit, the adversary can corrupt up to t wires in each region of each circuit produced by the stateless transformation. This means that every new circuit execution corresponds to adding more regions in the unwound circuit (see Fig. 7). However the adversary can move its probes between circuit executions; therefore in the unwound circuit C'', the probes corresponding to the i-th execution must be simulated without knowing the position of the probes from the $(i+1)$-th execution. To perform these successive simulations we must consider a slightly stronger definition than t-SNI security for mask refreshing between successive executions, where in a given gadget the set of input variables I that must be known for the simulation, does not depend on the set of output variables O to be simulated; we refer to the full version of this paper [CS21] for the definition, and a proof that the AND-based mask refreshing algorithm satisfies this stronger definition.

Theorem 7 (Perfect privacy, region stateful model). *There exists a perfectly t-private stateful circuit transformer secure in the region probing model* *which maps any stateful circuit C of size $|C|$ and depth d to a randomized state-ful circuit of size $\mathcal{O}(|C| \cdot t^2)$ and depth $\mathcal{O}(d \log t)$.*

4.2   Worst-Case Statistical Privacy in the Stateful Model and the ISW Construction

The definition of worst-case statistical privacy in the stateful model is the same as for perfect privacy, except that the simulator can now fail with negligible probability ε; we recall the definition in the full version of this paper [CS21]. We now recall the ISW construction. As for the stateless case, one proceeds in two steps, with each wire in the intermediate circuit C' being expanded into ℓ wires in the final circuit $\tilde{C}$, such that only one of the ℓ wires contains the original signal v_i from C', while the other wires contain only the dummy value \$.

However for the stateful construction we must add some additional counter-measure, because the adversary can move its probes between executions, and therefore could accumulate knowledge about the locations of the signal in $\tilde{C}$. This is easy to see in our stateless construction from Sect. 3.1: since the adversary can probe the index location j of a signal v at the end of an execution, he could directly probe v at the beginning of the next execution; this holds for memory cells that must be transmitted from one execution to the next. In ISW this is prevented by using a perfectly t-private encoding of a random cyclic shift for each pack of ℓ wires, for each signal v_i from C' that must be transmitted from one execution to the other. Such t-private encoding has complexity $\mathcal{O}(t^2)$, and since for every memory cell this cyclic shift requires a circuit of size $\mathcal{O}(\ell \log \ell)$, the additional complexity is $\mathcal{O}(st^2\ell \log \ell)$, which gives a complexity $\tilde{\mathcal{O}}(st^3)$ for s memory cells. We recall below the theorem from [ISW03].

Theorem 8 (Worst-case statistical privacy, stateful model). *There exists a statistically t-private stateful transformer $\tilde{T}$, such that $\tilde{T}(C, k)$ maps a circuit C with s memory cells to a circuit $\tilde{C}$ of size $\mathcal{O}(|C| \cdot t \log t + s \cdot t^3 \log t)$. The depth of $\tilde{C}$ is the same as that of C, up to* polylog *factors.*

5   Our Construction in the Statistical Stateful Model

In this section we describe two constructions in the worst-case statistical state-ful model that achieve a better complexity bound than the ISW construction recalled in the previous section. Recall that in our stateless construction from Sect. 3.1, the position $j \in [0, \ell - 1]$ of the signal v_i among the ℓ wires is explicitly computed; we can therefore assume that it is known to the adversary at the end of a given execution. For the stateful model, this means that without any additional countermeasure, the adversary could directly probe the signal v_i at the beginning of the next execution; this holds for the hidden state that must be transmitted from one execution to the other.

To handle the adaptive case of the stateful model, we extend Definition 6 by requiring that even after having observed t probes in the gadget, any set O of output probes can be simulated from scratch, except with probability at most $2t/\ell$. Note that the construction of Fig. 4 from the stateless case cannot satisfy this definition, since the adversary could directly probe the output position j'' of the signal.

Definition 9 (Strong ℓ-shuffling security). *We say that a randomized gate G achieves strong ℓ-shuffling security if any set S of t probes (excluding the input wires) and any set O of output probes, can be perfectly simulated from scratch, except with probability at most $2t/\ell$, where the set O is chosen adaptively from the value of the probes in S.*

As recalled in the previous section the authors of [ISW03] used a perfectly t-private random cyclic shift; this construction satisfies Definition 9, since from the t-privacy the adversary gets no information about the position of the output signal, and therefore for a total of $2t$ probes the probability to recover the signal is at most $2t/\ell$; the complexity of the ISW construction for a single gadget is $\tilde{O}(\ell t^2)$.

In the following we describe two improved constructions achieving the strong ℓ-shuffling security defined above. We then show that any construction satisfying Definition 9 enables to obtain worst-case statistical security in the stateful model.

5.1   First Construction: Iterated Cyclic Shifts

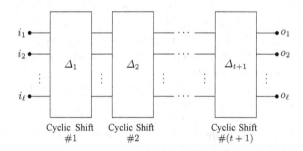

Fig. 8. First construction: sequence of $t + 1$ random cyclic shifts.

Our first construction consists of a sequence of $t + 1$ random cyclic shifts with uniformly and independently distributed shifts $\Delta_1, \ldots, \Delta_{t+1} \leftarrow [0, \ell - 1]$; see Fig. 8 for an illustration. As in [ISW03], the construction is used as output for every hidden state bit that must be transmitted from one execution to the next. As opposed to our stateless construction described in Fig. 4, the index position of the signal is not explicitly computed in the cyclic shifts; the position of the signal is only implicitly determined by the value of the wires in $\{0, 1, \$\}$, where $\$$ is the dummy value. At the end of a given execution, we must therefore convert from a representation with explicit signal index j to a representation with wire values in $\{0, 1, \$\}$; this can be done with complexity $\mathcal{O}(\ell)$. The index position of the signal is computed again explicitly as the beginning of the next execution.

The construction satisfies the strong ℓ-shuffling security (Definition 9), since with at most t internal probes, one of the $t+1$ random cyclic shifts is not probed, and therefore the adversary does not get information about the position of the output signal. We refer to the full version of this paper [CS21] for the proof of the following lemma. The cost of this first construction is $\tilde{O}(\ell t)$, instead of $\tilde{O}(\ell t^2)$ for the ISW construction with the perfectly t-private random cyclic shift.

Lemma 8. *The gadget described above is strong ℓ-shuffling secure.*

5.2   Second Construction: Randomizing Network

Our second construction consists of a network of $\log_2 \ell$ layers, where in the m-th layer for $0 \leq m < \log_2 \ell$ the information in all wires of index i and $i + 2^m$ is swapped with independent probability $1/2$; see Fig. 9 for an illustration; note that for simplicity we assume that ℓ is a power of 2. Letting $j' \in \{0, \ldots, \ell - 1\}$ be the index position of the signal before the randomizing network, at layer m the m-th bit of the signal position is therefore randomly flipped. Since this is done for all layers $0 \leq m < \log_2 \ell$, at the end the output index of the signal is randomly distributed in $\{0, \ldots, \ell - 1\}$.

As in the previous construction, the index position j' is only known as input and not computed explicitly during the swaps: the position of the signal is only implicitly determined by the value of the wires in $\{0, 1, \$\}$; the index position of the signal is computed again explicitly as the beginning of the next execution; see Fig. 10 for an illustration. For a single gadget, our second construction has complexity $\tilde{O}(\ell)$, instead of $\tilde{O}(\ell t)$ in our first construction and $\tilde{O}(\ell \cdot t^2)$ in [ISW03]. Moreover, our second construction has depth polylogarithmic in t, instead of linear in t in our first construction.

Finally, to satisfy the strong ℓ-shuffling security (Definition 9), we must prepend a random cyclic shift; otherwise, since in Definition 9 the input index j is fixed, the adversary could directly probe the j-th wire after the first layer, and learn the signal with probability $1/2$. We provide the proof of Lemma 9 in the full version of this paper [CS21].

Lemma 9. *The gadget described above is strong ℓ-shuffling secure, with circuit complexity $\mathcal{O}(\ell \cdot \log \ell)$.*

5.3   Composition in the Statistical Stateful Model

As in the stateless case, we show that the worst-case statistical privacy of $\tilde{C}$ in the stateful model follows from the p-random gate-probing security of C', based on the ℓ-shuffling security (Definition 6) and strong ℓ-shuffling security (Definition 9) of the gadgets. We provide the proof in the full version of this paper [CS21].

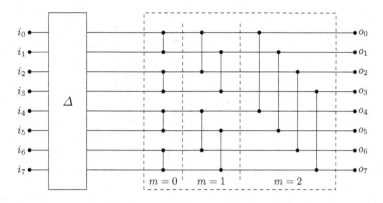

Fig. 9. Second construction: random cyclic shift and randomizing network for $\ell = 8$.

Lemma 10. *Suppose that C' is (p, ε)-random gate probing secure. Then, the circuit $\tilde{C}$ constructed as described above with $\ell := 3t/(2p)$ achieves stateful ε-statistical security in the worst case against t probes per execution.*

Eventually, thanks to the randomizing network construction with complexity $\mathcal{O}(\ell \log \ell)$, the complexity of the final circuit $\tilde{C}$ is $\mathcal{O}(|C| \cdot t \log t)$ instead of $\mathcal{O}(|C|t \log t + s \cdot t^3)$ in [ISW03]. Therefore as opposed to ISW our construction has quasi-linear complexity even for a large number s of memory cells. Moreover the construction applies without the RAM model as well, see the full version of this paper [CS21].

Theorem 9. *There exists a statistically t-private stateful transformer $\widetilde{T}$, such that $\widetilde{T}(C, k)$ maps a circuit C with s memory cells to a circuit $\tilde{C}$ with complexity $\mathcal{O}(|C| \cdot t \cdot \log t)$. The depth of $\tilde{C}$ is the same as that of C, up to* polylog *factors.*

Proof. From Lemma 10, the circuit $\tilde{C}$ achieves statistical privacy in the stateful worst-case model, with circuit complexity $\mathcal{O}(|C| \cdot \ell \log \ell)$. With $\ell = \mathcal{O}(t)$, the circuit complexity is finally $\mathcal{O}(|C| \cdot t \cdot \log t)$. $\qquad\square$

6   Implementation

Security Parameters. We consider the implementation of our stateless construction from Sect. 3.1 under the model from Sect. 3.3, that is worst-case statistical security against a total of t probes in the circuit. Recall that the construction proceeds in two steps. Starting from the original circuit C, we first construct an intermediate circuit C' based on the classical masking countermeasure with perfect security against k probes, where k is the security parameter. From Chernoff bound, the intermediate circuit C' is also secure in the random probing model; more precisely, according to Lemma 6, the circuit C' achieves the (μ, ε)-random

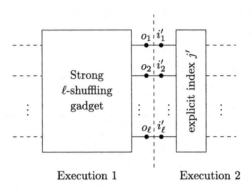

Fig. 10. Thanks to a strong ℓ-shuffling gadget, the adversary does not get information about the index position of the signal at the end of an execution.

Σ-gate-probing security with parameters $\mu(k) = k/4$ and $\varepsilon(k) = 2^{-k/(12\log 2)}$. Here $\mu(k) = k/4$ denotes the number of gates that are probed on average, and $\varepsilon(k) = 2^{-k/(12\log 2)}$ the probability of simulation failure (for the unlucky case when the number of leaking gates in C' is too large). Therefore, to get $\varepsilon = 2^{-80}$ security, we must fix $k = 668$. For the intermediate circuit C' we use $n = k + 1$ shares with appropriate mask refreshing, as in [BBD+16].

In the second step, every wire from the intermediate circuit C' must be expanded into ℓ wires in the final circuit $\tilde{C}$, where according to Lemma 7 we must take $\ell = \lceil t/\mu \rceil = \lceil 4t/k \rceil$ to get security against t probes. This implies that we get security against $t = k \cdot \ell/4$ probes as a function of ℓ. For $\varepsilon = 2^{-80}$ and $k = 668$, this gives security against $t = 167 \cdot \ell$ probes as a function of the parameter ℓ.[4] Since the running time of our construction is $\mathcal{O}(\ell)$, the running time is $\mathcal{O}(t)$ for security against t probes, instead of $\mathcal{O}(t^2)$ for the masking countermeasure.

Number of Operations. We compare the concrete number of operations between the masking countermeasure and our construction. For simplicity we consider a single AND gadget. From the gadget description in the full version of this paper [CS21], the AND gadget in the intermediate circuit C' performs a total of $n \cdot (7n - 5)/2$ operations, with $n = t + 1$ shares for perfect security against t probes. This includes $n \cdot (n-1)/2$ random generations, and $n \cdot (3n - 2)$ boolean operations. This gives $N_m = (t + 1) \cdot (7t + 2)/2 \simeq 7t^2/2$ operations as a function of the maximum number of probes t.

We now consider the circuit $\tilde{C}$ corresponding to the expansion of the AND gadget in C'. Every random generation in the intermediate circuit C' requires $\ell + 1$ operations in $\tilde{C}$. From Algorithm 1, every boolean operation in C' requires

---

[4] We see that it would not make sense to use $\ell \leq 4$, since the intermediate circuit C' already provides perfect security against $k = 668$ probes.

$5\ell + 3$ operations in $\tilde{C}$. The total number of operations is therefore:

$$N_s = n \cdot (n-1)/2 \cdot (\ell+1) + n \cdot (3n-2) \cdot (5\ell+3) \simeq \frac{31}{2} \cdot n^2 \cdot \ell$$

With $n = k+1$ and $\ell = 4t/k$, we get $N_s \simeq 62 \cdot k \cdot t$. Finally, with $k = 668$, the number of operations is therefore $N_s \simeq 41\,416 \cdot t$ for worst-case security against t probes. We refer to Table 2 for a summary of the operation count.

Since the masking countermeasure has complexity $7t^2/2$ and our shuffling countermeasure has complexity $41\,416 \cdot t$, the two countermeasures have equal complexity for $7t^2/2 = 41\,416 \cdot t$, which gives $t \simeq 12 \cdot 10^3$. Therefore we expect our shuffling countermeasure to beat the masking countermeasure for a number of probes $t \geq 12 \cdot 10^3$.

Table 2. Number of operations for worst-case security against t probes, where $n = t+1$ for the masking countermeasure, and $n = k+1$ and $\ell = 4t/k$ for the shuffling countermeasure, with $k = 668$; we only keep the high-order terms.

	Masking countermeasure	Shuffling countermeasure
#rand	$n^2/2$	$\frac{1}{2} \cdot n^2 \cdot \ell$
#bool	$3n^2$	$15n^2 \cdot \ell$
#op	$7n^2/2$	$\frac{31}{2} \cdot n^2 \cdot \ell$
#op	$\mathbf{7t^2/2}$	$\mathbf{41\,416 \cdot t}$

AES Implementation. We have performed an AES implementation of our shuffling countermeasure, which we compare with an AES implementation of the masking countermeasure, using the same parameters as above. We summarize the timings in Table 3; see also Fig. 11. We see that our shuffling construction outperforms the masking countermeasure for a number of probes $t \geq 6\,000$, with a running time of approximately 2 min for $t \simeq 6\,000$. We provide the source code in [Cor21].

Table 3. Running time of AES implementation, as a function of the number of probes t. We use $n = t+1$ for the masking countermeasure, and $\ell = 4t/k$ for the shuffling countermeasure. Implementation on a 3,2 GHz Intel processor, running on a single core.

t	668	2004	3340	4676	6012	7348	8684	10020
Masking (s)	1.4	12	34	70	111	187	235	310
Shuffling (s)	52	63	78	91	102	119	134	141

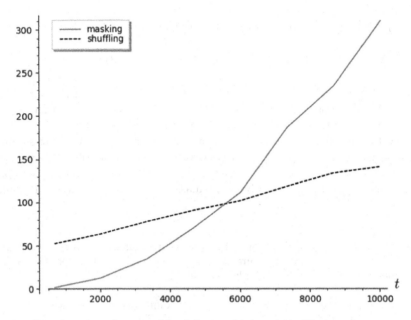

Fig. 11. Running time (in seconds) of the masking and shuffling countermeasure for AES, to get security against t probes. Implementation on a 3,2 GHz Intel processor, running on a single core.

7   Conclusion

We have described the first improvement of the wire shuffling countermeasure against side-channel attacks described by Ishai, Sahai and Wagner at Crypto 2003, with running time $\mathcal{O}(t)$ instead of $\mathcal{O}(t \log t)$ for worst-case security against t probes, and $\mathcal{O}(t^2)$ for the classical masking countermeasure. Our construction is somehow practical in that for an AES implementation we can beat the classical masking countermeasure for a reasonable running time. However the crossover point occurs for $t \simeq 6\,000$, so our countermeasure is probably unpractical for embedded implementations.

Acknowledgements. We thank the reviewers for insightful comments. The two authors were supported by the ERC Advanced Grant no. 787390.

References

ADF16. Andrychowicz, M., Dziembowski, S., Faust, S.: Circuit compilers with $O(1/\log(n))$ leakage rate. In: Fischlin, M., Coron, J.-S. (eds.) EUROCRYPT 2016. LNCS, vol. 9666, pp. 586–615. Springer, Heidelberg (2016). https://doi.org/10.1007/978-3-662-49896-5_21

AKS83. Ajtai, M., Komlós, J., Szemerédi, E.: An $O(n \log n)$ sorting network. In: Proceedings of the 15th Annual ACM Symposium on Theory of Computing, Boston, Massachusetts, USA, 25–27 April 1983 pp. 1–9 (1983)

BBD+16. Barthe, G.: Strong non-interference and type-directed higher-order masking. In: Proceedings of the 2016 ACM SIGSAC Conference on Computer and Communications Security, Vienna, Austria, 24–28 October 2016, pp. 116–129 (2016)

BDD+04. Biedl, T., Demaine, E.D., Duncanc, C.A., Fleischerd, R., Kobourove, S.G.: Tight bounds on maximal and maximum matchings. Discrete Math. **285**, 7–15 (2004)

CCD00. Clavier, C., Coron, J.-S., Dabbous, N.: Differential power analysis in the presence of hardware countermeasures. In: Koç, Ç.K., Paar, C. (eds.) CHES 2000. LNCS, vol. 1965, pp. 252–263. Springer, Heidelberg (2000). https://doi.org/10.1007/3-540-44499-8_20

CGP+12. Carlet, C., Goubin, L., Prouff, E., Quisquater, M., Rivain, M.: Higher-order masking schemes for s-boxes. In: FSE, pp. 366–384 (2012)

Cor14. Coron, J.-S.: Higher order masking of look-up tables. In: Nguyen, P.Q., Oswald, E. (eds.) EUROCRYPT 2014. LNCS, vol. 8441, pp. 441–458. Springer, Heidelberg (2014). https://doi.org/10.1007/978-3-642-55220-5_25

Cor21. Coron, J.-S.: Implementation of higher-order countermeasures 2021. https://github.com/coron/htable/

CS21. Coron, J.-S., Spignoli, L.: Secure wire shuffling in the probing model. Full version of this paper. Cryptology ePrint Archive, Report 2021/258 (2021). https://eprint.iacr.org/2021/258

FPS17. Faust, S., Paglialonga, C., Schneider, T.: Amortizing randomness complexity in private circuits. In: Takagi, T., Peyrin, T. (eds.) ASIACRYPT 2017. LNCS, vol. 10624, pp. 781–810. Springer, Cham (2017). https://doi.org/10.1007/978-3-319-70694-8_27

GJRS18. Goudarzi, D., Journault, A., Rivain, M., Standaert, F.-X.: Secure multiplication for bitslice higher-order masking: optimisation and comparison. In: Fan, J., Gierlichs, B. (eds.) COSADE 2018. LNCS, vol. 10815, pp. 3–22. Springer, Cham (2018). https://doi.org/10.1007/978-3-319-89641-0_1

HOM06. Herbst, C., Oswald, E., Mangard, S.: An AES smart card implementation resistant to power analysis attacks. In: Zhou, J., Yung, M., Bao, F. (eds.) ACNS 2006. LNCS, vol. 3989, pp. 239–252. Springer, Heidelberg (2006). https://doi.org/10.1007/11767480_16

ISW03. Ishai, Y., Sahai, A., Wagner, D.: Private circuits: securing hardware against probing attacks. In: Boneh, D. (ed.) CRYPTO 2003. LNCS, vol. 2729, pp. 463–481. Springer, Heidelberg (2003). https://doi.org/10.1007/978-3-540-45146-4_27

JS17. Journault, A., Standaert, F.-X.: Very high order masking: efficient implementation and security evaluation. In: Fischer, W., Homma, N. (eds.) CHES 2017. LNCS, vol. 10529, pp. 623–643. Springer, Cham (2017). https://doi.org/10.1007/978-3-319-66787-4_30

MS08. Mehlhorn, K., Sanders, P.: Algorithms and Data Structures: The Basic Toolbox. Springer (2008). https://doi.org/10.1007/978-3-540-77978-0

Pap18. Papagiannopoulos, K.: Low randomness masking and shuffling: an evaluation using mutual information. IACR Trans. Cryptogr. Hardw. Embed. Syst. **2018**(3), 524–546 (2018)

RP10. Rivain, M., Prouff, E.: Provably secure higher-order masking of AES. In: Mangard, S., Standaert, F.-X. (eds.) CHES 2010. LNCS, vol. 6225, pp. 413–427. Springer, Heidelberg (2010). https://doi.org/10.1007/978-3-642-15031-9_28

RPD09. Rivain, M., Prouff, E., Doget, J.: Higher-order masking and shuffling for software implementations of block ciphers. In: Clavier, C., Gaj, K. (eds.) CHES 2009. LNCS, vol. 5747, pp. 171–188. Springer, Heidelberg (2009). https://doi.org/10.1007/978-3-642-04138-9_13

THM07. Tillich, S., Herbst, C., Mangard, S.: Protecting AES software implementations on 32-bit processors against power analysis. In: Katz, J., Yung, M. (eds.) ACNS 2007. LNCS, vol. 4521, pp. 141–157. Springer, Heidelberg (2007). https://doi.org/10.1007/978-3-540-72738-5_10

VMKS12. Veyrat-Charvillon, N., Medwed, M., Kerckhof, S., Standaert, F.-X.: Shuffling against side-channel attacks: a comprehensive study with cautionary note. In: Wang, X., Sako, K. (eds.) ASIACRYPT 2012. LNCS, vol. 7658, pp. 740–757. Springer, Heidelberg (2012). https://doi.org/10.1007/978-3-642-34961-4_44

VML16. Veshchikov, N., Medeiros, S.F., Lerman, L.: Variety of scalable shuffling countermeasures against side channel attacks. J. Cyber Secur. Mobil. 5(3), 195–232 (2016)

Cryptanalysis

Differential-Linear Cryptanalysis from an Algebraic Perspective

Meicheng Liu[1,2]($\boxtimes$), Xiaojuan Lu[1,2], and Dongdai Lin[1,2]

[1] State Key Laboratory of Information Security, Institute of Information Engineering, Chinese Academy of Sciences, Beijing, People's Republic of China
liumeicheng@iie.ac.cn
[2] School of Cyber Security, University of Chinese Academy of Sciences, Beijing, People's Republic of China

Abstract. The differential-linear cryptanalysis is an important cryptanalytic tool in cryptography, and has been extensively researched since its discovery by Langford and Hellman in 1994. There are nevertheless very few methods to study the middle part where the differential and linear trail connect. In this paper, we study differential-linear cryptanalysis from an algebraic perspective. We first introduce a technique called Differential Algebraic Transitional Form (DATF) for differential-linear cryptanalysis, then develop a new theory of estimation of the differential-linear bias and techniques for key recovery in differential-linear cryptanalysis.

The techniques are applied to the CAESAR and LWC finalist Ascon, the AES finalist Serpent, and the eSTREAM finalist Grain v1. The bias of the differential-linear approximation is estimated for Ascon and Serpent. The theoretical estimates of the bias are more accurate than that obtained by the Differential-Linear Connectivity Table (Bar-On *et al.*, EUROCRYPT 2019), and the techniques can be applied with more rounds. Our general techniques can also be used to estimate the bias of Grain v1 in differential cryptanalysis, and have a markedly better performance than the Differential Engine tool tailor-made for the cipher. The improved key recovery attacks on round-reduced variants of these ciphers are then proposed. To the best of our knowledge, they are thus far the best known cryptanalysis of Serpent, as well as the best differential-linear cryptanalysis of Ascon and the best initialization analysis of Grain v1. The results have been fully verified by experiments. Notably, security analysis of Serpent is one of the most important applications of differential-linear cryptanalysis in the last two decades. The results in this paper update the differential-linear cryptanalysis of Serpent-128 and Serpent-256 with one more round after the work of Biham, Dunkelman and Keller in 2003.

Keyword: Cryptanalysis, Differential-linear, Truncated differential, Authenticated cipher, Block cipher, Stream cipher

This work was supported by the National Natural Science Foundation of China (Grant No. 61672516 and 61872359), the National Key R&D Program of China (Grant No. 2020YFB1805402), and the Youth Innovation Promotion Association of Chinese Academy of Sciences.

T. Malkin and C. Peikert (Eds.): CRYPTO 2021, LNCS 12827, pp. 247–277, 2021.
https://doi.org/10.1007/978-3-030-84252-9_9

1   Introduction

Differential cryptanalysis and linear cryptanalysis are the two best-known techniques for cryptanalysis of block ciphers. Differential-linear attack [LH94, BDK02] is a chosen plaintext two-stage technique of cryptanalysis in which the first stage is covered by differential cryptanalysis, which ensures propagation of useful properties midway through the block cipher. The second stage is then performed from the middle of the cipher to the ciphertext using linear cryptanalysis. The technique was discovered by Langford and Hellman [LH94] and demonstrated on the example of 8-round DES.

Theoretically, the differential-linear attack can be considered as a truncated differential or a multidimensional linear attack, but is an extreme case for both types, which is usually measured by the differential-linear bias. Recently, in 2017, Blondeau, Leander and Nyberg [BLN17] gave an exact expression of the bias under an assumption that the two parts of the cipher are independent, and revisited the previous treatments of differential-linear bias by Biham *et al.* in 2002–2003 [BDK02,BDK03], Liu *et al.* in 2009 [LGZL09], and Lu in 2012 [Lu12], and formulated assumptions under which a single differential-linear characteristic gives a close estimate of the bias.

More recently, at EUROCRYPT 2019, Bar-On *et al.* [BDKW19] showed that in many cases, dependency between two parts of the cipher significantly affects the complexity of the differential-linear attack, and might be exploited to make the attack more efficient. The authors of [BDKW19] presented the Differential-Linear Connectivity Table (DLCT) which allows to take into account the dependency between the two subciphers, and to choose the differential characteristic and the linear approximation in a way that takes advantage of this dependency. They then showed that the DLCT can be constructed efficiently using the Fast Fourier Transform, and demonstrated the strength of the DLCT by using it to improve differential-linear attacks on ICEPOLE and on 8-round DES, and to explain published experimental results on Serpent and on the CAESAR finalist Ascon which did not comply with the standard differential-linear framework.

In this paper, we study differential-linear cryptanalysis from an algebraic point of view. In theory, the bias of a differential-linear approximation can be determined by the algebraic normal forms of the output bits, with input bits as variables. Nevertheless, this is computationally infeasible for a cipher. In Sect. 3, we introduce an algebraic and feasible technique called Differential Algebraic Transitional Form (DATF) for differential-linear cryptanalysis, and then develop a new theory of estimation of the differential-linear bias and techniques for key recovery in differential-linear cryptanalysis. The algebraic transitional form (ATF) is similar to the algebraic normal form (ANF), but an algebraic expression in the ANF can be replaced by a transitional variable in the ATF. This ensures the feasibility of calculating the ATF by iteration. With the DATF technique, the ATF of the difference of output bits can be computed round by round, rather than from the derivative of the output function with respect to the input difference. Based on the DATF algorithm, we describe two feasible frameworks for estimating the differential-linear bias. One is efficient and has a moderate accuracy. The other is less efficient, but more accurate. Further we exploit an algorithm for key recovery. Unlike the convention, it is an organic combination of distinguisher searching and key guessing, and thus has an advantage over the existing techniques. We stress that our techniques are purely algebraic and quite different from the previous methods, including the DLCT [BDKW19] and its subsequent work [CKW19, CKL+19] as well as the techniques proposed for ARX ciphers [Leu16, BLT20].

As illustrations, we apply our theory and techniques to three different types of ciphers, the authenticated cipher Ascon [DEMS16], the block cipher Serpent [ABK98], and the stream cipher Grain v1 [HJMM08], respectively in Sect. 4, Sect. 5 and Sect. 6.

Ascon is a family of authenticated encryption and hashing algorithms designed by Dobraunig *et al.* [DEMS16, DEMS19] that has been selected as the primary choice for lightweight authenticated encryption in the final portfolio of the CAESAR competition and is currently competing in the NIST Lightweight Cryptography competition. In [DEMS15], Dobraunig *et al.* presented practical differential-linear attacks on up to 5 rounds of Ascon, including a 4-round differential-linear distinguisher. The authors of [DEMS15] stated that while the overall bias of the approximation is expected to be 2^{-20} by the theory of the classical differential-linear framework, experiments show that the bias is 2^{-2} which is significantly higher. Bar-On *et al.* [BDKW19] recomputed the bias of the distinguisher using the DLCT and obtained a theoretical bias of 2^{-5}.

The theory in this paper shows that the bias of this differential-linear approximation is estimated to be $2^{-2.365}$. This value is extremely close to the experimentally obtained bias of 2^{-2}, and much higher than the theoretical bias of 2^{-5} obtained in [BDKW19] using the DLCT. We also show a 5-round differential-linear approximation with a theoretical bias of $2^{-5.415}$ by imposing 9 conditions. Our experiments show that the bias is $2^{-4.54}$, when these conditions are satisfied.

We further propose in Sect. 4 a key recovery attack on 5-round Ascon-128, which is also applicable to Ascon-128a. The attack benefits from the above differential-linear approximation with an experimental bias of $2^{-5.5}$ using less conditions. The data complexity of the attack is on average 2^{26}, and the expected time complexity is about 2^{26}. This attack improves the existing differential-linear attack on 5-round Ascon-128 with complexity 2^{36} [DEMS15].

Serpent is a 128-bit block cipher designed by Anderson, Biham and Knudsen. It is a finalist in the Advanced Encryption Standard (AES) competition. In the past 20 years, there have been tremendous efforts devoted to cryptanalysis of Serpent, *e.g.*, [BDK03, DIK08, Lu12, Lu15, BLN17, BDKW19]. In 2003, Biham, Dunkelman and Keller [BDK03] presented the first differential-linear attack on 11-round Serpent, using a 9-round differential-linear distinguisher with bias of 2^{-60}. An improved attack was presented by Dunkelman *et al.* in [DIK08]. The authors of [DIK08] performed experiments with 4 rounds of Serpent, obtained the bias $2^{-13.75}$ for the 4-round approximation rather than 2^{-15}, and concluded that the actual bias of the 9-round approximation is $2^{-57.75}$ and not 2^{-60}. In

[BDKW19], Bar-On *et al.* recomputed the bias of the 4-round differential-linear distinguisher using the DLCT and obtained the value $2^{-13.68}$.

In Sect. 5, we revisit the analysis of the bias of this distinguisher by our theory, and show an estimate of $2^{-13.736}$. This value is closer to the experimental value even than that of [BDKW19]. We conjecture that the gap between the experimental value and our estimate is a statistical error. We further apply the DATF with one more round, and obtain the bias $2^{-17.736}$ for the 5-round distinguisher.

For an 11-round variant of Serpent from round 4 to round 14, we propose in Sect. 5 a key recovery attack with improved time complexities. The data complexity of the attack is $2^{125.7}$ chosen ciphertexts, the time complexity is $2^{125.7}$ memory accesses, and the memory complexity is 2^{99} bytes. The success probability of the attack is expected to be more than 99%. As far as we know, this is the first differential-linear attack on 11-round Serpent-128, through nearly 20 years of community efforts since the publication of its first 10-round attack of the same kind in 2003 [BDK03].

As mentioned in [BDKW19], the differential-linear technique yields the best known attacks on the AES finalist Serpent [DIK08, Lu15]. In Sect. 5.3, we nevertheless find that there is a same flaw in the attacks on 12-round Serpent-256 in [DIK08, Lu15] which leads to underestimated time complexity, up to a factor of 2^{16} or 2^{20} by our analysis, and the existing 12-round attacks are thus worse than a brute-force attack.

In Sect. 5.3, we extend the chosen ciphertext attack on 11-round Serpent to 12 rounds (starting from round 4 and ending at round 15). The attack on 12-round Serpent-256 has the data complexity of 2^{127} chosen ciphertexts, time complexity of 2^{251} memory accesses, and memory complexity of 2^{99} bytes. The success probability of the attack is expected to be more than 77%. To the best of our knowledge, this is the first correct attack on 12-round Serpent as well as the best known cryptanalysis on Serpent, almost 20 years after Biham, Dunkelman and Keller presented the first 11-round attack of different kind in 2001 [BDK01] and the first 11-round attack of the same kind in 2003 [BDK03].

The stream cipher Grain v1, proposed by Hell *et al.* [HJMM08], is an eSTREAM finalist in the hardware profile. At ASIACRYPT 2010, Knellwolf *et al.* [KMN10] proposed conditional differential attacks on NFSR-based cryptosystems, and applied the attack to Grain v1 with 104 rounds. Since the seminal work of [KMN10], there are a lot of efforts working towards the conditional differential attacks on Grain v1, *e.g.*, [Ban14, Ban16, MTQ17, LG19]. In the literature, the largest number of initialization rounds of Grain v1 that can be attacked is 120, proposed by Li and Guan [LG19] using a conditional differential approximation with an experimental bias $2^{-12.8}$.

In Sect. 6, we apply our theory and techniques to conditional differential attacks on the initialization of Grain v1, and finding an optimized key recovery attack on round-reduced Grain v1. Using the DATF, we revisit the analysis of the bias of the 120-round differential approximation of [LG19], and obtain an estimate of $2^{-13.39}$. This is very close to the experimental value $2^{-12.8}$, and much higher than the estimate of $2^{-18.13}$ obtained by the method called Differential Engine proposed by Banik [Ban14]. Further, a new differential with a theoretical bias $2^{-20.77}$ in the output difference of 125 rounds is found for Grain v1, by an exhaustive search over all the input differences up to 4 bits using the DATF. We have verified by experiments that the bias is $2^{-17.4}$. Our estimate of the bias is smaller than the experimental value, but much higher than the estimate $2^{-24.78}$ by the Differential Engine tool. By imposing 13 equations on the key bits and initial value, where 18 expressions of the key bits need to be guessed, we can mount a chosen IV attack to recover 20 key-bit information on 125-round Grain v1, with time complexity of about 2^{57}, data complexity of 2^{52} and negligible memory. The success probability of the attack is expected to be more than 92.5%. To the best of our knowledge, this is thus far the best key recovery attack in practical complexity as well as the best initialization analysis of Grain v1, in the single key setting.

Table 1. The differential-linear and differential bias

Cipher	Type	Rounds	Experimental value	Theoretical estimate		
				[BDK03]	DLCT [BDKW19]	DATF
Ascon	DL	4/12	2^{-2} [DEMS15]	2^{-20}	2^{-5}	$2^{-2.365}$
	CDL	5/12	$2^{-4.54}$ (Sect. 4)	-	-	$2^{-5.415}$
Serpent	DL	4/32	$2^{-13.75}$ [DIK08]	2^{-15}	$2^{-13.68}$	$2^{-13.736}$
	DL	5/32	$2^{-17.75}$ [DIK08]	2^{-19}	-	$2^{-17.736}$
				Differential Engine [Ban14]		DATF
Grain v1	CD	120/160	$2^{-12.8}$ [LG19]	$2^{-18.13}$		$2^{-13.39}$
	CD	125/160	$2^{-17.4}$ (Sect. 6)	$2^{-24.78}$		$2^{-20.77}$

The results on the differential-linear bias of Ascon and Serpent and the differential bias of Grain v1 are summarized in Table 1, with the comparisons of the previous results, where CDL means conditional differential-linear (DL) and CD means conditional differential. Compared with the DLCT tool, the DATF techniques can be applied with more rounds for Ascon and Serpent, and provide more accurate estimation of the DL bias. Besides, our techniques can also be applied to differential cryptanalysis. Compared with the Differential Engine method tailor-made for Grain-like ciphers, our techniques are more general and have a much better performance. Compared with the experimental approach, the algebraic techniques are more formalized and intelligent for conditional attacks and, in particular, much faster when the bias is low. This helps us find better conditional approximations for Ascon and Grain v1.

Our cryptanalytic results of Ascon, Serpent and Grain v1 are summarized in Table 2, with comparisons of the previous attacks. For Ascon, our attack outperforms the previous differential-linear one but not the cube-like attack [LDW17]. For Serpent, to the best of our knowledge, we provide the first correct attack on its 12-round variant, and the first differential-linear attack on its 11-round variant with 128-bit key. The best known theoretical attack on Grain v1

Table 2. Key recovery attacks on `Ascon`, `Serpent`, and `Grain v1`

Cipher	Key size	Type	Rounds	Time	Data	Space	Source
`Ascon`	128	diff.-linear	5/12	2^{36}	2^{36} bits	neg.	[DEMS15]
		diff.-linear	5/12	2^{26}	2^{26} bits	neg.	Section 4.2
		cube-like	7/12	$2^{103.9}$	$2^{77.2}$ words	-	[LDW17]
`Serpent`	192/256	diff.-linear	11/32	$2^{139.2}$ En	$2^{125.3}$ CP	2^{60} B	[BDK03]
	192/256	diff.-linear	11/32	$2^{135.7}$ En	$2^{121.8}$ CP	2^{76} B	[DIK08]
	192/256	diff.-linear	11/32	$2^{137.7}$ MA	$2^{113.7}$ CC	2^{99} B	[DIK08]
	all	diff.-linear	11/32	$2^{125.7}$ MA	$2^{125.7}$ CC	2^{99} B	Section 5.3
	256	diff.-linear	12/32	2^{251} MA	2^{127} CC	2^{99} B	Section 5.3
`Grain v1`	80	differential	104/160	2^{79}	2^{35}	neg.	[KMN10]
		differential	120/160	2^{68}	-	neg.	[LG19]
		differential	125/160	2^{60}	2^{52}	neg.	Section 6.2
		fast corr.	full	$2^{76.7}$	$2^{75.1}$	2^{69}	[TIM+18]

is the fast correlation attack on its full version proposed in [TIM+18], with time complexity of $2^{76.7}$, data complexity of $2^{75.1}$ and memory[1] of about 2^{69}. This attack targets at state recovery in the keystream generator, while our attack targets at key recovery in the initialization. Moreover, our attack on `Grain v1` has practical complexities and has been fully verified by experiments on the real cipher, compared with the impractical complexities of the fast correlation attack which was verified on a toy cipher in [TIM+18].

2   Differential-Linear Cryptanalysis

Differential-linear cryptanalysis consists of two stages. The first stage ensures propagation of useful properties in the middle of the cipher, which is covered by

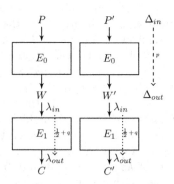

Fig. 1. Differential-linear cryptanalysis

---

[1] The space complexity of the attack was not provided in [TIM+18] and is assessed by our analysis.

differential cryptanalysis. The second stage is performed from the middle of the cipher to the ciphertext using linear cryptanalysis.

Let E be a cipher which can be described as a cascade of two subciphers E_0 and E_1, *i.e.*, $E = E_1 \circ E_0$. Let Δ_{in} and Δ_{out} be respectively the input and output differences of the differential characteristic for E_0, and λ_{in} and λ_{out} respectively the input and output masks of the linear characteristic for E_1, as shown in Fig. 1.

Assume that the differential $\Delta_{in} \rightarrow \Delta_{out}$ is satisfied with probability p, and the linear approximation $\lambda_{in} \rightarrow \lambda_{out}$ with probability $1/2 + q$ (or with bias q). In case the differential is not satisfied (probability $1 - p$) we assume a random behavior of the parities of the output subset. The probability that a pair with input difference Δ_{in} will satisfy $\lambda_{out} \cdot C = \lambda_{out} \cdot C'$ is in that case $p(1/2 + 2q^2) + (1 - p) \cdot 1/2 = 1/2 + 2pq^2$. The data complexity of the differential-linear attack/distinguisher is $O(p^{-2}q^{-4})$.

3 Algebraic Perspective of Differential-Linear Cryptanalysis

In this section, from an algebraic perspective, we discuss the estimation of the differential-linear bias as well as techniques for key recovery in differential-linear cryptanalysis, starting from some basic concepts and facts.

3.1 Basic Concepts and Facts

Let $\mathbb{F}_2$ denote the binary field and $\mathbb{F}_2^n$ the n-dimensional vector space over $\mathbb{F}_2$. An n-variable Boolean polynomial is a mapping from $\mathbb{F}_2^n$ into $\mathbb{F}_2$, which can be uniquely represented as a multivariate polynomial over $\mathbb{F}_2$,

$$f(x_1, x_2, \cdots, x_n) = \bigoplus_{c=(c_1,\cdots,c_n)\in\mathbb{F}_2^n} a_c \prod_{i=1}^{n} x_i^{c_i}, \ a_c \in \mathbb{F}_2,$$

called the algebraic normal form (ANF).

A variable is called *isolated* if it appears and only appears in the linear part of the ANF of f. For example, x_1 is an isolated variable in $x_1 \oplus x_2x_3 \oplus x_4x_5$.

For a variable x_i, the Boolean polynomial $f(x_1, x_2, \cdots, x_n)$ can uniquely be represented as $f = f''x_i \oplus f'$ with f' and f'' independent of x_i, which implies $f' = f|_{x_i=0}$ and $f'' = f|_{x_i=1} \oplus f|_{x_i=0}$. The partial derivative of f with respect to the variable x_i is the polynomial f'', denoted by $D_{x_i}f$. For example, $D_{x_2}(x_1 \oplus x_2x_3 \oplus x_4x_5) = x_3$.

For $\Delta \in \mathbb{F}_2^n$ and an n-variable Boolean polynomial f on X, the derivative of f with respect to Δ is the polynomial

$$D_\Delta f(X) = f(X) \oplus f(X \oplus \Delta),$$

and the polynomial f_Δ is defined as

$$f_\Delta(X, x) = f(X \oplus x\Delta),$$

where x is a binary variable that we introduce. Note that f_Δ is a Boolean polynomial on $n + 1$ variables. From the above definitions, it is clear that

$$D_x f_\Delta = D_\Delta f.$$

Example 1. Let $f(x_1, x_2, x_3) = x_1 \oplus x_2 x_3 \oplus x_3$ and $\Delta = (1, 1, 0)$. On one hand, the derivative of f with respect to Δ is

$$\begin{aligned} D_\Delta f &= f(X) \oplus f(X \oplus \Delta) = f(x_1, x_2, x_3) \oplus f(x_1 \oplus 1, x_2 \oplus 1, x_3) \\ &= (x_1 \oplus x_2 x_3 \oplus x_3) \oplus ((x_1 \oplus 1) \oplus (x_2 \oplus 1)x_3 \oplus x_3) = x_3 \oplus 1. \end{aligned}$$

On the other hand, by the definition of f_Δ we have

$$f_\Delta = f(x_1 \oplus x, x_2 \oplus x, x_3) = (x_1 \oplus x) \oplus (x_2 \oplus x)x_3 \oplus x_3 = (x_3 \oplus 1)x \oplus x_1 \oplus x_2 x_3 \oplus x_3$$

and the partial derivative of f_Δ with respect to x is $D_x f_\Delta = x_3 \oplus 1 = D_\Delta f$.

Given a Boolean polynomial f on $X = (x_1, x_2, \cdots, x_n)$, if the polynomial f can be represented as a polynomial g on $(y_1, y_2, \cdots, y_m)$, where each y_i can be seen as a polynomial on X, to say, $y_i = \phi_i(X)$, then the ANF of g is called in this paper an *algebraic transitional form* (ATF) of f. The variables $y_1, y_2, \cdots, y_m$ are called *transitional variables*. Note that the ATF of a Boolean polynomial is not unique. Actually, the polynomial f is a composition of g and $\Phi = (\phi_1, \phi_2, \cdots, \phi_m)$, that is, $f(X) = g(\Phi(X))$, denoted by $f = g \circ \Phi$.

Each polynomial ϕ_i can also be represented in terms of the ATF. From this point of view, an iterated cipher can be iteratively represented by the ATF in practical time if it is feasible to compute the ANF of its round function. It can be extended to iteratively computed the ATF of the difference of a cipher. To this end, we further introduce the following notations and basic facts.

For an input difference $\Delta \in \mathbb{F}_2^n$, $\phi_i(X \oplus x\Delta) = \phi_i \oplus (D_\Delta \phi_i)x$. By introducing transitional variables α_i's and β_i's, we represent $\phi_i(X \oplus x\Delta)$ as $\alpha_i \oplus x\beta_i$. Denote $\alpha = (\alpha_1, \alpha_2, \cdots, \alpha_m)$ and $\beta = (\beta_1, \beta_2, \cdots, \beta_m)$. Then the polynomial $f_\Delta = f(X \oplus x\Delta)$ can be represented as

$$g(\alpha \oplus x\beta) = g(\alpha_1 \oplus x\beta_1, \alpha_2 \oplus x\beta_2, \cdots, \alpha_m \oplus x\beta_m),$$

which is called a *differential algebraic transitional form* (DATF) of f with respect to Δ. More exactly, we have

$$f_\Delta = f(X \oplus x\Delta) = g(\Phi(X \oplus x\Delta)) = g(\Phi \oplus (D_\Delta \Phi)x) = g(\alpha \oplus x\beta) \circ \Psi,$$

where $\Psi = (\Phi, D_\Delta \Phi)$. Since Ψ is independent of x, we obtain

$$D_\Delta f = D_x f_\Delta = D_x(g(\alpha \oplus x\beta) \circ \Psi) = (D_x g(\alpha \oplus x\beta)) \circ \Psi.$$

Proposition 1. *If an n-variable Boolean polynomial f is a composition of an m-variable Boolean polynomial g and a function Φ from $\mathbb{F}_2^n$ into $\mathbb{F}_2^m$, i.e., $f = g \circ \Phi$, then the derivative of f with respect to Δ is a composition of the partial derivative of the DATF $g(\alpha \oplus x\beta)$ with respect to x and the function $\Psi = (\Phi, D_\Delta \Phi)$, i.e., $D_\Delta f = (D_x g(\alpha \oplus x\beta)) \circ \Psi$, where α and β are m-variable vectors and x is a binary variable.*

Example 2. Let $\Delta = (1, 1, 0, 0, 0)$ and $f = g \circ \Phi$ with $g(y_1, y_2, y_3) = y_1 \oplus y_2 y_3 \oplus y_3$, $\Phi(x_1, x_2, x_3, x_4, x_5) = (x_1 \oplus x_2 x_3 \oplus x_3, x_2 \oplus x_3 x_4 \oplus x_4, x_3 \oplus x_4 x_5 \oplus x_5)$. The ANF of f is $f(X) = x_1 \oplus x_2 x_4 x_5 \oplus x_2 x_5 \oplus x_4 x_5 \oplus x_5$.

On one hand, the derivative of f with respect to Δ is

$$D_\Delta f = f(X) \oplus f(X \oplus \Delta) = x_4 x_5 \oplus x_5 \oplus 1.$$

On the other hand, we have

$$
\begin{aligned}
D_x g(\alpha \oplus x\beta) &= D_x g(\alpha_1 \oplus x\beta_1, \alpha_2 \oplus x\beta_2, \alpha_3 \oplus x\beta_3) \\
&= D_x((\alpha_1 \oplus x\beta_1) \oplus (\alpha_2 \oplus x\beta_2)(\alpha_3 \oplus x\beta_3) \oplus (\alpha_3 \oplus x\beta_3)) \\
&= D_x((\beta_1 \oplus \beta_2(\alpha_3 \oplus \beta_3) \oplus \alpha_2\beta_3 \oplus \beta_3)x \oplus \alpha_1 \oplus \alpha_2\alpha_3 \oplus \alpha_3) \\
&= \beta_1 \oplus \beta_2(\alpha_3 \oplus \beta_3) \oplus \alpha_2\beta_3 \oplus \beta_3.
\end{aligned}
$$

Computing $D_\Delta \Phi = (x_3 \oplus 1, 1, 0)$ and substituting (α, β) with $\Psi = (\Phi, D_\Delta \Phi)$, *e.g.*, $\beta_1 = x_3 \oplus 1, \beta_2 = 1, \beta_3 = 0$ and $\alpha_3 = x_3 \oplus x_4 x_5 \oplus x_5$, it gives

$$D_x g(\alpha \oplus x\beta) \circ \Psi = (x_3 \oplus 1) \oplus (x_3 \oplus x_4 x_5 \oplus x_5) = x_4 x_5 \oplus x_5 \oplus 1 = D_\Delta f.$$

3.2   Calculation of the Differential-Linear Bias

In theory, the differential-linear bias can be determined by the algebraic normal forms (ANFs) of the output bits, with input bits as variables. Nevertheless, it is computationally infeasible to compute the ANFs of the output bits of a cipher. To make it feasible, we compute their algebraic transitional forms (ATFs) rather than the ANFs. More exactly, we compute the differential algebraic transitional forms (DATFs) of internal bits as well as output bits of a cipher, and then estimate the differential-linear bias.

For a cipher E, we consider it as a function from $\mathbb{F}_2^n$ into $\mathbb{F}_2^m$. The differential-linear bias corresponding to $(\Delta_{in}, \lambda_{out})$ describes the bias of differential-linear approximation $\lambda_{out} \cdot C \oplus \lambda_{out} \cdot C' = 0$, that is, $\lambda_{out} \cdot E(P) \oplus \lambda_{out} \cdot E(P \oplus \Delta_{in}) = 0$. Denoting $f = \lambda_{out} \cdot E$ gives $f(X) \oplus f(X \oplus \Delta_{in}) = 0$. The bias is determined by the Hamming weight of the partial derivative of $f_{\Delta_{in}} = f(X + x\Delta_{in})$ with respect to x. By Proposition 1 we know the derivative of f with respect to Δ_{in} can be computed from its DATF.

Now we show how to compute the DATF for an iterated cipher. Given the round function $\mathtt{R}$ of the cipher and an input difference Δ_{in}, the procedure for computing the DATF of the output bits is depicted in Algorithm 1. Note that we only concern the nonlinear operation and thus the first (last resp.) linear layer can be omitted in the procedure if it is performed before (after resp.) the nonlinear operation, and that the key and round keys can be taken as a part of the state that is treated as a vector of variables or polynomials.

For an input binary variable vector X, we first initialize $Y^{(0)} = X \oplus x\Delta_{in}$ where x is a binary variable. Any instance of $(Y^{(0)}|_{x=0}, Y^{(0)}|_{x=1})$ corresponds to a pair with difference Δ_{in} in the convention. Next we compute the algebraic normal form of the output of the first rounds, *i.e.*, $Y^{(1)} = \mathtt{R}(Y^{(0)})$. We then rewrite $Y^{(i-1)}$ as $Y'^{(i-1)} \oplus xY''^{(i-1)}$ with both $Y'^{(i-1)}$ and $Y''^{(i-1)}$ independent of x, introduce new variable vectors $\alpha^{(i-1)}$ and $\beta^{(i-1)}$, and record the expressions $\alpha^{(i-1)} = Y'^{(i-1)}$ and $\beta^{(i-1)} = Y''^{(i-1)}$ in an equation set Q. Noting that in this step we use the "**Transitional Rule**" described below as the rule for introducing transitional variable. That is, $\alpha^{(i-1)} \oplus x\beta^{(i-1)} = \mathtt{ATF}(Y^{(i-1)}, x)$. After this we compute the ATF of the output of the i-th round $Y^{(i)} = \mathtt{R}(\alpha^{(i-1)} \oplus x\beta^{(i-1)})$. Finally, we obtain the ATF of the output $Y^{(r)}$ together with an expression set Q. A diagram of the procedure is depicted in Fig. 2.

Transitional Rule: For a Boolean polynomial $u = u''x \oplus u'$ with u' and u'' independent with the variable x, if u' involves two or more variables, then replace u' with a new transitional variable; if u'' involves two or more variables, then replace u'' with another new transitional variable. The new expression derived from u is denoted by $\mathtt{ATF}(u, x)$, or $\mathtt{ATF}(u)$ for short. In other words, for any polynomial w not involving the variable x, we have

$$\mathtt{ATF}(w) = \begin{cases} \mathrm{var}_w, & \text{if } w \text{ involves two or more variables} \\ w, & \text{otherwise} \end{cases}$$

where var_w is a transitional variable identified by w, and thus $\mathtt{ATF}(w)$ is a constant or a variable up to a constant. By the rule, we know $\mathtt{ATF}(u, x) = \mathtt{ATF}(u'')x \oplus \mathtt{ATF}(u')$ has at most three variables including x. For a polynomial vector, $\mathtt{ATF}$ operates on each component of the vector. This rule ensures that $\mathtt{ATF}(f, x)$ is an ATF of f in a very simplified way that keeps x unchanged.

Remark 1. Our experiments show that the DATF techniques perform best when the **Transitional Rule** is applied before the nonlinear operations. Hereinafter, the rule is thus used before the nonlinear operations by default.

Algorithm 1: Differential Algebraic Transitional Form (DATF)

Input: An input difference Δ_{in}, the round function $\mathtt{R}$ of an iterated cipher, and the number r of rounds.
Output: Expressions $(Y^{(r)}, Q)$.
1: Initialize the input variable vector $Y^{(0)} = X \oplus x\Delta_{in}$, and set $Q = \emptyset$;
2: Compute the ANF of the first round, $Y^{(1)} = \mathtt{R}(Y^{(0)})$;
3: **for** i from 2 **to** r **do**
4:     $Y'^{(i-1)} \leftarrow Y^{(i-1)}|_{x=0}$;
5:     $Y''^{(i-1)} \leftarrow D_x Y^{(i-1)}$;
6:     $\alpha^{(i-1)} \leftarrow \mathtt{ATF}(Y'^{(i-1)})$;
7:     $\beta^{(i-1)} \leftarrow \mathtt{ATF}(Y''^{(i-1)})$; // each component of $\alpha^{(i)}$ and $\beta^{(i)}$ is a variable up to a constant or a constant
8:     Add the expressions $\alpha^{(i-1)} = Y'^{(i-1)}$ and $\beta^{(i-1)} = Y''^{(i-1)}$ to Q;
9:     Compute the ATF of the i-th round, $Y^{(i)} = \mathtt{R}(\alpha^{(i-1)} \oplus x\beta^{(i-1)})$;
10: Return $(Y^{(r)}, Q)$.

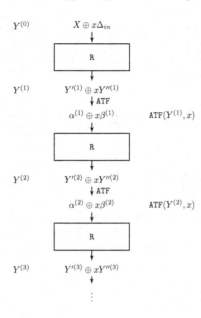

Fig. 2. Differential algebraic transitional form (Algorithm 1)

The polynomial $Y^{(r)}$ is a DATF of $E = R^r$ with respect to Δ_{in}, and thus $\lambda_{out} \cdot Y^{(r)}$ is a DATF of $f = \lambda_{out} \cdot E$. As analyzed previously, $D_{\Delta_{in}} f$ can be computed from $D_x(\lambda_{out} \cdot Y^{(r)}) = \lambda_{out} \cdot D_x Y^{(r)}$ and Q.

The Complexity of Algorithm 1. Let t_R be the complexity of computing the ANF of the round function R, and d the algebraic degree of R. The dominant step is Line 9 in the loop. Usually, after a few rounds, all the components of $Y'^{(i)}$ and $Y''^{(i)}$ involve at least two variables due to the propagation of both the value and difference. By the transitional rule, each component of the vectors $\alpha^{(i)}$ and $\beta^{(i)}$ is set to a transitional variable. Then the complexity for computing the ATF of $R(\alpha^{(i)} \oplus x\beta^{(i)})$ is at most $2^d t_R$. So the complexity of Algorithm 1 is $\mathcal{O}(2^d r t_R)$ in the worst case. Taking d and r as small constants, the complexity is then $\mathcal{O}(t_R)$. It is feasible to compute the algebraic expression of $R(\alpha^{(i)} \oplus x\beta^{(i)})$ if it is feasible to compute the ANF of the round function R with small degree. This is the case for most iterated ciphers without addition operations.

Next we show how to estimate the differential-linear bias. Given the ATF of the output $Y^{(r)}$ and the expression set Q generated by Algorithm 1, we target at estimating the differential-linear bias of the parity of the output pair with linear mask λ_{out}. First we compute the ATF of the parity $e = \lambda_{out} \cdot Y''^{(r)}$, where $Y''^{(r)} = D_x Y^{(r)}$ is the partial derivative of $Y^{(r)}$ with respect to x. Note that the bias will be 0 if there is an isolated variable in the ATF of e, assuming that all the variables follow uniform distribution and are independent of each other. Therefore, we compute the bias of the polynomial obtained by removing all the isolated variables from the ATF of e. For the sum of the isolated variables, we substitute the expressions Q and obtain a new polynomial. Then we update e with this new polynomial, and deal with this polynomial iteratively until it is zero. By the piling-up lemma, we finally obtain the bias ε. The whole procedure is depicted as Algorithm 2.

Algorithm 2: Estimation of the Differential-Linear Bias

Input: Linear mask λ_{out} and the expressions $(Y^{(r)}, Q)$.
Output: A bias ε.
1: Calculate the partial derivative of $Y^{(r)}$: $Y''^{(r)} \leftarrow D_x Y^{(r)}$;
2: Compute the ATF of the parity $e = \lambda_{out} \cdot Y''^{(r)}$, and set $\varepsilon = \frac{1}{2}$;
3: **while** $e \neq 0$ **do**
4:     Select the isolated variables in the ATF of e, and sum them to e_l;
5:     Compute the bias of $e^* = e - e_l$ by $\varepsilon^* = \texttt{Bias}(e^*)$, and calculate $\varepsilon = 2 \cdot \varepsilon^* \cdot \varepsilon$;
6:     Substitute the expressions Q into e_l, and update e with this new polynomial;
7: Return ε.
      /* The procedure for computing the bias from the ATF of f */
8: **procedure** Bias(f)
9:     $(f_1, f_2, \cdots, f_m) \leftarrow$ Separate(f);
10:    $\varepsilon \leftarrow \frac{1}{2}$;
11:    **for** i from 1 **to** m **do**
12:        **if** the number of variables in the expression of f_i is small **then**
13:            Compute the bias ε_i of f_i according to its Hamming weight;
14:        **else**
15:            Select a variable v minimizing the maximum cardinality of the variable
               sets of the polynomials in Separate($f_i|_{v=0}$) and Separate($f_i|_{v=1}$);
16:            Compute the bias of f_i by $\varepsilon_i = \frac{1}{2}\texttt{Bias}(f_i|_{v=0}) + \frac{1}{2}\texttt{Bias}(f_i|_{v=1})$;
17:        $\varepsilon \leftarrow 2 \cdot \varepsilon \cdot \varepsilon_i$;
18:        **if** $\varepsilon = 0$ **then**
19:            **break**
20:    **return** ε.
      /* The procedure for Separating the ATF of f */
21: **procedure** Separate(f)
22:    Separate the Boolean polynomial f as a sum of m polynomials f_i whose
       variable sets are mutually disjoint, and sort $f_1, f_2, \cdots, f_m$ in ascending order
       according to the number of terms in their ANFs;
23:    **return** $(f_1, f_2, \cdots, f_m)$.

In Algorithm 2, we use a procedure Bias() to compute the bias given an algebraic expression in binary variables, in which another procedure Separate() is used to separate the expression as a sum of m polynomials that have no common variables. For a polynomial that could not be separated, if it involves a small number of variables, e.g., 20, we can easily compute the bias from its Hamming weight; otherwise, we guess the values of the variables one by one, and apply Bias() repeatedly until all the polynomials have a small number of variables.

Lemma 2. *Given the ATF of f, if the variables are independent and identically distributed, then the output of* Bias(f) *gives the bias of f.*

Proof. Let ε_f be the bias of f, and it needs to prove $\varepsilon_f =$ Bias(f). Since $f = \sum_{i=1}^m f_i$ after the first step Separate(f) and f_i's are independent (because their variables are disjoint and independent), we have $\varepsilon_f = 2^{m-1}\varepsilon_{f_1}\varepsilon_{f_2}\cdots\varepsilon_{f_m}$ by the piling-up lemma. This is calculated by 2^{m-1}Bias(f_1)Bias$(f_2)\cdots$Bias(f_m) in Line 17 of the procedure. Therefore, it is sufficient to prove $\varepsilon_f =$ Bias(f) for the case $m = 1$. This is clearly true when the number n of variables is small. The rest can be proved by induction. Suppose that it is true that $\varepsilon_f =$ Bias(f) for any f with at most $n-1$ variables. Let v be a variable of f. Since $\frac{1}{2} + \varepsilon_f = \Pr(v = 0) \cdot (\frac{1}{2} + \varepsilon_{f|_{v=0}}) + \Pr(v = 1) \cdot (\frac{1}{2} + \varepsilon_{f|_{v=1}})$, we have

$$\varepsilon_f = \Pr(v = 0) \cdot \varepsilon_{f|_{v=0}} + \Pr(v = 1) \cdot \varepsilon_{f|_{v=1}} \tag{3.1}$$

and according the variable distribution and the inductive assumption it implies

$$\varepsilon_f = \frac{1}{2}\varepsilon_{f|_{v=0}} + \frac{1}{2}\varepsilon_{f|_{v=1}} = \frac{1}{2}\text{Bias}(f|_{v=0}) + \frac{1}{2}\text{Bias}(f|_{v=1}) = \text{Bias}(f).$$

Since the ATF of the parity with respect to the output linear mask λ_{out} is $e = e^* + e_l$ with $e^* = e - e_l$ and e_l sharing no common variables, where e_l is the sum of the isolated variables of e, the bias of e is twice the product of the biases of e^* and e_l. Substituting the expressions in Q into e_l gives a new Boolean polynomial, and its bias can be computed in a similarly way. From this observation, the following statement can be derived.

Theorem 3. *Assuming that all the variables of e^*'s in Algorithm 2 are independent and identically distributed, the output ε of Algorithm 2 is the bias of the differential-linear approximation $\Delta_{in} \rightarrowtail \lambda_{out}$.*

Proof. As the previous analysis of Algorithm 1, we know $Y^{(i)}$ is a DATF of R^i with respect to Δ_{in}, and thus $\lambda_{out} \cdot Y^{(r)}$ is a DATF of $f = \lambda_{out} \cdot R^r$. By Proposition 1, $D_x(\lambda_{out} \cdot Y^{(r)}) = \lambda_{out} \cdot D_x Y^{(r)} = e$ is an ATF of $D_{\Delta_{in}} f$. Suppose that Line 5 executes t and only t times in the algorithm. Let $e_l^{(i)}$ be the polynomial e_l after i executions of Line 5, and $e^{(i)}$ the polynomial obtained by substituting the expressions Q into $e_l^{(i)}$. Then $D_{\Delta_{in}} f$ can be represented as $e^* + \sum_{i=1}^{t-1} e^{*(i)} + e^{(t)}$, where $e^* = e - e_l^{(1)}$ and $e^{*(i)} = e^{(i)} - e_l^{(i+1)}$. Since Line 5 repeates only t times, we have $e^{(t)} = 0$ and thus $D_{\Delta_{in}} f$ is represented as $e^* + \sum_{i=1}^{t-1} e^{*(i)}$, in which the expressions e^* and $e^{*(i)}$'s have independent variables under the assumption of the theorem. By the piling-up lemma and Lemma 2, the bias of $D_{\Delta_{in}} f$ is equal to 2^{t-1}Bias$(e^*) \prod_{i=1}^{t-1}$Bias$(e^{*(i)})$, which is the output ε of Algorithm 2.

The Complexity of Algorithm 2. The complexity of Line 5 in the loop dominates the complexity, that is, the computation of Bias(e^*). The complexity of Bias(e^*) is at most 2^{m^*}, where m^* is the maximum cardinality of the variable sets of the polynomials in Separate(e^*). So the complexity of Algorithm 2 is

$\mathcal{O}(2^m)$ in the worst case, where m is the maximum of m^*. In the case for most iterated ciphers without addition operations, especially for lightweight ciphers using small S-boxes, m is small so that the algorithm is practical. In particular, when Line 5 executes only once, m is at most twice the size of S-boxes, since the algorithm treat the output of the last nonlinear operation as the output of the cipher.

In the following we propose a refined method for estimating the differential-linear bias. It follows the main framework of Algorithm 1 and Algorithm 2. The difference is that the assumption of uniform distribution of the transitional variables is removed and replaced by auxiliary computation. The procedure is depicted as Algorithm 3, and the different parts include Line 2, Line 6 and Line 12 (in blue). In Line 2, the probability distribution of each input variable is set. In Line 6, the probability distribution of each transitional variable is computed according to the probability distribution of previous variables. In Line 12 of the algorithm, each estimation of bias takes the probability distribution of transitional variables into account. This refined method usually gives a more accurate estimation of the bias, while it requires more computations.

With a probability distribution set $D = \{\Pr(X_i = 0) = \frac{1}{2} + \varepsilon_i | X_i \in X, 1 \leq i \leq n\}$, if X_i's are independent, then the probability that $f(X)$ equals zero is

$$\Pr(f(X) = 0) = \sum_{C \in \{X | f(X) = 0\}} \prod_{i=1}^{n} (\frac{1}{2} + (-1)^{C_i} \varepsilon_i). \tag{3.2}$$

According to (3.2), we execute Step 6 of the algorithm. Adapting the procedure Bias() with (3.2) and (3.1), we execute Step 12. The complexity of the adapted procedure is about n times the complexity of Bias(). Combining Algorithm 1 and Algorithm 2 with these steps, we obtain Algorithm 3.

Similarly as Theorem 3 for Algorithm 2, we conclude the following statement for Algorithm 3. Since the probability distribution of each transitional variable is calculated in the algorithm, the assumption of their distribution is removed.

Theorem 4. *Assuming that the variables of the DATF, i.e., $Y^{(i)}$, at each round are independent, the output ε of Algorithm 3 is the bias of the differential-linear approximation $\Delta_{in} \to \lambda_{out}$.*

Proof. Since the variables of each round are independent, it can proved by induction on the number i of rounds that all the probability distributions in D are correct according to (3.2). Then under the independence assumption of the variables of the last round, the theorem is proved by the correctness of the modified procedure that adjusts Bias() with (3.2) and (3.1).

The Complexity of Algorithm 3. Let T_1 and T_2 respectively be the complexity of Algorithm 1 and Algorithm 2, and n the state size. Then the complexity of Algorithm 3 is at most $T_1 + 2nT_2$, since the main difference between Algorithm 3 and the combination of Algorithm 1 and Algorithm 2 is generated by (3.2).

Algorithm 3: Refined Estimation of the Differential-Linear Bias

---

Input: An input difference Δ_{in}, output linear mask λ_{out}, the round function R of an iterated cipher, and the number r of rounds.
Output: A bias ε.

  1: Initialize the input variable vector $Y^{(0)} = X \oplus x\Delta_{in}$, and set $Q = \emptyset$;
  2: Initialize a probability distribution set $D = \{\Pr(X_i = 0) = \frac{1}{2} | X_i \in X\}$;
  3: Compute the ANF of the output of the first round $Y^{(1)} = \text{R}(Y^{(0)})$;
  4: **for** i from 2 **to** r **do**
  5:    Write $Y^{(i-1)} = Y'^{(i-1)} \oplus xY''^{(i-1)}$ with $Y'^{(i-1)}$ and $Y''^{(i-1)}$ independent of x, introduce new variable vectors $\alpha^{(i-1)}$ and $\beta^{(i-1)}$, and add the expressions $\alpha^{(i-1)} = Y'^{(i-1)}$ and $\beta^{(i-1)} = Y''^{(i-1)}$ to Q;
  6:    With D, compute the probabilities that $\alpha_j^{(i-1)}$ and $\beta_j^{(i-1)}$ are respectively zero for all j, and add to D;
  7:    Compute the ATF of the output of the i-th round $Y^{(i)} = \text{R}(\alpha^{(i-1)} \oplus x\beta^{(i-1)})$;
  8: Calculate the partial derivative of $Y^{(r)}$: $Y''^{(r)} \leftarrow D_x Y^{(r)}$;
  9: Compute the ATF of the parity $e = \lambda_{out} \cdot Y''^{(r)}$, and set $\varepsilon = \frac{1}{2}$;
10: **while** $e \neq 0$ **do**
11:    Select the isolated variables in the ATF of e, and sum them to e_l;
12:    With D, compute the bias ε^* of $e^* = e - e_l$, and calculate $\varepsilon = 2 \cdot \varepsilon^* \cdot \varepsilon$;
13:    Substitute the expressions Q into e_l, and update e with this new polynomial;
14: Return ε.

3.3 Key Recovery in Differential-Linear Cryptanalysis

To convert a differential-linear distinguisher to a key recovery attack, for a block cipher, we usually guess some key bits, perform partial encryption or decryption, and apply the distinguisher. In the previous work, the distinguisher and the process of key guessing are separately treated. Here we show an algebraic approach to deal with these two processes simultaneously. The approach also applies to iterated ciphers of other types, including stream ciphers and authenticated encryption ciphers.

A crucial stage of this approach is to impose some conditions on the internal bits of the cipher to make uncertain differences determined in the first rounds. Similar techniques were used in conditional differential cryptanalysis [BB93, KMN10] and conditional linear cryptanalysis [BP18], and a similar idea called the partitioning technique was applied to differential-linear cryptanalysis in [Leu16] with an application to Chaskey.

Our precomputation for the key recovery follows the main framework of estimating the differential-linear bias in Algorithm 3. The procedure is depicted as Algorithm 4. For the sake of brevity, here we only explain its differences with Algorithm 3, marked blue in the procedure. The main difference is that some conditions I are imposed in the first r_1 rounds. Note that in each computation of the ANFs and ATFs we reduce the polynomials over the ideal of I, denoted by "mod I".

After precomputation for the key recovery as shown in Algorithm 4, we obtain a set of expressions Q_I and a differential-linear bias ε. Then a system of equations $S = \{f = 0 | f \in Q_I\}$ is derived. Assume that the equations in S are

---

Algorithm 4: Key Recovery in Differential-Linear Cryptanalysis

---

Input: An input difference Δ_{in}, output linear mask λ_{out}, the round function R of an iterated cipher, the number r of rounds, and a parameter r_1.

Output: A set Q_I of expressions in key bits and a bias ε.

1: Initialize the input variable vector $Y^{(0)} = X \oplus x\Delta_{in}$, and set $Q = \emptyset$ and $I = \emptyset$;
2: Initialize a probability distribution set $D = \{\Pr(X_i = 0) = \frac{1}{2} | X_i \in X\}$;
3: Compute the ANF of the first round $Y^{(1)} = \mathtt{R}(Y^{(0)}) \mod I$;
4: **for** i from 2 **to** r **do**
5:     Write $Y^{(i-1)} = Y'^{(i-1)} \oplus xY''^{(i-1)}$ with $Y'^{(i-1)}$ and $Y''^{(i-1)}$ independent of x;
6:     **if** $i \leq r_1$ and $Y''^{(i-1)} \notin \{0, 1\}$ **then**
7:         Add $Y''^{(i-1)}$ to I, impose $Y''^{(i-1)} = 0$, and set $Y'^{(i-1)} = Y'^{(i-1)} \mod I$;
8:         Introduce new variable vectors $\alpha^{(i-1)}$ and $\beta^{(i-1)}$, and add the expressions $\alpha^{(i-1)} = Y'^{(i-1)}$ and $\beta^{(i-1)} = Y''^{(i-1)}$ to Q;
9:         With D, compute the probabilities that $\alpha_j^{(i-1)}$ and $\beta_j^{(i-1)}$ are zeros for j, and add to D;
10:    Compute the ATF of the i-th round $Y^{(i)} = \mathtt{R}(\alpha^{(i-1)} \oplus x\beta^{(i-1)}) \mod I$;
11: Calculate the partial derivative of $Y^{(r)}$: $Y''^{(r)} \leftarrow D_x Y^{(r)}$;
12: Compute the ATF of the parity $e = \lambda_{out} \cdot Y''^{(r)} \mod I$, and set $\varepsilon = \frac{1}{2}$;
13: **while** $e \neq 0$ **do**
14:    Select the isolated variables in the ATF of e, and sum them to e_l;
15:    With D, compute the bias of $e - e_l$, denoted by ε^*, and calculate $\varepsilon = 2 \cdot \varepsilon^* \cdot \varepsilon$;
16:    Substitute the expressions Q into e_l, and update e with this new polynomial (mod I);
17: Deal with I, and obtain a set of expressions in input bits, denoted by Q_I;
18: Return Q_I, ε.

---

independently and they are always consistent for an arbitrary fixed key. Denote by n the number of equations in S and by m the number of independent expressions of key bits in S. In the key recovery attack, the key is unknown, and thus we need to guess the values of the expressions that involve the key bits. For each guess of these expressions, $O(\frac{1}{\varepsilon^2})$ pairs of plaintexts with input difference Δ_{in} is sufficient to mount a distinguisher. We assume a random behavior of the parities of the output subset for a wrong key. Then the data complexity of the attack is $D = O(\frac{2^n}{\varepsilon^2})$. There are 2^m values for the m expressions that need to be guessed in the attack, so the attack time is $T = O(\frac{2^m}{\varepsilon^2})$.

The success probability of the attack is calculated according to analytical results of the success probability of linear attacks (also applicable to differential-linear attacks) in [Sel08, Theorem 2] as below.

Theorem 5. ([Sel08]) *Denote by Φ the cumulative distribution functions of the standard normal distribution. Let P_S be the probability that a linear attack on an m-bit subkey, with a linear approximation of probability p, with N known plaintext blocks, delivers an a-bit or higher advantage. Assuming that the linear approximation's probability to hold is independent for each key tried and is equal to $1/2$ for all wrong keys, we have, for sufficiently large m and N,*

$$P_S = \Phi(2\sqrt{N}|p - 1/2| - \Phi^{-1}(1 - 2^{-a-1})). \tag{3.3}$$

The Complexity of Algorithm 4. Excluding the cost of computing the ATF and bias that is almost the same as Algorithm 3, the running time of Algorithm 4 mainly depends on the cost t_I of each computation of mod I. The former is computed as $T_3 = T_1 + 2nT_2$ as previously. Then the complexity of Algorithm 4 is $\mathcal{O}(T_3 + nrt_I)$. Therefore Algorithm 4 is practical when Algorithm 3 is feasible and the size of I is small.

We have implemented Algorithm 4 in SageMath for `Ascon`, `Serpent`, and `Grain v1`. Our experiments show that the algorithm performs well when r_1 is small enough (such that the number of independent expressions in I is small), though it is slower than Algorithm 2 and Algorithm 3. It is a good choice to use Algorithm 2 and Algorithm 3 to screen differential-linear approximations. Especially for input difference and output linear mask with small Hamming weights, we can use Algorithm 2 to exhaust all possible differential-linear approximations, and use Algorithm 3 to further screen candidates. In the applications in conditional attacks, we can equip Algorithm 4 with Algorithm 2 for fast computation. As a general method, the algorithm can also be applied with a DL distinguisher obtained by other approaches, in particular when it can not detect a reasonable bias.

4 Applications to `Ascon`

In this section, we apply our techniques to `Ascon` for estimating the differential-linear bias, and then propose a key recovery attack to a 5-round variant. `Ascon` is a family of authenticated encryption and hashing algorithms designed by Dobraunig et al. [DEMS16, DEMS19]. It has been selected as the primary choice for lightweight authenticated encryption in the final portfolio of the CAESAR competition (2014–2019) and is currently competing in the NIST Lightweight Cryptography competition. The analysis in this paper is focused on `Ascon`-128, and the results are also applicable to `Ascon`-128a. Note that given the 64 bits of the output, one can invert the last linear layer. Hereinafter we thus consider the cipher without the last linear layer.

4.1 Differential-Linear Bias of `Ascon`

In [DEMS15], Dobraunig et al. presented practical differential-linear attacks on up to 5 rounds of the `Ascon` permutation, based on a 4-round differential-linear distinguisher. The authors of [DEMS15] stated that while the overall bias of the approximation is expected to be 2^{-20} by the theory of the differential-linear attack, experiments show that the bias is 2^{-2} which is significantly higher.

Recently, at EUROCRYPT 2019, Bar-On et al. [BDKW19] recomputed the bias of the distinguisher using the Differential-Linear Connectivity Table (DLCT) and obtained a higher bias of 2^{-5}. This value is significantly higher than the value 2^{-20} which follows from the classical differential-linear framework. On the other hand, it is still much lower than the experimentally obtained bias of 2^{-2}. The authors of [BDKW19] conjectured that it may be explained by the effect of other differentials and linear approximations.

In the following, we exploit the two algorithms, Algorithm 2 and Algorithm 3, as shown in Sect. 3 to estimate the differential-linear bias for `Ascon`.

Before applying Algorithm 2, we have to compute the DATF of `Ascon` by Algorithm 1. We divide the S-box of `Ascon` into two parts, p_{S_L} and p_{S_N}, and the permutation of `Ascon` is then divided into two parts, $p_A = p_{S_L} \circ p_C$ and $p_B = p_L \circ p_{S_N}$. The first part of the S-box, p_{S_L}, is actually a linear transform, as shown below.

$$\texttt{x0 \textasciicircum= x4;} \quad \texttt{x4 \textasciicircum= x3;} \quad \texttt{x2 \textasciicircum= x1;}$$

In Algorithm 1, we compute the ANF of a half round of p, i.e., $\text{R}^{\frac{1}{2}} = p_A$, instead of the entire first round. We then set $\text{R} = p_A \circ p_B$, and for the last round set $\text{R} = p_{S_N}$. A function of r rounds p^r without the last linear layer is exactly $p_{S_N} \circ \text{R}^{r-1} \circ p_A$. The 128-bit key and 128-bit nonce are set to 256 binary variables, and the IV is set to a constant defined by the cipher.

For the input difference Δ_{in} with differences in bit 63 of x_3 and x_4, by performing Algorithm 1 with $r = 4$, we obtain the ATF of the output $Y^{(4)}$ together with an expression set Q. Note that in Line 3 of Algorithm 1 the number i of rounds ranges from 1 to $r = 4$. Applying Algorithm 2 to a single-bit linear mask in bit 9 then gives a differential-linear bias $\varepsilon = 2^{-3}$.

Similarly as done in Algorithm 1, in Algorithm 3 we set $\text{R}^{\frac{1}{2}} = p_A$, $\text{R} = p_A \circ p_B$, and for the last round $\text{R} = p_{S_N}$. With the same input difference and output mask, applying Algorithm 3 to 4 rounds of `Ascon` permutation gives a bias $\varepsilon = 2^{-2.365}$. This result slightly improves the estimate of 2^{-3} obtained by Algorithm 2, at cost of computations of the probability distribution. It is very close to the experimentally obtained bias of 2^{-2}, and much higher than the theoretical bias of 2^{-5} obtained in [BDKW19] using the DLCT.

4.2 Differential-Linear Cryptanalysis of `Ascon`

Now we apply the key recovery algorithm, Algorithm 4, to 5-round `Ascon-128`. By performing Algorithm 4 with $r_1 = 2$ and $r = 5$ over all possible single-bit or two-bit input differences and all possible single-bit output masks, we obtain a differential-linear bias $\varepsilon = 2^{-5.415}$ for the input difference Δ_{in} with differences in bit 63 of x_3 and x_4 and the output mask λ_{out} in bit 36. The R function is the same as defined previously, and in Line 4 of Algorithm 4 the number i of rounds ranges from 1 to 5. The set of expressions Q_I has 9 polynomials, with algebraic degree at most 2. Among these 9 polynomials, 6 of them involve both the key and nonce bits, 2 polynomials involve only a single key bit (bit 63 and 127 respectively), and one involves only two nonce bits (bit 63 XOR bit 127). We impose bit 63 and bit 127 of the nonce to be equal, and run all the possible cases for the other 8 polynomials by experiments on random 2^{28} samples for each case. We then derive a bias of $2^{-4.5}$ when all the polynomials equals zero and a reasonable high bias of $2^{-5.5}$ when 5 of them equals zero. The 5 equations are listed as follows, where k_i means bit i of the key and v_i means bit i of the nonce.

$k_{63} = 0;$

$k_{127} = 0;$

$v_{52} = k_{12}v_{76} + k_{12} + k_{35}v_{99} + k_{42}v_{106} + k_{45} + k_{52} + k_{99} + k_{109} + k_{116}$
$\quad\quad + v_{12} + v_{42} + v_{45} + v_{76} + v_{106} + v_{109} + v_{116} + 1;$

$v_{74} = k_{10}k_{74} + k_{10}v_{10} + k_{10} + k_{32}k_{96} + k_{32}v_{32} + k_{32} + k_{35}k_{99} + k_{35}v_{35} + k_{35}$
$\quad\quad + k_{74}v_{10} + k_{74} + k_{96}v_{32} + k_{96} + k_{99}v_{35} + k_{99}$
$\quad\quad + v_{10} + v_{32} + v_{35} + v_{96} + v_{99} + 1;$

$v_{83} = k_{19}k_{83} + k_{19}v_{19} + k_{19} + k_{41}k_{105} + k_{41}v_{41} + k_{41} + k_{44}k_{108} + k_{44}v_{44} + k_{44}$
$\quad\quad + k_{83}v_{19} + k_{83} + k_{105}v_{41} + k_{105} + k_{108}v_{44} + k_{108}$
$\quad\quad + v_{19} + v_{41} + v_{44} + v_{105} + v_{108}.$

Our experiments show that the differential-linear bias is significantly smaller than $2^{-5.5}$ when one or more equations of the above equations are not satisfied. Fixing the values of $V_{\text{fix}} = \{v_{10}, v_{19}, v_{32}, v_{35}, v_{41}, v_{44}, v_{76}, v_{99}, v_{106}\}$, $2^{15.3+3}$ samples with v_{52}, v_{74}, v_{83} running over possible values are sufficient to distinguish $k_{63} = k_{127} = 0$ from the other cases. For the case $k_{63} = k_{127} = 0$, we can also recover 3 extra expressions on key bits. More exactly, in this case, we are able to derive the above 5 equations. We can further set up 9 more equations by flipping the values of V_{fix} bit by bit. By elimination of nonlinear terms in key bits and after simplification, we obtain 12 linear equations on key bits, that is, $k_{63} = 0, k_{127} = 0, k_{12} = c_0, k_{35} = c_1, k_{42} = c_2, k_{99} = c_3, k_{10}+k_{74} = c_4, k_{19}+k_{83} = c_5, k_{32} + k_{96} = c_6, k_{41} + k_{105} = c_7, k_{44} + k_{108} = c_8, k_{45} + k_{52} + k_{109} + k_{116} = c_9$. Since we know the value c_4 of the sum $k_{10} + k_{74}$, we can linearize the quadratic term $k_{10}k_{74}$ to $k_{10}(1 + k_{10} + k_{74}) = (1 + c_4)k_{10}$. By a similar way, the two nonlinear equations can be linearized, and they are linearly independent with the previous equations with a high probability.

Noting that the characteristics of Ascon are rotation-invariant within the 64-bit words, the same method can be used to set up other equations by placing differences in bit i of x_3, x_4 and observing the bias at position $(i + 37) \mod 64$. For each i, we can detect whether $k_i = k_{i+64} = 0$ is satisfied, and then set up 14 linear equations. We can obtain on average 16 i's with $k_i = k_{i+64} = 0$, and thus derive $16 \times 14 = 224$ linear equations on key bits, which is sufficient to recover the correct key. We have verified by experiments on thousands of keys that for most cases the linear system has at least 104 linearly independent equations.

The data complexity of the attack is on average $64 \times 2^{19.3} + 16 \times 9 \times 2^{17.3} \approx 2^{26}$ bits, and the expected time complexity is about 2^{26}, for most of the keys. The complexity has been practically verified. This attack significantly improves the existing differential-linear attack on 5-round Ascon-128 with complexity 2^{36} [DEMS15]. Our results are summarized in Table 3, with the comparisons of the previous differential-linear attacks.

Remark 2. We have made a lot of efforts to apply the method to Ascon for 6 and more rounds, e.g., performing an exhaustive search over all the possible DL approximations with low-weight differences and linear masks, but we did

Table 3. Differential-linear cryptanalysis on `Ascon`-128

Type	Rounds	Time	Data	Source
key recovery	4/12	2^{18}	2^{18}	[DEMS15]
key recovery	5/12	2^{36}	2^{36}	[DEMS15]
key recovery	5/12	2^{26}	2^{26}	Section 4.2

not find any approximation with bias larger than 2^{-64}. This probably enhances confidence that there does not exist valid DL approximation for 6-round `Ascon`, at least for low-weight differences and linear masks.

5   Applications to Serpent

In this section, we first give a brief description of the cipher `Serpent` [ABK98], as well as revisit the estimation of the differential-linear bias in [BDK03] by our techniques, and then propose key recovery attacks to round-reduced `Serpent`.

5.1   A Brief Description of Serpent

In [ABK98] Anderson, Biham and Knudsen presented the block cipher `Serpent`. `Serpent` is an AES finalist. `Serpent` has a block size of 128 bits and supports a key size of 128, 192 or 256 bits. The cipher is a 32-round SP-network operating on a block of four 32-bit words. Each round is composed of key mixing, a layer of S-boxes and a linear transformation.

In the following, we adopt the notations of [ABK98,BDK03] in the bitsliced version. The intermediate value of the round i is denoted by $\hat{B}_i$ (which is a 128-bit value). The rounds are numbered from 0 to 31. Each $\hat{B}_i$ is composed of four 32-bit words X_0, X_1, X_2, X_3. `Serpent` has 32 rounds, and a set of eight 4-bit to 4-bit S-boxes. Each round function $R_i (i \in \{0, \cdots, 31\})$ uses a single S-box 32 times in parallel. For example, R_0 uses S_0, 32 copies of which are applied in parallel. Thus, the first copy of S_0 takes the least significant bits from X_0, X_1, X_2, X_3 and returns the output to the same bits. This can be implemented as a Boolean expression of the 4 words. The set of eight S-boxes is used four times. S_0 is used in round 0, S_1 is used in round 1, *etc.* After using S_7 in round 7, S_0 is used again in round 8, then S_1 in round 9, and so on. In the last round (round 31) the linear transformation is omitted and another key is XORed.

5.2   Differential-Linear Bias of Serpent

One of the first applications of the differential-linear cryptanalysis is an attack on the AES finalist `Serpent` presented by Biham *et al.* in [BDK03]. The attack is based on a 9-round differential-linear distinguisher with bias of 2^{-60} and targets an 11-round variant of the cipher. In [DIK08], Dunkelman *et al.* performed experiments with reduced round variants of Serpent, and concluded that the actual bias of the approximation is $2^{-57.75}$ and not 2^{-60}. In [BDKW19], Bar-On *et al.* recomputed the bias of the distinguisher using the DLCT and obtained the value $2^{-57.68}$.

In this section, we revisit the analysis of the bias of this distinguisher by DATF techniques, and show an estimate of $2^{-57.736}$. This value is extremely close to the experimental value.

Before showing our results, we recall the analysis of [BDK03]. In the following, we adopt the notations of [BDKW19, BDK03], and refer the reader to [BDK03] for the exact difference and mask values. The differential-linear distinguisher of [BDK03] targets a 9-round reduced variant of Serpent that starts with round 2 of the cipher. This variant is denoted by E and decomposed as $E = E_1 \circ E_0$, where E_0 consists of rounds 2–4 and E_1 consists of rounds 5–10. For E_0, the distinguisher uses a differential characteristic of the form

$$\Delta_0 \xrightarrow[LT \circ S_2]{p_0 = 2^{-5}} \Delta_1 \xrightarrow[LT \circ S_3]{p_1 = 2^{-1}} \Delta_2 \xrightarrow[LT \circ S_4]{p_2 = 1} \Delta_3,$$

where Δ_2, Δ_3 are truncated differences. For E_1, the distinguisher uses a linear approximation of the form

$$\lambda_0 \xrightarrow[LT \circ S_5]{q_0 = 2^{-5}} \lambda_1 \xrightarrow[LT \circ S_6]{q_1 = 2^{-3}} \lambda_2 \xrightarrow[R^4]{q_1 = 2^{-21}} \lambda_6,$$

where all nonzero bits of the mask λ_0 are included in the bits that are known to be zero in Δ_3. The authors of [BDK03] found out by experiments that there are other differentials which also predict the difference in the bits of λ_0. Summing all the differentials, they got that the probability that $\lambda_0 \cdot \Delta_3 = 0$ is $1/2 + 2^{-7}$, and hence used $p = 2^{-7}$ in their analysis. Using the complexity analysis of the classical differential-linear framework, the authors of [BDK03] concluded that the overall bias of the approximation is $2 \times 2^{-7} \times (2^{-27})^2 = 2^{-60}$.

The authors of [DIK08] checked experimentally the first 4 rounds of the differential-linear distinguisher of [BDK03] (that is, a 4-round distinguisher which starts with the difference Δ_0 and ends with the mask λ_1) and found that its bias is $2^{-13.75}$, instead of the estimate $2 \cdot 2^{-7} \cdot (2^{-5})^2 = 2^{-16}$. They concluded that the bias of the 9-round distinguisher is $2^{-57.75}$ instead of 2^{-60}.

The authors of [BDKW19] considered a 3-round variant of Serpent that starts at round 3, denoted it by E', and found that its bias is $2^{-8.68}$. Hence they concluded that the bias of the 4-round distinguisher examined in [DIK08] is $2^{-5} \cdot 2^{-8.68} = 2^{-13.68}$.

We apply Algorithm 3 to the 3-round variant of Serpent E' considered in [BDKW19], with the input difference $\Delta_{in} = \Delta_1$ and output mask $\lambda_{out} = \lambda_1$, and obtain a bias $\varepsilon = 2^{-8.736}$. Therefore we conclude that the bias of the 4-round distinguisher examined in [DIK08] is $2^{-5} \cdot 2^{-8.736} = 2^{-13.736}$. This value is extremely close to the experimental value, and slightly more accurate than that of [BDKW19]. Note that the gap is $2^{-20.4}$ while the standard deviation of the bias was $2^{-18.87}$ in the experiment of [DIK08]. We conjecture that the gap between the experimental value and our estimate is a statistical error.

We further apply Algorithm 3 to a 4-round variant of Serpent that starts at round 3, with the input difference $\Delta_{in} = \Delta_1$ and output mask $\lambda_{out} = \lambda_2$, and obtain a bias $\varepsilon = 2^{-12.736}$. We thus conclude that the bias of the 5-round distinguisher is $2^{-5} \cdot 2^{-12.736} = 2^{-17.736}$.

5.3   Differential-Linear Cryptanalysis of 11-Round and 12-Round Serpent

In this section, we first point out the flaws in the previous attacks on 12-round Serpent, and then show our improved attack by applying Algorithm 4.

Comments on the Attacks on 12-round Serpent in [DIK08,Lu15]. The authors of [DIK08] found that the S-boxes 2, 3, 19, and 23 do not affect the active bits of $LT^{-1}(\Delta_0)$, and used this property to extend the 11-round attack to 12 rounds by partially encrypting plaintexts for one more round. Nevertheless, in Step 3(b) of the 11-round attack, the bits input to the 5 active S-boxes in round 1 are partially encrypted, and thus not only the differences but also the values of these bits must be taken into account. Our experiment shows that the S-boxes 2, 3, 19, and 23 affect their values, though they do not affect their differences. This implies that the attack on 12-round Serpent in [DIK08] has an underestimated time complexity, up to a factor of 2^{16}. The same issue exists in the 12-round attack on Serpent in [Lu15] with time complexity of $2^{244.9}$ encryptions. Instead, they used the property that the S-boxes 1, 8, 10, 30, and 14 of Round 0 do not affect the difference corresponding to the S-boxes 18, 22, 24 and 25 of Round 1, but our experiment shows that all the S-boxes of Round 0 affect their values. This means that the complexity was underestimated by a factor of 2^{20}. We therefore conclude that these attacks are thus worse than a brute-force attack.[2]

The Improved Attacks on 11-round Serpent. First, we consider a 6-round variant of Serpent that starts at round 1, using Algorithm 4. The input difference is set to $\Delta_{in} = \{11, 14, 18, 31, 46, 49, 50, 75, 78, 81, 82, 95, 107, 114, 127\}$, and the output mask $\lambda_{out} = \lambda_2$. With $r_1 = 2$, performing Algorithm 4, we obtain a bias $\varepsilon = 2^{-12.736}$. The set of expressions Q_I has 16 independent polynomials, 11 of which are generated in round 1. The remaining 5 polynomials are produced in round 2, and the probability that all of these 5 polynomials equal zeros is 2^{-5}. If we impose the 11 polynomials in round 1 to be zeros, which are all linear, then we obtain a differential-linear distinguisher with a bias of $2^{-5} \cdot 2^{-12.736} = 2^{-17.736}$, for 6-round Serpent. By assuming the piling-up lemma to hold for the linear approximation from round 7 to round 10

---

[2]   The authors of [DIK08] have confirmed the issue with the attacks after a long-time effort to find solution for fixing it. We are grateful to them for their helpful discussions and precious feedback on the issue. The flaw was found when we tried to apply our techniques to Serpent. We believe that the techniques can improve the 12-round attacks in [DIK08], but the "improved" attack is even worse than a brute-force attack. We were then aware that this is a contradiction.

$(\lambda_2 \xrightarrow[R^4]{q_1=2^{-21}} \lambda_6)$, we can obtain a 10-round differential-linear distinguisher with a bias $4 \cdot 2^{-17.736} \cdot 2^{-21} \cdot 2^{-21} = 2^{-57.736}$, by imposing 11 linear equations on the input bits and key bits in round 1. This is because imposing these equations makes the differential characteristic $\Delta_{in} \xrightarrow{LT \circ S_1} \Delta_0$ hold with probability one. Nevertheless, the technique of Sect. 3.3 can not be adopted directly, since the required data exceeds 2^{128}. As a trade off, the data complexity can be cut down by imposing less equations, at cost of increasing the attack time.

Based on the above observation, we improve the differential-linear attack on 11-round Serpent as follows.

In the attack, we use an input difference with 3 active S-boxes 11, 14, 18:

$$\Delta_{in} = \{11, 14, 18, 46, 50, 75, 78, 82, 107, 114\},$$

and impose the following 6 equations:

$$
\begin{aligned}
v_{11} &= k_{11}; \\
v_{14} &= k_{14} \oplus k_{78} \oplus v_{78} \oplus 1; \\
v_{18} &= k_{18} \oplus k_{50} \oplus v_{50}; \\
v_{43} &= k_{43} \oplus k_{107} \oplus v_{107} \oplus 1; \\
v_{46} &= k_{46} \oplus k_{78} \oplus v_{78} \oplus 1; \\
v_{82} &= v_{50} \oplus k_{50} \oplus k_{82} \oplus 1,
\end{aligned}
\tag{5.1}
$$

where v_i and k_i respectively denote bit i of plain-text input to round 1 and the 128-bit subkey K_1 of round 1.

The attack is described by the following procedure.

1. Select $N = 2^{125.6}$ pairs of plaintexts with difference Δ_{in}, consisting of $2^{111.6}$ structures, each is chosen by selecting:

(a) Any pairs of plaintexts $(P_0, P_0 \oplus \Delta_{in})$.
(b) The pairs of plaintexts $(P_i, P_i \oplus \Delta_{in})$ for $1 \leq i \leq 2^{14} - 1$, where $P_1, \cdots, P_{2^{14}-1}$ differ from P_0 by all the $2^{14} - 1$ possible (non-empty) subsets of the 6 bits $\{11, 14, 18, 43, 46, 82\}$, S-box 17 (bits $\{17, 49, 81, 113\}$) and S-box 31 (bits $\{31, 63, 95, 127\}$) in round 1.

2. Request the ciphertexts of these plaintext structures (encrypted under the unknown key K).
3. For each value of the 6 expressions of K_1, choose the $2^{119.6}$ pairs of plaintexts $(P, P \oplus \Delta_{in})$ with P satisfying (5.1), and perform the following steps for each value of the 8 bits of K_1 entering S-box 17 and S-box 31:

(a) Initialize an array of 2^{56} counters to zeros.
(b) Partially encrypt for each plaintext the S-boxes 17 and 31 in round 1, and find the pairs which satisfy the difference Δ_0 before round 2.
(c) Given those $2^{119.6}$ pairs, perform for each ciphertext pair: count over all pairs how many times each of the 2^{56} possibilities of the 56 bits entering the 7 active S-boxes in round 11 occurs.

(d) For each guess of the subkey entering these S-boxes, find how many pairs agree on the output subset parity, and how many disagree.

(e) The highest entry in the array should correspond to the 28 bits of K_{12} entering the 7 active S-boxes in round 11.

4. Each trial of the key gives us 42 bits of the subkeys (14 bits in round 1 and 28 bits in round 11), along with a measure for correctness. The correct value of the 40 bits is expected to be the most frequently suggested value.

5. The rest of the key bits are then recovered by auxiliary techniques.

The data complexity of the attack is $2^{126.6}$ chosen plaintexts, the time complexity of the attack is $2^{120.6} \cdot 2^{14} \cdot \frac{2}{352} = 2^{127.1}$ encryptions, and the memory complexity is 2^{60} bytes for the 11-round attack. Using the formula (3.3), the success probability of the attack is expected to be about 85%. As far as we know, this is the first differential-linear cryptanalysis on 11-round Serpent-128.

Further Improvements on the Attacks on Serpent. In [DIK08], Dunkelman *et al.* presented a 9-round differential-linear approximation in the inverse direction with a bias of 2^{-54}, starting from round 13 and ending at round 5, and showed an attack on 11-round Serpent with data complexity of $2^{113.7}$ chosen ciphertexts, time complexity of $2^{137.7}$ memory accesses, and memory complexity of 2^{99} bytes.

With the help of Algorithm 4, we can improve the attack on 11-round Serpent in the setting of chosen ciphertext attack, using the techniques as discussed previously. By imposing 12 linear equations on the ciphertext and the bits of subkey K_{15} that are XORed with the 6 active S-boxes in round 14, the 9-round differential-linear approximation in the inverse direction can be extended to 10 rounds with the same bias 2^{-54}, starting from round 14 and ending at round 5. Then the time complexity can be cut down by a factor of about 2^{-12}. The improved attack on 11-round Serpent has the data complexity of $2^{125.7}$ chosen ciphertexts, time complexity of $2^{125.7}$ memory accesses, and memory complexity of 2^{99} bytes. Using the Formula (3.3), the success probability of the attack is expected to be more than 99%.

Our experiment shows that there is one S-box in round 15 that does not affect either the differences or the values of the 6 active S-boxes in round 14. Based on this observation, we can extend the chosen ciphertext attack on 11-round Serpent to 12 rounds (starting from round 15 and ending at round 4), by guessing the bits of the subkey K_{16} that are XORed with the other 31 S-boxes. The attack on 12-round Serpent-256 has the data complexity of 2^{127} chosen ciphertexts, time complexity of $2^{127} \cdot 2^{124} = 2^{251}$ memory accesses, and memory complexity of 2^{99} bytes. The success probability of the attack is expected to be more than 77%. To the best of our knowledge, this is the first correct attack on 12-round Serpent.

The cryptanalytic results are summarized in Table 4, with the comparisons of the previous differential-linear attacks.

Table 4. Differential-linear cryptanalysis on `Serpent`

Key size	Rounds	Time	Data	Memory	Source
192 & 256	11/32	$2^{139.2}$ En	$2^{125.3}$ CP	2^{60} B	[BDK03]
192 & 256		$2^{135.7}$ En	$2^{121.8}$ CP	2^{76} B	[DIK08]
192 & 256		$2^{137.7}$ MA	$2^{113.7}$ CC	2^{99} B	[DIK08]
all	11/32	$2^{127.1}$ En	$2^{126.6}$ CP	2^{60} B	Section 5.3
all		$2^{125.7}$ MA	$2^{125.7}$ CC	2^{99} B	Section 5.3
256	12/32	2^{251} MA	2^{127} CC	2^{99} B	Section 5.3

6   Applications to `Grain v1`

As mentioned earlier, an extreme case of the differential-linear attack can be theoretically considered as a truncated differential attack, see also [BLN17]. The techniques we propose for differential-linear attack can also be used in a (truncated) differential attack. In this section, we apply the previous techniques to differential cryptanalysis of the stream cipher `Grain v1`, propose key recovery attacks to a round-reduced variant of the cipher, and also revisit the previous differential attacks.

`Grain v1` is an NFSR-based stream cipher proposed by Hell *et al.* [HJMM08]. The cipher is one of the finalists which has been selected in the eSTREAM hardware profile. `Grain v1` uses an 80-bit secret key $K = (k_0, k_1, \ldots, k_{79})$ and a 64-bit initial value $V = (v_0, v_1, \ldots, v_{63})$. It consists of three main building blocks: an 80-bit LFSR, an 80-bit NFSR and a non-linear output function. In this paper, round-reduced variants of `Grain v1` with r initialization rounds means the cipher outputs keystream after r rounds and the first keystream bit is z_r.

At ASIACRYPT 2010, Knellwolf *et al.* [KMN10] proposed conditional differential attacks on NFSR-based cryptosystems, with applications to 104-round `Grain v1`. The framework of this attack is as follows: First, in a chosen plaintext attack scenario, the authors choose a suitable difference that controls difference propagation as many rounds as possible. Second, they impose conditions to prevent the propagation of the difference to the newly generated state bits at first few rounds. Since the bias of the keystream is wanted to be tested, there is an important trade-off between the number of imposed conditions and the number of inputs that can be derived. Finally, depending on whether the conditions involve the initial value only, or also key variables, they obtain distinguishing and partial key recovering attacks. In the literature, the largest number of initialization rounds of `Grain v1` that can be attacked is 120, proposed by Li and Guan [LG19] using a conditional differential approximation with an experimental bias $2^{-12.8}$.

6.1   Searching the Differences of Round-Reduced `Grain v1`

In this section, we exploit the two algorithms, Algorithm 1 and Algorithm 2, as shown in Sect. 3 to estimate the differential-linear bias as well as search for good differences for `Grain v1`. We use Algorithm 2 rather than Algorithm 3 because of its efficiency. By an exhaustive search over all the differences in at most 4 bits of the initial value, the algorithms find a differential approximation with a theoretical bias $2^{-20.77}$ for 125-round `Grain v1`. For purposes of comparison, we have applied the existing method called Differential Engine proposed by Banik in [Ban14] to analyzing the bias of the same approximation, and detect a bias of $2^{-24.78}$, which is much smaller. The found input difference is a 2-bit difference, with differences in bit 21 and 46 of the initial value. The output linear mask is located in the first bit of the keystream. Note here that we use modified Algorithm 1 and Algorithm 2 which partially adopt the key recovery techniques of Algorithm 4 with $r_1 = 50$. From the algorithms we obtain 6 equations represented by the ATFs of the internal bits of `Grain v1`. The ANFs of the internal bits on the key and initial value are very complicated. Instead of directly converting the ATF into the ANF, we analyze these equations specifically one by one manually.

Using the same method, we revisit the analysis of the conditional differential bias of 120 rounds in [LG19], and obtain a theoretical estimate of $2^{-13.39}$. This is very close to the experimental value $2^{-12.8}$, and much higher than the estimate of $2^{-18.13}$ obtained by the Differential Engine method.

6.2   Analysis of 125-Round `Grain v1`

Imposing the appropriate conditions is the crucial part of conditional differential attack. It has a trade-off between the two aims: one is to prevent a maximum number of propagation, the other is to find enough IVs that satisfy the conditions. A condition that we assign a certain IV bit to fixed value 0 or 1 is called Type 0 condition, and a condition which is a function of IV bits and key bits is called Type 1 condition.

We now introduce the strategy of our conditions analysis. Since the updated symbolic expressions of `Grain v1` are rather complicated after few rounds, it is not easy to analyze conditions. A new variable is used to compute the updated expression and we store the original complex one and factor the condition expression as $f + \sum_{i=1}^{n} f_i g_i$. Thus it is easier to analyze expressions and impose simple conditions. To obtain enough IVs that satisfy the conditions, we allow Type 1 conditions to have the term $\sum_{i,j} k_i v_j$ and we guess the value of each k_i when we attack 125-round `Grain v1`. We finally impose 10 Type 0 conditions and 13 Type 1 conditions.

We have performed for 8 random keys each with 2^{40} pairs of initial values that satisfy the above equations, and observed a bias of $2^{-17.4}$ with standard deviation of $2^{-20.5}$. Hence we use the bias $2^{-17.4}$ in our attack.

In the above equations, there are in total 20 independent expressions of key bits that need to be guessed in the attack. A primary analysis of the attack gives a data complexity of $2 \cdot 2^{13} \cdot 2^{38} = 2^{52}$ chosen IVs and a time complexity of $2^{20} \cdot 2^{39} = 2^{59}$. Since 20 expressions of key bits are recovered, the full key recovery attack runs in time 2^{60}. Using the Formula (3.3), the success probability of the attack is expected to be more than 87.7%.

By imposing two extra bits of IV to be zeros, $e.g.$, $v_{47} = v_{50} = 0$, two less expressions of the key need to be guessed, and the time complexity of the attack can be cut down to $2^{18} \cdot 2^{39} = 2^{57}$, keeping the data complexity unchanged. After recovering the 18 expressions of the key, we can recover the other two key expressions, at cost of additional but negligible time and data. The success probability of the attack is expected to be more than 92.5%. To the best of our knowledge, this is the best known initialization analysis of `Grain v1` in the single key setting. The results are summarized in Table 5, with the comparisons of the previous differential attacks. Note here that this table does not include the distinguishing, related key or weak-key attacks.

Table 5. Differential cryptanalysis on `Grain v1` in the single key setting

Type	Rounds	Time	Data	Gain	Source
partial key recovery	104/160	2^{35}	2^{35}	1 bit	[KMN10]
full key recovery	105/160	2^{71}	-	9 bits	[Ban16]
partial key recovery	110/160	2^{47}	-	15 bits	[MTQ17]
partial key recovery	120/160	$2^{42.75}$	-	12 bits	[LG19]
partial key recovery	125/160	2^{57}	2^{52}	20 bits	Section 6.2
full key recovery	125/160	2^{60}	2^{52}	20 bits	Section 6.2

7 Discussions and Open Problems

Here we would like to discuss why our theoretical value is more accurate than that of the DLCT tool [BDKW19] and why the gap behaves different for `Ascon`, `Serpent` and `Grain v1`. As a general case, it has been proven in Theorem 4 that the theoretical value given by Algorithm 3 is accurate, under the assumption that the variables of each round are independent. The number of transitional variables in each round is at most twice the number of updated bits. Thus the assumption is competitive with the traditional assumption of differential-linear cryptanalysis, $i.e.$, round independence within E_0 and E_1 (see also [BLN17, BDKW19]). For a concrete case, especially in the case of low-weight differences and linear masks, a much weaker assumption might be required in the DATF techniques. Compared with round independence assumption, our assumption for `Ascon` and `Serpent` is weaker, which leads to more accurate estimation.

When applying Algorithm 3 to 3- and 4-round `Serpent`, we have two observations: (1) there are no isolated variables in the ATF of the parity e, that is, Line 12 of Algorithm 3 runs only once; (2) the number of transitional variables is small. The property (1) avoids using the piling-up lemma in Line 12 of Algorithm 3 and makes the assumption become a weaker one. The property (2) makes the assumption easy to be satisfied. They are the reasons that our value is extremely close to the experimental value and why we conjecture that the gap between the experimental value and our estimate is generated by the statistical error.

For the approximation of 4-round `Ascon`, Line 12 of Algorithm 3 runs twice, and the number of transitional variables is relatively small. This makes the assumption more valid, because a transitional variable in $e - e_l$ relies on the transitional variables of the expression obtained by substituting Q into e_l. This may produce an inaccurate estimation when using the piling-up lemma in Line 12. We conjecture this is the reason why there is still a gap in the case of `Ascon`.

For the application to `Grain v1`, it is much more complicated. Algorithm 2 rather than Algorithm 3 is applied in the key-dependent setting. For 120 rounds, Line 5 of Algorithm 2 runs twice, that is, the piling-up lemma in Line 5 is used once. For 125 rounds, Line 5 of Algorithm 2 runs three times, that is, the piling-up lemma in Line 5 is used twice. These produce a bigger gap between the assumption and the truth. Moreover, a significant difference between the theoretical analysis and experimental evaluation of the 125-round bias is the number of conditional equations, *i.e.*, 6 equations on the internal bits for the former and 23 conditions in the key and IV bits for the latter.

To conclude, the less the frequency of using the piling-up lemma and the smaller the number of transitional variables related to the approximation, the more accurate the theoretical estimation of its bias would be.

Usage and Limitation. The underlying idea of the DATF techniques is simple and easy implemented in symbolic computation software, *e.g.*, SageMath. All the algorithms are practical for almost iterated cipher without using addition operations reduced to a moderate number of rounds, *e.g.*, `Ascon` reduced to 4–5 out of 12 rounds, `Serpent` reduced to 4–6 out of 32 rounds, and `Grain v1` reduced to 125 out of 160 rounds. The running time ranges from a few seconds to dozens of minutes, for calculating the bias of one differential-linear or differential trail in SageMath. The techniques are superior to the DLCT in both the accuracy and the length of the trail, which has at least been illustrated in the above instances, and the new techniques proposed in this paper thus can be seen, at least, as a complementary analytical tool to the existing theory of differential-linear cryptanalysis as well as differential cryptanalysis. It seems that the DATF techniques are suitable for analysis of low-weight differential-linear or differential trails and not suitable for linear trails. Thus using the DATF together with the classical differential-linear cryptanalytic methods might be a good choice.

Open Problems and Future Work. In the future, it is worthy of working on the applications of the DATF techniques to more cryptographic primitives. The techniques can be applied to most iterated ciphers but not to ARX ciphers that use addition operations. A natural question is how to adjust the techniques applicable to a cipher using additions. It is also worthy of comparative study between the DLCT and DATF techniques. A main question raised is whether the DATF techniques are more efficient and more accurate than the DLCT tool in the general case. Though our estimates of the bias in the differential-linear approximation are close to the experimental values, there are still some gaps in some cases. These cases happen when the assumption is not satisfied. It is worthy of further study of the DATF techniques as well as exploration of new methods, for analysis of the differential-linear bias under weaker assumptions or without assumptions.

8   Conclusion

In this paper, we have shown a new theory of differential-linear cryptanalysis from an algebraic perspective, including the estimation of the differential-linear bias and techniques for key recovery. As illustrations, we applied it to the CAESAR finalist Ascon, the AES finalist Serpent, and the eSTREAM finalist Grain v1, and gained the most accurate estimation of the bias as well as the best known differential-linear or differential attacks. In particular, the results in this paper update the cryptanalysis of Serpent with one more round. Our technique for key recovery is an organic combination of distinguisher searching and key guessing, and thus outperforms the previous key recovery in differential-linear cryptanalysis. We believe that this new cryptanalytic tool is useful in both cryptanalysis and design of symmetric cryptosystems.

Acknowledgments. We are grateful to the anonymous reviewers of this manuscript for their valuable comments, and thank the authors of [DIK08, Lu15] for helpful discussions on their papers. We thank Anne Canteaut for her useful and helpful suggestions on our submission. We would also like to thank Shichang Wang for checking parts of the results of this paper.

References

[ABK98] Anderson, R., Biham, E., Knudsen, L.R.: Serpent: a proposal for the advanced encryption standard. NIST AES Proposal (1998). https://www.cl.cam.ac.uk/~rja14/serpent.html

[Ban14] Banik, S.: Some insights into differential cryptanalysis of Grain v1. In: Susilo, W., Mu, Y. (eds.) ACISP 2014. LNCS, vol. 8544, pp. 34–49. Springer, Cham (2014). https://doi.org/10.1007/978-3-319-08344-5_3

[Ban16] Banik, S.: Conditional differential cryptanalysis of 105 round Grain v1. Cryptograph. Commun. 8(1), 113–137 (2016)

[BB93] Ben-Aroya, I., Biham, E.: Differential cryptanalysis of Lucifer. In: Stinson, D.R. (ed.) CRYPTO 1993. LNCS, vol. 773, pp. 187–199. Springer, Heidelberg (1994). https://doi.org/10.1007/3-540-48329-2_17

[BDK01] Biham, E., Dunkelman, O., Keller, N.: Linear cryptanalysis of reduced round Serpent. In: Matsui, M. (ed.) FSE 2001. LNCS, vol. 2355, pp. 16–27. Springer, Heidelberg (2002). https://doi.org/10.1007/3-540-45473-X_2

[BDK02] Biham, E., Dunkelman, O., Keller, N.: Enhancing differential-linear cryptanalysis. In: Zheng, Y. (ed.) ASIACRYPT 2002. LNCS, vol. 2501, pp. 254–266. Springer, Heidelberg (2002). https://doi.org/10.1007/3-540-36178-2_16

[BDK03] Biham, E., Dunkelman, O., Keller, N.: Differential-linear cryptanalysis of Serpent. In: Johansson, T. (ed.) FSE 2003. LNCS, vol. 2887, pp. 9–21. Springer, Heidelberg (2003). https://doi.org/10.1007/978-3-540-39887-5_2

[BDKW19] Bar-On, A., Dunkelman, O., Keller, N., Weizman, A.: DLCT: a new tool for differential-linear cryptanalysis. In: Ishai, Y., Rijmen, V. (eds.) EURO-CRYPT 2019. LNCS, vol. 11476, pp. 313–342. Springer, Cham (2019). https://doi.org/10.1007/978-3-030-17653-2_11

[BDPV11] Bertoni, G., Daemen, J., Peeters, M.,Van Assche, G.: The Keccak reference. http://keccak.noekeon.org, January 2011. Version 3.0

[BLN17] Blondeau, C., Leander, G., Nyberg, K.: Differential-linear cryptanalysis revisited. J. Cryptol. 30(3), 859–888 (2017)

[BLT20] Beierle, C., Leander, G., Todo, Y.: Improved differential-linear attacks with applications to ARX ciphers. In: Micciancio, D., Ristenpart, T. (eds.) CRYPTO 2020. LNCS, vol. 12172, pp. 329–358. Springer, Cham (2020). https://doi.org/10.1007/978-3-030-56877-1_12

[BP18] Biham, E., Perle, S.: Conditional linear cryptanalysis - cryptanalysis of DES with less than 2^{42} complexity. IACR Trans. Symmetric Cryptol. 2018(3), 215–264 (2018)

[CKL+19] Canteaut, A., et al.: On the differential-linear connectivity table of vectorial Boolean functions. CoRR, abs/1908.07445 (2019)

[CKW19] Canteaut, A., Kölsch, L., Wiemer, F.: Observations on the DLCT and absolute indicators. IACR Cryptol. ePrint Arch. 2019, 848 (2019)

[DEMS15] Dobraunig, C., Eichlseder, M., Mendel, F., Schläffer, M.: Cryptanalysis of ASCON. In: Nyberg, K. (ed.) CT-RSA 2015. LNCS, vol. 9048, pp. 371–387. Springer, Cham (2015). https://doi.org/10.1007/978-3-319-16715-2_20

[DEMS16] Dobraunig, C., Eichlseder, M., Mendel, F., Schläffer, M.: Ascon v1.2. Submission to the CAESAR Competition (2016)

[DEMS19] Dobraunig, C., Eichlseder, M.,Mendel, F., Schläffer, M.: Ascon v1.2. Submission to the NIST Lightweight Cryptography competition (2019)

[DIK08] Dunkelman, O., Indesteege, S., Keller, N.: A differential-linear attack on 12-round Serpent. In: Chowdhury, D.R., Rijmen, V., Das, A. (eds.) INDOCRYPT 2008. LNCS, vol. 5365, pp. 308–321. Springer, Heidelberg (2008). https://doi.org/10.1007/978-3-540-89754-5_24

[HJMM08] Hell, M., Johansson, T., Maximov, A., Meier, W.: The Grain family of stream ciphers. In: Robshaw, M., Billet, O. (eds.) New Stream Cipher Designs. LNCS, vol. 4986, pp. 179–190. Springer, Heidelberg (2008). https://doi.org/10.1007/978-3-540-68351-3_14

[KMN10] Knellwolf, S., Meier, W., Naya-Plasencia, M.: Conditional differential cryptanalysis of NLFSR-based cryptosystems. In: Abe, M. (ed.) ASIACRYPT 2010. LNCS, vol. 6477, pp. 130–145. Springer, Heidelberg (2010). https://doi.org/10.1007/978-3-642-17373-8_8

[LDW17] Li, Z., Dong, X., Wang, X.: Conditional cube attack on round-reduced ASCON. IACR Trans. Symmetric Cryptol. 2017(1), 175–202 (2017)

[Leu16] Leurent, G.: Improved differential-linear cryptanalysis of 7-round Chaskey with partitioning. In: Fischlin, M., Coron, J.-S. (eds.) EUROCRYPT 2016. LNCS, vol. 9665, pp. 344–371. Springer, Heidelberg (2016). https://doi.org/10.1007/978-3-662-49890-3_14

[LG19] Li, J.-Z., Guan, J.: Advanced conditional differential attack on Grain-like stream cipher and application on Grain v1. IET Informat. Secur. 13(2), 141–148 (2019)

[LGZL09] Liu, Z., Gu, D., Zhang, J., Li, W.: Differential-multiple linear cryptanalysis. In: Bao, F., Yung, M., Lin, D., Jing, J. (eds.) Inscrypt 2009. LNCS, vol. 6151, pp. 35–49. Springer, Heidelberg (2010). https://doi.org/10.1007/978-3-642-16342-5_3

[LH94] Langford, S.K., Hellman, M.E.: Differential-linear cryptanalysis. In: Desmedt, Y.G. (ed.) CRYPTO 1994. LNCS, vol. 839, pp. 17–25. Springer, Heidelberg (1994). https://doi.org/10.1007/3-540-48658-5_3

[Lu12] Lu, J.: A methodology for differential-linear cryptanalysis and its applications - (extended abstract). In: Canteaut, A. (ed.) FSE 2012. LNCS, vol. 7549, pp. 69–89. (2012). https://doi.org/10.1007/s10623-014-9985-x

[Lu15] Jiqiang, L.: A methodology for differential-linear cryptanalysis and its applications. Des. Codes Cryptogr. **77**(1), 11–48 (2015)

[MTQ17] Ma, Z., Tian, T., Qi, W.-F.: Improved conditional differential attacks on Grain v1. IET Informat. Secur. **11**(1), 46–53 (2017)

[Sel08] Selçuk, A.A.: On probability of success in linear and differential cryptanalysis. J. Cryptology **21**(1), 131–147 (2008)

[TIM+18] Todo, Y., Isobe, T., Meier, W., Aoki, K., Zhang, B.: Fast correlation attack revisited - cryptanalysis on full Grain-128a, Grain-128, and Grain-v1. In: Shacham, H., Boldyreva, A. (eds.) CRYPTO 2018. LNCS, Part II, vol. 10992, pp. 129–159. Springer, Cham (2018). https://doi.org/10.1007/978-3-319-96881-0_5

Meet-in-the-Middle Attacks Revisited: Key-Recovery, Collision, and Preimage Attacks

Xiaoyang Dong[1], Jialiang Hua[1(✉)], Siwei Sun[2,3(✉)], Zheng Li[4,7],
Xiaoyun Wang[1,5,6], and Lei Hu[2,3]

[1] Institute for Advanced Study, BNRist, Tsinghua University, Beijing, China
{xiaoyangdong,huajl18,xiaoyunwang}@tsinghua.edu.cn
[2] State Key Laboratory of Information Security,
Institute of Information Engineering, Chinese Academy of Sciences, Beijing, China
[3] University of Chinese Academy of Sciences, Beijing, China
sunsiwei@ucas.ac.cn
[4] Faculty of Information Technology, Beijing University of Technology, Beijing, China
lizhengcn@bjut.edu.cn
[5] Key Laboratory of Cryptologic Technology and Information Security,
Ministry of Education, Shandong University, Jinan, China
[6] School of Cyber Science and Technology, Shandong University, Qingdao, China
[7] Beijing Key Laboratory of Trusted Computing, Beijing University of Technology,
Beijing, China

Abstract. At EUROCRYPT 2021, Bao et al. proposed an automatic method for systematically exploring the configuration space of meet-in-the-middle (MITM) preimage attacks. We further extend it into a constraint-based framework for finding exploitable MITM characteristics in the context of key-recovery and collision attacks by taking the subtle peculiarities of both scenarios into account. Moreover, to perform attacks based on MITM characteristics with nonlinear constrained neutral words, which have not been seen before, we present a procedure for deriving the solution spaces of neutral words without solving the corresponding nonlinear equations or increasing the overall time complexities of the attack. We apply our method to concrete symmetric-key primitives, including SKINNY, ForkSkinny, Romulus-H, Saturnin, Grøstl, WHIRLPOOL, and hashing modes with AES-256. As a result, we identify the first 23-round key-recovery attack on SKINNY-n-$3n$ and the first 24-round key-recovery attack on ForkSkinny-n-$3n$ in the single-key model. Moreover, improved (pseudo) preimage or collision attacks on round-reduced WHIRLPOOL, Grøstl, and hashing modes with AES-256 are obtained. In particular, employing the new representation of the AES key schedule due to Leurent and Pernot (EUROCRYPT 2021), we identify the first preimage attack on 10-round AES-256 hashing.

Keywords: Meet-in-the-Middle · Three-subset MITM · Preimage attack · Collision attack · AES-256 · MILP

The full version of the paper is available at https://eprint.iacr.org/2021/427.

© International Association for Cryptologic Research 2021
T. Malkin and C. Peikert (Eds.): CRYPTO 2021, LNCS 12827, pp. 278–308, 2021.
https://doi.org/10.1007/978-3-030-84252-9_10

1   Introduction

The meet-in-the-middle (MITM) approach is a generic technique for cryptanalysis of symmetric-key primitives, which was first introduced by Diffie and Hellman in 1977 for attacking block ciphers [18]. Many variants of this technique can be found in the literature [10,19–21,25]. Its basic idea is best illustrated by performing an MITM attack on a block cipher deliberately made susceptible to this type of attacks. Let $E_K(\cdot)$ be a block cipher whose block size is n-bit such that $C = E_K(P) = F_{K_2}(F_{K_1}(P))$, where $K = K_1\|K_2$, and K_1 and K_2 are independent key materials. Therefore, for a given pair of plaintext-ciphertext pair (P, C), the intermediate value V can be computed independently as $F_{K_1}(P)$ and $F_{K_2}^{-1}(C)$ with independent guesses of K_1 and K_2. The correct key guess necessarily satisfies $F_{K_1}(P) = F_{K_2}^{-1}(C)$. Therefore, by searching collisions on the intermediate values computed from P and C, one can reduce the search space from $2^{|K|} = 2^{|K_1|+|K_2|}$ to $2^{|K_1|+|K_2|-n}$ with time complexity $2^{|K_1|} + 2^{|K_2|}$. The remaining key space with $2^{|K_1|+|K_2|-n}$ candidates can be tested against several known plaintext-ciphertext pairs to identify the unique secret key.

However, in practice, it is rare that a target cipher can be clearly separated into two independent halves as the above doubly cascaded F with independent key materials. When a clear separation into two independent chunks is not possible, a variant of the basic MITM strategy (known as three-subset MITM attack) is available. This method was originally proposed by Bogdanov and Rechberger [12], applied to many ciphers [12,35,47,51], and was well summarized by Isobe [33]. Again, let us briefly demonstrate this technique on an ill-designed example with respect the three-subset MITM attack. Let $E_K(\cdot)$ be a block cipher whose block size is n-bit such that it can be divided into three chunks as $C = E_K(P) = H_{K_3\|K_2}(G_{K_1\|K_2\|K_3}(F_{K_1\|K_2}(P)))$, where $K = K_1\|K_2\|K_3$ and K_1, K_2, K_3 are independent. Moreover, some m-bit ($m < n$) information of a state value inside G can be partially computed along the forward direction from $F_{K_1\|K_2}(P)$ without the knowledge of K_3, or computed along the backward direction from $H_{K_3\|K_2}^{-1}(C)$ without the knowledge of K_1. The three-subset MITM attack partitions the search space with $2^{|K|} = 2^{|K_1|+|K_2|+|K_3|}$ elements into $2^{|K_2|}$ subspaces of equal size according to the value of $|K_2|$. For each subspace, where the value of $|K_2|$ is fixed, one can perform the basic MITM attack with partial match to reduce the size of the search space from $2^{|K_1|+|K_3|}$ to $2^{|K_1|+|K_3|-m}$ with time complexity $2^{|K_1|} + 2^{|K_3|}$. Under our terminology, which will be introduced in Sect. 2, one run of the basic version of the MITM attack with a fixed K_2 is called one MITM *episode*. To identify the correct key, $2^{|K_2|}$ episodes have to be performed. Therefore, the overall time complexity can be estimated as $2^{|K_2|}(2^{|K_1|} + 2^{|K_3|} + 2^{|K_1|+|K_3|-m})$. This technique has been applied to many block ciphers [10,12,33,34,47,51].

Although the MITM technique was originally introduced for attacking block ciphers, its development seems to be largely cultivated and promoted in the cryptanalysis of hash functions. In 2008, Sasaki and Aoki successfully achieved preimage attacks on several full versions of HAVAL by combining the MITM approach with the local collision technique [48]. From then on, many MITM preimage attacks together with their enhancements and improvements targeting various hash functions emerged in the literature [1,2,4,6,30,31,40,46,49,56,57]. Along the way, several important techniques arise which significantly enhance and enrich the MITM methodology, including the *splice-and-cut* technique [3], the concept of *initial structure* [49], *(indirect-)partial matching* [3,49], *sieve-in-the-middle* [15] and *match-box* technique [27]. Some techniques are formalized as *bicliques* [11,39] and further perceived from differential views [26,40]. These developments in the context of cryptanalysis of hash functions were finally found to be applicable in the MITM attacks on block ciphers. In [58], Wei et al. first applied the splice-and-cut technique to the MITM attacks on block ciphers by connecting the plaintext and ciphertext states with encryption or decryption oracles.

Despite that the principle of how to combine all these techniques in MITM attacks is quite clear, to actually apply them in practice effectively and efficiently is complicated, tedious, and error-prone. Recently, (semi) automatic tools are developed to explore the configuration space of MITM attacks in a more systematic approach. In [47], Sasaki proposed an MILP-based method to search for optimal independent key bits used in the three-subset MITM key-recovery attacks on GIFT [5]. However, Sasaki's model is not general enough and the possible positions of neutral words are prefixed. At EUROCRYPT 2021, the MITM preimage attacks on AES-like hashing was throughly modeled as constrained optimization problems which were solved with MILP techniques [6]. This approach outperforms previous work done manually, and many attacks on AES-like hashing [41,46,59] are shown to have room to be further improved. However, this method is described in a way specific to preimage attacks and do not translate directly to MITM-based key-recovery or collision attacks.

Our Contribution. We describe the MITM attacks[1] in a unified way as MITM attacks on the so-called *closed computation path*. This view has been long known to our community. Nevertheless, we believe that our treatment is more formal and general. In particular, by introducing some new concepts, we make the description of MITM attacks more expressive and accurate.

Then, we focus our attention on MITM key-recovery and collision attacks on block ciphers and hash functions. We identify the peculiarities specific to these scenarios and show how to deal with them automatically. For the MITM characteristics employed in key-recovery attacks, the degrees of freedom originated from the states in the key schedule data path must not be depleted, while the degrees of freedom originated from the encryption data path must be used up. Also, when searching for candidate configurations for the MITM key-recovery attacks, we should avoid those configurations that lead to attacks requiring the full codebook. We apply our methods to concrete block ciphers SKINNY and ForkSkinny. and we identify the first 23-round attack on SKINNY-n-$3n$ in the single-key model, penetrating one more round than the designers have

---

[1] We do not consider the Demirci-Selçuk MITM attacks [16,17,24,54] in this paper, which is a quite different technique.

expected: *We conclude that meet-in-the-middle attack may work up to at most 22 rounds* [9, Sect. 4.2, page 22]. Interestingly, the characteristics we employed in these attacks impose nontrivial constraints on the neutral words from the key states, which has not been seen before. For collision attacks, they are based on a generalized version of the t-cell partial target preimage attacks, where the words of the target value fulfill t (word-oriented) equations.

Finally, we perform MITM preimage and collision attacks on concrete hash functions (e.g., Romulus-H [36], Saturnin [14], WHIRLPOOL [8], and Grøstl [28]). In the attacks on certain hash functions, we encounter some special MITM characteristics where the neutral words are *nonlinearly* constrained. In previous work, the neutral words are linearly constrained and thus the solution space of the neutral words can be obtained efficiently by solving the corresponding system of linear equations. For nonlinear equations, this approach would significantly increase the complexities. We propose a technique that is applicable to both the non-linearly and linearly constrained neutral words, overcoming this difficulty without increasing the time complexity of the attacks. Based on this technique, we improve the (pseudo) preimage attacks on round-reduced Grøstl-256 and its output transformation by one round. For collision attacks, the first 6-round classical collision attack on WHIRLPOOL is provided, breaking a 10-year record for collision attacks on WHIRLPOOL in the classical setting. Also, we give the first 6-round collision attack and 8-round collision attack on the output transformations of Grøstl-256 and Grøstl-512, respectively. Interestingly, we notice that all competitive collision attacks on these AES-like hashings are based on the rebound technique [44]. In addition, we offer the first third-party cryptanalysis of Saturnin-Hash [14], a second round candidate of the NIST LWC project. A summary of our results on concrete primitives is given in Table 1 and Table 2. The source code of the paper is available at https://github.com/siweisun/mitm-attacks-revisited.

Table 1. Single-key attacks (SK) on SKINNY-n-$3n$ and ForkSkinny-n-$3n$, where ID and DS-MITM denote impossible differential and Demirci-Selçuk MITM attacks, respectively.

SKINNY							
Version	Rounds	Data	Time	Memory	Attack	Setting	Ref.
64-192	22	$2^{47.84}$	$2^{183.97}$	$2^{74.84}$	ID	SK	[55]
	23	2^{52}	2^{188}	2^4	MITM	SK	Sect. 4
128-384	22	2^{96}	$2^{382.46}$	$2^{330.99}$	DS-MITM	SK	[54]
	22	$2^{92.22}$	$2^{373.48}$	$2^{147.22}$	ID	SK	[55]
	23	2^{104}	2^{376}	2^8	MITM	SK	Sect. 4
ForkSkinny							
64-192	24	2^{52}	2^{188}	2^4	MITM	SK	Full Ver. [22]
128-384	24	2^{104}	2^{376}	2^8	MITM	SK	Full Ver. [22]
128-256	24	$2^{122.5}$	$2^{124.5}$	$2^{97.5}$	ID	RK	[7]
	26	2^{127}	$2^{250.3}$	2^{160}	ID	RK	[7]

Table 2. A Summary of the results. Note that we only consider preimage and collision attacks. Distinguishing attacks [13, 37, 42, 50] are not included. Also, note that the complexity of the preimage attack on `Romulus-H` is 2^{248}. This attack does not break 23-round `Romulus-H` since the designers only claim 128-bit security. However, this complexity is better than an exhaustive search, whose complexity is 2^{256}. Similarly, `Saturnin` claims only 224-bit security.

WHIRLPOOL						
Target	Attack	Rounds	Time	Memory	Setting	Ref.
Hash function	Collision	4	2^{120}	2^{16}	Classic	[44]
		5	2^{120}	2^{64}	Classic	[29,42]
		6	2^{228}	-	Quantum	[32]
		6	2^{248}	2^{248}	Classic	Sect. 6.2
	Preimage	5	2^{504}	2^{8}	Classic	[46]
		5	$2^{481.5}$	2^{64}		[59]
		6	2^{481}	2^{256}		[52]
Compression function	(Semi-) free-start	5	2^{120}	2^{16}	Classic	[44]
		7	2^{184}	2^{8}		[42]
		8	2^{120}	2^{8}		[52]
Grøstl-256						
Hash function	Collision	3	2^{64}	-	Classic	[53]
		5	2^{120}	2^{64}		[45]
	Pseudo preimage	5	$2^{244.8}$	2^{230}	Classic	[59]
		6	2^{252}	2^{251}		Full Ver. [22]
Compression function	Semi-free-start	6	2^{112}	2^{64}	Classic	[53]
Output transformation	Preimage	5	2^{206}	2^{48}	Classic	[59]
		6	2^{240}	2^{152}		Full Ver. [22]
	Collision	6	2^{124}	2^{124}	Classic	Full Ver. [22]
Grøstl-512						
Hash function	Collision	5	2^{240}	2^{64}	Quantum	[23]
Compression function		7	2^{152}	2^{56}	Classic	[50]
Output transformation		8	2^{248}	2^{248}	Classic	Full Ver. [22]
Hash function	Pseudo preimage	8	$2^{507.3}$	2^{507}	Classic	[59]
Saturnin-Hash						
Compression function	Preimage	7	2^{208}	2^{48}	Classic	Full Ver. [22]
Hash function		7	2^{232}	2^{48}		
SKINNY-128-384, Romulus-H, and AES hashing mode						
SKINNY-128-384-DM/MMO	Preimage	23	2^{120}	2^{8}	Classic	Full Ver. [22]
Romulus-H		23	2^{248}	2^{8}		Full Ver. [22]
AES-256		9	2^{120}	2^{8}		[6]
AES-256		10	2^{120}	2^{56}		Full Ver. [22]
Romulus-H compression function	Free-start	23	2^{124}	2^{124}		Full Ver. [22]

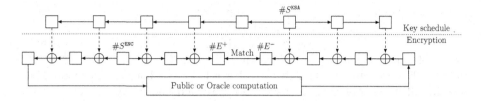

Fig. 1. A high-level overview of the MITM attacks

2   A Formal Description of the MITM Technique

We now formally describe the MITM attacks with the notations introduced by Bao et al.'s work [6] in a more unified way. We encourage the readers to carefully go through this section since it not only serves as a recall of Bao et al.'s work, but also introduces some new terminologies that enhance the expressiveness and accuracy of the descriptions of MITM attacks.

Given a computation path that forms a "closed loop", the ultimate goal of the meet-in-the-middle attack is to find a particular value for some intermediate states with which the values for all the states involved in the computation path can be determined, such that the values are compatible with the whole computation path (there are no conflicts between the values due to the involved computation). Let us descend from the abstract highland and consider the closed computation path shown in Fig. 1. The upper segment of the computation path constitutes an iterative block cipher with an iterative key schedule, and we assume that the states involved in the encryption data path and key schedule data path contains n and $\bar{n}$ w-bit words respectively, which are typically visualized as rectangles with n and $\bar{n}$ cells, respectively. The lower segment of the computation path can be arbitrary. In our context, it can be an oracle of the block cipher appearing in the upper segment of the computation path when we consider an MITM key-recovery attack, or a simple exclusive-or of a given target value when we consider preimage attacks. Before we can perform an MITM attack on the computation path, a configuration or an MITM *characteristic* has to be identified.

MITM Characteristics and Their Visualization. The MITM attack entails the identification of several special states: the starting state $\#S^{\mathrm{ENC}}$ (see Fig. 1) in the encryption data path, the starting state $\#S^{\mathrm{KSA}}$ in the key schedule data path, the ending state $\#E^+$ for the forward computation (the computation path starting from $(\#S^{\mathrm{ENC}}, \#S^{\mathrm{KSA}})$ leading to $\#E^+$), and the ending state $\#E^-$ for the backward computation (the computation path starting from $(\#S^{\mathrm{ENC}}, \#S^{\mathrm{KSA}})$ leading to $\#E^-$). Moreover, the cells of $(\#S^{\mathrm{ENC}}, \#S^{\mathrm{KSA}})$ are partitioned into different subsets with different meanings. Let $\mathcal{B}^{\mathrm{ENC}}$, $\mathcal{B}^{\mathrm{KSA}}$, $\mathcal{R}^{\mathrm{ENC}}$, $\mathcal{R}^{\mathrm{KSA}}$, $\mathcal{M}^+$, and $\mathcal{M}^-$ be some ordered subsets of $\mathcal{N} = \{0, 1, \cdots, n-1\}$ or $\overline{\mathcal{N}} = \{0, 1, \cdots, \bar{n}-1\}$ such that $\mathcal{B}^{\mathrm{ENC}} \cap \mathcal{R}^{\mathrm{ENC}} = \emptyset$, $\mathcal{B}^{\mathrm{KSA}} \cap \mathcal{R}^{\mathrm{KSA}} = \emptyset$, $\mathcal{G}^{\mathrm{ENC}} = \mathcal{N} - \mathcal{B}^{\mathrm{ENC}} \cup \mathcal{R}^{\mathrm{ENC}}$ and $\mathcal{G}^{\mathrm{KSA}} = \overline{\mathcal{N}} - \mathcal{B}^{\mathrm{KSA}} \cup \mathcal{R}^{\mathrm{KSA}}$. We will use these index sets to reference the cells of the states. For example, for a 16-cell state $\#S$ and $\mathcal{M}^+ = [0,1,3]$, we have $\#S[\mathcal{M}^+] = \#S[0,1,3] = (\#S[0], \#S[1], \#S[3])$.

The cells $(\#S^{\mathrm{ENC}}[\mathcal{B}^{\mathrm{ENC}}], \#S^{\mathrm{KSA}}[\mathcal{B}^{\mathrm{KSA}}])$, visualized as ■ cells, are called neutral words of the forward computation, and the cells $(\#S^{\mathrm{ENC}}[\mathcal{R}^{\mathrm{ENC}}], \#S^{\mathrm{KSA}}[\mathcal{R}^{\mathrm{KSA}}])$, visualized as ■ cells, are called neutral words of the backward computation. The initial degrees of freedom for the forward and backward computation are defined as $\lambda^+ = |\mathcal{B}^{\mathrm{ENC}}| + |\mathcal{B}^{\mathrm{KSA}}|$ and $\lambda^- = |\mathcal{R}^{\mathrm{ENC}}| + |\mathcal{R}^{\mathrm{KSA}}|$ respectively, that is, the numbers of ■ cells and ■ cells in the starting states. In addition, $E^+[\mathcal{M}^+]$ are visualized as ■ cells, and $E^-[\mathcal{M}^-]$ are visualized as ■ cells. Finally, $\#S^{\mathrm{ENC}}[\mathcal{G}^{\mathrm{ENC}}]$ and $\#S^{\mathrm{KSA}}[\mathcal{G}^{\mathrm{KSA}}]$ are visualized as ■ cells.

We then define a sequence of l^+ functions $\boldsymbol{\pi}^+ = (\pi_1^+, \cdots, \pi_{l^+}^+)$ whose values can be computed with the knowledge of the ■ cells $(\#S^{\mathrm{ENC}}[\mathcal{G}^{\mathrm{ENC}}], \#S^{\mathrm{KSA}}[\mathcal{G}^{\mathrm{KSA}}])$ and ■ cells $(\#S^{\mathrm{ENC}}[\mathcal{B}^{\mathrm{ENC}}], \#S^{\mathrm{KSA}}[\mathcal{B}^{\mathrm{KSA}}])$ in the starting states, where

$$\pi_i^+ : \mathbb{F}_2^{w \cdot (|\mathcal{G}^{\mathrm{ENC}}| + |\mathcal{G}^{\mathrm{KSA}}| + |\mathcal{B}^{\mathrm{ENC}}| + |\mathcal{B}^{\mathrm{KSA}}|)} \to \mathbb{F}_2^w$$

is a function mapping $(\#S^{\mathrm{ENC}}[\mathcal{G}^{\mathrm{ENC}}], \#S^{\mathrm{KSA}}[\mathcal{G}^{\mathrm{KSA}}], \#S^{\mathrm{ENC}}[\mathcal{B}^{\mathrm{ENC}}], \#S^{\mathrm{KSA}}[\mathcal{B}^{\mathrm{KSA}}])$ to a w-bit word $\pi_i^+(\#S^{\mathrm{ENC}}[\mathcal{G}^{\mathrm{ENC}}], \#S^{\mathrm{KSA}}[\mathcal{G}^{\mathrm{KSA}}], \#S^{\mathrm{ENC}}[\mathcal{B}^{\mathrm{ENC}}], \#S^{\mathrm{KSA}}[\mathcal{B}^{\mathrm{KSA}}])$. Similarly, we define a sequence of l^- functions $\boldsymbol{\pi}^- = (\pi_1^-, \cdots, \pi_{l^-}^-)$ whose values can be computed with the knowledge of the ■ cells $(\#S^{\mathrm{ENC}}[\mathcal{G}^{\mathrm{ENC}}], \#S^{\mathrm{KSA}}[\mathcal{G}^{\mathrm{KSA}}])$ and ■ cells $(\#S^{\mathrm{ENC}}[\mathcal{R}^{\mathrm{ENC}}], \#S^{\mathrm{KSA}}[\mathcal{R}^{\mathrm{KSA}}])$. $\boldsymbol{\pi}^+$ and $\boldsymbol{\pi}^-$ will be used to represent certain constraints on the neutral words of the forward and backward computations, respectively. A valid MITM characteristic satisfies the following property.

Property 1. For any fixed $\mathfrak{c}^+ = (a_1, \cdots, a_{l^+}) \in \mathbb{F}_2^{w \cdot l^+}$ and $\mathfrak{c}^- = (b_1, \cdots, b_{l^-}) \in \mathbb{F}_2^{w \cdot l^-}$, when the cells $(\#S^{\mathrm{ENC}}[\mathcal{G}^{\mathrm{ENC}}], \#S^{\mathrm{KSA}}[\mathcal{G}^{\mathrm{KSA}}])$ are fixed to an arbitrary constant, and the neutral words for the forward computation and backward computation paths fulfill the following systems of equations:

$$\begin{cases} \pi_1^+(\#S^{\mathrm{ENC}}[\mathcal{G}^{\mathrm{ENC}}], \#S^{\mathrm{KSA}}[\mathcal{G}^{\mathrm{KSA}}], \#S^{\mathrm{ENC}}[\mathcal{B}^{\mathrm{ENC}}], \#S^{\mathrm{KSA}}[\mathcal{B}^{\mathrm{KSA}}]) = a_1 \\ \pi_2^+(\#S^{\mathrm{ENC}}[\mathcal{G}^{\mathrm{ENC}}], \#S^{\mathrm{KSA}}[\mathcal{G}^{\mathrm{KSA}}], \#S^{\mathrm{ENC}}[\mathcal{B}^{\mathrm{ENC}}], \#S^{\mathrm{KSA}}[\mathcal{B}^{\mathrm{KSA}}]) = a_2 \\ \qquad \cdots \quad \cdots \\ \pi_{l^+}^+(\#S^{\mathrm{ENC}}[\mathcal{G}^{\mathrm{ENC}}], \#S^{\mathrm{KSA}}[\mathcal{G}^{\mathrm{KSA}}], \#S^{\mathrm{ENC}}[\mathcal{B}^{\mathrm{ENC}}], \#S^{\mathrm{KSA}}[\mathcal{B}^{\mathrm{KSA}}]) = a_{l^+} \end{cases} \quad (1)$$

and

$$\begin{cases} \pi_1^-(\#S^{\mathrm{ENC}}[\mathcal{G}^{\mathrm{ENC}}], \#S^{\mathrm{KSA}}[\mathcal{G}^{\mathrm{KSA}}], \#S^{\mathrm{ENC}}[\mathcal{R}^{\mathrm{ENC}}], \#S^{\mathrm{KSA}}[\mathcal{R}^{\mathrm{KSA}}]) = b_1 \\ \pi_2^-(\#S^{\mathrm{ENC}}[\mathcal{G}^{\mathrm{ENC}}], \#S^{\mathrm{KSA}}[\mathcal{G}^{\mathrm{KSA}}], \#S^{\mathrm{ENC}}[\mathcal{R}^{\mathrm{ENC}}], \#S^{\mathrm{KSA}}[\mathcal{R}^{\mathrm{KSA}}]) = b_2 \\ \qquad \cdots \quad \cdots \\ \pi_{l^-}^-(\#S^{\mathrm{ENC}}[\mathcal{G}^{\mathrm{ENC}}], \#S^{\mathrm{KSA}}[\mathcal{G}^{\mathrm{KSA}}], \#S^{\mathrm{ENC}}[\mathcal{R}^{\mathrm{ENC}}], \#S^{\mathrm{KSA}}[\mathcal{R}^{\mathrm{KSA}}]) = b_{l^-} \end{cases} \quad (2)$$

respectively, then the values of the cells $\#E^+[\mathcal{M}^+]$ can be derived from the starting states $(\#S^{\mathrm{ENC}}, \#S^{\mathrm{KSA}})$ along the forward computation path without the knowledge of the neutral words for the backward computation, and the values of the cells $\#E^-[\mathcal{M}^-]$ can be derived from the starting states $(\#S^{\mathrm{ENC}}, \#S^{\mathrm{KSA}})$ along the backward computation path without the knowledge of the neutral words for the forward computation. In short, computations for deriving $\#E^-[\mathcal{M}^+]$ and $\#E^-[\mathcal{M}^-]$ can be carried out independently.

Let us talk more about Property 1. For any given $(\#S^{\mathrm{ENC}}[\mathcal{G}^{\mathrm{ENC}}], \#S^{\mathrm{KSA}}[\mathcal{G}^{\mathrm{KSA}}])$ and $\mathfrak{c}^+ = (a_1, \cdots, a_{l^+})$, the solution space of $(\#S^{\mathrm{ENC}}[\mathcal{B}^{\mathrm{ENC}}], \#S^{\mathrm{KSA}}[\mathcal{B}^{\mathrm{KSA}}])$ induced by Eq. (1) is denoted by

$$\mathbb{B}(\#S^{\mathrm{ENC}}[\mathcal{G}^{\mathrm{ENC}}], \#S^{\mathrm{KSA}}[\mathcal{G}^{\mathrm{KSA}}], \mathfrak{c}^+).$$

Since there are $\lambda^+ = |\mathcal{B}^{\mathrm{ENC}}| + |\mathcal{B}^{\mathrm{KSA}}|$ w-bit variables and l^+ equations, we expect $2^{w \cdot (\lambda^+ - l^+)}$ solutions, and we call $\mathrm{DoF}^+ = \lambda^+ - l^+$ the *degrees of freedom for the forward computation*. Similarly, the solution space of $(\#S^{\mathrm{ENC}}[\mathcal{R}^{\mathrm{ENC}}], \#S^{\mathrm{KSA}}[\mathcal{R}^{\mathrm{KSA}}])$ induced by Eq. (2) is denoted by $\mathbb{R}(\#S^{\mathrm{ENC}}[\mathcal{G}^{\mathrm{ENC}}], \#S^{\mathrm{KSA}}[\mathcal{G}^{\mathrm{KSA}}], \mathfrak{c}^-)$. Since there are $\lambda^- = |\mathcal{R}^{\mathrm{ENC}}| + |\mathcal{R}^{\mathrm{KSA}}|$ w-bit variables and l^- equations, we expect $2^{w \cdot (\lambda^- - l^-)}$ solutions, and we call $\mathrm{DoF}^- = \lambda^- - l^-$ the *degrees of freedom for the backward computation*.

Let F^+ be the function computing $\#E^+[\mathcal{M}^+]$ from $(\#S^{\mathrm{ENC}}, \#S^{\mathrm{KSA}})$, that is, $\#E^+[\mathcal{M}^+]$ can be computed as

$$F^+(\#S^{\mathrm{ENC}}[\mathcal{G}^{\mathrm{ENC}}], \#S^{\mathrm{KSA}}[\mathcal{G}^{\mathrm{KSA}}], \#S^{\mathrm{ENC}}[\mathcal{B}^{\mathrm{ENC}}], \#S^{\mathrm{KSA}}[\mathcal{B}^{\mathrm{KSA}}], \#S^{\mathrm{ENC}}[\mathcal{R}^{\mathrm{ENC}}], \#S^{\mathrm{KSA}}[\mathcal{R}^{\mathrm{KSA}}]),$$

and similarly, $\#E^-[\mathcal{M}^-]$ can be computed as

$$F^-(\#S^{\mathrm{ENC}}[\mathcal{G}^{\mathrm{ENC}}], \#S^{\mathrm{KSA}}[\mathcal{G}^{\mathrm{KSA}}], \#S^{\mathrm{ENC}}[\mathcal{B}^{\mathrm{ENC}}], \#S^{\mathrm{KSA}}[\mathcal{B}^{\mathrm{KSA}}], \#S^{\mathrm{ENC}}[\mathcal{R}^{\mathrm{ENC}}], \#S^{\mathrm{KSA}}[\mathcal{R}^{\mathrm{KSA}}]).$$

Property 1 implies that

$$F^-(\alpha, x, \#S^{\mathrm{ENC}}[\mathcal{R}^{\mathrm{ENC}}], \#S^{\mathrm{KSA}}[\mathcal{R}^{\mathrm{KSA}}]) = F^-(\alpha, y, \#S^{\mathrm{ENC}}[\mathcal{R}^{\mathrm{ENC}}], \#S^{\mathrm{KSA}}[\mathcal{R}^{\mathrm{KSA}}])$$

for any given $x, y \in \mathbb{B}(\#S^{\mathrm{ENC}}[\mathcal{G}^{\mathrm{ENC}}], \#S^{\mathrm{KSA}}[\mathcal{G}^{\mathrm{KSA}}], \mathfrak{c}^+)$ and $\alpha \in \mathbb{F}_2^{|\mathcal{G}^{\mathrm{ENC}}| + |\mathcal{G}^{\mathrm{KSA}}|}$. Similarly, for any $u, v \in \mathbb{R}(\#S^{\mathrm{ENC}}[\mathcal{G}^{\mathrm{ENC}}], \#S^{\mathrm{KSA}}[\mathcal{G}^{\mathrm{KSA}}], \mathfrak{c}^-)$, we have

$$F^+(\alpha, \#S^{\mathrm{ENC}}[\mathcal{B}^{\mathrm{ENC}}], \#S^{\mathrm{KSA}}[\mathcal{B}^{\mathrm{KSA}}], u) = F^+(\alpha, \#S^{\mathrm{ENC}}[\mathcal{B}^{\mathrm{ENC}}], \#S^{\mathrm{KSA}}[\mathcal{B}^{\mathrm{KSA}}], v).$$

Consequently, for any given $(\#S^{\mathrm{ENC}}[\mathcal{G}^{\mathrm{ENC}}], \#S^{\mathrm{KSA}}[\mathcal{G}^{\mathrm{KSA}}]) = \alpha$, and $\mathfrak{c}^+$, and $\mathfrak{c}^-$, we can perform a matching process given in Algorithm 1.

In real MITM attacks, Algorithm 1 will be performed multiple times for many different α, $\mathfrak{c}^+$, and $\mathfrak{c}^-$, each time is called one MITM *episode*. Variables that remain constant within each episode are called *episodic constants*, and variables remain constant in the whole life cycle of an attack (remaining constant across different episodes) are called *global constants*. Thus *global constants* are always *episodic constants*. The ■ cells used in [6] and this work capture the episodic constants, whose values can change across different episodes.

Within each episode, $(2^w)^{\mathrm{DoF}^+}$ times of forward computation are carried out, and $(2^w)^{\mathrm{DoF}^-}$ times of backward computations are carried out, which are referred to as *forward threads* and *backward threads*. Each forward thread and backward thread *within the same episode* gives a pair of values for $(\#E^+[\mathcal{M}^+], \#E^-[\mathcal{M}^-])$ which are computed along the forward and backward computation paths from a *common value* of the starting states $(\#S^{\mathrm{ENC}}, \#S^{\mathrm{KSA}})$, and thus can be tested for match according to the computation connecting $\#E^+$ and $\#E^-$ in the closed loop. Note that testing pairs computed from different values of the starting point

---

Algorithm 1: One MITM episode

---

1 Fix $(\#S^{\text{ENC}}[\mathcal{G}^{\text{ENC}}], \#S^{\text{KSA}}[\mathcal{G}^{\text{KSA}}])$ to a constant α

2 Fix $\mathfrak{c}^+$, and $\mathfrak{c}^-$ to some constants

3 Fix x^* to be an element in $\mathbb{B}(\#S^{\text{ENC}}[\mathcal{G}^{\text{ENC}}], \#S^{\text{KSA}}[\mathcal{G}^{\text{KSA}}], \mathfrak{c}^+)$

4 Fix u^* to be an element in $\mathbb{R}(\#S^{\text{ENC}}[\mathcal{G}^{\text{ENC}}], \#S^{\text{KSA}}[\mathcal{G}^{\text{KSA}}], \mathfrak{c}^-)$

5 $L \leftarrow [\,]$

6 **for** *all* $(\#S^{\text{ENC}}[\mathcal{B}^{\text{ENC}}], \#S^{\text{KSA}}[\mathcal{B}^{\text{KSA}}]) \in \mathbb{B}(\#S^{\text{ENC}}[\mathcal{G}^{\text{ENC}}], \#S^{\text{KSA}}[\mathcal{G}^{\text{KSA}}], \mathfrak{c}^+)$ **do**

7    $\quad$ $E^+[\mathcal{M}^+] \leftarrow F^+(\alpha, \#S^{\text{ENC}}[\mathcal{B}^{\text{ENC}}], \#S^{\text{KSA}}[\mathcal{B}^{\text{KSA}}], u^*)$

8    $\quad$ Insert $E^+[\mathcal{M}^+]$ into L

9 **for** *all* $(\#S^{\text{ENC}}[\mathcal{R}^{\text{ENC}}], \#S^{\text{KSA}}[\mathcal{R}^{\text{KSA}}]) \in \mathbb{R}(\#S^{\text{ENC}}[\mathcal{G}^{\text{ENC}}], \#S^{\text{KSA}}[\mathcal{G}^{\text{KSA}}], \mathfrak{c}^-)$ **do**

10   $\quad$ $E^-[\mathcal{M}^-] \leftarrow F^-(\alpha, x^*, \#S^{\text{ENC}}[\mathcal{R}^{\text{ENC}}], \#S^{\text{KSA}}[\mathcal{R}^{\text{KSA}}])$

11   $\quad$ **for** $E^+[\mathcal{M}^+]$ *in* L *matching with* $E^-[\mathcal{M}^-]$ **do**

12   $\quad\quad$ Test for full match between $E^+[\mathcal{M}^+]$ and $E^-[\mathcal{M}^-]$

(e.g., pairs formed from different episodes) is meaningless. In each episode, we have $(2^w)^{\text{DoF}^+ + \text{DoF}^-}$ *paired threads*. If the computation connecting $\#E^+[\mathcal{M}^+]$ and $\#E^-[\mathcal{M}^-]$ forms an m-cell filter, then there are about $(2^w)^{\text{DoF}^+ + \text{DoF}^- - m}$ paired threads will pass the filter and be tested for a full match. We call DoM = m the degrees of match or the strength of the filter. Finally, we emphasize again that the MITM procedure given in Algorithm 1 is performed for some fixed $(\#S^{\text{ENC}}[\mathcal{G}^{\text{ENC}}], \#S^{\text{KSA}}[\mathcal{G}^{\text{KSA}}], \mathfrak{c}^+, \mathfrak{c}^-)$, and we say $(\#S^{\text{ENC}}[\mathcal{G}^{\text{ENC}}], \#S^{\text{KSA}}[\mathcal{G}^{\text{KSA}}], \mathfrak{c}^+, \mathfrak{c}^-)$ defines the *context* of the MITM episode.

Automatic Search for MITM Characteristics. For a given closed computation path shown in Fig. 1, a configuration of the states $\#S^{\text{ENC}}$, $\#S^{\text{KSA}}$, $\#E^+$, $\#E^-$, and the parameters $\mathcal{B}^{\text{ENC}}$, $\mathcal{B}^{\text{KSA}}$, $\mathcal{R}^{\text{ENC}}$, $\mathcal{R}^{\text{KSA}}$, $\mathcal{M}^+$, $\mathcal{M}^-$, DoF$^+$, DoF$^-$, π^+, π^-, and DoM satisfying Property 1 is called an MITM characteristic. At EURO-CRYPT 2021, Bao et al. presented an MILP-based method for finding optimal MITM characteristics for preimage attacks, and we refer the reader to [6] for more details. Here, we only mention that an MILP characteristic can be visualized with the following coloring scheme on the states of the closed computation path and the ith cell of a state $\#S$ is encoded with a pair of 0-1 variables $(x_i^{\#S}, y_i^{\#S})$ in the MILP models according to the following rule:

$\blacksquare$ Gray (G), $(x_i^{\#S}, y_i^{\#S}) = (1,1)$: known *episodic* constants.

$\blacksquare$ Red (R), $(x_i^{\#S}, y_i^{\#S}) = (0,1)$: neutral words for backward computation or dependent on $\blacksquare$ cells and neutral words for backward computation.

$\blacksquare$ Blue (B), $(x_i^{\#S}, y_i^{\#S}) = (1,0)$: neutral words for forward computation or dependent on $\blacksquare$ cells and neutral words for forward computation.

$\square$ White (W), $(x_i^{\#S}, y_i^{\#S}) = (0,0)$: dependent on $\blacksquare$ cells in the backward computation or dependent on $\blacksquare$ cells in the forward computation.

3   Automatic MITM Key-Recovery Attacks

We describe the MITM key-recovery attack on a block cipher based on Fig. 1 with the lower segment being an encryption or decryption oracle. Before going any further, we introduce some new notations. The initial degrees of freedom from the encryption and key schedule data paths for the forward computation are defined as $\lambda_{\text{ENC}}^+ = |\mathcal{B}^{\text{ENC}}|$ and $\lambda_{\text{KSA}}^+ = |\mathcal{B}^{\text{KSA}}|$, respectively. Similarly, The initial degrees of freedom from the encryption and key schedule data paths for the backward computation are defined as $\lambda_{\text{ENC}}^- = |\mathcal{R}^{\text{ENC}}|$ and $\lambda_{\text{KSA}}^- = |\mathcal{R}^{\text{KSA}}|$, respectively. Under these notations, we have $\lambda^+ = \lambda_{\text{ENC}}^+ + \lambda_{\text{KSA}}^+$ and $\lambda^- = \lambda_{\text{ENC}}^- + \lambda_{\text{KSA}}^-$.

For an MITM characteristic, we say that the degrees of freedom from the encryption data path for the forward computation is used up if for any given $(\#S^{\text{ENC}}[\mathcal{G}^{\text{ENC}}], \#S^{\text{KSA}}[\mathcal{G}^{\text{KSA}}], \mathfrak{c}^+)$, we partition the solution space

$$\mathbb{B}(\#S^{\text{ENC}}[\mathcal{G}^{\text{ENC}}], \#S^{\text{KSA}}[\mathcal{G}^{\text{KSA}}], \mathfrak{c}^+)$$

of $(\#S^{\text{ENC}}[\mathcal{B}^{\text{ENC}}], \#S^{\text{KSA}}[\mathcal{B}^{\text{KSA}}])$ due to Eq. (1) into subspaces according to the value of $\#S^{\text{KSA}}[\mathcal{B}^{\text{KSA}}]$, then each space contains exactly one element. That is, the values of the ■ cells in $\#S^{\text{ENC}}$ can be fully determined by the ■ cells in $\#S^{\text{KSA}}$ for a given $(\#S^{\text{ENC}}[\mathcal{G}^{\text{ENC}}], \#S^{\text{KSA}}[\mathcal{G}^{\text{KSA}}], \mathfrak{c}^+)$. Similarly, we say that the degrees of freedom from the encryption data path for the backward computation is used up if the values of the ■ cells in $\#S^{\text{ENC}}$ can be fully determined by the ■ cells in $\#S^{\text{KSA}}$ for a given $(\#S^{\text{ENC}}[\mathcal{G}^{\text{ENC}}], \#S^{\text{KSA}}[\mathcal{G}^{\text{KSA}}], \mathfrak{c}^-)$.

Now, Let us recall from Sect. 2 that the goal of the MITM attack is to find a particular value for some intermediate states in the closed computation path shown in Fig. 1 with which the values for all the states involved in the computation path can be determined, such that the values derived are compatible with the whole computation path. Specifically, in the context of MITM key-recovery attacks, our goal can be formulated as follows.

Goal 1. *Identify a value K for the key register hosting the master key, and a value for one full state in the encryption data path, with which we can derive the values of all states involved. We require that the values for all states are compatible and K equals to the secret key hiding in the oracle.*

The above goal indicates that in the MITM key-recovery attack, the full key space must be (implicitly) tested, since a compatible assignment of values to the states is not enough (unlike MITM preimage attacks), and we must identify the unique secret key. Secondly, in the key-recovery attack, we prefer not to exhaust the full codebook of the targeted cipher. These particularities result in the following requirements for the MITM characteristic:

I. The degrees of freedom for the forward computation or backward computation from $\#S^{\text{KSA}}$ cannot be depleted (i.e., $\text{DoF}^+ > 0$ and $\text{DoF}^- > 0$), while the degrees of freedom for *both* the forward computation and backward computation from $\#S^{\text{ENC}}$ should be used up.

II. In the MITM characteristic, we require that there is at least one ■ cell (*episodic constant*) in the plaintext state, which will be set to *global constant* in the actual attack to avoid using the full codebook.

To ensure (I), we require the corresponding systems of equations of the MITM characteristic given in Eqs. (1) and (2) to satisfy the following conditions. For Eq. (1), there are l_{KSA}^+ equations (without loss of generality, we assume these are the first l_{KSA}^+ equations) do not involve $\#S^{\text{ENC}}[\mathcal{G}^{\text{ENC}}]$ and $S^{\text{ENC}}[\mathcal{B}^{\text{ENC}}]$. The remaining $l^+ - l_{\text{KSA}}^+$ equations are used to exhaust the degrees of freedom from the encryption data path, and thus $|\lambda_{\text{ENC}}^+| = |\mathcal{B}^{\text{ENC}}| = l^+ - l_{\text{KSA}}^+$. Under this, we have $\text{DoF}^+ = \lambda_{\text{KSA}}^+ - l_{\text{KSA}}^+$. In addition, for each constant $(\#S^{\text{ENC}}[\mathcal{G}^{\text{ENC}}], \#S^{\text{KSA}}[\mathcal{G}^{\text{KSA}}], \mathfrak{c}^+)$, and each solution for $\#S^{\text{KSA}}[\mathcal{B}^{\text{KSA}}]$ of the first l_{KSA}^+ equations, we can derive one and only one solution for $\#S^{\text{ENC}}[\mathcal{B}^{\text{ENC}}]$ by solving the remaining equations. For Eq. (2), there are l_{KSA}^- equations (without loss of generality, we assume these are the first l_{KSA}^- equations) do not involve $\#S^{\text{ENC}}[\mathcal{G}^{\text{ENC}}]$ and $S^{\text{ENC}}[\mathcal{R}^{\text{ENC}}]$. The remaining $l^- - l_{\text{KSA}}^-$ equations are used to exhaust the degrees of freedom from the encryption data path, and thus $|\lambda_{\text{ENC}}^-| = |\mathcal{R}^{\text{ENC}}| = l^- - l_{\text{KSA}}^-$. Under this, we have $\text{DoF}^- = \lambda_{\text{KSA}}^- - l_{\text{KSA}}^-$. In addition, for each constant $(\#S^{\text{ENC}}[\mathcal{G}^{\text{ENC}}], \#S^{\text{KSA}}[\mathcal{G}^{\text{KSA}}], \mathfrak{c}^-)$, and each solution for $\#S^{\text{KSA}}[\mathcal{R}^{\text{KSA}}]$ of the first l_{KSA}^- equations, we can derive one and only one solution for $\#S^{\text{ENC}}[\mathcal{R}^{\text{ENC}}]$ by solving the remaining equations.

Requirement (I) may be less obvious than (II), and we will explain it by looking into the algorithmic framework given in Algorithm 2. But before we go into the details, we emphasize that due to these peculiarities, almost all MITM characteristics found by the the method presented in [6] are useless in the context of key-recovery attacks.

From now on, we use $|\#S|$ denote the number of cells in a state $\#S$. In Line 1 of Algorithm 2, we set $|\#S^{\text{ENC}}|$ gray cells, including all the gray cells in the plaintext state to global constants, where $|\#S^{\text{ENC}}|$ denotes the number of cells in $\#S^{\text{ENC}}$. Since the gray cells in the plaintext states are set to global constant, the attack will not use the full codebook. These $|\#S^{\text{ENC}}|$ gray cells are not necessarily within one single state along the computation path. Instead, they can be distributed over multiple states. Moreover, we require that the values of these cells can be set independently to *arbitrary* values without leading to a conflict along the computation path (excluding the computations connecting the ending states). When these constants are set, for any given key, we can derive the values of all the states (including $\#S^{\text{ENC}}$), along the computation path (excluding the computation connecting the ending states), which indicates that if the degrees of freedom of $\#S^{\text{ENC}}$ are not exhausted, this constant setting process may lead to conflicts, which is equivalent to setting more than $|\#S^{\text{ENC}}|$ cells of $\#S^{\text{ENC}}$ to constants. Then, each MITM episode is performed within the context defined by the outer loops surrounding the code segment from Line 8 to Line 15.

Complexity Analysis. In Line 2 of Algorithm 2, suppose there are ε gray cells in the plaintext state, then the data complexity $(2^w)^{n-\varepsilon}$. Suppose the states in the encryption data and key schedule data paths contains n and $\bar{n}$ cells, respectively, and the matching part forms an m-cell filter. According Algorithm 2, there

---

Algorithm 2: The MITM key-recovery attack on block ciphers

---

1   Set $|\#S^{\text{ENC}}|$ *independent* gray cells to constants, which should contain all the gray cells in the plaintext state

2   Collecting a structure of plaintext-ciphertext pairs and store them in a table H, which traverses the non-constant cells in the plaintext

3   **for** $\#S^{\text{KSA}}[\mathcal{G}^{\text{KSA}}] \in \mathbb{F}_2^{w \cdot |\mathcal{G}^{\text{KSA}}|}$ **do**

4   **for** $c_{\text{KSA}}^+ = (a_1, \cdots, a_{l_{\text{KSA}}^+}) \in \mathbb{F}_2^{w \cdot l_{\text{KSA}}^+}$ **do**

5   **for** $c_{\text{KSA}}^- = (b_1, \cdots, b_{l_{\text{KSA}}^-}) \in \mathbb{F}_2^{w \cdot l_{\text{KSA}}^-}$ **do**

6   Derive the the value of $\#S^{\text{ENC}}[\mathcal{G}^{\text{ENC}}]$

7        $L \leftarrow [\,]$

8   **for** $\#S^{\text{KSA}}[\mathcal{B}^{\text{KSA}}] \in \mathbb{B}^{\text{KSA}}(\#S^{\text{KSA}}[\mathcal{G}^{\text{KSA}}], c_{\text{KSA}}^+)$ **do**

9   Derive the the value of $\#S^{\text{ENC}}[\mathcal{B}^{\text{ENC}}]$ and compute $E^+[\mathcal{M}^+]$ along the forward computation path

10   Insert $\#S^{\text{KSA}}[\mathcal{B}^{\text{KSA}}]$ into L indexed by $E^+[\mathcal{M}^+]$

11   **for** $\#S^{\text{KSA}}[\mathcal{R}^{\text{KSA}}] \in \mathbb{R}^{\text{KSA}}(\#S^{\text{KSA}}[\mathcal{G}^{\text{KSA}}], c_{\text{KSA}}^-)$ **do**

12   Derive the the value of $\#S^{\text{ENC}}[\mathcal{R}^{\text{ENC}}]$ and Compute $E^-[\mathcal{M}^-]$ along the backward computation path by accessing H

13   **for** $\#S^{\text{KSA}}[\mathcal{B}^{\text{KSA}}] \in L[E^-[\mathcal{M}^-]]$ **do**

14   Reconstruct the (guessed) key value K' from $\#S^{\text{KSA}}[\mathcal{B}^{\text{KSA}}]$, $\#S^{\text{KSA}}[\mathcal{R}^{\text{KSA}}]$, and $\#S^{\text{KSA}}[\mathcal{G}^{\text{KSA}}]$

15   Test K' against several plaintext-ciphertext pairs

---

are $(2^w)^{\bar{n} - \lambda_{\text{KSA}}^+ - \lambda_{\text{KSA}}^-} \cdot (2^w)^{l_{\text{KSA}}^+} \cdot (2^w)^{l_{\text{KSA}}^-} = (2^w)^{\bar{n} - (\text{DoF}^+ + \text{DoF}^-)}$ MITM episodes, and in each episode $(2^w)^{\text{DoF}^+ + \text{DoF}^-}$ different keys are tested, where $(2^w)^{\text{DoF}^+ + \text{DoF}^- - m}$ of them will pass the m-cell filter. Therefore, the overall time complexity can be estimated as $(2^w)^{\bar{n} - \text{DoF}^+ - \text{DoF}^-}((2^w)^{\text{DoF}^+} + (2^w)^{\text{DoF}^-} + (2^w)^{\text{DoF}^+ + \text{DoF}^- - m})$, which is approximately

$$(2^w)^{\bar{n} - \min\{\text{DoF}^+, \text{DoF}^-, m\}}. \tag{3}$$

4   MITM Attacks on SKINNY and ForkSkinny

SKINNY is a family of lightweight block ciphers designed by Beierle et al. [9] based on the TWEAKEY framework [38]. In this section, we apply our method to SKINNY-n-$3n$ (The version with an n-bit block size, a $3n$-bit key, and a 0-bit tweak) with $n \in \{64, 128\}$. The overall structure of SKINNY-n-$3n$ and its round function are given in Fig. 2.

The internal state is viewed as a 4×4 square with 16 cells. In each round, the state is updated with five operations: SubCells (SC), AddConstants (AC), AddRoundTweakey (ART), ShiftRows (SR) and MixColumns (MC). The key register is arranged into three 4×4 squares denoted as TK_1, TK_2, and TK_3

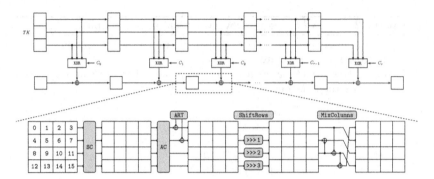

Fig. 2. The hight-level structure of SKINNY-n-$3n$ and its round function (Thanks to https://www.iacr.org/authors/tikz/).

respectively. Note that the in each round only the first two rows of the internal state are affected by ART, and the MC operation is non-MDS and thus quite different from the AES-like structures analyzed in [6]. Specifically, we have

$$
\text{MC} \begin{pmatrix} a \\ b \\ c \\ d \end{pmatrix} = \begin{pmatrix} a \oplus c \oplus d \\ a \\ b \oplus c \\ a \oplus c \end{pmatrix} \quad \text{and} \quad \text{MC}^{-1} \begin{pmatrix} \alpha \\ \beta \\ \gamma \\ \delta \end{pmatrix} = \begin{pmatrix} \beta \\ \beta \oplus \gamma \oplus \delta \\ \beta \oplus \delta \\ \alpha \oplus \delta \end{pmatrix}. \tag{4}
$$

4.1 Programming the MITM Attacks on SKINNY-n-$3n$ with MILP

Based on the analysis of Sect. 3, we show how to build the MILP model for finding MITM characteristics of SKINNY-n-$3n$ in the context of key-recovery attacks. We employ the same encoding scheme from [6], where the ith cell of a state $\#S$ is encoded with a pair of 0-1 variables $(x_i^{\#S}, y_i^{\#S})$ according to the rule given in Sect. 2. Firstly, due to the complexity estimation given by Eq. (3), $\min\{\text{DoF}^+, \text{DoF}^-, \text{DoM}\}$ should be maximized in our model. To this end, we introduce an auxiliary variable v_{Obj}, impose the constraints

$$\{v_{\text{Obj}} \leq \text{DoF}^+, v_{\text{Obj}} \leq \text{DoF}^-, v_{\text{Obj}} \leq \text{DoM}\}$$

and set the objective function to maximize v_{Obj}. In what follows, we describe the constraints for the starting states, ending states, and the states in the computation paths with a special focus on what is different from Bao et al.'s work [6]. First of all, the tweakey schedule algorithm of SKINNY-n-$3n$ only involves in-cell operations and permutations changing the positions of the cells in the tweakey register, which will not alter the color of a cell in our model (only their positions are changed). Therefore, we will not discuss the constraints imposed solely by the tweakey schedule algorithm in the following.

Constraints for the Starting States. As discussed in Sect. 3, we distinguish the sources of degrees of freedom from the encryption data path (denoted by λ_{ENC}^+

and λ_{ENC}^-) and the key schedule data path (denoted by λ_{KSA}^+ and λ_{KSA}^-), and the initial degrees of freedom satisfies $\lambda^+ = \lambda_{\text{ENC}}^+ + \lambda_{\text{KSA}}^+$ and $\lambda^- = \lambda_{\text{ENC}}^- + \lambda_{\text{KSA}}^-$, where $\lambda_{\text{ENC}}^+ = |\mathcal{B}^{\text{ENC}}|$, $\lambda_{\text{KSA}}^+ = |\mathcal{B}^{\text{KSA}}|$, $\lambda_{\text{ENC}}^- = |\mathcal{R}^{\text{ENC}}|$, and $\lambda_{\text{KSA}}^- = |\mathcal{R}^{\text{KSA}}|$. We introduce two variables α_i and β_i for each cell in $(\#S^{\text{ENC}}, \#S^{\text{KSA}})$, where $\alpha_i = 1$ if and only if $(x_i^{\#S}, y_i^{\#S}) = (1,0)$ and $\beta_i = 1$ if and only if $(x_i^{\#S}, y_i^{\#S}) = (0,1)$. Then we have the following constraints:

$$\lambda_{\text{ENC}}^+ = \sum_i \alpha_i^{\text{ENC}}, \ \lambda_{\text{KSA}}^+ = \sum_i \alpha_i^{\text{KSA}}, \ \lambda_{\text{ENC}}^- = \sum_i \beta_i^{\text{ENC}}, \ \lambda_{\text{KSA}}^- = \sum_i \beta_i^{\text{KSA}},$$

and

$$\begin{cases} x_i^{\#S^{\text{ENC}}} - \alpha_i^{\text{ENC}} \geq 0 \\ y_i^{\#S^{\text{ENC}}} - x_i^{\#S^{\text{ENC}}} + \alpha_i^{\text{ENC}} \geq 0 \\ y_i^{\#S^{\text{ENC}}} + \alpha_i^{\text{ENC}} \leq 1 \end{cases} , \quad \begin{cases} y_i^{\#S^{\text{ENC}}} - \beta_i^{\text{ENC}} \geq 0 \\ x_i^{\#S^{\text{ENC}}} - y_i^{\#S^{\text{ENC}}} + \beta_i^{\text{ENC}} \geq 0 \\ x_i^{\#S^{\text{ENC}}} + \beta_i^{\text{ENC}} \leq 1 \end{cases} ,$$

$$\begin{cases} x_i^{\#S^{\text{KSA}}} - \alpha_i^{\text{KSA}} \geq 0 \\ y_i^{\#S^{\text{KSA}}} - x_i^{\#S^{\text{KSA}}} + \alpha_i^{\text{KSA}} \geq 0 \\ y_i^{\#S^{\text{KSA}}} + \alpha_i^{\text{KSA}} \leq 1 \end{cases} , \quad \begin{cases} y_i^{\#S^{\text{KSA}}} - \beta_i^{\text{KSA}} \geq 0 \\ x_i^{\#S^{\text{KSA}}} - y_i^{\#S^{\text{KSA}}} + \beta_i^{\text{KSA}} \geq 0 \\ x_i^{\#S^{\text{KSA}}} + \beta_i^{\text{KSA}} \leq 1 \end{cases} .$$

Constraints for the Ending States. We assume that the matching only happens at the MixColumns. Let $(\#E^+[4j], \#E^+[4j+1], \#E^+[4j+2], \#E^+[4j+3])^T$ and $(\#E^-[4j], \#E^-[4j+1], \#E^-[4j+2], \#E^-[4j+3])^T$ be the jth column of the ending states $\#E^+$ and $\#E^-$ linked by the MC operation. Since MC is non-MDS, its constraints are quite different from Bao et al.'s model for MDS matrix, where there is a $(\Sigma - 4)$-cell filter if and only if $\Sigma \geq 5$ out of 8 cells of the two columns are ■ or ▨ cells (see [6, Property 1, page 14]).

For the MC operation of SKINNY, there may exist an m-cell ($m > 0$) filter even if $\Sigma < 5$. For example, according to Eq. (4), if $\#E^+[4j] = $ ■, $\#E^-[4j+1] = $ ■ and all other cells are □, we still get a 1-cell filter due to $\#E^+[4j] = \#E^-[4j+1]$. We can enumerate all possible patterns and convert these local constraints into linear inequalities using the convex hull computation method. In Fig. 3, we list some of the possible matching patterns with their filtering strength measured in cells. We introduce a variable $\gamma_j \geq 0$ for the j-th columns of $\#E^+$ and $\#E^-$ such that there is a γ_j-cell filter due to the coloring patterns of $\#E^+$ and $\#E^-$, then we get a DoM-cell filter at the matching point, where $\text{DoM} = \sum_j \gamma_j$ and should be positive according to the complexity analysis given by Eq. (3).

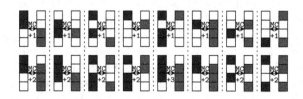

Fig. 3. Some possible coloring patterns at the matching point

Constraints Imposed by the Computation Paths. Along the computation paths leading to the ending states, the initial degrees of freedom are consumed according to the MITM characteristic. Forward computation consumes the degrees of freedom of the neutral words for backward computation while backward computation consumes the degrees of freedom of the neutral words for the forward computation. The consumption of degrees of freedom is counted in cells. Let σ^+_{ENC}, σ^+_{KSA} and σ^-_{ENC}, σ^-_{KSA} be the accumulated degrees of freedom that have been consumed in the backward and forward computation in the encryption and key schedule data paths. Since the degrees of freedom from the encryption data paths for both directions should be used up and the degrees of freedom originated from the key schedule data path should not be exhausted, we require

$$\begin{cases} \lambda^+_{\text{ENC}} - \sigma^+_{\text{ENC}} = 0, \quad \lambda^-_{\text{ENC}} - \sigma^-_{\text{ENC}} = 0 \\ \text{DoF}^+ = \lambda^+_{\text{KSA}} - \sigma^+_{\text{KSA}} \geq 1, \quad \text{DoF}^- = \lambda^-_{\text{KSA}} - \sigma^-_{\text{KSA}} \geq 1 \end{cases}.$$

According to the semantics of the colors, how a coloring pattern of the input and output states of an operation consumes the degrees of freedom should be be different for the forward and the backward computation paths. Therefore, we will give two sets of rules for different directions of the computation.

XOR. The XOR operations exist in the ART and MC, and we can reuse the XOR-RULE$^+$ (for forward computation) and XOR-RULE$^-$ (for backward computation) rules gvien in [6]. The coloring patterns and how the degrees of freedom are consumed are visualized in Fig. 4.

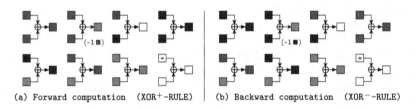

(a) Forward computation   (XOR$^+$-RULE)   (b) Backward computation   (XOR$^-$-RULE)

Fig. 4. Rules for XOR, where a "*" means that the cell can be any color

AddRoundTweakey. ART is the operation that the first two rows of the three tweakey states are XORed into the encryption data path. There are three XOR operations and four input cells (three from the tweakey state and one from the encryption data path) involved to produce an output cell. Certainly, we can use the XOR-RULE three times to get the constraints. However, this approach misses some important coloring patterns that may lead to better attacks. We take the forward computation for example as shown in Fig. 5. If we use XOR$^+$-RULE three times successively as shown in Fig. 5(a), when the ■ and ■ are the input cells of the XOR, the output cell will be □ , eventually leading to a □ output cell.

However, if we change the order of the XOR operations as shown in Fig. 5(b), then ■ ⊕ ■ may produce a ■ cell by consuming one degree of freedom, leading to a ■ output cell. To take this into account, we model the rule for three XORs as a whole, named as 3-XOR⁺-RULE, with Fig. 5(c) as an example.

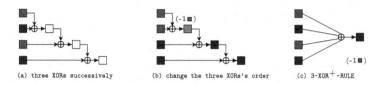

(a) three XORs successively   (b) change the three XORs's order   (c) 3-XOR⁺-RULE

Fig. 5. The inaccuracy of modeling 3-XOR⁺ by applying XOR⁺ successively

For the 3-XOR operation in the forward computation, we have the following set of rules (denoted by 3-XOR⁺-RULE):

▶ **3-XOR⁺-RULE-1.** If there are ■ cells but no □ and ■ cells in the input, the output cell is ■ or ■ (partially cancel the impacts of the input ■ cells by consuming λ_{ENC}^- or λ_{KSA}^-).

▶ **3-XOR⁺-RULE-2.** If there are ■ and ■ cells but no □ cells in the input, the output cell is □ or ■ (partially cancel the impacts from ■ on ■ by consuming λ_{ENC}^- or λ_{KSA}^-).

▶ **3-XOR⁺-RULE-3.** If there are ■ cells but no □ and ■ cells in the input, the output cell is ■.

▶ **3-XOR⁺-RULE-4.** If all the input cells are ■, then the output cell is ■.

▶ **3-XOR⁺-RULE-5.** If there is at least one □ cell in the input, the output is □.

We introduce variables δ_{ENC}^- and δ_{KSA}^- to denote the consumed degrees of freedom due to 3-XOR⁺-RULE. For example, $\delta_{\mathrm{ENC}}^- = 1$ means that we consume one degree of freedom from λ_{ENC}^- by applying the rule. In order to use up all the degrees of freedom from $\#S^{\mathrm{ENC}}$, we should consume λ_{ENC}^- first whenever possible. As shown in Fig. 6, when there are degrees of freedom in the encryption path, i.e., ■ cells, the consumption of degree of freedom is always from λ_{ENC}^-, i.e., $\delta_{\mathrm{ENC}}^- = 1$ and $\delta_{\mathrm{KSA}}^- = 0$.

Let $\#a$, $\#b$, $\#c$, $\#d$ be the input cells and $\#e$ be the output cell. Then, the set of rules 3-XOR⁺-RULE restricts $(x^{\#a}, y^{\#a}, x^{\#b}, y^{\#b}, x^{\#c}, y^{\#c}, x^{\#d}, y^{\#d}, x^{\#e}, y^{\#e}, \delta_{\mathrm{ENC}}^-)$ and $(x^{\#a}, y^{\#a}, x^{\#b}, y^{\#b}, x^{\#c}, y^{\#c}, x^{\#d}, y^{\#d}, x^{\#e}, y^{\#e}, \delta_{\mathrm{KSA}}^-)$ to subsets of $\mathbb{F}_2^{11}$, which can be described by a system of linear inequalities by using the convex hull computation method. Some valid coloring patterns due to 3-XOR⁺-RULE are given in Fig. 6. Note that 3-XOR⁻-RULE can be obtained from 3-XOR⁺-RULE by exchanging the ■ cells and ■ cells, since the meanings of ■ and ■ are dual for the forward and backward computations.

MixColumn. Since MC contains only XOR operations, we can use XOR-RULE to generate the set of rules MC-RULE for MC. According to Eq. (4), there exists one equation that XORs three cells together to get one cell. We use a similar approach

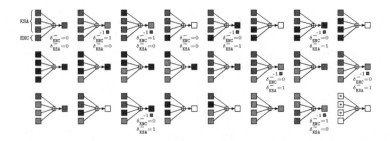

Fig. 6. 3-XOR$^+$-RULE, where a "*" means that the cell can be any color

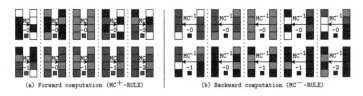

(a) Forward computation (MC$^+$-RULE)   (b) Backward computation (MC$^-$-RULE)

Fig. 7. MC-RULE

we employed for 3-XOR$^+$-RULE and 3-XOR$^-$-RULE to handle this special equation. Finally, we get the valid propogations of the coloring patterns and list some of them in Fig. 7. Note that there are no key additions involved in MC, and thus all the consumed degrees of freedom are from λ_{ENC}^+ and λ_{ENC}^-.

4.2 The MITM Key-Recovery Attack on SKINNY-n-$3n$

Solving the model built in Sect. 4.1, we identify a 23-round MITM characteristic as shown in Fig. 8. The starting states are $\#S^{\text{ENC}} = Y_1$ and the three tweakey words $\#S^{\text{KSA}} = (TK_1^{(1)}, TK_2^{(1)}, TK_3^{(1)})$. The matching process happens at the MC operation between the ending states $\#E^+ = Z_{12}$ and $\#E^- = X_{13}$. There are 3 ■ cells and 3 ▨ cells in $\#S^{\text{KSA}}$, providing $\lambda_{\text{KSA}}^- = \lambda_{\text{KSA}}^+ = 3$ cells of initial degrees of freedom originated from the key schedule data path. For $\#S^{\text{ENC}}$, Y_1 provides $\lambda_{\text{ENC}}^- = 8$ and $\lambda_{\text{ENC}}^+ = 1$ cells of initial degrees of freedom from the encryption data path. The $\lambda_{\text{ENC}}^+ = 1$ cells of degrees of freedom is used up when computing X_1 from Y_1 by XORing the subtweakey. In the forward computation, the $\lambda_{\text{ENC}}^- = 8$ cells of degrees of freedom are used up when computing Y_4 from Y_1. For the forward computation, we require $TK_1^{(6)}[7] \oplus TK_2^{(6)}[7] \oplus TK_3^{(6)}[7]$ and $TK_1^{(8)}[1] \oplus TK_2^{(8)}[1] \oplus TK_3^{(8)}[1]$ to be constants, consuming $\sigma_{\text{KSA}}^- = 2$ cells of degrees of freedom originated from the key schedule data path. Hence, we get $\text{DoF}^- = \lambda_{\text{KSA}}^- - \sigma_{\text{KSA}}^- = 1$. Similarly, we get $\text{DoF}^+ = \lambda_{\text{KSA}}^+ - \sigma_{\text{KSA}}^+ = 1$. At the matching point, we have $\text{DoM} = 2$ from the first two column of $\#E^+$ and $\#E^-$ with Eq. (4). The 23-round key-recovery attack is given in Algorithm 3. The data and memory complexity is bounded by Line 2, which is 2^{104} for SKINNY-128-384 and 2^{52} for SKINNY-64-192. According to Eq. (3), the time complexity is about 2^{376} for SKINNY-128-384 and 2^{188} for SKINNY-64-192.

Algorithm 3: The MITM key-recovery attack on SKINNY-n-$3n$

---

1 $X_0[3, 9, 13] \leftarrow 0$, $X_1[0, 2, 8, 10, 13] \leftarrow 0$, $X_2[1, 3, 9, 11] \leftarrow 0$, $Y_2[5] \leftarrow 0$,
   $X_3[0, 8] \leftarrow 0$, $Y_4[3] \leftarrow 0$

2 Collecting structure of plaintext-ciphertext pairs and store them in table H,
   which traverses the non-constant 16-3=13 cells in the plaintext

3 **for** *All possilbe values of the* ■ *cells in* $(TK_1^{(0)}, TK_2^{(0)}, TK_3^{(0)})$ **do**

4   **for** $(a_1, a_2, b_1, b_2) \in \mathbb{F}_2^{4w}$ **do**

5          $Y_0[3] \leftarrow TK_1^{(0)}[3] \oplus TK_2^{(0)}[3] \oplus TK_3^{(0)}[3]$, $Y_0[9, 13] \leftarrow X_0[9, 13]$,
           $Z_0[3, 11, 12] \leftarrow Y_0[3, 9, 13]$, $X_1[12] \leftarrow X_1[0] \oplus Z_0[12]$, $X_1[7] \leftarrow Z_0[3]$,
           $X_1[15] \leftarrow Z_0[3] \oplus Z_0[11]$, $X_2[15] \leftarrow X_2[3] \oplus Z_1[15]$, $X_3[4] \leftarrow Z_2[0]$

6   Derive the solution space of the ■ cells in the TK by

$$\begin{cases} TK_1^{(6)}[7] \oplus TK_2^{(6)}[7] \oplus TK_3^{(6)}[7] = a_1 \\ TK_1^{(8)}[1] \oplus TK_2^{(8)}[1] \oplus TK_3^{(8)}[1] = a_2 \end{cases}.$$

7   Derive the solution space of the ■ cells in the TK by

$$\begin{cases} TK_1^{(19)}[4] \oplus TK_2^{(19)}[4] \oplus TK_3^{(19)}[4] = b_1 \\ TK_1^{(21)}[6] \oplus TK_2^{(21)}[6] \oplus TK_3^{(21)}[6] = b_2 \end{cases}.$$

8   Initialize L to be an empty hash table

9   **for** *the value in the solution space of* ■ *cells in* TK **do**

10   Compute $X_{13}[8]$ along the backward computation path:
               $X_4 \rightarrow X_0 \rightarrow E_K(X_0) \rightarrow X_{13}$ by accessing H

11   Insert relative information into L indexed by $X_{13}[8]$

12   **for** *the value in the solution space of* ■ *cells in* TK **do**

13   Compute $Z_{12}[4]$ and $Z_{12}[8]$ along the forward computation path:
               $X_1 \rightarrow Z_{12}$

14   **for** *Candidate keys in* $L[Z_{12}[4] \oplus Z_{12}[8]]$ **do**

15   Test the guessed key with several plaintext-ciphertext pairs

---

Remark. The designers of SKINNY claimed that: *"We conclude that meet-in-the-middle attack may work up to at most 22 rounds (see [9], Sect. 4.2, page 22)"*. Our attack penetrates one more round than expected and is the first 23-round single-key attack on SKINNY-128-384 and SKINNY-64-192. Using the same method, we also analyze ForkSkinny (see the full version of the paper). In addition, we report on some results on Romulus-H as a by-product of the analysis of SKINNY (see the full version of the paper).

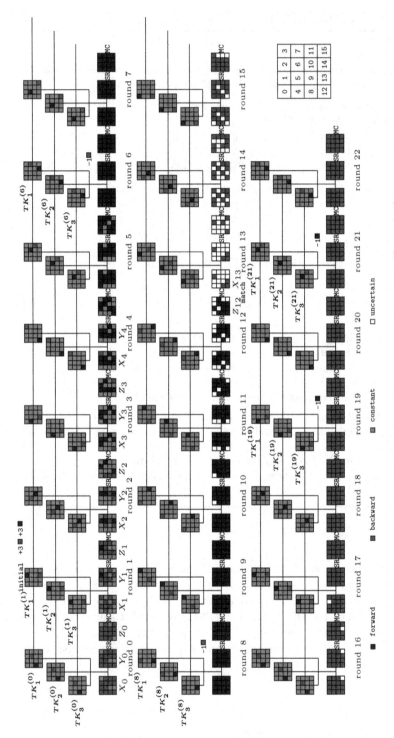

Fig. 8. An MITM key-recovery attack on 23-round SKINNY-n-$3n$

5 Exploiting Nonlinearly Constrained Neutral Words in MITM Attacks and Its Applications

According to Property 1 in Sect. 2, in order to compute the allowable values for the neutral words, one has to solve two systems of equations, i.e., Eq. (1) and (2). In previous MITM preimage attacks [6,46], the two systems of equations are linear (or can be reduced to linear equations involving certain cells not from the starting states that implicitly define the spaces of the neutral words). Hence, it is easy to derive the solution spaces $\mathbb{B}(\#S^{\mathrm{ENC}}[\mathcal{G}^{\mathrm{ENC}}], \#S^{\mathrm{KSA}}[\mathcal{G}^{\mathrm{KSA}}], \mathfrak{c}^{+})$ and $\mathbb{R}(\#S^{\mathrm{ENC}}[\mathcal{G}^{\mathrm{ENC}}], \#S^{\mathrm{KSA}}[\mathcal{G}^{\mathrm{KSA}}], \mathfrak{c}^{-})$ by solving the systems of equations, whose cost can be ignored compared with the overall complexity. However, in practice, we encounter many interesting MITM characteristics with nonlinear constrained neutral words, and there is no efficient method for solving them. We present a table based technique in Algorithm 4 which can be applied in attacks relying on such MITM characteristics without solving the equations or increasing the overall time complexities.

Algorithm 4: Computing the solution spaces of the neutral words

Input: $(\#S^{\mathrm{ENC}}[\mathcal{G}^{\mathrm{ENC}}], \#S^{\mathrm{KSA}}[\mathcal{G}^{\mathrm{KSA}}]) \in \mathbb{F}_2^{w \cdot (|\mathcal{G}^{\mathrm{ENC}}| + |\mathcal{G}^{\mathrm{KSA}}|)}$

Output: V, U

1 $V \leftarrow [\,], U \leftarrow [\,]$

2 **for** $(\#S^{\mathrm{ENC}}[\mathcal{B}^{\mathrm{ENC}}], \#S^{\mathrm{KSA}}[\mathcal{B}^{\mathrm{KSA}}]) \in \mathbb{F}_2^{w \cdot (|\mathcal{B}^{\mathrm{ENC}}| + |\mathcal{B}^{\mathrm{KSA}}|)}$ **do**

3 $\quad v \leftarrow \pi^+(\#S^{\mathrm{ENC}}[\mathcal{G}^{\mathrm{ENC}}], \#S^{\mathrm{KSA}}[\mathcal{G}^{\mathrm{KSA}}], \#S^{\mathrm{ENC}}[\mathcal{B}^{\mathrm{ENC}}], \#S^{\mathrm{KSA}}[\mathcal{B}^{\mathrm{KSA}}])$ by Equation 1

4 $\quad$ Insert $(\#S^{\mathrm{ENC}}[\mathcal{B}^{\mathrm{ENC}}], \#S^{\mathrm{KSA}}[\mathcal{B}^{\mathrm{KSA}}])$ into V at index v

5 **for** $(\#S^{\mathrm{ENC}}[\mathcal{R}^{\mathrm{ENC}}], \#S^{\mathrm{KSA}}[\mathcal{R}^{\mathrm{KSA}}]) \in \mathbb{F}_2^{w \cdot (|\mathcal{R}^{\mathrm{ENC}}| + |\mathcal{R}^{\mathrm{KSA}}|)}$ **do**

6 $\quad u \leftarrow \pi^-(\#S^{\mathrm{ENC}}[\mathcal{G}^{\mathrm{ENC}}], \#S^{\mathrm{KSA}}[\mathcal{G}^{\mathrm{KSA}}], \#S^{\mathrm{ENC}}[\mathcal{R}^{\mathrm{ENC}}], \#S^{\mathrm{KSA}}[\mathcal{R}^{\mathrm{KSA}}])$ by Equation 2

7 $\quad$ Insert $(\#S^{\mathrm{ENC}}[\mathcal{R}^{\mathrm{ENC}}], \#S^{\mathrm{KSA}}[\mathcal{R}^{\mathrm{KSA}}])$ into U at index u

---

Algorithm 4 obtains the solution spaces of the neutral words for all possible $\mathfrak{c}^+$ and $\mathfrak{c}^-$ under a given value of $(\#S^{\mathrm{ENC}}[\mathcal{G}^{\mathrm{ENC}}], \#S^{\mathrm{KSA}}[\mathcal{G}^{\mathrm{KSA}}])$ with time complexity $(2^w)^{\lambda^+} + (2^w)^{\lambda^-}$ and memory complexity $(2^w)^{\lambda^+} + (2^w)^{\lambda^-}$. After running Algorithm 4, $V[v]$ stores the solution space of

$$\pi^+(\#S^{\mathrm{ENC}}[\mathcal{G}^{\mathrm{ENC}}], \#S^{\mathrm{KSA}}[\mathcal{G}^{\mathrm{KSA}}], \#S^{\mathrm{ENC}}[\mathcal{B}^{\mathrm{ENC}}], \#S^{\mathrm{KSA}}[\mathcal{B}^{\mathrm{KSA}}]) = v,$$

which consists about $2^{w \cdot (\lambda^+ - l^+)} = 2^{w \cdot \mathrm{DoF}^+}$ values for the neutral words for the forward computation. Similarly, under each index u of U, there are about $2^{w \cdot (\lambda^- - l^-)} = 2^{w \cdot \mathrm{DoF}^-}$ values for the neutral words for the backward computation. Algorithm 4 can be plugged into the procedure for MITM attacks to deal with MITM characteristics with nonlinearly constrained neutral words. For example, applying the technique to the MITM preimage attack gives Algorithm 5. Next, we show the time complexity is not increased.

Algorithm 5: The framework of the MITM preimage attack on AES-like hashing with non-linearly constrained neutral words

---

1 **for** $(\#S^{\mathrm{ENC}}[\mathcal{G}^{\mathrm{ENC}}], \#S^{\mathrm{KSA}}[\mathcal{G}^{\mathrm{KSA}}]) \in \mathbb{G} \subseteq \mathbb{F}_2^{w \cdot (|\mathcal{G}^{\mathrm{ENC}}| + |\mathcal{G}^{\mathrm{KSA}}|)}$ **do**

2   Call Algorithm 4 to build V, U

3   **for** $\mathfrak{c}^+ = (a_1, \cdots, a_{l^+}) \in \mathbb{F}_2^{w \cdot l^+}$ **do**

4   **for** $\mathfrak{c}^- = (b_1, \cdots, b_{l^-}) \in \mathbb{F}_2^{w \cdot l^-}$ **do**

5             $L \leftarrow [\,]$

6   **for** $(\#S^{\mathrm{ENC}}[\mathcal{B}^{\mathrm{ENC}}], \#S^{\mathrm{KSA}}[\mathcal{B}^{\mathrm{KSA}}]) \in V[\mathfrak{c}^+]$ **do**

7   Compute $E^+[\mathcal{M}^+]$ along the forward computation path

8   Insert $(\#S^{\mathrm{ENC}}[\mathcal{B}^{\mathrm{ENC}}], \#S^{\mathrm{KSA}}[\mathcal{B}^{\mathrm{KSA}}])$ into L indexed by $E^+[\mathcal{M}^+]$

9   **for** $(\#S^{\mathrm{ENC}}[\mathcal{R}^{\mathrm{KSA}}], \#S^{\mathrm{KSA}}[\mathcal{R}^{\mathrm{KSA}}]) \in U[\mathfrak{c}^-],$ **do**

10   Compute $E^-[\mathcal{M}^-]$ along the backward computation path

11   **for** $(\#S^{\mathrm{ENC}}[\mathcal{B}^{\mathrm{ENC}}], \#S^{\mathrm{KSA}}[\mathcal{B}^{\mathrm{KSA}}]) \in L[E^-[\mathcal{M}^-]]$ **do**

12   Reconstruct the (candidate) message X

13   **if** X *is a preimage* **then**

14   Output X and Stop.

Complexity Analysis. In each MITM episode within the context defined by the "For" loops surrounding the code segment from Line 6 to Line 14 of Algorithm 5, we test $2^{w \cdot (\mathrm{DoF}^+ + \mathrm{DoF}^-)}$ messages and we expect $2^{w \cdot (\mathrm{DoF}^+ + \mathrm{DoF}^- - m)}$ of them to pass the m-cell filter, and averagely, there are about $2^{w \cdot (\mathrm{DoF}^+ + \mathrm{DoF}^- - h)}$ preimages passing the check at Line 13 for each episode. The time complexity to perform one MITM episode is

$$(2^w)^{\mathrm{DoF}^+} + (2^w)^{\mathrm{DoF}^-} + (2^w)^{\mathrm{DoF}^+ + \mathrm{DoF}^- - m}. \tag{5}$$

Then, we estimate the size of $\mathbb{G}$ in Line 1 of Algorithm 5, which determines the number of MITM episodes performed. Suppose $|\mathbb{G}| = (2^w)^x$, to produce one preimage, we require that $(2^w)^x \cdot (2^w)^{l^+ + l^-} \cdot (2^w)^{\mathrm{DoF}^+ + \mathrm{DoF}^-} = (2^w)^h$ or $x = h - (\lambda^+ + \lambda^-)$. Hence, we consider two situations depending on $\lambda^+ + \lambda^-$.

- $\lambda^+ + \lambda^- \geq h$: In this case, we set $x = 0$, then $|\mathbb{G}| = 1$. At Line 3 and Line 4 of Algorithm 5, we only need to traverse $(2^w)^{h - (\mathrm{DoF}^+ + \mathrm{DoF}^-)}$ values of $(\mathfrak{c}^+, \mathfrak{c}^-) \in \mathbb{F}_2^{w \cdot l^+ + w \cdot l^-}$, where $h - (\mathrm{DoF}^+ + \mathrm{DoF}^-) \leq l^+ + l^-$ due to $\lambda^+ + \lambda^- \geq h$, to find the preimage. Then, together with Eq. (5), we have the overall time complexity: $(2^w)^{\lambda^+} + (2^w)^{\lambda^-} + (2^w)^{h - \min(\mathrm{DoF}^+, \, \mathrm{DoF}^-, \, m)}$.

- $\lambda^+ + \lambda^- < h$: Set $x = h - (\lambda^+ + \lambda^-)$, and we need to build 2^x V and U in Line 2 of Algorithm 5. Hence, we get the overall complexity:

$$(2^w)^{h - \lambda^+} + (2^w)^{h - \lambda^-} + (2^w)^{h - \min(\mathrm{DoF}^+, \, \mathrm{DoF}^-, \, m)}. \tag{6}$$

Moreover, the memory complexity for both situations is

$$(2^w)^{\lambda^+} + (2^w)^{\lambda^-} + (2^w)^{\min(\mathrm{DoF}^+, \, \mathrm{DoF}^-)}. \tag{7}$$

We apply Algorithm 5 to Grøstl-256, Saturnin-Hash, and AES-256 hashing and improved cryptanalytic results are obtained (see the full version of the paper). In particular, employing the new representation of the AES key schedule due to Leurent and Pernot (EUROCRYPT 2021), we identify the first preimage attack on 10-round AES-256 hashing.

6   MITM-Based Collision Attacks and Its Applications

Suppose that there is an algorithm that can produce a different t-cell partial target preimage. Then we expect to find a collision by running the algorithm $2^{w \cdot (h-t)/2}$ times to identify a collision on the h-cell hash value. At FSE 2012 [43], Li, Isobe, and Shibutani employed this strategy to convert the MITM-based partial target preimage attacks into pseudo collision attacks. First, we consider a generalization of partial target preimage attacks.

Let $\mathbb{T}$ be the space of all possible values of the output of the hash function. For a predefined partition of $\mathbb{T}$ into $(2^w)^t$ subspaces with an equal size. We call an algorithm a t-cell partial target preimage attack if it can produce a message whose hash value is a random element in a given subspace. For example, an algorithm generating a message such that the first word of its hash value is always 0 is a 1-cell partial target preimage attack. An algorithm generating a message such that the XOR of the first and second words of its hash value is always 0 is also a 1-cell partial target preimage attack. Given an MITM characteristic, the framework for a collision attack is described in Algorithm 6. Note that the call to Algorithm 6 can be replaced by an ordinary equation solving procedure to save the memory if the involved equations are linear or easy to solve. To be clear on how to set the objective functions in our MILP models, we need to understand how the complexity of the attack is related to the parameters specified in the MITM characteristic.

Complexity Analysis. In the MITM t-cell partial target preimage attack, if the matching process results in an m-cell filter, then we have $m \le t$, because the matching information is derived from the known cells of the target T. To determine the overall complexity of the algorithm, we need to determine how many MITM episodes (Line 9 to 18 of Algorithm 6) are required. According to the analysis of Algorithm 4 in Sect. 5, the time complexity for building U and V is $(2^w)^{\lambda^+} + (2^w)^{\lambda^-}$. In each MITM episode within the context defined by the "For" loops surrounding the code segment from Line 9 to Line 18, we test $2^{w \cdot (\text{DoF}^+ + \text{DoF}^-)}$ messages and we expect $2^{w \cdot (\text{DoF}^+ + \text{DoF}^- - m)}$ of them to pass the m-cell filter, and averagely, there are about $2^{w \cdot (\text{DoF}^+ + \text{DoF}^- - t)}$ messages are inserted into the hash table H. Therefore, we need about $(2^w)^{\frac{h-t}{2} - (\text{DoF}^+ + \text{DoF}^- - t)}$ episodes to produce one collision. The time to perform one MITM episode is

$$(2^w)^{\text{DoF}^+} + (2^w)^{\text{DoF}^-} + (2^w)^{\text{DoF}^+ + \text{DoF}^- - m} + (2^w)^{\text{DoF}^+ + \text{DoF}^- - t}. \qquad (8)$$

Suppose in Line 3 of Algorithm 6 we have $\mathbb{G} = 2^{w \cdot x}$. Then, $(2^w)^x \cdot (2^w)^{l^+} \cdot (2^w)^{l^-}$ matching episodes are performed. Hence, we have

---

Algorithm 6: The framework of the MITM collision attack on AES-like hashing with non-linearly constrained starting states

---

1 Setting the selected t cells of $\#T$ to constants
2 $H \leftarrow [\,]$

3 **for** $(\#S^{\mathrm{ENC}}[\mathcal{G}^{\mathrm{ENC}}], \#S^{\mathrm{KSA}}[\mathcal{G}^{\mathrm{KSA}}]) \in \mathbb{G} \subseteq \mathbb{F}_2^{w \cdot (|\mathcal{G}^{\mathrm{ENC}}| + |\mathcal{G}^{\mathrm{KSA}}|)}$ **do**
4    $V \leftarrow [\,], U \leftarrow [\,]$
5   Call Algorithm 4 to populate V and U
6   **for** $\mathfrak{c}^+ = (a_1, \cdots, a_{l^+}) \in \mathbb{F}_2^{w \cdot l^+}$ **do**
7   **for** $\mathfrak{c}^- = (b_1, \cdots, b_{l^-}) \in \mathbb{F}_2^{w \cdot l^-}$ **do**
8        $L \leftarrow [\,]$

9   **for** $(\#S^{\mathrm{ENC}}[\mathcal{B}^{\mathrm{ENC}}], \#S^{\mathrm{KSA}}[\mathcal{B}^{\mathrm{KSA}}]) \in V[\mathfrak{c}^+]$ **do**
10   Compute $E^+[\mathcal{M}^+]$ along the forward computation path
11   Insert $(\#S^{\mathrm{ENC}}[\mathcal{B}^{\mathrm{ENC}}], \#S^{\mathrm{KSA}}[\mathcal{B}^{\mathrm{KSA}}])$ into L indexed by $E^+[\mathcal{M}^+]$

12   **for** $(\#S^{\mathrm{ENC}}[\mathcal{R}^{\mathrm{KSA}}], \#S^{\mathrm{KSA}}[\mathcal{R}^{\mathrm{KSA}}]) \in U[\mathfrak{c}^-]$, **do**
13   Compute $E^-[\mathcal{M}^-]$ along the backward computation path

14   **for** $(\#S^{\mathrm{ENC}}[\mathcal{B}^{\mathrm{ENC}}], \#S^{\mathrm{KSA}}[\mathcal{B}^{\mathrm{KSA}}]) \in L[E^-[\mathcal{M}^-]]$ **do**
15   Reconstruct the (candidate) message X
16   **if** X *is a t-cell partial target preimage* **then**
17   Insert X into H indexed by the hash value of X
18   Stop when there is a collision

$$(2^w)^x \cdot (2^w)^{l^+} \cdot (2^w)^{l^-} = (2^w)^{\frac{h-t}{2} - (\mathrm{DoF}^+ + \mathrm{DoF}^- - t)}.$$

We get $x = \frac{h}{2} - (\lambda^+ + \lambda^- - \frac{t}{2})$. Hence, we consider two situations:

- $\lambda^+ + \lambda^- \geq \frac{h+t}{2}$: In this case, we set $x = 0$. At Line 6 and Line 7 of Algorithm 6, we only need to traverse $(2^w)^{\frac{h-t}{2} - (\mathrm{DoF}^+ + \mathrm{DoF}^- - t)}$ values of $(\mathfrak{c}^+, \mathfrak{c}^-) \in \mathbb{F}_2^{w \cdot l^+ + w \cdot l^-}$, where $\frac{h-t}{2} - (\mathrm{DoF}^+ + \mathrm{DoF}^- - t) \leq l^+ + l^-$ due to $\lambda^+ + \lambda^- \geq \frac{h+t}{2}$, to find the collision. Then, together with Eq. 8, we have the overall time complexity:

$$(2^w)^{\lambda^+} + (2^w)^{\lambda^-} + (2^w)^{\frac{h}{2} - \min\{\mathrm{DoF}^+ - \frac{t}{2}, \ \mathrm{DoF}^- - \frac{t}{2}, \ m - \frac{t}{2}, \ \frac{t}{2}\}}. \tag{9}$$

- $\lambda^+ + \lambda^- < \frac{h+t}{2}$: Set $x = \frac{h}{2} - (\lambda^+ + \lambda^- - \frac{t}{2})$, and we need to build 2^x V and U in Line 5 of Algorithm 6. Hence, we get the overall complexity:

$$(2^w)^{\frac{h}{2} - (\lambda^+ - \frac{t}{2})} + (2^w)^{\frac{h}{2} - (\lambda^- - \frac{t}{2})} + (2^w)^{\frac{h}{2} - \min\{\mathrm{DoF}^+ - \frac{t}{2}, \ \mathrm{DoF}^- - \frac{t}{2}, \ m - \frac{t}{2}, \ \frac{t}{2}\}}, \tag{10}$$

which is approximately $(2^w)^{\frac{h}{2} - \min\{\mathrm{DoF}^+ - \frac{t}{2}, \ \mathrm{DoF}^- - \frac{t}{2}, \ m - \frac{t}{2}, \ \frac{t}{2}\}}$, since we always have $\mathrm{DoF}^+ \leq \lambda^+$ and $\mathrm{DoF}^- \leq \lambda^-$.

The memory complexity in both situations is

$$(2^w)^{\lambda^+} + (2^w)^{\lambda^-} + (2^w)^{\min\{\text{DoF}^+,\text{DoF}^-\}} + (2^w)^{\frac{h-t}{2}}. \tag{11}$$

where the $(2^w)^{\frac{h-t}{2}}$ is to store the t-cell partial target preimages in H. Consequently, for an attack efficient than the trivial birthday attack, we have $\min\{\text{DoF}^+ - \frac{t}{2}, \text{DoF}^- - \frac{t}{2}, m - \frac{t}{2}, \frac{t}{2}\} > 0$, $\lambda^+ < \frac{h}{2}$ and $\lambda^- < \frac{h}{2}$, or

$$\begin{cases} \text{DoF}^+ > \frac{t}{2}, \ \text{DoF}^- > \frac{t}{2} \\ \frac{t}{2} < m \leq t \\ \lambda^+ < \frac{h}{2}, \ \lambda^- < \frac{h}{2} \end{cases}.$$

6.1   Automatic Search for MITM-Based Collision Attacks

First of all, The objective function of the model is to maximize

$$\min(\text{DoF}^+ - \frac{t}{2}, \text{DoF}^+ - \frac{t}{2}, m - \frac{t}{2}, \frac{t}{2})$$

according to Eq. (10). In what follows, we only discuss the main particularity of MITM-based collision attacks, which lies in the matching part. To be more specific, the degree of match (DoM) is derived differently from other attacks discussed in the work. To be concrete, we consider AES-like hashings like WHIRLPOOL and Grøstl, which includes the MixColumn(MC) or MixRows(MR) operation in their last rounds. To determine the degree of match, we consider two situations according to the position where the match happens.

The Matching Point is Placed at the Last Round. Suppose that the MDS matrix of the MC operation at the matching point operates on k cells, which links the state Z in the last round to the XOR sum of the input state X of the first round and the target T, i.e., $MC(Z) = X \oplus T$. Suppose that from the forward and backward computation α ■ cells and β ■ cells are known. Without loss of generality, we assume $(Z[0], \cdots, Z[\alpha - 1])^T$ of Z is known as ■, and $(X[0], \cdots, X[\beta - 1])^T$ of X is known as ■. From

$$MC \cdot \begin{pmatrix} Z[0] \\ \vdots \\ Z[\alpha - 1] \\ \vdots \\ Z[k-1] \end{pmatrix} = \begin{pmatrix} X[0] \oplus T[0] \\ X[1] \oplus T[1] \\ \vdots \\ X[\beta - 1] \oplus T[\beta - 1] \\ \vdots \end{pmatrix},$$

we get β linear equations with k variables $Z[0], Z[1], \cdots, Z[k-1]$ on the left, and 2β variables $X[0], \cdots, X[\beta - 1], T[0], \cdots, T[\beta - 1]$ on the right. There are $k - \alpha$ unknowns $Z[\alpha], \cdots, Z[k - 1]$ on the left. Hence, if $\beta > k - \alpha$, we can represent the $k - \alpha$ unknowns by other variables by consuming $k - \alpha$ linear equations. At last, we have $\Sigma = \beta - (k - \alpha)$ linear equations left:

$$\begin{cases} \zeta_1(Z[0], \cdots, Z[\alpha - 1]) = \phi_1(X[0], \cdots, X[\beta - 1]) \oplus \varphi_1(T[0], \cdots, T[\beta - 1]), \\ \zeta_2(Z[0], \cdots, Z[\alpha - 1]) = \phi_2(X[0], \cdots, X[\beta - 1]) \oplus \varphi_2(T[0], \cdots, T[\beta - 1]), \\ \qquad\qquad\qquad \vdots \\ \zeta_\Sigma(Z[0], \cdots, Z[\alpha - 1]) = \phi_\Sigma(X[0], \cdots, X[\beta - 1]) \oplus \varphi_\Sigma(T[0], \cdots, T[\beta - 1]), \end{cases} \tag{12}$$

where $\zeta_i(\cdot)$, $\phi_i(\cdot)$, $\varphi_i(\cdot)$ are linear equations. By assigning $t \leq \Sigma = \beta + \alpha - k$ conditions on the target T in the Eq. (12):

$$\begin{cases} \varphi_1(T[0], \cdots, T[\beta-1]) = \tau_1, \\ \varphi_2(T[0], \cdots, T[\beta-1]) = \tau_2, \\ \quad \vdots \\ \varphi_t(T[0], \cdots, T[\beta-1]) = \tau_t, \end{cases} \tag{13}$$

where $\boldsymbol{\tau} = (\tau_1, \cdots, \tau_t) \in \mathbb{F}_2^{w \cdot t}$, we get a t-cell filter:

$$\begin{cases} \zeta_1(Z[0], \cdots, Z[\alpha-1]) = \phi_1(X[0], \cdots, X[\beta-1]) \oplus \tau_1, \\ \zeta_2(Z[0], \cdots, Z[\alpha-1]) = \phi_2(X[0], \cdots, X[\beta-1]) \oplus \tau_2, \\ \quad \vdots \\ \zeta_{\tau_t}(Z[0], \cdots, Z[\alpha-1]) = \phi_{\Sigma}(X[0], \cdots, X[\beta-1]) \oplus \tau_t. \end{cases}$$

In summary, we have the constraints DoF $= t \leq \Sigma = \beta + \alpha - k$ and $\beta + \alpha \geq k$. Therefore, in the MILP model for this case, we can ignore the coloring information of T. After identifying an MITM characteristic with configurations for (α, β, m, t), the t conditions on T can be derived accordingly with Eq. (13).

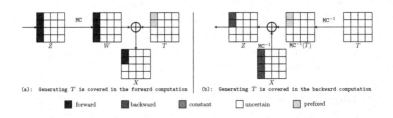

(a): Generating T is covered in the forward computation   (b): Generating T is covered in the backward computation

■ forward   ■ backward   ■ constant   □ uncertain   ▨ prefixed

Fig. 9. The matching point is not placed at the last round.

The Matching Point is not at the Last Round. In this case, the XOR of the target T can happen in the forward computation (see Fig. 9(a)) or in the backward computation (see Fig. 9(b)). The yellow cells are prefixed constants, which can be represented as 0-1 variables in the same way as the Gray (G) cells: If the ith cell of T is yellow, then $(x_i^T, y_i^T) = (1,1)$. Other cells of T are White (W), encoded as $(x_j^T, y_j^T) = (0,0)$.

In the case shown in Fig. 9(a), the rules of xoring the tag T is the same to the XOR$^+$-RULE by regarding the □ cells as ■ cells. Moreover, we require that the □ cells in T align with the ■ cells in X as shown in Fig. 9(a). Hence, the constraint $x_i^T \leq x_i^X$ is added to avoid the transition $□ \oplus □ \to □$. Therefore, for the number t of conditions imposed on T, we have $t = \sum_i x_i^T$.

In the case of Fig. 9(b), we consider the positions of □ cells in $\mathrm{MC}^{-1}(T)$. The rules of xoring the tag T is the same to the XOR$^+$-RULE by regarding the □ cells as ■ cells. In addition, we require that the □ cells in $\mathrm{MC}^{-1}(T)$ align with the ■ cells in Z. Hence, the constraint $y_i^{\mathrm{MC}^{-1}(T)} \leq y_i^Z$ is added to avoid the transition $□ \oplus □ \to □$. Therefore, for the number t of conditions imposed on T, we have

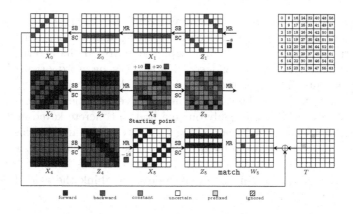

Fig. 10. An MITM attack on 6-round WHIRLPOOL

$$t = \sum_i y_i^{\text{MC}^{-1}(T)}.$$

6.2 Collision Attacks on WHIRLPOOL and Grøstl

The WHIRLPOOL hash function, designed by Barreto and Rijmen, is an ISO/IEC standard. Its compression function is built by plug an AES-like cipher into the Miyaguchi-Preneel construction . During the last 20 years, WHIRLPOOL has withstood extensive cryptanalysis [32,44,52] and the best collision attack in the classical setting reaches 5 rounds [29,42]. Recently, Hosoyamada and Sasaki introduced a quantum collision attack on 6-round WHIRLPOOL [32].

We give the first 6-round collision attack on WHIRLPOOL in the classical setting, breaking the 10-year record for collision attacks on WHIRLPOOL. Applying the automatic model of MITM collision attack to WHIRLPOOL, we find a new 6-round MITM characteristic shown in Fig. 10. We apply Algorithm 6 to WHIRLPOOL based on this MITM characteristic. The starting state is X_3. Then, we have $\lambda^+ = 10$ and $\lambda^- = 20$, $w = 8$. According to Property 1, we have $l^+ = 8$ and $\mathfrak{c}^+ = (a_1, \cdots, a_8) \in \mathbb{F}_2^{8 \times 8}$; $l^- = 16$ and $\mathfrak{c}^- = (b_1, \cdots, b_{16}) \in \mathbb{F}_2^{8 \times 16}$. Then we build similar equations in the attack on Grøstl (See Section D in the full version of the paper). Therefore, we call Algorithm 4 to build V and U. $\text{DoF}^+ = \lambda^+ - l^+ = 2$, $\text{DoF}^- = \lambda^- - l^- = 4$, $t = m = 2$ and $h = 64$. The time complexity is $(2^8)^{\frac{64}{2}-(10-\frac{2}{2})} + (2^8)^{\frac{64}{2}-(20-\frac{2}{2})} + (2^8)^{\frac{64}{2}-\min\{2-\frac{2}{2},\, 4-\frac{2}{2},\, 2-\frac{2}{2},\, \frac{2}{2}\}} \approx 2^{248}$ according to Eq. (10), and the memory complexity is about 2^{248}. We also apply the method to Grøstl, and the results are given in Section F of the full version of the paper.

7 Conclusion and Open Problems

We formulate the MITM attacks in a more formal, expressive, and accurate way. Based on this formulation, we investigate the peculiarities of MITM-based key-recovery attacks on block ciphers and collision attacks on AES-like hash functions and model them in the constraint programming paradigm. Now, we have a fairly powerful tool for finding exploitable MITM characteristics in key-recovery, (pseudo) preimage, and collision attacks on word oriented designs. Moreover, we present a generic procedure for dealing with nonlinearly constrained neutral words without increasing the overall time complexities of the attacks relying on them. We apply our method to concrete keyed and unkeyed primitives, leading to attacks improving the state-of-the-art. At this point, we would like propose an open problem: Is it possible to search for bit-level MITM characteristics automatically, and to what extent it can improve the current cryptanalytic results? For bit-oriented models, we think the work from Fuhr, Minaud, and Yu [27,47] is good starting point.

Acknowledgment. We thank the reviewers for their valuable comments. This work is supported by National Key R&D Program of China (2018YFA0704701, 2018YFA0704704), the Major Program of Guangdong Basic and Applied Research (2019B030302008), Major Scientific and Techological Innovation Project of Shandong Province, China (2019JZZY010133), Natural Science Foundation of China (61902207, 61772519) and the Chinese Major Program of National Cryptography Development Foundation (MMJJ20180101, MMJJ20180102).

References

1. AlTawy, R., Youssef, A.M.: Preimage attacks on reduced-round stribog. In: Pointcheval, D., Vergnaud, D. (eds.) AFRICACRYPT 2014. LNCS, vol. 8469, pp. 109–125. Springer, Cham (2014). https://doi.org/10.1007/978-3-319-06734-6_7
2. Aoki, K., Guo, J., Matusiewicz, K., Sasaki, Yu., Wang, L.: Preimages for step-reduced SHA-2. In: Matsui, M. (ed.) ASIACRYPT 2009. LNCS, vol. 5912, pp. 578–597. Springer, Heidelberg (2009). https://doi.org/10.1007/978-3-642-10366-7_34
3. Aoki, K., Sasaki, Yu.: Preimage attacks on one-block MD4, 63-step MD5 and more. In: Avanzi, R.M., Keliher, L., Sica, F. (eds.) SAC 2008. LNCS, vol. 5381, pp. 103–119. Springer, Heidelberg (2009). https://doi.org/10.1007/978-3-642-04159-4_7
4. Aoki, K., Sasaki, Yu.: Meet-in-the-middle preimage attacks against reduced SHA-0 and SHA-1. In: Halevi, S. (ed.) CRYPTO 2009. LNCS, vol. 5677, pp. 70–89. Springer, Heidelberg (2009). https://doi.org/10.1007/978-3-642-03356-8_5
5. Banik, Subhadeep, Pandey, Sumit Kumar, Peyrin, Thomas, Sasaki, Yu., Sim, Siang Meng, Todo, Yosuke: GIFT: a small Present - towards reaching the limit of lightweight encryption. In: Fischer, Wieland, Homma, Naofumi (eds.) CHES 2017. LNCS, vol. 10529, pp. 321–345. Springer, Cham (2017). https://doi.org/10.1007/978-3-319-66787-4_16
6. Bao, Z., et al.: Automatic search of meet-in-the-middle preimage attacks on AES-like hashing. Cryptology ePrint Archive, Report 2020/467 (2020)
7. Bariant, A., David, N., Leurent, G.: Cryptanalysis of Forkciphers. IACR Trans. Symmetric Cryptol. **2020**(1), 233–265 (2020)
8. Barreto, P.S.L.M., Rijmen, V.: The WHIRLPOOL Hashing Function (2000). Revised in 2003

9. Beierle, C., et al.: The SKINNY family of block ciphers and its low-latency variant MANTIS. In: Robshaw, M., Katz, J. (eds.) CRYPTO 2016. LNCS, vol. 9815, pp. 123–153. Springer, Heidelberg (2016). https://doi.org/10.1007/978-3-662-53008-5_5

10. Biham, E., Dunkelman, O., Keller, N., Shamir, A.: New attacks on IDEA with at least 6 rounds. J. Cryptol. 28(2), 209–239 (2015)

11. Bogdanov, A., Khovratovich, D., Rechberger, C.: Biclique cryptanalysis of the full AES. In: Lee, D.H., Wang, X. (eds.) ASIACRYPT 2011. LNCS, vol. 7073, pp. 344–371. Springer, Heidelberg (2011). https://doi.org/10.1007/978-3-642-25385-0_19

12. Bogdanov, A., Rechberger, C.: A 3-subset meet-in-the-middle attack: cryptanalysis of the lightweight block cipher KTANTAN. In: Biryukov, A., Gong, G., Stinson, D.R. (eds.) SAC 2010. LNCS, vol. 6544, pp. 229–240. Springer, Heidelberg (2011). https://doi.org/10.1007/978-3-642-19574-7_16

13. Boura, C., Canteaut, A., De Cannière, C.: Higher-order differential properties of KECCAK and Luffa. In: Joux, A. (ed.) FSE 2011. LNCS, vol. 6733, pp. 252–269. Springer, Heidelberg (2011). https://doi.org/10.1007/978-3-642-21702-9_15

14. Canteaut, A., et al.: Saturnin: a suite of lightweight symmetric algorithms for post-quantum security. IACR Trans. Symmetric Cryptol. 2020(S1), 160–207 (2020)

15. Canteaut, A., Naya-Plasencia, M., Vayssière, B.: Sieve-in-the-middle: improved MITM attacks. In: Canetti, R., Garay, J.A. (eds.) CRYPTO 2013. LNCS, vol. 8042, pp. 222–240. Springer, Heidelberg (2013). https://doi.org/10.1007/978-3-642-40041-4_13

16. Demirci, H., Selçuk, A.A.: A meet-in-the-middle attack on 8-round AES. In: Nyberg, K. (ed.) FSE 2008. LNCS, vol. 5086, pp. 116–126. Springer, Heidelberg (2008). https://doi.org/10.1007/978-3-540-71039-4_7

17. Derbez, P., Fouque, P.-A., Jean, J.: Improved key recovery attacks on reduced-round, in the single-key setting. In: Johansson, T., Nguyen, P.Q. (eds.) EUROCRYPT 2013. LNCS, vol. 7881, pp. 371–387. Springer, Heidelberg (2013). https://doi.org/10.1007/978-3-642-38348-9_23

18. Diffie, W., Hellman, M.E.: Special feature exhaustive cryptanalysis of the NBS data encryption standard. Computer 10(6), 74–84 (1977)

19. Dinur, I., Dunkelman, O., Keller, N., Shamir, A.: Key recovery attacks on 3-round even-mansour, 8-step LED-128, and full AES2. In: Sako, K., Sarkar, P. (eds.) ASIACRYPT 2013. LNCS, vol. 8269, pp. 337–356. Springer, Heidelberg (2013). https://doi.org/10.1007/978-3-642-42033-7_18

20. Dinur, I., Dunkelman, O., Keller, N., Shamir, A.: Cryptanalysis of iterated even-mansour schemes with two keys. In: Sarkar, P., Iwata, T. (eds.) ASIACRYPT 2014. LNCS, vol. 8873, pp. 439–457. Springer, Heidelberg (2014). https://doi.org/10.1007/978-3-662-45611-8_23

21. Dinur, I., Dunkelman, O., Keller, N., Shamir, A.: New attacks on feistel structures with improved memory complexities. In: Gennaro, R., Robshaw, M. (eds.) CRYPTO 2015. LNCS, vol. 9215, pp. 433–454. Springer, Heidelberg (2015). https://doi.org/10.1007/978-3-662-47989-6_21

22. Dong, X., Hua, J., Sun, S., Li, Z., Wang, X., Hu, L.: Meet-in-the-middle attacks revisited: Key-recovery, collision, and preimage attacks. Cryptology ePrint Archive, Report 2021/427 (2021). https://eprint.iacr.org/2021/427

23. Dong, X., Sun, S., Shi, D., Gao, F., Wang, X., Hu, L.: Quantum collision attacks on AES-like hashing with low quantum random access memories. In: Moriai, S., Wang, H. (eds.) ASIACRYPT 2020. LNCS, vol. 12492, pp. 727–757. Springer, Cham (2020). https://doi.org/10.1007/978-3-030-64834-3_25

24. Dunkelman, O., Keller, N., Shamir, A.: Improved single-key attacks on 8-round AES-192 and AES-256. In: Abe, M. (ed.) ASIACRYPT 2010. LNCS, vol. 6477, pp. 158–176. Springer, Heidelberg (2010). https://doi.org/10.1007/978-3-642-17373-8_10

25. Dunkelman, O., Sekar, G., Preneel, B.: Improved meet-in-the-middle attacks on reduced-round DES. In: Srinathan, K., Rangan, C.P., Yung, M. (eds.) INDOCRYPT 2007. LNCS, vol. 4859, pp. 86–100. Springer, Heidelberg (2007). https://doi.org/10.1007/978-3-540-77026-8_8

26. Espitau, T., Fouque, P.-A., Karpman, P.: Higher-order differential meet-in-the-middle preimage attacks on SHA-1 and BLAKE. In: Gennaro, R., Robshaw, M. (eds.) CRYPTO 2015. LNCS, vol. 9215, pp. 683–701. Springer, Heidelberg (2015). https://doi.org/10.1007/978-3-662-47989-6_33

27. Fuhr, T., Minaud, B.: Match box meet-in-the-middle attack against KATAN. FSE **2014**, 61–81 (2014)

28. Gauravaram, P., et al.: Grøstl - a SHA-3 candidate. In: Symmetric Cryptography (2009)

29. Gilbert, H., Peyrin, T.: Super-Sbox cryptanalysis: improved attacks for AES-like permutations. FSE **2010**, 365–383 (2010)

30. Guo, J., Ling, S., Rechberger, C., Wang, H.: Advanced meet-in-the-middle preimage attacks: first results on full tiger, and improved results on MD4 and SHA-2. In: Abe, M. (ed.) ASIACRYPT 2010. LNCS, vol. 6477, pp. 56–75. Springer, Heidelberg (2010). https://doi.org/10.1007/978-3-642-17373-8_4

31. Hong, D., Koo, B., Sasaki, Yu.: Improved preimage attack for 68-step HAS-160. In: Lee, D., Hong, S. (eds.) ICISC 2009. LNCS, vol. 5984, pp. 332–348. Springer, Heidelberg (2010). https://doi.org/10.1007/978-3-642-14423-3_22

32. Hosoyamada, A., Sasaki, Yu.: Finding hash collisions with quantum computers by using differential trails with smaller probability than birthday bound. In: Canteaut, A., Ishai, Y. (eds.) EUROCRYPT 2020. LNCS, vol. 12106, pp. 249–279. Springer, Cham (2020). https://doi.org/10.1007/978-3-030-45724-2_9

33. Isobe, T.: A single-key attack on the full GOST block cipher. J. Cryptol. **26**(1), 172–189 (2013)

34. Isobe, T., Shibutani, K.: Security analysis of the lightweight block ciphers XTEA, LED and piccolo. In: Susilo, W., Mu, Y., Seberry, J. (eds.) ACISP 2012. LNCS, vol. 7372, pp. 71–86. Springer, Heidelberg (2012). https://doi.org/10.1007/978-3-642-31448-3_6

35. Isobe, T., Shibutani, K.: Generic key recovery attack on feistel scheme. In: Sako, K., Sarkar, P. (eds.) ASIACRYPT 2013. LNCS, vol. 8269, pp. 464–485. Springer, Heidelberg (2013). https://doi.org/10.1007/978-3-642-42033-7_24

36. Iwata, T., Khairallah, M., Minematsu, K., Peyrin, T.: Romulus for Round 3. NIST Lightweight Crypto Standardization process (Round 2) (2020)

37. Jean, J., Naya-Plasencia, M., Peyrin, T.: Improved rebound attack on the finalist Grøstl. In: Canteaut, A. (ed.) FSE 2012. LNCS, vol. 7549, pp. 110–126. Springer, Heidelberg (2012). https://doi.org/10.1007/978-3-642-34047-5_7

38. Jean, J., Nikolić, I., Peyrin, T.: Tweaks and keys for block ciphers: the TWEAKEY framework. In: Sarkar, P., Iwata, T. (eds.) ASIACRYPT 2014. LNCS, vol. 8874, pp. 274–288. Springer, Heidelberg (2014). https://doi.org/10.1007/978-3-662-45608-8_15

39. Khovratovich, D., Rechberger, C., Savelieva, A.: Bicliques for preimages: attacks on Skein-512 and the SHA-2 family. IACR Cryptol. ePrint Arch. **2011**, 286 (2011)

40. Knellwolf, S., Khovratovich, D.: New preimage attacks against reduced SHA-1. In: Safavi-Naini, R., Canetti, R. (eds.) CRYPTO 2012. LNCS, vol. 7417, pp. 367–383. Springer, Heidelberg (2012). https://doi.org/10.1007/978-3-642-32009-5_22

41. Kölbl, S., Lauridsen, M.M., Mendel, F., Rechberger, C.: Haraka v2 - efficient short-input hashing for post-quantum applications. IACR Trans. Symmetric Cryptol. **2016**(2), 1–29 (2016)

42. Lamberger, M., Mendel, F., Rechberger, C., Rijmen, V., Schläffer, M.: Rebound distinguishers: results on the full whirlpool compression function. In: Matsui, M. (ed.) ASIACRYPT 2009. LNCS, vol. 5912, pp. 126–143. Springer, Heidelberg (2009). https://doi.org/10.1007/978-3-642-10366-7_8

43. Li, J., Isobe, T., Shibutani, K.: Converting meet-in-the-middle preimage attack into pseudo collision attack: application to SHA-2. In: Canteaut, A. (ed.) FSE 2012. LNCS, vol. 7549, pp. 264–286. Springer, Heidelberg (2012). https://doi.org/10.1007/978-3-642-34047-5_16

44. Mendel, F., Rechberger, C., Schläffer, M., Thomsen, S.S.: The rebound attack: cryptanalysis of reduced WHIRLPOOL and Grøstl. FSE **2009**, 260–276 (2009)

45. Mendel, F., Rijmen, V., Schläffer, M.: Collision attack on 5 rounds of Grøstl. FSE **2014**, 509–521 (2014)

46. Sasaki, Yu.: Meet-in-the-middle preimage attacks on AES hashing modes and an application to whirlpool. In: Joux, A. (ed.) FSE 2011. LNCS, vol. 6733, pp. 378–396. Springer, Heidelberg (2011). https://doi.org/10.1007/978-3-642-21702-9_22

47. Sasaki, Yu.: Integer linear programming for three-subset meet-in-the-middle attacks: application to GIFT. In: Inomata, A., Yasuda, K. (eds.) IWSEC 2018. LNCS, vol. 11049, pp. 227–243. Springer, Cham (2018). https://doi.org/10.1007/978-3-319-97916-8_15

48. Sasaki, Yu., Aoki, K.: Preimage attacks on 3, 4, and 5-pass HAVAL. In: Pieprzyk, J. (ed.) ASIACRYPT 2008. LNCS, vol. 5350, pp. 253–271. Springer, Heidelberg (2008). https://doi.org/10.1007/978-3-540-89255-7_16

49. Sasaki, Yu., Aoki, K.: Finding preimages in full MD5 faster than exhaustive search. In: Joux, A. (ed.) EUROCRYPT 2009. LNCS, vol. 5479, pp. 134–152. Springer, Heidelberg (2009). https://doi.org/10.1007/978-3-642-01001-9_8

50. Sasaki, Y., Li, Y., Wang, L., Sakiyama, K., Ohta,K.: Non-full-active super-sbox analysis: applications to ECHO and Grøstl. In: ASIACRYPT 2010, Proceedings, pp. 38–55 (2010)

51. Sasaki, Yu., Wang, L., Sakai, Y., Sakiyama, K., Ohta, K.: Three-subset meet-in-the-middle attack on reduced XTEA. In: Mitrokotsa, A., Vaudenay, S. (eds.) AFRICACRYPT 2012. LNCS, vol. 7374, pp. 138–154. Springer, Heidelberg (2012). https://doi.org/10.1007/978-3-642-31410-0_9

52. Sasaki, Yu., Wang, L., Wu, S., Wu, W.: Investigating fundamental security requirements on whirlpool: improved preimage and collision attacks. In: Wang, X., Sako, K. (eds.) ASIACRYPT 2012. LNCS, vol. 7658, pp. 562–579. Springer, Heidelberg (2012). https://doi.org/10.1007/978-3-642-34961-4_34

53. Schläffer, M.: Updated differential analysis of Grøstl. In: Grøstl Website (2011)

54. Shi, D., Sun, S., Derbez, P., Todo, Y., Sun, B., Hu, L.: Programming the Demirci-Selçuk meet-in-the-middle attack with constraints. In: Peyrin, T., Galbraith, S. (eds.) ASIACRYPT 2018. LNCS, vol. 11273, pp. 3–34. Springer, Cham (2018). https://doi.org/10.1007/978-3-030-03329-3_1

55. Tolba, M., Abdelkhalek, A., Youssef, A.M.: Impossible differential cryptanalysis of reduced-round SKINNY. In: AFRICACRYPT 2017, Proceedings, vol. 10239, pp. 117–134 (2017)

56. Wang, L., Sasaki, Yu.: Finding preimages of tiger Up to 23 Steps. In: Hong, S., Iwata, T. (eds.) FSE 2010. LNCS, vol. 6147, pp. 116–133. Springer, Heidelberg (2010). https://doi.org/10.1007/978-3-642-13858-4_7

57. Wang, L., Sasaki, Yu., Komatsubara, W., Ohta, K., Sakiyama, K.: (Second) preimage attacks on step-reduced RIPEMD/RIPEMD-128 with a new local-collision approach. In: Kiayias, A. (ed.) CT-RSA 2011. LNCS, vol. 6558, pp. 197–212. Springer, Heidelberg (2011). https://doi.org/10.1007/978-3-642-19074-2_14

58. Wei, L., Rechberger, C., Guo, J., Wu, H., Wang, H., Ling, S.: Improved meet-in-the-middle cryptanalysis of KTANTAN (poster). In: Parampalli, U., Hawkes, P. (eds.) ACISP 2011. LNCS, vol. 6812, pp. 433–438. Springer, Heidelberg (2011). https://doi.org/10.1007/978-3-642-22497-3_31

59. Shuang, W., Feng, D., Wenling, W., Guo, J., Dong, L., Zou, J.: (pseudo) Preimage attack on round-reduced Grøstl hash function and others. FSE **2012**, 127–145 (2012)

Revisiting the Security of DbHtS MACs: Beyond-Birthday-Bound in the Multi-user Setting

Yaobin Shen[1], Lei Wang[1(✉)], Dawu Gu[1], and Jian Weng[2]

[1] Shanghai Jiao Tong University, Shanghai, China
{yb_shen,wanglei_hb,dwgu}@sjtu.edu.cn
[2] Jinan University, Guangzhou, China

Abstract. Double-block Hash-then-Sum (DbHtS) MACs are a class of MACs that aim for achieving beyond-birthday-bound security, including SUM-ECBC, PMAC_Plus, 3kf9 and LightMAC_Plus. Recently Datta et al. (FSE'19), and then Kim et al. (Eurocrypt'20) prove that DbHtS constructions are secure beyond the birthday bound in the single-user setting. However, by a generic reduction, their results degrade to (or even worse than) the birthday bound in the multi-user setting.

In this work, we revisit the security of DbHtS MACs in the multi-user setting. We propose a generic framework to prove beyond-birthday-bound security for DbHtS constructions. We demonstrate the usability of this framework with applications to key-reduced variants of DbHtS MACs, including 2k-SUM-ECBC, 2k-PMAC_Plus and 2k-LightMAC_Plus. Our results show that the security of these constructions will not degrade as the number of users grows. On the other hand, our results also indicate that these constructions are secure beyond the birthday bound in both single-user and multi-user setting without additional domain separation, which is used in the prior work to simplify the analysis.

Moreover, we find a critical flaw in 2kf9, which is proved to be secure beyond the birthday bound by Datta et al. (FSE'19). We can successfully forge a tag with probability 1 without making any queries. We go further to show attacks with birthday-bound complexity on several variants of 2kf9.

Keywords: Message authentication codes · Beyond-birthday-bound security · Multi-user security

1 Introduction

Message Authentication Code (MAC) is a fundamental symmetric-key primitive to ensure the authenticity of data. A MAC is typically built from a blockcipher (e.g., CBC-MAC [6], OMAC [22], PMAC [11], LightMAC [27]), or from a hash function (e.g., HMAC [5], NMAC [5], NI-MAC [1]). At a high level, many of these

© International Association for Cryptologic Research 2021
T. Malkin and C. Peikert (Eds.): CRYPTO 2021, LNCS 12827, pp. 309–336, 2021.
https://doi.org/10.1007/978-3-030-84252-9_11

constructions generically follow the Hash-then-PRF paradigm. Firstly, a message is mapped by a universal hash function into an n-bit string. Then, the string is processed by a fixed-input-length Pseudo-Random Function (PRF) to produce the tag. This paradigm is simple and easy to analyze because (i) it does not require nonce or extra random coins, and hence is deterministic and stateless; (ii)the produced tag is a random string as long as the input to PRF is fresh. The security of this method is usually capped at the so-called birthday bound $2^{n/2}$, since a collision at the output of the universal hash function typically results in a forgery for the construction. However, the birthday-bound security margin might not be enough in practice, especially when a MAC is instantiated with a lightweight blockcipher such as PRESENT [12], PRINCE [13], and GIFT [2] whose block size is small. In such case, the birthday bound becomes 2^{32} as $n = 64$ and is vulnerable in certain practical applications. For example, Bhargavan and Leurent [9] have demonstrated two practical attacks that exploit collision on short blockciphers.

DOUBLE-BLOCK HASH-THEN-SUM CONSTRUCTION. To go beyond the birthday bound, a series of blockcipher-based MACs have been proposed, including SUM-ECBC [33], PMAC_Plus [34], 3kf9 [35] and LightMAC_Plus [30]. Interestingly, all of these MACs use a similar paradigm called Double-block Hash-then Sum (shorthand for DbHtS), where a message is first mapped into a $2n$-bit string by a double-block hash function and then the two encrypted values of each n-bit half are xor-summed to generate the tag. Datta et al. [17] abstract out this paradigm and divide it into two classes: (i) three-key DbHtS constructions, where apart from the hash key, two blockcipher keys are used in the finalization phase (including SUM-ECBC, PMAC_Plus, 3kf9 and LightMAC_Plus); (ii) two-key DbHtS constructions, where apart from the hash key, only one single blockcipher key is used in the finalization phase (including all the two-key variants, i.e., 2k-SUM-ECBC, 2k-PMAC_Plus, 2k-LightMAC_Plus and 2kf9). Under a generic framework, they prove that both three-key and two-key DbHtS constructions can achieve beyond-birthday-bound security with a bound $q^3/2^{2n}$ where q is the number of MAC queries. Leurent et al. [25] show attacks on all three-key DbHtS constructions with query complexity $2^{3n/4}$. Very recently, Kim et al. [24] give a tight provable bound $q^{4/3}/2^n$ for three-key DbHtS constructions.

MULTI-USER SECURITY. All the above beyond-birthday-bound results only consider a single user. Yet, as one of the most commonly used cryptographic primitives in practice, MACs are typically deployed in contexts with a great number of users. For instance, they are a core element of real-world security protocols such as TLS, SSH, and IPSec, which are used by major websites with billions of daily active users. A natural question is to what extent the number of users will affect the security bound of DbHtS constructions, or more specifically, can DbHtS constructions still achieve beyond-birthday-bound security in the multi-user setting?

The notion of multi-user (mu) security is introduced by Biham [10] in symmetric cryptanalysis and by Bellare, Boldyreva, and Micali [4] in the context of public-key encryption. Attackers can adaptively distribute its queries across multiple users with independent key. It considers attackers who succeed as long as they can compromise at least one user among many. As evident in a series of works [3,8,14,19–21,26,29,32], evaluating how security degrades as the number of users grows is a challenging technical problem even when the security is known in the single-user setting. Unfortunately, until now research on provable mu security for MACs has been somewhat missing. The notable exceptions are the works of Chatterjee et al. [15], very recently Andrew et al. [28], and Bellare et al. [3]. The first two consider a generic reduction for MACs and by using which the mu security of DbHtS constructions will be capped at (or even worse than) the birthday bound, which will be discussed below. The last considers a hash-function-based MAC which is quite different from our focus on blockcipher-based MACs.

Let us explain why the generic reduction does not help DbHtS constructions to go beyond the birthday bound in the mu setting. Suppose the number of users is u. By using the generic reduction [15,28] from single-user (su) security to mu security, the above beyond-birthday bound for two-key DbHtS constructions becomes

$$\frac{uq^3}{2^{2n}}$$

in the mu setting. If the adversary only issues one query per user, then the security bound becomes

$$\frac{uq^3}{2^{2n}} \leq \frac{q^4}{2^{2n}} \ , \tag{1}$$

which is still capped at the worrisome birthday bound. Even for three-key DbHtS constructions with a better bound $q^{4/3}/2^n$ [1] in the su setting, the mu security via generic reduction becomes

$$\frac{uq^{4/3}}{2^n} \leq \frac{q^{\frac{7}{3}}}{2^n} \ ,$$

which is worse than the birthday bound $2^{n/2}$. Thus it is worth directly analyzing the mu security of DbHtS constructions instead of relying on the generic reduction.

OUR CONTRIBUTIONS. We revisit the security of DbHtS constructions in the mu setting, with a focus on two-key DbHtS constructions. Two-key DbHtS constructions such as 2k-PMAC_Plus, 2k-LightMAC_Plus and 2kf9, only use two blockcipher keys in total. Assume the length of each key is $k = n$, then to resist a similar attack like Biham's key-collision attack on DES [10], two keys is the minimal number of keys to potentially achieve beyond-birthday-bound security.

We give a generic framework to prove beyond-birthday-bound security for two-key DbHtS constructions in the mu setting. Our framework is easy to use,

---

[1] This term is mainly due to the usage of Markov inequality and appears in all security bounds of three-key DbHtS constructions [24].

and can achieve much better security bound comparing with prior generic reduction method. Under this framework, one only needs to show that the abstracted double-block hash function satisfies two properties, namely ϵ_1-regular and ϵ_2-almost universal. The first property implies that for a message, the probability that the hashed value equals to any fixed string is small when the hash key is uniformly chosen from the key space. The second one implies that for any two distinct messages, the probability that the two hashed values collide is small when the hash key is uniformly chosen from the key space. These two properties are typically inherent in the hash part of DbHtS constructions.

We demonstrate the usability of this framework with applications to two-key DbHtS constructions. More specifically, we prove that all of 2k-SUM-ECBC, 2k-PMAC_Plus and 2k-LightMAC_Plus are still secure beyond the birthday bound in the mu setting. Our bounds are independent of the number of users, and imply that the security of two-key DbHtS constructions will not degrade as the number of users grows. On the other hand, during the proof of these three constructions, we do not rely on domain separating functions, which are used to simplify the su analysis while at the meantime complicate these constructions [17]. Thus our results also indicate these three constructions are secure beyond the birthday bound in both su and mu setting without additional domain separating functions.

Moreover, we find a critical flaw in 2kf9 in the su setting. Datta et al. [17] prove that 2kf9 without domain separating functions is secure beyond the birthday bound, and then based on it they claim that the other three two-key DbHtS constructions can also achieve the same security level without domain separation. However, we can successfully forge a tag with probability 1 without making any queries. The flaw is that any short message M that will become a single block after padding, the output of 2kf9 without domain separation is always zero. One may think that if we resume domain separation in 2kf9, then it can recover beyond-birthday-bound security. However, we go further to show that even with domain separation, 2kf9 cannot be secure beyond the birthday bound. We also investigate whether the common tricks help 2kf9 by modifying a blockcipher-based MAC to go beyond the birthday bound. Unfortunately, a similar attack with birthday-bound complexity always exists for these variants of 2kf9.

OUR BOUND. Our bound is interesting for beyond-birthday-bound security with practical interest. We show that for any adversary making q MAC queries and p ideal-cipher queries, the advantage of breaking DbHtS's mu security in the main theorem is of the order[2]

$$\frac{qp\ell}{2^{k+n}} + \frac{q^3}{2^{2n}} + \frac{q^2 p + qp^2}{2^{2k}}$$

by assuming H is $1/2^n$-regular and $1/2^n$-almost universal, where n and k are the length of the blockcipher block and key respectively, and ℓ is the maximal block length among these MAC queries. Note that our bound does not depend on the number of users u, which can be adaptively chosen by the adversary, and can be as large as q.

---

[2] Here we omit lower-order terms and small constant factors.

When the number of MAC queries q equals to the birthday bound, i.e., $q = 2^{n/2}$, the bound (1) obtained via the generic reduction will become moot. On the contrary, our bound becomes

$$\frac{p\ell}{2^{k+\frac{n}{2}}} + \frac{1}{2^{\frac{n}{2}}} + \frac{p}{2^{2k-n}} + \frac{p^2}{2^{2k-\frac{n}{2}}}$$

which is still reasonably small. More concretely, if for instance $n = 64, k = 128, q = 2^{32}$, then this requires the adversary to query at least 2^{38} bits $= 2^{35}$ bytes $\approx$ 32GB online data, yet the terms related to the local computation of the adversary become $\frac{p\ell}{2^{160}} + \frac{p}{2^{192}} + \frac{p^2}{2^{224}}$.

IDEAL CIPHER MODEL. The proofs of this paper are done in the ideal cipher model, which is common in most analyses for the mu security. In the mu setting, we are particularly concerned about how local computation (that is captured by the number of ideal cipher queries) affects security, which is a fundamental part of the analysis, and the standard model that regarding a blockcipher as a PRP is not helpful in this estimation. Moreover, in the ideal model, to break the security of DbHtS constructions, attackers must find key collisions among these keys (at least two) at the same time. While in the standard model, inherently we have an isolated term $\mathsf{Adv}_E^{\mathrm{muPRP}}(A)$, for which one key collision among these keys would solely make this term meaningless. Thus to prove beyond-birthday-bound security in the standard model, it may require longer keys, which is somewhat overly pessimistic.

OUTLINE OF THIS PAPER. We introduce basic notions and security definitions in the multi-user setting in Sect. 2. We propose a generic framework to prove beyond-birthday-bound security for DbHtS constructions in Sect. 3. Then, we show the usability of this framework with applications to key-reduced variants of DbHtS MACs in Sect. 4. Finally in Sect. 5, we discuss the flaw in the security proof of 2kf9, and show forgery attacks on it.

2 Preliminaries

NOTATION. Let ε denote the empty string. For an integer i, we let $\langle i \rangle_m$ denote the m-bit representation of i. For a finite set S, we let $x \leftarrow_\$ S$ denote the uniform sampling from S and assigning the value to x. Let $|x|$ denote the length of the string x. Let $|S|$ denote the size of the set S. If A is an algorithm, we let $y \leftarrow A(x_1, \ldots; r)$ denote running A with randomness r on inputs $x_1, \ldots$ and assigning the output to y. We let $y \leftarrow_\$ A(x_1, \ldots)$ be the result of picking r at random and letting $y \leftarrow A(x_1, \ldots; r)$. For a domain Dom and a range Rng, let Func(Dom, Rng) denote the set of functions $f : \text{Dom} \to \text{Rng}$. For integers $1 \le a \le N$, let $(N)_a$ denote $N(N-1) \ldots (N-a+1)$.

MULTI-USER PRF. Let $F : \mathcal{K} \times \mathcal{M} \to \{0,1\}^n$ be a function. For an adversary A, let

$$\mathsf{Adv}_F^{\mathrm{prf}}(A) = 2\Pr[\mathbf{G}_F^{\mathrm{prf}}(A)] - 1 \ ,$$

procedure INITIALIZE	**procedure** EVAL(i, M)
$K_1, K_2, \ldots, \leftarrow\!\!\$ \, \mathcal{K}; \; b \leftarrow\!\!\$ \, \{0,1\}$	$Y_1 \leftarrow F(K_i, M); \; Y_0 \leftarrow f_i(M)$
$f_1, f_2, \ldots, \leftarrow\!\!\$ \, \mathrm{Func}(\mathcal{M}, \{0,1\}^n)$	**return** Y_b
procedure FINALIZE(b')	
return $(b' = b)$	

Fig. 1. Game $\mathbf{G}_F^{\mathrm{prf}}$ defining multi-user PRF security of a function F.

be the advantage of the adversary against the multi-user PRF security of F, where game $\mathbf{G}_F^{\mathrm{prf}}$ is defined in Fig. 1. Note that for any function F of key length k, the PRF advantage is at least $pq/2^{k+2}$ by adapting Biham's key-collision attack on DES [10], where q is the number of queries and p is the number of calls to F.

THE H-COEFFICIENT TECHNIQUE. Following the notation from Hoang and Tessaro [19], it is useful to consider interactions between an adversary A and an abstract system $\mathbf{S}$ which answers A's queries. The resulting interaction can then be recorded with a transcript $\tau = ((X_1, Y_1), \ldots, (X_q, Y_q))$. Let $\mathsf{p_S}(\tau)$ denote the probability that $\mathbf{S}$ produces τ. It is known that $\mathsf{p_S}(\tau)$ is the description of $\mathbf{S}$ and independent of the adversary A. We say that a transcript is attainable for the system $\mathbf{S}$ if $\mathsf{p_S}(\tau) > 0$.

We now describe the H-coefficient technique of Patarin [16,31]. Generically, it considers an adversary that aims at distinguishing a "real" system $\mathbf{S}_1$ from an "ideal" system $\mathbf{S}_0$. The interactions of the adversary with those systems induce two transcript distributions X_1 and X_0 respectively. It is well known that the statistical distance $\mathsf{SD}(X_1, X_0)$ is an upper bound on the distinguishing advantage of A.

Lemma 1. *[16,31] Suppose that the set of attainable transcripts for the ideal system can be partitioned into good and bad ones. If there exists $\epsilon \geq 0$ such that $\frac{\mathsf{p_{S_1}}(\tau)}{\mathsf{p_{S_0}}(\tau)} \geq 1 - \epsilon$ for any good transcript τ, then*

$$\mathsf{SD}(X_1, X_0) \leq \epsilon + \Pr[X_0 \text{ is bad}] \ .$$

REGULAR AND AU HASH FUNCTION. Let $H : \mathcal{K}_h \times \mathcal{X} \to \mathcal{Y}$ be a hash function where $\mathcal{K}_h$ is the key space, $\mathcal{X}$ is the domain and $\mathcal{Y}$ is the range. Hash function H is said to be ϵ_1-*regular* if for any $X \in \mathcal{X}$ and $Y \in \mathcal{Y}$,

$$\Pr\left[K_h \leftarrow\!\!\$ \, \mathcal{K}_h : H_{K_h}(X) = Y\right] \leq \epsilon_1$$

and it is said to be ϵ_2-*almost universal* if for any two distinct strings $X, X' \in \mathcal{X}$,

$$\Pr\left[K_h \leftarrow\!\!\$ \, \mathcal{K}_h : H_{K_h}(X) = H_{K_h}(X')\right] \leq \epsilon_2 \ .$$

Sum of Two Identical Permutations. We will use the following result in some proofs, which is a special case of [18, Theorem 2] by setting the conditional set to be empty.

Lemma 2. *For any tuple* $(T_1, \ldots, T_q)$ *such that each* $T_i \neq 0^n$*, let* $U_1, \ldots, U_q$*,* $V_1, \ldots, V_q$ *be* $2q$ *random variables sampled without replacement from* $\{0,1\}^n$ *and satisfying* $U_i \oplus V_i = T_i$ *for* $1 \leq i \leq q$*. Denote by* S *the set of tuples of these* $2q$ *variables. Then*

$$|S| \geq \frac{(2^n)_{2q}}{2^{nq}}(1 - \mu) \ ,$$

where $\mu = \frac{6q^3}{2^{2n}}$ *and assuming* $q \leq 2^{n-2}$*.*

3 Multi-user Security Proof Framework for DbHtS MACs

In this section, we propose a generic proof framework for DbHtS MACs. We begin with the description of DbHtS constructions. Here we focus on two-key DbHtS constructions, including 2k-SUM-ECBC, 2k-LightMAC_Plus and 2k-PMAC_Plus.

The DbHtS construction. Let $H : \mathcal{K}_h \times \mathcal{M} \rightarrow \{0,1\}^n \times \{0,1\}^n$ be a $2n$-bit hash function with key space $\mathcal{K}_h$ and message space $\mathcal{M}$. We will always decompose H into two n-bit hash functions H^1 and H^2 for convenience, and thus have $H_{K_h}(M) = (H^1_{K_{h,1}}(M), H^2_{K_{h,2}}(M))$ where $K_h = (K_{h,1}, K_{h,2})$. Given a blockcipher $E : \mathcal{K} \times \{0,1\}^n \rightarrow \{0,1\}^n$ and a hash function H as defined above, one can define the DbHtS construction as follows

$$\mathsf{DbHtS}[H, E](K_h, K, M) = E_K(H^1_{K_{h,1}}(M)) \oplus E_K(H^2_{K_{h,2}}(M)) \ .$$

In blockcipher-based MACs, the hash function H is typically built from an n-bit blockcipher E. The message M (after padding) is always split into n-bit blocks without being more specific, namely $M = M[1] \| M[2] \| \ldots \| M[\ell]$ where $|M[i]| = n$. For message M, we denote by $X[i]$ the i-th input to the underlying blockcipher E of H.

Security analysis of DbHtS construction. Given that H is a good $2n$-bit hash function and the underlying blockcipher E is ideal, we have the following result.

Theorem 1. *Let* $E : \{0,1\}^k \times \{0,1\}^n \rightarrow \{0,1\}^n$ *be a blockcipher that we model as an ideal blockcipher. Suppose that each* n*-bit hash function of* $H = (H^1, H^2)$ *is* ϵ_1*-regular and* ϵ_2*-almost universal. Then for any adversary* A *that makes at most* q *evaluation queries and* p *ideal-cipher queries,*

$$\mathsf{Adv}^{\mathrm{prf}}_{\mathsf{DbHtS}}(A) \leq \frac{2q}{2^k} + \frac{q(3q+p)(6q+2p)}{2^{2k}} + \frac{2qp\ell}{2^{n+k}} + \frac{2qp\epsilon_1}{2^k} + \frac{4qp}{2^{n+k}}$$

$$+ \frac{4q^2\epsilon_1}{2^k} + \frac{2q^2\ell\epsilon_1}{2^k} + 2q^3(\epsilon_1 + \epsilon_2)^2 + \frac{8q^3(\epsilon_1 + \epsilon_2)}{2^n} + \frac{6q^3}{2^{2n}} \ ,$$

where ℓ *is the maximal block length among these evaluation queries and assuming* $p + q\ell \leq 2^{n-1}$*.*

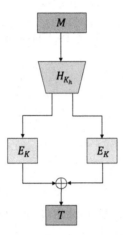

Fig. 2. The DbHtS construction. Here H is a $2n$-bit hash function from $\mathcal{K}_h \times \mathcal{M}$ to $\{0,1\}^n \times \{0,1\}^n$, and E is a n-bit blockcipher from $\mathcal{K} \times \{0,1\}^n$ to $\{0,1\}^n$.

---

procedure INITIALIZE

$(K_h^1, K_1), (K_h^2, K_2), \cdots, \leftarrow\!\!{}_\$ \, \mathcal{K}_h \times \mathcal{K}$

$f_1, f_2, \cdots, \leftarrow\!\!{}_\$ \, \mathrm{Func}(\mathcal{M}, \{0,1\}^n)$

$b \leftarrow\!\!{}_\$ \, \{0,1\}$

procedure PRIM(J, X)

if $X = (+, x)$ **then return** $E_J(x)$

if $X = (-, y)$ **then return** $E_J^{-1}(y)$

procedure EVAL(i, M)

$T_1 \leftarrow \mathsf{DbHtS}[H, E](K_h^i, K_i, M)$

$T_0 \leftarrow f_i(M)$

return T_b

procedure FINALIZE(b')

return $(b' = b)$

Fig. 3. Game $\mathbf{G}_{\mathsf{DbHtS}}^{\mathrm{prf}}$ defining multi-user prf security of the construction DbHtS.

Proof. Our proof is based on the H-coefficient technique. We will consider a computationally unbounded adversary, and without loss of generality assume that the adversary is deterministic and never repeats a prior query. Assume further that the adversary never makes a redundant query: if it queries $y \leftarrow E(J, x)$ then it won't query $E^{-1}(J, y)$ and vice versa. The security game is detailed in Fig. 3. The real system corresponds to game $\mathbf{G}_{\mathsf{DbHtS}}^{\mathrm{prf}}$ with challenge bit $b = 1$, and the ideal system corresponds to game $\mathbf{G}_{\mathsf{DbHtS}}^{\mathrm{prf}}$ with challenge bit $b = 0$.

SETUP. In both of the two worlds, after the adversary finishes querying, it obtains the following information:

- **Ideal-cipher queries:** for each query PRIM$(J, (x, +))$ with answer y, we associate it with an entry $(\mathtt{prim}, J, x, y, +)$. For each query PRIM$(J, (y, -))$ with answer x, we associate it with an entry $(\mathtt{prim}, J, x, y, -)$.
- **Evaluation queries:** for each query $T \leftarrow$ EVAL(i, M), we associate it with an entry $(\mathtt{eval}, i, M, T)$.

We denote by $(\mathsf{eval}, i, M_a^i, T_a^i)$ the entry obtained when the adversary makes the a-th query to user i. Denote by ℓ_a^i the block length of M_a^i and denote by ℓ the maximal block length among these q evaluation queries. During the computation of entry $(\mathsf{eval}, i, M_a^i, T_a^i)$, we denote by Σ_a^i and Λ_a^i the internal outputs of hash function H, namely $\Sigma_a^i = H_{K_{h,1}}^1(M_a^i)$ and $\Lambda_a^i = H_{K_{h,2}}^2(M_a^i)$ respectively, and denote by U_a^i and V_a^i the outputs of blockcipher E with inputs Σ_a^i and Λ_a^i respectively, namely $U_a^i = E(K_i, \Sigma_a^i)$ and $V_a^i = E(K_i, \Lambda_a^i)$ respectively. For a key $J \in \{0,1\}^k$, let $P(J)$ be the set of entries $(\mathsf{prim}, J, x, y, *)$, and let $Q(J)$ be the set of entries $(\mathsf{eval}, i, M_a^i, T_a^i)$ such that $K_i = J$. In the real world, after the adversary finishes all its queries, we will further give it: (i) the keys (K_h^i, K_i) where $K_h^i = (K_{h,1}^i, K_{h,2}^i)$ and (ii) the internal values U_a^i and V_a^i. In the ideal world, we will instead give the adversary truly random strings $(K_h^i, K_i) \leftarrow_\$ \mathcal{K}_h \times \mathcal{K}$, independent of its queries. In addition, we will give the adversary dummy values U_a^i and V_a^i computed as follows: for each set $Q(J)$, the simulation oracle $\mathrm{SIM}(Q(J))$ (depicted in Fig. 4) will be invoked and return corresponding values U_a^i and V_a^i to the adversary. These additional information can only help the adversary. Thus a transcript consists of the revealed keys (K_h^i, K_i), the internal values U_a^i and V_a^i, the ideal-cipher queries and evaluation queries. On the other hand, the internal values Σ_a^i and Λ_a^i during the computation of SIM are uniquely determined by message M_a^i and key (K_h^i, K_i).

DEFINING BAD TRANSCRIPTS. We now give the definition of bad transcripts. The goal of defining bad transcripts is to ensure that (i) for each user, at least one of its two keys is fresh, namely either the key of the blockcipher is fresh or the key of the hash function is fresh; (ii) for queries to the same user, at least one of two inputs to blockcipher E is fresh; (iii) for queries to different users, if the key of blockcipher E collides with that of other users or ideal-cipher queries, then the input to E should be fresh. We say a transcript is *bad* if one of the following happens:

1. There is an entry $(\mathsf{eval}, i, M_a^i, T_a^i)$ such that $K_i = K_{h,d}^i$ for $d \in \{1,2\}$.
2. There is an entry $(\mathsf{eval}, i, M_a^i, T_a^i)$ such that both K_i and $K_{h,d}^i$ for $d \in \{1,2\}$ have been used in other entries, namely either in entries $(\mathsf{eval}, j, M_b^j, T_b^j)$ or entries $(\mathsf{prim}, J, x, y, *)$.
   Conditions (1) and (2) are to guarantee that at least one of two keys of any user i is fresh. Note that in blockcipher-based MACs, hash function H is usually built from blockcipher E.
3. There is an entry $(\mathsf{eval}, i, M_a^i, T_a^i)$ such that $K_{h,d}^i = J$ for $d \in \{1,2\}$ and $x = X_a^i[j]$ for some entry $(\mathsf{prim}, J, x, y, -)$ and some $1 \le j \le \ell_a^i$.
   Condition (3) is to prevent that the adversary can somehow control the (partial) output of $H_{K_h}(M_a^i)$ by using its backward ideal-cipher queries for some $1 \le j \le \ell_a^i$ where $M_a^i = M_a^i[1] \| \ldots \| M_a^i[\ell_a^i]$ and $X_a^i[j]$ is the j-th corresponding input to the underlying blockcipher E of H.
4. There is an entry $(\mathsf{eval}, i, M_a^i, T_a^i)$ such that $K_i = J$, and either $\Sigma_a^i = x$ or $\Lambda_a^i = x$ for some entry $(\mathsf{prim}, J, x, y, *)$.

5. There is an entry $(\mathsf{eval}, i, M_a^i, T_a^i)$ such that $K_i = J$, and either $U_a^i = y$ or $V_a^i = y$ for some entry $(\mathsf{prim}, J, x, y, *)$.
   Conditions (4) and (5) are to remove the case that either the inputs or outputs of E_{K_i} collide with those in the ideal-cipher queries when $K_i = J$.

6. There is an entry $(\mathsf{eval}, i, M_a^i, T_a^i)$ such that $K_i = K_j$, and either $\Sigma_a^i = \Sigma_b^j$ or $\Sigma_a^i = \Lambda_b^j$ for some entry $(\mathsf{eval}, j, M_b^j, T_b^j)$.

7. There is an entry $(\mathsf{eval}, i, M_a^i, T_a^i)$ such that $K_i = K_j$, and either $\Lambda_a^i = \Lambda_b^j$ or $\Lambda_a^i = \Sigma_b^j$ for some entry $(\mathsf{eval}, j, M_b^j, T_b^j)$.
   Conditions (6) and (7) are to guarantee that when the key K_i collides with the key K_j, then all the inputs of E_{K_i} are distinct from those of E_{K_j}.

8. There is an entry $(\mathsf{eval}, i, M_a^i, T_a^i)$ such that $K_i = K_{h,1}^j$ and $\Sigma_a^i = X_b^j[k]$, or $K_i = K_{h,2}^j$ and $\Lambda_a^i = X_b^j[k]$ for some entry $(\mathsf{eval}, j, M_b^j, T_b^j)$ and $1 \leq k \leq \ell_b^j$.
   Condition (8) is to guarantee that when there is a collision between K_i and $K_{h,d}^j$ for $d \in \{1, 2\}$, then the inputs to E_{K_i} do not collide with the inputs in the hash part with key $K_{h,d}^j$, and thus keep the freshness of the final output.

9. There is an entry $(\mathsf{eval}, i, M_a^i, T_a^i)$ such that either $\Sigma_a^i = \Sigma_b^i$ or $\Sigma_a^i = \Lambda_b^i$, and either $\Lambda_a^i = \Lambda_b^i$ or $\Lambda_a^i = \Sigma_b^i$ for some entry $(\mathsf{eval}, i, M_b^i, T_b^i)$.
   Condition (9) is to guarantee that for any pair of entries $(\mathsf{eval}, i, M_a^i, T_a^i)$ and $(\mathsf{eval}, i, M_b^i, T_b^i)$ of the same user, at least one of Σ_a^i and Λ_a^i is fresh.

10. There is an entry $(\mathsf{eval}, i, M_a^i, T_a^i)$ such that either $\Sigma_a^i = \Sigma_b^i$ or $\Sigma_a^i = \Lambda_b^i$, and either $V_a^i = V_b^i$ or $V_a^i = U_b^i$ for some entry $(\mathsf{eval}, i, M_b^i, T_b^i)$.

11. There is an entry $(\mathsf{eval}, i, M_a^i, T_a^i)$ such that either $\Lambda_a^i = \Lambda_b^i$ or $\Lambda_a^i = \Sigma_b^i$, and either $U_a^i = U_b^i$ or $U_a^i = V_b^i$ for some entry $(\mathsf{eval}, i, M_b^i, T_b^i)$.
    Conditions (10) and (11) are to guarantee that the outputs of Φ_{K_i} in the ideal world are compatible with a permutation, namely when the inputs are distinct, then the corresponding outputs should also be distinct.

12. There is an entry $(\mathsf{eval}, i, M_a^i, T_a^i)$ such that either $\Sigma_a^i = \Sigma_b^i$ or $\Sigma_a^i = \Lambda_b^i$, and either $\Lambda_a^i = \Lambda_c^i$ or $\Lambda_a^i = \Sigma_c^i$ for some entries $(\mathsf{eval}, i, M_b^i, T_b^i)$ and $(\mathsf{eval}, i, M_c^i, T_c^i)$.
    Condition (12) is to guarantee that for any triple of entries $(\mathsf{eval}, i, M_a^i, T_a^i)$, $(\mathsf{eval}, i, M_b^i, T_b^i)$ and $(\mathsf{eval}, i, M_c^i, T_c^i)$, at least one of Σ_a^i and Λ_a^i is fresh.

13. There is an entry $(\mathsf{eval}, i, M_a^i, T_a^i)$ such that either $\Sigma_a^i = \Sigma_b^i$ or $\Sigma_a^i = \Lambda_b^i$, and either $V_a^i = V_c^i$ or $V_a^i = U_c^i$ for some entries $(\mathsf{eval}, i, M_b^i, T_b^i)$ and $(\mathsf{eval}, i, M_c^i, T_c^i)$.

14. There is an entry $(\mathsf{eval}, i, M_a^i, T_a^i)$ such that either $\Lambda_a^i = \Lambda_b^i$ or $\Lambda_a^i = \Sigma_b^i$, and either $U_a^i = U_c^i$ or $U_a^i = V_c^i$ for some entries $(\mathsf{eval}, i, M_b^i, T_b^i)$ and $(\mathsf{eval}, i, M_c^i, T_c^i)$.
    Conditions (13) and (14) are to guarantee that the outputs of Φ_{K_i} in the ideal world are compatible with a permutation, namely when the inputs are distinct, then the corresponding outputs should also be distinct.

If a transcript is not bad then we say it's *good*. Let X_1 and X_0 be the random variables for the transcript distributions in the real and ideal system respectively.

PROBABILITY OF BAD TRANSCRIPTS. We now bound the chance that X_0 is bad in the ideal world. Let Bad_i be the event that X_0 violates the i-th condition. By the union bound,

$$\Pr[X_0 \text{ is bad}] = \Pr[\text{Bad}_1 \vee \cdots \vee \text{Bad}_{14}]$$

$$\leq \sum_{i=1}^{3} \Pr[\text{Bad}_i] + \sum_{i=4}^{8} \Pr[\text{Bad}_i \mid \overline{\text{Bad}_2}] + \sum_{i=9}^{14} \Pr[\text{Bad}_i] \ .$$

We first bound the probability $\Pr[\text{Bad}_1]$. Recall that in the ideal world, K_i and $K_{h,d}^i$ are uniformly random, independent of each other and those entries. Thus the chance that $K_i = K_{h,d}^i$ is at most $1/2^k$. Summing over at most q evaluation queries and $d \in \{1,2\}$,

$$\Pr[\text{Bad}_1] \leq \frac{2q}{2^k} \ .$$

Next, we bound the probability $\Pr[\text{Bad}_2]$. Recall that in the ideal world, K_i and $K_{h,d}^i$ are uniformly random, independent of each other and those entries. Thus the probability that $K_i = K_j$ or $K_i = K_{h,d'}^j$ for at most $q-1$ other users and $d' \in \{1,2\}$, or $K_i = J$ for at most p ideal-cipher queries, is at most $(3q+p)/2^k$. For $d \in \{1,2\}$, the probability that $K_{h,d}^i = K_j$ or $K_{h,d}^i = K_{h,d'}^j$ for at most $q-1$ other users and $d' \in \{1,2\}$, or $K_{h,d}^i = J$ for at most p ideal-cipher queries, is also at most $(3q+p)/2^k$. Since K_i and $K_{h,d}^i$ are independent of each other, and summing over at most q evaluation queries,

$$\Pr[\text{Bad}_2] \leq \frac{q(3q+p)(6q+2p)}{2^{2k}} \ .$$

Next, we bound the probability $\Pr[\text{Bad}_3]$. Recall that in the ideal world, $K_{h,d}^i$ is uniformly random, independent of those entries. Thus the chance that $K_{h,d}^i = J$ for at most p ideal-cipher queries is at most $p/2^k$. On the other hand, for each ideal-cipher entry $(\texttt{prim}, J, x, y, -)$, the probability that $x = X_a^i[j]$ is at most $1/(2^n - p - q\ell) \leq 2/2^n$ by assuming $p + q\ell \leq 2^{n-1}$. Summing over at most q evaluation queries and $1 \leq j \leq \ell_a^i \leq \ell$,

$$\Pr[\text{Bad}_3] \leq \frac{2qp\ell}{2^{k+n}} \ .$$

Next, we bound the probability $\Pr[\text{Bad}_4 \mid \overline{\text{Bad}_2}]$. Recall that in the ideal world, K_i is uniformly random, independent of those entries. Thus for each entry $(\texttt{prim}, J, x, y, *)$, the chance that $K_i = J$ is $1/2^k$. On the other hand, conditioned on $\overline{\text{Bad}_2}$, the key $K_{h,d}^i$ is fresh for $d \in \{1,2\}$. The event that $\Sigma_a^i = x$ or $\Lambda_a^i = x$ is the same as

$$H_{K_{h,1}^i}^1(M_a^i) = x \vee H_{K_{h,2}^i}^2(M_a^i) = x \ ,$$

which holds with probability at most $2\epsilon_1$ by the assumption that H^1 and H^2 are both ϵ_1-regular. Summing over at most q evaluation queries and p ideal-cipher queries,

$$\Pr[\text{Bad}_4 \mid \overline{\text{Bad}_2}] \leq \frac{2qp\epsilon_1}{2^k} \ .$$

Bounding the probability $\Pr[\mathrm{Bad}_5 \mid \overline{\mathrm{Bad}_2}]$ is similar to handling $\Pr[\mathrm{Bad}_4 \mid \overline{\mathrm{Bad}_2}]$, but now the event $U_a^i = y$ or $V_a^i = y$ is the same as $\Phi_{K_i}(\Sigma_a^i) = y$ or $\Phi_{K_i}(\Lambda_a^i) = y$. The probability that $\Phi_{K_i}(\Sigma_a^i) = y$ is at most $1/(2^n - p - q\ell) \le 2/2^n$ by assuming $p + q\ell \le 2^{n-1}$. Similarly, the probability that $\Phi_{K_i}(\Lambda_a^i) = y$ is at most $2/2^n$. Thus, summing over at most q evaluation queries and p ideal-cipher queries

$$\Pr[\mathrm{Bad}_5 \mid \overline{\mathrm{Bad}_2}] \le \frac{4qp}{2^{n+k}} \ .$$

We now bound the probability $\Pr[\mathrm{Bad}_6 \mid \overline{\mathrm{Bad}_2}]$. Recall that in the ideal world, K_i is uniformly random, independent of those entries. Thus the chance that $K_i = K_j$ is $1/2^k$. On the other hand, conditioned on $\overline{\mathrm{Bad}_2}$, the key $K_{h,1}^i$ is fresh. The event that $\Sigma_a^i = \Sigma_b^j$ is the same as

$$H_{K_{h,1}^i}^1(M_a^i) = H_{K_{h,1}^j}^1(M_b^j)$$

which holds with probability at most ϵ_1 by the assumption that H^1 is ϵ_1-regular. Similarly, the event that $\Sigma_a^i = \Lambda_b^j$ holds with probability at most ϵ_1. Summing over at most q^2 pairs of i and j,

$$\Pr[\mathrm{Bad}_6 \mid \overline{\mathrm{Bad}_2}] \le \frac{2q^2\epsilon_1}{2^k} \ .$$

Bounding $\Pr[\mathrm{Bad}_7 \mid \overline{\mathrm{Bad}_2}]$ is similar to handling $\Pr[\mathrm{Bad}_6 \mid \overline{\mathrm{Bad}_2}]$, and thus

$$\Pr[\mathrm{Bad}_7 \mid \overline{\mathrm{Bad}_2}] \le \frac{2q^2\epsilon_1}{2^k} \ .$$

Next, we bound the probability $\Pr[\mathrm{Bad}_8]$. Recall that in the ideal world, K_i is uniformly random, independent of those entries. Thus the chance that $K_i = K_{h,1}^j$ for some other j is at most $1/2^k$. On the other hand, for each entry $(\mathrm{eval}, j, M_b^j, T_b^j)$, the probability that $\Sigma_a^i = X_b^j[k]$ is at most ϵ_1 by the assumption that H^1 is ϵ_1-regular. Hence the chance that $K_i = K_{h,1}^j$ and $\Sigma_a^i = X_b^j[k]$ is at most $\epsilon_1/2^k$. Similarly, the probability that $K_i = K_{h,2}^j$ and $\Lambda_a^i = X_b^j[k]$ is at most $\epsilon_1/2^k$. Summing over at most q^2 pairs of evaluation queries and $1 \le k \le \ell$,

$$\Pr[\mathrm{Bad}_8] \le \frac{2q^2\ell\epsilon_1}{2^k} \ .$$

Next, we bound the probability $\Pr[\mathrm{Bad}_9]$. The event $\Sigma_a^i = \Sigma_b^i$ or $\Sigma_a^i = \Lambda_b^i$ is the same as

$$H_{K_{h,1}^i}^1(M_a^i) = H_{K_{h,1}^i}^1(M_b^i) \vee H_{K_{h,1}^i}^1(M_a^i) = H_{K_{h,2}^i}^2(M_b^i) \ ,$$

which holds with probability at most $\epsilon_1 + \epsilon_2$ by the assumption that H^1 is ϵ_1-regular and ϵ_2-almost universal. Similarly, the probability of the event $\Lambda_a^i = \Lambda_b^i$ or $\Lambda_a^i = \Sigma_b^i$ is at most $\epsilon_1 + \epsilon_2$. Note that for each user i, there are at most q_i^2

pairs of (a, b). By the assumption that $K^i_{h,1}$ and $K^i_{h,2}$ are two independent keys, and summing among u users,

$$\Pr[\text{Bad}_9] \leq \sum_{i=1}^{u} q_i^2(\epsilon_1 + \epsilon_2)^2 \leq q^2(\epsilon_1 + \epsilon_2)^2 \ .$$

Next, we bound the probability $\Pr[\text{Bad}_{10}]$. The event $\Sigma^i_a = \Sigma^i_b$ or $\Sigma^i_a = \Lambda^i_b$ is the same as

$$H^1_{K^i_{h,1}}(M^i_a) = H^1_{K^i_{h,1}}(M^i_b) \vee H^1_{K^i_{h,1}}(M^i_a) = H^2_{K^i_{h,2}}(M^i_b) \ ,$$

which holds with probability at most $\epsilon_1 + \epsilon_2$. On the other hand, the event $V^i_a = V^i_b$ or $V^i_a = U^i_b$ is the same as

$$T^i_a \oplus U^i_a = V^i_b \vee T^i_a \oplus U^i_a = U^i_b \ ,$$

which holds with probability at most $2/2^n$ since T^i_a is a random string and independent of these entries. Summing among u users,

$$\Pr[\text{Bad}_{10}] \leq \sum_{i=1}^{u} \frac{2q_i^2(\epsilon_1 + \epsilon_2)}{2^n} \leq \frac{2q^2(\epsilon_1 + \epsilon_2)}{2^n} \ .$$

Bounding the probability $\Pr[\text{Bad}_{11}]$ is similar to handling $\Pr[\text{Bad}_{10}]$, and thus

$$\Pr[\text{Bad}_{11}] \leq \frac{2q^2(\epsilon_1 + \epsilon_2)}{2^n} \ .$$

Bounding the probability $\Pr[\text{Bad}_{12}]$ is similar to handling $\Pr[\text{Bad}_9]$, except that now for each user i, there are at most q_i^3 tuples of (a, b, c). Hence summing among these u users,

$$\Pr[\text{Bad}_{12}] \leq \sum_{i=1}^{u} q_i^3(\epsilon_1 + \epsilon_2)^2 \leq q^3(\epsilon_1 + \epsilon_2)^2 \ .$$

Bounding the probability $\Pr[\text{Bad}_{13}]$ is similar to handling $\Pr[\text{Bad}_{10}]$, except that now for each user i, there are at most q_i^3 tuples of (a, b, c). Hence summing among these u users,

$$\Pr[\text{Bad}_{13}] \leq \sum_{i=1}^{u} \frac{2q_i^3(\epsilon_1 + \epsilon_2)}{2^n} \leq \frac{2q^3(\epsilon_1 + \epsilon_2)}{2^n} \ .$$

Bounding the probability $\Pr[\text{Bad}_{14}]$ is similar to handling $\Pr[\text{Bad}_{13}]$, and thus

$$\Pr[\text{Bad}_{14}] \leq \frac{2q^3(\epsilon_1 + \epsilon_2)}{2^n} \ .$$

Summing up,

$$\Pr[X_0 \text{ is bad}] \leq \frac{2q}{2^k} + \frac{q(3q+p)(6q+2p)}{2^{2k}} + \frac{2qp\ell}{2^{k+n}} + \frac{2qp\epsilon_1}{2^k} + \frac{4qp}{2^{n+k}}$$
$$+ \frac{4q^2\epsilon_1}{2^k} + \frac{2q^2\ell\epsilon_1}{2^k} + 2q^3(\epsilon_1 + \epsilon_2)^2 + \frac{8q^3(\epsilon_1 + \epsilon_2)}{2^n} \ . \quad (2)$$

TRANSCRIPT RATIO. Let τ be a good transcript. Note that for any good transcript, at least one of Σ_a^i and Λ_a^i is fresh. Hence the set $R(J)$ in Fig. 4 is empty and the procedure will not abort. Recall that $|S|$ denotes the size of the set S. Among the set $H(J)$, there are exactly $|Q(J)| + |F(J)|$ fresh values, and $|Q(J)| - |F(J)|$ non-fresh values. For the entries in $G(J)$, suppose that there are g classes among the values Σ_a^i and Λ_a^i: the elements in the same class either connected by a value T_a^i such that $\Sigma_a^i \oplus \Lambda_a^i = T_a^i$, or connected by the equation such that $\Sigma_a^i = \Sigma_b^j$ or $\Sigma_a^i = \Lambda_b^j$, or $\Lambda_a^i = \Lambda_b^j$ or $\Lambda_a^i = \Sigma_b^j$. Note that each class contains at least three elements, and only has one sampled value in SIM of Fig. 4. Since τ is good, the corresponding samples U_a^i and V_a^i of these g distinct classes are compatible with the permutation, namely these g outputs are sampled in a manner such that they are distinct and do not collide with other values during the computation of the set $F(J)$.

Suppose that this transcript contains exactly u users. Then in the ideal world, since τ is good,

$$\Pr[X_0 = \tau]$$
$$= 2^{-2uk} \cdot 2^{-qn} \prod_{J \in \{0,1\}^k} \left(\frac{1}{|S(J)|} \cdot \frac{1}{(2^n - 2|F(J)|)_g} \cdot \prod_{i=0}^{|P(J)|-1} \frac{1}{2^n - 2|F(J)| - g - i} \right).$$

On the other hand, in the real world, the number of permutation outputs that we need to consider for each $J \in \{0,1\}^k$ is exactly $|Q(J)| + |F(J)| + g$. The reason is that, we have $|Q(J)| + |F(J)|$ fresh input-output tuples in total, and for each class in $G(J)$, we have one additional input-output tuple. Thus,

$$\Pr[X_1 = \tau]$$
$$= 2^{-2uk} \prod_{J \in \{0,1\}^k} \left(\frac{1}{(2^n)_{|Q(J)|+|F(J)|+g}} \cdot \prod_{i=0}^{|P(J)|-1} \frac{1}{2^n - |Q(J)| - |F(J)| - g - i} \right).$$

Hence,

$$\frac{\Pr[X_1 = \tau]}{\Pr[X_0 = \tau]} \geq 2^{qn} \prod_{J \in \{0,1\}^k} \frac{|S(J)| \cdot (2^n - 2|F(J)|)_g}{(2^n)_{|Q(J)|+|F(J)|+g}}$$

$$\geq \prod_{J \in \{0,1\}^k} \frac{2^{|Q(J)|n}(2^n - 2|F(J)|)_g (2^n)_{2|F(J)|}}{(2^n)_{|Q(J)|+|F(J)|+g} \cdot 2^{|F(J)|n}} \cdot \left(1 - \frac{6|F(J)|^3}{2^{2n}}\right)$$

$$\geq \prod_{J \in \{0,1\}^k} \frac{2^{n(|Q(J)|-|F(J)|)}}{(2^n - 2|F(J)| - g)_{|Q(J)|-|F(J)|}} \cdot \left(1 - \frac{6|F(J)|^3}{2^{2n}}\right)$$

$$\geq 1 - \frac{6q^3}{2^{2n}}, \tag{3}$$

where the second inequality comes from Lemma 2.

WRAPPING UP. From Lemma 1 and Eqs. (2) and (3), we conclude that

$$\mathsf{Adv}^{\mathrm{prf}}_{\mathsf{DbHtS}}(A) \leq \frac{2q}{2^k} + \frac{q(3q+p)(6q+2p)}{2^{2k}} + \frac{2qp\ell}{2^{k+n}} + \frac{2qp\epsilon_1}{2^k} + \frac{4qp}{2^{n+k}}$$
$$+ \frac{4q^2\epsilon_1}{2^k} + \frac{2q^2\ell\epsilon_1}{2^k} + 2q^3(\epsilon_1 + \epsilon_2)^2 + \frac{8q^3(\epsilon_1 + \epsilon_2)}{2^n} + \frac{6q^3}{2^{2n}} \ .$$

REMARK 1. In some applications, the amount of data processed by each user may be bounded by a threshold B. That is, when the amount of data exceeds the threshold B, the user may refresh its key. We leave it as an open problem to analyzing DbHtS constructions in this setting. On the other hand, in nonce-based authenticated encryption, it is useful to analyze the mu security in d-bounded model, namely each nonce can be re-used by at most d users in the encryption phase. This model is natural for nonce-based AE, as in practice such as TLS 1.3, AES-GCM is equipped with nonce randomization technique to improve nonce robustness [8,21]. While for DbHtS constructions, they do not require nonce. Thus analyzing DbHtS constructions in d-bounded model is not helpful here.

REMARK 2. It would be interesting to consider the relation between the multi-user framework and universal composability, as pointed out by a reviewer. That is, defining an ideal functionality to capture either a single user and then compose to get the multi-user security, or starting with an ideal functionality that handles multiple users. It is unclear how to define such ideal functionality for DbHtS constructions, as there exist some bad events that only occur in the mu setting; we leave it as an open problem.

4 Multi-user Security of Three Constructions

In this section, we demonstrate the usability of multi-user proof framework with applications to key-reduced DbHtS MACs, and prove that 2k-SUM-ECBC, 2k-LightMAC_Plus and 2k-PMAC_Plus are secure beyond the birthday bound in the mu setting.

4.1 Security of 2k-SUM-ECBC

We begin with the description of 2k-SUM-ECBC. The $2n$-bit hash function used in 2k-SUM-ECBC is the concatenation of two CBC MACs with two independent keys $K_{h,1}$ and $K_{h,2}$. Let $E : \{0,1\}^k \times \{0,1\}^n \rightarrow \{0,1\}^n$ be a blockcipher. For a message $M = M[1] \parallel M[2] \parallel \ldots \parallel M[\ell]$ where $|M[i]| = n$, the CBC MAC algorithm $\mathsf{CBC}[E](K, M)$ is defined as Y_ℓ, where

$$Y_i = E_K(M[i] \oplus Y_{i-1})$$

for $i = 1, \ldots, \ell$ and $Y_0 = 0^n$. Then 2k-SUM-ECBC is defined as $\mathsf{DbHtS}[H, E]$, where

$$H_{K_h}(M) = (H^1_{K_{h,1}}(M), H^2_{K_{h,2}}(M)) = (\mathsf{CBC}[E](K_{h,1}, M), \mathsf{CBC}[E](K_{h,2}, M)) \ ,$$

procedure $\text{SIM}(Q(J))$

$\forall\,(\text{eval}, i, M_a^i, T_a^i) \in Q(J) : (\Sigma_a^i, \Lambda_a^i) \leftarrow H_{K_h}(M_a^i)$

$I(J) = \{(i,a) : 1 \leq i \leq u, 1 \leq a \leq q_i, (\text{eval}, i, M_a^i, T_a^i) \in Q(J)\}$

$H(J) = \{(\Sigma_a^i, \Lambda_a^i) : (i,a) \in I(J)\}$

$F(J) = \{(i,a) : \text{both } \Sigma_a^i \text{ and } \Lambda_a^i \text{ are fresh in } H(J)\}$

$G(J) = \{(i,a) : \text{only one of } \Sigma_a^i \text{ and } \Lambda_a^i \text{ is fresh in } H(J)\}$

$R(J) = \{(i,a) : \text{neither } \Sigma_a^i \text{ nor } \Lambda_a^i \text{ is fresh in } H(J)\}$

$O(J)$: set of tuples of $2\,|F(J)|$ distinct values from $\{0,1\}^n \setminus \text{Rng}(\Phi_J)$

$S(J) = \{(W_a^i, X_a^i)_{(i,a)\in F(J)} \in O(J) : W_a^i \oplus X_a^i = T_a^i\}$

$(U_a^i, V_a^i)_{(i,a)\in F(J)} \leftarrow\!\!\text{\$}\ S(J)$

$\forall\,(i,a) \in F(J) : (\Phi_J(\Sigma_a^i), \Phi_J(\Lambda_a^i)) \leftarrow (U_a^i, V_a^i)$

$\forall\,(i,a) \in G(J) :$

   if Σ_a^i is not fresh in H **then**

      if $\Sigma_a^i \notin \text{Dom}(\Phi_J)$

         then $U_a^i \leftarrow\!\!\text{\$}\ \{0,1\}^n \setminus \text{Rng}(\Phi_J);\ \Phi_J(\Sigma_a^i) \leftarrow U_a^i$

      else $U_a^i \leftarrow \Phi_J(\Sigma_a^i)$

      $V_a^i \leftarrow T_a^i \oplus U_a^i$

   else

      if $\Lambda_a^i \notin \text{Dom}(\Phi_J)$

         then $V_a^i \leftarrow\!\!\text{\$}\ \{0,1\}^n \setminus \text{Rng}(\Phi_J);\ \Phi_J(\Lambda_a^i) \leftarrow V_a^i$

      else $V_a^i \leftarrow \Phi_J(\Lambda_a^i)$

      $U_a^i \leftarrow T_a^i \oplus V_a^i$

$\forall\,(i,a) \in R(J) :$ **return** $\perp$

return $(U_a^i, V_a^i)_{(i,a)\in I(J)}$

Fig. 4. Offline oracle in the ideal world. For each J, Φ_J is a partial function that used to simulate a random permutation. The domain and range of Φ_J are initialized to be the domain and range of E_J respectively.

and $K_{h,1}$ and $K_{h,2}$ are two independent keys. The specification of 2k-SUM-ECBC is illustrated in Fig. 5. For any two distinct messages M_1 and M_2 of at most $\ell \leq 2^{n/4}$ blocks, Bellare et al. [7] and Jha and Nandi [23] show that

$$\Pr\left[\,\text{CBC}[E](K, M_1) = \text{CBC}[E](K, M_2)\,\right] \leq \frac{2\sqrt{\ell}}{2^n} + \frac{16\ell^4}{2^{2n}}\ .$$

This directly implies that CBC MAC is ϵ_2-almost universal where $\epsilon_2 = \frac{2\sqrt{\ell}}{2^n} + \frac{16\ell^4}{2^{2n}}$.

Below we prove that CBC MAC is ϵ_1-regular, where $\epsilon_1 = \epsilon_2 = \frac{2\sqrt{\ell}}{2^n} + \frac{16\ell^4}{2^{2n}}$.

Lemma 3. *For any* $X \in \{0,1\}^{\ell n}$ *and* $Y \in \{0,1\}^n$, *we have*

$$\Pr\left[\,\text{CBC}[E](K, X) = Y\,\right] \leq \frac{2\sqrt{\ell}}{2^n} + \frac{16\ell^4}{2^{2n}}\ .$$

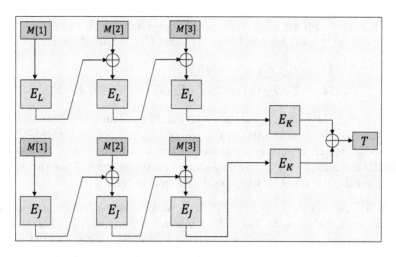

Fig. 5. The 2k-SUM-ECBC construction. It is built from a blockcipher E. Here the hash key is $H_{K_h} = (L, J)$.

Proof. Let $M_1 = X \| Y$ and $M_2 = 0^n$. Then the event $\mathsf{CBC}[E](K, X) = Y$ is the same as $\mathsf{CBC}[E](K, M_1) = \mathsf{CBC}[E](K, M_2)$. Hence

$$\Pr\left[\,\mathsf{CBC}[E](K, X) = Y\,\right] = \Pr\left[\,\mathsf{CBC}[E](K, M_1) = \mathsf{CBC}[E](K, M_2)\,\right]$$
$$\leq \frac{2\sqrt{\ell}}{2^n} + \frac{16\ell^4}{2^{2n}}\,,$$

where the last inequality comes from the fact that CBC MAC is ϵ_2-almost universal.

By using Theorem 1, we obtain the following result.

Theorem 2. *Let $E : \{0,1\}^k \times \{0,1\}^n \to \{0,1\}^n$ be a blockcipher that we model as an ideal blockcipher. Assume that $\ell \leq 2^{n/4}$. Then for any adversary A that makes at most q evaluation queries and p ideal-cipher queries,*

$$\mathsf{Adv}^{\mathrm{prf}}_{\text{2k-SUM-ECBC}}(A) \leq \frac{2q}{2^k} + \frac{q(3q+p)(6q+2p)}{2^{2k}} + \frac{6qp\ell}{2^{k+n}} + \frac{64q^2}{2^{n+k}} + \frac{36qp}{2^{n+k}}$$
$$+ \frac{44q^2\ell^{\frac{3}{2}}}{2^{n+k}} + \frac{576q^3\ell}{2^{2n}} + \frac{2304q^3}{2^{2n}}\,,$$

where $p + q\ell \leq 2^{n-1}$ by the assumption.

4.2 Security of 2k-LightMAC_Plus

The $2n$-bit hash function H used in 2k-LightMAC_Plus is the concatenation of two n-bit functions H^1 and H^2 where H^1 and H^2 are both based on a blockcipher E

with the same key, namely $K_{h,1} = K_{h,2} = L$. For a message $M = M[1]\| \dots \| M[\ell]$ where $M[i]$ is a $(n-m)$-bit block, $H^1_L(M)$ and $H^2_L(M)$ are defined as follows

$$H^1_L(M) = E_L(Y_1) \oplus \dots \oplus E_L(Y_\ell) \ ,$$
$$H^2_L(M) = 2^\ell \cdot E_L(Y_1) \oplus 2^{\ell-1} \cdot E_L(Y_2) \oplus \dots \oplus 2 \cdot E_L(Y_\ell)$$

where $Y_i = \langle i \rangle_m \| M[i]$ and $\langle i \rangle_m$ is the m-bit encoding of integer i. The description of hash function H is illustrated at the top of Fig. 6. Then 2k-LightMAC_Plus is defined as DbHtS$[H, E]$ and is illustrated at the bottom of Fig. 6. To prove that H^1 and H^2 are both ϵ_1-regular and ϵ_2-almost universal, we will use the following algebraic result, the proof of which can be found in [18].

Lemma 4. *[18] Let $Z = (Z_1, \dots, Z_\ell)$ be ℓ random variables that sampled from $\{0,1\}^n$ without replacement. Let A be a matrix of dimension $s \times \ell$ defined over $\mathsf{GF}(2^n)$. Then for any given column vector c of dimension $s \times 1$ over $\mathsf{GF}(2^n)$,*

$$\Pr[A \cdot Z^T = c] \le \frac{1}{(2^n - \ell + r)_r} \ ,$$

where r is the rank of the matrix A.

We first show that H^1 is ϵ_1-regular. Note that for any message M and any n-bit string $Y \in \{0,1\}^n$, the rank of equation

$$E_L(Y_1) \oplus \dots \oplus E_L(Y_\ell) = Y$$

is 1 since $Y_1, \dots, Y_\ell$ are all distinct from each other. Hence by Lemma 4, the equation $H^1_L(M) = Y$ holds with probability at most $1/(2^n - \ell + 1) \le 2/2^n$ by assuming $\ell \le 2^{n-2}$, namely H^1 is $2/2^n$-regular. Similarly, we can prove that H^2 is $2/2^n$-regular.

Next, we will show that H^1 is ϵ_2-almost universal. Note that for any two distinct messages M_1 and M_2, the equation $H^1_L(M_1) = H^1_L(M_2)$ can be written as

$$E_L(Y^1_1) \oplus \dots \oplus E_L(Y^1_{\ell_1}) = E_L(Y^2_1) \oplus \dots \oplus E_L(Y^2_{\ell_2}) \ ,$$

where $Y^1_i = \langle i \rangle_m \| M_1[i]$ and $Y^2_i = \langle i \rangle_m \| M_2[i]$. Without loss of generality, we assume $\ell_1 \le \ell_2$. If $\ell_1 = \ell_2$, then there must exist some i such that $M_1[i] \ne M_2[i]$. If $\ell_1 < \ell_2$, then $Y^2_{\ell_2}$ must be different from the values $Y^1_1, \dots, Y^1_{\ell_1}$. So in either of these two cases, the rank of above equation is exactly 1. By Lemma 4, the equation $H^1_L(M_1) = H^1_L(M_2)$ holds with probability at most $1/(2^n - \ell_1 - \ell_2 + 1) \le 2/2^n$ by assuming $\ell_1, \ell_2 \le 2^{n-2}$. Hence H^1 is $2/2^n$-almost universal. Similarly, we can prove that H^2 is $2/2^n$-almost universal.

However, we cannot directly apply Theorem 1 at this stage since the two hash keys $K_{h,1}$ and $K_{h,2}$ are identical in 2k-LightMAC_Plus while it is assumed that $K_{h,1}$ and $K_{h,2}$ are two independent keys in Theorem 1. The only problematic term in Theorem 1 is $(\epsilon_1 + \epsilon_2)^2$ since only this term relies on the independence of these two keys (i.e., condition 9 and condition 12 in the proof of Theorem 1).

To handle this issue, for condition 9, we should consider for any two distinct messages M_1 and M_2, the probability of equations

$$\begin{cases} E_L(Y_1^1) \oplus \cdots \oplus E_L(Y_{\ell_1}^1) = E_L(Y_1^2) \oplus \cdots \oplus E_L(Y_{\ell_2}^2) \\ 2^{\ell_1} \cdot E_L(Y_1^1) \oplus \cdots \oplus 2 \cdot E_L(Y_{\ell_1}^1) = 2^{\ell_2} \cdot E_L(Y_1^2) \oplus \cdots \oplus 2 \cdot E_L(Y_{\ell_2}^2) \ . \end{cases}$$

Note that since M_1 and M_2 are two distinct messages, by using the result in [30, Case A], we can always find two random variables $E_L(Y_i^a)$ and $E_L(Y_j^b)$ where $a, b \in \{1, 2\}$, $1 \le i \le \ell_a$, $1 \le j \le \ell_b$ such that the rank of above two equations is 2. By Lemma 4, the above two equations hold with probability at most $1/(2^n - \ell_1 - \ell_2 + 2)_2 \le 4/2^{2n}$ by assuming $\ell_1, \ell_2 \le 2^{n-2}$. For other three cases in condition 9, we can analyze them similarly. Hence condition 9 holds with probability at most $16q^2/2^{2n}$. For condition 12, we should consider for three distinct messages M_1, M_2 and M_3 such that

$$\begin{cases} E_L(Y_1^1) \oplus \cdots \oplus E_L(Y_{\ell_1}^1) = E_L(Y_1^2) \oplus \cdots \oplus E_L(Y_{\ell_2}^2) \\ 2^{\ell_1} \cdot E_L(Y_1^1) \oplus \cdots \oplus 2 \cdot E_L(Y_{\ell_1}^1) = 2^{\ell_3} \cdot E_L(Y_1^3) \oplus \cdots \oplus 2 \cdot E_L(Y_{\ell_3}^3) \ . \end{cases}$$

Similarly, it holds with probability at most $16q^3/2^{2n}$.

Therefore, by using Theorem 1 and combined with above analysis, we can obtain the multi-user security of 2k-LightMAC_Plus.

Theorem 3. *Let $E : \{0, 1\}^k \times \{0, 1\}^n \to \{0, 1\}^n$ be a blockcipher that we model as an ideal blockcipher. Assume that $\ell \le 2^{n-3}$. Then for any adversary A that makes at most q evaluation queries and p ideal-cipher queries,*

$$\mathrm{Adv}^{\mathrm{prf}}_{\text{2k-LightMAC\_Plus}}(A) \le \frac{2q}{2^k} + \frac{q(3q + p)(6q + 2p)}{2^{2k}} + \frac{2qp\ell}{2^{k+n}} + \frac{8qp}{2^{k+n}}$$

$$+ \frac{8q^2}{2^{k+n}} + \frac{4q^2\ell}{2^{k+n}} + \frac{70q^3}{2^{2n}} \ ,$$

where $p + q\ell \le 2^{n-1}$ by the assumption.

4.3 Security of 2k-PMAC_Plus

The $2n$-bit hash function H used in 2k-PMAC_Plus is the concatenation of two n-bit functions H^1 and H^2 where H^1 and H^2 are both based a blockcipher E with the same key, namely $K_{h,1} = K_{h,2} = L$. For a message $M = M[1] \| \ldots \| M[\ell]$ where $M[i]$ is a n-bit block, $H^1_L(M)$ and $H^2_L(M)$ are defined as follows

$$H^1_L(M) = E_L(Y_1) \oplus \cdots \oplus E_L(Y_\ell) \ ,$$
$$H^2_L(M) = 2 \cdot E_L(Y_1) \oplus \cdots \oplus 2^\ell \cdot E_L(Y_\ell)$$

where $Y_i = M[i] \oplus 2^i \cdot \Delta_0 \oplus 2^{2i} \cdot \Delta_1$, $\Delta_0 = E_L(0)$, and $\Delta_1 = E_L(1)$. The detailed code description of hash function H is illustrated at the top of Fig. 7. Then 2k-PMAC_Plus is defined as DbHtS$[H, E]$ and is illustrated at the bottom of Fig. 7.

```
procedure H(L, M)
 M[1] ‖ ... ‖ M[ℓ] ← M
 for i ← 1 to ℓ do
     Yᵢ ← ⟨i⟩ₘ ‖ M[i];  Zᵢ ← E_L(Yᵢ)
 Σ = Z₁ ⊕ Z₂ ⊕ ··· ⊕ Zℓ;  Λ = 2ℓ · Z₁ ⊕ 2^{ℓ-1} · Z₂ ⊕ ··· ⊕ 2 · Zℓ
 return (Σ, Λ)
```

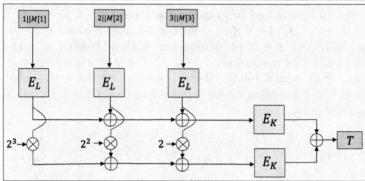

Fig. 6. Top. The $2n$-bit hash function used in 2k-LightMAC_Plus. Here the hash key is $K_h = (K_{h,1}, K_{h,2})$ where $K_{h,1} = K_{h,2} = L$. **Bottom.** The 2k-LightMAC_Plus construction built from a blockcipher E.

We now show that both H^1 and H^2 are ϵ_1-regular and ϵ_2-almost universal. For any message $M = M[1] \,\|\, \dots \,\|\, M[\ell]$, we denote by E_1 the event that $Y_i = Y_j$ for $1 \leq i, j \leq \ell$ and $i \neq j$. Note that the rank of equation

$$M[i] \oplus M[j] \oplus (2^i \oplus 2^j) \cdot \Delta_0 \oplus (2^{2i} \oplus 2^{2j}) \cdot \Delta_1 = 0$$

is 1. Hence by Lemma 4,

$$\Pr[\mathsf{E}_1] \leq \frac{\binom{\ell}{2}}{2^n - 2 + 1} \leq \frac{\ell^2}{2^n} \ .$$

For any n-bit string $Y \in \{0,1\}^n$, the rank of equation

$$E_L(Y_1) \oplus \cdots \oplus E_L(Y_\ell) = Y$$

is 1 when event E_1 does not happen. Hence by Lemma 4, the equation $H_L^1(M) = Y$ holds with probability at most

$$\begin{aligned}
\Pr\left[H_L^1(M) = Y \right] &= \Pr\left[H_L^1(M) = Y \wedge \overline{\mathsf{E}}_1 \right] + \Pr\left[H_L^1(M) = Y \wedge \mathsf{E}_1 \right] \\
&\leq \Pr\left[H_L^1(M) = Y \mid \overline{\mathsf{E}}_1 \right] + \Pr\left[\mathsf{E}_1 \right] \\
&\leq \frac{1}{2^n - \ell + 1} + \frac{\ell^2}{2^n} \leq \frac{2\ell^2}{2^n} \ ,
\end{aligned}$$

by assuming $\ell \leq 2^{n-1}$. Thus H^1 is $2\ell^2/2^n$-regular. Similarly, we can prove that H^2 is $2\ell^2/2^n$-regular.

Next, we will show that H^1 is ϵ_2-almost universal. For any two distinct messages $M_1 = M_1[1] \| \ldots \| M_1[\ell_1]$ and $M_2 = M_2[1] \| \ldots \| M_2[\ell_2]$, we denote by E_2 the event that $Y_i^a = Y_j^b$ for $a, b \in \{1, 2\}$ and $1 \leq i \leq \ell_a$, $1 \leq j \leq \ell_b$, $i \neq j$. Then similar to the analysis of event E_1, we have $\Pr[\mathsf{E}_2] \leq 4\ell^2/2^n$. Hence the rank of equation

$$E_L(Y_1^1) \oplus \cdots \oplus E_L(Y_{\ell_1}^1) = E_L(Y_1^2) \oplus \cdots \oplus E_L(Y_{\ell_2}^2)$$

is 1 when event E_2 does not happen. By Lemma 4, the equation $H_L^1(M_1) = H_L^1(M_2)$ holds with probability at most $1/(2^n - 2\ell + 1) + 4\ell^2/2^n \leq 6\ell^2/2^n$ by assuming $\ell \leq 2^{n-2}$. This implies that H^1 is $6\ell^2/2^n$-almost universal. By using similar argument, we can prove that H^2 is $6\ell^2/2^n$-almost universal.

Since H^1 and H^2 use the same key, similar to the case of 2k-LightMAC_Plus, we should handle the problematic term $(\epsilon_1 + \epsilon_2)^2$ in Theorem 1 before applying it. This term arises from condition 9 and condition 12. Denote by E_3 the event that among q evaluation queries, there exits some message M such that $E_L(Y_i) = 0$ for $1 \leq i \leq \ell$. It is easy to see that $\Pr[\mathsf{E}_3] \leq q\ell/(2^n - q\ell) \leq 2q\ell/2^n$ by assuming $q\ell \leq 2^{n-1}$. We proceed to analyze condition 9 and condition 12 when E_3 does not occur. For condition 9, we should consider for any two distinct messages M_1 and M_2, the probability of equations

$$\begin{cases} E_L(Y_1^1) \oplus \cdots \oplus E_L(Y_{\ell_1}^1) = E_L(Y_1^2) \oplus \cdots \oplus E_L(Y_{\ell_2}^2) \\ 2 \cdot E_L(Y_1^1) \oplus \cdots \oplus 2^{\ell_1} \cdot E_L(Y_{\ell_1}^1) = 2 \cdot E_L(Y_1^2) \oplus \cdots \oplus 2^{\ell_2} \cdot E_L(Y_{\ell_2}^2) \ . \end{cases}$$

Since M_1 and M_2 are two distinct messages, by using the result in [34, Case D], we can always find two random variables $E_L(Y_i^a)$ and $E_L(Y_j^b)$ where $a, b \in \{1, 2\}$ and $1 \leq i \leq \ell_a$, $1 \leq j \leq \ell_b$ such that the rank of above two equations is 2 when E_2 does not happen. On the other hand, if E_2 happens, then it is easy to see that the rank of above two equations is at least 1. By Lemma 4, the above two equations hold with probability at most

$$\frac{1}{(2^n - 2\ell + 2)_2} + \frac{4\ell^2}{2^n} \cdot \frac{1}{2^n - 2\ell + 1} \leq \frac{12\ell^2}{2^{2n}} \ .$$

For other three cases in condition 9, we can analyze them similarly. Hence condition 9 holds with probability at most $48q^2\ell^2/2^{2n} + 4q\ell/2^n$. For condition 12, we should consider for any there distinct messages M_1, M_2 and M_3

$$\begin{cases} E_L(Y_1^1) \oplus \cdots \oplus E_L(Y_{\ell_1}^1) = E_L(Y_1^2) \oplus \cdots \oplus E_L(Y_{\ell_2}^2) \\ 2 \cdot E_L(Y_1^1) \oplus \cdots \oplus 2^{\ell_1} \cdot E_L(Y_{\ell_1}^1) = 2 \cdot E_L(Y_1^3) \oplus \cdots \oplus 2^{\ell_3} \cdot E_L(Y_{\ell_3}^3) \ . \end{cases}$$

Denote by E_4 the event that $Y_i^a = Y_j^b$ for $a, b \in \{1, 2, 3\}$ and $1 \leq i \leq \ell_a$, $1 \leq j \leq \ell_b$, $i \neq j$. Then similar to the analysis of E_2, we have $\Pr[\mathsf{E}_4] \leq 9\ell^2/2^n$. By using the result in [34, Case D], we can always find two random variables $E_L(Y_i^a)$ and $E_L(Y_j^b)$ where $a, b \in \{1, 2, 3\}$ and $1 \leq i \leq \ell_a$, $1 \leq j \leq \ell_b$ such that the rank of above two equations is 2 when E_4 dose not occur. On the other hand,

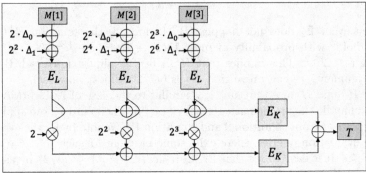

procedure $H(L, M)$
$M[1] \| \dots \| M[\ell] \leftarrow M$; $\Delta_0 \leftarrow E_L(0)$; $\Delta_1 \leftarrow E_L(1)$
for $i \leftarrow 1$ **to** ℓ **do**
$\quad Y_i \leftarrow M[i] \oplus 2^i \cdot \Delta_0 \oplus 2^{2i} \cdot \Delta_1$; $Z_i \leftarrow E_L(Y_i)$
$\Sigma = Z_1 \oplus Z_2 \oplus \dots \oplus Z_\ell$; $\Lambda = 2 \cdot Z_1 \oplus 2^2 \cdot Z_2 \oplus \dots \oplus 2^\ell \cdot Z_\ell$
return (Σ, Λ)

Fig. 7. Top. The $2n$-bit hash function used in 2k-PMAC_Plus. Here the hash key is $K_h = (K_{h,1}, K_{h,2})$ where $K_{h,1} = K_{h,2} = L$. **Bottom.** The 2k-PMAC_Plus construction built from a blockcipher E.eps

if E_4 happens, then it is easy to see that the rank of above two equations is at least 1. By Lemma 4, the above two equations hold with probability at most

$$\frac{1}{(2^n - 3\ell + 2)_2} + \frac{9\ell^2}{2^n} \cdot \frac{1}{2^n - 3\ell + 1} \leq \frac{22\ell^2}{2^{2n}},$$

by assuming $\ell \leq 2^{n-3}$. For other three cases in condition 12, we can analyze them similarly. Thus, condition 12 holds with probability at most $88q^3\ell^2/2^{2n} + 4q\ell/2^n$.

Therefore, by using Theorem 1 and combined with above analysis, we can obtain the multi-user security of 2k-PMAC_Plus.

Theorem 4. *Let* $E : \{0,1\}^k \times \{0,1\}^n \rightarrow \{0,1\}^n$ *be a blockcipher that we model as an ideal blockcipher. Assume that* $\ell \leq 2^{n-3}$. *Then for any adversary* A *that makes at most* q *evaluation queries and* p *ideal-cipher queries,*

$$\mathsf{Adv}^{\mathrm{prf}}_{\text{2k-PMAC\_Plus}}(A) \leq \frac{2q}{2^k} + \frac{q(3q + p)(6q + 2p)}{2^{2k}} + \frac{6qp\ell^2}{2^{n+k}} + \frac{4qp}{2^{n+k}} + \frac{20q^2\ell^3}{2^{n+k}}$$
$$+ \frac{200q^3\ell^2}{2^{2n}} + \frac{8q\ell}{2^n} + \frac{6q^3}{2^{2n}},$$

where $p + q\ell \leq 2^{n-1}$ *by the assumption.*

procedure 2kf9[E](L, K, M)
$M[1] \parallel \cdots \parallel M[\ell] \leftarrow M$; $Y_0 \leftarrow 0^n$
for $i \leftarrow 1$ to ℓ do
    $Y_i \leftarrow E_L(Y_{i-1} \oplus M[i])$
$\Sigma = Y_\ell$; $\Lambda = Y_1 \oplus Y_2 \oplus \cdots \oplus Y_\ell$
$(\Sigma, \Lambda) \leftarrow (\mathrm{fix}_0(\Sigma), \mathrm{fix}_1(\Lambda))$; $(U, V) \leftarrow (E_K(\Sigma), E_K(\Lambda))$
$T \leftarrow U \oplus V$; return T

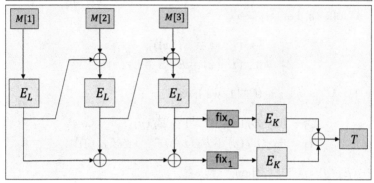

Fig. 8. The 2kf9[E] construction. It is built on top of a blockcipher $E : \{0,1\}^k \times \{0,1\}^n \to \{0,1\}^n$. Here fix_0 and fix_1 are two domain separating functions that fix the least significant bit of an n-bit string to 0 and 1 respectively.

5 Attack on 2kf9 Construction

In this section, we will show attacks on several variants of the 2kf9 construction, which is proposed by Datta et al. [17] to achieve beyond-birthday-bound security. We begin with the description of 2kf9 construction.

THE 2kf9 CONSTRUCTION. Let $E : \{0,1\}^k \times \{0,1\}^n \to \{0,1\}^n$ be a blockcipher. The 2kf9 construction is based on a blockcipher E with two keys L and K. Let fix_0 and fix_1 be two separating functions that fix the least significant bit of an n-bit string to 0 and 1 respectively. The specification of 2kf9 with domain separation is illustrated in Fig. 8.

5.1 Attack on 2kf9 Without Domain Separation

Datta et al. [17] prove that 2kf9 without domain separation can achieve beyond-birthday-bound security. In the proof, they claim that the collision probability between Σ and Λ (without fix_0 and fix_1) is small for any message M, namely $2/2^n$. However, this claim is essentially incorrect. For any short-block message M that will become a single block after 10* padded, i.e., $|M| < n$, the probability of Σ colliding with Λ is exactly 1, since they are both the outputs of blockcipher E_L with the same input M. Hence, for any short-block message M, $(M, 0^n)$ is always a valid forgery for this construction.

5.2 Attack on 2kf9 with Domain Separation

One may think that if we resume the domain separation in 2kf9 (Fig. 8), then it can recover beyond-birthday-bound security. However, our attack shows that even with domain separation, 2kf9 cannot be secure beyond the birthday bound. The attack is as follows.

For any two-block messages $M_1 = x \parallel z$ and $M_2 = y \parallel z \oplus 0^{n-1}1$ where $x, y \in \{0,1\}^n$, if $E_L(x) \oplus E_L(y) = 0^{n-1}1$, then $T_1 = T_2$ for any $z \in \{0,1\}^n$. The reason is as follows. For $M_1 = x \parallel z$, we have

$$\Sigma_1 = \text{fix}_0(E_L(z \oplus E_L(x)))$$
$$\Lambda_1 = \text{fix}_1(E_L(x) \oplus E_L(z \oplus E_L(x))) .$$

Similarly, for $M_2 = y \parallel z \oplus 0^{n-1}1$, we have

$$\Sigma_2 = \text{fix}_0(E_L(z \oplus 0^{n-1}1 \oplus E_L(y)))$$
$$\Lambda_2 = \text{fix}_1(E_L(y) \oplus E_L(z \oplus 0^{n-1}1 \oplus E_L(y))) .$$

If $E_L(x) \oplus E_L(y) = 0^{n-1}1$, then

$$E_L(z \oplus E_L(x)) = E_L(z \oplus 0^{n-1}1 \oplus E_L(y))$$
$$E_L(x) \oplus E_L(z \oplus E_L(x)) = E_L(y) \oplus E_L(z \oplus 0^{n-1}1 \oplus E_L(y)) \oplus 0^{n-1}1 .$$

Obviously it holds that $\Sigma_1 = \Sigma_2$. On the other hand, due to one-bit fixing function fix_1, it also holds that $\Lambda_1 = \Lambda_2$. Hence $E_K(\Sigma_1) \oplus E_K(\Lambda_1) = E_K(\Sigma_2) \oplus E_K(\Lambda_2)$, namely $T_1 = T_2$.

The detailed attack procedure is as follows. The adversary first chooses $2^{n/2+1}$ distinct n-bit strings $x_1, \ldots, x_{2^{n/2}}, y_1, \ldots, y_{2^{n/2}}$ from the set $\{0,1\}^n$. Fixing $z_1 \in \{0,1\}^n$, it then makes queries $x_i \parallel z_1$ and $y_i \parallel z_1 \oplus 0^{n-1}1$ to construction 2kf9, and receives the corresponding answers T_i^1 and T_i^2 for $1 \le i \le 2^{n/2}$. One can expect on average that there exists a pair of (x_i, y_j), such that $E_L(x_i) \oplus E_L(y_j) = 0^{n-1}1$ for $1 \le i, j \le 2^{n/2}$. The adversary can check it by looking at whether $T_i^1 = T_j^2$. To remove the case that $T_i^1 = T_j^2$ is not caused by $E_L(x_i) \oplus E_L(y_j) = 0^{n-1}1$, when $T_i^1 = T_j^2$ is found, the adversary will make two additional queries $x_i \parallel z_2$ and $y_j \parallel z_2 \oplus 0^{n-1}1$ to see whether the corresponding answers are identical. Finally, as soon as a desired pair (x_i, y_j) is obtained, the adversary makes query $x_i \parallel z_3$ to receive T. Then (M, T) where $M = y_j \parallel z_3 \oplus 0^{n-1}1$ is a valid forgery. The complexity of this attack is $O(2^{n/2})$.

REMARK 1. If Λ is multiplied by 2 before applying fix_1 function as is done in 2k-LightMAC_Plus and 2k-PMAC_Plus, then a similar birthday-bound attack as above still works. Instead of searching for a pair of (x, y) such that $E_L(x) \oplus E_L(y) = 0^{n-1}1$ for two-block messages $M_1 = x \parallel z$ and $M_2 = x \parallel z \oplus 0^{n-1}1$, here we need to find a pair of (x, y) such that $E_L(x) \oplus E_L(y) = d$ for two-block messages $M_1 = x \parallel z$ and $M_2 = x \parallel z \oplus d$, where d is the inverse of 2 in the finite field.

REMARK 2. Even if using more complicated multiplication in Λ, e.g. $\Lambda = 2^\ell \cdot Y_1 \oplus \cdots \oplus 2 \cdot Y_\ell$ as is used in 2k-LightMAC_Plus (or $\Lambda = 2 \cdot Y_1 \oplus \cdots \oplus 2^\ell \cdot Y_\ell$ as is used in 2k-PMAC_Plus), we can also propose a similar attack as above. The core idea of the attack is to find a pair of (x, y) such that $E_L(x) \oplus E_L(y) = u$ for two-block messages $M_1 = x \parallel z$ and $M_2 = y \parallel z \oplus u$, where u is the inverse of 4 in the finite field.

REMARK 3. The reason behind this flaw is that for 2kf9, we can always find a relation between variables Σ and Λ, regardless of the usage of field multiplication. By utilizing this relation, if there is a collision on Σ, then it will lead to another collision on Λ. So to forge a tag, we only need to search for a collision on Σ, which requires only birthday-bound complexity. While for other three two-key DbHtS constructions (i.e., 2k-SUM-ECBC, 2k-LightMAC_Plus and 2k-PMAC_Plus), there does not exist such relation or the chance that such relation occurs is negligible. For SUM-ECBC, the two variables Σ and Λ are produced by using two independent keys, thus being independent from each other. For 2k-LightMAC_Plus and 2k-PMAC_Plus, we can always prove that the probability of such relation occurrence is small, thus Σ and Λ are somewhat independent due to the usage of field multiplication.

Acknowledgments. Yaobin Shen is more than grateful to Viet Tung Hoang for motivating this work and many helpful discussions. We thank the anonymous reviewers for their useful feedback. Yaobin Shen and Lei Wang were supported partially by National Key Research and Development Program of China (No. 2019YFB2101601). Dawu Gu was supported partially by Natural Science Foundation of China (No. 62072307) and National Key Research and Development Project (No. 2020YFA0712300). Jian Weng was supported by National Natural Science Foundation of China (Grant Nos. 61825203, U1736203, 61732021), Major Program of Guangdong Basic and Applied Research Project (Grant No. 2019B030302008).

References

1. An, J.H., Bellare, M.: Constructing VIL-MACs from FIL-MACs: message authentication under weakened assumptions. In: Wiener, M. (ed.) CRYPTO 1999. LNCS, vol. 1666, pp. 252–269. Springer, Heidelberg (1999). https://doi.org/10.1007/3-540-48405-1_16

2. Banik, S., Pandey, S.K., Peyrin, T., Sasaki, Yu., Sim, S.M., Todo, Y.: GIFT: a small present. In: Fischer, W., Homma, N. (eds.) CHES 2017. LNCS, vol. 10529, pp. 321–345. Springer, Cham (2017). https://doi.org/10.1007/978-3-319-66787-4_16

3. Bellare, M., Bernstein, D.J., Tessaro, S.: Hash-function based PRFs: AMAC and its multi-user security. In: Fischlin, M., Coron, J.-S. (eds.) EUROCRYPT 2016, Part I. LNCS, vol. 9665, pp. 566–595. Springer, Heidelberg (2016). https://doi.org/10.1007/978-3-662-49890-3_22

4. Bellare, M., Boldyreva, A., Micali, S.: Public-key encryption in a multi-user setting: security proofs and improvements. In: Preneel, B. (ed.) EUROCRYPT 2000. LNCS, vol. 1807, pp. 259–274. Springer, Heidelberg (2000). https://doi.org/10.1007/3-540-45539-6_18

5. Bellare, M., Canetti, R., Krawczyk, H.: Keying hash functions for message authentication. In: Koblitz, N. (ed.) CRYPTO 1996. LNCS, vol. 1109, pp. 1–15. Springer, Heidelberg (1996). https://doi.org/10.1007/3-540-68697-5_1

6. Bellare, M., Kilian, J., Rogaway, P.: The security of the cipher block chaining message authentication code. J. Comput. Syst. Sci. **61**(3), 362–399 (2000). https://doi.org/10.1006/jcss.1999.1694

7. Bellare, M., Pietrzak, K., Rogaway, P.: Improved security analyses for CBC MACs. In: Shoup, V. (ed.) CRYPTO 2005. LNCS, vol. 3621, pp. 527–545. Springer, Heidelberg (2005). https://doi.org/10.1007/11535218_32

8. Bellare, M., Tackmann, B.: The multi-user security of authenticated encryption: AES-GCM in TLS 1.3. In: Robshaw, M., Katz, J. (eds.) CRYPTO 2016, Part I. LNCS, vol. 9814, pp. 247–276. Springer, Heidelberg (2016). https://doi.org/10.1007/978-3-662-53018-4_10

9. Bhargavan, K., Leurent, G.: On the practical (in-)security of 64-bit block ciphers: collision attacks on HTTP over TLS and OpenVPN. In: Weippl, E.R., Katzenbeisser, S., Kruegel, C., Myers, A.C., Halevi, S. (eds.) ACM CCS 2016, pp. 456–467. ACM Press, October 2016. https://doi.org/10.1145/2976749.2978423

10. Biham, E.: How to decrypt or even substitute DES-encrypted messages in 2^{28} steps. Inf. Process. Lett. **84**(3), 117–124 (2002)

11. Black, J., Rogaway, P.: A block-cipher mode of operation for parallelizable message authentication. In: Knudsen, L.R. (ed.) EUROCRYPT 2002. LNCS, vol. 2332, pp. 384–397. Springer, Heidelberg (2002). https://doi.org/10.1007/3-540-46035-7_25

12. Bogdanov, A., et al.: PRESENT: an ultra-lightweight block cipher. In: Paillier, P., Verbauwhede, I. (eds.) CHES 2007. LNCS, vol. 4727, pp. 450–466. Springer, Heidelberg (2007). https://doi.org/10.1007/978-3-540-74735-2_31

13. Borghoff, J., et al.: PRINCE – a low-latency block cipher for pervasive computing applications. In: Wang, X., Sako, K. (eds.) ASIACRYPT 2012. LNCS, vol. 7658, pp. 208–225. Springer, Heidelberg (2012). https://doi.org/10.1007/978-3-642-34961-4_14

14. Bose, P., Hoang, V.T., Tessaro, S.: Revisiting AES-GCM-SIV: multi-user security, faster key derivation, and better bounds. In: Nielsen, J.B., Rijmen, V. (eds.) EUROCRYPT 2018. LNCS, vol. 10820, pp. 468–499. Springer, Cham (2018). https://doi.org/10.1007/978-3-319-78381-9_18

15. Chatterjee, S., Menezes, A., Sarkar, P.: Another look at tightness. In: Miri, A., Vaudenay, S. (eds.) SAC 2011. LNCS, vol. 7118, pp. 293–319. Springer, Heidelberg (2012). https://doi.org/10.1007/978-3-642-28496-0_18

16. Chen, S., Steinberger, J.: Tight security bounds for key-alternating ciphers. In: Nguyen, P.Q., Oswald, E. (eds.) EUROCRYPT 2014. LNCS, vol. 8441, pp. 327–350. Springer, Heidelberg (2014). https://doi.org/10.1007/978-3-642-55220-5_19

17. Datta, N., Dutta, A., Nandi, M., Paul, G.: Double-block hash-then-sum: a paradigm for constructing BBB secure PRF. IACR Trans. Symm. Cryptol. **2018**(3), 36–92 (2018). https://doi.org/10.13154/tosc.v2018.i3.36-92

18. Datta, N., Dutta, A., Nandi, M., Paul, G., Zhang, L.: Single key variant of PMAC_Plus. IACR Trans. Symm. Cryptol. **2017**(4), 268–305 (2017). https://doi.org/10.13154/tosc.v2017.i4.268-305

19. Hoang, V.T., Tessaro, S.: Key-alternating ciphers and key-length extension: exact bounds and multi-user security. In: Robshaw, M., Katz, J. (eds.) CRYPTO 2016, Part I. LNCS, vol. 9814, pp. 3–32. Springer, Heidelberg (2016). https://doi.org/10.1007/978-3-662-53018-4_1

20. Hoang, V.T., Tessaro, S.: The multi-user security of double encryption. In: Coron, J.-S., Nielsen, J.B. (eds.) EUROCRYPT 2017, Part II. LNCS, vol. 10211, pp. 381–411. Springer, Cham (2017). https://doi.org/10.1007/978-3-319-56614-6_13

21. Hoang, V.T., Tessaro, S., Thiruvengadam, A.: The multi-user security of GCM, revisited: tight bounds for nonce randomization. In: Lie, D., Mannan, M., Backes, M., Wang, X. (eds.) ACM CCS 2018, pp. 1429–1440. ACM Press, October 2018. https://doi.org/10.1145/3243734.3243816

22. Iwata, T., Kurosawa, K.: OMAC: one-key CBC MAC. In: Johansson, T. (ed.) FSE 2003. LNCS, vol. 2887, pp. 129–153. Springer, Heidelberg (2003). https://doi.org/10.1007/978-3-540-39887-5_11

23. Jha, A., Nandi, M.: Revisiting structure graph and its applications to CBC-MAC and EMAC. Cryptology ePrint Archive, Report 2016/161 (2016). http://eprint.iacr.org/2016/161

24. Kim, Seongkwang., Lee, Byeonghak, Lee, Jooyoung: Tight security bounds for double-block hash-then-sum MACs. In: Canteaut, Anne, Ishai, Yuval (eds.) EURO-CRYPT 2020. LNCS, vol. 12105, pp. 435–465. Springer, Cham (2020). https://doi.org/10.1007/978-3-030-45721-1_16

25. Leurent, G., Nandi, M., Sibleyras, F.: Generic attacks against beyond-birthday-bound MACs. In: Shacham, H., Boldyreva, A. (eds.) CRYPTO 2018, Part I. LNCS, vol. 10991, pp. 306–336. Springer, Cham (2018). https://doi.org/10.1007/978-3-319-96884-1_11

26. Luykx, A., Mennink, B., Paterson, K.G.: Analyzing multi-key security degradation. In: Takagi, T., Peyrin, T. (eds.) ASIACRYPT 2017, Part II. LNCS, vol. 10625, pp. 575–605. Springer, Cham (2017). https://doi.org/10.1007/978-3-319-70697-9_20

27. Luykx, A., Preneel, B., Tischhauser, E., Yasuda, K.: A MAC mode for lightweight block ciphers. In: Peyrin, T. (ed.) FSE 2016. LNCS, vol. 9783, pp. 43–59. Springer, Heidelberg (2016). https://doi.org/10.1007/978-3-662-52993-5_3

28. Morgan, Andrew., Pass, Rafael, Shi, Elaine: On the adaptive security of MACs and PRFs. In: Moriai, Shiho, Wang, Huaxiong (eds.) ASIACRYPT 2020. LNCS, vol. 12491, pp. 724–753. Springer, Cham (2020). https://doi.org/10.1007/978-3-030-64837-4_24

29. Mouha, N., Luykx, A.: Multi-key security: the Even-Mansour construction revisited. In: Gennaro, R., Robshaw, M. (eds.) CRYPTO 2015, Part I. LNCS, vol. 9215, pp. 209–223. Springer, Heidelberg (2015). https://doi.org/10.1007/978-3-662-47989-6_10

30. Naito, Y.: Blockcipher-based MACs: beyond the birthday bound without message length. In: Takagi, T., Peyrin, T. (eds.) ASIACRYPT 2017, Part III. LNCS, vol. 10626, pp. 446–470. Springer, Cham (2017). https://doi.org/10.1007/978-3-319-70700-6_16

31. Patarin, J.: The "coefficients H" technique. In: Avanzi, R.M., Keliher, L., Sica, F. (eds.) SAC 2008. LNCS, vol. 5381, pp. 328–345. Springer, Heidelberg (2009). https://doi.org/10.1007/978-3-642-04159-4_21

32. Tessaro, S.: Optimally secure block ciphers from ideal primitives. In: Iwata, T., Cheon, J.H. (eds.) ASIACRYPT 2015, Part II. LNCS, vol. 9453, pp. 437–462. Springer, Heidelberg (2015). https://doi.org/10.1007/978-3-662-48800-3_18

33. Yasuda, K.: The sum of CBC MACs is a secure PRF. In: Pieprzyk, J. (ed.) CT-RSA 2010. LNCS, vol. 5985, pp. 366–381. Springer, Heidelberg (2010). https://doi.org/10.1007/978-3-642-11925-5_25

34. Yasuda, K.: A new variant of PMAC: beyond the birthday bound. In: Rogaway, P. (ed.) CRYPTO 2011. LNCS, vol. 6841, pp. 596–609. Springer, Heidelberg (2011). https://doi.org/10.1007/978-3-642-22792-9_34

35. Zhang, L., Wu, W., Sui, H., Wang, P.: 3kf9: enhancing 3GPP-MAC beyond the birthday bound. In: Wang, X., Sako, K. (eds.) ASIACRYPT 2012. LNCS, vol. 7658, pp. 296–312. Springer, Heidelberg (2012). https://doi.org/10.1007/978-3-642-34961-4_19

Thinking Outside the Superbox

Nicolas Bordes[1]([⊠]), Joan Daemen[2], Daniël Kuijsters[2], and Gilles Van Assche[3]

[1] Université Grenoble Alpes, Grenoble, France
`nicolas.bordes@univ-grenoble-alpes.fr`
[2] Radboud University, Nijmegen, The Netherlands
`{joan.daemen,Daniel.Kuijsters}@ru.nl`
[3] STMicroelectronics, Diegem, Belgium
`gilles-iacr@noekeon.org`

Abstract. Designing a block cipher or cryptographic permutation can be approached in many different ways. One such approach, popularized by AES, consists in grouping the bits along the S-box boundaries, e.g., in bytes, and in consistently processing them in these groups. This aligned approach leads to hierarchical structures like superboxes that make it possible to reason about the differential and linear propagation properties using combinatorial arguments. In contrast, an unaligned approach avoids any such grouping in the design of transformations. However, without hierarchical structure, sophisticated computer programs are required to investigate the differential and linear propagation properties of the primitive. In this paper, we formalize this notion of alignment and study four primitives that are exponents of different design strategies. We propose a way to analyze the interactions between the linear and the nonlinear layers w.r.t. the differential and linear propagation, and we use it to systematically compare the four primitives using non-trivial computer experiments. We show that alignment naturally leads to different forms of clustering, e.g., of active bits in boxes, of two-round trails in activity patterns, and of trails in differentials and linear approximations.

Keywords: Symmetric cryptography · Permutations · Block ciphers · Round functions

1 Introduction

Modern block ciphers and cryptographic permutations consist of the iteration of a round function. In many cases this round function consists of a layer of nonlinear S-boxes, a mixing layer, a shuffle layer (AKA a bit transposition or bit permutation), and the addition of a round key (in block ciphers) or constant (in cryptographic permutations).

Electronic supplementary material The online version of this chapter (https://doi.org/10.1007/978-3-030-84252-9_12) contains supplementary material, which is available to authorized users.

T. Malkin and C. Peikert (Eds.): CRYPTO 2021, LNCS 12827, pp. 337–367, 2021.
https://doi.org/10.1007/978-3-030-84252-9_12

Many papers investigate S-boxes and try to find a good compromise between implementation cost and propagation properties or provide a classification of all invertible S-boxes of a given width, see, e.g., [27,34]. Similarly, there is a rich literature on certain types of mixing layers. In particular, there have been many papers written about finding maximum-distance separable (MDS) mappings or near-MDS mappings with minimum implementation cost according to some metric, see, e.g., [28,37]. Building a good cipher starts with taking a good S-box and mixing layer and the rich cryptographic literature on these components provides us with ample choice. However, how these building blocks are combined in a round function and the resulting propagation properties has received much less systematic attention.

A standard way for designing a good round function from an S-box and an MDS mapping is the one followed in the Advanced Encryption Standard (AES) [32] and is known as the *wide trail strategy* [14,20]. This strategy gives criteria for the shuffle layer and comes with easy-to-verify bounds for the differential probability (DP) of differential trails (also known as characteristics) and the linear potential (LP) of linear trails. These bounds and its simplicity have made it one of the most applied design strategies, and AES has inspired a plethora of primitive designs, including lightweight ones. By adopting 4-bit S-boxes instead of 8-bit ones and modern lightweight MDS layers in a smart structure, multiple lightweight ciphers have been constructed. Many lessons were learned and this line of design has culminated in the block cipher of the NIST lightweight competition candidate SATURNIN [12], a truly modern version of AES.

Naturally, there are alternative design approaches. A popular design approach is the one underlying the 64-bit lightweight block cipher PRESENT [10]. Its round function has no MDS layer and simply consists of an S-box layer, a bit shuffle, and a key addition. It gets its diffusion from the combination of a smart choice of the bit shuffle and specific propagation criteria from its well-chosen S-box and doing many rounds. The PRESENT line of design has also been refined in the form of the GIFT (64- and 128-bit) block ciphers [1] and the cryptographic permutations of the SPONGENT lightweight hash function [9] that is used in ELEPHANT [7].

Another distinctive design approach is that of the cryptographic permutation of the SHA-3 standard [33], KECCAK-f. Unlike PRESENT, its round function does have a mixing layer, and it actually has all ingredients that AES has. Specifically, in their rationale, the designers also refer to the wide trail design strategy [6]. However, this wide-trail flavor does not appear to come with the simple bounds as in the case of AES, and designers have to resort to tedious and time-consuming programming efforts to obtain similar bounds. This is related to the fact that AES operates on *bytes* and KECCAK-f on *bits*. The KECCAK-f designers have discussed the difference between these two design approaches in [18]. In that paper, they have coined the term *alignment* to characterize this difference and supported it with some propagation experiments on KECCAK-f. The KECCAK-f line of design has also been refined and led to the 384-bit permutation that is used in XOODYAK [15], namely XOODOO [16], a truly modern version of KECCAK-f.

This treatment is not exhaustive and other distinctive design strategies exist. Some of them do not even use S-boxes or mixing layers, but they are based on alternating Additions with Rotations and XOR (ARX) such as SALSA [3], or they iterate very simple round functions many times such as SIMON [2].

In this paper we systematically analyze the impact of alignment on the differential and linear propagation properties of ciphers. We show that certain design choices regarding how the S-box and mixing layers are combined have a profound impact on the propagation properties. We identify and name a number of effects that are relevant in this context. Furthermore, we believe that this makes it possible to give a meaningful and non-ambiguous definition of the term alignment.

To illustrate this, we study the four primitives RIJNDAEL-256 [22], SATURNIN, SPONGENT-384, and XOODOO. They have comparable width and all have a non-linear layer consisting of equally-sized S-boxes that have the lowest known maximum DP and LP for their dimensions, see Sect. 2. They represent the three different design strategies, where we include both RIJNDAEL-256 and SATURNIN to illustrate the progress made in the last twenty years. We investigate their difference propagation and correlation properties, where for multiple rounds we adopt a *fixed-key* perspective. This, combined with the choice of relatively wide primitives, is geared towards their usage in permutation-based cryptography, but most findings are also relevant for the key-alternating block cipher case.

1.1   Outline and Contributions

After discussing notation and conventions, we review the notions of differential and linear cryptanalysis in Sect. 2. In Sect. 3 we show how the nonlinear layer defines a so-called *box partition*, and we present a non-ambiguous definition of alignment. In Sect. 4 we present our four ciphers from the perspective of alignment and compare the costs of their round functions. Surprisingly, SPONGENT, despite being specified at bit level like KECCAK-*f*, turns out to be aligned.

In Sect. 5 we recall the notions of bit and box weight as a measure of the mixing power of a linear layer. We report on this mixing power by means of *histograms* of states by their weight before and after the linear layer, rather than the usual *branch number* criterion. For all ciphers we observe a decay in mixing power from bit to box weight and describe and name the effect that causes this: *huddling*. This effect is more pronounced in aligned ciphers. This translates directly to the two-round differential and linear trail weight distributions, and we list them for all four ciphers. For the two most competitive proposals, we include histograms for three-round trails and a comparison for four rounds. Remarkably, despite the fact that SATURNIN has a more expensive S-box layer and a mixing layer with better bit-level mixing power, XOODOO has better differential and linear trail histograms for more than two rounds.

In Sect. 6, we show that trails that cluster necessarily share the same activity pattern, and we introduce the *cluster histogram* as a quantitative tool for the relation between the linear layer and the clustering of two-round trails in ciphers. We see that there is more clustering in the aligned than in the unaligned ciphers. We present the cluster histogram of the four primitives and, for three of them, we also analyze their two-round trail weight histograms. We conclude with a discussion on the clustering of trails in two and three rounds, and show that, at least up to weight 50, differentials over three rounds of XOODOO admit only one trail, hence they do not cluster.

Finally, in Sect. 7 we study the independence of round differentials in trails. We show that, again at least up to weight 50, three-round differentials of XOODOO are independent.

The generation of our histograms was non-trivial and the computation methods could be considered a contribution in themselves. Due to space restrictions we could not treat them in the paper but we have added their description in the supplementary material A after the paper. The related software is available at https://github.com/ongetekend/ThinkingOutsideTheSuperbox under the CC0 license (public domain).

1.2   Notation and Conventions

In this paper, we use the following conventions and notation. We write $\mathbb{Z}_{\geq 0}$ for the nonnegative integers and $\mathbb{Z}_{>0}$ for the positive integers. We write k with $k \in \mathbb{Z}_{\geq 0}$ for nonnegative integer variables. In other words, k is used as a placeholder for any nonnegative integer value.

Whenever we use indices, they always begin at 0. We define $[0, K-1] = \{i \in \mathbb{Z}_{\geq 0} : 0 \leq i \leq k-1\}$. Given a set S and an equivalence relation $\sim$ on S, we write $[a]_\sim$ for the equivalence class of $a \in S$. We denote the cardinality of S by $\#S$.

We study permutations $f : \mathbb{F}_2^b \to \mathbb{F}_2^b$. Any block cipher is transformed into a permutation by fixing the key, e.g., we fix all of its bits to 0.

We use the term *state* for a vector of b bits. It is either a vector that the permutation is applied to, a difference, or a linear mask (See Sect. 2). Given a state $a \in \mathbb{F}_2^b$, we refer to its ith component as a_i. In this paper, we consider index sets $B_i \subseteq [0, B-1]$ that form an *ordered* partition. We write $P_i(a) : \mathbb{F}_2^b \to \mathbb{F}_2^{\#B_i}$ for the *projection* onto the bits of a indexed by B_i.

We write e_i^k for the ith standard basis vector in $\mathbb{F}_2^k$, i.e., for $j \in [0, K-1]$ we have that $e_{ij}^k = 1$ if $i = j$ and 0 otherwise. We write $+$ for vector addition in $\mathbb{F}_2^k$.

Permutations are typically built by composing a number of lightweight *round functions*, i.e., $f = R_{r-1} \circ \cdots \circ R_1 \circ R_0$ for some $r \in \mathbb{Z}_{>0}$. We write $f[r] = R_{r-1} \circ \cdots \circ R_0$ and define $f[0] = id$ with id the identity function. A round function is composed of *step functions*, i.e., $R_i = \iota_i \circ L_i \circ N_i$, where N_i is a nonlinear map, L_i is a linear map, and ι_i is addition of a round constant. Apart from the round constant addition, these round functions are often, but not always, identical. For this reason, we will often simply write N or L, without reference to an index if the context allows for this, and we call N the nonlinear layer of f and L the linear layer of f. We write n for the number of S-boxes of N and denote their size by m. In this context, we suppose that $B_j = \{jm, \ldots, (j+1)m - 1\}$.

Permutations of the index space are written as $\tau : [0, b-1] \to [0, b-1]$. By *shuffle (layer)*, we mean a linear transformation $\pi : \mathbb{F}_2^b \to \mathbb{F}_2^b$ given by $\pi(a) = P_\tau a$, where P_τ is the permutation matrix associated with some τ, i.e., obtained by permuting the columns of the $(b \times b)$ identity matrix according to τ.

Given a linear transformation $L : \mathbb{F}_2^b \to \mathbb{F}_2^b$, there exists a matrix $M \in \mathbb{F}_2^{b \times b}$ such that $L(a) = Ma$. We define its transpose $L^\top : \mathbb{F}_2^b \to \mathbb{F}_2^b$ by $L^\top(a) = M^\top a$ and we denote the inverse of $L^\top$, when it exists, by $L^{-\top}$.

2   Differential and Linear Cryptanalysis

A major motivation behind the tools developed in this paper is better under-standing of the interplay between the linear and nonlinear layer in relation to differential and linear cryptanalysis. We want to be able to use the associated language freely when discussing these tools. Therefore, in this section, we go over the basic notions to make sure they are on hand when needed.

2.1   Differential Cryptanalysis

Differential cryptanalysis [8] is a chosen-plaintext attack that exploits the non-uniformity of the distribution of differences at the output of a permutation when it is applied to pairs of inputs with a fixed difference. We call an ordered pair of an input and output difference $(\Delta_{in}, \Delta_{out}) \in (\mathbb{F}_2^b)^2$ a differential.

Definition 1. *Let* $f \colon \mathbb{F}_2^b \to \mathbb{F}_2^b$ *be a permutation and define* $U_f(\Delta_{in}, \Delta_{out}) = \{x \in \mathbb{F}_2^b : f(x) + f(x + \Delta_{in}) = \Delta_{out}\}$. *We call* $U_f(\Delta_{in}, \Delta_{out})$ *the solution set of the differential* $(\Delta_{in}, \Delta_{out})$.

Definition 2. *The* differential probability *(DP) of a differential* $(\Delta_{in}, \Delta_{out})$ *over the permutation* $f \colon \mathbb{F}_2^b \to \mathbb{F}_2^b$ *is defined as* $\mathrm{DP}_f(\Delta_{in}, \Delta_{out}) = \frac{\#U_f(\Delta_{in}, \Delta_{out})}{2^b}$.

If there exists an ordered pair $(x, x + \Delta_{in})$ with $x \in U_f(\Delta_{in}, \Delta_{out})$, then it is said to follow the differential $(\Delta_{in}, \Delta_{out})$. In this case, we say that the input difference Δ_{in} is *compatible* with the output difference Δ_{out} through f and call $(\Delta_{in}, \Delta_{out})$ a *valid* differential.

Definition 3. *A sequence* $Q = (q^{(0)}, q^{(1)}, \ldots, q^{(k)}) \in (\mathbb{F}_2^b)^{k+1}$ *that satisfies* $\mathrm{DP}_{\mathrm{R}_i}(q^{(i)}, q^{(i+1)}) > 0$ *for* $0 \leq i \leq k-1$ *is called a* k-round *differential trail*.

Sometimes we specify a trail as $Q = (b_{-1}, a_0, b_0, \ldots, a_k, b_k)$ by giving the intermediate differences between N_i and L_i as well, where $b_i = \mathrm{L}_i(a_i) = q_{i+1}$. We write $\mathrm{DT}(\Delta_{in}, \Delta_{out})$ for the set of all differential trails in the differential $(\Delta_{in}, \Delta_{out})$, so with $q^{(0)} = \Delta_{in}$ and $q^{(k)} = \Delta_{out}$. We call $(\Delta_{in}, \Delta_{out})$ the *envelop-ing differential* of the trails in $\mathrm{DT}(\Delta_{in}, \Delta_{out})$. If $\#\mathrm{DT}(\Delta_{in}, \Delta_{out}) > 1$, then we say that trails *cluster* together in the differential $(\Delta_{in}, \Delta_{out})$.

By deleting the initial difference Δ_{in} and final difference Δ_{out} of a differential trail $(\Delta_{in}, q^{(1)}, \ldots, q^{(k-1)}, \Delta_{out})$ we are left with a *differential trail core*. A differential trail core obtained in this way is said to be in the differential $(\Delta_{in}, \Delta_{out})$. Note that a differential trail core actually defines a set of differential trails with the same inner differences.

We now define the DP of a differential trail. Each round differential $(q^{(i)}, q^{(i+1)})$ has a solution set $U_{\mathrm{R}_i}(q^{(i)}, q^{(i+1)})$. Consider the transformed set of points $U_i = f[i]^{-1}(U_{\mathrm{R}_i}(q^{(i)}, q^{(i+1)}))$ at the input of f. For an ordered pair $(x, x + q^{(0)})$ to follow the differential trail, it is required that $x \in U_f(Q) = \bigcap_{i=0}^{k-1} U_i$. The fraction of states x that satisfy this equation is the DP of the trail.

Definition 4. *The DP of a differential trail is defined as* $\mathrm{DP}_f(Q) = \frac{\#U_f(Q)}{2^b}$.

Definition 5. *The round differentials are said to be* independent *if*

$$\mathrm{DP}_f(Q) = \prod_{i=0}^{k-1} \mathrm{DP}_{R_i}(q^{(i)}, q^{(i+1)}).$$

Any given ordered pair $(x, x + \Delta_{\mathrm{in}})$ follows exactly one differential trail. Hence, the DP of the differential $(\Delta_{\mathrm{in}}, \Delta_{\mathrm{out}})$ is the sum of the DPs of all differential trails with initial difference Δ_{in} and final difference Δ_{out}.

$$\mathrm{DP}_f(\Delta_{\mathrm{in}}, \Delta_{\mathrm{out}}) = \sum_{Q \in \mathrm{DT}(\Delta_{\mathrm{in}}, \Delta_{\mathrm{out}})} \mathrm{DP}_f(Q).$$

Given any differential $(\Delta_{\mathrm{in}}, \Delta_{\mathrm{out}})$ over a round function R, it is easy to compute its DP value. By specifying the intermediate differences we obtain a differential trail $(\Delta_{\mathrm{in}}, b, c, \Delta_{\mathrm{out}})$. Thanks to the linearity of L, we have $c = L(b)$ and due to the fact that a difference is invariant under addition of a constant, all valid such differential trails are of the form $(\Delta_{\mathrm{in}}, L^{-1}(\Delta_{\mathrm{out}}), \Delta_{\mathrm{out}}, \Delta_{\mathrm{out}})$. Therefore, the differential $(\Delta_{\mathrm{in}}, \Delta_{\mathrm{out}})$ contains only a single trail and its DP is the DP of the differential $(\Delta_{\mathrm{in}}, L^{-1}(\Delta_{\mathrm{out}}))$ over the S-box layer:

$$\mathrm{DP}_R(\Delta_{\mathrm{in}}, \Delta_{\mathrm{out}}) = \prod_{0 \leq j < n} \mathrm{DP}_{S_j}(P_j(\Delta_{\mathrm{in}}), P_j(L^{-1}(\Delta_{\mathrm{out}}))).$$

Hence, the DP of a round differential is the product of the DP values of its S-box differentials.

Definition 6. *The* restriction weight *of a differential* $(\Delta_{in}, \Delta_{out})$ *that satisfies* $\mathrm{DP}_f(\Delta_{in}, \Delta_{out}) > 0$ *is defined as* $\mathrm{w_r}(\Delta_{in}, \Delta_{out}) = -\log_2 \mathrm{DP}_f(\Delta_{in}, \Delta_{out})$.

For a differential trail, we sum the weights of the round differentials.

Definition 7. *The* restriction weight *of a differential trail* $Q = (q^{(0)}, q^{(1)}, \ldots, q^{(k)})$ *is defined as*

$$\mathrm{w_r}(Q) = \sum_{i=0}^{k-1} \mathrm{w_r}(q^{(i)}, q^{(i+1)}).$$

If the round differentials are independent in the sense of Definition 5, then we have that $\mathrm{DP}_f(Q) = 2^{-\mathrm{w_r}(Q)}$.

2.2   Linear Cryptanalysis

Linear cryptanalysis [29] is a known-plaintext attack. It exploits large correlations (in absolute value) between linear combinations of input bits and linear combinations of output bits of a permutation.

Definition 8. *The (signed) correlation between the linear mask $u \in \mathbb{F}_2^b$ at the input and the linear mask $v \in \mathbb{F}_2^b$ at the output of a function $f \colon \mathbb{F}_2^b \to \mathbb{F}_2^b$ is defined as*

$$C_f(u, v) = \frac{1}{2^b} \sum_{x \in \mathbb{F}_2^b} (-1)^{u^\top x + v^\top f(x)} .$$

If $C_f(u, v) \neq 0$, then we say that u is compatible with v. We call the ordered pair of linear masks (u, v) a *linear approximation*. We note that in the literature (e.g., in the linear cryptanalysis attack by Matsui [29]) the term linear approximation has several meanings. It should not be confused with what we call a linear trail.

Definition 9. *A sequence $Q = (q^{(0)}, q^{(1)}, \ldots, q^{(k)}) \in (\mathbb{F}_2^b)^{k+1}$ that satisfies $C_{R_i}(q^{(i)}, q^{(i+1)}) \neq 0$ for $0 \leq i \leq k - 1$ is called a* linear trail.

We write $\mathrm{LT}(u, v)$ for the set of all linear trails in the linear approximation (u, v), so with $q^{(0)} = u$ and $q^{(k)} = v$. We call (u, v) the *enveloping linear approximation* of the trails in $\mathrm{LT}(u, v)$. If $\#\mathrm{LT}(u, v) > 1$, then we say that trails *cluster* together in the linear approximation (u, v).

By deleting the initial linear mask u and final linear mask v of a linear trail $(u, q^{(1)}, \ldots, q^{(k-1)}, v)$ we are left with a *linear trail core*. A linear trail core obtained in this way is said to be in the linear approximation (u, v). Note that a linear trail core actually defines a set of linear trails with the same inner linear masks.

Definition 10. *The* correlation contribution *of a linear trail Q over f equals*

$$C_f(Q) = \prod_{i=0}^{k-1} C_{R_i}(q^{(i)}, q^{(i+1)}) .$$

From the theory of correlation matrices [14], it follows that

$$C_f(u, v) = \sum_{Q \in \mathrm{LT}(u,v)} C_f(Q) .$$

Given any linear approximation (u, v) over a round function R, it is easy to compute its correlation. By specifying the intermediate linear masks we obtain a linear trail (u, b, c, v). Thanks to the linearity of L, we have $b = \mathrm{L}^\top(c)$ and due to the fact that a linear mask is invariant under addition of a constant, all valid such linear trails are of the form $(u, \mathrm{L}^\top(v), v, v)$. Hence the linear approximation (u, v) contains only a single trail and its correlation contribution is the correlation of the linear approximation $(u, \mathrm{L}^\top(v))$ over the S-box layer, where the round constant addition affects the sign:

$$C_R(u, v) = (-1)^{v^\top \iota(0)} \prod_{0 \leq j < n} C_{S_j}(P_j(u), P_j(\mathrm{L}^\top(v))) .$$

Definition 11. *The* linear potential *(LP) of a linear approximation (u, v) is defined as* $\mathrm{LP}_f(u, v) = \mathrm{C}_f(u, v)^2$.

Analogous to the differential cryptanalysis case, we define a weight metric.

Definition 12. *The* correlation weight *of a linear approximation (u, v) with $\mathrm{LP}_f(u, v) \neq 0$ is given by* $\mathrm{w_c}(u, v) = -\log_2 \mathrm{LP}_f(u, v)$.

Definition 13. *The correlation weight of a linear trail $Q = (q^{(0)}, q^{(1)}, \ldots, q^{(k)})$ is defined as*

$$\mathrm{w_c}(Q) = \sum_{i=0}^{k-1} \mathrm{w_c}(q^{(i)}, q^{(i+1)}).$$

3   Box Partitioning and Alignment

In this section, we consider the partition of the index space defined by the non-linear layer N. The *alignment* properties of the other step functions with respect to this partition have an important impact on the propagation properties of the round function.

The nonlinear layer N consists of the parallel application of n S-boxes of size m to disjoint parts of the state, indexed by B_i. Formally, this means that we can write N as $\mathrm{S}_0 \times \cdots \times \mathrm{S}_{n-1}$ and that it is characterized by

$$P_i \circ (\mathrm{S}_0 \times \cdots \times \mathrm{S}_{n-1}) = \mathrm{S}_i \circ P_i \text{ for } 0 \leq i \leq n - 1.$$

Hence, N defines a unique *ordered* partition $\varPi_{\mathrm{N}} = (\mathrm{B}_0, \ldots, \mathrm{B}_{n-1})$ of the index space $[0, b - 1]$. We call $\varPi_{\mathrm{N}}$ the *box partition* defined by N and the B_i N-boxes. If there is no ambiguity, we call the box partition $\varPi$ and its members boxes.

Besides the box partition, it is clearly possible to define other partitions of the index space as well. We call a partition *non-trivial* if it has at least two members. Between any two partitions of the index space there may be a relation that we denote as *refinement*.

Definition 14. *We call $\varPi$ a* refinement *of $\varPi'$ and write $\varPi \leq \varPi'$ if for every $(i, \mathrm{B}_i) \in \varPi$ there exists a $(j, \mathrm{B}'_j) \in \varPi'$ such that $\mathrm{B}_i \subseteq \mathrm{B}'_j$.*

Let $\varPi$ be a partition of the index space consisting of k boxes, each of size l. We call a shuffle layer a $\varPi$-shuffle if the associated permutation matrix can be partitioned into k identity matrices of dimension $(l \times l)$. If this is the case, then bit index permutation can be specified as a box index permutation.

Definition 15. *We call $\phi \colon \mathbb{F}_2^b \to \mathbb{F}_2^b$* aligned *to $\varPi$ if we can decompose it as*

$$\phi_0 \times \cdots \times \phi_{k-1} \colon \underset{i=0}{\overset{k-1}{\times}} \mathbb{F}_2^l \to \underset{i=0}{\overset{k-1}{\times}} \mathbb{F}_2^l,$$

In this case, we call the ϕ_i *box functions*.

Definition 16. *Given a round function that is composed of the parallel application* N *of equally-sized S-boxes, a linear layer* L, *and the addition* ι *of a round constant, we say it is* aligned *if it is possible to decompose the linear layer* L *as* L $= \pi \circ$ M *in such a way that*

- π *is a* Π_{N}-shuffle;
- M *is aligned to a non-trivial partition* Π_{M} *that satisfies* $\Pi_{\mathrm{N}} \leq \Pi_{\mathrm{M}}$.

We assume that the split between the linear and nonlinear layer is chosen so as to maximize the number of S-boxes in N.

Note that ι does not play a role in the alignment properties. If all of the round functions of a primitive are aligned, then we call the primitive aligned. If the primitive is *not* aligned, then we call it *unaligned*.

Any aligned primitive has a *superbox* structure [35], that is helpful when investigating distributions and bounds on the DP of two-round differentials and the LP of two-round trails. We explain what this means. Consider a two-round structure: $\pi \circ$ M $\circ$ N $\circ \pi \circ$ M $\circ$ N. The final two linear steps π and M have no effect on the distributions, so we can simplify this expression to N $\circ \pi \circ$ M $\circ$ N. Clearly, N $\circ \pi = \pi \circ$ N$'$, with N$' := \pi^{-1} \circ$ N $\circ \pi$. Hence, this is equivalent to $\pi \circ$ N$' \circ$ M $\circ$ N. Discarding the shuffle layer at the end gives N$' \circ$ M $\circ$ N. Since $\Pi_{\mathrm{N}'} = \Pi_{\mathrm{N}} \leq \Pi_{\mathrm{M}}$, we can view this as the parallel application of a number of superboxes. We call this a *superbox layer*. In a sequence of two rounds, N$' \circ$ M $\circ$ N is a (composite) nonlinear layer and $\pi \circ$ M $\circ \pi$ is a (composite) linear layer. If the latter is aligned to a non-trivial partition Π such that $\Pi_{\mathrm{M}} \leq \Pi$, then we call this two-round structure aligned to Π_{M}.

4   The Ciphers We Investigate

In this section we describe the round functions of the ciphers we investigate in this paper, their alignment properties, and compare their implementation cost.

4.1   Rijndael

RIJNDAEL [22] is a block cipher family supporting all block and key lengths of $b = 32k$ bits, with $4 \leq k \leq 8$, i.e., ranging from 128 up to and including 256 bits. The case $b = 128$ is of great importance as RIJNDAEL with that block length is the ubiquitous AES [32]. In this paper we investigate RIJNDAEL-256, the instance with $b = 256$, a width closer to those of the other ciphers we investigate. In the remainder of this paper we will write RIJNDAEL for RIJNDAEL-256.

The RIJNDAEL round function consists of four steps: a nonlinear layer SubBytes, a box shuffle ShiftRows, a mixing layer MixColumns, and round key addition AddRoundKey. As its name suggest, $\Pi_{\mathtt{SubBytes}}$ partitions the state in bytes and ShiftRows is a $\Pi_{\mathtt{SubBytes}}$-shuffle. The mixing layer, MixColumns, is aligned to a non-trivial partition $\Pi_{\mathtt{MixColumns}}$ that corresponds to the 8 *columns*, each containing 4 bytes, and we have $\Pi_{\mathtt{SubBytes}} \leq \Pi_{\mathtt{MixColumns}}$. It follows that RIJNDAEL is aligned. Figure 1 shows RIJNDAEL-128 that is easier to draw due to its dimensions, but the alignment properties for RIJNDAEL-256 are the same.

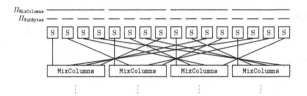

Fig. 1. Alignment properties of RIJNDAEL.

4.2 Saturnin

The SATURNIN [12] block cipher has a 256-bit key and block length. The state has several representations: three-dimensional, two-dimensional, and flat. In three dimensions, the 256-bit state is represented as a $4 \times 4 \times 4$ cube of 4-bit *nibbles*. Nibbles in the cube are indexed by triples (x, y, z). A *slice* is a subset of the nibbles with z constant. A *sheet* is a subset of the nibbles with x constant. A *column* is a subset of the nibbles with x and z constant.

The SATURNIN permutation is composed of a number of so-called super-rounds and a super-round consists of two consecutive rounds with indices $2r$ and $2r + 1$. Round $2r$ is composed as $\mathrm{MC} \circ \mathrm{S}$, where MC is a mixing layer and S is a nonlinear layer. There are two different rounds with odd indices. Round $4r + 1$ is composed as follows: $\mathrm{RC} \circ \mathrm{RK} \circ \mathrm{SR}_{\mathrm{slice}}^{-1} \circ \mathrm{MC} \circ \mathrm{SR}_{\mathrm{slice}} \circ \mathrm{S}$. Round $4r + 3$ consists of $\mathrm{RC} \circ \mathrm{RK} \circ \mathrm{SR}_{\mathrm{sheet}}^{-1} \circ \mathrm{MC} \circ \mathrm{SR}_{\mathrm{sheet}} \circ \mathrm{S}$. Here, RC denotes addition of a round constant, RK denotes addition of a round key, and $\mathrm{SR}_{\mathrm{slice}}$ and $\mathrm{SR}_{\mathrm{sheet}}$ shuffle nibbles. The partition Π_{S} divides the state into 64 nibbles. The shuffles $\mathrm{SR}_{\mathrm{slice}}$ and $\mathrm{SR}_{\mathrm{sheet}}$ are Π_{S}-shuffles. The mixing layer MC is aligned to a non-trivial partition Π_{MC} that divides the state into 16 columns, each consisting of 4 nibbles, and that satisfies $\Pi_{\mathrm{S}} \leq \Pi_{\mathrm{MC}}$. It follows that SATURNIN is aligned. In a super-round we identify the sequence $\mathrm{S} \circ \mathrm{MC} \circ \mathrm{S}$ as a superbox layer with partition Π_{MC} and the linear layer of such a round is $\mathrm{SR}_{\mathrm{slice}}^{-1} \circ \mathrm{MC} \circ \mathrm{SR}_{\mathrm{slice}}$. This is a mixing layer that is aligned to a non-trivial partition Π_{slice} that divides the state into 4 slices, each containing 4 columns, and we have $\Pi_{\mathrm{MC}} \leq \Pi_{\mathrm{slice}}$. Similarly, for the other type of super-round, the mixing layer is aligned to a non-trivial partition Π_{sheet} that divides the state into 4 sheets, and we have $\Pi_{\mathrm{MC}} \leq \Pi_{\mathrm{sheet}}$. It follows that the super-rounds of SATURNIN are aligned and hence have their own superboxes. These have width 64 bits and we call them *hyperboxes*. Figure 2 shows the alignment properties of the steps.

4.3 Spongent

SPONGENT [9] is a sponge-based hash function family that uses a PRESENT-like permutation. The permutation is defined for any b that is a multiple of 4. In this paper, we only consider the case $b = 384$, to match the state size of the largest of the other permutations that we investigate, XOODOO. The round function of SPONGENT consists of three steps: a round constant addition lCounter, a 4-bit S-box layer sBoxLayer, and a bit shuffle pLayer.

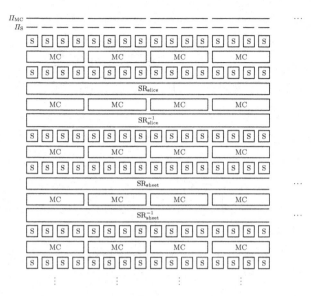

Fig. 2. Alignment properties of SATURNIN.

The index permutation of the bit shuffle `pLayer` is:

$$\texttt{pLayer}(j) = \begin{cases} 96j \bmod 383, & \text{if } j \in [0, 382] \\ 383, & \text{if } j = 383 \end{cases}$$

As indicated by the Spongent designers in [9], we can decompose it into a mixing layer, followed by a box shuffle:

1. `SpongentMixLayer` applies the same mixing function `SpongentMix` in parallel to the 24 *subgroups* (following the terminology of [9]). It is a bit shuffle associated with the index permutation $\tau_{\text{subgroup}} \colon [0, 15] \to [0, 15]$:

$$\tau_{\text{subgroup}}(j) = \begin{cases} 4j \bmod 15, & \text{if } j \in [0, 14] \\ 15, & \text{if } j = 15 \end{cases}$$

2. `SpongentBoxShuffle` is a box shuffle that is associated with the box index permutation $\tau_{\text{box}} \colon [0, 95] \to [0, 95]$ defined by:

$$\tau_{\text{box}}(j) = \left\lfloor \frac{j}{4} \right\rfloor + 24(j \bmod 4).$$

The `sBoxLayer` defines a box partition $\Pi_{\texttt{sBoxLayer}}$ corresponding to the 96 4-bit boxes. The box shuffle `SpongentBoxShuffle` is a $\Pi_{\texttt{sBoxLayer}}$-shuffle. The bit shuffle `SpongentMixLayer` is aligned to a non-trivial partition $\Pi_{\texttt{SpongentMixLayer}}$ that divides the state into 96 16-bit subgroups, each grouping four consecutive boxes, and we have $\Pi_{\texttt{sBoxLayer}} \leq \Pi_{\texttt{SpongentMixLayer}}$. It follows that SPONGENT is aligned. Figure 3 shows these steps and their alignment properties.

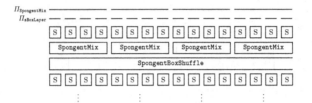

Fig. 3. Alignment properties of SPONGENT.

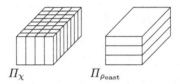

Fig. 4. Alignment properties of XOODOO.

4.4 Xoodoo

XOODOO [16] is a permutation with $b = 384$. The state consists of 3 equally sized horizontal *planes*, each one consisting of 4 parallel 32-bit *lanes*. Alternatively, the state can be seen as a set of 128 *columns* of 3 bits, arranged in a 4×32 array.

The round function of XOODOO consists of the following five steps: a mixing layer θ, a bit shuffle ρ_{east}, round constant addition ι, a nonlinear layer χ, and a bit shuffle ρ_{west}. The χ step applies the same 3-bit S-box to the columns of the state. The nonlinear layer χ defines a box partition Π_χ that corresponds to the 128 columns. The bit shuffles ρ_{east} and ρ_{west} perform translations of planes and are not aligned to Π_χ. The mixing layer θ defines no non-trivial box partition at all. Due to the properties of the ρ steps and θ it is impossible to split the linear layer in a column shuffle and a mixing layer that is aligned to a partition that Π_χ is a refinement of. In other words, XOODOO is unaligned. See Section E of the supplementary material for a more formal proof. Figure 4 shows the alignment properties of the steps.

4.5 Round Cost

In this section, we compare the implementation complexity of the round functions of the four ciphers. This depends on the platform and the requirements. Platforms may range from low-end 8-bit CPUs to multi-core high-end workstation CPUs, FPGAs, and even dedicated hardware. Requirements include throughput, latency, usage of resources such as power and energy consumption, area in hardware, and RAM/ROM usage in software. Moreover, protection against fault attacks and/or side channel attacks may be required.

In our comparison of the round functions we let their three layers guide us: the S-box layer, the mixing layer (if any), and the shuffle layer. We also discuss the presence of key addition in block ciphers and its relative cost.

Table 1. S-box computational cost comparison.

cipher	max DP/LP	operations in $\mathbb{F}_2$				2-layer nand circuit							
			# operations			# nand gates per # inputs						totals	
		ref	xor	and/or	not	2-in	3-in	4-in	5-in	6-in	7-in	gates	inp
RIJNDAEL	2^{-6}	[11,36]	81	32	4			?					
SATURNIN	2^{-2}	[12]	6	6	-	4	5	6	1	-	-	16	52
SPONGENT	2^{-2}		?			-	6	8	-	3	1	18	75
XOODOO	2^{-2}	[16]	3	3	3	3	6	-	-	-	-	9	24

S-Box Layer. Given that our ciphers have invertible S-boxes with lowest known maximum DP and LP values that can be achieved for their width, their implementation cost increases with width.

We report on the implementations with minimum number of binary XOR, binary AND/OR, and unary NOT operations that we found in the literature. For SPONGENT we found no such numbers. We have also determined a minimal sum-of-products (SOP) form in Boolean algebra of the S-boxes using the Espresso algorithm [30] for two-level logic optimization. For RIJNDAEL, finding the minimal SOP was infeasible. We refer to Section B of the supplementary material for the SOP expressions. Using De Morgan's laws, the SOP form can be implemented by two layers of nand gates. Table 1 lists the number of nand gates per bit for each of the S-boxes.

We can see in Table 1 that the cost of the SATURNIN and SPONGENT S-boxes is comparable. The cost of the XOODOO S-box is roughly half of that, but is only 3 bits wide instead of 4. The Rijndael S-box is a roughly a factor 10 more costly than that of SATURNIN and SPONGENT, a very high price for its better max DP/LP value. These numbers give an indication for the size of a hardware circuit and the number of cycles in bit-sliced software implementations. The number of and/or operations is related to the cost of masking countermeasures.

Mixing Layer. SPONGENT has no mixing layer, so there is no cost. XOODOO-θ requires 2 binary xor operations per bit, while SATURNIN's MC can be implemented with 2.25 binary xor operations per bit [12]. The circuit depth for these computations is in both cases 4 xor gates. Despite the difference in design philosophy, their computational costs are almost the same.

A simple implementation of RIJNDAEL's MixColumns takes 3.875 binary xor operations per bit and has a circuit depth of 3 xor gates. This was reduced to $97/32 \approx 3$ additions per bit [25] at the expense of a higher circuit depth. Despite the fact that both MixColumns and SATURNIN's MC implement an MDS mapping operating on 5 boxes, their costs diverge. The main difference between the two is that MixColumns operates on bytes while MC operates on nibbles. However, this is not the reason for the higher cost per bit of MixColumns. The reason is that there have been significant advances in building efficient MDS mappings and MC reaps the benefits of that.

Table 2. The cost of a round in cycles per byte on the ARM Cortex-M4.

Cipher	# cycles/byte
RIJNDAEL [38]	10.0
SATURNIN [13]	2.7
SPONGENT	?
XOODOO [5]	1.1

Shuffle Layer. RIJNDAEL, SPONGENT, and XOODOO consist of the iteration of a single round function. In a hardware architecture that implements the full round in combinatorial logic, a bit shuffle consists of wiring between gates. SATURNIN has three different rounds, so this is more complex in a hardware architecture in which a single round is implemented in combinatorial logic. However, in a combinatorial block that implements a sequence of four rounds, the shuffle operations do correspond to wiring.

We compare software implementation on a particular platform: the ARM Cortex-M4 processor. We choose this because it is a popular lightweight platform for benchmarks and for three of our ciphers there is assembly code available. On this platform, it is difficult to assess the cost of the shuffle layer in isolation due to the *barrel shifter*. This feature of the ARM architecture allows applying (cyclic) shift operations to one of the two operands in arithmetic and bitwise Boolean instructions at no additional cost. To compare, we measure the number of cycles of the entire round function, revealing the marginal cost of the shuffle layer. Table 2 lists the performance of the round functions of our four ciphers expressed in number of cycles per byte as measured on a Cortex-M4 processor. In addition, it includes references to the bit-sliced implementations that we have used in order to measure the cycle counts. In RIJNDAEL and SATURNIN we removed any operations related to the key addition to make a fair comparison possible and in SATURNIN we measured the number of cycles for 4 rounds and divided that by 4. We have not included SPONGENT because we do not have access to any (optimized) assembly code. However, considering that it was designed with hardware in mind, we do not believe it is competitive in software.

5   Huddling

In this section, we describe a phenomenon that we call *huddling*. We present the bit and box weight histograms as natural extensions of the bit and box branch numbers, respectively. Using these histograms, we analyze the huddling properties of the ciphers described in Sect. 4. We see that these properties are more pronounced in ciphers that are aligned. Finally, we look at the relation between huddling and the distribution of trail weights.

5.1   Definitions of Bit Weight, Box Weight and Their Histograms

The weight of a two-round trail $(q_{\text{in}}, a, b, q_{\text{out}})$ over $\text{N} \circ \text{L} \circ \text{N}$ can be bounded from below by the sum of the number of active boxes at the input and output of L. This number is fully determined by a as $b = \text{L}(a)$ in differential trails and $a = \text{L}^\top(b)$ in linear trails. The distribution of states a according to this number determines the *mixing power* of the linear layer with respect to Π_N.

First, we formally define what it means for a box to be active. To this end, we define an *indicator function* $1_i \colon \mathbb{F}_2^b \to \mathbb{F}_2$ with respect to a box partition Π by $1_i(a) = 0$ if $P_i(a) = 0$ and $1_i(a) = 1$ otherwise. We call the box B_i *active* in the difference or linear mask $a \in \mathbb{F}_2^b$ if $1_i(a) = 1$ and *passive* otherwise. The natural metric associated with box activity is the *box weight* of a, defined by $\text{w}_\Pi(a) = \#\{i \in [0,\, n-1] : 1_i(a) \neq 0\}$. Clearly, a box is active in a difference or linear mask if at least one of the bits in that box is non-zero. We call the bit i *active* in a if $a_i = 1$ and *passive* otherwise. The number of active bits is given by the *bit weight* of a, i.e., $\text{w}_2(a) = \#\{i \in [0,\, b-1] : a_i \neq 0\}$. The *activity pattern* of a is defined by $r_\Pi(a) = \sum_{i=0}^{n-1} 1_{\text{B}_i}(a) e_i^n$. It is the vector whose ith component is one if box B_i is active and zero otherwise.

In order to quantify the mixing power of a linear transformation L, we consider the weight distribution of $(a, \text{L}(a))$ over all differences or linear masks $a \in \mathbb{F}_2^b$ and embed it in a histogram. This is a well-known concept in coding theory, where weight distributions are embedded in so-called weight enumerator polynomials that classify the code [23].

Definition 17. *The* weight histogram *of a linear transformation* $\text{L} \colon \mathbb{F}_2^b \to \mathbb{F}_2^b$ *is a function* $\mathcal{N}_{\cdot, \text{L}} \colon \mathbb{Z}_{\geq 0} \to \mathbb{Z}_{\geq 0}$ *given by*

$$\mathcal{N}_{\cdot, \text{L}}(k) = \#\{a \in \mathbb{F}_2^b : \text{w}_\cdot(a) + \text{w}_\cdot(\text{L}(a)) = k\}.$$

The cumulative version on the same domain and codomain is given by

$$\mathcal{C}_{\cdot, \text{L}}(k) = \sum_{l \leq k} \mathcal{N}_\text{L}(l).$$

Here, $\cdot$ denotes either 2 or Π.

The *tail* of the histogram consists of the left-most values that correspond to low weight.

If the primitive is aligned, then π is a box shuffle and this implies that the box weight histograms of $\text{L} = \text{M} \circ \pi$ and M are the same. The superbox structure of an aligned primitive makes it possible to use a divide-and-conquer approach to compute the weight histograms. Indeed, let $S(\text{w}) = \{v \in \mathbb{Z}_{\geq 0}^s : \sum_{i=0}^{s-1} v_i = \text{w}\}$ with s the number of superboxes. Then we can compute the weight histograms of M by *convolving* the weight histograms of its box functions:

$$\mathcal{N}_{\cdot, \text{M}}(\text{w}) = \sum_{v \in S(\text{w})} \prod_{i=0}^{s-1} \mathcal{N}_{\cdot, \text{M}_i}(v_i). \tag{1}$$

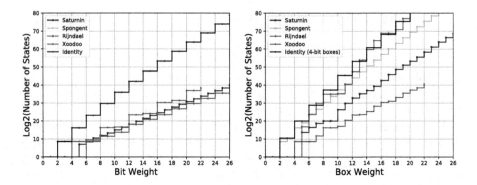

Fig. 5. Cumulative bit weight and box weight histograms.

We note that the *differential branch number* [14] is simply the smallest non-zero entry of this histogram, i.e., $\min\{w > 0 : \mathcal{N}_{\cdot,L}(w) > 0\}$. The linear branch number is the smallest non-zero entry in the corresponding histogram of $L^\top$ and can be different from its differential counterpart. This is not the case for the mappings in this paper and we will omit the qualifier in the remainder. A higher branch number typically implies higher mixing power. However, the weight histogram is more informative than just the branch number. The number of differences or linear masks meeting the branch number is valuable information as well. In general, the weight histogram allows a more nuanced comparison of mixing layers than the branch number.

The box weight histogram is the relevant histogram in the context of the wide trail design strategy [20]. A linear layer that systematically has lower values in the tail of its box weight histogram than the other does typically has fewer two-round trails with low weight, given equal nonlinear layers.

5.2 Bit and Box Weight Histograms

We discuss the cumulative bit and box weight histograms for the linear layers of our four ciphers, given in Fig. 5. We include the histogram for the identity function, assuming 4-bit S-boxes for the box weight to allow for comparison with SPONGENT and SATURNIN.

The bit weight histogram for SPONGENT coincides with that of the identity permutation. This is because its linear layer is a bit shuffle. As the identity permutation maps inputs to identical outputs, it has only non-zero entries for even bit weights. Its bit branch number is 2. In conclusion, its mixing power is the lowest possible.

The bit branch number of the mixing layer of RIJNDAEL, MixColumns, is 6, that of SATURNIN-MC is 5, and that of XOODOO-θ is 4.

Similar to SPONGENT, the bit weight histograms of RIJNDAEL and XOODOO have only non-zero entries at even bit weights. This is because both XOODOO-θ and RIJNDAEL-MixColumns can be modeled as $a \mapsto (I + M)a$ for some matrix

$M \in \mathbb{F}_2^{b \times b}$ with the property that the bit weight of Ma is even for all $a \in \mathbb{F}_2^b$. SATURNIN-MC cannot be modeled in that way and does have non-zero entries at odd bit weights.

The bit weight histograms of RIJNDAEL and SATURNIN are very close and that of XOODOO is somewhat higher. The ranking per bit weight histogram reflects the computational resources invested in the mixing layer: RIJNDAEL uses 3.5 additions per bit, SATURNIN 2.25, XOODOO 2, and SPONGENT 0.

In the box weight histograms we see the following. For SPONGENT the box branch number is 2, the same as the bit branch number. However, the box weight histogram of SPONGENT has a lower tail than the identity permutation. What it shows is the mixing power of `SpongentMixLayer` in our factorization of `pLayer`, operating on 4-box superboxes.

The box branch number of the linear layers of RIJNDAEL, `MixColumns`, and of SATURNIN-MC are both 5, while for XOODOO it is 4.

The discrepancy between the bit and box weight histogram brings us to the notion of *bit huddling*: many active bits huddle together in few active boxes. We say that the bit huddling in a linear layer is *high* if the concentration is high and we say that the bit huddling is *low* otherwise.

Huddling has an effect on the contribution of states a to the histogram, i.e., by definition we have that $w_{\Pi}(a) + w_{\Pi}(L(a)) \leq w_2(a) + w_2(L(a))$. In words, from bit to box weight, huddling moves states to the left in the histogram, thereby raising the tail. Huddling therefore results in the decay of mixing power at box level as compared to bit level. In the absence of huddling, the bit and box weight histogram would be equal. However, huddling cannot be avoided altogether as states do exist with multiple active bits in a box (note that $m \geq 2$).

We see RIJNDAEL has *high* bit huddling. In moving from bit weights to box weights, the branch number decreases from 6 to 5 and the tail rises from being the lowest of the four to the highest. This is a direct consequence of the large width of the RIJNDAEL S-boxes, namely 8, and the byte alignment. Indeed, `MixColumns` only mixes bits within the 32-bit columns. We call this the *superbox huddling effect*. Of course, there is a reason for these large S-boxes: they have low maximum DP/LP values. They were part of a design approach assuming table-lookup implementations where the main impact of the S-box size is the size of the lookup tables. Unfortunately table-lookups are expensive in dedicated hardware and on modern CPUs lookup tables are kept in cache making such implementations susceptible to cache-timing attacks [4].

SATURNIN, with its RIJNDAEL-like structure also exhibits the superbox huddling effect, though less pronounced than RIJNDAEL. From bits to boxes the branch number does not decrease and the tail rises less than for RIJNDAEL. Clearly, its smaller S-box size, namely 4, allows for less bit huddling. Due to its alignment, SPONGENT exhibits the superbox huddling effect, but less so than SATURNIN. The reason for this is the already high tail in the bit weight histogram, due to the absence of bit-level diffusion in the mixing layer.

Finally, Xoodoo has the *lowest* bit huddling of the four primitives studied. This is the consequence of two design choices: having very small S-boxes (3-bit) and the absence of alignment, avoiding the superbox huddling effect altogether.

5.3 Two-Round Trail Weight Histograms

We define the trail weight histogram analogous to Definition 17 with the change that $\mathcal{N}_{\cdot}(k) = \#\{\text{trails } Q : \text{w}_{\cdot}(Q) = k\}$, where $\cdot$ is either r for differential trails or c for linear trails. Like for the other diagrams, the lower the tail, the lower the number of states with small weights, the better.

Figure 6 reports on the distribution of the weight of two-round differential and linear trails of our four ciphers. To compute the trail weight histograms of the aligned ciphers, we convolved the histograms of the superbox structures (See Eq. 1). The distribution of the linear trails for Rijndael is an approximation that was obtained by first taking the integer part of the correlation weights of its S-box to allow for integer arithmetic. The other distributions are exact.

While Rijndael performed the worst with respect to the box weight metric, we see that it performs the best with respect to the trail weights. The reasons are the low maximum DP/LP value of its S-box and its high branch number. However, as seen in Sect. 4.5, one pays a price in terms of the implementation cost. The relative ranking of the other ciphers does not change in moving from box weight to trail weights. Still, Xoodoo loses some terrain due to its more lightweight S-box layer.

Despite the difference in design approach, Xoodoo and Saturnin have quite similar two-round trail weight histograms. It is therefore interesting how the trail weight histograms compare for three and four rounds.

5.4 Three-Round Trail Weight Histograms

We have computed the three-round differential and linear trail weight histograms for Saturnin and Xoodoo and give them in Fig. 7. We did not do it for Rijndael due to the prohibitively high cost of its round function and neither for Spongent due to its non-competitive bounds for multiple-round trails as reported in [9]. Hence, we focus on Saturnin and Xoodoo as exponents of the aligned and unaligned wide-trail design approaches. Computing the three-round Saturnin trail histograms turned out to be very computationally intensive for higher weights (see Subsect. A.3 for more details) and we were forced to stop at weight 36. Still, the diagrams show the big difference in histograms between Saturnin and Xoodoo.

Despite the fact that the box branch number of Xoodoo is 4 and that of Saturnin is 5, we see that for three-round trails, Xoodoo performs much better than Saturnin. In particular, Xoodoo has no trails with weight below 36, whereas Saturnin has about 2^{43} linear trails with weight below 36, starting from weight 18. Moreover, it has about 2^{47} differential trails with weight below

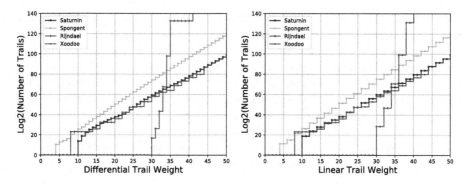

Fig. 6. Two rounds: cumulative differential and linear trail weight histograms.

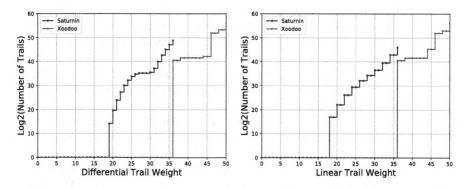

Fig. 7. Three rounds: cumulative differential and linear trail weight histograms.

36, starting from weight 19. This confirms the idea that branch number alone does not paint the whole picture and that these histograms prove to be very useful in comparing the different design approaches.

5.5   Four Rounds and Beyond

We did not conduct experiments for four or more rounds, but can make use of available information. According to [15], there exist no differential or linear trails over four rounds of XOODOO with weight below 74. In contrast, SATURNIN has roughly 2^{82} four-round differential trails with 25 active S-boxes and it has more than $2^{94.5}$ such linear trails. See Section C for a derivation of this estimate. Since each S-box has a weight of 2 or 3, this implies many four-round differential trails with weights in the range [50, 75]. The linear trails have weights in the range [50, 100] due to the fact that active S-boxes have weight 2 or 4. Naturally, in both cases there are also trails with $26, 27, \ldots$ active S-boxes and their number grows quickly with the box weight due to the additional degrees of freedom in building them. It follows that the trend we see in three-round trails persists for four-round trails: unaligned XOODOO has a significantly lower tail than aligned SATURNIN, despite its lighter round function and lower branch number.

For trails over five rounds and more we report on the known lower bounds on weight in Table 6 in Section D of the supplementary material. We see that up to 6 rounds XOODOO remains ahead of SATURNIN. For higher weights the trail scan programs in XOODOO reach their computational limit and SATURNIN overtakes XOODOO. Advances in trail scanning are likely to improve the bounds for XOODOO while for SATURNIN the currently known bounds are much more tight. For the whole range RIJNDAEL is well ahead and SPONGENT is invisible with its weight of 28 for 6 rounds.

6 Clustering

In this section, we investigate clustering of differential trails and of linear trails. The occurrence of such clustering in two-round differentials and linear approximations requires certain conditions to be satisfied. In particular, we define an equivalence relation of states with respect to a linear layer and an S-box partition that partitions the state space in candidate two-round trail cores and the size of its equivalence classes upper bounds the amount of possible trail clustering. This is the so-called cluster partition. We present the partitions of our four ciphers by means of their cluster histograms. For all four ciphers, we report on two-round trail clustering and for XOODOO in particular we look at the three-round case. With its unaligned structure, we found little clustering in XOODOO. However, the effects of clustering are apparent in the aligned primitives RIJNDAEL, SATURNIN, and SPONGENT, with them being most noticeable in RIJNDAEL.

6.1 The Cluster Histogram

To define the cluster histogram we need to define two equivalence classes.

Definition 18. *Two states are box-activity equivalent if they have the same activity pattern with respect to a box partition Π:*

$$a \sim a' \text{ if and only if } r_\Pi(a) = r_\Pi(a').$$

We denote the set of states that are box-activity equivalent with a by $[a]_\sim$ and call it the box-activity class *of a.*

Box-activity equivalence has an application in the relation between trail cores and differentials and linear approximations.

Lemma 1. *Two trail cores $(a_0, b_0 \ldots, a_{r-2}, b_{r-2})$ and $(a_0^*, b_0^* \ldots a_{r-2}^*, b_{r-2}^*)$ over a function $f = N_{r-1} \circ L_{r-2} \circ N_{r-2} \circ \cdots \circ L_0 \circ N_0$ that are in the same differential (or linear approximation) satisfy $a_0 \sim a_0^*$ and $b_{r-2} \sim b_{r-2}^*$.*

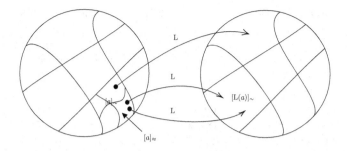

Fig. 8. Partitions of $\mathbb{F}_2^b$ defined by $\sim$ and $\approx$.

Proof. Let $(\Delta_{\text{in}}, \Delta_{\text{out}})$ be the differential over f that the trail cores are in. Since N_0 and N_{r-2} preserve activity patterns, we have that $\Delta_{\text{in}} \sim a_0$, and $\Delta_{\text{in}} \sim a_0^*$, and $\Delta_{\text{out}} \sim b_{r-2}$, and $\Delta_{\text{out}} \sim b_{r-2}^*$. From the symmetry and transitivity of $\sim$ it follows that $a_0 \sim a_0^*$ and $b_{r-2} \sim b_{r-2}^*$. □

Considering the case $r = 2$ in Lemma 1 immediately gives rise to a refinement of box-activity equivalence.

Definition 19. *Two states are cluster-equivalent with respect to a linear mapping* $L : \mathbb{F}_2^b \to \mathbb{F}_2^b$ *and a box partition* Π *if they are box-activity equivalent before* L *and after it (See Fig. 8):*

$$a \approx a' \text{ if and only if } a \sim a' \text{ and } L(a) \sim L(a').$$

We denote the set of states that are cluster-equivalent with a by $[a]_\approx$ and call it the cluster class *of a. The partition of $\mathbb{F}_2^b$ according to these cluster classes is called the* cluster partition.

Corollary 1. *If two two-round trail cores $(a, L(a))$ and $(a^*, L(a^*))$ over $f = N \circ L \circ N$ are in the same differential, then $a \approx a^*$.*

Proof. If we apply Lemma 1 to the case $r = 2$, we have $a \sim a^*$ and $L(a) \sim L(a^*)$. It follows that $a \approx a^*$. □

Corollary 1 shows that the defining differences of any two-round trail cores that cluster together are in the same cluster class. It follows that if these cluster classes are small, then there is little clustering.

For all $a' \in [a]_\approx$ the box weight $\text{w}_\Pi(a') + \text{w}_\Pi(L(a'))$ is the same. We denote this weight by $\widetilde{\text{w}}([a]_\approx)$.

Definition 20. *Let $L : \mathbb{F}_2^b \to \mathbb{F}_2^b$ be a linear transformation. Let $\approx$ be the equivalence relation given in Definition 19. The* cluster histogram $N_{\Pi,L} : \mathbb{Z}_{\geq 0} \times \mathbb{Z}_{\geq 0} \to \mathbb{Z}_{\geq 0}$ *of L with respect to the box partition Π is given by*

$$N_{\Pi,L}(k, c) = \#\{[a]_\approx \in \mathbb{F}_2^b / \approx : \widetilde{\text{w}}([a]_\approx) = k \wedge \#[a]_\approx = c\}.$$

For a fixed box weight, the cluster histogram shows the distribution of the sizes of the cluster classes with that box weight. Ideally, for small box weights, the cluster classes are all very small. Large cluster classes of small weight may lead to two-round trails with a large DP or LP.

Table 3. The cluster histograms of RIJNDAEL and SATURNIN.

		$N \times C_{m,n}$	
$\widetilde{w}$	RIJNDAEL superbox	SATURNIN superbox	SATURNIN hyperbox
	$m = 8, n = 4$	$m = 4, n = 4$	$m = 16, n = 4$
5	(56×255)	(56×15)	(56×65535)
6	$(28 \times 64005))$	(28×165)	(28×4294574085)
7	(8×16323825)	(8×2625)	$(8 \times 281444913315825)$
8	(1×4162570275)	(1×39075)	$(1 \times 18444492394151280675)$

Table 4. The cluster histogram of SpongentMix of SPONGENT.

$\widetilde{w}$	$N \times C$
2	(16×1)
3	(48×1)
4	$(32 \times 1)(36 \times 7)$
5	$(8 \times 1)(48 \times 25)$
6	$(12 \times 79)(16 \times 265)$
7	(8×2161)
8	(1×41503)

Table 5. Partial cluster histogram (up to translation equivalence) of XOODOO.

$\widetilde{w}$	$N \times C$
4	(3×1)
7	(24×1)
8	(600×1)
9	(2×1)
10	(442×1)
11	(10062×1)
12	(80218×1)
13	(11676×1)
14	$(228531 \times 1)(3 \times 2)$
15	$(2107864 \times 1)(90 \times 2)$
16	$(8447176 \times 1)(702 \times 2)$
$\vdots$	$\vdots$

6.2   The Cluster Histograms of Our Ciphers

Next, we present the cluster histograms of the superboxes of RIJNDAEL, SATURNIN, and SPONGENT and of the SATURNIN hyperbox. Moreover, we present a partial cluster histogram of XOODOO. The results for RIJNDAEL and SATURNIN are found in Table 3, for SPONGENT in Table 4, and for XOODOO in Table 5. In these tables, C denotes the cardinality of a cluster class and N denotes the number of cluster classes with that cardinality. For instance, an expression such as $(32 \times 1)(36 \times 7)$ means that there are 32 cluster classes of cardinality 1 and 36 classes of cardinality 7. Looking at $\widetilde{w} = 8$ across the three tables, we see that RIJNDAEL, SATURNIN, and SPONGENT have only a single cluster class containing all the states with $w_\Pi(a) + w_\Pi(L(a)) = 8$. In contrast, for XOODOO, each state a sits in its own cluster class. This means that $L(a)$ is in a different box activity class than $L(b)$ for any $b \in [a]_\sim$ and $b \neq a$.

Thanks to the fact that the mixing layers of RIJNDAEL and SATURNIN have the MDS property, the entries of their cluster histograms are combinatorial expressions of m, the box size, and n, the number of boxes. We describe these methods in detail in Subsection A.2 of the supplementary material.

Table 4 gives the cluster histogram of SPONGENT's superbox. For weights above 4 we see large cluster equivalence classes.

Now, consider the cluster histogram of XOODOO in Table 5. We see that up to and including box weight 13, we have $\#[a]_\approx = 1$. For box weight $14, 15$, and 16, we see that $\#[a]_\approx \leq 2$. Due to its unaligned structure, it is less likely that equal activity patterns are propagated to equal activity patterns. Therefore, many cluster classes contain only a single state.

6.3   Two-Round Trail Clustering

Two-round trail clustering in the keyed RIJNDAEL superbox was investigated in [19]. In that paper the *expected* DP values of trails and differentials are studied, where expected means averaged over all keys. We see considerable clustering in differentials with 5 active S-boxes. For these, the maximum expected DP of differentials is more than a factor 3 higher than the maximum expected DP of 2-round trails, with differentials containing up to 75 trails. For more active S-boxes the number of trails per differential is much higher and hence clustering is worse, but their individual contributions to the expected DP are much smaller and all differentials have expected DP very close to 2^{-32}. For fixed keys or in an unkeyed superbox these differentials and trails have a DP that is a multiple of 2^{-31}. For trails this effect was studied in [21].

In this section we report on our experiments on the other three of our ciphers where we compare two-round differentials with differential trails and linear approximations with linear trails. Figure 9 shows the number of differentials and differential trails up to a given weight of the SATURNIN and the SPONGENT superboxes. In both cases, we see that for low weight the histograms are close and as the weight grows, these histograms diverge. For SATURNIN there are roughly 50 times more differentials with weight 15 or less than differential trails with weight 15 or less. For SPONGENT this ratio is roughly 20. This divergence is due to two reasons: clustering and what we call *clipping*. Due to the large number of differential trails and the limited width of the superbox, the trails cluster. This effect is especially strong for trails with almost all S-boxes active and would give rise to many differentials with DP close to 2^{-16} as the superbox has width 16. What we observe is a majority of differentials with DP equal to 2^{-15}. This is the result of the fact that any differential over a superbox has an even number of ordered pairs and hence the minimum DP is 2^{-15}, yielding weight 15. We call this effect clipping: the weight of differentials cannot be strictly greater than 15. A trail over a k-bit superbox with weight $w > k - 1$ cannot have a DP $= 2^{-w}$ as this would imply a fractional number of pairs. This effect has been studied in AES and we refer to Sect. 7 for a discussion.

Figure 10 shows the weight histograms for two-round differentials and linear approximations. The full-state correlation weight histogram of SATURNIN was obtained from that of any of its columns by first rounding the correlation weights to the nearest integer to make integer arithmetic possible. The full-state correlation weight histogram of SPONGENT was obtained in a similar manner. The remainder of the histograms is exact. Table 5 shows that in XOODOO almost all

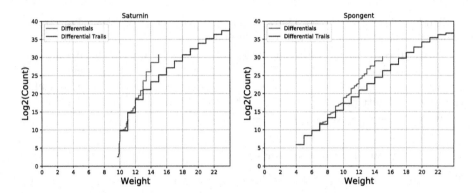

Fig. 9. Differentials and differential trails in the superboxes of SATURNIN and SPON-GENT.

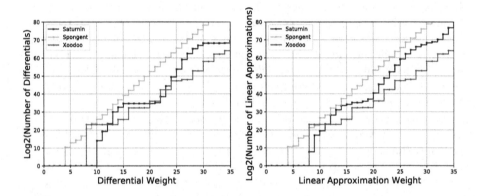

Fig. 10. Two rounds: cumulative restriction and correlation weight histograms.

differentials contain only a single trail. This means that the clustering is negligible. Therefore, there is no difference between Figs. 6 and 10 for XOODOO. For SATURNIN the clustering is the most striking. For linear trails we observe a similar effect. For SPONGENT the clustering is less outspoken due to the fact that the trail weight histogram is quite bad to start with.

The effect of clustering in four-round (or two super-round) SATURNIN is interesting. Four-round SATURNIN consists of the parallel application of four 64-bit hyperboxes. The consequence is that for a fixed key, the roughly $2^{127} \cdot 4$ differentials that are active in a single hyperbox and have non-zero DP, all have weight below 63. When computing expected DP values averaging the DP over all round keys, this is closer to 64.

The cluster classes also determine the applicability of the very powerful *truncated differential attacks* [24]. These attacks exploit sets of differentials that share the same box activity pattern in their input difference and the same box activity pattern in their output difference. Despite the fact that the individual trails in these truncated differentials may have very low DP, the joint probability can be significant due to the massive numbers. For two-round differentials the cluster classes are exactly the trail cores in a given truncated differential. In Table 3 we see that the cluster classes for the RIJNDAEL superbox and SATURNIN hyperbox are very large. This clustering leads to powerful distinguishers for e.g., 4-round AES and 8-round SATURNIN. The latter can be modeled as 4 hyperboxes followed by an MDS mixing layer followed by 4 hyperboxes and an input difference with a single active hyperbox will have 4 active hyperboxes after 8 rounds, with probability 1. In contrast, if the cluster classes are small, as in the case of the unaligned XOODOO permutation, it is very unlikely that truncated differential attacks would have an advantage over ordinary differential attacks.

6.4   Three-Round Trail Clustering in XOODOO

Recall that for XOODOO, no 4-round trails exist with weight below 74 and Table 5 showed that trail clustering in two-round differentials in XOODOO is negligible, as expected because of its unaligned design. We investigate the conjecture that it is also the case for three rounds.

First, we present a generic technique to find all trails that have an enveloping differential compatible with a given three-round trail core. We apply the technique to XOODOO, for which it is very efficient.

Given the trail core $(a_1^*, b_1^*, a_2^*, b_2^*)$, Lemma 1 shows that we can restrict ourselves to those (a_1, b_1, a_2, b_2) with $a_1 \sim a_1^*$ and $b_2 \sim b_2^*$. The difference a_1^* defines a vector space A' of all the states in which a box is passive whenever it is passive in a_1^*. If $a_1 \in [a_1^*]_\sim$, then $a_1 \in A'$. Similarly, b_2^* defines a vector space B'. If $b_2 \in [b_2^*]_\sim$, then $b_2 \in B'$. The vector space $B = \mathrm{L}(A')$ contains the candidate values for b_1. Similarly, the vector space $A = \mathrm{L}^{-1}(B')$ contains candidate values for a_2. Because it preserves activity patterns, N restricts the set of candidate values to those satisfying $b_1 \sim a_2$. Hence, we can limit the search to those $x \in B$ and $y \in A$ with $x \sim y$.

To find all valid trails of the form $(\Delta_{\mathrm{in}}, a_1, b_1, a_2, b_2, \Delta_{\mathrm{out}})$, we first reduce the size of the space of all trail cores (a_1, b_1, a_2, b_2) using a necessary condition. When this space is small enough, we exhaustively search for a valid trail.

We write $\overline{B}$ for a basis of B and $\overline{A}$ for a basis of A. To reduce the dimension of the spaces, we will apply an algorithm directly on their bases. First, we need the notion of *isolated active bit*.

Definition 21. *A bit i of $b \in \overline{B}$ is said to be an isolated active bit if $b_i = 1$ and $b_i' = 0$ for all $b' \in \overline{B} \setminus \{b\}$.*

A basis vector having an isolated active bit determines the box activity of any linear combination that includes it.

Lemma 2. *If $b \in \overline{B}$ has an isolated active bit in position i, then any vector in the affine space $b + \mathrm{span}(\overline{B} \setminus \{b\})$ has the corresponding box activated.*

Proof. If b has an isolated active bit in position i, then the ith bit of any vector in $b + \mathrm{span}(\overline{B} \setminus \{b\})$ is active. As a result, the box containing this bit is active. $\square$

Similar to how an isolated active bit always activates the corresponding box, a box is never activated if no basis vector activates it.

Lemma 3. *If the ith box is passive in every vector of $\overline{A}$, then the ith box is passive in all vectors of A. We say that box i is passive in $\overline{A}$.*

We define a condition that makes it possible to remove a basis vector from the basis without excluding potentially valid trails.

Condition 1 (reduction condition). *We say that a basis vector $b \in \overline{B}$ satisfies the reduction condition if and only if it has an isolated active bit in a box that is passive in $\overline{A}$. The same is true when swapping the role of $\overline{B}$ and $\overline{A}$.*

The following lemma shows that the reduction condition is sufficient to reduce the dimension of the vector space we consider.

Lemma 4. *If a basis vector $b \in \overline{B}$ satisfies Condition 1, then all valid differences before the N in the middle are in $span(\overline{B} \setminus \{b\})$. The same is true when swapping the role of $\overline{B}$ and $\overline{A}$.*

Proof. As a consequence of Lemma 2 and Lemma 3, a valid difference before the nonlinear layer cannot be constructed from $b^{(i)}$ because it would contradict the fact that the activity pattern is preserved through the nonlinear layer. $\square$

The algorithm now consists in repeatedly removing basis vectors from $\overline{B}$ and $\overline{A}$ that satisfy Condition 1 until this is no longer possible. This can be done efficiently by searching for pivots for a Gaussian elimination among indices of vectors from $\overline{A'}$ (respectively $\overline{B'}$) that correspond to never activated boxes in $\overline{B'}$ (respectively $\overline{A'}$). Indeed, these pivots can be used to row-reduce the corresponding basis along them, thus revealing an isolated active bit.

If the algorithm sufficiently decreased the dimensions, then we can exhaustively test all pairs $(b_1, a_2) \in B \times A$ (after reduction) according to the following criteria:

- (b_1, a_2) is a valid differential over N;
- There exists a Δ_{in} such that both $(\Delta_{\text{in}}, a_1^*)$ and $(\Delta_{\text{in}}, a_1)$ are valid differentials over N;
- There exists a Δ_{out} such that both $(b_2^*, \Delta_{\text{out}})$ and $(b_2, \Delta_{\text{out}})$ are valid differentials over N.

Applying our method to all three-round trail cores of XOODOO up to weight 50 [17] shows that there exists no cluster for all these trails.

7   Dependence of Round Differentials

In this section we study the dependence of round differentials in the sense of Definition 5 in Sect. 2.1. It has been found in [21] that the vast majority of trails over the RIJNDAEL superbox have dependent round differentials. We will investigate this for differential trails over three-round XOODOO. We expect that the dependence effects observed in RIJNDAEL disappear in an unaligned cipher. Hence, we now investigate this for differential trails over three-round XOODOO.

7.1 Masks for Differentials over Nonlinear Components

We note $V_N(\Delta_{in}, \Delta_{out})$ the set of output states that follow the differential $(\Delta_{in}, \Delta_{out})$ over N, i.e. $V_N(\Delta_{in}, \Delta_{out}) = N(U_N(\Delta_{in}, \Delta_{out}))$. From [21], we have that $U_N(\Delta_{in}, \Delta_{out})$ and $V_N(\Delta_{in}, \Delta_{out})$ are affine if $\#U_{S_i}(P_i(\Delta_{in}), P_i(\Delta_{out})) \leq 4$ for each S-box. Since this assumption holds for our four ciphers, both $U_N(\Delta_{in}, \Delta_{out})$ and $V_N(\Delta_{in}, \Delta_{out})$ are affine and can be described by a system of affine equations on the bits of the state x. Each affine equation can be written as $u^\top x + c$ with u a b-bit vector called mask and c a bit.

Given a three-round differential trail $Q = (\Delta_{in}, a_1, b_1, a_2, b_2, \Delta_{out})$, one can define four sets of masks:

- A_1, the masks that come from $V_N(\Delta_{in}, a_1)$;
- B_1, the masks that come from $U_N(b_1, a_2)$;
- A_2, the masks that come from $V_N(b_1, a_2)$;
- B_2, the masks that come from $U_N(b_2, \Delta_{out})$.

These masks are said to be all *independent* if

$$\#U_{\mathrm{NoLoNoLoN}}(Q) = 2^{b-(\#A_1 + \#B_1 + \#B_2)} = 2^{b-(\#A_1 + \#A_2 + \#B_2)} .$$

which is, per Definition 5, equivalent to the independence of round differentials.

We first present an efficient generic method for determining whether three-round trail masks are independent. Then we apply this method to XOODOO. Since L is linear, A_1 can be linearly propagated through it to obtain a set of masks A_1' at the input of the second nonlinear layer. Similarly, we can propagate B_2 through the inverse linear layer to obtain a set of masks B_2' at the output of the second nonlinear layer.

7.2 Independence of Masks over a Nonlinear Layer

B_1 and A_1' form sets of masks at the input of the second nonlinear layer. If the rank of $C_1 = B_1 \cup A_1'$ is the sum of the ranks of B_1 and A_1', then C_1 contains independent masks. The same strategy can be used to test for dependence of masks in $C_2 = A_2 \cup B_2'$.

As for the independence of masks of the complete trail, we need to check for dependence between C_1 and B_2' or between A_1' and C_2. We will apply an algorithm similar to the one we used in Sect. 6.4 to reduce bases. However, here we use it to reduce the cardinalities of the mask sets.

The following lemma makes this possible.

Lemma 5. *Let C_1 and B_2' be two sets of masks before and after an S-box layer. If a mask u in C_1 satisfies Condition 1, then the number of states that satisfy the equations associated with the masks in both $C_1 \setminus \{u\}$ and B_2' is exactly two times the number of states before removing u. The same is true by swapping the role of C_1 and B_2'.*

Proof. Since u satisfies Condition 1, let i be the index of the isolated bit, j be the index of the corresponding S-Box and k the number of masks in B'_2. No mask in B'_2 is putting a constraint on any of the m bits of the jth S-Box, thus the 2^{b-k} solutions can be seen as 2^{b-k-m} groups of 2^m different states that only differ in the m bits of the jth S-box. Since the S-box is invertible, the application of the inverse of the nonlinear layer to a whole group of 2^m vectors results in a group of 2^m different states that, again, only differ on the value of the jth S-box.

We can further divide those 2^{b-k-m} groups each into 2^{m-1} subgroups of 2 different states that only differ in the value of the ith bit. By definition on an isolated bit, either both or none of the two states inside a subgroup satisfy all equations associated with the masks in $C_1 \setminus \{u\}$. Finally, inside a subgroup exactly one of the two states will satisfy the equation associated with mask u. Thus, the number of solutions by removing u is multiplied by exactly two.   □

We first check for linear dependence inside C_1 by computing its associated rank. Then, we recursively check if some mask in either C_1 or B'_2 satisfies Condition 1 and if it is the case we remove them from the sets of masks.

There are three possible outcomes when applying this process to a three-round differential trail:

- If C_1 is not full rank, we can conclude that masks in B_1 and A'_1 are dependent;
- Else, if either set is empty, Lemma 5 applied at each step guarantees us that the number of states satisfying the equations associated with the masks in both C_1 and B'_2 is equal to $2^{b-(\#C_1+\#B'_2)}$, that is to say the masks are independent;
- If none of the two conditions above are met, we cannot directly conclude about (in)dependence between remaining masks but we can apply the same method to A_1 and C_2 and hope for a better outcome.

7.3   Application to Xoodoo

This process is used to check for independence in differential trails over three rounds of XOODOO. It has been applied to the same differential trails as processed in Sect. 6.4. In all cases, the masks, and thus round differentials, were found to be independent. This was not obtained by sampling, but instead by counting the number of solutions, hence this independence is exact in the sense of Definition 5. As a result, the DP of each such trail is the product of the DP values of its round differentials, which implies that $DP(Q) = 2^{-w_r(Q)}$.

8   Conclusion

We put forward alignment as a crucial property that characterizes the interactions between linear and nonlinear layers w.r.t. the differential and linear propagation properties. We conducted experiments on four S-box based primitives that otherwise represent different design approaches. We precisely defined what it means for a primitive to be aligned and showed that RIJNDAEL, SATURNIN, and SPONGENT are aligned, whereas XOODOO is unaligned. Through these examples, we highlighted and analyzed different effects of alignment on the propagation properties.

Acknowledgements. We thank Bart Mennink for helpful comments. Moreover, we would like to thank the anonymous reviewers of an earlier version of this paper for their useful feedback. Joan Daemen and Daniël Kuijsters are supported by the European Research Council under the ERC advanced grant agreement under grant ERC-2017-ADG Nr. 788980 ESCADA. This work is partially supported by the French National Research Agency in the framework of the *Investissements d'avenir* programme (ANR-15-IDEX-02).

References

1. Banik, S., Pandey, S.K., Peyrin, T., Sasaki, Y., Sim, S.M., Todo, Y.: GIFT: a small present - towards reaching the limit of lightweight encryption. In: CHES (2017)
2. Beaulieu, R., Shors, D., Smith, J., Treatman-Clark, S., Weeks, B., Wingers, L.: The SIMON and SPECK families of lightweight block ciphers. IACR Cryptol. ePrint Arch. **2013**, 404 (2013)
3. Bernstein, D.J.: The Salsa20 family of stream ciphers. In: Robshaw, M., Billet, O. (eds.) New Stream Cipher Designs. LNCS, vol. 4986, pp. 84–97. Springer, Heidelberg (2008). https://doi.org/10.1007/978-3-540-68351-3_8
4. Bernstein, D.J.: Cache-timing attacks on AES. Technical report (2005)
5. Bertoni, G., Daemen, J., Hoffert, S., Peeters, M., Van Assche, G., Van Keer, R.: Extended Keccak code package. https://github.com/XKCP/XKCP
6. Bertoni, G., Daemen, J., Peeters, M., Van Assche, G.: The Keccak reference (Jan 2011)
7. Beyne, T., Chen, Y.L., Dobraunig, C., Mennink, B.: Dumbo, jumbo, and delirium: Parallel authenticated encryption for the lightweight circus. IACR Trans. Symmetric Cryptol. **2020**(S1), 5–30 (2020). https://doi.org/10.13154/tosc.v2020.iS1.5-30
8. Biham, E., Shamir, A.: Differential cryptanalysis of DES-like cryptosystems. In: Menezes, A.J., Vanstone, S.A. (eds.) CRYPTO 1990. LNCS, vol. 537, pp. 2–21. Springer, Heidelberg (1991). https://doi.org/10.1007/3-540-38424-3_1
9. Bogdanov, A., Knezevic, M., Leander, G., Toz, D., Varici, K., Verbauwhede, I.: SPONGENT: the design space of lightweight cryptographic hashing. IACR Cryptol. ePrint Arch. **2011**, 697 (2011)
10. Bogdanov, A., et al.: PRESENT: an ultra-lightweight block cipher. In: Paillier, P., Verbauwhede, I. (eds.) CHES 2007. LNCS, vol. 4727, pp. 450–466. Springer, Heidelberg (2007). https://doi.org/10.1007/978-3-540-74735-2_31
11. Boyar, J., Peralta, R.: A new combinational logic minimization technique with applications to cryptology. In: Festa, P. (ed.) SEA 2010. LNCS, vol. 6049, pp. 178–189. Springer, Heidelberg (2010). https://doi.org/10.1007/978-3-642-13193-6_16
12. Canteaut, A., et al.: Saturnin: a suite of lightweight symmetric algorithms for post-quantum security. IACR ToSC (S1) (2020)
13. Canteaut, A., et al.: Saturnin implementations. https://project.inria.fr/saturnin/files/2019/05/saturnin.zip

14. Daemen, J.: Cipher and hash function design, strategies based on linear and differential cryptanalysis, PhD Thesis. K.U. Leuven (1995)
15. Daemen, J., Hoffert, S., Peeters, M., Van Assche, G., Van Keer, R.: Xoodyak, a lightweight cryptographic scheme. IACR ToSC (S1) (2020)
16. Daemen, J., Hoffert, S., Van Assche, G., Van Keer, R.: The design of Xoodoo and Xoofff. IACR Trans. Symmetric Cryptol. **2018**(4), 1–38 (2018)
17. Daemen, J., Hoffert, S., Van Assche, G., Van Keer, R.: XooTools (2018). https://github.com/KeccakTeam/Xoodoo/tree/master/XooTools
18. Daemen, J., Peeters, M., Van Assche, G., Bertoni, G.: On alignment in Keccak. Note (2011)
19. Daemen, J., Rijmen, V.: Understanding two-round differentials in AES. In: De Prisco, R., Yung, M. (eds.) SCN 2006. LNCS, vol. 4116, pp. 78–94. Springer, Heidelberg (2006). https://doi.org/10.1007/11832072_6
20. Daemen, J., Rijmen, V.: The wide trail design strategy. In: Honary, B. (ed.) Cryptography and Coding 2001. LNCS, vol. 2260, pp. 222–238. Springer, Heidelberg (2001). https://doi.org/10.1007/3-540-45325-3_20
21. Daemen, J., Rijmen, V.: Plateau characteristics. IET Inf. Secur. **1**(1), 11–17 (2007)
22. Daemen, J., Rijmen, V.: The Design of Rijndael - The Advanced Encryption Standard (AES), 2nd edn. Information Security and Cryptography. Springer, Berlin (2020). https://doi.org/10.1007/978-3-662-60769-5
23. Huffman, W.C., Pless, V.: Fundamentals of Error-Correcting Codes. Cambridge University Press, Cambridge (2003)
24. Knudsen, L.R.: Truncated and higher order differentials. In: Preneel, B. (ed.) FSE 1994. LNCS, vol. 1008, pp. 196–211. Springer, Heidelberg (1995). https://doi.org/10.1007/3-540-60590-8_16
25. Kranz, T., Leander, G., Stoffelen, K., Wiemer, F.: Shorter linear straight-line programs for MDS matrices. IACR Trans. Symmetric Cryptol. **2017**(4), 188–211 (2017)
26. Künzer, M., Tentler, W.: Zassenhaus-algorithmus. https://mo.mathematik.uni-stuttgart.de/inhalt/beispiel/beispiel1105/
27. Leander, G., Poschmann, A.: On the classification of 4 bit S-boxes. In: Carlet, C., Sunar, B. (eds.) WAIFI 2007. LNCS, vol. 4547, pp. 159–176. Springer, Heidelberg (2007). https://doi.org/10.1007/978-3-540-73074-3_13
28. Li, C., Wang, Q.: Design of lightweight linear diffusion layers from near-MDS matrices. IACR Trans. Symmetric Cryptol. **2017**(1), 129–155 (2017)
29. Matsui, M.: Linear cryptanalysis method for DES cipher. In: Helleseth, T. (ed.) EUROCRYPT 1993. LNCS, vol. 765, pp. 386–397. Springer, Heidelberg (1994). https://doi.org/10.1007/3-540-48285-7_33
30. McGeer, P.C., Sanghavi, J.V., Brayton, R.K., Sangiovanni-Vincentelli, A.L.: ESPRESSO-SIGNATURE: a new exact minimizer for logic functions. IEEE Trans. Very Large Scale Integr. Syst. **1**(4), 432–440 (1993)
31. Mella, S., Daemen, J., Van Assche, G.: New techniques for trail bounds and application to differential trails in Keccak. IACR ToSC (1) (2017)
32. NIST: Federal information processing standard 197, advanced encryption standard (AES) (Nov 2001)
33. NIST: Federal information processing standard 202, SHA-3 standard: Permutation-based hash and extendable-output functions (Aug 2015)
34. Nyberg, K.: Differentially uniform mappings for cryptography. In: Helleseth, T. (ed.) EUROCRYPT 1993. LNCS, vol. 765, pp. 55–64. Springer, Heidelberg (1994). https://doi.org/10.1007/3-540-48285-7_6

35. Park, S., Sung, S.H., Chee, S., Yoon, E.-J., Lim, J.: On the security of Rijndael-like structures against differential and linear cryptanalysis. In: Zheng, Y. (ed.) ASIACRYPT 2002. LNCS, vol. 2501, pp. 176–191. Springer, Heidelberg (2002). https://doi.org/10.1007/3-540-36178-2_11
36. Schwabe, P., Stoffelen, K.: All the AES you need on cortex-M3 and M4. In: Avanzi, R., Heys, H. (eds.) SAC 2016. LNCS, vol. 10532, pp. 180–194. Springer, Cham (2017). https://doi.org/10.1007/978-3-319-69453-5_10
37. Shamsabad, M.R.M., Dehnavi, S.M.: Dynamic MDS diffusion layers with efficient software implementation. Int. J. Appl. Cryptogr. **4**(1), 36–44 (2020)
38. Stoffelen, K.: AES implementations. https://github.com/Ko-/aes-armcortexm

Cryptanalysis of Full LowMC and LowMC-M with Algebraic Techniques

Fukang Liu[1,2(✉)], Takanori Isobe[2,3,4], and Willi Meier[5]

[1] East China Normal University, Shanghai, China
[2] University of Hyogo, Hyogo, Japan
`liufukangs@163.com, takanori.isobe@ai.u-hyogo.ac.jp`
[3] National Institute of Information and Communications Technology, Tokyo, Japan
[4] PRESTO, Japan Science and Technology Agency, Tokyo, Japan
[5] FHNW, Windisch, Switzerland
`willi.meier@fhnw.ch`

Abstract. In this paper, we revisit the difference enumeration technique for LowMC and develop new algebraic techniques to achieve efficient key-recovery attacks. In the original difference enumeration attack framework, an inevitable step is to precompute and store a set of intermediate state differences for efficient checking via the binary search. Our first observation is that Bar-On et al.'s general algebraic technique developed for SPNs with partial nonlinear layers can be utilized to fulfill the same task, which can make the memory complexity negligible as there is no need to store a huge set of state differences any more. Benefiting from this technique, we could significantly improve the attacks on LowMC when the block size is much larger than the key size and even break LowMC with such a kind of parameter. On the other hand, with our new key-recovery technique, we could significantly improve the time to retrieve the full key if given only a single pair of input and output messages together with the difference trail that they take, which was stated as an interesting question by Rechberger et al. at ToSC 2018. Combining both techniques, with only 2 chosen plaintexts, we could break 4 rounds of LowMC adopting a full S-Box layer with block size of 129, 192 and 255 bits, respectively, which are the 3 recommended parameters for Picnic3, an alternative third-round candidate in NIST's Post-Quantum Cryptography competition. We have to emphasize that our attacks do not indicate that Picnic3 is broken as the Picnic use-case is very different and an attacker cannot even freely choose 2 plaintexts to encrypt for a concrete LowMC instance. However, such parameters are deemed as secure in the latest LowMC. Moreover, much more rounds of seven instances of the backdoor cipher LowMC-M as proposed by Peyrin and Wang in CRYPTO 2020 can be broken without finding the backdoor by making full use of the allowed 2^{64} data. The above mentioned attacks are all achieved with negligible memory.

Keywords: LowMC · LowMC-M · Linearization · Key recovery · Negligible memory

© International Association for Cryptologic Research 2021
T. Malkin and C. Peikert (Eds.): CRYPTO 2021, LNCS 12827, pp. 368–401, 2021.
https://doi.org/10.1007/978-3-030-84252-9_13

1   Introduction

LowMC [5], a family of flexible Substitution-Permutation-Network (SPN) block ciphers aiming at achieving low multiplicative complexity, is a relatively new design in the literature and has been utilized as the underlying block cipher of the post-quantum signature scheme Picnic [3], which is an alternative third-round candidate in NIST's Post-Quantum Cryptography competition [1]. The feature of LowMC is that users can independently choose the parameters to instantiate it, from the number of S-boxes in each round to the linear layer, key schedule function and round constants.

To achieve a low multiplicative complexity, the construction adopting a partial S-box layer (only partial state bits will pass through the S-boxes and an identity mapping is applied for the remaining state bits) together with a random dense linear layer is most used. As such a construction is relatively new, novel cryptanalysis techniques are required. Soon after its publication, the higher-order differential attack and interpolation attack on LowMC were proposed [14,16], both of which required many chosen plaintexts. To resist these attacks, LowMC v2 was proposed, i.e. new formulas were used to determine the secure number of rounds. To analyse one of the most useful settings, namely a few S-boxes in each round with low allowable data complexities, the so-called difference enumeration technique [29], which we call difference enumeration attack, was proposed, which directly made LowMC v2 move to LowMC v3. The difference enumeration attack is a chosen-plaintext attack. The basic idea is to encrypt a pair (or more) of chosen plaintexts and then recover the difference evolutions between the plaintexts through each component in each round, i.e. to recover the differential trail. Finally, the secret key is derived from the recovered differential trail. As a result, the number of the required plaintexts can be as small as 4. For simplicity, LowMC represents LowMC v3 in the remaining part of this paper.

Recently, Picnic3 [21] has been proposed and alternative parameters have been chosen for LowMC. Specifically, different from Picnic2 where a partial S-box layer is adopted when instantiating LowMC, a full S-box layer is used when generating the three instances of LowMC in Picnic3. By choosing the number of rounds as 4, the designers found that the cost of signing time and verifying time can be reduced while the signature size is almost kept the same with that of Picnic2 [3]. By increasing the number of rounds to 5 for a larger security margin, the cost is still lower than that of Picnic2. Consequently, 4-round LowMC is recommended and 5-round LowMC is treated as an alternative choice.

As can be found in the latest source code [2] to determine the secure number of rounds, the 3 instances of 4-round LowMC used in Picnic3 are deemed as secure. However, there is no thorough study for the constructions adopting a full S-box layer and low allowable data complexities (as low as 2 plaintexts[1]).

---

[1] In the security proof of Picnic, 2 plaintexts are required, which can be found at footnote 11 in Page 10 in [10]. This is also our motivation to analyze such instances with only 2 allowed plaintexts. In the security proof, the parameters with 2 allowed plaintexts are treated as secure.

Therefore, it is meaningful to make an investigation in this direction. It should be mentioned that a recent guess-and-determine attack with 1 plaintext can only reach 2 rounds for the constructions with a full S-box layer [7]. Moreover, a parallel work [12] also shows that 2 out of 3 instances of the 4-round LowMC in the Picnic3 setting can be broken, though it requires a huge amount of memory.

Moreover, a family of tweakable block ciphers called LowMC-M [27] was proposed in CRYPTO 2020, which is built on LowMC and allows to embed a backdoor in the instantiation. It is natural to ask whether the additional available degrees of freedom of the tweak can give more power to an attacker. Based on the current cryptanalysis [14, 16, 29], the designers claim that all the parameters of LowMC-M are secure even if the tweak is exploitable by an attacker.

Related Techniques. For the SPNs with partial nonlinear layers, Bar-On et al. have described an efficient algebraic approach [8] to search for differential trails covering a large number of rounds, given that the predefined number of active S-boxes is not too large. First, the attacker introduces intermediate variables to represent the state difference after the first round. Then, traverse all possible differential patterns where the number of active S-boxes is below a predefined value. For each pattern, in the following consecutive rounds, introduce again intermediate variables to represent the output differences of all **active S-boxes**, whose positions have already been fixed. Finally, set up equations in terms of these variables according to the positions of the **inactive S-boxes** as their input and output differences must be 0 and all of them can be written as linear expressions in these variables. Such a strategy has been successfully applied to full Zorro [17].

For algebraic techniques, they seem to be prominent tools to analyze designs using low-degree S-boxes. The recent progress made in the cryptanalysis of Keccak is essentially based on algebraic techniques, including the preimage attacks [19, 22, 25], collision attacks [13, 18, 28, 30] and cube attacks [15, 20, 23].

A pure algebraic attack is to construct a multivariate equation system to describe the target problem and then to solve this equation system efficiently. When the equation system is linear, the well-known gaussian elimination can be directly applied. However, when the equation system is nonlinear, solving such an equation system is NP-hard even if it is quadratic. For the design of block ciphers, there may exist undesirable algebraic properties inside the design which can simplify the equation system and can be further exploitable to accelerate the solving of equations. Such an example can be found in the recent cryptanalysis of the initial version of MARVELLOUS [6] using Gröbner basis attacks [4]. Indeed, there was once a trend to analyze the security of AES against algebraic attacks [11, 26]. In the literature, the simple linearization and guess-and-determine methods are also common techniques to solve a nonlinear multivariate equation system.

Recently at CRYPTO 2020, a method is proposed to automatically verify a specified differential trail [24]. The core technique is to accurately capture the relations between the difference transitions and value transitions. We are inspired from such an idea and will further demonstrate that when the relations between the two transitions are special and when the difference transitions are special, under the difference enumeration attack framework [29], it is possible to utilize algebraic techniques to efficiently recover the differential trail for a single pair of (plaintext, ciphertext) and then to efficiently retrieve the full key from the recovered differential trail.

Our Contributions. This work is based on the difference enumeration attack framework and we developed several non-trivial techniques to significantly improve the cryptanalysis of LowMC. Our results are detailed as follows:

1. Based on Bar-On et al.'s general algebraic technique [8], it is feasible to efficiently check the compatibility of differential trails in the difference enumeration attack [29] by solving a linear equation system, which directly leads to negligible memory complexity. Moreover, it can be found that this technique will be more effective for LowMC due to a special property of the 3-bit S-box, especially when the partial nonlinear layer is close to a full nonlinear layer.
2. By studying the S-box of LowMC, we develop an efficient algebraic technique to retrieve the full key if given only a single pair of (plaintext, ciphertext) along with the corresponding differential trail that they take, which was stated as an interesting question by Rechberger et al. at ToSC 2018.
3. We further develop a new difference enumeration attack framework to analyze the constructions adopting a full S-box layer and low allowable data complexities.
4. Combining our techniques, we could break the 3 recommended parameters of 4-round LowMC used in Picnic3, which are treated as secure against the existing cryptanalysis techniques, though it cannot lead to an attack on Picnic3. In addition, much more rounds of 7 instances of LowMC-M can be broken without finding the backdoor, thus violating the security claim of the designers.

All our key-recovery attacks on LowMC only require 2 chosen plaintexts and negligible memory. For the attacks on LowMC-M, we will make full use of the allowed data to achieve more rounds. More details are displayed in Table 1, Table 2 and Table 3. To advance the understanding of the secure number of rounds for both LowMC and LowMC-M, we focus on the attacks reaching the largest number of rounds with the complexity below the exhaustive search.

Organization. A brief introduction of LowMC and LowMC-M is given in Sect. 2. We then revisit the difference enumeration attack framework in Sect. 3. In Sect. 4, we make a study on the S-box of LowMC. The techniques to reduce the memory complexity and to reduce the cost to retrieve the secret key from a differential trail are detailed in Sect. 5 and Sect. 6, respectively. The application of the two techniques to LowMC with a partial S-box layer and LowMC-M can be referred to Sect. 7. The attack on LowMC with a full S-box layer is explained in Sect. 8. The experimental results are reported in Sect. 9. Finally, we conclude the paper in Sect. 10.

2   Preliminaries

2.1   Notation

As there are many parameters for both LowMC [5] and LowMC-M [27], we use n, k, m and R to represent the block size in bits, the key size in bits, the number of S-boxes in each round and the total number of rounds, respectively. Besides, the number of allowed data under each key is denoted by 2^D. In addition, the following notations will also be used:

1. $Pr[\omega]$ represents the probability that the event ω happens.
2. $Pr[\omega|\chi]$ represents the conditional probability, i.e. the probability that ω happens under the condition that χ happens.
3. $x >> y$ represents that x is much larger than y.

2.2   Description of LowMC

LowMC [5] is a family of SPN block ciphers proposed by Albrecht et al. in Eurocrypt 2015. Different from conventional block ciphers, the instantiation of LowMC is not fixed and each user can independently choose parameters to instantiate LowMC.

LowMC follows a common encryption procedure as most block ciphers. Specifically, it starts with a key whitening (**WK**) and then iterates a round function R times. The round function at the $(i+1)$-th ($0 \leq i \leq R-1$) round can be described as follows:

1. SBoxLayer (**SB**): A 3-bit S-box $S(x_0, x_1, x_2) = (x_0 \oplus x_1 x_2, x_0 \oplus x_1 \oplus x_0 x_2, x_0 \oplus x_1 \oplus x_2 \oplus x_0 x_1)$ will be applied to the first $3m$ bits of the state in parallel, while an identity mapping is applied to the remaining $n - 3m$ bits.
2. MatrixMul (**L**): A regular matrix $L_i \in \mathbb{F}_2^{n \times n}$ is randomly generated and the n-bit state is multiplied with L_i.
3. ConstantAddition (**AC**): An n-bit constant $C_i \in \mathbb{F}_2^n$ is randomly generated and is XORed to the n-bit state.
4. KeyAddition (**AK**): A full-rank $n \times k$ binary matrix M_{i+1} is randomly generated. The n-bit round key K_{i+1} is obtained by multiplying the k-bit master key with M_{i+1}. Then, the n-bit state is XORed with K_{i+1}.

The whitening key is denoted by K_0 and it is also calculated by multiplying the master key with a random $n \times k$ binary matrix M_0.

It has been studied that there is an equivalent representation of LowMC by placing (**AK**) between (**SB**) and (**L**). In this way, the size of the round key K_i ($i > 0$) becomes $3m$, which is still linear in the k-bit master key and can be viewed as multiplying the master key with a $3m \times k$ random binary matrix. Notice that K_0 is still an n-bit value. We will use this equivalent representation throughout this paper for simplicity.

Moreover, for convenience, we denote the plaintext by p and the ciphertext by c. The state after **WK** is denoted by A_0. In the $(i+1)$-th round, the input state of **SB** is denoted by A_i and the output state of **SB** is denoted by A_i^S, as shown below:

$$p \xrightarrow{\textbf{WK}} A_0 \xrightarrow{\textbf{SB}} A_0^S \xrightarrow{\textbf{AK}}\xrightarrow{\textbf{L}}\xrightarrow{\textbf{AC}} A_1 \rightarrow \cdots \rightarrow A_{R-1} \xrightarrow{\textbf{SB}} A_{R-1}^S \xrightarrow{\textbf{AK}}\xrightarrow{\textbf{L}}\xrightarrow{\textbf{AC}} A_R.$$

In addition, we also introduce the notations to represent the xor difference transitions, as specified below:

$$\Delta_p \xrightarrow{\textbf{WK}} \Delta_0 \xrightarrow{\textbf{SB}} \Delta_0^S \xrightarrow{\textbf{AK}}\xrightarrow{\textbf{L}}\xrightarrow{\textbf{AC}} \Delta_1 \rightarrow \cdots \rightarrow \Delta_{R-1} \xrightarrow{\textbf{SB}} \Delta_{R-1}^S \xrightarrow{\textbf{AK}}\xrightarrow{\textbf{L}}\xrightarrow{\textbf{AC}} \Delta_R.$$

Specifically, in the $(i+1)$-th round, the difference of the input state of **SB** is denoted by Δ_i and the difference of the output state of **SB** is denoted by Δ_i^S. The difference of plaintexts is denoted by Δ_p, i.e. $\Delta_p = \Delta_0$.

Definition 1. A differential trail $\Delta_0 \rightarrow \Delta_1 \rightarrow \cdots \rightarrow \Delta_r$ is called a r-round **compact differential trail** when all (Δ_j, Δ_j^S) $(0 \leq j \leq r-1)$ and Δ_r are known.

LowMC-M [27] is a family of tweakable block ciphers built on LowMC, which was introduced by Peyrin and Wang at CRYPTO 2020. The feature of LowMC-M is that backdoors can be inserted in the instantiation. The only difference between LowMC and LowMC-M is that there is an addition operation AddSub-Tweak (**AT**) after **AK** and **WK** where the sub-tweaks are the output of an extendable-output-function (XOF) function by setting the tweak as the input. A detailed description can be referred to Appendix A.

3   The Difference Enumeration Techniques

In this section, we briefly revisit the difference enumeration techniques in [29]. The overall procedure can be divided into three phases, as depicted in Fig. 1.

Phase 1: Determine an input difference Δ_0 such that it will not activate any S-boxes in the first t_0 rounds, i.e. $Pr[\Delta_0 \rightarrow \Delta_{t_0}] = 1$.

Phase 2: Compute the corresponding Δ_{t_0} from Δ_0 obtained at Phase 1. Then, enumerate the differences forwards for t_1 consecutive rounds and collect all reachable values for $\Delta_{t_0+t_1}$. Store all possible values of $\Delta_{t_0+t_1}$ in a table denoted by D_f.

Phase 3: Encrypt a pair of plaintexts whose difference equals Δ_0 and compute the difference Δ_r of the corresponding two ciphertexts. Enumerate all reachable differences of $\Delta_{t_0+t_1}$ backwards for $t_2 = r - t_0 - t_1$ rounds staring from Δ_r and check whether it is in D_f.

For convenience, suppose the reachable differences of $\Delta_{t_0+t_1}$ obtained by computing backwards are stored in a table denoted by D_b, though there is no need to store them. To construct a distinguisher, one should expect that $|D_f| \times |D_b| < 2^n$. In this way, one could only expect at most one solution that can connect the difference transitions in both directions. Since there must be a solution, the solution

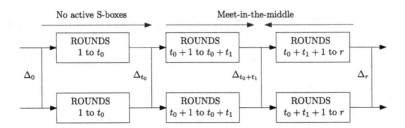

Fig. 1. The framework of the difference enumeration techniques

found with the above difference enumeration techniques is the actual solution. After the compact differential trail is determined, i.e. the difference transitions in each round are fully recovered, the attacker launches the key-recovery phase.

To increase the number of rounds that can be attacked, the authors exploited the concept of d-difference[2] [31], which can increase the upper bound for $|D_f| \times |D_b|$, i.e. $|D_f| \times |D_b| < 2^{nd}$ and $max(|D_f|, |D_b|) < 2^k$. The constraint $|D_f| \times |D_b| < 2^{nd}$ can ensure there is only one valid d-differential trail left since there are in total 2nd possible values for the n-bit d-difference. The remaining two constraints are used to ensure the time complexity to enumerate d-differences cannot exceed that of the brute-force attack. It should be noted that $|D_f| = \lambda_d^{mt_1}$ and $|D_b| = \lambda_d^{mt_2}$, where λ_d denotes the average number of reachable output d-differences over the S-box for a uniformly randomly chosen input d-difference. For the 3-bit S-box used in LowMC, $\lambda_1 \approx 3.62 \approx 2^{1.86}$ and $\lambda_2 \approx 6.58 \approx 2^{2.719}$. Therefore, a larger number of rounds can be covered with d-differences ($d > 1$) when $k \geq n$. As for $n > k$, it is thus more effective to use the standard difference ($d = 1$) rather than the d-difference ($d > 1$). This paper is irrelevant to the concept of d-difference [31] and hence we omit the corresponding explanation.

It is claimed in [29] that to efficiently recover the secret key based on the recovered compact differential trail, a few pairs of plaintexts are required to identify the unique secret key. As our key-recovery technique is quite different, we refer the interested readers to [29] for details.

3.1 The Extended Framework

It is stated in [29] that the above framework can be extended to more rounds if the allowed data are increased. Specifically, as depicted in Fig. 2, when the allowed data complexity is 2^D, after choosing a good starting input d-difference in the plaintexts, the attacker could construct $\lfloor \frac{2^D}{d+1} \rfloor$ different tuples of plaintexts satisfying the chosen input d-difference. For each tuple of plaintexts, the attacker can obtain the corresponding d-difference in the ciphertexts and check whether it will activate the S-boxes in the last r_3 rounds.

---

[2] For a tuple of $(d + 1)$ values $(u_0, u_1, \ldots, u_d)$, its d-difference is defined as $(\delta_0, \delta_1, \ldots, \delta_{d-1}) = (u_0 \oplus u_1, u_0 \oplus u_2, \ldots, u_0 \oplus u_d)$.

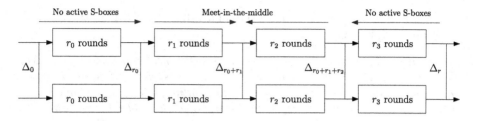

Fig. 2. The extended framework of the difference enumeration techniques

From now on, as shown in Fig. 2, it is assumed that there is a probability-1 differential trail covering the first r_0 rounds, and that the difference enumeration in the forward and backward directions will cover r_1 and r_2 rounds, respectively.

A simple extension of the original difference enumeration attack [29] is to consider larger r_1 and r_2. In this case, there will be much more candidates for compact differential trails, i.e. the number of which is $\lambda_1^{r_1+r_2} \times 2^{-n}$ for the standard xor difference. Then, it is essential to efficiently retrieve the full key from each compact differential trail, which is indeed an interesting question raised in [29].

Based on the method mentioned in [29], when only 2 plaintexts are allowed, the cost to retrieve the full key from each compact differential trail is lower bounded by $2^{k/3}$ as each non-zero difference transition through the 3-bit S-box will suggest two solutions and the master key is a k-bit value. The reason why it is a lower bound is that there may exist inactive S-boxes in the differential trails and the attacker has to try all the 8 values. Thus, an efficient method to retrieve the full key will allow us to enlarge $\lambda_1^{m(r_1+r_2)} \times 2^{-n}$, thus increasing the number of rounds that can be attacked.

Apart from the high cost of key recovery, in the original difference enumeration attack, it seems to be inevitable that the attacker needs to store a huge set of $\Delta_{r_0+r_1}$, whose size is about $\lambda_1^{mr_1}$ for the standard xor difference. We believe that attacks with negligible memory are more effective and meaningful if compared with a pure exhaustive key search.

4   Observations on the S-Box

Before introducing our linearization-based techniques for LowMC, it is necessary to describe our observations on the 3-bit S-box used in LowMC. Denote the 3-bit input and output of the S-box by (x_0, x_1, x_2) and (z_0, z_1, z_2), respectively. Based on the definition of the S-box, the following relations hold:

$$z_0 = x_0 \oplus x_1 x_2, \ z_1 = x_0 \oplus x_1 \oplus x_0 x_2, \ z_2 = x_0 \oplus x_1 \oplus x_2 \oplus x_0 x_1.$$

Therefore, for the inverse of the S-box, there will exist

$$x_0 = z_0 \oplus z_1 \oplus z_1 z_2, \ x_1 = z_1 \oplus z_0 z_2, \ x_2 = z_0 \oplus z_1 \oplus z_2 \oplus z_0 z_1.$$

According to the specification of the 3-bit S-box, we observed the following useful properties of the S-box.

Observation 1. *For each valid non-zero difference transition $(\Delta x_0, \Delta x_1, \Delta x_2) \to (\Delta z_0, \Delta z_1, \Delta z_2)$, the inputs conforming to such a difference transition will form an affine space of dimension 1. In addition, (z_0, z_1, z_2) becomes linear in (x_0, x_1, x_2), i.e. the S-box is freely linearized for a valid non-zero difference transition. A similar property also applies to the inverse of the S-box.*

Observation 2. *For each non-zero input difference $(\Delta x_0, \Delta x_1, \Delta x_2)$, its valid output differences form an affine space of dimension 2. A similar property also applies to the inverse of the S-box.*

Observation 3. *For an inactive S-box, the input becomes linear in the output after guessing two output bits. If guessing two input bits, the output also becomes linear in the input. The same property holds for its inverse.*

Example. The last observation is trivial and let us make a short explanation for the remaining observations. For example, when $(\Delta x_0, \Delta x_1, \Delta x_2) = (0, 0, 1)$ and $(\Delta z_0, \Delta z_1, \Delta z_2) = (0, 0, 1)$, it can be derived that $x_0 = 0$ and $x_1 = 0$. Therefore, the expressions of (z_0, z_1, z_2) become $z_0 = 0$, $z_1 = 0$ and $z_2 = x_2$. When the input difference is $(0, 1, 1)$, the corresponding valid output differences satisfy $\Delta z_1 \oplus \Delta z_2 = 1$. When the output difference is $(0, 1, 1)$, the corresponding valid input differences satisfy $\Delta x_1 \oplus \Delta x_2 = 1$. A full list of all the valid non-zero difference transitions along with the corresponding conditions on (x_0, x_1, x_2) as well as the updated expressions for (z_0, z_1, z_2) is given in Table 4 in Appendix D.

Generalization. It is easy to identify Observation 1 since it is a 2-differentially uniform 3-bit S-box. However, it is surprising that such a property has never been exploited in the cryptanalysis of LowMC. To generalise our results, we prove that the above 3 observations hold for all 3-bit almost perfect nonlinear (APN) S-boxes. Observation 3 is trivial and we only focus on the remaining 2 observations, especially on Observation 2.

To save space, we simply explain what a 3-bit APN S-box is. For simplicity, we still denote the input and output of the S-box by (x_0, x_1, x_2) and $(z_0, z_1, z_2) = S'(x_0, x_1, x_2)$, respectively. Formally, for a 3-bit APN S-box, for any valid nonzero difference transition $(\Delta x_0, \Delta x_1, \Delta x_2) \to (\Delta z_0, \Delta z_1, \Delta z_2)$, there are only 2 solutions of (x_0, x_1, x_2) to the following equation:

$$S'(x_0 \oplus \Delta x_0, x_1 \oplus \Delta x_1, x_2 \oplus \Delta x_2) \oplus S'(x_0, x_1, x_2) = (\Delta z_0, \Delta z_1, \Delta z_2).$$

For a 3-bit APN S-box, its algebraic degree must be 2. Hence, the S-box can be defined in the following way:

$$z_0 = \varphi_0(x_0, x_1, x_2) \oplus \kappa_0 x_0 x_1 \oplus \kappa_1 x_0 x_2 \oplus \kappa_2 x_1 x_2 \oplus \epsilon_0,$$
$$z_1 = \varphi_1(x_0, x_1, x_2) \oplus \kappa_3 x_0 x_1 \oplus \kappa_4 x_0 x_2 \oplus \kappa_5 x_1 x_2 \oplus \epsilon_1,$$
$$z_2 = \varphi_2(x_0, x_1, x_2) \oplus \kappa_6 x_0 x_1 \oplus \kappa_7 x_0 x_2 \oplus \kappa_8 x_1 x_2 \oplus \epsilon_2,$$

where $\varphi_i(x_0, x_1, x_2)$ $(0 \leq i \leq 2)$ are linear boolean functions and $\kappa_j \in \mathbb{F}_2$ $(0 \leq j \leq 8)$, $\epsilon_i \in \mathbb{F}_2$ $(0 \leq i \leq 2)$. For a specific 3-bit APN S-box, all $\varphi_i(x_0, x_1, x_2)$, κ_j and ϵ_i will be fixed.

First, consider the case when $(\Delta x_0, \Delta x_1, \Delta x_2) = (0, 0, 1)$. It can be found that there are four assignments to (x_0, x_1) that will influence the output difference, as shown below, where $\Delta\varphi_i$ $(0 \leq i \leq 2)$ represents the xor difference of the outputs of the linear function $\varphi_i(x_0, x_1, x_2)$.

$$(x_0, x_1) \rightarrow (\Delta z_0, \Delta z_1, \Delta z_2)$$
$$(0, 0) \rightarrow (\Delta\varphi_0, \Delta\varphi_1, \Delta\varphi_2),$$
$$(0, 1) \rightarrow (\Delta\varphi_0 \oplus \kappa_2, \Delta\varphi_1 \oplus \kappa_5, \Delta\varphi_2 \oplus \kappa_8),$$
$$(1, 0) \rightarrow (\Delta\varphi_0 \oplus \kappa_1, \Delta\varphi_1 \oplus \kappa_4, \Delta\varphi_2 \oplus \kappa_7),$$
$$(1, 1) \rightarrow (\Delta\varphi_0 \oplus \kappa_1 \oplus \kappa_2, \Delta\varphi_1 \oplus \kappa_4 \oplus \kappa_5, \Delta\varphi_2 \oplus \kappa_7 \oplus \kappa_8).$$

As the S-box is APN, the above four possible values of the output difference $(\Delta z_0, \Delta z_1, \Delta z_2)$ are the actual 4 distinct output differences for the input difference $(\Delta x_0, \Delta x_1, \Delta x_2) = (0, 0, 1)$. As the set

$$\{(0,0,0), (\kappa_2, \kappa_5, \kappa_8), (\kappa_1, \kappa_4, \kappa_7), (\kappa_1 \oplus \kappa_2, \kappa_4 \oplus \kappa_5, \kappa_7 \oplus \kappa_8)\}$$

forms a linear subspace of dimension 2 over $\mathbb{F}_2^3$, the 4 possible output differences for the input difference $(0, 0, 1)$ form an affine subspace of dimension 2. For each of the 4 valid difference transitions, there will be 2 linear conditions on the input bits and hence the S-box is always freely linearized, i.e. each output bit can be written as a linear expression in the input bits. Due to the symmetry of the expressions, the same holds for the input differences $(1, 0, 0)$ and $(0, 1, 0)$.

When $(\Delta x_0, \Delta x_1, \Delta x_2) = (0, 1, 1)$, we can write the accurate 4 distinct output differences in a similar way, as listed below:

$$(x_0, x_1 \oplus x_2) \rightarrow (\Delta z_0, \Delta z_1, \Delta z_2)$$
$$(0, 0) \rightarrow (\Delta\varphi_0 \oplus \kappa_2, \Delta\varphi_1 \oplus \kappa_5, \Delta\varphi_2 \oplus \kappa_8),$$
$$(0, 1) \rightarrow (\Delta\varphi_0, \Delta\varphi_1, \Delta\varphi_2),$$
$$(1, 0) \rightarrow (\Delta\varphi_0 \oplus \kappa_0 \oplus \kappa_1 \oplus \kappa_2, \Delta\varphi_1 \oplus \kappa_3 \oplus \kappa_4 \oplus \kappa_5, \Delta\varphi_2 \oplus \kappa_6 \oplus \kappa_7 \oplus \kappa_8),$$
$$(1, 1) \rightarrow (\Delta\varphi_0 \oplus \kappa_0 \oplus \kappa_1, \Delta\varphi_1 \oplus \kappa_3 \oplus \kappa_4, \Delta\varphi_2 \oplus \kappa_6 \oplus \kappa_7).$$

Therefore, for each valid difference transition, there are 2 linear conditions on the input bits and the S-box is freely linearized. In addition, it can be found that the set

$$\{(0,0,0), (\kappa_2, \kappa_5, \kappa_8),$$
$$(\kappa_0 \oplus \kappa_1, \kappa_3 \oplus \kappa_4, \kappa_6 \oplus \kappa_7), (\kappa_0 \oplus \kappa_1 \oplus \kappa_2, \kappa_3 \oplus \kappa_4 \oplus \kappa_5, \kappa_6 \oplus \kappa_7 \oplus \kappa_8)\}$$

forms a linear subspace of dimension 2 over $\mathbb{F}_2^3$, thus resulting in the fact that the 4 output differences form an affine subspace of dimension 2. Due to the symmetry, the same conclusion also holds for the input differences $(1, 1, 0)$ and $(1, 0, 1)$.

When $(\Delta x_0, \Delta x_1, \Delta x_2) = (1, 1, 1)$, the 4 distinct output differences can be written as follows:

$$(x_0 \oplus x_1, x_1 \oplus x_2) \rightarrow (\Delta z_0, \Delta z_1, \Delta z_2)$$

$$(0, 0) \rightarrow (\varphi_0 \oplus \kappa_0 \oplus \kappa_1 \oplus \kappa_2, \varphi_1 \oplus \kappa_3 \oplus \kappa_4 \oplus \kappa_5, \varphi_2 \oplus \kappa_6 \oplus \kappa_7 \oplus \kappa_8),$$

$$(0, 1) \rightarrow (\varphi_0 \oplus \kappa_0, \varphi_1 \oplus \kappa_3, \varphi_2 \oplus \kappa_6),$$

$$(1, 0) \rightarrow (\varphi_0 \oplus \kappa_2, \varphi_1 \oplus \kappa_5, \varphi_2 \oplus \kappa_8),$$

$$(1, 1) \rightarrow (\varphi_0 \oplus \kappa_1, \varphi_1 \oplus \kappa_4, \varphi_2 \oplus \kappa_7).$$

Therefore, for each valid difference transition, there are 2 linear conditions on the input bits and the S-box is freely linearized. Moreover, since the set

$$\{(0, 0, 0), (\kappa_1 \oplus \kappa_2, \kappa_4 \oplus \kappa_5, \kappa_7 \oplus \kappa_8),$$
$$(\kappa_0 \oplus \kappa_1, \kappa_3 \oplus \kappa_4, \kappa_6 \oplus \kappa_7), (\kappa_0 \oplus \kappa_2, \kappa_3 \oplus \kappa_5, \kappa_6 \oplus \kappa_8)\}$$

forms a linear subspace of dimension 2 over $\mathbb{F}_2^3$, the 4 distinct output differences must also form an affine subspace of dimension 2.

As the inverse of an APN S-box is also APN, Observation 1 and Observation 2 hold for all 3-bit APN S-boxes, thus completing the proof.

5 Reducing the Memory Complexity

As mentioned in the previous section, it seems to be inevitable to use a sufficiently large amount of memory to store some reachable differences to achieve efficient checking for the reachable differences computed backwards. It is commonly believed that attacks requiring too much memory indeed cannot compete with a pure exhaustive key search. Therefore, our first aim is to significantly reduce the memory complexity in both the original and extended frameworks.

The main underlying strategy in Bar-On et al.'s algorithm [8] is to introduce intermediate variables to represent the output differences of S-boxes. Then, each intermediate state difference can be written as linear expressions in terms of these variables. It is obvious that such a strategy can be used to efficiently check whether the reachable differences computed backwards can be matched. Specifically, for each reachable difference computed in the backward direction, we can construct an equation system whose solutions can correspond to the difference transitions in the forward direction.

As illustrated in Fig. 3, after we determine the differential trail in the first r_0 rounds, Δ_{r_0} is known and there should be at least one active S-box when taking two inputs with Δ_{r_0} as difference to the $(r_0 + 1)$-th round, otherwise we could extend the deterministic differential trail for one more round.

As in [8], we can introduce at most $3m$ variables $(d_0, \cdots, d_{3m-1})$ to denote the output difference of the m S-boxes for the input difference Δ_{r_0}. However, by exploiting Observation 2, it is sufficient to introduce at most $2m$ variables. Specifically, for an inactive S-box, the output difference is $(0, 0, 0)$, i.e. three

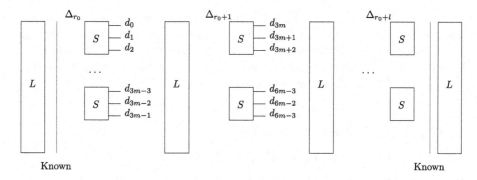

Fig. 3. Constructing the affine subspace of reachable differences

linear relations can be derived for these variables. When there is an active S-box, the valid output differences form an affine space of dimension 2 according to Observation 2, i.e. 1 linear relation can be obtained. In other words, we only need to introduce at most $3m - m = 2m$ variables to denote the output differences for Δ_{r_0}. For the next $l - 1$ rounds, since the input difference of the S-box is uncertain due to the diffusion of a random linear layer, we directly introduce $3m(l-1)$ variables $(d_{3m}, \cdots, d_{3ml-1})$ to represent the output differences for each S-box. In this way, Δ_{r_0+l} is obviously linear in the introduced $3m(l-1) + 2m = 3ml - m = m(3l - 1)$ variables. In other words, Δ_{r_0+l} can be written as linear expressions in terms of the introduced $m(3l - 1)$ variables.

Then, for the difference enumeration in the backward direction, after we obtain the output difference of the S-box for Δ_{r_0+l}, we start to construct the equation system to connect the output difference. If we directly use the idea in [8], at least $n - 3m$ linear equations can be constructed as there are m S-boxes in the nonlinear layer. However, according to Observation 2, once the output difference of the m S-boxes becomes known, it will leak at least m linear relations for the input difference. Specifically, when the S-box is inactive, the input difference is 0, i.e. three linear relations. When the S-box is active, according to Observation 2, one linear relation inside the input difference can be derived. In other words, we could collect at least $m + (n - 3m) = n - 2m$ linear equations in terms of the introduced $m(3l - 1)$ variables. When

$$m(3l - 1) \leq n - 2m \rightarrow n \geq m(3l + 1), \tag{1}$$

we can expect at most one solution of the equation system.

Once a solution is found, all output differences of the S-box in the middle l rounds become known and we can easily check whether the difference transitions are valid by computing forwards. If the transitions are valid, a connection between the difference transitions in both directions are constructed. Otherwise, we need to consider another enumerated output difference of the S-box for Δ_{r_0+l} in the backward direction. We have to stress that when enumerating the differences backwards for r_2 rounds, there are indeed $l + 1 + r_2$ rounds in the middle, i.e. $r_1 = l + 1$ if following the extended framework as shown in Fig. 2.

However, in some cases where m is large, there is no need to make such a strong constraint as in Eq. 1. Even with $n < m(3l+1)$, at the cost of enumerating all the solutions of the constructed linear equation system, more rounds can be covered. In this way, the time complexity to enumerate differences becomes $2^{1.86mr_2+m(3l+1)-n}$. Thus, the constraint becomes

$$1.86mr_2 + m(3l+1) - n < k. \tag{2}$$

As $l = r_1 - 1$, it can be derived that

$$m(1.86r_2 + 3r_1 - 2) < n + k \tag{3}$$

In addition, the following constraint on r_2 should hold as well.

$$1.86mr_2 < k \tag{4}$$

Therefore, when $r_1 + r_2$ is to be maximized, the above two inequalities should be taken into account. In this way, the time complexity of difference enumeration becomes

$$max(2^{1.86mr_2}, 2^{m(1.86r_2+3r_1-2)-n}). \tag{5}$$

Comparison. Due to Observation 2, we can introduce fewer variables and construct more equations to efficiently compute the compact differential trails if comparing our algorithm with the general algorithm in [8]. The advantage of such an optimized algorithm may be not evident when m is much smaller than n. However, as the nonlinear layer is closer to a full nonlinear layer, our algorithm will become more and more effective and may allow us to break one more round, which is essential to break the 4-round LowMC with a full S-box layer discussed in Sect. 8.

6   Efficient Algebraic Techniques for Key Recovery

In this section, we describe how to retrieve the full key from a compact differential trail with an algebraic method. Following the extended framework, we assume that there is no active S-box in the last r_3 rounds. As illustrated in Fig. 4, we could introduce $3mr_3$ variables to represent all the input bits of the S-boxes in the last r_3 rounds. Although A_r is the known ciphertext, the round key used in **AK** is unknown in the r-th round. Therefore, the input of the S-box is unknown in the r-th round and is quadratic in terms of the unknown secret key. By introducing variables $(v_0, \cdots, v_{3m-1})$ to represent the expressions of the inputs of the S-box when reversing the S-box, we could write A_{r-1} as linear expressions in terms of these variables[3]. Similarly, it can be derived that A_{r-r_3} can be written as linear expressions in terms of all the introduced $3mr_3$ variables $(v_0, \cdots, v_{3mr_3-1})$.

---

[3] If we use the equivalent representation of LowMC, such a statement is correct. If we do not use it, A_{r-1} can be written as linear expressions in terms of $(v_0, \cdots, v_{3m-1})$ and the key bits, which will not affect our attack as our final goal is to construct a linear equation system in terms of the $3mr_3$ variables and the key bits. For simplicity, we consider the equivalent representation.

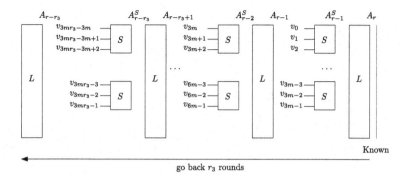

Fig. 4. Linearizing the last r_3 rounds

6.1 Exploiting the Leaked Linear Relations

Since all the S-boxes in the last r_3 rounds are inactive, we have to introduce $3mr_3$ variables to achieve linearization. However, we have not yet obtained any linear equations in terms of these variables. Therefore, we will focus on how to construct a sufficiently large number of linear equations such that there will be a unique solution of these introduced variables.

It should be noticed that the difference enumeration starts from Δ_{r-r_3} in the backward direction. For a valid r_2-round differential propagation $(\Delta_{r-r_3} \rightarrow \Delta_{r-r_3-1} \rightarrow \cdots \rightarrow \Delta_{r-r_3-r_2})$ enumerated in the backward direction, there should be one valid r_1-round differential propagation $(\Delta_{r_0} \rightarrow \Delta_{r_0+1} \rightarrow \cdots \rightarrow \Delta_{r_0+r_1})$ enumerated in the forward direction such that $\Delta_{r_0+r_1} = \Delta_{r-r_3-r_2}$. Once such a sequence is identified, i.e. $(\Delta_{r_0} \rightarrow \cdots \rightarrow \Delta_{r-r_3})$ is fully known, we start extracting linear equations from the difference transitions inside the S-boxes in the middle $r_1 + r_2$ rounds.

Specifically, for each active S-box, there will be two linear equations inside the 3-bit output according to Observation 1. In addition, the 3-bit S-box is freely linearized once it is active according to Observation 1, i.e. the 3-bit input can be written as linear expressions in terms of the 3-bit output. Note that A_{r-r_3} is linear in $(v_0, \cdots, v_{3mr_3-1})$.

As depicted in Fig. 5, denote the equivalent round key bits used in the $(r-r_3)$-th round by $(e_0, \cdots, e_{3m-1})$. For simplicity, assume that all the S-boxes are active when going back b rounds starting from A_{r-r_3}. The case when there are inactive S-boxes will be discussed later. Under such an assumption, we could derive $2m$ linear equations in terms of $(v_0, \cdots, v_{3mr_3-1}, e_0, \cdots, e_{3m-1})$ based on Observation 1. In addition, since the input becomes linear in the output for each active S-box, A_{r-r_3-1} becomes linear in $(v_0, \cdots, v_{3mr_3-1}, e_0, \cdots, e_{3m-1})$. Similarly, denote the equivalent round key bits used in the $(r-r_3-i)$-th round by $(e_{3mi}, \cdots, e_{3mi+3m-1})$ $(0 \leq i \leq b-1)$. Then, one could derive $2m$ linear equations in terms of $(v_0, \cdots, v_{3mr_3-1}, e_0, \cdots, e_{3mi+3m-1})$ in the $(r - r_3 - i)$-th round and A_{r-r_3-i-1} will be linear in $(v_0, \cdots, v_{3mr_3-1}, e_0, \cdots, e_{3mi+3m-1})$. Repeating such a procedure for b rounds backwards, we could collect in total $2mb$ linear equations

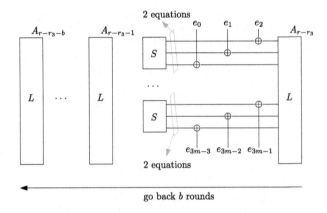

Fig. 5. Extract linear equations from the inactive S-boxes

in terms of $3mr_3 + 3mb$ variables $(v_0, \cdots, v_{3mr_3-1}, e_0, \cdots, e_{3mb-1})$. Since each equivalent round key bit is linear in the k-bit master key according to the linear key schedule function, we indeed succeed in constructing $2mb$ linear equations in terms of $(v_0, \cdots, v_{3mr_3-1})$ and the k-bit master key. To ensure that there is a unique solution to the equation system, the following constraint should hold:

$$2mb \geq k + 3mr_3. \tag{6}$$

As $2m$ linear equations will be leaked when going back 1 round, there may exist redundant linear equations, i.e. $2mb > k + 3mr_3$. Indeed, only

$$h = \lceil \frac{(k + 3mr_3) - 2m(b - 1)}{2} \rceil \tag{7}$$

active S-boxes are needed in the $(r - r_3 - b)$-th round. In this way, we only need in total

$$H = h + m(b - 1) \tag{8}$$

S-boxes to ensure that there exists a unique solution of the constructed equation system.

6.2   Linearizing the Inactive S-Boxes

After discussing the case when all the S-boxes are active when going back b rounds starting from A_{r-r_3}, consider the case when there are q inactive S-boxes among the required H S-boxes in these b rounds ($0 \leq q \leq H$). Specifically, we aim to compute the time complexity to recover the full key for such a case.

While 2 linear equations can be freely derived from the output of an active S-box and the input becomes freely linear in the output for an active S-box as explained previously, linearizing the inactive S-box will require additional cost when going backwards. For an inactive S-box, it can be linearized by guessing two bits of its input or output according to Observation 3. In other words, even for an inactive S-box, we could guess 2 linear equations for its output and then the input still becomes linear in the output. Therefore, the number of equations remain the same as in the case when all the S-boxes are active. The only cost is that we need to iterate 2^{2q} times of guessing. If Eq. 6 holds, for each time of guessing, one could only expect 1 unique solution of the k-bit master key.

Assuming there are N valid compact differential trails left in the extended framework, we can expect there are $N \times \sum_{q=0}^{H} (\frac{7}{8})^{H-q} \times (\frac{1}{8})^q \times \binom{H}{q}$ differential trails where there are q inactive S-boxes in the key-recovery rounds. Recovering the full key from each of these trails will require time complexity 2^{2q}. After the full key is recovered, we need to further verify it via the plaintext-ciphertext pair. Hence, the expected time to recover the full key from one random compact differential trail can be evaluated as follows:

$$T_0 = \sum_{q=0}^{H} (\frac{7}{8})^{H-q} \times (\frac{1}{8})^q \times \binom{H}{q} \times 2^{2q} = \sum_{q=0}^{H} (\frac{7}{8})^{H-q} \times (\frac{1}{2})^q \times \binom{H}{q} = 1.375^H.$$

Therefore, the total time complexity to recover the correct master key is

$$T_1 = N \times 1.375^H = N \times 2^{0.46H}. \tag{9}$$

Similar to the above method, we could also give a formula to compute the expected time to recover the correct key if following the simple method as discussed in [29]. It should be noted that there is no extra strategy used in the key-recovery phase in [29] if with only 2 plaintexts. Specifically, when the S-box is active, the attacker needs to try the two possible values. When the S-box is inactive, the attacker needs to try all the 8 possible values. However, since the attacker could always derive 3-bit information of the master key from one S-box in this way, he only needs to go back $b' = \lceil \frac{k-mr_3}{3m} \rceil$ rounds and the number of required S-boxes is $H' = \lceil \frac{k}{3} \rceil - mr_3$ in these b' rounds. Thus, the expected time T_2 can be formalized as follows:

$$T_2 = N \times 8^{mr_3} \times \sum_{q=0}^{H'} (\frac{7}{8})^{H'-q} \times (\frac{1}{8})^q \times \binom{H'}{q} \times 8^q \times 2^{H'-q}$$

$$= N \times 2^{3mr_3} \times \sum_{q=0}^{H'} (\frac{7}{8} \times 2)^{H'-q} \times (\frac{1}{8} \times 8)^q \times \binom{H'}{q}$$

$$= N \times 2^{3mr_3} \times (\frac{7}{4} + 1)^{H'}.$$

To explain the significant improvement achieved by our linearization techniques to recover the master key, we make a comparison between T_1 and T_2 as shown below:

$$\frac{T_2}{T_1} = \frac{2^{3mr_3} (\frac{7}{4} + 1)^{H'}}{1.375^H}.$$

Since $H = \lceil \frac{k+3mr_3}{2} \rceil$ and $H' = \lceil \frac{k}{3} \rceil - mr_3$, we have

$$\frac{T_2}{T_1} = \frac{2^{3mr_3}(\frac{7}{4}+1)^{H'}}{1.375^H} \approx \frac{2^{3mr_3+1.46(\frac{k}{3}-mr_3)}}{2^{0.46(0.5k+1.5mr_3)}} \approx 2^{0.256k+0.85mr_3}.$$

Obviously, our new key-recovery technique is much faster if compared with the method in [29].

6.3 Further Improvement

Indeed, one could further reduce the cost to retrieve the full key from a compact differential trail. Specifically, we first lower bound b as in Eq. 6. Then, when going back $r_3 + b - 1$ rounds from the ciphertext, there will be $2m(b-1)$ leaked equations and the last $r_3 + b - 1$ rounds are fully linearized. Since only $k + 3mr_3$ equations are needed and each active S-box will leak 2 equations, we only need to use

$$h = \lceil \frac{(k+3mr_3) - 2m(b-1)}{2} \rceil$$

active S-boxes in the $(r - r_3 - b)$-th round.

Therefore, in the $(r - r_3 - b)$-th round, when there are more than h active S-boxes, there is no need to guess extra equations but we still need to construct the equation system. However, when there are i ($i < h$) active S-boxes, it is necessary to guess $2h - 2i$ extra equations. Therefore, the expected time complexity can be refined as:

$$T_3 = N \times T_4 \times \sum_{i=0}^{h} \binom{m}{i} \times (\frac{7}{8})^i \times (\frac{1}{8})^{m-i} \times 2^{2h-2i}$$

$$+ N \times T_4 \times \sum_{i=h+1}^{m} \binom{m}{i} \times (\frac{7}{8})^i \times (\frac{1}{8})^{m-i}$$

$$\approx N \times T_4 \times 2^{2h} \times \sum_{i=0}^{h} \binom{m}{i} \times (\frac{7}{32})^i \times (\frac{1}{8})^{m-i}$$

$$+ N \times T_4 \times (1 - \sum_{i=0}^{h} \binom{m}{i} \times (\frac{7}{8})^i \times (\frac{1}{8})^{m-i})$$

$$< N \times T_4 \times (1 + 2^{2h} \times \sum_{i=0}^{h} \binom{m}{i} \times (\frac{7}{32})^i \times (\frac{1}{8})^{m-i})$$

where

$$T_4 = \sum_{q=0}^{m(b-1)} (\frac{7}{8})^{m(b-1)-q} \times (\frac{1}{8})^q \times \binom{m(b-1)}{q} \times 2^{2q} = 2^{0.46m(b-1)}.$$

There is no simple approximation for T_3 and we therefore provide a loose upper bound which can be easily calculated, as specified below:

$$T_3 < N \times T_4 \times (1 + 2^{2h} \times \sum_{i=0}^{m} \binom{m}{i} \times (\frac{7}{32})^i \times (\frac{1}{8})^{m-i}) = N \times T_4 \times (1 + 2^{2h-1.54m}).$$

Hence, in general, we can use the following formula Eq. 10 to calculate the time complexity to retrieve the full key from N compact differential trails.

$$T_3 \approx N \times 2^{0.46m(b-1)} \times (1 + 2^{2h-1.54m}). \tag{10}$$

It is not surprising that one could go back more than $b + r_3$ rounds to obtain more leaked linear equations if $b \leq r_1 + r_2$. However, the cost of linearization cannot be neglected, i.e. it is necessary to introduce more variables to represent the 3 input bits of an inactive S-box. In other words, although more linear equations can be derived, more variables are involved into the equation system. Note that we need to introduce 3 extra variables to linearize an inactive S-box and only 2 linear equations can be derived from an active S-box. For such a case, it is difficult to give a simple formula describing the expected time complexity to retrieve the full key. Thus, the formula Eq. 10 can be viewed as an upper bound.

7   Applications

The above two algebraic techniques can be utilized to further understand the security of LowMC as well as LowMC-M. LowMC is the underlying block cipher used in Picnic, which is an alternative third-round candidate in NIST's post-quantum cryptography competition. For LowMC-M, it is a family of block ciphers based on LowMC which allows to insert a backdoor.

7.1   Applications to LowMC with a Partial S-Box Layer

In this section, we describe how to apply our techniques to instantiations with a partial S-box layer. The results are summarized in Table 1. All these attacks only require 2 chosen plaintexts and negligible memory. For better understanding, we take the attack on the parameter $(n, k, m, D, R) = (128, 128, 10, 1, 20)$ for instance.

When $(n, k, m, D) = (128, 128, 10, 1)$, as explained in the extended framework, $r_3 = 0$ as there are only two allowed plaintexts for each instantiation and $r_0 = \lfloor \frac{128}{30} \rfloor = 4$. According to Eq. 6, $b = 7$. Therefore, the time complexity to retrieve the master key becomes $T_3 \approx 2^{1.86m(r_1+r_2)-128} \times 2^{0.46m(b-1)} = 2^{18.6(r_1+r_2)-81.8} < 2^{128}$ based on Eq. 10. The time complexity to enumerate differences is $max(1.86mr_2, m(1.86r_2 + 3r_1 - 2) - n) = max(18.6r_2, 18.6r_2 + 30r_1 - 148) < 2^{128}$ based on Eq. 5 while $18.6r_2 < 128$ (Eq. 4) and $18.6r_2 + 30r_1 < 276$ (Eq. 3) should hold. Therefore, we have $r_1 + r_2 \leq 11$, $r_2 \leq 6$, $18.6r_2 + 30r_1 \leq 276$. To maximize $r_1 + r_2$ and minimize the total time complexity, we can choose

$r_1 = 5$ and $r_2 = 6$. In this way, the time complexity to recover the master key is $2^{122.8}$ while the time complexity to enumerate differences is $max(2^{111.6}, 2^{111.8}) = 2^{111.8}$. Therefore, we could break 15 (out of 20) rounds of LowMC taking the parameter $(n, k, m, D) = (128, 128, 10, 1)$ with time complexity $2^{122.8}$ and only 2 chosen plaintexts.

Remark. It is not surprising to further extend r_1 by using a huge amount of memory when $n = k$ for some parameters. However, such attacks are indeed less effective compared with a pure exhaustive search. Therefore, we omit the simple extension of how to attack more rounds using huge memory.

On the other hand, when $n \gg k$, we could significantly improve r_1 as the constraint becomes $3r_1 < n$ when using our efficient technique to reduce the memory complexity, while the constraint is $\lambda_1^{r_1} < min(2^{nd}, 2^k)$ in the extended framework. For example, when attacking $(n, k, m, D) = (1024, 128, 1, 1)$, r_1 cannot reach 342 without our technique to reduce the memory complexity since $2^{1.86r_1} < 2^{128}$ has to be satisfied if simply enumerating the reachable differences.

Table 1. The results for LowMC with a partial S-box layer

n	k	m	D	R	r_0	r_1	r_2	r_3	r	Data	Time	Memory	Success Pro.
128	128	1	1	182	42	43	67	0	152	2	$2^{124.62}$	negligible	1
128	128	10	1	20	4	5	6	0	15	2	$2^{122.8}$	negligible	1
192	192	1	1	273	64	64	101	0	229	2	$2^{187.86}$	negligible	1
192	192	10	1	30	6	7	10	0	23	2	2^{186}	negligible	1
256	256	1	1	363	85	86	137	0	306	2	$2^{254.82}$	negligible	1
256	256	10	1	38	8	9	13	0	30	2	$2^{241.8}$	negligible	1
1024	128	1	1	776	341	342	66	0	749	2	$2^{122.76}$	negligible	1
1024	256	1	1	819	341	342	136	0	819	2	2^{253}	negligible	1

7.2   Applications to LowMC-M

The only difference between LowMC and LowMC-M is that there is an additional operation after the key addition, i.e. the sub-tweak addition. Since the sub-tweaks are generated with an XOF function, the attacker loses the capability to directly control the difference of the sub-tweaks. However, the additional degree of freedom provided by the tweak can still be utilized to further extend r_0.

Maximizing r_0 based on [9]. A very recent work [9] shows how to compute the maximal value of r_0 with a birthday search method. In a word, one could construct a probability-1 differential trail for the first r_0 rounds with time complexity $2^{\frac{3mr_0-n}{2}}$ and negligible memory in an offline phase. Therefore, r_0 should satisfy the following constraint:

$$\frac{3mr_0 - n}{2} < k. \tag{11}$$

A detailed description can be referred to Appendix B. We will use this method to maximize r_0 in our attacks.

Since the allowed data complexity is 2^{64} for all instances of LowMC-M, we can also construct a differential trail in the last r_3 rounds where no active S-boxes exist with 2^{3mr_3+1} attempts, i.e. $3mr_3 \leq 63$. Similar to the cryptanalysis of LowMC, we could compute (r_0, r_1, r_2, r_3) and the corresponding total time complexity, as summarized in Table 2. It should be mentioned that LowMC-M has moved to LowMC-M v2 by taking our attacks into account.

Table 2. The results for LowMC-M

n	k	m	D	R	r_0	r_1	r_2	r_3	r	Data	Time	Memory	Success Pro.
128	128	1	64	208	122	43	64	21	250	2^{64}	2^{120}	negligible	1
128	128	2	64	104	61	22	32	10	125	2^{61}	2^{120}	negligible	1
128	128	3	64	70	40	15	21	7	83	2^{64}	$2^{118.18}$	negligible	1
128	128	10	64	23	12	5	6	2	25	2^{61}	2^{118}	negligible	1
256	256	1	64	384	253	86	136	21	496	2^{64}	$2^{252.96}$	negligible	1
256	256	3	64	129	83	29	45	7	164	2^{64}	$2^{250.1}$	negligible	1
256	256	20	64	21	12	5	6	1	24	2^{61}	2^{232}	negligible	1

Comparison. Compared with the differential-linear attacks [9] on LowMC-M, our attacks are always better. As we utilized the idea in [9] to find a weak tweak pair, with the same time complexity to find a weak tweak pair, r_0 is always the same in their attacks and our attacks. Then, r_1 is also almost the same in their attacks and our attacks, though sometimes we will have a slightly larger r_1 according to Eq. 5. The most evident advantage of our attacks exists in r_2 and r_3. With the same data, there are extra r_3 rounds in our attacks while r_3 is always zero in differential-linear attacks [9]. For r_2, it is bounded by $1.86mr_2 < n$ in our attacks while it is bounded by $3mr_2 < n$ in [9] as $3m$ key bits are all guessed to reverse one round. Consequently, with the same data and the same time to find a weak tweak pair, our attacks are always better than the differential-linear attacks in [9], i.e. a larger number of rounds can be attacked.

8   A Refined Attack Framework for the Full S-Box Layer

The above two techniques are quite general and therefore they can be applied to arbitrary instances of LowMC. However, when it comes to a full S-Box layer, we need to make extra efforts to improve the extended attack framework developed by the designers of LowMC. Specifically, it is impossible to construct a probability-1 differential trail anymore in the first few rounds. On the other hand, the cost of difference enumeration becomes rather high as a full S-box layer is applied.

To overcome the obstacle that there is no probability-1 differential trail, we turn to consider how to choose a desirable input difference such that it will activate a small number of S-boxes as possible in the first two rounds. However, since the linear layer is randomly generated, it is difficult to provide an accurate answer. Thus, similar to the method to calculate the time complexity to retrieve the full key, the general case is taken into account and we calculate the expectation of the number of inactive S-boxes in the first two rounds and verify it via experiments.

To reduce the cost of the difference enumeration, we will demonstrate that it is possible to reduce the problem of enumerating differences to the problem of enumerating the solutions of a linear equation system by exploiting our observations on the S-box.

8.1   Maximizing the Number of Inactive S-Boxes

To maximize the number of inactive S-boxes in the first two rounds, we consider the case when there is only one active S-box in the first round, which can obviously reduce the total number of reachable differences after two rounds.

First, consider a simple related problem. Suppose there are two boolean vectors $\mu = (\mu_0, \mu_1, \mu_2) \in \mathbb{F}_2^3$ and $\gamma = (\gamma_0, \gamma_1, \gamma_2) \in \mathbb{F}_2^3$. For a random binary matrix M of size 3×3 satisfying

$$\gamma = M \times \mu,$$

it can be calculated that

$$Pr[(\gamma_0, \gamma_1, \gamma_2) = (0,0,0) | (\mu_0, \mu_1, \mu_2) \neq (0,0,0)] = 2^{-3}.$$

Note that $\Delta_1 = L_0 \times \Delta_0^S$, where Δ_1 and Δ_0^S are two Boolean vectors of size n and L_0 is a $n \times n$ invertible binary matrix. When there is only one active S-box in the first round, we can know that there is only one non-zero triple $(\Delta_0^S[3i], \Delta_0^S[3i+1], \Delta_0^S[3i+2])$ $(0 \leq i < \frac{n}{3})$.

Consider a randomly generated L_0 and a fixed value of Δ_0^S with only one non-zero triple $(\Delta_0^S[3i], \Delta_0^S[3i+1], \Delta_0^S[3i+2])$. Denote the event by α that $(\Delta_0^S[3i], \Delta_0^S[3i+1], \Delta_0^S[3i+2]) \neq (0,0,0)$. Denote by IA the number of inactive S-boxes in the second round. In this way, we could calculate the conditional probability that there are q inactive S-boxes under α happens, as specified below:

$$Pr[IA = q|\alpha] = \binom{\frac{n}{3}}{q} \times 2^{-3q} \times (\frac{7}{8})^{\frac{n}{3}-q},$$

Since that there are 7 assignments for a non-zero triple $(\Delta_0^S[3i], \Delta_0^S[3i+1], \Delta_0^S[3i+2])$ and there are $\frac{n}{3}$ such triples, there are in total $7 \times \frac{n}{3}$ assignments for Δ_0^S satisfying that there is only one active S-box in the first round. Hence, we can expect to find

$$V(n, q) = \frac{n}{3} \times 7 \times Pr[IA = q|\alpha]. \tag{12}$$

required assignments for Δ_0^S which can ensure q inactive S-boxes in the second round. In other words, when $V(n, q) > 1$, it is expected to find more than 1 assignments for Δ_0^S such that there are q inactive S-boxes in the second round.

8.2   Enumerating Differences via Solving Equations

Assuming Δ_i and Δ_{i+1}^S are fixed and known, our aim is to enumerate all the solutions for Δ_i^S such that they can reach Δ_{i+1}^S.

First, consider the case where all the S-boxes in the $(i+1)$-th and $(i+2)$-th rounds are active. In this case, there are $4^{\frac{n}{3}}$ possible reachable differences for Δ_{i+1} and each reachable difference of Δ_{i+1} can reach Δ_{i+1}^S with probability $2^{-\frac{n}{3}}$ as each output difference can correspond to 4 different input differences through the 3-bit S-box of LowMC. Thus, it is expected to find the valid $2^{\frac{n}{3}}$ solutions of Δ_{i+1} in $4^{\frac{n}{3}}$ time using the simple difference enumeration.

However, similar to our technique to reduce the memory complexity, based on Observation 2, we could introduce $2 \times \frac{n}{3}$ variables to represent the possible values of Δ_i^S. In this way, Δ_{i+1} will be linear in these variables. Furthermore, based on Observation 2, there will be $\frac{n}{3}$ linear constraints on Δ_{i+1}. Therefore, an equation system of size $\frac{n}{3}$ in terms of $2 \times \frac{n}{3}$ variables is constructed and each solution of the equation system will correspond to a valid connection between Δ_i and Δ_{i+1}^S. Thus, we could find the valid $2^{\frac{n}{3}}$ solutions in only $2^{\frac{n}{3}}$ time.

After discussing the case where all the S-boxes are active, we consider the general case. Specifically, assume there are w random pairs $(\Delta_i, \Delta_{i+1}^S)$. The expected time complexity to enumerate all the valid difference transitions $\Delta_i \rightarrow \Delta_{i+1}^S$ for these w random pairs using our techniques can be formalized as follows.

$$T_5 = \left(\sum_{t=0}^{\lfloor 0.5m \rfloor} \binom{m}{t} \times \left(\frac{1}{8}\right)^t \times \left(\frac{7}{8}\right)^{m-t} \times \sum_{j=0}^{\lfloor 0.5m \rfloor - t} \binom{m}{j} \times \left(\frac{1}{8}\right)^j \times \left(\frac{7}{8}\right)^{m-j} \times 2^{m-2j-2t} \right) w$$

$$+ \left(1 - \sum_{t=0}^{\lfloor 0.5m \rfloor} \binom{m}{t} \times \left(\frac{1}{8}\right)^t \times \left(\frac{7}{8}\right)^{m-t} \times \sum_{j=0}^{\lfloor 0.5m \rfloor - t} \binom{m}{j} \times \left(\frac{1}{8}\right)^j \times \left(\frac{7}{8}\right)^{m-j} \right) w$$

$$\approx \left(\sum_{t=0}^{\lfloor 0.5m \rfloor} \binom{m}{t} \times \left(\frac{1}{8}\right)^t \times \left(\frac{7}{8}\right)^{m-t} \times \sum_{j=0}^{\lfloor 0.5m \rfloor - t} \binom{m}{j} \times \left(\frac{1}{8}\right)^j \times \left(\frac{7}{8}\right)^{m-j} \times 2^{m-2j-2t} \right) w + w.$$

Specifically, when there are t and j inactive S-boxes in the $(i+2)$-th round and $(i+1)$-th round, respectively, the equation system is of size $3t + (m-t) = m + 2t$ and in terms of $2(m-j)$ variables. Thus, for the case $2(m-j) - (m+2t) = m - 2j - 2t < 0 \rightarrow 2j + 2t > m$, there is no need to enumerate the solutions and we only need to construct the equation system with time 1. However, for the case $2j + 2t \leq m$, we need to construct the equation system as well as enumerate the $2^{m-2j-2t}$ solutions.

As $m > 1$, a loose upper bound for T_5 can be as follows:

$$T_5 < w + w \times 2^m \times \left(\frac{29}{32}\right)^m \times \left(\frac{29}{32}\right)^m \approx w \times 2^{0.716m} \tag{13}$$

A fixed random Δ_{i+1}^S. We also feel interested in that Δ_{i+1}^S takes a fixed random value while Δ_i takes w random values, which is exactly the case in our attack on 4-round LowMC with a full S-box layer.

When there are $t \leq \lfloor 0.5m \rfloor$ inactive S-boxes in the $(i+2)$-th round, the time complexity T_5 to enumerate all the valid difference transitions can be refined as below:

$$
T_5 = (\sum_{j=0}^{\lfloor 0.5m \rfloor - t} \binom{m}{j} \times (\frac{1}{8})^j \times (\frac{7}{8})^{m-j} \times 2^{m-2j-2t})w
$$

$$
+ (1 - \sum_{j=0}^{\lfloor 0.5m \rfloor - t} \binom{m}{j} \times (\frac{1}{8})^j \times (\frac{7}{8})^{m-j})w
$$

$$
= (\sum_{j=0}^{\lfloor 0.5m \rfloor - t} \binom{m}{j} \times (\frac{1}{8})^j \times (\frac{7}{8})^{m-j} \times 2^{m-2j-2t})w + w.
$$

Similarly, a bound for T_5 can be as follows:

$$
T_5 < w + w \times 2^{m-2t} \times (\frac{29}{32})^m \approx w + w \times 2^{0.858m-2t}. \tag{14}
$$

When there are $t > \lfloor 0.5m \rfloor$ inactive S-boxes in the $(i+2)$-th round, the time complexity T_5 to enumerate all the valid difference transitions can be refined as below:

$$
T_5 = (\sum_{j=0}^{m} \binom{m}{j} \times (\frac{1}{8})^j \times (\frac{7}{8})^{m-j})w = w \tag{15}
$$

Combining Eq. 14 and Eq. 15, we can know that whatever value t takes, the following bound for T_5 holds

$$
T_5 < w + w \times 2^{0.858m-2t}. \tag{16}
$$

8.3 Applications to 4-Round LowMC with a Full S-Box Layer

As can be found in the latest released Picnic3 document, three recommended parameters $(n, k, m, D) \in \{(129, 129, 43, 1), (192, 192, 64, 1), (255, 255, 85, 1)\}$ with $R = 4$ are adopted to achieve the required security. By increasing the number of rounds by 1, i.e. $R = 5$, the designers claim that Picnic3 will provide stronger security. Anyway, 4-round LowMC with a full S-box layer is the recommended instance and such three parameters are deemed as secure against the existing attacks [2]. In the following, we explain how to break such 3 parameters with our linearization techniques under the difference enumeration attack framework.

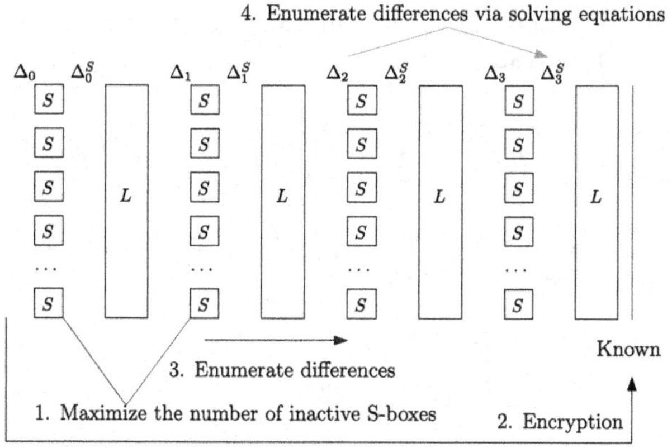

Fig. 6. The attack framework for 4-round LowMC with a full S-box layer

As depicted in Fig. 6, our attack procedure consists of 4 steps:

Step 1: According to Eq. 12, we find a suitable assignment for Δ_0^S such that the number of inactive S-boxes in the 2nd round can be maximized and there is only one active S-box in the first round. Denote the number of inactive S-boxes in the 2nd round by q.

Step 2: Choose a value for Δ_0 such that it can reach Δ_0^S and encrypt two arbitrary plaintexts whose difference equals Δ_0. Collect the corresponding ciphertexts and compute Δ_3^S.

Step 3: Enumerate 4^{m-q} possible difference transitions from Δ_1 to Δ_2. For each possible difference transition, move to Step 4.

Step 4: For each obtained Δ_2, we enumerate the possible difference transitions from Δ_2 to Δ_3^S via solving a linear equation system, as detailed above. For each solution of the equation system, a compact differential trail is obtained and we retrieve the full key from it using our linearization techniques.

Although the formula to calculate the time complexity to retrieve the full key has been given, we should refine it for the attack on 4-round LowMC with a full S-box layer. As can be observed in our attack procedure, once guessing Δ_0^S from its 4 possible values, we already collect two linear equations in terms of the master key and the plaintexts which can ensure that $\Delta_0 \to \Delta_0^S$ is deterministic based on Observation 1.

On the other hand, due to a sufficiently large number of S-boxes in each round, for the last round, we can introduce extra variables to represent the output bits of the inactive S-boxes. In this way, it is required to extract more than $k-2$ linear equations when a compact differential trail is confirmed. Specifically, assuming that there are t inactive S-boxes in the 4th round, the required number of equations becomes $3t + k - 2$. Therefore, we try to extract linear equations from the active S-boxes in the 3rd round and 2nd round, which requires that all the S-boxes in the 3rd are linearized. Therefore, the following formula can be used to estimate the expected time complexity to retrieve the full key from all compatible differential trails:

$$
\begin{aligned}
T_6 = 4^{m-q} \times (& \sum_{t=0}^{\lfloor \frac{6m-k+2-2q}{5} \rfloor} \binom{m}{t} \times (\tfrac{1}{8})^t \times (\tfrac{7}{8})^{m-t} \\
& \times \sum_{j=0}^{m} \binom{m}{j} \times (\tfrac{1}{8})^j \times (\tfrac{7}{8})^{m-j} \times 2^{2j} \times 2^{m-2j-2t} \\
& + \sum_{t=\lfloor \frac{6m-k+2-2q}{5} \rfloor +1}^{m} \binom{m}{t} \times (\tfrac{1}{8})^t \times (\tfrac{7}{8})^{m-t} \\
& \times \sum_{j=0}^{m} \binom{m}{j} \times (\tfrac{1}{8})^j \times (\tfrac{7}{8})^{m-j} \times 2^{2j} \\
& \times 2^{(3t+k-2)-(2(m-t)+2m+2(m-q))} \times 2^{m-2j-2t})
\end{aligned}
$$

Specifically, when there are t and j inactive S-boxes in the 4th and 3rd round, respectively, the equation system used to retrieve the master key will be of size $2+2(m-t)+2m+2(m-q)$ and in terms of $3t+k$ variables. More specifically, from the assumed difference transition $\Delta_0 \rightarrow \Delta_0^S$, two linear equations in terms of the master key and the plaintext can be obtained. From the 4th round, as there are $(m-t)$ active S-boxes, $2(m-t)$ equations are obtained. For the 3rd round, we linearize all the j inactive S-boxes by guessing two extra equations based on Observation 3, i.e. guessing two output bits of each inactive S-box. In this way, there will always be $2m$ equations derived from the 3rd round. For the 2nd round, as the 4th round and 3rd round are fully linearized and there are $(m-q)$ active S-boxes, we can obtain $2(m-q)$ linear equations in the 2nd round. Thus, if $3t+k-(2+2(m-t)+2m+2(m-q)) < 0 \rightarrow 5t < 6m-k+2-2q$, the cost is to establish the equation system. When $5t \geq 6m - k + 2 - 2q$, it is necessary to enumerate all the $2^{(3t+k-2)-(2(m-t)+2m+2(m-q))}$ solutions and check them via the plaintext-ciphertext pair.

Δ_3^S **is a fixed random value.** In our attack using only two chosen plaintexts, Δ_3^S is a random fixed value while Δ_2^S behaves randomly. Similar to computing the upper bound for the time complexity to enumerate differences for this case, i.e. Eq. 14 and Eq. 15, we also try to deal with the time complexity T_6 to retrieve the master key for this case. Similarly, we assume that there are t inactive S-boxes in the 4th round.

When $t \leq \lfloor \frac{6m-k+2-2q}{5} \rfloor$, we have

$$
T_6 = 4^{m-q} \times \sum_{j=0}^{m} \binom{m}{j} \times (\tfrac{1}{8})^j \times (\tfrac{7}{8})^{m-j} \times 2^{2j} \times 2^{m-2j-2t} = 2^{3m-2q-2t} \quad (17)
$$

When $t > \lfloor \frac{6m-k+2-2q}{5} \rfloor$, we have

$$T_6 = 4^{m-q} \times \sum_{j=0}^{m} \binom{m}{j} \times (\frac{1}{8})^j \times (\frac{7}{8})^{m-j} \times 2^{2j}$$

$$\times 2^{-6m+k-2+2q+5t} \times 2^{m-2j-2t} = 2^{-3m+3t+k-2}$$

As $k = 3m$ for the construction using a full s-box layer, when $t > \lfloor \frac{6m-k+2-2q}{5} \rfloor$, we indeed have

$$T_6 = 2^{3t-2}. \tag{18}$$

Remark. Indeed, when $t \leq \lfloor \frac{6m-k+2-2q}{5} \rfloor$, Eq. 17 is an overestimation of the time complexity to retrieve the key. Specifically, when there are a sufficient number of active S-boxes in the 3rd round, there is no need to linearize the nonactive S-boxes in the 3rd round. Formally, assuming that there are j inactive S-boxes in the 3rd round, when $2 \times (m - j + m - t) + 2 \geq k + 3 \times t$, i.e. $5t \leq 4m - k + 2 - 2j < 6m - 2q - k + 2$, the time complexity to retrieve the key is 1 rather than 2^{2j}. Therefore, Eq. 17 is an overestimation of the time complexity in order to achieve a simple approximation of the time complexity.

Attacks on $(129, 129, 43, 1, 4)$. For $(n, k, m, D, R) = (129, 129, 43, 1, 4)$, we have $V(129, 11) > 1$ based on Eq. 12, i.e. we can expect to find an assignment to Δ_0^S such that there will be $q = 11^4$ inactive S-boxes in the 2nd round. After such a Δ_0^S is chosen, we randomly choose Δ_0 such that $\Delta_0 \to \Delta_0^S$ is valid. There are 4 different values of Δ_0^S for such a Δ_0 and one of Δ_0^S is expected to inactivate 11 S-boxes in the second round.

The time complexity to retrieve the master key from all valid 4-round compact differential trails is related to the value of (t, q). As $t \sim \mathcal{B}(m, \frac{1}{8})$ where $\mathcal{B}$ represents the binomial distribution, we can expect $t = 5$. In this way, we have $5t = 25 < 6m - k + 2 - 2q = 131 - 2q$ whatever value q $(0 \leq q \leq m)$ takes. In other words, for the expected case $q = 11$, the time complexity to retrieve the master key is $2^{3m-2q-2t} = 2^{97}$ based on Eq. 17. By taking the remaining 3 different possible values of Δ_0^S into account, even for the worst case $(q = 0)$, the total time complexity to retrieve the master key for all 4 possible values of Δ_0^S will not exceed $3 \times 2^{3m-2t} = 2^{120.6}$, i.e. less than exhaustive key search.

For the time complexity to enumerate the difference, for the expected case $q = 11$, we have $T_5 < 2^{2m-2q} \times (1 + 2^{0.858m-2t}) = 2^{2.858m-2q-2t} + 2^{2m-2q} = 2^{90.9}$ based on Eq. 16. For the worst case $q = 0$, we have $T_5 < 2^{2.858m-2t} = 2^{112.9}$. Therefore, the total time complexity to enumerate the difference will not exceed $3 \times 2^{112.9} \approx 2^{114.5}$, i.e. less than exhaustive key search.

As t increases, T_5 will become smaller. However, when $5t \geq 6m - k + 2 - 2q = 132 - 2q$, we need to use another formula to calculate the time complexity to retrieve the master key, i.e. $T_6 = 2^{3t-2}$ as shown in Eq. 18. As $3t < 3m = k$ must

---

[4] Experiments show that it is better to choose $q = 11$, though $V(129, 12) > 1$.

holds, it means that the time complexity T_6 is always smaller than that of the exhaustive search.

As $Pr[t \geq 4] \approx 0.62$ and $Pr[42 \leq t \leq 43] \approx 0$, we conclude that with success probability 0.62, the total time complexity to retrieve the master key will be $max(3 \times 2^{3m-2t}, 4 \times 2^{3 \times 41-2}) = 2^{122.6}$ and the total time complexity to enumerate differences will not exceed $3 \times 2^{2.858m-2t} < 2^{117.5}$. Thus, we can break the parameter $(n, k, m, D, R) = (129, 129, 43, 1, 4)$ with time complexity less than $2^{122.6}$ and success probability 0.62.

As $Pr[t \geq 2] \approx 0.97$ and $Pr[36 \leq t \leq 43] \approx 0$, if further reducing the success probability to $0.97 \times 0.25 = 0.24$, i.e. $\Delta_0 \rightarrow \Delta_0^S$ is assumed to be deterministic and we expect $q = 11$, the time complexity to enumerate the difference will not exceed $2^{2m-2q} + 2^{2.858m-2q-2t} \approx 2^{96.9}$ and the time complexity to retrieve the master key be $max(2^{3m-2q-2t}, 2^{3t-2}) < 2^{104}$.

A similar detailed description of our attacks on another two parameters can be referred to Appendix C. All the results are summarized in Eq. 3. We remark that for the construction with a full S-box layer, if more data is allowed, our technique may not be competitive with the higher-order differential attack. Indeed, as the number of allowed data increases, such a construction will have much more rounds [2].

Table 3. The results for 4-round LowMC with a full S-box layer

n	k	m	D	R	Data	Time	Memory	Success Pro.
129	129	43	1	4	2	$2^{122.6}$	negligible	0.62
129	129	43	1	4	2	2^{104}	negligible	0.24
192	192	64	1	4	2	$2^{187.6}$	negligible	0.99
192	192	64	1	4	2	2^{180}	negligible	0.82
192	192	64	1	4	2	2^{156}	negligible	0.247
255	255	85	1	4	2	$2^{246.6}$	negligible	0.986
255	255	85	1	4	2	$2^{236.6}$	negligible	0.848
255	255	85	1	4	2	2^{208}	negligible	0.2465

9   Experiments

To confirm the correctness of our methods, we performed experiments[5] on two toy LowMC instances with parameters $(n, k, m, D, R) = (20, 20, 1, 1, 23)$ and $(n, k, m, D, R) = (21, 21, 7, 1, 4)$, respectively.

For the first parameter, $R = 23$ is the largest number of rounds that can be attacked, i.e. $r_0 = 6$, $r_1 = 7$ and $r_2 = 10$. The expected number of iterations to enumerate the differences is estimated as $2^{1.86r_2} \approx 397336$. The expected number

---
[5] See https://github.com/LFKOKAMI/LowMC_Diff_Enu.git for the code.

of valid compact differential trails is $2^{1.86(r_1+r_2)-n} \approx 3147$. Experimental results indeed match well with the estimated values[6]. As the guessing times to recover the key is affected by the number of inactive S-boxes, for each valid compact differential trail obtained in the experiments, we counted the number of inactive S-boxes in the last 10 rounds, which will dominate the time to recover the key as each S-box will give us 2 equations and there are 10 S-boxes in the last 10 rounds. The distribution of the number of inactive S-boxes is somewhat better than expected, thus resulting that the guessing times to recover the key is better than the estimated guessing times $3147 \times 2^{0.46 \times 10} \approx 76319$. Anyway, the total time complexity is dominated by the backward difference enumeration.

For the parameter $(n, k, m, D, R) = (21, 21, 7, 1, 4)$, we constrained that the difference transition in the first round follows our expectation by checking Δ_0^s when encrypting two plaintexts, i.e. the number of inactive S-boxes in the second round will be maximized. Based on the generated matrix L_0, there will be 3 inactive S-boxes in the second round. Then, the output difference of the first round is fixed and we enumerate the output differences of the second round and compute all possible compact differential trails by solving an equation system. In several experiments with 10000 tests each, the number of iterations to enumerate all compact differential trails is smaller than the upper bound computed based on Eq. 16 with probability higher than 0.99 and they are almost the same in the remaining tests. Then, the guessing times to recover the key is computed based on the number of active S-boxes in the last 3 rounds for each valid compact differential trail by summing the costs of guesses[7] or enumerating solutions. It is found that the obtained value is almost the same with the theoretical value computed based on Eq. 17 or Eq. 18.

10   Conclusion

Benefiting from the low-degree S-box and the linear key schedule function of LowMC, we developed an efficient algebraic technique to solve a general problem of how to retrieve the key if given a single pair of (plaintext, ciphertext) along with its compact differential trail. Such a technique is quite meaningful as much more differential trail candidates are allowed to exist under the difference enumeration attack framework. As a result, we could significantly extend the number of attacked rounds even with only 2 chosen plaintexts.

On the other hand, based on Bar-On et al.'s algorithm and our observation on the property of the 3-bit S-box in LowMC, the difference enumeration in the original difference enumeration attack is optimized and can be achieved with negligible memory. The new strategy to enumerate differences performs quite well for the cases when the block size is much larger and when a full S-box layer is adopted. Especially for the latter case, much more invalid difference transitions

---

[6] In several experiments with 1000 random tests each, the average number of iterations to enumerate differences is 392500 ± 12500 and the average number of valid compact differential trails is 3425 ± 125.

[7] The S-boxes in the 3rd round will be fully linearized, though it is an overestimation.

can be filtered out in advance as all valid difference transitions are constrained by a linear equation system.

Combining all our techniques, we violate the security claim for some instances of LowMC. Especially, the 3 recommended parameters of LowMC used in Picnic3 are shown to be insecure against our attacks. As the backdoor cipher LowMC-M is built on LowMC, making progress in the cryptanalysis of LowMC directly threatens the security claim for 7 instances of LowMC-M even without finding the backdoor.

Acknowledgement. We thank the reviewers of EUROCRYPT 2021 and CRYPTO 2021 for their insightful comments. Especially, we thank one reviewer for suggesting that we generalize our observations to an arbitrary 3-bit APN S-box. We also thank Itai Dinur for his advice to significantly improve this paper. Moreover, we thank Gaoli Wang for pointing out some typos. Fukang Liu is supported by the National Key Research and Development Program of China (Grant No. 2020YFA0712300), the National Natural Science Foundation of China (Grant No.61632012, No. 62072181), the Peng Cheng Laboratory Project of Guangdong Province (Grant No. PCL2018KP004), the International Science and Technology Cooperation Projects (No. 61961146004) and the Invitation Programs for Foreigner-based Researchers of NICT. Takanori Isobe is supported by JST, PRESTO Grant Number JPMJPR2031, Grant-inAid for Scientific Research (B) (KAKENHI 19H02141) for Japan Society for the Promotion of Science, and Support Center for Advanced Telecommunications Technology Research (SCAT).

A   Description of LowMC-M

LowMC-M [27] is a family of tweakable block ciphers built on LowMC, which is introduced by Peyrin and Wang at CRYPTO 2020. The feature of LowMC-M is that backdoors can be inserted in the instantiation. The only difference between LowMC and LowMC-M is that there is an addition operation AddSubTweak (**AT**) after **AK** and **WK**. In other words, the round function in the $(i + 1)$-round $(0 \leq i \leq R - 1)$ can be described as follows:

1. SBoxLayer (**SB**): Same with LowMC.
2. LinearLayer (**L**): Same with LowMC.
3. ConstantAddition (**AC**): Same with LowMC.
4. KeyAddition (**AK**): Same with LowMC.
5. AddSubTweak (**AT**): Add an n-bit sub-tweak TW_{i+1} to the n-bit state.

For the state after **WK**, it will also be XORed with an n-bit sub-tweak TW_0.

To strengthen the security of the backdoors, TW_i $(0 \leq i \leq R)$ are generated via an extendable-output-function (XOF) function. SHAKE-128 and SHAKE-256 are used as the XOF functions in LowMC-M for 128-bit and 256-bit security respectively. Specifically, the tweak TW is the input of the XOF function and the corresponding $n(R+1)$-bit output will be split into $(R+1)$ sub-tweaks TW_i, i.e. $(TW_0, TW_1, \cdots, TW_R) \leftarrow \mathrm{XOF}(TW)$.

B   Exploiting the Tweak to Maximize r_0 for LowMC-M

In brief, when there is no active S-box in the first r_0 rounds, an attacker can construct a linear equation system of size $3mr_0$ and in terms of Δ_0 as well as the difference of the sub-tweaks $(\Delta TW_0, \cdots, \Delta TW_{r_0-1})$. When the sub-tweaks are fixed, the equation system is thus only in terms of Δ_0, i.e. n variables. Therefore, when $3mr_0 > n$, the equation system is consistent with probability 2^{n-3mr_0}. Thus, the attacker needs to find an assignment for $(\Delta TW_0, \cdots, \Delta TW_{r_0-1})$ such that the constructed equation system is consistent.

To achieve this goal, the equation system will be first re-organized by placing $(\Delta TW_0, \cdots, \Delta TW_{r_0-1})$ on the right-hand of the equation system and placing Δ_0 on the left-hand of the equation system. In other words, the equation system becomes

$$A \cdot \Delta_0 = B \cdot (\Delta TW_0, \cdots, \Delta TW_{r_0-1}),$$

where A is a binary matrix of size $3mr_0 \times n$ and B is a binary matrix of size $3mr_0 \times nr_0$. To ensure that there is a solution to Δ_0, one can derive an equation system of size $3mr_0 - n$ and only in terms of $(\Delta TW_0, \cdots, \Delta TW_{r_0-1})$. Specifically, apply a transform $A'_{3mr_0 \times 3mr_0}$ to both A and B such that the first n rows of $A' \cdot A$ is an identity matrix and the remaining $(3mr_0 - n)$ rows of $A' \cdot A$ are all zero. In this way, we only need to focus on the last $(3mr_0 - n)$ rows of $A' \cdot B$, i.e. a linear equation system of size $3mr_0 - n$ and in terms of $(\Delta TW_0, \cdots, \Delta TW_{r_0-1})$ can be derived to ensure that there is always a solution to Δ_0. Thus, with a parallel collision search [32], it is expected to find $(\Delta TW_0, \cdots, \Delta TW_{r_0-1})$ with time complexity $2^{\frac{3mr_0-n}{2}}$ and negligible memory satisfying such an equation system. Therefore, the constraint for r_0 becomes

$$\frac{3mr_0 - n}{2} < k. \tag{19}$$

In this way, one could find the desirable pair of tweaks as well as the plaintext difference Δ_0 with time complexity $2^{\frac{3mr_0-n}{2}}$. This is the method given in [9] to maximize r_0.

C   Explanation of the Attacks on LowMC with a Full S-box Layer

Attacks on $(192, 192, 64, 1, 4)$. Similar to the above analysis, we first confirm q. As $V(192, 15) > 1$ based on Eq. 12, we can expect to always find an assignment to Δ_0^S such that there will be $q = 15^8$ inactive S-boxes in the 2nd round.

As $Pr[t \geq 3] \approx 0.99$ and $Pr[62 \leq t \leq 64] \approx 0$, based on Eq. 17 and Eq. 18, the time complexity to retrieve the master key will be $max(3 \times 2^{3m-2t}, 4 \times 2^{3t-2}) <$

---

[8] It can be found that $V(192, 16)$ is only slightly greater than 1. Experiments show that it is better to choose $q = 15$.

$2^{187.6}$. Based on Eq. 16, the time complexity to enumerate the difference is less than $3 \times (2^{2m} + 2^{2m-2t+0.858m}) = 3 \times (2^{2m} + 2^{2.858m-2t}) < 2^{178.5}$. Therefore, we could break $(n, k, m, D, R) = (192, 192, 64, 1, 4)$ with time complexity less than $2^{187.6}$ and success probability 0.99.

As $Pr[t \geq 6] = 0.82$ and $Pr[61 \leq t \leq 64] \approx 0$, the time complexity to retrieve the master key will be $max(3 \times 2^{3m-2t}, 4 \times 2^{3t-2}) = 2^{180}$, while the time complexity to enumerate the differences will not exceed $3 \times (2^{2m} + 2^{2.858m-2t}) < 2^{170.9}$. Therefore, we could break $(n, k, m, D, R) = (192, 192, 64, 1, 4)$ with time complexity less than 2^{180} and success probability 0.82.

To further reduce the success probability, we focus on the expected case $q = 15$ and $3 \leq t \leq 52$. As $Pr[t \geq 3] \approx 0.99$ and $Pr[53 \leq t \leq 64] \approx 0$, we have $Pr[3 \leq t \leq 52] \approx 0.99$. The time complexity to retrieve the master key becomes $max(2^{3m-2t-2q}, 2^{3t-2}) < 2^{156}$. The time complexity to enumerate the difference is less than $2^{2m-2q} + 2^{2.858m-2t-2q} < 2^{146.9}$. Therefore, we could break $(n, k, m, D, R) = (192, 192, 64, 1, 4)$ with time complexity less than 2^{156} and success probability $0.99 \times 0.25 = 0.247$.

Attacks on $(255, 256, 85, 1, 4)$. For $(n, k, m, D, R) = (255, 255, 85, 1, 4)$, we have $V(255, 19) > 1$ based on Eq. 12, i.e. we can expect to always find an assignment to Δ_0^S such that there will be $q = 19$[9] inactive S-boxes in the 2nd round.

As $Pr[t \geq 5] \approx 0.986$ and $Pr[79 \leq t \leq 85] \approx 0$, based on Eq. 17 and Eq. 18, the time complexity to retrieve the master key will be $max(3 \times 2^{3m-2t}, 4 \times 2^{3t-2}) < 2^{246.6}$. Based on Eq. 16, the time complexity to enumerate the difference is less than $3 \times (2^{2m} + 2^{2m-2t+0.858m}) = 3 \times (2^{2m} + 2^{2.858m-2t}) < 2^{234.53}$. Therefore, we could break $(n, k, m, D, R) = (255, 255, 85, 1, 4)$ with time complexity less than $2^{246.6}$ and success probability 0.986.

As $Pr[t \geq 8] = 0.848$ and $Pr[79 \leq t \leq 85] \approx 0$, the time complexity to retrieve the master key will be $max(3 \times 2^{3m-2t}, 4 \times 2^{3t-2}) < 2^{240.6}$, while the time complexity to enumerate the differences will not exceed $3 \times (2^{2m} + 2^{2.858m-2t}) < 2^{228.53}$. Therefore, we could break $(n, k, m, D, R) = (255, 255, 85, 1, 4)$ with time complexity less than $2^{240.6}$ and success probability 0.848.

To further reduce the success probability, we focus on the expected case $q = 19$ and $5 \leq t \leq 85$. As $Pr[t \geq 5] \approx 0.986$ and $Pr[70 \leq t \leq 85] \approx 0$, we have $Pr[5 \leq t \leq 69] \approx 0.986$. The time complexity to retrieve the master key becomes $max(2^{3m-2t-2q}, 2^{3t-2}) < 2^{208}$. The time complexity to enumerate the difference is less than $2^{2m-2q} + 2^{2.858m-2t-2q} < 2^{194.93}$. Therefore, we could break $(n, k, m, D, R) = (255, 255, 85, 1, 4)$ with time complexity less than 2^{208} and success probability $0.986 \times 0.25 = 0.2465$.

---

[9] It can be found that $V(255, 20)$ is only slightly greater than 1. Experiments show that it is better to choose $q = 19$.

D   A Table

Table 4. The full list for all valid non-zero difference transitions

$(\Delta x_0, \Delta x_1, \Delta x_2)$	$(\Delta z_0, \Delta z_1, \Delta z_2)$	Conditions	z_0	z_1	z_2
(0,0,1)	(0,0,1)	$x_0 = 0, x_1 = 0$	0	0	x_2
	(0,1,1)	$x_0 = 1, x_1 = 0$	1	$1 \oplus x_2$	$1 \oplus x_2$
	(1,0,1)	$x_0 = 0, x_1 = 1$	x_2	1	$1 \oplus x_2$
	(1,1,1)	$x_0 = 1, x_1 = 1$	$1 \oplus x_2$	x_2	$1 \oplus x_2$
(0,1,0)	(0,1,0)	$x_0 = 1, x_2 = 0$	1	$x_1 + 1$	1
	(0,1,1)	$x_0 = 0, x_2 = 0$	0	x_1	x_1
	(1,1,0)	$x_0 = 1, x_2 = 1$	$1 \oplus x_1$	x_1	0
	(1,1,1)	$x_0 = 0, x_2 = 1$	x_1	x_1	$1 \oplus x_1$
(1,0,0)	(1,0,0)	$x_1 = 1, x_2 = 1$	$1 \oplus x_0$	1	0
	(1,0,1)	$x_1 = 0, x_2 = 1$	x_0	0	$1 \oplus x_0$
	(1,1,0)	$x_1 = 1, x_2 = 0$	x_0	$1 \oplus x_0$	1
	(1,1,1)	$x_1 = 0, x_2 = 0$	x_0	x_0	x_0
(0,1,1)	(0,0,1)	$x_1 = x_2 \oplus 1, x_0 = 1$	1	0	x_1
	(0,1,0)	$x_1 = x_2 \oplus 1, x_0 = 0$	0	x_1	1
	(1,0,1)	$x_1 = x_2, x_0 = 1$	$1 \oplus x_1$	1	$1 \oplus x_1$
	(1,1,0)	$x_1 = x_2, x_0 = 0$	x_1	x_1	0
(1,1,0)	(0,1,0)	$x_0 = x_1 \oplus 1, x_2 = 1$	1	x_1	0
	(0,1,1)	$x_0 = x_1, x_2 = 1$	0	x_1	$1 \oplus x_1$
	(1,0,0)	$x_0 = x_1 \oplus 1, x_2 = 0$	x_1	1	1
	(1,0,1)	$x_0 = x_1, x_2 = 0$	x_1	0	x_1
(1,0,1)	(0,0,1)	$x_1 = 1, x_0 = x_2$	0	1	$1 \oplus x_2$
	(1,0,0)	$x_1 = 0, x_0 = x_2$	x_2	0	0
	(0,1,1)	$x_1 = 1, x_0 = x_2 \oplus 1$	1	$1 \oplus x_2$	$1 \oplus x_2$
	(1,1,0)	$x_1 = 0, x_0 = x_2 \oplus 1$	$1 \oplus x_2$	$1 \oplus x_2$	1
(1,1,1)	(0,0,1)	$x_1 = x_2, x_0 = x_2 \oplus 1$	1	1	x_0
	(0,1,0)	$x_1 = x_2, x_0 = x_2$	0	x_0	0
	(1,0,0)	$x_1 = x_2 \oplus 1, x_0 = x_2 \oplus 1$	x_0	0	1
	(1,1,1)	$x_1 = x_2 \oplus 1, x_0 = x_2$	x_0	$1 \oplus x_0$	$1 \oplus x_0$

References

1. https://csrc.nist.gov/projects/post-quantum-cryptography
2. Reference Code (2017). https://github.com/LowMC/lowmc/blob/master/determine_rounds.py
3. The Picnic signature algorithm specification (2019). https://microsoft.github.io/Picnic/
4. Galbraith, S.D., Moriai, S. (eds.): Algebraic cryptanalysis of STARK-friendly designs: application to MARVELLOUS and MiMC. In: ASIACRYPT 2019. LNCS, vol. 11923, pp. 371–397. Springer, Cham (2019). https://doi.org/10.1007/978-3-030-34618-8_13

5. Albrecht, M.R., Rechberger, C., Schneider, T., Tiessen, T., Zohner, M.: Ciphers for MPC and FHE. In: Oswald, E., Fischlin, M. (eds.) EUROCRYPT 2015. LNCS, vol. 9056, pp. 430–454. Springer, Heidelberg (2015). https://doi.org/10.1007/978-3-662-46800-5_17

6. Aly, A., Ashur, T., Ben-Sasson, E., Dhooghe, S., Szepieniec, A.: Design of symmetric-key primitives for advanced cryptographic protocols. Cryptology ePrint Archive, Report 2019/426 (2019). https://eprint.iacr.org/2019/426

7. Banik, S., Barooti, K., Durak, F.B., Vaudenay, S.: Cryptanalysis of LowMC instances using single plaintext/ciphertext pair. IACR Trans. Symmetric Cryptol. **2020**(4), 130–146 (2020)

8. Bar-On, A., Dinur, I., Dunkelman, O., Lallemand, V., Keller, N., Tsaban, B.: Cryptanalysis of SP networks with partial non-linear layers. In: Oswald, E., Fischlin, M. (eds.) EUROCRYPT 2015. LNCS, vol. 9056, pp. 315–342. Springer, Heidelberg (2015). https://doi.org/10.1007/978-3-662-46800-5_13

9. Beyne, T., Li, C.: Cryptanalysis of the MALICIOUS Framework. Cryptology ePrint Archive, Report 2020/1032 (2020). https://eprint.iacr.org/2020/1032

10. Chase, M., et al.: Post-quantum zero-knowledge and signatures from symmetric-key primitives. Cryptology ePrint Archive, Report 2017/279 (2017). https://eprint.iacr.org/2017/279

11. Courtois, N.T., Pieprzyk, J.: Cryptanalysis of block ciphers with overdefined systems of equations. In: Zheng, Y. (ed.) ASIACRYPT 2002. LNCS, vol. 2501, pp. 267–287. Springer, Heidelberg (2002). https://doi.org/10.1007/3-540-36178-2_17

12. Dinur, I.: Cryptanalytic applications of the polynomial method for solving multivariate equation systems over GF(2). Cryptology ePrint Archive, Report 2021/578 (2021). To appear at EUROCRYPT 2021. https://eprint.iacr.org/2021/578

13. Dinur, I., Dunkelman, O., Shamir, A.: New attacks on Keccak-224 and Keccak-256. In: Canteaut, A. (ed.) FSE 2012. LNCS, vol. 7549, pp. 442–461. Springer, Heidelberg (2012). https://doi.org/10.1007/978-3-642-34047-5_25

14. Dinur, I., Liu, Y., Meier, W., Wang, Q.: Optimized interpolation attacks on LowMC. In: Iwata, T., Cheon, J.H. (eds.) ASIACRYPT 2015. LNCS, vol. 9453, pp. 535–560. Springer, Heidelberg (2015). https://doi.org/10.1007/978-3-662-48800-3_22

15. Dinur, I., Morawiecki, P., Pieprzyk, J., Srebrny, M., Straus, M.: Cube attacks and cube-attack-like cryptanalysis on the round-reduced Keccak sponge function. In: Oswald, E., Fischlin, M. (eds.) EUROCRYPT 2015. LNCS, vol. 9056, pp. 733–761. Springer, Heidelberg (2015). https://doi.org/10.1007/978-3-662-46800-5_28

16. Dobraunig, C., Eichlseder, M., Mendel, F.: Higher-order cryptanalysis of LowMC. In: Kwon, S., Yun, A. (eds.) ICISC 2015. LNCS, vol. 9558, pp. 87–101. Springer, Cham (2016). https://doi.org/10.1007/978-3-319-30840-1_6

17. Gérard, B., Grosso, V., Naya-Plasencia, M., Standaert, F.-X.: Block ciphers that are easier to mask: how far can we go? In: Bertoni, G., Coron, J.-S. (eds.) CHES 2013. LNCS, vol. 8086, pp. 383–399. Springer, Heidelberg (2013). https://doi.org/10.1007/978-3-642-40349-1_22

18. Guo, J., Liao, G., Liu, G., Liu, M., Qiao, K., Song, L.: Practical collision attacks against round-reduced SHA-3. IACR Cryptology ePrint Archive 2019:147 (2019)

19. Guo, J., Liu, M., Song, L.: Linear structures: applications to cryptanalysis of round-reduced KECCAK. In: Cheon, J.H., Takagi, T. (eds.) ASIACRYPT 2016. LNCS, vol. 10031, pp. 249–274. Springer, Heidelberg (2016). https://doi.org/10.1007/978-3-662-53887-6_9

20. Huang, S., Wang, X., Xu, G., Wang, M., Zhao, J.: Conditional cube attack on reduced-round Keccak sponge function. In: Coron, J.-S., Nielsen, J.B. (eds.) EUROCRYPT 2017. LNCS, vol. 10211, pp. 259–288. Springer, Cham (2017). https://doi.org/10.1007/978-3-319-56614-6_9
21. Kales, D., Zaverucha, G.: Improving the performance of the picnic signature scheme. IACR Trans. Cryptogr. Hardw. Embed. Syst. **2020**(4), 154–188 (2020)
22. Li, T., Sun, Y.: Preimage attacks on round-reduced KECCAK-224/256 via an allocating approach. In: Ishai, Y., Rijmen, V. (eds.) EUROCRYPT 2019. LNCS, vol. 11478, pp. 556–584. Springer, Cham (2019). https://doi.org/10.1007/978-3-030-17659-4_19
23. Li, Z., Dong, X., Bi, W., Jia, K., Wang, X., Meier, W.: New conditional cube attack on Keccak keyed modes. IACR Trans. Symmetric Cryptol. **2019**(2), 94–124 (2019)
24. Liu, F., Isobe, T., Meier, W.: Automatic verification of differential characteristics: application to reduced Gimli. In: Micciancio, D., Ristenpart, T. (eds.) CRYPTO 2020. LNCS, vol. 12172, pp. 219–248. Springer, Cham (2020). https://doi.org/10.1007/978-3-030-56877-1_8
25. Liu, F., Isobe, T., Meier, W., Yang, Z.: Algebraic attacks on round-reduced Keccak/Xoodoo. Cryptology ePrint Archive, Report 2020/346 (2020). To appear at ACISP 2021. https://eprint.iacr.org/2020/346
26. Murphy, S., Robshaw, M.J.B.: Essential algebraic structure within the AES. In: Yung, M. (ed.) CRYPTO 2002. LNCS, vol. 2442, pp. 1–16. Springer, Heidelberg (2002). https://doi.org/10.1007/3-540-45708-9_1
27. Peyrin, T., Wang, H.: The MALICIOUS framework: embedding backdoors into tweakable block ciphers. In: Micciancio, D., Ristenpart, T. (eds.) CRYPTO 2020. LNCS, vol. 12172, pp. 249–278. Springer, Cham (2020). https://doi.org/10.1007/978-3-030-56877-1_9
28. Qiao, K., Song, L., Liu, M., Guo, J.: New collision attacks on round-reduced Keccak. In: Coron, J.-S., Nielsen, J.B. (eds.) EUROCRYPT 2017. LNCS, vol. 10212, pp. 216–243. Springer, Cham (2017). https://doi.org/10.1007/978-3-319-56617-7_8
29. Rechberger, C., Soleimany, H., Tiessen, T.: Cryptanalysis of low-data instances of full LowMC v2. IACR Trans. Symmetric Cryptol. **2018**(3), 163–181 (2018)
30. Song, L., Liao, G., Guo, J.: Non-full Sbox linearization: applications to collision attacks on round-reduced KECCAK. In: Katz, J., Shacham, H. (eds.) CRYPTO 2017. LNCS, vol. 10402, pp. 428–451. Springer, Cham (2017). https://doi.org/10.1007/978-3-319-63715-0_15
31. Tiessen, T.: Polytopic cryptanalysis. In: Fischlin, M., Coron, J.-S. (eds.) EUROCRYPT 2016. LNCS, vol. 9665, pp. 214–239. Springer, Heidelberg (2016). https://doi.org/10.1007/978-3-662-49890-3_9
32. van Oorschot, P.C., Wiener, M.J.: Parallel collision search with cryptanalytic applications. J. Cryptol. **12**(1), 1–28 (1999)

The Cost to Break SIKE: A Comparative Hardware-Based Analysis with AES and SHA-3

Patrick Longa[1(✉)], Wen Wang[2], and Jakub Szefer[2]

[1] Microsoft Research, Redmond, USA
plonga@microsoft.com
[2] Yale University, New Haven, USA
{wen.wang.ww349,jakub.szefer}@yale.edu

Abstract. This work presents a detailed study of the classical security of the post-quantum supersingular isogeny key encapsulation (SIKE) protocol using a realistic budget-based cost model that considers the actual computing and memory costs that are needed for cryptanalysis. In this effort, we design especially-tailored hardware accelerators for the time-critical multiplication and isogeny computations that we use to model an ASIC-powered instance of the van Oorschot-Wiener (vOW) parallel collision search algorithm. We then extend the analysis to AES and SHA-3 in the context of the NIST post-quantum cryptography standardization process to carry out a parameter analysis based on our cost model. This analysis, together with the state-of-the-art quantum security analysis of SIKE, indicates that the current SIKE parameters offer higher practical security than currently believed, closing an open issue on the suitability of the parameters to match NIST's security levels. In addition, we explore the possibility of using significantly smaller primes to enable more efficient and compact implementations with reduced bandwidth. Our improved cost model and analysis can be applied to other cryptographic settings and primitives, and can have implications for other post-quantum candidates in the NIST process.

Keywords: Cost model · Cryptanalysis · SIKE · Efficient hardware and software implementations

1 Introduction

The post-quantum cryptography (PQC) standardization process organized by the National Institute of Standards and Technology (NIST) has recently entered its third round with the selection of 15 key encapsulation mechanisms (KEM) and digital signature schemes [29]. Among them, the Supersingular Isogeny Key Encapsulation (SIKE) protocol [3] stands out by featuring the smallest public key sizes of all of the encryption and KEM candidates and by being the only isogeny-based submission. In its second round status report, NIST highlights that it sees SIKE "as a strong candidate for future standardization with continued improvements" [30].

© International Association for Cryptologic Research 2021
T. Malkin and C. Peikert (Eds.): CRYPTO 2021, LNCS 12827, pp. 402–431, 2021.
https://doi.org/10.1007/978-3-030-84252-9_14

SIKE's Security History. SIKE is the actively-secure version of Jao-De Feo's Supersingular Isogeny Diffie-Hellman (SIDH) key exchange proposed in 2011 [16]. SIDH, in contrast to preceding public-key isogeny-based protocols [9,37,40], bases its security on the difficulty of computing an isogeny between two isogenous *supersingular* elliptic curves defined over a field of characteristic p. This problem continues to be considered hard, as no algorithm is known to reduce its classical and quantum exponential-time complexity. More precisely, SIDH and SIKE are based on a problem—called the computational supersingular isogeny (CSSI) problem in [10]—that is more special than the general problem of constructing an isogeny between two supersingular curves. In these protocols, the degree of the isogeny is smooth and public, and both parties in the key exchange each publish two images of some fixed points under their corresponding secret isogenies. However, so far no passive attack has been able to advantageously exploit this extra information. Hence, it is still the case that the CSSI problem can be seen as an instance of the general *claw problem*, as originally suggested by the SIDH authors back in 2011. The black-box claw problem, and thus CSSI, can be solved with asymptotic exponential complexities $\mathcal{O}(p^{1/4})$ and $\mathcal{O}(p^{1/6})$ on classical and quantum computers, respectively [16].

SIKE's Parameter Selection. Since 2011, parameters for SIDH, and later for SIKE, have been selected following the above classical and quantum complexities [3,7,16]. Accordingly, the initial SIKE submission to the NIST PQC effort in 2017 [3] included the parameter sets SIKEp503, SIKEp751 and SIKEp964,[1] to match or exceed the computational resources required for key searches on AES128, AES192 and AES256, respectively. These, in turn, correspond to NIST's security levels 1, 3 and 5 [31]. Levels 2 and 4 are defined by matching or exceeding the computational resources required for collision searches on SHA3-256 and SHA3-384, respectively. It was not until 2019 that Adj, Cervantes-Vázquez, Chi-Domínguez, Menezes and Rodríguez-Henríquez [1] showed that the van Oorschot-Wiener (vOW) parallel collision finding algorithm [43] is the best classical algorithm for CSSI in practice. This was based on the observation that the vOW algorithm allows a time-memory trade-off that enables the reduction of the significant memory requirements (also of $\mathcal{O}(p^{1/4})$) of the meet-in-the-middle attack against the claw problem. Shortly afterwards, after studying the best known quantum algorithms for CSSI, Jaques and Schank [18] confirmed that the classical vOW algorithm should be used to establish the post-quantum security of SIKE and to choose its parameters; see [8] for a posterior study with recent cryptanalytic results. Accordingly, the SIKE team updated their parameter selection for Round 2 of the NIST PQC process, proposing SIKEp434, SIKEp503, SIKEp610 and SIKEp751 for levels 1, 2, 3 and 5, respectively [3].[2]

One problem that arises, and pointed out by NIST in [30, pp. 14], is that the studies mentioned above arbitrarily limit the total amount of memory available to an attacker. In [1,8], that memory limit is set to 2^{80} memory units, while in [18]

---

[1] The name of the parameter set is assembled by concatenating "SIKEp" and the bitlength of the underlying prime p.

[2] We note that there were no parameter changes for Round 3.

it is set to 2^{96} bits. Moreover, in some cases the security estimates from these works either match exactly or even fall below the classical gate requirements of the NIST levels (see [3, Table 5.1]).[3] This is justified in the SIKE specification document by conjecturing that "the corresponding conversion to gate counts would see these parameters comfortably exceed NIST's requirements". But no further explanation is provided.

Cost Models for Cryptographic Schemes. There are several approaches in the literature to assess the security of cryptographic schemes. A standard and platform-independent method is the random access machine (RAM) model. A simplistic abstraction of this model estimates security directly from the query complexity of the corresponding attacks, while refined versions incorporate algorithmic time complexity, instruction or cycle counts corresponding to an implementation of the atomic operations in the cryptanalysis. For example, in the case of SIKE, Adj et al. [1] derived security directly from the query complexity of the vOW algorithm, assuming $2^{e/2}$-isogenies as the unit of time. Later refinements by Jaques and Schank [18] and Costello et al. [8] incorporated estimates of the algorithmic complexity of the half-degree isogeny computation in the first case, and the number of x64 instructions to implement the same computation in the second case. One main drawback of these approaches based on the RAM model is that they ignore the cost of memory and do not capture the significant cost of memory access of algorithms with large shared-memory requirements, as is the case of SIKE. It is also unclear how precisely counting the number of gates, instructions or cycles relates to actual attacks.

Wiener [46] gave a step forward by considering a 3-dimensional machine model and analyzing its cost in terms of the processing, storage and wiring (communication) components that are required by an attack. This approach is slightly more complex but gives a more precise approximation of the actual security of a given cryptosystem. A positive side-effect of this more holistic approach is that, for example, it permits to identify parallel attacks that are *practically* more efficient than the serial versions.[4] This, in general, motivates cryptographers to use the most efficient attacks when evaluating security.

We note, however, that Wiener was only "concerned with asymptotics". In his model, the different components (processors, memory, wires) are assigned the same cost or "weight". Moreover, an algorithm's total cost is estimated by multiplying the total number of components by the number of steps that are executed per processing unit, giving both sides an equal weight.[5]

Some works in the literature apply an even more realistic *budget-based* cost model that avoids the issues above and is still relatively simple (e.g., see van

---

[3] The issue is particularly problematic for level 5 for which the gap between the security estimates for SIKEp751 and AES256 is relatively large.

[4] A point emphasized by Bernstein [4], for example, is that some studies focus on serial attacks and their improvement, ignoring the existence of better parallel attacks.

[5] Wiener's approach is unable to identify the best attack if, for example, an algorithm takes $\mathcal{O}(n^{1/2})$ steps per processor and $\mathcal{O}(n^{1/2})$ components, while another algorithm takes $\mathcal{O}(n^{2/3})$ steps per processor and $\mathcal{O}(n^{1/3})$ components.

Oorschot and Wiener [42,43]): Assume a fixed budget for the attacker and then let her/him allocate the money to get all the necessary hardware in such a way that the time it takes to break a scheme is minimized. The strength of the scheme is determined by such a lower bound for the attack time.

This approach has several advantages. First, it motivates searching for the most cost-effective solution for a problem to help establish a good practical approximation of the security of a scheme (expressed in terms of the time it takes to break it). Thus, it promotes the use of the most efficient algorithms in practice, in place of slower ones (e.g., parallel versus serial attacks). Economically, it motivates the use of the most cost-efficient hardware to achieve a successful break in the least amount of time. More to the point, most effective cryptanalytic efforts aimed at breaking cryptographically strong schemes are expected to use application-specific integrated circuits (ASICs), which demand high non-recurring engineering expenses but are the best alternative in large production volumes. Establishing lower bounds for security using ASICs guarantees that any other approach taken by an attacker (e.g., using an army of hijacked PCs over the Internet or renting cloud infrastructure or using GPUs) is going to take either more time or money (or both).

As Wiener [46] argued, one potential disadvantage of considering the cost of the various hardware components required in an attack is the risk of overestimating security if new cryptanalytic attacks are discovered that are able to reduce the memory and communication requirements without increasing the number of processing steps. However, by not including all the large costs in the analysis of the best known attacks, one is left chasing "future" attacks that could never materialize in practice. In our opinion, if our understanding of the underlying hardness problem of a scheme is *mature enough*, it is preferable to estimate the *actual* cost of the best known attacks and then decide on the security margin we want to add on top—one can argue that this is actually the role of having different security levels—, instead of disregarding some costs and assuming this provides a security margin.

Contributions. In this paper, taking advantage of the relatively stable history of SIKE's underlying hardness problem, we analyze its security under a budget-based cost model. Compared to previous work on cryptanalytic costs, the robustness of the model is strengthened by carrying out an analysis of historical price data of semiconductors and memory, and by making simple yet informative projections to the future.

To determine actual hardware costs for the model, we design especially-tailored, ASIC-friendly hardware accelerators for the multiplication in $\mathbb{F}_{p^2}$ and the large-degree isogeny computation, which are the most critical operations in the cryptanalysis of SIKE. The architectures, which are of independent interest for constructive purposes, are optimized for area-time (AT) product, matching the requirements in a real cryptanalytic setup. Using ASIC synthesis results, we estimate the cost of running the vOW algorithm on SIKE and produce security estimates for the SIKE Round 3 parameters and for a set of new parameters that we introduce.

To verify the soundness of our design, we implemented a proof-of-concept hardware/software co-design of the vOW algorithm on FPGA, leveraging the software developed by Costello, Longa, Naehrig, Renes and Virdia [8]. We hope that this implementation serves as basis for real-world, large-scale cryptanalytic efforts intended to assess the security of isogeny-based cryptosystems.

The cost model is also applied to AES [33] and SHA-3 [34], yielding more realistic security estimates for these primitives that are relevant for the ongoing NIST PQC process. A comparison with our SIKE estimates—complemented by the state-of-the-art results for quantum attacks—leads us to conclude that the current SIKE parameters are conservative and exceed the security required by their intended NIST levels by wide margins. This solves an open issue about the practical security of the SIKE parameters.

In addition, to explore the potential of using parameters that match more closely the NIST security targets, we generate the following *three* new alternative parameters:

- SIKEp377, with $p = 2^{191}3^{117} - 1$ (Level 1),
- SIKEp546, with $p = 2^{273}3^{172} - 1$ (Level 3),
- SIKEp697, with $p = 2^{356}3^{215} - 1$ (Level 5).

Finally, we report optimized implementations of these parameters for x64 platforms that show the potential improvement in performance. For example, SIKEp377, which is intended for level 1, is roughly 1.4× faster than the Round 3 parameter SIKEp434 on an x64 Intel processor. In addition, the public key size is reduced by roughly 13%. Even smaller key sizes would be possible with compressed variants of the parameters [3,28,35].

All our implementations and scripts have been publicly released and can be found at https://github.com/microsoft/vOW4SIKE_on_HW and https://caslab.csl.yale.edu/code/sikehwcryptanalysis.

Outline. After giving some preliminary background about SIKE and the vOW algorithm in Sect. 2, we describe the details of our improved budget-based cost model in Sect. 3. In Sect. 4, we describe the attack setup of the vOW algorithm on SIKE, present the design of our cryptanalysis hardware accelerators, as well as the hardware/software co-design of vOW, and summarize the synthesis results that are used to determine the cost of attacking SIKE. In Sect. 5, we revisit the cost analysis of attacking AES and SHA-3. Finally, the comparative security analysis of SIKE, AES and SHA-3 appears in Sect. 6, together with an analysis of SIKE parameters and their optimized implementations on x64 platforms.

2   Preliminaries

2.1   SIKE and the CSSI Problem

SIKE is a key encapsulation mechanism that is an actively-secure variant of the SIDH protocol [3], i.e., it offers resistance against indistinguishability under adaptive chosen ciphertext (IND-CCA2) attacks. In practice, this means that SIDH keys are *ephemeral* while SIKE's do not need to be.

Fix a prime $p = 2^{e_2}3^{e_3} - 1$ with $2^{e_2} \approx 3^{e_3}$. The protocol works with the roughly $p/12$ isomorphism classes of supersingular elliptic curves that exist in characteristic p and that are all defined over $\mathbb{F}_{p^2}$. Each of these classes is uniquely identified by its $\mathbb{F}_{p^2}$-rational j-invariant. If we define an isogeny as a *separable* non-constant rational map between two elliptic curves, its degree is assumed to be equal to the number of elements in its kernel. Let E be a (supersingular) elliptic curve defined over $\mathbb{F}_{p^2}$, for which $\#E = (p+1)^2$, and G be any subgroup of E. Then, there is a one-to-one correspondence (up to isomorphism) between subgroups $G \subset E$ and isogenies $\phi : E \to E/G$ whose kernel are G. Vélu's formulas can be used to compute these isogenies [44].

SIKE has as public parameters the two positive integers e_2 and e_3 that define p and the finite field $\mathbb{F}_{p^2}$, a starting supersingular elliptic curve $E_0/\mathbb{F}_{p^2}$, and bases $\{P_2, Q_2\}$ and $\{P_3, Q_3\}$ for the 2^{e_2}- and 3^{e_3}-torsion groups $E_0[2^{e_2}]$ and $E_0[3^{e_3}]$, respectively. A simplified version of the computational supersingular isogeny (CSSI) problem can then be described as follows [1].

Definition 1. *(CSSI). Let $(\ell, e) \in \{(2, e_2), (3, e_3)\}$. Given the public parameters $e_2, e_3, E_0/\mathbb{F}_{p^2}, P_\ell, Q_\ell$ and the elliptic curve E_0/G defined over $\mathbb{F}_{p^2}$, where G is an order-ℓ^e subgroup of $E_0[\ell^e]$, compute the degree-ℓ^e isogeny $\phi : E_0 \to E_0/G$ with kernel G or, equivalently, find a generator for G.*

2.2   The vOW Parallel Collision Finding Algorithm

Let $f : S \to S$ be a (pseudo-)random function on a finite set S. The van Oorschot-Wiener (vOW) algorithm finds collisions $f(r) = f(r')$ for distinct values $r, r' \in S$.

Define *distinguished points* as elements in S that have a distinguishing property that is easy to test, and denote by θ the proportion of points of S that are distinguished. The vOW algorithm proceeds by executing collision searches in parallel, where each search starts at a freshly chosen point $x_0 \in S$ and produces a trail of points $r_i = f(r_{i-1})$, for $i = 1, 2, \ldots$, until a distinguished point r_d is reached. Let a shared memory have capacity to collect up to w triples of the form (r_0, r_d, d), where each triple represents a distinguished point and its corresponding trail. Also assume that a given triple is stored at a memory address that is a function of its distinguished point. Every time in a search that a distinguished point is reached, two cases arise: (i) if the respective memory address is empty or holds a triple with a distinct distinguished point, the new triple (r_0, r_d, d) is added to memory and a new search is launched with a new starting point r_0, or (ii) if the distinguished point in the respective address is a match, a collision was detected. Note that it is possible that trails fall into loops that do not lead to distinguished points. To handle these cases, [43] suggests to abandon trails that exceed certain maximum length (e.g., $20/\theta$). The expected length d of the trails is $1/\theta$ on average.

In [43], van Oorschot and Wiener classified different cryptanalytic applications according to whether collision searches are required to find a *small* or a *large* number of collisions. Relevant to this work is that the first case matches collision-search on SHA-3 while the second one applies to golden collision-search for SIKE; see Sect. 5.2 and Sect. 4 for the application of each case.

Finding One (or a Small Number of) Collision(s). In this case, since $\sqrt{\pi|S|/2}$ points are expected to be produced before one trail touches another, the work required by each search engine is $\sqrt{\pi|S|/2}/m$ when m search engines are running in parallel. If we add to this the cost to reach a distinguished point after a useful collision has been detected (i.e., $1/\theta$ steps) and the cost of locating the initial point of collision (i.e., $1.5/\theta$ steps),[6] the total runtime to locate the first useful collision with probability close to 1 is [43]

$$T = \left(\frac{1}{m} \sqrt{\pi|S|/2} + \frac{2.5}{\theta} \right) t, \tag{1}$$

where t is the time for one run of f.

Finding a Large Number of Collisions. For the case where a large number of collisions exist, we follow convention and call *golden collision* to the unique collision that leads to solving the targeted cryptanalytic problem. In this case, since the number of collisions for f is approximately $|S|/2$, one would expect to have to detect this same number of collisions on average before finding the golden collision. However, the golden collision might have a low probability of detection for a given f. This suggests that the best performance on average should be achieved by using different function versions, each one running for a fixed period of time, until the golden collision is found. In the remainder, we denote the different function versions by f_n, with $n \in \mathbb{Z}^+$.

Assisted by a heuristic analysis, van Oorschot and Wiener determined that the total runtime of the algorithm is minimized when fixing $w \geq 2^{10}$ and $\theta = 2.25\sqrt{w/|S|}$, and the total number of distinguished points generated by each function version is set to $10w$, where, as before, w represents the number of memory units that are available to store the triples (r_0, r_d, d). Under these conditions, the total runtime to find a golden collision is estimated as

$$T = \left(\frac{2.5}{m} \sqrt{|S|^3/w} \right) t \tag{2}$$

where t is the time for one run of f_n and m is the number of search engines that are run in parallel.

3   Budget-Based Cost Model

In this section, we describe the budget-based cost model that we use to estimate the security of SIKE in Sect. 4 and the security of AES and SHA-3 in Sect. 6.

The basic idea under this model is that the attacker is assigned a fixed budget that he/she then uses to get computing and storage resources.[7] The specific amount of each of these two resources is determined such that the time to

---

[6] As pointed out in [43], some applications such as discrete logarithms do not require locating the initial point of collision of two colliding trails. In these cases, it suffices to detect that the trails merged.

[7] We use U.S. dollars (USD) as currency, without loss of generality.

successfully break the targeted scheme is *minimized*. The security of the scheme is given by the time it takes to break it.[8]

While our model is inspired by the analysis in [42,43], we expand it by considering historical price information of semiconductors and memory components. As we argue later on, an analysis of technological and economic trends gives confidence to using this data to help determine the strength of cryptographic schemes.

The Cost Model. The time in years that it takes to break a cryptographic scheme, under a budget of B dollars, is given by

$$Y = \left(\frac{\#par\_ops}{m} + \#ser\_ops \right) \cdot \frac{1}{ct}, \tag{3}$$

where:

- m represents the number of processing engines,
- ct is the computing throughput expressed in terms of the number of operations computed per year by one processing engine,
- $\#par\_ops$ is the total number of operations that can be perfectly parallelized, and
- $\#ser\_ops$ is the total number of serial operations.

The number of processing engines (m) and memory units (w) are constrained according to

$$B = m \cdot c_m + w \cdot c_w, \tag{4}$$

where c_m and c_w represent the cost (in dollars) of *one* processing engine and *one* memory unit, respectively.

The Cost of Computation Power and Memory. The inclusion of the costs of memory and computing resources is a key ingredient to better reflect the true cost of cryptanalysis. This is particularly relevant for memory-intensive cryptanalytic attacks (such as the vOW-based attack against SIKE), especially when analyzed in relation to attacks that require negligible use of memory (such as brute-force attacks against AES).

An important aspect commonly overlooked is how these computing/memory costs have behaved historically and how they are expected to behave in the future. Most analyses in the literature use costs that correspond to *one* specific point in history (typically, the "present time" for a certain study). But providing security estimates for different security levels involves an attempt at predicting the future looking at lifespans of 10, 15, 20 years or more. Thus, a natural question that arises is how a budget-based estimate could vary or is expected to vary over time.[9]

---

[8] We use "years" as the unit of security strength, without loss of generality.

[9] More generally, the question is how the security of a given cryptosystem is expected to change over time due to technological advances and increases in capital, which is an aspect that is frequently ignored.

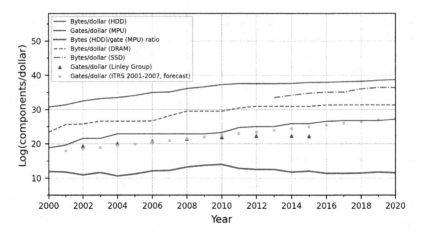

Fig. 1. Historical release prices of Intel and AMD MPUs in terms of number of gates per dollar, and prices of memory in terms of bytes per dollar. The prices are scaled by dividing the values by 7.4 (see [23, App. A]). Data corresponds to the lowest price found for each category (MPU, HDD, DRAM or SSD) per year from 2000 to 2020. Refer to Appendix A for the original price values and their respective sources. To estimate the number of gates, we use the standard assumption that each gate consists of four transistors. The (forecast) values by the Linley Group and the ITRS are taken from [14].

One imperfect but practical approach to predict such a future is to observe the historical evolution of transistors and memory prices. Specifically, we use the public release prices of microprocessor units (MPUs) from Intel and AMD, together with their corresponding transistor counts, to derive an approximation of the cost an attacker would have to pay to fabricate his/her own ASIC chips. As is standard, to get gate counts we assume that a so-called *gate equivalent (GE)* represents a 2-input NAND gate in CMOS technology, and that in turn each of these gates consists of *four* transistors. Similarly, we use the public prices of memory technologies that are most suitable for the task, including hard disk drive (HDD), dynamic random-access memory (DRAM) and solid-state drive (SSD), to get memory costs per byte. These costs are depicted in Fig. 1. It is important to note that to deal with the relatively small gap between *release prices* and the actual production cost of fabricating a chip at very large scale, we apply a scaling factor to the transistor and memory prices, which was calculated from the estimates in [20]; see the full paper version [23, App. A] for the exact derivation of the factor value.

It can be observed that, historically, the bytes to gates cost ratio has been quite stable, which highlights the strong correlation between the cost of transistors (gates) and memory (bytes). This is not surprising since, in general, semiconductors—including transistors for logic and memory means such as DRAM—have evolved under the same economic and technological stress forces, and have followed the same fundamental projections such as those dictated by

Moore's law [27] and Dennard scaling [11]. Over time the development of the different processes involved in the fabrication of semiconductor devices has been coordinated under the umbrella of so-called "technological roadmaps" [13,15,39]. These large coordination efforts—in part responsible for the meteoric progress of semiconductors—have led to a steady and uniform progress in the miniaturization of transistors and other related components that, in turn, has led to a steady and uniform reduction in the cost of semiconductors overall [14].[10]

Figure 1 also includes a forecast of the transistor prices for "high-performance MPUs" done by the ITRS in 2007 for the years between 2000 and 2020 (see Tables 7a and 7b of the "Executive Summary", 2007 edition [14]), and includes the costs of transistors reported by the Linley Group for the years between 2002 and 2012 and its forecast for the years 2014 and 2015 (see §8 in the "More Moore – ITRS 2.0" white paper [14]). Overall, the stability of the data and its consistency across different sources suggest that the adjusted prices of MPUs for logic and HDDs for memory can be used as good approximations to the lower bounds of the costs a real attacker would encounter in practice.

4   Cost of Attacking SIKE

In this section, we describe and adapt the vOW attack to Round-3 SIKE, and produce operation counts corresponding to the different parameter sets. Then, we describe the cryptanalysis design strategy, introduce our hardware implementation that covers efficient accelerators for the multiplication in $\mathbb{F}_{p^2}$ and the isogeny computation, and describe the proof-of-concept HW/SW co-design of vOW on SIKE. The synthesis results that we produce are used in combination with our operation counts to give area/time estimates that are later used in Sect. 6 to estimate the cost of breaking SIKE on ASICs.

4.1   vOW on SIKE

We start by adapting the attack setup in [8] to Round-3 SIKE for the most commonly found scenario, i.e., $\ell = 2$ with even e_2. Refer to the full paper version [23, App. B] for the details for the cases $\ell = 2$ with odd e_2, and $\ell = 3$ with odd e_3.

The SIKE Round 3 specification sets the Montgomery curve $E_6/\mathbb{F}_{p^2} : y^2 = x^3 + 6x^2 + x$ with $j(E_6) = 287496$ as the starting curve of the protocol. Fix $\ell = 2$ and assume e_2 is even. Let the final curve be defined as $E = E_6/G$, where G is an order-2^{e_2} subgroup of $E_6[2^{e_2}]$. Taking into account the use of E_6 and the savings in the final step of the large-degree isogeny computation [8, §3.1], attackers are left with the task of finding the isogeny of degree 2^{e_2-2} between E_6 and a certain challenge curve E_A.

Let $S = \{0, 1, \ldots, 2^{e_2/2-1} - 1\}$. In an efficient version of the attack, the attacker can fix bases $\{P, Q\}$ and $\{U, V\}$ for $E_6[2^{e_2/2}]$ and $E_A[2^{e_2/2-2}]$, where

---

[10] Although the core technology behind HDDs is not based on semiconductors, they have also followed a similar pattern of growth and cost reduction, arguably because of being under similar economic and technological forces.

$\pi(P) = -P$ and $\pi(Q) = Q$ with π representing the Frobenius endomorphism. We use the efficient instantiation for f_n proposed in [8]. They define $f_n : S \to S$ by $f_n(r) = g_n(h(r))$, where g_n is a hash function with index n and h is given by

$$h : r \mapsto \begin{cases} j, & \text{if lsb}(b) = 0 \text{ for } j = a + b \cdot i \in \mathbb{F}_{p^2} \\ \bar{j}, & \text{otherwise} \end{cases},$$

where

$$j = \begin{cases} j(E_6 / \langle P + [r \gg 1]Q \rangle), & \text{if lsb}(r) = 0 \\ j(E_A / \langle U + [r \gg 1]V \rangle), & \text{if lsb}(r) = 1 \end{cases}.$$

As can be seen, the function h uses a canonical representation of the conjugate classes in $\mathbb{F}_{p^2}$, such that it is always the case that we land on a j-invariant where the least significant bit of the imaginary part is 0. Note that $\gg$ represents the right shift operator. Thus, the least significant bit of r is used to select whether we compute an isogeny from E_6 or from E_A and, therefore, we have that $r \in \{0, 1, \ldots, 2^{e_2/2-2} - 1\}$.

The kernels $P + [r]Q$ determine degree-$2^{e_2/2}$ isogenies from E_6. However, by exploiting the Frobenius endomorphism [8, §3.1], it follows that the search space reduces to $2^{e_2/2-1}$ distinct equivalence classes of j-invariants. The kernels $U + [r]V$ determine degree-$2^{e_2/2-2}$ isogenies from E_A, leading to $2^{e_2/2-2}$ distinct equivalence classes of j-invariants. In the remainder, we slightly underestimate the attack cost and only consider the use of $2^{e_2/2-2}$-isogenies as the core operation that is needed to approximate the cost of f. This also means that we ignore the cost of the hash function g_n, in an effort to be conservative in our security estimates.

Another crucial ingredient to estimate the cost of attacking SIKE is the memory required to store distinguished point triples (Sect. 2.2). For a triple (r_0, r_d, d) the starting and distinguished points have a length of $\log |S| = e_2/2 - 1$ bits. However, if we apply van Oorschot and Wiener's recommendation of defining a fixed number of top 0 bits as the distinguishing property [43, §4.1], distinguished points can be efficiently stored using only $\log |S| + \log \theta$ bits, where θ is the distinguished point rate. If we fix the maximum length of the trails to $20/\theta$ then the counter d can be represented with $\log (20/\theta)$ bits. Thus, a *memory unit* in a vOW attack against SIKE requires approximately the following number of bytes

$$\lceil (2 \log |S| + \log 20)/8 \rceil. \tag{5}$$

Operation Counts. The two operations that make up the computation of a *full* large-degree isogeny as described above are the construction of kernels with the form $P + [r]Q$ and the computation of the half-degree isogeny itself. Hence, estimating their computing time and plugging the total "t" into Eq. (2) is expected to give a good approximation to a practical lower bound of the attack runtime.

For the kernel computation, it is standard to use the efficient Montgomery ladder, which computes $\chi(P + [r]Q)$ given input values $\chi(P), \chi(Q), \chi(Q - P)$ for elliptic curve points $P, Q, Q - P$, where $\chi(\cdot)$ represents the x-coordinate of a given point. We note that the vOW implementation reported in [8] makes use

Table 1. Operation counts for the isogeny and elliptic curve operations in the kernel and isogeny tree traversal computations corresponding to a $2^{e_2/2-2}$-isogeny for even exponent (resp. $2^{(e_2-3)/2}$-isogeny for odd exponent, omitting single 2-isogenies). Tree traversal uses an optimal strategy consisting of point quadrupling and 4-isogeny steps; ADD denotes a differential point addition, DBL a point doubling, 4-get a 4-isogeny computation, and 4-eval a 4-isogeny evaluation. Round 3 parameters appear at the top, while the new parameters proposed in this work are at the bottom.

	Kernel	Tree traversal		
	ADD	DBL	4-get	4-eval
SIKEp434	106	282	53	166
SIKEp503	123	352	61	187
SIKEp610	151	434	75	255
SIKEp751	184	548	92	334
SIKEp377	94	236	47	147
SIKEp546	135	394	67	211
SIKEp697	176	516	88	318

of the 3-point Montgomery ladder for variable input points proposed by Faz et al. [12]. However, for cryptanalysis one can employ the ladder version that exploits precomputations [12, Alg. 3], since the input points are fixed in this case. This algorithm speeds up the kernel computation by roughly 2 times at the expense of storing about $e_2/2$ points.

Recall that $\ell \in \{2, 3\}$. For the case of the half-degree isogeny itself, the computation can be visualized as traversing a tree, from top to bottom, doing point multiplications by ℓ and ℓ-isogeny computations which are guided by a so-called *optimal strategy* [10, §4.2.2]. This optimal strategy is derived by using the relative cost of point multiplication by ℓ and ℓ-isogeny evaluation.

Table 1 summarizes the operation counts for a full large-degree isogeny operation as required for cryptanalysis. The table only includes the 2-power torsion case which is the preferable option for cryptanalysis as it is more efficient than the 3-power torsion case for all the SIKE parameters under study. For the kernel, we take into account the optimization using a fixed-point Montgomery ladder. In contrast to [8, §5], we include the cost of the kernel computation as well as the costs of both the ℓ-isogeny computation and the ℓ-isogeny evaluation when assessing the cost of the full isogeny.

4.2 Hardware Implementation of the Attack

"Ideal" Cryptanalysis Design. Here we discuss our *idealized* design of a full attack, under the assumption that the main goal of the analysis is to help define *conservative* lower bounds for the cost of cryptanalyzing SIKE on ASICs. Likewise, with the budget-based cost model in mind, the main optimization goal for a hardware implementation of the attack is the minimization of the area-time (AT) product.

One core aspect of setting up a real-world, large-scale attack on SIKE using vOW is the configuration of the shared memory that stores the distinguished points. Each of the standard options, e.g., the use of a centralized database or a peer-to-peer system, has its advantages and disadvantages, and introduces non-negligible bottlenecks (see [8, App. C] for a discussion). In our analysis of the attack runtime, we abstract away from these engineering complexities and only consider the CPU time (i.e., we ignore communication costs for memory access).

A second core aspect is related to the hardware implementation of the "processing engine" that runs vOW on SIKE. While the critical part of this vOW engine is the isogeny step in the random function iteration for searching distinguished points and in the collision detection mechanism (a.k.a. backtracking), other associated costs include, for example, the pseudorandom sampling of starting points and the hashing of the j-invariants. There is also the cost associated to all the control circuitry to manage the algorithm flow outside the isogeny step (e.g., see [8, App. C] for a discussion about the synchronization of function versions across engines). Thus, by focusing the area and timing analysis on the isogeny function only, one can safely produce lower bounds for the attack cost.

It remains to discuss parallelization opportunities for the isogeny computation itself. In a typical setup that facilitates synchronization across engines, the pre-fixed number of distinguished points per function version can be evenly split between those engines, which then get to work to collect them. Beyond that, the parallel searches hardly stay in-sync at the arithmetic level, which makes difficult to save area by using controllers that manage multiple isogeny engines simultaneously, or by batching elliptic curve and small-degree isogeny operations from different engines (e.g., using Montgomery's inversion batching trick).

Internally, one can try to parallelize operations in the kernel computation $P + [r]Q$ and the isogeny tree traversal operation. However, existing approaches offer poor area utilization, which conflicts with our goal of minimizing the AT product. In contrast, we note that the elliptic curve and small-degree isogeny formulas, as well as the underlying arithmetic over $\mathbb{F}_{p^2}$, do offer good opportunities for parallelization of multiplications in $\mathbb{F}_{p^2}$ and $\mathbb{F}_p$.

Following this discussion, we designed a flexible and efficient hardware accelerator for the cost-intensive large-degree isogeny computation. This includes the hardware acceleration of the kernel construction as well as the isogeny computation itself. In turn, this accelerator is built on top of an efficient multiplier architecture that exploits a novel approach to optimize and exploit internal parallelism in the multiplication over $\mathbb{F}_{p^2}$ in hardware.

We describe our accelerators next, starting with the critical $\mathbb{F}_{p^2}$ multiplication.

Multiplier Core. The basic idea of our design is to merge the inner multiplications in a schoolbook-like computation of the $\mathbb{F}_{p^2}$ multiplication using a radix-r Montgomery multiplication algorithm. This allows us to parallelize digit multiplications while saving a full Montgomery reduction. Thus, the method can be seen as an application of lazy reduction to radix-r multiplication algorithms. While it is possible to apply the approach to most of the several radix-r variants

Algorithm 1. Modified FIOS algorithm for Montgomery multiplier in $\mathbb{F}_{p^2}$
▷ for computing: $c_0 = (a_0 \cdot b_0 - a_1 \cdot b_1) \bmod p$, where p is a SIKE prime.

Require: operands a_0, a_1, b_0, b_1, each of n digits, each digit $\in [0, 2^r)$ for radix of r bits; $m = p + 1$ and λ represents the number of 0 digits in m.
Ensure: $[t_0, \ldots, t_{n-1}] \leftarrow \text{MontRed}(a_0 \cdot b_0 - a_1 \cdot b_1)$

1: $t_i = 0$ for $i = 0, \ldots, n-1$
2: **for** $i = 0, \ldots, n-1$ **do**
3:      $(C, S) = a_{0,0} \cdot b_{0,i} - a_{1,0} \cdot b_{1,i} + t_0$
4:      $mm = S$
5:      **for** $j = 1, \ldots, n-1$ **do**
6:          **if** $j < \lambda$ **then**   // optimization for 0 digits in m
7:              $(C, S) = a_{0,j} \cdot b_{0,i} - a_{1,j} \cdot b_{1,i} + t_j + C$
8:          **else**   // mult. integrated with reduction
9:              $(C, S) = a_{0,j} \cdot b_{0,i} - a_{1,j} \cdot b_{1,i} + mm \cdot m_j + t_j + C$
10:        $t_{j-1} = S$
11:    $t_{n-1} = C$

---

of the Montgomery multiplication, in our application we use the finely integrated operand scanning (FIOS) algorithm [22]. In hardware, this algorithm allows us to maximize the number of parallel multiplications, while minimizing the control circuitry.

The proposed algorithm is depicted in Algorithm 1. We assume that, given inputs $a = (a_0, a_1)$ and $b = (b_0, b_1)$ in $\mathbb{F}_{p^2}$, $a \cdot b$ is computed as $(a_0 \cdot b_0 - a_1 \cdot b_1, a_0 \cdot b_1 + a_1 \cdot b_0)$. We only show the computation of the left-half of the result (the right-half computation easily follows). The algorithm also includes an additional optimization to save multiplications when the corresponding digit of the modulus is 0, as first noted by Costello et al. [7] in the context of SIDH. Ignoring this optimization, the method reduces the number of digit multiplications in one $\mathbb{F}_{p^2}$ multiplication from $2 \cdot 2 \cdot (2n^2 - n) = 8n^2 - 4n$ (using the standard approach on a SIKE prime) to $2 \cdot (3n^2 - n) = 6n^2 - 2n$. We note that, in comparison, the Karatsuba method is able to trade one $\mathbb{F}_p$ multiplication with a few much cheaper $\mathbb{F}_p$ additions and subtractions, roughly matching the number of digit multiplications of our method. However, as discussed in [24], when mapping the Karatsuba algorithm to hardware, there are more data dependencies that can easily lead to complex data scheduling in pipelined architectures.

A simplified diagram depicting our hardware multiplier core $\mathbb{F}_{p^2}$_Multiplier is presented in Fig. 2a. The input operands a_0, a_1, b_0, b_1 as well as the constant value m are all stored in memory blocks of width r and depth n, where r is the size of the radix and n is the number of digits per operand. Two separate modules step_sub and step_add are implemented for realizing the two inner loop variants in Algorithm 1, which gives a total of six digit multipliers and two digit adders for optimal parallel execution. Finally, a Controller module is responsible for coordinating the memory accesses as well as the interactions between the memory blocks and the computation units. Since our design is fully pipelined, step_sub

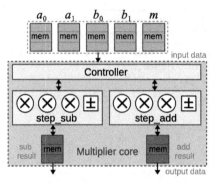

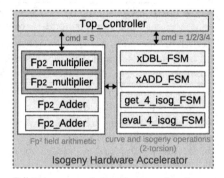

(a) Diagram of the $\mathbb{F}_{p^2}$ multiplier core.

(b) Diagram of the isogeny hardware accelerator.

Fig. 2. Simplified diagrams of the $\mathbb{F}_{p^2}$_Multiplier and the isogeny hardware accelerator.

and `step_add` execute their computations in one cycle on average, which means that a full $\mathbb{F}_{p^2}$ multiplication is completed in approximately n^2 cycles.

As desired for the cryptanalysis application, our approach gives great flexibility to balance area and computing time by tuning the value of the radix.

Isogeny Hardware Accelerator. Figure 2b shows the diagram of our isogeny hardware accelerator. A lightweight `Top_Controller` module sitting at the top of the design contains a state machine that implements the kernel and isogeny computations as described in the subsection "Operation counts" (Sect. 4.1). Accordingly, it supports all the necessary elliptic curve and small-degree isogeny computations for the 2-power torsion case, including doubling, differential addition, 4-isogeny evaluation and 4-isogeny computation. Separate compact state machines (called `xDBL_FSM`, `xADD_FSM`, `get_4_isog_FSM` and `eval_4_isog_FSM`) were designed for accelerating the respective operations above. As shown in the figure, these computations are carried out by the accelerator depending on the value of the `cmd` signal.

In our design, the $\mathbb{F}_{p^2}$-level arithmetic underlying these sub-modules is supported by two parallel blocks of our novel $\mathbb{F}_{p^2}$_Multiplier core, as well as two parallel $\mathbb{F}_{p^2}$_Adder blocks. This setup is optimal to minimize the AT product when using the Montgomery formulas for the small-degree isogeny and elliptic curve operations. As shown in Fig. 2b, the `Top_Controller` can also directly trigger $\mathbb{F}_{p^2}$ multiplications and additions using the `cmd` signal. This is done in order to accelerate these functions when invoked outside the elliptic curve and isogeny computations.

Comparison with Other Implementations. A relevant task for our analysis is to determine the suitability of using the proposed isogeny hardware accelerator for analyzing the security of SIKE under a realistic cost model. The main challenge that we face is that our implementation appears to be the first one intended for ASICs for cryptanalytic purposes. Nevertheless, we exploit the fact that a large-degree isogeny operation is also the main part of a typical hardware implementation of SIKE to carry out a *first-order* comparison between our isogeny accelerator and the most efficient open-source FPGA implementations of SIKE in the literature: the area-efficient implementation by Massolino et al. [24] and the speed-oriented implementation by Koziel et al. [21]. While ours is not a full SIKE implementation we argue that the resources and timing information it provides only introduce a small error. The isogeny function is by far the most resource and time-consuming operation in SIKE, and implementations like the ones from [21,24] only incorporate a specialized, lightweight controller to provide the rest of the functionality. Note that to have a more fair comparison we eliminated the SHAKE circuitry from the implementations of both works.

Another issue is that the implementations above are specialized for FPGA and, hence, make use of the internal digital signal processors (DSPs). However, what matters for our security analysis is the performance on ASICs. Therefore, to make the results more comparable to what would be observed on an ASIC, we have synthesized the implementations *without* DSPs.

Table 2 summarizes the resource utilization and encapsulation timing results for our and the aforementioned SIKE implementations.[11] As can be seen, our accelerator using radix 2^{32} achieves the lowest values for the slices/time product in comparison with [21] and [24]. More importantly, we achieve so for *both* the smallest and the largest SIKE Round 3 parameter sets, while the competing implementations do not scale as efficiently for different parameters. This is due to the efficiency and flexibility of our multiplier and isogeny designs, which have been especially tailored to achieve a low area-time product. We remark that this first-order comparison is conservative because it ignores some costly resources like Block RAMs.[12]

Synthesis Results. We now proceed to obtain area and timing synthesis results for our isogeny accelerator, which are used in Sect. 6 to determine the cost and performance of a "processing engine" to run vOW on SIKE.

We use Synopsis version Q-2019.12-SP1 with the NanGate 45 nm open-cell library v1.3 (v2010.12) [38]. Table 3 summarizes the cycle counts obtained for each of the individual elliptic curve and small-degree isogeny operations. To estimate conservative lower bounds for the computing cost of the full isogeny, we treat the individual accelerators (xDBL_FSM, xADD_FSM, get_4_isog_FSM, and eval_4_isog_FSM) as independent units, ignoring the controller computation cost and the timing overhead due to data communication. That is, the cycle counts from Table 3 are multiplied with the operation counts in Table 1 to calculate the total cycle counts for a full isogeny (see Table 4). The total time (msec) is then calculated by multiplying the isogeny cycle count by the clock period. Table 4 also reports the area (kGEs) occupied by our isogeny hardware accelerator.

---

[11] We only compare the encapsulation operation, as this is the only high-level function in SIKE that fully works on the 2^{e_2}-torsion subgroup, as in our isogeny accelerator.

[12] Each Block RAM on the Virtex-7 consists of 36Kb which our accelerator uses very scarcely (see Table 2).

Table 2. Comparison of our isogeny HW accelerator with SIKE implementations (encapsulation function Enc only, w/o SHAKE) on a Xilinx Virtex 7 690T FPGA of partname XC7VX690TFFG1157-3. Synthesis results were obtained with Vivado Software Version 2018.3. The use of FPGA DSPs was disallowed during synthesis.

Design	$\log p$	Resources				Freq (MHz)	Enc (msec.)	Slices × Time
		Slices	LUTs	FFs	RAMs			
This work (radix $= 2^{32}$)	434	6260	22347	4023	6.5	164.00	19.70	**123.7**
This work (radix $= 2^{64}$)		19120	69636	8808	12.5	116.84	10.51	200.9
[21]		20620	64553	21064	37.0	146.91	6.33	**130.5**
[24], 128-bit ALU		7472	24855	8477	23.5	162.20	22.88	171.0
[24], 256-bit ALU		24400	82143	18509	20.5	163.85	10.21	249.0
This work (radix $= 2^{32}$)	751	6031	21745	3273	19.5	161.00	94.31	**568.8**
This work (radix $= 2^{64}$)		18587	67699	6925	38.5	115.92	40.36	750.1
[21]		52941	151411	46095	45.5	116.88	18.91	1001.1
[24], 128-bit ALU		7472	24855	8477	23.5	162.20	81.09	**605.9**
[24], 256-bit ALU		24400	82143	18509	20.5	163.85	25.38	619.3

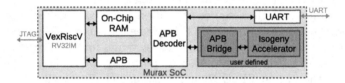

Fig. 3. Diagram of the HW/SW co-design for SIKE cryptanalysis based on Murax SoC. Blue box represents the user-defined logic, including the dedicated isogeny hardware accelerator and the APB bridge module `ApbController`.

HW/SW Co-design Prototype. To validate the soundness of our cryptanalytic design as well as the hardware accelerators, we devised a hardware prototype of the vOW algorithm on SIKE using HW/SW co-design based on the popular RISC-V platform [36]. An approach based on HW/SW co-design facilitates prototyping and analyzing cryptanalytic targets by combining the flexibility and portability of a processor like RISC-V with the power of rapidly-reprogrammable hardware acceleration on FPGA. The design uses as basis the software implementation of vOW by Costello, Longa, Naehrig, Renes and Virdia [8, 26]. Since their software targets SIKE Round 1 parameters, our first task was to adapt it to the Round 3 parameters and to the parameters proposed in this work, as described in Sect. 4.1. The HW/SW co-design is based on an open-source RISC-V platform, namely, VexRiscv [45]. It supports the RV32IM instruction set and implements a 5-stage in-order pipeline. The VexRiscv ecosystem also provides a complete predefined processor setup called "Murax SoC" that has a compact and modular design and aims at small resource usage. Due to the modularity of the VexRiscv implementation, dedicated hardware modules can be easily integrated to the system as an APB peripheral before synthesis of the System-on-a-Chip (SoC).

Figure 3 depicts the high-level view of the HW/SW co-design. As we can see, the dedicated isogeny hardware accelerator was integrated to the Murax SoC as an APB peripheral, and the communication between the two was realized by implementing a dedicated memory-mapped bridge module `ApbController`.

Table 3. Cycle results from synthesis for the isogeny and elliptic curve operations in the kernel and tree traversal computations using our hardware accelerators based on two $\mathbb{F}_{p^2}$ parallel multipliers. The parallel formula for ADD costs $3\mathbf{M} + 3\mathbf{add} + 3\mathbf{sub}$, for DBL it costs $3\mathbf{M} + 2\mathbf{add} + 2\mathbf{sub}$, for 4-get it costs $2\mathbf{M} + 4\mathbf{add} + 1\mathbf{sub}$, and for 4-eval it costs $4\mathbf{M} + 3\mathbf{add} + 3\mathbf{sub}$, where $\mathbf{M}$ denotes multiplication, $\mathbf{add}$ addition and $\mathbf{sub}$ subtraction in $\mathbb{F}_{p^2}$. Each case reports the results for the radix that achieves the lowest AT product.

		Kernel		Tree traversal	
	Radix	ADD	DBL	4-get	4-eval
SIKEp434	2^{32}	874	841	598	1105
SIKEp503	2^{32}	1088	1051	742	1383
SIKEp610	2^{64}	518	496	360	649
SIKEp751	2^{64}	684	658	472	863
SIKEp377	2^{32}	684	655	470	859
SIKEp546	2^{32}	1326	1288	904	1697
SIKEp697	2^{64}	634	610	438	800

5   Cost of Attacking Symmetric Primitives

In this section, we revisit the cost of cryptanalyzing AES and SHA-3 using efficient ASIC implementations from the literature. The analysis results are applied in Sect. 6 to produce estimates for the security of these primitives using the budget-based cost model.

5.1   Cost of Attacking AES

We revisit the problem of how costly it is for an attacker to find a secret key k that was used to encrypt a plaintext P as $C = E_k(P)$ using a block cipher E, assuming knowledge of the plaintext/ciphertext pair (P, C). In this scenario, one of the most efficient key-extraction algorithms is the *rainbow chains* method by Oechslin [32]. Herein, we treat E as a black box since the attack applies generically to block ciphers.

Let $f_n(r) = g_n(h(r))$ define a function where $h(r) = E_r(P)$ for a fixed plaintext P and g_n is a function with index n that produces (pseudo-)random values. The attack works as follows. In the precomputation stage, the attacker first chooses a random value k_0, then generates a rainbow chain of values $k_{i+1} = f_i(k_i)$ for $i = 0, \ldots, t - 2$ (the term "rainbow" precisely originates from the use of distinct function versions at each step of the chain generation), and finally stores the starting and ending values k_0 and k_{t-1}. This process is repeated to create a table with l entries, corresponding to l rainbow chains of length t each.

In the online stage, the attacker tries to determine if the key k used to encrypt P as $C = E_k(P)$ is among all the keys k_i used during the precomputation stage. To do so, he/she generates a new chain of length t starting from $g_n(C)$, and proceeds to compare the intermediate key values with the ending values k_{t-1}

Table 4. Area and timing synthesis results for a full $2^{e_2/2-2}$-isogeny (for even exponent) and a full $2^{(e_2-3)/2}$-isogeny (for odd exponent; omitting single 2-isogenies), using NanGate 45 nm technology. The estimated computing time ignores the controller computation and the data communication overhead. Total cycles are estimated using the operation counts from Table 1 and the cycle counts for each individual elliptic curve and small-degree isogeny operation (Table 3). The total time (msec) is calculated by multiplying the total cycle count by the clock period. Total area (kGEs) corresponds to the full isogeny hardware accelerator. For each case, results are reported for the radix that achieves the lowest AT product.

	Radix	Area (kGE)	Freq (MHz)	Period (nsec)	Speed Cycles	msec
SIKEp434	2^{32}	372.2	167.5	5.97	544930	3.253
SIKEp503	2^{32}	409.5	167.8	5.96	807659	4.814
SIKEp610	2^{64}	748.0	83.75	11.94	485977	5.803
SIKEp751	2^{64}	822.3	84.32	11.86	818106	9.703
SIKEp377	2^{32}	341.3	156.5	6.39	367239	2.347
SIKEp546	2^{32}	441.1	155.8	6.42	1105117	7.095
SIKEp697	2^{64}	798.9	83.68	11.95	719288	8.595

stored in the table. If one of those values was indeed used to construct the table, a collision with one of the ending values k_{t-1} will be detected and the attacker can proceed to reconstruct the stored chain using its corresponding starting value k_0. The key k is expected to be found in the step right before computing the value $g_n(C)$.

To implement the function g_n one can exploit that the block cipher itself can be used to generate pseudo-random values. Let β be a value chosen randomly. Since each execution of g_n is preceded by a computation of the form $E_r(P)$, we can use the pair (β, i) to represent the index n, for $i = 1, \ldots, t-2$, and set $g_{\beta,i}(x) = x \oplus (\beta \,||\, i)$ using a simple logical XOR operation.

The probability of finding k with the rainbow chains method is roughly $l \cdot t / 2^b$, where b is the cipher key bitlength. To increase this probability *efficiently* (i.e., without increasing the memory requirement excessively), the attacker can repeat the procedure above as many times as required, each time with a new table and a fresh value for β.

Cost of Parallel Attack. The precomputation and online key search stages can be perfectly parallelized and distributed across multiple processors with minimal communication. The sorting process for collision search of the precomputed and online key values can be done serially using some efficient sorting algorithm. The cost of this part can be made negligible in comparison to the rest of the computation for suitably chosen parameters.

The regeneration of the chain after a collision is detected needs to be executed serially. Therefore, to guarantee that this cost is relatively negligible we need

Table 5. Area and timing synthesis results for the AES implementation by Ueno et al. [41] and the Keccak-f[1600] implementation by Akin et al. [2] using 45 nm technology. InvThr represents the inverse throughput given in nanoseconds per operation (nsec/op). The latency for the Keccak-f[1600] (90 nm) implementation is scaled using the factor $1.5 \cdot (45/90)^2 = 0.375$ to approximate it to SHA-3 on 45 nm. The area is scaled by the factor 1.2.

	Area (kGE)	Freq (GHz)	Latency (nsec)	InvThr (nsec/op)
AES128	11.59	787.40	13.97	12.70
AES192	13.32	757.58	17.16	15.84
AES256	13.97	775.19	19.35	18.06
SHA-3	12.60	–	20.61	20.61

$t \ll \frac{l \cdot t}{m}$ to hold or, equivalently, $m \ll l$, for m key-search engines. In this case, the time to find k with probability close to 1 using m engines is approximately

$$T = \frac{2^b}{m} \cdot t, \tag{6}$$

where t denotes the time to compute one iteration of E.

Hardware Cost. The main building block in the attack is the targeted cipher itself. In the case of AES, there is a plethora of implementations in the literature ranging in scope from low-power/low-area to high-throughput/low-latency applications. As explained before, in a budget-based cost model trying to replicate a real-world setup the focus shifts instead to implementations that minimize the area-time product and are efficient on ASICs.

In that direction, we use the efficient round-based AES implementation by Ueno et al. [41]. A summary of their results for AES128/192/256, using the exact same Synopsis synthesis tool with the NanGate 45 nm library that we use for the case of SIKE in Sect. 4.2, is given in Table 5.

5.2 Cost of Attacking SHA-3

Finding hash collisions in SHA-3 can be done efficiently using the vOW algorithm in the scenario targeting a small number of collisions [43, 4.1]; see Sect. 2.2. In this case, the total runtime to locate the first useful collision with probability close to 1 using m collision-search engines is given by Eq. (1). However, this estimate is slightly optimistic since it does not consider that in a real setting an attacker runs out of memory at some point and new distinguished points need to replace old ones. See [43, §6.5] for an analysis for MD5 that also applies to SHA-3.

Hardware Cost. Similar to the case of AES, the main building block of the attack is the targeted primitive itself. For our analysis, we use the efficient, ASIC-friendly implementation of Keccak by Akin, Aysu, Can Ulusel and Savaş [2]. Their single-message hash (SMH) approach takes one cycle per round and achieves, to our knowledge, the lowest AT product on ASIC in the literature.

Akin et al. only report synthesis results for the Keccak-f[1600] permutation function with rate $r = 1088$—which corresponds to the standardized instance SHA3-256—on 90 nm technology. Table 5 presents the timing results scaled to 45 nm using the factor $(45/90)^2 = 0.25$ and scaled with a factor 1.5 to account for the initialization and absorb stages not considered by Akin et al. To account for the extra area required by the standardized instances SHA3-256 and SHA3-384, we scale the results by the factor 1.2.

6   Security Estimation: A Comparative Analysis

We now proceed to put all the pieces together and estimate the security strength of SIKE, AES and SHA-3 using the budget-based cost model described in Sect. 3.

To get security estimates we set fixed budgets of *ten million, one hundred million* and *one billion* dollars. Arguably, these choices apply to the vast majority of scenarios that involve sufficiently motivated actors.[13]

To estimate the security provided by SIKE, AES and SHA-3, we first proceed to calculate the cost of *one* processing engine using the area information (in GEs) from Tables 4 and 5 and multiplying it by the adjusted cost per gate of a given year (Tables 8 and 9 in Appendix A). We proceed to do a similar calculation to get the cost of *one* memory unit; in the case of SIKE we use Eq. (5). Our setup for the attacks against AES and SHA-3 guarantees that the total cost of memory is significantly smaller than the cost of computing power.

Recall that the operation complexity for SIKE, AES and SHA-3 is given by Eqs. (2), (6) and (1), respectively (after setting $t = 1$). The security strength in terms of years is then estimated as follows. We fix B to a given budget value in Eq. (4) and determine the optimal values for the number of processing engines and memory units that minimize Eq. (3) using the respective operation complexity and the costs for the processing and memory units established above. The minimal value found for Eq. (3), in years, is set as our security estimate.

In a first calculation, we use the yearly historical prices of MPUs and HDDs from 2000 to 2020 to determine the costs of processing and memory units. In each case we consider the lowest price per component (dollar/GE and dollar/byte) that we found per year. The exact prices as well as the respective sources are detailed in Table 8, Appendix A.

In a second calculation, we make projections of the prices of MPUs and HDDs for the years 2025, 2030, 2035 and 2040 by assuming a *constant* reduction rate starting at year 2020 and estimated from data for the latest 5-year period, i.e., 2015–2020. Specifically, the reduction rate for MPUs is taken as the ratio between a gate cost in 2015 and its cost in 2020. Similarly, for HDDs it is taken as the ratio between the cost of a byte of SSD memory in 2015 and its cost in 2020.[14] The projected prices that we derived are detailed in Table 9, Appendix A.

---

[13] As a relevant point of reference, the annual budget of the NSA in 2013 was estimated at US$10.8 billion https://en.wikipedia.org/wiki/National_Security_Agency.

[14] The use of SSD memory for calculating the cost reduction rate is to be conservative in our estimates: HDD memory is currently cheaper, but SSD is expected to become more cost-effective in the next years.

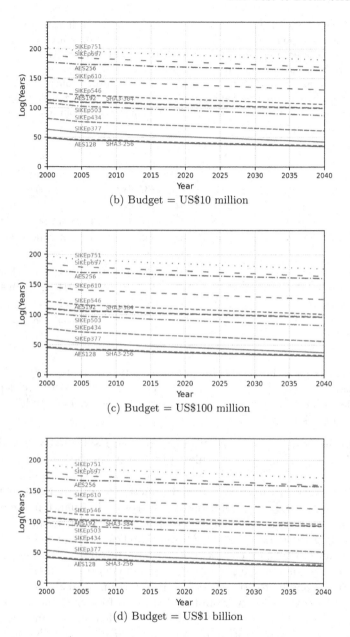

Fig. 4. Security estimates using historical GEs/HDDs prices from 2000 to 2020 and using projections of the same prices from 2025 to 2040, at intervals of five years. Security estimates are expressed as the base-2 logarithms of the number of years required to break a given primitive under a fixed budget. AES is depicted in red, SHA-3 in brown and SIKE in blue. SIKEp377 (new) and SIKEp434 (Round 3) are intended for level 1 (AES128), SIKEp546 (new) and SIKEp610 (Round 3) are intended for level 3 (AES192), and SIKEp697 (new) and SIKEp751 (Round 3) are intended for level 5 (AES256). SIKEp503 (Round 3) is for level 2 (SHA3-128). SHA3-384 determines level 4.

Table 6. Quantum security estimates in terms of gate (G) and depth-width (DW) costs. Results correspond to key-search on AES [17], collision-search on SHA-3 [6,19] and golden collision-search on SIKE. The displayed values for SIKE are the lowest achieved for the respective circuit Maxdepth (MD) assumption and cost metric by either Jaques-Schanck [18] (Grover and Tani), Jaques-Schrottenloher [19] (parallel local prefix-based walk and parallel local multi-Grover) or Biasse-Pring [5] (improved Grover oracle). Estimates for the alternative SIKE parameters were obtained using Jaques-Schrottenloher's script.

Metric	MD	AES key-search Security level			SHA-3 coll. Security level		SIKE collisions log p				log p (This work)		
		1	3	5	2	4	434	503	610	751	377	546	697
G-cost	∞	83	116	148	124	184	109	124	147	178	96	133	166
	2^{96}	83	126	191	134	221	110	134	179	234	96	152	213
	2^{64}	93	157	222	148	268	145	181	235	307	116	203	279
	2^{40}	117	181	246	187	340	184	219	274	345	155	241	318
DW-cost	∞	87	119	152	134	201	126	148	170	211	116	159	198
	2^{96}	87	130	194	145	239	131	158	189	244	116	169	223
	2^{64}	97	161	225	159	285	163	198	252	322	134	219	295
	2^{40}	121	185	249	198	357	187	222	276	346	158	243	319

The estimates for the various budget options for the years 2000–2020, as well as the estimates using projected data for the years 2025–2040, are depicted in Fig. 4 (refer to the full paper version [23, App. D] for extreme budget scenarios of up to one trillion dollars).

Quantum Security. Initially, SIDH and SIKE proposals used Tani's algorithm (of $\mathcal{O}(p^{1/6})$ time and memory complexity) to establish the quantum security of their parameters [3,7,16]. In 2019, Jaques and Schanck [18] established that the complexity of this algorithm is expected to actually achieve a time complexity of $\mathcal{O}(p^{1/4})$ due to costly random memory accesses in the quantum circuit model. More recently, Jaques and Schrottenloher [19] proposed efficient parallel golden collision finding algorithms that use Grover searches and a quantum analogue of vOW to achieve lower gate complexities, also in the quantum circuit model.

In Table 6, we summarize the gate (G-cost) and depth-width (DW-cost) complexities corresponding to all the SIKE parameters under analysis, as well as the respective complexities for AES and SHA-3 taken from [17] and [6,19], respectively. We present the lowest values achieved by either Jaques and Schanck [18] using Grover or Tani's algorithm, Jaques and Schrottenloher's parallel local prefix-based walk or parallel local multi-Grover method [19], or Biasse and Pring's improved Grover oracle for very deep maxdepths (beyond 2^{115}) [5]. Note that the maxdepth values suggested by NIST in [31] are 2^{40}, 2^{64} and 2^{96}. The estimates for our newly proposed parameters use the same procedure followed in [19, §6] and were obtained with Jaques and Schrottenloher's script.

Security Levels. We now have the tools to assess the security of the various SIKE parameters under our model. After observing the estimates in Fig. 4 and

Table 7. Performance results comparing SIKE Round 3 parameters and the alternative parameters proposed in this work. The speed results (rounded to 10^5 cycles) were obtained on a 3.4GHz Intel Core i7-6700 (Skylake) processor for the three SIKE operations: key generation (Gen), encapsulation (Enc), and decapsulation (Dec). Public keys are measured in bytes B.

| NIST sec level | Round 3 SIKE [3,25] | | Speed ($\times 10^6$ cc) | | | Proposed (this work) | | Speed ($\times 10^6$ cc) | | |
	$\log p$	PK	Gen	Enc	Dec	$\log p$	PK	Gen	Enc	Dec
1	434	330 B	5.9	9.7	10.3	377	288 B	3.9	7.3	7.2
2	503	378 B	8.2	13.5	14.4	–	–	–	–	–
3	610	462 B	14.9	27.3	27.4	546	414 B	11.5	19.9	19.9
5	751	564 B	25.2	40.7	43.9	697	528 B	19.8	33.3	35.0

Table 6 (also see the summary of results in Table 10, Appendix B), we can conclude that the SIKE Round 3 parameters achieve higher security than previously assumed. For example, if we look at the calculation for year 2040 with a billion dollar budget (worst case analyzed in Table 10), the security margin is of at least 2^{15} years (case between SIKEp751 and AES256 at level 5) and as high as 2^{48} years (case between SIKEp503 and SHA3-256 at level 2).

When we examine the case of our alternative parameters it can be seen that they approximate levels 1, 3 and 5 more closely. For example, the classical and quantum security of SIKEp377 meets the requirements for level 1, even when considering our most stringent budget scenarios. If we assume the case for the year 2020 with a billion dollar budget, SIKEp377 achieves a security estimate of 2^{40} years, which is above the estimate of 2^{33} for AES128. For the year 2040, AES128 is projected to provide a security of 2^{28} years, while SIKEp377 would achieve 2^{32}. Similar observations hold for SIKEp546 and SIKEp697 with respect to levels 3 (AES192) and 5 (AES256), respectively. SIDHp503 appears to hold its Round 3 position (i.e., level 2), although with a very large margin.[15]

Our results show that the gap between SIKE and AES reduces over time and with larger budgets. Nevertheless, security estimates for the Round 3 and our alternative parameters stay above or virtually match the corresponding AES estimates even for unrealistic budgets [23, App. D] and taking into account that our approach is still conservative and favors SIKE attackers.

Benchmarking Results. To assess the potential impact of using the alternative smaller parameters, we wrote hand-optimized x64 assembly implementations of the field arithmetic for p377, p546 and p697, and integrated them into the SIDH library, version 3.4 [25]. The implementations are written in *constant time*, i.e., there are no secret memory accesses and no secret data branches. Therefore, the software is protected against timing and cache attacks.

---

[15] The classical security of SIKEp503 is actually closer to that of AES192 and SHA3-384. It would be interesting to investigate if further analysis can reduce or eliminate the small gap.

The results on a 3.4 GHz Intel Core i7-6700 (Skylake) processor are shown in Table 7. Following standard practice, TurboBoost was disabled during the tests. For compilation we used clang v3.8.0 with the command `clang -O3`.

Our results show that the new parameters introduce large speedups in the range 1.25–1.40 (comparing the total costs), in addition to reductions in the public key and ciphertext sizes. For example, SIKEp377 is shown to be about 1.4× faster than SIKEp434, while reducing the public key size by $\sim 13\%$.

A   Price Data

Table 8 summarizes the price information that we collected per year for memory (HDD, DRAM and SSD) and Intel/AMD MPUs. For our security estimates, we used the lowest prices available per byte, which in all the cases considered correspond to HDDs. To estimate the cost per gate we considered the MPU (Intel or AMD) that provided the cheapest cost per transistor for a given year. We used the standard assumption that one gate equivalent consists of four transistors. The rows with the "adjusted" costs per byte or gate are obtained by dividing the corresponding costs by the factor 7.40 which approximates the release prices to the chip production cost, as described in the full paper version [23, App. A].

Table 9 summarizes our projections of HDD memory and gate costs for the years between 2025 and 2040. To obtain these values we used a constant cost reduction rate applied starting at the year 2020's prices. Specifically, the reduction rate that we used for MPUs is taken as the ratio between a gate cost in 2015 and its cost in 2020. Similarly, for HDDs it is taken as the ratio between the cost of a byte on SSD memory in 2015 and its cost in 2020. The use of data from SSD memory in this case is to derive conservative estimates, so that SSD is expected to become more cost-effective than HDD in the next years.

The "adjusted" costs were used to calculate the costs of the memory and processing units that are needed to set up the cryptanalytic attacks against SIKE, AES and SHA-3 (see Sect. 6).

Sources. We used the following sources for data collection:

- https://en.wikipedia.org/wiki/List_of_Intel_Core_2_microprocessors
- https://en.wikipedia.org/wiki/List_of_Intel_Core_i3_microprocessors
- https://en.wikipedia.org/wiki/List_of_Intel_Core_i5_microprocessors
- https://en.wikipedia.org/wiki/List_of_Intel_Celeron_microprocessors
- https://en.wikipedia.org/wiki/List_of_Intel_Pentium_D_microprocessors
- https://en.wikipedia.org/wiki/List_of_AMD_Athlon_microprocessors
- https://en.wikipedia.org/wiki/List_of_AMD_Ryzen_microprocessors
- https://en.wikichip.org
- https://www.cpu-world.com
- https://www.newegg.com
- http://jcmit.net/memoryprice.htm
- http://jcmit.net/diskprice.htm
- http://jcmit.net/flashprice.htm

And other several chip manufacturer websites.

Table 8. Historical release prices collected for memory (HDD, DRAM and SSD) and Intel/AMD MPUs from 2000 to 2020. To estimate the cost per gate we considered the MPU (Intel or AMD) that provided the cheapest cost per transistor ("trans.") for a given year. We used the standard assumption that one gate equivalent consists of four transistors. "Adjusted" costs approximate costs based on release prices to costs at production by dividing the corresponding costs by the factor 7.4 (see [23, App. A]).

	2000	2001	2002	2003	2004	2005	2006	2007	2008	2009	2010	2011	2012	2013	2014	2015	2016	2017	2018	2019	2020
HDD (US$)	125.00	259.00	146.00	89.99	97.50	130.00	69.99	99.99	99.99	69.99	89.99	54.99	54.99	54.99	104.99	84.99	221.63	99.99	93.49	149.99	129.99
HDD ($\times 10^{10}$ bytes)	3.1	10	12	12	16	32	32	50	100	100	200	150	150	150	300	300	800	400	400	800	800
Cost (US$) / byte ($\times 10^{-10}$)	40.72	25.90	12.17	7.50	6.09	4.06	2.19	2.00	1.00	0.70	0.45	0.37	0.37	0.37	0.35	0.28	0.28	0.25	0.23	0.19	0.16
"Adjusted" cost ($\times 10^{-11}$)	55.03	35.00	16.45	10.14	8.23	5.49	2.96	2.70	1.35	0.95	0.61	0.50	0.50	0.50	0.47	0.38	0.38	0.34	0.31	0.26	0.22
DRAM (US$)	89.00	18.89	34.19	39.00	39.00	39.00	148.99	49.95	39.99	39.99	39.99	41.99	29.99	29.99	29.99	29.99	44.99	44.99	44.99	44.99	44.99
DRAM ($\times 10^{8}$ bytes)	1.31	1.31	2.62	5.24	5.24	5.24	20.97	20.97	41.94	41.94	41.94	83.89	83.89	83.89	83.89	83.89	167.77	167.77	167.77	167.77	167.77
Cost (US$) / byte ($\times 10^{-10}$)	6793.9	1442.0	1305.0	744.3	744.3	744.3	710.5	238.2	95.4	95.4	95.4	50.1	35.7	35.7	35.7	35.7	26.8	26.8	26.8	26.8	26.8
"Adjusted" cost ($\times 10^{-10}$)	918.1	194.9	176.4	100.6	100.6	100.6	96.0	32.2	12.9	12.9	12.9	6.8	4.8	4.8	4.8	4.8	3.6	3.6	3.6	3.6	3.6
SSD (US$)	-	-	-	-	-	-	-	-	-	-	-	-	-	159.99	179.99	194.99	194.99	49.99	49.99	75.99	75.99
SSD ($\times 10^{11}$ bytes)	-	-	-	-	-	-	-	-	-	-	-	-	-	2.56	4.80	2.40	9.60	9.60	4.80	9.60	9.60
Cost (US$) / byte ($\times 10^{-10}$)	-	-	-	-	-	-	-	-	-	-	-	-	-	6.25	3.75	2.50	2.03	2.03	1.04	0.79	0.79
"Adjusted" cost ($\times 10^{-11}$)	-	-	-	-	-	-	-	-	-	-	-	-	-	8.45	5.07	3.38	2.74	2.74	1.41	1.07	1.07
Intel MPU (US$)	112.0	64.0	33.0	33.0	30.0	30.0	30.0	30.0	30.0	30.0	70.0	42.0	42.0	122.0	42.0	42.0	-	-	-	-	-
Intel MPU ($\times 10^{6}$ trans.)	28.1	28.1	55	55	125	125	125	125	125	125	382	624	1400	1400	1400	1400	-	-	-	-	-
AMD MPU (US$)	-	-	-	-	-	-	-	-	-	-	-	79.0	71.0	71.0	101.0	79.0	58.0	51.0	51.0	51.0	60.0
AMD MPU ($\times 10^{6}$ trans.)	-	-	-	-	-	-	-	-	-	-	-	1178	1303	1303	2410	2410	3100	3100	3100	3100	4940
Cost (US$) / gate ($\times 10^{-8}$)	1594.3	911.0	240.0	240.0	96.0	96.0	96.0	96.0	96.0	96.0	73.3	26.8	21.8	21.8	12.0	12.0	7.48	6.58	6.58	6.58	4.86
"Adjusted" cost ($\times 10^{-9}$)	2154.5	1231.1	324.3	324.3	129.7	129.7	129.7	129.7	129.7	129.7	99.1	36.2	29.5	29.5	16.2	16.2	10.1	8.89	8.89	8.89	6.57
Bytes/gate	3915.6	3517.5	1972.6	3200.4	1575.4	2363.1	4389.2	4800.5	9601.0	13716.2	16290.3	7317.3	5945.4	5945.4	3428.9	4235.8	2701.4	2632.5	2815.6	3509.9	2990.0

Table 9. Projected prices for HDD memory and gates for 2025–2040, at 5-year intervals. The values were obtained by applying a constant reduction factor starting at the adjusted cost in 2020. For MPUs the factor (2.47) is computed by diving a gate cost in 2015 by its cost in 2020. For HDDs the factor (3.16) is computed by dividing the cost of an SSD byte in 2015 by its cost in 2020.

	2025	2030	2035	2040
"Adjusted" cost (US$)/byte ($\times 10^{-13}$)	6.95	2.20	0.70	0.22
"Adjusted" cost (US$)/gate ($\times 10^{-9}$)	2.66	1.08	0.44	0.18
Bytes/gate		3822.5	4886.9	6247.7	7987.4

B   Security Estimates

Table 10. Security estimates in terms of years produced by the budget-based cost model and following the procedure from Sect. 6. The estimates are expressed as the base-2 logarithms of the number of years required to break a given primitive under a fixed budget. Results correspond to key-search on AES using Oechslin's rainbow chains, collision-search on SHA-3 using vOW (case of small number of collisions) and golden collision-search on SIKE using vOW (case of large number of collisions). The hardware (computing power and memory) costs used for the analysis can be found in Appendix A.

Budget	Year	AES key-search Security level 1	3	5	SHA-3 coll. Security level 2	4	SIKE collisions log p 434	503	610	751	log p (This work) 377	546	697
US$10 mill.	2020	39	104	168	41	105	69	95	139	189	50	114	177
	2030	37	101	166	38	102	65	91	134	185	46	110	173
	2040	34	99	163	35	99	60	87	130	181	42	106	168
US$100 mill.	2020	36	101	165	37	105	64	90	134	184	45	109	172
	2030	33	98	162	35	99	60	86	129	180	41	105	168
	2040	31	95	160	32	96	55	82	125	176	37	101	163
US$1 billion	2020	33	97	162	34	98	59	85	129	179	40	104	167
	2030	30	95	159	31	95	55	81	124	175	36	100	163
	2040	28	92	156	29	93	51	77	120	171	32	96	158

References

1. Adj, G., Cervantes-Vázquez, D., Chi-Domínguez, J.-J., Menezes, A., Rodríguez-Henríquez, F.: On the cost of computing isogenies between supersingular elliptic curves. In: Cid, C., Jacobson, M.J., Jr. (eds.) SAC 2018. LNCS, vol. 11349, pp. 322–343. Springer, Cham (2019). https://doi.org/10.1007/978-3-030-10970-7_15

2. Akin, A., Aysu, A., Ulusel, O.C., Savaş, E.: Efficient hardware implementations of high throughput SHA-3 candidates Keccak, Luffa and Blue Midnight Wish for single- and multi-message hashing. In: Makarevich, O.B., et al. (eds.) International Conference on Security of Information and Networks (SIN 2010), pp. 168–177. ACM (2010)

3. Azarderakhsh, R., et al.: Supersingular Isogeny Key Encapsulation (SIKE), 2017–2020. Latest specification available at https://sike.org. Round 1 submission available at https://csrc.nist.gov/CSRC/media/Projects/Post-Quantum-Cryptography/documents/round-1/submissions/SIKE.zip. Round 2 submission available at https://csrc.nist.gov/CSRC/media/Projects/Post-Quantum-Cryptography/documents/round-2/submissions/SIKE-Round2.zip

4. Bernstein, D.J.: Understanding brute force. In: Workshop Record of ECRYPT STVL Workshop on Symmetric Key Encryption, eSTREAM report 2005/036 (2005)

5. Biasse, J.-F., Pring, B.: A framework for reducing the overhead of the quantum oracle for use with Grover's algorithm with applications to cryptanalysis of SIKE. In: MathCrypt 2019 (2019)

6. Chailloux, A., Naya-Plasencia, M., Schrottenloher, A.: An efficient quantum collision search algorithm and implications on symmetric cryptography. In: Takagi, T., Peyrin, T. (eds.) ASIACRYPT 2017. LNCS, vol. 10625, pp. 211–240. Springer, Cham (2017). https://doi.org/10.1007/978-3-319-70697-9_8

7. Costello, C., Longa, P., Naehrig, M.: Efficient algorithms for supersingular isogeny Diffie-Hellman. In: Robshaw, M., Katz, J. (eds.) CRYPTO 2016. LNCS, vol. 9814, pp. 572–601. Springer, Heidelberg (2016). https://doi.org/10.1007/978-3-662-53018-4_21

8. Costello, C., Longa, P., Naehrig, M., Renes, J., Virdia, F.: Improved classical cryptanalysis of SIKE in practice. In: Kiayias, A., Kohlweiss, M., Wallden, P., Zikas, V. (eds.) PKC 2020. LNCS, vol. 12111, pp. 505–534. Springer, Cham (2020). https://doi.org/10.1007/978-3-030-45388-6_18

9. Couveignes, J.-M.: Hard homogeneous spaces. Cryptology ePrint Archive, Report 2006/291 (2006). http://eprint.iacr.org/2006/291

10. De Feo, L., Jao, D., Plût, J.: Towards quantum-resistant cryptosystems from supersingular elliptic curve isogenies. J. Math. Cryptology **8**(3), 209–247 (2014)

11. Dennard, R.H., Gaensslen, F., Yu, H.-N., Rideout, L., Bassous, E., LeBlanc, A.: Design of ion-implanted MOSFET's with very small physical dimensions. IEEE J. Solid-State Circuits **SC-9**(5), 256–268 (1974)

12. Faz-Hernández, A., Hernandez, J.L., Ochoa-Jiménez, E., Rodríguez-Henríquez, F.: A faster software implementation of the supersingular isogeny Diffie-Hellman key exchange protocol. IEEE Trans. Comput. **67**(11), 1622–1636 (2018)

13. International Roadmap for Devices and Systems (IRDS), 2016–2020. https://irds.ieee.org/

14. The International Technology Roadmap for Semiconductors (ITRS). ITRS reports, 2001–2015. http://www.itrs2.net/itrs-reports.html

15. Gargini, P.: The International Technology Roadmap for Semiconductors (ITRS): "Past, present and future". In: IEEE Gallium Arsenide Integrated Circuits (GaAs IC) Symposium, pp. 3–5. IEEE (2000)

16. Jao, D., De Feo, L.: Towards quantum-resistant cryptosystems from supersingular elliptic curve isogenies. In: Yang, B.-Y. (ed.) PQCrypto 2011. LNCS, vol. 7071, pp. 19–34. Springer, Heidelberg (2011). https://doi.org/10.1007/978-3-642-25405-5_2

17. Jaques, S., Naehrig, M., Roetteler, M., Virdia, F.: Implementing grover Oracles for quantum key search on AES and LowMC. In: Canteaut, A., Ishai, Y. (eds.) EURO-CRYPT 2020. LNCS, vol. 12106, pp. 280–310. Springer, Cham (2020). https://doi.org/10.1007/978-3-030-45724-2_10

18. Jaques, S., Schanck, J.M.: Quantum cryptanalysis in the RAM model: claw-finding attacks on SIKE. In: Boldyreva, A., Micciancio, D. (eds.) CRYPTO 2019. LNCS, vol. 11692, pp. 32–61. Springer, Cham (2019). https://doi.org/10.1007/978-3-030-26948-7_2

19. Jaques, S., Schrottenloher, A.: Low-gate quantum golden collision finding. In: Selected Areas in Cryptography - SAC 2020 (2020). http://eprint.iacr.org/2020/424

20. Khan, S.M., Mann, A.: AI chips: what they are and why they matter. Center for Security and Emerging Technology (2020)

21. Koziel, B., Ackie, A.-B., El Khatib, R., Azarderakhsh, R., Kermani, M.M.: SIKE'd Up: fast and secure hardware architectures for supersingular isogeny key encapsulation. IEEE Trans. Circuits Syst. I: Regular Papers (2020). Software Available at https://github.com/kozielbrian/VHDL-SIKE_R2

22. Koç, Ç.K., Acar, T., Kaliski, B.S., Jr.: Analyzing and comparing Montgomery multiplication algorithms. IEEE Micro **16**(3), 26–33 (1996)

23. Longa, P., Wang, W., Szefer, J.: The cost to break SIKE: a comparative hardware-based analysis with AES and SHA-3 (full paper version). Cryptology ePrint Archive, Report 2020/1457 (2020). https://eprint.iacr.org/2020/1457

24. Massolino, P.M.C., Longa, P., Renes, J., Batina, L.: A compact and scalable hardware/software co-design of SIKE. IACR Trans. Cryptogr. Hardw. Embed. Syst. **2020**(2), 245–271 (2020). Software Available at https://github.com/pmassolino/hw-sike

25. Microsoft. SIDH Library v3.4 (2015–2021). https://github.com/Microsoft/PQCrypto-SIDH

26. Microsoft. vOW4SIKE Library (2020). https://github.com/microsoft/vOW4SIKE

27. Moore, G.E.: Cramming more components onto integrated circuits. Electronics **38**(8), 114–117 (1965)

28. Naehrig, M., Renes, J.: Dual isogenies and their application to public-key compression for isogeny-based cryptography. In: Galbraith, S.D., Moriai, S. (eds.) ASIACRYPT 2019. LNCS, vol. 11922, pp. 243–272. Springer, Cham (2019). https://doi.org/10.1007/978-3-030-34621-8_9

29. National Institute of Standards and Technology (NIST). Post-quantum cryptography standardization - round 3 submissions (2020). https://csrc.nist.gov/Projects/Post-Quantum-Cryptography/Round-3-Submissions

30. National Institute of Standards and Technology (NIST). Status report on the second round of the NIST post-quantum cryptography standardization process (2020). https://nvlpubs.nist.gov/nistpubs/ir/2020/NIST.IR.8309.pdf

31. National Institute of Standards and Technology (NIST). Submission requirements and evaluation criteria for the post-quantum cryptography standardization process, December 2016. https://csrc.nist.gov/CSRC/media/Projects/Post-Quantum-Cryptography/documents/call-for-proposals-final-dec-2016.pdf

32. Oechslin, P.: Making a faster cryptanalytic time-memory trade-off. In: Boneh, D. (ed.) CRYPTO 2003. LNCS, vol. 2729, pp. 617–630. Springer, Heidelberg (2003). https://doi.org/10.1007/978-3-540-45146-4_36

33. National Institute of Standards and Technology (NIST). Advanced Encryption Standard (AES. Federal Inf. Process. Stds. (FIPS PUBS) - 197 (2001). https://nvlpubs.nist.gov/nistpubs/FIPS/NIST.FIPS.197.pdf

34. National Institute of Standards and Technology (NIST). SHA-3 standard: Permutation-based hash and extendable-output functions. Federal Inf. Process. Stds. (FIPS PUBS) - 202 (2015). https://nvlpubs.nist.gov/nistpubs/FIPS/NIST.FIPS.202.pdf
35. Geovandro, C.C.F.P., Doliskani, J., Jao, D.: X-only point addition formula and faster compressed SIKE. J. Cryptogr. Eng. **11**(1), 57–69 (2021)
36. RISC-V, 2010–2020. https://riscv.org/
37. Rostovtsev, A., Stolbunov, A.: Public-key cryptosystem based on isogenies. Cryptology ePrint Archive, Report 2006/145 (2006). http://eprint.iacr.org/2006/145
38. Silvaco. NanGate FreePDK45 open-cell library. https://si2.org/open-cell-library/. Accessed Sept 2020
39. Spencer, W.J., Seidel, T.E.: National technology roadmaps: the U.S. semiconductor experience. In: International Conference on Solid-State and IC Technology (ICSICT). IEEE (1995)
40. Stolbunov, A.: Constructing public-key cryptographic schemes based on class group action on a set of isogenous elliptic curves. Adv. Math. Commun. **4**(2), 215–235 (2010)
41. Ueno, R., et al.: High throughput/gate AES hardware architectures based on datapath compression. IEEE Trans. Comput. **69**(4), 534–548 (2020)
42. van Oorschot, P.C., Wiener, M.J.: Parallel collision search with application to hash functions and discrete logarithms. In: Denning, D.E., Pyle, R., Ganesan, R., Sandhu, R.S. (eds.) ACM Conference on Computer and Communications Security - CCS 1994, pp. 210–218. ACM (1994)
43. van Oorschot, P.C., Wiener, M.J.: Parallel collision search with cryptanalytic applications. J. Cryptology **12**(1), 1–28 (1999)
44. Vélu, J.: Isogénies entre courbes elliptiques. Comptes Rendus de l'Académie des Sciences des Paris **273**, 238–241 (1971)
45. VexRiscv, 2017–2020. https://github.com/SpinalHDL/VexRiscv/
46. Wiener, M.J.: The full cost of cryptanalytic attacks. J. Cryptology **17**(2), 105–124 (2004)

Improved Torsion-Point Attacks on SIDH Variants

Victoria de Quehen[1]([✉]), Péter Kutas[2], Chris Leonardi[1], Chloe Martindale[3], Lorenz Panny[4], Christophe Petit[2,5], and Katherine E. Stange[6]

[1] ISARA Corporation, Waterloo, Canada
chris.leonardi@isara.com
[2] School of Computer Science, University of Birmingham, Birmingham, UK
P.Kutas@bham.ac.uk
[3] Department of Computer Science, University of Bristol, Bristol, UK
chloe.martindale@bristol.ac.uk
[4] Institute of Information Science, Academia Sinica, Taipei, Taiwan
lorenz@yx7.cc
[5] Laboratoire d'Informatique, Université Libre de Bruxelles, Brussels, Belgium
christophe.petit@ulb.be
[6] Department of Mathematics, University of Colorado Boulder, Boulder, CO, USA
kstange@math.colorado.edu

Abstract. SIDH is a post-quantum key exchange algorithm based on the presumed difficulty of finding isogenies between supersingular elliptic curves. However, SIDH and related cryptosystems also reveal additional information: the restriction of a secret isogeny to a subgroup of the curve (torsion-point information). Petit [31] was the first to demonstrate that torsion-point information could noticeably lower the difficulty of finding secret isogenies. In particular, Petit showed that "overstretched" parameterizations of SIDH could be broken in polynomial time. However, this did not impact the security of any cryptosystems proposed in the literature. The contribution of this paper is twofold: First, we strengthen the techniques of [31] by exploiting additional information coming from a dual and a Frobenius isogeny. This extends the impact of torsion-point attacks considerably. In particular, our techniques yield a classical attack that completely breaks the n-party group key exchange of [2], first introduced as GSIDH in [17], for 6 parties or more, and a quantum attack for 3 parties or more that improves on the best known asymptotic complexity. We also provide a Magma implementation of our attack for 6 parties.

Author list in alphabetical order; see https://www.ams.org/profession/leaders/culture/CultureStatement04.pdf. Lorenz Panny was a PhD student at Technische Universiteit Eindhoven while this research was conducted. Péter Kutas and Christophe Petit's work was supported by EPSRC grant EP/S01361X/1. Katherine E. Stange was supported by NSF-CAREER CNS-1652238. This work was supported in part by the Commission of the European Communities through the Horizon 2020 program under project number 643161 (ECRYPT-NET) and in part by NWO project 651.002.004 (CHIST-ERA USEIT). Date of this document: 2021-06-25. ©IACR 2021. This article is the final version submitted by the author(s) to the IACR and to Springer-Verlag on June 25, 2021. The version published by Springer-Verlag is available at <DOI>.".

We give the full range of parameters for which our attacks apply. Second, we construct SIDH variants designed to be weak against our attacks; this includes backdoor choices of starting curve, as well as backdoor choices of base-field prime. We stress that our results do not degrade the security of, or reveal any weakness in, the NIST submission SIKE [20].

1   Introduction

With the advent of quantum computers, commonly deployed cryptosystems based on the integer-factorization or discrete-logarithm problems will need to be replaced by new post-quantum cryptosystems that rely on different assumptions. Isogeny-based cryptography is a relatively new field within post-quantum cryptography. An *isogeny* is a non-zero rational map between elliptic curves that also preserves the group structure, and isogeny-based cryptography is based on the conjectured hardness of finding isogenies between elliptic curves over finite fields.

Isogeny-based cryptography stands out amongst post-quantum primitives due to the fact that isogeny-based key-exchange achieves the smallest key sizes of all candidates. Isogeny-based schemes also appear to be fairly flexible; for example, a relatively efficient post-quantum non-interactive key agreement protocol called CSIDH [8] is built on isogeny assumptions.

The *Supersingular Isogeny Diffie–Hellman* protocol, or *SIDH*, was the first practical isogeny-based key-exchange protocol, proposed in 2011 by Jao and De Feo [22]. The security of SIDH relies on the hardness of solving (a special case of) the following problem:[1]

Problem 1 (Supersingular Isogeny with Torsion (SSI-T)). For a prime p and smooth coprime integers A and B, given two supersingular elliptic curves $E_0/\mathbb{F}_{p^2}$ and $E/\mathbb{F}_{p^2}$ connected by an unknown degree-A isogeny $\varphi: E_0 \to E$, and given the restriction of φ to the B-torsion of E_0, recover an[2] isogeny φ matching these constraints.

SSI-T is a generalization of the "Computational Supersingular Isogeny problem", or CSSI for short, defined in [22]. Although the CSSI problem that appears in the literature also includes torsion information, we use the name SSI-T to stress the importance of the additional torsion information. Additionally, we consider more flexibility in the parameters than CSSI to challenge the implicit assumption that even with torsion information the hardness of the protocol always scales with the degree of the isogenies and the characteristic p of the field.

The best known way to break SIDH by treating it as a pure isogeny problem is a claw-finding approach on the isogeny graph having classical complexity $O(\sqrt{A} \cdot$

---

[1] See Sect. 2.2 for how the objects discussed are represented computationally.

[2] These constraints do not necessarily uniquely determine φ, but any efficiently computable isogeny from E_0 to E is usually enough to recover the SIDH secret [18,37]. Moreover, φ is unique whenever $B^2 > 4A$ [28, §4].

polylog(p)) and no known quantum speedups viable in reality [23].[3] However, it is clear that SSI-T provides the attacker with more information than the "pure" supersingular isogeny problem, where the goal is to find an isogeny between two given supersingular elliptic curves without any further hints or restrictions.

The first indication that additional torsion-point information could be exploited to attack a supersingular isogeny-based cryptosystem was an active key-reuse attack against SIDH published in 2016 [18] by Galbraith, Petit, Shani, and Ti. In [18] the attacker sends key-exchange messages with manipulated torsion points and detects whether the key exchange succeeds. This allows recovery of the secret key within $O(\log A)$ queries. To mitigate this attack, [18] proposes using the Fujisaki–Okamoto transform, which generically renders a CPA-secure public-key encryption scheme CCA-secure, and therefore thwarts those so-called *reaction attacks*. The resulting scheme *Supersingular Isogeny Key Encapsulation*, or *SIKE* [20] for short, is the only isogeny-based submission to NIST's standardization project for post-quantum cryptography [29], and is currently a Round 3 "Alternate Candidate".

However, SSI-T can be easier than finding isogenies in general. Indeed, a line of work [7,31] revealed a separation between the hardness of the supersingular isogeny problem and SSI-T for some parameterizations. This is potentially concerning because several similar schemes have been proposed that are based on the more general SSI-T, and in particular, not clearly based on the CSSI problem as stated in [22] due to CSSI's restrictions on A and B [2,5,11,14,17,34]. For example, for the security of the GSIDH n-party group key agreement [2,17], SSI-T must hold for $B \approx A^{n-1}$.

A particular choice made in SIKE is to fix the "starting curve" E_0 to be a curve defined over $\mathbb{F}_p$ that has small-degree non-scalar endomorphisms; these are very rare properties within the set of all supersingular curves defined over $\mathbb{F}_{p^2}$. On its own, such a choice of starting curve does not seem to have any negative security implications for SIKE. However, in addition to their active attack, [18] shows that given an explicit description of *both* curves' endomorphism rings, it is (under reasonable heuristic assumptions) possible to recover the secret isogeny in SIKE. The argument in [18] does not use torsion-point information, but only applies if the curves are sufficiently close; recently [37] showed that if torsion-point information is provided the two curves do not need to be close.

The approach for solving SSI-T introduced by Petit in 2017 [31] exploits both torsion-point information and knowledge of the endomorphism ring of the special starting curve. This attack is efficient for certain parameters, for which the "pure" supersingular isogeny problem still appears to be hard. It uses the knowledge of the secret isogeny restricted to a large torsion subgroup to recover the isogeny itself, giving a *passive* heuristic polynomial-time attack on non-standard variants of SIDH satisfying $B > A^4 > p^4$. However, in practice, for all the SIDH-style schemes proposed in the literature so far, both A and B are

---

[3] Note that the naïve meet-in-the-middle approach has prohibitively large memory requirements. Collision finding à la van Oorschot–Wiener thus performs better in practice, although its time complexity is worse in theory [1].

taken to be divisors of $p^2 - 1$, allowing torsion points to be defined over small field extensions, which makes the resulting scheme more efficient. One of the contributions of this work is extending torsion-point attacks to have a stronger impact on parameterizations where A and B are divisors of $p \pm 1$ or $p^2 - 1$.

1.1 Our Contributions

We improve upon and extend Petit's 2017 *torsion-point attacks* [31] in several ways. Our technical results have the following cryptographic implications:

- We give an attack on n-party group key agreement [2,17], see Sect. 7.1 and in particular Table 1. This attack applies to the GSIDH protocol of [17], not to the SIBD procotol of [17]. Our attack yields, under Heuristic 2:
  - A polynomial-time break for $n \geq 6$.
  - An improved classical attack for $n \geq 5$.
  - An improved quantum attack for $n \geq 3$ (compared to the asymptotic complexity for quantum claw-finding computed in [23]).

  We provide a Magma [6] implementation of our attack on 6-party group key agreement, see https://github.com/torsion-attacks-SIDH/6party.
- We give an attack on B-SIDH [11] that, under Heuristic 1, is asymptotically better than quantum claw-finding (with respect to [23]), although it does not weaken the security claims of [11] (see Sect. 7.2).
- We show that setting up a B-SIDH group key agreement in the natural way would yield a polynomial-time attack for 4 or more parties (see Sect. 7.3).
- More generally, we solve Problem SSI-T (under plausible explicit heuristics) in (Fig. 1):
  1. Polynomial time when
     - $j(E_0) = 1728$, $B > pA$, $p > A$, A has (at most) $O(\log \log p)$ distinct prime factors, and B is at most polynomial in A (Proposition 9 and Corollary 7).
     - $j(E_0) = 1728$, $B > \sqrt{p}A^2$, $p > A$, A has (at most) $O(\log \log p)$ distinct prime factors, and B is at most polynomial in A (Proposition 11 and Corollary 8).
     - E_0 is a specially constructed "backdoor curve", $B > A^2$, and A has (at most) $O(\log \log p)$ distinct prime factors (Theorem 15 and Algorithm 3).
     - $j(E_0) = 1728$ and p is a specially constructed backdoor prime (Sects. 5.3 and 5.4).
  2. Superpolynomial time but asymptotically more efficient than meet-in-the-middle on a classical computer when
     - $j(E_0) = 1728$, $B > \max\left\{\sqrt{p}A^{\frac{3}{4}}, A, p\right\}$, A has (at most) $O(\log \log p)$ distinct prime factors, and B is at most polynomial in A (Corollary 26).
     - $j(E_0) = 1728$, $B > \sqrt{p}A$, A has (at most) $O(\log \log p)$ distinct prime factors, and B is at most polynomial in A (Corollary 28).

- E_0 is a specially constructed "backdoor curve" and A has (at most) $O(\log \log p)$ distinct prime factors (Proposition 31).
3. Superpolynomial time but asymptotically more efficient than quantum claw-finding (with respect to [23]) when $j(E_0) = 1728$, $B > \sqrt{p}$, A has (at most) $O(\log \log p)$ distinct prime factors, and B is at most polynomial in A (Corollary 28).

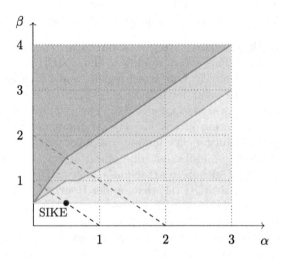

Fig. 1. Performance of our attacks for $j(E_0) = 1728$. Here $A \approx p^\alpha$ and $B \approx p^\beta$. Parameters above the red, orange and yellow curves are parameters admitting a polynomial-time attack, an improvement over the best classical attacks, and an improvement over the best quantum attacks respectively. Parameters below the upper dashed line are those allowing $AB \mid (p^2 - 1)$ as in [11]. Parameters below the lower dashed line are those allowing $AB \mid (p-1)$ as in [20,21]. The blue dot corresponds to SIKE parameters. (Color figure online)

These cryptographic implications are consequences of the following new mathematical results:

- In Sect. 3, we formalize the hardness assumption and reduction implicit in [31]. We call this hardness assumption the *Shifted Lollipop Endomorphism* (SLE) Problem.
- In Sect. 4, we give two improved reductions to SLE (leading to our *dual isogeny attack* and *Frobenius isogeny attack*).
- In Sect. 5, we:
    - Introduce "backdoor" curves, which, when used as E_0, allows us to solve SSI-T in polynomial time if $B > A^2$.
    - Give a method to construct backdoor curves and study their frequency.
    - Introduce "backdoor" primes, which, when used for p, allows us to solve SSI-T in polynomial time.

- In Sect. 6, we show how to extend both the dual isogeny attack and the Frobenius isogeny attack to allow for superpolynomial attacks.

We emphasize that none of our attacks apply to the NIST candidate SIKE: for each attack described in this paper, at least one aspect of SIKE needs to be changed (e.g., the balance of the degrees of the secret isogenies, the starting curve, or the base-field prime).

1.2   Comparison to Earlier Work

In [2], the authors estimated that the attack from [31] would render their scheme insecure for 400 parties or more. In contrast, we give a complete break when there are at least 6 parties.

The cryptanalysis done by Bottinelli et al. [7] also gave a reduction in the same vein as Petit's 2017 paper [31]. Our work overlaps with theirs (only) in Corollary 8, and the only similarity in techniques is in the use of "triangular decomposition" [7, §5.1], see the middle diagram in Fig. 4. Although their improvement is akin to the one given by our dual isogeny attack, they require additional (shifted lollipop) endomorphisms; unfortunately, we have not found a way to combine the two methods. Moreover, our results go beyond [7] in several ways: we additionally introduce the Frobenius isogeny attack (in particular giving rise to our attack on group key agreement). We consider multiple trade-offs for both the dual and the Frobenius isogeny attacks by allowing for superpolynomial attacks, as well as considering other starting curves and base-field primes.

1.3   Outline

In Sect. 2 we go over various preliminaries, including reviewing SIDH. In Sect. 3 we define the relevant hard isogeny problems and give a technical preview; we also outline the idea behind our attacks and how they give rise to reductions of the SSI-T Problem. In Sect. 4 we prove our reductions and give two new algorithms to solve SSI-T in polynomial time for certain parameter sets. In Sect. 5 we introduce backdoor curves E_0 and backdoor primes p for which we can solve SSI-T in polynomial time for certain parameter sets. In Sect. 6 we extend the attacks of Sects. 4 and 5 to superpolynomial attacks. In Sect. 7 we give the impact of our attacks on cryptographic protocols in the literature. In Sect. 8 we pose an open question on constructing new reductions.

2   Preliminaries

2.1   The Supersingular Isogeny Diffie–Hellman Protocol Family

We give a somewhat generalized high-level description of SIDH [22]. Recall that $E[N]$ denotes the N-torsion subgroup of an elliptic curve E and $[m]$ denotes scalar multiplication by m. The public parameters of the system are two smooth coprime numbers A and B, a prime p of the form $p = ABf - 1$, where f is a small cofactor, and a supersingular elliptic curve E_0 defined over $\mathbb{F}_{p^2}$ together with points $P_A, Q_A, P_B, Q_B \in E_0$ such that $E_0[A] = \langle P_A, Q_A \rangle$ and $E_0[B] = \langle P_B, Q_B \rangle$. The protocol then proceeds as follows:

1. Alice chooses a random cyclic subgroup of $E_0[A]$ as $G_A = \langle P_A + [x_A]Q_A \rangle$ and Bob chooses a random cyclic subgroup of $E_0[B]$ as $G_B = \langle P_B + [x_B]Q_B \rangle$.
2. Alice computes the isogeny $\varphi_A : E_0 \to E_0/\langle G_A \rangle =: E_A$ and Bob computes the isogeny $\varphi_B : E_0 \to E_0/\langle G_B \rangle =: E_B$.
3. Alice sends the curve E_A and the two points $\varphi_A(P_B), \varphi_A(Q_B)$ to Bob. Similarly, Bob sends $\big(E_B, \varphi_B(P_A), \varphi_B(Q_A)\big)$ to Alice.
4. Alice and Bob use the given torsion points to obtain the shared secret curve $E_0/\langle G_A, G_B \rangle$. To do so, Alice computes $\varphi_B(G_A) = \varphi_B(P_A) + [x_A]\varphi_B(Q_A)$ and uses the fact that $E_0/\langle G_A, G_B \rangle \cong E_B/\langle \varphi_B(G_A) \rangle$. Bob proceeds analogously.

The SIKE proposal [20] suggests various choices of (p, A, B) depending on the targeted security level: All parameter sets use powers of two and three for A and B, respectively, with $A \approx B$ and $f = 1$. For example, the smallest parameter set suggested in [20] uses $p = 2^{216} \cdot 3^{137} - 1$. Other constructions belonging to the SIDH "family tree" of protocols use different types of parameters [2,11,17,34].

We may assume knowledge of $\mathrm{End}(E_0)$: The only known way to construct supersingular elliptic curves is by reduction of elliptic curves with CM by a small discriminant (which implies small-degree endomorphisms: see [9,27]), or by isogeny walks starting from such curves (where knowledge of the path reveals the endomorphism ring, thus requiring trusted setup). A common choice when $p \equiv 3 \pmod 4$ is $j(E_0) = 1728$ or a small-degree isogeny neighbour of that curve [20]. Various variants of SIDH exist in the literature. We will call a variant an *SIDH-like* protocol if its security can be broken by solving SSI-T for some values of A and B.

In [2] the authors propose the following n-party key agreement, first introduced as GSIDH in [17].[4] The idea is to use primes of the form $p = f \prod_{i=1}^{n} \ell_i^{e_i} - 1$ where ℓ_i is the i-th prime number, the i-th party's secret isogeny has degree $\ell_i^{e_i}$, the i-th participant provides the images of a basis of the $\prod_{j=1}^{n} \ell_j^{e_j}/\ell_i^{e_i}$ torsion, and f is a small cofactor. They choose the starting curve to be of j-invariant 1728 and choose the e_i in such a way that all the $\ell_i^{e_i}$ are of roughly the same size. This is an example of an SIDH-like protocol; for this protocol to be secure it is required that SSI-T be hard when $A = \ell_1^{e_1}$ and $B = f \prod_{i=2}^{n} \ell_i^{e_i}$. However, we prove in Theorem 33 that SSI-T can be solved in polynomial time for 6 or more parties; also see Table 1 for the complexity of our attack for any number of parties.

Another example of a SIDH-like scheme is B-SIDH [11]. In B-SIDH, the prime has the property that $p^2 - 1$ is smooth (as opposed to just $p - 1$ being smooth) and $A \approx B \approx p$. It would seem that choosing parameters this way one has to work over $\mathbb{F}_{p^4}$ but in fact the scheme simultaneously works with the curve and its quadratic twist (i.e., a curve which is not isomorphic to the original

---

[4] [17] also proposes a different group key agreement, SIBD, to which our attack does not apply.

curve over $\mathbb{F}_{p^2}$ but has the same j-invariant) and avoids the use of extension fields. The main advantage of B-SIDH is that the base-field primes used can be considerably smaller than the primes used in SIDH. We discuss the impact of our attacks of B-SIDH in Subsect. 7.2; although we give an improvement on the quantum attack of [23] the parameter choices in [11] are not affected as they were chosen with a significant quantum security margin.

The general concept of using primes of this form extends beyond the actual B-SIDH scheme. As a final example of an SIDH-like scheme, consider the natural idea of using B-SIDH in a group key agreement context. The reason that this construction is a natural choice is that a large number of parties implies a large base-field prime, which is an issue both in terms of efficiency and key size. Using a B-SIDH prime could in theory enable the use of primes of half the size. However, as we show in Corollary 35, such a scheme is especially susceptible to our attacks and is broken in polynomial time for 4 or more parties.

2.2 Notation

Throughout this paper, we work with the field $\mathbb{F}_{p^2}$ for a prime p. In our analysis we often want to omit factors polynomial in $\log p$; as such, from this point on we will abbreviate $O(g \cdot \text{polylog}(p))$ by $O^*(g)$.[5] Similarly, a number is called *smooth*, without further qualification, if all of its prime factors are $O^*(1)$. *Polynomial time* without explicitly mentioning the variables means "polynomial in the representation size of the input" — usually the logarithms of integers. An algorithm is called *efficient* if its runs in polynomial time.

We let $\mathcal{B}_{p,\infty}$ denote the quaternion algebra ramified at p and ∞, for which we use a fixed $\mathbb{Q}$-basis $\langle 1,\mathbf{i},\mathbf{j},\mathbf{ij}\rangle$ such that $\mathbf{j}^2 = -p$ and $\mathbf{i}$ is a nonzero endomorphism of minimal norm satisfying $\mathbf{ij} = -\mathbf{ji}$. Quaternions are treated symbolically throughout; they are simply formal linear combinations of $1,\mathbf{i},\mathbf{j},\mathbf{ij}$.

For any positive integer N we write $\text{sqfr}(N)$ for the squarefree part of N.

Representation of Elliptic-Curve Points and Isogenies. We will generally require that the objects we are working with have "compact" representation (that is, size $\text{polylog}(p)$ bits), and that maps can be evaluated at points of representation size $\text{polylog}(p)$ in time $\text{polylog}(p)$.

In the interest of generality, we will not force a specific choice of representation, but for concreteness, the following data formats are examples of suitable instantiations:

- For an elliptic curve E defined over an extension of $\mathbb{F}_p$ and an integer N, a point in $E[N]$ may be stored as a tuple consisting of one point in $E[q_i^{e_i}]$ for each prime power $q_i^{e_i}$ in the factorization of N, each represented naïvely as coordinates. This "CRT-style" representation has size $\text{polylog}(p)$ when N is powersmooth and polynomial in p. (In some cases, storing points in $E[N]$

---

[5] Each occurrence of $\text{polylog}(p)$ is shorthand for a concrete, fixed polynomial in $\log p$. (The notation is *not* meant to imply that all instances of $\text{polylog}(p)$ be the same).

naïvely may be more efficient, for instance in the beneficial situation that $E[N] \subseteq E(\mathbb{F}_{p^k})$ for some small extension degree k.)

- A smooth-degree isogeny may be represented as a sequence (often of length one) of isogenies, each of which is represented by an (often singleton) set of generators of its kernel subgroup.
- Endomorphisms of a curve E_0 with known endomorphism ring spanned by a set of efficiently evaluatable endomorphisms may be stored as a formal $\mathbb{Z}$-linear combination of such "nice" endomorphisms. Evaluation is done by first evaluating each basis endomorphism separately, then taking the appropriate linear combination of the resulting points.

In some of our algorithms, we will deal with the *restriction* of an isogeny to some N-torsion subgroup, where N is smooth. This object is motivated by the auxiliary points $\varphi_A(P_B), \varphi_A(Q_B)$ given in the SIDH protocol (Sect. 2.1), and it can be represented in the same way: The restriction of an isogeny $\varphi \colon E \to E'$ to the N-torsion subgroup $E[N]$ is stored as a tuple of points $(P, Q, \varphi(P), \varphi(Q)) \in E^2 \times E'^2$, where $\{P, Q\}$ forms a basis of $E[N]$. Then, to evaluate φ on any other N-torsion point $R \in E[N]$, we first decompose R over the basis $\{P, Q\}$, yielding a linear combination $R = [i]P + [j]Q$. (This two-dimensional discrete-logarithm computation is feasible in polynomial time as N was assumed to be smooth.) Then, we may simply recover $\varphi(R)$ as $[i]\varphi(P) + [j]\varphi(Q)$, exploiting the fact that φ is a group homomorphism.

2.3   Quantum Computation Cost Assumptions

In the context of NIST's post-quantum cryptography standardization process [29], there is a significant ongoing effort to estimate the quantum cost of fundamental cryptanalysis tasks in practice. In particular, while it seems well-accepted that Grover's algorithm provides a square-root quantum speedup, the complexity of the claimed cube-root claw-finding algorithm of Tani [38] has been disputed by Jaques and Schanck [23], and the topic is still subject to ongoing research [24].

Several attacks we present in this paper use claw-finding algorithms as a subroutine, and the state-of-the-art algorithms against which we compare them are also claw-finding algorithms. We stress, however, that the insight provided by our attacks is independent of the choice of the quantum computation model. For concreteness we chose the RAM model studied in detail by Jaques and Schanck in [23], in which it is argued that quantum computers do not seem to offer a significant speedup over classical computers for the task of claw-finding. Adapting our various calculations to other existing and future quantum computing cost models, in particular with respect to claw-finding, is certainly possible.

3   Overview

Standard attacks on SIDH follow two general approaches: they either solve the supersingular isogeny problem directly, or they reduce finding an isogeny to computing endomorphism rings. However, SIDH is based on SSI-T introduced above, where an adversary is also given the restriction of the secret isogeny to the B-torsion of the starting curve E_0. Exploiting this B-torsion information led to a new line of attack as first illustrated in [31].

In Subsect. 3.1 we discuss the Supersingular Isogeny Problem and SSI-T. Petit's work was the first to show an apparent separation between the hardness of SSI-T and the hardness of the Supersingular Isogeny Problem in certain settings. In this work we introduce a new isogeny problem, the Shifted Lollipop Endomorphism Problem (SLE). This problem was implicit in Petit's work [31], which contained a purely algebraic reduction from SSI-T to this new hard problem. We improve upon the work of [31] by giving two significantly stronger reductions. In Subsect. 3.2 we sketch the main idea behind the reduction obtained by Petit. In Subsect. 3.3 we present a technical overview which covers the ideas behind our two improved reduction variants.

In Sect. 4 we will present and analyze our two reductions, and give algorithms to solve SLE for certain parameter sets. As we will see, the combination of our reductions and our algorithms to solve particular parameter sets of SLE give rise to two families of improvements on the torsion-point attacks of [31] on SIDH-like protocols; these attacks will additionally exploit the dual of the secret isogeny and the Frobenius isogeny.

3.1 Hard Isogeny Problems

We first review the most basic hardness assumption in isogeny-based cryptography:

Problem 2 (Supersingular Isogeny). Given a prime p, a smooth integer A, and two supersingular elliptic curves $E_0/\mathbb{F}_{p^2}$ and $E/\mathbb{F}_{p^2}$ guaranteed to be A-isogenous, find an isogeny $\varphi \colon E_0 \to E$ of degree A.

In SIDH, we denote Alice's secret isogeny $\varphi_A : E_0 \to E_A$, but in general we will denote some unknown isogeny by $\varphi : E_0 \to E$.

Recall that Alice's public key contains not only the curve E but also the points $\varphi(P), \varphi(Q)$ for a fixed basis $\{P, Q\}$ of $E_0[B]$. Since B is smooth, knowing $\varphi(P)$ and $\varphi(Q)$ allows us to efficiently compute the restriction of φ to the torsion subgroup $E_0[B]$ [33]. Hence, it is more accurate to say that the security of SIDH is based on SSI-T, which includes this additional torsion information.

One additional fact that is often overlooked is that the hardness of SIDH is not based on a *random* instance of SSI-T, because the starting curve is fixed and has a well-known endomorphism ring with small degree endomorphisms. It is known that given an explicit description of both endomorphism rings $\text{End}(E)$ and $\text{End}(E_0)$, it is (under reasonable heuristic assumptions) possible to recover the secret isogeny [18,37]. However, it is not clear if knowing only one of $\text{End}(E)$ and $\text{End}(E_0)$ makes the isogeny problem easier.

Petit was the first to observe that knowing $\text{End}(E_0)$ could be useful to show an apparent separation between the hardness of the Supersingular Isogeny Problem and the hardness of SSI-T. In particular, in [31] Petit gave a reduction from SSI-T to the following problem, which we will call the *Shifted Lollipop Endomorphism* (SLE) Problem, where $N = B$.

Problem 3 (Shifted Lollipop Endomorphism ($\text{SLE}_{N,\lambda}$)). Let p be a prime, A and B be smooth coprime integers, and a supersingular elliptic curve $E_0/\mathbb{F}_{p^2}$. Given a positive integer N, find the restriction of a trace-zero endomorphism $\theta \in \text{End}(E_0)$ to $E_0[B]$, an integer d coprime to B, and a smooth integer $0 < e < \lambda$ such that

$$A^2 \deg \theta + d^2 = Ne. \tag{1}$$

When λ is left unspecified we let SLE_N denote $\text{SLE}_{N,O^*(1)}$.

Notice that SLE_N only depends on the parameters (p, A, B, E_0). It does not depend on an unknown isogeny (it depends on A, which in practice will be the degree of the unknown isogeny). Thus solving SLE_N can be completed in a pre-computation phase and applied to any unknown isogeny in a fixed SIDH protocol. In [31], Petit was able to show solutions to SLE_N where $N = B$ in certain cases, where $\text{End}(E_0)$ was known and has small-degree, non-scalar endomorphisms.

The goal of this work is to further investigate for which parameters there exists a separation between SSI-T and the Supersingular Isogeny Problem. Intuitively, SLE_N should become easier to solve as N increases, however, this is not true in general and it is unclear how to find efficient reductions to SLE_N for most values of N. To this end, we will give two reductions: one reduction from SSI-T to $\text{SLE}_{N,\lambda}$ where $N = B^2$, and the other where $N = B^2p$. Both reductions run in $O^*(\lambda^{\frac{1}{2}})$, assuming A has only $O(\log \log p)$ distinct prime factors, see Theorems 3 and 5. We then investigate their impact on supersingular isogeny-based protocols.

3.2   Petit's Torsion-Point Attack

We begin this subsection by sketching Petit's reduction from SSI-T to SLE_N where $N = B$. Suppose we are given an instance of SSI-T, that is, $(p, A, B, E_0, E, \varphi|_{E[B]})$, where the goal is to recover the unknown isogeny φ. We call an endomorphism on E that has the form $\varphi \circ \theta \circ \widehat{\varphi}$ for some endomorphism θ on E_0 a **lollipop endomorphism**, and an endomorphism of the form $\varphi \circ \theta \circ \widehat{\varphi} + [d]$ for $d \in \mathbb{Z}$ a **shifted lollipop endomorphism**; see Fig. 2 (this is the motivation for the name of Problem SLE). We will now discuss how to find a shifted lollipop endomorphism, as we will show in Lemma 4 how to use the resulting shifted lollipop endomorphism to recover the secret isogeny.

The main idea of Petit's original attack is that if (θ, d, e) forms a solution to SLE_B, then $\tau = \varphi \circ \theta \circ \hat{\varphi} + [d]$ is a shifted lollipop endomorphism of degree Be where e is smooth. Since $\deg \tau = Be$, it follows that τ also decomposes as $\tau = \eta \circ \varphi$ for two isogenies $\varphi : E \to E_1$ and $\eta : E_1 \to E$ of degrees B and e; see Fig. 3.

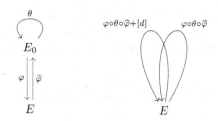

Fig. 2. Lollipop and Shifted Lollipop endomorphisms. The name "lollipop" endomorphism was inspired by the diagram on the left.

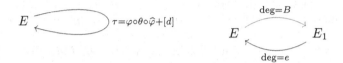

Fig. 3. A decomposition of τ in Petit's original attack

The restriction of φ to $E_0[B]$ given in Alice's public key can be used to construct the B-isogeny in the decomposition (the green arrow in Fig. 3), see [31] for details. This can be done efficiently if θ is in a representation that can be efficiently evaluated on $E_0[B]$. As e is smooth, the e-isogeny in the decomposition (the blue arrow) can be found via brute-force in time $O^*(e^{\frac{1}{2}})$. This gives us τ. Subtracting $[d]$ from τ gives $\varphi \circ \theta \circ \hat{\varphi}$.

Suppose the lollipop endomorphism $\rho = \varphi \circ \theta \circ \hat{\varphi}$ is cyclic. Then $\ker(\rho) \cap E_1[A] = \ker \hat{\varphi}$. (The kernel of ρ can be calculated as A is smooth.) Once we have found $\hat{\varphi}$, it is easy to find the unknown isogeny φ. If ρ is not cyclic, then one can still recover φ if A has $O(\log \log p)$ distinct prime factors by using a technical approach developed in [31, Section 4.3], for further details see Lemma 4. Thus we have a reduction from SSI-T to SLE_N where $N = B$, which is formalized in the following theorem.

Theorem 1. *Suppose we are given an instance of SSI-T where A has $O(\log \log p)$ distinct prime factors. Assume we are given the restriction of a trace-zero endomorphism $\theta \in \text{End}(E_0)$ to $E_0[B]$, an integer d coprime to B, and a smooth integer e such that*

$$\deg(\varphi \circ \theta \circ \hat{\varphi} + [d]) = Be.$$

Then we can compute φ in time $O^*(\sqrt{e}) = O(\sqrt{e} \cdot \text{polylog}(p))$.

3.3 Technical Preview

Although the attack of [31] was the first to establish an apparent separation between the hardness of SSI-T and the hardness of supersingular isogeny problem, it did not affect the security of any cryptosystems that appear in the literature. In this paper, we give two attacks improving upon [31] by additionally exploiting the dual and the Frobenius conjugate of the secret isogeny respectively.

The first attack, which we call the **dual isogeny attack**, corresponds to reducing SSI-T to SLE_N where $N = B^2$.[6] The second attack, which we call the **Frobenius isogeny attack**, corresponds to reducing SSI-T to SLE_N where $N = B^2 p$. The run-time of each attack depends on the parametrization of the cryptosystem, and one may perform better than the other for some choices of parameters. We show the details in Theorem 3 and Theorem 5. We begin by sketching the main ideas behind the reductions.

In the dual isogeny attack, finding a solution (θ, d, e) to SLE_N with $N = B^2$ corresponds to finding a shifted lollipop endomorphism $\tau = \varphi \circ \theta \circ \widehat{\varphi} + [d]$ on E of degree $B^2 e$, with e smooth. Assume τ is cyclic (only for simplicity in this overview; the general case is Theorem 3). Then since $\deg \tau = B^2 e$, it follows that τ also decomposes as $\tau = \varphi' \circ \eta \circ \varphi$ for three isogenies φ, η and φ' of degrees B, e and B, respectively: see the middle diagram in Fig. 4.

In the Frobenius isogeny attack, finding a solution (θ, d, e) to SLE_N with $N = B^2 p$ corresponds to finding a shifted lollipop endomorphism $\tau = \varphi \circ \theta \circ \widehat{\varphi} + [d]$ that has degree $B^2 p e$, with e smooth. Assume τ is cyclic (only for simplicity in this overview; the general case is Theorem 5). Since $\deg \tau = B^2 p e$, it follows that τ also decomposes as $\tau = \varphi' \circ \eta \circ \pi \circ \varphi$ for four isogenies φ, π, η and φ' of degrees B, p, e and B, respectively, where the isogeny of degree p is the Frobenius map $(x, y) \rightarrow (x^p, y^p)$: see the right-hand diagram in Fig. 4.

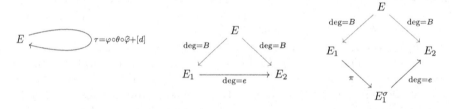

Fig. 4. A decomposition of τ in our two new attacks. Note: we take the dual of one isogeny in the middle and right-hand diagrams to reverse its arrow. (Color figure online)

In both attacks we find τ by calculating each isogeny in the decomposition of τ. In particular, we will use the restriction of φ to $E_0[B]$ given by Alice's public key to construct the two B-isogenies in the decomposition (the green arrows in Fig. 4). Again this can be done efficiently if θ is in a representation that can be efficiently evaluated on $E_0[B]$. As e is smooth we can calculate the e-isogeny in the decomposition (the blue arrow) via brute-force in time $O^*(e^{\frac{1}{2}})$. As we can always construct the Frobenius map π (the purple arrow), this gives us τ. The rest of the proof proceeds as with Petit's original attack assuming A has $O(\log \log p)$ distinct prime factors, see Lemma 4 for details.

Remark 2. These methods are an improvement over Petit's original attack, which only utilized a shifted lollipop endomorphism τ of degree Be. There τ could only be decomposed into two isogenies of degree B and e as in Fig. 3. Intuitively, Petit's original attack was less effective as a smaller proportion of τ could be calculated

---

[6] See also [7] for a different reduction to SLE_{B^2}, cf. Subsect. 1.2.

directly, and hence a much larger (potentially exponential) proportion of the endomorphism needed to be brute forced. It is not clear how to find a better decomposition with more computable isogenies than those given in Fig. 4 using the fixed parameters and public keys given in SIDH protocols. Furthermore, we give reductions both to SLE_{B^2} and $\mathrm{SLE}_{B^2 p}$, as increasing the degree of τ does not necessarily make a shifted lollipop endomorphism τ easier to find.

Once an appropriate (θ, d, e) is found for a particular setting (that is, a particular choice of p, A, B, E_0), then the reduction outlines an algorithm that can be run to find any unknown isogeny $\varphi : E_0 \to E$. In other words, there is first a precomputation needed to solve SLE_N and find a particular (θ, d, e). Using this (θ, d, e), the above reduction gives a key-dependent algorithm to find a particular unknown isogeny $\varphi : E_0 \to E$.

We now outline how to solve SLE_N when $N = B^2 p$ for a particular choice of E_0, see Algorithm 2 for details. A similar technique works when $N = B^2$, see Algorithm 1. In most supersingular isogeny-based protocols, the endomorphism ring of E_0 is known. A common choice of starting curve, in SIKE for example[7], is where E_0 has j-invariant 1728. We show that in the Frobenius isogeny attack finding a shifted lollipop endomorphism of degree $B^2 pe$ reduces to finding a solution of

$$A^2(a^2 + b^2) + pc^2 = B^2 e. \tag{2}$$

To proceed choose c and e such that $pc^2 = B^2 e$ modulo A^2. The remaining equation $a^2 + b^2 = \frac{Be - pc^2}{A^2}$ can be solved by Cornacchia's algorithm a large percentage of time; else the procedure is restarted with a new choice of e or c.

This method of solving SLE_N can be used to attack the n-party group key agreement [2]. We analyze this attack in Sect. 7.1, and show that it can be expected, heuristically, to run in polynomial time for $n \geq 6$. The results are summarized in Table 1, and an implementation of this attack for $n = 6$ can be found at https://github.com/torsion-attacks-SIDH/6party.

While we use the Frobenius isogeny attack to highlight vulnerabilities in the isogeny-based group key agreement, we use the ideas from the dual isogeny attack to investigate situations, namely different starting curves and base fields, which would result in insecure schemes.

4   Improved Torsion-Point Attacks

In this section, we generalize and improve upon the torsion-point attacks from Petit's 2017 paper [31]; in our notation, Petit's attack can be viewed as a reduction of SSI-T to $\mathrm{SLE}_{B,\lambda}$ together with $O^*(1)$-time algorithm to solve $\mathrm{SLE}_{B,\lambda}$ for certain parameter sets. In Subsect. 4.1, we introduce two new reductions from SSI-T to $\mathrm{SLE}_{N,\lambda}$, where $N = B^2$ and $N = B^2 p$, respectively. The runtime of both reductions is $O^*(\lambda^{\frac{1}{2}})$. The reductions exploit two new techniques: a dual isogeny and the Frobenius isogeny.

---

[7] Note that the newest version of SIKE [20] changed the starting curve to a 2-isogenous neighbour of $j = 1728$, but this does not affect the asymptotic complexity of any attack.

In Subsect. 4.2 we give an algorithm to solve SLE_N for $N = B^2$ and $N = B^2 p$, for specific starting curve[8] E_0 under explicit, plausible heuristics (Heuristic 1 and 2, respectively). For certain parameters these algorithms solve $\mathrm{SLE}_{N,\lambda}$ for $N = B^2$ for $\lambda = O^*(1)$ in polynomial time and SLE_N for $N = B^2 p$ for $\lambda = O(\log p)$ in polynomial time. For these parameters, this solves SSI-T in time $O^*(1)$.

4.1   Improved Torsion-Point Attacks

The main ingredient in Petit's [31] attack can be viewed as a reduction of SSI-T to SLE_B. In this section we introduce our first extension of this attack: the *dual isogeny attack*, which works by exploiting the dual isogeny of the (shifted lollipop) endomorphism τ on E. We begin by giving the reduction for the dual isogeny attack.

Theorem 3. *Suppose we are given an instance of SSI-T where A has $O(\log\log p)$ distinct prime factors. Assume we are given the restriction of a trace-zero endomorphism $\theta \in \mathrm{End}(E_0)$ to $E_0[B]$, an integer d coprime to B, and a smooth integer e such that*

$$\deg(\varphi \circ \theta \circ \hat{\varphi} + [d]) = B^2 e.$$

Then we can compute φ in time $O^*(\sqrt{e}) = O(\sqrt{e} \cdot \mathrm{polylog}(p))$.

We first state a technical lemma which mostly follows from [31, Section 4.3].

Lemma 4. *Let A be a smooth integer with $O(\log\log p)$ distinct prime factors, and let $E_0/\mathbb{F}_{p^2}$ and $E/\mathbb{F}_{p^2}$ be two supersingular elliptic curves connected by an unknown degree-A isogeny φ. Suppose we are given the restriction of some $\tau \in \mathrm{End}(E)$ to $E[A]$, where τ is of the form $\tau = \varphi \circ \theta \circ \hat{\varphi} + [d]$ such that if $E[m] \subseteq \ker\tau$ then $m \mid 2$. Then we can compute $\ker\varphi$ in time $O^*(1)$.*

Proof. See the full version [13, Appendix A.1].

Proof (of Theorem 3). Suppose we have d, e and the restriction of θ to $E[B]$ satisfying the conditions above. We wish to find an explicit description of $\tau = \varphi \circ \theta \circ \hat{\varphi} + [d]$. Let m be the largest integer dividing B such that $E[m] \subseteq \ker\tau$. Since the degree of τ is $B^2 e$, there exists a decomposition of the form $\tau = \psi' \circ \eta \circ \psi \circ [m]$, where ψ and ψ' are isogenies of degree B/m, ψ is cyclic, and η is an isogeny of degree e.

We proceed by deriving the maps in this decomposition. Since τ factors through $[m]$, this implies m divides $\mathrm{tr}(\tau) = 2d$. As we chose d coprime to B, this shows $m \in \{1, 2\}$.

To compute ψ and ψ', we start by finding the restriction of τ to the B-torsion. This can be computed from what we are given: the restrictions of θ, $[d]$, φ, hence $\hat{\varphi}$, to the B-torsion of the relevant elliptic curves. This also allows us to compute m explicitly, as the largest integer dividing B such that $E[m] \subseteq \ker\tau \cap E[B]$.

Let $\tau' = \psi' \circ \eta \circ \psi$. The isogeny ψ can now be computed from the restriction of τ to $E[B]$ via

---

[8] More generally, these attacks apply for any "special" starting curve in the sense of [26].

$$\ker \psi = \ker \tau' \cap ([m] \cdot E[B]) = (\ker \tau \cap E[B])/E[m].$$

From the cyclicity of ψ, we can also deduce that $\ker \hat{\psi}' = \tau(E[B])$, which gives ψ' explicitly.

Finally, we recover the isogeny η by a generic meet-in-the-middle algorithm, which runs in time $O^*(\sqrt{e})$ since e is smooth. Note that if $e = O^*(1)$, then the entire algorithm runs in time polylog(p). In this way we have found τ explicitly, and by Lemma 4 can compute φ.   □

Next we give the reduction for the *Frobenius isogeny attack*, which works by exploiting the Frobenius isogeny on E to improve, or at least alter, the dual attack.

Theorem 5. *Suppose we are given an instance of SSI-T where A has at most $O(\log \log p)$ distinct prime factors. Assume we are given the restriction of a trace-zero endomorphism $\theta \in \text{End}(E_0)$ to $E_0[B]$, an integer d coprime to B, and a smooth integer e such that*

$$\deg(\varphi \circ \theta \circ \hat{\varphi} + [d]) = B^2 pe.$$

Then we can compute φ in time $O^*(\sqrt{e}) = O(\sqrt{e} \cdot \text{polylog}(p))$.

Proof. Let $\tau = \varphi \circ \theta \circ \hat{\varphi} + [d]$. As in the proof of Theorem 3, we can decompose τ as $\psi' \circ \eta \circ \psi \circ [m]$, where η has degree pe, and compute ψ and ψ' efficiently.

We are left to recovering η. Instead of using a generic meet-in-the-middle algorithm, we observe that η has inseparable degree p (since we are in the super-singular case). Thus, $\eta = \eta' \circ \pi$, where π is the p-power Frobenius isogeny, and η' is of degree e. We use the meet-in-the-middle algorithm on η' and recover the specified runtime.   □

Remark 6. It is a natural question why we stick to the p-power Frobenius and why the attack doesn't give a better condition for a higher-power Frobenius isogeny. The reason is that for supersingular elliptic curves defined over $\mathbb{F}_{p^2}$, the p^2-power Frobenius isogeny is just a scalar multiplication followed by an isomorphism (since every supersingular j-invariant lies in $\mathbb{F}_{p^2}$), and hence would already be covered by the method of Theorem 3.

More generally, see Sect. 8 for a more abstract viewpoint that subsumes both of the reductions given above (but has not led to the discovery of other useful variants thus far).

The complexity of both attacks relies on whether one can find a suitable endomorphism θ with e as small as possible. In the next subsection we will establish criteria when we can find a suitable θ when the starting curve has j-invariant 1728.

4.2   Solving Norm Equations

In Subsect. 4.1 we showed two reductions (Theorem 3 and Theorem 5) from SSI-T to SLE$_N$ where $N = B^2$ and $N = B^2 p$. To complete the description of our attacks, we discuss how to solve SLE_N in these two cases; that is, we want to find solutions (θ, d, e) to

$$\deg(\varphi \circ \theta \circ \hat{\varphi} + [d]) = A^2 \deg \theta + d^2 = Ne,$$

where $N = B^2$ or $N = B^2 p$.

The degree of any endomorphism of E_0 is represented by a quadratic form that depends on E_0. To simply our exposition we choose $E_0/\mathbb{F}_p: y^2 = x^3 + x$ (having $j = 1728$), where p is congruent to 3 (mod 4). In this case the endomorphism ring $\text{End}(E_0)$ has a particularly simple norm form. To complete the dual isogeny attack, it suffices to find a solution to the norm Eq. (3):

Corollary 7. *Let $p \equiv 3$ (mod 4) and $j(E_0) = 1728$. Consider coprime smooth integers A, B such that A has (at most) $O(\log \log p)$ distinct prime factors and suppose that we are given an integer solution (a, b, c, d, e), with e smooth, to the equation*

$$A^2(pa^2 + pb^2 + c^2) + d^2 = B^2 e. \tag{3}$$

Then we can solve SSI-T with the above parameters in time $O^*(\sqrt{e})$.

Proof. Let $\iota \in \text{End}(E_0)$ be such that $\iota^2 = [-1]$ and let π be the Frobenius endomorphism of E_0. Let φ be as in Theorem 3. The endomorphism $\theta = a\iota\pi + b\pi + c\iota$ and the given choice of d satisfies the requirements of Theorem 3. □

To complete the Frobenius isogeny attack, we find a solution to the norm Eq. (8):

Corollary 8. *Let $p \equiv 3$ (mod 4) and $j(E_0) = 1728$. Consider coprime smooth integers A, B such that A has (at most) $O(\log \log p)$ distinct prime factors and suppose that we are given an integer solution (a, b, d, e), with e smooth, to the equation*

$$A^2(a^2 + b^2) + pd^2 = B^2 e. \tag{4}$$

Then we can solve SSI-T with the above parameters in time $O^*(\sqrt{e})$.

Proof. With ι and π as in the proof of Corollary 7, and φ as in Theorem 5, the endomorphism $\theta = a\iota\pi + b\pi$, together with the choice $c = 0$ satisfies the requirements of Theorem 5 (to see this, multiply (4) through by p). □

Now we present two algorithms for solving each norm Eq. (3) and (4). The algorithms are similar in nature but they work on different parameter sets. See Algorithms 1 and 2.

4.3   Runtime and Justification for Algorithms 1 and 2

The remainder of this section is devoted to providing justification that the algorithms succeed in polynomial time.

Algorithm 1: Solving norm equation 3.

Input: SIDH parameters p, A, B.
Output: A solution (a, b, c, d, e) to (3).

1 Set $e := 2$.
2 **If** e is a quadratic non-residue mod A^2 **then**
3 $\quad\lfloor$ Set $e := e + 1$ and go to Step 2.
4 Compute d such that $d^2 \equiv eB^2 \pmod{A^2}$.
5 **If** $eB^2 - d^2$ is a quadratic non-residue mod p **then**
6 $\quad\lfloor$ Set $e := e + 1$ and go to Step 2.
7 Compute c as the smallest positive integer such that $c^2 A^2 \equiv eB^2 - d^2$ $\pmod{p}$.
8 **If** $eB^2 > d^2 + c^2 A^2$ **then**
9 $\quad$ **If** $\frac{eB^2 - d^2 - c^2 A^2}{A^2 p}$ is prime **then**
10 $\quad\quad$ **If** $\frac{eB^2 - d^2 - c^2 A^2}{A^2 p} \equiv 1 \pmod 4$ **then**
11 $\quad\quad\quad$ Find $a, b \in \mathbb{Z}$ such that $a^2 + b^2 = \frac{eB^2 - d^2 - c^2 A^2}{A^2 p}$.
12 $\quad\quad\quad$ **Return** (a, b, c, d, e).
13 $\quad\lfloor$ Set $e := e + 1$ and go to Step 2.
14 **else**
15 $\quad\lfloor$ **Return** Failure.

Algorithm 2: Solving norm equation 4.

Input: SIDH parameters p, A, B.
Output: A solution (a, b, c, e) to (4).

1 Set $e := 1$.
2 **While** $\frac{eB^2}{p}$ is a quadratic non-residue mod A^2 **do**
3 $\quad\lfloor$ Set $e := e + 1$.
4 Compute c such that $eB^2 \equiv pc^2 \pmod{A^2}$.
5 **If** $eB^2 > pc^2$ **then**
6 $\quad$ **If** $\frac{eB^2 - pc^2}{A^2}$ is prime **then**
7 $\quad\quad$ **If** $\frac{eB^2 - pc^2}{A^2} \equiv 1 \pmod 4$ **then**
8 $\quad\quad\quad$ Find $a, b \in \mathbb{Z}$ such that $a^2 + b^2 = \frac{eB^2 - pc^2}{A^2}$.
9 $\quad\quad\quad$ **Return** (a, b, c, e).
10 $\quad\lfloor$ Set $e := e + 1$ and go to Step 2.
11 **else**
12 $\quad\lfloor$ **Return** Failure.

Heuristic 1. *Let p, A, B be SIDH parameters. Note that for each e, the equation*

$$eB^2 \equiv d^2 + c^2 A^2 \pmod{A^2 p}, \tag{5}$$

may or may not have a solution (c, d). We assert two heuristics:

1. *Amongst invertible residues e modulo $A^2 p$, which are quadratic residues modulo A^2, the probability of the existence of a solution is approximately $1/2$.*
2. *Amongst those e for which there is a solution, and for which the resulting integer*

$$\frac{B^2 e - d^2 - c^2 A^2}{A^2 p} \tag{6}$$

is positive, the probability that (6) is a prime congruent to 1 modulo 4 is expected to be approximately the same as the probability that a random integer of the same size is prime congruent to 1 modulo 4.

Justification. By the Chinese remainder theorem, solving (5) amounts to solving $eB^2 \equiv d^2 \pmod{A^2}$ and $eB^2 \equiv d^2 + c^2 A^2 \pmod{p}$. If e is a quadratic residue modulo A^2, then the first of these equations has a solution d. Using this d, the second equation has either no solutions or two, with equal probability. This justifies the first item.

For the second item, this is a restriction of the assertion that the values of the quadratic function $B^2 e - d^2 - c^2 A^2$, in terms of variables e, c and d, behave, in terms of their factorizations, as if they were random integers. In particular, the conditional probability that the value has the form $A^2 pq$ for a prime $q \equiv 1$ (mod 4), given that it is divisible by $A^2 p$, is as for random integers.

Proposition 9. *Let $\epsilon > 0$. Under Heuristic 1, if $B > pA$ and $p > A$, but B is at most polynomial in A, then Algorithm 1 returns a solution (a, b, c, d, e) with $e = O(\log^{2+\epsilon}(p))$ in polynomial time.*

Proof. Checking that a number is a quadratic residue modulo p can be accomplished by a square-and-multiply algorithm. Checking that a certain number is prime can also be accomplished in polynomial-time. Representing a prime as a sum of two squares can be carried out by Cornacchia's algorithm. Suppose one iterates e a total of X times.

For the algorithm to succeed, we must succeed in three key steps in reasonable time: first, that e such that e is a quadratic residue modulo A^2 (Step 2) and second, that $eB^2 - d^2$ is a quaratic residue modulo p (Step 5), and third, that $\frac{eB^2 - d^2 - c^2 A^2}{A^2 p}$ is a prime congruent to 1 modulo 4 (Step 9–10). Suppose we check values of e up to size X.

For Step 2, it suffices to find e an integer square, which happens $1/\sqrt{X}$ of the time. When this is satisfied, the resulting d can be taken so $d < A^2$. For Step 5, under Heuristic 1 Part 1, the probability that a corresponding c exists is $1/2$. Such a c can be taken with $c < p$. Under the given assumption that $B > pA$ and $p > A$, then

$$eB^2 \geq 2B^2 > 2p^2 A^2 > p^2 A^2 + A^4 > c^2 A^2 + d^2.$$

So the quantity in Heuristic 1 Part 2 is positive. We can bound it by eB^2/pA^2. Since B is at worst polynomial in A, the quantity B^2/pA^2 is at worst polynomial in p, say p^k. Hence, for Step 9–10, one expects at a proportion $1/\log(p^k X)$ of successes to find a prime congruent to 1 modulo 4. Such a prime is a sum of two squares, and the algorithm succeeds.

Finally, we set $X = \log^{2+\epsilon}(p)$ to optimize the result. If one iterates e at most $\log^{2+\epsilon}(p)$ times, one expects to succeed at Step 2 at least $\log^{1+\epsilon}(p))$ times, to succeed at Step 5 half of those times, and to succeed at Steps 9 and 10 at least $1/\log(p^k \log^{2+\epsilon}(p))$ of those times. This gives a total probability of success, at any one iteration, of $1/4k \log^{2+\epsilon}(p)$. Hence we expect to succeed with polynomial probability.

For the analysis of Algorithm 2, the following technical lemma is helpful.

Lemma 10. *Let M be an integer. Let r be an invertible residue modulo M. Then the pattern of e such that re is a quadratic residue repeats modulo $N = 4\,\mathrm{sqfr}(M)$, four times the squarefree part of M. Among residues modulo $4\,\mathrm{sqfr}(M)$, a proportion of $1/2^\ell$ of them are solutions, where ℓ is the number of distinct primes dividing M.*

Proof. Suppose M has prime factorization $M = \prod_i l_i^{e_i}$. A residue x modulo M is a quadratic residue if and only if it is a quadratic residue modulo $l_i^{e_i}$ for every i. For odd l_i, a residue modulo $l_i^{e_i}$ is a quadratic residue if and only if it is a quadratic residue modulo l_i, by Hensel's lemma. And a residue modulo 2^e, $e \geq 3$, is a quadratic residue if and only if it is a quadratic residue modulo 8. By the Chinese remainder theorem, re is a quadratic residue modulo M if and only if re is a quadratic residue modulo $4\,\mathrm{sqfr}(M)$.

Heuristic 2. *Let p, A, B be SIDH parameters. Let ℓ be the number of distinct prime divisors of A. Note that for each e, the equation*

$$eB^2 = pc^2 \pmod{A^2} \tag{7}$$

may or may not have solutions c. We assert two heuristics:

1. *As e varies, the probability that it has solutions is $1/2^\ell$.*
2. *Amongst those e for which there is a solution, and for which the resulting integer*

$$\frac{B^2 e - pc^2}{A^2} \tag{8}$$

is positive, the probability that (8) is a prime congruent to 1 modulo 4 is expected to be approximately the same as the probability that a random integer of the same size is prime congruent to 1 modulo 4.

Justification. Consider the first item. Modulo each prime dividing A^2, the quadratic residues vs. non-residues are expected to be distributed "randomly", resulting in a random distribution modulo 4 $\mathrm{sqfr}(A)$, by Lemma 10.

For the second item, this is a restriction of the assertion that the values of the quadratic function $B^2 e - pc^2$, in terms of variables e and c, behave, in terms of their factorizations, as if they were random integers. In particular, the conditional probability that the value has the form $A^2 q$ for a prime $q \equiv 1 \pmod 4$, given that it is divisible by A^2, is as for random integers.

Proposition 11. *Under Heuristic 2, if $B > \sqrt{p} A^2$, A has $O(\log \log p)$ distinct prime factors, B is at most polynomial in A, and[9] $p > A$, then Algorithm 2 returns a solution (a, b, c, e) with $e = O(\log p)$ in polynomial time.*

Proof. Checking that a number is a quadratic residue can be accomplished by a square-and-multiply algorithm. Checking that a certain number is prime can also be accomplished in polynomial-time. Representing a prime as a sum of two squares can be carried out by Cornacchia's algorithm.

For the algorithm to succeed, we must succeed in two key steps in reasonable time: first, that e such that eB^2/p is a quadratic residue (Step 2) and second, that $\frac{eB^2 - pc^2}{A^2}$ is a prime congruent to 1 modulo 4 (Step 6–7). Suppose we check values of e up to size X.

By Heuristic 2 Part 1, we expect to succeed at Step 2 with probability $1/2^\ell$, where ℓ is the number of distinct prime divisors of A.

When this is satisfied, the resulting c can be taken so $c < A^2$. Under the given assumption that $B > \sqrt{p} A$, then

$$eB^2 \geq B^2 > pA^4 > pc^2.$$

So the quantity in Heuristic 2 Part 2 is positive. We can bound it above by eB^2/A^2, and using the assumption that B is at most polynomial in A, we bound this by $< p^k X$ for some k. So we expect to succeed in Step 6–7 with probability $1/2 \log(p^k X)$. The resulting prime is a sum of two squares, and the algorithm succeeds. Thus, taking $X = O(\log p)$ suffices for the statement.

Remark 12. In practice, in Algorithm 2 it may be more efficient to increment c by multiples of A^2 in place of incrementing e. This however makes the inequalities satisfied by A, B, and p slightly less tight so for the sake of cleaner results we opted for incrementing only e.

Remark 13. If parameters A and B are slightly more unbalanced (i.e., $B > rA^2 \sqrt{p}$ for some $r > 100$), then instead of increasing e it is better to fix e and increase c by A^2 in each step.

5   Backdoor Instances

In this section we give a method to specifically create instantiations of the SIDH framework for which we can solve SSI-T more efficiently. So far all of our results were only considering cases where the starting curve E_0 has j-invariant 1728.

---

[9] In the proof, it suffices to take $p^k > A$ for any k.

In Sect. 5.1 we explore the question: For given A, B can we construct starting curves for which we can solve SSI-T with a better balance? We will call such curves *backdoor curves* (see Definition 14), and quantify the number of backdoor curves in Sect. 5.2. In Sects. 5.3 and 5.4, we also consider backdoored choices of (p, A, B), for which we can solve SSI-T more efficiently even when starting from the curve with j-invariant 1728.

5.1 Backdoor Curves

This section introduces the concept of *backdoor curves* and how to find such curves. Roughly speaking, these are specially crafted curves which, if used as starting curves for the SIDH protocol, are susceptible to our dual isogeny attack by the party which chose the curve, under only moderately unbalanced parameters A, B; in particular, the imbalance is independent of p. In fact, when we allow for non-polynomial time attacks we get an asymptotic improvement over meet-in-the-middle for balanced SIDH parameters (but starting from a backdoor curve). These curves could potentially be utilized as a backdoor, for example by suggesting the use of such a curve as a standardized starting curve. We note that it does not seem obvious how backdoored curves, such as those generated by Algorithm 3, can be detected by other parties: The existence of an endomorphism of large degree which satisfies Eq. 3 does not seem to be detectable without trying to recover such an endomorphism, which is hard using all currently known algorithms. The notion of backdoor curves is dependent on the parameters A, B, which motivates the following definition:

Definition 14. *Let A, B be coprime positive integers. An (A, B)-backdoor curve is a tuple (E_0, θ, d, e), where E_0 is a supersingular elliptic curve defined over some $\mathbb{F}_{p^2}$, an endomorphism $\theta \in \mathrm{End}(E_0)$ in an efficient representation, and two integers d, e such that Algorithm 5 solves SSI-T for that particular E_0 in time polynomial in $\log p$ when given (θ, d, e).*

The main result of this section is Algorithm 3 which computes (A, B)-backdoor curves in heuristic polynomial time, assuming we have a factoring oracle (see Theorem 15).

Theorem 15. *Given an oracle for factoring, if A has (at most) $O(\log \log p)$ distinct prime factors, then Algorithm 3 can heuristically be expected to succeed in polynomial time.*

Remark 16. The imbalance $B > A^2$ is naturally satisfied for a group key agreement in the style of [2] with three or more participants; we can break (in polynomial time) such a variant when starting at an (A, B)-backdoor curve.

Before proving Theorem 15 we need the following easy lemma:

Lemma 17. *Let p be a prime congruent to 3 modulo 4. Let D be a positive integer. Then the quadratic form $Q(x_1, x_2, x_3, x_4) = px_1^2 + px_2^2 + x_3^2 - Dx_4^2$ has a nontrivial integer root if and only if D is a quadratic residue modulo p.*

Algorithm 3: Generating (A, B)-backdoor curves.

Input: A prime $p \equiv 3 \pmod 4$ and smooth coprime integers A, B with $B > A^2$.

Output: An (A, B)-backdoor curve (E_0, θ, d, e) with $E_0/\mathbb{F}_{p^2}$.

1 Set $e := 1$.
2 **While true do**
3 | Find an integer d such that $d^2 \equiv B^2 e \pmod{A^2}$.
4 | **If** d *is coprime to* B **then**
5 | | **If** $\frac{B^2 e - d^2}{A^2}$ *is square modulo* p **then**
6 | | | Find rational a, b, c such that $pa^2 + pb^2 + c^2 = \frac{B^2 e - d^2}{A^2}$.
7 | | | **break**
8 | Set e to the next square.
9 Set $\vartheta = a\mathbf{ij} + b\mathbf{j} + c\mathbf{i} \in B_{p,\infty}$.
10 Compute a maximal order $\mathcal{O} \subseteq B_{p,\infty}$ containing θ.
11 Compute an elliptic curve E_0 whose endomorphism ring is isomorphic to $\mathcal{O}$.
12 Construct an efficient representation of the endomorphism θ of E_0 corresponding to ϑ.
13 **Return** (E_0, θ, d, e).

Proof. The proof is essentially a special case of [36, Proposition 10], but we give a brief sketch of the proof here. If D is a quadratic residue modulo p, then $px_1^2 + px_2^2 + x_3^2 - Dx_4^2$ has a solution in $\mathbb{Q}_p$ by setting $x_1 = x_2 = 0$ and $x_4 = 1$ and applying Hensel's lemma to the equation $x_3^2 = D$. The quadratic form Q also has local solutions everywhere else (the 2-adic case involves looking at the equation modulo 8 and applying a 2-adic version of Hensel's lemma). If on the other hand D is not a quadratic residue modulo p, then one has to choose x_3 and x_4 to be divisible by p. Dividing the equation $Q(x_1, x_2, x_3, x_4) = 0$ by p and reducing modulo p yields $x_1^2 + x_2^2 \equiv 0 \pmod p$. This does not have a solution as $p \equiv 3 \pmod 4$. Finally, one can show that this implies that Q does not have a root in $\mathbb{Q}_p$. □

Proof (of Theorem 15). The main idea is to apply Theorem 3 in the following way: using Algorithm 3, we find integers D, d, and e, with e polynomially small and D a quadratic residue mod p, such that $A^2 D + d^2 = B^2 e$, and an element $\theta \in B_{p,\infty}$ of trace zero and such that $\theta^2 = -D$. We then construct a maximal order $\mathcal{O} \subseteq B_{p,\infty}$ containing θ and an elliptic curve E_0 with $\mathrm{End}(E_0) \cong \mathcal{O}$.

Most steps of Algorithm 3 obviously run in polynomial time, although some need further explanation. We expect $d^2 \approx A^4$ since we solved for d modulo B^2, and we expect e to be small since heuristically we find a quadratic residue after a small number of tries. Then the right-hand side in step 6 should be positive since $B > A^2$, so by Lemma 17, step 6 returns a solution using Simon's algorithm [36], assuming an oracle for factoring $\frac{B^2e-d^2}{A^2}$. For step 10, we can apply either of the polynomial-time algorithms [19,39] for finding maximal orders containing a fixed order in a quaternion algebra, which again assume a factoring oracle. Steps 11 and 12 can be accomplished using the heuristically polynomial-time algorithm from [16,32] which returns both the curve E_0 and (see [16, § 5.3, Algorithm 5]) an efficient representation of θ.   □

Remark 18. The algorithm uses factorization twice (once in solving the quadratic form and once in factoring the discriminant of the starting order). In the full version [13, Appendix C] we discuss how one can ensure in practice that the numbers to be factored have an easy factorization.

Remark 19. Denis Simon's algorithm [36] is available on his webpage.[10] Furthermore, it is implemented in MAGMA [6] and PARI/GP [3]. The main contribution of Simon's paper is a polynomial-time algorithm for finding nontrivial zeroes of (not necessarily diagonal) quadratic forms which does not rely on an effective version of Dirichlet's theorem. In our case, however, we only need a heuristic polynomial-time algorithm for finding a nontrivial zero (x, y, z, u) of a form $px^2 + py^2 + z^2 - Du^2$. We sketch an easy way to do this: Suppose that D is squarefree, and pick a prime $q \equiv 1 \pmod 4$ such that $-pq$ is a quadratic residue modulo every prime divisor of D. It is then easy to see that the quadratic equations $px^2 + py^2 = pq$ and $Du^2 - z^2 = pq$ both admit a nontrivial rational solution which can be found using [12].

There are two natural questions that arise when looking at Theorem 15:

- Why are we using the dual attack and not the Frobenius attack?
- Why do we get a substantially better balance than we had before?

The answer to the first question is that we get a better result in terms of balance. In the Frobenius version we essentially get the same bound for backdoor curves as for the curve with j-invariant 1728. The answer to the second question is that by not restricting ourselves to one starting curve we only have the condition that $pa^2 + pb^2 + c^2$ is an integer and a, b, c can be rational numbers.

Remark 20. Backdoor curves also have a constructive application: An improvement on the recent paper [14] using Petit's attack to build a one-way function "SÉTA". In this scheme, the secret key is a secret isogeny to a curve E_s that starts from the elliptic curve with j-invariant 1728 and the message is the end point of a secret isogeny from E_s to some curve E_m, together with the image of some torsion points. The reason for using j-invariant 1728 is in order to apply Petit's attack constructively. One could instead use a backdoor curve; this provides more flexibility to the scheme as one does not need to disclose the starting curve and the corresponding norm equation is easier to solve.

---

[10] https://simond.users.lmno.cnrs.fr/.

5.2 Counting Backdoor Curves

Having shown how to construct backdoor curves and how to exploit them, a natural question to ask is how many of these curves we can find using the methods of the previous section. Recall that the methods above search for an element $\vartheta \in \mathcal{B}_{p,\infty}$ with reduced norm D. Theorem 21 below suggests they can be expected to produce exponentially (in $\log D$) many different maximal orders, and using Lemma 22 we can prove this rigorously for the (indeed interesting) case of (A, B)-backdoor curves with $AB \approx p$ and $A^2 < B < A^3$ (cf. Theorem 15).

We first recall some notation from [30]. The set $\rho(\mathcal{E}\ell\ell(\mathcal{O}))$ consists of the reductions modulo p of all elliptic curves over $\overline{\mathbb{Q}}$ with complex multiplication by $\mathcal{O}$. Each curve $E = \mathcal{E} \bmod p$ in this set comes with an optimal embedding $\iota \colon \mathcal{O} \hookrightarrow \operatorname{End}(E)$, referred to as an "orientation" of E, and conversely, [30, Prop. 3.3] shows that — up to conjugation — each oriented curve (E, ι) defined over $\overline{\mathbb{F}}_p$ is obtained by the reduction modulo p of a characteristic-zero curve; in other words, either (E, ι) or $(E^{(p)}, \iota^{(p)})$ lies in $\rho(\mathcal{E}\ell\ell(\mathcal{O}))$. The following theorem was to our knowledge first explicitly stated and used constructively in [10] to build the "OSIDH" cryptosystem. The proof was omitted,[11] but later published by Onuki [30], whose formulation we reproduce here:

Theorem 21. *Let K be an imaginary quadratic field such that p does not split in K, and $\mathcal{O}$ an order in K such that p does not divide the conductor of $\mathcal{O}$. Then the ideal class group $\operatorname{cl}(\mathcal{O})$ acts freely and transitively on $\rho(\mathcal{E}\ell\ell(\mathcal{O}))$.*

Thus, it follows from well-known results about imaginary quadratic class numbers [35] that asymptotically, there are $h(-D) \in \Omega(D^{\frac{1}{2}-\varepsilon})$ many backdoor elliptic curves *counted with multiplicities* given by the number of embeddings of $\mathcal{O}$. However, it is not generally clear that this corresponds to many distinct *curves* (or maximal orders). As an (extreme) indication of what could go wrong, consider the following: there seems to be no obvious reason why in some cases the entire orbit of the group action of Theorem 21 should *not* consist only of one elliptic curve with lots of independent copies of $\mathcal{O}$ in its endomorphism ring.

We can however at least prove that this does not always happen. In fact, in the case that D is small enough relative to p, one can show that there cannot be more than one embedding of $\mathcal{O}$ into any maximal order in $\mathcal{B}_{p,\infty}$, implying that the $h(-D)$ oriented supersingular elliptic curves indeed must constitute $h(-D) \approx \sqrt{D}$ distinct quaternion maximal orders:

Lemma 22. *Let $\mathcal{O}$ be a maximal order in $\mathcal{B}_{p,\infty}$. If $D \equiv 3, 0 \pmod 4$ is a positive integer smaller than p, then there exists at most one copy of the imaginary quadratic order of discriminant $-D$ inside $\mathcal{O}$.*

Proof. This follows readily from Theorem 2' of [25].

This lemma together with Theorem 15 shows that there are $\Theta(h(-D))$ many (A, B)-backdoor maximal orders under the restrictions that $B > A^2$ and $D < p$.

---

[11] In [10] the theorem was referred to as a classical result, considered to be folklore.

Consider the case (of interest) in which $AB \approx p$: Following the same line of reasoning as in the proof of Theorem 15 we have that $B^2/A^2 - A^2 \approx D$, which if $D < p \approx AB$ implies that $B \lesssim A^3$. Hence, as advertised above, Lemma 22 suffices to prove that there are $\Theta(h(-D))$ many (A, B)-backdoor maximal orders under the restriction that $AB \approx p$ and roughly $A^2 < B < A^3$. For larger choices of B, it is no longer true that there is only one embedding of $\mathcal{O}$ into a quaternion maximal order: indeed, at some point $h(-D)$ will exceed the number $\Theta(p)$ of available maximal orders, hence there must be repetitions. While it seems hard to imagine cases where the orbit of $\mathrm{cl}(\mathbb{Z}[\theta])$ covers only a negligible number of curves (recall that θ was our endomorphism of reduced norm D), we do not currently know how (and under which conditions) to rule out this possibility.

Remark 23. Having obtained any one maximal order $\mathfrak{O}$ that contains θ, it is efficient to compute more such orders (either randomly or exhaustively): For any ideal $\mathfrak{a}$ in $\mathbb{Z}[\theta]$, another maximal order with an optimal embedding of $\mathbb{Z}[\theta]$ is the right order of the left ideal $\mathcal{I} = \mathfrak{O}\mathfrak{a}$. (One way to see this: $\mathfrak{a}$ defines a horizontal isogeny with respect to the subring $\mathcal{O}$; multiplying by the full endomorphism ring does not change the represented kernel subgroup; the codomain of an isogeny described by a quaternion left ideal has endomorphism ring isomorphic to the right order of that ideal. Note that this is similar to a technique used by [9] in the context $\mathcal{O} \subseteq \mathbb{Q}(\pi)$.)

5.3   Backdoored p for Given A and B with Starting Vertex $j = 1728$

Another way of constructing backdoor instances of an SIDH-style key exchange is to keep the starting vertex as $j = 1728$ (or close to it), keep A and B smooth or powersmooth (but not necessarily only powers of 2 and 3 as in SIKE), and construct the base-field prime p to turn $j = 1728$ into an (A, B)-backdoor curve. In this section, let E_0 denote the curve $E_0\colon y^2 = x^3 + x$.

An easy way of constructing such a p is to perform steps 1 and 3 of Algorithm 3, and then let $D := \frac{B^2 e - d^2}{A^2}$. Then we can solve

$$D = p(a^2 + b^2) + c^2$$

in variables $a, b, c, p \in \mathbb{Z}$, p prime, as follows. Factor $D - c^2$ for small c until the result is of the form pm where p is a large prime congruent to 3 modulo 4 and m is a number representable as a sum of squares.[12]

Then, with $\theta = a\iota\pi + b\pi + c\iota$ the tuple (E_0, θ, d, e) is (A, B)-backdoor. (Note that, in this construction, we cannot expect to satisfy a relationship such as $p = ABf - 1$ with small $f \in \mathbb{Z}$.)

As an (unbalanced) example, let us choose $A = 2^{216}$ and $B = 3^{300}$ and set $e = 1$. Then we can use $d = B \bmod A^2$. Let $D = \frac{B^2 - d^2}{A^2}$, for which we will now produce two primes: First, pick $c = 53$, then $D - c^2$ is a prime number (i.e.,

---

[12] Some choices of A and B result in $D \equiv 2 \pmod 4$ which is an obstruction to this method.

$a = 1$, $b = 0$). Second, pick $c = 355$, then $D - c^2$ is 5 times a prime number (i.e., $a = 2$, $b = 1$). Both of these primes are congruent to 3 modulo 4.

For a powersmooth example, let A be the product of every other prime from 3 up through 317, and let B be the product of all remaining odd primes ≤ 479. With $e = 4$, we can again use $d = B \bmod A^2$ and compute D as above. Then $D - 153^2$ is prime and congruent to 3 modulo 4 (i.e., $a = 1$, $b = 0$).

5.4   Backdoored p for Given $A \approx B$ with Starting Vertex $j = 1728$

For $A \approx B$, finding (A, B)-backdoor curves seems difficult. However, in this section we show that certain choices of (power)smooth parameters A and B allow us to find f such that $j = 1728$ can be made insecure over any $\mathbb{F}_{p^2}$ with $p = ABf - 1$.

One approach to this is to find Pythagorean triples $A^2 + d^2 = B^2$ where A and B are coprime and (power)smooth; then $E_0 : y^2 = x^3 + x$ is a backdoor curve with $\theta = \iota$, the d value from the Pythagorean triple, and $e = 1$. With this construction, we can then use *any* $p \equiv 3 \pmod{4}$, in particular one of the form $p = ABf - 1$.

Note that given the isogeny degrees A, B, it is easy for anyone to detect if this method has been used by simply checking whether $B^2 - A^2$ is a square; hence, an SIDH key exchange using such degrees is simply *weak* and not just backdoored.[13]

Problem 4. Find Pythagorean triples $B^2 = A^2 + d^2$ such that A and B are coprime and smooth (or powersmooth).

Pythagorean triples can be parameterized in terms of Gaussian integers. To be precise, primitive integral Pythagorean triples $a^2 = b^2 + c^2$ are in bijection with Gaussian integers $z = m + ni$ with $\gcd(m, n) = 1$ via the correspondence $(a, b, c) = \left(N(z), \operatorname{Re}(z^2), \operatorname{Im}(z^2) \right)$. The condition that m and n are coprime is satisfied if we take z to be a product of split Gaussian primes, i.e., $z = \prod_i w_i$ where $N(w) \equiv 1 \pmod{4}$ is prime, taking care to avoid simultaneously including a prime and its conjugate. Thus the following method applies provided that B is taken to be an integer divisible only by primes congruent to 1 modulo 4, and $B > A$.

In order to guarantee that $B = N(z)$ is powersmooth, one may take many small w_i. In order to guarantee that B is smooth, it is convenient to take $z = w^k$ for a single small Gaussian prime w, and a large composite power k.

It so happens that the sequence of polynomials $\operatorname{Re}(z^k)$ in variables n and m (recall $z = n + mi$) factors generically into relatively small factors for composite k, so that, when $B^2 = A^2 + d^2$, we can expect that A is frequently smooth or powersmooth. In practice, running a simple search using this method, one very readily obtains example insecure parameters:

---

[13] We resist the temptation of referring to such instantiations as "door" instead of "backdoor".

$$B = 5^{105}$$

$$A = 2^2 \cdot 11 \cdot 19 \cdot 29 \cdot 41 \cdot 59 \cdot 61 \cdot 139 \cdot 241 \cdot 281 \cdot 419 \cdot 421 \cdot 839 \cdot 2381 \cdot 17921$$
$$\cdot \, 21001 \cdot 39761 \cdot 74761 \cdot 448139 \cdot 526679 \cdot 771961 \cdot 238197121$$

$$d = 3^2 \cdot 13 \cdot 79 \cdot 83 \cdot 239 \cdot 307 \cdot 2801 \cdot 3119 \cdot 3361 \cdot 3529 \cdot 28559 \cdot 36791 \cdot 53759$$
$$\cdot \, 908321 \cdot 3575762705759 \cdot 23030958433523039$$

For this example, if we take $p = 105AB - 1$, we obtain a prime which is 3 modulo 4. Note that here $B \approx 2^{244}$ and $A \approx 2^{238}$. Many other primes can easily be obtained (replacing 105 with 214, 222, etc.).

Remark 24. When choosing parameter sets to run B-SIDH [11], if the user is very unlucky, they could hit an instance of such a weak prime. With this in mind, it would be prudent to check that a given combination of A, B, and p does not fall into this category before implementing such a B-SIDH instance.

6 Non-polynomial-time Attacks

So far we focused on polynomial-time algorithms both for the starting curve E_0 with j-invariant 1728 and for backdoor curves, which required the integer e occuring in the attack to be polynomial in $\log p$. However, the attack still works when e is bigger, with decent scaling behaviour. Hence, we may (and will in this section) consider algorithms which are exponential-time, yet improve on the state of the art. The best known classical and quantum attacks for retrieving an isogeny of degree A take time $O^*(A^{\frac{1}{2}})$; recall that we discussed quantum claw-finding in Subsect. 2.3. We will adapt both the dual and the Frobenius isogeny attacks of Sect. 4 to allow for some brute-force in order to attack balanced parameters. We will also adapt the definition of backdoor curves to include curves for which there exists an exponential dual isogeny attack that improves on the state of the art, thus increasing the pool of backdoor curves.

6.1 Non-polynomial Time Dual Isogeny Attack for $E_0 : y^2 = x^3 + x$

Recall from Sect. 4 that the dual isogeny attack consists of a "precomputation" phase and a "key-dependent" phase. The precomputation phase (Algorithm 1) was to find a solution to Eq. (3) — notably, this depends only on the parameters (p, A, B) and not on the concrete public key under attack. The "key-dependent" phase utilized said solution to recover the secret isogeny via Theorem 3 for a specific public key. Our modifications to the dual isogeny attack come in three independent guises, and the resulting algorithm is shown in Algorithm 6:

- Precomputation phase:
  - **Larger d:** When computing a solution to Eq. (3), we fix e and then try up to A^δ values for d until the equation has solutions. This allows us to further relax the constraints between A, B, and p, at the price of an exhaustive search of classical cost $O^*(A^\delta)$ or quantum cost $O^*(A^{\frac{\delta}{2}})$ using Grover's algorithm.

- Key-dependent phase:
  - **Larger e:** We search for a solution to Eq. (3) where e is any smooth number $\leq A^\epsilon$ with $\epsilon \in [0, 1]$, whereas in [31] the integer e was required to be polynomial in $\log p$. This relaxes the constraints on A and B, at a cost of a $O^*(e^{\frac{1}{2}}) = O^*(A^{\frac{\epsilon}{2}})$ computation, both classically and quantumly, via a meet-in-the-middle or claw-finding algorithm (to retrieve the endomorphism η defined in the proof of Theorem 3).
  - **Smaller A:** We first naïvely guess part of the secret isogeny and then apply the dual isogeny attack only on the remaining part for each guess; see Fig. 5. More precisely, we iterate through isogenies of degree $A^\gamma \mid A$, with $\gamma \in [0, 1]$, and for each possible guess we apply the dual isogeny attack to SSI-T with $A' := A^{1-\gamma}$ in place of A. The Diophantine equation to solve thus turns into

$$A'^2(pa^2 + pb^2 + c^2) + d^2 = B^2 e. \qquad (9)$$

The cost of using A' in place of A is the cost of iterating over the isogenies of degree A^γ multiplied by the cost T of running the dual isogeny attack (possibly adapted as above to allow for larger e). This is an exhaustive search of cost $O^*(A^\gamma \cdot T) = O^*(A^{\gamma+\frac{\epsilon}{2}})$ classically or $O^*(A^{\frac{\gamma}{2}} \cdot T) = O^*(A^{\frac{\gamma+\epsilon}{2}})$ quantumly using Grover's algorithm.[14]

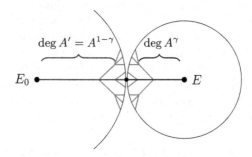

$$\deg A' = A^{1-\gamma} \qquad \deg A^\gamma$$

$$E_0 \qquad\qquad E$$

Fig. 5. Brute-force guessing the degree A^γ part of Alice's isogeny φ from Alice's curve E and the dual isogeny attack to find the remaining degree A' part of φ from E_0.

Proposition 25. *Define α and β by setting $A = p^\alpha$ and $B = p^\beta$ and fix $0 < \alpha \leq \beta$. Under Heuristic 1, if*

$$2\beta + \alpha\epsilon \geq \max\{4\alpha + 2\alpha\delta - 4\alpha\gamma, \ 2 + 2\alpha - 2\alpha\delta - 2\alpha\gamma\},$$

---

[14] For the reader who is wondering exactly how to apply Grover's algorithm in this context: Let $\langle P_A, Q_A \rangle = E_0[A^\gamma]$. The input for Grover's algorithm here is an integer $n < A^\gamma$ and all of the input of Algorithm 5. Attempt Steps 2 and 3 for φ_g such that $\ker(\varphi_g) = \langle P_A + nQ_A \rangle$; the output will be success or failure. Every subroutine of Steps 2 and 3 can be broken down into basic elliptic curve arithmetic for which there are known quantum algorithms of similar complexity to their classical counterparts.

Algorithm 4: Solving the norm equation; precomputation.

Input: • SIDH parameters $p, A = p^\alpha, B = p^\beta$.
   • Attack parameters $\delta, \gamma, \epsilon \in [0, 1]$, with $A^\gamma \mid A$.
Output: A solution (a, b, c, d, e) to (9) with $A' = A^{1-\gamma}$ and $e \leq A^\epsilon$ smooth.

1 Pick a smooth number $e \leq A^\epsilon$ which is a square modulo A'^2.
2 Compute d_0 such that $d_0^2 \equiv eB^2 \pmod{A'^2}$.
3 **For** $d' = 1, 2, ..., \lfloor A^\delta \rfloor$ *such that* $d_0 + A'^2 d' < \sqrt{e}B$ **do**
4   Let $d = d_0 + A'^2 d'$.
5   Find the smallest positive integer c such that $c^2 A'^2 = eB^2 - d^2$ $\pmod{p}$, or **continue** if no such c exists.
6   **If** $eB^2 > d^2 + c^2 A'^2$ **then**
7   Try finding (a, b) such that $a^2 + b^2 = \frac{eB^2 - d^2 - c^2 A'^2}{A'^2 p}$.
      If a solution is found, **return** (a, b, c, d, e).

Algorithm 5: Recovering the secret isogeny; key-dependent phase.

Input: • All the inputs of Algorithm 4.
   • An instance of SSI-T with those parameters, namely a curve E and points $P, Q \in E[B]$ where there exists a degree-A isogeny $\varphi : E_0 \to E$ such that P, Q are the images by φ of a canonical basis of $E_0[B]$.
   • $\theta \in \text{End}(E_0)$ and $d, e \in \mathbb{Z}$ such that $\deg(A'\theta + d) = B^2 e$ with $e \leq A^\epsilon$ smooth.
Output: An isogeny φ matching the constraints given by the input.

1 **For** $\varphi_g : E \to E'$ an A^γ-isogeny **do**
2   Compute $P' = [A^{-\gamma} \mod B] \varphi_g(P)$ and $Q' = [A^{-\gamma} \mod B] \varphi_g(Q)$.
3   Use Theorem 3 to compute $\varphi' : E_0 \to E'$ of degree $A' = A^{1-\gamma}$, assuming that P' and Q' are the images by φ' of the canonical basis of $E_0[B]$, or conclude that no such isogeny exists.
4   **If** φ' *is found* **then**
5   **Return** $\varphi = \widehat{\varphi_g} \circ \varphi'$.

Algorithm 6: Solving SSI-T.

1 Invoke Algorithm 4, yielding $a, b, c, d, e \in \mathbb{Z}$, and then Algorithm 5 with $\theta = a\iota\pi + b\pi + c\iota$.

A has (at most) $O(\log \log p)$ distinct prime factors, and B is at most polynomial in A, then Algorithm 6 solves SSI-T in time $O^*(A^\Gamma)$ on a classical computer and time $O^*(A^{\Gamma/2})$ on a quantum computer, where

$$\Gamma := \max\left\{\frac{1 + 3\alpha - 2\beta}{3\alpha}, \frac{2\alpha - \beta}{2\alpha}, \frac{1 + \alpha - \beta}{2\alpha}\right\}.$$

Proof. See the full version [13, Appendix A.2]. □

Corollary 26. *Suppose that B is at most polynomial in A and that A has (at most) $O(\log \log p)$ distinct prime factors. When run on a classical computer, Algorithm 6 is asymptotically more efficient than meet-in-the-middle — disregarding memory concerns, so more efficient than $O^*(A^{\frac{1}{2}})$ — whenever*

$$B > \max\left\{\sqrt{p}A^{\frac{3}{4}}, A, p\right\}.$$

When run on a quantum computer, Algorithm 6 is asymptotically more efficient than quantum claw-funding — according to the model in [23], so more efficient than $O^*(A^{\frac{1}{2}})$ — whenever

$$B > \max\left\{\sqrt{p}, A^{-1}p\right\}.$$

6.2 Non-polynomial Time Frobenius Isogeny Attack for $E_0 : y^2 = x^3 + x$

Recall the Frobenius isogeny attack from Sect. 4. In a similar way to the previous section, we allow for some brute-force to improve the balance of our parameters. More precisely, we consider again:

- **Smaller A:** Iterate through isogenies of degree $A^\gamma | A$; in the precomputation we solve instead

$$A'^2(a^2 + b^2) + pc^2 = B^2 e, \tag{10}$$

  where $A' = A^{1-\gamma}$.

Algorithm 7 describes how to adapt the Frobenius isogeny attack of Sect. 4 in this way.

Algorithm 7: Solving SSI-T.

---

1 (Precomputation) Invoke Algorithm 2 with inputs p, A', B, yielding $a, b, c, e \in \mathbb{Z}$.
2 (Key-dependent) Run Algorithm 5 except that $\theta = a\iota\pi + b\pi \in \text{End}(E_0)$ instead satisfies the equation $\deg(A'\theta + c) = B^2 ep$ and we use Theorem 5 in place of Theorem 3.

Proposition 27. *Define α and β by $A = p^\alpha$ and $B = p^\beta$, fix $B \geq A$ and B at most polynomial in A, and suppose that $A' = A^{1-\gamma}$ has (at most) $O(\log \log p)$ distinct prime factors. Under Heuristic 2, Algorithm 7 has complexity $O^*(A^\gamma) = O^*\left(A^{\frac{1+4\alpha-2\beta}{4\alpha}}\right)$ classically and $O^*\left(A^{\frac{1}{2}}\right) = O^*\left(A^{\frac{1+4\alpha-2\beta}{8\alpha}}\right)$ quantumly. Moreover, the precomputation step runs in time $O^*(1)$.*

Proof. See the full version [13, Appendix A.3].

Corollary 28. *Suppose that B is at most polynomial in A and that A has (at most) $O(\log \log p)$ distinct prime factors. When run on a classical computer, Algorithm 7 is asymptotically more efficient than meet-in-the-middle — disregarding memory concerns, so more efficient than $O^*(A^{\frac{1}{2}})$ — whenever $B > \sqrt{p}A$. When run on a quantum computer, Algorithm 7 is asymptotically more efficient than quantum claw-funding — according to the model in [23], so more efficient than $O^*(A^{\frac{1}{2}})$ — whenever $B > \sqrt{p}$.*

Remark 29. It may seem natural to also allow for larger e as in the dual isogeny attack. However, this limits how small A' can be, and the gain from reducing A' is strictly better than the gain from increasing e. Intuitively this is because A' appears in Eq. 10 as a square, which doubles the gain compared to gain from increasing e.

6.3 Non-polynomial Time Dual Isogeny Attack for Backdoor Curves

Recall the definition of an (A, B)-backdoor curve (E_0, θ, d, e) from Definition 14; we now extend this to define backdoor curves that give rise to a torsion-point attack of complexity $O^*(A^{\mathscr{C}})$. In this section we explain how to modify Algorithm 3 to compute these more general backdoor curves, and apply Algorithm 6 with such a backdoored starting curve E_0 by replacing the precomputation step with the modified Algorithm 3.

Definition 30. *Let A, B be coprime positive integers and $0 \leq \mathscr{C} \leq 1/2$. An $(A, B, \mathscr{C})$-backdoor curve is a tuple (E_0, θ, d, e) of a supersingular elliptic curve E_0 over some $\mathbb{F}_{p^2}$, an endomorphism $\theta \in \mathrm{End}(E_0)$ in an efficient representation, and two integers d, e, such that Algorithm 5 solves SSI-T for that particular E_0 in time $O^*(A^{\mathscr{C}})$ when given (θ, d, e). An $(A, B, 0)$-backdoor curve is then an (A, B)-backdoor curve in the sense of Definition 14.*

To construct $(A, B, \mathscr{C})$-backdoor curves, we modify Algorithm 3 as follows:

- Use $A' = A^{1-\gamma}$ instead of A, namely we will guess part of the isogeny with degree $A^\gamma \mid A$.
- Instead of starting from $e = 1$, choose $A^{e'}$ random values of $A'^4 B^{-2} < e \leq A^e$ (note e is not necessarily an integer square) until there exists d such that $d^2 = B^2 e \bmod (A')^2$,

$$B^2 e - d^2 > 0 \tag{11}$$

and $B^2 e - d^2$ is a square modulo p. Once these values of d and e are found, continue like in Algorithm 3, Step 6.

Proposition 31. *Heuristically, if A has (at most) $O(\log \log p)$ distinct prime factors:*

- Let $\mathscr{C} \in [0, 0.4]$. For A, B such that $B > A^{2-\frac{5}{2}\cdot\mathscr{C}}$, Algorithm 3 modified as above constructs a $(A, B, \mathscr{C})$-backdoor curve in time $O^*(A^{\mathscr{C}})$ on a classical computer, assuming an oracle for factoring.
- Let $\mathscr{C} \in [0, 0.25]$. For every A, B such that $B > A^{2-4\cdot\mathscr{C}}$, Algorithm 3 constructs a $(A, B, \mathscr{C})$-backdoor curve in polynomial time on a quantum computer.

Proof. See the full version [13, Appendix A.4].

Corollary 32. *When $A \approx B$ (e.g. as in SIKE [21]), the modified Algorithm 3 computes a $(A, B, \frac{2}{5})$-insecure curve in time $O^*(A^{\frac{2}{5}})$ on a classical computer and computes a $(A, B, \frac{1}{4})$-insecure curve in polynomial time on a quantum computer. In particular, when $A \approx B \approx \sqrt{p}$, there exist backdoor curves E_0 for which we can solve SSI-T on a classical computer in time $O^*(p^{\frac{1}{5}})$ and for which we can solve SSI-T on a quantum computer in time $O^*(p^{\frac{1}{8}})$.*

7 Impact on Unbalanced SIDH, Group Key Agreement, and B-SIDH

We summarize how the results of Sects. 4, 6.1, and 6.2 impact unbalanced SIDH with $p \approx AB$, the GSIDH multiparty group key agreement [2,17], and B-SIDH [11].

7.1 Frobenius Isogeny Attack on Group Key Agreement and Unbalanced SIDH

Let us consider unbalanced SIDH with $p \approx AB$. More precisely, we study instances of SSI-T with $p = AB \cdot f - 1$, where f is a small cofactor and where A has (at most) $O(\log\log p)$ distinct prime factors. Then by Proposition 11 and Theorem 5, under Heuristic 2, the Frobenius isogeny attack of Sect. 4 gives a polynomial-time attack on SSI-T when $B > \sqrt{p}A^2$. Since in this section we restrict to the case $p \approx AB$, this inequality simplifies to $B \geq A^5$. In particular, this gives us one of our main results:

Theorem 33. *Under Heuristic 2, the Frobenius isogeny attack presented in Sect. 4 breaks the GSIDH n-party group key agreement protocol presented in [2,17] in time polynomial in $\log p$ for all $n \geq 6$.*

Proof. Recall from Subsect. 2.1 that the cryptanalytic challenge underlying the n-party group key agreement as presented in [2,17] can be modelled as an instance of SSI-T with $A = \ell_1^{e_1}$, $B = \ell_2^{e_2} \cdots \ell_n^{e_n}$, and $p = AB \cdot f - 1$, where $\ell_1, \ldots, \ell_n$ are primes such that for all i, j we have $\ell_i^{e_i} \approx \ell_j^{e_j}$ and f is a small cofactor chosen such that p is prime. Thus the security of the n-party group key agreement is similar to that of unbalanced SIDH with the same p, A, B. Suppose $n \geq 6$. Since A is a prime power (hence has $1 = O(\log\log p)$ prime divisors) and $B \geq A^5$, the Frobenius isogeny attack on the group key agreement is polynomial-time when there are 6 or more parties. $\qquad\square$

We have implemented this attack in Magma [6] for 6 parties, see the code at https://github.com/torsion-attacks-SIDH/6party. The code is written to attack the power-of-3 torsion subgroup, when $p + 1$ is powers of the first 6 primes, and uses cryptographically large parameters.

We know the Frobenius isogeny attack is polynomial on unbalanced SIDH when $B \geq A^5$ (and the n-party group key agreement when $n \geq 6$); it remains to investigate the non-polynomial analogue. To this end, consider the attack presented in Subsect. 6.2. As above, suppose given an instance of SSI-T with $p = AB \cdot f - 1$, where f is a small cofactor, such that A has (at most) $O(\log \log p)$ distinct prime factors, and now additionally suppose that $B \approx A^{1+\epsilon}$, where $0 < \epsilon < 4$. To apply this attack to n-party group key agreement with $n = 2, 3, 4, 5$, just set $\epsilon = n - 2$.

Proposition 34 demonstrates an improvement on the asymptotic complexity for quantum claw-finding as analyzed in [23] for any level of imbalance (i.e., for any $\epsilon > 0$). However, note that the only quantum subroutine used in our Frobenius isogeny attack is Grover's algorithm, so our complexity computation is independent of the choice of quantum computation model used for claw-finding. As such, using a more nuanced model working with concrete complexities, such as the one presented in [24], will make our quantum attack start to "improve on the state of the art" at different levels of imbalance. As our work currently only presents asymptotic complexities, we are leaving an analysis of this for future work.

Proposition 34. *Let A, B be coprime smooth numbers where $B > A^{1+\epsilon}$, and let p be a prime congruent to 3 (mod 4). Furthermore, suppose that $p = ABf - 1$ for some small cofactor f, and that the number of distinct prime factors of A is (at most) $O(\log \log p)$. Let $E_0/\mathbb{F}_p$ be the supersingular elliptic curve with j-invariant 1728. Algorithm 7 solves SSI-T with these parameters in time $O^* \left(A^{1-\frac{\epsilon}{4}} \right)$ when run on a classical computer and time $O^* \left(A^{\frac{1}{2}-\frac{\epsilon}{8}} \right)$ when run on a quantum computer.*

Proof. Let $\alpha = \frac{1}{2+\epsilon}$ and $\beta = \frac{1+\epsilon}{2+\epsilon}$. Proposition 27 proves that Algorithm 7 runs classically in time

$$O^* \left(A^{\frac{1+4\alpha-2\beta}{4\alpha}} \right) = O^* \left(A^{\frac{(2+\epsilon)+4-2(1+\epsilon)}{4}} \right) = O^* \left(A^{1-\frac{\epsilon}{4}} \right).$$

Similarly, Proposition 27 proves that Algorithm 7 runs quantumly in time

$$O^* \left(A^{\frac{1+4\alpha-2\beta}{8\alpha}} \right) = O^* \left(A^{\frac{(2+\epsilon)+4-2(1+\epsilon)}{8}} \right) = O^* \left(A^{\frac{1}{2}-\frac{\epsilon}{8}} \right).$$

$\square$

As stated above, akin to the polynomial-time attack, substituting $n = \epsilon+2$ in Proposition 34 gives us the complexity of the non-polynomial Frobenius isogeny attack on n-party group key agreement for $n = 2, 3, 4, 5$ parties, see Table 1.

Table 1. Asymptotic complexities of our Frobenius isogeny attack on n-party key agreement and comparison with the state of the art, i.e., meet-in-the-middle and claw-finding. (As justified above, we take [23] for the "state-of-the-art" numbers for quantum claw-finding here rather than [24]). Numbers given are the logarithm to base A of the complexity, ignoring factors polynomial in $\log p$.

# parties	This work (classical)	This work (quantum)	MitM (classical)	[23] (quantum)
2	1	1/2		
3	3/4	3/8		
4	1/2	1/4	1/2	1/2
5	1/4	1/8		
≥ 6	0	0		

7.2 Dual Isogeny Attack Applied to B-SIDH

A recent proposal called *B-SIDH* [11] consists of instantiating SIDH with parameters where AB is a divisor of $p^2 - 1$. By Proposition 25, under Heuristic 1, when $A \approx B \approx p$ (that is, $\alpha \approx \beta \approx 1$), Algorithm 6 yields a quantum attack on these parameters of complexity $O^*(A^{\frac{1}{3}}) = O^*(p^{\frac{1}{3}})$. This compares to other attack complexities in the literature as follows:

- Tani's quantum claw-finding algorithm [38] was claimed to have complexity $O^*(p^{\frac{1}{3}})$, but [23] argues that the complexity is actually no lower than $O^*(p^{\frac{2}{3}})$ when the cost of data-structure operations is properly accounted for.
- A quantum algorithm due to Biasse, Jao, and Sankar [4] finds *some* isogeny between the start and end curve in time $O^*(p^{\frac{1}{4}})$. While there is a heuristic argument for "standard" SIDH/SIKE that any isogeny suffices to find the correct isogeny [18], this argument relies on the fact that the isogeny sought in SIKE has relatively small degree compared to p, which is was not believed to be true for B-SIDH. The B-SIDH paper [11] conservatively views [4] as the best quantum attack. Since the publication of B-SIDH, it has been shown [37] that [4] does in fact apply, so this is currently the best known quantum attack against B-SIDH.
- The cost of known classical attacks is no lower than $O^*(A^{\frac{1}{2}})$, which is achieved by meet-in-the-middle techniques (using exponential memory) and potentially memoryless by Delfs and Galbraith [15] when $A \approx p$ assuming a sufficiently efficient method to produce *the* isogeny from some isogeny.

Thus, assuming Heuristic 1 holds, Algorithm 6 is asymptotically better than quantum claw-finding but is not the best known quantum attack against B-SIDH at the moment.

Note that for $1/2 < \alpha \approx \beta < 1$, the (quantum) attack cost in terms of p may be lower than $O^*(p^{\frac{1}{3}})$, but it does not get smaller than $O^*(p^{\frac{1}{4}})$ and hence does not improve on [4] for $\alpha \approx \beta$.

7.3   Impact on B-SIDH Group Key Exchange

As an example of how care should be taken when constructing new SIDH-style schemes, we also include a scheme that does not exist in the literature: group key agreement instantiated with B-SIDH parameters. This is a natural scheme to consider: The size of the base-field prime used in group key agreement grows with the number of parties, and optimally chosen B-SIDH parameters (with respect to efficiency) halves the bit-length of the base-field prime. Corollary 35 shows that such an instantiation is insecure for 4 or more parties:

Corollary 35. *Let A, B be coprime smooth numbers and let p be a prime congruent to 3 (mod 4). Furthermore, suppose that $p^2 - 1 = ABf$ for some small cofactor f and that $B > A^3$. Let E_0 be the supersingular elliptic curve with j-invariant 1728. Then, assuming Heuristic 1, SSI-T can be solved in polynomial time.*

Proof. The result follows from Proposition 9.

Finally, in Corollary 36 we give the complexity of our dual isogeny attack on an instantiation of B-SIDH 3-party group key agreement with minimal base-field prime:

Corollary 36. *Let A, B be coprime smooth numbers and let p be a prime congruent to 3 (mod 4). Furthermore, suppose that $p^2 - 1 = ABf$ for some small cofactor f and that $B > A^2$. Let E_0 be the supersingular elliptic curve with j-invariant 1728. Then, assuming Heuristic 1, Algorithm 6 solves SSI-T in time $O^*(A^{\frac{1}{4}}) = O^*(p^{\frac{1}{6}})$ when run on a classical computer and time $O^*(A^{\frac{1}{8}}) = O^*(p^{\frac{1}{12}})$ when run on a quantum computer.*

Proof. This follows from plugging $\alpha = 2/3$ and $\beta = 4/3$ into Proposition 25.

8   Open Question

The two attack variants given in Theorems 3 and 5 may seem somewhat ad hoc at first. In this Section, we describe a common abstraction for both variants and discuss potential generalizations.

The core idea is to relax the choice of τ as an *endo*morphism of E, instead allowing τ to be an isogeny from E to another curve E':

Theorem 37. *Suppose given an instance of SSI-T where A has $O(\log \log p)$ distinct prime factors. Let $\omega : E \to E'$ be a known isogeny to some curve E'. Furthermore, assume we are given the restriction to $E_0[B]$ of an isogeny $\psi : E_0 \to E'$, and an integer $d \in \mathbb{Z}$ such that the isogeny $\tau = \psi\widehat{\varphi} + d\omega \in \mathrm{Hom}(E, E')$ has degree $B^2 e$, where e is smooth. Then, we can compute a matching isogeny φ in time $O^*(\sqrt{e})$.*

Proof. The proof is completely analogous to Theorems 3 and 5.

The specific instantiations obtained as special cases earlier can be recovered as follows:

- For Theorem 3, we simply use $E' = E$, the map ω is the identity morphism on E, and the isogeny ψ is an element of the set $M' = \varphi M \subseteq \text{Hom}(E_0, E)$, where $M \leq \text{End}(E_0)$ is the subgroup of trace-zero endomorphisms of E_0.
- For Theorem 5, we use the Galois conjugate $E' = E^\sigma$ of E, the map $\omega \colon E \to E^\sigma$ is the p-power Frobenius isogeny, and the isogeny ψ is an element of the set $M' = \varphi^\sigma M \subseteq \text{Hom}(E_0, E^\sigma)$, where $M \leq \text{End}(E_0)$ is the subgroup orthogonal to Frobenius $\pi \in \text{End}(E_0)$.[15]

In both cases, the choice of M' and ω is such that the resulting degree form for the subgroup $M' + \omega\mathbb{Z}$ of $\text{Hom}(E_0, E')$ has a sufficiently nice shape to be solved efficiently using techniques such as those shown in Subsect. 4.2.

It is unclear whether there are any other choices of M' and ω which lead to an efficiently solvable norm equation and potentially improved attacks. However, so far we have not found any other ways to exploit this viewpoint beyond using φ itself or its Galois conjugate. Finding other useful generalizations is an interesting open problem.

Acknowledgements. Thanks to Daniel J. Bernstein for his insight into estimating sizes of solutions to Eq. 3, to John Voight for answering a question of ours concerning Subsect. 5.2, and to Boris Fouotsa for identifying errors in Proposition 34 and its proof. We would also like to thank Filip Pawlega and the anonymous reviewers for their careful reading and helpful feedback.

References

1. Adj, G., Cervantes-Vázquez, D., Chi-Domínguez, J.-J., Menezes, A., Rodríguez-Henríquez, F.: On the cost of computing isogenies between supersingular elliptic curves. In: Cid, C., Jacobson Jr, M. (eds.) SAC 2018. LNCS, vol. 11349, pp. 322–343. Springer, Cham (2018). https://doi.org/10.1007/978-3-030-10970-7_15
2. Azarderakhsh, R., Jalali, A., Jao, D., Soukharev, V.: Practical supersingular isogeny group key agreement. IACR Cryptology ePrint Archive 2019/330 (2019)
3. Batut, C., Belabas, K., Bernardi, D., Cohen, H., Olivier, M.: User's Guide to PARI-GP. Université de Bordeaux I. https://pari.math.u-bordeaux.fr/
4. Biasse, J.-F., Jao, D., Sankar, A.: A quantum algorithm for computing isogenies between supersingular elliptic curves. In: Meier, W., Mukhopadhyay, D. (eds.) INDOCRYPT 2014. LNCS, vol. 8885, pp. 428–442. Springer, Cham (2014). https://doi.org/10.1007/978-3-319-13039-2_25
5. Boneh, D., Kogan, D., Woo, K.: Oblivious pseudorandom functions from isogenies. In: Moriai, S., Wang, H. (eds.) ASIACRYPT 2020, Part II. LNCS, vol. 12492, pp. 520–550. Springer, Cham (2020). https://doi.org/10.1007/978-3-030-64834-3_18
6. Bosma, W., Cannon, J., Playoust, C.: The Magma algebra system I: the user language. J. Symbolic Comput. **24**(3–4), 235–265 (1997). https://magma.maths.usyd.edu.au/

---

[15] The way Theorem 5 is presented differs from Theorem 37 here; this is merely a change in notation.

7. Bottinelli, P., de Quehen, V., Leonardi, C., Mosunov, A., Pawlega, F., Sheth, M.: The dark SIDH of isogenies. IACR Cryptology ePrint Archive 2019/1333 (2019)
8. Castryck, W., Lange, T., Martindale, C., Panny, L., Renes, J.: CSIDH: an efficient post-quantum commutative group action. In: Peyrin, T., Galbraith, S. (eds.) ASIA-CRYPT 2018, Part III. LNCS, vol. 11274, pp. 395–427. Springer, Cham (2018). https://doi.org/10.1007/978-3-030-03332-3_15
9. Castryck, W., Panny, L., Vercauteren, F.: Rational isogenies from irrational endomorphisms. In: Canteaut, A., Ishai, Y. (eds.) EUROCRYPT 2020, Part II. LNCS, vol. 12106, pp. 523–548. Springer, Cham (2020). https://doi.org/10.1007/978-3-030-45724-2_18
10. Colò, L., David, K.: Orienting supersingular isogeny graphs. J. Math. Cryptology **14**(1), 414–437 (2020)
11. Costello, C.: B-SIDH: supersingular isogeny Diffie-Hellman using twisted torsion. In: Moriai, S., Wang, H. (eds.) ASIACRYPT 2020, Part II. LNCS, vol. 12492, pp. 440–463. Springer, Cham (2020). https://doi.org/10.1007/978-3-030-64834-3_15
12. Cremona, J., David, R.: Efficient solution of rational conics. Math. Comput. **72**(243), 1417–1441 (2003)
13. de Quehen, V., et al.: Improved torsion-point attacks on SIDH variants. Full version of this article. IACR Cryptology ePrint Archive 2020/633 (2021). https://ia.cr/2020/633
14. Delpech de Saint Guilhem, C., Kutas, P., Petit, C., Silva, J.: SÉTA: supersingular encryption from torsion attacks. IACR Cryptology ePrint Archive 2019/1291 (2019)
15. Delfs, C., Galbraith, S.D.: Computing isogenies between supersingular elliptic curves over $\mathbb{F}_p$. Des. Codes Crypt. **78**(2), 425–440 (2016)
16. Eisenträger, K., Hallgren, S., Lauter, K., Morrison, T., Petit, C.: Supersingular isogeny graphs and endomorphism rings: reductions and solutions. In: Nielsen, J.B., Rijmen, V. (eds.) EUROCRYPT 2018, Part III. LNCS, vol. 10822, pp. 329–368. Springer, Cham (2018). https://doi.org/10.1007/978-3-319-78372-7_11
17. Furukawa, S., Kunihiro, N., Takashima, K.: Multi-party key exchange protocols from supersingular isogenies. In: ISITA, pp. 208–212. IEEE (2018)
18. Galbraith, S.D., Petit, C., Shani, B., Ti, Y.B.: On the security of supersingular isogeny cryptosystems. In: Cheon, J.H., Takagi, T. (eds.) ASIACRYPT 2016, Part I. LNCS, vol. 10031, pp. 63–91. Springer, Heidelberg (2016). https://doi.org/10.1007/978-3-662-53887-6_3
19. Ivanyos, G., Rónyai, L.: Finding maximal orders in semisimple algebras over $\mathbb{Q}$. Comput. Complex. **3**(3), 245–261 (1993)
20. Jao, D., et al.: Supersingular isogeny key encapsulation. Updated version of [21] for round 3 of [29] (2020)
21. Jao, D., et al.: Supersingular isogeny key encapsulation. Submission to [29] (2017). https://sike.org
22. Jao, D., De Feo, L.: Towards quantum-resistant cryptosystems from supersingular elliptic curve isogenies. In: Yang, B.-Y. (ed.) PQCrypto 2011. LNCS, vol. 7071, pp. 19–34. Springer, Heidelberg (2011). https://doi.org/10.1007/978-3-642-25405-5_2
23. Jaques, S., Schanck, J.M.: Quantum cryptanalysis in the RAM model: claw-finding attacks on SIKE. In: Boldyreva, A., Micciancio, D. (eds.) CRYPTO 2019, Part I. LNCS, vol. 11692, pp. 32–61. Springer, Cham (2019). https://doi.org/10.1007/978-3-030-26948-7_2
24. Jaques, S., Schrottenloher, A.: Low-gate quantum golden collision finding. In: SAC 2020. Springer (2020)

25. Kaneko, M.: Supersingular j-invariants as singular moduli mod p. Osaka J. Math. **26**(4), 849–855 (1989)
26. Kohel, D., Lauter, K., Petit, C., Tignol, J.-P.: On the quaternion ℓ-isogeny path problem. LMS J. Comput. Math. **17A**, 418–432 (2014)
27. Love, J., Boneh, D.: Supersingular curves with small non-integer endomorphisms. In: Galbraith, S. (ed.) ANTS XIV: Proceedings of the Fourteenth Algorithmic Number Theory Symposium (2020)
28. Martindale, C., Panny, L.: How to not break SIDH. In: CFAIL 2019 (2019)
29. National Institute of Standards and Technology: Post-quantum cryptography standardization, December 2016. https://csrc.nist.gov/Projects/Post-Quantum-Cryptography/Post-Quantum-Cryptography-Standardization
30. Onuki, H.: On oriented supersingular elliptic curves. Finite Fields Appl. **69**, 101777 (2021)
31. Petit, C.: Faster algorithms for isogeny problems using torsion point images. In: Takagi, T., Peyrin, T. (eds.) ASIACRYPT 2017, Part II. LNCS, vol. 10625, pp. 330–353. Springer, Cham (2017). https://doi.org/10.1007/978-3-319-70697-9_12
32. Petit, C., Lauter, K.E.: Hard and easy problems for supersingular isogeny graphs. IACR Cryptology ePrint Archive 2017/962 (2017)
33. Pohlig, S., Hellman, M.: An improved algorithm for computing logarithms over GF(p) and its cryptographic significance (corresp.). IEEE Trans. Inf. Theory **24**(1), 106–110 (1978)
34. Sahu, R.A., Gini, A., Pal, A.: Supersingular isogeny-based designated verifier blind signature. IACR Cryptology ePrint Archive 2019/1498 (2019)
35. Siegel, C.L.: Über die Classenzahl quadratischer Zahlkörper. Acta Arithmetica, pp. 83–86 (1935)
36. Simon, D.: Quadratic equations in dimensions 4, 5 and more. Preprint (2005). https://simond.users.lmno.cnrs.fr/maths/Dim4.pdf
37. Tako, B.F., Kutas, P., Merz, S.-P.: On the isogeny problem with torsion point information. IACR Cryptology ePrint Archive 2021/153
38. Tani, S.: An improved claw finding algorithm using quantum walk. In: Kučera, L., Kučera, A. (eds.) MFCS 2007. LNCS, vol. 4708, pp. 536–547. Springer, Heidelberg (2007). https://doi.org/10.1007/978-3-540-74456-6_48
39. Voight, J.: Identifying the matrix ring: algorithms for quaternion algebras and quadratic forms. In: Alladi, K., Bhargava, M., Savitt, D., Tiep, P. (eds.) Quadratic and Higher Degree Forms, pp. 255–298. Springer, New York (2013). https://doi.org/10.1007/978-1-4614-7488-3_10

Codes and Extractors

Smoothing Out Binary Linear Codes and Worst-Case Sub-exponential Hardness for LPN

Yu Yu[1,2,3($\boxtimes$)] and Jiang Zhang[4]

[1] Department of Computer Science and Engineering, Shanghai Jiao Tong University, 800 Dongchuan Road, Shanghai 200240, China
[2] Shanghai Qi Zhi Institute, 701 Yunjin Road, Shanghai 200232, China
[3] Shanghai Key Laboratory of Privacy-Preserving Computation, 701 Yunjin Road, Shanghai 200232, China
[4] State Key Laboratory of Cryptology, P.O. Box 5159, Beijing 100878, China

Abstract. Learning parity with noise (LPN) is a notorious (average-case) hard problem that has been well studied in learning theory, coding theory and cryptography since the early 90's. It further inspires the Learning with Errors (LWE) problem [Regev, STOC 2005], which has become one of the central building blocks for post-quantum cryptography and advanced cryptographic primitives. Unlike LWE whose hardness can be reducible from worst-case lattice problems, no corresponding worst-case hardness results were known for LPN until very recently. At Eurocrypt 2019, Brakerski et al. [BLVW19] established the first feasibility result that the worst-case hardness of nearest codeword problem (NCP) (on balanced linear code) at the extremely low noise rate $\frac{\log^2 n}{n}$ implies the quasi-polynomial hardness of LPN at the high noise rate $1/2 - 1/\mathsf{poly}(n)$. It remained open whether a worst-case to average-case reduction can be established for standard (constant-noise) LPN, ideally with sub-exponential hardness.

We start with a simple observation that the hardness of high-noise LPN over large fields is implied by that of the LWE of the same modulus, and is thus reducible from worst-case hardness of lattice problems. We then revisit [BLVW19], which is the main focus of this work. We first expand the underlying binary linear codes (of the NCP) to not only the balanced code considered in [BLVW19] but also to another code (with a minimum dual distance). At the core of our reduction is a new variant of smoothing lemma (for both binary codes) that circumvents the barriers (inherent in the underlying worst-case randomness extraction) and admits tradeoffs for a wider spectrum of parameter choices. In addition to similar worst-case hardness result obtained in [BLVW19], we show that for any constant $0 < c < 1$ the constant-noise LPN problem is ($T = 2^{\Omega(n^{1-c})}, \epsilon = 2^{-\Omega(n^{\min(c,1-c)})}, q = 2^{\Omega(n^{\min(c,1-c)})}$)-hard assuming that the NCP at the low-noise rate $\tau = n^{-c}$ is ($T' = 2^{\Omega(\tau n)}, \epsilon' = 2^{-\Omega(\tau n)}, m = 2^{\Omega(\tau n)}$)-hard in the worst case, where T, ϵ, q and m are time complexity, success rate, sample complexity, and codeword length respectively. Moreover, refuting the worst-case hardness assumption would imply arbitrary polynomial speedups over the current state-of-the-art algorithms for solving the NCP

© International Association for Cryptologic Research 2021
T. Malkin and C. Peikert (Eds.): CRYPTO 2021, LNCS 12827, pp. 473–501, 2021.
https://doi.org/10.1007/978-3-030-84252-9_16

(and LPN), which is a win-win result. Unfortunately, public-key encryptions and collision resistant hash functions need constant-noise LPN with $(T = 2^{\omega(\sqrt{n})}, \epsilon' = 2^{-\omega(\sqrt{n})}, q = 2^{\sqrt{n}})$-hardness (Yu et al. CRYPTO 2016 & ASIACRYPT 2019), which is almost (up to an arbitrary $\omega(1)$ factor in the exponent) what is reducible from the worst-case NCP when $c = 0.5$. We leave it as an open problem whether the gap can be closed or there is a separation in place.

Keywords: Foundations of cryptography · Worst-case to average-case reduction · Learning parity with noise · Smoothing lemma

1   Introduction

1.1   Learning Parity with Noise

Learning parity with noise (LPN) [12] represents a noisy version of the "parity learning problem" in machine learning as well as the "decoding random linear codes" in coding theory. The conjectured hardness of the LPN problem implies various cryptographic applications, such as symmetric encryption and authentication [4,19,22,33,38–40,43], zero-knowledge proof for commitment schemes [37], oblivious transfer [21], public-key cryptography [1] and collision resistant hash functions [18,52]. Regev [46] introduced the problem of learning with errors (LWE) by generalizing LPN to larger moduli and to a broader choice of noise distributions. Both LPN and LWE are believed to be hard problems not succumbing to quantum algorithms and thus constitute promising candidates for post-quantum cryptography. For the past fifteen years LWE has shown great success in founding upon worst-case hard lattice problems [17,45,46] and as a versatile building block for advanced cryptographic algorithms (such as fully homomorphic encryption [28] and attribute-based encryption [14,32]). In contrast, its twelve-year elder cousin LPN remains much less understood. For instance, it was not until recently did we get the first feasibility result about its root of worst-case hardness [18].

The computational version of the Learning Parity with Noise (LPN) problem with secret size $n \in \mathbb{N}$ and noise rate $0 < \mu < 1/2$ asks to recover the random secret $\mathbf{x}$ given $(\mathbf{A}, \mathbf{A} \cdot \mathbf{x} + \mathbf{e})$, where $\mathbf{x} \xleftarrow{\$} \mathbb{F}_2^n$, $\mathbf{A}$ is a random $q \times n$ Boolean matrix, $\mathbf{e}$ follows the q-fold Bernoulli distribution with parameter μ (i.e., taking the value 1 with probability μ and the value 0 with probability $1 - \mu$), '·' and '+' denote (matrix-vector) multiplication and addition modulo 2 respectively.[1] The decisional version of LPN challenges to distinguish $(\mathbf{A}, \mathbf{A} \cdot \mathbf{x} + \mathbf{e})$ from uniform randomness. In terms of hardness, the two LPN versions are polynomially equivalent [6,27,39].

---

[1] Another equivalent formulation is to find out **s** given as many (up to one's resource capacity) random noisy inner product $\langle \mathbf{a}_i, \mathbf{s} \rangle + \mathbf{e}_i$ as possible. In this paper we use the $\mathbf{Ax} + \mathbf{e}$ representation that is consistent with that of the decoding problems.

LPN has been extensively studied in learning theory, and it was shown in [26] that an efficient algorithm for LPN would allow to learn several important function classes such as 2-DNF formulas, juntas, and any function with a sparse Fourier spectrum. Typically, the noise rate μ of LPN is constant (i.e., independent of secret size n). The BKW (Blum, Kalai and Wasserman) algorithm [13] solves LPN in time/sample complexity $2^{O(n/\log n)}$. Lyubashevsky [42] introduced "sample amplification" trick to obtain a variant of the BKW attack with time complexity $2^{O(n/\log\log n)}$ and sample complexity $q = n^{1+\epsilon}$. If further restricted to linearly many samples (i.e., $q = O(n)$) then the best attacks run in exponential time. Alekhnovich's work [1] implies an interesting variant of LPN (referred to as low-noise LPN) in the noise regime of $\mu = 1/\sqrt{n}$ (or more generally $\mu = n^{-c}$ for $1/2 \leq c < 1$) that can be used to construct public-key crypto-systems. More recently, Brakerski et al. [18] shows that LPN for noise rate $\mu = \frac{\log^2 n}{n}$ (called extremely low-noise LPN) implies collision resistant hash functions. Note that the best solvers for low-noise LPN runs in time $\mathsf{poly}(n) \cdot e^{\mu n}$ [7,10,41], so the LPN at noise rate $\mu = \frac{\log^2 n}{n}$ is still polynomially hard despite the existence of quasi-polynomial attacks. Alternatively, public-key encryption [51] and collision resistant hash functions [52] can be constructed under the assumption that the constant-noise LPN problem is $2^{\omega(\sqrt{n})}$-hard given $2^{\sqrt{n}}$ samples, known as the sub-exponential LPN assumption.

1.2 Nearest Codeword Problem and Worst-Case Hardness

Quite naturally, the worst-case decoding problem considered in [18] and this work is the worst-case analogue of the LPN problem, known as the promise version of the Nearest Codeword Problem (NCP). Informally, the problem is about finding out $\mathbf{s}^{\mathsf{T}} \in \mathbb{F}_2^n$ given a generator matrix $\mathbf{C} \in \mathbb{F}_2^{n \times m}$ for some $[m,n]$ binary linear code $(m > n)$ and a noisy codeword $\mathbf{t}^{\mathsf{T}} = (\mathbf{s}^{\mathsf{T}}\mathbf{C} + \mathbf{x}^{\mathsf{T}}) \in \mathbb{F}_2^m$ with the promise that the error vector $\mathbf{x} \in \mathbb{F}_2^m$ has exact Hamming weight $|\mathbf{x}| = w$, as opposed to the general requirement $|\mathbf{x}| \leq w$. Note that the difference is not substantial since having smaller weight can only make the problem easier (seen by a simple reduction), and one can enumerate all possible values for w and invoke the corresponding solver (for the exact weight). The non-promise version of the NCP problem is known to be NP-hard even to approximate [7] and the promise version is also NP-hard in the high-noise regime where the Hamming weight of error vector $|\mathbf{x}| \geq (1/2+\epsilon)d$ for minimal distance d of the code and any arbitrarily small constant ϵ [25]. As for the algorithms, Berman and Karpinski [9] showed how to search for the $O(n/\log n)$-approximate nearest codeword in polynomial time and Alon, Panigrahy and Yekhanin [2] gives a deterministic algorithm with the same parameters, which is the current state-of-the-art for solving NCP.

1.3 Worst-Case to Average-Case Reductions for LPN

We start with the "sample amplification" technique [42] that bears some resemblance to the smoothing lemma in [18]. The idea is to use polynomially many

LPN samples, say $(\mathbf{C}, \mathbf{t}^\mathsf{T} = (\mathbf{s}^\mathsf{T}\mathbf{C} + \mathbf{x}^\mathsf{T}))$, as a basis to generate much more samples (with a higher noise), which enables meaningful tradeoff between sample and time complexities for the BKW algorithm. In more details, a "sample amplification" oracle take as input $(\mathbf{C}, \mathbf{t}^\mathsf{T})$ and responds with $(\mathbf{C}\mathbf{r}_i, \mathbf{t}^\mathsf{T}\mathbf{r}_i = \mathbf{s}^\mathsf{T}\mathbf{C}\mathbf{r}_i + \mathbf{x}^\mathsf{T}\mathbf{r}_i)$ as the i-th re-randomized LPN sample, where $\mathbf{r}_i \leftarrow R$ and $(\mathbf{C}, \mathbf{C}\mathbf{r}_i, \mathbf{x}^\mathsf{T}\mathbf{r}_i)$ is statically close to $(\mathbf{C}, \mathbf{U}_n, \mathbf{x}^\mathsf{T}\mathbf{r}_i)$ by the leftover hash lemma. Preferably distribution R should be maximized with min-entropy (of more than n bits) while keeping as small Hamming weight as possible (to make $\mathbf{x}^\mathsf{T}\mathbf{r}_i$ biased) at the same time, so a natural candidate can be a random length-m-weight-d distribution or similar (e.g., m-fold Bernoulli distribution for parameter $\frac{d}{m}$), where $d \ll m$ is a tunable parameter. Döttling [23] used a computational version of this technique which yields better parameters by relying on the dual-LPN assumption (in place of the leftover hash lemma) for pseudorandomness generation.

In the context of reducing worst-case hard promise-NCP to average-case hard LPN [18], let $(\mathbf{C}, \mathbf{t}^\mathsf{T} = (\mathbf{s}^\mathsf{T}\mathbf{C} + \mathbf{x}^\mathsf{T}))$ be an NCP instance, where $\mathbf{C} \in \mathbb{F}_2^{n\times m}$, $\mathbf{s} \in \mathbb{F}_2^n$, $\mathbf{x} \in \mathbb{F}_2^m$ with $|\mathbf{x}| = w$ are all fixed values, and the goal to generate randomized LPN sample $(\mathbf{C}\mathbf{r}_i, \mathbf{t}^\mathsf{T}\mathbf{r}_i + \mathbf{u}^\mathsf{T}\mathbf{C}\mathbf{r}_i = (\mathbf{s}^\mathsf{T} + \mathbf{u}^\mathsf{T})\mathbf{C}\mathbf{r}_i + \mathbf{x}^\mathsf{T}\mathbf{r}_i)$ with random $\mathbf{u} \xleftarrow{\$} \mathbb{F}_2^n$ and each $\mathbf{r}_i$ drawn from a random weight-d distribution[2]. The difference is that $\mathbf{C}$ is a generator matrix for a specific code (instead of being sampled from uniform), and $\mathbf{s}$ is masked by random $\mathbf{u}$. Brakerski et al. [18] showed that if $\mathbf{C}$ belongs to a β-balanced code for $\beta = O(\sqrt{n/m})$, i.e., the Hamming distance lies in between $(1/2 - \beta)m$ and $(1/2 + \beta)m$, then $(\mathbf{C}\mathbf{r}_i, \mathbf{x}^\mathsf{T}\mathbf{r}_i)$ is $2^{\frac{n}{2}} \cdot (\frac{2w}{m} + \beta)^d$ close to $(\mathbf{U}_n, \mathbf{x}^\mathsf{T}\mathbf{r}_i)$, where $\Pr[\mathbf{x}^\mathsf{T}\mathbf{r}_i = 1] = 1/2 - e^{-\Theta(\frac{w}{m}d)}$ is noise rate of the LPN. As a main result[3], the worst-case hardness of the NCP on balanced code of noise rate $\frac{w}{m} = \frac{\log^2 n}{n}$ implies the average-case hardness of LPN of noise rate $\mu = 1/2 - 1/\mathrm{poly}(n)$. This was the only known result for basing LPN on worst-case hardness assumptions. It mainly establishes the feasibility result, i.e., assuming polynomial hardness for extremely low-noise NCP (for which quasi-polynomial attacks are known) only to reach the conservative conclusion that extremely high-noise LPN is quasi-polynomially hard. Therefore, it remained open whether worst-hardness guarantee can be secured for LPN of a lower noise, such as constant-noise LPN with sub-exponential hardness shown in this paper.

Curiously, one can investigate existentially (using probabilistic method) the possibility of extending the reduction to constant-noise LPN. Think of a uniformly random $\mathbf{C} \xleftarrow{\$} \mathbb{F}_2^{n\times m}$, and by the leftover hash lemma $(\mathbf{C}, \mathbf{C}\mathbf{r}, \mathbf{x}^\mathsf{T}\mathbf{r})$ is 2^{-n}-close to $(\mathbf{C}, \mathbf{U}_n, \mathbf{x}^\mathsf{T}\mathbf{r})$ provided that the random m-choose-d distribution $\mathbf{r}$ has sufficient min-entropy $d\log(m/d) = \Omega(n)$. It follows by Markov inequality that there exists at least a $(1 - 2^{-n/2})$-fraction of "good" $\mathbf{C}$ satisfying $(\mathbf{C}\mathbf{r}, \mathbf{x}^\mathsf{T}\mathbf{r})$ is $2^{-n/2}$-close to $(\mathbf{U}_n, \mathbf{x}^\mathsf{T}\mathbf{r})$. Take into account that $\mathbf{x}$ has $\binom{m}{w}$ possible values, the fraction of "bad" $\mathbf{C}$ amounts up to $\binom{m}{w}2^{-\frac{n}{2}}$. In terms of parameters, we set $\frac{w}{m}d = \Theta(1)$ for constant-noise LPN, noise rate $\frac{w}{m} = \omega(\frac{\log n}{n})$ is necessary for the

---

[2] Strictly speaking, $\mathbf{r}_i$ is sampled from $R_{d,m}$ whose definition is deferred to Sect. 2.1.

[3] More generally, as an end result [18] proves the $n^{O(\lambda)}$-hardness of LPN at noise rate $1/2 - 2^{-\Omega(\lambda)}$ for tunable parameter $\lambda = \omega(1)$, see Remark 2 for discussions.

hardness assumption to hold and recall the entropy condition $d \log(m/d) = \Omega(n)$, which implies $d = o(\frac{n}{\log n})$ and thus

$$\log \binom{m}{w} \approx w \log(m/w) = \Omega(\frac{m}{d} \log d) = 2^{\Omega(n/d)} \log d = n^{\omega(1)} \ .$$

This means the upper bound $\binom{m}{w} 2^{-O(n)}$ on the fraction of "bad" $\mathbf{C}$ is useless (i.e., greater than 1). In other words, we don't have a straightforward non-constructive proof that the worst-case hardness of NCP problem (on any binary linear codes) implies the hardness of constant-noise LPN, and solving this problem needs new ideas to beat the union bound.

1.4 Our Contributions

Prior to our main work, we give a worst-case hardness result for LPN over large fields, which was introduced in [35] and used in various works, e.g., [3,5,15, 16,24,29,36,50]. Informally, the large-field LPN extends the original LPN to a prime field $\mathbb{F}_p$ with a generalized Bernoulli distribution $\mathcal{B}_{r,p}$, which samples a random element from $\mathbb{F}_p$ with probability r and sets to 0 with probability $1 - r$. We show that the hardness of large-field LPN with noise $r = 1 - \Omega(1/\alpha p)$ is implied by that of LWE with the same dimension n and modulus p and parameter αp for the discrete Gaussian distribution. In composition with known worst-case to average-case reductions for LWE, this ensures worst-case hardness for LPN with field size $p \geq \mathsf{poly}(n)$ and high noise rate $r = 1 - \Omega(1/\sqrt{n})$. To our best knowledge, this result doesn't seem to be known previously despite a simple proof. However, similar to the end result of [18], it establishes worst-case hardness guarantee only for LPN whose noise is inversely polynomial ($\Omega(1/\sqrt{n})$ more precisely) close to uniform.

Next we start our investigation on the original LPN (over the binary field). We consider the promise version of NCP on two classes of binary linear codes, i.e., balanced code considered in [18] and (a relaxed form of) independent code. Informally, a β-balanced $[m, n]$ code is a strengthened form of $[m, n, m(1/2 - \beta)]$ code with maximal distance $m(1/2 + \beta)$, and a k-independent $[m, n]$ code is dual to a $[m, m - n, k + 1]$ code. Instead of sampling $\mathbf{r}$ from a random weight-d distribution, we let $\mathbf{r}$ follow Bernoulli distribution $\mathcal{B}_{\frac{d}{m}}^m$ (i.e., with expected Hamming weight d). While this looks like a weakening of the distribution ($\mathbf{r}$ is now only $2^{-\Omega(d)}$-close to a random weight-roughly-d distribution), the condition that all bits of $\mathbf{r}$ are independent is crucial for proving a tighter version of smooth lemma that avoids the accumulative loss due to union bound. For proper parameter choice that guarantees: (1) $\mathbf{r}$ is $2^{-\Omega(d)}$-close to having min-entropy $d \log(m/d) = \Omega(n)$ and (2) the code exists in overwhelming abundance, we prove for each code a corresponding smooth lemma that $(\mathbf{Cr}, \mathbf{x}^\mathsf{T}\mathbf{r})$ is $\frac{2^{-\Omega(d)}}{1-2\mu}$-close to $(\mathbf{U}_n, \mathbf{x}^\mathsf{T}\mathbf{r})$, where $\mu \overset{\mathrm{def}}{=} \Pr[\mathbf{x}^\mathsf{T}\mathbf{r} = 1] = 1/2 - 2^{-\Theta(\frac{w}{m}d)}$ is the noise rate of the LPN. Compared to the unconditional case where (it can be shown that) $\mathbf{Cr}$ is $2^{-\Omega(d)}$-close to $\mathbf{U}_n$, the result is worsened by only a factor of $\frac{1}{1-2\mu}$, rather than suffering from the multiplicative factor $\binom{m}{w}$ in the aforementioned non-constructive analysis. The result of [18] falls into a corollary by setting $\frac{w}{m} = \frac{\log^2 n}{n}$, $m = \mathsf{poly}(n)$, $d = 2n/\log n$ such that $\mu = 1/2 - 1/\mathsf{poly}(n)$. Furthermore, our smoothing lemma allows to transform sub-exponential worst-case hardness of NCP into the sub-exponential average-case hardness for constant-LPN, where the underlying NCP lies in the low-noise regime $\frac{w}{m} = n^{-c}$ ($0 < c < 1$). In particular, we assume there exists some constant $0 < \varepsilon < 1$ such that NCP problem is $2^{\varepsilon \frac{w}{m} n}$-hard on either code of codeword length, say[4] $m = 2^{\frac{\varepsilon}{8} \frac{w}{m} n}$. To our best knowledge, the state-of-the-art algorithms [2,9] solve the worst-case NCP with complexity $\mathsf{poly}(n, m) e^{\frac{w}{m} n}$, and we are not aware of any algorithms with additional accelerations for the balanced/independent codes. In fact, we don't even know a much better algorithm for its average-case analogue, i.e., the LPN problem of noise rate $\mu = n^{-c}$ ($0 < c < 1$) needs time $\mathsf{poly}(n) e^{\mu n}$ to solve with overwhelming success [41, Appendix C]. Falsifying our assumption would imply arbitrary polynomial speedups over the current state-of-the-art, i.e., for every constant $\varepsilon > 0$ there exists an algorithm that runs in time $2^{\varepsilon \frac{w}{m} n}$ and solves the problem in worst case (for at least infinitely many values of n), which is a win-win situation.

Theorem 1 (main result, informal). *Assume that the NCP problem at noise rate $\frac{w}{m} = n^{-c}$, on either balanced code or independent code, is ($T = 2^{\Omega(n^{1-c})}, m = 2^{\Omega(n^{1-c})}$)-hard. Then,*

(1) for $0 < c < 1/2$, the constant-noise LPN is ($T = 2^{\Omega(n^{1-c})}, \epsilon = 2^{-\Omega(n^c)}, q = 2^{\Omega(n^c)}$)-hard;

(2) for $1/2 \leq c < 1$, the constant-noise LPN is ($T = 2^{\Omega(n^{1-c})}, \epsilon = 2^{-\Omega(n^{1-c})}, q = 2^{\Omega(n^{1-c})}$)-hard.

Here the (T,ϵ,q)-hardness of LPN refers to that no algorithm of time T can solve LPN of q samples with probability better than ϵ. The constant-noise LPN with sub-exponential hardness already implies efficient symmetric-key cryptographic applications, and we further discuss possibilities of going beyond minicrypt[5]. Unfortunately, for whatever reason that could be interesting, public-key cryptography and collision resistant hash functions require constant-noise LPN with ($T = 2^{\omega(n^{0.5})}, \epsilon = 2^{-\omega(n^{0.5})}, q = 2^{n^{0.5}}$)-hardness [51,52], in contrast to the ($T = 2^{\Omega(n^{0.5})}, \epsilon = 2^{-\Omega(n^{0.5})}, q = 2^{\Omega(n^{0.5})}$)-hardness we established for LPN when $c = 0.5$, where $\omega(\cdot)$ omits a (arbitrarily small) super-constant (see more discussions in Sect. 3.7). One might try to set $c = 0.5 - \delta$ to obtain ($T = 2^{\Omega(n^{0.5+\delta})}, \epsilon = 2^{-\Omega(n^{0.5-\delta})}, q = 2^{\Omega(n^{0.5-\delta})}$)-hard LPN, and then rebalance T and $1/\epsilon$ to be of the same order (as in a typical hardness assumption). However, we don't know if such a time/success-rate tradeoff for LPN can be obtained in

---

[4] We just need $T \geq \mathsf{poly}(m, n)$. One may replace $m = 2^{\frac{\varepsilon}{8} \frac{w}{m} n}$ with $m = 2^{\delta \varepsilon \frac{w}{m} n}$ for any small constant δ. In general, the hardness of NCP (resp., LPN) is insensitive to codeword length m (resp., sample complexity q).

[5] minicrypt is Impagliazzo's [34] hypothetical world where one-way functions exist but public-key cryptography does not.

general (without sacrificing q). We leave it as an open problem whether such a gap can be closed with tighter proofs or there's in a strict hierarchy in place. On the other hand, the attempt to use our reduction for cryptanalysis, i.e., to turn the BKW algorithm (for LPN) into a worst-case solver for constant-noise NCP (i.e., $\frac{w}{m} = O(1)$), is not successful again due to some small gap. We refer to Sect. 3.7 for further details.

2   Preliminaries

2.1   Notations, Definitions and Inequalities

Column vectors are represented by bold lower-case letters (e.g., $\mathbf{s}$), row vectors are denoted as their transpose (e.g., $\mathbf{s}^{\mathsf{T}}$), and matrices are denoted by bold capital letters (e.g., $\mathbf{A}$). $|\mathbf{s}|$ refers to the Hamming weight of bit string $\mathbf{s}$. We use notations for sets and distributions as follows.

- $\mathcal{R}_d^m$: the uniform distribution over set $\mathcal{R}_d^m \stackrel{\text{def}}{=} \{\mathbf{r} \in \mathbb{F}_2^m : |\mathbf{r}| = d\}$.
- $R_{d,m}$: the distribution that first samples $\mathbf{t}_1, \cdots, \mathbf{t}_m$ uniformly and independent from $\mathcal{R}_1^m$ and then produces as output their XOR sum $\bigoplus_{i=1}^m \mathbf{t}_i$.
- $\mathcal{B}_\mu^q \stackrel{\text{def}}{=} \underbrace{\mathcal{B}_\mu \times \cdots \times \mathcal{B}_\mu}_{q}$, where $\mathcal{B}_\mu$ is Bernoulli distribution with parameter μ.

We use e for the natural constant and $\log(\cdot)$ for binary logarithm. $\mathbf{x} \stackrel{\$}{\leftarrow} \mathcal{X}$ refers to drawing $\mathbf{x}$ from set $\mathcal{X}$ uniformly at random, and $\mathbf{x} \leftarrow X$ means drawing $\mathbf{x}$ according to distribution X. $X \sim Y$ denotes that X and Y are identically distributed. The collision probability of Y is defined as $\mathsf{Col}(Y) \stackrel{\text{def}}{=} \sum_y \Pr[Y = y]^2$. We denote by $\mathbf{H}_\infty(Y)$ the min-entropy of random variable Y. $\mathsf{poly}(\cdot)$ refers to a certain polynomial. The *statistical distance* between X and Y, denoted by $\mathsf{SD}(X, Y) \stackrel{\text{def}}{=} \frac{1}{2}\sum_x |\Pr[X = x] - \Pr[Y = x]|$. We say that X and Y are ε-close if $\mathsf{SD}(X, Y) \leq \varepsilon$. We refer to Appendix A for proofs omitted in the main body and Appendix B for the inequalities, lemmas and theorems used in this paper.

2.2   Binary Linear Codes

Coding theory terminology typically refers to a linear code as $[n, k]$-code or $[n, k, d]$-code, but we choose to use $[m,n]$-code ($m > n$) in order to be more compatible with the LPN problem and [18], where n is the size of message (secret to be decoded) and m is codeword length.

Definition 1 (binary linear code). *A binary (m,n)-code is a set of codewords $\mathcal{C} \subset \mathbb{F}_2^m$ with $|\mathcal{C}| = 2^n$ ($n < m$), and a binary linear $[m,n]$-code $\mathcal{C}$ is a binary (m,n)-code that is the row span of some generator matrix $\mathbf{C} \in \mathbb{F}_2^{n \times m}$, i.e., $\mathcal{C} \stackrel{\text{def}}{=} \{\mathbf{s}^{\mathsf{T}}\mathbf{C} \in \mathbb{F}_2^m | \mathbf{s}^{\mathsf{T}} \in \mathbb{F}_2^n\}$.*

Definition 2 (dual code/distance). *The dual code of a binary linear $[m,n]$-code $\mathcal{C}$, denoted by $\mathcal{C}^\perp$, is a binary $[m,m-n]$-code $\mathcal{C}^\perp \stackrel{\text{def}}{=} \{\mathbf{d} \in \mathbb{F}_2^m | \forall \mathbf{c} \in \mathcal{C} : \mathbf{d}^{\mathsf{T}}\mathbf{c} = \mathbf{0}\}$. The dual distance of $\mathcal{C}$, denoted by $d^\perp$, is the minimum distance of $\mathcal{C}^\perp$.*

Definition 3 (minimum/maximum distance). *The minimum (resp., maximum) distance of a binary linear code C refers to $\min_{\mathbf{x} \neq \mathbf{y} \in C}\{|\mathbf{x} - \mathbf{y}|\}$ (resp., $\max_{\mathbf{x},\mathbf{y} \in C}\{|\mathbf{x} - \mathbf{y}|\}$). A linear $[m,n]$-code with minimum distance d is called a $[m,n,d]$-code.*

A β-balanced code is a $[m,n,\frac{1}{2}(1-\beta)m]$ code with maximal distance bounded by $\frac{1}{2}(1+\beta)m$. A binary linear code is k-independent if and only if its minimum dual distance is at least $k+1$ (i.e., its generator matrix has k-wise independent columns). In the extreme case $k = n$, k-independent $[m,n]$ code becomes a maximum distance separable (MDS) code, but since binary MDS codes are trivial we use $k < n$ with further relaxed conditions.

Definition 4 (balanced code). *A binary linear $[m,n]$ code $C \subseteq \mathbb{F}_2^m$ is β-balanced if its minimum distance is at least $\frac{1}{2}(1-\beta)m$ and maximum distance is at most $\frac{1}{2}(1+\beta)m$.*

Definition 5 (independent code). *For a binary linear $[m,n]$ code $C \subseteq \mathbb{F}_2^m$,*

- *C is k-independent iff. every k columns of its generator matrix $\mathbf{C}$ are linearly independent, i.e., $\forall i \in [1,\ldots,k] : \Pr[\mathbf{C}\mathbf{r} = \mathbf{0} : \mathbf{r} \leftarrow R_i^m] = 0$.*
- *C is (k,ζ)-independent iff. $\forall i \in \{\frac{k}{2}, \frac{k}{2}+1, \ldots, k\} : \Pr[\mathbf{C}\mathbf{r} = \mathbf{0} : \mathbf{r} \leftarrow R_i^m] \leq 2^{-n}(1+\zeta)$.*

The latter relaxes the independence condition by only enforcing it for $i \in [k/2, k]$ (instead of for all $i \in (0, k]$) and even for $i \in [k/2, k]$ a slackness of ζ is allowed, in the spirit of almost universal hash functions [48]. Note that there is nothing special with the cut-off point $k/2$, which can be replaced with δk for any constant $0 < \delta < 1$ without affecting our results asymptotically.

The following lemmas assert that balanced code and independent code exist in abundance and they both account for an overwhelming portion of linear code (for the parameter choices of this paper). In other words, it is very likely that a random matrix is both balanced and independent at the same time. The proof of Lemma 1 follows a simple probabilistic argument (already given in [18]) while as for the proof of Lemma 2 we exploit the pairwise independence in order to apply the Chebyshev's inequality. We refer interested readers to Appendix A and Remark 3 for its proof and discussions. A similar result with $k \approx n/2$ was stated in [20, Theorem 6].

Lemma 1 (Existence of balanced code [18]). *A random binary linear $[n,m]$-code is β-balanced with probability at least $1 - 2^{n+1}e^{-\frac{\beta^2 m}{4}}$. In particular, for $\beta \geq 2\sqrt{n/m}$ the random binary linear code is β-balanced with probability $1 - 2^{-\Omega(n)}$.*

Remark 1 (existence vs. abundance). Lemma 1 states that $\beta \geq 2\sqrt{n/m}$ ensures the overwhelming abundance rather than the mere existence of balanced codes. We remark that the difference is not substantial, e.g., for any arbitrarily small

$\varepsilon > 0$ by setting $\beta \geq \sqrt{\frac{4(n+1+\varepsilon \log(e))}{(\log e)m}} \approx 1.66\sqrt{n/m}$ we derive a corollary of Lemma 1 that β-balanced $[n,m]$-code exists with a fraction of at least

$$1 - 2^{n+1}e^{-\frac{\beta^2 m}{4}} \geq 1 - e^{-\varepsilon} \approx \varepsilon .$$

The above is essentially the Gilbert-Varshamov bound that asserts the existence of certain codes[6], and it is almost tight for binary linear codes [11].

Lemma 2 (Existence of independent code). *A random binary linear $[m,n]$ code $\mathcal{C}$ is (k, ζ)-independent with probability at least $(1 - \frac{k2^{n+\frac{\log m}{2} - \frac{k}{2}\log\frac{m}{k}}}{\zeta^2})$. In particular, for $k\log(m/k) \geq 16n$ and $\log m = o(n)$ the random binary linear code is $(k, 2^{-n})$-independent with probability at least $1 - 2^{-4n}$.*

2.3 The NCP and LPN Problem

Throughout, n is the main security parameter, and other parameters, e.g., $\mu = \mu(n)$, $q = q(n)$, $m = m(n)$ and $T = T(n)$, can be seen as functions of n.

Definition 6 (Nearest Codeword Problem (NCP)). *The nearest codeword problem $\mathsf{NCP}_{n,m,w}$ for $n, m, w \in \mathbb{N}$ refers to that given the input of a matrix $\mathbf{C} \in \mathbb{F}_2^{n \times m}$ of a binary linear code $\mathcal{C}$ and a noisy codeword $\mathbf{t}^\mathsf{T} = \mathbf{s}^\mathsf{T}\mathbf{C} + \mathbf{x}^\mathsf{T}$ for some $\mathbf{s} \in \mathbb{F}_2^n$ and $\mathbf{x} \in \mathcal{R}_w^m$, and the challenge is to find out a solution $\mathbf{s}'$ such that $\mathbf{s}^\mathsf{T}\mathbf{C} + \mathbf{x}^\mathsf{T} = \mathbf{s}'^\mathsf{T}\mathbf{C} + \mathbf{x}'^\mathsf{T}$ for some $\mathbf{x}' \in \mathcal{R}_w^m$. In particular, we consider the NCP on the following codes:*

- *(Balanced NCP).* *The balanced nearest codeword problem, referred to as* $\mathsf{balNCP}_{n,m,w,\beta}$, *is the* $\mathsf{NCP}_{n,m,w}$ *on β-balanced linear $[m,n]$-code.*
- *(Independent NCP).* *The independent nearest codeword problem, denoted by* $\mathsf{indNCP}_{n,m,w,k,\zeta}$, *refers to the* $\mathsf{NCP}_{n,m,w}$ *on (k,ζ)-independent linear $[m,n]$-code.*

Similar to one-way function, an instance of the NCP is considered solved as long as a decoding algorithm comes up with any legitimate solution $\mathbf{x}'$, which does not necessarily equal the original $\mathbf{x}$. In general, linear codes have unique solutions except for a $2^{-m+n+2w\log m}$ fraction (see Lemma 3), which is super-exponentially small for our parameter setting $w\log m = O(n)$ and $m = \Omega(n^{1+\varepsilon})$. Moreover, $\mathsf{balNCP}_{n,m,w,\beta}$ has unique solution for $w < \frac{1}{4}(1 - \beta)m$. Decisional and computational LPN are polynomially equivalent even for the same sample complexity [6].

---

[6] Strictly speaking, Gilbert-Varshamov bound concerns with the existence of a code with minimum distance $m(1/2 - \beta)$ while the balanced code we consider requires minimum/maximum distance $m(1/2 \mp \beta)$ at the same time, where the difference can be omitted due to the symmetry of binomial coefficient $\binom{m}{m(1/2 \mp \beta)}$ centered on $m/2$.

Definition 7 (Learning Parity with Noise (LPN)). *The (computational) LPN problem with secret length n, noise rate $\mu \in (0, 1/2)$ and sample complexity q, denoted by $\mathsf{LPN}_{n,\mu,q}$, asks to find out $\mathbf{x}$ given $(\mathbf{A}, \mathbf{A} \cdot \mathbf{x} + \mathbf{e})$; and the decisional LPN problem $\mathsf{DLPN}_{n,\mu,q}$ challenges to distinguish $(\mathbf{A}, \mathbf{A} \cdot \mathbf{x} + \mathbf{e})$ and $(\mathbf{A}, \mathbf{U}_q)$, where matrix $\mathbf{A} \xleftarrow{\$} \mathbb{F}_2^{q \times n}$, $\mathbf{x} \xleftarrow{\$} \mathbb{F}_2^n$, $\mathbf{y} \xleftarrow{\$} \mathbb{F}_2^q$, and $\mathbf{e} \leftarrow \mathcal{B}_\mu^q$.*

COMPUTATIONAL HARDNESS. We say that a computational/decisional problem is (T,ϵ)-hard, if every probabilistic algorithm running in time T solves it with probability/advantage at most ϵ. We say that NCP (resp., LPN) is (T,ϵ,q)-hard if the problem is (T,ϵ)-hard when the codeword length (resp., sample complexity) does not exceed q. When the success-rate term $\epsilon = 1/T$ we often omit ϵ. Recall that standard polynomial hardness requires that $T > \mathsf{poly}(n)$ and $\epsilon < 1/\mathsf{poly}(n)$ for every poly and all sufficiently large n's.

Lemma 3 (Unique decoding of binary LPN). *For $w/m < 1/4$,*

$$\Pr_{\mathbf{C} \xleftarrow{\$} \mathbb{F}_2^{m \times n}} \left[\exists \mathbf{s}_1 \neq \mathbf{s}_2 \in \mathbb{F}_2^n, \exists \mathbf{x}_1, \mathbf{x}_2 \in \mathbb{F}_2^m : |\mathbf{x}_1|, |\mathbf{x}_2| \leq w \wedge \left(\mathbf{s}_1^\mathsf{T} \mathbf{C} + \mathbf{x}_1^\mathsf{T} = \mathbf{s}_2^\mathsf{T} \mathbf{C} + \mathbf{x}_2^\mathsf{T} \right) \right]$$

is upper bounded by $2^{-m+n+2w \log m}$.

3   Worst-Case to Average-Case Reductions for LPN

3.1   Worst-Case Hardness for Large-Field LPN

Denote with $\mathsf{LWE}_{n,p,\alpha}$ and $\mathsf{LPN}_{n,r}(\mathbb{F}_p)$ the LWE problem and the large-field LPN problem respectively, both of dimension n and over prime modulus p, where the LWE's noise follows the discrete Gaussian distribution $\mathcal{D}_{\mathbb{Z},\alpha p}$ of standard deviation parameter αp, and the LPN's noise distribution returns a random element over $\mathbb{F}_p$ with probability r, and is set to 0 otherwise.

Lemma 4 (LWE implies high-noise LPN over $\mathbb{F}_p$). *Assume that $\mathsf{LWE}_{n,p,\alpha}$ with prime p, $\alpha = o(1)$, $\alpha p = \omega(\log n)$ is hard, then $\mathsf{LPN}_{n,r}(\mathbb{F}_p)$ with $r = 1 - \Omega(\frac{1}{\alpha p})$ is hard.*

Proof. Every LWE sample $(\mathbf{a}_i, \langle \mathbf{a}_i, \mathbf{s} \rangle + e_i)$ can be transformed into an LPN sample $(\mathbf{a}_i', \langle \mathbf{a}_i', \mathbf{s} \rangle + e_i')$ (over the same field) by multiplying with a random $m_i \xleftarrow{\$} \mathbb{F}_p \setminus \{0\}$, where $\mathbf{a}_i'$ is the scalar-vector product $m_i \mathbf{a}_i$, and $e_i' = m_i e_i$. For any $e_i \neq 0$ we have $(\mathbf{a}_i', e_i')$ is uniformly distributed over $\mathbb{F}_p^n \times (\mathbb{F}_p \setminus \{0\})$, and for $e_i = 0$ it is uniform over $\mathbb{F}_p^n \times \{0\}$. Thus, overall $(\mathbf{a}_i', e_i')$ is an $\mathsf{LPN}_{n,r}(\mathbb{F}_p)$ sample with

$$1 - r = \Pr[e_i = 0] - \frac{1 - \Pr[e_i = 0]}{p - 1} \geq \Omega(1/\alpha p) - \frac{2}{p} \geq \Omega(1/\alpha p) \ .$$

Lemma 4 puts no lower bounds on the size of p, and recall that the LPN problem becomes a special case of LWE for $p = 2$ (for which no reductions are needed). However, in order for the LWE to be quantumly reducible from worst-case lattice problems, we need $q = \mathsf{poly}(n)$ and $\alpha p = \Omega(\sqrt{n})$. The reduction can be made classical at the cost of either a much larger modulus $q \geq 2^{n/2}$ or relying on a non-standard variant of GapSVP [45].

Theorem 2 ([46]). *For any $p \leq \mathsf{poly}(n)$, any $\alpha p \geq 2\sqrt{n}$ and $0 < \alpha < 1$, solving the (decisional) $\mathsf{LWE}_{n,p,\alpha}$ problem is at least as hard as quantumly solving GapSVP_γ and SIVP_γ on arbitrary n-dimensional lattices, for some $\gamma = \tilde{O}(n/\alpha)$.*

To summarize, based on the (quantum or even classical) worst-case hardness of lattice problems, we establish up to $2^{O(n)}$-(average-case)-hardness of large-field LPN for modulus $p \geq \mathsf{poly}(n)$ and noise rate $r = 1 - \Omega(1/\sqrt{n})$. Next, we will revisit [18] and show worst-case to average-case reductions for constant-noise LPN (over the binary field), which is the main focus of this work.

3.2   The Worst-Case to Average-Case Reduction from [18]

Brakerski et al. [18] showed that the worst-case hardness of the extremely low-noise NCP problem on balanced code implies the (average-case) hardness of extremely high-noise LPN.

Theorem 3 ([18]). *Assume that $\mathsf{balNCP}_{n,m,w,\beta}$ is hard in the worst case for noise rate $\frac{w}{m} = \frac{\log^2 n}{n}$, $m = 4n^2$, $\beta = 1/\sqrt{n}$ then $\mathsf{LPN}_{n,\mu,q}$ is hard (in the average case) for $\mu = 1/2 - \frac{1}{n^{O(1)}}$ and any $q = \mathsf{poly}(n)$.*

As detailed in Algorithm 1, the idea is to convert an NCP instance $(\mathbf{C}, \mathbf{t}^\mathsf{T})$ into LPN samples. By Theorem 4, the conversion produces q LPN samples of noise rate μ up to error $q\delta$, where

$$\mu = \frac{1}{2} - \frac{1}{2}(1 - \frac{2w}{m})^d, \quad q\delta = O(q)2^{\frac{n}{2}} \cdot (\frac{2w}{m} + \beta)^d .$$

Thus, the conclusion follows by setting $\frac{w}{m} = \frac{\log^2 n}{n}$, $\beta = 2\sqrt{n/m} = 1/\sqrt{n}$, $d = 2n/\log n$ such that $\mu = 1/2 - 1/n^{O(1)}$ and $q\delta = \mathsf{negl}(n)$.

Remark 2 (possibilities and limitations). Other possible parameter choices are also discussed in [18], e.g., assume that $\mathsf{balNCP}_{n,m,w,\beta}$ is $2^{\Omega(\sqrt{n})}$-hard for $\frac{w}{m} = \frac{1}{\sqrt{n}}$ (while keeping $\beta = \frac{1}{\sqrt{n}}$ and $d = 2n/\log n$) then $\mathsf{LPN}_{n,\mu,q}$ is $2^{\Omega(\sqrt{n})}$-hard for noise $\mu = 1/2 - 2^{-\sqrt{n}/\log n}$ and $q = 2^{\Omega(\sqrt{n})}$. This result is non-trivial since the noise rate μ (although quite close to uniform already) isn't high enough for the conclusion to hold statistically. However, it does not seem to yield efficient (a.k.a. polynomial-time) cryptographic applications due to the high noise rate. In fact, the barriers are inherent in its smoothing lemma Theorem 4. Informally, assume that NCP at noise rate $\frac{w}{m} = \frac{\log n \cdot \lambda}{n}$ is $n^{O(\lambda)}$-hard[7] on β-balanced code, then the LPN of noise rate $\mu = \frac{1}{2} - \frac{1}{2}(1 - \frac{2w}{m})^d$ is (at most) $n^{O(\lambda)}$-hard provided that $(\frac{2w}{m} + \beta)^d < 2^{-n/2}$. Therefore, we need to set $\lambda = \omega(1)$ for the worst-case hardness assumption to hold. Further, regardless of the value of β it requires $d = \Omega(n/\log n)$ to make $(\frac{2w}{m} + \beta)^d < 2^{-n/2}$. This lower bounds the noise rate of LPN, i.e., $\mu = \frac{1}{2} - \frac{1}{2}(1 - \frac{2w}{m})^d = 1/2 - 2^{-\Omega(\lambda)}$. Raising the value of λ brings better

---

[7] We recall the known attacks [2,9] of time complexity $2^{O(\frac{w}{m}n)}$ on NCP of noise rate $\frac{w}{m}$.

hardness, but at the same time it makes the noise of LPN closer to uniform (and hence renders the result less interesting). A reasonable compromise seems to let $\lambda = \log n$ which was the main choice of [18].

Algorithm 1. Converting an NCP instance to LPN samples.

Input: $(\mathbf{C}, \mathbf{t}^\top = \mathbf{s}^\top \mathbf{C} + \mathbf{x}^\top)$, where $\mathbf{C} \in \mathbb{F}_2^{n \times m}$, $\mathbf{s} \in \mathbb{F}_2^n$, $\mathbf{x} \in \mathcal{R}_w^m$

$\mathbf{u} \overset{\$}{\leftarrow} \mathbb{F}_2^n$

Sample $\mathbf{R} \overset{\text{def}}{=} [\mathbf{r}_1, \ldots, \mathbf{r}_q] \in \mathbb{F}_2^{m \times q}$, where every column $\mathbf{r}_i \leftarrow R_{d,m}$ $(1 \leq i \leq q)$

Output: $(\mathbf{CR}, \mathbf{t}^\top \mathbf{R} + \mathbf{u}^\top \mathbf{CR}) = (\mathbf{CR}, (\mathbf{s}^\top + \mathbf{u}^\top)\mathbf{CR} + \mathbf{x}^\top \mathbf{R})$

Theorem 4 (W/A-case reduction via code smoothing [18]). *Assume that* $\mathsf{balNCP}_{n,m,w,\beta}$ *is* T-*hard in the worst case, then* $\mathsf{LPN}_{n,\mu,q}$ *is* $(T - O(nmq), \frac{1}{T} + q\delta)$-*hard (in the average case) for any* $w, d \leq m$, *any* q *and*

$$\delta = \max_{\mathbf{x} \in \mathcal{R}_{m,w}} \mathsf{SD}\Big((\mathbf{Cr}, \mathbf{x}^\top \mathbf{r}) , (\mathbf{U}_n, \mathbf{x}^\top \mathbf{r}) \Big) \leq 2^{\frac{n+1}{2}} \cdot \big(\frac{2w}{m} + \beta\big)^d , \qquad (1)$$

$$\mu = \max_{\mathbf{x} \in \mathcal{R}_{m,w}} \Pr[\mathbf{x}^\top \mathbf{r} = 1] = \frac{1}{2} - \frac{1}{2}\big(1 - \frac{2w}{m}\big)^d . \qquad (2)$$

where $\mathbf{r} \leftarrow R_{d,m}$, $\mathbf{C} \in \mathbb{F}_2^{n \times m}$ *is a generator matrix of any* β-*balanced* $[m, n]$ *code and* $O(mnq)$ *accounts for the complexity of Algorithm 1.*

The authors of [18] proved the above smoothing lemma using harmonic analysis. We give an alternative proof via Vazirani's XOR lemma [30,49]. We stress that the approach serves to simplify the presentation to readers by establishing the proof under a well-known theorem. In other words, the proof below is not essentially different from that in [18] after unrolling out the proof of the XOR lemma.

Lemma 5 (Vazirani's XOR lemma [30,49]). *For any r.v.* $\mathbf{v} \in \mathbb{F}_2^n$, *we have*

$$\mathsf{SD}(\mathbf{v}, \mathbf{U}_n) \leq \sqrt{\sum_{0 \neq \mathbf{a} \in \mathbb{F}_2^n} \mathsf{SD}(\mathbf{a}^\top \mathbf{v}, \mathbf{U}_1)^2} .$$

A SIMPLIFIED PROOF FOR THEOREM 4. We denote with $\mathbf{C}_{\mathbf{x}} \in \mathbb{F}_2^{n \times (m-w)}$ and $\mathbf{r}_{\mathbf{x}} \in \mathbb{F}_2^{m-w}$ be the submatrix and substring of $\mathbf{C}$ and $\mathbf{r}$ respectively by keeping columns and bits that correspond to the positions of 0's in $\mathbf{x}^\top$. Recall that $\mathbf{r} \leftarrow R_{d,m}$ refers to $\mathbf{r} := \oplus_{i=1}^d \mathbf{t}_i$ for random weight-1 strings $\mathbf{t}_1, \cdots, \mathbf{t}_d \in \mathbb{F}_2^m$. Similarly, let $\mathbf{t}_i^{\bar{\mathbf{x}}}$ denote $\mathbf{t}_i$'s w-bit substring corresponding to the positions of 1's in $\mathbf{x}^\top$. Further, let $\mathcal{E}_j$ denote the event that the Hamming weight sum $\sum_{i=1}^d |\mathbf{t}_i^{\bar{\mathbf{x}}}| = j$, and thus $\mathbf{r}_{\mathbf{x}}$ conditioned on $\mathcal{E}_j$, denoted by $\mathbf{r}_{\mathbf{x},j}$, follows distribution $R_{d-j,m-w}$.

$$\mathsf{SD}\Big((\mathbf{Cr}, \mathbf{x}^\mathsf{T}\mathbf{r}) , (\mathbf{U}_n, \mathbf{x}^\mathsf{T}\mathbf{r})\Big)$$

$$\leq \mathsf{SD}\Big((\mathbf{C_x r_x}, \mathbf{t}_1^{\bar{\mathbf{x}}}, \ldots, \mathbf{t}_d^{\bar{\mathbf{x}}}) , (\mathbf{U}_n, \mathbf{t}_1^{\bar{\mathbf{x}}}, \ldots, \mathbf{t}_d^{\bar{\mathbf{x}}})\Big)$$

$$\leq \sum_{j=0}^{d} \Pr[\mathcal{E}_j] \cdot \sqrt{\sum_{0 \neq \mathbf{a} \in \mathbb{F}_2^n} \mathsf{SD}\Big(\mathbf{a}^\mathsf{T} \mathbf{C_x r}_{\mathbf{x},j}, \ \mathbf{U}_1\Big)^2}$$

$$\leq \sum_{j=0}^{d} \Pr[\mathcal{E}_j] \cdot \sqrt{2^n \cdot \left((\frac{w + \beta m}{m - w})^{d-j}\right)^2}$$

$$= 2^{\frac{n}{2}} \sum_{j=0}^{d} \underbrace{\binom{d}{j}(\frac{w}{m})^j (1 - \frac{w}{m})^{d-j}}_{\Pr[\mathcal{E}_j]} \cdot (\frac{w + \beta m}{m - w})^{d-j} = 2^{\frac{n}{2}} (\beta + \frac{2w}{m})^d ,$$

where the first inequality is due to that $\mathbf{x}^\mathsf{T}\mathbf{r}$ is implied by $\mathbf{t}_1^{\bar{\mathbf{x}}}, \ldots, \mathbf{t}_d^{\bar{\mathbf{x}}}$ (i.e., $\mathbf{x}^\mathsf{T}\mathbf{r}$ is the parity bit of $\oplus_{i=1}^{d} \mathbf{t}_i^{\bar{\mathbf{x}}}$), the second inequality follows from Vazirani's XOR lemma and the third inequality is due to Piling-up lemma, in particular, $\mathbf{a}^\mathsf{T}\mathbf{C} \in \mathbb{F}_2^m$ is a balanced string with $\frac{(1 \pm \beta)m}{2}$ 1's and thus its substring $\mathbf{a}^\mathsf{T}\mathbf{C_x} \in \mathbb{F}_2^{m-w}$ has $(\frac{m-w}{2}) \pm (\frac{w+\beta m}{2})$ 1's and each bit 1 of $\mathbf{r}_{\mathbf{x},j}$ hits the 1's in $\mathbf{a}^\mathsf{T}\mathbf{C_x}$ with probability $\frac{1}{2} \pm \frac{w+\beta m}{2(m-w)}$. Finally, we compute noise rate μ by the following:

$$1 - 2\mu = \Pr[\mathbf{x}^\mathsf{T}\mathbf{r} = 0] - \Pr[\mathbf{x}^\mathsf{T}\mathbf{r} = 1] = \sum_{i=0}^{d} \binom{d}{i}(\frac{-w}{m})^i (1 - \frac{w}{m})^{d-i} = (1 - \frac{2w}{m})^d .$$

3.3   On the Non-triviality of Code Smoothing

As discussed in Remark 2, the worst-case to average-case reduction in [18] may only give rise to the $n^{O(\lambda)}$-hardness of LPN on noise rate $\mu = 1/2 - 2^{-\Omega(\lambda)}$. Ideally, the dependency of μ on λ would be removed such that the noise rate of LPN μ can be kept constant while assigning a large value to λ to enjoy subexponential hardness for LPN. This will be goal of this paper.

Before we proceed, it is worth to repeat what we pointed out in the introduction that a better smoothing lemma is non-trivial without new ideas. The possibilities of smoothing linear binary codes can be investigated existentially using a probabilistic argument. The code smoothing lemma, as stated in Eq. 1, can be seen as deterministic randomness extractor from Bernoulli-like distributions. Consider $\mathbf{C}$ to be uniform over $\in \mathbb{F}_2^{n \times m}$ instead of a fixed one, then $\mathbf{r}$ has average min-entropy roughly $d \log(m/d)$ even given the single bit leakage $\mathbf{x}^\mathsf{T}\mathbf{r}$, and thus by the leftover hash lemma $\mathsf{SD}\Big((\mathbf{C}, \mathbf{Cr}, \mathbf{x}^\mathsf{T}\mathbf{r}), (\mathbf{C}, \mathbf{U}_n, \mathbf{x}^\mathsf{T}\mathbf{r})\Big) \leq 2^{-n}$ for $d \log(m/d) = 3n$. It follows by Markov inequality that there exists at least a $(1 - 2^{-n/2})$-fraction of "good" $\mathbf{C}$ satisfying $\mathsf{SD}\Big((\mathbf{Cr}, \mathbf{x}^\mathsf{T}\mathbf{r}), (\mathbf{U}_n, \mathbf{x}^\mathsf{T}\mathbf{r})\Big) \leq 2^{-n/2}$. This seemingly opens new possibilities especially in the sub-exponential hardness regime. For example, assume the NCP problem on a "good" code is $2^{\Omega(\sqrt{n})}$-hard (in the worst case) for noise rate $\frac{w}{m} = \frac{1}{\sqrt{n}}$, $d = O(\sqrt{n})$, and $m = 2^{O(\sqrt{n})}$ then $\mathsf{LPN}_{n,\mu,q}$ is $2^{\Omega(\sqrt{n})}$-hard against constant noise (see Eq. 2). However, so far we only consider a specific value of $\mathbf{x}$ for which there is a $2^{-n/2}$ fraction of $\mathbf{C}$ that fails the randomness extraction, and by summing over all the possible $\mathbf{x} \in \mathcal{R}_w^m$ the fraction of "bad" $\mathbf{C}$ amounts up to $\binom{m}{w} 2^{-n/2}$, which is useless since $\binom{m}{w}$ is super-exponential for $w = O(2^{\sqrt{n}}/\sqrt{n})$. To summarize, the existence of more meaningful smoothing lemma for binary linear code crucially relies on tighter proof techniques and better exploitation of the actual code/distribution in consideration to beat the union bound (so that "bad" $\mathbf{C}$ for different values of $\mathbf{x}$ mostly coincide and they jointly constitute only a negligible fraction).

3.4   Worst-Case Sub-exponential Hardness for LPN

We obtain the following worst-case to average-case reductions for LPN, where $d \log(m/d) = \Omega(n)$ is a necessary entropy condition (which is implicit in Eq. 1 of Theorem 4) and the values of β, k, and ζ are chosen to ensure the existence of respective codes (Lemma 1 and Lemma 2).

Theorem 5 (W/A-reduction for β-balanced codes). *Assume that the* $\mathsf{balNCP}_{n,m,w,\beta}$ *is (T,ϵ)-hard in the worst case for $\beta = 2\sqrt{n/m}$, then $\mathsf{LPN}_{n,\mu,q}$ is* $(T - O(nmq),\ \epsilon + \frac{q \cdot 2^{-\Omega(d)}}{1-2\mu})$-*hard for $\mu = \frac{1}{2} - \frac{1}{2}(1 - \frac{2d}{m})^w$, any m and d satisfying* $d \log(m/d) \geq 4n$.

Theorem 6 (W/A-reduction for independent codes). *Assume that the* $\mathsf{indNCP}_{n,m,w,k,\zeta}$ *is (T,ϵ)-hard in the worst case for $k = \frac{16d}{7}$ and $\zeta = 2^{-n}$, then* $\mathsf{LPN}_{n,\mu,q}$ *is $(T - O(nmq),\ \epsilon + \frac{q \cdot 2^{-\Omega(d)}}{1-2\mu})$-hard for $\mu = \frac{1}{2} - \frac{1}{2}(1 - \frac{2d}{m})^w$, any m and d satisfying $d \log(m/d) \geq 7n$.*

Proof Sketch. The proofs of Theorem 5 and Theorem 6 use the NCP instance to LPN sample conversion as described in Algorithm 1 except for sampling every $\mathbf{r}_i \leftarrow \mathcal{B}_{\frac{d}{m}}$ instead of $\mathbf{r}_i \leftarrow \mathcal{R}_{d,m}$. The conclusions follow from the respective smoothing lemmas (Lemma 9 and Lemma 12). While replacing $\mathcal{R}_{d,m}$ with $\mathcal{B}_{\frac{d}{m}}$ seems equivalent in terms of the resulting noise rate μ (almost same as Eq. 2 except that d and w are swapped), the fact that bits of $\mathbf{r}_i$ are all independent is crucial in obtaining more generic security bounds for δ that allow for a wider range of parameter choices.   □

A Comparison with [18]. With appropriate parameter assignment to Theorem 5, we obtain comparable results to [18] (see Theorem 3). Following [18], we consider balanced code with noise rate $w/m = \log^2 n/n$. As explained in Remark 1, while $\beta \geq 2\sqrt{n/m}$ ensures the overwhelming abundance of the balanced code, the existence condition does not impose much less, i.e., $\beta \geq 1.66\sqrt{n/m}$. It is convenient to fix $\beta = 2\sqrt{n/m}$ as larger values for β can only lead to larger d and renders LPN's noise μ closer to uniform. We give the comparison in Table 1 with various values for $m \geq n^{1+\epsilon}$. Note that the NCP is hard up to $T = n^{O(\log n)}$ due to known attacks, and the reduction requires $T' = T - O(nmq) > 0$, so here we let $m = \mathsf{poly}(n)$, and $q = \mathsf{poly}(n)$. In [18] the constraint on d is implied by Eq. 1, i.e.,

$$2^{\frac{n+1}{2}} \cdot (\frac{2w}{m} + \beta)^d = 2^{\frac{n+1}{2}} \cdot (\frac{2\log^2 n}{n} + \beta)^d = \mathsf{negl}(n) \tag{3}$$

while Theorem 5 explicitly sets $d\log(m/d) = 4n$. Substituting d into the noise rate of LPN, which is roughly $\mu \approx 1/2 - e^{-\frac{2w}{m}d + O(1)}$ in both cases, yields

$$\mu \approx \begin{cases} 1/2 - n^{\frac{-2.88\log n}{(\log m - \log n)}} & \text{for } \frac{n^3}{\log^4 n} > m \geq n^{1+\epsilon} \\ 1/2 - n^{-1.44} & \text{for } m \geq \frac{n^3}{\log^4 n} \end{cases}$$

for [18], and $\mu \approx 1/2 - n^{\frac{-11.54\log m}{(\log m - \log n)}}$ for $m \geq n^{1+\epsilon}$ in our case. As we can see from Table 1, our result is slightly (by a factor of 4 in the exponent) worse than [18] for $m < n^3$, and the gap decreases from $m \geq n^3$. Our result starts to show its advantage for $m \geq n^9$. In other words, [18] stays at $\mu \approx 1/2 - n^{-1.4}$ and ceases to improve for $m \geq n^3$. This is because for $m \geq n^3$ it is $2\log^2 n/n$ (instead of $\beta \leq 2\sqrt{n/m} \leq 2/n$) that dominates the term in Eq. 3, and thus one can no longer trade β for better μ regardless how small β is.

Table 1. Restate Theorem 5 and its analogue in [18] as "T-wc-hardness of "$\mathsf{NCP}(n, m, \frac{w}{m})$ on β-balanced code implies T'-ac-hardness of $\mathsf{LPN}(n, q, \mu)$" for $m \in \{n^{1.2}, n^2, \ldots, 100\}$, where $\frac{w}{m} = \frac{\log^2 n}{n}$, $\beta = 2\sqrt{n/m}$, $T' = T - O(nmq)$, $q = \mathsf{poly}(n)$.

m	LPN's noise rate μ from [18] (see Theorem 3)	LPN's noise rate μ from our Theorem 5
$n^{1.2}$	$\frac{1}{2} - n^{-14}$	$\frac{1}{2} - n^{-58}$
n^2	$\frac{1}{2} - n^{-3}$	$\frac{1}{2} - n^{-12}$
n^3	$\frac{1}{2} - n^{-1.4}$	$\frac{1}{2} - n^{-6}$
n^6	$\frac{1}{2} - n^{-1.4}$	$\frac{1}{2} - n^{-2.3}$
n^9	$\frac{1}{2} - n^{-1.4}$	$\frac{1}{2} - n^{-1.4}$
n^{10}	$\frac{1}{2} - n^{-1.4}$	$\frac{1}{2} - n^{-1.3}$
n^{100}	$\frac{1}{2} - n^{-1.4}$	$\frac{1}{2} - n^{-0.1}$

Our result admits a wider range of trade-offs between m and μ. More importantly, when m goes beyond $\mathsf{poly}(n)$ it enables to guarantee sub-exponential hardness for constant-noise LPN. In particular, we now assume that there exists constant ε such that the NCP problem is is $2^{\varepsilon\frac{w}{m}n}$-hard at noise rate $\frac{w}{m}$ and codeword length $m = 2^{\frac{\varepsilon}{8}\frac{w}{m}n}$. Note that refuting this assumption means that we can do arbitrary polynomial speedup over the current best known algorithms in solving the respective NCPs, which is a win-win situation.

Theorem 7 (Sub-exponential hardness for LPN). *Assume that either (1)* balNCP$_{n,m,w,\beta}$ *with* $\beta = 2\sqrt{n/m}$, *or (2)* indNCP$_{n,m,w,k,\zeta}$ *with* $k = \frac{16d}{7}$ *and* $\zeta = 2^{-n}$, *is* $2^{\Omega(n^{1-c})}$*-hard at noise rate* $\frac{w}{m} = n^{-c}$ *and codeword size* $m = 2^{\Omega(n^{1-c})}$, *then depending on the value of c we have*

Case $0 < c < 1/2$: LPN$_{n,\mu,q}$ *is* $(2^{\Omega(n^{1-c})}, 2^{-\Omega(n^c)})$*-hard for* $0 < \mu = O(1) < 1/2$
  and $q = 2^{\Omega(n^c)}$;
Case $1/2 \leq c < 1$: LPN$_{n,\mu,q}$ *is* $2^{\Omega(n^{1-c})}$*-hard for* $0 < \mu = O(1) < 1/2$ *and*
  $q = 2^{\Omega(n^{1-c})}$.

Proof Sketch. This is a corollary of Theorem 5 and Theorem 6 (from the respective assumptions) for $\frac{w}{m} = n^{-c}$, $\mu = O(1)$ (s.t. $\frac{w}{m}d = O(1)$), $d\log(m/d) = O(n)$ and $T = \Omega(n^{1-c})$. Note that $1/T + q2^{-\Omega(d)} = 2^{-\Omega(n^{1-c})} + 2^{-\Omega(n^c)}$, which is why the value of c is considered. $\qquad\qquad\qquad\qquad\qquad\qquad\qquad\qquad\quad\square$

3.5   Smoothing Balanced Codes

Our smoothing lemma benefits from Lemma 7 which tightly relates the bound on the conditional case $\mathsf{SD}\big((\mathbf{Cr}, \mathbf{x}^\mathsf{T}\mathbf{r}), (\mathbf{U}_n, \mathbf{x}^\mathsf{T}\mathbf{r})\big)$ to that of the unconditional case $\mathsf{SD}(\mathbf{Cr}, \mathbf{U}_n)$, regardless of which $\mathbf{x}$ is used. Note that this would not have been possible if $\mathbf{r}$ were not sampled from the Bernoulli distribution that is coordinate-wise independent. We first introduce Lemma 6 based on which Lemma 7 is built.

Lemma 6. *Let* $\mathbf{p}$ *be a random variable over* $\mathbb{F}_2^n$, *and let* $\mathbf{c}$ *be any constant vector over* $\mathbb{F}_2^n$. *Then, we have*

$$\mathsf{SD}(\mathbf{p} \oplus (e_1\mathbf{c}), \mathbf{U}_n) \geq (1 - 2a) \cdot \mathsf{SD}(\mathbf{p}, \mathbf{U}_n) \ ,$$

where $e_1 \xleftarrow{\$} \mathcal{B}_a$ $(0 \leq a \leq 1/2)$ *and* $e_1\mathbf{c}$ *denotes scalar vector multiplication between* e_1 *and* $\mathbf{c}$.

Proof. We use the shorthand $p_x \stackrel{\mathrm{def}}{=} \Pr[\mathbf{p} = x] - 2^{-n}$ for any $x \in \mathbb{F}_2^n$. Observe that any non-zero $\mathbf{c}$ divides $\mathbb{F}_2^n$ into two disjoint equal-size subsets $\mathcal{S}_1, \mathcal{S}_2 \subset \mathbb{F}_2^n$ such that every $\mathbf{p} \in \mathcal{S}_1$ implies $(\mathbf{p} + \mathbf{c}) \in \mathcal{S}_2$ and vice versa. Therefore,

$$\mathsf{SD}\big(\mathbf{p} \oplus (e_1\mathbf{c}), \mathbf{U}_n\big) = \frac{1}{2}\sum_{x \in \mathbb{F}_2^n} \Big| p_x(1 - a) + p_{x\oplus\mathbf{c}}a \Big|$$

$$\geq \frac{1}{2}\sum_{x \in \mathbb{F}_2^n} \Big(|p_x|(1 - a) - |p_{x\oplus\mathbf{c}}|a \Big)$$

$$= \frac{1}{2}\sum_{x \in \mathbb{F}_2^n} \Big(|p_x|(1 - 2a) \Big) = (1 - 2a) \cdot \mathsf{SD}(\mathbf{x}, \mathbf{U}_n) \ .$$

Lemma 7. *For any matrix* $\mathbf{C} \in \mathbb{F}_2^{n \times m}$, *any* $\mathbf{x} \in \mathcal{R}_w^m$ *and any* $0 \le a \le 1/2$ *we have*

$$\mathsf{SD}(\mathbf{C_x r_x}, \mathbf{U}_n) \le \frac{\mathsf{SD}(\mathbf{Cr}, \mathbf{U}_n)}{(1-2a)^w} \ ,$$

where $\mathbf{r} \leftarrow \mathcal{B}_a^m$, $\mathbf{C_x} \in \mathbb{F}_2^{n \times (m-w)}$ *(resp.,* $\mathbf{r_x} \in \mathbb{F}_2^{m-w}$*) denotes the submatrix of* $\mathbf{C}$ *(resp., subvector of* $\mathbf{r}$*) by keeping only columns (resp., bits) corresponding to the positions of bit-0 in* $\mathbf{x}$ *respectively.*

Proof. We have $\mathbf{Cr} = \mathbf{C_x r_x} + \bigoplus_{i=1}^w e_i \mathbf{c}_i$ where $e_i \leftarrow \mathcal{B}_a$ and $\mathbf{c}_i$ is the i-th column vector of $\mathbf{C} \setminus \mathbf{C_x}$ (i.e., the columns of $\mathbf{C}$ that are excluded from $\mathbf{C_x}$). By applying Lemma 6 w times we get

$$\mathsf{SD}(\mathbf{Cr}, \mathbf{U}_n) \ge (1-2a)^w \cdot \mathsf{SD}(\mathbf{C_x r_x}, \mathbf{U}_n) \ .$$

We need the following corollary of two-source extractors to prove the smoothing lemma. Recall that two-source extractor distills almost uniform randomness from pair-wise independent sources $\mathbf{b}^\mathsf{T}$ and $\mathbf{r}$, while Corollary 1 shows that the result holds even when $\mathbf{b}^\mathsf{T}$ is fixed (has no entropy at all) as long as certain conditioned are met.

Lemma 8 (Two-source extraction via inner product). *For independent random variables* $\mathbf{b}^\mathsf{T}$, $\mathbf{r} \in \mathbb{F}_2^m$ *with* $\mathbf{H}_\infty(\mathbf{b}^\mathsf{T}) = k_b$ *and* $\mathbf{H}_\infty(\mathbf{r}) = k_r$ *we have*

$$\mathsf{SD}\Big((\mathbf{b}^\mathsf{T}, \mathbf{b}^\mathsf{T}\mathbf{r}), (\mathbf{b}^\mathsf{T}, U_1) \Big) \le 2^{-(\frac{k_b + k_r - m}{2} + 1)} \ .$$

Corollary 1. *For random variable* $\mathbf{r}$ *and distribution* D *defined over* $\mathbb{F}_2^m$ *and* $\mathbb{F}_2$ *respectively, define set* $\mathcal{B}_{D,\mathbf{r}} \stackrel{\text{def}}{=} \{\mathbf{b}^\mathsf{T} : \mathbf{b}^\mathsf{T}\mathbf{r} \sim D\}$, *where* $\mathbf{H}_\infty(\mathbf{r}) = k_r$, *and* $|\mathcal{B}_{D,\mathbf{r}}| \ge 2^{k_b}$. *Then, for any* $\mathbf{b}^\mathsf{T} \in \mathcal{B}_{D,\mathbf{r}}$ *it holds that*

$$\mathsf{SD}(\mathbf{b}^\mathsf{T}\mathbf{r}, U_1) \le 2^{-(\frac{k_b + k_r - m}{2} + 1)} \ .$$

Proof. Fix an arbitrary $\mathbf{b}^\mathsf{T} \in \mathcal{B}_{D,\mathbf{r}}$, and let $\mathbf{b}'^\mathsf{T}$ be a random variable that is uniform over $\mathcal{B}_{D,\mathbf{r}}$, we have

$$\mathsf{SD}(\mathbf{b}^\mathsf{T}\mathbf{r}, U_1) = \mathsf{SD}(D, U_1) = \mathsf{SD}\Big((\mathbf{b}'^\mathsf{T}, \mathbf{b}'^\mathsf{T}\mathbf{r}), (\mathbf{b}'^\mathsf{T}, U_1) \Big) \le 2^{-(\frac{k_b + k_r - m}{2} + 1)} \ ,$$

where the equalities are simply by the definitions of $\mathcal{B}_{D,\mathbf{r}}$ and $\mathbf{b}'^\mathsf{T}$, and the inequality follows from the two source extractor lemma below.

Lemma 9 (Smoothing lemma for balanced codes). *Let* $\beta \le 2\sqrt{n/m}$, $d \log(m/d) \ge 4n$, $d = O(n)$, *and let* $\mathbf{C} \in \mathbb{F}_2^{n \times m}$ *be any generator matrix for a* β-*balanced* $[m, n]$-*linear code, then for every* $\mathbf{x} \in \mathcal{R}_w^m$ *and* $\mathbf{r} \leftarrow \mathcal{B}_{\frac{d}{m}}^m$ *it holds that* $\mu = \Pr[\mathbf{x}^\mathsf{T}\mathbf{r} = 1] = \frac{1}{2} - \frac{1}{2}(1 - \frac{2d}{m})^w$ *and*

$$\delta_{\mathbf{C},\mathbf{x}} = \mathsf{SD}\Big((\mathbf{Cr}, \mathbf{x}^\mathsf{T}\mathbf{r}), (\mathbf{U}_n, \mathbf{x}^\mathsf{T}\mathbf{r}) \Big) \le \frac{2^{-\Omega(d)}}{1 - 2\mu} \ .$$

Proof. The noise rate μ directly follows from the Piling-up lemma.

$$\begin{aligned}
&\mathrm{SD}(\mathbf{Cr}, \mathbf{U}_n) \\
&\leq \mathrm{SD}(\mathbf{Cr'}, \mathbf{U}_n) + 2^{-\Omega(d)} \\
&\leq \sqrt{\sum_{0 \neq \mathbf{a} \in \mathbb{F}_2^n} \mathrm{SD}\left(\underbrace{\mathbf{a}^\mathsf{T}\mathbf{C}}_{\mathbf{b}^\mathsf{T}}\mathbf{r'},\ \mathbf{U}_1 \right)^2} + 2^{-\Omega(d)} \\
&\leq \sqrt{\sum_{0 \neq \mathbf{a} \in \mathbb{F}_2^n} \mathrm{SD}\left((\mathbf{b'}^\mathsf{T}, \mathbf{b'}^\mathsf{T}\mathbf{r'}),\ (\mathbf{b'}^\mathsf{T}, \mathbf{U}_1) \right)^2} + 2^{-\Omega(d)} \\
&\leq 2^{\frac{n}{2}} \cdot 2^{\frac{(\log e)\beta^2}{2} m + \frac{\log m}{2} - d(1-\delta) \log(\frac{m}{d(1-\delta)})}{2}} + 2^{-\Omega(d)} \\
&= 2^{-\Omega(d)}
\end{aligned}$$

where the first inequality follows from a Chernoff bound that $\mathbf{r}$ is $2^{-\Omega(d)}$-close to some $\mathbf{r'}$ that is a convex combination of $R_{d(1-\delta)}^m$, $R_{d(1-\delta)+1}^m$, $\cdots$, $R_{d(1+\delta)}^m$ for any small constant $\delta > 0$, the second is due to Vazirani's XOR lemma. By the definition of balanced code $\mathbf{b}^\mathsf{T} \overset{\text{def}}{=} \mathbf{a}^\mathsf{T}\mathbf{C} \in \mathbb{F}_2^m$ satisfies $\frac{(1-\beta)m}{2} \leq |\mathbf{b}^\mathsf{T}| \leq \frac{(1+\beta)m}{2}$ and we assume WLOG $|\mathbf{b}^\mathsf{T}| = \frac{(1-\beta)m}{2}$ so that $\mathbf{b}^\mathsf{T}\mathbf{r'}$ is maximally biased. The third and fourth inequalities follow from Corollary 1 based on two-source extractors. In particular, let $\mathbf{b'}^\mathsf{T}$ be a random variable uniformly drawn from $\mathcal{R}_{\frac{(1-\beta)m}{2}}^m$, i.e., the set of all values with the same Hamming weight as $\mathbf{b}^\mathsf{T}$. We observe that $\mathbf{r'} \sim R_j^m$ implies that every $\mathbf{b}_1^\mathsf{T}$ and $\mathbf{b}_2^\mathsf{T}$ with $|\mathbf{b}_1^\mathsf{T}| = |\mathbf{b}_2^\mathsf{T}|$ must satisfy $\mathbf{b}_1^\mathsf{T}\mathbf{r'} \sim \mathbf{b}_2^\mathsf{T}\mathbf{r'}$ and therefore $\mathrm{SD}(\mathbf{b}^\mathsf{T}\mathbf{r'},\ U_1) = \mathrm{SD}\left((\mathbf{b'}^\mathsf{T}, \mathbf{b'}^\mathsf{T}\mathbf{r'}),\ (\mathbf{b'}^\mathsf{T}, U_1) \right)$. This allows to apply the strong two-source extractor, where Fact 2 is used to estimate the entropy of $\mathbf{b'}^\mathsf{T}$, i.e., $\log \left(\frac{m}{(1-\beta)m} \right)$. Finally, we set $\beta = 2\sqrt{n/m}$, $d \log(m/d) = 4n$ and sufficiently small δ to complete the proof. Following the proof of Theorem 4, let $\mathbf{C_x} \in \mathbb{F}_2^{n \times (m-w)}$ and $\mathbf{C_{\bar{x}}} \in \mathbb{F}_2^{n \times w}$ denote the submatrices of $\mathbf{C}$ by keeping columns corresponding to the 0's and 1's in $\mathbf{x}^\mathsf{T}$ respectively, and let $\mathbf{r_x} \in \mathbb{F}_2^{m-w}$ and $\mathbf{r_{\bar{x}}} \in \mathbb{F}_2^w$ denote the subvectors of $\mathbf{r}$ that correspond to the positions of 0's and 1's in $\mathbf{x}^\mathsf{T}$ respectively. This allows to complete the proof by

$$\begin{aligned}
\mathrm{SD}\left((\mathbf{Cr}, \mathbf{x}^\mathsf{T}\mathbf{r}),\ (\mathbf{U}_n, \mathbf{x}^\mathsf{T}\mathbf{r}) \right) &\leq \mathrm{SD}\left((\mathbf{C_x}\mathbf{r_x}, \mathbf{r_{\bar{x}}}),\ (\mathbf{U}_n, \mathbf{r_{\bar{x}}}) \right) \\
&= \mathrm{SD}(\mathbf{C_x}\mathbf{r_x}, \mathbf{U}_n) \leq \frac{\mathrm{SD}(\mathbf{Cr}, \mathbf{U}_n)}{(1 - \frac{2d}{m})^w} = \frac{2^{-\Omega(d)}}{(1 - \frac{2d}{m})^w} \ .
\end{aligned}$$

where the first inequality is due to that $(\mathbf{Cr}, \mathbf{x}^\mathsf{T}\mathbf{r})$ is implied by $(\mathbf{C_x}\mathbf{r_x}, \mathbf{r_{\bar{x}}})$, i.e., $\mathbf{Cr} = \mathbf{C_x}\mathbf{r_x} + \mathbf{C_{\bar{x}}}\mathbf{r_{\bar{x}}}$ and $\mathbf{x}^\mathsf{T}\mathbf{r} = \langle 1^w, \mathbf{r_{\bar{x}}} \rangle$, and so is $(\mathbf{U}_n, \mathbf{x}^\mathsf{T}\mathbf{r})$ by $(\mathbf{U}_n, \mathbf{r_{\bar{x}}})$, the equality is due to the independence of $\mathbf{r_x}$ and $\mathbf{r_{\bar{x}}}$, and the last inequality follows from Lemma 7.

As stated in Lemma 10, it is not hard to see a lower bound on smoothing any binary linear code (i.e., not just the balanced code considered above) with respect to $\mathbf{r} \leftarrow \mathcal{B}^m_{\frac{d}{m}}$. This means that our smoothing lemmas (Lemma 9 and Lemma 12) are optimal (up to some constant factor in the exponent) for $\mu \le 1/2 - 2^{-O(d)}$.

Lemma 10 (Lower bound on code smoothing). *For any* $\mathbf{C} \in \mathbb{F}_2^{n \times m}$, *for any* $\mathbf{x} \in \mathbb{F}_2^m$ *and* $\mathbf{r} \leftarrow \mathcal{B}^m_{\frac{d}{m}}$ *with* $\frac{d}{m} = o(1)$ *it holds that*

$$\mathsf{SD}\Big((\mathbf{Cr}, \mathbf{x}^\mathsf{T}\mathbf{r})\ ,\ (\mathbf{U}_n, \mathbf{x}^\mathsf{T}\mathbf{r})\Big) \ge 2^{-O(d)} \ .$$

Proof. Denote the first row of $\mathbf{C}$ by $\mathbf{c}_1^\mathsf{T}$

$$\mathsf{SD}\Big((\mathbf{Cr}, \mathbf{x}^\mathsf{T}\mathbf{r})\ ,\ (\mathbf{U}_n, \mathbf{x}^\mathsf{T}\mathbf{r})\Big) \ge \mathsf{SD}(\mathbf{c}_1^\mathsf{T}\mathbf{r}, \mathbf{U}_1) = \frac{(1 - \frac{2d}{m})^{|\mathbf{c}_1^\mathsf{T}|}}{2} \ge 2^{-O(d)} \ ,$$

where the equality is the piling-up lemma, and the last inequality is due to $|\mathbf{c}_1^\mathsf{T}| \le m$ and $1 - x = 2^{-O(x)}$ for $x = o(1)$.

3.6 Smoothing Independent Codes

The proof of the smoothing lemma relies on following Lemma 11, which is abstracted out from the leftover hash lemma (see Appendix A for its proof).

Lemma 11 (Generalized Hash Lemma). *For any function* $h : \mathbb{F}_2^m \to \mathbb{F}_2^n$ *and any random variable* $\mathbf{r}$ *over* $\mathbb{F}_2^m$ *we have*

$$\mathsf{SD}\Big(h(\mathbf{r}),\ \mathbf{U}_n\Big) \le \frac{1}{2}\sqrt{2^n \cdot \mathsf{Col}(h(\mathbf{r})) - 1} \ .$$

Lemma 12 (Smoothing lemma for independent codes). *Let* $d\log(m/d) \ge 7n$ *and* $\log m = o(n)$, *and let* $\mathbf{C} \in \mathbb{F}_2^{n \times m}$ *be any generator matrix for a* $(k = \frac{16d}{7}, 2^{-n})$-*independent* $[m, n]$-*linear code* $\mathcal{C} \in \mathbb{F}_2^m$, *then for every* $\mathbf{x} \in \mathcal{R}_{m,w}$ *and* $\mathbf{r} \leftarrow \mathcal{B}^m_{\frac{d}{m}}$ *it holds that*

$$\delta_{\mathbf{C},\mathbf{x}} = \mathsf{SD}\Big((\mathbf{Cr}, \mathbf{x}^\mathsf{T}\mathbf{r})\ ,\ (\mathbf{U}_n, \mathbf{x}^\mathsf{T}\mathbf{r})\Big) \le \frac{2^{-\Omega(d)}}{(1 - \frac{2d}{m})^w} \ ,$$

$$\mu = \Pr[\mathbf{x}^\mathsf{T}\mathbf{r} = 1] = \frac{1}{2} - \frac{1}{2}(1 - \frac{2d}{m})^w \ .$$

Proof. For any constant $0 < \delta < 1$, $\mathbf{r}$ is $2^{-\Omega(d)}$-close to some convex combination of $R^m_{d(1-\delta)}, R^m_{d(1-\delta)+1}, \cdots, R^m_{d(1+\delta)}$, which is denoted by $\mathbf{r}'$. By Lemma 11,

$$\mathsf{SD}(\mathbf{Cr}\ ,\ \mathbf{U}_n) \le 2^{-\Omega(d)} + \sqrt{2^n \cdot \mathsf{Col}(\mathbf{Cr}') - 1} \ .$$

We assume WLOG $\mathbf{r}' \leftarrow R^m_{d(1-\delta)}$ and consider i.i.d. $\mathbf{r}_1, \mathbf{r}_2 \leftarrow R^m_{d(1-\delta)}$ such that

$$\mathsf{Col}(\mathbf{Cr}') = \Pr[\mathbf{Cr}_1 = \mathbf{Cr}_2] = \Pr[\mathbf{C\ddot{r}}]$$

where for constant $0 < \Delta < 1$ variable $\ddot{\mathbf{r}} \overset{\text{def}}{=} \mathbf{r}_1 - \mathbf{r}_2$ follows a convex combination of $R^m_{2d(1-\delta)(1-\Delta)}, R^m_{2d(1-\delta)(1-\Delta)+1}, \cdots, R^m_{2d(1-\delta)}$ whose weights lie in between[8]

$$k/2 = 2d(1-\delta)(1-\Delta) \leq \text{weight} \leq 2d(1+\delta) = k$$

for $\delta = 1/7$ and $\Delta = 1/3$ except with error

$$\sum_{i=d(1-\delta)\Delta}^{d(1-\delta)} \frac{\binom{d(1-\delta)}{i}\binom{m-d(1-\delta)}{d(1-\delta)-i}}{\binom{m}{d(1-\delta)}} \leq \frac{2^{d(1-\delta)(1-\Delta)\log\frac{m}{d(1-\delta)(1-\Delta)}}}{2^{d(1-\delta)\log\frac{m}{d(1-\delta)}}} \leq 2^{-d(1-\delta)\Delta\log\frac{m}{d(1-\delta)}} .$$

The error is upper bounded by 2^{-2n} (for $\delta = 1/7$ and $\Delta = 1/3$). Thus,

$$\sqrt{2^n \cdot \mathsf{Col}(\mathbf{Cr}') - 1} \leq \sqrt{2^n \cdot (2^{-n}(1+2^{-n}) + 2^{-2n}) - 1} = 2^{-\Omega(n)} .$$

and $\mathsf{SD}(\mathbf{Cr}, \mathbf{U}_n) \leq 2^{-\Omega(d)}$. The rest follow the same steps as in the proof of Lemma 9.

3.7   Discussions

We conclude that the constant-noise LPN problem is $(T = 2^{\Omega(n^{1-c})}, \epsilon = 2^{-\Omega(n^{\min(c,1-c)})}, q = 2^{\Omega(n^{\min(c,1-c)})})$-hard assuming that the NCP (on the balanced/independent code) at the low-noise rate $\tau = n^{-c}$ is $(T' = 2^{\Omega(\tau n)}, \epsilon' = 2^{-\Omega(\tau n)}, m = 2^{\Omega(\tau n)})$-hard in the worst case. Unfortunately, we need $(T = 2^{\omega(n^{0.5})}, \epsilon = 2^{-\omega(n^{0.5})}, q = 2^{\Omega(n^{0.5})})$-hardness for constructing collision resistant hash functions and public-key encryptions [51,52], where the super-constant omitted by $\omega(\cdot)$ (representing the gap between what we prove for $c = 0.5$ and what is needed for PKE/CRH) can be arbitrarily small.[9] We explain in details below.

Theorem 8 ([52]). *Let n be the security parameter, and let $\mu = \mu(n)$, $k = k(n)$, $q = q(n)$, $t = t(n)$ and $T = T(n)$ such that $t^2 \leq q \leq T = 2^{\frac{8\mu t}{\ln 2(1-2\mu)}}$. For each $\mathbf{A} \in \mathbb{F}_2^{n \times q}$, define compressing function $h_\mathbf{A} : \mathbb{F}_2^{\log(\frac{q}{t})t} \to \mathbb{F}_2^n$ with $\log(\frac{q}{t})t > n$ by $h_\mathbf{A}(\mathbf{x}) = \mathbf{A} \cdot \mathsf{Expand}(\mathbf{x})$, where Expand expands any string of length $\log(\frac{q}{t})t$ into one of length q with Hamming weight no greater than t, and $h_\mathbf{A}$ is computable in time $O(q \log q)$ (see [52, Construction 3.1] for concrete instantiation of $h_\mathbf{A}$). Assume that the $\mathsf{DLPN}_{n,\mu,q}$ is T-hard, then for every probabilistic adversary $\mathcal{A}$ of running time $T' = 2^{\frac{4\mu t}{\ln 2(1-2\mu)} - 1}$*

$$\Pr_{\mathbf{A} \overset{\$}{\leftarrow} \mathbb{F}_2^{n \times q}} [(\mathbf{y}, \mathbf{y}') \leftarrow \mathcal{A}(\mathbf{A}) : \mathbf{y} \neq \mathbf{y}' \wedge h_\mathbf{A}(\mathbf{y}) = h_\mathbf{A}(\mathbf{y}')] \leq \frac{1}{T'} .$$

---

[8] For up limit on $|\ddot{\mathbf{r}}|$ we need to consider the other extreme case $\mathbf{r}' \leftarrow R^m_{d(1+\delta)}$, where the corresponding $\ddot{\mathbf{r}}$ is a convex combination of $R^m_{2d(1+\delta)(1-\Delta)}, R^m_{2d(1+\delta)(1-\Delta)+1}, \cdots, R^m_{2d(1+\delta)}$ up to small error.

[9] The difference between decisional and computational LPN is omitted since 2^p-hard $\mathsf{LPN}_{n,\mu,q}$ implies $2^{\Omega(p)}$-hard $\mathsf{DLPN}_{n,\mu,q}$ for any $p = \omega(\log n)$, $\mu = O(1)$ and $q \geq \mathsf{poly}(n)$ due to the sample-preserving reduction [6].

Note that the above theorem does not state "$h_\mathbf{A}$ is a T'-hard collision resistant hash (CRH)" as it is computable in time $O(q \log q)$ while $q = 2^{\Omega(\sqrt{n})}$ is not polynomial in the security parameter n. In particular, length requirement $q \leq T$ (any adversary making q queries runs in time at least q) implies, by taking a logarithm, $\log(q) = O(t)$ (recall that μ is constant). Since the compressing condition requires $\log(\frac{q}{t})t > n$ we need to set q and t to be at least $2^{\Omega(\sqrt{n})}$ and $\Omega(\sqrt{n})$ respectively. The authors of [52] offers a remedy to solve this problem. Switch to a new security parameter $\lambda = q$, and let $t = \log \lambda \cdot \omega(1)$ for any arbitrarily small $\omega(1)$. This ensures that $h_\mathbf{A}$ is computable in time $\mathsf{poly}(\lambda)$ while remaining $\lambda^{\omega(1)}$-collision resistant. Therefore, we need $(T = 2^{\omega(n^{0.5})}, \epsilon = 2^{-\omega(n^{0.5})}, q = 2^{\Omega(n^{0.5})})$-hardness for constant-noise LPN to construct collision resistant hash functions, where $\omega(\cdot)$ omits an arbitrary super constant.

Neither can we construct public-key encryptions from $(T = 2^{\Omega(n^{0.5})}, \epsilon = 2^{-\Omega(n^{0.5})}, q = 2^{\Omega(n^{0.5})})$-hard LPN due to the same $\omega(1)$ gap factor (see Theorem 9). The reason is essentially similar to the case of CRH. In fact, in some extent CRH and PKE are dual to each when being constructed from LPN. The authors of [51] already minimized the hardness needed for LPN to construct PKE, and also used the parameter switching technique. We restate the main results of [51] below.

Theorem 9 ([51]). *Assume that* $\mathsf{DLPN}_{n,\mu,q}$ *is* $(T = 2^{\omega(n^{0.5})}, \epsilon = 2^{-\omega(n^{0.5})}, q = 2^{n^{0.5}})$-*hard for any constant* $0 < \mu \leq 1/10$, *there exist IND-CCA secure public-key encryption schemes.*

We also mention that our result fails to transform the BKW algorithm (for LPN) into a worst-case solver for constant-noise NCP (i.e., $\frac{w}{m} = O(1)$) again due to some small gap. In particular, we recall the variant of BKW algorithm in Theorem 10 below, and we informally state our reduction results (Theorem 5 and Theorem 6) in Lemma 13. In order for Lemma 13 to compose with Theorem 10, we need $q = n^{1+\varepsilon}$ and $d = O(\log n)$ to make $\frac{q \cdot 2^{-\Omega(d)}}{1-2\mu} < 1$ and thus $\mu = \frac{1}{2} - e^{-O(\frac{w}{m}d)} = \frac{1}{2} - 2^{-O(\log n)}$, which does not meet the noise rate needed by Theorem 10, i.e., $\mu = 1/2 - 2^{-(\log n)^\delta}$ for any constant $0 < \delta < 1$.

Theorem 10 ([42]). *Let* $q = n^{1+\varepsilon}$ *and* $\mu = 1/2 - 2^{-(\log n)^\delta}$ *for any constants* $\varepsilon > 0$ *and* $0 < \delta < 1$. $\mathsf{LPN}_{n,\mu,q}$ *can be solved in time* $2^{O(n/\log\log n)}$ *with overwhelming probability.*

Lemma 13 (Our reduction, informal). *Any algorithm that solves* $\mathsf{LPN}_{n,\mu,q}$ *in time* T *with success rate* p, *implies another worst-case algorithm (for the NCP considered in Theorem 5 and Theorem 6) of running time* $T + O(nmq)$ *with success rate* $p - \frac{q \cdot 2^{-\Omega(d)}}{1-2\mu}$, *where* $\mu = \frac{1}{2} - e^{-O(\frac{w}{m}d)}$.

4   Concluding Remarks

We first show that the hardness of high-noise large-field LPN is reducible from the worst-case hardness of lattice problems via a simple reduction from LWE to

LPN over the same modulus. We then show that constant-noise LPN is $(T = 2^{\Omega(n^{1-c})}, \epsilon = 2^{-\Omega(n^{\min(c,1-c)})}, q = 2^{\Omega(n^{\min(c,1-c)})})$-hard assuming that the NCP (on the balanced/independent code) at the low-noise rate $\tau = n^{-c}$ is $(T' = 2^{\Omega(\tau n)}, \epsilon' = 2^{-\Omega(\tau n)}, m = 2^{\Omega(\tau n)})$-hard in the worst case, improving upon the work of [18]. However, the result is not strong enough to imply collision resistant hash functions or public-key encryptions due to the $\omega(1)$ gap term. We leave it as an open problem whether the gap can be closed.

Acknowledgement. Yu Yu, the corresponding author, was supported by the National Key Research and Development Program of China (Grant Nos. 2020YFA0309705 and 2018YFA0704701) and the National Natural Science Foundation of China (Grant Nos. 61872236 and 61971192). Jiang Zhang is supported by the National Natural Science Foundation of China (Grant Nos. 62022018, 61932019), the National Key Research and Development Program of China (Grant No. 2018YFB0804105). This work is also supported by the Major Program of Guangdong Basic and Applied Research (Grant No. 2019B030302008), Shandong Provincial Key Research and Development Program (Major Scientific and Technological Innovation Project, Grant No. 2019JZZY010133), Shandong Key Research and Development Program (Grant No. 2020ZLYS09) and in part by the Anhui Initiative in Quantum Information Technologies under Grant No. AHY150100.

A   Proofs Omitted

Proof of Lemma 2. For $\mathbf{C} \xleftarrow{\$} \mathbb{F}_2^{n \times m}$ and every $\mathbf{r} \in \mathbb{F}_2^m$ define

$$z_{\mathbf{C},\mathbf{r}} \overset{\text{def}}{=} \begin{cases} 1, & \text{if} \qquad \mathbf{C} \cdot \mathbf{r} = 0 \\ 0, & \text{otherwise } \mathbf{C} \cdot \mathbf{r} \neq 0 \end{cases}$$

For every $\mathbf{r} \neq 0$, the expectation $\mathbb{E}_{\mathbf{C} \xleftarrow{\$} \mathbb{F}_2^{n \times m}}[z_{\mathbf{C},\mathbf{r}}] = 2^{-n}$, and for every two distinct $\mathbf{r}_1 \neq \mathbf{r}_2$ variables $z_{\mathbf{C},\mathbf{r}_1}$ and $z_{\mathbf{C},\mathbf{r}_2}$ are pair-wise independent. For any $k/2 \leq i \leq k$,

$$\Pr_{\mathbf{C} \xleftarrow{\$} \mathbb{F}_2^{n \times m}} \left[\sum_{\mathbf{r} \in \mathcal{R}_i^m} z_{\mathbf{C},\mathbf{r}} \geq N \cdot 2^{-n}(1 + \zeta) \right]$$

$$\leq \Pr_{\mathbf{C} \xleftarrow{\$} \mathbb{F}_2^{n \times m}} \left[\left| \sum_{\mathbf{r} \in \mathcal{R}_i^m} z_{\mathbf{C},\mathbf{r}} - N \cdot 2^{-n} \right| \geq N 2^{-n} \zeta \right]$$

$$\leq \frac{Var\left[\sum_{\mathbf{r} \in \mathcal{R}_i^m} z_{\mathbf{C},\mathbf{r}} \right]}{(N 2^{-n} \zeta)^2}$$

$$= \frac{N 2^{-n}(1 - 2^{-n})}{(N 2^{-n} \zeta)^2} \leq \frac{1}{N 2^{-n} \zeta^2} \leq \frac{2^{n + \frac{\log m}{2} - \frac{k}{2}\log(m/k)}}{\zeta^2},$$

where $N \overset{\text{def}}{=} |\mathcal{R}_i^m| \geq \binom{m}{k/2}$, the second inequality is by Chebyshev, and the equality is due to the following: denote $z = \sum_{\mathbf{r} \in \mathcal{R}_i^m} z_{\mathbf{C},\mathbf{r}}$ and $\mu = \mathbb{E}[z]$ and therefore

$$Var[z] = \mathbb{E}[(z - \mu)^2]$$
$$= \mathbb{E}[z^2] - 2\mu\mathbb{E}[z] + \mu^2$$
$$= \mathbb{E}[z^2] - \mu^2$$
$$= \mathbb{E}[z^2] - N^2 2^{-2n} \ ,$$

$$\mathbb{E}[z^2] = \mathbb{E}\Big[(z_1 + z_2 + \ldots + z_N)^2\Big]$$
$$= \mathbb{E}\Big[\sum_{u \neq v} z_u \cdot z_v\Big] + \mathbb{E}\Big[\sum_u z_u^2\Big]$$
$$= \sum_{u \neq v} \mathbb{E}[z_u] \cdot \mathbb{E}[z_v] + \sum_u 2^{-n}$$
$$= 2^{-2n}(N^2 - N) + N2^{-n} = N^2 2^{-2n} + N2^{-n}(1 - 2^{-n}) \ .$$

We complete the proof by a union bound on all possible values of i.   □

Remark 3 (Why not $i \in (0, k/2)$). Note that the above considers only $i \geq k/2$. As we can see from the above proof, this is because $\log N = \log |\mathcal{R}_i^m| = \log \binom{m}{i}$ needs to be $\Omega(n)$ to make the bound meaningful. For small values of i, it is not possible since m is only sub-exponential.

Proof of Lemma 3. Let $\mathbf{s} \overset{\text{def}}{=} \mathbf{s}_1 - \mathbf{s}_2$ and $\mathbf{x} \overset{\text{def}}{=} \mathbf{x}_1 - \mathbf{x}_2$. For any $\mathbf{s} \neq \mathbf{0}$ the random variable $\mathbf{s}^\mathsf{T}\mathbf{C}$ is uniform over $\mathbb{F}_2^m$ and thus it hits $\{\mathbf{x} \in \mathbb{F}_2^m : |\mathbf{x}| \leq 2w\}$ with probability at most $\sum_{i=0}^{2w} \binom{m}{i}/2^m$. The conclusion follows by a union bound on all possible $\mathbf{s} \in \mathbb{F}_2^n$.   □

Proof of Lemma 11. We denote $\mathcal{S} \overset{\text{def}}{=} \mathbb{F}_2^n$ and $p_s = \Pr[h(\mathbf{r}) = s]$.

$$\mathsf{SD}\Big(h(\mathbf{r}), \mathbf{U}_n\Big)$$
$$= \frac{1}{2}\sum_{s \in \mathcal{S}} |p_s - \frac{1}{|\mathcal{S}|}|$$
$$= \frac{1}{2}\sum_{s \in \mathcal{S}} \sqrt{\frac{1}{|\mathcal{S}|}} \cdot \Big(\sqrt{|\mathcal{S}|} \cdot \Big|p_s - \frac{1}{|\mathcal{S}|}\Big|\Big)$$
$$\leq \frac{1}{2}\sqrt{\sum_{s \in \mathcal{S}}(\frac{1}{|\mathcal{S}|}) \cdot \sum_{s \in \mathcal{S}}|\mathcal{S}|(p_s - \frac{1}{|\mathcal{S}|})^2}$$
$$= \frac{1}{2}\sqrt{2^n(\sum_{s \in \mathcal{S}} p_s^2) - 1}$$
$$= \frac{1}{2}\sqrt{2^n \cdot \mathsf{Col}(h(\mathbf{r})) - 1} \ ,$$

where the first inequality is Cauchy-Schwartz, i.e., $|\sum_i a_i b_i| \leq \sqrt{(\sum_i a_i^2) \cdot (\sum_i b_i^2)}$.   □

B   Inequalities, Theorems and Lemmas

Lemma 14 (Piling-up lemma). *For $0 < \mu < 1/2$ and $\ell \in \mathbb{N}^+$ we have*

$$\Pr\left[\bigoplus_{i=1}^{\ell} E_i = 0 : E_1, \ldots, E_\ell \leftarrow \mathcal{B}_\mu\right] = \frac{1}{2}(1 + (1 - 2\mu)^\ell) \ .$$

Lemma 15 (Chebyshev's inequality). *Let Y be any random variable (taking real values) with expectation μ and standard deviation σ (i.e., $Var[Y] = \sigma^2 = \mathbb{E}[(Y - \mu)^2]$). Then, for any $\delta > 0$ we have $\Pr[\ |Y - \mu| \geq \delta\sigma] \leq 1/\delta^2$.*

Lemma 16 (Chernoff bound). *Let $X_1, \ldots, X_n$ be independent random variables and let $\bar{X} = \sum_{i=1}^n X_i$, where $\Pr[0 \leq X_i \leq 1] = 1$ holds for every $1 \leq i \leq n$. Then, for any $\Delta_1 > 0$ and $0 < \Delta_2 < 1$,*

$$\Pr[\ \bar{X} > (1 + \Delta_1) \cdot \mathbb{E}[\bar{X}]\ ] < e^{-\frac{\min(\Delta_1, \Delta_1^2)}{3}\mathbb{E}[\bar{X}]} \ ,$$

$$\Pr[\ \bar{X} < (1 - \Delta_2) \cdot \mathbb{E}[\bar{X}]\ ] < e^{-\frac{\Delta_2^2}{2}\mathbb{E}[\bar{X}]} \ .$$

Fact 1. *For any $0 \leq x \leq 1$, $\log(1 + x) \geq x$; and for any $x > -1$ we have $\log(1 + x) \leq x/\ln 2$.*

Fact 2. *For $k = o(m)$ we have $\log \binom{m}{k} = (1 + o(1))k \log \frac{m}{k}$; and for $\beta = o(1)$, $\log \binom{m}{\frac{m}{2}(1-\beta)} = m(1 - \frac{\beta^2}{2}(\log e + o(1))) - \frac{\log m}{2} + O(1)$.*

Proof of Fact 2. The first inequality follows from the approximation $\log(n!) = \log\left(O(\sqrt{n}(\frac{n}{e})^n)\right) = \frac{1}{2}\log n + n \log n - n \log e + O(1)$ and for the second one we have

$$\log\binom{m}{\frac{m}{2}(1-\beta)} = \log \frac{m!}{\left(\frac{m}{2}(1-\beta)\right)!\left(\frac{m}{2}(1+\beta)\right)!}$$

$$= m \log m - \frac{m}{2}(1-\beta)\log\left(\frac{m}{2}(1-\beta)\right)$$

$$\qquad - \frac{m}{2}(1+\beta)\log\left(\frac{m}{2}(1+\beta)\right) - \frac{1}{2}\log m + O(1)$$

$$= m\left(1 - \frac{\log e}{2}(1-\beta)\left(-\beta - \frac{1}{2}\beta^2 + o(\beta^2)\right)\right.$$

$$\qquad \left. - \frac{\log e}{2}(1+\beta)\left(\beta - \frac{1}{2}\beta^2 + o(\beta^2)\right)\right) - \frac{1}{2}\log m + O(1)$$

$$= m(1 - \frac{\log e}{2}\beta^2 + o(\beta^2)) - \frac{1}{2}\log m + O(1) \ ,$$

where we use the approximation of $\log(n!)$ and for $x = o(1)$, $\log(1 + x) = \log e(x - \frac{1}{2}x^2 + o(x^2))$. $\qquad\square$

Lemma 17 (Sample-preserving reduction [6]**).** *Any distinguisher* $\mathcal{D}$ *of running time* T *with*

$$\Pr_{\mathbf{A}\xleftarrow{\$}\mathbb{F}_2^{q\times n},\mathbf{s}\leftarrow S,\mathbf{e}\leftarrow E} [\mathcal{D}(\mathbf{A}, \mathbf{As} + \mathbf{e}) = 1] - \Pr[\mathcal{D}(\mathbf{A}, \mathbf{U}_n) = 1] \geq \varepsilon$$

implies another algorithm $\mathcal{D}'$ *of running time* $T + O(nq)$ *such that*

$$\Pr_{\mathbf{A}\xleftarrow{\$}\mathbb{F}_2^{q\times n},\mathbf{s}\leftarrow S,\mathbf{e}\leftarrow E} [\mathcal{D}'(\mathbf{A}, \mathbf{As} + \mathbf{e}, \mathbf{r}^\mathsf{T}) = \mathbf{r}^\mathsf{T}\mathbf{s}] \geq \frac{1}{2} + \frac{\varepsilon}{2} \ ,$$

where S *and* E *are any distributions over* $\mathbb{F}_2^n$ *and* $\mathbb{F}_2^q$ *respectively.*

Lemma 18 (Goldreich-Levin Theorem [31]**).** *Any algorithm* $\mathcal{D}$ *of running time* T *with*

$$\Pr[\mathcal{D}(f(\mathbf{s}), \mathbf{r}^\mathsf{T}) = \mathbf{r}^\mathsf{T}\mathbf{s}] \geq \frac{1}{2} + \varepsilon$$

implies algorithm $\mathcal{A}$ *of running time* $O(\frac{n^2}{\varepsilon^2}T)$ *such that* $\Pr_{\mathbf{s}\leftarrow S}[\mathcal{A}(f(\mathbf{s})) = f^{-1}(f(\mathbf{s})))] = \frac{\Omega(\varepsilon^3)}{n}$, *where* f *is any function on input* $s \leftarrow S \in \mathbb{F}_2^n$ *and* $\mathbf{r} \xleftarrow{\$} \mathbb{F}_2^n$.

References

1. Alekhnovich, M.: More on average case vs approximation complexity. In: 44th FOCS, Cambridge, MA, USA, 11–14 October 2003, pp. 298–307. IEEE Computer Society Press (2003). https://doi.org/10.1109/SFCS.2003.1238204
2. Alon, N., Panigrahy, R., Yekhanin, S.: Deterministic approximation algorithms for the nearest codeword problem. In: Dinur, I., Jansen, K., Naor, J., Rolim, J. (eds.) APPROX/RANDOM-2009. LNCS, vol. 5687, pp. 339–351. Springer, Heidelberg (2009). https://doi.org/10.1007/978-3-642-03685-9_26
3. Applebaum, B., Avron, J., Brzuska, C.: Arithmetic cryptography: extended abstract. In: Roughgarden, T. (ed.) ITCS 2015, Rehovot, Israel, 11–13 January 2015, pp. 143–151. ACM (2015). https://doi.org/10.1145/2688073.2688114
4. Applebaum, B., Cash, D., Peikert, C., Sahai, A.: Fast cryptographic primitives and circular-secure encryption based on hard learning problems. In: Halevi, S. (ed.) CRYPTO 2009. LNCS, vol. 5677, pp. 595–618. Springer, Heidelberg (2009). https://doi.org/10.1007/978-3-642-03356-8_35
5. Applebaum, B., Damgård, I., Ishai, Y., Nielsen, M., Zichron, L.: Secure arithmetic computation with constant computational overhead. In: Katz, J., Shacham, H. (eds.) CRYPTO 2017, Part I. LNCS, vol. 10401, pp. 223–254. Springer, Heidelberg (2017). https://doi.org/10.1007/978-3-319-63688-7_8
6. Applebaum, B., Ishai, Y., Kushilevitz, E.: Cryptography with constant input locality. J. Cryptol. **22**(4), 429–469 (2009). https://doi.org/10.1007/s00145-009-9039-0
7. Arora, S., Babai, L., Stern, J., Sweedyk, Z.: The hardness of approximate optima in lattices, codes, and systems of linear equations. J. Comput. Syst. Sci. **54**(2), 317–331 (1997)

8. Becker, A., Joux, A., May, A., Meurer, A.: Decoding random binary linear codes in $2^{n/20}$: how $1 + 1 = 0$ improves information set decoding. In: Pointcheval, D., Johansson, T. (eds.) EUROCRYPT 2012. LNCS, vol. 7237, pp. 520–536. Springer, Heidelberg (2012). https://doi.org/10.1007/978-3-642-29011-4_31

9. Berman, P., Karpinski, M.: Approximating minimum unsatisfiability of linear equations. In: Eppstein, D. (ed.) 13th SODA, San Francisco, CA, USA, 6–8 January 2002, pp. 514–516. ACM-SIAM (2002)

10. Bernstein, D.J., Lange, T., Peters, C.: Smaller decoding exponents: ball-collision decoding. In: Rogaway, P. (ed.) CRYPTO 2011. LNCS, vol. 6841, pp. 743–760. Springer, Heidelberg (2011). https://doi.org/10.1007/978-3-642-22792-9_42

11. Blinovsky, V.M.: Proof of tightness of Varshamov - Gilbert bound for binary codes. CoRR arXiv:1606.01592 (2016)

12. Blum, A., Furst, M.L., Kearns, M.J., Lipton, R.J.: Cryptographic primitives based on hard learning problems. In: Stinson, D.R. (ed.) CRYPTO 1993. LNCS, vol. 773, pp. 278–291. Springer, Heidelberg (1994). https://doi.org/10.1007/3-540-48329-2_24

13. Blum, A., Kalai, A., Wasserman, H.: Noise-tolerant learning, the parity problem, and the statistical query model. In: 32nd ACM STOC, Portland, OR, USA, 21–23 May 2000, pp. 435–440. ACM Press (2000). https://doi.org/10.1145/335305.335355

14. Boneh, D., et al.: Fully key-homomorphic encryption, arithmetic circuit ABE and compact garbled circuits. In: Nguyen, P.Q., Oswald, E. (eds.) EUROCRYPT 2014. LNCS, vol. 8441, pp. 533–556. Springer, Heidelberg (2014). https://doi.org/10.1007/978-3-642-55220-5_30

15. Boyle, E., Couteau, G., Gilboa, N., Ishai, Y.: Compressing vector OLE. In: Lie, D., Mannan, M., Backes, M., Wang, X. (eds.) ACM CCS 2018, Toronto, ON, Canada, 15–19 October 2018, pp. 896–912. ACM Press (2018). https://doi.org/10.1145/3243734.3243868

16. Boyle, E., et al.: Efficient two-round OT extension and silent non-interactive secure computation. In: ACM CCS 2019, pp. 291–308. ACM Press (2019). https://doi.org/10.1145/3319535.3354255

17. Brakerski, Z., Langlois, A., Peikert, C., Regev, O., Stehlé, D.: Classical hardness of learning with errors. In: Boneh, D., Roughgarden, T., Feigenbaum, J. (eds.) 45th ACM STOC, Palo Alto, CA, USA, 1–4 June 2013, pp. 575–584. ACM Press (2013). https://doi.org/10.1145/2488608.2488680

18. Brakerski, Z., Lyubashevsky, V., Vaikuntanathan, V., Wichs, D.: Worst-case hardness for LPN and cryptographic hashing via code smoothing. In: Ishai, Y., Rijmen, V. (eds.) EUROCRYPT 2019, Part III. LNCS, vol. 11478, pp. 619–635. Springer, Heidelberg (2019). https://doi.org/10.1007/978-3-030-17659-4_21

19. Cash, D., Kiltz, E., Tessaro, S.: Two-round man-in-the-middle security from LPN. In: Kushilevitz, E., Malkin, T. (eds.) TCC 2016-A, Part I. LNCS, vol. 9562, pp. 225–248. Springer, Heidelberg (2016). https://doi.org/10.1007/978-3-662-49096-9_10

20. Chen, H., Cramer, R., Goldwasser, S., de Haan, R., Vaikuntanathan, V.: Secure computation from random error correcting codes. In: Naor, M. (ed.) EUROCRYPT 2007. LNCS, vol. 4515, pp. 291–310. Springer, Heidelberg (2007). https://doi.org/10.1007/978-3-540-72540-4_17

21. David, B., Dowsley, R., Nascimento, A.C.A.: Universally composable oblivious transfer based on a variant of LPN. In: Gritzalis, D., Kiayias, A., Askoxylakis, I.G. (eds.) CANS 14. LNCS, vol. 8813, pp. 143–158. Springer, Heidelberg, Germany (2014). https://doi.org/10.1007/978-3-319-12280-9_10

22. Dodis, Y., Kiltz, E., Pietrzak, K., Wichs, D.: Message authentication, revisited. In: Pointcheval, D., Johansson, T. (eds.) EUROCRYPT 2012. LNCS, vol. 7237, pp. 355–374. Springer, Heidelberg (2012). https://doi.org/10.1007/978-3-642-29011-4_22

23. Döttling, N.: Low noise LPN: KDM secure public key encryption and sample amplification. In: Katz, J. (ed.) PKC 2015. LNCS, vol. 9020, pp. 604–626. Springer, Heidelberg (2015). https://doi.org/10.1007/978-3-662-46447-2_27

24. Döttling, N., Ghosh, S., Nielsen, J.B., Nilges, T., Trifiletti, R.: TinyOLE: Efficient actively secure two-party computation from oblivious linear function evaluation. In: Thuraisingham, B.M., Evans, D., Malkin, T., Xu, D. (eds.) ACM CCS 2017, Dallas, TX, USA, 31 October–2 November 2017, pp. 2263–2276. ACM Press (2017). https://doi.org/10.1145/3133956.3134024

25. Dumer, I., Micciancio, D., Sudan, M.: Hardness of approximating the minimum distance of a linear code. In: 40th FOCS, New York, NY, USA, 17–19 October 1999, pp. 475–485. IEEE Computer Society Press (1999). https://doi.org/10.1109/SFFCS.1999.814620

26. Feldman, V., Gopalan, P., Khot, S., Ponnuswami, A.K.: New results for learning noisy parities and halfspaces. In: 47th FOCS, Berkeley, CA, USA, 21–24 October 2006, pp. 563–574. IEEE Computer Society Press (2006). https://doi.org/10.1109/FOCS.2006.51

27. Fischer, J.-B., Stern, J.: An efficient pseudo-random generator provably as secure as syndrome decoding. In: Maurer, U. (ed.) EUROCRYPT 1996. LNCS, vol. 1070, pp. 245–255. Springer, Heidelberg (1996). https://doi.org/10.1007/3-540-68339-9_22

28. Gentry, C.: Fully homomorphic encryption using ideal lattices. In: Mitzenmacher, M. (ed.) 41st ACM STOC, Bethesda, MD, USA, 31 May–2 June 2009, pp. 169–178. ACM Press (2009). https://doi.org/10.1145/1536414.1536440

29. Ghosh, S., Nielsen, J.B., Nilges, T.: Maliciously secure oblivious linear function evaluation with constant overhead. In: Takagi, T., Peyrin, T. (eds.) ASIACRYPT 2017, Part I. LNCS, vol. 10624, pp. 629–659. Springer, Heidelberg (2017). https://doi.org/10.1007/978-3-319-70694-8_22

30. Goldreich, O.: Three XOR-lemmas — an exposition. In: Goldreich, O. (ed.) Studies in Complexity and Cryptography. Miscellanea on the Interplay between Randomness and Computation. LNCS, vol. 6650, pp. 248–272. Springer, Heidelberg (2011). https://doi.org/10.1007/978-3-642-22670-0_22

31. Goldreich, O., Levin, L.A.: A hard-core predicate for all one-way functions. In: 21st ACM STOC, Seattle, WA, USA, 15–17 May 1989, pp. 25–32. ACM Press (1989). https://doi.org/10.1145/73007.73010

32. Gorbunov, S., Vaikuntanathan, V., Wee, H.: Attribute-based encryption for circuits. In: Boneh, D., Roughgarden, T., Feigenbaum, J. (eds.) 45th ACM STOC, Palo Alto, CA, USA, 1–4 June 2013, pp. 545–554. ACM Press (2013). https://doi.org/10.1145/2488608.2488677

33. Hopper, N.J., Blum, M.: Secure human identification protocols. In: Boyd, C. (ed.) ASIACRYPT 2001. LNCS, vol. 2248, pp. 52–66. Springer, Heidelberg (2001). https://doi.org/10.1007/3-540-45682-1_4

34. Impagliazzo, R.: A personal view of average-case complexity. In: Structure in Complexity Theory Conference, pp. 134–147 (1995)

35. Ishai, Y., Prabhakaran, M., Sahai, A.: Secure arithmetic computation with no honest majority. In: Reingold, O. (ed.) TCC 2009. LNCS, vol. 5444, pp. 294–314. Springer, Heidelberg (2009). https://doi.org/10.1007/978-3-642-00457-5_18

36. Jain, A., Lin, H., Sahai, A.: Indistinguishability obfuscation from well-founded assumptions. Cryptology ePrint Archive, Report 2020/1003 (2020). https://eprint.iacr.org/2020/1003

37. Jain, A., Krenn, S., Pietrzak, K., Tentes, A.: Commitments and efficient zero-knowledge proofs from learning parity with noise. In: Wang, X., Sako, K. (eds.) ASIACRYPT 2012. LNCS, vol. 7658, pp. 663–680. Springer, Heidelberg (2012). https://doi.org/10.1007/978-3-642-34961-4_40

38. Juels, A., Weis, S.A.: Authenticating pervasive devices with human protocols. In: Shoup, V. (ed.) CRYPTO 2005. LNCS, vol. 3621, pp. 293–308. Springer, Heidelberg (2005). https://doi.org/10.1007/11535218_18

39. Katz, J., Shin, J.S.: Parallel and concurrent security of the HB and HB+ protocols. In: Vaudenay, S. (ed.) EUROCRYPT 2006. LNCS, vol. 4004, pp. 73–87. Springer, Heidelberg (2006). https://doi.org/10.1007/11761679_6

40. Kiltz, E., Pietrzak, K., Cash, D., Jain, A., Venturi, D.: Efficient authentication from hard learning problems. In: Paterson, K.G. (ed.) EUROCRYPT 2011. LNCS, vol. 6632, pp. 7–26. Springer, Heidelberg (2011). https://doi.org/10.1007/978-3-642-20465-4_3

41. Kirchner, P., Fouque, P.A.: An improved BKW algorithm for LWE with applications to cryptography and lattices. In: Gennaro, R., Robshaw, M.J.B. (eds.) CRYPTO 2015, Part I. LNCS, vol. 9215, pp. 43–62. Springer, Heidelberg (2015). https://doi.org/10.1007/978-3-662-47989-6_3

42. Lyubashevsky, V.: The parity problem in the presence of noise, decoding random linear codes, and the subset sum problem. In: Chekuri, C., Jansen, K., Rolim, J.D.P., Trevisan, L. (eds.) APPROX/RANDOM-2005. LNCS, vol. 3624, pp. 378–389. Springer, Heidelberg (2005). https://doi.org/10.1007/11538462_32

43. Lyubashevsky, V., Masny, D.: Man-in-the-middle secure authentication schemes from LPN and weak PRFs. In: Canetti, R., Garay, J.A. (eds.) CRYPTO 2013, Part II. LNCS, vol. 8043, pp. 308–325. Springer, Heidelberg (2013). https://doi.org/10.1007/978-3-642-40084-1_18

44. May, A., Meurer, A., Thomae, E.: Decoding random linear codes in $\tilde{\mathcal{O}}(2^{0.054n})$. In: Lee, D.H., Wang, X. (eds.) ASIACRYPT 2011. LNCS, vol. 7073, pp. 107–124. Springer, Heidelberg (2011). https://doi.org/10.1007/978-3-642-25385-0_6

45. Peikert, C.: Public-key cryptosystems from the worst-case shortest vector problem: extended abstract. In: Mitzenmacher, M. (ed.) 41st ACM STOC, Bethesda, MD, USA, 31 May–2 June 2009, pp. 333–342. ACM Press (2009). https://doi.org/10.1145/1536414.1536461

46. Regev, O.: On lattices, learning with errors, random linear codes, and cryptography. In: Gabow, H.N., Fagin, R. (eds.) 37th ACM STOC, Baltimore, MA, USA, 22–24 May 2005, pp. 84–93. ACM Press (2005). https://doi.org/10.1145/1060590.1060603

47. Stern, J.: A method for finding codewords of small weight. In: Cohen, G., Wolfmann, J. (eds.) Coding Theory and Applications, 1988. LNCS, vol. 388, pp. 106–113. Springer, Heidelberg (1989). https://doi.org/10.1007/BFb0019850

48. Stinson, D.R.: Universal hash families and the leftover hash lemma, and applications to cryptography and computing. J. Comb. Math. Comb. Comput. **42**, 3–31 (2002)

49. Vazirani, U.V.: Randomness, Adversaries and Computation (Random Polynomial Time). Ph.D. thesis (1986). aAI8718194

50. Weng, C., Yang, K., Katz, J., Wang, X.: Wolverine: fast, scalable, and communication-efficient zero-knowledge proofs for boolean and arithmetic circuits. Cryptology ePrint Archive, Report 2020/925 (2020). https://eprint.iacr.org/2020/925

51. Yu, Y., Zhang, J.: Cryptography with auxiliary input and trapdoor from constant-noise LPN. In: Robshaw, M., Katz, J. (eds.) CRYPTO 2016. LNCS, vol. 9814, pp. 214–243. Springer, Heidelberg (2016). https://doi.org/10.1007/978-3-662-53018-4_9

52. Yu, Y., Zhang, J., Weng, J., Guo, C., Li, X.: Collision resistant hashing from sub-exponential learning parity with noise. In: Galbraith, S.D., Moriai, S. (eds.) ASIACRYPT 2019. LNCS, vol. 11922, pp. 3–24. Springer, Cham (2019). https://doi.org/10.1007/978-3-030-34621-8_1

Silver: Silent VOLE and Oblivious Transfer from Hardness of Decoding Structured LDPC Codes

Geoffroy Couteau[1]($\boxtimes$), Peter Rindal[2], and Srinivasan Raghuraman[2]

[1] CNRS, IRIF, Université de Paris, Paris, France
couteau@irif.fr
[2] Visa Research, Palo Alto, USA

Abstract. We put forth new protocols for oblivious transfer extension and vector OLE, called *Silver*, for SILent Vole and oblivious transfER. Silver offers extremely high performances: generating 10 million random OTs on one core of a standard laptop requires only 300 ms of computation and 122 KB of communication. This represents 37% less computation and $\sim$1300$\times$ less communication than the standard IKNP protocol, as well as $\sim$4$\times$ less computation and $\sim$14$\times$ less communication than the recent protocol of Yang et al. (CCS 2020). Silver is *silent*: after a one-time cheap interaction, two parties can store small seeds, from which they can later *locally* generate a large number of OTs *while remaining offline*. Neither IKNP nor Yang et al. enjoys this feature; compared to the best known silent OT extension protocol of Boyle et al. (CCS 2019), upon which we build up, Silver has 19$\times$ less computation, and the same communication. Due to its attractive efficiency features, Silver yields major efficiency improvements in numerous MPC protocols.

Our approach is a radical departure from the standard paradigm for building MPC protocols, in that we do *not* attempt to base our constructions on a well-studied assumption. Rather, we follow an approach closer in spirit to the standard paradigm in the design of symmetric primitives: we identify a set of fundamental structural properties that allow us to withstand all known attacks, and put forth a candidate design, guided by our analysis. We also rely on extensive experimentations to analyze our candidate and experimentally validate their properties. In essence, our approach boils down to constructing new families of linear codes with (plausibly) high minimum distance and extremely low encoding time. While further analysis is of course welcomed in order to gain total confidence in the security of Silver, we hope and believe that initiating this approach to the design of MPC primitives will pave the way to new secure primitives with extremely attractive efficiency features.

Electronic supplementary material The online version of this chapter (https://doi.org/10.1007/978-3-030-84252-9_17) contains supplementary material, which is available to authorized users.

T. Malkin and C. Peikert (Eds.): CRYPTO 2021, LNCS 12827, pp. 502–534, 2021.
https://doi.org/10.1007/978-3-030-84252-9_17

1   Introduction

Secure multiparty computation (MPC) allows n parties to jointly evaluate a function f, while leaking no information on their own input beyond the output of the function. It is a fundamental problem in cryptography, which has received considerable attention since its introduction in the seminal works of Yao [Yao86], and Goldreich, Micali, and Wigderson [GMW87b, GMW87a]. While early feasibility results for MPC were mainly of theoretical interest, MPC protocols have enjoyed tremendous improvements in the past decade.

Oblivious transfers (OT) are perhaps the most fundamental building block for MPC protocols. In a random OT, two parties receive respectively (s_0, s_1) and (s_b, b), where (s_0, s_1) are two random *strings*, and b is a random *selection bit*. Random OT is a complete primitive for secure computation [Kil88] , and modern MPC protocols rely on it. Efficiency improvements in protocols for generating OTs directly translate into improvements for a plethora of MPC protocols.

OT Extension. A long line of work, initiated with the breakthrough work of [IKNP03], has therefore sought to develop increasingly efficient protocols for generating a large number of random OTs. At a high level, OT extension protocols [IKNP03, KOS15, KKRT16, OOS17] turns a small number of base OTs into a near-arbitrary number of OTs, using only cheap operations. The latest generation of these protocols, initiated in [BCG+17], leverages the notion of pseudorandom correlation generators (PCGs) [BCGI18, BCG+19b] to enable the construction of extremely efficient OT extension protocols. This line of work recently culminated with the protocols of [BCG+19a, SGRR19, WYKW20, YWL+20].

Silent OT Extension. While PCGs allow for very efficient constructions of OT extension, this is not their main *claim to fame*: perhaps their most remarkable feature is that they allow the construction of *silent* OT extension protocols. A silent protocol has the property that: after a short interaction, with communication and computation essentially independent of the target number of OTs, the parties can locally store small correlated seeds. Then, the parties can later retrieve these seeds, and *without any further interaction* stretch them into a very large number of OTs. Unfortunately, while the protocols of [BCG+19a] enjoy the silent feature, the running time improvements in [SGRR19, WYKW20, YWL+20] were achieved at the cost of sacrificing this crucial property.

1.1   Our Results

In this work, we design new protocols for silent oblivious transfer extension and silent vector oblivious linear evaluation (VOLE). The latter is defined over a field $\mathbb{F}$ and allows a receiver with input $x \in \mathbb{F}$ to obtain $x \cdot \mathbf{a} + \mathbf{b}$ from a sender with input vectors $(\mathbf{a}, \mathbf{b})$ over $\mathbb{F}$. VOLE is another important building block in some of the most prominent secure computation tasks; e.g. the current most efficient private set intersection [RS21]. We call our (family of) protocols *Silver*, which stands for SILent Vole and oblivious transfER. In addition its silent feature, Silver exhibits extremely good performances, significantly outperforming the most efficient OT extension protocols [IKNP03, YWL+20] on all fronts.

At the heart of our results is a radical departure from previous works on secure computation. To put it bluntly, *we decidedly give up on provable security reductions to any well-studied assumption*. Instead, our protocols are based on the conjectured hardness of decoding new, *heuristically designed* linear codes (or, equivalently, the hardness of a new learning parity with noise (LPN) variant). Our approach for building these new linear codes is much closer in spirit to the de facto standard approach for building efficient block ciphers and hash functions in symmetric cryptography: using a general framework that encompasses essentially all known attacks on LPN and syndrome decoding, we identify the core properties that guarantee resistance of our new assumptions against existing attacks. Then, we extract a number of fundamental design criteria which guide the design of codes with these properties. Eventually, we rely on these design criteria together with extensive simulations to experimentally identify, with good confidence, the codes that exhibit the best properties for our constructions, while plausibly leading to very hard instances of the syndrome decoding problem.

1.2   Philosophy of Our Approach

The construction of a cryptographic primitive or protocol can follow two complementary design strategies: a *top-down* approach, which starts from well-established cryptographic assumptions and aims at finding the most efficient construction whose security provably reduces to these assumptions, or a *bottom-up* approach, which tries to find the minimal construction that resists all known attacks, and relies on heuristic design criteria to build an intuition about the concrete security. Traditionally, secure computation has focused on the former, while symmetric cryptography (e.g. block cipher design) followed the latter.

The top-down approach has many attractive features – it deepens our theoretical understanding of the feasibility of cryptographic primitives, enlightens their relation to other primitives, and allows us to spend cryptanalytic efforts on a small set of assumptions. However, this sometimes comes at a huge cost in terms of efficiency: there is often a large gap between the best efficiency which can be achieved from well-established assumptions, and the efficiency which can be achieved with heuristic designs (consider the efficiency gap between SHA-256 and discrete-logarithm-based hash functions). When (our theoretical understanding of) a cryptographic primitive reaches a sufficient level of maturity, it is natural to envision the alternative bottom-up approach, in order to achieve real-world efficiency. This is the position that we advocate for in this work.

In the same way that symmetric cryptography has identified core families of attacks (e.g. linear and differential) and extracted a set of design principles for constructing primitives which plausibly resists them (e.g. substitution-permutation networks), our aim is to initiate the study of the most fundamental MPC primitives, oblivious transfer and its variants, under this angle. Pursuing this approach has the potential of yielding considerable efficiency improvements for MPC and strikes us as a natural next step for putting the efficiency of MPC primitives on par with that of symmetric primitives.

Our work being the first (to our knowledge) to study OT under the lens of heuristic cryptographic design, our constructions should of course be treated with the necessary caution. We invested a considerable effort in developing a rigorous understanding of which design criteria are likely to yield secure and efficient constructions, and relied on extensive experimental simulations to validate that our candidates satisfy these criteria; however, further study is welcomed in order to gain total confidence in their security. Given that Silver withstands the test of time, it will allow for significant improvements for numerous MPC protocols. And if not, we are confident that our analysis will motivate further constructions and analyses from which secure and efficient candidates will emerge.

1.3   Overview of Our Methodology

Our starting point is the recent line of work on pseudorandom correlation generators (PCG) [BCG+17,BCGI18,BCG+19b]. PCGs allow to securely generate long, pseudorandom correlated strings, using minimal communication. Among the most remarkable achievements of this line of work is *silent oblivious transfer extensions* (SOT extension) [BCG+19a,SGRR19]. These protocols have two phases: (1) the two parties interact to distributively generate short correlated seeds with communication/computation essentially independent of the target number of OTs; (2) the parties locally expand the seeds, without any interaction, into a large number of pseudorandom OTs. Afterwards, these OTs can be converted into chosen-input OTs using standard methods. Very recently, efficiency improvements were obtained by [YWL+20,WYKW20]. However, this came at the cost of sacrificing the silent feature. In practice, the ability to confine the bulk of the computation to an entirely offline phase, is a crucial efficiency feature.

The SOT Protocol of [BCG+19a]**.** Our approach builds upon the protocol of [BCG+19a]. Let us briefly recall its high level intuition:

1. the parties generate additive shares of $x \cdot \mathbf{e}$, where $x \in \mathbb{F}$ is known to the sender, and $\mathbf{e} \in \mathbb{F}^n$ is a random *sparse* vector, known to the receiver.
2. they multiply the shares of $x \cdot \mathbf{e}$ with a public matrix G, obtaining shares of $x \cdot \mathbf{a}$, for $\mathbf{a} = \mathbf{e} \cdot G^\mathsf{T}$. Given a uniform G, $\mathbf{a}$ is pseudorandom under LPN.
3. Optionally, the shares can be hashed to generate pseudorandom OTs.

Generating additive shares of $x \cdot \mathbf{e}$ is extremely efficient, requiring merely two calls to AES for each entry of the vector. The matrix-vector multiplication, however, is the bulk of the computation: in [BCG+19a], G is a matrix over $\mathbb{F}_2^{k \times n}$, where k is the target number of OTs and $n = c \cdot k$ for some small constant $c > 1$. MPC protocols commonly require a number of OTs in the millions (if not more), making this step impractical unless G has some structure that allows for fast matrix-vector multiplication. This leads to a tradeoff between efficiency and confidence in the security: when H is a truly random matrix, the multiplication is impractical, but security reduces to the standard syndrome decoding/LPN assumption. Structured matrices give better efficiency, but security reduces to syndrome decoding variants which are less well-understood.

[BCG+19a] settled for a reasonable middle ground, by letting G be a random matrix with a quasi-cyclic structure. On the one hand, this structure allows for matrix-vector multiplication in quasilinear time using fast Fourier transform; on the other hand, the underlying assumption (hardness of decoding quasi-cyclic linear codes) has been used in candidate post-quantum code-based cryptographic primitives submitted to the NIST competition, and are therefore relatively well studied. While this choice leads to a reasonably efficient construction, it remains somewhat unsatisfying: it seems very likely that there exists alternative choices for G which have significantly better efficiency, yet still are secure.

However, the particular set of constraints of silent OT extension is very different from all previous coding theory primitives: typically the dimension of the code is minimized, allow high noise rate, and rely on codes with a hidden structure to enable efficient decoding given a secret. In contrast, in the SOT application, the code dimension scales with the target number of OTs (hence typically millions), the noise rate must remain very low, and no hidden structure or efficient decoding property is required. As a result, there exists no well-established assumption regarding codes tailored for our unusual set of constraints.

Our Approach: A Design Methodology for Constructing G. In this work, we choose to approach the problem differently. Let us call a public matrix $G \in \mathbb{F}_2^{k \times n}$ *SOT-friendly* if it satisfies the following two properties:

- Security: it is infeasible to distinguish $\mathbf{e} \cdot G^\mathsf{T}$ from uniform (for sparse $\mathbf{e}$).
- Efficiency: the mapping $\mathbf{x} \rightarrow \mathbf{x} \cdot G^\mathsf{T}$ can be computed in *strict linear time*.

We develop a methodology for constructing SOT-friendly matrices by directly identifying some core structural properties of G which guarantee that distinguishing $\mathbf{e} \cdot G^\mathsf{T}$ from random cannot be done using essentially all known attacks on LPN and code-based cryptographic primitives. Yet the mapping $\mathbf{x} \rightarrow \mathbf{x} \cdot G^\mathsf{T}$ can be computed in strict linear time. Our methodology does not "start from zero": it builds upon well-known results related to breaking these assumptions.

1.4   Our Design Criteria

The first property can be stated in one sentence: G *should generate a code with large minimum distance*. For the second property, we focus on the following sufficient condition: we restrict our attention to matrices G which have a *sparse parity-check matrix H* (i.e., H is a sparse matrix in $\mathbb{F}_2^{m \times n}$ such that $H^\mathsf{T} G = 0$) such that H are in *approximate lower triangular form*.

Large Minimum Distance and Security. Given a matrix G, the problem of distinguishing $\mathbf{e} \cdot G^\mathsf{T}$ from random (for a random sparse vector $\mathbf{e}$) is the *decisional syndrome decoding problem* with respect to G^T. The name LPN is commonly used to denote the syndrome decoding assumption in the cryptographic community. As such, we will use both terms interchangeably. It is well-known that distinguishing $\mathbf{e} \cdot G^\mathsf{T}$ reduces to the following problem: given a parity-check matrix

H of G, distinguish the distribution $\{\mathbf{b} = \mathbf{x} \cdot H + \mathbf{e}\}$ (where $\mathbf{x}$ is a uniformly random vector over $\mathbb{F}_2^m$ and $\mathbf{e}$ is a random length-n sparse vector) from the uniform distribution (indeed, if $\mathbf{b}$ is indistinguishable from random, then so is $\mathbf{b} \cdot G^\mathsf{T} = (\mathbf{x} \cdot H + \mathbf{e}) \cdot G^\mathsf{T} = \mathbf{e} \cdot G^\mathsf{T})$, which is the learning parity with noise assumption, with dimension n and number of samples m, for the code matrix H. Both LPN and the syndrome decoding problem have been heavily studied in the past decades, and many attacks have been developed. A core observation (which is folklore, and was made explicitly e.g. in [BCG+20]) is that essentially all known attacks share a common high level structure: *the distinguisher computes a linear function in the samples $\mathbf{b}$* (but can depend arbitrarily on the matrix H). But if the code generated by G has large minimum distance d, the distribution $H \cdot \mathbf{x}$ for random $\mathbf{x}$ must be d-wise independent, which implies that no weight-$t \leq d$ linear function $\mathbf{v}^\mathsf{T} \cdot \mathbf{b}$ of $\mathbf{b} = \mathbf{x} \cdot H + \mathbf{e}$ can possibly distinguish it from random. However, if $\mathbf{v}$ has high weight, then the distribution of $\mathbf{v}^\mathsf{T} \cdot \mathbf{e}$ for a random sparse vector $\mathbf{e}$ is close to uniform, and so is $\mathbf{v}^\mathsf{T} \cdot \mathbf{b}$. In this work, we formalize this folklore observation, and use it to derive a concrete heuristic for choosing the parameters of an SOT-friendly matrix. Our concrete heuristic is the following:

If two codes have the same minimum distance & dimensions, their decision syndrome decoding problems likely have the same level of security.

Therefore, when choosing concrete parameters, we will use as a baseline the codes underlying well-studied syndrome decoding variants (e.g. random linear codes in syndrome decoding, or LDPC codes in Alekhnovich's assumption [Ale03]) and set parameters to achieve the same minimum distance that these codes exhibit. We make two additional comments before moving on to the second property:

- In practice, it is generally very hard to compute the minimum distance of a family of codes. We will provide some efficient concrete choices where provable bounds exists. However, in our most efficient instantiations, we will instead rely on extensive simulations to analyze the minimum distance of the code family using an optimized *minimum distance estimator*, from which we will heuristically derive the minimum distance on large dimensions.
- In existing attacks against LPN/syndrome decoding, the number of noisy coordinates plays a crucial role. However, it has a small impact on the overall efficiency of the SOT: scaling the noise by some factor increases the (very small) amount of communication and computation in the first phase, but has no impact on the second phase. Therefore, even if our hypothesis turns out to be too aggressive, we can actually significantly increase the security level, by increasing the number of coordinates, at a minor cost.

Linear-Time Encodable LDPC Codes. Low-density parity-check codes (LDPC) have a sparse parity-check H, were introduced in the seminal work of Gallagher [Gal62], and are among the most well-studied objects in coding theory. Certain random LDPC codes are known to exhibit a good minimum distance [Gal62] and can be decoded efficiently. On the other hand, their encoding time (i.e., the time to evaluate the mapping $\mathbf{x} \rightarrow \mathbf{x} \cdot G$) grows quadratically with the dimension in general. Due to the transposition principle (Sect. 4), our linear map $\mathbf{x} \to \mathbf{x} \cdot G^{\mathsf{T}}$ is efficient if and only if LDPC encoding $\mathbf{x} \to \mathbf{x} \cdot G$ is. Hence, finding LDPC codes whose generating matrix is SOT-friendly boils down to finding linear-time LDPC codes with large distance.

Achieving Fast Encoding and High Minimum Distance. Guided by the above, we therefore seek to construct new families of structured LDPC codes which simultaneously appear to achieve high minimum distance, yet can be encoded extremely efficiently with (our optimized variant of) the g-ALT encoder of Richardson and Urbanke [RU01] as presented in Sect. 4. Here, we use as a starting point the Tillich-Zémor (TZ) family of codes [TZ06]. TZ codes have appealing features in our setting: they provably achieve *almost* linear minimum distance, and can be encoded in linear time. However, their structure is also sub-optimal in our specific setting: their code is not cache friendly and has sublinear distance due to degree-2 variable nodes. In [TZ06], the presence of these degree-2 variable nodes is motivated by the fact that they allow for high performance iterative decoding. In contrast, our application does not require any decoding property whatsoever. Hence, in Sect. 6 we refine the TZ codes to tailor them to our setting, improving the concrete minimum distance and encoding time.

We achieve this by iteratively refining our design, using extensive simulations to track the presence of *bad local structures* which, when they show up, lead to worse minimum distance guarantees. We fine-tune the structure of the matrix to minimize the number of cache misses in the encoding algorithm, which have a significant performance impact. To fine-tune the best possible choices of parameters in the low cache-misses setting, we compute, for many randomly generated choices of parameters, the average minimum distance and worst-case minimum distance over 10,000+ random samples of the code matrix.

1.5 Efficiency

After performing this iterative sequence of refinements, we end up with a variety of candidate new LDPC codes, which we call *Silver codes*. We use our Silver codes to instantiate the code matrix in the silent OT extension protocol of [BCG+19a], which we also generalize to the setting of VOLE. We implemented Silver, our protocol for SILent Vole and oblivious transfER, using our most optimized code; our implementation is available at libOTe [Rin]. We compare Silver to the best existing OT extension protocols: the standard IKNP protocol [IKNP03], which remains to date the most efficient protocol in the "unlimited bandwidth" setting, the recent protocol of Yang et al. [YWL+20], which provides the best concrete performance in natural bandwidth settings (from 10 Mbps to 5 Gbps), and the silent OT extension protocol of Boyle et al. [BCG+19a], which is the most efficient protocol that enjoys the silent feature. When generating 10^7 OTs on one core of a standard laptop, our protocol requires only 300 ms of computation and 122 KB of communication. In comparison, IKNP requires 58% more computation and ~1300× more communication, [YWL+20] requires ~4× more computation and ~14× more communication, and [BCG+19a] requires 19× more computation (since our protocol is essentially their SOT with a Silver code, the communication is identical). In a setting with 100 Mbps of bandwidth, Silver is at least 50 times more efficient than IKNP even when ignoring all costs beyond those of communication, and at least 4× and 19× more efficient than [YWL+20] and [BCG+19a] respectively, even when ignoring all communication costs.

2 Preliminaries

Throughout the work we will using $[a, b]$ to denote the set $\{a, ..., b\}$. $[n]$ is short-hand for $[1, n]$. $=$ will denote mathematical equality while $x := y$ denotes defining x to be equal to y. $|\mathbf{v}|$ denotes the Hamming weight of vector $\mathbf{v}$. Matrix and vector horizontal concatenation is denoted as $[X|Y]$. Due to space restriction, we defer preliminaries on the silent OT extension protocol of [BCG+19a] to Appendix A of the Supplementary Material.

2.1 Preliminaries on Bias

Definition 1 (Bias of a Distribution). *Given a distribution $\mathcal{D}$ over $\mathbb{F}^n$ and a vector $\mathbf{u} \in \mathbb{F}^n$, the bias of $\mathcal{D}$ with respect to $\mathbf{u}$, denoted $\mathsf{bias}_{\mathbf{u}}(\mathcal{D})$, is equal to*

$$\mathsf{bias}_{\mathbf{u}}(\mathcal{D}) = |\mathbb{E}_{\mathbf{x} \sim \mathcal{D}}[\mathbf{u}^\mathsf{T} \cdot \mathbf{x}] - \mathbb{E}_{\mathbf{x} \sim \mathcal{U}_n}[\mathbf{u}^\mathsf{T} \cdot \mathbf{x}]| = \left| \mathbb{E}_{\mathbf{x} \sim \mathcal{D}}[\mathbf{u}^\mathsf{T} \cdot \mathbf{x}] - \frac{1}{|\mathbb{F}|} \right|,$$

where $\mathcal{U}_n$ denotes the uniform distribution over $\mathbb{F}^n$. The bias of $\mathcal{D}$, denoted $\mathsf{bias}(\mathcal{D})$, is the maximum bias of $\mathcal{D}$ with respect to any nonzero vector $\mathbf{u}$.

Given t distributions $(\mathcal{D}_1, \cdots, \mathcal{D}_t)$ over $\mathbb{F}_2^n$, we denote by $\bigoplus_{i \leq t} \mathcal{D}_i$ the distribution obtained by *independently* sampling $\mathbf{v}_i \xleftarrow{\$} \mathcal{D}_i$ for $i = 1$ to t and outputting $\mathbf{v} \leftarrow \mathbf{v}_1 \oplus \cdots \oplus \mathbf{v}_t$. We will use the following bias of the exclusive-or (cf. [Shp09]).

Lemma 2. *Let $t \in \mathbb{N}$ be an integer, and let $(\mathcal{D}_1, \cdots, \mathcal{D}_t)$ be t independent distributions over $\mathbb{F}_2^n$. Then $\mathsf{bias}(\bigoplus_{i \leq t} \mathcal{D}_i) \leq 2^{t-1} \cdot \prod_{i=1}^t \mathsf{bias}(\mathcal{D}_i) \leq \min_{i \leq t}\mathsf{bias}(\mathcal{D}_i)$.*

Eventually, let $\mathsf{Ber}_r(\mathbb{F}_2)$ denote the Bernoulli distribution that outputs 1 with probability r, and 0 otherwise. More generally, we denote by $\mathsf{Ber}_r(\mathbb{F})$ the distribution that outputs a uniformly random element of $\mathbb{F}$ with probability r, and 0 otherwise. We will use a standard simple lemma for computing the bias of a XOR of Bernoulli samples:

Lemma 3 (Piling-up lemma). *For any $0 < r < 1/2$ and any integer n, given n random variables $X_1, \cdots, X_n$ i.i.d. to $\mathsf{Ber}_r(\mathbb{F}_2)$, it holds that $\Pr[\bigoplus_{i=1}^n X_i = 0] = 1/2 + (1 - 2r)^n/2$.*

2.2 Syndrome Decoding and Learning Parity with Noise

Our constructions will rely on new variants of the learning parity with noise (LPN) assumption (more accurately, a variant of the syndrome decoding assumption). The LPN assumption over a field $\mathbb{F}$ states, informally, that no adversary can distinguish $(A, A \cdot \mathbf{s} + \mathbf{e})$ from $(A, \mathbf{b})$, where A is sampled from the set of generating matrices of some linear code ensemble, $\mathbf{s}$ is a uniform secret vector over $\mathbb{F}$, $\mathbf{e}$ is a *noise vector* sampled from some distribution over $\mathbb{F}$-vectors and typically sparse. $\mathbf{b}$ is a uniform vector over $\mathbb{F}$. More formally, we define the LPN assumption over a ring $\mathcal{R}$ with dimension k, number of samples n, w.r.t. a code generation algorithm $\mathbf{C}$, and a noise distribution $\mathcal{D}$:

Definition 4 (Primal LPN). *Let* $\mathcal{D}(\mathcal{R}) = \{\mathcal{D}_{k,n}(\mathcal{R})\}_{k,n \in \mathbb{N}}$ *denote a family of efficiently sampleable distributions over a ring* $\mathcal{R}$, *such that for any* $k, n \in \mathbb{N}$, $\mathsf{Im}(\mathcal{D}_{k,n}(\mathcal{R})) \subseteq \mathcal{R}^n$. *Let* $\mathbf{C}$ *be a probabilistic code generation algorithm such that* $\mathbf{C}(k, n, \mathcal{R})$ *outputs a matrix* $A \in \mathcal{R}^{n \times k}$. *For dimension* $k = k(\lambda)$, *number of samples (or block length)* $n = n(\lambda)$, *and ring* $\mathcal{R} = \mathcal{R}(\lambda)$, *the (primal)* $(\mathcal{D}, \mathbf{C}, \mathcal{R})$-$\mathsf{LPN}(k, n)$ *assumption states that*

$$\{(A, \mathbf{b}) \mid A \xleftarrow{\$} \mathbf{C}(k, n, \mathcal{R}), \mathbf{e} \xleftarrow{\$} \mathcal{D}_{k,n}(\mathcal{R}), \mathbf{s} \xleftarrow{\$} \mathbb{F}^k, \mathbf{b} \leftarrow A \cdot \mathbf{s} + \mathbf{e}\}$$

$$\overset{c}{\approx} \{(A, \mathbf{b}) \mid A \xleftarrow{\$} \mathbf{C}(k, n, \mathcal{R}), \mathbf{b} \xleftarrow{\$} \mathcal{R}^n\}.$$

The above definition is very general, and captures in particular not only the standard LPN assumption and its variants, but also assumptions such as LWE or the multivariate quadratic assumption. However, we will typically restrict our attention to assumptions where the noise distribution outputs sparse vectors with high probability. The standard LPN assumption with dimension k, noise rate r, and n samples is obtained by setting A to be a uniformly random matrix over $\mathbb{F}_2^{n \times k}$, and the noise distribution to be the Bernoulli distribution $\mathsf{Ber}_r^n(\mathbb{F}_2)$, where each coordinate of $\mathbf{e}$ is independently set to 1 with probability r and to 0 with probability $1 - r$. The term "primal" in the above definition comes from the fact that the assumption can come in two equivalent form: the primal form as above, but also a *dual form*: viewing A as the transpose of the parity check matrix H of a linear code generated by G a matrix, i.e. $A = H^\mathsf{T}$, the hardness of distinguishing $H^\mathsf{T} \cdot \mathbf{x} + \mathbf{e}$ from random is equivalent to the hardness of distinguishing $G \cdot (H^\mathsf{T} \cdot \mathbf{x} + \mathbf{e}) = G \cdot \mathbf{e} = \mathbf{e} \cdot G^\mathsf{T}$ from random (since $G^\mathsf{T} \cdot H = 0$).

3 On the Hardness of LPN for Structured LDPC Codes

The learning parity with noise assumption is one of the most fundamental assumptions of cryptography, introduced in the work of [BFKL94]; related problems were used even earlier [McE78]. The hardness of syndrome decoding and its variants (which is equivalent to LPN under our definition – see above) has also been intensely studied in coding theory, starting with the seminal work of Prange [Pra62] (under the name the of syndrome decoding), in learning theory (see e.g. [FGKP09] and references therein), and in random CSP theory (starting with the seminal work of Feige [Fei02]) – all with many follow ups.

Over the past few decades, a tremendous number of attacks against LPN have been proposed. These attacks include, but are not limited to, attacks based on Gaussian elimination and the BKW algorithm [BKW00,Lyu05,LF06,EKM17] and variants based on covering codes [ZJW16, BV16, BTV16, GJL20], information set decoding attacks [Pra62, Ste88, FS09, BLP11, MMT11, BJMM12, MO15, EKM17, BM18], statistical decoding attacks [AJ01, FKI06, Ove06, DAT17], generalized birthday attacks [Wag02, Kir11], linearization attacks [BM97, Saa07], attacks based on finding low weight code vectors [Zic17], or on finding correlations with low-degree polynomials [ABG+14, BR17].

A Unified Framework for Attacks Against LPN. In light of this situation, it would be excessively cumbersome, when introducing a new variant of LPN, to go over the entire literature of existing attacks and analyze their potential impact on the new variant. The crucial observation, however, is that this is not necessary, as *all the above attacks* (and more generally, essentially all known attacks against LPN and its variants) fit in a common framework, usually denoted the *linear test framework*. Furthermore, the asymptotic resistance of any LPN variant against any attack from the linear test framework can be deduced from two simple properties of the underlying code ensemble and noise distribution. Informally, if

- the code generated by G has high minimum distance, and
- for any large enough subset S of coordinates, with high probability over the choice of $\mathbf{e} \leftarrow \mathcal{D}$, at least one of the coordinates in S of $\mathbf{e}$ will be nonzero,

then the LPN assumption with code matrix G and noise distribution $\mathcal{D}$ cannot be broken by any attack from the linear test framework. We will formalize this and build on it to analyze the asymptotic security of our new LPN variants.

We stress that this crucial observation is not new to our work: a similar observation was explicitly made in previous works [ADI+17, BCG+20], where it was also used to analyze the security of new LPN variants. Even long before these works, distributions whose outputs look random to linear tests, called *low-bias sample spaces,* have been the subject of a rich and fruitful line of work which was initiated in the seminal work of Naor and Naor [NN90], and the relevance of linear tests to the security analysis LPN assumptions seems to have been at least somewhat folklore. Still, we believe that it will be beneficial and instructive to the reader to present this argument in a unified way with explicit bounds.

3.1   The Linear Test Framework

The common feature of essentially all known attacks against LPN and its variants is that the distinguisher can be implemented as a (nonzero) *linear function of the samples* (the linear test), where the coefficients of the linear combination can depend arbitrarily on the code matrix. Therefore, all these attacks can be formulated as distinguishing LPN samples from random samples by checking whether the output of some linear test (with coefficients depending arbitrarily on the code matrix) is biased away from the uniform distribution. Formally,

Definition 5 (Security against Linear Test). *Let $\mathbb{F}$ be an arbitrary finite field, and let $\mathcal{D} = \{\mathcal{D}_{m,n}\}_{m,n \in \mathbb{N}}$ denote a family of noise distributions over $\mathbb{F}^n$. Let $\mathbf{C}$ be a probabilistic code generation algorithm such that $\mathbf{C}(m,n)$ outputs a matrix $A \in \mathbb{F}^{n \times m}$. Let $\varepsilon, \delta : \mathbb{N} \mapsto [0,1]$ be two functions. We say that the*

$(\mathcal{D}, \mathbf{C}, \mathbb{F})$-LPN$(m, n)$ *assumption with dimension* $m = m(\lambda)$ *and* $n = n(\lambda)$ *samples is* (ε, δ)-*secure against linear tests if for any (possibly inefficient) adversary* $\mathcal{A}$ *which, on input a matrix* $A \in \mathbb{F}^{n \times m}$, *outputs a nonzero* $\mathbf{v} \in \mathbb{F}^n$, *it holds that*

$$\Pr[A \xleftarrow{\$} \mathbf{C}(m, n), \mathbf{v} \xleftarrow{\$} \mathcal{A}(A) \; : \; \mathsf{bias_v}(\mathcal{D}_A) \geq \varepsilon(\lambda)] \leq \delta(\lambda),$$

where $\mathcal{D}_A$ *denotes the distribution induced by sampling* $\mathbf{s} \xleftarrow{\$} \mathbb{F}_2^m$, $\mathbf{e} \leftarrow \mathcal{D}_{m,n}$, *and outputting the LPN samples* $A \cdot \mathbf{s} + \mathbf{e}$.

The following observation is folklore, and was made explicitly e.g. in [BCG+20]:

Observation 1. *Existing attacks against LPN (as listed above) can be cast as instances of the linear test framework. Therefore, none of these attacks can provide a polynomial-time distinguisher against any LPN assumption that is provably* (ε, δ)-*secure against linear tests, for any negligible functions* (ε, δ).

[ADI+17] went even further and explicitly conjectured that for any LPN variant with a sparse code matrix, the runtime of the best possible attack against LPN is essentially $\mathsf{poly}(1/\varepsilon)$, *i.e.*, the number of times a linear test attack must be repeated until the bias becomes noticeable. See Assumption 1.

3.2   Dual Distance and Security Against Linear Tests

Following [ADI+17], we call *dual distance* of a matrix M, and write $\mathsf{dd}(M)$, the largest integer d such that every subset of d rows of M is linearly independent. The name "dual distance" stems from the fact that the $\mathsf{dd}(M)$ is also the minimum distance of the dual of the code generated by M (*i.e.*, the code generated by the left null space of M). The following lemma is folklore:

Lemma 6. *Let* $\mathcal{D} = \{\mathcal{D}_{m,n}\}_{m,n \in \mathbb{N}}$ *denote a family of noise distributions over* $\mathbb{F}^n$. *Let* $\mathbf{C}$ *be a probabilistic code generation algorithm s.t.* $\mathbf{C}(m, n) \to A \in \mathbb{F}^{n \times m}$. *Then for any* $d \in \mathbb{N}$, *the* $(\mathcal{D}, \mathbf{C}, \mathbb{F})$-LPN$(m, n)$ *assumption with dimension* $m = m(\lambda)$ *and* $n = n(\lambda)$ *samples is* $(\varepsilon_d, \delta_d)$-*secure against linear tests, where*

$$\varepsilon_d = \max_{|\mathbf{v}| > d} \mathsf{bias_v}(\mathcal{D}_{m,n}), \qquad and \qquad \delta_d = \Pr_{A \xleftarrow{\$} \mathbf{C}(m,n)} [\mathsf{dd}(A) \geq d].$$

Proof. The proof is straightforward: fix any integer d. Then with probability at least δ_d, $\mathsf{dd}(A) \geq d$. Consider any (possibly unbounded) adversary $\mathcal{A}$ outputting $\mathbf{v}$. Two cases can occur:

- Either $|\mathbf{v}| \leq d \leq \mathsf{dd}(A)$. In this case, the bias with respect to $\mathbf{v}$ of the distribution $\{A \cdot \mathbf{s} \mid \mathbf{s} \xleftarrow{\$} \mathbb{F}^m\}$ is 0 (since this distribution is d-wise independent). Since the bias of the XOR of two distribution is at most the smallest bias among them (see Lemma 2; the same holds for the bias with respect to any fixed $\mathbf{v}$), we get $\mathsf{bias}(\mathcal{D}_A) = 0$.
- Or $|\mathbf{v}| > d$; in which case, applying Lemma 2 again, $\mathsf{bias}(\mathcal{D}_A) \leq \mathsf{bias}(\mathcal{D}_{m,n})$.

Security of LPN with Random Codes. An instructive example is to consider the case of LPN with a uniformly random code matrix over $\mathbb{F}_2$, and a Bernoulli noise distribution $\mathcal{D}_{m,n} = \mathsf{Ber}_r^n(\mathbb{F}_2)$, for some noise rate r. The probability that d random vectors over $\mathbb{F}_2^m$ are linearly independent is at least

$$\prod_{i=0}^{d-1} \frac{2^m - 2^i}{2^m} \geq (1 - 2^{d-1-m})^d \geq 1 - 2^{2d-m}.$$

Therefore, by a union bound, the probability that a random matrix $A \xleftarrow{\$} \mathbb{F}_2^{n \times m}$ satisfies $\mathsf{dd}(A) \geq d$ is at least $1 - \binom{n}{d} \cdot 2^{2d-m} \geq 1 - 2^{(2+\log n)d - m}$. On the other hand, for any d and any $\mathbf{v}$ with $|\mathbf{v}| > d$, we have by Lemma 3:

$$\Pr[\mathbf{e} \leftarrow \mathsf{Ber}_r^n(\mathbb{F}_2) \; : \; \mathbf{v}^\mathsf{T} \cdot \mathbf{e} = 1] = \frac{1 - (1 - 2r)^d}{2},$$

hence $\mathsf{bias}_\mathbf{v}(\mathsf{Ber}_r^n(\mathbb{F}_2)) = (1-2r)^d \leq e^{-2rd}$. In particular, setting $d = O(m/\log n)$ suffices to guarantee that with probability at least $\delta_d = 1 - 2^{-O(m)}$, the LPN samples will have bias (with respect to any possible nonzero vector $\mathbf{v}$) ε_d at most $e^{-O(rm/\log n)}$. Hence, any attack that fits in the linear test framework against the standard LPN assumption with dimension m and noise rate r requires of the order of $e^{O(rm/\log n)}$ iterations. Note that this lower bound still leaves a gap with respect to the best known linear attacks, which require time of the order of $e^{O(rm)}$, $e^{O(rm/\log\log m)}$, and $e^{O(rm/\log m)}$ when $n = O(m)$, $n = \mathsf{poly}(m)$, and $n = 2^{O(m/\log m)}$ respectively [BKW00, Lyu05, EKM17].

3.3 SOT from Asymptotically Good Linear-Time Encodable Codes

Abstracting out the unnecessary details, recall that the construction of silent oblivious transfer extension introduced in [BCG+19b, BCG+19a] and recalled in Appendix A, relies on the following assumption: given a large public matrix $G \in \mathbb{F}_2^{k \times n}$, is such that $n = c \cdot k$ for some small constant $c > 1$ (e.g. $c = 2$), it should be infeasible to distinguish $\mathbf{e} \cdot G^\mathsf{T}$ from random, where $\mathbf{e}$ is a uniformly random weight-t vector. This corresponds to the dual-LPN assumption, which is equivalent to the primal-LPN assumption with matrix $H \in \mathbb{F}_2^{m \times n}$, where H is the parity check for generator G; i.e., $G^\mathsf{T} \cdot H = 0$.

A Selection Principle for LPN with Structured Code. Based on the previous discussions, for any linear code ensemble $\mathbf{C}$ which outputs matrices $H \xleftarrow{\$} \mathbf{C}$ having a large distance w.h.p., it is reasonable to conjecture that the corresponding primal-LPN assumption will hold (since a contradiction would imply a fundamentally different type of attack than existing ones). This conjecture was formally stated in [ADI+17] for the case of all *sparse* code ensembles:

Assumption 1 (Assumption 6 in [ADI+17]). *For every prime-order field* $\mathbb{F}$, *every polynomial* $m(\lambda), n(\lambda)$, *every constant* t, *every real* $r \in (0, 1/2)$, *and every t-sparse matrix* $A \in \mathbb{F}^{n \times m}$, *the following holds: Any circuit of size* $T = \exp(\Omega_r(\mathsf{dd}(A)))$ *cannot distinguish* $(A \cdot \mathbf{s} + \mathbf{e})$ *for* $\mathbf{s} \xleftarrow{\$} \mathbb{F}_2^m, \mathbf{e} \leftarrow \mathsf{Ber}_r(\mathbb{F})$ *from* *the uniform distribution with advantage better than $1/T$ ($\Omega_r(x)$ denotes $\Omega(x)$, where the hidden constant may depend on the noise rate r).*

Noise Weight versus Minimum Distance. The above discussions allows to make a simple, yet powerful observation: for typical noise distributions, including the Bernoulli distribution with parameter t/n, the *regular* noise distribution (concatenations of t length-n/t unit vectors), and the *exact* noise distribution (random t-sparse vectors), the running time of linear attacks is lower bounded by a term of the form $e^{c \cdot rd}$ for some constant c, where $r = t/n$ is the noise rate and d is the minimum distance. This suggests the following *safeguard*: if a SOT code exhibits a much worse typical minimum distance behavior than estimated (which in our case would be very surprising but theoretically possible), say, the true distance d is v times shorter than estimated, then same conjectured security level as before can be obtained by *scaling the number of noisy coordinates t by a factor v*. Crucially, in our SOT construction, the impact of this scaling vanishes when the number of OTs is large: it only impacts the complexity of distributing the seed (which increases by a factor v), but has no influence whatsoever, neither on the matrix multiplication part (which is the bulk of the computation) nor on the sparse vector expansion (which is the only other component whose cost scales with the target number of OTs).

Our Approach: Structured LDPC Codes. Asymptotically good families of linear-time encodable codes have been studied in the literature, with probabilistic constructions given in [GDP73, Spi96]. However, these works only targeted asymptotic efficiency. Our aim, on the other hand, is to focus on concrete efficiency, and to find codes with a large concrete minimum distance, and extremely efficient encoding. We choose to focus on structured families of LDPC codes (*i.e.*, codes whose parity-check matrix is sparse), which have been widely studied in the coding theory literature. Our rationale is based on the following observations:

- Most LDPC codes have linear minimum distance;
- Some structured families of LDPC codes admit efficient encoding algorithms;
- Some structured families of LDPC codes provably achieve both fast linear time encoding and *almost* linear minimum distance;
- Structured families of LDPC codes in the literature which do *not* exhibit linear or close-to-linear minimum distance typically satisfy a specific constraint: their Tanner graph contains a large number of degree-2 variable nodes. In contrast, we suggest candidates which admit extremely fast encoding, but do *not* exhibit this structural weakness, and can be experimentally verified to exhibit a very good minimum distance growth.
- For *random* LDPC codes, the corresponding assumption (primal LPN with a random sparse code matrix) is the Alekhnovich assumption [Ale03], an important and well-studied assumption.

3.4 Most Sparse Matrices Have Linear Dual Distance

In this section, we show that for any integer $t > 2$, most matrices in $\mathbb{F}_2^{n \times m}$ with rows of Hamming weight t have dual distance linear in m; more precisely, the fraction of such matrices with dual distance at least $\gamma \cdot k$ (for some constant γ) is at least $1 - m^{2.1-t}$. In coding-theoretic terms, it says that most *column-regular* LDPC codes have linear minimum distance, where the parity check matrix has fixed column weight. Let $W_t(\mathbb{F}_2^m)$ denote the set of all vectors in $\mathbb{F}_2^m$ with Hamming weight exactly t; we also denote by $W_t(\mathbb{F}_2^{n \times m})$ the set of all matrices in $\mathbb{F}_2^{n \times m}$ with exactly t ones per column.

Theorem 7 (Most sparse matrices have dual distance $O(m)$). *For any constant $c > 1$ and integer $t > 2$, there is a constant $\gamma = \gamma(c,t)$ such that for any large enough m, denoting $n = c \cdot m$,*

$$\Pr\left[A \xleftarrow{\$} W_t(\mathbb{F}_2^{n \times m}) \ : \ \frac{dd(A)}{m} < \gamma \right] \leq 1 - m^{2.1-t}.$$

For completeness, we provide the proof in Appendix C of the Supplementary Material; the proof is a direct adaptation to our setting of the analysis of [MST03, Section 5.3]. Building upon our analysis, we also make a key observation: random LDPC codes over *large fields* have linear minimum distance with high probability, *even when their parity-check matrix is randomly sampled with $\{0,1\}$ entries*. We discuss the implications of this observation for one of our applications, as well as its relation to previous assumptions from the literature, in Appendix C.

4 Fast LDPC Encoding

We begin with an overview of how to perform fast encoding of LDPC codes by leveraging the sparsity/structure of H. Let us first review the naive encoding method. Recall H defines the code $\mathcal{C} = \{\mathbf{c} \mid H\mathbf{c}^\mathsf{T} = 0\}$. As such, define the systematic form H' for the same code by performing elementary row operations on H to obtain $H' = [-P^T | I_{n-k}]$. Since elementary row operations do not change the null-space, we have $\mathcal{C} = \{\mathbf{c} \mid H\mathbf{c}^\mathsf{T} = 0\} = \{\mathbf{c} \mid H'\mathbf{c}^\mathsf{T} = 0\}$. Although H is sparse, $P \in \mathbb{F}^{k \times m}$ is likely dense. Let $G := [I_k|P]$ be the symmetric form generator and then encoding can be achieved by computing $\mathbf{c} := \mathbf{x}G$ for $\mathbf{x} \in \mathbb{F}^k$. The cost of this is $O(n^3)$ time to compute P and $O(n^2)$ time to compute $\mathbf{x}P$.

However, we can also use the fact that $H\mathbf{c}^\mathsf{T} = 0$ to encode $\mathbf{x}$ into $\mathbf{c}$. Recall that $c = \mathbf{x}G = [\mathbf{x}|\mathbf{c}']$ for $\mathbf{c}' := \mathbf{x}P$. Therefore we can rewrite this as

$$0 = H\mathbf{c}^\mathsf{T} = H[\mathbf{x}|\mathbf{c}']^\mathsf{T} = T\mathbf{x}^\mathsf{T} + S\mathbf{c}'^\mathsf{T} \qquad \Longleftrightarrow \qquad -T\mathbf{x}^\mathsf{T} = S\mathbf{c}'^\mathsf{T}$$

where $H = [T|S]$ and $T \in \mathbb{F}^{m \times k}, S \in \mathbb{F}^{m \times m}$. Given $\mathbf{x}$, we can compute $\mathbf{y} := -T\mathbf{x}^\mathsf{T}$ in $O(k)$ time since T is sparse. We then solve the sparse system $\mathbf{y} = S\mathbf{c}'^\mathsf{T}$. Using Gaussian elimination, this would naively require $O(m^3) = O(n^3)$ time. However, we can try to leverage the sparsity of H to achieve better efficiency.

Our starting point is the somewhat standard LDPC solving technique known as g-Approximate Lower Triangularization (g-ALT) [RU01,DP15,KS12]. The basic intuition is that this system can be solved in linear time if S is a lower triangular matrix. In particular, the entries along the diagonal should all be set to one. Later we will discuss how to ensure this is the case. The system can be solved by solving each row "independently" starting with row 1 and working down. This idea can be generalized to allow all but the last g rows of H to be triangular (see Fig. 9 in Appendix D). The last g rows are said to be part of the *gap*. As discussed in Appendix D, a parity check matrix with this form allows for encoding $\mathbf{x}$ as $\mathbf{c} = \mathbf{x}G$ in $O(n + g^2)$ time. Therefore, this remains linear so long as $g = O(\sqrt{n})$. Additionally, we present an optimization in Appendix E which reduces this to $O(n)$ at the expense of $O(g)$ communication in the protocol.

Recall that in dual LPN we wish to compute $\mathbf{u} := \mathbf{e} \cdot G^{\mathsf{T}}$ which is equivalent to primal LPN where $\mathbf{u} := \mathbf{x} \cdot H + \mathbf{e}$. Yet, the encoding algorithm described above is for computing $\mathbf{x} \cdot G$. By the transposition principle [Bor57, IKOS08], we can achieve our goal at effectively the same cost. Roughly, the transformation works by first expressing the circuit which computes $\mathbf{x} \cdot G$ as a series of matrix multiplication, $\mathbf{s}_1 := M_1 \cdot \mathbf{x}, \mathbf{s}_2 := M_2 \cdot \mathbf{s}_1, ..., \mathbf{e} := M_n \cdot \mathbf{s}_{n-1}$ such that $\mathbf{e}$ is the final output. Any circuit can be expressed in this way. Then $\mathbf{e} \cdot G^{\mathsf{T}}$ can be computed as $\mathbf{s}_{n-1} := M_n^{\mathsf{T}} \cdot \mathbf{e}, \mathbf{s}_{n-2} := M_{n-1}^{\mathsf{T}} \cdot \mathbf{s}_{n-1}, ..., \mathbf{x} := M_1^{\mathsf{T}} \cdot \mathbf{s}_1$. Refer to Appendix D for a detailed description of all the algorithms discussed in this section.

5   Estimating the Minimum Distance Empirically

Crucial to our construction is the ability to accurately determine the minimum distance of the LDPC matrix H that is employed. Computing the exact minimum distance is known to be NP-Complete [Var97] and typically infeasible for our parameter region, e.g. $n = 2^{20}$. For some LDPC distributions, it is possible to derive an asymptotic bound on the minimum distance; however, many of these have drawbacks in efficiency or distance.

To overcome this, we resort to computational approaches for estimating the minimum distance of an LDPC code ensemble. For relatively small values of n, say less than 200, we compute the exact minimum distance using the approach presented in [HIQO19]. For larger n, say less than 4000, we fall back to a standard heuristic, the noisy impulse method of [BVJD02], for upper bounding the minimum distance (which we have verified does in fact closely agree with exact minimum distance for smaller values of n). We then extrapolate the asymptotic behavior of the minimum distance for larger values of n.

5.1   Exact Minimum Distance

For computing the exact minimum distance we make use of the so-called Brouwer-Zimmerman algorithm as described in [Gra06], and implemented in [HIQO19]. Loosely speaking, this approach iteratively refines a lower and upper bound until they are equal. First, the generator matrix G is placed in systematic form $G' = [I_k | P]$. Recall that for all $\mathbf{x} \in \mathbb{F}^k \setminus \{0\}$, the corresponding codeword is $\mathbf{c} = [\mathbf{x} | \mathbf{x}P]$ and therefore clearly $|\mathbf{c}| \geq |\mathbf{x}|$. Using this observation, the algorithm proceeds by initializing the lower bound $\ell = 1$ and upper bound $u = m + 1$. All x with $|\mathbf{x}| = \ell$ are encoded as $\mathbf{c} = \mathbf{x}G$ and the upper bound u is replaced as the minimum weight over all codewords considered. While $u \neq \ell$, ℓ is incremented and the process is repeated. See [Gra06,HIQO19] for details.

The running time remains exponential in the size of the code. With careful optimizations, the implementation of [HIQO19] is capable of computing the minimum distance up to about $n = 160$. Since this is relatively small compared to the codes our protocol employs, this approach is primarily used to validate the accuracy of the so-called *noisy impulse method* which we describe next.

5.2   Upper Bounding the Minimum Distance

Our second approach for evaluating the minimum distance of a LDPC family is known as the noise impulse method [BVJD02]. Very roughly speaking, this approach tries to decode the zero codeword when one or more of the bits have been flipped. The intuition is that if the right bits are flipped, then the next closest codeword will correspond to a close-to-minimum weight codeword.

In more details, and including improvements from [XFE04], this approach considers all vectors $\mathbf{c} \in \{0, 1\}^n$ with $|\mathbf{c}| \leq w$ for some small constant w, e.g. 1 or 2. Each $\mathbf{c}$ is input into a belief propagation decoder, typically Min-Sum, which output the decoders estimates on the likelihood that each bit of $\mathbf{c}$ should be error corrected to zero or one. Since at most w bits in $\mathbf{c}$ are one and the actually minimum distance d is almost certainly more than twice w, the most likely codeword will in fact be the original all zero codeword.

However, the likelihood information contained in the decoder output can be leveraged to aid in the search of nearby non-zero codewords. Loosely speaking, belief propagation (BP) decoders work by assigning each bit of $\mathbf{c}$ a likelihood of being zero or one and updating these likelihoods in an iterative process. The initial likelihood values could be that the decoder is 95% certain that each bit is as specified by $\mathbf{c}$, i.e. an error rate of 0.05. Intuitively, at each iteration the likelihood information for each bit of $\mathbf{c}$ is updated based on how many of the corresponding parity checks pass or fail. An interpretation of this is that it reduces the likelihood values for the zero positions of $\mathbf{c}$ when they are closely related to the positions of $\mathbf{c}$ which were set to one.

The idea is then to sort the positions of $\mathbf{c}$ such that the positions which are most confidently zero are to the right. The same permutation is applied to the columns of G. Partial Gaussian elimination is applied to G s.t. the left $k \times k$ submatrix is lower triangular with ones along the diagonal. Some of the first k columns are likely linearly dependent, preventing us from making the left k columns of G lower diagonal. In this case, the dependent columns are permuted right and replaced with the next left most column of G. We then consider all (permuted) codewords with the form $\mathbf{c}^* = [\mathbf{c}_1 | \mathbf{c}_2 | 0^{n-k-t}]$ where $\mathbf{c}_2 \in \{0, 1\}^t$ has some maximum weight u, e.g. $t = 50, u = 10$. For each choice of $\mathbf{c}_2$, it is possible to compute $\mathbf{c}_1 \in \{0, 1\}^k$ via the left lower diagonal submatrix of G. The estimated upper bound the distance as the minimum weight over all $\mathbf{c}^*$ (Table 1).

Table 1. The minimum $d_{\min}$, average d_{avg} and maximum $d_{\max}$ minimum distance obtained over 100 trials for weight 5 uniform LDPC codes.

m	method	w	$d_{\min}$	d_{avg}	$d_{\max}$
20	impulse	1	2	5	6
	exact	-	2	5	6
40	impulse	1	4	8.3	10
	exact	-	4	8.3	10
60	impulse	1	8	11.44	14
	impulse	2	8	11.38	14
	exact	-	8	11.38	14
80	impulse	1	12	16.48	20
	impulse	2	12	14.86	18
	exact	-	12	14.86	18
100	impulse	1	16	22.28	26
	impulse	2	14	18.2	20

6 Code Design

Designing an efficient LDPC code for large dimension LPN offers many unique challenges. Our primary two design goals are to achieve large minimum distance, ideally linear in n, and linear time encoding. However, unlike many existing codes from the coding community, we do not care about its decoding performance or other error correcting properties. All our codes have rate $1/2$, i.e. $n/2 = m = k$.

In this section we review two existing LDPC codes, namely uniform and Tillich-Zémor Codes. After describing various benefits and drawbacks of each, we design a new highly efficient LDPC code which achieves an extremely fast linear encoding time and plausibly linear minimum distance.

6.1 Uniform LDPC

As described in Sect. 3.4, the family $W_t(\mathbb{F}_2^{n \times m})$ of uniform LDPC codes with fixed column weight t are known to have linear minimum distance with good probability. We consider the family of codes parameters by $t \in \{5, 11\}$. While the theoretical bound applies to all $t > 2$, we observe that $t = 3$ experiences very poor concrete minimum distance performance and often do not correspond to a code that can be made systematic. For $t = 5$ we observe a concrete linear minimum distance growth rate of $d_{\mathrm{avg}} = 0.28m$, $d_{\min} = 0.19m$ over 100 trials. These growth rates were obtained for $n \in [200, 800]$. Since we are interested in the worse case performance, we are mostly interested in $d_{\min}$. By increasing the weight to $t = 11$ we obtain a minimum distance growth rate of $d_{\mathrm{avg}} = 0.38m$, $d_{\min} = 0.36m$.

The hardness of syndrome decoding for uniform LDPC codes was the basis of recent proposals [BCGI18, YWL+20], and corresponds to the well-established

Alekhnovich assumption [Ale03]. While these codes turn out to be inappropriate efficiency-wise in our setting (see below), we will rely on the following heuristic to select the concrete parameters of our new codes: when we experimentally observe, with high confidence, that a distribution over codes achieves a similar average minimum distance, with a similar variance, compared to uniform LDPC codes, we heuristically estimate that the corresponding assumptions should provide a comparable level of hardness. We note that, if it turns out that this heuristic is too optimistic (which would intuitively require finding new attacks radically different from all known attacks), increasing the noise (as described in Sect. 3.3, Noise weight versus minimum distance) can be used to adjust the hardness level of the underlying assumption without significantly harming efficiency.

Shortcoming of Uniform LDPC Codes. The choice of basing security on the hardness of decoding uniform LDPC codes was motivated in previous works [BCGI18, YWL+20] by the fact that they correspond to the relatively well-established Alekhnovich assumption. However, they turn out to be a relatively poor choice in our setting. At a high level, the reason is that for distributions over random LDPC codes which do not enforce any particular structure beyond guaranteeing some conditions on the number of ones per row and column (*i.e.*, which sample the parity-check matrix uniformly conditioned on constraints on the fractions of variable and check nodes from the Tanner graph which must have a given degree), having a high minimum distance with good probability, and being linear-time encodable with the g-approximate lower triangularization algorithm, appear to be at odd, according to a conjecture of Richardson and Urbanke [RU01] (we will discuss this conjecture in more details in Sect. 6.2). This effectively justifies moving towards *structured* ensembles of LDPC codes, which also enforce some structure on the *shape* of the parity-check matrix. A prime example of codes achieving a sweet spot between having high minimum distance with good probability, and very fast encoding, is given by the Tillich-Zémor code ensemble.

6.2   Tillich-Zémor Codes

As discussed before, in order to design codes that have efficient encoders as well as good minimum distance, one must move away from random codes and consider more structured codes. As such, structured codes would offer an immediate handle on efficient encoding purely by design. On the other hand, this approaches leaves much for the desire of a more rigorous theoretical understanding of the minimum distance of such structured codes. Such questions have been posed in the past amongst the members of the coding theory and communications communities. One such work is that of Tillich and Zémor [TZ06]. They investigate the minimum distance of structured LDPC codes with two variable nodes of degree-2 per parity-check equation. In the design of LDPC codes with high iterative decoding performance the variable nodes of degree-2 play a very important role, and this is their motivation for investigating the minimum distance of such codes. Concretely, they investigate codes with $m \times n$ parity check matrices of the form $H = [L|R]$, where R is the $m \times m$ matrix defined by

$$R = \begin{pmatrix} 1 & 1 & & & \\ & 1 & 1 & & \\ & & \ddots & \ddots & \\ & & & 1 & 1 \\ 1 & & & & 1 \end{pmatrix}$$

and L is an $m \times k$ matrix such that all of its columns/rows have weight constant t. As such, H is in g-ALT form for $g = 1$. Tillich and Zémor prove that if H was generated at random subject to these structural constraints, then the minimum distance of the corresponding code is at most $\alpha n^{1-\frac{2}{t}}$ with probability $\mathcal{O}(n^{\frac{2}{t}-1}) + \mathcal{O}(\alpha^{\frac{t}{2}})$ for even t, and $\mathcal{O}(n^{\frac{2}{t}-1}) + \mathcal{O}(\alpha^t)$ for odd t. In fact, they also show that for *any* H that has the aforementioned structure, the corresponding code will have minimum distance upper bounded by a quantity of order $\mathcal{O}(n^{1-\frac{1}{t}})$. Thus, such codes always have sub-linear distance.

Looking at the structure of H, there are a few observations we can make. Let n_2 denote the number of variable nodes of degree 2. A principal quantity of interest is the ratio n_2/m. It can be shown that if $n_2/m > 1$, then the minimum distance of the corresponding LDPC code cannot be larger than a logarithmic function of n. If $n_2/m < 1$, then it is possible for the minimum distance to be a linear function of n. The codes considered by Tillich and Zémor achieve $n_2/m = 1$ (for $t \neq 2$) and offer readily a simple linear-time encoding algorithm for the corresponding code. Yet, as mentioned before, these codes always have sub-linear (albiet, close to linear) minimum distance. In the next section we will empirically verify that the sub-linear growth is in fact the case.

Other works, e.g. [OTA07, DRU06], have looked at the sub-graph $\mathcal{G}_2$ of the Tanner graph formed by only the degree-2 variable nodes (columns of H with weight 2) and certain structural properties can lead to poor minimum distance. For example, it is a common practice to ensure that there are no cycles in the Tanner graph involving only variable nodes of degree 2. Also, Otmani, Tillich and Andriyanova [OTA07] proved that if $\mathcal{G}_2$ is slightly dense (has average degree greater than 2), then the minimum distance is only at most logarithmic in n. They also consider several other conditions for ensuring sub-linear distance.

Another work regarding $\mathcal{G}_2$ is that of Di, Richardson and Urbanke [RU01, DRU06] and regard the quantity $Q = \lambda'(0)\rho'(1)$ (λ and ρ are polynomials describing specific weight distributions of the rows/columns respectively) and how it impacts the minimum distance. $\lambda'(0)$ is the fraction of edges in the Tanner graph connecting to degree-2 variable nodes. They show that if $Q > 1$, then the minimum distance grows sub-linearly with n and linear time encoding. A question that is left open and remains to be answered is whether a linear encoding complexity necessarily implies sub-linear minimal distance.

We end this section with a few concluding remarks regarding our new codes and how they compare against the several techniques laid out in this section. Firstly, our codes have designed to ensure fast/linear encoding complexity while also having high (potentially linear) minimum distance. However, the approach to ensure linear encoding complexity is different from the works described in this section, since we actually have zero columns with weight 2. Thus, none the sufficient conditions for sub-linear minimal distance described above are satisfied by our codes. Based on these observations, we conclude that our codes do not provably have sub-linear minimal distance. We leave open the task of formally proving claims regarding the minimum distance of our codes.

6.3   LDPC Silver Codes

We now present our new LDPC constructions, which we dub Silver Codes (codes for SILent Vole and oblivious transfER). The goal of these codes is to obtain (plausible) linear minimum distance and extremely efficient encoding. Unlike in the traditional setting, our codes need to perform well (encoding-wise) when n is on the order of millions (but do not need to admit efficient decoding algorithms). Ideally our code would have a very compact representation. If a large preprocessing/sampling procedure must be performed, then the codes will likely need to be stored in memory, possibly requiring more memory than the rest of the protocol. Therefore we aim to design codes with a very succinct description.

Our second goal is to have a very efficient memory access structure. Recall that the encoding algorithm will have to access "memory locations" j and i whenever there is a 1 located at $H_{j,i}$. Therefore we would ideally like H to have some additional structure which maintains some memory locality. For example, having a bounded distance between sequential memory accesses. In the case of TZ codes, for example, the left matrix is uniformly distributed, which significantly harms the performances in terms of memory access. When n is on the order of millions, performing random access into an array of length n can quickly dominate the running time as we will see in Sect. 7.

Despite this shortcoming, we take TZ as our starting point and iteratively improve it (sacrificing decoding performance, but trying to optimize minimum distance and encoding time) with the (heuristic) guidance of our minimum distance estimators. It will be useful to partition H into left and right halves $[L|R] := H$ which are each of size $m \times m$. For TZ, L is therefore a uniform column/row weight t matrix while R has column/row weight 2 where all ones are effectively on a diagonal band. Recall that we only consider rate $1/2$ codes where $k = m = n/2$.

It is also a well known phenomenon that odd column weight t LDPC codes achieve better minimum distance performance (for examples, the bounds on the minimum distance achieved in [TZ06] are much better for odd t). Hence, we restrict ourselves to odd values of t. In particular, we focus on $t \in \{5, 11\}$.

Slv1. Our first observations is that the structure of R in TZ plays a crucial role in the proof of sub-linear distance. For TZ, this structure was desirable as it enables a very efficient linear time encoder. However, using the more general g-ALT encoder we are still able to have linear time encoding for any $g = O(\sqrt{n})$. Our first alteration is then to increase the gap g and ensure all columns of R have weight t. There are several possible values for g and we experimentally settle on $g \in \{24, 32\}$ as they will provide good concrete performance.

The next question is how should the ones be distributed in R. Our g-ALT encoder require ones along the diagonal which leaves $t - 1$ degrees of freedom per column. While one could distribute these uniformly over the lower half of R, we opt to place them uniformly in the g positions below the main diagonal. An example of $g = 2, t = 2$ is shown in Fig. 1a. We consider two choices of these parameters, $(g, t) \in \{(24, 5), (32, 11)\}$, which are respectively used in our weight 5 and 11 codes. We note that other parameter choices are possible and that we settled on these as a good trade off between efficiency and distance.

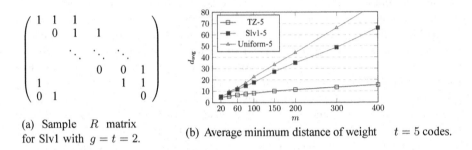

(a) Sample R matrix for Slv1 with $g = t = 2$.

(b) Average minimum distance of weight $t = 5$ codes.

Fig. 1. Example of R and distance of Slv1, uniform, TZ for weight $t = 5$.

We denote this code family as Slv1-t. Slv1 immediately gives a significant improvement over TZ as shown in Fig. 1b. Consider the structure of minimum codewords in TZ: They are often composed of several columns from L which when added together result in small distances between the non-zero elements, e.g. 1001000...000100010 which has distances 3, 4 between the ones. The small distances can then be "bridged" by including the corresponding columns of R, e.g. 7 columns in the case above. However, this strategy does not work for our codes due to R having larger column weight which are randomly distributed.

Moreover, this code performs remarkably similar to uniform of the same column weight $t = 5$. With $m = n/2 = 200$ rows, the average (estimated) minimum distance over 100 trials of this code is 35 while uniform is 45.

Although this code represents a significant improvement over TZ for our particular application, we observe that some samples of the Slv1 code have significantly lower distance that others. In particular, the variance in this code can result in samples with as low as $d_{min} \approx 0.55 d_{avg}$ while uniform has a much smaller variance, with $d_{min} \approx 0.95 d_{avg}$ over 100 samples.

Slv2. Through experimentation and inspecting the Slv1 instances which perform unusually poorly, we identified that key contributors are bad local structures in the main diagonal of R which can at times result in low weight codewords. To prevent this, we observed that adding additional weight one diagonals below the main diagonal prevents these structures. Intuitively they work by increasing the expanding property of each column by guaranteeing they span more than g rows. Moreover, these structures add almost no computational overhead.

Additionally, we remove the first g columns of R such that its a $m \times m - g$ matrix and the portion of the band which wraps around is removed. In Appendix

E we will use a different technique to restore R to being square. An example of the Slv2 distribution of R is in Fig. 2a with $g = t = 2$ and a single diagonal.

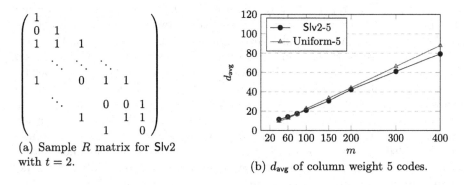

(a) Sample R matrix for Slv2 with $t = 2$.

(b) d_{avg} of column weight 5 codes.

Fig. 2. The alterations in Slv2 along with the minimum distance performance.

Through experimentation we observe that adding two weight 1 diagonal bands at distances 5 and 31 below the main diagonal significantly reduces the variance and improves the average distance. As shown in Fig. 2b the performance of the second code which we denote as Slv2. We note that the uniform code also had the n dimension reduced by g in order to maintain a fair comparison. Remarkably, the Slv2 code has average performance almost identical to that of uniform codes. Moreover, the variance of Slv2 is significantly reduced, with $d_{\text{min}} = 0.88 d_{\text{avg}}$ compared to $d_{\text{min}} = 0.91 d_{\text{avg}}$ for uniform over 100 trials.

Slv3. Next we turn our attention to the distribution of L after which we will further optimize R. While the current distribution of L gives good minimum distance, its memory locality properties are extremely poor since it is uniform. For each non-zero $L_{i,j}$, the g-ALT encoder must access two arrays at i, j respectively. This effectively means one of them is always a cache miss and can quickly dominate the running time as see in Fig. 5 of Sect. 7.

We investigated numerous methods of improving the memory locality of L. For instances, an L consisting of random non-zero submatrixes with various dimensions. However, for the most part this line of thinking was ineffective. Core to a high performing L is an expanding property. In particular, each column of L should have non-zero locations which are somewhat unique and spread out. This is particularly important since the distribution of R is more or less a single band along the diagonal. If both L and R consists of clumps of ones, then it is more likely that cancellation can occur.

However, we identified a surprisingly simple and highly efficient structure which can possess the exact properties we desire. In particular, we will distribute L such that each column is a cyclic shift of exactly one over the previous. This effectively results in t weight one diagonals wrapping around L.

We observe that the exact distribution of the diagonal plays a very crucial role in the minimum distance performance of L. For instance, if they are sampled uniformly, then with some noticeable probability the diagonals can be clumped together. In these cases the code can perform extremely poorly due to L and R being too similarly distributed. One also might think that to achieve a good expanding property that distributing the diagonals evenly over L would be optimal. However, in this case it is possible for two columns of L to equal.

We have experimentally identified that a compromise between these two extremes achieves very good minimum distance performance (both in terms of average distance and variance). In particular, the diagonals should be somewhat evenly distributed while still being irregularly spaced. To identify such distributions we sampled many L at random and evaluate the resulting minimum distance over hundreds of trials and various values of n. An instances of a well performing L with weight $t = 5$ is to distribute the ones of the first column as $\{0m, 0.049m, 0.43m, 0.60m, 0.73m\}$. Other well performing instances have a similar distribution where some diagonals are relatively close while overall they are evenly distributed over the range.

Our methodology for selecting the exact parameters was to evaluate 10,000 random choices at $m \in \{40, 60, 80, 100, 150, 200, 300, 400\}$ and select the top 100 best performing. Out of these, we then ran 100 trials for each $m \in [40, 400]$ with independently sampled R and selected the parameters which maximized d_{min}/d_{avg} for each m. As such, our selection didn't achieve the highest average distance d_{avg} but instead was "consistently well performing." We note that one has to be careful with the selection of L as a poorly chosen one can result in bad/erratic minimum distance performance. That being said, we observed that most randomly sampled chooses performed well.

The minimum distance performance of this code is depicted in Fig. 3a. Interestingly, this code out performs uniform with an average (estimated) minimum distance of $d_{avg} = 94$ at $m = 400$ compared to $d_{avg} = 91$ for uniform. Moreover, the variance of this code is quite low, with $d_{min} = 0.94d_{avg}$ at $m = 400$ compared to $d_{min} = 0.91d_{avg}$ for uniform over 100 trials.

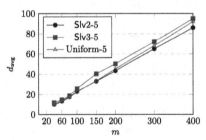

(a) Average minimum distance of Slv2, Slv5 vs uniform with $t = 5$.

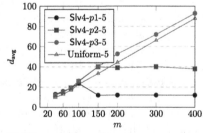

(b) The negative effect on average minimum distance of having repeats of $p \in \{1, 2\}$ vs $p \geq 3$.

Fig. 3. Performance of Slv3 and Slv4 with $p \in \{1, 2, 3\}$ vs uniform.

Slv4. We now return our attention to improving the distribution of R. Generating R is effectively sampling $O(m)$ random sets of $\binom{g}{t}$, which correspond to the location of the ones on the main diagonal. While linear time, this sampling can be quite expensive. We therefore experiment with the idea of letting the diagonal repeat ever p columns. While one has to be careful with repeated structures in a code, for a sufficiently large p we conjecture and experimentally confirm that it should not harm the minimum distance. We consider a repeat of $p \in \{1, 2, 3, ..., g\}$ and observe the repeating structure only introduces a weakness for $p \in \{1, 2\}$. The case of $p = 1$ is clearly problematic due to R now effectively being $t + 2$ diagonal lines of width one which structurally is too similar to L. Our experiments reflect this with minimum distances being effectively upper bounded by 12 as seen in Fig. 4. For $p = 2$ we observe a similar trend with the distance being upper bounded by 40. However, for $p \geq 3$ we observe no negative effects over all of the trials. To be slightly conservative, we opt to set $p = g$ which for our weight 5 code results in $p = 24$.

We further propose selecting a concrete instance of the diagonal, and validating its performance on the range of experimentally testable values of n. This can in turn give us confidence that the repeating structure does not happen to correspond to a weak instances, e.g. a $p = 1$ instance. Moreover, by selecting a concrete instance, it is possible to hardcode the indices into the program and get a very significant performance improvement.

Slv5. This leads us to our final modification. For the case of $p = g$ we restrict our selection of R such that each row[1] and column has fixed weight $t - 1$ with respect to these random indices. The reason for this alteration is purely to improve the computational efficiency of computing xG^T via the transposed circuit. In particular, the encoding algorithm will process R in a row by row manner. This alteration allows the weight of each row to be not be hard coded improved the performance of the branch predictor, etc. We observe that restricting R to be row regular does not decrease the minimum distance performs. See Appendix F for a detailed description.

Eventually, we further consider a variant of Slv5, called Slv5'. This variant is entirely identical, with the sole exception that the parity-check matrix is now viewed as the parity-check matrix *over a field* $\mathbb{F}$ which might not be equal to $\mathbb{F}_2$ – while the parity-check matrix still has $\{0, 1\}$ entries. We do not use this

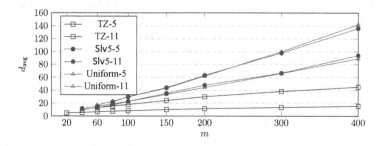

Fig. 4. Average minimum distance of uniform, Slv5 and TZ for weight $t \in \{5, 11\}$.

---

[1] Excluding edge cases for the first and last set of g rows.

variant in our main application to silent OT, but it can be used to provide strong efficiency improvements for VOLE over larger fields. We provide support for this modification in Appendix C of the Supplementary Material.

7 Performance Evaluation

We now evaluate the concrete running times of our LDPC codes along with our Silent OT and Vole implementations (available at [Rin]). With respect to our OT protocol we compare with [IKNP03, BCG+19a, YWL+20]. We also compare our Vole implementation (a direct generalization of [BCG+19a] with our LDPC code) with the implementation of [WYKW20]. All implementations target $\kappa = 128$ bits of computational security and $\lambda = 40$ bits of statistical security.

All performance evaluations were perform on a single consumer laptop with an i7 9750H CPU and 16 GB of RAM. Networking is performed via localhost. Each party is restricted to a single thread. We note that due to silent property of our protocol, it is very conducive to a multi-threaded implementation but that we only consider single thread performing for simplicity. All numbers reported exclude a setup phase where 128 base OTs are perform.

LDPC Encoding Performance. In previous protocols for silent OT and Vole, the running time was dominated by the compression of the noisy vectors generated in the setup. We now compare our new algorithms with the bit polynomial multiplication encoding used in [BCG+19a].

For $n = 2^{20}$, our most optimized code is 31× faster than [BCG+19a, CCK+18]. This improved running time is not merely due to using an LDPC code as demonstrate by the running time of TZ, which is only between 1.1 and 2× faster than [BCG+19a, CCK+18]. Moreover, the initial strengthening of the TZ minimum distance by the Slv1 code results in a significant running time increase of 1.5×.

The first major performance improvement is achieved by the Slv3 code which changes the distribution of L to have an extremely efficient memory access structure. This change reduces the running time of the L encoding by around 25×. The Slv5 code then optimizes the distribution of R to have a repeating structure along with ensuring that it is row regular. These changes allow for very significant memory and system level optimization.

Oblivious Transfer Performance. We now turn our attention to analysing the concrete performance of our OT protocol in comparison to [BCG+19a, YWL+20, IKNP03] as shown in Fig. 7. All protocols output m instances of correlated OT where the receiver obtains a per instance bit b and message $m_b \in \{0,1\}^{128}$ while the sender obtains a global $\Delta \in \{0,1\}^{128}$ and a per instance message $m_0 \in \{0,1\}^{128}$ such that $m_b = m_0 + b\Delta$. Random and chosen message OTs can then be obtained via standard techniques. Our protocol is based on that of [BCG+19a] and we inherit their $O(\log m)$ communication overhead.

Encoder	weight t	2^{16}	2^{20}	2^{24}
[BCG+19a]	-	10.2	194.2	4180
TZ	5	4.5	77.4	1943
	11	4.9	145.2	3971
Slv1	5	7.3	153.2	3632
	11	7.9	241.7	5414
Slv3	5	5.8	88.2	1688
	11	6.1	97	1792
Slv5	5	0.2	6.3	134
	11	0.5	11.3	234

Fig. 5. Running times (ms) of encoding algorithms for LPN with n length vector.

We observe that both our weight 5 and 11 Slv5 codes out perform *all* existing protocol in terms of computational overhead while matching the best communication overhead of [BCG+19a]. In particular, our protocol is as much as 1.5× faster than the highly optimized [IKNP03,Rin] protocol which has stood as the most computationally efficient protocol for almost two decades. All this is achieved while communicating exponentially less data. We argue that this is a landmark achievement given the central role OT plays in countless protocols.

The next most efficient protocol is that of Yang et al. [YWL+20] which also achieves a sub-linear (but not logarithmic) communication overhead. This protocol is based on Primal LPN and therefore requires a one time setup sub-protocol in which correlated randomness is constructed. Given this, their protocol can then generate correlated OTs on demand. In Fig. 7 we distinguish their setup and online protocols as $x + y$ respectively. However, even if only the online protocol is considered, our protocol is more than 4× more efficient in terms of running time and communication. If their setup phase is included then our protocol requires 13× less communication for $m = 10^7$. What is more, their setup phase requires a relatively complicated parameter select procedure which limited us to only performing $m = 10^7$ OTs with their implementation. One reason their only implement this size is that their setup phase has a relatively fixed cost regardless of m. On the other hand, our protocol can easily be executed with any value of m with running times that scales proportionally (Fig. 6).

Vole Performance. We implement the generalization of [BCG+19a] for performing vole. The protocol is largely the same as the OT variant except that f more OTs on strings of length $O(\kappa f)$ need to be performed where f is the log of the field size, i.e. $f = 128$. For our protocol we use the binary Slv5 code while the noise vector is distributed over the while field. The security of this optimization is discussed in Section C.2. We compare with the vole protocol of [WYKW20] (a generalization of [YWL+20]) which is based on Primal LPN and therefore requires a one time setup sub-protocol. We also compare to the 1-out-of-N OT protocol of [OOS17] due to vole also supporting this functionality via hashing.

Protocol:	weight t:	Time (ms) m				Comm (KB) m			
		2^{16}	2^{20}	10^7	2^{24}	2^{16}	2^{20}	10^7	2^{24}
[BCG+19a]	-		25	510	5,121	1,0432			
This	5	1	29	268	488	75	94	122	126
	11	2	33	324	591				
[YWL+20]	10	-	-	44+1,134	-	-	-	1,130+550	-
[IKNP03]	-	4	45	423	692	1,048	16,777	160,038	268,435

Fig. 6. Single thread running time (ms) and communication (KB) to perform m correlated oblivious transfers in the LAN setting.

We observe that our protocol significantly out performs both of these works. Moreover, [WYKW20] performs a vole over a field of size $2^{61} - 1$ while our implementation is for the Galois field of size 2^{128}. As such, this effectively halves their communication. Similarly, [OOS17] has an analogous field size of 2^{79}. Despite working over a larger field, the running time of our protocol $4\times$ faster than [WYKW20] at $m = 4 \times 10^7$ and $22\times$ faster than [OOS17]. Similarly, at $m = 4 \times 10^7$ our protocols requires between 5 to $8\times$ less communication than [WYKW20] depending on if their setup is include and $6200\times$ less than [OOS17].

Protocol:	weight t:	$\log|\mathbb{F}|$	Time (ms) m				Comm (KB) m			
			2^{16}	2^{20}	2^{24}	$4 \cdot 10^7$	2^{16}	2^{20}	2^{24}	$4 \cdot 10^7$
This	5	128	10	50	616	1,390	339	373	405	409
	11	128	11	53	750	1,660				
[WYKW20]	10	61	-	-	-	260+5,699	-	-	-	1,130+2,101
[OOS17]	-	79	15	218	3,499	31,219	4,219	67,137	1,073,832	2,561,551

Fig. 7. Single thread running time (ms) and communication (KB) to perform m voles (or 1-out-of-N OTs for [OOS17]) in the LAN setting.

Applications. The applications of our new protocol are extremely broad. Two of the most compelling are binary triple generation for the GMW[GMW87b] protocol and private set intersection. The former allows generic secure computation of binary circuit at the expense of performing $2|C|$ OTs and sending $2|C|$ bits where $|C|$ is the number of AND gates in the circuit. Due to the extreme efficiency of our protocol, the cost of the OTs is like dominated by the other costs in the GMW protocol, i.e. simply sending the bits. More generally, since our OT protocol is faster than all prior works in effectively all metrics, our protocol should be the de facto choice for generating OTs and binary triples.

The recent semi-hones/malicious secure PSI protocol of [RS21] directly builds on vole and achieved the lowest communication and very fast running times compared to all prior works. This protocol performs a vole of size $2.4n$ where the sets are of size n. Their implementation makes use of the vole protocol of [SGRR19] along with optimizations of [WYKW20]. As such, integrating our vole protocol gives a good example of the speed ups that can be obtained.

For sets of size $n = 2^{16}$ to $n = 2^{24}$ we observe that our vole protocol improves the running time of [RS21] by between 40 and 45% and 25 to 1% reduction in communication. Concretely, the semi-honest variant of their PSI protocol for $n = 2^{20}$ with our vole implementation would require 3.1 s compared to 2.4 s of [KKRT16] while at the same time sending 2.5× less data than [KKRT16]. As such, in effectively all real world situation the PSI protocol of [RS21] with our vole is the optimal protocol to use. Moreover, the malicious variant of [RS21] with our vole achieves the fastest running time and lowest communication by a factor of 1.7× and 4× respectively compared to then next most efficient protocol [PRTY20].

References

ABG+14. Akavia, A., Bogdanov, A., Guo, S., Kamath, A., Rosen, A.: Candidate weak pseudorandom functions in AC^0 o MOD2, pp. 251–260 (2014)

ADI+17. Applebaum, B., Damgård, I., Ishai, Y., Nielsen, M., Zichron, L.: Secure arithmetic computation with constant computational overhead. In: Katz, J., Shacham, H. (eds.) CRYPTO 2017. LNCS, vol. 10401, pp. 223–254. Springer, Cham (2017). https://doi.org/10.1007/978-3-319-63688-7_8

AJ01. Jabri, A.A.: A statistical decoding algorithm for general linear block codes. In: Honary, B. (ed.) Cryptography and Coding 2001. LNCS, vol. 2260, pp. 1–8. Springer, Heidelberg (2001). https://doi.org/10.1007/3-540-45325-3_1

Ale03. Alekhnovich, M.: More on average case vs approximation complexity, pp. 298–307 (2003)

BCG+17. Boyle, E., Couteau, G., Gilboa, N., Ishai, Y., Orrù, M.: Homomorphic secret sharing: optimizations and applications, pp. 2105–2122 (2017)

BCG+19a. Boyle, E., et al.: Efficient two-round OT extension and silent non-interactive secure computation, pp. 291–308 (2019)

BCG+19b. Boyle, E., Couteau, G., Gilboa, N., Ishai, Y., Kohl, L., Scholl, P.: Efficient pseudorandom correlation generators: silent OT extension and more. In: Boldyreva, A., Micciancio, D. (eds.) CRYPTO 2019. LNCS, vol. 11694, pp. 489–518. Springer, Cham (2019). https://doi.org/10.1007/978-3-030-26954-8_16

BCG+20. Boyle, E., Couteau, G., Gilboa, N., Ishai, Y., Kohl, L., Scholl, P.: Correlated pseudorandom functions from variable-density LPN, pp. 1069–1080 (2020)

BCGI18. Boyle, E., Couteau, G., Gilboa, N., Ishai, Y.: Compressing vector OLE, pp. 896–912 (2018)

BFKL94. Blum, A., Furst, M., Kearns, M., Lipton, R.J.: Cryptographic primitives based on hard learning problems. In: Stinson, D.R. (ed.) CRYPTO 1993. LNCS, vol. 773, pp. 278–291. Springer, Heidelberg (1994). https://doi.org/10.1007/3-540-48329-2_24

BGI14. Boyle, E., Goldwasser, S., Ivan, I.: Functional signatures and pseudorandom functions. In: Krawczyk, H. (ed.) PKC 2014. LNCS, vol. 8383, pp. 501–519. Springer, Heidelberg (2014). https://doi.org/10.1007/978-3-642-54631-0_29

BJMM12. Becker, A., Joux, A., May, A., Meurer, A.: Decoding Random Binary Linear Codes in $2^n/20$: How $1 + 1 = 0$ improves information set decoding. In: Pointcheval, D., Johansson, T. (eds.) EUROCRYPT 2012. LNCS, vol. 7237, pp. 520–536. Springer, Heidelberg (2012). https://doi.org/10.1007/978-3-642-29011-4_31

BKW00. Blum, A., Kalai, A., Wasserman, H.: Noise-tolerant learning, the parity problem, and the statistical query model, pp. 435–440 (2000)

BLP11. Bernstein, D.J., Lange, T., Peters, C.: Smaller decoding exponents: ball-collision decoding. In: Rogaway, P. (ed.) CRYPTO 2011. LNCS, vol. 6841, pp. 743–760. Springer, Heidelberg (2011). https://doi.org/10.1007/978-3-642-22792-9_42

BM97. Bellare, M., Micciancio, D.: A new paradigm for collision-free hashing: incrementality at reduced cost. In: Fumy, W. (ed.) EUROCRYPT 1997. LNCS, vol. 1233, pp. 163–192. Springer, Heidelberg (1997). https://doi.org/10.1007/3-540-69053-0_13

BM18. Both, L., May, A.: Decoding linear codes with high error rate and its impact for LPN security. In: Lange, T., Steinwandt, R. (eds.) PQCrypto 2018. LNCS, vol. 10786, pp. 25–46. Springer, Cham (2018). https://doi.org/10.1007/978-3-319-79063-3_2

Bor57. Bordewijk, J.L.: Inter-reciprocity applied to electrical networks. Appl. Sci. Res. **6**, 1–74 (1957). https://doi.org/10.1007/BF02410413

BR17. Bogdanov, A., Rosen, A.: Pseudorandom functions: three decades later. Cryptology ePrint Archive, Report 2017/652 (2017). http://eprint.iacr.org/2017/652

BTV16. Bogos, S., Tramèr, F., Vaudenay, S.: On solving LPN using BKW and variants. Cryptogr. Commun. **8**(3), 331–369 (2015). https://doi.org/10.1007/s12095-015-0149-2

BV16. Bogos, S., Vaudenay, S.: Optimization of LPN solving algorithms. In: Cheon, J.H., Takagi, T. (eds.) ASIACRYPT 2016. LNCS, vol. 10031, pp. 703–728. Springer, Heidelberg (2016). https://doi.org/10.1007/978-3-662-53887-6_26

BVJD02. Berrou, C., Vaton, S., Jezequel, M., Douillard, C.: Computing the minimum distance of linear codes by the error impulse method (2002)

BW13. Boneh, D., Waters, B.: Constrained pseudorandom functions and their applications. In: Sako, K., Sarkar, P. (eds.) ASIACRYPT 2013. LNCS, vol. 8270, pp. 280–300. Springer, Heidelberg (2013). https://doi.org/10.1007/978-3-642-42045-0_15

CCK+18. Chen, M.-S., Cheng, C.-M., Kuo, P.-C., Li, W.-D., Yang, B.-Y.: Multiplying Boolean polynomials with Frobenius partitions in additive fast Fourier transform (2018)

CG90. Coffey, J.T., Goodman, R.M.: The complexity of information set decoding. IEEE Trans. Inf. Theory **36**, 1031–1037 (1990)

DAT17. Debris-Alazard, T., Tillich, J.-P.: Statistical decoding (2017)

DP15. Dutta, A., Pramanik, A.: Modified approximate lower triangular encoding of LDPC codes (2015)

DRU06. Di, C., Richardson, T.J., Urbanke, R.L.: Weight distribution of low-density parity-check codes. IEEE Trans. Inf. Theory **52**, 4839–4855 (2006)

EKM17. Esser, A., Kübler, R., May, A.: LPN decoded. In: Katz, J., Shacham, H. (eds.) CRYPTO 2017. LNCS, vol. 10402, pp. 486–514. Springer, Cham (2017). https://doi.org/10.1007/978-3-319-63715-0_17

Fei02. Feige, U.: Relations between average case complexity and approximation complexity, pp. 534–543 (2002)

FGKP09. Feldman, V., Gopalan, P., Khot, S., Ponnuswami, A.K.: On agnostic learning of parities, monomials, and halfspaces. SIAM J. Comput. **39**, 606–645 (2009)

FKI06. Fossorier, M.P.C., Kobara, K., Imai, H.: Modeling bit flipping decoding based on nonorthogonal check sums with application to iterative decoding attack of McEliece cryptosystem (2006)

FS09. Finiasz, M., Sendrier, N.: Security bounds for the design of code-based cryptosystems. In: Matsui, M. (ed.) ASIACRYPT 2009. LNCS, vol. 5912, pp. 88–105. Springer, Heidelberg (2009). https://doi.org/10.1007/978-3-642-10366-7_6

Gal62. Gallager, R.: Low-density parity-check codes. IRE Trans. Inf. Theory **8**(1), 21–28 (1962)

Gal13. Galbraith, S.D.: Space-efficient variants of cryptosystems based on learning with errors (2013)

GDP73. Gelfand, S.I., Dobrushin, R.L., Pinsker, M.S.: On the complexity of coding (1973)

GJL20. Guo, Q., Johansson, T., Löndahl, C.: Solving LPN using covering codes. J. Cryptol. **33**(1), 1–33 (2019). https://doi.org/10.1007/s00145-019-09338-8

GMW87a. Goldreich, O., Micali, S., Wigderson, A.: How to play any mental game or a completeness theorem for protocols with honest majority, pp. 218–229 (1987)

GMW87b. Goldreich, O., Micali, S., Wigderson, A.: How to prove all NP statements in zero-knowledge and a methodology of cryptographic protocol design (extended abstract). In: Odlyzko, A.M. (ed.) CRYPTO 1986. LNCS, vol. 263, pp. 171–185. Springer, Heidelberg (1987). https://doi.org/10.1007/3-540-47721-7_11

Gra06. Grassl, M.: Searching for linear codes with large minimum distance. In: Bosma, W., Cannon, J. (eds.) Discovering Mathematics with Magma. AACIM, vol. 19, pp. 287–313. Springer, Heidelberg (2006). https://doi.org/10.1007/978-3-540-37634-7_13

HIQO19. Hernando, F., Igual, F.D., Quintana-Ortí, G.: Algorithm 994: fast implementations of the Brouwer-Zimmermann algorithm for the computation of the minimum distance of a random linear code. ACM Trans. Math. Softw. **45**, 1–28 (2019)

HM17. Herold, G., May, A.: LP solutions of vectorial integer subset sums – cryptanalysis of Galbraith's binary matrix LWE. In: Fehr, S. (ed.) PKC 2017. LNCS, vol. 10174, pp. 3–15. Springer, Heidelberg (2017). https://doi.org/10.1007/978-3-662-54365-8_1

HS13. Hamdaoui, Y., Sendrier, N.: A non asymptotic analysis of information set decoding (2013)

IKNP03. Ishai, Y., Kilian, J., Nissim, K., Petrank, E.: Extending oblivious transfers efficiently. In: Boneh, D. (ed.) CRYPTO 2003. LNCS, vol. 2729, pp. 145–161. Springer, Heidelberg (2003). https://doi.org/10.1007/978-3-540-45146-4_9

IKOS08. Ishai, Y., Kushilevitz, E., Ostrovsky, R., Sahai, A.: Cryptography with constant computational overhead, pp. 433–442 (2008)

Kil88. Kilian, J.: Founding cryptography on oblivious transfer (1988)

Kir11. Kirchner, P.: Improved generalized birthday attack. Cryptology ePrint Archive, Report 2011/377 (2011). https://eprint.iacr.org/2011/377

KKRT16. Kolesnikov, V., Kumaresan, R., Rosulek, M., Trieu, N.: Efficient batched oblivious PRF with applications to private set intersection, pp. 818–829 (2016)

KOS15. Keller, M., Orsini, E., Scholl, P.: Actively secure OT extension with optimal overhead. In: Gennaro, R., Robshaw, M. (eds.) CRYPTO 2015. LNCS, vol. 9215, pp. 724–741. Springer, Heidelberg (2015). https://doi.org/10.1007/978-3-662-47989-6_35

KPTZ13. Kiayias, A., Papadopoulos, S., Triandopoulos, N., Zacharias, T.: Delegatable pseudorandom functions and applications, pp. 669–684 (2013)

KS12. Kobayashi, K., Shibuya, T.: Generalization of Lu's linear time encoding algorithm for LDPC codes (2012)

KT17. Kachigar, G., Tillich, J.-P.: Quantum information set decoding algorithms. In: Lange, T., Takagi, T. (eds.) PQCrypto 2017. LNCS, vol. 10346, pp. 69–89. Springer, Cham (2017). https://doi.org/10.1007/978-3-319-59879-6_5

LF06. Levieil, É., Fouque, P.-A.: An improved LPN algorithm. In: De Prisco, R., Yung, M. (eds.) SCN 2006. LNCS, vol. 4116, pp. 348–359. Springer, Heidelberg (2006). https://doi.org/10.1007/11832072_24

Lyu05. Lyubashevsky, V.: The parity problem in the presence of noise, decoding random linear codes, and the subset sum problem. In: Chekuri, C., Jansen, K., Rolim, J.D.P., Trevisan, L. (eds.) APPROX/RANDOM -2005. LNCS, vol. 3624, pp. 378–389. Springer, Heidelberg (2005). https://doi.org/10.1007/11538462_32

McE78. McEliece, R.J.: A public-key cryptosystem based on algebraic (1978)

MMT11. May, A., Meurer, A., Thomae, E.: Decoding random linear codes in $\tilde{\mathcal{O}}(2^{0.054n})$. In: Lee, D.H., Wang, X. (eds.) ASIACRYPT 2011. LNCS, vol. 7073, pp. 107–124. Springer, Heidelberg (2011). https://doi.org/10.1007/978-3-642-25385-0_6

MO15. May, A., Ozerov, I.: On computing nearest neighbors with applications to decoding of binary linear codes. In: Oswald, E., Fischlin, M. (eds.) EUROCRYPT 2015. LNCS, vol. 9056, pp. 203–228. Springer, Heidelberg (2015). https://doi.org/10.1007/978-3-662-46800-5_9

MST03. Mossel, E., Shpilka, A., Trevisan, L.: On e-biased generators in NC0, pp. 136–145 (2003)

NN90. Naor, J., Naor, M.: Small-bias probability spaces: efficient constructions and applications, pp. 213–223 (1990)

NPC+17. Niebuhr, R., Persichetti, E., Cayrel, P.-L., Bulygin, S., Buchmann, J.A.: On lower bounds for information set decoding over $\mathbb{F}_q$ and on the effect of partial knowledge (2017)

OOS17. Orrù, M., Orsini, E., Scholl, P.: Actively secure 1-out-of-N OT extension with application to private set intersection. In: Handschuh, H. (ed.) CT-RSA 2017. LNCS, vol. 10159, pp. 381–396. Springer, Cham (2017). https://doi.org/10.1007/978-3-319-52153-4_22

OTA07. Otmani, A., Tillich, J.-P., Andriyanova, I.: On the minimum distance of generalized LDPC codes (2007)

Ove06. Overbeck, R.: Statistical decoding revisited. In: Batten, L.M., Safavi-Naini, R. (eds.) ACISP 2006. LNCS, vol. 4058, pp. 283–294. Springer, Heidelberg (2006). https://doi.org/10.1007/11780656_24

Pet10. Peters, C.: Information-set decoding for linear codes over $\mathbf{F}_q$. In: Sendrier, N. (ed.) PQCrypto 2010. LNCS, vol. 6061, pp. 81–94. Springer, Heidelberg (2010). https://doi.org/10.1007/978-3-642-12929-2_7

Pra62. Prange, E.: The use of information sets in decoding cyclic codes. IRE Trans. Inf. Theory **8**, 5–9 (1962)

PRTY20. Pinkas, B., Rosulek, M., Trieu, N., Yanai, A.: PSI from PaXoS: fast, malicious private set intersection. In: Canteaut, A., Ishai, Y. (eds.) EUROCRYPT 2020. LNCS, vol. 12106, pp. 739–767. Springer, Cham (2020). https://doi.org/10.1007/978-3-030-45724-2_25

Rin. Rindal, P.: libOTe: an efficient, portable, and easy to use Oblivious Transfer Library. https://github.com/osu-crypto/libOTe

RS21. Rindal, P., Schoppmann, P.: VOLE-PSI: fast OPRF and circuit-PSI from vector-OLE. In: Canteaut, A., Standaert, F.-X. (eds.) EUROCRYPT 2021. LNCS, vol. 12697, pp. 901–930. Springer, Cham (2021). https://doi.org/10.1007/978-3-030-77886-6_31

RU01. Richardson, T.J., Urbanke, R.L.: Efficient encoding of low-density parity-check codes. IEEE Trans. Inf. Theory **47**, 638–656 (2001)

Saa07. Saarinen, M.-J.O.: Linearization attacks against syndrome based hashes. In: Srinathan, K., Rangan, C.P., Yung, M. (eds.) INDOCRYPT 2007. LNCS, vol. 4859, pp. 1–9. Springer, Heidelberg (2007). https://doi.org/10.1007/978-3-540-77026-8_1

SGRR19. Schoppmann, P., Gascón, A., Reichert, L., Raykova, M.: Distributed vector-OLE: improved constructions and implementation, pp. 1055–1072 (2019)

Shp09. Shpilka, A.: Constructions of low-degree and error-correcting ε-biased generators. Comput. Complex. **18**, 495 (2009). https://doi.org/10.1007/s00037-009-0281-5

SNDM18. Sanyashi, T., Nahata, S., Dhanesha, R., Menezes, B.: Learning plaintext in Galbraith's LWE cryptosystem (2018)

Spi96. Spielman, D.A.: Linear-time encodable and decodable error-correcting codes. IEEE Trans. Inf. Theory **42**, 1723–1731 (1996)

Ste88. Stern, J.: A method for finding codewords of small weight. In: Cohen, G., Wolfmann, J. (eds.) Coding Theory 1988. LNCS, vol. 388, pp. 106–113. Springer, Heidelberg (1989). https://doi.org/10.1007/BFb0019850

SVA+19. Sanyashi, T., Venkatesh, M., Agarwal, K., Verma, M., Menezes, B.: A new hybrid lattice attack on Galbraith's binary LWE cryptosystem (2019)

TS16. Canto Torres, R., Sendrier, N.: Analysis of information set decoding for a sub-linear error weight. In: Takagi, T. (ed.) PQCrypto 2016. LNCS, vol. 9606, pp. 144–161. Springer, Cham (2016). https://doi.org/10.1007/978-3-319-29360-8_10

TZ06. Tillich, J.-P., Zémor, G.: On the minimum distance of structured LDPC codes with two variable nodes of degree 2 per parity-check equation (2006)

Var97. Vardy, A.: The intractability of computing the minimum distance of a code. IEEE Trans. Inf. Theory **43**, 1757–1766 (1997)

Wag02. Wagner, D.: A generalized birthday problem. In: Yung, M. (ed.) CRYPTO 2002. LNCS, vol. 2442, pp. 288–304. Springer, Heidelberg (2002). https://doi.org/10.1007/3-540-45708-9_19

WYKW20. Weng, C., Yang, K., Katz, J., Wang, X.: Wolverine: fast, scalable, and communication-efficient zero-knowledge proofs for Boolean and arithmetic circuits (2020)

XFE04. Hu, X.-Y., Fossorier, M.P.C., Eleftheriou, E.: On the computation of the minimum distance of low-density parity-check codes (2004)

Yao86. Yao, A.C.-C.: How to generate and exchange secrets (extended abstract), pp. 162–167 (1986)

YWL+20. Yang, K., Weng, C., Lan, X., Zhang, J., Wang, X.: Ferret: fast extension for correlated OT with small communication, pp. 1607–1626 (2020)

Zic17. Zichron, L.: Locally computable arithmetic pseudorandom generators (2017)

ZJW16. Zhang, B., Jiao, L., Wang, M.: Faster algorithms for solving LPN. In: Fischlin, M., Coron, J.-S. (eds.) EUROCRYPT 2016. LNCS, vol. 9665, pp. 168–195. Springer, Heidelberg (2016). https://doi.org/10.1007/978-3-662-49890-3_7

Non-malleable Codes for Bounded Parallel-Time Tampering

Dana Dachman-Soled[1]([⊠]), Ilan Komargodski[2], and Rafael Pass[3]

[1] University of Maryland, College Park, USA
danadach@ece.umd.edu
[2] Hebrew University of Jerusalem and NTT Research, Jerusalem, Israel
ilank@cs.huji.ac.il
[3] Cornell Tech, New York City, USA
rafael@cs.cornell.edu

Abstract. Non-malleable codes allow one to encode data in such a way that once a codeword is being tampered with, the modified codeword is either an encoding of the original message, or a completely unrelated one. Since the introduction of this notion by Dziembowski, Pietrzak, and Wichs (ICS '10 and J. ACM '18), there has been a large body of works realizing such coding schemes secure against various classes of tampering functions. It is well known that there is no efficient non-malleable code secure against all polynomial size tampering functions. Nevertheless, no code which is non-malleable for *bounded* polynomial size attackers is known and obtaining such a code has been a major open problem.

We present the first construction of a non-malleable code secure against all polynomial size tampering functions that have bounded parallel time. This is an even larger class than all bounded polynomial size functions. In particular, this class includes all functions in non-uniform **NC** (and much more). Our construction is in the plain model (i.e., no trusted setup) and relies on several cryptographic assumptions such as keyless hash functions, time-lock puzzles, as well as other standard assumptions. Additionally, our construction has several appealing properties: the complexity of encoding is independent of the class of tampering functions and we can obtain (sub-)exponentially small error.

D. Dachman-Soled—Supported in part by NSF grants #CNS-1933033, #CNS-1453045 (CAREER), and by financial assistance awards 70NANB15H328 and 70NANB19H126 from the U.S. Department of Commerce, National Institute of Standards and Technology. R. Pass—Supported in part by NSF Award SATC-1704788, NSF Award RI-1703846, AFOSR Award FA9550-18-1-0267, and a JP Morgan Faculty Award. This material is based upon work supported by DARPA under Agreement No. HR00110C0086 and Office of the Director of National Intelligence (ODNI), Intelligence Advanced Research Projects Activity (IARPA), via 2019-19-020700006. The views and conclusions contained herein are those of the authors and should not be interpreted as necessarily representing the official policies, either expressed or implied, of DARPA, ODNI, IARPA, or the U.S. Government. The U.S. Government is authorized to reproduce and distribute reprints for governmental purposes notwithstanding any copyright annotation therein.

T. Malkin and C. Peikert (Eds.): CRYPTO 2021, LNCS 12827, pp. 535–565, 2021.
https://doi.org/10.1007/978-3-030-84252-9_18

1   Introduction

A non-malleable code is a fascinating concept that (informally) allows one to encode messages such that it is impossible to modify the underlying message of a given codeword without decoding it first. More precisely, the operation applied to the codeword is called the *tampering function*, and the guarantee is that, with "high probability", decoding a tampered codeword results in either the original message or an unrelated one. We refer to the probability that the attacker succeeds in coming up with a tampered codeword of a related messages as its *distinguishing advantage*, and we typically require this advantage to be negligible (i.e., smaller than the inverse of any polynomial). Note that in contrast to standard error-correcting (or detecting) codes, non-malleable codes can achieve security against tampering functions that modify *every* part of a codeword.

Non-malleable codes have proven to be a fundamental concept, giving rise to many beautiful connections and results, both in complexity theory (e.g., two-source extractors [23,26,57,58] and additive combinatorics [2,3]) as well as in cryptography (e.g., non-malleable encryption and commitments [31,32,47]).

In the paper that introduced non-malleable codes, Dziembowski, Pietrzak, and Wichs [37,38], observed that it is impossible to construct a non-malleable code secure against arbitrary tampering functions, since a tampering function which first decodes the codeword and then re-encodes a related message breaks security. By the same principle, it is impossible to construct a code with polynomial-time decoding which is secure against all polynomial-time tampering functions.[1] Therefore, the class of tampering functions has to be limited in some way—either in terms of computational power or in the way the functions can access the codeword. One natural limitation is by restricting the available computational complexity resources (e.g., running time, space, etc.).

Already in the original work of Dziembowski et al. [38] (see also [27] for a followup), it was shown that (with high probability) a random function is a non-malleable code secure against all circuits of size (say) $2^{n/2}$, where n is the size of a codeword. However, the code is clearly inefficient. Faust et al. [42] gave an efficient version of that result, but it is still not an explicit construction: For any polynomial bound S, there is an efficiently samplable *family* of codes such that (with high probability) a random member of the family is a non-malleable code secure against all functions computable by a circuit of size S. Stated differently, the result can be seen as an explicit construction (i.e., a single code) assuming an untamperable *common reference string* (CRS) which is longer than the running time of the tampering function. In the random oracle model (which can be thought of as an exponential size common random string), Faust et al. [41] constructed non-malleable codes secure against space-bounded tampering. Ball et al. [7] constructed a non-malleable code secure against bounded depth circuits with constant fan-in (which includes $\mathbf{NC}^0$). Several works were able to get non-

---

[1] Here is the attack: the tampering function can decode the codeword and if it contains some pre-defined message (say all 0s), then it replaces it with garbage (which might not even correspond to a valid codeword), and otherwise it does not change the input.

malleable codes secure against $\mathbf{AC}^0$ tampering functions [5,8,11,25] (actually even circuits of depth $O(\log n/\log\log n)$).

Arguably, the holy grail in this line of works is to construct an explicit non-malleable code which is secure against all tampering functions from the class of bounded polynomial-size circuits. Specifically, for a size bound S, we would like to get an efficient code which is non-malleable for all tampering functions that can be described by an arbitrary circuit of size S. Ideally, only decoding should require running-time greater than S and encoding should run in some a-priori fixed polynomial-time, independent of S.

> *Does there exist an explicit construction (in the plain model) of an efficient non-malleable code which is secure against all bounded polynomial-size attackers?*

Ball et al. [8] made an important step towards this goal by using computational assumptions. Concretely, using public-key encryption and non-interactive zero-knowledge (NIZK), they gave a generic way to construct non-malleable codes secure against tampering classes $\mathcal{F}$ using sufficiently strong average-case hardness for $\mathcal{F}$. This construction, however, still requires a CRS (for the public key of the encryption scheme and the CRS of the NIZK) albeit it is short (polynomial in the the security parameter and independent of the class $\mathcal{F}$).

In a recent follow-up work, Ball et al. [6] managed to get rid of the CRS, but at the cost of (a) using non-standard assumptions, and (b) limiting the class of attacks and the level of security. In more detail, they showed a construction of an efficient non-malleable codes secure against all (uniform) tampering functions computable in an a-priori fixed polynomial-time. But:

- Their construction relies (amongst other assumptions) on sub-exponentially sound **P**-certificates[2] which is a very strong and non-standard assumption. In particular, the *only* known instantiation requires *assuming* soundness of a non-trivial argument system (Micali's CS proofs [67]), which is true in the Random Oracle model.
- Their scheme is non-malleable only with respect to *uniform* polynomial-time tampering as opposed to the standard model of polynomial-*size* tampering. In other words, the tampering attacker is restricted to being a *uniform* polynomial-time algorithm, in contrast to the standard model of non-uniform polynomial-time attackers.
- Their scheme achieves only *a-priori bounded* inverse polynomial-distinguishing advantage, as opposed to achieving "full" security (i.e., negligble distinguishing advantage).
- Finally, both their encoding procedure, as well as the decoding procedure, run *longer* than the allowed tampering functions (i.e., the adversary can neither encode nor decode). In contrast, as mentionned, in principle encoding could be "efficient" in the sense that it is independent of the size/running-time of the tampering attacker.

---

[2] These are "succinct" one-message arguments for languages in **P**, with proof length which is a fixed polynomial, independent of the time it takes to decide the language [28].

To summarize, despite several beautiful steps towards resolving the above question, the answer is still largely unknown. Known partial solutions either require a CRS or strong and non-standard cryptographic assumptions that are only known to be instantiated in the Random Oracle model (and even then only achieve a weaker form of non-malleability).

1.1   Our Results

We give the first full affirmative answer to the aforementioned question. Specifically, we construct an efficient non-malleable code that is (computationally) secure against tampering functions computable by any bounded polynomial-size circuit. Our construction is in the plain model and relies on several generic and well-studied cryptographic building blocks: a time-lock puzzle [77], a non-interactive non-malleable commitment [20,49,52,63], and a non-interactive SPS (super-polynomial-time simulatable) zero-knowledge protocol [14,20] (all in the plain model). While we cannot use the aforementioned primitives in their most general form, we identify certain additional properties from them that will be needed in our construction; additionally, we note that particular known constructions of them satisfy the additional desired properties; see below and in Sect. 2 for more details.

Our construction actually captures an even larger class of tampering functions. Specifically, we give a non-malleable code secure against all tampering functions that can be computed by *arbitrary* (unbounded) polynomial-size circuit of *bounded polynomial-depth*. We emphasize that while the circuit depth of the tampering function is bounded a priori by some fixed polynomial in the security parameter, the size of the circuit is *unbounded* and can be any polynomial in the security parameter.

Theorem 1 (Informal Meta Theorem). *Assume the existence of a "special-purpose" time-lock puzzle, one-message non-malleable commitment, and one-message SPS zero-knowledge protocol. For any $\overline{T} \in \mathsf{poly}(\lambda)$, there exists an explicit code where encoding takes time $\mathsf{poly}(\lambda)$, decoding takes time $\mathsf{poly}(\overline{T}, \lambda)$, and it is non-malleable against all tampering functions computable by a non-uniform arbitrary polynomial-size (in λ) circuit of depth $\overline{T}$.*

Our result is the first to handle all bounded polynomial-size tampering functions (and in fact much more). In particular, as a special case, we capture all tampering functions in non-uniform **NC** (while previously there was no construction even for **NC^1**). We emphasize that our scheme is efficiently encodable, namely, encoding time depends only on the security parameter and not on the (depth) complexity of the decoder. Furthermore, our construction readily extends to withstand (sub-)exponential size tampering functions (of depth $\overline{T}$) without affecting the complexity of neither encoding nor decoding. Lastly, we note that the distinguishing advantage of any tampering function in our scheme can be made sub-exponentially small in λ at essentially no cost (since in any case we need to rely on sub-exponential hardness of the underlying building blocks).

In comparison, as mentioned, prior to this work, even dealing with just bounded polynomial-size tampering was not known. The only approach towards polynomial-size tampering [6] captured only *uniform* polynomial-time tampering, but as mentioned above, even for this restricted class of tampering, their result has additional drawbacks: (1) it relies on a strong non-standard assumption (**P**-certificates) that we only know how to satisfy in the random oracle model, and (2) it only gives inverse-polynomial distinguishing advantage (as opposed to negligible distinguishing advantage).

We instantiate the time-lock puzzle using the construction of Rivest et al. [77] and we show how to further use results of Bitansky and Lin [20] and Lin et al. [63] to instantiate the required non-malleable commitment and zero-knowledge protocol. Thus, assuming the repeated squaring assumption [77] (i.e., there is no way to significantly speed-up repeated squarings in a hidden-order group), a keyless multi-collision resistant hash function [19] (i.e., a single function for which any PPT attacker with $\ell(\lambda)$ bits of non-uniform advice cannot find more than $\ell(\lambda)^c$ collisions for a constant $c \in \mathbb{N}$),[3] as well as other standard assumptions, we obtain the following theorem.

Theorem 2 (Informal). *Assume a keyless multi-collision resistant hash function, the repeated squaring assumption, an injective one-way function, and non-interactive witness-indistinguishable proofs,[4] all being sub-exponentially secure. Then, for any $\overline{T} \in \mathsf{poly}(\lambda)$, there exists an explicit code where encoding takes time $\mathsf{poly}(\lambda)$, decoding takes time $\mathsf{poly}(\overline{T}, \lambda)$, and it is non-malleable against all tampering functions computable by a non-uniform arbitrary polynomial-size (in λ) circuit of depth $\overline{T}$.*

We refer to Sect. 1.2 for more details about the above assumptions.

Non-malleable Time-Lock Puzzle. Our non-malleable code construction is secure for all bounded polynomial-depth tampering functions and additionally it is efficiently encodable, meaning that encoding time is fixed as a function of the security parameter, but is otherwise independent of the time it takes to decode. We observe that the combination of these two properties actually implies a *time-lock puzzle* which is additionally *non-malleable*.[5] In other words, under the same assumptions as in Theorems 1 and 2, we get a *non-malleable* time-lock puzzle.

---

[3] While keyless multi-collision resistance is a relatively new assumption, it is a natural and simple security property for keyless cryptographic hash functions, which in particular is satisfies by a random function.

[4] Non-interactive witness-indistinguishable proofs are known to exist based on various assumptions: trapdoor permutations and a particular derandomization-type assumption [13], cryptographic bilinear maps [48], or indistinguishability obfuscation and one-way permutations [21].

[5] Recall that time-lock puzzles are a cryptographic mechanism for sending messages "to the future", by allowing a sender to quickly generate a puzzle with an underlying message that remains hidden until a receiver spends a moderately large amount of time solving it. Non-malleability guarantees that not only the puzzle hides the underlying message, but actually it is hard to "maul" it into a puzzle with a different "related" message.

We emphasize that the non-malleable time-lock puzzle that we obtain here is in the plain model, i.e., does not require any trusted setup.

Related Followup or Concurrent Work. We mention the following related followup or concurrent work [15,16,40,50]. Katz et al. [50] construct non-malleable non-interactive timed-commitments relying in the security proof on the algebraic group model [44] and on trusted setup. Ephraim et al. [40] focus on efficiency and applications; specifically, they give a more efficient construction than the one given in this work (which is proven secure in the auxiliary-input random oracle model) and further show how to use it to obtain desirable crypto-graphic protocols such as fair multiparty coin flipping. Lastly, Baum et al. [15,16] construct UC-secure time-lock puzzles while relying on a programmable random oracle, which they show to be necessary. Most recently, Ball et al. [10] (see [4, Theorem 32]) showed that the derandomization assumption that there is a lan-guage that can be computed in exponential deterministic time and requires expo-nential size nondeterministic circuits implies explicit codes for bounded polyno-mial size circuits (without any setup assumptions) with inverse polynomial secu-rity. The construction of [10] requires an encoding procedure that runs in time larger than the a priori polynomial upper bound on the size of the tampering circuit.

1.2   Related Work

Since the work of Dziembowski, Pietrzak, and Wichs [37,38] which introduced non-malleable codes, there has been a quite a significant amount of works on this subject in various different directions (for example, [1–3,22,23,25,34,53,59,60] to mention only a few in addition to the ones we mentioned earlier). Notably, various different classes of tampering functions were considered. The original work of [37] presented a construction of non-malleable codes against bit-wise tampering functions. Also, Liu and Lysyanskaya [65] were the first to consider the class of split state tampering functions, where left and right halves of a codeword may be tampered arbitrarily, but independently. There has been a very long line of works on getting optimal constructions against such tampering functions (see the references above).

Next, we give more information about the building blocks used in our con-structions and mention relevant related work.

Time-Lock Puzzles. These are puzzles that can be solved by "brute-force" in time $\overline{T}$, but cannot be solved significantly faster even using parallel pro-cessors. This concept was proposed by Rivest, Shamir, and Wagner [77] (fol-lowing May's work [66] on timed-release cryptography), and they have been used quite extensively studied since. The most popular instantiation relies on the *repeated squaring assumption* that postulates that $\overline{T}$ repeated squarings mod N, where $N = pq$ is a product of two secret primes, require "roughly" $\overline{T}$ parallel time/depth. Bitansky et al. [18] gave a construction of a time-lock puzzle from (strong) assumptions related to program obfuscation.

Our construction requires a "weak" notion of (sub-exponential) security that guarantees that the puzzle cannot be solved by sub-exponential size attackers that have depth $\overline{T}^\epsilon$. Therefore, using the instantiation that relies on repeated squarings, we only need to assume that there are no huge improvements in the parallel complexity of repeated squaring algorithms even for very large attackers. It is worth mentioning that there are known algorithms for factoring that run in sub-exponential time. The best known algorithm has running time roughly $2^{n^{1/3}}$, where n is the input size (see [35,78]). In contrast, our assumption stipulates that there is no algorithm with running time 2^{n^ϵ} for any $\epsilon > 0$ (for concreteness, think about $\epsilon = 0.001$). This is similar to the assumption being made in any construction that relies on sub-exponential factoring or discrete log.

Non-malleable Commitments. Non-malleable commitments, introduced by Dolev, Dwork and Naor [36], guarantee *hiding* (the committed value is kept secret from the receiver), *binding* ("opening" can yield only a single value determined in the commit phase), and *non-malleability* (guaranteeing that it is hard to "maul" a commitment to a given value into a commitment to a related value). Non-malleable commitments are extremely well studied with huge body of works trying to pin down the exact round complexity and minimal assumptions needed to obtain them [12,29,30,45–47,49,51,52,61–64,71,73–75,79].

We need a *non-interactive* (i.e., one-message) non-malleable commitment, of which relatively few constructions are known. Pandey et al. [71] formulated a concrete property of a random oracle and showed that it suffices for non-interactive non-malleable commitments. This is a non-standard and non-falsifiable (Naor [68]) assumption. Lin et al. [63] showed a construction that satisfies non-malleability against uniform attackers assuming a keyless collision resistant hash function, time-lock puzzles, non-interactive commitments, and NIWI proofs, all with sub-exponential hardness. Bitansky and Lin [20] were able to get non-malleability against all attackers (i.e., even non-uniform ones) by either replacing the keyless collision resistant hash function with a keyless *multi*-collision resistant hash function,[6] or using a new assumption regarding sub-exponentially secure one-way functions admitting some strong form of hardness amplification. Most recently, Kalai and Khurana [49] gave a construction of a non-interactive non-malleable commitment from sub-exponential hardness of factoring or discrete log, and sub-exponential *quantum* hardness of Learning With Errors (LWE) or Learning Parity with Noise (LPN).

We will use the construction of Bitansky and Lin [20] and Lin et al. [63] both of which rely on time-lock puzzles. Various properties of their non-malleable commitments will be crucial for our construction.

---

[6] Actually, Bitansky and Lin [20] formulate an assumption about incompressible functions which is implied by keyless multi-collision resistant hash functions.

One-Message SPS Zero-Knowledge. This is a one-message proof system for every language in **NP** in the plain model and without any setup assumptions that satisfies a relaxed notion of zero-knowledge referred to as super-polynomial-time simulation (SPS) zero-knowledge [72]. This concept was introduced by Barak and Pass [14] who also gave a construction assuming a keyless collision resistance hash function,[7] non-interactive commitments, and NIWI proofs, all with sub-exponential hardness. Their construction however satisfies soundness only against uniform attackers. Bitansky and Lin [20] showed how to overcome this limitation using keyless *multi*-collision resistant hash functions,[8] at the cost of obtaining a weaker soundness (allowing any attacker to output some bounded number of convincing proofs for false statements).

Non-malleable Codes vs. Commitments. (Non-interactive) non-malleable commitments and codes seem very similar. The only difference is that in the latter decoding should be efficient, while in the former it should be hard. There has been some evidence that the objects are not only syntactically related. For instance, non-malleable codes were used to construct non-malleable commitments [22,47]. In the reverse direction, some works used ideas from the (vast) literature on non-malleable commitments to get new non-malleable codes [6,24,70]. Our work continues the latter line of works and shows yet again that the notions are intimately related.

Lower Bounds for Non-malleability. We mentioned that there cannot be a non-malleable code secure against a class of tampering functions that includes the decoding procedures. In a very recent work, Ball et al. [9] gave various new lower bounds. The most related lower bound to this work is the one regarding (in)existence of non-malleable codes for $\mathbf{NC}^1$ ($\subseteq \mathbf{NC}$) in the standard model (a class that our construction captures). Their result introduces a notion of black-box reductions tailored for the setting of non-malleable codes and rules out such reductions for certain classes of tampering functions $\mathcal{F}$. Importantly, their impossibility results hold for constructions that rely only on the *minimal assumption* that there exists a distributional problem that is hard for the tampering class $\mathcal{F}$, but easy for **P**. Our result bypasses the impossibility since we—in addition to an assumption of the above type (i.e. time-lock puzzles)—rely on standard cryptographic assumptions such as keyless multi-collision resistant hash functions, injective one-way functions, and non-interactive witness-indistinguishable proofs.

The Magic of the Repeated Squaring Assumption. In the past several years the repeated squaring assumption has played an important role in many works. In addition to the work about non-malleable commitments [63] that we have already mentioned and the current work, this assumption was also used in

---

[7] Actually, Barak and Pass [14] formulate an assumption regarding the existence of a language in **P** which is hard to sample in slightly super-polynomial-time but easy to sample in a slightly larger super-polynomial-time. The existence of a keyless collision resistance hash function with sub-exponential hardness implies such a language.

[8] See Footnote 6.

several constructions of verifiable delay functions [39,76,80]. These functions are, roughly speaking, a publicly verifiable version of time-lock puzzles. The reason why this assumption has been so successful is that it brings a new dimension of hardness to the table, i.e., parallel-time, which is different from the type of hardness that standard cryptographic assumptions give.

(Multi-)collisions Resistance. Collision resistant hash functions are (a family of) compressing functions where no efficient attacker can find a colliding pair in a random function from the family. The existence of such a family is a standard cryptographic assumption which is implied by many of the most classical assumptions such as factoring, discrete log, and more. A *keyless* collision resistant hash function is a *single* function where the above is hard for *uniform* attackers. Such functions exist in the random oracle model and may be heuristically instantiated using common constructions of cryptographic hash functions, such as SHA-3, where collisions are simply not known.

Multi-collision resistance [17,19,54,55] is a relaxation of collision resistance where the goal of the attacker is to find a collection of *many* inputs (rather than just two) to a random function in the family that collide. The keyless version, introduced by [19], is again a single function but now the security guarantee can be formulated so that it holds for all efficient attackers, even non-uniform ones. Concretely, the security guarantee is that while an attacker of size s can find about s inputs that collide, it cannot find many more, say s^5 (i.e., multi-collisions cannot be compressed). Again, such functions exist in the random oracle model and may be heuristically instantiated using common constructions of cryptographic hash functions, such as SHA-3.

2   Technical Overview

At a very high level, as in several previous related works (e.g., [6,8]), we follow the Naor-Yung [69] paradigm that achieves CCA security of encryption by concatenating two instances of a CPA secure public key encryption scheme, followed by a (non-interactive) zero-knowledge proof of the equality of encrypted values. The novelty in this work stems from the way we instantiate and prove soundness of this approach in the context of non-malleable codes.

Concretely, the three main components in our construction are: a time-lock puzzle, a non-malleable commitment, and a one-message SPS zero-knowledge proof of consistency. As we will see later, these building blocks need to be instantiated in a very careful way to guarantee security. The construction NMCode = (NMCode.E, NMCode.D) for a message space $\{0,1\}^\lambda$ and depth bound $\overline{T}$ is informally described in Algorithm 1.

Let us provide some intuition and state some simple observations. Recall that a time-lock puzzle can be solved by "brute-force" in depth $\overline{T}$, but cannot be solved in depth $\ll \overline{T}$. However, time-lock puzzles may be malleable (in fact, the construction based on repeated squaring [77] is easily malleable). Non-malleable commitments are, by definition, non-malleable but as opposed to time-lock puzzles, cannot be "brute-force" opened in polynomial time. Intuitively, adding the

NMCode.E(m):	NMCode.D(Z, c, π):
1. Let Z be a time-lock puzzle with hardness $\overline{T}$ and underlying message m. 2. Let c be a non-malleable commitment to m. 3. Let π be a zero-knowledge proof of consistency between Z and c. 4. Output $\hat{Z} := (Z, c, \pi)$.	1. Verify the proof π. 2. If verifies, solve the puzzle Z and output the underlying message. Otherwise, output 0.

Algorithm 1: Our non-malleable code (*Informal*).

zero-knowledge proof of consistency in the above construction ties the hands of the attacker and achieves the desired properties of each of the primitives. The scheme inherits non-malleability from the non-malleable commitment while preserving the ability of solving the time-lock puzzle in polynomial time, which allows extraction of the underlying message and thereby decoding in polynomial time.

For efficiency, time-lock puzzles have a built-in trapdoor that allows one to generate puzzles *very fast* (while solving them requires many sequential resources). Thus, the running time of step 3 (generation of the zero-knowledge proof) takes fixed polynomial time (in the security parameter), independent of the depth bound $\overline{T}$. This is why NMCode.E has a fixed running time, polynomial in the security parameter, independent of $\overline{T}$. Negligible soundness of our construction, at a high level, is inherited from the security of the underlying primitives. Lastly, as we will explain shortly, we use the non-interactive non-malleable commitments of Lin et al. [63] and Bitansky and Lin [20] both of which are based on time-lock puzzles (and keyless collision resistant hash functions or keyless multi-collision resistant hash functions, respectively) and so this will work nicely with our usage of the time-lock puzzle in our construction.

While the intuition described above is rather solid, proving that the above construction satisfies non-malleability turns out to be challenging. We explain the high-level approach next.

2.1 Overview of the Proof

We will first explain the high-level approach when considering only uniform tampering functions and later explain how to handle non-uniform ones.

Since we only handle uniform tampering functions (for now), it will suffice to rely (in addition to time-lock puzzles) on a non-malleable commitment for uniform tampering functions and a one-message SPS zero-knowledge proof which satisfies uniform soundness. For the commitment scheme we will use the one of Lin, Pass, and Soni [63] and for the zero-knowledge we will use the one of Barak and Pass [14]. We remark again that while the scheme of Lin et al. [63] is also based on a time-lock puzzle, it will be convenient to use it not only in terms of assumptions, but to actually use specific properties of the scheme that will help us carry out the proof.

The proof is, naturally, by a hybrid argument where we start with the standard non-malleability game with a message m_0 and in the last hybrid we will play the non-malleability game with a message m_1. Recall that the non-malleability game (a.k.a. Man-In-Middle game) consists of two stages. In the first stage, the adversary gets a codeword and it tries to maul it into a code with a related message. Then, roughly, the distribution of the underlying message in that tampered codeword should be simulatable without knowing the message itself.

In a high level, here are the sequence of hybrids that we consider. We describe the changes incrementally, namely, each hybrid starts with the scheme from the previous hybrid and makes a modification.

- Hybrid 0: The original scheme.
- Hybrid 1: Instead of using the zero-knowledge prover, we use the simulator.
- Hybrid 2: Instead of committing to m, we commit to 0.
- Hybrid 3: Instead of decoding by solving the time-lock puzzle, we decode by extracting from the commitment.
- Hybrid 4: Instead of using m as the underlying message in the time-lock puzzle, use 0.

Showing that hybrids 0, 1, and 2 are indistinguishable is simple. Hybrids 0 and 1 are indistinguishable due to the zero-knowledge property, and hybrids 1 and 2 are indistinguishable due to the hiding of the commitment scheme. The most challenging part is showing that hybrids 2 and 3 and hybrids 3 and 4 are indistinguishable.

Hybrids 2 and 3. The modification in this transition is from decoding via brute-force opening the time-lock puzzle, to decoding via extraction from the non-malleable commitment. To prove indistinguishability, we show that the distribution of the underlying value in the right commitment does not change throughout the hybrids when considering both methods of decoding.

A careful inspection of the schemes in each hybrid reveals that in order for the proof to go through, we need to satisfy two conditions simultaneously:

1. The extractor of the commitment scheme (whose size is S_{Ext}) cannot break zero-knowledge (which holds for all attackers of size at most S_{ZK}). That is,

$$S_{\mathsf{Ext}} \ll S_{\mathsf{ZK}}.$$

2. The simulator of the zero-knowledge scheme (whose size is S_{Sim}) cannot break non-malleability of the commitment (which holds for all attackers of size at most S_{NMCom}). That is,

$$S_{\mathsf{Sim}} \ll S_{\mathsf{NMCom}}.$$

It also holds that $S_{\mathsf{NMCom}} \ll S_{\mathsf{Ext}}$ since the commitment extractor can definitely break non-malleability (by extracting and re-committing to a related value).

Therefore, the only way to satisfy the above two inequalities is if $S_{\mathsf{Sim}} \ll S_{\mathsf{ZK}}$, namely, a one-message zero-knowledge scheme where the simulator runs faster than the distinguisher![9] Unfortunately, no such scheme is known as in all known schemes the simulator needs to "break" the underlying cryptographic primitives and so it has to have more resources than the distinguishers.

Our idea to make this go through is to introduce another axis of hardness which will allow us to satisfy both "inequalities" simultaneously—the axes of total size and depth. Namely, we think of algorithms as parallelizable machines and measure their complexity by counting their total size and parallel time (size and time/depth, in short). We will set the complexities of the above procedures as follows, where λ denotes the security parameter and where $0 < c_1 < c_2 < c_3 < 1$:

- S_{Ext} (extraction from the non-malleable commitment): in quasi-polynomial size and depth.
- S_{ZK} (zero-knowledge security): for all $2^{\lambda^{c_1}}$ size (and depth) attackers.
- S_{Sim} (ZK simulator complexity): in $2^{\lambda^{c_2}}$ size but fixed polynomial depth.
- S_{NMCom} (non-malleability): for all $2^{\lambda^{c_3}}$ size attackers with arbitrary polynomial depth.

With this choice of parameters, it is evident that the commitment extractor cannot break zero-knowledge and also the zero-knowledge simulator cannot break non-malleability. It is also not too hard to instantiate the primitives with the above properties. The zero-knowledge scheme of Barak and Pass [14] readily satisfies the above properties if it is sub-exponentially hard. To get the required non-malleable commitment, we need to slightly adjust the scheme of Lin et al. [63] (as they did not consider such tampering functions), but the changes are relatively minor.

Hybrids 3 and 4. In this hybrid, we change the time-lock puzzle's underlying value and we want to use its hiding property. While seemingly being a relatively simple hybrid, it turns out that some complications arise. Specifically, to reduce to the underlying security of the time-lock puzzle, we need to come up with a bounded time attacker while there are two procedures that we need to run which seem to be of *arbitrary* depth. Specifically, in the reduction we need to simulate the whole experiment and use the distinguisher to break the security of the time-lock puzzle. The two procedures that seem to require arbitrary large depth are:

- The distinguisher itself, denoted D from now on.
- The extraction procedure of the non-malleable commitment (which we should execute as part of decoding).

We have *no* control over the depth (or size) of the distinguisher D, except that it is of arbitrary polynomial size and depth. However, we do know that its

---

[9] This kind of zero-knowledge simulation is known as *strong* super-polynomial simulation. Recently, Khurana and Sahai [52] managed to obtain it in two rounds, but we need a non-interactive scheme.

input, the message underlying the tampered code, is of bounded length. So, we *modify* the distinguisher and write it as a *truth table* which has hardcoded all of D's outputs on every possible input. Call this distinguisher $\tilde{D}$. Observe that $\tilde{D}$ (1) has the same input-output functionality as that of D (and so it serves as a good distinguisher), and (2) while $\tilde{D}$'s size is now exponential in the security parameter, its depth is some fixed polynomial in the security parameter!

For the extraction procedure, we intuitively make a similar modification. We rely on the fact that there is another brute-force extractor that requires exponential size but only fixed polynomial time. Note that for this to go through, the size of the extraction procedure has to smaller than the hardness of the time-lock puzzle (and this can be achieved by making the time-lock puzzle sufficiently long and using sub-exponential security). So, we switch to this alternate extractor. Now, we can simulate the whole experiment in fixed polynomial depth and reduce to the security game of the underlying time-lock puzzle.

The Non-uniform Case. Extending to handle non-uniform tampering functions is challenging in the fully non-interactive setting and in the plain model. While it is relatively straight-forward to replace the non-malleable commitment scheme of Lin et al. [63] (which is uniformly non-malleable) with the one of Bitansky and Lin [20], the challenge stems from finding an appropriate non-uniform analogue for the uniformly sound one-message zero-knowledge scheme of Barak and Pass [14]. Indeed, in the plain model and allowing only one message *there is no* non-uniformly sound zero-knowledge scheme (as accepting proofs for false statements just exist).

The closest candidate is the one of Bitansky and Lin [20] who constructed a non-uniformly *weakly* sound one-message zero-knowledge scheme. This notion captures all non-uniform attackers but the soundness guarantee is weak: every attacker *can* output some number of accepting proofs for false statements but not too many of those. Unfortunately, if we use this scheme directly in our construction instead of the current zero-knowledge scheme, the above proof outline fails. Specifically, when we switch to alternate decoding (which extracts from the commitment rather than breaks the time-lock puzzle), if the adversary uses such a maliciously crafted proof (which verifies), it can easily distinguish the two hybrids (as their outputs will be different). Another thing that makes the situation even harder is that the bad set of proofs is not global but actually attacker-dependent so we cannot just "black-list" some set of proofs in the decoding procedure.

To this end, we observe that in the security reduction, the attacker *is* fixed and so the set of "bad" proofs is *non-uniformly* known. Therefore, we can modify the alternate decoding procedure to check whether the tampered proof is one of some (polynomial size) non-uniformly hardcoded set of bad proofs—the ones that the given attacker can find. If it is one of these bad proofs, we output a fixed message, the one underlying the time-lock puzzle that corresponds to the false statement. In this way, we are guaranteed that even when switch to alternate decoding, for those maliciously crafted proofs, the attacker will not see any difference between the two hybrids.

3   Preliminaries

Model of Computation. We consider uniform and non-uniform algorithms and we distinguish between their size and parallel time. The amount of non-uniformity is usually denoted by κ, the parallel time by T, and the size by S. We think of those algorithms as (possibly probabilistic) Turing machines with multiple heads that can operate in parallel. A non-uniform algorithm $\mathcal{A}$ is described by a family of of algorithms $\{\mathcal{A}_\lambda\}_{\lambda \in \mathbb{N}}$, one per security parameter λ. Each $\mathcal{A}_\lambda$ corresponds to an algorithm that has input size $n(\lambda)$ for some function $n \colon \mathbb{N} \to \mathbb{N}$. We say that $\mathcal{A}$ is T-time, denoted $\mathsf{Time}\,[\mathcal{A}] = T(\lambda)$, if for every $\lambda \in \mathbb{N}$, the parallel running time of $\mathcal{A}_\lambda$ is at most $T(\lambda)$. We say that $\mathcal{A}$ is S-size, denoted $\mathsf{Size}\,[\mathcal{A}] = S(\lambda)$, if for every $\lambda \in \mathbb{N}$, the total work that the algorithm $\mathcal{A}_\lambda$ does is at most $S(\lambda)$. Lastly, the mount of non-uniformity κ is chosen such that $\kappa(\lambda)$ is an upper bound on the size of advice used per λ.

Additional necessary but standard preliminaries appear in the full version [33]. There, the reader can find standard notation that we use and standard definitions related to non-malleable commitments (following Lin, Pass, and Soni [63]), one-message zero-knowledge proofs (following Barak and Pass [14]), and time-lock puzzles (following Rivest, Shamir, and Wagner [77]).

4   Definition of Non-Malleable Codes

In this section we give our definition of non-malleable codes. Our definition follows closely the definition of [8]. One difference though is that, rather than defining non-malleability for an abstract class of tampering functions, we define non-malleability directly for the class of tampering functions that we consider in this work .

Let Σ and Σ' be sets of strings. A *coding scheme* consists of two algorithms $\mathsf{NMCode} = (\mathsf{NMCode.E}, \mathsf{NMCode.D})$ such that $\mathsf{NMCode.E} \colon \Sigma \to \Sigma'$ and $\mathsf{NMCode.D} \colon \Sigma' \to \Sigma$. In words, $\mathsf{NMCode.E}$ ("encoding") maps messages to codewords and $\mathsf{NMCode.D}$ ("decoding") maps codewords to messages. The algorithm $\mathsf{NMCode.E}$ can be randomized and $\mathsf{NMCode.D}$ is assumed to be deterministic. For *correctness*, we require that for every message $m \in \Sigma$, it holds that

$$\Pr_{\mathsf{NMCode.E}}[\mathsf{NMCode.D}(\mathsf{NMCode.E}(m)) = m] = 1.$$

$\mathsf{NMCode.E}$ may also accept as an explicit input a security parameter in unary (in which case the syntax is $\mathsf{NMCode.E}(1^\lambda, m)$).

Non-malleability. Intuitively, this notion requires that given a codeword, as long as one cannot decode it, it is hard to generate a codeword with a different related underlying message. A function that takes a codeword and tries to generate a codeword for a related message out of it is called a *tampering function*. As mentioned, we have to limit the possible tampering functions in some way. Otherwise, a tampering function could decode a codeword and re-encode a related message.

Definition 1 (Tampering Experiment). *For an algorithm* $\mathcal{A} = \{\mathcal{A}_\lambda\}_{\lambda \in \mathbb{N}}$, *a security parameter* $\lambda \in \mathbb{N}$, *and a string* $s \in \{0,1\}^\lambda$, *define the tampering experiment:*

$$\mathsf{Tamper}_{\mathcal{A},s}^{\mathsf{NMCode}}(\lambda) = \left\{ \begin{array}{c} Z \leftarrow \mathsf{NMCode.E}(1^\lambda, s); \ \tilde{Z} = \mathcal{A}_\lambda(Z); \ \tilde{s} = \mathsf{NMCode.D}(\tilde{Z}) \\ \textit{Output: } \tilde{s} \end{array} \right\},$$

where the randomness of the above experiment comes from the randomness of $\mathsf{NMCode.E}$.

Definition 2 ((S, T, κ)-Non-malleability). *We say that a code* NMCode *is* (S, T, κ)-*non-malleable if for every* S-*size* T-*time algorithm* $\mathcal{A} = \{\mathcal{A}_\lambda\}_{\lambda \in \mathbb{N}}$ *with* κ *bits of non-uniformity, there exists a (uniform) probabilistic polynomial-time simulator* Sim *such that*

$$\{\mathsf{Tamper}_{\mathcal{A},s}^{\mathsf{NMCode}}(\lambda)\}_\lambda \approx \{\mathsf{Ideal}_{\mathsf{Sim},s}(\lambda)\}_\lambda,$$

where

$$\mathsf{Ideal}_{\mathsf{Sim},s}(\lambda) = \left\{ \begin{array}{c} \tilde{s} \cup \{same\} \leftarrow \mathsf{Sim}^{\mathcal{A}_\lambda}(1^\lambda) \\ \textit{Output: } s \textit{ if output of } \mathsf{Sim} \textit{ is same and otherwise } \tilde{s} \end{array} \right\}.$$

Medium Non-malleability. We next define a different notion of non-malleability, referred to as *medium* non-malleability, which implies the one above (Definition 2) but is slightly easier to work with [6,56]. The difference between the definitions is that the medium non-malleability experiment allows to output same* only when some predicate g evaluated on an original codeword and a tampered one is satisfied. On the other hand, plain non-malleability (as defined above) does not impose restrictions on when the experiment is allowed to output same*.

Definition 3 ((S, T, κ)-Medium Non-malleability). *We say that a code* NMCode *is* (S, T, κ)-*medium non-malleable if there exists a function* g *such that for every* $s_0, s_1 \in \{0,1\}^\lambda$ *and every* S-*size* T-*time algorithm* $\mathcal{A} = \{\mathcal{A}_\lambda\}_{\lambda \in \mathbb{N}}$ *with* κ *bits of non-uniformity, it holds that*

$$\{\mathsf{MedTamper}_{\mathcal{A},s_0}^{\mathsf{NMCode}}(\lambda)\}_{\lambda \in \mathbb{N}} \approx \{\mathsf{MedTamper}_{\mathcal{A},s_1}^{\mathsf{NMCode}}(\lambda)\}_{\lambda \in \mathbb{N}},$$

where the tampering experiment (whose randomness comes from the randomness of $\mathsf{NMCode.E}$) *is defined as follows:*

$$\mathsf{MedTamper}_{\mathcal{A},s}^{\mathsf{NMCode}}(\lambda) = \left\{ \begin{array}{c} Z \leftarrow \mathsf{NMCode.E}(1^\lambda, s); \ \tilde{Z} = \mathcal{A}_\lambda(Z); \ \tilde{s} = \mathsf{NMCode.D}(\tilde{Z}) \\ \textit{Output: } \mathbf{same}^* \textit{ if } g(Z, \tilde{Z}) = 1, \textit{ and } \tilde{s} \textit{ otherwise} \end{array} \right\},$$

and where $g(\cdot, \cdot)$ *is a predicate such that for every* $\mathcal{A}$ *as above,* $\lambda \in \mathbb{N}$, *and* $s \in \{0,1\}^\lambda$,

$$\Pr_{Z \leftarrow \mathsf{NMCode.D}(1^\lambda, s)} [g(Z, \mathcal{A}_\lambda(Z)) = 1 \ \wedge \ \mathsf{NMCode.D}(\mathcal{A}_\lambda(Z)) \neq s] \leq \mathsf{negl}(\lambda).$$

5 The Building Blocks

5.1 Time-Lock Puzzle

Theorem 3. *Assuming the sub-exponential hardness of the repeated squaring assumption, there exists a time-lock puzzle which is $(S^{\mathsf{TL}}, \epsilon)$-hard for a fixed $\epsilon \in (0,1)$ and where $S^{\mathsf{TL}} = 2^{3\lambda}$.*

We need a time-lock puzzle which, when instantiated with difficulty parameter t, is hard for machines that have parallel time at most t^ϵ for some fixed $\epsilon \in (0,1)$, even if their total size is $2^{3\lambda}$. We instantiate this primitive by relying on the repeated squaring assumption with sub-exponential hardness. The latter says that for some $\epsilon, \epsilon' \in (0,1)$ and any large enough t the following holds: any $2^{\lambda^{\epsilon'}}$-size t^ϵ-time algorithm cannot distinguish $(g, N, t, g^{2^t} \bmod N)$ from (g, N, t, g') for uniform $g, g' \in Z_{p \cdot q}^*$, where p and q are two random λ-bit primes. Note that it is common to assume the above assumption even for $((1 - \epsilon) \cdot t)$-time algorithms–our assumption is much weaker.

To generate a puzzle Z with difficulty t and a message m, one does the following (we assume here for simplicity that m is short enough but it is easy to extend this): Sample an RSA modulus $N = pq$ to be a product of two random $\mathsf{poly}(\lambda)$-bit primes (with some large enough polynomial; see below), and computes $Z = (g, N, t, m + g^{2^t} \bmod N)$, where g is a randomly chosen element in Z_N^*. Note that using p and q it is possible to compute $g^{2^t} \bmod N$ in fixed polynomial time in λ (and $\log t$ which is absorbed by the $\mathsf{poly}(\lambda)$ term) by first computing $a = 2^t \bmod \phi(N)$ (where $\phi(N) = (p-1)(q-1)$) and then computing $Z = g^a \bmod N$.

Assuming the sub-exponential hardness of the repeated squaring assumption, we want a time-lock puzzle whose guarantee is that the underlying value is completely hidden as long as the attacker has size less than $2^{3\lambda}$ size and t^ϵ time. To achieve this, the bit-length of p and q needs to be large enough. That is, we need to instantiate our primes with say $\tilde{\lambda} = (3\lambda)^{1/\epsilon}$ bits which would give security for attackers of size $2^{3\lambda}$ and t^ϵ time.

5.2 Non-malleable Commitment

Theorem 4. *Assume that there is a keyless multi-collision resistant hash function, the repeated squaring assumption, NIWI proof for all* **NP***, and injective one-way functions, all with sub-exponential hardness. Then, there exists a non-interactive commitment which is $(S^{\mathsf{NMCom}}, T^{\mathsf{NMCom}})$-hiding, $(S_{\mathsf{Ext}_1}^{\mathsf{NMCom}}, T_{\mathsf{Ext}_1}^{\mathsf{NMCom}})$-extractable via $\mathsf{NMCom.Ext}_1$ and $(S_{\mathsf{Ext}_2}^{\mathsf{NMCom}}, T_{\mathsf{Ext}_2}^{\mathsf{NMCom}})$-extractable via $\mathsf{NMCom.Ext}_2$, and $(S_{NM}^{\mathsf{NMCom}}, T_{NM}^{\mathsf{NMCom}})$-non-malleable for all polynomial functions T^{NMCom} and T_{NM}^{NMCom}, and where $S^{\mathsf{NMCom}}(\lambda) = 2^{\lambda^{\eta''}}$ for an appropriate constant η'', $S_{\mathsf{Ext}_1}^{\mathsf{NMCom}}(\lambda) = T_{\mathsf{Ext}_1}^{\mathsf{NMCom}}(\lambda) = 2^{\log^2 \lambda}$, $S_{\mathsf{Ext}_2}^{\mathsf{NMCom}}(\lambda) = 2^{2\lambda}$, $T_{\mathsf{Ext}_2}^{\mathsf{NMCom}}(\lambda) = \lambda^3$, and $S_{NM}^{\mathsf{NMCom}} = 2^\lambda$.*

Theorem 5. *Assume that there is a keyless collision resistant hash function, the repeated squaring assumption, NIWI proof for all* **NP**, *and injective one-way functions, all with sub-exponential hardness. Then, there exists a non-interactive commitment which is* $(S^{\mathsf{NMCom}}, T^{\mathsf{NMCom}})$-*hiding,* $(S^{\mathsf{NMCom}}_{\mathsf{Ext}_1}, T^{\mathsf{NMCom}}_{\mathsf{Ext}_1})$-*extractable via* $\mathsf{NMCom.Ext}_1$ *and* $(S^{\mathsf{NMCom}}_{\mathsf{Ext}_2}, T^{\mathsf{NMCom}}_{\mathsf{Ext}_2})$-*extractable via* $\mathsf{NMCom.Ext}_2$, *and* $(S^{\mathsf{NMCom}}_{NM}, T^{\mathsf{NMCom}}_{NM}, \kappa^{\mathsf{NMCom}}_{NM})$-*non-malleable for all polynomial functions* T^{NMCom} *and* T^{NMCom}_{NM}, *and where* $S^{\mathsf{NMCom}}(\lambda) = 2^{\lambda^{\eta''}}$ *for an appropriate constant* η'', $S^{\mathsf{NMCom}}_{\mathsf{Ext}_1}(\lambda) = T^{\mathsf{NMCom}}_{\mathsf{Ext}_1}(\lambda) = 2^{\log^2 \lambda}$, $S^{\mathsf{NMCom}}_{\mathsf{Ext}_2}(\lambda) = 2^{2\lambda}$, $T^{\mathsf{NMCom}}_{\mathsf{Ext}_2}(\lambda) = \lambda^3$, $S^{\mathsf{NMCom}}_{NM} = 2^{\lambda}$, *and* $\kappa^{\mathsf{NMCom}}_{NM} = 0$.

The difference between the two theorems are that in the former we obtain non-malleability for non-uniform attackers but using a keyless multi-collision resistant hash, while in the latter we obtain non-malleability only for uniform attackers but we are using a keyless (plain) collision resistant hash.

We need a one-message non-malleable tag-based commitment scheme which is hiding for all (non-uniform) polynomial-size distinguishers, extractable either in size and time $2^{\log^2 \lambda}$ or in 2^{λ}-size and λ^3-time, and non-malleable for all exponential size and polynomial time tampering functions.

The Uniform Scheme. To get the scheme satisfying the properties listed in Theorem 5 we use the scheme of Lin et al. [63]. Let us review their scheme and explain why and how it satisfies the above properties. In a high-level, they use two types of commitment scheme, each with a different "axis" of hardness. From sub-exponentially secure injective one-way functions, they obtain a sub-exponentially secure commitment scheme Com^s. By instantiating Com^s with different security parameters, one can obtain a family of γ commitment schemes $\{\mathsf{Com}^s_i\}_{i \in [\gamma]}$ such that Com^s_{i+1} is harder than Com^s_i for all $1 \le i \le \gamma - 1$ in the *axis of size*. Namely, using size which is sufficient to extract from Com^s_i it is still hard to break Com^s_{i+1}. Also, the extraction procedure is essentially a brute force algorithm that "tries all option" and so it is highly parallelizable and requires fixed parallel time (depth).

A similar trick is performed using time-lock puzzles. They are used to obtain a family of γ commitment schemes $\{\mathsf{Com}^t_i\}_{i \in [\gamma]}$ such that Com^t_{i+1} is harder than Com^t_i for all $1 \le i \le \gamma - 1$ in the *axis of time*. Namely, in time which is sufficient to extract from Com^t_i it is still hard to break Com^t_{i+1}. The extraction procedure is highly sequential and requires very small total size. In particular, in size which is sufficient to extract from any Com^t it is still hard to break any Com^s.

To construct a non-malleable commitment scheme NMCom, their key idea is to combine a Com^s and Com^t scheme with opposite strength. That is,

$$\mathsf{NMCom}(1^{\lambda}, m, \mathsf{tag}) = \mathsf{Com}^s_{\mathsf{tag}}(1^{\lambda}, s) \| \mathsf{Com}^t_{\gamma - \mathsf{tag}}(1^{\lambda}, s \oplus m) \text{, where } s \leftarrow \{0, 1\}^{|m|}.$$

The hiding and non-malleability proofs are the same as in [63]. Hiding is immediate from hiding of the two underlying commitments, and we sketch the main idea behind the proof of non-malleability next. Non-malleability holds by considering two cases. First, if the left tag i is smaller than the right tag j, the Com_j^t commitment on the right remains hiding for attackers of size and time enough for extracting from both Com_i^t and Com_j^s. Therefore the right committed value remains hidden, while the right is extracted. Otherwise, if the left tag i is larger than the right commitment j, then the Com_i^s commitment on the left remains hiding for attackers of size and time enough for extracting from both Com_j^s and $\mathsf{Com}_{\gamma-j}^t$. Thus, the left committed value remains hidden, while the right is extracted.

Lastly, we explain how to implement the two extraction procedures that we need. Recall that we need one extraction procedure that works in quasi-linear size and time and another procedure that works in exponential size and fixed polynomial time. The former is implemented by extracting from the right commitment (by breaking the time-lock puzzles) and the latter is implemented by breaking the left commitment (by checking in parallel all possible openings).

Of course, the above construction is not the final construction of [63] as it supports only a small number of tags (while our goal is to support an exponential number of tags). To get around this they present a tag-amplification technique that is based on a tree-like structure and the way they avoid blow-up in the commitment size is by using a (keyless) collision resistant hash function (which causes the final construction to be non-malleable only with respect to uniform attackers). We refer to [63] for the precise details.

The Non-uniform Scheme. To get the scheme satisfying the properties listed in Theorem 4 we use the scheme of Bitansky and Lin [20] (which in turns is based on the scheme of [63]). Here, they present a new tag-amplification technique, inspired by a interactive tag-amplification technique of Khurana and Sahai [52], where they make it non-interactive using their one-message zero-knowledge protocol (which is based on keyless multi-collision resistant hash functions).

For our purposes, the details of this transformation are not very relevant—the only thing that is important is the structure of thier final commitment. Indeed, it consists of the same time or space hard commitments of [63] (along with various proofs). These are extractable in the same manner, either in quasi-linear time or in exponential size and polynomial time.

5.3   One-Message Zero-Knowledge

Theorem 6. *Assume the existence of a one-way permutation, a NIWI proof systems for all NP, a keyless multi-collision resistant hash function, all sub-exponentially secure. Then, there exists a one-message SPS zero-knowledge argument system satisfying (S_P, K)-weak-soundness and $(S_D, S_{\mathsf{Sim}}, T_{\mathsf{Sim}})$-zero-knowledge for all polynomials $S_P(\lambda)$, and where $K \in \mathsf{poly}(\lambda)$ is a fixed polynomial, $S_D(\lambda) = 2^{\lambda^\eta}$ and $S_{\mathsf{Sim}}(\lambda) = 2^{\lambda^{\eta'}}$ for some constants $\eta, \eta' \in (0, 1)$, and $T_{\mathsf{Sim}}(\lambda) = \lambda^2$.*

Theorem 7. *Assume the existence of a one-way permutation, a NIWI proof systems for all NP, a collision resistant hash function secure against uniform polynomial-time algorithms, all sub-exponentially secure. Then, there exists a* *one-message SPS zero-knowledge argument system satisfying (S_P, κ)-soundness and $(S_D, S_{\mathsf{Sim}}, T_{\mathsf{Sim}})$-zero-knowledge for all polynomial $S_P(\lambda)$, and where $\kappa(\lambda) = 0$, $S_D(\lambda) = 2^{\lambda^\eta}$ and $S_{\mathsf{Sim}}(\lambda) = 2^{\lambda^{\eta'}}$ for some constants $\eta, \eta' \in (0,1)$, and $T_{\mathsf{Sim}}(\lambda) = \lambda^2$.*

The difference between the two theorems are that in the former we obtain weak-soundness for non-uniform attackers but using a keyless multi-collision resistant hash, while in the latter we obtain (plain) soundness only for uniform attackers but we are using a keyless (plain) collision resistant hash.

Barak and Pass [14] showed that a one-message zero-knowledge system exists assuming a collection of sub-exponentially hard primitives: a one-way permutation, a NIWI for all NP, and a keyless collision resistant hash function. Intuitively, their construction follows the Feige-Lapidot-Shamir paradigm [43] where the protocol consists of a commitment to 0 and a WI argument for the statement that either the prover knows a witness for the given instance, or it used a commitment to a special (hard to guess) value. The special value which is hard to guess is, intuitively, a collision in an appropriately chosen hash function and this is why soundness only applies to uniform malicious provers. The simulator is a parallel machine that can find such a collision by brute force using a super-polynomial size procedure which has only fixed polynomial time (it tries all possibilities in parallel). Their construction gives Theorem 7.

Bitansky and Lin [20] constructed a one-message zero-knowledge argument system by replacing the uniform hash function used by Barak and Pass with a *keyless* multi collision resistant hash function [19]. Their construction gives Theorem 6.

6   The Non-malleable Code

In this section, we present a construction of a non-malleable code that satisfies non-malleability against all (non-uniform) polynomial size attackers that have bounded polynomial depth. In other words, the only way to maul a codeword is by having high depth.

Our construction relies on several building blocks on which we elaborate next.

1. A time-lock puzzle (Theorem 3) $\mathsf{TL} = (\mathsf{TL.Gen}, \mathsf{TL.Sol})$ which, for all large enough difficulty parameters t, allows to generate puzzles which are hard for any (non-uniform) machine whose parallel time/depth is at most t^ϵ, even it has size $2^{3\lambda}$.
   More precisely, for a difficulty parameter t, it is $(S^{\mathsf{TL}}, \epsilon)$-hard for a fixed $\epsilon \in (0,1)$ and for $S^{\mathsf{TL}}(\lambda) = 2^{3\lambda}$.
2. A one-message SPS zero-knowledge argument system (Theorem 6) $\mathsf{ZK} = (\mathsf{ZK.P}, \mathsf{ZK.V})$ which is weakly sound w.r.t. all (non-uniform) polynomial-size attackers, there is a (uniform) simulator that requires sub-exponential size and fixed polynomial time, and zero-knowledge holds w.r.t. sub-exponential size adversaries.

More precisely, it is $(S_P^{\mathsf{ZK}}, K^{\mathsf{ZK}})$-sound and $(S_D^{\mathsf{ZK}}, S_{\mathsf{Sim}}^{\mathsf{ZK}}, T_{\mathsf{Sim}}^{\mathsf{ZK}})$-zero-knowledge for all polynomial functions S_P^{ZK} and where $K^{\mathsf{ZK}} \in \mathsf{poly}(\lambda)$ is a fixed polynomial, $S_D^{\mathsf{ZK}}(\lambda) = 2^{\lambda^\eta}$, $S_{\mathsf{Sim}}^{\mathsf{ZK}}(\lambda) = 2^{\lambda^{\eta'}}$, and $T_{\mathsf{Sim}}^{\mathsf{ZK}}(\lambda) = \lambda^2$.

3. A one-message non-malleable tag-based commitment scheme (Theorem 4) $\mathsf{NMCom} = (\mathsf{NMCom.C}, \mathsf{NMCom.O})$ which is hiding for all (non-uniform) polynomial-size distinguishers, extractable either in size and time $2^{\log^2 \lambda}$ or in 2^λ size and λ^3 time, and non-malleable for all exponential size and polynomial time tampering functions.

   More precisely, it is $(S^{\mathsf{NMCom}}, T^{\mathsf{NMCom}})$-hiding, $(S_{\mathsf{Ext}_1}^{\mathsf{NMCom}}, T_{\mathsf{Ext}_1}^{\mathsf{NMCom}})$-extractable via $\mathsf{NMCom.Ext}_1$ and $(S_{\mathsf{Ext}_2}^{\mathsf{NMCom}}, T_{\mathsf{Ext}_2}^{\mathsf{NMCom}})$-extractable via $\mathsf{NMCom.Ext}_2$, and $(S_{NM}^{\mathsf{NMCom}}, T_{NM}^{\mathsf{NMCom}})$-non-malleable for all polynomial functions T^{NMCom} and T_{NM}^{NMCom}, and where $S^{\mathsf{NMCom}}(\lambda) = 2^{\lambda^{\eta''}}$ where $\eta'' > \eta'$, $S_{\mathsf{Ext}_1}^{\mathsf{NMCom}}(\lambda) = T_{\mathsf{Ext}_1}^{\mathsf{NMCom}}(\lambda) = 2^{\log^2 \lambda}$, $S_{\mathsf{Ext}_2}^{\mathsf{NMCom}}(\lambda) = 2^{2\lambda}$, $T_{\mathsf{Ext}_2}^{\mathsf{NMCom}}(\lambda) = \lambda^3$, and $S_{NM}^{\mathsf{NMCom}} = 2^\lambda$.

4. $\mathsf{Sig} = (\mathsf{Sig.G}, \mathsf{Sig.S}, \mathsf{Sig.V})$. A one-time signature scheme, unforgeable for polynomial-size attackers.

We show that assuming the existence of the above primitives, there is a code which is non-malleable for *all* polynomial-size attackers that run in bounded polynomial depth. We denote the latter $\overline{T}$. Our main result is summarized in the following theorem.

Theorem 8. *Assume a time-lock puzzle* TL, *a one-message SPS zero knowledge system* ZK, *a one-message non-malleable commitment scheme* NMCom, *and a one-time signature scheme* Sig, *as above. Then, there exist constants* $\alpha, \beta, \gamma \in \mathbb{N}$ *such that for any large enough polynomial* $\overline{T}$, *there is a code* $\mathsf{NMCode} = (\mathsf{NMCode.E}, \mathsf{NMCode.D})$ *(described below in Algorithms 2, 3, and 4) with the following properties:*

1. *The input of* $\mathsf{NMCode.E}$ *is a message from* $\{0,1\}^\lambda$ *and it outputs a codeword in* $\{0,1\}^{\lambda^\alpha}$.
2. *The running time of* $\mathsf{NMCode.E}$ *is* λ^β *and the running time of* $\mathsf{NMCode.D}$ *is* $(\overline{T} \cdot \lambda)^\gamma$.
3. *It is* $(S, \overline{T})$-non-malleable for all polynomials $S(\lambda)$.

The Construction. Fix $\overline{T}$, the upper bound on the depth of the tampering function. The high level idea of the construction is to combine the hardness for parallel machines that comes from a time-lock puzzle together with non-malleability that comes from a non-malleable commitment. Specifically, the way we combine them is so that an encoding of a message m consists of a time-lock puzzle for m, a non-malleable commitment for m, and a zero-knowledge proof that ties them together and asserts that they have the same underlying message. The construction is described formally in Algorithms 2, 3, and 4

Sub-exponential Security. The theorem extends to show that the resulting non-malleable code cannot be mauled in depth better than $\overline{T}$ even if the total size of the solver is exponential in λ. For that, we need to make all of our

---

Algorithm NMCode.E($1^\lambda, m$) for $m \in \{0,1\}^\lambda$:

1. $(\mathsf{vk}, \mathsf{sk}) \leftarrow \mathsf{Sig.G}(1^\lambda)$.
2. $Z \leftarrow \mathsf{TL.Gen}(1^\lambda, \overline{T}^{2/\epsilon}, m; r_{\mathsf{TL}})$ with uniformly random r_{TL}.
3. $(c, r_{\mathsf{NMCom}}) \leftarrow \mathsf{NMCom.C}(1^\lambda, m, tag = \mathsf{vk})$.
4. Compute a ZK proof $\pi \leftarrow \mathsf{ZK.P}(\cdot, \cdot, 1^\lambda)$ for the relation $\mathcal{R}_u$ from Algorithm 4 using (vk, Z, c) as the instance and $(r_{\mathsf{TL}}, m, r_{\mathsf{NMCom}})$ as the witness.
5. $\sigma \leftarrow \mathsf{Sig.S}(\mathsf{sk}, (Z, c, \pi))$.
6. Output $\hat{Z} = (\mathsf{vk}, Z, c, \pi, \sigma)$.

Algorithm 2: The encoding procedure NMCode.E.

Algorithm NMCode.D($\mathsf{vk}, Z, c, \pi, \sigma$):

1. Verify the signature σ:
$$\mathsf{Sig.V}(\mathsf{vk}, (Z, c, \pi), \sigma) \overset{?}{=} 1.$$

2. Verify the proof π:
$$\mathsf{ZK.V}((\mathsf{vk}, Z, c), \pi) \overset{?}{=} 1.$$

3. If both accept, output $\mathsf{TL.Sol}(Z)$. Otherwise, output 0^λ.

Algorithm 3: The decoding procedure NMCode.D.

underlying building blocks sub-exponentially secure (in particular, they have to remain secure in the presence of an exponential size adversary). We focus on the polynomial regime for simplicity.

Organization. The proof of Theorem 8 consists of two parts: (1) efficiency analysis showing that the encoding and decoding procedures can be implemented with the required complexities and (2) showing that the code is non-malleable. Part (1) is proven in Sect. 6.1 and Part (2) is proven in Sect. 6.2.

6.1 Efficiency Analysis

Fix a security parameter $\lambda \in \mathbb{N}$ and a message $m \in \{0,1\}^\lambda$. The encoding (i.e., the output of NMCode.E($1^\lambda, m$) consists of a verification key of a signature scheme, a time-lock puzzle, a non-malleable commitment scheme, a zero-knowledge proof, and a signature. All of these are of fixed polynomial size in λ.

The procedure NMCode.E, on input $(1^\lambda, s)$, runs in time $\mathsf{poly}(\log \overline{T}, \lambda)$. Indeed, steps 1,3, and 5 are independent of $\overline{T}$ and take $\mathsf{poly}(\lambda)$ time. Step 2, by definition of time-lock puzzles, takes time $\mathsf{poly}(\log \overline{T}, \lambda)$. Finally, step 4 takes time $\mathsf{poly}(\log \overline{T}, \lambda)$ due to the running time of the verification procedure of the underlying language. The procedure NMCode.D can be computed in time $\overline{T}^{2/\epsilon} \cdot \mathsf{poly}(\lambda)$. Indeed, verifying the proof and the signature both take fixed polynomial time $\mathsf{poly}(\lambda)$ and the last step takes time $\overline{T}^{2/\epsilon} \cdot \mathsf{poly}(\lambda)$, by definition.

Relation $\mathcal{R}_u\left((\mathsf{vk}, Z, c), (r_{\mathsf{TL}}, m, r_{\mathsf{NMCom}})\right)$:

- <u>Instance</u>: a verification key vk, a puzzle generated by $\mathsf{TL.Gen}(1^\lambda, \overline{T}^{2/\epsilon}, m)$, and a commitment c.
- <u>Witness</u>: a string $t_{\mathsf{TL}} \in \{0, 1\}^*$, a string $m \in \{0, 1\}^\lambda$, and a string $r_{\mathsf{NMCom}} \in \{0, 1\}^*$.
- <u>Statement</u>: $\mathsf{TL.Gen}(1^\lambda, \overline{T}^{2/\epsilon}, m; r_{\mathsf{TL}}) = Z$ and $\mathsf{NMCom.O}(c, m, r_{\mathsf{NMCom}}, tag = \mathsf{vk}) = 1$.

Algorithm 4: The Relation $\mathcal{R}_u$.

6.2 Proof of Non-malleability

In what follows, we prove that the coding scheme from Algorithms 2 and 3 is medium-non-malleable for all polynomial-size S and bounded polynomial-time $\overline{T}$ tampering functions. Let $g(Z, Z')$ be the procedure defined in Algorithm 5.

$g(Z, Z')$:

1. Parse Z as $(\mathsf{vk}, Z, c, \pi, \sigma)$ and Z' as $(\mathsf{vk}', Z', c', \pi', \sigma')$.
2. If $\mathsf{vk} = \mathsf{vk}'$ and σ' verifies (that is, $\mathsf{Sig.V}(\mathsf{vk}', (Z, c', \pi'), \sigma') = 1$), output 1. Otherwise output 0.

Running time: The procedure g has fixed polynomial size (and time) in its input size.

Algorithm 5: The procedure g.

Claim 9. *For every non-uniform polynomial-size tampering function $\mathcal{A} = \{\mathcal{A}_\lambda\}_{\lambda \in \mathbb{N}}$, every difficulty parameter t, and every $m \in \{0, 1\}^\lambda$, it holds that*

$$\Pr_{\hat{Z} \leftarrow \mathsf{NMCode.E}(1^\lambda, m)} \left[g(\hat{Z}, \mathcal{A}_\lambda(\hat{Z})) = 1 \land \mathsf{NMCode.D}(\mathcal{A}_\lambda(\hat{Z})) \neq m \right] \leq \mathsf{negl}(\lambda).$$

Proof. Let $\hat{Z} = (\mathsf{vk}, Z, c, \pi, \sigma)$ and $\mathcal{A}_\lambda(\hat{Z}) = \hat{Z}' = (\mathsf{vk}', Z', c', \pi', \sigma')$. If $g(\hat{Z}, \hat{Z}') = 1$, then $\mathsf{vk} = \mathsf{vk}'$ and $\mathsf{Sig.V}(\mathsf{vk}', Z', c', \pi'), \sigma') = 1$. Also, recall that Z is a puzzle with underlying message m. Thus, if $\mathsf{NMCode.D}(\hat{Z}') \neq m$, it means that $(Z, c, \pi) \neq (Z', c', \pi')$. Thus, $\mathcal{A}_\lambda$ can be used to create (in polynomial-time) a valid signature σ' w.r.t. verification key vk for a new statement which is a contradiction to the security of the one-time signature.

We next show that w.r.t. the above g (Algorithm 5), for any polynomial-size algorithm $\mathcal{A} = \{\mathcal{A}_\lambda\}_{\lambda \in \mathbb{N}}$ such that $\mathsf{Time}[\mathcal{A}] \leq \overline{T}$ and any $m_0, m_1 \in \{0, 1\}^\lambda$, it holds that

$$\{\mathsf{MedTamper}_{\mathcal{A}, m_0}^{\mathsf{NMCode}}(\lambda)\}_{\lambda \in \mathbb{N}} \approx \{\mathsf{MedTamper}_{\mathcal{A}, m_1}^{\mathsf{NMCode}}(\lambda)\}_{\lambda \in \mathbb{N}},$$

where

$$\mathsf{MedTamper}_{\mathcal{A},m}^{\mathsf{NMCode}}(\lambda) = \left\{ \begin{array}{l} \hat{Z} \leftarrow \mathsf{NMCode.E}(1^\lambda, m); \quad \tilde{m} = \mathsf{NMCode.D}(\mathcal{A}_\lambda(\hat{Z})) \\ \text{Output: same* if } g(Z, \mathcal{A}_\lambda(Z)) = 1, \text{ and } \tilde{m} \text{ otherwise} \end{array} \right\}.$$

We do so by defining a sequence of hybrid experiments where we slowly change how NMCode.E and NMCode.D work and showing that every two consecutive hybrids are indistinguishable. For consistency of notation with what follows, we denote the non-malleable code from Algorithms 2 and 3 used in the original scheme by $\mathsf{NMCode}_0 = (\mathsf{NMCode}_0.\mathsf{E}, \mathsf{NMCode}_0.\mathsf{D})$, where $\mathsf{NMCode}_0.\mathsf{E} \equiv \mathsf{NMCode.E}$ and $\mathsf{NMCode}_0.\mathsf{D} \equiv \mathsf{NMCode.D}$. The first experiment that we define corresponds to the experiment $\{\mathsf{MedTamper}_{\mathcal{A},m_0}^{\mathsf{NMCode}_0}(\lambda)\}_{\lambda \in \mathbb{N}}$ and the last one corresponds to an experiment where we encode m_1. From that point, one can "reverse" the sequence of experiment to reach the experiment $\{\mathsf{MedTamper}_{\mathcal{A},m_1}^{\mathsf{NMCode}_0}(\lambda)\}_{\lambda \in \mathbb{N}}$. We omit this part to avoid repetition.

Throughout the following sequence of hybrids, we treat $\mathcal{A}$ and m_0, m_1 as fixed. Some of the proofs are deferred to the full version [33].

Experiment $\mathcal{H}_0(\lambda)$. This is the original experiment, where we encode m_0 under NMCode_0 (see Algorithms 2 and 3) and execute the experiment $\{\mathsf{MedTamper}_{\mathcal{A},m_0}^{\mathsf{NMCode}_0}(\lambda)\}_{\lambda \in \mathbb{N}}$.

Experiment $\mathcal{H}_1(\lambda)$. This experiment is the same as Experiment $\mathcal{H}_0(\lambda)$ except that we use the simulator of the ZK proof to generate π. This gives rise to the scheme $\mathsf{NMCode}_1 = (\mathsf{NMCode}_1.\mathsf{E}, \mathsf{NMCode}_0.\mathsf{D})$, where $\mathsf{NMCode}_1.\mathsf{E}$ is describer in Algorithm 6. Using this scheme we execute the experiment $\{\mathsf{MedTamper}_{\mathcal{A},m_0}^{\mathsf{NMCode}_1}(\lambda)\}_{\lambda \in \mathbb{N}}$. By the zero-knowledge property of ZK, this hybrid is indistinguishable from $\mathcal{H}_0(\lambda)$.

Algorithm $\mathsf{NMCode}_1.\mathsf{E}(m)$ for $m \in \{0,1\}^\lambda$:

1. $(\mathsf{vk}, \mathsf{sk}) \leftarrow \mathsf{Sig.G}(1^\lambda)$.
2. $Z \leftarrow \mathsf{TL.Gen}(1^\lambda, \overline{T}^{2/\epsilon}, m)$.
3. $(c, r) \leftarrow \mathsf{NMCom.C}(1^\lambda, m, tag = \mathsf{vk})$.
4. Use the simulator Sim to simulate a proof for the relation $\mathcal{R}_u$ using (vk, Z, c) as the instance.
5. $\sigma \leftarrow \mathsf{Sig.S}(\mathsf{sk}, (Z, c, \pi))$.
6. Output $\hat{Z} = (\mathsf{vk}, Z, c, \pi, \sigma)$.

Algorithm 6: The encoding procedure $\mathsf{NMCode}_1.\mathsf{E}$ used in $\mathcal{H}_1(\lambda)$.

Claim 10. *It holds that*

$$\{\mathsf{MedTamper}_{\mathcal{A},m_0}^{\mathsf{NMCode}_0}(\lambda)\}_{\lambda \in \mathbb{N}} \approx \{\mathsf{MedTamper}_{\mathcal{A},m_0}^{\mathsf{NMCode}_1}(\lambda)\}_{\lambda \in \mathbb{N}}.$$

Experiment $\mathcal{H}_2(\lambda)$. This experiment is the same as Experiment $\mathcal{H}_1(\lambda)$ except that instead of committing to m_0 with a non-malleable commitment, we commit to 0^λ. This gives rise to the scheme $\mathsf{NMCode}_2 = (\mathsf{NMCode}_2.\mathsf{E}, \mathsf{NMCode}_0.\mathsf{D})$ which is described in Algorithm 6. Using this scheme we execute the experiment $\{\mathsf{MedTamper}_{\mathcal{A},m_0}^{\mathsf{NMCode}_2}(\lambda)\}_{\lambda \in \mathbb{N}}$. By the hiding property of NMCom, this hybrid is indistinguishable from $\mathcal{H}_1(\lambda)$.

Algorithm $\mathsf{NMCode}_2.\mathsf{E}(m)$ for $m \in \{0,1\}^\lambda$:

1. $(\mathsf{vk}, \mathsf{sk}) \leftarrow \mathsf{Sig.G}(1^\lambda)$.
2. $Z \leftarrow \mathsf{TL.Gen}(1^\lambda, \overline{T}^{2/\epsilon}, m)$.
3. $(c, r) \leftarrow \mathsf{NMCom.C}(1^\lambda, 0^\lambda, tag = \mathsf{vk})$.
4. Use the simulator Sim to simulate a proof for the relation $\mathcal{R}_u$ using (vk, Z, c) as the instance.
5. $\sigma \leftarrow \mathsf{Sig.S}(\mathsf{sk}, (Z, c, \pi))$.
6. Output $\hat{Z} = (\mathsf{vk}, Z, c, \pi, \sigma)$.

Algorithm 7: The encoding procedure $\mathsf{NMCode}_2.\mathsf{E}$ used in $\mathcal{H}_2(\lambda)$.

Claim 11. *It holds that*

$$\{\mathsf{MedTamper}_{\mathcal{A},m_0}^{\mathsf{NMCode}_1}(\lambda)\}_{\lambda \in \mathbb{N}} \approx \{\mathsf{MedTamper}_{\mathcal{A},m_0}^{\mathsf{NMCode}_2}(\lambda)\}_{\lambda \in \mathbb{N}}.$$

Experiment $\mathcal{H}_3(\lambda)$. This experiment is the same as Experiment $\mathcal{H}_2(\lambda)$ except that we use an alternate decoding procedure. The alternate decoding procedure does not solve the time-lock puzzle in order to decode the secret m, but rather it "breaks" the commitment scheme and extracts m from it using $\mathsf{NMCom.Ext}_1$ *unless* the (tampered) proof is one of a fix set of "bad" proofs.

Concretely, recall that by weak-soundness of ZK, every algorithm (and in particular $\mathcal{A}$) can come up with some small bounded number of proofs that are verified yet are for false statements. If the proof on the right size is one of those proofs, we will output a hard coded value instead of trying to extract the value from the commitment.

More precisely, the adversary $\mathcal{A}$ can find a set $\mathcal{Z}'$ (that depends on the adversary and the hybrid) of size at most $K \triangleq K^{\mathsf{ZK}}(|\mathcal{A}_\lambda| + O(1)) \in \mathsf{poly}(\lambda)$ of proofs that are verified yet are for false statements. We denote by $\mathcal{Z}$ the augmented set of proofs (for false statements) together with the instance and with the values underlying the time-lock puzzle in each such statements. Namely, $\mathcal{Z}$ is a set that consists of tuples of the form $(\pi, \mathsf{vk}, Z, c, \tilde{m})$, where π is a proof from $\mathcal{Z}'$ for the instance (vk, Z, c) and $\tilde{m}$ is the message underlying Z.

This gives rise to the scheme $\mathsf{NMCode}_3 = (\mathsf{NMCode}_2.\mathsf{E}, \mathsf{NMCode}_1.\mathsf{D})$ which is described in Algorithm 8. Using this scheme we execute the experiment $\{\mathsf{MedTamper}_{\mathcal{A},m_0}^{\mathsf{NMCode}_3}(\lambda)\}_{\lambda \in \mathbb{N}}$.

Algorithm $\mathsf{NMCode}_1.\mathsf{D}(\mathsf{vk}, Z, c, \pi, \sigma)$:

1. Verify the signature σ:
$$\mathsf{Sig.V}(\mathsf{vk}, (Z, c, \pi), \sigma) \overset{?}{=} 1.$$

2. Verify the ZK proof π:
$$\mathsf{ZK.V}((\mathsf{vk}, Z, c), \pi) \overset{?}{=} 1.$$

3. If either test from Steps 1 or 2 does not pass or $c = \bot$, output 0^λ and terminate.
4. If π is a proof which is in $\mathcal{Z}$, output the corresponding message $\tilde{m}$ and terminate.
5. Otherwise (both tests pass, $c \neq \bot$, and $\pi \notin \mathcal{Z}'$), use the extractor $\mathsf{NMCom.Ext}_1(c)$ to get the underlying value $\tilde{m}$. Output $\tilde{m}$ (if extraction fails, $\tilde{m} = \bot$).

Algorithm 8: The decoding procedures $\mathsf{NMCode}_1.\mathsf{D}$ used in $\mathcal{H}_3(\lambda)$.

Claim 12. *It holds that*
$$\{\mathsf{MedTamper}^{\mathsf{NMCode}_2}_{\mathcal{A},m}(\lambda)\}_{\lambda \in \mathbb{N}} \approx \{\mathsf{MedTamper}^{\mathsf{NMCode}_3}_{\mathcal{A},m}(\lambda)\}_{\lambda \in \mathbb{N}}.$$

Experiment $\mathcal{H}_4(\lambda)$. This experiment is the same as Experiment $\mathcal{H}_3(\lambda)$ except that we modify the alternate decoding procedure to use the extractor $\mathsf{NMCom.Ext}_2$ instead of $\mathsf{NMCom.Ext}_1$. Namely, we execute the experiment $\{\mathsf{MedTamper}^{\mathsf{NMCode}_4}_{\mathcal{A},m_1}(\lambda)\}_{\lambda \in \mathbb{N}}$. This gives rise to the scheme $\mathsf{NMCode}_4 = (\mathsf{NMCode}_2.\mathsf{E}, \mathsf{NMCode}_2.\mathsf{D})$ which is described in Algorithm 9. Using this scheme we execute the experiment $\{\mathsf{MedTamper}^{\mathsf{NMCode}_4}_{\mathcal{A},m_0}(\lambda)\}_{\lambda \in \mathbb{N}}$.

Algorithm $\mathsf{NMCode}_2.\mathsf{D}(\mathsf{vk}, Z, c, \pi, \sigma)$:

1. Verify the signature σ:
$$\mathsf{Sig.V}(\mathsf{vk}, (Z, c, \pi), \sigma) \overset{?}{=} 1.$$

2. Verify the ZK proof π:
$$\mathsf{ZK.V}((\mathsf{vk}, Z, c), \pi) \overset{?}{=} 1.$$

3. If either test from Steps 1 or 2 does not pass or $c = \bot$, output 0^λ and terminate.
4. If π is a proof which is in $\mathcal{Z}$, output the corresponding message $\tilde{m}$ and terminate.
5. Otherwise (both tests pass, $c \neq \bot$, and $\pi \notin \mathcal{Z}'$), use the extractor $\mathsf{NMCom.Ext}_2(c)$ to get the underlying value $\tilde{m}$. Output $\tilde{m}$ (if extraction fails, $\tilde{m} = \bot$).

Algorithm 9: The decoding procedures $\mathsf{NMCode}_2.\mathsf{D}$ used in $\mathcal{H}_4(\lambda)$.

Claim 13. *It holds that* $\{\mathsf{MedTamper}^{\mathsf{NMCode}_3}_{\mathcal{A},m_0}(\lambda)\}_{\lambda \in \mathbb{N}}$ *and* $\{\mathsf{MedTamper}^{\mathsf{NMCode}_4}_{\mathcal{A},m_0}(\lambda)\}_{\lambda \in \mathbb{N}}$ *are identically distributed.*

Experiment $\mathcal{H}_5(\lambda)$. This experiment is the same as Experiment $\mathcal{H}_4(\lambda)$ except that we use m_1 as the underlying message for $\mathsf{TL.Gen}$ (rather than m_0), namely, we execute the experiment $\{\mathsf{MedTamper}^{\mathsf{NMCode}_4}_{\mathcal{A},m_1}(\lambda)\}_{\lambda \in \mathbb{N}}$.

Claim 14. *It holds that*

$$\{\mathsf{MedTamper}_{\mathcal{A},m_0}^{\mathsf{NMCode_4}}(\lambda)\}_{\lambda\in\mathbb{N}} \approx \{\mathsf{MedTamper}_{\mathcal{A},m_1}^{\mathsf{NMCode_4}}(\lambda)\}_{\lambda\in\mathbb{N}}.$$

7   The Case of Uniform Tampering

In Sect. 6 we gave a construction of a non-malleable code secure against all tampering functions that can be described as non-uniform polynomial size algorithm with *bounded* polynomial depth. In this section we focus on the natural class of tampering functions that consists of *uniform* polynomial size algorithm with bounded polynomial parallel running time. This is the class that was considered in the work of Ball et al. [6].

The construction is essentially the same as the one for non-uniform tampering functions and the main differences are in how we instantiate the building blocks and how the security proof goes through. Let us precisely list the building blocks with which we use the scheme from Sect. 6 (Algorithms 2, 3, and 4). We note that the time-lock puzzle and the signature scheme that we use (Items 1. and 4. below) are the same as the one we used in Sect. 6.

1. A time-lock puzzle (Theorem 3) $\mathsf{TL} = (\mathsf{TL.Gen}, \mathsf{TL.Sol})$ which, for all large enough difficulty parameters t, allows to generate puzzles which are hard for any (non-uniform) machine whose parallel time is at most t^ϵ, even it has size $2^{3\lambda}$.
   More precisely, for a difficulty parameter t, it is $(S^{\mathsf{TL}}, \epsilon)$-hard for a fixed $\epsilon \in (0,1)$ and for $S^{\mathsf{TL}}(\lambda) = 2^{3\lambda}$.
2. A one-message zero-knowledge argument system (Theorem 7) $\mathsf{ZK} = (\mathsf{ZK.P}, \mathsf{ZK.V})$ which is sound w.r.t. all uniform polynomial-size attackers, there is a (uniform) simulator that requires sub-exponential size and fixed polynomial time, and zero-knowledge holds w.r.t. sub-exponential size adversaries.
   More precisely, it is $(S_P^{\mathsf{ZK}}, \kappa^{\mathsf{ZK}})$-sound and $(S_D^{\mathsf{ZK}}, S_{\mathsf{Sim}}^{\mathsf{ZK}}, T_{\mathsf{Sim}}^{\mathsf{ZK}})$-zero-knowledge for all polynomial functions S_P^{ZK} and where $\kappa^{\mathsf{ZK}} = 0$, $S_D^{\mathsf{ZK}}(\lambda) = 2^{\lambda^{\eta}}$, $S_{\mathsf{Sim}}^{\mathsf{ZK}}(\lambda) = 2^{\lambda^{\eta'}}$, and $T_{\mathsf{Sim}}^{\mathsf{ZK}}(\lambda) = \lambda^2$.
3. A one-message non-malleable tag-based commitment scheme (Theorem 5) $\mathsf{NMCom} = (\mathsf{NMCom.C}, \mathsf{NMCom.O})$ which is hiding for all (non-uniform) polynomial-size distinguishers, extractable either in size and time $2^{\log^2 \lambda}$ or in 2^λ size and λ^3 time, and non-malleable for all *uniform* exponential size and polynomial time tampering functions.
   More precisely, it is $(S^{\mathsf{NMCom}}, T^{\mathsf{NMCom}})$-hiding, $(S_{\mathsf{Ext}_1}^{\mathsf{NMCom}}, T_{\mathsf{Ext}_1}^{\mathsf{NMCom}})$-extractable via $\mathsf{NMCom.Ext}_1$ and $(S_{\mathsf{Ext}_2}^{\mathsf{NMCom}}, T_{\mathsf{Ext}_2}^{\mathsf{NMCom}})$-extractable via $\mathsf{NMCom.Ext}_2$, and $(S_{NM}^{\mathsf{NMCom}}, T_{NM}^{\mathsf{NMCom}}, \kappa_{NM}^{\mathsf{NMCom}})$-non-malleable for all polynomial functions T^{NMCom} and T_{NM}^{NMCom}, and where $S^{\mathsf{NMCom}}(\lambda) = 2^{\lambda^{\eta''}}$ for $\eta'' > \eta'$, $S_{\mathsf{Ext}_1}^{\mathsf{NMCom}}(\lambda) = T_{\mathsf{Ext}_1}^{\mathsf{NMCom}}(\lambda) = 2^{\log^2 \lambda}$, $S_{\mathsf{Ext}_2}^{\mathsf{NMCom}}(\lambda) = 2^{2\lambda}$, $T_{\mathsf{Ext}_2}^{\mathsf{NMCom}}(\lambda) = \lambda^3$, $S_{NM}^{\mathsf{NMCom}} = 2^\lambda$, and $\kappa_{NM}^{\mathsf{NMCom}} = 0$.
4. $\mathsf{Sig} = (\mathsf{Sig.G}, \mathsf{Sig.S}, \mathsf{Sig.V})$. A one-time signature scheme, unforgeable for polynomial-size attackers.

Overview of the Proof. The proof works by defining a sequence of hybrid experiments, where in the first the Man-In-the-Middle game is played with a message m_0 and in the last with a message m_1. The sequence of experiments is analogous to the one described in Sect. 6 except that we do not need worry about "weak-soundness" of the ZK scheme and so some transitions follow due to slightly different reasons. We refer to the full version [33] for details.

References

1. Aggarwal, D., Agrawal, S., Gupta, D., Maji, H.K., Pandey, O., Prabhakaran, M.: Optimal computational split-state non-malleable codes. In: TCC, pp. 393–417 (2016)
2. Aggarwal, D., Dodis, Y., Kazana, T., Obremski, M.: Non-malleable reductions and applications. In: STOC, pp. 459–468 (2015)
3. Aggarwal, D., Dodis, Y., Lovett, S.: Non-malleable codes from additive combinatorics. SIAM J. Comput. **47**(2), 524–546 (2018)
4. Ball, M.: On Resilience to Computable Tampering. Ph.D. thesis, Columbia University (2021). https://academiccommons.columbia.edu/doi/10.7916/d8-debr-bw49
5. Ball, M., Dachman-Soled, D., Guo, S., Malkin, T., Tan, L.: Non-malleable codes for small-depth circuits. In: FOCS, pp. 826–837 (2018)
6. Ball, M., Dachman-Soled, D., Kulkarni, M., Lin, H., Malkin, T.: Non-malleable codes against bounded polynomial time tampering. In: Ishai, Y., Rijmen, V. (eds.) EUROCRYPT 2019. LNCS, vol. 11476, pp. 501–530. Springer, Cham (2019). https://doi.org/10.1007/978-3-030-17653-2_17
7. Ball, M., Dachman-Soled, D., Kulkarni, M., Malkin, T.: Non-malleable codes for bounded depth, bounded fan-in circuits. In: Fischlin, M., Coron, J.-S. (eds.) EUROCRYPT 2016. LNCS, vol. 9666, pp. 881–908. Springer, Heidelberg (2016). https://doi.org/10.1007/978-3-662-49896-5_31
8. Ball, M., Dachman-Soled, D., Kulkarni, M., Malkin, T.: Non-malleable codes from average-case hardness: AC^0, decision trees, and streaming space-bounded tampering. In: Nielsen, J.B., Rijmen, V. (eds.) EUROCRYPT 2018. LNCS, vol. 10822, pp. 618–650. Springer, Cham (2018). https://doi.org/10.1007/978-3-319-78372-7_20
9. Ball, M., Dachman-Soled, D., Kulkarni, M., Malkin, T.: Limits to non-malleability. In: ITCS, pp. 80:1–80:32 (2020)
10. Ball, M., Dachman-Soled, D., Loss, J.: Explicit non-malleable codes for polynomial size circuit tampering. (unpublished manuscript)
11. Ball, M., Guo, S., Wichs, D.: Non-malleable codes for decision trees. In: Boldyreva, A., Micciancio, D. (eds.) CRYPTO 2019. LNCS, vol. 11692, pp. 413–434. Springer, Cham (2019). https://doi.org/10.1007/978-3-030-26948-7_15
12. Barak, B.: Constant-round coin-tossing with a man in the middle or realizing the shared random string model. In: FOCS, pp. 345–355 (2002)
13. Barak, B., Ong, S.J., Vadhan, S.P.: Derandomization in cryptography. SIAM J. Comput. **37**(2), 380–400 (2007)
14. Barak, B., Pass, R.: On the possibility of one-message weak zero-knowledge. In: TCC, pp. 121–132 (2004)
15. Baum, C., David, B., Dowsley, R., Nielsen, J.B., Oechsner, S.: Craft: composable randomness and almost fairness from time. Cryptology ePrint Archive, Report 2020/784 (2020)

16. Baum, C., David, B., Dowsley, R., Nielsen, J.B., Oechsner, S.: TARDIS: a foundation of time-lock puzzles in UC. In: Canteaut, A., Standaert, F.-X. (eds.) EUROCRYPT 2021. LNCS, vol. 12698, pp. 429–459. Springer, Cham (2021). https://doi.org/10.1007/978-3-030-77883-5_15

17. Berman, I., Degwekar, A., Rothblum, R.D., Vasudevan, P.N.: Multi-collision resistant hash functions and their applications. In: Nielsen, J.B., Rijmen, V. (eds.) EUROCRYPT 2018. LNCS, vol. 10821, pp. 133–161. Springer, Cham (2018). https://doi.org/10.1007/978-3-319-78375-8_5

18. Bitansky, N., Goldwasser, S., Jain, A., Paneth, O., Vaikuntanathan, V., Waters, B.: Time-lock puzzles from randomized encodings. In: ITCS, pp. 345–356 (2016)

19. Bitansky, N., Kalai, Y.T., Paneth, O.: Multi-collision resistance: a paradigm for keyless hash functions. In: STOC, pp. 671–684 (2018)

20. Bitansky, N., Lin, H.: One-message zero knowledge and non-malleable commitments. In: TCC, pp. 209–234 (2018)

21. Bitansky, N., Paneth, O.: Zaps and non-interactive witness indistinguishability from indistinguishability obfuscation. In: TCC, pp. 401–427 (2015)

22. Chandran, N., Goyal, V., Mukherjee, P., Pandey, O., Upadhyay, J.: Block-wise non-malleable codes. In: ICALP, pp. 31:1–31:14 (2016)

23. Chattopadhyay, E., Goyal, V., Li, X.: Non-malleable extractors and codes, with their many tampered extensions. Electron. Colloq. Comput. Complex. (ECCC) **22**, 75 (2015)

24. Chattopadhyay, E., Goyal, V., Li, X.: Non-malleable extractors and codes, with their many tampered extensions. In: STOC, pp. 285–298 (2016)

25. Chattopadhyay, E., Li, X.: Non-malleable codes and extractors for small-depth circuits, and affine functions. In: STOC, pp. 1171–1184 (2017)

26. Chattopadhyay, E., Zuckerman, D.: Explicit two-source extractors and resilient functions. In: STOC, pp. 670–683 (2016)

27. Cheraghchi, M., Guruswami, V.: Capacity of non-malleable codes. IEEE Trans. Inf. Theory **62**(3), 1097–1118 (2016)

28. Chung, K., Lin, H., Pass, R.: Constant-round concurrent zero knowledge from P-certificates. In: FOCS, pp. 50–59 (2013)

29. Ciampi, M., Ostrovsky, R., Siniscalchi, L., Visconti, I.: Concurrent non-malleable commitments (and more) in 3 rounds. In: Robshaw, M., Katz, J. (eds.) CRYPTO 2016. LNCS, vol. 9816, pp. 270–299. Springer, Heidelberg (2016). https://doi.org/10.1007/978-3-662-53015-3_10

30. Ciampi, M., Ostrovsky, R., Siniscalchi, L., Visconti, I.: Four-round concurrent non-malleable commitments from one-way functions. In: Katz, J., Shacham, H. (eds.) CRYPTO 2017. LNCS, vol. 10402, pp. 127–157. Springer, Cham (2017). https://doi.org/10.1007/978-3-319-63715-0_5

31. Coretti, S., Dodis, Y., Tackmann, B., Venturi, D.: Non-malleable encryption: simpler, shorter, stronger. In: TCC, pp. 306–335 (2016)

32. Coretti, S., Maurer, U., Tackmann, B., Venturi, D.: From single-bit to multi-bit public-key encryption via non-malleable codes. In: TCC, pp. 532–560 (2015)

33. Dachman-Soled, D., Komargodski, I., Pass, R.: Non-malleable codes for bounded polynomial depth tampering. IACR Cryptol. ePrint Arch. **2020**, 776 (2020)

34. Dachman-Soled, D., Liu, F., Shi, E., Zhou, H.: Locally decodable and updatable non-malleable codes and their applications. In: TCC, pp. 427–450 (2015)

35. Dixon, J.D.: Asymptotically fast factorization of integers. Math. Comput. **36**(153), 255–260 (1981)

36. Dolev, D., Dwork, C., Naor, M.: Non-malleable cryptography (extended abstract). In: STOC, pp. 542–552 (1991)

37. Dziembowski, S., Pietrzak, K., Wichs, D.: Non-malleable codes. In: ICS, pp. 434–452 (2010)
38. Dziembowski, S., Pietrzak, K., Wichs, D.: Non-malleable codes. J. ACM **65**(4), 20:1–20:32 (2018)
39. Ephraim, N., Freitag, C., Komargodski, I., Pass, R.: Continuous verifiable delay functions. In: Canteaut, A., Ishai, Y. (eds.) EUROCRYPT 2020. LNCS, vol. 12107, pp. 125–154. Springer, Cham (2020). https://doi.org/10.1007/978-3-030-45727-3_5
40. Ephraim, N., Freitag, C., Komargodski, I., Pass, R.: Non-malleable time-lock puzzles and applications. IACR Cryptol. ePrint Arch. **2020**, 779 (2020)
41. Faust, S., Hostáková, K., Mukherjee, P., Venturi, D.: Non-malleable codes for space-bounded tampering. In: Katz, J., Shacham, H. (eds.) CRYPTO 2017. LNCS, vol. 10402, pp. 95–126. Springer, Cham (2017). https://doi.org/10.1007/978-3-319-63715-0_4
42. Faust, S., Mukherjee, P., Venturi, D., Wichs, D.: Efficient non-malleable codes and key derivation for poly-size tampering circuits. IEEE Trans. Inf. Theory **62**(12), 7179–7194 (2016)
43. Feige, U., Lapidot, D., Shamir, A.: Multiple non-interactive zero knowledge proofs based on a single random string (extended abstract). In: FOCS, pp. 308–317 (1990)
44. Fuchsbauer, G., Kiltz, E., Loss, J.: The algebraic group model and its applications. In: Shacham, H., Boldyreva, A. (eds.) CRYPTO 2018. LNCS, vol. 10992, pp. 33–62. Springer, Cham (2018). https://doi.org/10.1007/978-3-319-96881-0_2
45. Goyal, V.: Constant round non-malleable protocols using one way functions. In: Fortnow, L., Vadhan, S.P. (eds.) STOC, pp. 695–704 (2011)
46. Goyal, V., Lee, C., Ostrovsky, R., Visconti, I.: Constructing non-malleable commitments: a black-box approach. In: FOCS, pp. 51–60 (2012)
47. Goyal, V., Pandey, O., Richelson, S.: Textbook non-malleable commitments. In: STOC, pp. 1128–1141 (2016)
48. Groth, J., Ostrovsky, R., Sahai, A.: Non-interactive zaps and new techniques for NIZK. In: Dwork, C. (ed.) CRYPTO 2006. LNCS, vol. 4117, pp. 97–111. Springer, Heidelberg (2006). https://doi.org/10.1007/11818175_6
49. Kalai, Y.T., Khurana, D.: Non-interactive non-malleability from quantum supremacy. In: Boldyreva, A., Micciancio, D. (eds.) CRYPTO 2019. LNCS, vol. 11694, pp. 552–582. Springer, Cham (2019). https://doi.org/10.1007/978-3-030-26954-8_18
50. Katz, J., Loss, J., Xu, J.: On the security of time-lock puzzles and timed commitments. In: TCC, pp. 390–413 (2020)
51. Khurana, D.: Round optimal concurrent non-malleability from polynomial hardness. In: TCC, pp. 139–171 (2017)
52. Khurana, D., Sahai, A.: How to achieve non-malleability in one or two rounds. In: FOCS, pp. 564–575 (2017)
53. Kiayias, A., Liu, F., Tselekounis, Y.: Practical non-malleable codes from l-more extractable hash functions. In: CCS, pp. 1317–1328 (2016)
54. Komargodski, I., Naor, M., Yogev, E.: Collision resistant hashing for paranoids: dealing with multiple collisions. In: Nielsen, J.B., Rijmen, V. (eds.) EUROCRYPT 2018. LNCS, vol. 10821, pp. 162–194. Springer, Cham (2018). https://doi.org/10.1007/978-3-319-78375-8_6
55. Komargodski, I., Naor, M., Yogev, E.: White-box vs. black-box complexity of search problems: ramsey and graph property testing. J. ACM **66**(5), 34:1–34:28 (2019)

56. Kulkarni, M.R.: Extending the Applicability of Non-Malleable Codes. Ph.D. thesis, The University of Maryland (2019). https://drum.lib.umd.edu/bitstream/handle/1903/25179/Kulkarni_umd_0117E_20306.pdf?sequence=2

57. Li, X.: Non-malleable extractors, two-source extractors and privacy amplification. In: 53rd Annual IEEE Symposium on Foundations of Computer Science, FOCS, pp. 688–697 (2012)

58. Li, X.: New independent source extractors with exponential improvement. In: STOC, pp. 783–792 (2013)

59. Li, X.: Improved non-malleable extractors, non-malleable codes and independent source extractors. In: STOC, pp. 1144–1156. ACM (2017)

60. Li, X.: Non-malleable extractors and non-malleable codes: partially optimal constructions. arXiv preprint arXiv:1804.04005 (2018)

61. Lin, H., Pass, R.: Non-malleability amplification. In: STOC, pp. 189–198 (2009)

62. Lin, H., Pass, R.: Constant-round non-malleable commitments from any one-way function. In: STOC, pp. 705–714 (2011)

63. Lin, H., Pass, R., Soni, P.: Two-round and non-interactive concurrent non-malleable commitments from time-lock puzzles. In: FOCS, pp. 576–587 (2017)

64. Lin, H., Pass, R., Venkitasubramaniam, M.: Concurrent non-malleable commitments from any one-way function. In: TCC, pp. 571–588 (2008)

65. Liu, F.-H., Lysyanskaya, A.: Tamper and leakage resilience in the split-state model. In: Safavi-Naini, R., Canetti, R. (eds.) CRYPTO 2012. LNCS, vol. 7417, pp. 517–532. Springer, Heidelberg (2012). https://doi.org/10.1007/978-3-642-32009-5_30

66. May, T.: Timed-release crypto (1992)

67. Micali, S.: Computationally sound proofs. SIAM J. Comput. **30**(4), 1253–1298 (2000)

68. Naor, M.: On cryptographic assumptions and challenges. In: Boneh, D. (ed.) CRYPTO 2003. LNCS, vol. 2729, pp. 96–109. Springer, Heidelberg (2003). https://doi.org/10.1007/978-3-540-45146-4_6

69. Naor, M., Yung, M.: Public-key cryptosystems provably secure against chosen ciphertext attacks. In: STOC, pp. 427–437 (1990)

70. Ostrovsky, R., Persiano, G., Venturi, D., Visconti, I.: Continuously non-malleable codes in the split-state model from minimal assumptions. In: Shacham, H., Boldyreva, A. (eds.) CRYPTO 2018. LNCS, vol. 10993, pp. 608–639. Springer, Cham (2018). https://doi.org/10.1007/978-3-319-96878-0_21

71. Pandey, O., Pass, R., Vaikuntanathan, V.: Adaptive one-way functions and applications. In: Wagner, D. (ed.) CRYPTO 2008. LNCS, vol. 5157, pp. 57–74. Springer, Heidelberg (2008). https://doi.org/10.1007/978-3-540-85174-5_4

72. Pass, R.: Simulation in quasi-polynomial time, and its application to protocol composition. In: Biham, E. (ed.) EUROCRYPT 2003. LNCS, vol. 2656, pp. 160–176. Springer, Heidelberg (2003). https://doi.org/10.1007/3-540-39200-9_10

73. Pass, R., Rosen, A.: Concurrent non-malleable commitments. In: FOCS, pp. 563–572 (2005)

74. Pass, R., Rosen, A.: New and improved constructions of non-malleable cryptographic protocols. In: STOC, pp. 533–542 (2005)

75. Pass, R., Wee, H.: Constant-round non-malleable commitments from sub-exponential one-way functions. In: Gilbert, H. (ed.) EUROCRYPT 2010. LNCS, vol. 6110, pp. 638–655. Springer, Heidelberg (2010). https://doi.org/10.1007/978-3-642-13190-5_32

76. Pietrzak, K.: Simple verifiable delay functions. In: ITCS, pp. 60:1–60:15 (2019)

77. Rivest, R.L., Shamir, A., Wagner, D.A.: Time-lock puzzles and timed-release crypto. Technical Report. Massachusetts Institute of Technology, Cambridge, MA, USA (1996)
78. Shoup, V.: A Computational Introduction to Number Theory and Algebra. Cambridge University Press, Cambridge (2006)
79. Wee, H.: Black-box, round-efficient secure computation via non-malleability amplification. In: FOCS, pp. 531–540 (2010)
80. Wesolowski, B.: Efficient verifiable delay functions. In: Ishai, Y., Rijmen, V. (eds.) EUROCRYPT 2019. LNCS, vol. 11478, pp. 379–407. Springer, Cham (2019). https://doi.org/10.1007/978-3-030-17659-4_13

Improved Computational Extractors
and Their Applications

Dakshita Khurana[1]([✉]) and Akshayaram Srinivasan[2]

[1] University of Illinois Urbana-Champaign, Champaign, USA
[2] Tata Institute of Fundamental Research, Bengaluru, India

Abstract. Recent exciting breakthroughs have achieved the first two-source extractors that operate in the low min-entropy regime. Unfortunately, these constructions suffer from non-negligible error, and reducing the error to negligible remains an important open problem. In recent work, Garg, Kalai, and Khurana (GKK, Eurocrypt 2020) investigated a meaningful relaxation of this problem to the computational setting, in the presence of a common random string (CRS). In this relaxed model, their work built explicit two-source extractors for a restricted class of unbalanced sources with min-entropy n^γ (for some constant γ) and negligible error, under the sub-exponential DDH assumption.

In this work, we investigate whether computational extractors in the CRS model be applied to more challenging environments. Specifically, we study network extractor protocols (Kalai et al., FOCS 2008) and extractors for adversarial sources (Chattopadhyay et al., STOC 2020) in the CRS model. We observe that these settings require extractors that work well for balanced sources, making the GKK results inapplicable.

We remedy this situation by obtaining the following results, all of which are in the CRS model and assume the sub-exponential hardness of DDH.

- We obtain "optimal" computational two-source and non-malleable extractors for balanced sources: requiring both sources to have only poly-logarithmic min-entropy, and achieving negligible error. To obtain this result, we perform a tighter and arguably simpler analysis of the GKK extractor.
- We obtain a single-round network extractor protocol for poly-logarithmic min-entropy sources that tolerates an optimal number of adversarial corruptions. Prior work in the information-theoretic setting required sources with high min-entropy rates, and in the computational setting had round complexity that grew with the number of parties, required sources with linear min-entropy, and relied on exponential hardness (albeit without a CRS).
- We obtain an "optimal" *adversarial source extractor* for poly-logarithmic min-entropy sources, where the number of honest sources is only 2 and each corrupted source can depend on either one of the honest sources. Prior work in the information-theoretic setting had to assume a large number of honest sources.

© International Association for Cryptologic Research 2021
T. Malkin and C. Peikert (Eds.): CRYPTO 2021, LNCS 12827, pp. 566–594, 2021.
https://doi.org/10.1007/978-3-030-84252-9_19

1   Introduction

Randomness is fundamental in the design of algorithms and cryptographic systems. For many problems (such as Polynomial Identity Testing), the fastest known algorithms use randomness. The role of randomness is more pronounced in the design of cryptographic systems such as bit commitment, encryption, etc., as one needs unbiased random bits to achieve security [DOPS04].

Most sources of randomness found in nature are not perfect. The amount of randomness in a source is usually formalized via the notion of min-entropy. The min-entropy of a random source X is defined as the $\max_{x \in \mathsf{Supp}(X)} \log 1/\Pr[X = x]$. A natural, fundamental question is: Can we extract uniform random bits out of these weak sources? The answer is: Yes, and this is achieved by a tool called as randomness extractors. However, it is well-known that it is impossible to extract uniform random bits given only a single weak source. To side step this impossibility, two notions have been considered. One is the seeded setting where you assume the existence of a uniform short seed that is independent of the weak source. The other setting is the independence source setting. The independence setting is weaker than the seeded setting as it only needs independent sources $X_1, \ldots, X_p$ such that each have sufficient min-entropy. In this work, we are interested in the independent source setting.

Independent Source Extractor. Starting with the seminal work of Chor and Goldreich [CG88], there has been a long line of work on constructing better independent source extractors.[1] A recent breakthrough work of Chattopadhyay and Zuckerman [CZ16] gave a construction of two-source extractor for poly logarithmic min-entropy sources. However, the error of the extractor was inverse polynomial. Even though the subsequent works [Li16, Coh16a, Coh16b, Coh16c, Coh16d, Li17, BADTS16] improved the min-entropy of the sources to nearly logarithmic, none of these works achieved negligible error (which is important for cryptographic applications).

A recent work of Garg, Kalai, and Khurana [GKK20] considered the problem of constructing two-source computational extractors with negligible error. They additionally assumed the existence of a common random string that is sampled once and for all, and the weak sources can depend on the CRS. This precludes constructions where the common random string can be used as a seed to extract uniform random bits from these weak sources. They provided a construction of a computational two-source extractor with negligible error in the CRS model for sources with min-entropy $\Omega(n^\gamma)$ (for some constant $\gamma \in (0, 1)$) under the sub-exponential hardness of the DDH assumption.

---

[1] The quality of an independent source extractor is determined by three parameters, (i) the number of independent sources, (ii) the min-entropy of these sources, and (iii) the error which is the statistical distance between the output of the extractor and the uniform distribution.

Challenges. The independent source setting makes two crucial assumptions. First, it assumes that each of the sources $X_1, \ldots, X_p$ are independently generated. Second, it assumes that each of these sources have sufficient min-entropy. However, neither of these assumptions may be true in general for many sources found in nature. For instance, it could be possible that one or more of these weak sources are biased and have little or no min-entropy. It could also be the case that some of these sources are adversarially corrupted so as to introduce an artificial dependence between them. Hence, it is only safe to assume that some of these sources have sufficient min-entropy and are independent whereas other sources might have low min-entropy and might also depend on these honest sources. The main challenge is that we do not know a-priori which sources are honest and which ones are corrupted.

Can we nevertheless construct an extractor that outputs uniform random bits given a sample from such sources?

This question is not new and has already been previously investigated in two types of contexts: network extractor protocols [DO03, GSV05, KLRZ08, KLR09] and extractors for adversarial sources [CGGL20].

Network Extractor Protocols. Consider a setting where there are multiple parties and each party has an independent weak random source. The parties want to communicate with each other over a public channel and at the end of the protocol, each party outputs uniform random bits. These random bits could be used to run a distributed computation protocol or for securely computing a multiparty functionality. The challenge, however, is that some of these parties may be corrupted by a malicious adversary that may instruct them to deviate arbitrarily from the protocol. Can honest parties still end up with uniform random bits under such an adversarial attack? This is precisely what is achieved by a network extractor protocol [DO03, GSV05, KLRZ08, KLR09].

Here, the key barrier is that adversarial messages may be derived from sources that have little or no min-entropy and furthermore, these messages may depend on the messages from the honest parties. In the information-theoretic setting, the work of Kalai et al. [KLRZ08] provided constructions of network extractor protocol for sources that have min-entropy of $2^{\log^\beta n}$ (for some constant $\beta < 1$). However, the main drawback is that they could guarantee that only a fraction of the honest parties end up with uniform random bits. In a recent work, Goyal et al. [GSZ21] gave a protocol that did not have this limitation, but their protocol only works in a setting where the min-entropy of the sources was very high. Specifically, they required that for any p number of parties, there exists a constant γ such that min-entropy was $n(1 - \gamma)$. In the computational setting, the work of Kalai et al. [KLR09] gave a protocol for sources with min-entropy $\Omega(n)$ but relied on exponential hardness of one-way permutations and the round complexity of the protocol grew with the number of parties.

Extractors for Adversarial Sources. In this setting, we consider a distribution of p sources $(X_1, \ldots, X_p)$ where some them are guaranteed to be independent and have sufficient min-entropy (called as honest sources) and the others are adversarially generated and could depend on the honest sources in some limited ways (called as corrupt sources). Given a sample from this distribution, we need to extract bits that are close to the uniform distribution. Of course, the main challenge here is that we do not know apriori which sources are honest and which sources are corrupt and how the corrupt sources depend on the honest sources. The work of Chattopadhyay et al. [CGGL20] formally studied this primitive[2] and gave constructions (in the information-theoretic setting) where the number of honest sources K is at least $p^{1-\gamma}$ (for some contant γ), their min-entropy is poly logarithmic and each corrupted source could depend on at most K^γ honest sources.

Our Work. We continue the line of work initiated by Garg et al. [GKK20] on constructing computational extractors in the CRS model and provide new constructions that extract uniform bits in the setting of network extractors and from adversarial sources.

1.1 Our Results

The key technical tool that allows us to obtain the above applications is a *better* construction of computational two-source extractor in the CRS model.

The construction from [GKK20] had two drawbacks: first, it required sources that have min-entropy of $\Omega(n^\gamma)$ (for some constant $\gamma \in (0, 1)$) and second, it worked only for sources that were heavily imbalanced: requiring that one of the sources have entropy equal to the size of the other source.

Our first result is a much cleaner analysis of this construction. Our improved analysis essentially shows, somewhat surprisingly, that the extractor from [GKK20] actually does not suffer from either of the limitations stated above. That is, it works for *balanced* sources that are each only required to have *poly logarithmic* min-entropy, and achieves negligible error.

Informal Theorem 1. *Let λ denote the security parameter. Assuming the sub-exponential hardness of DDH, there exists a constant $c > 1$ such that for any $\lambda \leq n_1, n_2 \leq \text{poly}(\lambda)$, there exists a construction of a negligible error, two-source computational extractor in the CRS model where sources have lengths n_1, n_2 respectively and min-entropy $O(\log^c n)$.*

Our tighter analysis is also arguably *simpler* than the one in [GKK20]. As a corollary, we use the transformation from [GKK20] to obtain a construction of

---

[2] In a work that is concurrent and independent to Chattopadhyay et al., Aggarwal et al. [AOR+20b] studied another model of adversarial sources called as SHELA sources. They showed that it is impossible to extract uniform random bits from SHELA sources and gave constructions of extractors whose output is somewhere random. In another work, Dodis et al. [DVW20] studied a notion of extractor dependent sources which arise in the setting where the source sampler could depend on the output of the previous invocations of the extractor using the same seed.

a negligible-error, *non-malleable* two-source extractor for balanced sources with polylogarithmic min-entropy, where one source can be tampered an arbitrary polynomial number of times (this is called a one-sided non-malleable extractor). Specifically, in the one-sided setting, the adversary gets access to a tampering oracle and can specify any efficiently computable tampering function on one of the sources. The oracle responds with the output of the extractor computed on the first source and the tampered second source.

Informal Theorem 2. *Let λ denote the security parameter. Assuming the sub-exponential hardness of the DDH assumption, there exists a constant $c > 1$ such that for any $\lambda \leq n_1, n_2 \leq \mathrm{poly}(\lambda)$, there exists a construction of a negligible error, two-source, one-sided computational non-malleable extractor in the CRS model where both sources have lengths n_1, n_2 respectively and have min-entropy $O(\log^c n)$.*

We then use the above non-malleable extractor as the main building block and give a construction of network extractor protocol that has a single round of communication, works with poly logarithmic min-entropy sources and can tolerate an optimum number of malicious corruptions.

Informal Theorem 3. *Let λ be the security parameter. Assuming sub-exponential hardness of the DDH assumption, there exists a constant $c > 1$ s.t. for any $\lambda \leq n \leq \mathrm{poly}(\lambda)$, there exists a construction of a single round, negligible error, computational network extractor protocol in the CRS model for any p (which is a polynomial in the security parameter) number of parties each having an independent source of length n and min-entropy $O(\log^c n)$. The protocol tolerates $p - 2$ corruptions by a malicious adversary (which is optimum). Furthermore, all the honest parties end up with an output that is computationally indistinguishable to the uniform distribution given the view of the adversary.*

We also give a construction of an adversarial source extractor that works in the extreme setting where there are only two honest sources and every corrupted source can depend on either one of the honest sources. This construction uses our computational two-source extractor as the main building block.

Informal Theorem 4. *Let $p \in \mathbb{N}$ be fixed and let λ be the security parameter. Assuming that sub-exponential hardness of DDH assumption, there exists some constant $c > 1$ s.t. for $\Omega(\lambda) \leq n \leq \mathrm{poly}(\lambda)$, there exists a construction of negligible error adversarial source extractor in the CRS model that works for an arbitrary adversarial p-source distribution where (i) each source has length n, (ii) there are two honest independent sources with min-entropy $O(\log^c \lambda)$, and (iii) every other source is the output of an (efficient) function of either one of the two honest sources.*

Comparison with [AOR+20a]. We now compare our results with the prior work of Aggarwal et al. [AOR+20a]. While both papers build on [GKK20] and obtain new types of computational non-malleable extractors, there are some important differences in the results. In the setting where only one of the sources is tamperable and the number of tamperings is unbounded,

- Techniques in [AOR+20a] give non-malleable extractors for linear min-entropy (min-entropy greater than 0.46n) based on quasi-polynomial DDH. To achieve poly-logarithmic min-entropy, they additionally assume the existence of near optimal (exponentially hard) collision-resistant hash functions.
- Our work gives a construction for poly-logarithmic min-entropy based on sub-exponential DDH.

We remark that [AOR+20a] also (primarily) considers a setting where both sources can be tampered but the number of tamperings is bounded. Among other results, they provide new constructions in this setting for linear min-entropy (min-entropy greater than 0.46n) based on quasi-polynomial DDH and for poly-logarithmic min-entropy based on near-optimal (exponential) hardness of collision-resistant hash functions.

An important objective of our work is to achieve new applications: these applications require a setting where the number of tamperings is unbounded, with only one source being tampered. For this setting, as discussed above, our work shows that the [GKK20] construction achieves poly-logarithmic min-entropy for balanced sources from sub-exponential DDH.

2   Technical Overview

In this section, we provide an overview of our results.

2.1   Improved Two-Source and Non-malleable Extractors

We start with an overview of our improved two-source and non-malleable extractors. The key technical bulk of this part of our work is an improved two-source extractor, and plugging in the resulting extractor into the work of [GKK20] also immediately yields an improved non-malleable extractor, as we will discuss below.

Background: The Blueprints of [BHK11, BACD+17, GKK20]. As a first step, we recall the construction of two-source extractors in [GKK20], which itself combines the blueprint of [BHK11] with that of [BACD+17]. As discussed above, we will show that essentially the same construction serves as a strong computational extractor even for *balanced sources*, and even in settings where sources have only *polylogarithmic min-entropy*. In contrast, the techniques in [GKK20] limited them to highly unbalanced sources and required λ^ϵ min-entropy

At a high level, [GKK20] obtain two-source extractors with low error via two steps.

Step 1. Following a blueprint suggested in [BHK11, GKK20] build a computational non-malleable extractor in the CRS model, in a setting where one of the sources has min entropy rate larger than 1/2. We use the same blueprint in this work also, and therefore we describe it below.

First, start with any 2-source extractor

$$2\mathsf{Ext} : \{0,1\}^{n_1} \times \{0,1\}^{n_2} \to \{0,1\}^m,$$

with negligible error (e.g., [Bou05, Raz05]), min-entropy (poly $\log n_1$) for one of the sources and min-entropy rate of about $1/2$ for the other.

The construction makes use of the following cryptographic primitives, which can be obtained based on the (sub-exponential) hardness of DDH.

1. A collision resistant function family $\mathcal{H}$, where for each $h \in \mathcal{H}$, $h : \{0,1\}^{n_2} \to \{0,1\}^k$, where k is significantly smaller than the min-entropy of the second source of 2Ext.
2. A family of lossy functions $\mathcal{F}$, where for each $f \in \mathcal{F}$, $f : \{0,1\}^{n_1} \to \{0,1\}^{n_1}$. A lossy function family consist of two types of functions: injective and lossy. Each lossy function loses most of the information about the input (i.e., image size is very small). It is hard to distinguish between a random injective and a random lossy function in the family.

The actual construction is as follows. The CRS consists of a random function $h \leftarrow \mathcal{H}$ from the collision-resistant hash family, and consists of $2k$ random family $\mathcal{F}$, denoted by

$$f_{1,0}, f_{2,0}, \dots, f_{k,0}$$
$$f_{1,1}, f_{2,1}, \dots, f_{k,1}$$

where for a randomly sampled $b \leftarrow \{0,1\}^k$, for all $i \in [k]$, f_{i,b_i} are injective, and $f_{i,1-b_i}$ are lossy.

The computational non-malleable extractor (in the CRS model) is defined by

$$\mathsf{cnm\text{-}Ext}(x, y, \mathsf{crs}) := 2\mathsf{Ext}(f_{\mathsf{crs},h(y)}(x), y),$$

where

$$f_{\mathsf{crs},s}(x) := f_{1,s_1} \circ \dots \circ f_{k,s_k}(x)$$

Consider any polynomial size adversary $\mathcal{A}$ that obtains either ($\mathsf{cnm\text{-}Ext}(x, y)$, y, crs) or (U, y, crs), together with an oracle $\mathcal{O}$ that has (x, y, crs) hardwired, and on input y' outputs $\perp$ if $y' = y$, and otherwise outputs $\mathsf{nm\text{-}Ext}(x, y', \mathsf{crs})$. By the collision resistance property of h, $\mathcal{A}$ queries the oracle on input y' s.t. $h(y') = h(y)$ only with negligible probability. Therefore, the oracle $\mathcal{O}$ can be replaced by a different oracle, that only hardwires ($\mathsf{crs}, h(y), x$) and on input y' outputs $\perp$ if $h(y') = h(y)$, and otherwise outputs $\mathsf{cnm\text{-}Ext}(x, y')$.

It is observed in [BHK11, GKK20] that access to this oracle can be simulated entirely given only $\mathsf{crs}, h(y)$ and ($Z_1, \dots Z_k$), where for every i, $Z_i = f_{1,1-h(y)_1}(f_{2,1-h(y)_2}(\dots f_{i,h(y)_i}, (\dots f_{k,h(y)_k}(x)))$. Now suppose that the functions $\{f_{i,1-h(y)_i}\}_{i \in [k]}$ were all lossy – then it is easy to see that (for small enough k), Y has high min-entropy conditioned on $h(y)$ and $Z = (Z_1, \dots, Z_k)$. At the same time, as long as the functions $\{f_{i,h(y)_i}\}_{i \in [k]}$ are all injective, the output $f_{\mathsf{crs},h(y)}(x)$ continues to have high entropy conditioned on $h(y)$ and Z. Then one could use the fact that 2Ext is a (strong) 2-source extractor, to argue that the output of our non-malleable extractor is close to uniform.

Moreover, since the adversary $\mathcal{A}$ cannot distinguish between random injective functions and random lossy ones, it should be possible to (indistinguishably) change the CRS to ensure that functions $f_{1,h(y)_1}, \ldots, f_{k,h(y)_k}$ are injective, whereas the functions $f_{1,1-h(y)_1}, \ldots, f_{k,1-h(y)_k}$ are all lossy.

This intuition is converted into a formal proof by [BHK11, GKK20]. In summary, these works show that the resulting non-malleable extractor (very roughly) inherits the entropy requirements of the underlying two-source extractor. Moreover, the resulting extractor is non-malleable w.r.t. *arbitrarily many* tampering functions (this is impossible to achieve information theoretically).

Looking ahead, this transformation appears to be fairly tight, and is *not* why [GKK20] are limited to unbalanced sources and λ^ϵ min-entropy. These restrictions appear to be a result of the next transformation, which converts non-malleable extractors with high entropy for one source, to two-source extractos with low min-entropy for both sources. We describe this next.

Step 2. Next, [GKK20] convert the resulting non-malleable extractor (for a setting where one source has high min-entropy rate) to a two-source extractor for a setting where both sources have low min-entropy, by following a blueprint of [BACD+17].

An important difference between [BACD+17] and [GKK20] is that the reduction in [BACD+17] is not efficient: specifically, even given an efficient adversary that contradicts the security of the 2-source extractor, [BACD+17] obtain an *inefficient* adversary that contradicts the security of the underlying non-malleable extractor.

To better understand this issue, we briefly summarize the transformation of [BACD+17]. Their transformation uses a disperser as a building block.

A (K, K') disperser is a function

$$\Gamma : \{0,1\}^{n_2} \times [t] \to \{0,1\}^d$$

such that for every subset A of $\{0,1\}^{n_2}$ that is of size $\geq K$, it holds that the size of the set of neighbors of A under Γ is at least K'.

The [BACD+17]-transformation starts with a seeded non-malleable extractor nm-Ext : $\{0,1\}^{n_1} \times \{0,1\}^d \to \{0,1\}^m$ and a disperser $\Gamma : \{0,1\}^{n_2} \times [t] \to \{0,1\}^d$, and constructs the following 2-source extractor 2Ext : $\{0,1\}^{n_1} \times \{0,1\}^{n_2} \to \{0,1\}^m$, defined by

$$2\text{Ext}(x_1, x_2) = \bigoplus_{y:\exists i \text{ s.t. } \Gamma(x_2,i)=y} \text{nm-Ext}(x_1, y)$$

Intuitively, by the definition of an (information-theoretic) t-non-malleable extractor nm-Ext, for a random $y \in \{0,1\}^d$, for all $y'_1, \ldots, y'_t$ that are distinct from y, it holds that

$$(\text{nm-Ext}(X_1, y), \text{nm-Ext}(X_1, y'_1), \ldots, \text{nm-Ext}(X_1, y'_t))$$

$$\equiv (U, \text{nm-Ext}(X_1, y'_1), \ldots, \text{nm-Ext}(X_1, y'_t)).$$

This means that for "most" y, nm-Ext(X_1, y) is statistically close to uniform, even given nm-Ext$(X_1, \Gamma(x_2, j))$ for every $j \in [t] \setminus \{i\}$ such that $\Gamma(x_2, j) \neq y$, which in turn implies that the XOR of these (distinct) values is close to uniform, which implies that 2Ext(X_1, x_2) is close to uniform.

But to formally prove that the resulting extractor is a strong (information-theoretic) non-malleable extractor, one would need to construct a reduction $\mathcal{R}$ that breaks the non-malleable extractor, given any adversary $\mathcal{A}$ that breaks the two-source extractor. In the computational setting, $\mathcal{R}$ is required to be efficient, which causes the bulk of the technical difficulty in [GKK20].

In more detail, $\mathcal{R}$ obtains input $(\alpha, \widehat{y})$, where $\widehat{y}$ is a random seed for the non-malleable extractor and where α is either chosen according to cnm-Ext$(X_1, \widehat{y})$ or is chosen uniformly at random. In addition, $\mathcal{R}$ obtains an oracle that outputs cnm-Ext(X_1, y') on input $y' \neq \widehat{y}$. $\mathcal{R}$ must *efficiently* distinguish between the case where $\alpha \leftarrow$ cnm-Ext$(X_1, \widehat{y})$ and the case where α is chosen uniformly at random. In order to use the (two-source extractor adversary) $\mathcal{A}$, $\mathcal{R}$ needs to generate a challenge for $\mathcal{A}$ that corresponds either to the output of the 2-source extractor (if α was the output of cnm-Ext) or uniform (if α was uniform). In addition, the reduction $\mathcal{R}$ must generate a corresponding x_2 for $\mathcal{A}$, that is sampled according to X_2. This is easy to do in unbounded time by simply sampling $x_2 \leftarrow X_2$ conditioned on the existence of i such that $\Gamma(x_2, i) = y$.

To enable a reduction in the computational setting, [GKK20] view the inefficient computation involved; i.e. sampling $x_2 \leftarrow X_2$ conditioned on the existence of i such that $\Gamma(x_2, i) = y$; as the output of a leakage function. They *simulate* this leakage by running in time exponential in the length of the leakage. Unfortunately, this means that the running time of the reduction grows as $2^{|x_2|}$, which restricts $|x_2|$ to being extremely small, in fact much smaller than the size of the first source. This also restricts the sources in such a way that the min-entropy in the first source is required to be larger than the size of the second source. As discussed above, the highly asymmetric state of affairs does not bode well for many natural applications of two-source and non-malleable extractors.

Our Key Ideas. To remedy this situation, we develop a completely different analysis for essentially the same construction. In contrast with [GKK20], our analysis is arguably simpler, does not impose any artificial restrictions on the size of each source, and leads to significantly improved min-entropy parameters.

First, we do not split the analysis of the resulting two-source extractor into two steps as described above. In other words, unlike [GKK20], we *do not* attempt to prove that the [BACD+17] template as described in Step 2, when applied to *any computational non-malleable extractor*, yields a good two-source extractor with low min-entropy and low error.

Instead, we apply the [BHK11] transform to an *information-theoretic* two-source extractor with low error but min-entropy rate of $1/2$ for one of the sources (e.g., [Bou05, Raz05]). Next, we consider the [BACD+17] transform applied to the result of this extractor. We then give a monolithic proof that the result of applying these transformations one after the other, results in a two-source extractor for balanced sources, polylogarithmic min-entropy and negligible error.

At a very high level, this monolithic approach enables us to *strip off* all computational components one by one, to eventually end up with a purely information theoretic experiment. This allows us to sidestep the need to invert the disperser in any of our computational reductions; limiting our use of inefficient reductions to the information-theoretic step in the proof.

We now discuss our proof strategy in additional detail. We will start with an experiment where the adversary obtains either the output of the (final) two-source extractor, which we will denote by $\mathsf{c2Ext}(x_1, x_2)$ or a uniformly random value (in each case the adversary also obtains the sample x_2). As discussed above, we will modify this experiment in steps, slowly stripping off computational assumptions until we end up in an experiment that does not require any assumptions.

Discarding Hash Collisions. Recall that the [BHK11] blueprint uses $z = h(y)$ to choose a subset of functions f_{i,z_i} to apply to the first source. As a first step, we will modify the experiment so that if in the process of computing $\mathsf{c2Ext}(x_1, x_2)$, a hash collision is encountered, then we simply outputs a uniformly random sample instead of $\mathsf{c2Ext}(x_1, x_2)$. In more detail, the output of the two-source extractor $\mathsf{c2Ext}$ is replaced by a slightly modified $\mathsf{c2Ext}'$. The replacement $\mathsf{c2Ext}'(x_1, x_2)$ first checks if $\exists (i_1, i_2)$ such that $\Gamma(x_2, i_1) \neq \Gamma(x_2, i_2)$ but $h(\Gamma(x_2, i_1)) = h(\Gamma(x_2, i_2))$. If such (i_1, i_2) exist, then $\mathsf{c2Ext}'$ outputs a uniformly random value.

At the same time, the oracle $\mathcal{O}$ is replaced with $\mathcal{O}'$ that is identical to $\mathcal{O}$, except that on input any y' such that $h(y') = h(y)$, $\mathcal{O}'$ outputs $\bot$.

We rely on the collision resistance of the hash function family to argue that as long as the sources are efficiently sampleable, this experiment is statistically indistinguishable from the previous one. This argument will allow us to simply discard hash collisions throughout the rest of this overview. The other remaining assumption is that of the lossy function family.

Working Around Lossy Functions. Recall that the approach in [GKK20] is to (indistinguishably) switch the crs so that the functions $\{f_{i,1-h(y)_i}\}_{i \in [k]}$ are all lossy, and the rest are injective. This 'nicely distributed' CRS allows them to efficiently "simulate" the output of the oracle $\mathcal{O}$, and prove that the resulting construction is a non-malleable extractor[3] But this approach runs into the barriers described above, as the eventual two-source extractors do not support balanced sources or poly-logarithmic min-entropy.

In this work, as a first stab, we attempt to make statistical arguments about the sources in an (imagined) experiment where the CRS is assumed to be 'nicely

---

[3] There are many other subtleties involved, most importantly, a circularity: the CRS must be programmed according to $h(y)$, but y is sampled as a function of the CRS. The work of [GKK20] develops techniques to avoid these subtleties, but we do not discuss them here as they are less relevant to the current approach.

distributed'. In more detail, we say that the random variable y takes a "bad" value if it becomes possible for an oracle-aided *unbounded* adversary to distinguish the output of the [BHK11] non-malleable extractor from uniform, *when conditioned on the CRS being 'nicely distributed' for y*. That is, for a function $\epsilon = \epsilon(\lambda)$, we define the set BAD-seed$_\epsilon$ (roughly) as the set of y, for which the following holds: conditioned on the CRS being such that functions at positions indexed by $h(y)$ are injective and the others are lossy, the output of the non-malleable extractor is at least ϵ-statistically distinguishable from a uniformly random value in presence of the oracle $\mathcal{O}'$.

Bounding BAD-seed$_\epsilon$. We prove that for large enough (but still negligible) ϵ, the size of the set BAD-seed$_\epsilon$ is negligibly small. Fortunately, since the definition of BAD-seed$_\epsilon$ already conditions on the CRS being nicely distributed, this argument does not involve any computational assumptions, and follows by a reduction to the underlying *information-theoretic* two-source extractor of [Bou05, Raz05], as long as the number of tampering queries is polynomially bounded. Intuitively, conditioned on the CRS being nice, we can establish that the sources (for the non-malleable extractor) retain high entropy even in the presence of the oracle $\mathcal{O}'$, and therefore, the output of the two-source extractor, applied to $(f_{\text{crs},h(y)}(x), y)$ is statistically indistinguishable from uniform. Then a simple averaging argument allows us to prove that BAD-seed$_\epsilon$ is small.

From Non-malleable to Two-Source Extractors. Next, we aim to use the definition of BAD-seed$_\epsilon$ to derive a meaningful (statistical) conclusion about the final two-source extractor. Specifically, we fix a (large enough, but still negligible) ϵ.

We consider a game that samples sources (x_1, x_2) for the final two-source extractor, and samples $i \leftarrow [t]$, *conditioned on* $y = \Gamma(x_2, i)$ lying outside the set BAD-seed$_\epsilon$. By definition of the set BAD-seed$_\epsilon$, for any y outside this set, the output of the non-malleable extractor is *statistically* indistinguishable from uniform, even given (polynomial-query) access to the tampering oracle. Recall that the output of the two-source extractor is

$$2\text{Ext}(x_1, x_2) = \bigoplus_{y:\exists i \text{ s.t. } \Gamma(x_2,i)=y} \text{nm-Ext}(x_1, y)$$

This means that for $y \notin$ BAD-seed$_\epsilon$, for all $y'_1, \ldots, y'_t$ that are distinct from y, it holds that

$$(\text{nm-Ext}(X_1, y), \text{nm-Ext}(X_1, y'_1), \ldots, \text{nm-Ext}(X_1, y'_t)) \text{ and}$$

$$(U, \text{nm-Ext}(X_1, y'_1), \ldots, \text{nm-Ext}(X_1, y'_t))$$

are at most ϵ-statistically distinguishable.

This means that for such y, nm-Ext(X_1, y) is statistically close to uniform, even given nm-Ext$(X_1, \Gamma(x_2, j))$ for every $j \in [t] \setminus \{i\}$ such that $\Gamma(x_2, j) \neq y$, which in turn implies that the XOR of these (distinct) values is close to uniform, which implies that $2\text{Ext}(X_1, x_2)$ statistically is close to uniform.

Because we carefully conditioned on $y = \Gamma(x_2, i) \notin$ BAD-seed$_\epsilon$, we are able to (again, *statistically*) argue that the output of the *two-source* extractor in this game will be statistically indistinguishable from uniform, even given x_2.

At this point, we have argued that in an idealized game where the CRS is conditioned on being nicely distributed, the output of the (strong) two-source extractor will be indistinguishable from uniform. But the in the actual construction, the CRS is distributed in such a way that for a random $b \leftarrow \{0,1\}^k$ the functions $f_{i,1-b_i}$ are lossy, and the others are injective. This only very rarely matches the idealized game (where we essentially condition on $b = h(y)$). At this point, we would like to use the fact that lossy functions are indistinguishable from injective ones, to argue that the adversary cannot distinguish an actual game from the idealized game. Formalizing this intuition runs into a few subtle issues, that we briefly describe next.

The Computational Argument. Note that in the idealized game described above, (x_2, i) are sampled conditioned on:

- The crs being such that functions indexed by $\Gamma(x_2, i)$ are injective and the others are lossy.
- $\Gamma(x_2, i) \notin$ BAD-seed, and

We begin by removing the first requirement, and moving to a game where we *only* condition on $\Gamma(x_2, i) \notin$ BAD-seed. We prove that removing the first conditioning does not (significantly) affect a PPT distinguisher's ability to distinguish between the output of the extractor and uniform. The proof of this makes careful use of Chernoff bounds and the leakage lemma [GW11, JP14, CLP15], to show that if the two games are different, then one can *guess* which functions in the CRS are injective and which ones are lossy, with advantage better than what is allowed by the security of the lossy function family.

At this point, we have moved to a game where (x_2, i) are sampled only subject to the restriction that $\Gamma(x_2, i) \notin$ BAD-seed. Next, we prove that this restriction can also be removed without (significantly) affect an unbounded distinguisher's ability to distinguish between the output of the extractor and uniform. Intuitively, this follows because of the disperser and because the set BAD $-$ seed$_\epsilon$ is small. Recall that the disperser maps every "large enough" set of x_2's to a "large enough" set of y's. This implies that if the set of y's for which $y \in$ BAD $-$ seed$_\epsilon$ is small, their inverses (under the disperser) are also small. We show that as long as the source x_2 has polylogarithmic min-entropy, the probability that x_2 is such that $\Gamma(x_2, i) \notin$ BAD-seed for *any* i will be negligibly small.

This allows us to argue that the output of the strong two-source extractor is indistinguishable from uniform. A careful separation of the information-theoretic and computational components allows us to set parameters so that the entropy loss from the first source is only polylogarithmic. As discussed above, existing dispersers (e.g., from [GUV09]) already suffice in a setting where the second source also has polylogarithmic min-entropy.

Here, we clarify that the exact min-entropy loss depends on our computational assumptions. In more detail, we assume that there exists a constant

$0 < \epsilon < 1$ such that DDH with security parameter λ is hard against $\text{poly}(2^{\lambda^\epsilon})$-size machines. The exact polylogarithmic min-entropy requirement on our sources then depends on ϵ.

This completes a high-level picture of our new proof strategy. For the sake of conceptual simplicity, we swept a few details under the rug. We refer the reader to the full version for a detailed formal proof.

From Two-Source to Non-malleable Extractors. Once we obtain two-source extractors as discussed above, we directly invoke a theorem from [GKK20] (that builds on the [BHK11] blueprint) to bootstrap our low entropy, low error two-source extractors to low entropy, low error *non-malleable extractors*. Since this follows almost immediately from prior work (modulo a few parameter choices), we omit details in this overview.

2.2   Network Extractor Protocol

In the network extractor setting, there are p parties and each party P_i for $i \in [p]$ has an independent weak random source X_i. There is a centralized adversary that controls an arbitrary subset $M \subset [p]$ of the parties. This adversary is malicious, which means that it can instruct the corrupted parties to deviate arbitrarily from the protocol specification and is rushing which means that in each round of the protocol, it can wait until it receives all the messages from the honest parties before sending its own message on behalf of the corrupted parties. We consider the parties to be connected via public channels and the adversary can view all the communication sent by honest parties. At the end of the protocol, we want all the honest parties to output uniform random bits that are independent of the view of the adversary.

In the computational setting, we restrict the adversary to be computationally bounded and independence mentioned above is required to hold in the computational sense. The quality of the network extractor protocol is determined by three parameters, (i) the number of corrupted parties $|M|$, (ii) the min-entropy of the weak random source available with the parties $H_\infty(X_i)$, and (iii) the number of rounds of the protocol. It is easy to observer that if $|M| = p - 1$, then we cannot construct a network extractor protocol as this task amounts to extracting uniform random bits from a single weak random source. So, the best we can hope for is the case where $|M| \leq p - 2$. In this work, we give a construction of network extractor protocol in the computational setting in the CRS model that tolerates $|M| \leq p - 2$ corruptions, runs in a single round, and works with polylogarithmic min-entropy for each $i \in [p]$.

Key Challenge. To understand the key challenge, let us first weaken the requirements from the network extractor protocol. Let us assume for now that the first party P_1 is never corrupted but the identity of the other honest party is not known at the beginning of the protocol. Furthermore, we only require the output of honest P_1 to be uniform and independent of the view of the adversary. Can we construct a single round protocol for this weaker setting?

We observe that the techniques developed in the work of Goyal et al. [GSZ21] gives such a protocol based on any two-source non-malleable extractor. Specifically, we ask every party to send its source in the clear to the first party P_1. For every $j \neq 1$, P_1 applies the two-source non-malleable extractor on its source and the source received from P_j and outputs the XOR of all such computations. We now argue that the output of P_1 is uniform and independent of the view of the adversary if the non-malleable extractor is strong and is multi-tamperable. Let us assume that P_i for some $i \neq 1$ is the other honest party. Now, the messages sent by the adversarial parties are an efficiently computable function of P_i's source. Thus, one can view the messages from the adversarial parties as a tampering of the honest source. The security of the non-malleable extractor guarantees that the output of the extractor on the good source is close to uniform even conditioned on its output on the tampered sources. This allows us to argue that the output of P_1 is close to uniform given the view of the adversary (which includes the other honest source and that is why we require the extractor to be strong).

However, we quickly run into trouble if we want to extend this to the setting where we require the outputs of two honest parties to be uniform and independent of the view of the adversary. Indeed, if P_1 were to send its source in the clear, then we cannot use the security of the non-malleable extractor to argue that the output of P_1 is close to uniform. In the "very high" min-entropy setting, the work of [GSZ21] gave a method to overcome this barrier. Specifically, party P_i divides its source into p slices, retains the i-th slice with itself and broadcasts the rest of the slices. It now uses the i-th slice received from the other parties along with its own slice to compute the output as mentioned above. It was argued in their work that if the min-entropy source was "very high", then the outputs of the all honest parties are close to uniform and independent of the view of the adversary. However, we cannot extend their argument to the setting where the min-entropy of each weak source $\delta \cdot n$ for some universal constant δ.

Our Approach. In order to overcome this barrier, we rely on computational tools (namely, lossy functions) to artificially create independence between the messages transmitted by each party and the sources used to compute their outputs. We now elaborate on this.

For each $i \in [p]$ and $b \in \{0, 1\}$, we sample $f_{i,b}$ uniformly in the injective mode and include the descriptions of these functions as part of the CRS. In the protocol, party P_i first computes $f_{i,b}(X_i)$ for each $b \in \{0, 1\}$ and broadcasts $f_{i,1}(X_i)$ and retains $f_{i,0}(X_i)$ with itself. To compute the output, it evaluates the non-malleable extractor with one source as $f_{i,0}(X_i)$ and the other source as $f_{j,1}(X_j)$ for each $j \neq i$. It then outputs the XOR of these evaluations. We now show how to use the security of lossy functions to argue that the joint distribution of the outputs of the honest parties are close to uniform conditioned on the view of the adversary.

We consider a sequence of hybrids where the first hybrid in the sequence consists of the outputs of the honest parties as computed in the protocol along with the view of the adversary and last hybrid is the distribution where the outputs of all the honest parties are replaced with uniform and independent bits. In the i-th intermediate hybrid, we replace the outputs of the first i uncorrupted parties with uniform. By a standard averaging argument, it is sufficient to show that the i-th hybrid in this sequence is computationally indistinguishable to the $(i-1)$-th hybrid. Let us assume that the i-th honest party is k_i and the identity of the other honest party is k'_i.

We first consider an intermediate distribution where we sample $f_{k_i,1}$ and $f_{k'_i,0}$ in the CRS using the lossy mode instead of the injective mode. It follows from the computational indistinguishability of the injective and the lossy modes that this intermediate distribution is indistinguishable to the $(i-1)$-th hybrid. Since $f_{k_i,1}$ and $f_{k'_i,0}$ are sampled in the lossy mode, we can view these as bounded leakages from the source X_{k_i} and $X_{k'_i}$. Now, conditioned on these leakages, we can argue that $f_{k_i,0}(X_{k_i})$ and $f_{k'_i,1}(X_{k'_i})$ are independent and have sufficient min-entropy (since $f_{k_i,0}$ and $f_{k'_i,1}$ are sampled in the injective mode). Now, we can rely on the argument sketched above and view the adversarial messages as tamperings of the honest source $f_{k'_i,1}(X_{k'_i})$ and use the security of the non-malleable extractor to replace the output of P_{k_i} with uniform bits independent of the view of the adversary. To show this distribution is indistinguishable to the i-th hybrid, we again rely on the indistinguihability of the lossy and injective modes and switch sampling $f_{k_i,1}$ and $f_{k'_i,0}$ in the CRS to the injective mode. This allows us to show that the $(i-1)$-th hybrid is computationally indistinguishable to the i-th hybrid.

2.3 Extractors for Adversarial Sources

An adversarial source distribution [CGGL20] is a sequence of p random variables $(X_1, \ldots, X_p)$ such that a subset of them are independent and have sufficient min-entropy (called as the honest sources) and the rest can depend on the honest sources in a limited way (called as the corrupt sources). The goal is to construct an extractor such that given a sample from the adversarial source distribution, it outputs a string that is close to random. Here, the parameters of interest are the (i) number of honest sources in the distribution, and (ii) the min-entropy of the honest sources. We are interested in constructing extractors that work in the extreme setting where the number of honest sources is only 2 and every corrupted source is an (efficiently computable) function of either one of the honest sources.

Challenge with the Prior Approaches. The works of Chattopadhyay et al. [CGGL20] and Goyal et al. [GSZ21] gave a method of constructing such an extractor using a non-malleable extractor that satisfies an additional security property. Specifically, the adversary is allowed to specify a set of tampering functions $\{(f_i, g_i)\}_{i \in [t]}$ as well as a sequence of bits $\{b_i\}_{i \in [t]}$. If $b_i = 0$, then the adversary receives the output of the non-malleable extractor applied on $f_i(X)$ and $g_i(Y)$. Otherwise, it receives the output of the extractor on $g_i(Y)$ and $f_i(X)$. Unfortunately, we do not know how to show that the non-malleable extractor constructions in the works of [GKK20, AOR+20a] satisfy this additional property. Hence, in this work, we take new approach towards this problem that is partly inspired by our network extractor construction and relies only on a computational two-source extractor (rather than a non-malleable extractor).

Our Construction. We first explain why a network extractor protocol doesn't directly give rise to an extractor for adversarial source distribution. In the case of a network extractor protocol, only the messages sent by the corrupted parties depend on the honest party's messages whereas in the case of the adversarial sources, the corrupted source could depend on the honest source. This difference precludes a direct construction. However, we use the techniques developed for the network extractor construction to construct an extractor for adversarial sources.

Our extractor for adversarial sources is similar to our network extractor construction except that we replace the non-malleable extractor with a computational two-source extractor. Specifically, we consider p parties and provide the i-th source X_i to party P_i and run the network extractor construction described above using a two-source extractor. Once we have obtained the outputs of each of the parties, we XOR them together to output a single string. We now argue that the distribution of the output string is close to the uniform distribution.

To show this, it is sufficient to show that the output of one of the honest parties is close to uniform and is independent of the outputs of every other party. Let us assume that X_i and X_j are honest sources. We first consider an intermediate distribution where we sample $f_{k,b}$ for every $(k, b) \notin \{(i, 0), (j, 1)\}$ in the lossy mode. It again follows from the indistinguishability of the injective and the lossy modes that this distribution is computationally close to the original output. Now, for every corrupted source k that is derived from X_i, we can view $\{f_{k,b}(X_k)\}_{b \in \{0,1\}}$ as bounded leakage from the honest source X_i. Similarly, for every source k that is derived from X_j, we can view $\{f_{k,b}(X_k)\}_{b \in \{0,1\}}$ as bounded leakage from the honest source X_j. We can additionally leak $f_{i,1}(X_i)$ and $f_{j,0}(X_j)$. This allows us to argue that conditioned on these leakages, the sources $f_{i,0}(X_i)$ and $f_{j,1}(X_j)$ are independent and have sufficient min-entropy. We can now invoke the two-source extractor security to argue that the output of the i-th party is close to uniform even conditioned on the outputs of every other party.[4]

This completes an overview of our techniques.

Roadmap. We list some preliminaries in Sect. 3, and defer standard definitions of collision-resistant hash functions, lossy functions, the leakage lemma and dispersers, as well as their standard instantiations, to the full version. We recall definitions of computational extractors in Sect. 3.1. In Sect. 4 we derive theorems and corollaries for improved two-source and non-malleable extractors. Due to space constraints, we defer their proofs to the full version. Finally, in Sects. 5 and 6, we describe improved constructions of network and adversarial source

---

[4] The reason why two-source extractor is sufficient in this case but non-malleable extractor was needed in the previous case is that the parties here can be thought of as following the protocol whereas in the previous case, they could deviate arbitrarily from the protocol specification.

extractors respectively. The proofs of these constructions are deferred to the full version.

3   Preliminaries

In this section, we discuss some preliminaries needed for the later sections. This includes facts about min-entropy, lossy functions and dispersers. Many parts of this section are taken from [GKK20].

Definition 5. *A distribution X over a domain D is said to have min-entropy k, denoted by $H_\infty(X) = k$, if for every $z \in D$,*

$$\Pr_{x \leftarrow X}[x = z] \leq 2^{-k}.$$

In this paper, we consider sources with average conditional min entropy, as defined in [DORS08] (and also in the quantum information literature). This notion is less restrictive than worst case conditional min-entropy (and therefore this strengthens our results), and is sometimes more suitable for cryptographic applications.

Definition 6. *[DORS08] Let X and Y be two distributions. The average conditional min-entropy of X conditioned on Y, denoted by $H_\infty(X|Y)^5$ is*

$$H_\infty(X|Y) = -\log E_{y \leftarrow Y} \max_x \Pr[X = x|Y = y] = -\log(\mathbb{E}_{y \leftarrow Y}[2^{-H_\infty(X|Y=y)}])$$

Note that $2^{-H_\infty(X|Y)}$ is the highest probability of guessing the value of the random variable X given the value of Y.

We will rely on the following useful claims about average conditional min-entropy.

Claim 1 [DORS08]. Let X, Y and Z be three distributions, where 2^b is the number of elements in the support of Y. Then,

$$H_\infty(X|Y, Z) \geq H_\infty(X, Y|Z) - b$$

Claim 2 ([GKK20]). Let X, Y and Z be three (arbitrary) distributions, then

$$H_\infty(X|Y) \geq H_\infty(X|Y, Z)$$

We defer the standard definitions of collision-resistant hash functions, lossy functions, the leakage lemma and dispersers, as well as their standard instantiations, to the full version.

---

[5] This is often denoted by $\widetilde{H}_\infty(X|Y)$ in the literature.

3.1   Computational Extractors: Definitions

In this section, we recall definitions of extractors in the computational setting with a CRS. We define both a 2-source extractor and a non-malleable extractor in this setting.

Like [GKK20], in both defintions, we allow the min-entropy sources to depend on the CRS, but require that they are efficiently sampleable conditioned on the CRS (where the efficiency is specified by a parameter T). We also allow each source to partially leak, as long as the source has sufficient min-entropy conditioned on the CRS and the leakage.

As discussed in [GKK20], it may seem that there is no need to consider leakage explicitly. However, in general a source conditioned on fixed leakage may not be efficiently sampleable. Therefore, in the defintions below we consider leakage explicitly. More specifically, for two sources X and Y we allow leakage on Y, which we will denote by L_{init}; and then allow leakage on X (that can also depend on L_{init}), which we will denote by L_{final}. Moreover, both L_{init} and L_{final} can depend on the CRS.

For technical reasons, and specifically to enable a proof of security for their two-source extractor, [GKK20] included an additional source of auxiliary information, AUX, that could be sampled jointly with Y. We do not require this auxiliary source in any of our applications or proofs. The following definitions are essentially identical to [GKK20], except we omit AUX for notational convenience.

Definition 7 (T-Admissible Leaky (n_1, n_2, k_1, k_2) Source Distribution).
A T-admissible leaky (n_1, n_2, k_1, k_2) source distribution with respect to a CRS distribution $\{\text{CRS}_\lambda\}_{\lambda \in \mathbb{N}}$ consists of an ensemble of sources $X = \{X_\lambda\}_{\lambda \in \mathbb{N}}$, $Y = \{Y_\lambda\}_{\lambda \in \mathbb{N}}$, and leakage $L = \{L_\lambda\}_{\lambda \in \mathbb{N}}$, such that $\forall \lambda \in \mathbb{N}$, the following holds:

- *For every $\text{crs} \in \text{Supp}(\text{CRS}_\lambda)$, $\text{Supp}(X_\lambda|\text{crs}) \subseteq \{0,1\}^{n_1(\lambda)}$ and $\text{Supp}(Y_\lambda|\text{crs}) \subseteq \{0,1\}^{n_2(\lambda)}$.*
- *The leakage L_λ consists of two parts, L_{init} and L_{final}, such that for every $\text{crs} \in \text{Supp}(\text{CRS})$, $(Y, L_{\text{init}}|\text{crs})$ is sampleable in time $\text{poly}(T)$, and for every $\ell_{\text{init}} \in \text{Supp}(L_{\text{init}}|\text{crs})$, $(X, L_{\text{final}}|\text{crs}, \ell_{\text{init}})$ is sampleable in time $\text{poly}(T)$.*
- $H_\infty(X_\lambda|\text{CRS}_\lambda, L_\lambda) \geq k_1$ *and* $H_\infty(Y_\lambda|\text{CRS}_\lambda, L_\lambda) \geq k_2$.
- *For every $\text{crs} \in \text{CRS}_\lambda$ and $\ell \in \text{Supp}(L_\lambda|\text{crs})$, the distributions $(X_\lambda|\text{crs}, \ell)$ and $(Y_\lambda|\text{crs}, \ell)$ are independent.[6]*

Definition 8 (Computational Strong 2-source Extractors). *For functions $n_1 = n_1(\lambda)$, $n_2 = n_2(\lambda)$, $c = c(\lambda)$, and $m = m(\lambda)$, a function ensemble $2\text{Ext} = \{2\text{Ext}_\lambda\}_{\lambda \in \mathbb{N}}$, where*

$$2\text{Ext}_\lambda : \{0,1\}^{n_1(\lambda)} \times \{0,1\}^{n_2(\lambda)} \times \{0,1\}^{c(\lambda)} \to \{0,1\}^{m(\lambda)},$$

is said to be a (n_1, n_2, k_1, k_2) strong T-computational 2-source extractor in the CRS model if there is an ensemble $\{\text{CRS}_\lambda\}_{\lambda \in \mathbb{N}}$ where $\text{CRS}_\lambda \in \{0,1\}^{c(\lambda)}$, such that the following holds:

---

[6] This condition follows from the way X and Y are sampled, and like [GKK20], we add it only for the sake of being explicit.

For every T-admissible leaky (n_1, n_2, k_1, k_2) source distribution (X, Y, L) with respect to CRS, for every polynomial p, there exists a negligible function $\nu(\cdot)$ s.t. for every λ and every $p(T(\lambda))$-size adversary $\mathcal{A}$,

$$\left| \Pr\left[\mathcal{A}\left(2\mathsf{Ext}_\lambda(x, y, \mathsf{crs}), y, \mathsf{crs}, \ell\right) = 1\right] \right.$$

$$\left. - \Pr\left[\mathcal{A}\left(U, y, \mathsf{crs}, \ell\right) = 1\right] \right| = \nu(T(\lambda)),$$

where the probabilities are over the randomness of sampling $(\mathsf{crs}, x, y, \ell) \leftarrow (\mathrm{CRS}_\lambda, X_\lambda, Y_\lambda, L_\lambda)$, and over U which is uniformly distributed over $\{0, 1\}^{m(\lambda)}$ independent of everything else.

Definition 9 (Computational Strong Non-malleable Extractors). *For functions $n_1 = n_1(\lambda)$, $n_2 = n_2(\lambda)$, $c = c(\lambda)$, and $m = m(\lambda)$, a function ensemble $\mathsf{cnm\text{-}Ext} = (\mathsf{cnm\text{-}Ext}_\lambda)_{\lambda \in \mathbb{N}}$, where*

$$\mathsf{cnm\text{-}Ext}_\lambda : \{0, 1\}^{n_1(\lambda)} \times \{0, 1\}^{n_2(\lambda)} \times \{0, 1\}^{c(\lambda)} \rightarrow \{0, 1\}^{m(\lambda)}$$

is said to be a (n_1, n_2, k_1, k_2) strong T-computational non-malleable extractor in the CRS model if there is an ensemble $\{\mathrm{CRS}_\lambda\}_{\lambda \in \mathbb{N}}$, where $\mathrm{CRS}_\lambda \in \{0, 1\}^{c(\lambda)}$, such that the following holds:

For every T-admissible leaky (n_1, n_2, k_1, k_2) source distribution (X, Y, L) with respect to CRS, for every polynomial p, there exists a negligible function $\nu(\cdot)$ such that for every λ and every $p(T(\lambda))$-size adversary $\mathcal{A}$,

$$\left| \Pr\left[\mathcal{A}^{\mathcal{O}^y_{x,\mathsf{crs}}}\left(\mathsf{cnm\text{-}Ext}(x, y, \mathsf{crs}), y, \mathsf{crs}, \ell\right) = 1\right] \right.$$

$$\left. - \Pr\left[\mathcal{A}^{\mathcal{O}^y_{x,\mathsf{crs}}}\left(U, y, \mathsf{crs}, \ell\right) = 1\right] \right| = \nu(T(\lambda)),$$

where the oracle $\mathcal{O}^y_{x,\mathsf{crs}}$ on input $y' \neq y$ outputs $\mathsf{cnm\text{-}Ext}(x, y, \mathsf{crs})$, and otherwise outputs $\bot$; and where the probabilities are over the randomness of sampling $(\mathsf{crs}, x, y, \ell) \leftarrow (\mathrm{CRS}_\lambda, X_\lambda, Y_\lambda, L_\lambda)$, and over U which is uniformly distributed over $\{0, 1\}^{m(\lambda)}$ independent of everything else.

We will occasionally need to impose a different requirement on the error distribution. In such cases we specify the error requirement explicitly. Specifically, we say that a (n_1, n_2, k_1, k_2) strong T-computational two source (or non-malleable) extractor has error $\mathsf{neg}(\gamma(\lambda))$ if it satisfies Definition 8 (or Definition 9), where the adversary's distinguishing advantage is required to be at most negligible in $\gamma(\lambda)$.

We will also rely on the following theorem from [Raz05] (simplified to our setting). This is a statistical 2-source extractor; i.e., one that considers sources that are sampled in unbounded time, and fools adversaries with unbounded running time.

Theorem 10. *[Raz05] There exists a* (n_1, n_2, k_1, k_2) *strong statistical 2-source extractor with output length* $O(k_2)$ *according to Definition 8 where* $n_2 = \omega(\log n_1)$, $k_1 \geq \log n_1$, *and* $k_2 \geq \alpha n_2$ *for any constant* $\alpha > \frac{1}{2}$, *and error* $\exp^{-\Theta(\min\{k_1, k_2\})}$.

Finally, we recall the following result from [GKK20] that transforms any two-source extractor in the CRS model to a non-malleable extractor.

Theorem 11 ([GKK20]). *Let* $T, T', n_1, n_2, k_1, k_2, k_3, w : \mathbb{N} \to \mathbb{N}$ *be functions of the security parameter where* $T \geq 2^{k_3}$, *such that the following primitives exist.*

- *A* (n_1, n_2, k_1, k_2) *strong* T-*computational 2-source extractor in the CRS model.*
- *A* (T, n_1, n_1, w)-*lossy function family.*
- T'-*secure collision resistant hash functions mapping* $\{0, 1\}^{n_2} \to \{0, 1\}^{k_3}$.

Then, there exists a (n_1, n_2, K_1, K_2) *strong* T'-*computational non-malleable extractor satisfying Definition 9 where* $K_1 = k_1 + k_3(n_1 - w + 1) + 1$ *and* $K_2 = k_2 + k_3 + 1$.

4   Computational Strong Two-Source Extractors in the CRS Model

In this section, we describe our construction of computational two-source extractors in the CRS model. We have the following theorem.

Theorem 12. *Let* $T, T', n_1, n_2, k_1, k_2, k_3, d, t, w, K_1, K_2 : \mathbb{N} \to \mathbb{N}$ *be functions of the security parameter, where* $T \geq 2^{k_3}$, *and such that the following primitives exist.*

- *A* $(n_1, d, k_1, d - k_3 - 1)$ *strong information-theoretic 2-source extractor denoted by:*
$$2\mathsf{Ext}_\lambda : \{0, 1\}^{n_1(\lambda)} \times \{0, 1\}^{d(\lambda)} \times \{0, 1\}^{c(\lambda)} \to \{0, 1\}^{m(\lambda)}$$
- *A* (T, n_1, n_1, w)-*lossy function family* $\mathcal{F} = \{\mathcal{F}_\lambda\}_{\lambda \in \mathbb{N}}$, *where* $w = n_1 - n_1^\gamma$ *for some constant* $\gamma \in (0, 1)$.
- *A* T'-*secure family of collision resistant hash functions* $\mathcal{H} = \{\mathcal{H}_\lambda\}_{\lambda \in \mathbb{N}}$ *with* $h : \{0, 1\}^d \to \{0, 1\}^{k_3}$.
- *A* $\left(\frac{2^{K_2/2}}{T' \log T'}, 2^{d-1}\right)$ *disperser*

$$\Gamma : \{0, 1\}^{n_2} \times [t] \to \{0, 1\}^d$$

Then there exists a (n_1, n_2, K_1, K_2) *strong* T'-*computational two-source extractor, satisfying Definition 9, where* $K_1 = k_1 + k_3(n - w) + k_3 + 1$.

Corollary 13. *Assuming the sub-exponential hardness of DDH, there exists constants* $c_0 > 1$ *and* c' *such that for all* $c > c_0$, *for every* $\Omega(\lambda) \leq n_1 \leq \text{poly}(\lambda), \Omega(\log \lambda) \leq n_2 \leq \text{poly}(\lambda)$, *there exists an* (n_1, n_2, K_1, K_2) λ-*computational strong two-source extractor in the CRS model, with* $K_1 = O(\log \lambda)^c$, $K_2 = O(\log \lambda)^c$ *and output length* $O(\log \lambda)^{c'}$.

Proof. The sub-exponential hardness of DDH implies that there exists a constant $0 < \epsilon < 1$ such that DDH with security parameter λ is hard against poly(2^{λ^ϵ})-sized adversaries.

- This implies that for all $c_1 \geq \frac{1}{\epsilon}$, there exist lossy functions with equal domain and co-domain, where $w = n_1 - (\log \lambda)^{c_1}$, and where no $T = \text{poly}(2^{\log \lambda^{c_1 \cdot \epsilon}})$-sized adversary can distinguish the lossy mode from the injective mode. This follows by setting, e.g., $\log q = (\log \lambda)^{c_1}$ in the construction of lossy functions from DDH in [BHK11].
- This also implies that for all $c_2 \geq \frac{1}{\epsilon}$, there exist collision-resistant hash functions with range $k_3 = (\log \lambda)^{c_2}$, and where no $T' = \text{poly}(2^{\log \lambda^{c_2 \cdot \epsilon}})$-sized adversary can find collisions.

Setting $c_2 = \frac{1}{\epsilon}, c_1 = \frac{1}{\epsilon^2}$, we get $T' = \lambda, k_3 = (\log \lambda)^{\frac{1}{\epsilon}}$ and $T = (2^{\log \lambda^{\frac{1}{\epsilon}}})$.

By the disperser construction in [GUV09], there exists a polynomial $t = \text{poly}(\lambda)$ for which there exists a $\left(\frac{2^{K_2/2}}{T'^{(\log T')}}, 2^{d-1}\right)$ disperser

$$\Gamma : \{0,1\}^{n_1} \times [t] \rightarrow \{0,1\}^d$$

for any d, k_2, T' that satisfy

$$K_2 \geq 4d + 2 \log^2 T' \tag{1}$$

Set $d = (\log \lambda)^{\frac{1}{\epsilon^2}}$. By Theorem 10, there exists a $(n_1, d, k_1, d - k_3 - 1)$ strong statistical 2-source extractor for $k_1 = (\log \lambda)^{\frac{1}{\epsilon^2}}$, with error $\exp^{-\Theta(\min(k_1, d-k_3-1))} = \text{neg}(2^{k_3})$. In particular, this extractor is a $(n_1, d, k_1, d - k_3 - 1)$ strong T-computational 2-source extractor in the CRS model (where the CRS is empty), with error $\text{neg}(2^{k_3})$.

Setting $d = (\log \lambda)^{\frac{1}{\epsilon^2}}$ and $T' = \lambda$ in Eq. (2), we have $K_2 \geq 4(\log \lambda)^{\frac{1}{\epsilon^2}} + 2 \log^2 \lambda$. Fixing K_2 to be $5(\log \lambda)^{\frac{1}{\epsilon^2}}$ satisfies this inequality. From Theorem 12, we have $K_1 \geq k_1 + k_3(n-w) + k_3 + 1 \geq (\log \lambda)^{\frac{1}{\epsilon^2}} + (\log \lambda)^{\frac{1}{\epsilon}} \cdot (\log \lambda)^{\frac{1}{\epsilon^2}} + (\log \lambda)^{\frac{1}{\epsilon}} + 1$. Fixing $K_1 \geq 2(\log \lambda)^{\frac{1}{\epsilon^3}}$ satisfies this inequality.

This completes the proof.

Corollary 14. *Assuming the sub-exponential hardness of DDH, there exists constants $c_0 > 1$ and c' such that for all $c > c_0$, for every $\Omega(\lambda) \leq n_1 \leq \text{poly}(\lambda), \Omega(\log \lambda) \leq n_2 \leq \text{poly}(\lambda)$, there exists an (n_1, n_2, K_1, K_2) λ-computational non-malleable extractor in the CRS model, with $K_1 = O(\log \lambda)^c$, $K_2 = O(\log \lambda)^c$ and output length $O(\log \lambda)^{c'}$.*

Proof. This corollary can be obtained by combining Theorem 12 with 11, as follows.

- First, we apply Theorem 12 but with somewhat scaled-up parameters than in the previous corollary, to obtain an (n_1, n_2, k_1, k_2) T-computational non-malleable extractor in the CRS model, with error $\text{neg}(2^{k_3})$. This extractor will be parameterized by a (small enough) constant $0 < \epsilon < 1$. It will have $T = 2^{(\log \lambda^{1/\epsilon})}$, and $k_3 = \log \lambda^{1/\epsilon}$.

The sub-exponential hardness of DDH implies that there exists a constant $0 < \epsilon < 1$ such that DDH with security parameter λ is hard against $\text{poly}(2^{\lambda^{\epsilon}})$-sized adversaries.

- This implies that for all $c_1 \geq \frac{1}{\epsilon}$, there exist (T, n_1, n_1, w)-lossy functions with equal domain and co-domain, where $w = n_1 - (\log \lambda)^{c_1}$, and where no $\text{poly}(T)$ for $T = (2^{\log \lambda^{c_1 \cdot \epsilon}})$ sized adversary can distinguish the lossy mode from the injective mode. This follows by setting, e.g., $\log q = (\log \lambda)^{c_1}$ in the construction of lossy functions from DDH in [BHK11].

- This also implies that for all $c_2 \geq \frac{1}{\epsilon}$, there exist collision-resistant hash functions with range $k_3 = (\log \lambda)^{c_2}$, and where no $\text{poly}(T')$ for $T' = 2^{\log \lambda^{c_2 \cdot \epsilon}}$-sized adversary can find collisions.

Setting $c_2 = \frac{1}{\epsilon^2}, c_1 = \frac{1}{\epsilon^3}$, we get $T' = 2^{\log \lambda^{\frac{1}{\epsilon}}}, k_3 = (\log \lambda)^{\frac{1}{\epsilon^2}}$ and $T = (2^{\log \lambda^{\frac{1}{\epsilon^2}}})$.

By the disperser construction in [GUV09], there exists a polynomial $t = \text{poly}(\lambda)$ for which there exists a $\left(\frac{2^{K_2/2}}{T'^{(\log T')}}, 2^{d-1}\right)$ disperser

$$\Gamma : \{0,1\}^{n_1} \times [t] \to \{0,1\}^d$$

for any d, k_2, T' that satisfy

$$K_2 \geq 4d + 2\log^2 T' \tag{2}$$

Set $d = (\log \lambda)^{\frac{1}{\epsilon^3}}$. By Theorem 10, there exists a $(n_1, d, k_1, d - k_3 - 1)$ strong statistical 2-source extractor for $k_1 = (\log \lambda)^{\frac{1}{\epsilon^3}}$, with error $\exp^{-\Theta(\min(k_1, d-k_3-1))} = \text{neg}(2^{k_3})$. In particular, this extractor is a $(n_1, d, k_1, d - k_3 - 1)$ strong T-computational 2-source extractor in the CRS model (where the CRS is empty), with error $\text{neg}(2^{k_3})$.

Setting $d = (\log \lambda)^{\frac{1}{\epsilon^3}}$ and $T' = 2^{\log \lambda^{\frac{1}{\epsilon}}}$ in Eq. (2), we can set $K_2 \geq 4(\log \lambda)^{\frac{1}{\epsilon^3}} + 2(\log \lambda)^{\frac{2}{\epsilon}}$. Fixing $K_2 \geq 5(\log \lambda)^{\frac{1}{\epsilon^3}}$ satisfies the above inequality. From Theorem 12, we can set $K_1 \geq k_1 + k_3(n - w) + k_3 + 1$ or $K_1 \geq (\log \lambda)^{\frac{1}{\epsilon^3}} + (\log \lambda)^{\frac{1}{\epsilon}} \cdot (\log \lambda)^{\frac{1}{\epsilon^3}} + (\log \lambda)^{\frac{1}{\epsilon^2}} + 1$. Fixing $K_1 \geq 2(\log \lambda)^{\frac{1}{\epsilon^4}}$ satisfies the above inequality.

- Re-defining some variables, we say that previous step results in a T-strong computational (n_1, n_2, k_1, k_2) non-malleable extractor in the CRS model, with $\Omega(\lambda) \leq n_1 \leq \text{poly}(\lambda), \Omega(\log \lambda) \leq n_2 \leq \text{poly}(\lambda), T = 2^{\log \lambda^{1/\epsilon}}$, $k_1 = 2(\log \lambda)^{\frac{1}{\epsilon^4}}, k_2 \geq 5(\log \lambda)^{\frac{1}{\epsilon^3}}$, and error $\text{neg}(T) = \text{neg}(2^{(\log \lambda)^{\frac{1}{\epsilon}}})$. Next, we apply Theorem 11 to this extractor.

As before, the subexponential hardness of DDH implies that for all $c_1' \geq \frac{1}{\epsilon}$, there exist (T, n_1, n_1, w)-lossy functions with equal domain and co-domain, where $w = n_1 - (\log \lambda)^{c_1'}$, and where no $\text{poly}(T)$ for $T = (2^{\log \lambda^{c_1' \cdot \epsilon}})$ sized adversary can distinguish the lossy mode from the injective mode. We will set $c_1' = \frac{1}{\epsilon^2}$. We also set $k_3 = (\log \lambda)^{\frac{1}{\epsilon}}$, and by subexponential DDH, there exists a T'-secure family of collision resistant hash functions mapping $\{0,1\}^{n_2} \to \{0,1\}^{k_3}$ for $T' = \lambda$.

Then, by Theorem 11, there exists an (n_1, n_2, K_1, K_2) strong T'-computational non-malleable extractor satisfying Definition 9 where $K_1 = k_1 + k_3(n_1 - w + 1) + 1 = 2(\log \lambda)^{\frac{1}{c^4}} + (\log \lambda)^{\frac{1}{c}} \cdot (\log \lambda)^{\frac{1}{c^2}} + 1$, or $K_1 \geq 3(\log \lambda)^{\frac{1}{c^4}}$ and $K_2 = k_2 + k_3 + 1 = 5(\log \lambda)^{\frac{1}{c^3}} + (\log \lambda)^{\frac{1}{c}} + 1$, or $K_2 \geq 6(\log \lambda)^{\frac{1}{c^3}}$.

This completes the proof.

4.1 Construction

As discussed above, we will prove that the construction of two-source extractors in [GKK20] is a strong non-malleable extractor for balanced sources, and additionally only requires polylogarithmic min-entropy. We first recall the construction in [GKK20], and begin by defining the CRS distribution.

Generating the Common Reference String (CRS). For a given security parameter $\lambda \in \mathbb{N}$, the common reference string is generated as follows.

1. Sample $h \leftarrow \mathcal{H}_\lambda$.
2. Sample $b = (b_1, \ldots, b_{k_3}) \leftarrow \{0,1\}^{k_3}$.
3. Sample independently k_3 pairs of random injective functions from $\mathcal{F}_\lambda$,

$$f_{1,b_1}, f_{2,b_2}, \ldots, f_{k_3,b_{k_3}} \leftarrow \mathsf{Gen}_{\mathsf{inj}}(1^\lambda).$$

4. Sample independently k_3 pairs of random lossy functions from $\mathcal{F}_\lambda$,

$$f_{1,1-b_1}, f_{2,1-b_2}, \ldots, f_{k_3,b_1-k_3} \leftarrow \mathsf{Gen}_{\mathsf{loss}}(1^\lambda).$$

Output

$$\mathsf{crs} = \left(h, \begin{array}{c} f_{1,0}, f_{2,0}, \ldots, f_{k_3,0} \\ f_{1,1}, f_{2,1}, \ldots, f_{k_3,1} \end{array} \right)$$

The (Computational) Two-Source Extractor: Construction.
The computational two-source extractor $\mathsf{c2Ext} = \{\mathsf{c2Ext}_\lambda\}_{\lambda \in \mathbb{N}}$ is defined as follows.
For any $\lambda \in \mathbb{N}$, denote by $c = c(\lambda) = |\mathsf{crs}|$, then

$$\mathsf{c2Ext}_\lambda : \{0,1\}^c \times \{0,1\}^{n_1} \times \{0,1\}^{n_2} \to \{0,1\}^m,$$

where $\forall (\mathsf{crs}, x_1, x_2) \in \{0,1\}^c \times \{0,1\}^{n_1} \times \{0,1\}^{n_2}$,

$$\mathsf{c2Ext}_\lambda(\mathsf{crs}, x_1, x_2) = \bigoplus_{y : \exists i \text{ s.t. } \Gamma(x_2,i)=y} \mathsf{cnm\text{-}Ext}_\lambda(\mathsf{crs}, x_1, y)$$

where $\Gamma : \{0,1\}^{n_2} \times [t] \to \{0,1\}^d$ is a $(\frac{2^{k_2}}{T' \log T'}, 2^{d-1})$ disperser, and $\forall (\mathsf{crs}, x_1, y) \in \{0,1\}^c \times \{0,1\}^{n_1} \times \{0,1\}^d$, and crs parsed as $\left(h, \begin{array}{c} f_{1,0}, f_{2,0}, \ldots, f_{k_3,0} \\ f_{1,1}, f_{2,1}, \ldots, f_{k_3,1} \end{array} \right)$,

$$\mathsf{cnm\text{-}Ext}_\lambda(\mathsf{crs}, x_1, y) = 2\mathsf{Ext}_\lambda \left(f_{1,h(y)_1} \circ f_{2,h(y)_2} \circ \cdots \circ f_{k_3,h(y)_{k_3}}(x_1), y \right)$$

Due to space constraints, we defer the proof to the full version.

5   Network Extractor Protocol in the CRS Model

We start with the definition of the T-admissible leaky (p, n, k)-source distribution.

Definition 15 (T-Admissible Leaky (p, n, k) Source Distribution). *A T-admissible leaky (p, n, k) source distribution with respect to a CRS distribution $\{CRS_\lambda\}_{\lambda \in \mathbb{N}}$ consists of an ensemble of sources $X = \{X_{i,\lambda}\}_{i \in [p], \lambda \in \mathbb{N}}$, and leakage $L = \{L_{i,\lambda}\}_{i \in [p], \lambda \in \mathbb{N}}$ such that for every $\lambda \in \mathbb{N}$, the following holds:*

- *For every $crs \in \mathsf{Supp}(CRS_\lambda)$, $\mathsf{Supp}(X_{i,\lambda} | crs) \subseteq \{0, 1\}^{n(\lambda)}$ for every $i \in [p]$.*
- *For every $crs \in \mathsf{Supp}(CRS_\lambda)$, $(X_{i,\lambda}, L_{i,\lambda} | crs)$ is sampleable in time $\mathrm{poly}(T(\lambda))$ for every $i \in [p]$.*
- *For every $i \in [p]$, $H_\infty(X_{i,\lambda} | CRS_\lambda, L_\lambda) \geq k(\lambda)$ where $L_\lambda = \{L_{i,\lambda}\}_{i \in [p]}$.*
- *For every $crs \in CRS_\lambda$, $\ell \in \mathsf{Supp}(L_\lambda | crs)$ and for every distinct $i, j \in [p]$, the distributions $(X_{i,\lambda} | crs, \ell)$ and $(X_{j,\lambda} | crs, \ell)$ are independent.[7]*

We now provide the definition of network extractor protocol in the CRS model adapting the definitions from [KLRZ08, KLR09].

Definition 16. *A protocol for p processors is a (T, t, g) network extractor with respect to CRS distribution $\{CRS_\lambda\}_{\lambda \in \mathbb{N}}$ with source length $n(\lambda)$, min-entropy $k(\lambda)$ and output length $m(\lambda)$ if for any T-admissible leaky (p, n, k) source distribution (X, L) w.r.t. $\{CRS_\lambda\}_{\lambda \in \mathbb{N}}$ (see Definition 15) and any choice M of t faulty processors, after running the protocol, there exists a set $G \in [p] \setminus T$ of size at least g such that*

$$|CRS, B, \{X_i\}_{i \notin G}, \{L_i\}_{i \in [p]}, \{Z_i\}_{i \in G} - CRS, B, \{X_i\}_{i \notin G}, \{L_i\}_{i \in [p]}, U_{gm}| < \mathsf{negl}(\lambda)$$

Here, $(CRS, \{X_i, L_i\}_{i \in [p]}) \leftarrow (CRS_\lambda, \{X_{i,\lambda}, L_{i,\lambda}\}_{i \in [p]})$, B is the transcript of the protocol and Z_i denote the output of the i-th party in the protocol, U_{gm} is the uniform distribution on gm bits independent of B, $\{X_i\}_{i \notin G}$ and $\{L_i\}_{i \in [p]}$.

5.1   Building Blocks

We use the following building blocks in the construction.

1. A (n, n_1, w)-lossy function family $\mathcal{F} = \{\mathcal{F}_\lambda : \{0, 1\}^{n(\lambda)} \to \{0, 1\}^{n_1(\lambda)}\}_{\lambda \in \mathbb{N}}$.
2. A (n_1, k_1) T-strong computational non-malleable extractor in the CRS model denoted by

$$\mathsf{NMExt}_\lambda : \{0, 1\}^{n_1(\lambda)} \times \{0, 1\}^{n_1(\lambda)} \times \{0, 1\}^{c(\lambda)} \to \{0, 1\}^{m(\lambda)}$$

5.2   Construction

We give the construction of the network extractor protocol in Fig. 1.

---

[7] This condition follows from the way X and Y are sampled, and we add it only for the sake of being explicit.

- CRSGen(1^λ):
    1. Sample $\mathsf{CRS}_{\mathsf{NMExt}}$ for the non-malleable extractor NMExt.
    2. For each $i \in [p]$ and $b \in \{0,1\}$, sample $f_{i,b} \leftarrow \mathsf{Gen}_{\mathsf{inj}}(1^\lambda)$.
    3. Output $\mathsf{CRS} := (\mathsf{CRS}_{\mathsf{NMExt}}, \{f_{i,b}\}_{i \in [p], b \in \{0,1\}})$.
- **Description of the Protocol.** Party P_i on input $x_i \in \{0,1\}^n$ does the following:
    1. For each $b \in \{0,1\}$, it computes $f_{i,b}(x_i)$ and broadcasts $f_{i,1}(x_i)$.
    2. It receives $\{f_{j,1}(x_j)\}_{j \neq i}$ from the other parties.
    3. It outputs $\bigoplus_{j \neq i} \mathsf{NMExt}(f_{i,0}(x_i) \circ i, f_{j,1}(x_j) \circ j, \mathsf{CRS}_{\mathsf{NMExt}})$.

Fig. 1. Network extractor protocol in the CRS model

Theorem 17. *Let $\gamma \in (0,1)$ be a fixed constant and let $k(\lambda)$ be an arbitrary polynomial larger than $n_1(\lambda) - w(\lambda)$. Assuming the existence of the following primitives:*

- *A (n, n_1, w)-lossy function family $\mathcal{F} = \{\mathcal{F}_\lambda : \{0,1\}^{n(\lambda)} \rightarrow \{0,1\}^{n_1(\lambda)}\}_{\lambda \in \mathbb{N}}$, where $w(\lambda) = n_1(\lambda) - (n_1(\lambda))^\gamma$.*
- *A (n_1, k_1) T-strong computational non-malleable extractor in the CRS model denoted by*

$$\mathsf{NMExt}_\lambda : \{0,1\}^{n_1(\lambda)} \times \{0,1\}^{n_1(\lambda)} \times \{0,1\}^{c(\lambda)} \rightarrow \{0,1\}^{m(\lambda)}$$

where $k_1(\lambda) \geq k(\lambda) - (n_1(\lambda) - w(\lambda))$.

Then, the construction given in Fig. 1 is a $(T, p-2, 2, \mathsf{negl})$ network extractor with respect to the CRS distribution in Fig. 1 and min-entropy $k(\lambda)$.

Due to space constraints, we defer the proof of Theorem 17 to the full version.

5.3 Instantiation

We instantiate the non-malleable extractor from Corollary 14 and the lossy functions from [PW08,BHK11] Specifically, we set the constant c of the non-malleable extractor to be $\max(c_0, c_1)$ (where c_1 is the parameter for the lossy functions). Thus, we obtain the following corollary.

Corollary 18. *Assuming the sub-exponential hardness of the DDH assumption, there exist constants $c > 1$ and c' such that for any p number of players, there exists a construction of $(\lambda, p-2, 2)$ network extractor protocol in the CRS model with sources of length $\Omega(\lambda) \leq n(\lambda) \leq \mathsf{poly}(\lambda)$, min-entropy $O(\log \lambda)^c$ and output length $O(\log \lambda)^{c'}$.*

6   Extractor for Adversarial Sources in the CRS Model

We start with the definition of the adversaial source distribution.

Definition 19. *A T-admissible leaky (p, n, k) adversarial sources with respect to CRS distribution $\{CRS_\lambda\}_\lambda$ is a tuple $(i, j, (X, Y, L), I, \{x_k\}_{k \in I}, I_i, I_j, \{f_k\}_{k \in I_i \cup I_j})$ where $i, j \in [p]$, (X, Y, L) is T-admissible leaky (n, k)-source distribution w.r.t. $\{CRS_\lambda\}_{\lambda \in \mathbb{N}}$, $I \cup I_i \cup I_j = [p]$ and $f_k : \{0, 1\}^n \to \{0, 1\}^n$ are T-time computable functions.*

We now give the definition of the extractor for adversarial sources below.

Definition 20. *For any $p \in \mathbb{N}$, and functions $n = n(\lambda)$, $c = c(\lambda)$ and $m = m(\lambda)$, a function ensemble $\mathsf{AdvExt} = \{\mathsf{AdvExt}_\lambda\}_{\lambda \in \mathbb{N}}$, where*

$$\mathsf{AdvExt}_\lambda : (\{0, 1\}^{n(\lambda)})^p \times \{0, 1\}^{c(\lambda)} \to \{0, 1\}^{m(\lambda)}$$

is said to be a (p, n, k) T-computational adversarial source extractor in the CRS model if there exists an ensemble $\{CRS_\lambda\}_{\lambda \in \mathbb{N}}$ such that the following holds:

For every T-admissible leaky (p, n, k) adversarial sources $(i, j, (X, Y, L), I, \{x_k\}_{k \in I}, I_i, I_j, \{f_k\}_{k \in I_i \cup I_j})$ wrt CRS, the following two distributions are computationally indistinguishable:

$$\{\mathsf{AdvExt}_\lambda((x'_1, \ldots, x'_p), \mathsf{crs}), \mathsf{crs}, \ell\} \approx_c \{U_m, \mathsf{crs}, \ell\}$$

where $\mathsf{crs} \leftarrow CRS_\lambda$, $(x_i, x_j, \ell) \leftarrow (X, Y, L | \mathsf{crs})$, for every $k \in I$, $x'_k = x_k$, for every $k \in I_i$, $x'_k = f_k(x_i)$, and for every $k \in I_j$, $x'_k = f_k(x_j)$.

6.1   Building Blocks

We use the following building blocks in the construction.

1. A (n, n_1, w)-lossy trapdoor function family $\mathcal{F} = \{\mathcal{F}_\lambda : \{0, 1\}^{n(\lambda)} \to \{0, 1\}^{n_1(\lambda)}\}_{\lambda \in \mathbb{N}}$.
2. A (n_1, k_1) T-strong computational 2-source extractor in the CRS model denoted by

$$\mathsf{cExt}_\lambda : \{0, 1\}^{n_1(\lambda)} \times \{0, 1\}^{n_1(\lambda)} \times \{0, 1\}^{c(\lambda)} \to \{0, 1\}^{m(\lambda)}$$

6.2   Construction

We give the construction of our extractor for adversarial sources in Fig. 2.

Theorem 21. *Let $p \in \mathbb{N}$ be fixed and let $m(\cdot)$ be an arbitrary polynomial. Let $k(\cdot)$ be an arbitrary polynomial such that for every $\lambda \in \mathbb{N}$, $k(\lambda) \geq (2p-1)(n_1(\lambda) - w(\lambda)) + m(\lambda)$. Let $n(\cdot)$ be another polynomial such that $n(\lambda) \geq k(\lambda)$ for every $\lambda \in \mathbb{N}$. Assuming the existence of the following primitives:*

- *A (n, n_1, w)-lossy function family $\mathcal{F} = \{\mathcal{F}_\lambda : \{0, 1\}^{n(\lambda)} \to \{0, 1\}^{n_1(\lambda)}\}_{\lambda \in \mathbb{N}}$.*

- CRSGen(1^λ):
    1. Sample CRS_{cExt} for the non-malleable extractor cExt.
    2. For each $i \in [p]$ and $b \in \{0, 1\}$, sample $f_{i,b} \leftarrow Gen_{inj}(1^\lambda)$.
    3. Output $CRS := (CRS_{cExt}, \{f_{i,b}\}_{i \in [p], b \in \{0,1\}})$.
- **Description of the Extractor.** On input $(x_1, \ldots, x_p) \in (\{0, 1\}^n)^p$, the extractor does the following:
    1. For each $j \in [p]$ and $b \in \{0, 1\}$, it computes $f_{j,b}(x_j)$.
    2. For each $i \in [p]$, it computes
    $$r_i := \bigoplus_{j \neq i} cExt(f_{i,0}(x_i) \circ i, f_{j,1}(x_j) \circ j, CRS_{cExt}).$$
    3. It outputs $\bigoplus_{i \in [p]} r_i$.

Fig. 2. Extractor for adversarial sources

- *A (n_1, k_1) T-strong computational non-malleable extractor in the CRS model denoted by*

$$cExt_\lambda : \{0, 1\}^{n_1(\lambda)} \times \{0, 1\}^{n_1(\lambda)} \times \{0, 1\}^{c(\lambda)} \rightarrow \{0, 1\}^{m(\lambda)}$$

where $k_1(\lambda) \geq k(\lambda) - (2p - 1)(n_1(\lambda) - w(\lambda)) - m(\lambda)$.

Then, the construction given in Fig. 2 is a (p, n, k) adversarial source extractor with respect to the CRS distribution described in Fig. 2.

Due to space constraints, we defer the proof of this theorem to the full version.

6.3   Instantiation

We instantiate the two-source extractor from Corollary 13 and the lossy functions from [PW08, BHK11]. Specifically, for any fixed p, we set c for the two-source extractor to be large enough such that min-entropy of the two source extractor $(2p-1)O(\log^{c_1} \lambda) < \log^c \lambda$. We set $m(\lambda) < \log^c \lambda$. We, thus, obtain the following corollary.

Corollary 22. *Fix any $p \in \mathbb{N}$. Assuming the sub-exponential hardness of DDH assumption, there exists constants $c > 1$ and $c' < c$ such that for any $\Omega(\lambda) \leq n(\lambda) \leq poly(\lambda)$, $k(\lambda) = O(\log^c \lambda)$ and $m(\lambda) \leq O(k(\lambda))$, there exists a construction of a (p, n, k) λ-computational adversarial two-source extractor in the CRS model with output length $O(\log \lambda)^{c'}$.*

References

[AOR+20a] Aggarwal, D., Obremski, M., Ribeiro, J.L., Simkin, M., Siniscalchi, L.: Two-source non-malleable extractors and applications to privacy amplification with tamperable memory. IACR Cryptol. ePrint Arch., 2020, p. 1371 (2020). https://eprint.iacr.org/2020/1371

[AOR+20b] Aggarwal, D., Obremski, M., Ribeiro, J., Siniscalchi, L., Visconti, I.: How to extract useful randomness from unreliable sources. In: Canteaut, A., Ishai, Y. (eds.) EUROCRYPT 2020. LNCS, vol. 12105, pp. 343–372. Springer, Cham (2020). https://doi.org/10.1007/978-3-030-45721-1_13

[BACD+17] Ben-Aroya, A., Chattopadhyay, E., Doron, D., Li, X., Ta-Shma, A.: Low-error, two-source extractors assuming efficient non-malleable extractors. In: CCC (2017)

[BADTS16] Ben-Aroya, A., Doron, D., Ta-Shma, A.: Explicit two-source extractors for near-logarithmic min-entropy. In: Electronic Colloquium on Computational Complexity (ECCC), vol. 23, p. 88 (2016)

[BHK11] Braverman, M., Hassidim, A., Kalai, Y.T.: Leaky pseudo-entropy functions. In: Innovations in Computer Science (2011)

[Bou05] Bourgain, J.: More on the sum-product phenomenon in prime fields and its applications. Int. J. Number Theory 1, 1–32 (2005)

[CG88] Chor, B., Goldreich, O.: Unbiased bits from sources of weak randomness and probabilistic communication complexity. SIAM J. Comput. 17(2), 230–261 (1988). https://doi.org/10.1137/0217015

[CGGL20] Chattopadhyay, E., Goodman, J., Goyal, V., Li, X.: Extractors for adversarial sources via extremal hypergraphs. In: Makarychev, K., Makarychev, Y., Tulsiani, M., Kamath, G., Chuzhoy, J. (eds.) Procceedings of the 52nd Annual ACM SIGACT Symposium on Theory of Computing, STOC 2020, Chicago, IL, USA, 22–26 June, 2020, pp. 1184–1197. ACM (2020). https://doi.org/10.1145/3357713.3384339

[CLP15] Chung, K.-M., Lui, E., Pass, R.: From weak to strong zero-knowledge and applications. In: Dodis, Y., Nielsen, J.B. (eds.) TCC 2015. LNCS, vol. 9014, pp. 66–92. Springer, Heidelberg (2015). https://doi.org/10.1007/978-3-662-46494-6_4

[Coh16a] Cohen, G.: Local correlation breakers and applications to three-source extractors and mergers. SIAM J. Comput. 45(4), 1297–1338 (2016)

[Coh16b] Cohen, G.: Making the most of advice: new correlation breakers and their applications. In: 2016 IEEE 57th Annual Symposium on Foundations of Computer Science (FOCS), pp. 188–196. IEEE (2016)

[Coh16c] Cohen, G.: Non-malleable extractors-new tools and improved constructions. In: LIPIcs-Leibniz International Proceedings in Informatics, vol. 50. Schloss Dagstuhl-Leibniz-Zentrum fuer Informatik (2016)

[Coh16d] Cohen, G.: Two-source extractors for quasi-logarithmic min-entropy and improved privacy amplification protocols. In: Electronic Colloquium on Computational Complexity (ECCC), vol. 23, p. 114 (2016)

[CZ16] Chattopadhyay, E., Zuckerman, D.: Explicit two-source extractors and resilient functions. In: Proceedings of the Forty-Eighth Annual ACM Symposium on Theory of Computing, pp. 670–683. ACM (2016)

[DO03] Dodis, Y., Oliveira, R.: On extracting private randomness over a public channel. In: Arora, S., Jansen, K., Rolim, J.D.P., Sahai, A. (eds.) APPROX/RANDOM -2003. LNCS, vol. 2764, pp. 252–263. Springer, Heidelberg (2003). https://doi.org/10.1007/978-3-540-45198-3_22

[DOPS04] Dodis, Y., Ong, S.J., Prabhakaran, M., Sahai, A.: On the (im)possibility of cryptography with imperfect randomness. In: Proceedings of the 45th Symposium on Foundations of Computer Science (FOCS 2004), Rome, Italy, 17–19 October 2004, pp. 196–205 (2004). https://doi.org/10.1109/FOCS.2004.44

[DORS08] Dodis, Y., Ostrovsky, R., Reyzin, L., Smith, A.D.: Fuzzy extractors: how to generate strong keys from biometrics and other noisy data. SIAM J. Comput. **38**(1), 97–139 (2008). https://doi.org/10.1137/060651380

[DVW20]   Dodis, Y., Vaikuntanathan, V., Wichs, D.: Extracting randomness from extractor-dependent sources. In: Canteaut, A., Ishai, Y. (eds.) EURO-CRYPT 2020. LNCS, vol. 12105, pp. 313–342. Springer, Cham (2020). https://doi.org/10.1007/978-3-030-45721-1_12

[GKK20]   Garg, A., Kalai, Y.T., Khurana, D.: Low error efficient computational extractors in the CRS model. In: Canteaut, A., Ishai, Y. (eds.) EURO-CRYPT 2020. LNCS, vol. 12105, pp. 373–402. Springer, Cham (2020). https://doi.org/10.1007/978-3-030-45721-1_14

[GSV05]   Goldwasser, S., Sudan, M., Vaikuntanathan, V.: Distributed computing with imperfect randomness. In: Fraigniaud, P. (ed.) DISC 2005. LNCS, vol. 3724, pp. 288–302. Springer, Heidelberg (2005). https://doi.org/10.1007/11561927_22

[GSZ21]   Goyal, V., Srinivasan, A., Zhu, C.: Multi-source non-malleable extractors and applications. To appear in Eurocrypt, 2021, p. 157 (2021). https://eprint.iacr.org/2020/157

[GUV09]   Guruswami, V., Umans, C., Vadhan, S.: Unbalanced expanders and randomness extractors from parvaresh-vardy codes. J. ACM (JACM) **56**(4), 20 (2009)

[GW11]   Gentry, C., Wichs, D.: Separating succinct non-interactive arguments from all falsifiable assumptions. In: Fortnow, L., Vadhan, S.P. (eds.) Proceedings of the 43rd ACM Symposium on Theory of Computing, STOC 2011, San Jose, CA, USA, 6–8 June 2011, pp. 99–108. ACM (2011). https://doi.org/10.1145/1993636.1993651

[JP14]   Jetchev, D., Pietrzak, K.: How to fake auxiliary input. In: Lindell, Y. (ed.) TCC 2014. LNCS, vol. 8349, pp. 566–590. Springer, Heidelberg (2014). https://doi.org/10.1007/978-3-642-54242-8_24

[KLR09]   Kalai, Y.T., Li, X., Rao, A.: 2-source extractors under computational assumptions and cryptography with defective randomness. In: 50th Annual IEEE Symposium on Foundations of Computer Science, FOCS 2009, Atlanta, Georgia, USA, 25–27 October, 2009, pp. 617–626. IEEE Computer Society (2009). https://doi.org/10.1109/FOCS.2009.61

[KLRZ08] Kalai, Y.T., Li, X., Rao, A., Zuckerman, D.: Network extractor protocols. In: 49th Annual IEEE Symposium on Foundations of Computer Science, FOCS 2008, Philadelphia, PA, USA, 25–28 October, 2008, pp. 654–663. IEEE Computer Society (2008). https://doi.org/10.1109/FOCS.2008.73

[Li16]   Li, X.: Improved two-source extractors, and affine extractors for poly-logarithmic entropy. In: Dinur, I. (ed.) IEEE 57th Annual Symposium on Foundations of Computer Science, FOCS 2016, Hyatt Regency, New Brunswick, New Jersey, USA, 9–11 October 2016, pp. 168–177. IEEE Computer Society (2016). https://doi.org/10.1109/FOCS.2016.26

[Li17]   Li, X.: Improved non-malleable extractors, non-malleable codes and independent source extractors. In: Proceedings of the 49th Annual ACM SIGACT Symposium on Theory of Computing, pp. 1144–1156. ACM (2017)

[PW08]   Peikert, C., Waters, B.: Lossy trapdoor functions and their applications. In: STOC, pp. 187–196 (2008)

[Raz05]   Raz, R.: Extractors with weak random seeds. In: STOC, pp. 11–20 (2005)

Adaptive Extractors and Their Application to Leakage Resilient Secret Sharing

Nishanth Chandran[1]($\boxtimes$), Bhavana Kanukurthi[2],
Sai Lakshmi Bhavana Obbattu[1], and Sruthi Sekar[3]

[1] Microsoft Research, Bangalore, India
{nichandr,t-saobb}@microsoft.com
[2] Indian Institute of Science, Research Supported by Microsoft Research Grant,
Bangalore, India
bhavana@iisc.ac.in
[3] Indian Institute of Science, Research Supported by TCS Research Grant,
Bangalore, India
sruthisekar@iisc.ac.in

Abstract. We introduce Adaptive Extractors, which unlike traditional randomness extractors, guarantee security even when an adversary obtains leakage on the source *after* observing the extractor output. We make a compelling case for the study of such extractors by demonstrating their use in obtaining adaptive leakage in secret sharing schemes.

Specifically, at FOCS 2020, Chattopadhyay, Goodman, Goyal, Kumar, Li, Meka, Zuckerman, built an adaptively secure leakage resilient secret sharing scheme (LRSS) with both rate and leakage rate being $\mathcal{O}(1/n)$, where n is the number of parties. In this work, we build an adaptively secure LRSS that offers an interesting trade-off between rate, leakage rate, and the total number of shares from which an adversary can obtain leakage. As a special case, when considering t-out-of-n secret sharing schemes for threshold $t = \alpha n$ (constant $0 < \alpha < 1$), we build a scheme with a constant rate, constant leakage rate, and allow the adversary leakage from all but $t - 1$ of the shares, while giving her the remaining $t - 1$ shares completely in the clear. (Prior to this, constant rate LRSS scheme tolerating adaptive leakage was unknown for *any* threshold.)

Finally, we show applications of our techniques to both non-malleable secret sharing and secure message transmission.

Keywords: Randomness extractors · Leakage resilient secret sharing · Information theoretic cryptography

1 Introduction

Randomness extractors [28] are a fundamental primitive in the world of theoretical computer science, which have found widespread applications in derandomization techniques, cryptography, and so on. A randomness extractor Ext is a

© International Association for Cryptologic Research 2021
T. Malkin and C. Peikert (Eds.): CRYPTO 2021, LNCS 12827, pp. 595–624, 2021.
https://doi.org/10.1007/978-3-030-84252-9_20

function that takes as input an n-bit entropic source W, a uniformly random d-bit string S (seed) and outputs $\mathsf{Ext}(W;S)$ such that $\mathsf{Ext}(W;S)$ "looks uniform" to an unbounded eavesdropper Eve even given the seed S. Unfortunately, the standard notion of extractors offers no guarantees whatsoever if the adversary Eve obtains some information about W, after observing, the output of the extractor. In this work, we address this gap.

Does the security of extractors hold even after the adversary obtains some information on W, "after the fact"?

Naturally, we have to be careful about what information Eve can learn about W and S, after the fact. For instance, the function f, which on input w, s and the extractor challenge y, outputs 1 if and only if $y = \mathsf{Ext}(w;s)$, is an after the fact leakage function, which can break extractor security, with high probability, with only 1 bit of leakage. Hence, one needs to define the leakage function family carefully.

In this work, we introduce the notion of *adaptive extractors* with respect to an after the fact leakage family $\mathcal{F}$. Formally, we say that an extractor is an adaptive extractor with respect to a function family $\mathcal{F}$, if for each $f \in \mathcal{F}$, an adversary cannot (statistically) distinguish $(S, f(W, \mathsf{Ext}(W;S)), \mathsf{Ext}(W;S))$ from $(S, f(W, U), U)$. Our notion of adaptive extractors can be seen as a generalization of exposure-resilient extractors introduced by Zimand [33] (Zimand's extractors allow the adversary to adaptively learn up to n^δ bits of the source, for some $\delta < 1$ bits; the adversary can determine which bits to query based on an arbitrary function of the extractor output.), and of the notion of adaptive non-malleable extractors introduced by Aggarwal *et al.* in [2] (where adaptive non-malleability particularly guarantees that the adversary cannot distibuish between $(S, \mathsf{Ext}(W;g(S, \mathsf{Ext}(W;S))), \mathsf{Ext}(W;S))$ and $(S, \mathsf{Ext}(W;g(S, U)), U)$). We then observe that every randomness extractor is also an adaptive extractor with respect to a leakage family depending arbitrarily on the source and the output, with some loss in parameters. We note that this observation is similar to how the authors in [2, Lemma 3.5] show that every non-malleable extractor is adaptive non-malleable, with some loss in parameters. We demonstrate that, in spite of the loss in parameters that adaptivity incurs, such extractors can be powerful. In particular, we use them to build constant-rate secret sharing schemes resilient to adaptive leakage. We now describe these contributions in greater detail.

Secret Sharing. Secret sharing schemes [10,30] are a fundamental cryptographic primitive and have many applications, such as in multi-party computation [7,14], and leakage-resilient circuit compilers [19,23,29]. These are cryptographic primitives that allow a dealer to distribute a secret to n parties, such that only an authorized subset of parties can reconstruct the original secret and any unauthorized set of parties have no information about the underlying secret (*privacy*). For instance, in a $t-$out-of-n threshold secret sharing scheme, there are n parties, and any collection of t $(t \leq n)$ or more parties would correspond to an authorized set, and any collection of less than t parties would be unauthorized.

Note that an implicit assumption is that the unauthorized set of parties has no information about secrets of the remaining shares. A rich study on leakage attacks initiated by Kocher [24] tells us that this is an idealized assumption that may not hold in practice. Such leakage can be dangerous and completely break the security of the underlying primitive[1].

Leakage Resilient Secret Sharing (LRSS). Dziembowski and Pietrzak in [17] introduced the problem of leakage resilience in secret sharing schemes. This problem has received much attention (for example, [1,3,9,12,15,18,20,25,27,31], [11,13]), wherein researchers have strived to improve various parameters such as its rate (defined as (message length)/(length of longest share)), leakage model as well as leakage rate (defined as (number of bits of leakage allowed)/(the size of a share)).

At a high level, in an LRSS, the adversary is allowed leakage on shares of the secret. This is captured by permitting the adversary to specify functions $\ell_1, \ell_2, \ldots$, and receive, in response, $\ell_i(sh_i)$ (where sh_i denotes the ith share). Informally, security of an LRSS requires that privacy should hold even given this leakage. In our work, we explore the stronger setting where the adversary specifies which share to receive leakage from, in an adaptive manner - i.e., the adversary specifies i, ℓ_i and upon learning $\ell_i(sh_i)$, it may make the next leakage query by specifying j, ℓ_j. In this adaptive leakage setting[2], the construction of [13] achieved a rate of $\mathcal{O}(1/n)$ as well as a leakage rate of $\mathcal{O}(1/n)$. A consequence of this is that there currently does not exist a scheme with constant rate and leakage rate for any threshold in this strong leakage model, whereas we do know of such constructions for the non-adaptive leakage model. Our work fills this gap precisely.

1.1 Our Results

Our first and main result on the LRSS scheme in the adaptive leakage model is as follows. Here n denotes the number of parties, t denotes the threshold and l denotes the message length.

Result 1: *We build an LRSS scheme, tolerating ψ adaptive queries, each dependent on X shares (with $\psi \cdot X \leq n - t + 1$) and the reveal of the remaining $t - 1$ shares, such that it achieves a rate of $(X^{\Theta(\psi X/t)})^{-1}$, while allowing $\Theta(l)$ bits of leakage per query, for threshold access structures. In particular, for a constant X and $n = \Theta(t)$, this gives the first constant-rate adaptive LRSS scheme for the threshold access structure. Finally, we also generalize our constructions to the first constant-rate adaptive LRSS for general access structures.*

---

[1] For example, Guruswami and Wooters [22] show that Shamir's secret sharing scheme is completely insecure when the adversary gets some $t - 1$ shares and just one-bit of leakage from other shares.

[2] We note that here we only compare in an adaptive leakage model, without any joint leakage queries on multiple shares (which is called the *bounded collusion protocols* (BCP) model), for ease of expostion, and discuss the joint model in the technical section later.

Further, in the full version of our paper, we also show the following applications of our LRSS scheme.

Result 2: *As an application of our LRSS, we show compilers to get a leakage resilient non-malleable secret sharing (LRNMSS) scheme (which are LRSS schemes, additionally resilient to tampering attacks), and an information-theoretic secure message transmission protocol (SMT), tolerant against leakage and tampering attacks. The rates of both these schemes translate appropriately from the rate of the LRSS. In particular, for a constant LRSS, we get constant-rate schemes for both LRNMSS and SMTs.*

1.2   Our Techniques

We begin by describing the leakage model for LRSS and then give a technical overview of our scheme. For simplicity, we provide our technical overview for threshold access structures (which we can extend to general access structures as well). Let t denote the threshold and n, the number of parties.

Leakage Model. We allow the adversary to obtain adaptive leakage on $n-(t-1)$ shares and then reveal the full shares of the remaining $t-1$ shares. Each adaptive query can be on a set of at most X shares (where X is some value between 1 and $t-1$), and different queries must be on sets that are disjoint from the prior queries. For the purposes of this exposition, we make the following restriction to our model: we assume that the adversary makes adaptive queries but only on a single share each time, i.e., it doesn't make any leakage query on multiple shares.

Warm-up Construction. To motivate our construction, we consider the following modification[3] of a construction due to Srinivasan and Vasudevan in [31, Section 3.2.1]. Take any t-out-of-n secret sharing scheme (MShare, MRec) and then do as follows:

- Sample shares $(m_1, .., m_n)$ of the message m using MShare.
- Choose an extractor seed s and split s into $(sd_1, .., sd_n)$ using a t-out-of-n secret sharing scheme.
- Now, for every m_i, choose an extractor source w_i uniformly and compute $y_i = m_i \oplus \mathsf{Ext}(w_i; s)$.
- Finally, output the final shares $\{sh_i\}$ as $\{(w_i, y_i, sd_i)\}$.

For now, consider a weak model, where the adversary obtains only non-adaptive and independent leakage from a total of (say) $t-1$ shares, in addition to $t-1$ full shares. The hope is to show that the $t-1$ leakage queries are independent of the message shares m_i, following which the privacy of MShare can be used to get the $t-1$ full shares. One might hope to show this independence of leakage from the m_i's, using the security of the extractor as follows: Pick sd_i uniformly at random

---

[3] We note that the original construction of [31] only aimed to achieve non-adaptive security, and we consider a modification, with the aim to expand to adaptive security.

and independent of s; then the leakage function on $\{sh_i\}$, can be answered as an auxiliary leakage query on the source w_i. Once s is revealed in the extractor security game, the reduction can pick the other sd_j values in a consistent manner. However, this proof strategy has a flaw. For extractor security, it is important that the auxiliary leakage query on w is independent of s; however, there is a dependence on s via y_i. In other words, it is unclear how to prove that this construction satisfies leakage resilience even in a weak model where the adversary obtains leakage only independently and non-adaptively.

Fortunately, with adaptive extractors, we can show that this construction is secure not only in this weak model but also in a stronger model where the adversary is allowed to leak from $t-1$ shares adaptively, before receiving $t-1$ full shares. Furthermore, this construction even has a constant rate! The high-level idea of security is as follows. We wish to reduce the adaptive leakage queries on the shares to an adaptive extractor leakage query. Since the adaptive leakage query on w_j cannot depend on the seed, we need to first show that the share sd_j in the corresponding query is independent of the seed s. Indeed, using the privacy of secret sharing[4], we can show that for the first $t-1$ queries, the shares sd_j in sh_j can be replaced with shares of 0 (hence removing the dependence on s). Then, using the adaptive extractor security, we can replace the y_j's (for the first $t-1$ queries) with uniform, where the leakage can be asked on the w_j's. Now, the privacy of MShare can be invoked to get the $t-1$ full shares.

Main Construction. Our next goal is to leverage adaptive extractors to go beyond leaking from just $t-1$ shares. The main bottleneck is that for any subsequent leakage query (beyond $t-1$), the sd_j's will reveal s, and hence the adaptive leakage query on subsequent w_j's will no longer remain independent of the seed s. Thus, extractor security fails. This is the challenge we must address to achieve our main result where the adversary is allowed to obtain adaptive leakage on $n-(t-1)$ shares (in total) and reveal $t-1$ of the remaining shares.

One approach to facilitating leakage from more than $t-1$ shares could be to use independent extractor seeds to extract independent random masks. Consider the following modification of the above construction: mask the share of a message m_i not just with one extractor output but with many. In particular, let $y_i = m_i \oplus \mathsf{Ext}(w_i; s^1) \oplus \mathsf{Ext}(w_i; s^2) \ldots \oplus \mathsf{Ext}(w_i; s^h)$, for some parameter h, where $s^1 \ldots s^h$ are independent seeds. We might hope that because we are using h seeds, we could hope to leak from $h(t-1)$ shares and use the security of each seed per batch of $t-1$ shares. Unfortunately, this doesn't work for the following reason: reconstruction is only possible if we recover all h seeds. This means that we ultimately need to somehow share all the seeds in a manner where they can be reconstructed from $t-1$ shares. In other words, once we leak from $t-1$ shares, we can no longer argue security by leveraging any of the seeds because they can all be reconstructed from $t-1$ shares. We overcome this challenge by carefully using a multi-layered approach for both masking the message shares as well as for reconstructing the seeds.

---

[4] Since the leakage queries are adaptive, we require adaptive privacy of the underlying secret sharing scheme, and we show instantiations of the same.

Construction Overview:

1. Pick h extractor seeds $s^1, \ldots, s^h$ and hn extractor sources $w_1^1, \ldots w_1^h, \ldots, w_n^1, \ldots, w_n^h$.
2. Secret share each of the h seeds using a t-out-of-n secret sharing scheme to obtain shares; let the share of s^j be $sd_1^j, \ldots, sd_n^j$
3. Each share m_j is masked using the h seeds in a layered manner as follows:
   (a) In level $h+1$: Set $y_j^{h+1} = m_j$.
   (b) For every subsequent lower level $i(i \geq 1)$, compute $x_j^i = y_j^{i+1} \oplus \mathsf{Ext}^i(w_j^i; s_i)$ and set $y_j^i = (x_j^i || sd_j^i)$. [Note that we use a different extractor per-level since the length of the extractor outputs (and the length of y_js they mask) increase with level.]
   Finally set $Sh_j = (w_j^1, \cdots, w_j^h, y_j^1)$.
4. Output $(Sh_1, \cdots, Sh_n)$

A pictorial representation of the construction can be found in Fig. 1. In order to give an overview of the proof, we first recall that we are in a setting where each adaptive query of an adversary is a query on a single share – we can extend our results to the case of joint leakage but, for the sake of simplicity, we don't focus on that for now.

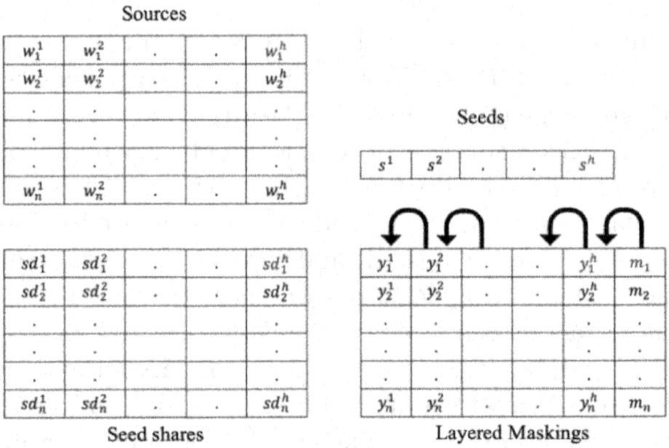

Each entry of the layered maskings matrix appropriately uses the corresponding entries of the sources, seeds and seed shares matrices. In addition, each entry y_i^j $(j \leq h)$ also depends on the subsequent value i.e., y_i^{j+1}. Example:
$$y_1^h = m_1 \oplus \mathsf{Ext}^h(w_1^h; s^h) || sd_1^h \text{ (colored red)}$$

Fig. 1. The main construction. (Color figure online)

At a high-level, the idea of the security proof is that we view the leakage queries in batches of $t - 1$ queries. For the first set of $t - 1$ queries, we rely on the adaptive security of the extractor outputs evaluated using seed s^1 and, in particular, all of these outputs can be replaced by uniform. (This also relies on the *adaptive* privacy of the secret sharing scheme, a notion we define and instantiate.) For the second set of $t - 1$ queries, we can no longer assume that s^1 is hidden, since we can not use the privacy of the secret sharing scheme any more. However, two things come to our rescue: first, the second batch of queries helps unmask at most $t-1$ shares of s^2 and therefore, adaptive extractor security on seed s^2 can be leveraged; second, the extractor outputs $\mathsf{Ext}(w_j^1; s^1)$ (where j was a share that was leaked from in the first batch) continue to remain uniform. The reason for the latter is that all extractor sources are uniformly chosen, and our model requires a disjoint set of indices to be leaked from across batches. In short, for the first batch of queries, we use adaptive security of the extractor outputs evaluated on the first seed and, for every subsequent batch, we move to argue extractor security using the subsequent seed. Since we have h independent seeds, we can do this h times and therefore answer h batches of queries, i.e., we can obtain leakage on $h(t - 1)$ shares.

1.3   Related Work

We first list out some of the parameters that are relevant to LRSS schemes:

- *Rate*: This is defined as $\frac{\text{messagelength}}{\text{sharelength}}$.
- *Global Limit*: This refers to the total number of shares on which the leakage queries can depend on.
- *Per-query Limit*: This refers to the number of shares that a specific query can depend on.
- *Per-query Leakage Rate*: This is the ratio of the total allowable leakage from a single leakage query to the size of a share.

The problems of leakage resilient and non-malleable secret sharing have seen a flurry of activity in recent times [1,5,9,11–13,18,20,25–27,31]. Here we compare our work with only the most relevant works in this area. The only prior LRSS schemes allowing for a joint and adaptive leakage model are [13,25]. While our model allows adaptive queries on up to $n - t + 1$ shares, each dependent on at most X shares (where X is some value between 1 and $t - 1$), before fully revealing the remaining $t - 1$ shares, [13] allows adaptive queries on all n shares, each dependent on at most $t-1$ shares before revealing $t-1$ full shares. Both the schemes require the adaptive queries to be on disjoint sets of shares. However, our scheme/analysis offers a more fine-grained trade-off between the various parameters and allows us to obtain better results for certain settings. In particular, when we consider the instance where X is constant (and $t = \alpha n$, for a constant $\alpha < 1$), we get a constant-rate adaptive LRSS achieving a constant leakage rate, while [13] gets a rate and leakage rate of $\mathcal{O}(1/n)$ each, in all instances. To put this in context, even if [13] makes independent adaptive leakage queries on all shares, their rate is $\mathcal{O}(1/n)$ and the maximum number of bits they can leak is at most a constant fraction of the size of a single share, while we can leak close $(n - t + 1)$ times a constant fraction of the size of a single share!

The work of [13] also consider a variant of joint leakage, allowing overlap of the query sets, the detailed parameters of which are given in Table 1. We give a detailed comparison of the parameters achieved by the various schemes in Table 1, for the threshold setting with $t = \alpha n$ (for a constant $\alpha < 1$).

Table 1. LRSS prior work

Work*	Rate	Joint Leakage	Global Limit	Per Query Limit	Leakage Rate (per query)	Adaptive	Full shares
[SV19]	$1/3$	No	n	1	≈ 1	No	Unauthorized
[ADN+19]	$O(1/n)$	No	n	1	$\approx (1-c)$	No	Unauthorized
[KMS19]	$O\left(\frac{1}{poly(n)}\right)$	Yes (overlapping)	n	$\log(n)$	$\approx \Theta\left(\frac{1}{poly(n)}\right)$	Yes	$\log(n)$
[CGG+20]	$O\left(\frac{1}{n}\right)$	Yes	n	$t-1$	$\approx \Theta\left(\frac{1}{n}\right)$	Yes	Unauthorized
[CGG+20] (threshold)	$O\left(\frac{1}{poly(n)}\right)$	Yes (overlapping)	n	$O\left(\frac{t}{\log(t)}\right)$	$\approx \Theta\left(\frac{1}{poly(n)}\right)$	Yes	Unauthorized
[CGG+20] (n-out of-n)	$O\left(\frac{1}{poly(l_{msg})}\right)$	Yes (overlapping)	n	$0.99n$	$\approx \Theta\left(\frac{1}{poly(l_{msg})}\right)$	Yes	Unauthorized
Our result	$\Theta(1)$	Yes	$n-t+1$	$constant$	$\approx \Theta(1)$	Yes	Unauthorized**

- *All works mentioned here are information-theoretic. We write all comparisons for the threshold setting with threshold $t = \alpha n$ (where $\alpha < 1$ is a constant and n denotes the total number of parties).
- ** For our result, the unauthorized queries cannot overlap with the leakage queries.
- c is a small constant and l_{msg} is the message length.
- All schemes (except the joint overlapping schemes of [13] (threshold and n-out-of-n) actually work for general access structures.
- **Full Shares**: Number of complete shares that an adversary can see (at the end of all leakage queries, in the adaptive schemes).

Open Problems. We believe that it would be interesting to explore the direction of building adaptive extractors against restricted classes of leakage families such as those captured by computational/bounded depth circuits, local functions, etc.

1.4 Organization of the Paper

We provide the preliminaries and definitions in Sect. 2. Then, we define and build adaptive extractors in Sect. 3. We define and build leakage resilient secret sharing schemes in Sect. 4.

2 Preliminaries and Definitions

2.1 Notation

We denote the security parameter by κ. For any two sets S and S', $S \backslash S'$ denotes the set of elements that are present in S, but not in S'. For any natural number n, $[n]$ denotes the set $\{1, 2, \cdots, n\}$ and $[0]$ denotes a null set. $s \in_R S$ denotes uniform sampling from set S. $x \leftarrow X$ denotes sampling from a probability distribution X. The notation $\Pr_X[x]$ denotes the probability assigned by X to the value x. $x \| y$ represents concatenation of two binary strings x and y. $|x|$ denotes length of binary string x. U_l denotes the uniform distribution on $\{0,1\}^l$. All logarithms are base 2. If S is a subset of $[n]$:

- If $x_1, .., x_n$ are some variables or elements, then x_S denotes the set $\{x_i$ such that $i \in S\}$.

- For some function f outputting n values $y_1, \cdots, y_n$ on input x, $f(x)_S$ denotes $(y_i)_{i \in S}$.
- If $T_1, .., T_n$ are sets, then T_S denotes the union $\cup_{i \in S} T_i$.

Statistical Distance. Let X_1, X_2 be two probability distributions over some set S. Their *statistical distance* is

$$\mathbf{SD}\,(X_1, X_2) \stackrel{\text{def}}{=} \max_{T \subseteq S}\{\Pr[X_1 \in T] - \Pr[X_2 \in T]\} = \frac{1}{2} \sum_{s \in S} \left| \Pr_{X_1}[s] - \Pr_{X_2}[s] \right|$$

(they are said to be ε-*close* if $\mathbf{SD}\,(X_1, X_2) \leq \varepsilon$ and denoted by $X_1 \approx_\varepsilon X_2$). For an event E, $\mathbf{SD}_E(A; B)$ denotes $\mathbf{SD}\,(A|E; B|E)$.

Entropy. The *min-entropy* of a random variable W is $\mathbf{H}_\infty(W) = -\log(\max_w \Pr[W = w])$.

For a joint distribution (W, Z), following [16], we define the *(average) conditional min-entropy* of W given Z as

$$\widetilde{\mathbf{H}}_\infty(W \mid Z) = -\log(\mathop{\mathbf{E}}_{e \leftarrow Z}(2^{-\mathbf{H}_\infty(W|Z=z)}))$$

(here the expectation is taken over e for which $\Pr[E = e]$ is nonzero).

For any two random variable W, Z, $(W|Z)$ is said to be an (n, t')-average source if W is over $\{0, 1\}^n$ and $\widetilde{\mathbf{H}}_\infty(W|Z) \geq t'$.

We require some basic properties of entropy and statistical distance, which are given by the following lemmata.

Lemma 1. *[16] Let A, B, C be random variables. Then if B has at most 2^λ possible values, then $\widetilde{\mathbf{H}}_\infty(A \mid B) \geq \mathbf{H}_\infty(A, B) - \lambda \geq \mathbf{H}_\infty(A) - \lambda$ and, more generally, $\widetilde{\mathbf{H}}_\infty(A \mid B, C) \geq \widetilde{\mathbf{H}}_\infty(A, B \mid C) - \lambda \geq \widetilde{\mathbf{H}}_\infty(A \mid C) - \lambda$.*

Lemma 2. *[32] For any random variables A, B, if $A \approx_\epsilon B$, then for any function f, $f(A) \approx_\epsilon f(B)$.*

Lemma 3. *For any random variables A, B over $\mathcal{A}$, and events E, E' with nonzero probabilities,*

$$\mathbf{SD}\,(A \wedge E, B \wedge E') \leq |\Pr[E] - \Pr[E']| + \Pr[E'] \cdot \mathbf{SD}\,(A|E, B|E')$$

where,

$$\mathbf{SD}\,(A \wedge E, B \wedge E') \stackrel{\text{def}}{=} \frac{1}{2} \sum_{a \in \mathcal{A}} |\Pr[A = a \wedge E] - \Pr[B = a \wedge E']|$$

and

$$\mathbf{SD}\,(A|E, B|E') \stackrel{\text{def}}{=} \frac{1}{2} \sum_{a \in \mathcal{A}} |\Pr[A = a|E] - \Pr[B = a|E']|$$

Lemma 4 *[4]   Let X, Y, X', Y' be random variables such that $\mathbf{SD}\,((X, Y), (X', Y')) \leq \epsilon$ and S be any set such that $\Pr[Y \in S] > 0$ and $\Pr[Y' \in S] > 0$, then*

$$\mathbf{SD}\,(X|Y \in S, X'|Y' \in S) \leq \frac{2\epsilon}{\Pr[Y' \in S]}$$

2.2   Secret Sharing Schemes

Secret sharing schemes provide a mechanism to distribute a secret into shares such that only an authorized subset of shares can reconstruct the secret and any unauthorized subset of shares has "almost" no information about the secret. We now define secret sharing schemes formally.

Definition 1. *Let $\mathcal{M}$ be a finite set of secrets, where $|\mathcal{M}| \geq 2$. Let $[n]$ be a set of identities (indices) of n parties. A sharing function* Share : $\mathcal{M} \to (\{0,1\}^l)^n$ *is a $(\mathcal{A}, n, \epsilon_s)$- **secret sharing scheme** with respect to a monotone access structure[5] $\mathcal{A}$ if the following two properties hold :*

1. **Correctness:** *The secret can be reconstructed by any set of parties that are part of the access structure $\mathcal{A}$. That is, for any set $T \in \mathcal{A}$, there exists a deterministic reconstruction function* Rec : $(\{0,1\}^l)^{|T|} \to \mathcal{M}$ *such that for every $m \in \mathcal{M}$,*
$$\Pr[\mathsf{Rec}(\mathsf{Share}(m)_T) = m] = 1$$
   where the probability is over the randomness of the Share *function and if $(sh_1, .., sh_n) \leftarrow$ Share(m), then* Share$(m)_T$ *denotes $\{sh_i\}_{i \in T}$. We will slightly abuse the notation and denote* Rec *as the reconstruction procedure that takes in $T \in \mathcal{A}$ and* Share$(m)_T$ *as input and outputs the secret.*

2. **Statistical Privacy:** *Any collusion of parties not part of the access structure should have "almost" no information about the underlying secret. More formally, for any unauthorized set $U \notin \mathcal{A}$, and for every pair of secrets $m, m' \in \mathcal{M}$,*
$$\Delta((\mathsf{Share}(m))_U ; (\mathsf{Share}(m'))_U) \leq \epsilon_s$$

An access structure $\mathcal{A}$ is said to be (n,t)-threshold if and only if $\mathcal{A}$ contains all subsets of $[n]$ of size at least t.
Rate *of a secret sharing scheme is defined as $\frac{message\ size}{share\ size}$ (which would be equal to $\frac{\log |\mathcal{M}|}{l}$).*

We now study a stronger privacy requirement, *adaptive privacy* (introduced by Bellare and Rogaway [6][6]).

2.2.1   Adaptive Privacy
Statistical privacy captures privacy against any non-adaptively chosen unauthorized set U. *Adaptive privacy* preserves privacy even when the choice of U to be adaptive, which means the following. Let $U = \{i_1, .., i_q\}$. We say i_j is chosen adaptively, if its choice depended on $\{share_j\}_{j \in \{i_1, .., i_{j-1}\}}$. The choice of which share to query next depends on all the previously observed shares. We give the formal definition below.

---

[5] $\mathcal{A}$ is a monotone access structure if for all A, B such that $A \subset B \subseteq [N]$ and $A \in \mathcal{A}$, it holds that $B \in \mathcal{A}$. Throughout this paper whenever we consider a general access structure, we mean a monotone access structure.

[6] In [6], the authors refer to adaptive privacy as privacy against dynamic adversaries.

We say a $(\mathcal{A}, n, \epsilon_s)$-secret sharing scheme satisfies adaptive privacy with error ϵ_{adp} if, for any distinguisher $\mathcal{D}$, the advantage in the following game is at most ϵ_{adp}.

$\mathsf{Game}_{\mathsf{Ad-Privacy}}$: For any arbitrary distinct messages $m_0, m_1 \in \mathcal{M}$

1. $(share_1, \cdots, share_n) \leftarrow \mathsf{Share}(m_b)$ where $b \in_R \{0, 1\}$
2. For $j = 1$ to q [7]
   - $\mathcal{D}$ queries on a distinct index i_j (such that $i_{[j]} \notin \mathcal{A}$) and receives $share_{i_j}$
3. $\mathcal{D}$ outputs the guess b' for b and wins if $b = b'$

While generally, any secret sharing scheme may not be adaptively private, we can show that for the threshold setting, the scheme of [30] and for the general access structures, the scheme of [8] are both adaptively private (which is proved in the full version of our paper). We use them to instantiate our schemes.

Consistent Re-sampling. For any $(\mathcal{A}, n, \epsilon_s)$-secret sharing scheme (Share, Rec), for any message m and a subset $\mathcal{L} \subseteq [n]$, when we say "$(sh_1, .., sh_n) \leftarrow \mathsf{Share}(m)$ consistent with $sh_{\mathcal{L}}^*$ on $\mathcal{L}$" or "$(sh_1, .., sh_n) \leftarrow \mathsf{Share}(m|sh_{\mathcal{L}}^*)$" we mean the following procedure:

- Sample and output $(sh_1, .., sh_n)$ uniformly from the distribution $\mathsf{Share}(m)$ conditioned on the event that $sh_{\mathcal{L}} = sh_{\mathcal{L}}^*$
- If the above event is a zero probability event then output a string of all zeroes (of appropriate length).

We require the following consistent re-sampling feature[8], which informally states that for any $(\mathcal{A}, n, \epsilon_s)$-secret sharing scheme and any message m, the distribution of shares which are re-sampled as shares of m, conditioned on some set T of shares (which are also generated as shares of m) chosen adaptively, is identical to the distribution of shares of m generated directly.

Lemma 5. *For any $(\mathcal{A}, n, \epsilon_s)$-secret sharing scheme* (Share, Rec) *and for any message m, the following two distributions are identical.*

$\mathcal{D}_1$:	$\mathcal{D}_2$:
- $(sh_1', .., sh_n') \leftarrow \mathsf{Share}(m)$ - $(sh_1, .., sh_n) \leftarrow \mathsf{Share}(m\|sh_T')$ - Output $(sh_1, .., sh_n)$	- $(sh_1, .., sh_n) \leftarrow \mathsf{Share}(m)$ - Output $(sh_1, .., sh_n)$

Here, $T \subseteq [N]$ can be any subset chosen as: every index (except the first) depends arbitrarily on the shares corresponding to all the previous indices.

We give a full proof of the above lemma in the full version of our paper.

---

[7] q is arbitrary and chosen by $\mathcal{D}$. It need not be chosen a-priori. We only use it to denote the total number queries made by $\mathcal{D}$

[8] Note that we only use the re-sampling in proofs and do not require the procedure to be efficient.

3   Adaptive Extractors

Extractors (introduced by Nissan and Zuckerman [28]) output a near uniform string y, from a source w that only has min-entropy, using a short uniform string s, called the *seed*, as a catalyst. Average-case extractors are extractors whose output remains close to uniform, even given the seed and some auxiliary information (or leakage) about the source (independent of the seed), as long as the source has enough average entropy given this leakage. We give their formal definition below.

Definition 2. *[16] Let* $\mathsf{Ext} : \{0,1\}^\eta \times \{0,1\}^d \to \{0,1\}^l$ *be a polynomial time computable function. We say that* Ext *is an efficient average-case* $(\eta, \mu, d, l, \epsilon)$*- strong extractor if for all pairs of random variables* (W, Z) *such that* W *is an* η*-bit string satisfying* $\widetilde{\mathbf{H}}_\infty(W|Z) \geq \mu$, *we have*

$$\mathsf{Ext}(W; U_d), U_d, Z \approx_\epsilon U_l, U_d, Z$$

3.1   Definition

Average-case extractors, unfortunately, provide no guarantees on the extractor output being uniform when an adversary can obtain an 'adaptive' leakage on the source, that is *dependent on the extractor output* and the seed. This is not surprising, as if an adversary can obtain *arbitrary adaptive leakage* on the source, then we cannot hope for the extractor output to remain uniform. For example, given $y = \mathsf{Ext}(w, s)$, an adversary can distinguish the extractor output from uniform with high probability by querying a single bit of auxiliary information that tells her whether $\mathsf{Ext}(w, s) = y$. However, as we will see later, in many applications, the adaptive leakage that the adversary obtains comes from a specific function family. Hence, by carefully defining this function family, we show how to obtain useful notions of extractors that guarantee security even in the presence of an adaptive auxiliary information. We introduce and call this notion *adaptive extractors* and now proceed to formally define them.

Definition 3. *An* $(\eta, \mu, d, l, \epsilon)$*- extractor* Ext *is said to be an* $(\mathcal{F}, \delta)$*-adaptive extractor if for all pairs of random variables* (W, Z) *such that* W *is an* η*-bit string satisfying* $\widetilde{\mathbf{H}}_\infty(W|Z) \geq \mu$, *and any function* f *in the function family* $\mathcal{F}$, *it holds that*

$$Z, U_d, f(W, \mathsf{Ext}(W; U_d), U_d), \mathsf{Ext}(W; U_d) \approx_\delta Z, U_d, f(W, U_l, U_d), U_l$$

We call δ, *the* **adaptive error** *of the extractor.*

3.2   Construction

Generic Relation. We show that every extractor is in fact an adaptive extractor for the family of leakage functions where the adaptive leakage depends only on the source and the extractor output (i.e., it doesn't depend on the seed except via the extractor output), with some loss in security. This loss, in fact, depends only on the number of bits of the extractor output that the adaptive leakage function depends on. For ease of exposition, we omit auxiliary information z that depends only on the source (but not on the extractor output or seed) from the notation below. We now explicitly define this family below:

$$\mathcal{F}_{a,\zeta} \subseteq \{f' : \{0,1\}^\eta \times \{0,1\}^l \to \{0,1\}^\zeta\}$$

such that for every $f' \in \mathcal{F}_{a,\zeta}$ there exists two functions $f : \{0,1\}^l \to \{0,1\}^a$ and

$$g : \{0,1\}^{\eta+a} \to \{0,1\}^\zeta \text{ such that } \forall w, y, \; f'(w,y) = g(w, f(y))\}$$

Here, 'ζ' denotes the number of bits of adaptive leakage and 'a' denotes the number of bits of the extractor output (or the uniform string) that the adaptive leakage depends on. This is captured by requiring that every function f' has an equivalent representation in terms of some g and f such that $f'(w,y) = g(w, f(y))$ where f's output is only a bits long. w and y should be interpreted as the source and the extractor output (or the uniform string) respectively.

The following theorem shows that any $(\eta, \mu, d, l, \epsilon)$- average case extractor can be shown to be adaptive secure against the above family $\mathcal{F}_{a,\zeta}$, with an adaptive error of $2^{a+2}\epsilon$. Informally, we can reduce the adaptive security to the extractor security (as in Definition 2) in the following way: to answer the adaptive leakage query, the reduction makes a guess, v, for the extractor challenge dependent value $f(y_b)$ (where, y_b is the extractor challenge), which is of a-bits, and gets the leakage $g(w, v)$ from the source. Now, it gets the challenge y_b from the extractor challenger and if $f(y_b)$ matches the guess v, then the reduction can successfully simulate the challenge and the adaptive leakage response, else it cannot proceed (and aborts). Hence, the winning probability in the extractor game is the probability of a correct guess (2^{-a}), multiplied with the winning probability of the adaptive extractor adversary. We formalize this proof in the theorem below.

Theorem 1. *Every $(\eta, \mu, d, l, \epsilon)$- average case extractor* Ext *is an $(\eta, \mu + \zeta, d, l, \epsilon)$- extractor that is $(\mathcal{F}_{a,\zeta}, 2^{a+2}\epsilon)$-adaptive, for any $\mu + \zeta \leq \eta$ and $a \leq l$.*

Proof. For simplicity, we omit the auxiliary information Z, that depends only on the source (and not on the extractor output). Let W be the source of η bits, such that $\mathbf{H}_\infty(W) \geq \mu + \zeta$. Consider $f' \in \mathcal{F}_{a,\zeta}$, with the corresponding functions (f, g) (recall $f'(w, y) = g(w, f(y))$, where f outputs a bits and g outputs ζ bits). To prove adaptive security (Definition 3), we need to show that:

$$U_d, f'(W, Y), Y \approx_{2^{a+2}\epsilon} U_d, f'(W, U_l), U_l,$$

where Y is the random variable $\mathsf{Ext}(W; U_d)$. Expanding the description of f', this gives:

$$U_d, g(W, f(Y)), Y \approx_{2^{a+2}\epsilon} U_d, g(W, f(U_l)), U_l$$

To prove this, we consider the following two sets $\mathcal{B} = \{b : \Pr[f(Y) = b] > 0\}$ and $\mathcal{A} = \{0,1\}^{d+\zeta+l}$. For each $b \in \mathcal{B}$, we begin by using the statistical distance Lemma 3 with random variables A, B and events E, E' set as $(U_d, g(W, f(Y)), Y)$, $(U_d, g(W, f(U_l)), U_l)$, $f(Y) = b$ and $f(U_l) = b$, respectively. By use of law of total probability and Lemma 3, we get:

$$\mathbf{SD}((U_d, g(W, f(Y)), Y), \ (U_d, g(W, f(U_l)), U_l))$$

$$\leq \Pr[f(U_l) \notin \mathcal{B}] + \sum_{b \in \mathcal{B}} \mathbf{SD}\left(A \wedge E, B \wedge E'\right)$$

$$\leq \Pr[f(U_l) \notin \mathcal{B}] + \sum_{b \in \mathcal{B}} ((|\Pr[E] - \Pr[E']|) + \Pr[E'] \cdot \mathbf{SD}\left(A|E, B|E'\right))$$

But now, note that, by extractor security, since $Y \approx_\epsilon U_l$, by applying Lemma 2, we have $f(Y) \approx_\epsilon f(U_l)$. Further, by the definition of statistical distance, we have that, for each $b \in \mathcal{B}$, $|\Pr[f(Y) = b] - \Pr[f(U_l) = b]| \leq \epsilon$ and $\Pr[f(U_l) \notin \mathcal{B}] \leq \epsilon$ (since $\Pr[f(Y) \notin \mathcal{B}] = 0]$). Applying this to above inequality, we get:

$$\mathbf{SD}((U_d, g(W, f(Y)), Y), \ (U_d, g(W, f(U_l)), U_l))$$

$$\leq \epsilon + \sum_{b \in \mathcal{B}} (\epsilon + \Pr[E'] \cdot \mathbf{SD}\left(A|E, B|E'\right))$$

$$= (|\mathcal{B}| + 1)\epsilon + \sum_{b \in \mathcal{B}} \Pr[E'] \cdot \mathbf{SD}(A|E, \ B|E')$$

Finally, we apply the statistical distance Lemma 4 on the random variables $(A, f(Y))$ and $(B, f(U_l))$ with set $S = \{b\}$. Note that, given events E and E' the value of $f(Y)$ and $f(U_l)$ are fixed to a b, which means the leakage $g(W, b)$ is only a leakage on W. Thus, we can use extractor security to get: $(U_d, g(W, b), Y) \approx_\epsilon (U_d, g(W, b), U_l)$. Hence, applying this to the above inequality, we get:

$$\mathbf{SD}((U_d, g(W, f(Y)), Y), \ (U_d, g(W, f(U_l)), U_l))$$

$$\leq (|\mathcal{B}| + 1)\epsilon + \sum_{b \in \mathcal{B}} \Pr[E'] \cdot \frac{2\epsilon}{\Pr[f(U_l) = b]}$$

$$\leq 4|\mathcal{B}|\epsilon \leq 2^{a+2}\epsilon$$

Concrete Instantiation. We show that the extractor due to Guruswami *et al.* [21] is an adaptive extractor even when the leakage depends on the entire extractor output. We state the result from [21] below.

Lemma 6. *[21] For every constant $\nu > 0$ all integers $\eta \geq \mu$ and all $\epsilon \geq 0$, there is an explicit (efficient) $(\eta, \mu, d, l, \epsilon)-$strong extractor with $l = (1 - \nu)\mu - \mathcal{O}(\log(\eta) + \log(\frac{1}{\epsilon}))$ and $d \leq \mathcal{O}(\log(\eta) + \log(\frac{1}{\epsilon}))$.*

Let Full_ζ $(= \mathcal{F}_{l,\zeta})$, denote the leakage function family which computes leakage (of size ζ) dependent on the entire extractor output and the source. The following lemma shows that one can appropriately set the parameters of the [21] extractor to get negligible error, while extracting a constant fraction of the bits from the source, and while adaptively leaking a constant fraction of bits from it.

Lemma 7. *For all positive integers l, ζ, every constant $\nu > 1$ and $\epsilon \geq 0$, there is an explicit (efficient) $(\eta, \mu + \zeta, d, l, \epsilon)$-extractor that is $(\mathsf{Full}_\zeta, \delta)$-adaptive with $d = \mathcal{O}(\log(\frac{\eta}{\epsilon}))$, $\mu = \nu l + \mathcal{O}(\log(\frac{\eta}{\epsilon}))$, any $\eta \geq \mu + \zeta$ and $\delta = \epsilon \cdot 2^{l+2}$.*
On further implication, for any $c > 1$, there exists constants α, β such that $d \leq \alpha l$, $\mu \leq \beta l$, $\eta \geq \beta l + \zeta$, $\epsilon = 2^{-cl}$ and $\delta = 2^{(1-c)l+2}$ when $l = \omega(\log \eta)$.

Proof. The proof of the first part of the lemma follows directly from Theorem 1 and Lemma 6 and the further implication can be obtained by simple substitution.

Further, we use the following generalization of adaptive extractors: for an adaptive extractor Ext, if we consider k independent sources $W_1, \cdots, W_k$ and a single seed S, all the extractor outputs $(\mathsf{Ext}(W_i; S))_{i \in [k]}$ look uniform, even given adaptive leakage on each W_i, dependent on not just $\mathsf{Ext}(W_i; S)$ (or uniform), but also all the prior extractor outputs and adaptive leakages (queried before i). As the sources are independent, this lemma can be proved using a simple hybrid argument (the detailed proof is given in our full version).

Lemma 8. *Let k be an arbitrary positive integer, $W_1, \cdots, W_k$ be k independent $(\eta, \mu + \zeta)$ sources and S be the uniform distribution on $\{0,1\}^d$. Let Ext be an $(\eta, \mu + \zeta, d, l, \delta')$-extractor that is $(\mathsf{Full}_\zeta, \delta)$-adaptive. For each $i \in [k]$, let E_i^0 denotes $\mathsf{Ext}(W_i; S)$, E_i^1 denotes uniform distribution on $\{0,1\}^l$. For $b \in \{0,1\}$, we define AdLeak^b as follows. Then for any stateful distinguisher $\mathcal{D}'$ we have $\mathsf{AdLeak}^0 \approx_{k\delta} \mathsf{AdLeak}^1$.*
AdLeak^b :

- *Let Tr and $\mathcal{S}$ be a null string and null set respectively.*
- *For upto k times*
  - *$(j, g_j) \leftarrow \mathcal{D}'(Tr)$ where $j \in [k] \backslash \mathcal{S}$ and $g_j : \{0,1\}^{\eta+l} \to \{0,1\}^\zeta$.*
  - *Append $(j, g_j, g_j(w_j, E_j^b), E_j^b)$ to Tr.*
  - *Add j to $\mathcal{S}$.*
- *Output Tr.*

4 Leakage Resilient Secret Sharing

Leakage-resilience of a secret sharing scheme is defined specific to a leakage model/ leakage family. We begin by formally defining leakage-resilience and then describe the leakage model.

Definition 4. *An $(\mathcal{A}, n, \epsilon_s)$-secret sharing scheme is said to be an $(\mathcal{A}, n, \epsilon_s, \epsilon_l)$-**leakage resilient secret sharing scheme** against a leakage family $\mathcal{F}$ if for all functions $f \in \mathcal{F}$ and for any two messages m, m', $\mathbf{SD}\left(f(Share(m)), f(Share(m'))\right) \leq \epsilon_l$.*

4.1   Leakage Models

We consider two leakage models in this paper. For now, we restrict our discussion to an (n, t)-threshold access structure.

- **Adaptive Leakage and Reveal Model**: The adversary can adaptively obtain leakage on individual shares for any $n - t + 1$ shares. After this, he can additionally even get all the remaining $t - 1$ shares in their entirety.
- **Joint Leakage and Reveal Model**: The adversary can ask any number of joint leakage queries on disjoint sets of size X (a parameter). After this, he can additionally get any (at most $t - 1$) of the remaining shares in their entirety. While this model completely subsumes the adaptive leakage and reveal model, the amount of leakage per share supported in the latter would be lesser.

We provide a formal description of the adaptive leakage and reveal model and the joint leakage and reveal model in Sect. 4.1.1 and Sect. 4.5 respectively. We give a construction that is leakage resilient with respect to both these models in Sect. 4.2. We prove leakage resilience of this scheme in the adaptive leakage and reveal model in Sect. 4.3. We provide a proof sketch of leakage resilience in the joint adaptive and reveal model in Sect. 4.5.2.

4.1.1   Adaptive Leakage and Reveal Model $\mathcal{F}_{leak}^{\psi, \tau}$

The model allows for leakage on individual shares and then also reveals at most $t - 1$ of the remaining shares in clear. We have two parameters in the model τ and ψ where τ denotes the amount of leakage provided in each leakage query and ψ captures the maximum number of leakage queries allowed. We allow ψ ranging from 1 to $n - t + 1$. Though we allow ψ to be $n - t + 1$, we have it as an explicit parameter because lower ψ would imply a weaker leakage model and possibly have better constructions. In fact, our multi-layered construction in Sect. 4.2 becomes compact (and offers better rate) as ψ decreases.

Leak_{Share}^m:

- Initialize Z to be a null string and $\mathcal{S}$ to be a null set.
- $(Sh_1, \cdots, Sh_n) \leftarrow Share(m)$
- **Leakage Phase:**
    For upto ψ times
    - $(j, f_j) \leftarrow \mathcal{D}(Z)$ where $f_j : \{0, 1\}^\gamma \rightarrow \{0, 1\}^\tau$
    - If $j \in [n] \backslash \mathcal{S}$, add j to $\mathcal{S}$ and append $(j, f_j, f_j(Sh_j))$ to Z
- **Reveal phase**

    For upto $t - 1$ times
    - $j \leftarrow \mathcal{D}(Z)$
    - If $j \in [n] \backslash \mathcal{S}$, append (j, Sh_j) to Z
- $\mathcal{D}$ updates Z with any relevant state information.
- Output Z.

Fig. 2. LRSS definition- Leak_{Share}^m distribution

Let $(Share, Rec)$ (where $Share : \{0,1\}^l \to (\{0,1\}^\gamma)^n$) be a t-out-of-n secret sharing scheme. We formalize leakage obtained in this model on shares of a message m as Leak^m_{Share} in Fig. 2, where an arbitrary stateful distinguisher $\mathcal{D}$ makes the queries. For any two messages m and m', we require $\mathsf{Leak}^m_{Share} \approx_{\epsilon_{lr}} \mathsf{Leak}^{m'}_{Share}$, for $(Share, Rec)$ to be ϵ_{lr} leakage resilient against the adaptive leakage and reveal model.

4.2 LRSS Construction for the Adaptive Leakage and Reveal Model

We refer the reader to the Introduction (Sect. 1.2) for a high-level overview of the construction and proof. We proceed to describe the construction in detail in Fig. 3 and prove its security in Sect. 4.3.

Let n be the number of parties and t be the reconstruction threshold. Let $h > 0$ be a parameter guaranteed to be less than $\lceil n/(t-1) \rceil$.

Building Blocks. Let $(\mathsf{MShare}, \mathsf{MRec})$ be an $((n,t), \varepsilon, \epsilon)$-adaptive secret sharing scheme for messages in $\{0,1\}^l$ with share space being $\{0,1\}^{l'}$. For $i \in [h]$, let $(\mathsf{SdShare}^i, \mathsf{SdRec}^i)$ be an $((n,t), \varepsilon'_i, \epsilon'_i)$-adaptive secret sharing scheme for messages in $\{0,1\}^{d_i}$ with share space being $\{0,1\}^{d'_i}$. For $i \in [h]$, let Ext^i be an $(\eta_i, \mu_i + \tau, d_i, \ell_i, \delta'_i)$-extractor that is $(\mathsf{Full}_\tau, \delta_i)$-adaptive. We set $\ell_1 = l'$ and for $i \in [h]\backslash\{1\}$ we set $l_i = l_{i-1} + d'_{i-1}$.

$\mathsf{Share}^h(m)$:

- $(m_1, \cdots, m_n) \leftarrow \mathsf{MShare}(m)$.
- For $i \in [h]$, pick seeds $s^i \in_R \{0,1\}^{d_i}$ and compute their shares $(sd^i_1, \cdots, sd^i_n) \leftarrow \mathsf{SdShare}^i(s^i)$.
- For $i \in [h]$ and $j \in [n]$, pick sources $w^i_j \in_R \{0,1\}^{\eta_i}$.
- For $j \in [n]$:
  - Define $y^{h+1}_j = m_j$.
  - For $i \leftarrow h$ to 1, compute $x^i_j = y^{i+1}_j \oplus \mathsf{Ext}^i(w^i_j; s^i)$ and $y^i_j = (x^i_j \| sd^i_j)$.
- For $j \in [n]$, define $Sh_j = (w^1_j, \cdots, w^h_j, y^1_j)$.
- Output $(Sh_1, \cdots, Sh_n)$.

$\mathsf{Rec}^h(Sh_T)$: (where T is the reconstruction set)

- For $j \in T$, parse Sh_j as $(w^1_j, \cdots, w^h_j, y^1_j)$, where $y^1_j = x^1_j \| sd^1_j$.
- For $i \leftarrow 1$ to h:
  - $s^i = \mathsf{SdRec}^i(sd^i_T)$.
  - For each $j \in T$, $y^{i+1}_j = x^i_j \oplus \mathsf{Ext}^i(w^i_j; s^i)$. For each $i \in [h-1]$, parse y^{i+1}_j as $x^{i+1}_j \| sd^{i+1}_j$.
- Parse y^{h+1}_j as m_j. Recover $m = \mathsf{MRec}(m_T)$.
- Output m.

Fig. 3. LRSS construction

4.3   Proof of Leakage Resilience in the Adaptive Leakage and Reveal Model

Theorem 2. *For any $\psi \leq n - t + 1$ and $l, \tau > 0$, (Share^h, Rec^h) is an $((n,t), \varepsilon)$- secret sharing scheme for l bit messages and is $2(\epsilon + h(\epsilon' + (t-1)\delta))$-leakage resilient in the Adaptive Leakage and Reveal model $\mathcal{F}_{leak}^{\psi, \tau}$ where $h = \lceil \psi/(t-1) \rceil$. Further, there exists an instantiation of the scheme with rate is $(2^{\Theta(h)} + h\tau/l)^{-1}$. When $\tau = \Theta(l)$ and either $n = \Theta(t)$ or h is a constant, the scheme achieves constant rate and constant leakage rate asymptotically.*

Proof. The correctness of the scheme follows directly from the correctness of underlying extractors and secret sharing schemes. The (adaptive) privacy of the scheme is directly implied by the leakage resilience (against the adaptive leakage and reveal model).

Leakage Resilience. For any message m we define the following the sequence of hybrids. In these hybrids we assume that $\mathcal{D}$ always asks legitimate queries as per the model and won't write explicit checks for legitimacy (for example, we assume that $\mathcal{D}$ doesn't ask leakage on same share twice).

We analyze the leakage queries made by $\mathcal{D}$ as bunches of $(t-1)$ queries. We now introduce some useful notation. Let $\mathcal{S}_1, \cdots, \mathcal{S}_h$ denote the sets of indices queried by $\mathcal{D}$, where $\mathcal{S}_i$ contains the indices queried by $\mathcal{D}$ from the $((i-1)(t-1)+1)^{th}$ query to $i(t-1)^{th}$ leakage queries (i.e., $\mathcal{S}_1$ contains the first $t-1$ queries, $\mathcal{S}_2$ the next $t-1$ queries and so on). For $i \in [h]$, we use $\mathcal{S}_{[i]}$ to denote $\bigcup_{j=1}^{i} \mathcal{S}_j$, which captures the set of indices queried in the first $i(t-1)$ leakage queries. For $i \in [h]$, let $Z_{[i]}$ denotes the set of leakage queries and the corresponding responses to the first $i(t-1)$ leakage queries. $Z_{[h+1]}$ denotes $Z_{[h]}$ together with the final reveal queries as well as any relevant state information. We prove leakage resilience using a hybrid argument, with the following sequence of hybrids, LeakB$_0^m$, {LeakA$_q^m$, LeakB$_q^m$}$_{q \in [h]}$ and LeakC^m. The order of the hybrids is LeakB$_0^m$, LeakA$_1^m$, LeakB$_1^m$, $\cdots$, LeakA$_h^m$, LeakB$_h^m$, LeakC^m, where we will show that LeakC^m is independent of m, and LeakB$_0^m$ will correspond to the distribution Leak$_{Share^h}^m$. This will allow us to show that Leak$_{Share^h}^m$ is indistinguishable from Leak$_{Share^h}^{m'}$. We begin by giving an informal description of these hybrids.

LeakA$_q^m$: We start with $q = 1$. LeakA$_1^m$ follows the actual leakage game i.e., Leak$_{Share^h}^m$ ($\equiv$ LeakB$_0^m$) except for the following change: we replace the shares sd_j^1, for each $j \in \mathcal{S}_1$ (the shares of s^1 corresponding to the first $t-1$ leakage queries), with shares of a dummy seed $\widetilde{s}^1 = 0^d$. In general, for each $1 < q \leq h$, the only change we make in LeakA$_q^m$ (in comparison to the previous hybrid LeakB$_{q-1}^m$) is that we replace the shares sd_j^q, for each $j \in \mathcal{S}_q$ (the shares of s^q corresponding to the q-th set of $t-1$ leakage queries), with shares of a dummy seed $\widetilde{s}^q$. After answering the leakage queries corresponding to $\mathcal{S}_q$, shares of s^q are re-sampled consistent with the dummy seed shares used so far. The hybrid is formally described in Fig. 4.

LeakA_q^m:

1. Initialize Z to be a null string and $\mathcal{S}_1, \cdots, \mathcal{S}_h$ to be null sets.
2. $(m_1, \cdots, m_n) \leftarrow \mathsf{MShare}(m)$
3. For $i \in [h]$, choose $s^i \in_R \{0,1\}^{d_i}$
4. For $i \in [h]$ and $j \in [n]$, choose $w_j^i \in_R \{0,1\}^{\eta_i}$
5. For $i \in [h]\backslash[q]$, compute $(sd_1^i, \cdots, sd_n^i) \leftarrow \mathsf{SdShare}^i(s^i)$
6. For $i \in [q]$, let $\widetilde{s}^i = 0^d$
7. For $j \in [n]$, define $y_j^{h+1} = m_j$
8. **Leakage Phase:**
   (a) For $c \leftarrow 1$ to q
       i. $(\widetilde{sd}_1^c, \cdots, \widetilde{sd}_n^c) \leftarrow \mathsf{SdShare}^c(\widetilde{s}^c)$
       ii. For up to $(t-1)$ times
           A. $(j, f_j) \leftarrow \mathcal{D}(Z)$
           B. If $c < q$,
              * Choose $x_j^c \in_R \{0,1\}^{l_c}$ and compute $y_j^c = (x_j^c || \widetilde{sd}_j^c)$
              * For $i \leftarrow c-1$ down to 1,
                compute $x_j^i = y_j^{i+1} \oplus \mathsf{Ext}^i(w_j^i; s^i)$ and $y_j^i = (x_j^i || sd_j^i)$
           C. If $c = q$, for $i \leftarrow h$ down to 1 compute
              $$\begin{cases} x_j^i = y_j^{i+1} \oplus \mathsf{Ext}^i(w_j^i; s^i) \text{ and } y_j^i = (x_j^i || sd_j^i) \text{ when } i \neq q \\ x_j^i = y_j^{i+1} \oplus \mathsf{Ext}^i(w_j^i; s^i) \text{ and } y_j^i = (x_j^i || \widetilde{sd}_j^i) \text{ when } i = q \end{cases}$$
           D. Define $Sh_j = (w_j^1, \cdots, w_j^h, y_j^1)$

           E. Add j to $\mathcal{S}_c$ and append $(j, f_j, f_j(Sh_j))$ to Z
       iii. $(sd_1^c, \cdots, sd_n^c) \leftarrow \mathsf{SdShare}^c(s^c | \widetilde{sd}_{\mathcal{S}_c}^c)$
   (b) For $j \in [n]\backslash(\mathcal{S}_{[q]})$ and $i \leftarrow h$ down to 1,
       compute $x_j^i = y_j^{i+1} \oplus \mathsf{Ext}^i(w_j^i; s^i)$ and $y_j^i = (x_j^i || sd_j^i)$
   (c) Define $Sh_j = (w_j^1, \cdots, w_j^h, y_j^1)$
   (d) For $c \leftarrow q+1$ to h
       i. For upto $t-1$ times
          A. $(j, f_j) \leftarrow \mathcal{D}(Z)$
          B. Add j to $\mathcal{S}_c$ and append $(j, f_j, f_j(Sh_j))$ to Z
9. **Reveal phase**
   (a) For upto $t-1$ times
       i. $j \leftarrow \mathcal{D}(Z)$
       ii. Append (j, Sh_j) to Z
10. $\mathcal{D}$ updates Z with any relevant state information.
11. Output Z.

Fig. 4. Hybrid LeakA_q^m

LeakB_q^m: For $q = 1$, LeakB_1^m follows the hybrid LeakA_1^m except for the following change: in LeakB_1^m, we replace the values x_j^1, for each $j \in \mathcal{S}_1$ with random, instead of evaluating the h layers of masking to get x_j^1 (and hence x_j^1's for $j \in \mathcal{S}_1$ are independent of $m_{\mathcal{S}_1}$, s^i and the shares of s^i, for each $1 < i \leq h$). Note that in LeakA_1^m, the shares Sh_j corresponding to $\mathcal{S}_1$ no longer depend on the seed s^1. We carefully use the adaptive extractor security of Ext^1 to move to LeakB_1^m. In general, for each $1 < q \leq h$, the only change we make in LeakB_q^m (in comparison

---

LeakB_q^m

1. Initialize Z to be a null string and $\mathcal{S}_1, \cdots, \mathcal{S}_h$ to be null sets.
2. $(m_1, \cdots, m_n) \leftarrow \mathsf{MShare}(m)$
3. For $i \in [h]$, choose $s^i \in_R \{0,1\}^{d_i}$
4. For $i \in [h]$ and $j \in [n]$, choose $w_j^i \in_R \{0,1\}^{n_i}$
5. For $i \in [h] \backslash [q]$, compute $(sd_1^i, \cdots, sd_n^i) \leftarrow \mathsf{SdShare}^i(s^i)$
6. For $i \in [q]$, let $\widetilde{s}^i = 0^d$
7. For $j \in [n]$, define $y_j^{h+1} = m_j$
8. **Leakage Phase:**
   (a) For $c \leftarrow 1$ to q
      i. $(\widetilde{sd}_1^c, \cdots, \widetilde{sd}_n^c) \leftarrow \mathsf{SdShare}^c(\widetilde{s}^c)$
      ii. For upto $(t-1)$ times
         A. $(j, f_j) \leftarrow \mathcal{D}(Z)$
         B. Choose $x_j^c \in_R \{0,1\}^{l_c}$ and compute $y_j^c = (x_j^c \| \widetilde{sd}_j^c)$
         C. For $i \leftarrow c - 1$ down to 1
            compute $x_j^i = y_j^{i+1} \oplus \mathsf{Ext}^i(w_j^i; s^i)$ and $y_j^i = (x_j^i \| sd_j^i)$
         D. Define $Sh_j = (w_j^1, \cdots, w_j^h, y_j^1)$
         E. Add j to $\mathcal{S}_c$ and append $(j, f_j, f_j(Sh_j))$ to Z
      iii. $(sd_1^c, \cdots, sd_n^c) \leftarrow \mathsf{SdShare}^c(s^c | \widetilde{sd}_{\mathcal{S}_c}^c)$
   (b) For $j \in [n] \backslash \mathcal{S}_{[q]}$ and $i \leftarrow h$ to 1, ($\mathcal{S}_{[q]}$ denotes a null set when $q = 0$)
      compute $x_j^i = y_j^{i+1} \oplus \mathsf{Ext}^i(w_j^i; s^i)$ and $y_j^i = (x_j^i \| sd_j^i)$
   (c) Define $Sh_j = (w_j^1, \cdots, w_j^h, y_j^1)$
   (d) For $c \leftarrow q + 1$ to h
      i. For upto $t - 1$ times
         A. $(j, f_j) \leftarrow \mathcal{D}(Z)$

         B. Add j to $\mathcal{S}_c$ and append $(j, f_j, f_j(Sh_j))$ to Z
9. **Reveal phase**
   (a) For upto $t - 1$ times
      i. $j \leftarrow \mathcal{D}(Z)$
      ii. Append (j, Sh_j) to Z
10. $\mathcal{D}$ updates Z with any relevant state information.
11. Output Z.

Fig. 5. Hybrid LeakB_q^m

to the previous hybrid LeakA_q^m) is that we replace the values x_j^q, for each $j \in \mathcal{S}_q$ with random, instead of evaluating the $h - (q - 1)$ layers of masking to get x_j^q (and hence, for these queries in $\mathcal{S}_q$, s^i and the shares of s^i, for each $q < i \leq h$, and the shares m are not used to evaluate x_j^q). Further, we continue the steps of masking to evaluate $x_j^{q-1}, x_j^{q-2}, \cdots, x_j^1$, for each $j \in \mathcal{S}_q$ as in the previous hybrid. The hybrid is formally described in Fig. 5.

LeakC^m: In the hybrid LeakB_h^m, all the shares used in the leakage phase are independent of the shares of the message m. Hence, the only part of the view of $\mathcal{D}$ that depends on the shares of m corresponds to the reveal phase. In the final hybrid LeakC^m, we replace the $t - 1$ shares of m used in the reveal phase by shares of 0^l. This hybrid is formally described in Fig. 6.

The formal descriptions of all hybrids are given below with the change from the prior hybrid highlighted in red color.

LeakC^m

1. Initialize Z to be a null string and $\mathcal{S}_1, \cdots, \mathcal{S}_h$ to be null sets.
2. Let $\tilde{m} = 0^l$ and $(\tilde{m}_1, \cdots, \tilde{m}_n) \leftarrow \mathsf{MShare}(\tilde{m})$
3. For $i \in [h]$, choose $s^i \in_R \{0, 1\}^{d_i}$
4. For $i \in [h]$, let $\tilde{s}^i = 0^d$
5. For $i \in [h]$ and $j \in [n]$, choose $w_j^i \in_R \{0, 1\}^{\eta_i}$
6. **Leakage Phase:**
   (a) For $c \leftarrow 1$ to h
       i. $(\tilde{sd}_1^c, \cdots, \tilde{sd}_n^c) \leftarrow \mathsf{SdShare}^c(\tilde{s}^c)$
       ii. For upto $(t - 1)$ times
           A. $(j, f_j) \leftarrow \mathcal{D}(Z)$
           B. Choose $x_j^c \in_R \{0, 1\}^{l_c}$ and compute $y_j^c = (x_j^c || \tilde{sd}_j^c)$
           C. For $i \leftarrow c - 1$ down to 1
              compute $x_j^i = y_j^{i+1} \oplus \mathsf{Ext}^i(w_j^i; s^i)$ and $y_j^i = (x_j^i || sd_j^i)$
           D. Define $Sh_j = (w_j^1, \cdots, w_j^h, y_j^1)$
           E. Add j to $\mathcal{S}_c$ and append $(j, f_j, f_j(Sh_j))$ to Z
       iii. $(sd_1^c, \cdots, sd_n^c) \leftarrow \mathsf{SdShare}^c(s^c | \tilde{sd}_{\mathcal{S}_c}^c)$
7. **Reveal phase**
   (a) For upto $t - 1$ times
       i. $j \leftarrow \mathcal{D}(Z)$
       ii. Define $y_j^{h+1} = \tilde{m}_j$
       iii. For $i \leftarrow h$ to 1, compute $x_j^i = y_j^{i+1} \oplus \mathsf{Ext}^i(w_j^i; s^i)$ and $y_j^i = (x_j^i || sd_j^i)$
       iv. Define $Sh_j = (w_j^1, \cdots, w_j^h, y_j^1)$
       v. Append (j, Sh_j) to Z
8. $\mathcal{D}$ updates Z with any relevant state information.
9. Output Z.

Fig. 6. Hybrid LeakC^m. (Color figure online)

We begin by proving the statistical closeness of LeakA_q^m and LeakB_{q-1}^m, for each $q \in [h]$, which follows from adaptive privacy of $\mathsf{SdShare}^q$, as atmost only $t-1$ dummy seed shares are used.

Claim 1. *For $q \in [h]$, if $\mathsf{SdShare}^q$ is ϵ_q'-adaptively private against (n,t)-threshold access structures, then $\mathsf{LeakA}_q^m \approx_{\epsilon_q'} \mathsf{LeakB}_{q-1}^m$.*

Proof. **Answering the first $(q-1)$ sets of leakage queries (when $q > 1$):** Observe that the hybrids are identical up to answering the first $(q-1)(t-1)$ leakage queries and differ in answering the remaining queries. For any $k \in [q-1]$ and, $j \in \mathcal{S}_k$ the leakage response only depends on $\widetilde{sd}_j^k, w_j^1, \cdots, w_j^h$ and $\{s^i, sd_j^i\}_{1 \leq i < k}$ (as x_j^k is chosen uniformly). We let Pre denote the union of these random variables upon which the leakage responses to $j \in \mathcal{S}_{[q-1]}$ depend.

Answering the qth Set of Leakage Queries: Consider $j \in \mathcal{S}_q$. To answer this leakage query, it suffices to compute $Sh_j = (w_j^1, \cdots, w_j^h, y_j^1)$. The hybrids only differ in computation of y_j^1 (particularly in computation of y_j^q, which is used to compute y_j^1) and the distribution of extractor sources is identical in both. We highlight the differences here. LeakA_q^m (Step 8-(a)-ii-C), iteratively computes $y_j^h, \cdots, y_j^q, \cdots, y_j^1$ as follows.

- $(y_j^h, \cdots, y_j^{q+1})$ are computed using y_j^{h+1} and $\{w_j^i, sd_j^i, s^i\}_{i \in [h] \setminus [q]}$. Note that the distribution of $y_j^h, \cdots, y_j^{q+1}$ is identical in both hybrids.
- x_j^q is computed using y_j^{q+1}, w^q and s^q. x_j^q is also identical in both hybrids.
- y_j^q is computed as $x_j^q || \widetilde{sd}_j^q$ (where $\widetilde{sd}_{[n]}^q$ are shares of a dummy seed $\widetilde{s}^q$ which are generated before answering any queries in $\mathcal{S}_q$ in Step 8-(a)-i (when $c = q$)). Whereas in LeakB_{q-1}^m, $y_j^q = x_j^q || sd_j^q$ (where $sd_{[n]}^q$ are shares of s^q)
- $(y_j^{q-1}, \cdots, y_j^1)$ are computed using y_j^q and $\{sd_j^i, w_j^i, s^i\}_{i \in [q-1]}$. The computation of $(y_j^{q-1}, \cdots, y_j^1)$ given the later random variables is again identical to LeakB_{q-1}^m.
- Now LeakA_q^m defines $Sh_j = (w_j^1, \cdots, w_j^h, y_j^1)$

For convenience, in this proof we distinguish (whenever necessary) the random variables that have same literal in both the hybrids but are distributionally different with subscripts A and B respectively. For example, $y_{j,A}^q$ and $y_{j,B}^q$ denote the distributions of y_j^q in LeakA_q^m and, LeakB_{q-1}^m respectively.

Let $\mathsf{Pre}' = (\{w_j^q, \{sd_j^i, w_j^i, s^i\}_{i \in [h] \setminus \{q\}}\}_{j \in [n] \setminus \mathcal{S}_{[q-1]}})$. Pre' captures the information required to answer all queries after the first $q-1$ sets of leakage queries, except for any information regarding $s^q, \widetilde{s}^q$ and their shares. Note that Pre' is identical in both hybrids[9]. Since, $|\mathcal{S}_q| \leq t-1$, with a reduction to adaptive privacy of $\mathsf{SdShare}^q$ we have

---

[9] Pre' possibly repeats some information already there in Pre. For example for $q = 2$, s^1 is there in both Pre and Pre'. It is for the ease of exposition that we have this repetition.

$$\mathsf{Pre}, \mathsf{Pre}', s^q, \widetilde{s}^q, \{\widetilde{sd}_j^q\}_{j \in \mathcal{S}_{q,A}} \approx_{\epsilon_q'} \mathsf{Pre}, \mathsf{Pre}', s^q, \widetilde{s}^q, \{sd_j^q\}_{j \in \mathcal{S}_{q,B}}$$

as $(\mathsf{Pre}, \mathsf{Pre}')$ is independent of the randomness used to generate the shares of $\widetilde{s}^q$ and s^q. Note that the information on LHS suffices to answer the first q sets of queries as per LeakA_q^m. Similarly, RHS suffices to answer queries in $\mathcal{S}_{[q]}$ as per LeakB_{q-1}^m. Therefore, we have,

$$\mathsf{Pre}, \mathsf{Pre}', s^q, \widetilde{s}^q, \{\widetilde{sd}_j^q\}_{j \in \mathcal{S}_{q,A}}, Z_{[q],A} \approx_{\epsilon_q'} \mathsf{Pre}, \mathsf{Pre}', s^q, \widetilde{s}^q, \{sd_j^q\}_{j \in \mathcal{S}_{q,B}}, Z_{[q],B} \quad (1)$$

Answering the Leakage and Reveal Queries Made After the qth Set of Leakage Queries: After all the qth set leakage queries are answered, LeakA_q^m computes $(sd_1^q, \cdots, sd_n^q) \leftarrow \mathsf{SdShare}^q(s^q | \widetilde{sd}_{\mathcal{S}_{q,A}}^q)$. Given $(sd_1^q, \cdots, sd_n^q), s^q, \mathsf{Pre}$ and Pre', for any $j \in [n] \backslash \mathcal{S}_q$, Sh_j is easily computed (Steps 8-(b) and 8-(c)). With this, any further queries can be correctly answered as per LeakA_q^m. Let $(\widehat{sd}_1^q, \cdots, \widehat{sd}_n^q) \leftarrow \mathsf{SdShare}^q(s^q | sd_{\mathcal{S}_{q,B}}^q)$. By Lemma 2, we have

$$\mathsf{Pre}, \mathsf{Pre}', s^q, \widetilde{s}^q, Z_{[q],A}, sd_{[n],A}^q \approx_{\epsilon_q'} \mathsf{Pre}, \mathsf{Pre}', s^q, \widetilde{s}^q, Z_{[q],B}, \widehat{sd}_{[n],B}^q$$

Note that $\widehat{sd}_{[n]}^q$ is identical to $sd_{[n],B}^q$ (of LeakB_{q-1}^m) even given s^q and $\{sd_j^q\}_{j \in \mathcal{S}_q}$ by the property of consistent resampling in Claim 5. Therefore, we have,

$$\mathsf{Pre}, \mathsf{Pre}', s^q, Z_{[q],A}, sd_{[n],A}^q \approx_{\epsilon_q'} \mathsf{Pre}, \mathsf{Pre}', s^q, Z_{[q],B}, sd_{[n],B}^q$$

Since the above LHS and RHS are sufficient to answer any further queries, we have

$$Z_{[h+1],A} \approx_{\epsilon_q'} Z_{[h+1],B}$$

which proves the claim.

Now, we prove the statistical closeness of LeakA_q^m and LeakB_q^m, for each $q \in [h]$ using the adaptive extractor security. The high-level idea behind the reduction is that in hybrid LeakA_q^m, the shares corresponding to the first $q(t-1)$ queries (i.e., $\mathcal{S}_{[q]}$) no longer depend on the seed s^q and hence, we can use the adaptive extractor security of Ext^q to move to LeakB_q^m.

Claim 2. *For $q \in [h]$, if Ext^q is an $(\eta_q, \mu_q + \tau, d_q, l_q, \delta_q')$- extractor that is $(\mathsf{Full}_\tau, \delta_q)$-adaptive, then $\mathsf{LeakA}_q^m \approx_{(t-1)\delta_q} \mathsf{LeakB}_q^m$*

Proof. Observe that the hybrids are identical up to answering the first $(q-1)(t-1)$ leakage queries and differ in answering the qth set of queries. Further, after answering the qth set of leakage queries, the responses to all remaining leakage/reveal queries are answered identically in both hybrids.

Answering the first $(q-1)$ Sets of Leakage Queries (when $q > 1$):
For any $k \in [q-1]$ and $j \in \mathcal{S}_k$ the leakage response only depends on $\widetilde{sd}_j^k$, $w_j^1, \cdots, w_j^h, \{s^i, sd_j^i\}_{1 \leq i < k}$ and x_j^k, where the latter is uniformly chosen. We let

Pre denote the leakage responses $Z_{[q-1]}$ and the union of these random variables upon which the leakage responses to $j \in \mathcal{S}_{[q-1]}$ depend.

Answering the qth Set of Leakage Queries:

Consider $j \in \mathcal{S}_q$ and f_j be the corresponding leakage function. To answer this leakage query, we require computing $f_j(Sh_j)$ where $Sh_j = (w_j^1, \cdots, w_j^h, y_j^1)$. The hybrids only differ in computation of y_j^1 (particularly in computation of x_j^q, which is used to compute y_j^1) and the distribution of extractor sources is identical in both. The hybrids iteratively computes $y_j^q, \cdots, y_j^1$ as follows.

- x_j^q is chosen uniformly from $\{0,1\}^{l_q}$ in LeakB_q^m. In contrast, x_j^q of LeakA_q^m depended on $\mathsf{Ext}^q(w_j^q; s^q)$ and y_j^{q+1}.
- $(y_j^q, \cdots, y_j^1)$ is determined given $x_j^q, \tilde{sd}_j^q$ and $\{sd_j^i, w_j^i, s^i\}_{i \in [q-1]}$ in both the hybrids.
- Both hybrids define $Sh_j = (w_j^1, \cdots, w_j^h, y_j^1)$

Let $\mathsf{Pre'} = \{w_j^i, sd_j^i, s^i, y_j^{h+1}, \tilde{sd}_j^q\}_{i \in [h] \backslash \{q\}, j \in [n] \backslash \mathcal{S}_{[q-1]}}$. We capture $\mathsf{Pre'}$ as the information which along with $\{w_j^q, s^q\}_{j \in \mathcal{S}_q}$ is sufficient to answer any leakage queries on $j \in \mathcal{S}_q$. Also, $\mathsf{Pre'}$ is identical in both hybrids.

Let $j_1, \cdots, j_{t-1}$ be the order of indices in which leakage queries are made in $\mathcal{S}_q$. Firstly, we prove that $(\mathsf{Pre}, \mathsf{Pre'}, f_{j_1}(Sh_{j_1}))$ of both hybrids are statistically close. After that we proceed to show that $(\mathsf{Pre}, \mathsf{Pre'}, f_{j_1}(Sh_{j_1}), \cdots, f_{j_{(t-1)}}(Sh_{j_{(t-1)}}))$ of both the hybrids are statistically close, which implies that the hybrids are statistically close up to answering first q sets of queries. For convenience, in this proof we distinguish (whenever necessary) the random variables that have same literal in the hybrids but are distributionally different with subscripts A and B respectively. For example, $x_{j,A}^q$ and $x_{j,B}^q$ denote the distributions of x_j^q in LeakA_q^m and LeakB_q^m respectively.

Firstly, in both hybrids the distribution of (j_1, f_{j_1}) only depends on $Z_{[q-1]}$ (and any internal randomness of $\mathcal{D}$) and hence are identical. Note that given $\mathsf{Pre'}$, $f_{j_1}(Sh_{j_1})$ in LeakA_q^m, can be captured as Full_r-adaptive leakage on the extractor source $w_{j_1}^q$ and $(x_{j_1,A}^q =) \mathsf{Ext}^q(w_{j_1}^q; s^q) \oplus y_{j_1}^{q+1}$. This is because $(y_{j_1}^{q+1}, \mathsf{Pre'})$ are independent of $(w_{j_1}^q, s^q)$. Let g_1 be a function that takes $\mathsf{Pre'}, w_{j_1}^q$ and $x_{j_1,A}^q$ (or $x_{j_1,B}^q$) as input, computes $y_{j_1,A}^1$ (or $y_{j_1,B}^1$) and outputs $f_j(w_{j_1}^1, \cdots, w_{j_1}^h, y_{j_1,A}^1)$ (or $f_j(w_{j_1}^1, \cdots, w_{j_1}^h, y_{j_1,B}^1)$). With a reduction to adaptive security of Ext^q we have

$$\mathsf{Pre}, \mathsf{Pre'}, s^q, g_1(\mathsf{Pre'}, w_{j_1}^q, \mathsf{Ext}^q(w_{j_1}^q; s^q) \oplus y_j^{q+1})$$
$$\approx_{\delta_q} \mathsf{Pre}, \mathsf{Pre'}, s^q, g_1(\mathsf{Pre'}, w_{j_1}^q, U_{l_q} \oplus y_j^{q+1})$$
$$\equiv \mathsf{Pre}, \mathsf{Pre'}, s^q, g_1(\mathsf{Pre'}, w_{j_1}^q, x_{j_1,B}^q)$$

Therefore

$$\mathsf{Pre}, \mathsf{Pre'}, s^q, f_{j_1}(Sh_{j_1,A}) \approx_{\delta_q} \mathsf{Pre}, \mathsf{Pre'}, s^q, f_{j_1}(Sh_{j_1,B})$$

With this, we showed that the hybrids are statistically close up to responding to the first query in the qth set. Although, superficially, it may seem that all the leakage responses corresponding to $j \in \mathcal{S}_q$ can be captured as adaptive extractor leakage on the source w_j^q, but it's not the case because of the following subtlety. The extractor sources used in each query are independent of each other, but the seed is the same. For example, one cannot directly capture $f_{j_2}(Sh_{j_2})$ as Full_τ-adaptive leakage (as we did with $f_{j_1}(Sh_{j_1})$). This is because the choice of j_2, f_{j_2} depends on $f_{j_1}(Sh_{j_1})$ which in turn depends on $\mathsf{Ext}^q(w_j^q; s^q)$, and hence is not independent of the seed s^q. We observe in Lemma 8 that adaptive extractors allow us to handle even such (stronger) form of adaptive leakages across different sources with same seed.

Proceeding, with a reduction to Lemma 8 with $k = (t-1), \{W_i = W_{j_i}^q :$ $i \in [k]\}$, $S = s^q$ and $\mathsf{Ext} = \mathsf{Ext}^q$ and the ith leakage function being g_i such that g_i (hardwired with $\mathsf{Pre}', y_{j_i}^{q+1}$) takes $w_{j_i}^q$ and $\mathsf{Ext}^q(w_{j_i}^q; s^q)$ (resp. U_{l_q}) as input, computes $y_{j_i,A}^1$ (resp. $y_{j_i,B}^1$) and outputs $f_{j_i}(w_{j_i}^1, \cdots, w_{j_i}^h, y_{j_i,A}^1)$ (resp. $f_{j_i}(w_{j_i}^1, \cdots, w_{j_i}^h, y_{j_i,B}^1)$).

$$\mathsf{Pre}, \mathsf{Pre}', s^q, \{f_{j_i}, f_{j_i}(Sh_{j_i,A})\}_{j_i \in \mathcal{S}_{q,A}}, \mathcal{S}_{q,A}$$

$$\approx_{(t-1)\delta_q} \mathsf{Pre}, \mathsf{Pre}', s^q, \{f_{j_i}, f_{j_i}(Sh_{j_i,B})\}_{j_i \in \mathcal{S}_{q,B}}, \mathcal{S}_{q,B}$$

This shows that the hybrids are statistically close up to answering the first q sets of leakage queries.

Answering the Leakage and Reveal Queries Made After the qth Set of Leakage Queries: After all the qth set of leakage queries are answered, both hybrids compute $(sd_1^q, \cdots, sd_n^q) \leftarrow \mathsf{SdShare}(s^q | \widetilde{sd}_{\mathcal{S}_q}^q)$. Let $\mathsf{Pre}'' = \{w_j^q, sd_j^q, s^q\}_{j \in [n] \setminus \mathcal{S}_q}$. Note that Pre' in conjunction with Pre'' completely defines Sh_j for any $j \in [n] \setminus \mathcal{S}_{[q]}$. Since Pre'' corresponding to LeakA_q^m (resp. LeakB_q^m) is only correlated to $\mathcal{S}_q, s^q$ and $\widetilde{sd}_{\mathcal{S}_q}^q$ (which is in Pre') of the respective hybrids, we have

$$\mathsf{Pre}, \mathsf{Pre}', \mathsf{Pre}''_A, s^q, \{f_{j_i}, f_{j_i}(Sh_{j_i,A})\}_{j_i \in \mathcal{S}_{q,A}}, \mathcal{S}_{q,A}$$

$$\approx_{(t-1)\delta_q} \mathsf{Pre}, \mathsf{Pre}', \mathsf{Pre}''_B, s^q, \{f_{j_i}, f_{j_i}(Sh_{j_i,B})\}_{j_i \in \mathcal{S}_{q,B}}, \mathcal{S}_{q,B}$$

Since responses to leakage/reveal queries after the qth set are can be derived from the LHS and RHS respectively depending on the hybrid, we have

$$Z_{[h+1],A} \approx_{(t-1)\delta_q} Z_{[h+1],B}$$

This proves the claim.

Finally, we use the adaptive security of MShare to show that LeakC^m is statistically close to LeakB_h^m.

Claim 3. *If MShare is ϵ-adaptively private against (n,t)-threshold access structures, then $\mathsf{LeakC}^m \approx_\epsilon \mathsf{LeakB}_h^m$.*

Proof. The hybrids answer the leakage queries identically and differ only in answering the reveal queries.

Answering the Leakage Queries:

For any $k \in [h]$ and $j \in \mathcal{S}_k$ the leakage response only depends on $\widetilde{sd}_j^k$, $w_j^1, \cdots, w_j^h$, $\{s^i, sd_j^i\}_{1 \le i < k}$ and x_j^k, where the latter is uniformly chosen. We let Pre denote the leakage responses $Z_{[h]}$ and the union of these random variables upon which the leakage responses to $j \in \mathcal{S}_{[h]}$ depend.

Answering the Reveal Queries: Let $\mathsf{Pre}' = \{w_j^i, sd_j^i, s^i\}_{i \in [h], j \in [n] \setminus \mathcal{S}_{[h]}}$. Note that given y_j^{h+1} for all j queried in the reveal phase, $(\mathsf{Pre}, \mathsf{Pre}')$ has sufficient information to answer all the reveal queries.

- LeakB_h^m samples $(m_1, \cdots, m_n) \leftarrow \mathsf{MShare}(m)$ and sets $y_j^{h+1} = m_j$ for all j queried in the reveal phase.
- LeakC^m samples $(\tilde{m}_0, \cdots, \tilde{m}) \leftarrow \mathsf{MShare}(\tilde{m})$ and sets $y_j^{h+1} = \tilde{m}_j$ for all j queried in the reveal phase.

Let $\mathsf{RevealB}$ and $\mathsf{RevealC}$ denote the sets of indices queried in the reveal phase of LeakB_h^m and LeakC^m respectively. As reveal queries are at most $t-1$ in number, we now invoke adaptive privacy of MShare and get

$$\mathsf{Pre}, \mathsf{Pre}', \tilde{m}, m, \{m_j\}_{j \in \mathsf{RevealB}} \approx_\epsilon \mathsf{Pre}, \mathsf{Pre}', \tilde{m}, m, \{\tilde{m}_j\}_{j \in \mathsf{RevealC}}$$

Note that $(\mathsf{Pre}, \mathsf{Pre}')$ is independent of the randomness used in generating shares of m and $\tilde{m}$, therefore adaptive privacy of MShare can be invoked even given these random variables.

Since Sh_j for j queried in reveal phase of LeakB_h^m (resp. LeakC^m) is determined by the above LHS (resp. RHS) we have

$$\underbrace{Z_{[h+1]}}_{of\ \mathsf{LeakB}_q^m} \approx_\epsilon \underbrace{Z_{[h+1]}}_{of\ \mathsf{LeakC}^m}$$

With the above claims and use of triangle inequality we know that for any message m, $\mathsf{Leak}_{Share^h}^m \approx_{\epsilon + \sum_{i \in [h]}((t-1)\delta_i + \epsilon_i')} \mathsf{LeakC}^m$. Note that the description of LeakC^m is independent of m. Hence for any message $m \ne m'$, we have $\mathsf{LeakC}^m \equiv \mathsf{LeakC}^{m'}$. Since, $\mathsf{Leak}_{Share^h}^{m'} \approx_{h\epsilon' + h(t-1)\delta + \epsilon} \mathsf{LeakC}^{m'}$ we get

$$\mathsf{Leak}_{Share^h}^m \approx_{2\epsilon + 2\sum_{i \in [h]}((t-1)\delta_i + \epsilon_i')} \mathsf{Leak}_{Share^h}^{m'}$$

4.4   Parameters

For $i \in [h]$, we instantiate $\mathsf{SdShare}^i$ on seeds of length d_i with the (adaptively) private Shamir secret sharing scheme, which results in individual seed share length being d_i. We instantiate MShare on messages of length l_i with the (adaptively) private Shamir secret sharing scheme, which results in individual seed share length being l_i.

Recall Lemma 7 which states that for any $c > 1$, there exists constants α, β such that $d \leq \alpha l$, $\mu \leq \beta l$, $\eta \geq \beta l + \tau$, $\epsilon = 2^{-cl}$ and $\delta = 2^{-(c-1)l+2}$ when $l = \omega(\log \eta)$. Fix any $c > 1$, and constants α, β corresponding to this c given by Lemma 7. For each $i \in [h]$, we instantiate $(\eta_i, \mu_i + \tau, d_i, l_i, \delta_i')$-extractor Ext^i that is $(\mathsf{Full}_\tau, \delta_i)$-adaptive as per this lemma as follows:

- We set $l_1 = l$, $\delta_1' = 2^{-cl}$, $\delta_1 = 2^{-\Omega(l)}$, $d_1 \leq \alpha l_1$, $\mu_1 \leq \beta l_1$ and $\eta_1 = \beta l_1 + \tau$.
- For $i > 1$, we set $l_i = l_{i-1} + d_{i-1}$, $\delta_i' = 2^{-cl_i}$, $\delta_i = 2^{-\Omega(l_i)}$, $d_i \leq \alpha l_i$, $\mu_i \leq \beta l_i$ and $\eta_i = \beta l_i + \tau$.

With this setting, individual share length of Share^h is $l_h + d_h + \sum_{i \in [h]} \eta_i = h\tau + \Theta((1+\alpha)^h l)$. Therefore, Share^h acheives constant rate and constant leakage rate whenever $\tau = \mathcal{O}(l)$ and either $n = \Theta(t)$ or h is a constant.

As our instantiations of $\mathsf{SdShare}^i$'s and MShare are perfectly adaptively private, we have Share^h to be a perfectly adaptively private secret sharing scheme which is $t \cdot 2^{-\Omega(l)}$-leakage resilient against the adaptive leakage and reveal model.

4.5 LRSS for Joint Leakage and Reveal Model

4.5.1 Joint Leakage and Reveal Model $\mathcal{J}^{X, \psi, \tau}$

The model allows for ψ number of joint leakage queries on disjoint sets where each query depends on X number of shares and additionally also reveals $t - 1$ of the remaining shares (on which leakage isn't queried) in clear. The parameter τ captures the amount of leakage provided in each leakage query.

Let $(Share, Rec)$ (where $Share : \{0,1\}^l \rightarrow (\{0,1\}^\gamma)^n$) be a secret sharing scheme for an (n, t)- threshold access structure. We formalize leakage obtained in this model on shares of a message m as JLeak^m_{Share} in Fig. 7, where an arbitrary stateful distinguisher $\mathcal{D}$ makes the queries. For any two messages m and m', we require $\mathsf{JLeak}^m_{Share} \approx_{\epsilon_{lr}} \mathsf{JLeak}^{m'}_{Share}$, for $(Share, Rec)$ to be ϵ_{lr} leakage resilient against this model.

JLeak^m_{Share}:

- Initialize Z be a null string and $\mathcal{S}$ to be a null set.
- $(Sh_1, \cdots, Sh_n) \leftarrow Share(m)$
- **Leakage Phase:**
  For upto ψ times
  - $(Q_j, f_j) \leftarrow \mathcal{D}(Z)$ where $Q_j \subseteq [n]$ and $f_j : \{0,1\}^{|Q_j|\gamma} \rightarrow \{0,1\}^\tau$
  - If $Q_j \in [n] \backslash \mathcal{S}$ and $|Q_j| \leq X$,
    add elements of Q_j to $\mathcal{S}$ and append $(Q_j, f_j, f_j(Sh_{Q_j}))$ to Z
- **Reveal phase**
  For upto $t - 1$ times
  - $j \leftarrow \mathcal{D}(Z)$
  - If $j \in [n] \backslash \mathcal{S}$, append (j, Sh_j) to Z
- $\mathcal{D}$ updates Z to include any relevant state information.
- Output Z

Fig. 7. Joint LRSS definition- JLeak^m_{Share} distribution

4.5.2   Leakage Resilience of (Share^h, Rec^h) in $\mathcal{J}^{X,\psi,\tau}$ Model

Theorem 3. *For any $\psi, X > 0$ such that $\psi \cdot X \leq n - t + 1$ and $l, \tau > 0$, (Share^h, Rec^h) is an $((n,t), \varepsilon)$-secret sharing scheme for l bit messages and is ϵ_{lr}-leakage resilient in the joint leakage and reveal model $\mathcal{J}^{X,\psi,\tau}$ where $h = \lceil \frac{\psi}{\lfloor (t-1)/X \rfloor} \rceil$ and $\epsilon_{lr} = 2(\epsilon + h\epsilon' + (t - 1) \sum_{i \in [h]} 2^{Xl_i} \delta'_i))$.*

Further, there exists an instantiation of the scheme with rate is $(X^{\Theta(h)} + h\tau/l)^{-1}$. When $\tau = \Theta(l)$, X is a constant and when either $n = \Theta(t)$ or h is a constant, the scheme achieves constant rate and leakage rate asymptotically.

The proof for the joint leakage setting is very similar to the proof of Theorem 2 for the adaptive setting (on single shares). We give a complete proof of this in our full version.

Further, we can also extend our construction to get LRSS for general access structures as well, the details of which are given in the full version of our paper.

Acknowledgement. We thank all the anonymous reviewers who provided their valuable comments on an earlier version of this manuscript.

References

1. Aggarwal, D., Damgård, I., Nielsen, J.B., Obremski, M., Purwanto, E., Ribeiro, J., Simkin, M.: Stronger leakage-resilient and non-malleable secret sharing schemes for general access structures. In: Boldyreva, A., Micciancio, D. (eds.) CRYPTO 2019. LNCS, vol. 11693, pp. 510–539. Springer, Cham (2019). https://doi.org/10.1007/978-3-030-26951-7_18

2. Aggarwal, D., Dodis, Y., Jafargholi, Z., Miles, E., Reyzin, L.: Amplifying privacy in privacy amplification. In: Garay, J.A., Gennaro, R. (eds.) CRYPTO 2014. LNCS, vol. 8617, pp. 183–198. Springer, Heidelberg (2014). https://doi.org/10.1007/978-3-662-44381-1_11

3. Aggarwal, D., Dodis, Y., Kazana, T., Obremski, M.: Non-malleable reductions and applications. In: Proceedings of the Forty-Seventh Annual ACM on Symposium on Theory of Computing, STOC 2015 (2015). https://doi.org/10.1145/2746539.2746544

4. Aggarwal, D., Dodis, Y., Lovett, S.: Non-malleable codes from additive combinatorics. In: Symposium on Theory of Computing, STOC 2014 (2014). https://doi.org/10.1145/2591796.2591804

5. Badrinarayanan, S., Srinivasan, A.: Revisiting non-malleable secret sharing. In: Ishai, Y., Rijmen, V. (eds.) EUROCRYPT 2019. LNCS, vol. 11476, pp. 593–622. Springer, Cham (2019). https://doi.org/10.1007/978-3-030-17653-2_20

6. Bellare, M., Rogaway, P.: Robust computational secret sharing and a unified account of classical secret-sharing goals. In: Proceedings of the 14th ACM Conference on Computer and Communications Security. CCS 2007, Association for Computing Machinery (2007). https://doi.org/10.1145/1315245.1315268

7. Ben-Or, M., Goldwasser, S., Wigderson, A.: Completeness theorems for non-cryptographic fault-tolerant distributed computation (extended abstract). In: Simon, J. (ed.) Proceedings of the 20th Annual ACM Symposium on Theory of Computing, Chicago, Illinois, USA, 2–4 May 1988, pp. 1–10. ACM (1988). https://doi.org/10.1145/62212.62213

8. Benaloh, J., Leichter, J.: Generalized secret sharing and monotone functions. In: Goldwasser, S. (ed.) CRYPTO 1988. LNCS, vol. 403, pp. 27–35. Springer, New York (1990). https://doi.org/10.1007/0-387-34799-2_3

9. Benhamouda, F., Degwekar, A., Ishai, Y., Rabin, T.: On the local leakage resilience of linear secret sharing schemes. In: Shacham, H., Boldyreva, A. (eds.) CRYPTO 2018. LNCS, vol. 10991, pp. 531–561. Springer, Cham (2018). https://doi.org/10.1007/978-3-319-96884-1_18

10. Blakley, G.: Safeguarding cryptographic keys. In: Proceedings of the 1979 AFIPS National Computer Conference. AFIPS Press (1979)

11. Brian, G., Faonio, A., Obremski, M., Simkin, M., Venturi, D.: Non-malleable secret sharing against bounded joint-tampering attacks in the plain model. In: Micciancio, D., Ristenpart, T. (eds.) CRYPTO 2020. LNCS, vol. 12172, pp. 127–155. Springer, Cham (2020). https://doi.org/10.1007/978-3-030-56877-1_5

12. Brian, G., Faonio, A., Venturi, D.: Continuously non-malleable secret sharing for general access structures. In: Hofheinz, D., Rosen, A. (eds.) TCC 2019. LNCS, vol. 11892, pp. 211–232. Springer, Cham (2019). https://doi.org/10.1007/978-3-030-36033-7_8

13. Chattopadhyay, E., et al.: Extractors and secret sharing against bounded collusion protocols. In: 61st IEEE Annual Symposium on Foundations of Computer Science, FOCS 2020 (2020). https://doi.org/10.1109/FOCS46700.2020.00117

14. Chaum, D., Crépeau, C., Damgård, I.: Multiparty unconditionally secure protocols (extended abstract). In: Simon, J. (ed.) Proceedings of the 20th Annual ACM Symposium on Theory of Computing, Chicago, Illinois, USA, 2–4 May 1988, pp. 11–19. ACM (1988). https://doi.org/10.1145/62212.62214

15. Davì, F., Dziembowski, S., Venturi, D.: Leakage-resilient storage. In: 7th International Conference on Security and Cryptography for Networks, SCN 2010 (2010). https://doi.org/10.1007/978-3-642-15317-4_9

16. Dodis, Y., Ostrovsky, R., Reyzin, L., Smith, A.: Fuzzy extractors: how to generate strong keys from biometrics and other noisy data. SIAM J. Comput. 38(1), 97–139 (2008), arXiv:cs/0602007

17. Dziembowski, S., Pietrzak, K.: Intrusion-resilient secret sharing. In: Proceedings of the 48th Annual IEEE Symposium on Foundations of Computer Science, FOCS 2007 (2007). https://doi.org/10.1109/FOCS.2007.35

18. Faonio, A., Venturi, D.: Non-malleable secret sharing in the computational setting: adaptive tampering, noisy-leakage resilience, and improved rate. In: Boldyreva, A., Micciancio, D. (eds.) CRYPTO 2019. LNCS, vol. 11693, pp. 448–479. Springer, Cham (2019). https://doi.org/10.1007/978-3-030-26951-7_16

19. Faust, S., Rabin, T., Reyzin, L., Tromer, E., Vaikuntanathan, V.: Protecting circuits from leakage: the computationally-bounded and noisy cases. In: Gilbert, H. (ed.) EUROCRYPT 2010. LNCS, vol. 6110, pp. 135–156. Springer, Heidelberg (2010). https://doi.org/10.1007/978-3-642-13190-5_7

20. Goyal, V., Kumar, A.: Non-malleable secret sharing. In: Proceedings of the 50th Annual ACM SIGACT Symposium on Theory of Computing, STOC 2018 (2018). https://doi.org/10.1145/3188745.3188872

21. Guruswami, V., Umans, C., Vadhan, S.P.: Unbalanced expanders and randomness extractors from Parvaresh-Vardy codes. In: IEEE Conference on Computational Complexity, pp. 96–108 (2007)

22. Guruswami, V., Wootters, M.: Repairing reed-solomon codes. In: Proceedings of the Forty-eighth Annual ACM Symposium on Theory of Computing. STOC 2016. ACM, New York (2016). https://doi.org/10.1145/2897518.2897525

23. Ishai, Y., Sahai, A., Wagner, D.: Private circuits: securing hardware against probing attacks. In: Boneh, D. (ed.) CRYPTO 2003. LNCS, vol. 2729, pp. 463–481. Springer, Heidelberg (2003). https://doi.org/10.1007/978-3-540-45146-4_27

24. Kocher, P.C.: Timing attacks on implementations of Diffie-Hellman, RSA, DSS, and other systems. In: Koblitz, N. (ed.) CRYPTO 1996. LNCS, vol. 1109, pp. 104–113. Springer, Heidelberg (1996). https://doi.org/10.1007/3-540-68697-5_9

25. Kumar, A., Meka, R., Sahai, A.: Leakage-resilient secret sharing against colluding parties. In: 60th IEEE Annual Symposium on Foundations of Computer Science, FOCS 2019 (2019). https://doi.org/10.1109/FOCS.2019.00045

26. Lin, F., Cheraghchi, M., Guruswami, V., Safavi-Naini, R., Wang, H.: Non-malleable secret sharing against affine tampering. CoRR abs/1902.06195 (2019). http://arxiv.org/abs/1902.06195

27. Liu, F.-H., Lysyanskaya, A.: Tamper and leakage resilience in the split-state model. In: Safavi-Naini, R., Canetti, R. (eds.) CRYPTO 2012. LNCS, vol. 7417, pp. 517–532. Springer, Heidelberg (2012). https://doi.org/10.1007/978-3-642-32009-5_30

28. Nisan, N., Zuckerman, D.: Randomness is linear in space. J. Comput. Syst. Sci. **52**(1), 43–53 (1996)

29. Rothblum, G.N.: How to compute under $\mathcal{AC}^0$ leakage without secure hardware. In: Safavi-Naini, R., Canetti, R. (eds.) CRYPTO 2012. LNCS, vol. 7417, pp. 552–569. Springer, Heidelberg (2012). https://doi.org/10.1007/978-3-642-32009-5_32

30. Shamir, A.: How to share a secret. Commun. ACM **22**(11), 612–613 (1979)

31. Srinivasan, A., Vasudevan, P.N.: Leakage resilient secret sharing and applications. In: Boldyreva, A., Micciancio, D. (eds.) CRYPTO 2019. LNCS, vol. 11693, pp. 480–509. Springer, Cham (2019). https://doi.org/10.1007/978-3-030-26951-7_17

32. Vadhan, S.: Pseudorandomness. Foundations and Trends in Theoretical Computer Science. Now Publishers (2012). http://people.seas.harvard.edu/~salil/pseudorandomness/

33. Zimand, M.: Exposure-resilient extractors. In: 21st Annual IEEE Conference on Computational Complexity (CCC 2006). IEEE Computer Society (2006). https://doi.org/10.1109/CCC.2006.19

Secret Sharing

Upslices, Downslices, and Secret-Sharing with Complexity of 1.5^n

Benny Applebaum[(✉)] and Oded Nir

Tel Aviv University, Tel Aviv, Israel
bennyap@post.tau.ac.il, odednir@mail.tau.ac.il

Abstract. A secret-sharing scheme allows to distribute a secret s among n parties such that only some predefined "authorized" sets of parties can reconstruct the secret, and all other "unauthorized" sets learn nothing about s. The collection of authorized/unauthorized sets can be captured by a monotone function $f : \{0,1\}^n \rightarrow \{0,1\}$. In this paper, we focus on monotone functions that all their min-terms are sets of size a, and on their duals – monotone functions whose max-terms are of size b. We refer to these classes as (a,n)-*upslices* and (b,n)-*downslices*, and note that these natural families correspond to monotone a-regular DNFs and monotone $(n-b)$-regular CNFs. We derive the following results.

1. (General downslices) Every downslice can be realized with total share size of $1.5^{n+o(n)} < 2^{0.585n}$. Since every monotone function can be cheaply decomposed into n downslices, we obtain a similar result for general access structures improving the previously known $2^{0.637n+o(n)}$ complexity of Applebaum, Beimel, Nir and Peter (STOC 2020). We also achieve a minor improvement in the exponent of linear secrets sharing schemes.

2. (Random mixture of upslices) Following Beimel and Farràs (TCC 2020) who studied the complexity of random DNFs with constant-size terms, we consider the following general distribution F over monotone DNFs: For each width value $a \in [n]$, uniformly sample k_a monotone terms of size a, where $\mathbf{k} = (k_1, \ldots, k_n)$ is an arbitrary vector of non-negative integers. We show that, except with exponentially small probability, F can be realized with share size of $2^{0.5n+o(n)}$ and can be linearly realized with an exponent strictly smaller than $2/3$. Our proof also provides a candidate distribution for "exponentially-hard" access structure.

We use our results to explore connections between several seemingly unrelated questions about the complexity of secret-sharing schemes such as worst-case vs. average-case, linear vs. non-linear and primal vs. dual access structures. We prove that, in at least one of these settings, there is a significant gap in secret-sharing complexity.

© International Association for Cryptologic Research 2021
T. Malkin and C. Peikert (Eds.): CRYPTO 2021, LNCS 12827, pp. 627–655, 2021.
https://doi.org/10.1007/978-3-030-84252-9_21

1   Introduction

Secret-sharing schemes, introduced by Shamir [32] and Blakley [12], are a central cryptographic tool with a wide range of applications including secure multiparty computation protocols [9,14], threshold cryptography [17], access control [28], attribute-based encryption [22,36], and oblivious transfer [33,35]. In its general form [24], an n-party secret-sharing scheme for a family of authorized sets $F \subseteq 2^{[n]}$ (referred to as *access structure*) allows to distribute a secret s into n shares, $s_1, \ldots, s_n$, one for each party, such that: (1) every authorized set of parties, $A \in F$, can reconstruct s from its shares; and (2) every unauthorized set of parties, $A \notin F$, cannot reveal any partial information on the secret even if the parties are computationally unbounded. For example, in the canonical case of threshold secret sharing the family F contains all the sets whose cardinality exceeds some certain threshold. For this case, Shamir's scheme [32] provides a solution whose complexity, measured as the total share-size $\sum_i |s_i|$, is quasi-linear, $O(n \log n)$, in the number of parties n. Moreover, Shamir's scheme is *linear*, that is, each share can be written as a linear combination of the secret and the randomness that are taken from a finite field. This form of linearity turns to be useful for many applications. (See the full version of the paper for a formal definition of secret sharing and linear secret sharing.)

The complexity of general secret-sharing schemes. Determining the complexity of general access structures is a basic, well-known, open problem in information-theoretic cryptography. Formally, given a (monotone) access structure[1] F we let $\mathsf{SSize}(F) := \min_{\mathcal{D} \text{ realizes } F} |\mathcal{D}|$, where $|\mathcal{D}|$ denotes the total share size of a secret-sharing scheme $\mathcal{D}$. For over 30 years, since the pioneering work of Ito et al. [24], all known upper-bounds on $\mathsf{SSize}(F)$ are tightly related to the computational complexity of the characteristic function F. Here we think of F as the monotone function that given a vector $x \in \{0,1\}^n$ outputs 1 if and only if the corresponding characteristic set $A = \{i : x_i = 1\}$ is an authorized set. Specifically, it is known that the complexity of an access structure is at most polynomial in the representation size of F as a monotone CNF or DNF [24], as a monotone formula [10], as a monotone span program [25], or as a multi-target monotone span program [11]. This leads to an exponential upper-bound of $2^{n(1-o(1))}$ for any n-party access structure F.

On the other hand, despite much efforts, the best known lower-bound on the complexity of an n-party access structure is $\Omega(n^2 / \log n)$ due to [15]. Moreover, we have no better lower-bounds even for *non-explicit* functions! This leaves a huge exponential gap between the upper-bound and the lower-bound. For the case of linear schemes, a counting argument (see, e.g., [8]) shows that for most monotone functions $F : \{0,1\}^n \to \{0,1\}$, the complexity of the best linear secret-

---

[1] Monotonicity here means that for any $A \subset B$ it holds that $A \in F \Rightarrow B \in F$. It is not hard to see that a non-monotone access structure does not admit a secret-sharing scheme, and therefore this requirement is necessary.

sharing (LSS) scheme, denoted by $\mathsf{LSSize}(F)$, is at least $2^{n/2-o(n)}$.[2] Furthermore, Pitassi and Robere [30] (building on results of [29,31]) prove that for every n there exists an explicit n-input function F such that $\mathsf{LSSize}(F) = 2^{\Omega(n)}$. In his 1996 thesis [4], Beimel conjectured that an exponential lower-bound of $2^{\Omega(n)}$ also holds for the general case. Resolving this conjecture has remained one of the main open problems in the field of secret sharing [5]. Taking a broader view, similar exponential communication-complexity gaps exist for a large family of information-theoretic secure computation tasks [3,6,19,21,23]. Among these, secret-sharing is of special interest due to its elementary nature: Secret data is only *stored and revealed* without being processed or manipulated.

Recent advances: slices, multislices and general access structures. In the past three years, the seemingly tight correspondence between computational complexity and secret-sharing complexity was challenged by several works. In a breakthrough result, Liu, Vaikuntanathan and Wee [26,27] showed that *any general access structure* can be realized with complexity of $2^{0.994n}$, thus breaking the formula-size (or even circuit-size) barrier of $2^{n-o(n)}$. The exponent was further reduced to 0.64 in follow-up works of Applebaum, Beimel, Farràs, Nir and Peter [1,2]. From a technical point of view, all these works reduced the problem of realizing a general monotone function F to the problem of realizing the simpler case of *slice functions* and *multislice functions* (originally referred to as "fat slices" by [26]). Formally, $(a : b, n)$-*multislices* are monotone functions that are unconstrained on inputs x of weight $\mathrm{wt}(x) \in [a, b]$, but must take the value 0 on lighter inputs, and the value 1 on heavier inputs. An $(a : a, n)$-multislice is referred to as an (a, n)-*slice*. Roughly, the results of [26] were obtained by a sequence of 3 reductions: (1) Secret sharing for slice functions with sub-exponential share size of $2^{\tilde{O}(\sqrt{n})}$ based on constructions of Conditional Disclosure of Secrets (CDS) [27]; (2) Secret sharing for $((0.5 - \epsilon)n, (0.5 + \epsilon)n, n)$-multislices (aka ϵ-midslice) with non-trivial cost of 2^{cn} for some $c < 1$ based on slice functions; and (3) Secret sharing for general access structures with 2^{cn} complexity based on midslice secret sharing. The work of [1] showed how to improve Step 3 based on combinatorial covers, and the work of [2] improved the second step by presenting and constructing *robust-CDS* schemes. A combination of these results allows us to realize any n-party access structure by a secret sharing scheme of complexity $2^{0.64n+o(n)}$ and by a linear secret sharing scheme of complexity $2^{0.762n+o(n)}$.

Intriguing questions. This state of affairs leaves open several intriguing questions. Firstly, what is the best-achievable *exponent* of secret-sharing schemes? Secondly, which access structures are the hardest to realize? While the above results do not seem to yield sub-exponential share size, they also do not give rise to a candidate "hard" access structure. That is, to the best of our knowledge, we

---

[2] The bound holds for any finite field. From now on when the field is unspecified we take it, by default, to be the binary field. This only makes our positive results stronger.

do not have an explicit candidate distribution over access structures whose cost is $2^{\Omega(n)}$ even if one restricts the attention to the current schemes. Indeed, it was recently observed by Beimel and Farràs [7] that a randomly chosen monotone function is likely to be a $(n/2 - 1, n/2 + 2, n)$-multislice, and therefore it can be realized with sub-exponential complexity.

2   Our Contribution

We make progress towards answering the above questions by shifting the focus from slices and multislices to *downslices* and *upslices*. Before stating our results, let us introduce these new access structures.

2.1   Upslice and Downslices

A monotone function $f : \{0,1\}^n \to \{0,1\}$ is an (a,n)-upslice if all its min-terms are of size exactly a. Similarly to (a,n)-slice functions, an (a,n)-upslice is unconstrained for inputs of weight a and takes the value 0 on lighter inputs, however, in contrast to slice functions, an input y of weight larger than a takes the value 1 only if there exists a *smaller* input $x \leq y$ of weight a on which the function takes the value 1.[3] This means that f is the pointwise *smallest* function among all the monotone functions that agree with f on inputs of weight a. Downslices are defined in a dual way. That is, a monotone function f is a (b,n)-downslice if all its *max-terms* are of size exactly b. This means that f is unconstrained over b-weight inputs, takes the value 1 on heavier inputs, and (unlike slice functions) evaluates to 0 on an input y of weight smaller than b only if there exists a *larger* input $x \geq y$ of weight b on which the function evaluates to 0. Accordingly, f is the pointwise *largest* function among all the monotone functions that agree with f on inputs of weight b. (An example of upslices and downslices is depicted in Fig. 1).

Why Upslices and Downslices? Upslices and downslices are natural classes of monotone functions. Indeed, (a,n)-upslices (resp., (b,n)-downslices) are exactly the functions that can be represented by logical formulas in a Disjunctive Normal Form (resp., Conjunctive Normal Form) in which each term (resp., clause) consists of exactly a variables (resp., $n - b$ variables). Therefore, these function families capture the basic computational models of regular monotone-DNFs and regular monotone-CNFs. Additionally, every monotone function can be decomposed into a disjunction of its upslices, i.e., $f = \bigvee_{a \in [n]} f_a$ where f_a is the (a,n)-slice function that agrees with f on its a-weight inputs (hereafter referred to as the a-*upslice of* f). Similarly, f can be written as a conjunction of its downslices. Using standard closure properties of secret sharing, we conclude that the secret-sharing complexity of worst-case monotone functions is at most n times larger

---

[3] We use the standard partial order over strings that is induced by inclusion over the corresponding characteristic sets. That is, $x \leq y$ if for every index i it holds that $x_i \leq y_i$.

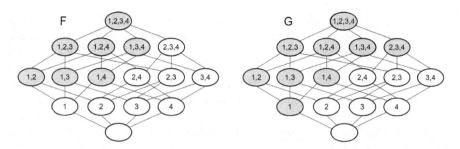

Fig. 1. An example of a 2-upslice access structure F and a 2-downslice access structure G. Both access structures are defined over 4 parties and colored nodes correspond to authorized sets. Note that in this example F and G agree on sets of size 2.

than the secret-sharing complexity of downslices/upslices. This should be contrasted with the status of "simple" slice functions whose complexity seems significantly smaller (i.e., sub-exponential) than the complexity of general monotone functions. Indeed, one can show that the complexity of an a-slice function f is the smallest among all monotone functions that agree with f on inputs of weight a (ignoring low-order terms).[4] For general values of a and b, the best known secret sharing schemes of (a, n)-upslices and (b, n)-downslices are based on their DNF and CNF representations and therefore have total share size of $\binom{n}{a}$ and $\binom{n}{b}$, respectively. Up to logarithmic improvements, these worst-case bounds have remained unchanged even for the special case of $(2, n)$-upslices that correspond to *graph* access structures [13] (not to be confused with *forbidden graph* access structures [34] that correspond to $(2, n)$-slices). See [7] for additional references.

2.2 Worst-Case Downslices

In Sect. 4 we show that every (b, n)-downslice admits a secret sharing scheme with complexity of $(3/2)^{n+o(n)}$. Using the completeness of downslices this allows us to improve the complexity of general access structures. Formally, following [2], we define the *secret-sharing exponent* of a monotone function $f : \{0, 1\}^n \to \{0, 1\}$, denoted by $\mathbf{S}(f) := n^{-1} \cdot \log_2 \mathrm{SSize}(f)$ and define the (worst-case) *secret-sharing exponent* $\mathbf{S}$ to be $\mathbf{S} = \limsup_{n\to\infty} \max_{f \in \mathcal{M}(n)} \mathbf{S}(f)$, where $\mathcal{M}(n)$ is the family of all monotone functions over $\{0, 1\}^n$ (equivalently, all n-party access structures). We prove the following theorem.

Theorem 2.1 (Main theorem). *Every access structure over n parties can be realized by a secret-sharing scheme with a total share-size of $1.5^{n+o(n)}$. That is,* $\mathbf{S} \le \log \frac{3}{2} < 0.585$.

---

[4] To see this, observe that if f is the a-slice of a monotone function g, we can write f as $f = (g \wedge T_{a-1}) \vee T_{a+1}$ where T_k is the k threshold function over n-bit inputs. By using standard closure properties of secret sharing, one can therefore transform a secret sharing for g into a secret sharing for f with an additive cost of $O(\log n)$.

Recall that the previous best exponent, due to [2], was 0.637. The proof of the theorem is based on two schemes for $(\beta n, n)$-downslices. The first scheme is tailored to low downslices with $\beta \leq 1/2$ and achieves an exponent of β, and the second scheme is tailored to high downslices with $\beta \geq 1/2$ and achieves an exponent of $H_2(\beta) - (1 - \beta)$ where H_2 is the binary entropy function. The most expensive downslice corresponds to the case where $\beta = 2/3$ and has an exponent of $\log(\frac{3}{2})$. (See Fig. 2 in Sect. 4.) The two schemes are based on adaptation of previous tools, such as robust-CDS and combinatorial covers, to the current setting. See Sect. 4 for details.

Linear schemes. We also obtain a minor improvement for the exponent of linear secret-sharing schemes. Let $\mathbf{S}_\ell$ denote the *linear exponent*, that is defined analogously to $\mathbf{S}$, except that $\mathsf{SSize}(F)$ is replaced with $\mathsf{LSSize}(F)$, the minimal complexity of a linear scheme that realizes F.

Theorem 2.2 (Worst-case linear exponent). *Every access structure over n parties can be realized by a linear secret sharing scheme with a total share-size of $2^{0.7576n+o(n)}$. That is, the linear exponent $\mathbf{S}_\ell$ is at most 0.7576.*

Recall that the previous best linear exponent, due to [2], was 0.762. Again the theorem is based on LSS for $(\beta n, n)$-downslices for an arbitrary density β. Unfortunately, a naive approach that mimics the proof of Theorem 2.2 yields an exponent of $\frac{1}{2} + \frac{\beta}{2}$ or, for $\beta > 0.5$, an exponent of $H_2(\beta) - \frac{1}{2}(1 - \beta)$. For densities larger than $1/2$, the exponent can be as large as 0.772 which is strictly larger than the exponent 0.762 that is achieved by [2]. To overcome this difficulty, we introduce several additional tools that are tailored to the linear setting. Most notably, we present a bootstrapping technique that starts with an LSS for a target downslice with a given density γ, transforms it into an LSS for upslices of various densities and then exploits the new schemes, to obtain a better LSS for the target $(\gamma n, n)$-downslice. We apply this procedure iteratively to several key values of γ, and use these pivots to propagate the improvement to all other values of β. See Sect. 5 for details.

2.3   Random Upslices and Mixed DNFs

Following [7], we study the complexity of randomly-chosen upslices. For this we define a family of distributions over monotone-DNFs that is parameterized by an arbitrary vector $\mathbf{k} = (k_1, \ldots, k_n)$ of non-negative integers. We sample a DNF from the $\mathbf{k}$-DNF distribution as follows: For each width parameter a, select k_a random clauses uniformly at random from the set of all possible $\binom{n}{a}$ monotone a-clauses. We prove the following theorem.

Theorem 2.3 (Average case exponents). *For every non-negative vector $\mathbf{k}$, a randomly chosen $\mathbf{k}$-DNF f can be realized with complexity of $2^{0.5n+o(n)}$ except with exponentially small probability of $2^{-\Omega(n)}$. For linear schemes, we get an exponent which is strictly smaller than $2/3$.*

Observe that there is a polynomial gap between the average-case complexity and the best-known worst-case complexity. It is instructive to compare this gap with the results of Beimel and Farràs [7] who considered (1) The uniform distribution over all access structures, and (2) the uniform distribution over $(a = O(1), n)$-upslices with exactly k_a min-terms for an arbitrary value of k_a. For these distributions, [7] have established *super-polynomial* gaps between the average case complexity and the best-known worst-case complexity. Our results may indicate that such dramatic gaps are an artifact of the chosen distribution. Technically, the proof of Theorem 2.3 extends the ideas of [7] to handle arbitrary large values of $a \in [n]$. (We note that the proof of [7] suffers from an a^a dependency and so it cannot be applied to $(a = \Omega(n), n)$-upslices.)

Candidate hard distribution. We believe that random upslices form a good candidates for *exponentially-hard* distributions. Concretely, the proof of Theorem 2.3 suggests that the hardest case (for existing schemes) corresponds to the uniform distribution over $(n/2, n)$-upslices with $\sqrt{\binom{n}{n/2}} = 2^{n/2+o(n)}$ min-terms. (Equivalently, random DNF that contains $\sqrt{\binom{n}{n/2}}$ random monotone terms of width $n/2$). We believe that identifying such a candidate hard distribution is a valuable first step towards achieving further progress either at the upper-bound front or at the lower-bound front.

Is the worst-case/average-case gap real? Recall that in the average-case, we derive an exponent of 0.5 for general schemes and an exponent slightly better than 2/3 for linear schemes, whereas the worst-case exponents are $\log(3/2)$ and slightly over 3/4 respectively. Admittedly, we do not know whether this gap is "real", and as far as we can see, there may be a way to reduce the worst-case exponents to the average-case ones. (We do not have good candidates for separation either.) While we cannot prove the existence of such a gap, we can relate it to other central questions in the complexity of secret sharing like the power of *non-linearity* and closure under *duality*. Define the *dual* access structure of an n-party access structure f to be the n-party access structure that accepts of all sets x whose complements $\bar{x}$ are unauthorized under f, i.e., $\mathrm{DUAL}(f)(x) = 1 - f(\bar{x})$. We prove the following gap theorem.

Theorem 2.4 (Gap theorem). *At least one of the following gaps hold:*

1. *(Duality gap) There exists an n-party monotone access structure[5] f whose secret-sharing exponent is strictly smaller than the secret-sharing exponent of its dual.*
2. *(Non-linearity gap) The (general) secret sharing exponent $\mathbf{S}$ is strictly smaller than the linear secret sharing exponent $\mathbf{S}_\ell$.*
3. *(Average-case gap) Every $\mathbf{k}$-DNF distribution can be realized, except with exponentially small probability, with an exponent $\bar{\mathbf{S}}$ that is strictly smaller than the worst-case secret sharing exponent $\mathbf{S}$.*

---

[5] Formally, for asymptotic purposes one should think of f as a sequence of access structures $\{f_n : \{0,1\}^n \to \{0,1\}\}_{n \in \mathbb{N}}$.

Let us elaborate on the first two possibilities. The first item asserts that $\mathsf{SSize}(f) < \mathsf{SSize}(\mathrm{DUAL}(f)) \cdot 2^{\Omega(n)}$. The *absence* of a duality gap, hereafter referred to as the *duality hypothesis*, asserts that $\mathsf{SSize}(f) = \mathsf{SSize}(\mathrm{DUAL}(f)) \cdot 2^{o(n)}$. That is, the primal and dual access structure have similar secret-sharing complexity up to sub-exponential difference. This hypothesis is known to hold for LSS, and, to the best of our knowledge, its status for general secret-sharing schemes is wide open. In fact, a recent paper of Csirmaz [16] refers to a stronger version of this hypothesis (e.g., $\mathsf{SSize}(f) = \mathsf{SSize}(\mathrm{DUAL}(f))$) as a long-standing open problem. Item 1 asserts that the complexity-gap between primal and dual structures may be exponentially large.

The second item asserts that there is an exponential gap between linear-schemes and non-linear schemes even in the worst-case! While we can prove such a result for concrete cases (e.g., random slice functions), we do not know whether non-linearity significantly helps for worst-case functions, and one may guess that eventually the two exponents $\mathbf{S}_\ell$ and $\mathbf{S}$ will collapse to, say $1/2$. Item 2 asserts that this is not the case.

Proving Theorem 2.4. To prove the theorem, we show that, under the duality hypothesis, one can improve Theorem 2.3 so that a random DNF, that is sampled from an arbitrary $\mathbf{k}$-DNF distribution, can be realized with an exponent that is strictly smaller than 0.5, except with exponentially small probability. If, in addition, there is no Average-case gap, we get that the worst-case exponent $\mathbf{S}$ is smaller than 0.5. Since it is known that the linear exponent $\mathbf{S}_\ell$ cannot be smaller that 0.5 (e.g., by counting), we conclude that the linear exponent must be strictly larger than the general exponent. (See Sect. 6).

3   Preliminaries

General. By default, all logarithms are taken to base 2. For positive integers $k \leq n$, we let $\binom{n}{\geq a} := \sum_{a \leq i \leq n} \binom{n}{i}$. We use the following standard estimate for the binomial coefficients

$$\binom{n}{k} = \Theta(k^{-1/2} 2^{\mathrm{H}_2(k/n)n}) \tag{1}$$

where $\mathrm{H}_2(\cdot)$, denotes the *binary entropy function*, that maps a real number $\alpha \in (0,1)$ to $\mathrm{H}_2(\alpha) = -\alpha \log \alpha - (1-\alpha)\log(1-\alpha)$ and is set to zero for $\alpha \in \{0,1\}$.

Secret sharing. Standard background on secret-sharing schemes is deferred to the full version of the paper, while formal definitions of slices, multislices, downslices, and upslices can be found in Appendix A. Let us just mention the following complexity conventions. Given a (monotone) access structure $f : \{0,1\}^n \to \{0,1\}$ we let $\mathsf{SSize}(f) := \min_{\mathcal{D} \text{ realizes } f} |\mathcal{D}|$, where $|\mathcal{D}|$ denotes the total share size of a secret-sharing scheme $\mathcal{D}$. The *exponent* of f is $n^{-1} \cdot \log_2 \mathsf{SSize}(f)$, and it is denoted by $\mathbf{S}(f)$. If $\mathcal{F}$ is a collection of n-party access structures then

$$\mathsf{SSize}(\mathcal{F}) := \max_{f \in \mathcal{F}} \mathsf{SSize}(f), \qquad \text{and} \qquad \mathbf{S}(\mathcal{F}) := \max_{f \in \mathcal{F}} \mathbf{S}(f).$$

When $\mathcal{F} = \{\mathcal{F}_n\}$ is a sequence of collections $\mathcal{F}_n$ of n-party access structures we think of $\mathsf{SSize}(\mathcal{F})$ as a function of n, and define the *secret-sharing exponent* $\mathbf{S}(\mathcal{F})$ to be $\mathbf{S}(\mathcal{F}) := \limsup_{n\to\infty} \mathbf{S}(\mathcal{F}_n)$. All these definitions naturally extend to the linear setting as well.

We denote by $\mathbf{D}(b,n)$ (resp., $\mathbf{D}_\ell(b,n)$) the secret-sharing exponent (resp., the LSS exponent) of (b,n)-downslices and by $\mathbf{D}(\beta)$ (resp., $\mathbf{D}_\ell(\beta)$) the secret-sharing exponent (resp., the LSS exponent) of $(\beta n, n)$-downslices. The notation $\mathbf{U}(a,n), \mathbf{U}_\ell(a,n), \mathbf{U}(\alpha)$ and $\mathbf{U}_\ell(\alpha)$ is defined analogously for the secret-sharing exponents and LSS exponents of (a,n)-upslices and $(\alpha n, n)$-upslices. The secret-sharing exponents and LSS exponents of $(a : b, n)$-multislices and $(\alpha n : \beta n, n)$-multislices are denoted by $\mathbf{M}(a : b, n), \mathbf{M}_\ell(a : b, n), \mathbf{M}(\alpha : \beta)$ and $\mathbf{M}_\ell(\alpha : \beta)$.

3.1 Covers

We will make use of the following combinatorial concept of "covers".

Definition 3.1 (Covering a slice). We say that a collection of subsets $\mathcal{G} = \{G_i\}$ over a ground set $[n]$ *upcovers* a *slice* t if for every set A of size t, exists a set $G_i \in \mathcal{G}$ such that $A \subseteq G_i$. Analogously, we say that $\mathcal{G}$ *downcovers* a slice t, if for every set A of size t, exists a set $G_i \in \mathcal{G}$ such that $G_i \subseteq A$.

We start by introducing a fact about *combinatorial covering designs* by Erdős and Spenser:

Fact 3.2 ([18]). *For every positive integers $a \leq b \leq n$, there exists a family $\mathcal{G} = \{G_i\}_{i=1}^L$ of b-subsets of $[n]$ that upcovers the slice a where $\mathcal{G}$ is of size $L = L(n,a,b) \leq \left[\binom{n}{a}/\binom{b}{a}\right]\left[1 + \log\binom{b}{a}\right].$*

We will make use of the following dual fact.

Fact 3.3. *For every positive integers $a \leq b \leq n$, there exists a family $\mathcal{G} = \{G_i\}_{i=1}^L$ of a-subsets of $[n]$ that downcovers the slice b where $\mathcal{G}$ is of size $L = L(n,a,b) \leq \left[\binom{n}{n-b}/\binom{n-a}{n-b}\right]\left[1 + \log\binom{n-a}{n-b}\right].$*

Moreover, for some constant $C > 1$, a random family $\mathcal{G}$ of a-subsets of n of size at least $\bar{L}(n,a,b) = \left[\binom{n}{a}/\binom{b}{a}\right] \cdot n$ downcovers the slice b except with probability C^{-n}.

The reader should note that $\left[\binom{n}{a}/\binom{b}{a}\right] = \left[\binom{n}{n-b}/\binom{n-a}{n-b}\right]$.

Proof. Whenever a collection $\{G_i\}_{i=1}^L$ upcovers the slice a, the collection of complement sets $\{\bar{G}_i\}_{i=1}^L$ downcovers the slice $n - a$. Fact 3.2 therefore implies the first part.

For the "Moreover" part. Sample $\mathcal{G}$ by sampling each G_i uniformly at random among all a-subsets of $[n]$. Fix some b-subset $B \subseteq [n]$. For every $i \in [L]$, the probability that $G_i \subseteq B$ is $p = \binom{b}{a}/\binom{n}{a}$, and therefore

$$\Pr[\forall i, G_i \not\subseteq B] \leq (1-p)^L = (1-p)^{n/p} < e^{-n},$$

where the equality follows by noting that $\bar{L}(n, a, b) \cdot p = n$. Therefore, by a union bound over all sets of size b, the probability that there is some b-set that does not contain any G_i is at most $\binom{n}{b} \cdot e^{-n} < 2^n \cdot e^{-n} = 1/C^n$ for $C = e/2$.   □

4   General Secret-Sharing for Downslices

Recall that $\mathbf{D}(\beta)$ and $\mathbf{D}_\ell(\beta)$ denote the secret-sharing exponent and LSS exponent of $(\beta n, n)$-downslices. The classical CNF-based scheme [24] that enumerates over all of the max-terms of size βn, yields an LSS exponent of $\mathrm{H}_2(\beta)$. One can also get an exponent of 0.637 via the general-purpose secret-sharing scheme of [2]. In this section, we improve these results and show that $\mathbf{D}(\beta) \leq \log(3/2)$ for any β.

Theorem 4.1. *Every n-party downslice access structure can be realized with complexity of $2^{\log(3/2)n+o(n)}$. Additionally, for LSS, $\mathbf{D}_\ell(\beta) \leq \frac{1}{2} + \frac{\beta}{2}$ and, for $\beta > 0.5$, it holds that $\mathbf{D}_\ell(\beta) \leq \mathrm{H}_2(\beta) - \frac{1}{2}(1 - \beta)$.*

The linear exponent will be improved in the next section. Before proving Theorem 2.1, we will need the following simple observation whose proof is deferred to the full version of the paper,.

Observation 4.2. *Let f be an access structures over n parties, and assume that F_i, the i-downslice of f, can be realized (resp., linearly realized) with total share size of S_i for every $i \in [0, n]$. Then, f can be realized (resp., linearly realized) with share size of $\sum_{i=0}^{n} S_i \leq n \max_i S_i$.*

We can now prove Theorem 2.1.

Proof (Proof of Theorem 2.1). Fix some access structure f over n parties and let F_b denote the (b, n)-downslice of f. By Theorem 4.1 the access structure F_b can be realized with total share size S_b of at most $2^{\log(\frac{3}{2})n+o(n)}$, and so by Observation 4.2, f can be realized with complexity of $\max_b(S_b) \cdot n \leq 2^{\log(\frac{3}{2})n+o(n)}$.   □

The proof of Theorem 4.1 is based on the following two lemmas.

Lemma 4.3 (low-density downslices). *Secret sharing for (b, n)-downslices can be realized (resp., linearly realized) with share size of $2^{b+o(n)}$ (resp., $2^{b/2+n/2+o(n)}$). Consequently, for any constant $\beta \in [0, 1]$, it holds that*

$$\mathbf{D}(\beta) \leq \beta \qquad and \qquad \mathbf{D}_\ell(\beta) \leq \frac{1}{2} + \frac{\beta}{2}.$$

The proof of Lemma 4.3 appears in Sect. 4.1 and it is based on a scheme for multislices that will be employed also in the next sections. Lemma 4.3 presents an improvement over previously known schemes for (b, n)-downslices in the regime $b \in [0, 0.637n]$, i.e., as long as the level b is smaller than the exponent of [2]. Higher levels, for which Lemma 4.3 provides no improvement, are treated by the following lemma.

Lemma 4.4 (high-density downslices). *For every integers n and $b \in (0.5n, n]$, every (b, n)-downslice can be realized with share size of*

$$\left[\binom{n}{n-b} / \binom{2n-2b}{n-b} \right] \cdot 2^{n-b+o(n)},$$

and can be realized by a linear scheme with share size

$$\left[\binom{n}{n-b} / \binom{2n-2b}{n-b} \right] \cdot 2^{(3n-3b)/2+o(n)}.$$

Consequently, for every constant $\beta \in (0.5, 1]$, it holds that

$$\mathbf{D}(\beta) \le \mathrm{H}_2(\beta) - (1 - \beta) \qquad and \qquad \mathbf{D}_\ell(\beta) \le \mathrm{H}_2(\beta) - \frac{1}{2}(1 - \beta).$$

We note that the maximal value of $\mathbf{D}(\beta)$ is $\log\left(\frac{3}{2}\right)$ and it is obtained when $\beta = 2/3$. Therefore, a combination of Lemma 4.3 and Lemma 4.4 yield Theorem 4.1. The proof Lemma 4.4 is deferred to Sect. 4.2 and is based on a general cover-reduction that will be also useful for the next sections.

The exponents of the above lemmas together with the CNF-based exponent and the exponent of [2] are depicted in Fig. 2.

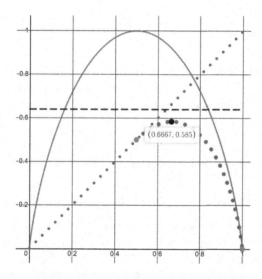

Fig. 2. A description of the exponents of four general schemes for $(\beta n, n)$-downslices. The horizontal axis represents the density β of the slice, and the vertical axis represents the resulting exponents. The solid red curve corresponds to the exponent of the CNF-based scheme. The constant exponent of the general access structures scheme of [2] appears as the dashed blue line. The dotted green straight line represents the exponent that is achieved by the scheme of Lemma 4.3, and the dotted green curve which starts at $x = 0.5$ represents the scheme for downslices of Lemma 4.4. (Color figure online)

4.1   Low-Density Downslices via Multislices

Secret sharing schemes for $(a : b, n)$ multislice access structures were considered in [1,2,26], for the special cases of "mid-slices" where $a = \left(\frac{1}{2} - \delta\right) n$, $b = \left(\frac{1}{2} + \delta\right) n$ for some constant $\delta \in [0, 0.5]$. It is possible to generalize the scheme of [2] that was originally designed to handle mid-slices to handle any pair $a < b \in [n]$ as follows. Recall that, for every constants $0 \le \alpha < \beta \le 1$, we let $\mathbf{M}(\alpha : \beta)$ (resp., $\mathbf{M}_\ell(\alpha : \beta)$) denote the exponent (resp., LSS exponent) of $(\alpha n : \beta n, n)$-multislice access structures.

Lemma 4.5 (multislice lemma). *For every $a < b \in [n]$, every $(a : b, n)$-multislice access structure can be realized by a secret-sharing scheme with share size $\binom{b}{\ge a} \cdot 2^{o(n)}$ and by a linear scheme with share size $\sqrt{\binom{b}{\ge a}} \cdot 2^{n/2 + o(n)}$. Consequently, for every constants $0 \le \alpha < \beta \le 1$, the exponent $\mathbf{M}(\alpha : \beta)$ of $(\alpha n : \beta n, n)$-multislice access structures satisfies*

$$\mathbf{M}(\alpha : \beta) \le \begin{cases} \beta \, \mathrm{H}_2\left(\frac{\alpha}{\beta}\right) & \text{if } \alpha > \beta/2 \\ \beta & \text{if } \alpha \le \beta/2 \end{cases},$$

and, for the linear case, the exponent $\mathbf{M}_\ell(\alpha : \beta)$ satisfies

$$\mathbf{M}_\ell(\alpha : \beta) \le \begin{cases} \frac{1}{2} + \frac{\beta}{2} \cdot \mathrm{H}_2\left(\frac{\alpha}{\beta}\right) & \text{if } \alpha > \beta/2 \\ \frac{1}{2} + \frac{\beta}{2} & \text{if } \alpha \le \beta/2 \end{cases}.$$

The proof follows the exact steps of the proof of Lemma 5.10 from [2] except that we use a more general setting of parameters. See the full version of the paper, for details. By using multislices to implement downslices, we derive Lemma 4.3.

Proof (Proof of Lemma 4.3). Let F be a (b, n)-downslice and let F' be the $(0 : b, n)$-multislice of F. Observe that F equals F', and so by Lemma 4.5 it can be implemented with the desired share sizes since $\binom{b}{\ge 0} = 2^b$.   □

4.2   Reducing High-Density Downslices to Low Downslices

In order to prove Lemma 4.4 we reduce the problem of realizing (b, n)-downslices for $b > 0.5n$ to the problem of realizing (b', n')-downslices over a smaller set of parties $n' < n$ and for density $b' = n'/2$. This is, in fact, a special case of the following more general reduction that will be also applied in its full power later in Sect. 5.

Lemma 4.6 (cover reduction lemma). *Let $v < b \le n$ be positive integers. If $(b - v, n - v)$-downslices can be realized (resp., linearly realized) with share size $z(b - v, n - v)$ then (b, n)-downslices can be realized (resp., linearly realized) with share size of*

$$\left[\binom{n}{n-b} \Big/ \binom{n-v}{n-b}\right] \left[1 + \log\binom{n-v}{n-b}\right] \cdot z(b - v, n - v) \tag{2}$$

Consequently, for every constants $0 < \alpha \leq \beta < 1$, if $(\alpha m, m)$-downslices can be realized (resp., linearly realized) with exponent of $z'(\alpha)$ then $(\beta n, n)$-downslices can be realized with an exponent of

$$H_2(\beta) - (1 - \beta)\left(\frac{H_2(\alpha) - z'(\alpha)}{1 - \alpha}\right). \tag{3}$$

The proof of Lemma 4.6 is deferred to Sect. 4.3.

Remark 4.7 (Generalizations of Lemma 4.6 and completeness of downslices). The proof of Lemma 4.6 relies on downcovers. One can use upcovers to prove a similar lemma that reduces low-density downslices to high-density downslices. Moreover, both, Lemma 4.6 and its low-to-high variant, can be also proved for the dual setting of upslices. So overall, Lemma 4.6 represents four possible transformations. (The other three will not be used in this work.) By combining these reductions with the completeness of downslices/upslices (Observation 4.2), we conclude that it is possible to reduce a general access structure to downslices or upslices of specific density.

We are now ready to realize high-density downslices.

Proof (Proof of Lemma 4.4). Let f be a (b, n)-downslice with $b \in (0.5n, n]$. Let $v = 2b - n$, and observe that $v \in (0, b]$ since $b \in (0.5n, n]$. We use the *cover reduction lemma* (Lemma 4.6) to realize f based on secret-sharing scheme for downslices with parameters $(b - v, n - v) = (n - b, 2n - 2b)$.[6] The latter can be realized (non-linearly) with share size of $2^{n-b+o(n)}$ by Lemma 4.3. Overall, Lemma 4.6 yields a (non-linear) scheme for f with total share size of

$$\left[\binom{n}{n-b} \Big/ \binom{2n-2b}{n-b}\right]\left[1 + \log\binom{2n-2b}{n-b}\right] \cdot 2^{n-b+o(n)}$$

which equals $\left[\binom{n}{n-b} \Big/ \binom{2n-2b}{n-b}\right] \cdot 2^{n-b+o(n)}$. In the linear case, we realize $(n-b, 2(n-b))$-downslices using the linear secret-sharing scheme promised by Lemma 4.3. This results in the desired share size:

$$\left[\binom{n}{n-b} \Big/ \binom{2n-2b}{n-b}\right]\left[1 + \log\binom{2n-2b}{n-b}\right] \cdot 2^{(3n-3b)/2+o(n)}$$

which equals $\left[\binom{n}{n-b} \Big/ \binom{2n-2b}{n-b}\right] \cdot 2^{(3n-3b)/2+o(n)}$. If we plug in $b = \beta n$ for a constant $\beta \in (0.5, 1]$ and make use of (1), the general and linear share sizes translate to $2^{(H_2(\beta)-2(1-\beta)+(1-\beta))n+o(n)}$ and $2^{(H_2(\beta)-2(1-\beta)+\frac{3}{2}(1-\beta))n+o(n)}$, leading to the desired exponents. $\qquad\square$

---

[6] This choice of v can be shown to be optimal for both for the general and linear case.

4.3 Proof of the Cover Reduction

The proof of Lemma 4.6 is based on the following construction.

Construction 4.8. *Let F be a (b,n)-downslice. We share the secret s according to F as follows:*

1. *Pick a family $\mathcal{G} = \{G_i\}_{i=1}^{L}$ of sets of size v that downcovers the slice b.*
2. *For every $G_i \in \mathcal{G}$ define the access structure F_i over the participant's set $[n] \setminus G_i$ as follows:*
$$F_i(x') = F(x' \cup G_i)$$
   where x' is viewed as a subset of $[n] \setminus G_i$.
3. *Split the secret s with an $(L\text{-out-of-}L)$ LSS scheme to random shares $s_1, \ldots, s_L \in \{0,1\}$ such that $s_1 \oplus \cdots \oplus s_L = s$. For every $1 \le i \le L$ share s_i according to the access structure F_i.*

Claim 4.9. *Construction 4.8 realizes the access structure F.*

Proof. It suffices to show that $F = \bigwedge_i F_i$. Assume that x is authorized under F, we will show that it is also authorized by F_i for every i. Fix i and let $x' = x \cap \bar{G}_i$, we claim that x' is authorized under F_i. Indeed, by definition, $F_i(x') = F(x' \cup G_i)$ which is 1 since $x' \cup G_i$ contains x and is therefore authorized under F.

Next, assume that x is unauthorized under F. Since F is a (b,n)-downslice, x must be a subset of some unauthorized set B of size b, and by the down-covering property there exists an index $i \in [L]$ such that G_i is a subset of the same set B. Again letting $x' = x \cap \bar{G}_i$, we then get that $x' \cup G_i \subseteq B$, and therefore $F_i(x') = F(x' \cup G_i) = 0$. The claim follows. $\square$

Claim 4.10. *For every $1 \le i \le L$, F_i is a $(b-v, n-v)$-downslice access structure.*

Proof. Fix a maximal unauthorized set $x' \subset [n] \setminus G_i$ of F_i. We show that x' contains exactly $b-v$ parties. For this, it suffices to show that $x = x' \cup G_i$ is a maximal unauthorized set of F. By definition, $x' \cup G_i$ is unauthorized under F. Moreover, every strict super-set y of $x' \cup G_i$ must be F-authorized. Otherwise, if y is F-unauthorized then the set $y' = y \cap \bar{G}_i$ must be also F_i-unauthorized and since y' is a strict-super set of x', this contradicts the fact that x' is max-unauthorized under F_i. Finally, since any max-term of F is of size b, the max-terms of F_i is of size $b-v$. $\square$

Share size analysis: Due to Fact 3.3 we can pick a family $\mathcal{G}$ for step 1 of the scheme of size
$$L = \left[\binom{n}{n-b} / \binom{n-v}{n-b}\right]\left[1 + \log\binom{n-v}{n-b}\right],$$

and for every set in $\mathcal{G}$ we use a secret sharing scheme with share size $z(b-v, n-v)$, which results in the desired share size. This completes the proof of the first part of Lemma 4.6.

The "Consequently" part follows immediately by plugging-in $b = \lceil \beta n \rceil$, $v = \lceil \frac{\beta - \alpha}{1 - \alpha} n \rceil$, and noting that $\alpha_n = \frac{b - v}{n - v}$ converges to α when n goes to infinity. Observe that the exponent of $(\alpha_n(n - v), (n - v))$-downslices is the same as the exponent, $z'(\alpha)$, of α-downslice.[7] Now, by applying (1) and noting that $\beta_n = b/n = \lceil \beta n \rceil / n$ converges to β when n grows, we derive an exponent of

$$H_2(\beta) - \frac{1 - \beta}{1 - \alpha} H_2(1 - \alpha) + z'(\alpha) \cdot \frac{1 - \beta}{1 - \alpha},$$

which equals the expression in (3), as required.   □

5   Linear Secret Sharing for Downslices

In this section we present a LSS for general access structures with an exponent of 0.7576 (Theorem 2.2). As in Sect. 4, this is done by showing that downslices can be linearly realized with this exponent.

Theorem 5.1. *Every n-party downslice access structure can be linearly realized with complexity of $2^{0.7576n + o(n)}$.*

The proof of Theorem 5.1 is based on a bootstrapping procedure which strongly exploits the *duality* properties of LSS.

Section Organization. In Sect. 5.1 we describe a property of linear schemes for *dual access structures*. In Sect. 5.2 we reduce downslices to upslices and vice versa. In Section 5.3 we iteratively employ these reductions together with tools from the previous section, to obtain a LSS for downslices with lower exponents than before. Lastly in Sect. 5.4 we prove Theorem 2.2. Some additional optimizations for low downslices (that do not affect Theorem 5.1) appear in the full version of the paper.

5.1   Exploiting Duality

Definition 5.2 (Dual Access structures). *The* dual *access structure of an n-party access structure f is an n-party access structure, denoted by $\mathrm{DUAL}(f)$, that consists of all sets x whose complements $\bar{x}$ are unauthorized under f. Viewing f as a function, this means that for every input x*

$$\mathrm{DUAL}(f)(x) = 1 - f(\bar{x}).$$

Consequently, the complement of every min-term of f is a max-term of the dual $\mathrm{DUAL}(f)$, and the complement of every max-term of f is a min-term of $\mathrm{DUAL}(f)$.

---

[7] More generally, whenever $|g(n) - g'(n)| = o(n)$, the exponent of $(g(n), n)$-downslices is equal to the exponent of $(g'(n), n)$-downslices. To see this, observe that $(g(n), n)$-downslices can be written as a sub-exponential formula over $(g'(n), n)$-downslices.

We make the following observation.

Fact 5.3 (Duals of slice access structures). *Let f be an access structure. Then:*

1. *If f is an (a, n)-slice then its dual is an $((n - a), n)$-slice.*
2. *If f is an (a, n)-upslice then its dual is a $((n - a), n)$-downslice, and vice versa.*
3. *If f is an $(a : b, n)$-multislice then its dual is an $(n - b : n - a, n)$-multislice.*

It is known that for linear schemes the total share size of an access structure is equal to the total share size of its dual.

Fact 5.4 ([20]). *A linear secret sharing scheme for an access structure f can be converted into a linear scheme for the dual access structure $\mathrm{DUAL}(f)$ with the same total share size.*

By Fact 5.4, Fact 5.3, Lemma 4.3, and Lemma 4.4, we get the following corollary.

Corollary 5.5 (Duality reduction). *For every integers $a \le n$, the LSS complexity of the family of (a, n)-downslices equals to the LSS complexity of the family $(n - a, n)$-upslices.*

By Lemma 4.4 and Lemma 4.3, for any constant $0 < \alpha < 1$, the family of $(\alpha n, n)$-upslices can be linearly realized with an exponent of

$$\mathbf{U}_\ell(\alpha) \le \begin{cases} H_2(\alpha) - \frac{1}{2}(\alpha) & \text{if } \alpha < \frac{1}{2} \\ \frac{1}{2} + \frac{1-\alpha}{2} & \text{if } \alpha \ge \frac{1}{2} \end{cases}.$$

5.2 High-Density Downslices from Low-Density Upslices and Mid-Range Multislices

In the following lemma we improve the exponent of a (c, n)-downslice f by decomposing it into two access structures: one that has the same min-terms as f up to a specific size u (which will be realized using low-density upslices), and one that is simply the $(u : c, n)$ multislice of f.

Lemma 5.6 (Reducing downslices to upslices). *Let $u \le c < n$ be integers. Given a LSS that realizes (a, n)-upslices with an exponent of $\mathbf{U}'_\ell(a, n)$ and a LSS that realizes the $(u : c, n)$-multislices with an exponent of $\mathbf{M}'_\ell(u : c, n)$, there exists a LSS that realizes (a, n)-downslices with an exponent of*

$$\mathbf{D}_\ell(c, n) \le \min_u \left[\max \left(\max_{i \le u} \{\mathbf{U}'_\ell(i, n)\}, \mathbf{M}'_\ell(u : c, n) \right) \right] + o(1),$$

where $o(1)$ stands for a quantity that tends to zero as n increases, regardless of the values of u and c.

Proof. It suffices to show that for every $u \leq c$ any downward-induced (c, n) access structure f can be realized with an exponent of

$$\max\left(\max_{i \leq u}\{\mathbf{U}'_\ell(i, n)\}, \mathbf{M}'_\ell(u : c, n)\right) + o(1). \qquad (4)$$

Fix some $u \in [0, c]$. Define $f_{u,c}$ to be the $(u : c, n)$-multislice of f, and $f^{\text{up}}_{0,u}$ as the disjunction of the first u upslices of f. More formally, $f^{\text{up}}_{0,u} := \bigvee_{i=0}^{u} f_i$ where f_i is the i-upslice of f. Clearly, $f^{\text{up}}_{0,u}$ can be linearly realized with an exponent of $\max_{i \leq u}\{\mathbf{U}'_\ell(i, n)\} + O(n^{-1}\log n)$ (just duplicate the secret u times and deal the i-th copy via the access structure f_i). Consequently, the access structure $f^{\text{up}}_{0,u} \vee f_{u,c}$ can be linearly realized with an exponent of (4). We complete the proof by showing that $f = f^{\text{up}}_{0,u} \vee f_{u,c}$.

For inputs x such that $|x| \leq u$, $f(x) = f^{\text{up}}_{0,u}(x)$ and $f_{u,c}(x) = 0$. For inputs x such that $u < |x| \leq c$, it holds that (1) $f(x) = f_{u,c}(x)$, and (2) $f^{\text{up}}_{0,u} \leq f$ since the min-terms of $f^{\text{up}}_{0,u}$ are a subset of those of f. We therefore conclude that for such inputs $f(x) = f^{\text{up}}_{0,u}(x) \vee f_{u,c}(x)$. Finally, for inputs x with $|x| > c$, both $f(x)$ and $f_{u,c}(x)$ take the value 1, and so equality holds in this case as well. □

5.3   Bootstrapping (c, n)-downslices

In this section we construct an LSS for (c, n)-downslices via an iterative process. In each iteration, we will start with an LSS for (c, n)-downslices and end-up with a new LSS for (c, n)-downslices whose exponent is at least as good as the one achieved in the previous iteration. Each iteration i is composed of three steps: (1) We generate LSS for all downslices of density larger than c; (2) We generate LSS for all upslices of density smaller than $n - c$; (3) We use the current schemes for (u, n)-upslices for $u < u_i$ for some parameter u_i to obtain a new LSS for (c, n)-downslices. Note that the target slice c is kept fixed across iterations. The structure of a single iteration that consists of the three reductions is depicted below. The process is formally defined in Construction 5.7.

Construction 5.7 (Bootstrapping downslices). *Given integer n, a target slice $c < n$, and time-bound $t \in \mathbb{N}$, initialize an LSS for (c, n)-downslice based on Theorem 4.1 and set $\mathbf{D}_\ell(c, n)[0]$ to be its exponent, and repeat the following steps for $i \in [t]$ iterations:*

1. *For every $d \in (c, n]$, apply the cover reduction (Lemma 4.6) and transform the current LSS for (c, n)-downslices to an LSS for (d, n)-downslices with exponent*

$$\mathbf{D}_\ell(d, n)[i + 1] = H_2(d/n) - (1 - d/n)\left(\frac{H_2(c/n) - \mathbf{D}_\ell(c, n)[i]}{1 - c/n}\right) + o(1). \quad (5)$$

2. *For every $d \in (c, n]$, apply the duality reduction (Corollary 5.5) and transform the LSS for (d, n)-downslices to an LSS for $(n - d, n)$-upslices with an exponent of*

$$\mathbf{U}_\ell(n - d, n)[i + 1] = \mathbf{D}_\ell(d, n)[i + 1]. \quad (6)$$

Three reductions of Construction 5.7

1. The cover reduction (Lemma 4.6): Transform a scheme for (c, n)-downslices with to a scheme for downslices with higher density.

2. Duality reduction: Transform high downslices to low upslices (Corollary 5.5): Transform a scheme for downslices of high density in $(c, n]$ to a scheme for upslices with low density in $[0, n - c)$.

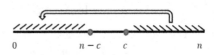

3. Reducing high downslices to low upslices (Lemma 5.6): For an integer $u \leq c$, transform a scheme for upslices in the range $[0, u]$ and a scheme for the $(u : c, n)$-multislice to a scheme for the c-downslice.

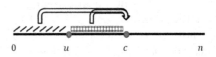

Fig. 3. We place all slices on an horizontal axis with an arrow which represents the direction of the transformation.

3. *Construct an LSS for (c, n)-downslices by applying Lemma 5.6 where (j, n)-upslices for every $j < n - c$ are instantiated with the LSS that were derived in the previous step. Accordingly, the new LSS for (c, n)-downslices has an exponent of*

$$\mathbf{D}_\ell(c, n)[i + 1] = \min_{u \leq c} \left[\max \left(\max_{j \leq u} \mathbf{U}_\ell(j, n)[i + 1], \mathbf{M}_\ell^0(u : c, n) \right) \right] + o(1). \quad (7)$$

where $\mathbf{M}_\ell^0(a : b, n)$ denotes the linear exponent of $(a : b, n)$-multislice access structures that is achieved in Lemma 4.5.

Now by Lemma 4.6, Corollary 5.5 and Lemma 5.6, for any parameter t, Construction 5.7 yields an LSS for (c, n)-downslices. For a given $\gamma \in [0, 1]$ and constant t, we can define a function $\Phi_t(\gamma)$ that captures the asymptotic exponent that is achieved for $(\gamma n, n)$-downslices after running Construction 5.7 for t iterations. Formally,

$$\Phi_0(\gamma) := \begin{cases} \frac{1}{2} + \frac{1}{2}\gamma & \text{if } \gamma \leq \frac{1}{2} \\ H_2(\gamma) - \frac{1}{2}(1 - \gamma) & \text{if } \gamma > \frac{1}{2} \end{cases}$$

is set to be the exponent derived from Theorem 4.1. Then by (5), (6) and (7)

$$\Phi_{i+1}(\gamma) := \min_{v \in [0, \gamma]} \left[\max \left(\max_{\chi \in [0, v]} (\mathbf{U}_\ell'(\chi, \gamma), \mathbf{M}_\ell'(v, \gamma)) \right) \right],$$

where

$$\mathbf{U}_\ell'(\chi, \gamma) := H_2(\chi) - \chi \left(\frac{H_2(\gamma) - \Phi_i(\gamma)}{1 - \gamma} \right),$$

and

$$\mathbf{M}'_\ell(v, \gamma) := \begin{cases} \frac{1}{2} + \frac{1}{2}\gamma\, \mathrm{H}_2(v/\gamma) & \text{if } \gamma/2 < v < \gamma \\ \frac{1}{2} + \frac{1}{2}\gamma & \text{if } v < \gamma/2 \end{cases}.$$

We therefore conclude that

Lemma 5.8. *For every constant $t \in \mathbb{N}$ and constant $\gamma \in [0, 1]$, and for all n's, the LSS constructed by invoking Construction 5.7 for t steps on $(\gamma n, n)$, has an exponent of $\Phi_t(\gamma) + \epsilon(n)$ where $\epsilon(n)$ tends to zero when n grows.*

Lemma 5.8 suffices for proving Theorem 5.1 (see Sect. 5.4).

Remark 5.9. Assuming the *duality hypothesis*, the same bootstraping idea can be employed for general (non-linear) schemes. However, it does not yield better general exponents than the ones shown in the previous section for any downwslice.

5.4   Proof of Theorem 5.1

A natural approach for proving Theorem 5.1 would be to run the bootstrapping scheme for each possible target $c \in [n]$, and then glue together all the (c, n)-downslices. This approach fails since the exponents of some slices will still be too high. Instead we will apply Construction 5.7 for only two concrete values of c and use the cover reduction to handle downslices of higher densities. Downslices with low density will be treated by Lemma 4.5. Details follow.

By applying Construction 5.7 with $\gamma_1 = 0.5$ and $\gamma_2 = 0.535$ for $t = 7$ times, we derive the following claim from Lemma 5.8.

Claim 5.10. *Set $\gamma_1 = 0.5$ and $\gamma_2 = 0.535$. The family of $(\gamma_1 n, n)$-downslices and the family of $(\gamma_2 n, n)$-downslices can be linearly realized with exponents of $z_1 = 0.736$ and $z_2 = 0.748$.*

Let f be a (d, n)-downslice. We distinguish between the following cases.

1. For $d \in [0, 0.5n]$ linearly realize f by Lemma 4.3 with a maximal exponent of 0.75.
2. For $d \in [0.5n, 0.535n]$ linearly realize f by applying the cover reduction (Lemma 4.6) instantiated with the LSS for $(0.5n, n)$-downslices of Claim 5.10. This yields an exponent of

$$\mathrm{H}_2(d/n) - (1 - d/n)\frac{\mathrm{H}_2(\gamma_1) - z_1}{1 - \gamma_1} < \mathrm{H}_2(d/n) - 0.528(1 - d/n) \quad (8)$$

   which is upper-bounded by 0.751 for $d \in [0.5n, 0.535n]$.
3. For $d \in [0.535n, n]$ linearly realize f by applying the cover reduction (Lemma 4.6) instantiated with the LSS for $(0.535n, n)$-downslices of Claim 5.10. This yields an exponent of

$$\mathrm{H}_2(d/n) - (1 - d/n)\frac{\mathrm{H}_2(\gamma_2) - z_2}{1 - \gamma_2} < \mathrm{H}_2(d/n) - 0.534(1 - d/n) + o(1) \quad (9)$$

   which is upper-bounded by 0.7576 for $d \in [0.535n, n]$.

The proof of Theorem 5.1 follows.   □

Remark 5.11. A more careful analysis allows to obtain a better exponent for values of $d \leq 0.535n$. We sketch this result in the full version of the paper.

6   Random Upslices

Recall that, for a vector of non-negative integers $\mathbf{k} = (k_1, \ldots, k_n)$, the $\mathbf{k}$-DNF distribution is defined by selecting, for each parameter a, k_a clauses uniformly at random from the set of all possible $\binom{n}{a}$ monotone a-clauses. (We allow repetitions though this choice does not change the results.) When $\mathbf{k} = (0^{a-1}k_a 0^{n-a})$ is supported on a single level a, we refer to this distribution as a random (a, k_a, n)-upslice. Observe that this special case is *complete* in the following sense.

Observation 6.1. *For every $\mathbf{k} = (k_1, \ldots, k_n)$ the following holds. If, for every $a \in [n]$, a random (a, k_a, n)-upslice can be realized (resp., linearly realized) with total share size of at most S_a except with probability ϵ, then, a random $\mathbf{k} = (k_1, \ldots, k_n)$ can be realized (resp., linearly realized) with an complexity of at most $\sum S_a$ except with probability $n\epsilon$.*

Proof. A random $\mathbf{k}$-DNF f can be written as $f = \bigvee_a f_a$ where each f_a is a random (a, k_a, n)-upslice. Hence, we can share f by duplicating the secret n times and sharing the ath copy according to f_a. The claim follows by applying union-bound.   □

We can therefore reduce Theorem 2.3 to the following refined statements (Theorem 6.2 and Theorem 6.3) about random (a, k_a, n)-upslices. Specifically, we prove the following theorem in Sect. 6.1.

Theorem 6.2 (random upslices). *Let $a \in [n]$, $k \leq \binom{n}{a}$ and let f be a randomly chosen (a, k_a, n)-upslice. Then, with probability $1 - 2^{-\Omega(n)}$,*

$$\mathsf{SSize}(f) \leq \begin{cases} \sqrt{\binom{n}{\alpha^* n}} \cdot 2^{o(n)} & \text{if } a \in [0, \alpha^* n] \\ \sqrt{\binom{n}{a}} \cdot 2^{o(n)} & \text{if } a \in [\alpha^* n, n] \end{cases},$$

where $\alpha^* \sim 0.157$ is the root of $0.25\, \mathrm{H}_2(\alpha) - \alpha$. Moreover, under the duality hypothesis, with probability $1 - 2^{-\Omega(n)}$, the function f can be realized with an exponent of at most $\frac{1}{2}\mathrm{H}_2(\lambda) \sim 0.491$, where λ is the root of $\frac{1}{2}\mathrm{H}_2(\lambda) - (1 - \lambda)\mathrm{H}_2(\frac{\lambda}{1-\lambda})$.

The first part of the theorem (without the duality hypothesis), shows that, for every density $\alpha \in [0, 1]$, a random $(\alpha n, n)$-upslice can be realized, whp, with an exponent of 0.5. Thus, by Observation 6.1, the non-linear part of Theorem 2.3 follows. We further mention that we did not attempt to optimize the exponent for $a \leq \alpha^* n$, and indeed a better exponent can be achieved in this case.

Moving on to the second ("Moreover") part of the theorem, recall that the duality hypothesis asserts that for every $f = \{f_n\}$, it holds that $\mathsf{SSize}(f) \leq \mathsf{SSize}(\mathrm{DUAL}(f)) \cdot 2^{o(n)}$[8] and note that this part implies the gap Theorem (2.4), based on Observation 6.1 and the outline given in Sect. 2.

We move on to handle the linear case.

Theorem 6.3 (LSS for random upslices). *Let $a \in [n]$, $k \leq \binom{n}{a}$ and let f be a randomly chosen (a, k_a, n)-upslice. Then, with probability $1 - 2^{-\Omega(n)}$, it holds that*

$$\mathsf{LSSize}(f) \leq \binom{n}{a}^{1/3} \cdot 2^{\frac{n}{3}+o(n)}.$$

Moreover, with probability $1 - 2^{-\Omega(n)}$, f can be realized with an exponent of at most $0.6651 < 2/3$, where $0.6651 = H_2(\lambda) - (1 - \lambda) H_2(\frac{\lambda}{1-\lambda})$ for the λ which is the root of $H_2(\lambda) - \frac{3}{2}(1 - \lambda) H_2(\frac{\lambda}{1-\lambda}) - \frac{1}{2}$.

Together with Observation 6.1, Theorem 6.3 implies the non-linear part of Theorem 2.3. The proof of Theorem 6.3 appears in Sect. 6.2.

6.1   Proof of Theorem 6.2

Given a random (a, k_a, n)-upslice f we realize f via one of the following two schemes depending on k_a. Let t be some threshold parameter that will be chosen later.

1. If $k_a \leq t$ realize f via a DNF scheme with complexity of k_a.
2. If $k_a > t$, set b to be the smallest integer solution of the inequality

$$t \geq \left[\binom{n}{a} \bigg/ \binom{b}{a} \right] \cdot n. \tag{10}$$

If the min-terms of f downcover the slice b (that is, $f(x) = 1$ for every x of weight at least b) realize f via the $(a : b, n)$-multislice of f with the general scheme for multislices promised by Lemma 4.5. Otherwise, realize f via DNF and call this event "failure".

We analyze the complexity of the construction. We set t to $\sqrt{\binom{n}{a}}$. For $k_a \leq t$ we rely on the first scheme and get complexity of at most $t = \sqrt{\binom{n}{a}}$, as required. We move on to the case where $k_a \geq t$. By Fact 3.3, the probability of "failure" is $2^{-\Omega(n)}$ and so by Lemma 4.5, the complexity in this case is $\binom{b}{\geq a} \cdot 2^{o(n)}$. We will show that

$$\binom{b}{\geq a} \leq \begin{cases} \sqrt{\binom{n}{\alpha^* n}} \cdot 2^{o(n)} & \text{if } a \in [0, \alpha^* n] \\ \sqrt{\binom{n}{a}} \cdot 2^{o(n)} & \text{if } a \in [\alpha^* n, n] \end{cases}, \tag{11}$$

---

[8] In fact, a weaker hypothesis suffices that applies duality only to the family of $(a : b, n)$-multislices; See Lemma 6.4.

Let us start with the case of $a \geq \alpha^* n$. We claim that

$$\binom{b}{\geq a} \leq \binom{b}{a} \cdot 2^{o(n)} \underset{\star}{\leq} \sqrt{\binom{n}{a}} \cdot 2^{o(n)}. \tag{12}$$

Indeed, by plugging $t = \sqrt{\binom{n}{a}}$ into (10) and rearranging the terms, we get that b is the smallest integer that satisfies $\binom{b}{a} \geq n \cdot \sqrt{\binom{n}{a}}$. Therefore, $(\star)$ holds. To establish the first inequality, it suffices to show that $a + o(n) \geq b/2$, or, equivalently, that $\binom{2a}{a} \cdot 2^{o(n)} \geq \binom{b}{a}$. By $(\star)$ it suffices to show that $\binom{2a}{a} \cdot 2^{o(n)} \geq \sqrt{\binom{n}{a}}$. Taking logarithms from both sides, the inequality holds whenever $2a + o(n) > 0.5\, H_2(a/n)n$ which is indeed the case for any $a > \alpha^* n$.

Next we deal with the case where $a < \alpha^* n$. By (10), in this regime, b grows monotonically with a and so in this case it holds that $b < 2\alpha^*$. Therefore

$$\binom{b}{\geq a} \leq \binom{2\alpha^* n}{\geq a} \leq \binom{2\alpha^* n}{\alpha^* n} \cdot 2^{o(n)} \leq \sqrt{\binom{n}{\alpha^* n}} \cdot 2^{o(n)},$$

where the last inequality follows from the previous case. This completes the proof of the first part of Theorem 6.2 (without the "Moreover" part.)

Proving the "Moreover" part under the duality hypothesis. Now we assume the duality hypothesis and derive the last part of the proof. We will need the following lemma that is implied by the duality conjecture and the multislice lemma (Lemma 4.5).

Lemma 6.4. *Assuming the duality hypothesis, if $(a : b, n)$-multislices can be realized with share size of S, then the dual $(n - b : n - a, n)$-multislices can be realized with share size of $S \cdot 2^{o(n)}$. Specifically, $(a : b, n)$-multislice can be realized with share size of $\binom{n-a}{\geq n-b} \cdot 2^{o(n)}$.*

It can be verified that the above lemma outperforms the original $(a : b, n)$-multislice construction (Lemma 4.5) whenever $b > n - a$.

Getting back to the proof of Theorem 6.2, we will now realize random (a, n)-upslices with the same scheme but with different parameters and ingredients. We will analyze this scheme for $a \in [0, \alpha^{**} n]$, where $\alpha^{**} \sim 0.686$ is the solution of the equation

$$H_2(\alpha) + (1 - \alpha^*)\, H_2\left(\frac{\alpha}{1 - \alpha^*}\right) - \frac{1}{2}\, H_2(\alpha^*) = 0$$

and $\alpha^* \sim 0.157$ is defined as before to be the root of $0.25\, H_2(\alpha) - \alpha$. For a random (a, n)-upslice f, we will run the previous scheme with the following changes. In step (2) we will set b to be the smallest integer solution of the inequality

$$\sqrt{\binom{n}{n-b}} \geq \left[\binom{n}{a} \Big/ \binom{b}{a}\right] \cdot n = \left[\binom{n}{n-b} \Big/ \binom{n-a}{n-b}\right] \cdot n. \tag{13}$$

If in step (2) the min-terms of f downcover the slice b, we realize the $(a : b, n)$-multislice of f by the new construction (Lemma 6.4) with share size $\binom{n-a}{\geq n-b} \cdot 2^{o(n)}$. If the min-terms do not downcover the slice b, the process fails (and we use DNF-based secret sharing). In addition, we set the threshold t to $\sqrt{\binom{n}{b}}$.

Claim. Under the duality hypothesis, for any $a \in [0, \alpha^{**}n]$ and any k, the above scheme realizes a randomly chosen (a, k, n)-upslice with total share size of $\sqrt{\binom{n}{n-b}} \cdot 2^{o(n)}$ except with probability $2^{-\Omega(n)}$.

Proof. First observe that, by Fact 3.3, the scheme fail with probability at most $2^{-\Omega(n)}$. Conditioned on not failing, the share size is $\max(\binom{n-a}{\geq n-b}, t)$ and since $t = \sqrt{\binom{n}{b}} = \sqrt{\binom{n}{n-b}}$ it suffices to prove the following inequalities

$$\binom{n-a}{\geq n-b} \leq \binom{n-a}{n-b} \cdot 2^{o(n)} \underset{\star\star}{\leq} \sqrt{\binom{n}{n-b}} \cdot 2^{o(n)}.$$

Indeed, since b is the minimal integer that satisfies (13), we conclude that ($\star\star$) holds. The first inequality can be established by showing that $n - b + o(n) \geq (n-a)/2$, or, equivalently, that $\binom{2(n-b)}{n-b} \cdot 2^{o(n)} \geq \binom{n-a}{n-b}$. By ($\star\star$) it suffices to show that $\binom{2(n-b)}{n-b} \cdot 2^{o(n)} \geq \sqrt{\binom{n}{n-b}}$. Taking logarithms from both sides and dividing by n, we get that the inequality holds whenever $2(1 - b/n) + o(1) \geq 0.5 \, H_2(b/n)$ which holds whenever $b/n \leq 1 - \alpha^* + o(1)$. We conclude the argument by showing that $b/n \leq 1 - \alpha^* + o(1)$. Since b is monotonically increasing with a (by (13)) and since $a \leq \alpha^{**}n$, we may focus on the case where $a = \alpha^{**}n$. Let $\beta = b/n$. Taking logarithms from both sides of (13) and dividing by n, we can write $\frac{1}{2} H_2(\beta) = H_2(\alpha^{**}) - \beta H_2(\alpha^{**}/\beta) + o(1)$, which, by the definition of α^{**}, guarantees that $\beta \leq 1 - \alpha^* + o(1)$, as required. This completes the proof of Sect. 6.1.

Combining the two schemes together. Overall we now can realize random (a, n) upslices where $a \in [\alpha^*n, \alpha^{**}n]$ with share size

$$\min\left(\sqrt{\binom{n}{a}} \cdot 2^{o(n)}, \sqrt{\binom{n}{n-b}} \cdot 2^{o(n)}\right) \tag{14}$$

where $b = b(a, n)$ is the minimal integer that satisfies (13). Denote by a_0 the value for which the two expressions in (14) are equal, i.e., $b(a_0, n) = n - a_0$. We will later calculate a_0 and show that it is about $0.421n$. For now let us record the fact that $a_0 < n/2$ and that, consequently, for any $a > a_0$ it holds that $b(a, n) > b(a_0, n) = n - a_0 > n/2$ (since $b(a, n)$ monotonically increases with a). Next, observe that, the bound (14) on the complexity for an (a, n) upslice simplifies to $\sqrt{\binom{n}{a}} \cdot 2^{o(n)}$ when $a \leq a_0$ and to $\sqrt{\binom{n}{n-b}} \cdot 2^{o(n)}$ when $a > a_0$. Furthermore, the first expression monotonically increases with a for $a < a_0 < n/2$, and the second expression monotonically decreases with a for $a > a_0$ (since $b(a, n) > n/2$

and since $b(a, n)$ increases with a). Hence, the upslice with the maximal share size in the given range will be the (a_0, n)-upslice. We move on to calculate a_0. Let $a = \alpha n$ and $b = \beta n$, by plugging (13) into the equation $b(a, n) = n - a$, we conclude that $\alpha_0 = a_0/n$ is the solution to the equation

$$\frac{1}{2} H_2(1 - \alpha) = H_2(1 - \alpha) - (1 - \alpha) H_2\left(\frac{\alpha}{1 - \alpha}\right),$$

and therefore $\alpha_0 \sim 0.421$. Therefore (14) is upper-bounded by $\sqrt{\binom{n}{a_0}} \cdot 2^{o(n)} \leq 2^{0.5 H_2(\alpha_0)n + o(n)}$. We conclude that random (a, n)-upslices can be realized with an exponent of $0.5 H_2(\alpha_0) \leq 0.491$ whenever $a \in [\alpha^* n, \alpha^{**} n]$. We complete the proof by noting that all random upslices below $\alpha^* n$ and above $\alpha^{**} n$ can also be realized with exponents below 0.491 due to the first scheme.   □

□

6.2   Proof of Theorem 6.3

We begin by proving the first part of Theorem 6.3 (without the moreover part). The construction is identical to the first construction presented in Sect. 6.1, except that the threshold t is selected differently to be $\binom{n}{a}^{1/3} \cdot 2^{n/3}$. Again for $k_a \leq t$ we rely on the first scheme and get complexity of at most $t = \binom{n}{a}^{1/3} \cdot 2^{n/3}$, as required. For $k_a \geq t$, by Fact 3.3 failure happens with $2^{-\Omega(n)}$ probability, and, by Lemma 4.5, conditioned on not failing, the share complexity is at most $2^{n/2+o(n)} \cdot \sqrt{\binom{b}{\geq a}}$. To complete the first part of the proof, it suffices to show that the latter quantity is at most $\binom{n}{a}^{1/3} \cdot 2^{\frac{n}{3}+o(n)}$. This follows from the following claim

$$\binom{b}{\geq a} \leq \binom{b}{a} \cdot 2^{o(n)} \underset{\star}{\leq} \binom{n}{a}^{2/3} \cdot 2^{-n/3+o(n)}.$$

Indeed, by plugging $t = \binom{n}{a}^{1/3} \cdot 2^{n/3}$ into (10) and rearranging the terms, we get that b is the smallest integer that satisfies $\binom{b}{a} \geq n \cdot \binom{n}{a}^{2/3} \cdot 2^{-n/3}$. Therefore, $(\star)$ holds. To establish the first inequality, it suffices to show that $a + o(n) \geq b/2$, or, equivalently, that $\binom{2a}{a} \cdot 2^{o(n)} \geq \binom{b}{a}$. By $(\star)$ it suffices to show that $\binom{2a}{a} \cdot 2^{o(n)} \geq \binom{n}{a}^{2/3} \cdot 2^{-n/3}$. Taking logarithms from both sides, the inequality holds whenever $2a + o(n) > (\frac{2}{3} H_2(a/n) - 1/3)n$ which is indeed the case for every $a \in [n]$. This completes the proof of the first part of the theorem (without the moreover part).

To prove the "Moreover" part, we make use of the following lemma which is implied by the multislice construction (Lemma 4.5) and the duality closure of linear schemes (Fact 5.4):

Lemma 6.5 (LSS for multislices). *Let $a, b \in [0, n]$ be integers, then the family of $(a : b, n)$-multislices can be linearly realized with share size* $\sqrt{\binom{n-a}{\geq n-b}} \cdot 2^{n/2+o(n)}$.

It can be verified that the above lemma outperforms the original linear $(a : b, n)$-multislice construction (Lemma 4.5) whenever $b > n - a$.

This time for a random (a, n)-upslice f, we will run the previous linear scheme with the following changes. In step (2), we will set b to be the smallest integer solution of the inequality

$$\binom{n}{b}^{1/3} \cdot 2^{n/3} \geq \left[\binom{n}{a} / \binom{b}{a}\right] \cdot n = \left[\binom{n}{n-b} / \binom{n-a}{n-b}\right] \cdot n. \tag{15}$$

In addition, we set the threshold t to $\binom{n}{b}^{1/3} \cdot 2^{n/3}$.

Claim. For any $a \in [n]$ and any k, the above scheme realizes a randomly chosen (a, k, n)-upslice with total share size of $\binom{n}{n-b}^{1/3} \cdot 2^{n/3}$.

Proof. First observe that by Fact 3.3 we fail with probability at most $2^{-\Omega(n)}$. Conditioned on not failing, the share size is $\max(\sqrt{\binom{n-a}{\geq n-b}} \cdot 2^{n/2+o(n)}, t)$ and since $t = \binom{n}{b}^{1/3} \cdot 2^{n/3} = \binom{n}{n-b}^{1/3} \cdot 2^{n/3}$ it suffices to show that

$$\sqrt{\binom{n-a}{\geq n-b}} \cdot 2^{n/2+o(n)} \leq \binom{n}{n-b}^{1/3} \cdot 2^{n/3} \cdot 2^{o(n)}. \tag{16}$$

We prove (16) by establishing the following inequalities

$$\binom{n-a}{\geq n-b} \leq \binom{n-a}{n-b} \cdot 2^{o(n)} \underset{\star\star}{\leq} \binom{n}{n-b}^{2/3} \cdot 2^{-n/3+o(n)}.$$

Indeed, since b is the minimal integer that satisfies (15), we conclude that $(\star\star)$ holds. The first inequality can be established by showing that $n - b + o(n) \geq (n - a)/2$, or, equivalently, that $\binom{2(n-b)}{n-b} \cdot 2^{o(n)} \geq \binom{n-a}{n-b}$. By $(\star\star)$ it suffices to show that $\binom{2(n-b)}{n-b} \cdot 2^{o(n)} \geq \binom{n}{n-b}^{2/3} \cdot 2^{-n/3}$. Taking logarithms from both sides and dividing by n, we get that the inequality holds whenever $2(1 - b/n) + o(1) \geq (\frac{2}{3} H_2(b/n) - 1/3)$ which is indeed the case for every $b \in [n]$. This completes the proof of Sect. 6.2.

Combining the two schemes together. Overall we now can linearly realize random (a, n) upslices with share size of

$$\min\left(\binom{n}{a}^{1/3} \cdot 2^{n/3+o(n)}, \binom{n}{n-b}^{1/3} \cdot 2^{n/3+o(n)}\right) \tag{17}$$

where $b = b(a, n)$ is the smallest integer that satisfies (15). Similarly to the analysis in the proof for the general (non-linear) case, denote by a_0 the value for which the two expressions in (17) are equal, i.e., $b(a_0, n) = n - a_0$. We will later calculate a_0 and show that it is about $0.4595n$. For now let us record the fact that $a_0 < n/2$ and that, consequently, for any $a > a_0$ it holds that $b(a, n) > b(a_0, n) = n - a_0 > n/2$ (since $b(a, n)$ monotonically increases with a). Getting back to (17) observe that the complexity for an (a, n)-upslice is $\binom{n}{a}^{1/3} \cdot 2^{n/3 + o(n)}$ when $a \leq a_0$ and $\binom{n}{n-b}^{1/3} \cdot 2^{n/3 + o(n)}$ when $a > a_0$. Furthermore, the first expression monotonically increases with a for $a < a_0 < n/2$, and the second expression monotonically decreases with a for $a > a_0$ (since $b(a, n) > n/2$ and since $b(a, n)$ increases with a). Hence, the upslice with the maximal share size in the given range will be the (a_0, n)-upslice. We move on to calculate a_0. Let $a = \alpha n$ and $b = \beta n$, by plugging (15) into the equation $b(a, n) = n - a$, we conclude that $\alpha_0 = a_0/n$ is the solution to the equation

$$\frac{1}{3} + \frac{1}{3} H_2(1 - \alpha) = H_2(1 - \alpha) - (1 - \alpha) H_2\left(\frac{\alpha}{1 - \alpha}\right),$$

and therefore $\alpha_0 \sim 0.4595$. It follows that (17) is upper-bounded by $\binom{n}{a_0}^{1/3} \cdot 2^{n/3 + o(n)} \leq 2^{n \frac{H_2(\alpha_0) + 1}{3} + o(n)}$. We conclude that a random (a, n)-upslice can be linearly realized with an exponent of $\frac{H_2(\alpha_0) + 1}{3} \leq 0.6651$ for any a, and the "Moreover" part of Theorem 6.3 follows.   □

Acknowledgement. We thank Amos Beimel and Naty Peter for valuable discussions. Research supported by the European Union's Horizon 2020 Programme (ERC-StG-2014-2020) under Grant Agreement No. 639813 ERC-CLC.

A   Omitted Preliminaries

We formally define four different types of "slice access structures" that will be used as key components in our general constructions. Throughout this section, we fix some complete access structure f over n parties. The following definitions were extensively used by [26]. For string $x, x' \in \{0, 1\}^n$, we write $x \leq x'$ if for every $i \in [n]$, $x_i \leq x'_i$. We let $\text{wt}(x)$ denote the Hamming weight of x.

Definition A.1 (Slices and Multislices). *For $a \leq b \in [n]$, we define the $(a : b)$-multislice of f to be the access structure $F : \{0, 1\}^n \to \{0, 1\}$ for which*

$$F(x) = \begin{cases} 0 & \text{if wt}(x) < a \\ f(x) & \text{if wt}(x) \in [a, b] \\ 1 & \text{if wt}(x) > b \end{cases}.$$

We say that F is $(a : b, n)$-multislice access-structure (or just $(a : b, n)$-slice) if F is an $(a : b)$-multislice of some n-party access structure f. An $(a : a)$-multislice is refereed to as an a-slice.

As already mentioned, our constructions strongly exploit the following fine-grained variants of slice access structures.

Definition A.2 (Upslices). *For $a \in [n]$, we define the a-upslice of f to be the access structure $F : \{0, 1\}^n \to \{0, 1\}$ for which*

$$F(x) = \begin{cases} 0 & \textit{if } \mathrm{wt}(x) < a \\ f(x) & \textit{if } \mathrm{wt}(x) = a \\ 1 \iff \quad \exists x' : \mathrm{wt}(x') = a, x' \le x, f(x') = 1 & \textit{if } \mathrm{wt}(x) > a \end{cases} .$$

We say that F is an (a, n)-upslice access structure (or just (a, n)-upslice) if F is an (a, n)-upslice of some n-party access structure f.

Observe that F is (a, n)-upslice if and only if all its min-terms are at level a.

Definition A.3 (Downslices). *For $b \in [n]$, we define the b-downslice of f to be the access structure $F : \{0, 1\}^n \to \{0, 1\}$ for which*

$$F(x) = \begin{cases} 0 \iff \exists x' : \mathrm{wt}(x') = b, x \le x', f(x') = 0 & \textit{if } \mathrm{wt}(x) < b \\ f(x) & \textit{if } \mathrm{wt}(x) = b \\ 1 & \textit{if } \mathrm{wt}(x) > b \end{cases} .$$

We say that F is a (b, n)-downslice access structure (or just (b, n)-downslice) if F is a b-slice of some n-party access structure f.

Observe that F is a (b, n)-downslice if and only if all its max-terms are at level b.

References

1. Applebaum, B., Beimel, A., Farràs, O., Nir, O., Peter, N.: Secret-sharing schemes for general and uniform access structures. In: Ishai, Y., Rijmen, V. (eds.) EURO-CRYPT 2019. LNCS, vol. 11478, pp. 441–471. Springer, Cham (2019). https://doi.org/10.1007/978-3-030-17659-4_15
2. Applebaum, B., Beimel, A., Nir, O., Peter, N.: Better secret sharing via robust conditional disclosure of secrets. In: Makarychev, K., Makarychev, Y., Tulsiani, M., Kamath, G., Chuzhoy, J. (eds.) Proceedings of the 52nd Annual ACM SIGACT Symposium on Theory of Computing, STOC 2020, Chicago, IL, USA, 22–26 June 2020, pp. 280–293. ACM (2020). https://doi.org/10.1145/3357713.3384293
3. Beaver, D., Feigenbaum, J., Kilian, J., Rogaway, P.: Security with low communication overhead. In: Menezes, A.J., Vanstone, S.A. (eds.) CRYPTO 1990. LNCS, vol. 537, pp. 62–76. Springer, Heidelberg (1991). https://doi.org/10.1007/3-540-38424-3_5
4. Beimel, A.: Secure Schemes for Secret Sharing and Key Distribution. Ph.D. thesis, Technion (1996)
5. Beimel, A.: Secret-sharing schemes: a survey. In: Chee, Y.M., et al. (eds.) IWCC 2011. LNCS, vol. 6639, pp. 11–46. Springer, Heidelberg (2011). https://doi.org/10.1007/978-3-642-20901-7_2
6. Beimel, A., Gabizon, A., Ishai, Y., Kushilevitz, E.: Distribution design. In: Proceedings of the 2016 ACM Conference on Innovations in Theoretical Computer Science, pp. 81–92. ACM (2016)

7. Beimel, A., Farràs, O.: The share size of secret-sharing schemes for almost all access structures and graphs. In: Pass, R., Pietrzak, K. (eds.) TCC 2020. LNCS, vol. 12552, pp. 499–529. Springer, Cham (2020). https://doi.org/10.1007/978-3-030-64381-2_18

8. Beimel, A., Farràs, O., Mintz, Y., Peter, N.: Linear secret-sharing schemes for forbidden graph access structures. In: Kalai, Y., Reyzin, L. (eds.) TCC 2017. LNCS, Part II, vol. 10678, pp. 394–423. Springer, Cham (2017). https://doi.org/10.1007/978-3-319-70503-3_13

9. Ben-Or, M., Goldwasser, S., Wigderson, A.: Completeness theorems for noncryptographic fault-tolerant distributed computations. In: 20th STOC, pp. 1–10. ACM (1988)

10. Benaloh, J., Leichter, J.: Generalized secret sharing and monotone functions. In: Goldwasser, S. (ed.) CRYPTO 1988. LNCS, vol. 403, pp. 27–35. Springer, New York (1990). https://doi.org/10.1007/0-387-34799-2_3

11. Bertilsson, M., Ingemarsson, I.: A construction of practical secret sharing schemes using linear block codes. In: Seberry, J., Zheng, Y. (eds.) AUSCRYPT 1992. LNCS, vol. 718, pp. 67–79. Springer, Heidelberg (1993). https://doi.org/10.1007/3-540-57220-1_53

12. Blakley, G.R.: Safeguarding cryptographic keys. In: Proceedings of the 1979 AFIPS National Computer Conference. AFIPS Conference Proceedings, vol. 48, pp. 313–317. AFIPS Press (1979)

13. Blundo, C., Santis, A.D., Gargano, L., Vaccaro, U.: On the information rate of secret sharing schemes (extended abstract). In: Advances in Cryptology - CRYPTO 1992, 12th Annual International Cryptology Conference, 16–20 August 1992, Santa Barbara, California, USA, Proceedings, pp. 148–167 (1992)

14. Chaum, D., Crépeau, C., Damgård, I.: Multiparty unconditionally secure protocols. In: 20th STOC, pp. 11–19. ACM (1988)

15. Csirmaz, L.: The size of a share must be large. J. Cryptol. **10**(4), 223–231 (1997)

16. Csirmaz, L.: Secret sharing and duality. J. Math. Cryptol. **15**(1), 157–173 (2020). https://doi.org/10.1515/jmc-2019-0045

17. Desmedt, Y., Frankel, Y.: Shared generation of authenticators and signatures. In: Feigenbaum, J. (ed.) CRYPTO 1991. LNCS, vol. 576, pp. 457–469. Springer, Heidelberg (1992). https://doi.org/10.1007/3-540-46766-1_37

18. Erdos, P., Spencer, J.: Probabilistic Methods in Combinatorics. Academic Press, Cambridge (1974)

19. Feige, U., Kilian, J., Naor, M.: A minimal model for secure computation. In: 26th STOC, pp. 554–563. ACM (1994)

20. Gal, A.: Combinatorial methods in Boolean function complexity. Ph.D. thesis, University of Chicago (1996)

21. Göös, M., Pitassi, T., Watson, T.: Zero-information protocols and unambiguity in Arthur-Merlin communication. Algorithmica **76**(3), 684–719 (2016)

22. Goyal, V., Pandey, O., Sahai, A., Waters, B.: Attribute-based encryption for fine-grained access control of encrypted data. In: 13th CCS, pp. 89–98. ACM (2006)

23. Ishai, Y., Kushilevitz, E.: On the hardness of information-theoretic multiparty computation. In: Cachin, C., Camenisch, J.L. (eds.) EUROCRYPT 2004. LNCS, vol. 3027, pp. 439–455. Springer, Heidelberg (2004). https://doi.org/10.1007/978-3-540-24676-3_26

24. Ito, M., Saito, A., Nishizeki, T.: Secret sharing schemes realizing general access structure. In: Globecom 87, pp. 99–102. IEEE (1987), Journal version: Multiple assignment scheme for sharing secret. J. Cryptol. **6**(1), 15–20 (1993)

25. Karchmer, M., Wigderson, A.: On span programs. In: 8th Structure in Complexity Theory, pp. 102–111. IEEE Computer Society (1993)
26. Liu, T., Vaikuntanathan, V.: Breaking the circuit-size barrier in secret sharing. In: Diakonikolas, I., Kempe, D., Henzinger, M. (eds.) Proceedings of the 50th Annual ACM SIGACT Symposium on Theory of Computing, STOC 2018, Los Angeles, CA, USA, 25–29 June 2018, pp. 699–708. ACM (2018). https://doi.org/10.1145/3188745.3188936
27. Liu, T., Vaikuntanathan, V., Wee, H.: Towards breaking the exponential barrier for general secret sharing. In: Nielsen, J.B., Rijmen, V. (eds.) EUROCRYPT 2018. LNCS, Part I, vol. 10820, pp. 567–596. Springer, Cham (2018). https://doi.org/10.1007/978-3-319-78381-9_21
28. Naor, M., Wool, A.: Access control and signatures via quorum secret sharing. In: 3rd CCS, pp. 157–167. ACM (1996)
29. Pitassi, T., Robere, R.: Strongly exponential lower bounds for monotone computation. In: 49th STOC, pp. 1246–1255. ACM (2017)
30. Pitassi, T., Robere, R.: Lifting Nullstellensatz to monotone span programs over any field. In: 50th STOC, pp. 1207–1219. ACM (2018)
31. Robere, R., Pitassi, T., Rossman, B., Cook, S.A.: Exponential lower bounds for monotone span programs. In: 57th FOCS, pp. 406–415. IEEE Computer Society (2016)
32. Shamir, A.: How to share a secret. Commun. ACM **22**, 612–613 (1979)
33. Shankar, B., Srinathan, K., Rangan, C.P.: Alternative protocols for generalized oblivious transfer. In: Rao, S., Chatterjee, M., Jayanti, P., Murthy, C.S.R., Saha, S.K. (eds.) ICDCN 2008. LNCS, vol. 4904, pp. 304–309. Springer, Heidelberg (2007). https://doi.org/10.1007/978-3-540-77444-0_31
34. Sun, H., Shieh, S.: Secret sharing in graph-based prohibited structures. In: Proceedings IEEE INFOCOM 1997, The Conference on Computer Communications, Sixteenth Annual Joint Conference of the IEEE Computer and Communications Societies, Driving the Information Revolution, Kobe, Japan, 7–12 April 1997, pp. 718–724 (1997)
35. Tassa, T.: Generalized oblivious transfer by secret sharing. Des. Codes Cryptograph. **58**(1), 11–21 (2011)
36. Waters, B.: Ciphertext-policy attribute-based encryption: an expressive, efficient, and provably secure realization. In: Catalano, D., Fazio, N., Gennaro, R., Nicolosi, A. (eds.) PKC 2011. LNCS, vol. 6571, pp. 53–70. Springer, Heidelberg (2011). https://doi.org/10.1007/978-3-642-19379-8_4

Asymptotically-Good Arithmetic Secret Sharing over $\mathbb{Z}/p^\ell\mathbb{Z}$ with Strong Multiplication and Its Applications to Efficient MPC

Ronald Cramer[1,2(✉)], Matthieu Rambaud[3(✉)], and Chaoping Xing[4,5(✉)]

[1] Cryptology Group, CWI Amsterdam, Amsterdam, The Netherlands
ronald.cramer@cwi.nl
[2] Leiden University, Leiden, The Netherlands
[3] Telecom Paris, Institut Polytechnique de Paris, Paris, France
rambaud@enst.fr
[4] School of Electronic Information and Electric Engineering,
Shanghai Jiao Tong University, Shanghai, China
[5] State Key Laboratory of Cryptology, Beijing, China

Abstract. This paper studies information-theoretically secure multiparty computation (MPC) over rings $\mathbb{Z}/p^\ell\mathbb{Z}$. In the work of [Abs+19a, TCC'19], a protocol based on the Shamir secret sharing over $\mathbb{Z}/p^\ell\mathbb{Z}$ was presented. As in the field case, its limitation is that the share size grows as the number of players increases. Then several MPC protocols were developed in [Abs+20, Asiacrypt'20] to overcome this limitation. However, (i) their offline multiplication gate has super-linear communication complexity in the number of players; (ii) the share size is doubled for the most important case, namely over $\mathbb{Z}/2^\ell\mathbb{Z}$ due to infeasible lifting of self-orthogonal codes from fields to rings; (iii) most importantly, the BGW model could not be applied via the secret sharing given in [Abs+20, Asiacrypt'20] due to lack of strong multiplication.

In this paper we overcome all the drawbacks mentioned above. Of independent interest, we establish an arithmetic secret sharing with strong multiplication, which is the most important primitive in the BGW model. Incidentally, our solution to (i) has some advantages over the concurrent one of [PS21, EC'21], since it is direct, is only one-page long, and furthermore carries over $\mathbb{Z}/p^\ell\mathbb{Z}$. Finally, we lift Reverse Multiplication Friendly Embeddings (RMFE) from fields to rings, with same (linear) complexity. Note that RMFE has become a standard technique for communication complexity in MPC in the regime over many instances of the same circuit, as in [Cas+18, Crypto'18] and [DLN19, Crypto'19]. We thus recover the same amortized complexity of MPC over $\mathbb{Z}/2^\ell\mathbb{Z}$ than over fields.

To obtain our theoretical results, we use the existence of lifts of curves over rings, then use the known results stating that Riemann-Roch spaces

Supported by Horizon 2020 74079 (ALGSTRONGCRYPTO) and NSFC under grant 12031011 and the National Key Research and Development Project 2020YFA0712300.

T. Malkin and C. Peikert (Eds.): CRYPTO 2021, LNCS 12827, pp. 656–686, 2021.
https://doi.org/10.1007/978-3-030-84252-9_22

are free modules. To make our scheme practical, we start from good alge-braic geometry codes over finite fields obtained from existing computa-tional techniques. Then we present, and implement, an efficient algorithm to Hensel-lift the generating matrix of the code, such that the multiplica-tive conditions are preserved over rings. On the other hand, a random lifting of codes over rings does not preserve multiplicativity in general. Finally we provide efficient methods for sharing and reconstruction over rings.

1 Introduction

MPC over rings $\mathbb{Z}/p^\ell\mathbb{Z}$, is a model relevant for secure computation of functions which are naturally expressed over rings of integers $\mathbb{Z}/p^\ell\mathbb{Z}$. The most important case is $\mathbb{Z}/2^\ell\mathbb{Z}$ with ℓ (a multiple of) the length of machines integers. In this model, the computation complexity is counted in terms of elementary additions and multiplications in $\mathbb{Z}/p^\ell\mathbb{Z}$, and the communication complexity is the number of elements of $\mathbb{Z}/p^\ell\mathbb{Z}$ sent. By contrast, the previous model of MPC are arithmetic circuits in $\mathbb{F}_p$. But computations modulo p are not natively done by processors. Unless $p = 2$, which is the case studied by MPC for the functions expressed naturally as binary circuits. It appears from the literature that emulating MPC over the integers, from MPC in $\mathbb{F}_p$, incurs a substantial overhead in complexity. For instance, the protocol of [Dam+06] for bit decomposition of numbers mod-ulo a large p, in order to perform secure comparisons, costs $\log(p)\log(\log(p))$ secure multiplications modulo p. Whereas comparisons directly between integers modulo a power of 2 are much more efficient [Ara+18].

1.1 Related Works

In a recent line of work on efficient MPC over $\mathbb{Z}/p^\ell\mathbb{Z}$, significant advances have been made in order to avoid the overhead incurred by this emulation, by redesign-ing basic arithmetic MPC so as to work "more directly" over the ring in question. The first published paper [Cra+18] in this line introduces the SPDZ$_{2^k}$ proto-col, a full redesign of the well-known SPDZ-protocol [Dam+12], the benchmark for the case of cryptographic security with dishonest majority in Beaver's pre-processing model, that works directly over the rings in question and that is essentially as efficient as the most efficient SPDZ-incarnation. See also the com-pilers of [DOS18, Abs+19b] from passive security over rings to active security over rings. For more discussion about practical advantages, see [Cra+18] and its follow-up [Dam+19], which also reports on applications to machine-learning that significantly outperform approaches from field-based MPC. Maliciously secure machine learning directly over the integers is now becoming the standard (e.g. [PS20]).

Closer to us is the line of work [Abs+19a, Abs+20], that aims at answering the question if information theoretically secure MPC over $\mathbb{Z}/p^\ell\mathbb{Z}$, has complexity equal to the one of MPC over $\mathbb{F}_p$. The issue is simple: suppose that one has the choice between two protocols with the same complexities: measured over $\mathbb{F}_p$ for the former, and over $\mathbb{Z}/p^\ell\mathbb{Z}$ for the latter. Then the latter protocol is automatically the most efficient to securely compute any function over $\mathbb{Z}/p^\ell\mathbb{Z}$, since no emulation is needed. The present paper firstly addresses this question mainly in the plain model [CDN15, §5], denoted "BGW", that is: assuming only authenticated channels and requiring perfect security. So in particular, we have that the number of malicious corruptions is $t < n/3$, since no broadcast channel is available beyond this bound in the BGW model. [Abs+19a] considers MPC in the BGW model over rings. It adapts the protocol of [BH08], including the secret sharing over $\mathbb{Z}/p^\ell\mathbb{Z}$ adapted from Shamir, and thus inherits the amortized suboptimal $O(n\log(n))$ communication complexity of [BH08].

We then consider the setting of Rabin&Ben-Or, denoted as "honest majority", which assumes a broadcast and requires unconditional statistical security, tolerating $t < n/2$ corruptions. Until recently the best amortized communication complexity over fields was [BFO12], in $n\log(n)$, plus a term in n^2 times the depth of the circuit. Let us first discuss the n^2 term, which was removed over fields by [GSZ20]. As noticed in [Abs+20] (at the beginning of §6), the main tool of [GSZ20] is the Batched Triple Sacrifice protocol of [BFO12], that checks correctness of shared Beaver triples. It runs in the offline phase, and has $O(n\log(n))$ communication complexity (to be sure, the notation ϕ in [GSZ20] stands for the log of the size of the field, it is required to be $\phi \geq \log(n)$). This Batched Triple Sacrifice was then carried over rings in [Abs+20], resulting in an overall amortized communication complexity in $O(n\log(n))$ also over rings.

Let us now discuss the $\log(n)$ overhead. Concurrently to our paper, it has been removed by [PS21, EC'21], over fields. Their technique use as black box the RMFE with optimal rate of [Cas+18], which come from algebraic curves.

In addition to the above super-linear offline communication complexity, there are some other drawbacks in [Abs+20]: (i) their secret sharing schemes with (standalone) Multiplication are constructed with a double sharing, which thus doubles the size (ii) their way around this doubling, only for $p \geq 3$, uses asymptotically good families of self-dual codes, for which no practical construction is known (by contrast with good families of codes from algebraic curves/function fields, whose computation is widely studied); (iii) most importantly, the secret sharing scheme given in [Abs+20] cannot be adopted for the BGW model due to lack of Strong multiplication.

1.2   Our Focus

Our main focus are the two fundamental primitives for MPC in the BGW model. We also deal with the asymptotic complexity of MPC under honest majority, especially the Batched Triple Sacrifice which costs the so-far $\log(n)$ communication overhead. We are finally concerned by the computational efficiency of general reconstruction methods of linear secret sharing schemes over rings, which was not dealt with at all in previous works.

The first primitive for MPC in the BGW model is *arithmetic secret sharing with Strong multiplication* (ASSSM). Recall that such a scheme with respect to adversary bound t, guarantees both: secrecy from any t shares, and, reconstruction of the product of two shared secrets, from any list of $n-t$ products of pairwise shares of these secrets. By contrast, secret sharing with (standalone) Multiplication only, requires *all* the n pairwise products of shares for reconstruction of the product. The simplest example is the Verifiable secret sharing of BGW itself. Importance of Strong multiplication is formalized in the Theorem 3 of [CDM00], as the building block of error-free MPC protocols. Namely, it is emphasized in [CDN15, p114] as the tool enabling not to restart the execution of the protocol, even when a player openly misbehaves. Notice that the $\log(n)$ overhead is inherited from Shamir's secret sharing, which operates in finite fields of cardinality *at least as large* as the number of players. This limitation was removed in the series of papers [CC06, Cas+09, CCX11] using algebraic geometric codes over fields. Notice that these state of the art ASSSM and constant size of shares, motivated the "MPC in the head technique" [Ish+07], see [Cas16, §5] for other applications. In this paper we ask if the same tight size of shares is achievable over rings. We also ask if the same efficiency of constructions is achievable as over fields [Hes02, Khu04, Shu+01, SG20]. Also, much optimisation has been made for sharing/reconstruction algorithms over fields [SW99, GS99, NW17].

The second primitive are *Reverse multiplication friendly embeddings* (RMFE). They enable to emulate several circuits in parallel over small finite fields $\mathbb{F}_p$, from a single circuit over a large extension $\mathbb{F}_{p^m}$. They are introduced in [Cas+18], and are the main tool for the upper bounds of [DLN19, BMN18, DLS20, CG20, PS21]. RMFE enable to linearize the amortized communication complexity of perfectly secure MPC, over multiple instances of the same circuit (with possibly different inputs), while preserving an *optimal* corruption tolerance. Recall that a RMFE [Cas+18, Definition 1] (recalled in Sect. 5.4), is an embedding from some vector space $\mathbb{F}_q^k$ over $\mathbb{F}_q$, into some field extension $\mathbb{F}_{q^m}$, which "carries" the multiplication in $\mathbb{F}_{q^m}$ into the component-wise multiplication of vectors in $\mathbb{F}_q^k$ (the same one as for multiplicative secret sharing). The larger the ratio k/m, the better the complexity of MPC is amortized. Again, RMFE with polynomial encoding (as in Shamir secret sharing) exist up to $k \leq q+1$. And again, this limit of the field size was removed in [Cas+18, Theorem 3] with constructions from algebraic geometry coding. Namely, they achieve for any fix q, a slowly growing infinite family of parameters k, m such that the ratios k/m are lower bounded by a *constant*, which is optimal. We thus ask if the same ratios are achievable over rings, and if constructions are as efficient.

1.3   Our Contributions

1.3.1   Asymptotically Optimal Strong Multiplication over Rings

Main Theorem 1. For every p and ℓ, for any fixed even r larger than some $\hat{r}(p)$, we have a slowly growing infinite family of number of integers n, such that there exists an ASSSM over the fixed ring $\mathbb{Z}/p^\ell\mathbb{Z}$, with n shares, with constant size of shares r and t-adversary bound such that $1/3 - t/n > 0$ a constant arbitrarily close to 0 (in $O(p^{-r/2})$).

More precisely and generally: all parameters $(n, p, \hat{r}(p), t)$ published in [CC06, Cas+09] over fields $\mathbb{F}_p$, *also* hold over rings. We have stronger than privacy: *uniformity* of the projection on any t shares of the space of vectors of shares of any given fixed secret. Moreover, the scheme obtained by reduction modulo p may be assumed to be asymptotically good as well. [1] Last but not least, sharing and reconstruction over $\mathbb{Z}/p^\ell\mathbb{Z}$ have the *same computational complexity* than for ASSSM over fields $\mathbb{F}_p$.

This thus closes the gap between the complexity of ASSSM over fields, and over rings. Since this result is tight, we do not further justify why our construction uses "Galois rings" extensions as an intermediary step. Although we hope that it will be clear from Sect. 1.4, Sect. 2.1 (and also [Abs+19a, Abs+20]) that these objects play the same auxiliary role over rings, as finite fields extensions do over fields. Concretely, under the hood is that $\mathbb{F}_p$ is embedded into $\mathbb{F}_{p^r}$ in order to access ASSSM/RMFE with good properties, which are then lifted over Galois ring extensions, then seen as free modules over $\mathbb{Z}/p^\ell\mathbb{Z}$. But for simplicity, we refrained from stating that the above theorem also holds for any Galois ring extension of degree r, with the same parameters $(n, p, r(p), t)$ than [CC06, Cas+09] over $\mathbb{F}_{p^r}$. We also kept simple the formula and made explicit only the case where t is close to $n/3$. To be sure, the parameters of [Cas+09] also enable smaller sizes of shares, at the cost of a lower t (using multiplication friendly embeddings). The last claim, on efficiency, will follow from the algorithms of Theorem 5 below. Technically, Theorem 5 applies here since the componentwise squares (see Sect. 3.1) of the codes constructed are included in "free codes" of dimension as small as the codes of the ASSSM over finite fields.

1.3.2 Optimal Communication of MPC Under Honest Majority

We remove the so-far aforementioned amortized $\log(n)$ communication overhead, which also held over fields. The bottleneck comes from the offline phase, in the subprotocol of [BFO12] checking triples, e.g., as transposed over rings in [Abs+20, §6.6]. Recall that the baseline method of [BFO12] proceeds by encoding many triples in three polynomials, then succinctly check the multiplicative relation between these polynomials. We start by replacing it by an alternative construction of Batched Triple Sacrifice over fields of fixed size. This construction is closely related to the strong multiplication property, it is stated and proven in Proposition 16. It enables to recover the main result of [PS21] in only one page. We then lift the construction over rings with the same methods as before.

Main Theorem 2. In the model of [RB89]: honest majority and assuming broadcast, then there exists a statistically secure MPC protocol with guaranteed output delivery and amortized communication complexity (both online and offline) linear in the number of players per multiplication gate.

---

[1] This fact is quite useful in some practical protocol applications but it is not strictly necessary for general arithmetic MPC.

Anticipating on the next result, notice that we could also have directly lifted over rings the construction of [PS21]. Indeed, theirs is based on the RMFE of [Cas+18], which we lift over rings with the same asymptotic rates.

1.3.3   Amortized Complexity of MPC over Rings

We construct, in Sect. 5.2 an infinite family of RMFE over rings with same *constant* asymptotic ratio as the ones of [Cas+18]. Combined with the tight complexities of general LSSS proven in Theorem 5, this enables to carry over rings the results of [Cas+18] with the same computational and communication complexities:

Main Theorem 3. In the BGW-model, there is an efficient MPC protocol for n parties secure against the maximal number of active corruptions $t < n/3$ that computes $\Omega(\log n)$ evaluations of a single circuit over $\mathbb{Z}/p^\ell\mathbb{Z}$ in parallel with an amortized communication complexity (per instance) of $O(n)$ elements of $\mathbb{Z}/p^\ell\mathbb{Z}$ per gate, and same computational complexity than in [Cas+18, Thm 1 & 2]. Combining with the Franklin-Yung paradigm [FY92], we get:

In the BGW-model, for every $\epsilon > 0$, there is an efficient MPC protocol for n parties secure against a submaximal number of active corruptions $t < (1-\epsilon)n/3$ that computes $\Omega(n\log n)$ evaluations of a single circuit over $\mathbb{Z}/p^\ell\mathbb{Z}$ in parallel with an amortized communication complexity (per instance) of $O(1)$ elements of $\mathbb{Z}/p^\ell\mathbb{Z}$ per gate.

1.3.4   Optimal Share Sizes and Computability Under Honest Majority

The asymptotically good ASSSM of Theorem 1 have a fortiori standalone Multiplication. So they can be used as a replacement for the schemes constructed in [Abs+20, §4.1]. Especially for $p = 2$, recall that Multiplication of their schemes is obtained via a double sharing, which thus doubles the size of the shares (as stressed in the roadmap of [Abs+20, §3]). Our construction thus *divides their sizes of shares by 2 for $p = 2$*. A corollary of above, is that the active protocol presented in Section 6 of [Abs+20], which requires standalone Multiplication, now works with share sizes reduced to half, and now using *computable* families of codes, including from AG/function fields.

1.3.5   Practical Computability (continued)

Main Theorems 1, 2 and 3 rely on objects (ASSSM or RMFE or the related ones of Proposition 16) with good asymptotic properties of which we prove existence. We then describe in Sect. 4 efficient algorithms to construct these objects.

Theorem 4. *Starting from any ASSSM over any fixed field $\mathbb{F}_p$ considered in [CC06, Cas+09, CCX11], then, obtaining the lifts over $\mathbb{Z}/p^\ell\mathbb{Z}$ for any ℓ, as predicted by Main Theorem 1, boils down to solving ℓ instances of a linear system over $\mathbb{F}_p$ with $\Omega(n^6)$ coefficients. Alternatively, $\log(\ell)$ linear systems: modulo $p, p^2, p^4, \ldots, (p^\ell)^{\frac{1}{2}}$.*

We have an analogous system to obtain the RMFE predicted by Main Theorem 3, from the ones of [Cas+18, Theorem 5].

A formal description is given in Sect. 4 (for ASSSM) and Sect. 5.4 (for RMFE), a toy example in Sect. 3.1. A proof of Theorem 4 is given in the long version. It requires to prove that AG codes have a free lift whose square is also free, which requires additional methods than those given in Sect. 3.3. We illustrate efficiency of our method in Sect. 4.1 by lifting a strongly multiplicative secret sharing scheme over $\mathbb{F}_{16}$ for 64 players and adversary threshold $t = 13$, into a scheme over the Galois extension of degree four of $\mathbb{Z}/2^{100}\mathbb{Z}$, in a minute on a single processor.

1.3.6   Tight Computational Complexity of Linear Secret Sharing Schemes (LSSS) over Rings

Although theoretical results for error correction over rings are shown in [Abs+19a, Construction 1 & Proposition 1], it is not yet clear in the literature if there exists *effective algorithms* for even the simple task of reconstruction of a secret with only erasures. We fill this gap by providing algorithms for sharing and reconstruction of linear secret sharing schemes (LSSS) over rings that arize from *free* codes. In particular it proves our efficiency claims in the Main Theorems above. A free code C over $\mathbb{Z}/p^\ell\mathbb{Z}$ is by definition the linear span of independent vectors with coordinates in $\mathbb{Z}/p^\ell\mathbb{Z}$, in particular it is of same dimension than its reduction $\overline{C}$ modulo p, which is a code over $\mathbb{F}_p$. In particular, all the ASSSM constructed in this paper have this property, as well as the objects studied in [Abs+20] and in [Abs+19a] (which considers the specific case of Shamir secret sharing over rings). On the other hand, LSSS arising from nonfree codes have bad computational complexity, as we illustrate in Counterexample 10. We provide computational complexities that match the ones over finite fields, so which are *tight*. For simplicity the following theorem is stated over $\mathbb{Z}/p^\ell\mathbb{Z}$, but it will be clear from the proof that it obviously also holds over any Galois ring extension.

Theorem 5. *Let n, ℓ be integers, consider a free code C in $(\mathbb{Z}/p^\ell\mathbb{Z})^{n+1}$ and let ψ the corresponding (LSSS) with n shares in $\mathbb{Z}/p^\ell\mathbb{Z}$, such that (without loss of generality) the secret is encoded in the 0-th coordinate of codewords. Denote $\overline{C}$ the code reduced modulo p and $\overline{\psi}$ the corresponding LSSS (which is ψ modulo p) over $\mathbb{F}_p$. We have:*

(A) *The task of computing a generating matrix of C in systematic form, from any generating matrix of C and, more generally, Gauss pivot, has same computational complexity as modulo p, plus $O((\dim C)(\log \ell))$.*

(A') *Then, sharing a secret using ψ (thus of bitsize ℓ times larger) has same computational complexity than using $\overline{\psi}$. As for sharewise multiplication.*

(B) *Let $I \subset \{1, \ldots, n\}$ be a set of $n - d(\overline{C}) + 2$ indices of shares. Then, there exists a linear map $\phi_I : (\mathbb{Z}/p^\ell\mathbb{Z})^{|I|} \longrightarrow \mathbb{Z}/p^\ell\mathbb{Z}$ that reconstructs the secret, with the same complexity than a reconstruction map $\overline{\phi_I}$ for $\overline{\psi}$. Moreover, ϕ_I can be compiled from a reconstruction map $\overline{\phi_I}$ for the LSSS modulo p, essentially for the cost of one matrix inversion in $(\mathbb{Z}/p^\ell\mathbb{Z})^{|I| \times |I|}$.*

Notice that the matrix inversion required in (B) can be computed using the Gauss pivot of (A).

1.4   Difficulties and Intuitions of the Constructions

Only algebraic-geometric (AG) constructions such as in [CC06] are so far known to enable ASSSM over fields of constant sizes for an arbitrarily large number of shares. They follow the same pattern than the scheme of Shamir, which is a particular case. First, select an algebraic curve (e.g. all the points in $\mathbb{F}_q$ plus the "point at infinity", in the case of Shamir). Second, select a "Riemann-Roch" vector space of functions (e.g. the polynomials of degree $\leq d$ in the case of Shamir: said otherwise, the space $\mathcal{L}(d\infty)$ of polynomials "vanishing at order at least d at infinity"). Then, select a particular point P_0 on the curve (e.g. the point 0 in Shamir). To share a secret s, select a function at random in the Riemann-Roch space that evaluates to s at P_0. Then evaluate it on n predefined points of the curve to obtain the shares. In what follows we will instead take a coding-based approach. This has both the advantage to make proofs which are more black box in the AG codes used, and also, our efficient methods will actually directly lift the generating matrices of such AG codes over fields.

For C a code (over a field or a ring), we denote as *componentwise square* C^{*2} the code of same length which is generated by all the products of any two codewords of C component by component. Strong multiplication of the LSSS from C thus requires that C^{*2} has large distance, thus be of small size. The central problem of this paper is thus brought down to: starting from a free code C over a ring (typically a finite field) which has free square of small dimension, then find a code $\widetilde{C}$ in a larger ring, that reduces to C mod p^ℓ, and has square contained in a free code of small size. On the one hand, it is trivial to lift Reed-Solomon (RS) codes over rings, in a way that preserves their remarkably small componentwise square. Indeed, lifts of RS codes are given for free: these are the RS codes over rings. RS codes over rings were studied in [Abs+19a], but, as over finite fields, these RS codes have a $\log(n)$ size overhead. This inefficiency is one of the main motivations of the present paper. On the other hand, when trying to lift AG codes with larger genus, in order to remove this overhead, we hit the main difficulty of this paper. Namely, we illustrate in Sect. 3.1 that lifting at random (as done in [Abs+20]) almost certainly *fails* to preserve the small dimension of the square.

But our theoretical results imply that a solution exists, which we are able to compute efficiently. Anticipating on them, we first present a toy example in Sect. 3.2. Recall that RS codes are the simplest case of AG codes, namely, over the curve $\mathbf{P}^1$ (the "projective line"), which is of genus 0. This is why our toy example Sect. 3.2 illustrates the simplest nontrivial example, which is a curve of genus 1.

To obtain our theoretical results over rings, we first use known theorems that state the existence of lifts of curves over rings. We then apply results of Judy Walker that state that Riemann Roch spaces are free modules, and also, the codes deduced from their injective evaluation at points of the curve. On the other hand, to compute the codes concretely, we will follow a direct approach. Namely, instead of lifting curves over rings, we will directly lift a generating matrix of the code, such that the multiplicative conditions are preserved. On the face of it, there are more constraints than variables. But a result is always returned. Proving this fact requires strictly more than that C lifts with a small square. Indeed, it also requires *freeness* of the square of the lift $\widetilde{C}^{*2}$, which is harder. This is why we prove it in the long version only.

The reader may wonder why we did not directly compute lifts of the curves. The reason is that the theoretical results require that the curves be represented with "smooth" equations, in particular, with many variables. But in practice, good curves are expressed in terms of equations with two variables only. And there is no efficient method today to compute smooth lifts of such "plane" models, that have many "non smooth" points. Let alone computing Riemann-Roch spaces of smooth models curves over rings, which is out of the scope of existing research (except Walker-Voloch, for smooth curves in the plane).

1.5   Roadmap

In Sect. 2 we show that LSSS derived from free codes over Galois rings have same privacy and reconstruction threshold as over the field modulo p. In Sect. 2.3 and Sect. 2.4 we present efficient sharing and reconstruction algorithms (proof of Theorem 5 (A) (A') and (B)). We show conversely in Counterexample 10 that *there does not exist a linear reconstruction map* for a large class of linear codes over rings which are not free. This is why we focus on LSSS derived from free codes. Let us mention for the hurry reader that the results in Sect. 2.3 and Sect. 2.5 are not used for the proof of Main Theorem 1.

In Sect. 3 we highlight the nontriviality of Main Theorem 1 on a toy example in Sect. 3.1, then illustrate in Sect. 3.2 how to compute a multiplicative lift of it. We then prove the Theorem in Sect. 3.3.

In Sect. 4 we elaborate more on the Hensel lifting method illustrated in the toy example.

In Sect. 5 we prove the aforementioned applications of the theory to MPC. First with a proof of Proposition 16 (the triples sacrifice algorithm over a field-/ring of constant size), then with a proof of Main Theorem 3. The proof involves RMFE over rings with same asymptotically constant rate than over fields: we also describe the effective algorithm to construct them in Sect. 5.4.

2   LSSS from *Free* Codes have Optimal Complexity

In Sect. 2.1 we introduce Galois ring extensions, and highlight that they the same size and computational overhead over $\mathbb{Z}/p^\ell\mathbb{Z}$, than finite field extensions have over $\mathbb{F}_{p^r}$. The presentation should be self-contained, but the reader can also refer to [Abs+20, Abs+19a]. In Sect. 2.2 and Sect. 2.3 we consider general LSSS from free codes over rings, and prove the tight complexity claims (A') and (B) of Theorem 5 for sharing and reconstruction. In Sect. 2.5 we show that free codes are generated from any lift of any basis. All the basics are recalled, but the reader can alternatively refer to [Abs+20, §2-§4]

2.1 Optimal Complexities in Galois Rings Extensions $R_\ell(r)$

2.1.1 Equal Computational and Sizes for Elementary Operations

Let p be a positive prime number and $\mathbb{F}_p := \mathbb{Z}/p\mathbb{Z}$ the finite field. Then, when operating on objects with coordinates in $\mathbb{F}_p$, we say that the *computational complexity* is the number of *elementary operations in $\mathbb{F}_p$* (where one can possibly weight differently additions, scalar multiplications and bilinear multiplications). Now, $\ell \geq 1$ denoting an integer, the second context encountered in this paper are objects with coordinates in $\mathbb{Z}/p^\ell\mathbb{Z}$ the ring of integers modulo p^ℓ. In these cases, we say that the computation complexity is the number of *elementary operations in $\mathbb{Z}/p^\ell\mathbb{Z}$* (where one gives the same weights as before to additions, scalar multiplications and bilinear multiplications). Likewise, the *communication (or size) complexity* is, in the first context: the number of elements in $\mathbb{F}_p$ which are sent by honest players; whereas in the second context it is the number of elements in $\mathbb{Z}/p^\ell\mathbb{Z}$ which are sent.

Galois-rings are defined as follows. Let $r \geq 1$ be a positive integer and $\overline{f(X)} \in \mathbb{F}_p[X]$ a monic irreducible polynomial of degree r. This defines the finite field extension or degree r:

$$\mathbb{F}_{p^r} = \mathbb{F}_p < \delta > := \mathbb{F}_p[X]/\overline{f(X)}$$

which is a vector space of dimension r over $\mathbb{F}_p$ with basis $1, \delta, \ldots, \delta^{r-1}$ and multiplication rule defined by the multiplication modulo $\overline{f(X)}$. Now, consider any monic polynomial $f(X) \in \mathbb{Z}/p^\ell\mathbb{Z}$ which reduces to $\overline{f(X)}$ modulo p. Then this defines the Galois ring extension of degree r:

$$(1) \qquad R_\ell(r) = \mathbb{Z}/p^\ell\mathbb{Z} < \Delta > := \mathbb{Z}/p^\ell\mathbb{Z}[X]/f(X)$$

which is in particular equal to $\mathbb{Z}/p^\ell\mathbb{Z}$ when $r = 1$. This is a *free module* over $\mathbb{Z}/p^\ell\mathbb{Z}$ of dimention r. That is: it is isomorphic to $(\mathbb{Z}/p^\ell\mathbb{Z})^r$, with basis $1, \Delta, \ldots, \Delta^{r-1}$. Multiplication in $R_\ell(r)$ is defined by the multiplication modulo $f(X)$. Notice that an equivalent definition of $R_\ell(r)$ is to consider the unramified extension of degree r of the ring $\mathbb{Z}_p$ of p-adic integers, which is denoted $W(\mathbb{F}_{p^r})$ the "Witt ring", then reduce it modulo p^ℓ. This will be used in Sect. 3.3, and is also a useful point of view for the Hensel lifting algorithm of Sect. 4.

We say that an element $x \in R_\ell(r)$ is invertible modulo p if its reduction $\bar{x} \in \mathbb{F}_{p^r}$ is invertible. A key property of Galois rings is that an element invertible modulo p, is then also invertible in $R_\ell(r)$. Indeed, consider an arbitrary lift y of $\bar{x}^{-1}$. Then we have a formula $xy = 1 - p\lambda$ which holds in $R_\ell(r)$ for some λ. But the right hand side of the equation is invertible, of inverse $1 + p\lambda + \cdots + (p\lambda)^{\ell-1}$. From this formula we see that inversion in $R_\ell(r)$ costs essentially one inversion in $\mathbb{F}_{p^r}$, and $O(\log(\ell))$ squarings in $R_\ell(r)$.

2.1.2   Embeddings, and Their Equal Complexities Than over Fields

From the previous, we see that considering $\mathbb{Z}/p^\ell\mathbb{Z}$ as *embedded* in $R_\ell(r)$, multiplies by r the size (an element x is mapped to the vector $(x, 0, \ldots, 0)$ with r coordinates) by the same factor than when embedding $\mathbb{F}_p$ in $\mathbb{F}_{p^r}$. It follows from the definition (1) that the naive schoolboy multiplication algorithm in $R_\ell(r)$ has the same complexity than the one in $\mathbb{F}_{p^r}$. For large Galois rings, we have efficient multiplication algorithms, which are motivated by their usage in LWE. Hence, the references pointed in [Abs+19a, page 4] and [PC] show that they have also the same complexity than in $\mathbb{F}_{p^r}$.

Finally, one may also need to make the converse operation, and "descend" from secret sharing schemes over $R_\ell(r)$, to secret sharing schemes over $\mathbb{Z}/p^\ell\mathbb{Z}$. The technique to do this over fields is introduced in [Cas+09, Theorem 7 & 8], and based on linear maps called "multiplication friendly embeddings (MFE)": $\mathbb{F}_{p^m} \longrightarrow \mathbb{F}_p^{2m-1}$, which have the property to bring the multiplication in $\mathbb{F}_{p^m}$, into the componentwise product in $\mathbb{F}_p^{2m-1}$. For the same reason as Reed Solomon codes lift trivially over rings, we have that the MFEs of [Cas+09, Theorem 8] carry over $\mathbb{Z}/p^\ell\mathbb{Z}$ with the same parameters, and thus we have exactly the same "expansion rates" $((2m-1)/m)$.

2.2   General LSSS and ASSSM over Rings

Let R be any finite ring (including $R = \mathbb{F}_{p^r}$ or $R_\ell(r)$), and n, k be positive integers. To share a secret s in R, one samples uniformly an element $\boldsymbol{w} \in R^{k-1}$ (the randomness space) then applies a certain linear map ψ on the whole to obtain n "shares" : $\psi(s, \boldsymbol{w}) \in R^n$. For $I \subset \{1, \ldots n\}$ a set of indices, we denote $|I|$ the size of I and $\pi_I : R^n \to R^I$ the projection on these components. For any vector $\boldsymbol{x} \in R^n$, we denote for short $\boldsymbol{x}_I := \pi_I(\boldsymbol{x})$ this projection, i.e., the components of $\boldsymbol{x}$ in I, and likewise, for any linear map ψ in R^n, we denote for short $\psi_I := \pi_I \circ \psi$ the "components of ψ in I". Let $0 \le t < n$ be a positive integer. Let $k, n \ge 1$ be integers, we say that a *linear secret sharing scheme* (LSSS) over R with n shares and randomness space R^{k-1}, is an R-linear map:

$$\psi : R \times R^{k-1} \longrightarrow R^n$$
$$(s, \boldsymbol{w}) \longrightarrow \psi(s, \boldsymbol{w})$$

We say that it has t-privacy if for any share vector, any t coordinates are independent of the secret, and it has *rec-reconstruction* if any *rec* coordinates of a vector of shares determine the secret s.

Definition 6. We say that a LSSS with privacy threshold t, is furthermore Arithmetic with Strong multiplication (ASSSM), if for any two secrets $s, s' \in R$, consider any sharings of them: $(s_i) = \psi(s, \boldsymbol{u})$ and $(s'_i) = \psi(s', \boldsymbol{u}')$, then for any set I of indices of size $n - t$, the data of the "sharewise" products $(\psi(s_i)\psi(s'_i))_{i \in I}$ determines uniquely ss'. Said otherwise, I is a "reconstruction set" for $\psi \times \psi$.

Notice that this a fortiori implies $n - t$ reconstruction threshold. If one replaces $n-t$ by n in the definition above, then this is the weaker *Multiplication* property.

2.3   Complexity of Sharing

From now on we specialize to a Galois ring $R := R_\ell(r)$ as defined in (1), e.g., equal to $\mathbb{Z}/p^\ell\mathbb{Z}$ when $r = 1$.

2.3.1   Proof of Theorem 5 (A): Systematic Form

Let $C \subset R_\ell(r)^{n+1}$ be a *free* submodule of rank k, i.e., which is isomorphic to $R_\ell(r)^k$. Making a choice of $n + 1$ coordinates in $R_\ell(r)^{n+1}$, we denote this a "free code". Likewise, we say that k elements in $R_\ell(r)^{n+1}$ form a *free* family if they generate a submodule isomorphic to $R_\ell(r)^k$ (we then say: "freely generate"). Recall that this implies that the reduction $\overline{C}$ of C modulo p is a vector space of *same dimension* k. [This follows immediately from the fact that if a square matrix with entries in $R_\ell(r)$ is invertible, then its reduction $\bmod\, p$ is invertible.] For the same reason, in the other direction, starting from a code $\overline{C}$ over $\mathbb{F}_{p^r}$ of dimension k, and considering any basis, then arbitrary lifts in $R_\ell(r)$ of these basis vectors generate a free code C of same rank k.

We denote that a matrix $G \in R_\ell(r)^{k\times(n+1)}$ is in *echelon form*, if for each row $i \in \{1,\dots,k\}$, there exists a column $j_i \in \{0,\dots,n\}$ containing a 1 entry on row i and 0 everywhere else. We say in particular that G is in *systematic form* if of the form $(\mathrm{Id}_k|N)$. We say that matrix G' is deduced from matrix G by "elementary row operations", if there exists a sequence of elementary row operations that transforms G into G'. Equivalently, if there exists an invertible matrix $E \in R_\ell(r)^{k\times k}$ such that $G' = EG$. Let us restate for convenience existence the systematic form of free codes, which is used at least since Calderbank-Sloane [CS95] (see also [SAS17, §5.1.1]). We re-prove it with an explicit construction, which has same complexity than over fields, which thus proves Theorem 5 (A).

Proposition 7. *Let $G \in R_\ell(r)^{k\times(n+1)}$ be a matrix such that the rows form a free family. Then there exists a matrix in echelon form which is obtained from G by elementary row operations. And thus, up to reordering the $n+1$, coordinates, in systematic form.*

Proof. Consider the reduction of $\overline{G}$ in $\mathbb{F}_{p^r}$. By the Gauss pivot, there exists an invertible $k \times k$ matrix $\overline{E}$ and a matrix $\overline{G'}$ in echelon form, such that $\overline{G'} = \overline{EG}$. Let $E \in R_\ell(r)^{k\times k}$ be an arbitrarily lift of $\overline{E}$. E being invertible (since its determinant is invertible modulo p), the matrix $G' := EG$ is deductible from G by elementary row operations. G' being a lift of $\overline{G'}$, we have furthermore, for each row i, existence of a column j_i such that the entry G'_{i,j_i} is a lift of 1, and thus *invertible* in $R_\ell(r)$. Using this entry as a pivot, we anihilate all the other entries on this column j_i by elementary row operations. Finally, we divide the row i by G'_{i,j_i}, thus entry (i,j_i) becomes 1. Repeating for all i yields a matrix G'' deduced from G' by elementary row operations.

2.3.2   Sharing

Up to permutation of the coordinates, we may now assume $G \in R_\ell(r)^{k\times(n+1)}$ of C in *systematic form*. By Theorem 5 (A) (Proposition 7), the (one-shot) complexity of computing this form is essentially the same as over fields. Then, sharing a secret $s \in R_\ell(r)$ with respect to the 0-th coordinate of C, boils down to the following. First, sample a vector $w \in R_\ell(r)^{k-1}$, uniformly at random. This has complexity $O(k)$ (or in terms of bits: $O(\ell k \log_2(p))$). Then, deduce the vector of shares from the left multiplication:

$$(2) \qquad\qquad \psi : R_\ell(r) \times R_\ell(r)^{k-1} \longrightarrow R_\ell(r)^n$$

$$(3) \qquad\qquad (s, w) \longrightarrow (s, w)G_{[1,\dots,n]}.$$

Where $G_{[1,\dots,n]}$ denotes the n last columns of G. The complexity claim of Theorem 5(A') then follows from the fact that $\dim(\overline{C}) = \mathrm{rk}\,(C) = k$, and thus that the generating matrices have the same sizes, combined with the fact pointed in Sect. 2.1, that complexity of the multiplication in $R_\ell(r)$ (by definition relatively to elementary operations in $\mathbb{Z}/p^\ell\mathbb{Z}$) is the same as the one in $\mathbb{F}_{p^r}$ (by definition relatively to $\mathbb{F}_p$).

2.4 Privacy (with Uniformity) and Efficient Reconstruction from *Free* Codes

Let us now bound privacy and reconstruction. The following states that Theorem 11.77 and Corollary 11.79 [CDN15] also hold over rings. Moreover, we will also prove computational efficiency of (4) (reconstruction) along the proof.

Proposition 8. *Let C be a free code in $R_\ell(r)^{n+1}$ of rank k. Denote $\overline{C}$ the code over $\mathbb{F}_{p^r}$ obtained by reduction modulo p, $\overline{C}^\perp$ the dual, and $d(\overline{C})$, $d(\overline{C}^\perp)$ the minimal distances. Consider the LSSS with n shares in $R_\ell(r)$ obtained from C. Recall that rec denotes the reconstruction threshold. Then we have:*

$$(4) \qquad\qquad \mathrm{rec} \leq n + 1 - (d(\overline{C}) - 1) = n - d(\overline{C}) + 2$$

$$(5) \qquad\qquad \text{For all }\ t \geq d(\overline{C}^\perp) - 2, \quad \text{we have that:}$$

each set of t shares is uniformly random in $R_\ell(r)^t$, in particular we have t-privacy.

2.4.1 Reconstruction: Constructive Proof of (4), Thus of Thm 5 (B)

Notice that Eq. (4) is proven on a specific case in [Abs+20, Theorem 6]. But it actually holds in general. Let us take the opportunity to make a constructive proof, which will thus support our complexity claim of Theorem 5 (B). We keep the notations of Eq. (2).

Let $I \subset \{1, \dots, n\}$ be a subset of $n + 1 - (d(\overline{C}) - 1)$ indices. By definition of the minimal distance, the linear map $\overline{\psi_I} : \mathbb{F}_{p^r} \times \mathbb{F}_{p^r}^{k-1} \longrightarrow \mathbb{F}_{p^r}^I$ is injective. Since it is defined over fields, it thus has a *linear left inverse*. We conclude by applying Lemma 9 to $M := R_\ell(r)^k$, $m := |I|$ and $f := \psi_I$.

Lemma 9. Let M be a free $R_\ell(r)$-module (say of rank v) and $f : M \to R_\ell(r)^m$ be a R-linear map. Assume that the map modulo p:

$$\overline{f} : (M \bmod p) = \mathbb{F}_{p^r}^v \longrightarrow \mathbb{F}_{p^r}^m$$

is an injection. Then f has a linear left inverse $g : R_\ell(r)^m \longrightarrow M$. In particular, the image of f is a free $R_\ell(r)$-module.

Proof. The matrix mat_f of f, of size $m \times v$ is such that, by assumption, when we reduce it modulo p, then it contains a $v \times v$ invertible minor. But then this minor in mat_f is also invertible (recall that $(1 + \lambda p)^{-1} = 1 + \sum_i \lambda^i p^i$). Inverting this minor (e.g. with Gauss pivot over $R_\ell(r)$, for efficiency), and completing with $m - v$ zero columns, yields a map $g : R_\ell(r)^m \longrightarrow R_\ell(r)^v$ such that $g \circ f = \mathrm{Id}_v$.

The last claim follow from the fact that f is in particular injective, so defines an isomorphism between M, which is free, and its image inside $R_\ell(r)^m$.

Our claim about the computational complexity then follows as previously from *linearity* of the reconstruction map ψ_I, and the fact (Sect. 2.1) that multiplications in $R_\ell(r)$ has same complexity than in $\mathbb{F}_{p^r}$.

2.4.2   Warning: Loss of Efficient Reconstruction for Non-free Codes

Recall that reconstructibility of a code means that, for any set of $d - 1$ coordinates, the map consisting in puncturing these coordinates is an injection; and that *efficient* reconstruction means that it has a *linear left-inverse*, which we denote a *retraction*, as known as the *reconstruction map*. In the following Counterexample 10 we show that, without the assumption to be free, there exists submodules of $R_\ell(r)^{n+1}$ for which the puncturing map is an injection, but for which *there does not exists any linear retraction*. This motivates why we restrict to *free* codes in $R_\ell(r)^{n+1}$ in order to construct LSSS.

Counterexample 10. Let C be a code in $R_\ell(r)^{n+1}$ with $\overline{d} := d(\overline{C}) \geq 2$ such that there exists a punctured $C^* \subset R_\ell(r)^{n+1-(\overline{d}-1)}$ which is not free. [For example

$$C = \langle (p, p, p, 0), (1, 0, 0, 1) \rangle \in R_\ell(r)^4, \quad (e.g. \ R_\ell(r) := \mathbb{Z}/p^\ell\mathbb{Z})$$

with $d(\overline{C}) = 2$ and injectivity in $R_\ell(r)^3$ when puncturing the last coordinate.] Then there does not exist any linear reconstruction map, i.e., any retraction $R_\ell(r)^{n+1-(\overline{d}-1)} \longrightarrow C$.

The proof is that, supposing such a retraction, then, composing it on the left with the puncturing map, yields a left-inverse to the inclusion $C^* \subset R_\ell(r)^{n+1-(\overline{d}-1)}$. Denoting $G^* \in R_\ell(r)^{k \times (n+1-(\overline{d}-1))}$ a generating matrix of C^* (in rows) and $L \in R_\ell(r)^{(n+1-(\overline{d}-1)) \times k}$ the matrix of this left-inverse, we would thus have by assumption $G^* L = \mathrm{Id}_k$. In particular $\overline{G^*}$ modulo p would be of maximal dimension, k, thus G^* would generate a *free* module, a contradiction.

2.4.3   Privacy (with Uniformity): Proof of (5)

The bound (5) is proven in [Abs+20, Theorem 6]: although on a specific LSSS, the arguments actually apply in general. The key to prove this formula over rings is their Lemma 3. Let us recall it here, and provide a both shorter and self-contained proof for it.

Lemma 11. *Let C be a submodule of $R_\ell(r)^n$, denote $\overline{d}^\perp$ the dual distance of the reduction $\overline{C}$ modulo p. Let $\mathcal{I}$ be a set of indices with $|\mathcal{I}| = \overline{d}^\perp - 1$. Then, projection of C on the indices in $\mathcal{I}$ is the full space $R_\ell(r)^{\mathcal{I}}$.*

Proof. By assumption, $\overline{C}_{\mathcal{I}} = \mathbb{F}_q^{\mathcal{I}}$. Hence $C_{\mathcal{I}}$ contains $|\mathcal{I}|$ vectors so that the matrix formed by them has an invertible determinant, thus has an inverse, thus these vectors generate $R_\ell(r)^{\mathcal{I}}$.

Then, the bound (5) follows by applying the Lemma to any set $\mathcal{I}_A$ of t indices, to which we add the index $\{0\}$. Indeed, we then have surjectivity of the projection $C \longrightarrow C_{\{0\}} \times C_{\mathcal{I}_A}$. In particular, for any fixed secret $s \in R_\ell(r)$ (0th coordinate), we have surjectivity of the projection from the affine submodule C_s of codewords with 0th coordinate equal to s, onto any subset of t shares. Thus by definition the shares of s under the LSSS are such that any t of them vary uniformly in $R_\ell(r)^t$, which was to be proven.

2.5   (Free) Generation from Any Lift of *Any* Basis

The following important fact is not formalized in the literature to our knowledge:

Theorem 12. *Let C be a free code in $R_\ell(r)^{n+1}$. Consider the reduced code modulo p: $\overline{C} \subset \mathbb{F}_{p^r}$, and any basis $(\overline{e'}_i)$ of $\overline{C}$. Then C is freely generated by any lift of $(\overline{e'}_i)$ inside C.*

Proof. Let k denote the rank of C. The "freely" claim again follows from the fact that a family whose reduction modulo p is free, is itself free (the generating matrix containing an invertible $k \times k$ determinant). Now, consider $(e'_{i=1\ldots k})$ an arbitrary lift of the $(\overline{e'}_i)$ inside C. It generates a submodule in C, which is free of rank k by the first part of the proof. But C is itself a free module of rank k. Thus this defines an injection $R_\ell(r)^k \hookrightarrow R_\ell(r)^k$, which is by assumption also an injection modulo k. Thus by Lemma 9 it has a left inverse, thus it is a bijection.

Corollary 13. *If $E \subset G$ are two lifts R^n of the same code $\overline{G}$, and G is free, then they are equal (in particular E is also free).*

Proof. Indeed E contains a lift of a basis of $\overline{G}$ which, by Theorem 12, generate the whole G. $\qquad\square$

3   Main Theorem 1

3.1   A Random Free Lift of a Code of *Small Square* Mostly *Fails* to Have a Small Square

For C a code (over a field or a ring), we denote as *componentwise square* C^{*2} the code of same length which is generated by all the products of any two codewords of C component by component. Strong multiplication of the LSSS from C thus requires that C^{*2} has large distance, thus be of small size. The central problem of this paper is, starting from a free code $C \in R_\ell(r)^n$ (typically $\ell = 1$, i.e., $R_\ell(r)$ is a finite field) which has free square of small dimension, then find a code $\widetilde{C}$ in a larger ring than C, that reduces to C mod p^ℓ, is also free, and has square of small size. Ideally, the square $\widetilde{C}^{*2}$ is desired to be also *free*, in which case it is automatically of same rank as C^{*2} (since the determinant is invertible mod p^ℓ). We denote this desirable object informally as a "multiplication friendly lift" in the exposition, whereas in the statements it will be replaced by precise specifications. Let us revisit the family of [Abs+20, Example 2], and explain why they provide also counterexamples where arbitrarily lifting *fails* to yield a multiplication friendly lift.

Counterexample 14. *Let $\bar{C}$ and $\bar{D}$ be codes over $\mathbb{F}_{p^r}$ of same dimension and let us assume that $\dim \bar{D}^{*2} < \dim \bar{C}^{*2}$. Let us now build a code E over $R_\ell(r)$ with $\ell \geq 3$ and of length equal to the sum of the lengths of $\bar{C}$ and $\bar{D}$. Let $(\bar{c}_i)_i$ and $(\bar{d}_i)_i$ be bases of $\bar{C}$ and $\bar{D}$, let $(c_i)_i$ and $(d_i)_i$ be arbitrary lifts and define E the code generated by the vectors $(d_i, pc_i)_i$. Then E is free, because of dimension $\dim \bar{D} = \dim \bar{E}$, and is a lift of $\bar{E}$. Suppose by contradiction that the square E^{*2} would be free, then we would have:*

$$\dim E^{*2} \geq \dim \bar{C}^{*2} > \dim \bar{D}^{*2} = \dim \bar{E}^{*2} .$$

On the other hand if it was free, then it would be of same rank than $\bar{E}^{*2}$ by Theorem 12. So we have a contradiction. Thus E^{*2} is not free, thus it is strictly larger than some free lift of $\bar{E}^{*2}$ inside him.

3.1.1   The Desirable Case of Small Square: Sparsity of Solutions, if Any, Illustrated on a Toy Example

Let us now illustrate hardness of the multiplicative lifting problem on a tiny AG code. Consider the elliptic curve $y^2 + xy + y - x^3 + 1$ over

$$\mathbb{F}_{2^3} = \mathbb{F}_2 < \delta > \text{ with polynomial } \delta^3 + \delta + 1 = 0,$$

with 14 places, P_0 the place at infinity, the divisor $D_0 = 4P_0$ and the Riemann-Roch space $L(4P_0)$, with basis $\overline{e}_i{}_{i=1...4}$ equal to the functions $(1, x, x^2, y)$. Let us define the evaluation code $C(D_0)$ at the $P_1, \ldots, P_{13}$, (not at P_0, for simplicity). We compute the following generating matrix:

$$\overline{G} = \begin{bmatrix} 1 & 1 & 1 & 1 & 1 & 1 & 1 & 1 & 1 & 1 & 1 & 1 & 1 \\ \delta & \delta & \delta^2 & \delta^2 & \delta^3 & \delta^3 & \delta^4 & \delta^4 & \delta^5 & \delta^5 & \delta^6 & \delta^6 & 1 \\ \delta^2 & \delta^2 & \delta^4 & \delta^4 & \delta^6 & \delta^6 & \delta & \delta & \delta^3 & \delta^3 & \delta^5 & \delta^5 & 1 \\ 1 & \delta & 1 & \delta^2 & \delta^2 & \delta^4 & 1 & \delta^4 & \delta & \delta^2 & \delta & \delta^4 & 0 \end{bmatrix}$$

Let us consider the 10 componentwise products $\overline{e_i} * \overline{e_j}$, with indices (i,j) ordered as: $(1,1),(1,2),(1,3),(1,4),(2,2),(2,3)$ etc. (i.e.: j increases first). They generate by definition $C(D_0)^{*2}$. We verify that, removing $(2,2)$ and $(4,4)$ from the indices in this list, then the remaining 8 products: $\overline{B} := (\overline{e_k} * \overline{e_l})_{(k,l) \in B}$ generate $C(D_0)^{*2}$, where B denotes the remaining indices ordered as before. In particular $\overline{e_2} * \overline{e_2}$ and $\overline{e_4} * \overline{e_4}$ decompose themselves on this basis $\overline{B}$, with decomposition coefficients $(\lambda_{2,2,k,l})_{k,l \in B}$ and $(\lambda_{4,4,k,l})_{k,l \in B}$ given by the following 2×8 matrix, called "Reduc" in the implementation:

$$(6) \qquad \left(transp(\overline{\lambda_{2,2,k,l}}, \overline{\lambda_{4,4,k,l}}) \right)_{(k,l) \in B} = \begin{bmatrix} 0 & 0 & 1 & 0 & 0 & 0 & 0 & 0 \\ 1 & 0 & 0 & 1 & 1 & 1 & 0 & 0 \end{bmatrix}$$

Then we repeated the following experiment 10^8 times: *randomly* lift the $(\overline{e_i})_i$ modulo 2^2, to obtain vectors $(e_i)_i$ with coordinates in $R_2(3) = \mathbb{Z}/2^2\mathbb{Z} < \Delta >$. Let C_{bad} the code generated by these lifts. By Theorem 12, it is always *free*. But we observed in *all the experiments* that $e_2 * e_2$ and $e_4 * e_4$ do *not* anymore decompose themselves on the lifts of the previous basis of $C(D_0)^{*2}$: $\mathcal{B} := (e_k * e_l)_{(k,l) \in B}$—see two paragraphs later for an explanation of how this checks were done efficiently with linear algebra. So in these situations C_{bad}^{*2} *is not a free lift* of the square $C(D_0)^{*2}$, because if it were, then by Theorem 12 the lifted basis $\mathcal{B}$ *would* generate it.

3.1.2   Why Solutions May Likely Not Exist at All

Let us give a feeling of why most codes with small squares are likely to have no multiplication friendly lift. Let $\overline{C}$ be a code over, say, $\mathbb{F}_p = \mathbb{Z}/p\mathbb{Z}$ of dimension k and length n, such that the square $\overline{C}^2$ has *small* dimension, say, $3k < n$. We would like to find a code C over $\mathbb{Z}/p^2\mathbb{Z}$ (namely: a free submodule of $(\mathbb{Z}/p^2\mathbb{Z})^n$) of same rank k, that lifts $\overline{C}$ modulo p^2, and such that the square C^2 is also a free lift of $\overline{C}^2$. As argued with the toy example, it follows from Theorem 12 that these requirements are equivalent to the following: let $(e_i)_i$ be any basis of C lifting a basis $(\overline{e_i})$ of $\overline{C}$; let $\overline{B}$ be *any* basis of $\overline{C}^2$; then $\overline{B}$ lifts modulo p^2 to a basis of the square C^2, in particular generates the componentwise products $(e_i * e_j)_{i,j}$. To fix ideas let us choose a basis of the form $\overline{B} = (\overline{e_k} * \overline{e_l})_{(k,l) \in B}$ as in the toy example. Then the previous equivalent condition translates itself into the fact that the equations expressing $\overline{e_i} * \overline{e_j}$ on this basis:

$$(7) \qquad \overline{e_i} * \overline{e_j} = \sum_{(k,l) \in B} \overline{\lambda_{i,j,k,l}} \, \overline{e_k} * \overline{e_l} \quad (\text{mod } p)$$

lift modulo p^2. The number of degrees of freedom (the unknowns) are: (i) the choices of lifts for the $\overline{e_i}$, so a total of nk coordinates to lift in $\mathbb{Z}/p^2\mathbb{Z}$; (ii) and lifts for the coefficients $\lambda_{i,j,k,l}$: a total of $3k \times k(k+1)/2$ unknowns in $\mathbb{Z}/p^2\mathbb{Z}$. So the number of unknowns is asymptotically equivalent to (ii): $3k \times k(k+1)/2$. Whereas the number of equations is $nk(k+1)/2$ (namely: $k(k+1)/2$ vectorial equations with n coordinates in $\mathbb{Z}/p^2\mathbb{Z}$ each). Notice that $3k < n$, so that there are more constraints than variables. Finally, as will be detailed in the next paragraph, and then further in Sect. 4 notice that this *quadratic* system over a *ring* simplifies modulo p^2 to a *linear system* over the *field* $\mathbb{F}_p$. Thus, the system being *overdetermined*, then *a priori no solution is likely to exist.*

3.2   A Technique to Find Them When They Exist, Illustrated on the Toy Example

We will formalize the general technique in Sect. 4. Existence of a solution to the system for AG codes, is further evidence that these codes are *highly non-generic* among those with small square.

First, fix a free lift C_{bad} of $C(D_0)$ by lifting arbitrarily the basis to $(e_i')_i$, for example by lifting the coordinates from $\mathbb{F}_2 < \delta >$ to $\mathbb{Z}/2^2\mathbb{Z} < \Delta >$ by the dummy rule: $1 \to 1$ and $\delta \to \Delta$. This gives formally the same generating matrix as $\overline{G}$, with δ replaced by Δ. With the same dummy rule, lift the decomposition coefficients $(\overline{\lambda}_{2,2,k,l})_{(k,l)\in B}$ and $(\overline{\lambda}_{4,4,k,l})_{(k,l)\in B}$ to $\lambda'_{2,2,k,l}$ and $\lambda'_{4,4,k,l}$, so that their matrix is formally the same as in (6). As the case for the huge majority of arbitrarily chosen lifts (and illustrated with random tests two paragraphs above), the vectors $e_2' * e_2'$ and $e_4' * e_4'$ do *not* decompose themselves on $B :=$ $(e_k' * e_l')_{(k,l)\in B}$, let alone with coefficients equal to $\lambda'_{2,2,k,l}$ and $\lambda'_{4,4,k,l}$. As a matter of fact, we encounter nonzero error vectors $2D_{2,2}$ and $2D_{4,4}$ when trying to write the decompositions in $\mathbb{Z}/2^2\mathbb{Z} < \Delta >$:

$$(8) \qquad e_2' * e_2' = \sum_{(k,l)\in B} \lambda'_{2,2,k,l} e_k' * e_l' + 2D_{2,2} \text{ and likewise for } e_4' * e_4'$$

Let us insist on the remarkable fact that the error vectors are multiples of 2, since the equalities (8) do hold without error term modulo 2. "Dividing" by 2, their coefficients are

$$transp(D_{2,2}, D_{4,4}) = \begin{bmatrix} 0 & 0 & \delta^4 & \delta^4 & \delta & \delta & 1 & 1 & \delta^5 & \delta^5 & \delta & \delta & 0 \\ 0 & 0 & \delta & \delta & 0 & 1 & \delta^2 & \delta^2 & \delta^4 & 0 & 0 & \delta^5 & 1 \end{bmatrix}$$

Which we express in $\mathbb{F}_{2^3}$ by abuse of notation (remember that an element $2x \in \mathbb{Z}/2^2\mathbb{Z} < \Delta >$ is determined by the residue $\overline{x} \in \mathbb{F}_{2^3}$ mod 2). Now, let us look for corrective terms $2f_i'$ and $2\mu'_{i,j,k,l}$, which we need only to find modulo 2:

$$(9) \qquad\qquad e_i = e_i' + 2f_i' \text{ and } \lambda_{i,j,k,l} = \lambda'_{i,j,k,l} + 2\mu'_{i,j,k,l}$$

So that, replacing e_i' in (8) by the corrected e_i of (9)—where the corrective terms are treated as unknowns—, simplifying and removing the terms that are multiples of 2^2—because they vanish in $\mathbb{Z}/2^2\mathbb{Z} < \Delta >$—, we observe that all the terms remaining in the system are multiples of 2. So "dividing" the system by 2, we fall back to a *linear* system in $\mathbb{F}_{2^3}$:

$$(10) \ \overline{e_2} * f_2' + \overline{e_2} * f_2' - D_{2,2} = \sum_{(k,l)\in B} \mu'_{2,2,k,l} \overline{e_k} * \overline{e_l} + \overline{\lambda}_{2,2,k,l}(\overline{e_k} * f_l' + \overline{e_l} * f_k')$$

(and likewise for $\overline{e_4} * \overline{e_4}$) as could be expected from Hensel's Lemma. Solving this system for the corrective terms, we deduce the corrected basis $(e_i)_i$ defined as in (9), that define the corrected code C_{good}, whose coordinates are given in the big left-hand rotated matrix on the first formula page of the Appendix.

Likewise we deduce the corrected decomposition coefficients $(\lambda_{2,2,k,l})_{k,l \in B}$ and $(\lambda_{4,4,k,l})_{k,l \in B}$ as given in the centered right-hand formula.

We can finally check straightforwardly that, with these corrected values, then $e_2 * e_2$ and $e_4 * e_4$ now decompose themselves on $\mathcal{B}$ with the corrected coefficients, without anymore parasitic error vectors. So with these corrected lifts $(e_i)_i$, we have now that the square of the corrected code C_{good} is also a free lift. That is, we have succeeded in modifying the free lift C_{bad} into a *multiplication-friendly* lift C_{good}.

3.3   Proof of Main Theorem 1

3.3.1   Roadmap of the Proof

First. Consider a smooth curve over $\mathbb{F}_{p^r}$ and a divisor D_0 on this curve (that is: a set of points with multiplicities), such that the degree (the sum of the multiplicities) is $\deg(D_0) < n$. Then, the curve has a lift defined over the ring $R_\ell(r)$ (provided it is given under an equivalent form where equations have no singular points). Lifting the points then applying Judy Walker's results, we have the existence of lifts of the Riemann-Roch spaces: $L(D)$ and $L(2D)$ which are *free* modules, and such that we have inclusions of products of spaces of global sections

$$(11) \qquad\qquad L(D)^{\otimes 2} = L(2D) \,,$$

where the traditional notation $L(D)^{\otimes 2}$ stands for the space generated by all products fg of pairs of sections (f, g) in $L(D)$. Then, from Judy Walker's Theorem 15 below, we deduce that the evaluation codes over rings $C(D)$ and $C(2D)$, arising from evaluation of these free lifts of Riemann-Roch spaces, are also *free*. We will detail this material in the two next subsections

Next. The key property of these free lifts is that they behave well with respect to inclusions and squares:

$$(12) \qquad\qquad C(D)^{*2} \subset C(2D) \,.$$

Here the code $C(2D)$ is free for the same reasons, with same rank as the classical AG code $\overline{C}(2D_0)$ below modulo p. So this forces the square $C(D)^{*2}$ to stay small, contrary to the square of an arbitrary free lift, which may "spread out" too much (as seen in Counterexample 14).

Deducing the Parameters. By freeness of $C(D)$, Proposition 8 (5) implies that a LSSS from $C(D)$ has privacy threshold at least as large as a LSSS from the code below modulo p: $\overline{C}(D_0)$.

Likewise, by Proposition 8 (4), a LSSS from the *free* code $C(2D)$ has *full reconstruction* from any $n - d(\overline{C}(2D_0)) + 2$ shares. Thus, by inclusion (12), so does a LSSS from the subcode $C(D)^{*2}$. Said otherwise, a LSSS from $C(D)$ has *reconstruction of the product*, from a number of pairwise products of shares which is *as small* as for a LSSS from $\overline{C}(D_0)$.

For sake of completeness we review the concrete parameters of these schemes in Sect. 3.4, exemplified on the ones of [CC06].

3.3.2 Lift of Curves, Divisors and Riemann-Roch Spaces

Let us follow Walker's [Wal99] notations. Note $R = R_\ell(r)$ the (Artinian local) Galois ring, with residue ring $R/(p) = \mathbb{F}_{p^r}$. X_0 being a smooth projective curve over $\mathbb{F}_{p^r}$, then from [Ill05, Theorem 5.19 ii)] (or [SGA1, III Corollaire 7.4]), X_0 has a smooth projective lift over the ring of Witt vectors $W(\mathbb{F}_{p^r})$. Which, after reduction mod p^ℓ, yields a projective lift X over R (because these properties are preserved by base change). Also, R being local, $\mathbb{F}_{p^r}$-points of X_0 lift to R-points of X by the formal smoothness criterion (see [Wal99, Remark 4.5] or next paragraph for details). As a consequence, divisors with support on rational points (actually any divisor) lift to X—and thus also do the line bundles $\mathcal{L}_0$ arising from them.

An Explicit Procedure for Simultaneous Compatible Free Lifts of Line Bundles. By [Wal99, Lemma 4.4] we can construct lifts of divisors D_0 on X from the following recipe. First, for every rational point $P_0^{(j)}$ of X_0, fix a closed point of degree one $P^{(j)}$ of X above P_0, as described in [Wal99, Remark 4.5] (lift arbitrarily $P_0^{(j)}$ to an R-point, then choose $P^{(j)}$ inside the image).

Then we can simultaneously lift divisors D_0 and $2D_0$ on X_0 as follows. For every rational point P_0 of X_0 in the support of the line bundle D_0, let m be the valuation of D_0 at P_0 and let P be the closed point lying above P_0 as fixed earlier. Deduce from it a divisor mP, then sum over the points P_0 in the support of D_0, to obtain a lift D of D_0. Likewise for the divisor $2D$, equal to the same formal sum of R-points as in D and with twice the multiplicities. In particular, note $\mathcal{L} := \mathcal{L}(D)$ the line bundle associated to D, and likewise for $\mathcal{L}(2D)$.

Proof of (11). This formula well known for curves over fields. Let us justify that it also holds over rings. The reason is that, by smoothness of the lift of the curve, this guarantees that, in a small enough neighborhood U of P, we also have a *uniformizer* denoted t_U (see [Wal, Proposition 4.9]). Thus, as long as U does not contain the other points of the support of D, we have:

$$(13) \qquad\qquad \mathcal{L}_U = t_U^{-m}\mathcal{O}_U .$$

Thus $t_U^{-m}t_U^{-m} \in \mathcal{L}_U(2D)$, hence the claimed inclusion of products of global sections (11).

3.3.3 Deducing AG Codes by Evaluation of Global Sections.

For any divisor D on X, we denote as the "Riemann-Roch space" $\Gamma(X, \mathcal{L})$ the space of global sections. In the rest of the paper it is denoted instead $L(D)$. By the argument above [Wal99, Theorem 4.7], f is a *free* R-module that reduces modulo p to $\Gamma(X_0, \mathcal{L}_0)$. With slightly narrower conditions on the degree, then have the following compatibilities, as wrapped-up in [Wal99, Theorem 5.5]:

Theorem 15 (Lifts of Riemann-Roch spaces and AG codes). *Consider n rational points $\mathcal{P}_0 = \left(P_0^{(j)}\right)_{j=1\ldots n}$ on X_0, D_0 a divisor of degree:*

$$2g - 2 < \deg D_0 < n$$

with associated line bundle $\mathcal{L}_0$, and the injective evaluation map γ_0 yielding an algebraic geometry code $\overline{C}$ in $\mathbb{F}_{p^r}^n$. Then this data lifts to objects over R: X, $\mathcal{P}$ and D, with associated line bundle $\mathcal{L}$, yielding an evaluation code C, such that we have the following commutative diagram:

(14)

$$
\begin{array}{ccccc}
\Gamma(X, \mathcal{L}) & \longrightarrow & \Gamma(X, \mathcal{L}) \otimes_R \mathbb{F}_{p^r} & \xrightarrow{\ \widetilde{\ \ }\ } & \Gamma(X_0, \mathcal{L}_0) \\
{\scriptstyle eval} \big\uparrow & & & & {\scriptstyle eval} \big\uparrow \\
\oplus_j \Gamma(P^{(j)}, \mathcal{L}|_{P^{(j)}}) & & & & \oplus_j \Gamma(P_0^{(j)}, \mathcal{L}_0|_{P_0^{(j)}}) \\
\cong \big\downarrow {\scriptstyle \gamma} & & & & \cong \big\downarrow {\scriptstyle \gamma_0} \\
R^n & & \xrightarrow{\ \bullet \otimes_R \mathbb{F}_{p^r}\ } & & \mathbb{F}_{p^r}^n
\end{array}
$$

Where: - the top left horizontal arrow and the bottom horizontal arrow are tensorisation by $\otimes_R \mathbb{F}_{p^r}$ - the top right isomorphism is constructed canonically as in the proofs of [Wal99, Lemma 4.6 & proof of Theorem 4.7]

- the top vertical arrows are the canonical restriction maps - the bottom left vertical arrow is a collection of arbitrary isomorphisms for all j:

$$\gamma_j : \Gamma(P^{(j)}, \mathcal{L}|_{P^{(j)}}) \longrightarrow A$$

that reduce to γ_0 by tensorisation by $\otimes_R \mathbb{F}_{p^r}$ (and if not, then redefine γ_0 accordingly without changing the code in $\mathbb{F}_{p^r}^n$).

Notice that the name "evaluation maps" of the top vertical arrows is abusive in general (because of poles, etc.: see the first example of Sect. 4.1), but they do play this role.

In conclusion, as explained in [Wal99], the code $C(D)$ (likewise $C(2D)$) is free because it is the image of a free module: $\Gamma(X, \mathcal{L})$, under the evaluation map which is an injection modulo (p), and thus its image is a *free* submodule of $R_\ell(r)^n$ by Lemma 9.

3.4   Reminders on the Asymptotic Parameters

Recall first the tradeoff of [CC06, §5] for secret sharing in finite fields $\mathbb{F}_p$. Let us cast a secret in $\mathbb{F}_p$, into the extension $\mathbb{F}_{p^r}$ of degree r, such that

$$p^r \geq 49 \ .$$

Then for adversary threshold $1/3 - \epsilon$, and for infinitely many number of players, there exists an ASSSM over $\mathbb{F}_{p^r}$ and size r of shares, such that:

$$\epsilon < \frac{4}{3(p^{r/2} - 1)} \ ,$$

[CC06, §5] In particular, choosing $\hat{r}(\epsilon) = -2\log(\epsilon)$ yields an adversary bound $1/3 - \epsilon$ when ϵ is sufficiently small.

Notice that the classical bound for the dual distance of AG codes over fields is not stated explicitly in [Cas+09, CCX11]. But its parameters are well known since Goppa (recalled e.g. in [Wal99, Theorem 2.1]), and also asymptocially optimal in our regime $2g - 2 < \deg D_0 < n$. Which supports the claims of [Cas+09, CCX11], and thus ours by Proposition 8.

4   Computing Hensel Lift of a Code with a Small Square

Starting from any code $\overline{C} \subset \mathbb{F}_{p^r}$, for any positive L, the following Hensel lift algorithm lifts the code to a free code $C_L \subset R_L(r)^n$ such that the square remains generated by a lift of a basis of the square $\overline{C}^{*2}$. It proceeds in L recursive steps. Each of the steps consists in solving one instance of the same linear system over $\mathbb{F}_{p^r}$, of size $O(n^3) \times O(n^3)$. Thus the overall complexity is linear in L and polynomial in n. The algorithm was already illustrated in Sect. 3.2, let us formalize it.

Let $(\overline{e_i})_{i\in[\dim\overline{C}]}$ be a basis of the code $C_1 := \overline{C}$. By definition, the square $\overline{C}^{*2}$ is generated by the $n(n+1)/2$ distinct componentwise products $(\overline{e_i} * \overline{e_j})_{(i,j)}$. $\overline{C}_1^{*2}$ being a vector space, one can extract a basis from the previous family, which we denote $(\overline{e_k} * \overline{e_l})_{(k,l)\in B}$, where $|B| = \dim\overline{C}_1^{*2}$.

A recursive step is as follows. The input is a free lift $C_\ell \in R_\ell(r)^n$ of $\overline{C}$, together with a basis $(e_i)_{i\in[\dim\overline{C}]}$, and coefficients $\left(\lambda_{i,j,k,l}\right)_{i\leq j,\,(k,l)\in B}$ in $R_\ell(r)$, such that we have the following invariant. The family of componentwise products $(e_k * e_l)_{(k,l)\in B}$ *generates* the square C_ℓ^{*2}. The coefficients express the larger generating family $(e_i * e_j)_{(i\leq j)}$ on the smaller generating family, namely:

$$(15) \qquad e_i * e_j = \sum_{(k,l)\in B} \lambda_{i,j,k,l}\, e_k * e_l \quad \text{for all } i \leq j$$

The output of a step is a lift $C_{\ell+1} \in R_{\ell+1}(r)^n$, together with a basis $(e_i'')_{i\in[\dim\overline{C}]}$ that lifts $(e_i)_{i\in[\dim\overline{C}]}$, and coefficients $\left(\lambda_{i,j,k,l}''\right)_{i\leq j,\,(k,l)\in B}$ in

$R_{\ell+1}(r)$ that lift the $\left(\lambda_{i,j,k,l}\right)_{i \leq j,\,(k,l) \in B}$ such that the same invariant holds (this time with respect to the square $C^{*2}_{\ell+1}$).

The computation of a step is as follows. Fix *arbitrary* lifts $\boldsymbol{e_i}'$ of the $\boldsymbol{e_i}$ in $R_{\ell+1}(r)^n$, and $\lambda'_{i,j,k,l}$ of the $\lambda_{i,j,k,l}$ in $R_{\ell+1}(r)$. We obtain error terms $p^\ell D_{i,j}$ when evaluating the equations in $R_{\ell+1}(r)^n$:

$$(16) \qquad \boldsymbol{e_i}' * \boldsymbol{e_j}' = \sum_{k,l} \lambda'_{i,j,k,l} \boldsymbol{e_k}' * \boldsymbol{e_l}' + p^\ell D_{i,j} \text{ for all } i \leq j$$

Solving the system means finding correct lifts $\boldsymbol{e_i}''$ and $\lambda''_{i,j,k,l}$ such that the error terms $p^\ell D_{i,j}$ are all equal to 0. We express $\boldsymbol{e_i}''$ and $\lambda''_{i,j,k,l}$ from $\boldsymbol{e_i}'$ and $\lambda'_{i,j,k,l}$, added with corrective terms $p^\ell \boldsymbol{f_i'}$ and $p^\ell \mu'_{i,j,k,l}$:

$$(17) \qquad \boldsymbol{e_i}'' = \boldsymbol{e_i}' + p^\ell \boldsymbol{f_i'} \text{ and } \lambda''_{i,j,k,l} = \lambda'_{i,j,k,l} + p^\ell \mu'_{i,j,k,l}$$

So that, replacing $\boldsymbol{e_i}'$ in (16) by the corrected $\boldsymbol{e_i}''$ of (17) (where the corrective terms are treated as unknows), simplifying and moding out the terms that are multiples of $p^{\ell+1}$, we observe (Hensel's trick) that all the terms remaining in the system are multiples of p^ℓ. Thus, dividing by p^ℓ, we fall back to the following *linear* system in $\mathbb{F}_{p^r}$:

$$(18) \quad \overline{\boldsymbol{e_i}} * \boldsymbol{f_j'} + \overline{\boldsymbol{e_j}} * \boldsymbol{f_i'} - D_{i,j} = \sum_{k,l} \mu'_{i,j,k,l} \overline{\boldsymbol{e_k}} * \overline{\boldsymbol{e_l}} + \overline{\lambda_{i,j,k,l}} (\overline{\boldsymbol{e_k}} * \boldsymbol{f_l'} + \overline{\boldsymbol{e_l}} * \boldsymbol{f_k'}) \; \forall i \leq j$$

which we notice is the *same* system for all steps. Finally, as for the size of the system, each vectorial equation for (i,j) expands itself in n scalar equations, so a total of $nk(k+1)/2$. The lifts of the $(e_i)_i$ are n unknowns and the lifts of $\lambda_{i,j,k,l}$ are $k(k+1).\dim\left(\overline{C}^{*2}\right)$ unknowns.

Complexity in $\log(L)$. It was suggested by a reviewer of Eurocrypt that, applying the Hensel lifting method in its full version would enable a lifting complexity in only $O(\log_2 L)$ steps. This comes from the possibility to lift (15) directly modulo $p^{2\ell}$ (full Hensel method). However, this requires to determine the corrective terms modulo p^ℓ, and not anymore just modulo p as in (18). This thus requires the task of solving a linear system modulo p^ℓ, not anymore just modulo p. This task is efficiently computable, as proven in Sect. 5 (A). But for simplicity, we nevertheless implemented the method in L steps.

4.1   Example of a Multiplication Friendly Lift Modulo 2^{100}

Here we illustrate efficiency of our method by lifting a strongly multiplicative secret sharing scheme over $\mathbb{F}_{16}$ for 64 players and adversary threshold $t = 13$, into a scheme over $\mathbb{Z}/2^{100}\mathbb{Z}$, in a minute on a single processor.

Let X_0 be the "Hermitian" plane curve over $\mathbb{F}_{16}$ defined by equation $f(x,T) = T^4 + T - x^{4+1}$. Then it is well known that this curve has genus $g = 4(4-1)/2 = 6$

and $n + 1 := |X_0(\mathbb{F}_{16})| = 1 + 4^3 = 65$ rational points (which reaches the Hasse-Weil upper-bound). Let us denote these points $P_0, \ldots, P_{n=64}$, consider the divisor $D_0 = 25P_0$, whose Riemann-Roch space $L(D_0)$ is of dimension 20. Let $\overline{C}$ be the algebraic geometry code $\overline{C}$ of length $n + 1$ defined as evaluations of $L(D_0)$ on all the rational points of X_0, *including the support* $\{P_0\}$ of D_0. Phrased with the notations of [CC06, §3], this means that we allow in addition to evaluate at Q. We do this to enable $+1$ on the adversary bound t. Evaluate at a point P_0 of the support of D_0, simply proceeds by pre-multiplying the function to be evaluated, by a uniformizer of P_0 to the power the order of P_0 in D_0. For the sake of illustration notice that, with $t = 13$, we have $\deg D_0 = 2g + t$ so that the condition $39 = 3t < n - 4g = 40$ of [CC06, Proposition 2] is satisfied, thus from $\overline{C}$ we can deduce a secret sharing scheme with strong multiplication for adversary bound $t = 13$.

Before going on, we compute the square code $\overline{C}^2$ and the (a priori larger) AG code associated to $L(2D_0)$, and check that both are equal. By the Riemann-Roch formula we have that $\overline{C(2D_0)}$ is of dimension $2.25 + 1 - 6 = 45$. From the generating set $(\overline{e_i} * \overline{e_j})_{i \leq j}$ of $\overline{C}^2$ we extract a basis $(\overline{e_k} * \overline{e_l})_{(k,l) \in B}$. We now look at the matrix expressing the $(\overline{e_i} * \overline{e_j})_{i \leq j}$ in terms of this basis (with the previous notations, this is the matrix of the coefficients $\overline{\lambda_{i,j,k,l}}$). It has $(\dim(C)(\dim(C) + 1))/2 = 210$ lines (all ordered pairs $i \leq j$). Obviously the lines where the index (i, j) belongs to B contain a single coefficient, equal to one. And obviously these coefficients will remain equal to one in every lift mod p^ℓ so we can remove these $n \dim \overline{C}^2 = 64 \times 45$ relations (and the corresponding variables) from the system from now on. This means that equality actually holds in (12). It is left outside of the scope of the paper to prove why this equality is actually implied by the condition $\deg D_0 \geq 2g + 1$.

After some optimizations outside of the scope of this paper, we end up with a system (18) of 10725 equations with 3305 unknowns but, surprisingly, of (still) very large kernel: dimension 83 (dimension 200 before applying the trick). We solve it in one second on a single processor.

Finally we repeat the operation, following the Hensel-lift algorithm: we reinject the solution (the lifted vectors e_i and coefficients $\lambda_{i,j,k,l}$) in a system mod 2^3 (as in (15)), which is a multiple of 2^2 after simplification, thus falls back to a system mod 2 after "division by 2^2". Note the general fact that the matrix of the new system obtained is exactly the same as the initial one (18), because the coefficients depend only on the values modulo 2 of $\overline{e_i}$ and $\overline{\lambda_{i,j,k,l}}$. To which we find again a solution (the mysterious lucky heuristic)—in one second as expected—then repeat exactly 97 times (always the lucky heuristic) to reach a multiplication friendly lift over $R_{100}(4)$.

5   Applications to MPC

5.1   Proof of Main Theorem 2

Proposition 16. *For any fixed p and ℓ, consider any fix number n of players, and choose any fixed even integer r such that $p^r \geq 64$, and security parameter κ.*

Then there exists a slowly growing infinite *sequence of integers N such that: for any set of N triples a_i, b_i, c_i in $\mathbb{Z}/p^\ell\mathbb{Z}$ (resp. in $\mathbb{F}_p$), which are shared between the players using any linear secret sharing scheme, then there exists a protocol that has the following properties*

- *The protocol consumes an additional number of triples, which is asymptotically $N(1 + 2p^{-r/2})$, that are opened (so cannot be used anymore);*
- *Either all triples considered are correct: $a_i b_i = c_i$ then it outputs* true, *or at least one is incorrect, then it outputs* false *except with probability $O(p^{-(r\kappa-1)/2}(1 + 4p^{-\kappa/2}))$*
- *The communication complexity is $nr(N + 2\kappa^2)$ of elements of $\mathbb{Z}/p^\ell\mathbb{Z}$ (resp. of $\mathbb{F}_p$) sent, the computational complexity is $O(N)$ linear operations in $\mathbb{Z}/p^\ell\mathbb{Z}$ (resp. in $\mathbb{F}_p$) per player.*

For simplicity we prove it over finite fields. Then the same methods to lift it over rings as in Main Theorem 1 apply. Consider the finite field extension $\mathbb{F}_{p^r}$ and an optimal family of algebraic curves over $\mathbb{F}_{p^r}$ with genera slowly growing to infinity. The best existing asymptotic ratio of the number of rational points divided by the genus, is denoted $A(p^r)$ "the Ihara constant". When r is *even* then Ihara showed existence of infinitely many curves with slowly growing genera such that it matches the upper-bound of Drinfeld-Vladuts: $A(p^r) = p^{r/2} - 1$. Recall that this bound is one order of magnitude lower than the Weil upper bound (which is relevant only for finite genera). Fix a curve $\mathcal{C}$ in this family, with genus $\mathfrak{g}$, such that it has at least $2(N + 2\mathfrak{g} - 1)$ points (which is possible for all N large enough since $p^r \geq 64$). Consider a fixed set of points $P_1, \ldots, P_N$ on this curve, and G a point of degree $N + 2\mathfrak{g} - 1$ (existence is guaranteed by [Sti09, Theorem 5.2.10 c)]). Then there exists an interpolation formula with coefficients linear in the a_i (resp. the b_i), that builds rational functions f (resp. g) in the Riemann Roch space $\mathcal{L}(G)$, such that they take the values a_i (resp. b_i) at the points $P_1, \ldots, P_N$. [The technique for this is as in Lagrange's interpolation formula: one considers for every point P_i a fixed public function χ_i that vanishes at all the P_j for $j \neq i$ but not at P_i. Existence of χ_i is guaranteed by a consequence of the Riemann-Roch formula: $\ell(G - \sum_{i \neq j} P_j) - \ell(G - \sum_j P_j) > 0$. Then, the function f is deduced as the linear combination $\sum_i (a_i/\chi_i(P_i)) f_i$]. The players can thus obtain a secret sharing of coefficients of f seen as a linear combination of the public χ_i's (same for g). Define $h = fg$ in $\mathcal{L}(2G)$. Consider the remaining points of the curve: $P_{N+1}, \ldots, P_{2(N+2\mathfrak{g}-1)}$. Players sacrifice $N + 2\mathfrak{g} - 1$ auxiliary triples (possibly incorrect), in order to compute with the Beaver passively-secure protocol (so possibly incorrectly) secret sharings of the products $\widetilde{c}_i = f(P_i)g(P_i)$ at all those remaining points. At this point, if all triples are correct and no cheating occurred, then we should have $h(P_i) = c_i$ for all $i = 1 \ldots N$ and $h(P_i) = \widetilde{c}_i$ for all $i = N + 1 \ldots 2(N + 2\mathfrak{g} - 1)$ As above, players compute a secret sharing of the unique function $\widetilde{h}$ in $\mathcal{L}(2G)$ such that $\widetilde{h}(P_i) = c_i$ for all $i = 1 \ldots N$ and $\widetilde{h}(P_i) = \widetilde{c}_i$ (namely they locally compute a secret sharing of the coefficients of the linear decomposition of $\widetilde{h}$ along the public χ_i). Then they sample a random secret shared challenge value $\lambda \in \mathbb{F}_{p^{r\kappa}}$, compute locally secret sharings of the evaluations $f(\lambda), g(\lambda)$ and $\widetilde{h}(\lambda)$, compute a (possibly false) secret sharing of the product $f(\lambda)g(\lambda)$ by sacrificing $2\kappa^2$ triples (multiplication in $\mathbb{F}_{p^{r\kappa}}/\mathbb{F}_{p^r}$ being done with the schoolboy algorithm), then perform a equal-to-zero check on $f(\lambda)g(\lambda) - \widetilde{h}(\lambda)$. If it passes, then they return accept.

5.2   Existence of Lifts of RMFE over Rings, with Constant Rate

Let p be a prime and r, k, $m \geq 1$ be positive integers. $*$ denotes the component-wise product. We adapt over rings [Cas+18, Definition 1] (where $q = p^r$).

Definition 17. A pair (ϕ, ψ) is called an $(k, m)_{p^r}$ -Reverse Multiplication Friendly Embedding (RMFE) if $\phi : R_\ell(r)^k \to R_\ell(rm)$ and $\psi : R_\ell(rm) \to R_\ell(r)^k$ are two $R_\ell(r)$-linear maps satisfying

$$(19) \qquad x * y = \psi(\phi(x)\phi(y)) \qquad \text{for all } x, y \in R_\ell(r)^k$$

Theorem 18. Consider the family of "Reverse multiplication friendly embeddings" (RMFE) of [Cas+18, Theorem 5] (where $q := p^r$), then there exists a family of RMFE of $(R_\ell(r))^k$ into $R_\ell(rm)$, with k slowly growing to infinity and the same constant asymptotic expansion rates m/k.

Let us review the construction over fields of [Cas+18, Lem 6 & Cor 1] that provides [Cas+18, Theorem 5], and use the tools of Sect. 3.3 to show that it lifts. We consider a smooth curve over $\mathbb{F}_q$ of genus g, with k distinct rational points denoted $P_1, P_2, \ldots, P_k$. Let G be a divisor such that $\deg G \geq k + 2g + 1$ (and for simplicity, with support outside of $\{P_1, \ldots, P_k\}$). By the Riemann-Roch formula we thus have $\dim_{\mathbb{F}_q} L(G) - \dim_{\mathbb{F}_q} L(G - \sum_i P_i) = k$. By Sect. 3.3, the Riemann Roch spaces in this equality lift to free modules of same rank. Consider the evaluation map $\pi : L(G) \longrightarrow \mathbb{F}_q^k : f \longrightarrow (f(P_i))_{i \in [k]}$, which has kernel $L(G - \sum_i P_i)$. Then π is surjective, since $\dim_{\mathbb{F}_q} \text{Im}(\pi) = \dim_{\mathbb{F}_q} L(G) - \dim_{\mathbb{F}_q} L(G - \sum_i P_i) = k$. Surjectivity is preserved over rings (by the invertible determinant mod p trick).

Choose a subspace W of $L(G)$ of dimension k such that π induces an isomorphism between W and $\mathbb{F}_q^k$. Choose R a point of degree $m > 2\deg(G)$, which exists for m large enough by [Sti09, Theorem 5.2.10 c)]. For any $f \in L(G)$, we denote by c_f the evaluation vector $(f(P_i))$, and by $f(R)$ the evaluation. The previous isomorphism induces the $\mathbb{F}_q$-linear map $\phi : \pi(V) = \mathbb{F}_q^k \longrightarrow \mathbb{F}_{q^m}$: $c_f \to f(R)$. Then ϕ is injective, since $\deg(R) > \deg(G)$. Thus the lift over rings is also injective, by Lemma 9.

Define the $\mathbb{F}_q$ -linear map $\tau : L(2G) \longrightarrow \mathbb{F}_{q^m} : f \to f(R)$. Then τ is injective, since $m = deg(R) > deg(2G)$, and likewise for the lift by Lemma 9. Bijectivity of $\text{Im}(\tau)$ with $L(2G)$ induces the $\mathbb{F}_q$-linear map $\psi' : \text{Im}(\tau) \subseteq \mathbb{F}_{q^m} \longrightarrow \mathbb{F}_q^k$: $f(R) \to (f(P_i))$. Then ψ' surjective (but not injective), by the same degree reason than π, and likewise for surjectivity of the lift. We extend ϕ' from $\text{Im}(\tau)$ to all of $\mathbb{F}_{q^m}$ linearly, and denote the resulting map ψ.

Finally, RMFE follows from the fact that, for any $c_f, c_g \in \mathbb{F}_q^k$ we have:

$$\psi(\phi(c_f)\phi(c_g)) = \psi(f(R)g(R)) = \psi((f.g)(R)) = c_{fg} = c_f * c_g$$

where $f, g \in W$ are uniquely determined from c_f, c_g by the injectivities above. Note that $(fg)(R)$ belongs to $\operatorname{Im}(\tau)$ since $fg \in L(2G)$.

5.3   Proof of Main Theorem 3

We can now compile a protocol for a circuit over a large Galois ring $R_\ell(r)$, into a protocol for many evaluations in parallel of this circuit in $\mathbb{Z}/p^\ell\mathbb{Z}$ by casting over rings the protocols of [Cas+18]. Since we choose to restrict ourselves to the case of optimal adversary rate, we really need hyperinvertible matrices over Galois rings for any number of players (not the alternative with suboptimal adversary bound discussed in [Cas+18, §2.4]). Fortunately their construction is straightforward, see e.g. [Abs+19a]. We can thus cast the original protocol of Beerliova-Hirt over Galois rings, then compensate their bad asymptotic communication overhead by amortizing it over several instances in parallel, exactly as done in [Cas+18, Theorem 1 & 2]. Namely, the main tool are RMFE over rings with asymptotically *linear* rate, which is solved above in Sect. 5.2. Whereas the "tensoring-up" trick carries over rings without any technical difficulty.

5.4   An Analogous Efficient Hensel Lift for RMFE

Again we consider for simplicity only the base field $\mathbb{F}_p$, instead of $\mathbb{F}_{p^r}$. Let us make the following useful rephrasing of the definition of a *reverse multiplication embedding* (RMFE) of $\mathbb{F}_p^k$ into $\mathbb{F}_{p^m}$ Consider the field extension $\mathbb{F}_{p^m}$, equipped with its internal multiplication law. Denoting the dual over $\mathbb{F}_p$ with $*$, this law is captured by what is denoted as the *multiplication tensor* $T \in \mathbb{F}_{p^m}^* \otimes \mathbb{F}_{p^m}^* \otimes \mathbb{F}_{p^m}$ Its components $T_{i=1..m}$ are $\mathbb{F}_p$-bilinear forms from $\left(\mathbb{F}_{p^m} \times \mathbb{F}_{p^m}\right)$ to $\mathbb{F}_p$. Now fix a linear map

$$\phi : \mathbb{F}_p^k \longrightarrow \mathbb{F}_{p^m}$$

The pull back of T :

$$\phi^* T = T(\phi(.), \phi(.))$$

decomposes in $\mathbb{F}_{p^m}$ in m components which are symmetric bilinear forms

$$\phi^* T_i = T_i(\phi(.), \phi(.)) \, , i = 1..m$$

belonging by definition to the symmetric tensor space of the linear forms $S^2((\mathbb{F}_p^k)^*)$.

Definition 19. Consider the (nonintegral) algebra $\mathbb{F}_p^k$, equipped with the multiplication law component-by-component. This law is captured by what is denoted as the "multiplication tensor", belonging to $\left(\mathbb{F}_p^k\right)^* \otimes \left(\mathbb{F}_p^k\right)^* \otimes \mathbb{F}_p^k$. We say that ϕ is a reverse multiplication embedding iff these m bilinear forms $\phi^* T_i$ generate the components $(x_1^* \otimes x_1^*, ...x_k^* \otimes x_k^*)$ of the multiplication tensor.

Lifting of an Algorithm ϕ Modulo p^2: Suppose we are given a reverse multiplication friendly embedding ϕ, over $\mathbb{F}_p$ ($r = 1$ to make notations simple): for each $j = 1 \ldots k$, we have coefficients $\lambda_{i,j}$ such that:

$$(20) \qquad x_j^* \otimes x_j^* = \sum_{i=1}^{m} \lambda_{i,j} \cdot \phi^* T_i$$

(it is a tensorial equality: it takes place in the space of symmetric bilinear forms of length k, so expands on coordinates as a set of $k(k+1)/2$ equations). We want to lift ϕ and the coefficients $\lambda_{i,j}$ such that the equalities (20) hold modulo p^2. (So we have $mk + mk$ unknowns and m equations, each of them taking place in a symmetric tensor space of dimension $k(k+1)/2$). Consider arbitrary lifts ϕ' and $\lambda'_{i,j}$ of ϕ and $\lambda_{i,j}$ over $\mathbb{Z}/p^2\mathbb{Z}$, we thus obtain the (tensorial) equalities modulo p^2 for $j = 1..k$:

$$x_j^* \otimes x_j^* = \sum_{i=1}^{m} \lambda'_{i,j} \phi'^* T_i + p\Delta_j$$

and we would like to eliminate the error terms $p\Delta_j$ modulo p^2 by choosing better lifts of ϕ and of $\lambda_{i,j}$:

$$(21) \qquad \phi' + p\psi \text{ and } \lambda'_{i,j} + p\mu_{i,j}$$

After replacing (21) in (20) then simplification, the equation becomes the following (tensorial) *linear* equation modulo p (so with coordinates in $\mathbb{F}_p$):

$$\sum_{i=1}^{m} 2\lambda'_{i,j} T_i\big(\phi'(.), \psi(.)\big) + \mu'_{i,j} T_i\big(\phi'(), \phi'_i(.)\big) = -\Delta_j$$

where the unknowns are ψ and $\mu'_{i,j}$.

How to repeat and compute higher lifts modulo p^ℓ then proceeds as in Sect. 4.

Ackowledgements. Matthieu Rambaud would like to thank Luc Illusie, Alberto Arabia, Stéphane Ballet, Mark Abspoel and Alain Couvreur.

References

[Abs+19a] Abspoel, M., Cramer, R., Damgård, I., Escudero, D., Yuan, C.: Efficient information-theoretic secure multiparty computation over $\mathbb{Z}/p^k\mathbb{Z}$ via Galois rings. In: Hofheinz, D., Rosen, A. (eds.) TCC 2019. LNCS, vol. 11891, pp. 471–501. Springer, Cham (2019). https://doi.org/10.1007/978-3-030-36030-6_19

[Abs+19b] Abspoel, M., Dalskov, A., Escudero, D., Nof, A.: An efficient passive-to-active compiler for honest-majority MPC over rings. In: Sako, K., Tippenhauer, N.O. (eds.) ACNS 2021. LNCS, vol. 12727, pp. 122–152. Springer, Cham (2021). https://doi.org/10.1007/978-3-030-78375-4_6

[Abs+20] Abspoel, M., et al.: Asymptotically good multiplicative LSSS over Galois rings and applications to MPC over $\mathbb{Z}/p^k\mathbb{Z}$. In: Moriai, S., Wang, H. (eds.) ASIACRYPT 2020. LNCS, vol. 12493, pp. 151–180. Springer, Cham (2020). https://doi.org/10.1007/978-3-030-64840-4_6

[Ara+18] Araki, T., et al.: Generalizing the SPDZ compiler for other protocols. In: CCS (2018)

[BFO12] Ben-Sasson, E., Fehr, S., Ostrovsky, R.: Near-linear unconditionally-secure multiparty computation with a dishonest minority. In: Safavi-Naini, R., Canetti, R. (eds.) CRYPTO 2012. LNCS, vol. 7417, pp. 663–680. Springer, Heidelberg (2012). https://doi.org/10.1007/978-3-642-32009-5_39

[BH08] Beerliová-Trubíniová, Z., Hirt, M.: Perfectly-secure MPC with linear communication complexity. In: Canetti, R. (ed.) TCC 2008. LNCS, vol. 4948, pp. 213–230. Springer, Heidelberg (2008). https://doi.org/10.1007/978-3-540-78524-8_13

[BMN18] Block, A.R., Maji, H.K., Nguyen, H.H.: Secure computation with constant communication overhead using multiplication embeddings. In: Chakraborty, D., Iwata, T. (eds.) INDOCRYPT 2018. LNCS, vol. 11356, pp. 375–398. Springer, Cham (2018). https://doi.org/10.1007/978-3-030-05378-9_20

[Cas+09] Cascudo, I., Chen, H., Cramer, R., Xing, C.: Asymptotically good ideal linear secret sharing with strong multiplication over *any* fixed finite field. In: Halevi, S. (ed.) CRYPTO 2009. LNCS, vol. 5677, pp. 466–486. Springer, Heidelberg (2009). https://doi.org/10.1007/978-3-642-03356-8_28

[Cas+18] Cascudo, I., Cramer, R., Xing, C., Yuan, C.: Amortized complexity of information-theoretically secure MPC revisited. In: Shacham, H., Boldyreva, A. (eds.) CRYPTO 2018. LNCS, vol. 10993, pp. 395–426. Springer, Cham (2018). https://doi.org/10.1007/978-3-319-96878-0_14

[Cas16] Cascudo, I.: Secret sharing schemes with algebraic properties and applications. In: Beckmann, A., Bienvenu, L., Jonoska, N. (eds.) CiE 2016. LNCS, vol. 9709, pp. 68–77. Springer, Cham (2016). https://doi.org/10.1007/978-3-319-40189-8_7

[CC06] Chen, H., Cramer, R.: Algebraic geometric secret sharing schemes and secure multi-party computations over small fields. In: Dwork, C. (ed.) CRYPTO 2006. LNCS, vol. 4117, pp. 521–536. Springer, Heidelberg (2006). https://doi.org/10.1007/11818175_31

[CCX11] Cascudo, I., Cramer, R., Xing, C.: The torsion-limit for algebraic function fields and its application to arithmetic secret sharing. In: Rogaway, P. (ed.) CRYPTO 2011. LNCS, vol. 6841, pp. 685–705. Springer, Heidelberg (2011). https://doi.org/10.1007/978-3-642-22792-9_39

[CDM00] Cramer, R., Damgård, I., Maurer, U.: General secure multi-party computation from any linear secret-sharing scheme. In: Preneel, B. (ed.) EUROCRYPT 2000. LNCS, vol. 1807, pp. 316–334. Springer, Heidelberg (2000). https://doi.org/10.1007/3-540-45539-6_22

[CDN15] Cramer, R., Damgård, I.B., Nielsen, J.B.: Secure Multiparty Computation and Secret Sharing. Cambridge University Press, New York (2015)

[CG20] Cascudo, I., Gundersen, J.S.: A secret-sharing based MPC protocol for Boolean circuits with good amortized complexity. In: Pass, R., Pietrzak, K. (eds.) TCC 2020. LNCS, vol. 12551, pp. 652–682. Springer, Cham (2020). https://doi.org/10.1007/978-3-030-64378-2_23

[Cra+18] Cramer, R., Damgård, I., Escudero, D., Scholl, P., Xing, C.: SPD$\mathbb{Z}_{2^k}$: efficient MPC mod 2^k for dishonest majority. In: Shacham, H., Boldyreva, A. (eds.) CRYPTO 2018. LNCS, vol. 10992, pp. 769–798. Springer, Cham (2018). https://doi.org/10.1007/978-3-319-96881-0_26

[CS95] Calderbank, A.R., Sloane, N.J.A.: Modular and p-adic cyclic codes. Des. Codes Crypt. **6**, 21–35 (1995). https://doi.org/10.1007/BF01390768

[Dam+06] Damgård, I., Fitzi, M., Kiltz, E., Nielsen, J.B., Toft, T.: Unconditionally secure constant-rounds MPC for equality, comparison, bits and exponentiation. In: TCC (2006)

[Dam+12] Damgård, I., Pastro, V., Smart, N., Zakarias, S.: Multiparty computation from somewhat homomorphic encryption. In: Safavi-Naini, R., Canetti, R. (eds.) CRYPTO 2012. LNCS, vol. 7417, pp. 643–662. Springer, Heidelberg (2012). https://doi.org/10.1007/978-3-642-32009-5_38

[Dam+19] Damgård, I., Escudero, D., Frederiksen, T., Keller, M., Scholl, P., Volgushev, N.: New primitives for actively-secure MPC over rings. In: IEEE S&P (2019)

[DLN19] Damgård, I., Larsen, K.G., Nielsen, J.B.: Communication lower bounds for statistically secure MPC, with or without preprocessing. In: Boldyreva, A., Micciancio, D. (eds.) CRYPTO 2019. LNCS, vol. 11693, pp. 61–84. Springer, Cham (2019). https://doi.org/10.1007/978-3-030-26951-7_3

[DLS20] Dalskov, A., Lee, E., Soria-Vazquez, E.: Circuit amortization friendly encodings and their application to statistically secure multiparty computation. In: Moriai, S., Wang, H. (eds.) ASIACRYPT 2020. LNCS, vol. 12493, pp. 213–243. Springer, Cham (2020). https://doi.org/10.1007/978-3-030-64840-4_8

[DOS18] Damgård, I., Orlandi, C., Simkin, M.: Yet another compiler for active security or: efficient MPC over arbitrary rings. In: Shacham, H., Boldyreva, A. (eds.) CRYPTO 2018. LNCS, vol. 10992, pp. 799–829. Springer, Cham (2018). https://doi.org/10.1007/978-3-319-96881-0_27

[FY92] Franklin, M., Yung, M.: Communication complexity of secure computation (extended abstract). In: STOC (1992)

[GS99] Guruswami, V., Sudan, M.: Improved decoding of Reed-Solomon and algebraic-geometry codes. IEEE Trans. Inf. Theory **45**, 1757–1767 (1999)

[GSZ20] Goyal, V., Song, Y., Zhu, C.: Guaranteed output delivery comes free in honest majority MPC. In: Micciancio, D., Ristenpart, T. (eds.) CRYPTO 2020. LNCS, vol. 12171, pp. 618–646. Springer, Cham (2020). https://doi.org/10.1007/978-3-030-56880-1_22

[Hes02] Hess, F.: Computing Riemann-Roch spaces in algebraic function fields and related topics. J. Symb. Comput. **35**, 425–445 (2002)

[Ill05] Illusie, L.: Grothendieck's existence theorem in formal geometry. In: Fundamental Algebraic Geometry: Grothendieck's FGA Explained. Ed. by AMS (2005)

[Ish+07] Ishai, Y., Kushilevitz, E., Ostrovsky, R., Sahai, A.: Zero-knowledge from secure multiparty computation. In: STOC (2007)

[Khu04] Khuri-Makdisi, K.: Linear algebra algorithms for divisors on an algebraic curve. Math. Comput. **73**(245), 333–357 (2004)

[NW17] Narayanan, A.K., Weidner, M.: Subquadratic time encodable codes beating the Gilbert-Varshamov bound. CoRR (2017). http://arxiv.org/abs/1712.10052

[PC] Keskinkurt Paksoy, İ., Cenk, M.: TMVP-based multiplication for polynomial quotient rings. eprint 2020/1302 (2020)

[PS20] Patra, A., Suresh, A.: BLAZE: blazing fast privacy-preserving machine learning. In: NDSSS (2020)

[PS21] Polychroniadou, A., Song, Y.: Constant-overhead unconditionally secure multiparty computation over binary fields. In: Canteaut, A., Standaert, F.-X. (eds.) EUROCRYPT 2021. LNCS, vol. 12697, pp. 812–841. Springer, Cham (2021). https://doi.org/10.1007/978-3-030-77886-6_28

[RB89] Rabin, T., Ben-Or, M.: Verifiable secret sharing and multiparty protocols with honest majority. In: STOC (1989)

[SAS17] Shi, M., Alahmadi, A., Solé, P.: Codes and Rings. Academic Press, Cambridge (2017)

[SG20] Spaenlehauer, P.-J., le Gluher, A.: A fast randomized geometric algorithm for computing Riemann-Roch spaces. Math. Comput. **89**, 2399–2433 (2020)

[SGA1] Grothendieck, A.: SGA 1. LNM, vol. 224. Springer, Heidelberg (1964)

[Shu+01] Shum, K.W., Aleshnikov, I., Kumar, P.V., Stichtenoth, H., Deolalikar, V.: A low-complexity algorithm for the construction of algebraic-geometric codes better than the Gilbert-Varshamov bound. IEEE Trans. Inf. Theory **47**, 2225–2241 (2001)

[Sti09] Stichtenoth, H.: Algebraic Function Fields and Codes. GTM, vol. 254, 2nd edn. Springer, Heidelberg (2009). https://doi.org/10.1007/978-3-540-76878-4

[SW99] Shokrollahi, M.A., Wasserman, H.: List decoding of algebraicgeometric codes. IEEE Trans. Inf. Theory **45**, 432–437 (1999)

[Wal] Walker, J.: Algebraic geometry codes over rings. Ph.D. thesis. Univ Illinois Champain (1996)

[Wal99] Walker, J.L.: Algebraic geometric codes over rings. J. Pure Appl. Algebra **144**(1), 91–110 (1999)

Large Message Homomorphic Secret Sharing from DCR and Applications

Lawrence Roy[(✉)] and Jaspal Singh[(✉)]

Oregon State University, Corvallis, USA
ldr709@gmail.com, singjasp@oregonstate.edu

Abstract. We present the first homomorphic secret sharing (HSS) construction that simultaneously (1) has negligible correctness error, (2) supports integers from an exponentially large range, and (3) relies on an assumption not known to imply FHE—specifically, the Decisional Composite Residuosity (DCR) assumption. This resolves an open question posed by Boyle, Gilboa, and Ishai (Crypto 2016). Homomorphic secret sharing is analogous to fully-homomorphic encryption, except the ciphertexts are shared across two non-colluding evaluators. Previous constructions of HSS either had non-negligible correctness error and polynomial-size plaintext space or were based on the stronger LWE assumption. We also present two applications of our technique: a two server ORAM with constant bandwidth overhead, and a rate-1 trapdoor hash function with negligible error rate.

1 Introduction

Homomorphic secret sharing is a relaxation of fully-homomorphic encryption (FHE) where the ciphertexts are shared across two non-colluding evaluators, who may homomorphically evaluate functions on their shares. In FHE, if $c \leftarrow \mathsf{Enc}(x)$ then $\mathsf{Hom}(f, c)$ is an encryption of $f(x)$. In HSS, if $s_0, s_1 \leftarrow \mathsf{Share}(x)$ then $\mathsf{Hom}(f, s_1)$ and $\mathsf{Hom}(f, s_0)$ (computed independently) are a sharing of $f(x)$.

Boyle, Gilboa, and Ishai [BGI16] initiated the line of work on secure computation from HSS with a construction based on the Decisional Diffie–Hellman (DDH) assumption. They used their scheme to achieve the first secure two-party computation protocol with *sublinear communication* from an assumption not known to imply FHE. Though their HSS only supports restricted multiplication straight-line (RMS) programs, this is enough at least to evaluate polynomial-size branching programs. All known HSS constructions (including ours) that aren't based on FHE have this same limitation.

The HSS of [BGI16] has two main limitations. First, it achieves correctness with probability only $1 - p$ (for $p = 1/\mathrm{poly}$). Second, it can only support a message space of polynomial size M, as it requires $O(M/p)$ time for a step they call "share conversion". [FGJS17] constructed a similar HSS scheme based on

---

L. Roy—Supported by a DoE CSGF fellowship.

T. Malkin and C. Peikert (Eds.): CRYPTO 2021, LNCS 12827, pp. 687–717, 2021.
https://doi.org/10.1007/978-3-030-84252-9_23

Paillier encryption (from the DCR assumption), with the same limitations and $O(M/p)$-time share conversion technique. The cost of share conversion was later improved to $O(\sqrt{M/p})$ by [DKK18], which they proved is optimal for these schemes unless faster interval discrete logarithm algorithms are found.

These limitations were eventually removed by [BKS19], using lattice-based cryptography. Their scheme is based the Learning With Errors (LWE) assumption, and achieves homomorphic secret sharing with exponentially small correctness error and exponentially large plaintext space. The LWE assumption is strong enough to construct FHE [BV11], although their HSS scheme uses simpler techniques and can be more efficient than FHE.

Why is correctness error important? Besides the theoretical distinction, it increases the overhead for secure computation: the 2PC protocol of [BGI16] needs to repeat homomorphic evaluation polynomially many times and take a majority vote (using another MPC protocol) on the outcome. Longer programs have higher chance for error, as if any operation errors then the whole computation will fail. Consequently, when evaluating an n-step program on plaintexts bounded by M, they require $O(Mn^2)$ time to get a constant error rate (or $O(Mn^2t)$ time after repeating for $O(t)$ tries to get a negligible error rate of 2^{-t}). The reduced error rate from [DKK18] allows this to be improved to $O(M^{1/2}n^{3/2})$. Ideally, we would want the computation cost of a 2PC protocol to be linear in n.

Supporting exponentially large plaintext space can also improve the 2PC protocol's computational complexity, because it is necessary to represent the HSS scheme's key inside of its messages. [BGI16] manage this by taking the bit-decomposition of the key, though this multiplies the computational cost by the key size. When M can be exponentially large, however, the key can directly fit inside the plaintext space. Additionally, computations can be performed on large chunks of data at a time, further improving efficiency. Finally, there may be some computations that can only be performed with the larger message space bound. Specifically, RMS programs with a polynomial bound on memory values are sufficient to evaluate branching programs [BGI16], while with a large enough message space algebraic branching programs over $\mathbb{Z}$ can be evaluated.

The question of whether negligible correctness error could be achieved from an assumption not known to imply FHE was left as an open problem by [BGI16].[1]

1.1   Our Results

We give an affirmative answer this open question. We construct an HSS scheme based on Damgård–Jurik encryption (under the DCR assumption) that achieves negligible correctness error and exponentially large message space. When our HSS is used for 2PC, there is no need for repeated HSS evaluation to amplify correctness. We can therefore securely evaluate n-step RMS programs in $O(n)$ time. Previous constructions required a polynomial bound on the size of the

---

[1] A concurrent work [OSY21] has also independently solved this problem.

values in the RMS computation, while our construction natively supports arithmetic operations over exponentially large values.

The main insight in our construction is to define a new "distance function", the key step used for share conversion in HSS schemes. Ours is based on the algebraic properties of the ciphertext group $(\mathbb{Z}/N^{s+1}\mathbb{Z})^{\times}$, while existing distance functions use the generic technique of searching for a randomly chosen subset of ciphertexts. This allows us to extract an exponentially large result from our distance function, and achieve share conversion with a negligible error rate.

We also present several other applications of our new result and techniques:

ORAM. We propose a novel 2-server malicious secure Oblivious RAM (ORAM) protocol that achieves constant bandwidth. An ORAM protocol allows the client to hide its access pattern on a database outsourced to untrusted server(s). Our protocol is closely based on the single server Onion ORAM protocol [DvDF+16], which leverages server side computation to achieve constant bandwidth blowup. We replace this server side computation with a number of RMS programs, which can be evaluated by the two servers using our HSS scheme.

While there already exist multi-server ORAM constructions with constant client-server bandwidth overhead (*e.g.*, [DvDF+16,FNR+15,HOY+17]), they all require either super-constant server-server communication or a minimum block size of $\Omega(\log^6 N)$, where N is the number of blocks in the ORAM. Whereas, our HSS based 2-server ORAM achieves constant bandwidth for block of size $\omega(\log^4 N)$ and with no server-server communication.

Trapdoor hash functions. Beyond HSS, another construction based on the notion of a distance function is trapdoor hash functions (TDH) [DGI+19]. Rate-1 TDHs are a kind of hash function that have additional properties useful for two-party computation. Specifically, if Alice has some f in a limited class of predicates and Bob has a message x, if Bob sends the hash of x and Alice sends a key generated based on f, they can each compute a single-bit share of $f(x)$. [DGI+19] use rate-1 TDHs to build rate-1 string oblivious transfer (OT), from which they construct efficient private information retrieval and semi-compact homomorphic encryption. They also present several other constructions based on TDHs.

Prior work [DGI+19] constructed rate-1 TDHs from a variety of assumptions (DDH, QR, DCR, and LWE), but only their QR and LWE instantiations achieve negligible correctness error. For DDH and DCR, they had to compensate by using error correcting codes in their construction of rate-1 string OT. We can directly construct a rate-1 trapdoor hash function from DCR using our distance function, achieving negligible correctness error. Our construction also generalizes beyond TDHs, in that it can handle functions f outputting more than a single bit.

HSS definition. We extend the definition of HSS to allow (generalized, to represent RMS operations) circuits to be evaluated one gate at a time. One benefit of this approach is that it allows secure evaluation of online algorithms, which may take input and produce output many times, while maintaining some secret state. The function to evaluate may be chosen adaptively based on previous outputs or shares. We also define malicious security of HSS, in the form of share authentication. These definitions are directly useful for our application to ORAM.

1.2 Technical Overview

Introduction to HSS. HSS schemes work through the interaction of two different homomorphic schemes: additively homomorphic encryption and additive secret sharing. Following the notation of [BGI16], let $[\![x]\!]$ denote an encryption of x. Let $\langle y \rangle$ denote additive shares of y, meaning that party 0 has $\langle y \rangle_0$ and party 1 has $\langle y \rangle_1$ such that $\langle y \rangle_1 - \langle y \rangle_0 = y$. Then $\langle x \rangle + \langle y \rangle \equiv \langle x + y \rangle$, where $\equiv$ means shares that decode to the same value, or ciphertexts that decrypt to the same plaintext. We will write the group operation on the homomorphic encryption multiplicatively, so $[\![x]\!][\![y]\!] \equiv [\![x + y]\!]$. Any additively homomorphic encryption supports multiplication by constants, so we have $[\![x]\!]^c \equiv [\![cx]\!]$.

We have two different additively homomorphic schemes; what happens if we let them interact? If the parties compute $[\![x]\!]^{\langle y \rangle}$, they get $\langle\!\langle [\![xy]\!] \rangle\!\rangle$, where $\langle\!\langle z \rangle\!\rangle$ denotes multiplicative shares of z. More precisely, party i has $\langle\!\langle [\![x]\!]^y \rangle\!\rangle_i = [\![x]\!]^{\langle y \rangle_i}$, and $\langle\!\langle [\![x]\!]^y \rangle\!\rangle_1 / \langle\!\langle [\![x]\!]^y \rangle\!\rangle_0 = [\![x]\!]^{\langle y \rangle_1 - \langle y \rangle_0} \equiv [\![xy]\!]$. What's interesting here is that by combining the two encryption schemes we get a representation of the product. That is, we have a bilinear map. However, we would really like to be able to perform multiple operations in sequence. Is there any way we could make the result instead be $\langle xy \rangle$?

Luckily, many additively homomorphic encryption schemes perform decryption through exponentiation, the same operation as was used for homomorphically multiplying by a constant. For Paillier, decryption is $\phi^{-1}([\![z]\!]^\varphi) = z$, where $\phi(z) = 1 + N\varphi z$ is a homomorphism from the plaintext space to the ciphertext space, and N and φ are the public and private keys. Therefore, if we have shares $\langle \varphi y \rangle$ then we can compute $[\![x]\!]^{\langle \varphi y \rangle} \equiv \langle\!\langle \phi(x)^y \rangle\!\rangle \equiv \langle\!\langle \phi(xy) \rangle\!\rangle$. For ElGamal, the decryption of a ciphertext $[\![z]\!] = (A, B)$ is $\phi^{-1}(A^{-k}B)$, where $\phi(z) = g^z$ for a public generator g. Again, ϕ is a homomorphism from the plaintext space. This is slightly more complicated in that it's taking a dot product "in the exponent" with the private key vector $\vec{k} = [-k \ 1]$, but if we take the secret shares to be vectors $\langle \vec{k} y \rangle$ then still we have $[\![x]\!]^{\langle \vec{k} y \rangle} \equiv \langle\!\langle \phi(x)^y \rangle\!\rangle \equiv \langle\!\langle \phi(xy) \rangle\!\rangle$.

The last step of decryption for both schemes is to compute ϕ^{-1}. For HSS we need to do the same, but on the multiplicative shares $\langle\!\langle \phi(z) \rangle\!\rangle$ split across the two parties performing HSS. This is done with a *distance function*, with the property that $\mathrm{Dist}(a\phi(z)) - \mathrm{Dist}(a) = z$, ideally for any ciphertext a and plaintext z. Then $\mathrm{Dist}(*)\langle\!\langle \phi(xy) \rangle\!\rangle_i \equiv \langle xy \rangle_i$ gives additive shares of the multiplication result. The idea from [BGI16] for constructing Dist is that both parties agree on a common set of "special points", which they choose randomly. They iteratively compute $a\phi(-1)^j$, starting at $j = 0$ and continuing until $c = a\phi(-1)^j$ is special, then set $\mathrm{Dist}(a)$ to be the distance j. If they find the same special point c,

$$\mathrm{Dist}(a\phi(z)) - \mathrm{Dist}(a) = \mathrm{Dist}(c\phi(j + z)) - \mathrm{Dist}(c\phi(j)) = j + z - j = z,$$

so their distances are additive shares of z. When the special points are chosen randomly and z is small, $\mathrm{Dist}(a\phi(z))$ and $\mathrm{Dist}(a)$ will usually pick the same c.

Putting this all together, HSS consists of a way of homomorphically multiplying a ciphertext $[\![x]\!]$ by a share $\langle y \rangle$, or rather $\langle ky \rangle$ for some private key k, to get $\langle\!\langle \phi(xy) \rangle\!\rangle$, then finally using a distance function to find $\langle xy \rangle$. A circularly secure encryption scheme allows ky to be encrypted, so then $\text{Dist}\left([\![ky]\!]^{kx}\right) \equiv \langle kxy \rangle$, which can feed the input of another multiplication operation, and so on.

Paillier distance function. We now present a simplified version of our main HSS construction. It uses a variant of Paillier encryption, where instead of encrypting messages as $r^N(1 + Nz) \bmod N^2$ for public key N and uniformly random r, it encrypts them as $r^{N^3}(1 + N^2z) \bmod N^4$. This is to allow the plaintext size to be bigger than the private key. We have $\left(r^{N^3}(1 + N^2z)\right)^{\varphi} = 1 + N^2\varphi z = \phi(z)$. To find $\phi^{-1}(a)$, compute $(a - 1)/N^2$, as $a - 1$ must be a multiple of N^2, then multiply by $\varphi^{-1} \bmod N^2$.

It turns out that we can design a distance function that is based on this ϕ^{-1}. A prior construction of HSS from Paillier encryption, [FGJS17], had a minor optimization based on $\langle\!\langle \phi(z) \rangle\!\rangle_1 = \langle\!\langle \phi(z) \rangle\!\rangle_0 \bmod N^2$, since $\langle\!\langle \phi(z) \rangle\!\rangle_1 / \langle\!\langle \phi(z) \rangle\!\rangle_0 = \phi(z) = 1 + N^2\varphi z$. Therefore both parties will have something in common, and they can use it as their common point $c = \langle\!\langle \phi(z) \rangle\!\rangle_0 \bmod N^2 = \langle\!\langle \phi(z) \rangle\!\rangle_1 \bmod N^2$. On input a, let the distance function pick a canonical representative $c = a \bmod N^2 \in [-\frac{N-1}{2}, \frac{N-1}{2}]$. Then $a/c = 1 + N^2w$, and we let $\text{Dist}(a) = w$. This means that our "special points" are $[-\frac{N-1}{2}, \frac{N-1}{2}]$, instead of a random set like [BGI16]. We then have $\text{Dist}(a\phi(z)) - \text{Dist}(a) = \varphi z$, because $a\phi(z)/c = (1 + N^2\varphi z)(1 + N^2w) = 1 + N^2(\varphi z + w)$. This is a slightly different property than what we specified for distance functions, but it is actually even better as we don't need to use circularly secure encryption to get $\langle \varphi xy \rangle$ as the result of multiplication—φ will already be multiplied in the output.

However, there's one last step before we have an HSS. The result from Dist will be in the form of additive shares modulo N^2, and we need them to be additive shares in $\mathbb{Z}$ so that we can use them as an exponent in the next operation. Exponentiating to a power that is modulo N^2 would not make sense, as the multiplicative order of almost any ciphertext does not divide N^2. We use a trick from the LWE HSS construction: additive shares modulo N^2 of a value z much smaller than N^2 (so $|z|/N^2$ is negligible) have overwhelming probability of being additive shares over $\mathbb{Z}$, *without any modulus*. Therefore we can make a distance function that has only negligible failure probability and supports an exponentially large bound on the plaintext.

1.3 Other Related Work

We compare our proposed ORAM construction to Onion ORAM [DvDF+16], which is also based on the Damgård–Jurik public-key encryption. To ensure malicious security and achieve constant bandwidth overhead, the scheme allows for blocks of size $\tilde{\omega}(\log^6 N)$, with $\tilde{O}(B\log^4 N)$ client computation and $\tilde{\omega}(B\log^4 N)$ server computation. For comparison, our proposed ORAM construction allows for blocks of size $\tilde{\omega}(\log^4 N)$, with $\tilde{O}(B\log^4 N)$ client computation and

$\widetilde{O}(B \log^5 N)$ server computation. To ensure the integrity of server side storage, Onion ORAM uses a verification algorithm that relies on probabilistic checking and error correcting codes. This integrity check adds an overhead to the communication and computation. In our protocol we get this verification check "for free", as the HSS shares held by the two servers satisfy the authenticated property—which ensures that a single corrupt server cannot modify its share without it being detected by the client during the decoding process. This gives major savings in our protocol's communication and client side computation compared to Onion ORAM.

Bucket ORAM proposed by Fletcher et al. [FNR+15] proposes a single server ORAM with constant bandwidth overhead for blocks of size $\widetilde{\Omega}(\log^6 N)$. It's a constant round protocol, but asymptotically its client and server computation match that of Onion ORAM. S^3ORAM [HOY+17] proposes a multi-server ORAM construction with constant client-server bandwidth overhead. It avoid the evaluation of homomorphic operations on the server side and is based on Shamir Secret Sharing. However, this protocol incurs $O(\log N)$ overhead in server-server communication, which makes the overall communication overhead logarithmic. Another interesting work on designing 2-server ORAMs optimized for secure computation is due to Doerner and Shelat [DS17]. Their construction is based on the notion of function secret sharing, which is closely related to HSS. However, it also incurs an $O(\log N)$ server-server communication overhead.

1.4   Concurrent Result

A concurrent and independent work [OSY21] also constructs an HSS from the DCR assumption and achieves negligible correctness error for an exponentially large plaintext space. Qualitatively, our distance function, which is the main construction we base our results on, matches theirs. There are two main aspects in which our work improves on theirs.

We use Damgård–Jurik encryption, which allows the plaintext space to be significantly larger than the whole private key. OSY instead uses Paillier encryption. They consequently have to split their private key into chunks, requiring either a circular security assumption or a provably circular secure encryption scheme. OSY needs to use around 6 chunks, assuming circular security, or $\Theta(\log(N))$ without. While our ciphertexts are somewhat bigger, we only need a single ciphertext for an input to our HSS scheme. We therefore have either a constant or $\Theta(\ell(\kappa))$ speedup in both computation and communication relative to OSY's HSS scheme, depending on the assumption. While their scheme more naturally supports additive decoding, a variant of our scheme also has this property.

We also give novel HSS definitions and proofs that support running online algorithms, and adaptively choosing functions to evaluate based on previous ciphertexts. We define authenticated HSS, and prove that our construction is authenticated, allowing its use in maliciously secure protocols such as our ORAM.

2   Preliminaries

2.1   Notation

Modular arithmetic. Let $\mathbb{Z}/N\mathbb{Z}$ be the ring of integers modulo N and $(\mathbb{Z}/N\mathbb{Z})^+$ be its additive group. Let $(\mathbb{Z}/N\mathbb{Z})^\times$ be the multiplicative group of all units x of $\mathbb{Z}/N\mathbb{Z}$, i.e. all x coprime to N. Normally multiplication of $\bar{x} = x + N\mathbb{Z} \in \mathbb{Z}/N\mathbb{Z}$ by some integer $K \in \mathbb{Z}$ will just be $K\bar{x} = Kx + N\mathbb{Z} \in \mathbb{Z}/N\mathbb{Z}$; however, we overload this to mean $Kx + KN\mathbb{Z} \in \mathbb{Z}/KN\mathbb{Z}$ as well. We will notate the quotient map from $\mathbb{Z}/KN\mathbb{Z}$ to $\mathbb{Z}/N\mathbb{Z}$ as $\cdot + N\mathbb{Z}$, or omit it when it is clear from context. To say that two values a and b are the same modulo N, i.e., that $a + N\mathbb{Z} = b + N\mathbb{Z}$, we write $a \equiv_N b$. For modulus we assume round to nearest, so $\cdot \bmod N : \mathbb{Z}/N\mathbb{Z} \to [-\frac{N}{2}, \frac{N}{2}) \cap \mathbb{Z}$ and $x = (x \bmod N) + N\mathbb{Z}$ for all x.

Algorithm notation. We write our constructions in pseudocode. While the notation should be mostly self-explanatory, there are a few things to take note of. The boolean AND and OR operations are $\wedge$ and $\vee$, and the compliment of a bit b is $\bar{b} = 1 - b$. We give equality testing its own symbol, $\overset{?}{=}$, so $x \overset{?}{=} y$ is 1 if $x = y$, and 0 otherwise. Assignment statements are written as $x := 1$, while sampling is written as $x \leftarrow \{0, 1\}$, to indicate that x is uniformly random in the set $\{0, 1\}$. We use $\rho \leftarrow \$$ to represent sampling a uniformly random bit stream ρ. This notation also applies to subroutine calls, so if f is deterministic then the notation is $y := f(x)$, but if f is randomized then it is $y \leftarrow f(x)$.

We will also write our definitions in pseudocode, expressing our security properties as indistinguishability of two randomized algorithms. Often the adversary $\mathcal{A}$ gets to choose some x partway through a randomized algorithm. To preserve the adversary's state and give it to the distinguisher we use $(\text{view}, x) \leftarrow \mathcal{A}$ and return view from the distribution along with everything else. This way $\mathcal{A}$ can put its state in view and the distinguisher will see it.

2.2   Damgård–Jurik Encryption

Our construction is based on the Damgård–Jurik public-key encryption scheme [DJ01], a generalization of Paillier encryption [Pai99]. At a high level, the plaintexts of Damgård–Jurik are members of an additive group $(\mathbb{Z}/N^s\mathbb{Z})^+$. Encryption applies an isomorphism exp from $(\mathbb{Z}/N^s\mathbb{Z})^+$ to a subgroup of $(\mathbb{Z}/N^{s+1}\mathbb{Z})^\times$, then hides the plaintext by multiplying by a random perfect power of N^s in $(\mathbb{Z}/N^{s+1}\mathbb{Z})^\times$. Decryption uses the private key to cancel out this random value, then applies log, the inverse of exp. This requires that the discrete logarithm be efficiently computable for the subgroup.

This is possible by taking advantage of N being nilpotent in $\mathbb{Z}/N^{s+1}\mathbb{Z}$. Power series in N can have at most $s+1$ nonzero terms because $N^{s+1} \equiv_{N^{s+1}} 0$, allowing us to use the usual Taylor series for e^{Nx} and $\frac{1}{N}\ln(x)$ to define $\exp(x)$ and $\log(x)$.

$$\exp(x) = \sum_{k=0}^{s} \frac{(Nx)^k}{k!} \qquad \log(1 + Nx) = \sum_{k=1}^{s} \frac{(-N)^{k-1}x^k}{k}.$$

exp is an isomorphism from $(\mathbb{Z}/N^s\mathbb{Z})^+$ to $1 + N(\mathbb{Z}/N^{s+1}\mathbb{Z})$, the subgroup consisting of all $u \in (\mathbb{Z}/N^{s+1}\mathbb{Z})^\times$ such that $u \equiv_N 1$. Specifically, exp and log are inverse functions and $\exp(x+y) = \exp(x)\exp(y)$ (see full version of the paper for the proof of these properties). These functions are sufficient to define Damgård–Jurik encryption.

Definition 1. *Given a security parameter κ and a message size s, define the Damgård–Jurik encryption scheme as follows.*[2]

$(N, \varphi) \leftarrow$ DJ.KeyGen(1^κ): *Generate an RSA modulus $N = pq$ where $2^{\ell(\kappa)-1} < p, q < 2^{\ell(\kappa)}$, and ℓ is a polynomial chosen to make the scheme achieve κ-bit security. Let the public key be N and the private key be $\varphi = \varphi(N)$, where $\varphi(N) = (p-1)(q-1)$ is Euler's totient function.*

$c \leftarrow$ DJ.Enc$_{N,s}(x)$: *Given $x \in \mathbb{Z}/N^s\mathbb{Z}$, choose a uniformly random $r \in (\mathbb{Z}/N^{s+1}\mathbb{Z})^\times$ and output $c = r^{N^s}\exp(x)$.*

$x :=$ DJ.Dec$_{N,s,\varphi}(c)$: *Given $c \in (\mathbb{Z}/N^{s+1}\mathbb{Z})^\times$, output $x = \frac{1}{\varphi}\log(c^\varphi) \in \mathbb{Z}/N^s\mathbb{Z}$.*

Encryption is clearly additively homomorphic, since $r_1^{N^s} r_2^{N^s} \exp(x)\exp(y) = (r_1 r_2)^{N^s}\exp(x+y)$. Decryption is well defined because $c^\varphi \equiv_N 1$ by Euler's theorem, and because $p-1$ and $q-1$ are each coprime to N since p and q have the same bit length. The order of $(\mathbb{Z}/N^{s+1}\mathbb{Z})^\times$ is $\varphi(N^{s+1}) = p^s(p-1)q^s(q-1) = \varphi N^s$, so $\log(c^\varphi) = \log(r^{\varphi N^s}\exp(x)^\varphi) = \log(\exp(\varphi x)) = \varphi x$, which implies the correctness of decryption.

The security of this encryption scheme is based on the decisional composite residuosity assumption (DCR).

Definition 2. *The* decisional composite residuosity (DCR) *assumption is that the uniform distribution on $(\mathbb{Z}/N^2\mathbb{Z})^\times$ is indistinguishable from the uniform distribution on the subgroup of perfect powers of N in $(\mathbb{Z}/N^2\mathbb{Z})^\times$.*

We will not use the assumption directly, as it will be more convenient use the CPA security of Damgård–Jurik encryption as the basis for our security proofs.

Theorem 3 (Damgård and Jurik [DJ01, Theorem 1]). *Damgård–Jurik encryption is CPA secure if and only if the DCR assumption holds. That is, the oracles $\mathcal{O}_{i,N,s}(x_0, x_1) =$ DJ.Enc$_{N,s}(N, x_i)$ for $i \in \{0,1\}$ must be indistinguishable, meaning that for any PPT $\mathcal{A}$ the following probability must be negligibly different between the two values of i.*

$$\Pr[(N, \varphi) \leftarrow \text{DJ.KeyGen}(1^\kappa); \mathcal{A}^{\mathcal{O}_{i,N,s}}(N) = 1]$$

---

[2] Damgård–Jurik was originally defined using $\exp(x) = (1+N)^x$, which required log to use Hensel lifting. We instead chose to use Taylor series because it simplifies the description of log, and only require $O(s)$ additions and multiplications to evaluate with Horner's rule, while the Hensel lifting algorithm took $O(s^2)$ arithmetic operations.

$$\begin{array}{|l|}
\hline
\text{SELECT}(b, x_0, x_1): \\
\hline
v := b(x_1 - x_0) \\
w := v + x_0 \\
\text{return } w \\
\hline
\end{array}$$

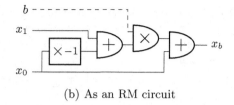

(a) As an RMS program

(b) As an RM circuit

Fig. 1. The selection function x_b represented as an RMS program (left, Definition 4) and a RM circuit (right, Definition 8). In the RM circuit, dashed wires (wire type IN) correspond to inputs in an RMS program, while solid wires (wire type REG) correspond to registers.

2.3 Universal Hashing

In our ORAM construction we will assume a family of hash function $H = \{h : U \to [m]\}$, which satisfied the *uniform difference property*, which states: for any two unequal $x, y \in U$, the number $(h(x) - h(y)) \mod m$ is uniformly random over all hash functions $h \in H$.

3 Circuit Homomorphic Secret Sharing

In this section we present a definition of homomorphic secret sharing (HSS) based on evaluating (generalized) circuits. We first present a notion of circuit that is general enough to capture the operations that our HSS scheme can perform, Restricted Multiplication Straight-line programs. Then we define a notion of HSS based on replacing each gate in a circuit with an operation that works on shares. We will only need to specify properties of a single gate at a time; these properties compose to become secure evaluation of a whole circuit.

The benefits of this approach are threefold. The piecewise definition allows the evaluation of online algorithms, where some output may need to be produced before the rest of the inputs can be taken, with state maintained throughout. It also allows the circuit to be chosen adaptively, based on previous outputs or even shares. Finally, it simplifies the proof of our HSS construction to be able to prove properties of individual gates and have them compose.

3.1 Restricted Multiplication Circuits

First, we give a definition for restricted multiplication straight-line programs, which were first defined in [Cle90]. We give a slight generalization however, allowing inputs to be added together before multiplication with a register. Polynomially sized RMS programs under the new definition could still be written in polynomial size in the traditional definition by applying the distributive property, but this may multiply the number of steps by n.

Definition 4. *A* Restricted Multiplication Straight-line (RMS) *program over a ring* $\mathbb{K}$ *is a sequential program taking with inputs* $x_1, \ldots, x_n \in \mathbb{K}$ *and registers* $z_1, \ldots,$ *where the outputs are a subset of the registers. Each instruction must take the form*

$$z_k := \left(A_0 + \sum_{i \le n} A_i x_i\right)\left(B_0 + \sum_{i < k} B_i z_i\right),$$

for some constants $A_0, \ldots, A_N, B_0, \cdots B_{k-1}$.

For convenience we take the first n registers to be the inputs, to avoid explicitly writing out a conversion like $z_1 := 1$; $z_{i+1} := x_i z_1$. An example of an RMS program is shown in Fig. 1a. We want to define a kind of circuit that captures the allowed operations in RMS programs. In an RMS program there are two types of values: inputs and registers. This suggests defining circuits with two types of wire, called IN and REG. The circuit for the example is shown in Fig. 1b, where IN wires are drawn with a dashed line, and REG wires are drawn with a solid line. Gates representing linear operations (addition and multiplication-by-constant) are allowed for either type of wire, and both wire types allow sources for the value 1. However, multiplication is only allowed between the IN wire type and the REG wire type, and must always produce a REG wire.

Typed circuits. To make this formal, we need to define circuits with multiple types of wire. First we define circuit prototypes, which specify what types of wires and gates are allowed, then we define circuits for a given prototype.

Definition 5. *A circuit prototype* (types, gates, in, out) *consists of a set* types $\subseteq \{0,1\}^*$ *of wire types and a set* gates $\subseteq \{0,1\}^*$ *of gate types, together with maps* in: gates $\to$ types* *and* out: gates $\to$ types *assigning to each gate type the wire types of its inputs and output.*

Definition 6. *A typed circuit* (nodes, wires, inputs, outputs, type, gate) *for a circuit prototype* (types, gates, in, out) *consists of **a**) a directed acyclic graph* (nodes, wires), ***b**) a total order on* wires, ***c**) subsets* inputs, outputs $\subseteq$ nodes, ***d**) a node labeling* type: nodes $\to$ types, *and **e**) a non-input node labeling* gate: nodes \ inputs $\to$ gates. *A non-input node is called a gate. We require the circuit to be well-formed: for any gate* v, type(v) = out$($gate$(v))$, *and if* $(v_1, v), (v_2, v), \ldots, (v_n, v)$ *are* v*'s incoming wires in sorted order,* type(v_1) type$(v_2) \cdots$ type(v_n) = in$($gate$(v))$.

Note that in the above definition we followed the more common practice of only using single output gates and letting fan-out be an implicit operation represented by a gate having multiple outgoing edges. A more general definition would allow gates with multiple outputs and disallow implicit fanout, so that fanout can be controlled by what gates are allowed. The simplified definition is enough for our application, but e.g. quantum circuits would be better represented by a more general definition.

We would like to evaluate typed circuits, just like any other kind of circuit. To do this, we to need a semantics to define what each gate does.

```
Run(f, s, x):
    (nodes, wires, inputs, outputs, type, gate) := f
    (values, eval) := s
    for v ∈ nodes \ inputs in topological order:
        u := empty list
        for e ∈ wires in sorted order:
            if (w, v) = e: append w to u
        x_v := eval(gate(g))(x_{u[1]}, x_{u[2]}, ..., x_{u[|u|]})
    return {x_v}_{v∈outputs}
```

Fig. 2. Algorithm for evaluating a circuit f with a semantics s. The circuit and the semantics must share the same circuit prototype.

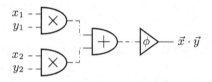

Fig. 3. A bounded RM circuit for computing the dot product of a pair of two element vectors. The new wire type MUL is drawn with a _._ line, and the new conversion operation ϕ with a triangle.

Definition 7. *A* semantics (values, eval) *for a circuit prototype* (types, gates, in, out) *assigns each wire type* $w \in$ types *a set of values* values(w), *and assigns each gate type* $g \in$ gates *a function* eval(g): values$(w_1)\times$values$(w_2)\times\cdots\times$values$(w_n) \to$ values$(\text{out}(g))$, *where* $w_1 w_2 \cdots w_n = \text{in}(g)$ *are the input wire types of the gate.*

We can evaluate a typed circuit using a semantics. Given values $x_v \in$ values$($type$(v))$ for all circuit inputs $v \in$ inputs, the evaluation proceeds in topological order. The inputs of each gate are its incoming wires, and the input order is given by the total order on the edges. Every gate $g \in$ nodes $\setminus$ inputs gets evaluated as $x_g = \text{eval}(\text{gate}(g))(x_{v_1}, x_{v_2}, \ldots, x_{v_n})$ where $(v_1, g), (v_2, g), \ldots, (v_n, g) \in$ wires are the incoming wires of g in sorted order. The outputs are then x_v for $v \in$ outputs. See Fig. 2 for the formal algorithm.

Restricted multiplication (RM) circuits. We can now define restricted multiplication circuits using the above definitions.

Definition 8. *The* RM circuit prototype *over a ring* $\mathbb{K}$ *has wire types* types $=$ $\{$IN, REG$\}$, *gate types for constants and linear operations* $\{1_{\text{IN}}, 1_{\text{REG}}, +_{\text{IN}}, +_{\text{REG}}, \times_{\text{IN}} c, \times_{\text{REG}} c\}$ *for all* $c \in \mathbb{K}$, *and a single nonlinear multiplication operation* $\times$: IN $\times$ REG $\to$ REG. *An* RM circuit *is a circuit for this circuit prototype.*

An RM circuit can be evaluated just like an RMS program.

Definition 9. *The* evaluation semantics *for RM circuits over* $\mathbb{K}$ *has* values(IN) = values(REG) = $\mathbb{K}$ *and performs each gate operation in the ring* $\mathbb{K}$.

However, this is not the only semantics assigned to RM programs. In fact, our HSS definition is based on the idea of giving multiple different semantics to the same circuit: one for the plaintexts and one for the shares. The latter define what shares are and how homomorphic operations are evaluated on them.

Bounded RM circuits. Unfortunately, our construction will not be capable of evaluating all RM circuits. Similarly to [BGI16], we have a share conversion step that only works for values of bounded size. This conversion step is normally done on the output of every multiplication, but it can be delayed until after further linear operations. We generalize RM circuits with another wire type to represent unconverted values.

Definition 10. *The* bounded RM circuit prototype *over a ring* $\mathcal{R}$ *has wire types* types = {IN, REG, MUL} *and gate types for a) the constant 1 for all wire types, b) linear operations for all wire types, c) a multiplication operation* $\times$: IN $\times$ REG $\rightarrow$ MUL, *and d) a conversion operation* ϕ: MUL $\rightarrow$ REG. *A bounded RM circuit is a circuit for this circuit prototype.*

An example of this new kind of circuit is illustrated in Fig. 3.

Definition 11. *The* evaluation semantics *for bounded RM circuits over* $\mathbb{K}$, *given a bound* $M \subseteq \mathbb{K}$, *sets* values(IN) = values(REG) = values(MUL) = $\mathbb{K} \cup \{\bot\}$ *and assigns the usual operations in* $\mathbb{K}$ *for linear operations and multiplication.* eval(ϕ)(x) *is* x *if* $x \in M$, *or* $\bot$ *otherwise.* $\bot$ *is an absorbing element for all operations, so if any input is* $\bot$ *then the output is* $\bot$.

The value $\bot$ allows the circuit evaluation to fail if the input to the conversion operation isn't bounded. This idea is generalized by the following definition.

Definition 12. *A* semantics (values, eval) *is called a* failure semantics *if, for all wire types* $w \in$ types, *there is a special value* $\bot \in$ values(w) *called* failure *that is absorbing for all functions in* eval(gates). *That is, for any* $g \in$ gates, eval(g)($\ldots, \bot, \ldots$) = $\bot$, *no matter what the other arguments are.*

The evaluation semantics of bounded RM circuits is a failure semantics.

3.2   Homomorphic Secret Sharing

Instead of taking a whole circuit to evaluate at once, our two-server HSS definition works piecemeal, by assigning three different semantics to the same circuit prototype. The first semantics is the usual one that works over the plaintexts, while the other two define, for each of the two servers, the what values the shares may take and how homomorphic operations may be computed on them. In a sense, these share semantics define compilers that turn the circuit into something that can be evaluated on shares, one gate at a time. The idea is that if we require that the plaintext semantics and share semantics be compatible with each other in a certain way, it implies that the homomorphic operations correctly evaluate the circuit to the sames result as if it were evaluated on the plaintext.

In our construction we are using Damgård–Jurik encryption, so $\mathbb{K}$ will be $\mathbb{Z}/N^s\mathbb{Z}$, which depends on the public key N and cannot be fixed in advance. This means that the operations we can perform have to be sampled randomly, at the same time as the public key, even though it is more usual to define homomorphic secret sharing in terms of some fixed operations (see e.g. [BGI+17]). Therefore, the plaintext evaluation will depend on the public key. We give the homomorphic operations access to shares of the secret key as well, as some of our operations (such as getting shares of 1) will depend on them.

Definition 13. *A $(1-p)$-correct two-server Homomorphic Secret Sharing (HSS) scheme with public-key setup consists of PPT algorithms:*

- $(\mathsf{pk}, \mathsf{sk}_0, \mathsf{sk}_1) \leftarrow \mathsf{Setup}(1^\kappa)$ *outputs the keys and the circuit prototype, where κ is the security parameter.*
- $((\mathsf{types}, \mathsf{gates}, \mathsf{in}, \mathsf{out}), (\mathsf{values}, \mathsf{eval})) := \mathsf{Eval}(\mathsf{pk})$ *gives the circuit prototype and the plaintext evaluation semantics. This must be a failure semantics.*
- $(\mathsf{values}_j, \mathsf{eval}_j) := \mathsf{Hom}(j, \mathsf{pk}, \mathsf{sk}_j)$ *outputs the homomorphic evaluation semantics for server j, except that eval_j takes an extra argument r, which is a stream of random coins.*
- $(s_0, s_1) \leftarrow \mathsf{Share}(\mathsf{pk}, \mathsf{sk}_0, \mathsf{sk}_1, w, x)$, *given a wire type $w \in \mathsf{types}$ and a value $x \in \mathsf{values}(w)$, outputs shares $s_j \in \mathsf{values}_j(w)$.*
- $y \leftarrow \mathsf{Decode}(\mathsf{pk}, \mathsf{sk}_0, \mathsf{sk}_1, w, s_0, s_1)$ *decodes an output $y \in \mathsf{values}(w)$ from shares $s_j \in \mathsf{values}_j(w)$, where $w \in \mathsf{types}$.*

The following conditions are imposed.

- *Correctness: Running Decode on the shares from Share must output the original input x when x is not failure. More precisely, the following distribution outputs TRUE with probability at least $1 - p$, for any PPT adversary $\mathcal{A}$.*

$$
\begin{aligned}
&(\mathsf{pk}, \mathsf{sk}_0, \mathsf{sk}_1) \leftarrow \mathsf{Setup}(1^\kappa) \\
&(w, x) \leftarrow \mathcal{A}(\mathsf{pk}, \mathsf{sk}_0, \mathsf{sk}_1) \\
&(s_0, s_1) \leftarrow \mathsf{Share}(\mathsf{pk}, \mathsf{sk}_0, \mathsf{sk}_1, w, x) \\
&y \leftarrow \mathsf{Decode}(\mathsf{pk}, \mathsf{sk}_0, \mathsf{sk}_1, w, s_0, s_1) \\
&\text{return } x \overset{?}{=} y \vee x \overset{?}{=} \bot
\end{aligned}
$$

- *Homomorphism: The semantics must commute with Decode. That is, the following distributions are indistinguishable except with advantage p, for any PPT adversary $\mathcal{A}$ such that the first distribution never returns $\bot$.*

$(\mathsf{pk}, \mathsf{sk}_0, \mathsf{sk}_1) \leftarrow \mathsf{Setup}(1^\kappa)$
$(\mathsf{proto}, (\mathsf{values}, \mathsf{eval})) := \mathsf{Eval}(\mathsf{pk})$
$(\mathsf{view}, g, \{(s_{i0}, s_{i1})\}_i) \leftarrow \mathcal{A}(\mathsf{pk}, \mathsf{sk}_0, \mathsf{sk}_1)$
$r \leftarrow \$$
for $i := 1$ to n:
$\quad x_i \leftarrow \mathsf{Decode}(\mathsf{pk}, \mathsf{sk}_0, \mathsf{sk}_1, \mathsf{in}(g)_i, s_{i0}, s_{i1})$
$y := \mathsf{eval}(g)(x_1, \ldots, x_n)$
return view, r, y

$(\mathsf{pk}, \mathsf{sk}_0, \mathsf{sk}_1) \leftarrow \mathsf{Setup}(1^\kappa)$
$(\mathsf{proto}, (\mathsf{values}, \mathsf{eval})) := \mathsf{Eval}(\mathsf{pk})$
$(\mathsf{view}, g, \{(s_{i0}, s_{i1})\}_i) \leftarrow \mathcal{A}(\mathsf{pk}, \mathsf{sk}_0, \mathsf{sk}_1)$
$r \leftarrow \$$
$(\mathsf{values}_j, \mathsf{eval}_j) := \mathsf{Hom}(j, \mathsf{pk}, \mathsf{sk}_j), \forall j \in \{0, 1\}$
$s'_j := \mathsf{eval}_j(g, r)(s_1, \ldots, s_n), \forall j \in \{0, 1\}$
$y \leftarrow \mathsf{Decode}(\mathsf{pk}, \mathsf{sk}_0, \mathsf{sk}_1, \mathsf{out}(g), s'_0, s'_1)$
return view, r, y

– *Privacy:* Share *must give each server no information about* x. *More precisely, we need the oracles* $\mathcal{O}_{0,\mathsf{pk},\mathsf{sk}_0,\mathsf{sk}_1}$ *and* $\mathcal{O}_{1,\mathsf{pk},\mathsf{sk}_0,\mathsf{sk}_1}$ *to be indistinguishable, for any PPT adversary* $\mathcal{A}$ *and any compromised server* $j \in \{0, 1\}$.

$$
\begin{array}{l}
\underline{\mathcal{O}_{i,\mathsf{pk},\mathsf{sk}_0,\mathsf{sk}_1}(w, x_0, x_1)\text{:}} \\
\quad (s_0, s_1) \leftarrow \mathsf{Share}(\mathsf{pk}, \mathsf{sk}_0, \mathsf{sk}_1, w, x_i) \\
\quad \text{return } s_j
\end{array}
$$

Formally, $\Pr[(\mathsf{pk}, \mathsf{sk}_0, \mathsf{sk}_1) \leftarrow \mathsf{Setup}(1^\kappa);\ \mathcal{A}^{\mathcal{O}_{i,\mathsf{pk},\mathsf{sk}_0,\mathsf{sk}_1}}(\mathsf{pk}, \mathsf{sk}_j) = 1]$ *must be negligibly different between* $i = 0$ *and* $i = 1$.

There are some important differences from the existing HSS definition such as [BGI+17]. In order to split the evaluation up into gates, we give a definition of homomorphism correctness that works on individual gates. We cannot simply use their definition for each gate, because their correctness property assumes that the shares input to Eval come directly from Share, not from other homomorphic operations. By allowing the shares to be chosen adversarially, we can accurately model online computation, where the adversary may dynamically choose what to evaluate based on the shares and keys.

However, HSS is not 100% correct. What's to stop the adversary from choosing shares (or even a sequence of gates that would generate those shares) that cause the HSS to fail? In [BGI16] this is solved by sampling a PRF provided to both parties, as part of Share, and using it to randomize the conversion operation. This works since the circuit is chosen before the shares. But our adversary gets to choose the shares, so we have to explicitly introduce into the homomorphism property a stream of randomness r that is sampled after the input shares have been determined. It could be instantiated with a shared PRG, reseeded whenever the circuit might be chosen adaptively based on the previous seed. If it were necessary to somehow adaptively change the circuit without using any communication at all, a random oracle evaluated on a description of the current gate and where the input shares came from would be an alternative.

For compatibility with existing constructions of HSS, we include an error probability p in our definition, even though in our HSS scheme p is negligible. The DDH-based construction of [BGI16] satisfies our definition with $p = \frac{1}{\mathrm{poly}(\kappa)}$. We do not prove this, but it should become clear that the same techniques we use to prove that our HSS scheme satisfies the definition would also work when applied to theirs. The LWE-based construction of [BKS19] should also work— this time with p a negligible function of κ.

The homomorphism property requires that decoding then performing a plaintext operation must work the same as doing the operation homomorphically, then decoding.[3] Why not go the other way round using Share and Hom, by requiring

---

[3] This structure may seem familiar to readers interested in category theory. In fact, we hit on these definitions by thinking of circuit semantics as functors. The homomorphism property then requires that Decode be a natural transformation from the homomorphic evaluation semantics to the plaintext evaluation semantics.

that the output of the homomorphic operation be indistinguishable from sharing the plaintext value? It turns out that this property is harder to achieve, as it is actually a form of circuit privacy. It asserts that the real distribution, where the shares are produced from a homomorphically evaluated circuit, is indistinguishable from an ideal distribution where the shares are simulated just using Share. Unfortunately, we cannot achieve this property because our construction involves holding shares of integers that may grow in size as they pass through the circuit. There's no way for Share to always produce shares of the right size.

Since our correctness and homomorphism definitions are in terms of performing a single operation, we need to prove that they can be composed into correctly evaluating a whole circuit.

Lemma 14. *In any $(1 - p)$-correct two-server HSS scheme, evaluating an arbitrary circuit on shares and then decoding the result vs. decoding the inputs and evaluating the circuit has distinguisher advantage at most np if the circuit has n gates. More precisely, following distributions are distinguishable with advantage at most np if the PPT $\mathcal{A}$ outputs a circuit f of at most n gates.*

$(\mathsf{pk}, \mathsf{sk}_0, \mathsf{sk}_1) \leftarrow \mathsf{Setup}(1^\kappa)$
$(\mathsf{proto}, \mathsf{sem}_{pt}) := \mathsf{Eval}(\mathsf{pk})$
$(\mathsf{view}, f, \{(s_{0v}, s_{1v})\}_v) \leftarrow \mathcal{A}(\mathsf{pk}, \mathsf{sk}_0, \mathsf{sk}_1)$
$(\mathsf{nodes}, \mathsf{wires}, \mathsf{inputs}, \mathsf{outputs}, \mathsf{type}, \mathsf{gate}) := f$
$r \leftarrow \$$
for $v \in$ inputs:
$\quad x_v \leftarrow \mathsf{Decode}(\mathsf{pk}, \mathsf{sk}_0, \mathsf{sk}_1, \mathsf{type}(v), s_{0v}, s_{1v})$
return $\mathsf{view}, r, \mathsf{Run}(f, \mathsf{sem}_{pt}, \{x_v\}_v)$

$(\mathsf{pk}, \mathsf{sk}_0, \mathsf{sk}_1) \leftarrow \mathsf{Setup}(1^\kappa)$
$(\mathsf{proto}, \mathsf{sem}_{pt}) := \mathsf{Eval}(\mathsf{pk})$
$(\mathsf{view}, f, \{(s_{0v}, s_{1v})\}_v) \leftarrow \mathcal{A}(\mathsf{pk}, \mathsf{sk}_0, \mathsf{sk}_1)$
$r \leftarrow \$$
for $j \in \{0, 1\}$:
$\quad s'_j := \mathsf{Run}(f, \mathsf{Hom}(j, \mathsf{pk}, \mathsf{sk}_j), \{s_{jv}\}_v, r)$
for $v \in$ outputs:
$\quad y_v \leftarrow \mathsf{Decode}(\mathsf{pk}, \mathsf{sk}_0, \mathsf{sk}_1, \mathsf{type}(v), s'_{0v}, s'_{1v})$
return view, r, y

In the second distribution, the extra parameter r to Run *represents giving each homomorphic gate evaluating its own piece of the random stream r.*

Proof. We give a hybrid proof starting from the right distribution and going to the left. Partition the circuit f into two parts g and h, where everything in g comes before everything in h in topological order. The circuit g is evaluated using Hom, then its outputs are fed into Decode and used to evaluate h in plaintext. Initially g is the whole circuit and h is nothing, and in each hybrid we shift a gate from g into h, picking a gate that comes last in topological order. The difference caused by the change is that before the gate was evaluated homomorphically, then decoded, while afterwards its inputs are decoded and then it is evaluated in plaintext. Since r is a freshly random string for each gate, the homomorphism property shows that this change has advantage at most p.

After all gates have been moved from g to h, we are at the left distribution. Since there are n gates to shift over, the total advantage is bounded by np.

An important property of our HSS scheme is that Decode authenticates its shares, at least for some wire types. More precisely, we can set up an experiment where shares are provided honestly to both the adversary and an honest server, the honest server performs some homomorphic operations on its shares, then they each provide an input to a decode operation. The adversary wins if it manages to obtain a different result than would be obtained with two honest servers.

$$\boxed{\begin{array}{l}
\hline
\qquad\qquad\qquad\qquad \textsf{AuthGame} \\
\hline
\textsc{init}(j \in \{0,1\})\text{:} \\
\quad (\textsf{pk}, \textsf{sk}_0, \textsf{sk}_1) \leftarrow \textsf{Setup}(1^\kappa) \\
\quad ((\textsf{types}, \textsf{gates}, \textsf{in}, \textsf{out}), (\textsf{values}, \textsf{eval})) := \textsf{Eval}(\textsf{pk}) \\
\quad (\textsf{values}_k, \textsf{eval}_k) := \textsf{Hom}(k, \textsf{pk}, \textsf{sk}_k), \forall k \in \{0,1\} \\
\quad U, W := \text{empty list} \\
\quad \text{return } \textsf{pk}, \textsf{sk}_j \\
\textsc{share}(w \in \textsf{types}, x \in \textsf{values}(w))\text{:} \\
\quad (s_0, s_1) \leftarrow \textsf{Share}(\textsf{pk}, \textsf{sk}_0, \textsf{sk}_1, w, x) \\
\quad \text{append } (s_0, s_1) \text{ to } U \text{ and } w \text{ to } W \\
\quad \text{return } s_j \\
\textsc{eval}(g \in \textsf{gates}, i_1, \ldots, i_n)\text{:} \\
\quad \text{assert } W[i_1] W[i_2] \cdots W[i_n] = \textsf{in}(g) \\
\quad r \leftarrow \$ \\
\quad s_k := \textsf{eval}_k(g, r)(U[i_1]_k, \ldots, U[i_n]_k), \forall k \in \{0,1\} \\
\quad \text{append } (s_0, s_1) \text{ to } U \text{ and } \textsf{out}(g) \text{ to } W \\
\quad \text{return } r \\
\textsc{guess}(i, s_j \in \textsf{values}_j(W[i]))\text{:} \\
\quad \text{assert } W[i] \in A \\
\quad s_{\bar{j}} := U[i]_{\bar{j}} \\
\quad y \leftarrow \textsf{Decode}(\textsf{pk}, \textsf{sk}_0, \textsf{sk}_1, W[i], U[i]_0, U[i]_1) \\
\quad z \leftarrow \textsf{Decode}(\textsf{pk}, \textsf{sk}_0, \textsf{sk}_1, W[i], s_0, s_1) \\
\quad \text{win if } y \overset{?}{\neq} z \wedge y \overset{?}{\neq} \bot \wedge z \overset{?}{\neq} \bot \\
\hline
\end{array}}$$

Fig. 4. Game defining authentication for wire types $A \subseteq \textsf{types}$. An adversary $\mathcal{A}$ is given oracle access to the interface of AuthGame, which emulates an honest party. $\mathcal{A}$ is required to call init exactly once, before calling anything else in AuthGame, and only wins by making a successful call to guess.

Definition 15. *An HSS scheme is* authenticated *for wire types $A \subseteq$ types if it is impossible for a single party to find a share of a wire type in A that decodes to a different result than would be obtained if they were honest. Formally, PPTs can only win* AuthGame *(Fig. 4) with negligible probability.*

Some applications have a single trusted client, who can run the Share and Decode operations themselves. Others might not trust the client, or have numerous mutually distrusting clients and so need to implement these algorithms with MPC. We define a couple special cases where these operations can be implemented more easily, without the need for generic MPC.

Definition 16. *A* two-server HSS scheme has public-key sharing *if there is a UC secure 3-party protocol to compute $(s_0, s_1) \leftarrow \textsf{Share}(\textsf{pk}, \textsf{sk}_0, \textsf{sk}_1, w, x)$, where x is provided by the client, $\textsf{sk}_j$ is input by server j, all parties know $\textsf{pk}$ and w, and s_j is output to server j. All protocol messages must come from the client.*

Definition 17. *A two-server HSS scheme has* additive decoding *for wire type* w *if* values(w) *is an abelian group and there are PPT algorithms* f_0, f_1 *such that*

$$\mathsf{Decode}(\mathsf{pk}, \mathsf{sk}_0, \mathsf{sk}_1, w, s_0, s_1) = f_1(\mathsf{pk}, \mathsf{sk}_1, s_1) - f_0(\mathsf{pk}, \mathsf{sk}_0, s_0).$$

4 Main Construction

4.1 Distance Function

Similarly to [BGI16], share conversion for our HSS scheme works by picking a subset of ciphertexts to be "special", and measuring the "distance" from the nearest special point. Here "distance" means the number of times some generator must be divided to reach the special point. We pick the subset of values in $\left[-\frac{N}{2}, \frac{N}{2}\right)$ to be special, i.e. those $c \in \mathbb{Z}/N^{s+1}\mathbb{Z}$ where $c = c \bmod N$. The generator in our case is $\exp(1)$. The only special point that can be reached is $c \bmod N$ because $\exp(1) \bmod N = 1$. This choice of generator allows the distance to be computed efficiently using log.

$$\mathsf{Dist}_{N,s} \colon (\mathbb{Z}/N^{s+1}\mathbb{Z})^\times \to \mathbb{Z}/N^s\mathbb{Z}$$
$$c \mapsto \log\left(\frac{c}{c \bmod N}\right)$$

This is justified by the following theorem, which shows that $\mathsf{Dist}_{N,s}$ preserves the distance between two ciphertexts.

Theorem 18. *For any* $c \in (\mathbb{Z}/N^{s+1}\mathbb{Z})^\times$ *and* $x \in \mathbb{Z}/N^s\mathbb{Z}$,

$$\mathsf{Dist}_{N,s}(c\exp(x)) - \mathsf{Dist}_{N,s}(c) = x.$$

Proof. First, we need to show that $\mathsf{Dist}_{N,s}(c)$ is always well defined. We have $\frac{c}{c \bmod N} \equiv_N \frac{c}{c} \equiv_N 1$, so $\log\left(\frac{c}{c \bmod N}\right)$ is well defined. Then,

$$\mathsf{Dist}_{N,s}(c\exp(x)) - \mathsf{Dist}_{N,s}(c)$$
$$= \log\left(\frac{c\exp(x)}{c\exp(x) \bmod N}\right) - \log\left(\frac{c}{c \bmod N}\right)$$
$$= \log\left(\frac{c\exp(x)}{c \bmod N}\right) - \log\left(\frac{c}{c \bmod N}\right) = x.$$

Note that we have only shown the correctness of the distance function modulo N^s. Our construction will in fact need to convert its outputs to be in $\mathbb{Z}$, as there is no consistent way to exponentiate to a power that is in $\mathbb{Z}/N^s\mathbb{Z}$ when the multiplicative order of the base does not divide N^s. The following lemma will be used to show that using $\cdot \bmod N^s$ to convert shares to $\mathbb{Z}$ works with all but negligible probability.

Lemma 19. *For any* $N \in \mathbb{Z}^+$, $x \in \mathbb{Z}$, *and uniformly random* $r \in \mathbb{Z}/N\mathbb{Z}$, *we have*

$$\Pr\left[x = (r + x) \bmod N - r \bmod N\right] = \max\left(1 - \frac{|x|}{N}, 0\right).$$

$$
\begin{array}{ll}
\hline
\textbf{Setup}(1^\kappa): & \text{values}_j(\mathsf{IN}) = (\mathbb{Z}/N^{s+1}\mathbb{Z})^\times \\
\quad (N, \varphi) \leftarrow \mathsf{DJ.KeyGen}(1^\kappa) & \text{values}_j(\mathsf{REG}) = \mathbb{Z} \\
\quad \varphi_0 \leftarrow [0, N) & \text{values}_j(\mathsf{MUL}) = \mathbb{Z}/N^s\mathbb{Z} \\
\quad \varphi_1 := \varphi_0 + \varphi & \text{eval}_j(\times, r)(c, s_j) = \mathsf{Dist}_{N,s}(c^{s_j}) \\
\quad \text{return } N, \varphi_0, \varphi_1 & \text{eval}_j(\phi, r)(s_j) = (s_j + r) \bmod N^s
\end{array}
$$

$\textbf{Share}(N, \varphi_0, \varphi_1, \mathsf{IN}, x):$
  $c \leftarrow \mathsf{DJ.Enc}_{N,s}(x_j)$
  return c, c

$\textbf{Share}(N, \varphi_0, \varphi_1, \mathsf{REG}, x):$
  $s_0 \leftarrow [0, N^{s+1}2^\kappa)$
  $x' := x \bmod N^s$
  return $s_0, s_0 + (\varphi_1 - \varphi_0)x'$

$\textbf{Share}(N, \varphi_0, \varphi_1, \mathsf{MUL}, x):$
  $s_0 \leftarrow \mathbb{Z}/N^s\mathbb{Z}$
  return $s_0, s_0 + (\varphi_1 - \varphi_0)x$

$\textbf{Decode}(N, \varphi_0, \varphi_1, \mathsf{IN}, s_0, s_1):$
  if $s_0 \neq s_1$: return $\bot$
  return $\mathsf{DJ.Dec}_{N,s,\varphi_1-\varphi_0}(s_0)$

$\textbf{Decode}(N, \varphi_0, \varphi_1, \mathsf{REG}, s_0, s_1):$
  if $s_1 - s_0 \notin (\varphi_1 - \varphi_0)\mathbb{Z}$:
    return $\bot$
  return $(s_1 - s_0)/(\varphi_1 - \varphi_0) + N^s\mathbb{Z}$

$\textbf{Decode}(N, \varphi_0, \varphi_1, \mathsf{MUL}, s_0, s_1):$
  return $(s_1 - s_0)/(\varphi_1 - \varphi_0)$

Fig. 5. Our HSS scheme for bounded RM circuits. In the top left the encryption is setup and the secret key shared between the two parties. The secret share sets are in the top right, along with the non-trivial homomorphic that may be performed on them. The linear operations are given by the abelian group structure that the shares are in, so we omit them. Share and Decode for the three types of shares are shown in the bottom.

Proof. The condition may equivalently be written as

$$
r \bmod N + x = (r \bmod N + x) \bmod N.
$$

This clearly holds if and only if $-\frac{N}{2} \leq r \bmod N + x < \frac{N}{2}$, i.e. if it is already reduced so taking the modulus will not change it. If $x \geq 0$ then this is equivalent to $r \in [-\frac{N}{2}, \frac{N}{2} - x)$, which contains $N - x$ (or none, if $x > N$) of the N possible integer values for $r \bmod N$. The case of negative x is symmetric, so the probability is either $\frac{N - |x|}{N} = 1 - \frac{|x|}{N}$, or 0 if it would otherwise be negative.

4.2 HSS Construction

Now we have everything required to define our main HSS scheme, which will be parameterized by a ciphertext size s and a bound M on the values. To start, we generate a random Damgård–Jurik key pair (N, φ) and share φ between the two parties in Setup (Fig. 5). The plaintext evaluation semantics $\mathsf{Eval}(N)$ are then the evaluation semantics (Definition 11) for bounded RM circuits over $\mathbb{Z}/N^s\mathbb{Z}$ bounded in $[-M, M]$.

Our three types of shares of a value x will be ciphertexts in $(\mathbb{Z}/N^{s+1}\mathbb{Z})^\times$, additive shares of φx in $\mathbb{Z}$, and additive shares of φx in $\mathbb{Z}/N^s\mathbb{Z}$ (see values in Fig. 5). We let Share encrypt or generate these shares and Decode decrypt or decode them, while checking for consistency between the two parties' shares. The share types are all abelian groups, allowing the circuit's linear operations to be defined on the shares easily. We omit these, other than noting that constructing 1_{REG} and 1_{MUL} requires secret shares of the private key φ. In fact, additive secret shares of φ are exactly the same as our REG and MUL shares of 1.

The homomorphic multiplication function $\mathsf{eval}_j(\times, r)$ in Fig. 5 is based on $c^{\varphi x}$ essentially decrypting x times the plaintext, so when performed on additive shares s_0, s_1 of φx this gives multiplicative shares of the decryption. We then use the distance function to convert them to additive shares. As these shares are only in $\mathbb{Z}/N^s\mathbb{Z}$, we define $\mathsf{eval}_j(\phi, r)$ to pick a representative in $\mathbb{Z}$, allowing the result to be converted to shares in $\mathbb{Z}$.

Theorem 20. *Figure 5 describes a $(1 - MN^{1-s})$-correct HSS scheme (Definition 13) under DCR.*

Proof. There are three properties to be proved.

Correctness: For the IN wire type, this is just the correctness of Damgård–Jurik encryption. For REG and MUL we have $s_1 - s_0 = (\varphi_1 - \varphi_0)x$, so dividing out $\varphi_1 - \varphi_0$ inside Decode gives the correct decoding.

Homomorphism: We omit the trivial proofs for the linear operations allowed in bounded RM circuits. For multiplication, we have

$$\frac{c^{s_1}}{c^{s_0}} = c^{s_1 - s_0} = c^{\varphi y} = \exp(\varphi x)^y = \exp(\varphi x y),$$

where $x = \mathsf{DJ.Dec}_{N,s,\varphi}(c)$ and $y = \frac{s_1 - s_0}{\varphi}$ are the two input share decodings. Then Theorem 18 shows that $\mathsf{eval}_1(\times, r)(c, s_1) - \mathsf{eval}_0(\times, r)(c, s_0) = \varphi x y$.

The correctness of share conversion $\mathsf{eval}_j(\times, r)(\phi)$ with probability $1 - \frac{\varphi M}{N^s}$ follows directly from Lemma 19. Adding r to both shares before taking the modulus guarantees that s_0 is uniformly random, as is required by the lemma, and does not change $s_1 - s_0 \equiv_{N^s} \varphi x$. This is the only step with imperfect correctness, so because $\varphi < N$ we get that the overall scheme is $(1 - MN^{1-s})$-correct.

Privacy: We must show that Share leaks nothing about the value being shared to any individual server. We present a hybrid proof, starting with the adversary $\mathcal{A}$ having access to $\mathcal{O}_{0,\mathsf{pk},\mathsf{sk}_0,\mathsf{sk}_1}$, and ending $\mathcal{A}$ accessing $\mathcal{O}_{1,\mathsf{pk},\mathsf{sk}_0,\mathsf{sk}_1}$.

1. Use dummy shares of 0 in Share for wire types REG and MUL. For MUL, s_0 and s_1 individually are uniformly random, independent of x, so this is indistinguishable to the adversary, who only gets to see s_j. Similarly, the distribution for s_0 when sharing a REG value does not depend on x, while s_1 is uniform in the range $[\varphi x', \varphi x' + N^{s+1}2^\kappa)$, which is statistically indistinguishable from being uniform in $[0, N^{s+1}2^\kappa)$ because the distributions are identical in all but a negligible fraction $\frac{|\varphi x'|}{N^{s+1}2^\kappa} < 2^{-\kappa}$ of the possibilities. After this change, φ is unused by Share.

2. Instead of setting $\varphi_1 = \varphi_0 + \varphi$, sample $\varphi_1 \leftarrow [N, 2N)$. This is indistinguishable because φ_0 is uniform in $[0, N)$, the adversary only gets to see

φ_j, and $[N, 2N)$ and $[\varphi, \varphi + N)$ overlap in all but $N - \varphi = p + q - 1$ out of N possibilities. Therefore, the adversary has advantage at most $\frac{p+q-1}{N} \leq \frac{2^{\ell(\kappa)+1}}{2^{2(\ell(\kappa)-1)}} = 2^{-\ell(\kappa)+3}$, which is negligible.

3. Notice that the private key φ is now totally unused. Therefore, swapping the oracle to $\mathcal{O}_{1,\mathsf{pk},\mathsf{sk}_0,\mathsf{sk}_1}$ is indistinguishable. Specifically, Share for wire types REG and MUL already ignores its input, while for wire type IN, Theorem 3 shows that Share encrypts its input securely.

4. Undo hybrids 2 and 1. We are now at a distribution where $\mathcal{A}$ is given oracle access to $\mathcal{O}_{1,\mathsf{pk},\mathsf{sk}_0,\mathsf{sk}_1}$, and Setup and Share once more have their real implementations.

We proved that each operation in our HSS scheme has an error rate of at most MN^{1-s}. Normally s should be chosen to be the smallest such that $MN^{1-s} \leq 2^{-k}$, to make the error rate negligible. For many applications (including ORAM), $M \leq 2^{-\kappa}N$, in which case $s = 2$ is most efficient. Concretely, at the 128-bit security level $N \approx 2^{3072}$, so $s = 2$ is sufficient for plaintexts of up to 2944 bits.

Authentication. Shares of type IN are trivially authenticated, as both parties always have the same share. REG values are always multiples of φ, so to create a fake share the adversary would have to guess a multiple of φ to offset their share by. Finding a multiple of φ would give an attack against privacy.

Theorem 21. *The HSS scheme in Fig. 5 is authenticated for wire types* {IN, REG}.

Proof. See the full version of this paper.

Public-key sharing. Our construction also satisfies public-key sharing (Definition 16). This is easiest to see for IN shares, because they are just encryptions under the public key N. We can build public-key sharing for the other share types from this. To share out a MUL share of x, just give out IN shares of x, then run the RM circuit to compute $x \times 1_{\mathsf{REG}}$, which produces MUL wire type shares. Finally, REG shares of x can be given out by splitting x into pieces small enough to guarantee that ϕ will succeed (so $x = \sum_i x_i M^i$), then doing public key sharing on every x_i. Then they are converted back to REG type with ϕ, and $x = \sum_i x_i M^i$ is then computed inside an RM circuit. Note that in all cases the client only needs to send a message to both servers, who then do some local computation to find the shares.

4.3   Additive Decoding

Notice how in the previous HSS scheme, decoding REG shares is almost additive. The only flaw is that we need to divide by φ. With circular security we could simply encrypt φ^{-1} and multiply it as the last step. It's a little trickier without.

Instead, we generate a second key (N', φ') and use it to encrypt $\varphi^{-1} \bmod N'^{s'}$, avoiding the need for a circular security assumption. But then how do we decrypt this ciphertext? If the shares were multiplied by $\varphi'(\varphi'^{-1} \bmod N'^{s'})$ then

$\text{values}_j(\text{REG}) = \mathbb{Z} \times \mathbb{Z} \times \mathbb{Z}$	$\text{values}_j(\text{MUL}) = \mathbb{Z}/N^s\mathbb{Z} \times \mathbb{Z}/N^s\mathbb{Z}$

Setup(1^κ):
$\quad (N, \varphi) \leftarrow \text{DJ.KeyGen}(1^\kappa)$
$\quad (N', \varphi') \leftarrow \text{DJ.KeyGen}(1^\kappa)$
$\quad \mu := \varphi^{-1} \bmod N'^{s-2}$
$\quad \nu := (N'^{s-2})^{-1} \bmod \varphi'$
$\quad c' \leftarrow \text{DJ.Enc}_{N',s-2}(\mu)$
$\quad \varphi_0, \varphi_0' \leftarrow [0, NN'2^\kappa)$
$\quad \text{return } (N, N', c'), (\varphi_0, \varphi_0'), (\varphi_0 + \varphi, \varphi_0' + \varphi\nu)$

Share($\ldots, \text{REG}, x$):
$\quad x' := x \bmod N^s$
$\quad s_0, s_0' \leftarrow [0, N^{s+1}N'2^\kappa)$
$\quad v_0 \leftarrow [0, N^s 2^\kappa)$
$\quad s_1 := s_0 + (\varphi_1 - \varphi_0)x'$
$\quad s_1' := s_0' + (\varphi_1' - \varphi_0')x'$
$\quad \text{return } (s_0, s_0', v_0), (s_1, s_1', v_1)$

Share($\ldots, \text{MUL}, x$):
$\quad (s_0, s_0', v_0), (s_1, s_1', v_1) \leftarrow \text{Share}(\ldots, \text{REG}, x)$
$\quad \text{return } (s_0, s_0'), (s_1, s_1')$

eval$_j(\times, r)(c, (s_j, s_j'))$:
$\quad \text{return } \text{Dist}_{N,s}(c^{s_j}), \text{Dist}_{N,s}(c^{s_j'})$

eval$_j(\phi, r \parallel r' \parallel r'')((t_j, t_j'))$:
$\quad s_j := (t_j + r) \bmod N^s$
$\quad s_j' := (t_j' + r') \bmod N^s$
$\quad v_j := \text{Dist}_{N',s-2}\left(c'^{s_j - N'^{s-2}s_j'}\right)$
$\quad v_j := (v_j + r'') \bmod N'^{s-2}$
$\quad \text{return } (s_j, s_j', v_j)$

Decode($\ldots, \text{REG}, (s_0, s_0', v_0), (s_1, s_1', v_1)$):
$\quad \text{if } (s_1 - s_0) \neq (\varphi_1 - \varphi_0)(v_1 - v_0)$
$\qquad \vee (s_1' - s_0') \neq (\varphi_1' - \varphi_0')(v_1 - v_0):$
$\qquad \text{return } \bot$
$\quad \text{return } v_1 - v_0 + N^s\mathbb{Z}$

Decode($\ldots, \text{MUL}, (s_0, s_0'), (s_1, s_1')$):
$\quad \nu := (\varphi_1' - \varphi_0')/(\varphi_1 - \varphi_0)$
$\quad \text{if } (s_1' - s_0') \neq \nu(s_1 - s_0):$
$\qquad \text{return } \bot$
$\quad \text{return } (s_1 - s_0)/(\varphi_1 - \varphi_0)$

Fig. 6. Modifications to the HSS scheme in Fig. 5 needed to support additive decoding. Only those functions that have been modified are shown. For compactness, the public and private keys in Share and Decode have been omitted with an ellipsis, rather than writing out $(N, N', c'), (\varphi_0, \varphi_0'), (\varphi_1, \varphi_1')$ every time.

during decryption the $\varphi'\varphi'^{-1}$ would cancel, since it is modulo $N'^{s'}$, and similarly φ would cancel with φ^{-1}. But $\varphi'^{-1} \bmod N'^{s'}$ is nearly as large as $N'^{s'}$, requiring s to be around double s' and making the scheme less efficient.

There's a trick to avoid this, however. Let $\nu = N'^{-s'} \bmod \varphi'$. Then,

$$1 - N'^{s'}\nu \equiv_{\varphi'N'^{s'}} \varphi'(\varphi'^{-1} \bmod N'^{s'})$$

by the Chinese remainder theorem, since modulo φ' they are both 0, and modulo $N'^{s'}$ they are both 1. Therefore, $1 - N'^{s'}\nu$ is just as good for decoding the result, because the final decryption is of a ciphertext in $(\mathbb{Z}/N'^{s'}\mathbb{Z})^\times$, which has order $\varphi'N'^{s'}$. If for every value x we maintain shares of φx and $\varphi\nu x$ (which are both relatively small), we can do additive decoding by first computing shares of $\varphi(1 - N'^{s'}\nu)x$, then doing a final multiply by the encryption of φ^{-1} to get additive shares of x.

We show the modified HSS scheme in Fig. 6. Setup now computes the second key pair (N', φ') and gives out an encryption c' of $\mu = \varphi^{-1}$ under the second key. It also returns secret shares $\varphi_1' - \varphi_0' = \varphi\nu$ alongside the secret shares of φ. The REG shares have the biggest changes. Not only does they keep track of shares of both φx and $\varphi\nu x$, but they also keep shares (v_0, v_1) of x. This is because the only time we have an upper bound on the size of a plaintext value x is during $\text{eval}_j(\phi, r)$, so we compute additive shares of x then and cache them. The MUL shares also needed to be changed to keep shares of both φx and $\varphi\nu x$. We set

$s' = s - 2$ because the additive decoding value x is much smaller (by a factor of nearly NN') than $\varphi\nu x$. The former is computed modulo N'^{s-2} while the latter is found modulo N^s, which makes the error probabilities similar.

Theorem 22. *Assuming DCR, the modified scheme in Fig. 6 is a $(1-p)$-correct HSS scheme that is authenticated for all wire types and has additive decoding for* REG *wires, where $p = MN'(N^{1-s} + N'^{1-s})$.*

Proof. See the full version of this paper.

Choosing s to achieve a negligible error rate is essentially the same as for the previous construction. Because N and N' are of approximately the same size, s should be chosen such that $p \approx 2MN^{2-s} \leq 2^{-k}$. Roughly, s just needs to be incremented. Public key sharing works for this new protocol in exactly the same way as before, since we did not change the sharing process for IN shares, and public key sharing of everything else was based on that one share type.

5   Distributed Oblivious RAM

An oblivious RAM (ORAM) allows a client to outsource its data (a sequence of N blocks) to an untrusted server, such that it can access any sequence of data blocks on the server while hiding the access pattern [Ost92, Gol87]. While traditionally ORAM protocols were designed assuming a single server which stores data passively, recent works have considered more general settings, allowing for multiple servers with computational capabilities [DvDF+16, HOY+17, FNR+15]. Given the result in [Gol87], all passive server ORAM protocols incur at least $\Omega(\log N)$ bandwidth overhead. However, if we allow for server side computation, constant bandwidth blowup can be achieved for large block sizes [DvDF+16]. In this section we propose a new malicious secure ORAM construction based on 2 party HSS. Our construction achieves constant bandwidth blowup for blocks of size at least $\Omega(\log^4 N)$ bits.

5.1   Definition: Distributed ORAM

We consider a 3 party distributed ORAM model with a single client and 2 non-colluding servers. All the parties maintain a state (st_c, st_{s0}, st_{s1}) which is updated after each ORAM operation, where st_c is the client state and st_{s0}, st_{s1} are the states of the two servers respectively.

Definition 23. *A distributed 2-server ORAM construction with security parameter κ consists of the following two interactive protocols:*

- $(st_c', st_{s0}', st_{s1}') \leftarrow \mathsf{Setup}(D)$: *The client inputs an N sized array D of blocks, where each block is of length B bits. This function initializes the ORAM with the array D.*

– $(data, st'_c, st'_{s0}, st'_{s1}) \leftarrow$ Access$(in, st_c, st_{s0}, st_{s1})$: The client receives as input an ORAM operation $in = (op, idx, data)$, where $op = \{read, write\}$, $idx \in [1 \ldots N]$ and $data \in \{0, 1\}^B \cup \{\perp\}$. If $op = read$ then the client should return the block $D[idx]$. If $op = write$, then this protocol should update the content of block $D[idx]$ in the ORAM with $data$.

We use the simulation based definition for a malicious secure ORAM as was considered in [DvDF+16] (see the full version of this paper for details).

5.2   An Overview of Bounded Feedback and Onion ORAM

Our protocol is inspired by the Onion ORAM protocol proposed in [DvDF+16], which in turn is based on the passive server Bounded Feedback ORAM protocol from the same paper. In this subsection we describe Bounded Feedback ORAM and how it can be modified to give the single server Onion ORAM construction.

Bounded Feedback ORAM. Similar to other tree-based ORAMs, its server memory is organized in the form of an L depth binary tree T, where each node of the tree (also referred to as a *bucket*) contains Z blocks. The leaves of the tree are numbered from 0 to $2^L - 1$. $\mathcal{P}(l)$ represent the blocks on the path to leaf l on this tree and $\mathcal{P}(l, k)$ represents the kth bucket from the root node on this same path respectively.

As is the case for all tree based ORAMs, each block is mapped to a unique random leaf node in this tree. And this mapping is stored in a position map (PosMap) by the client. The **key invariant** that's maintained is that each block (with index $addr$) is present in some bucket on the path $\mathcal{P}(\text{PosMap}[addr])$.

For each block in the tree, the server also stores the corresponding metadata $(addr, label)$, where $addr$ is the logical address of the block and $label = \text{PosMap}[addr]$. The corresponding metadata tree is referred to as md. We use the shorthand md$[l]$ to represent the list of all metadata present on the path l in md.

ORAM Access. To read/write a block $addr$ the client looks up the corresponding leaf label PosMap$[addr]$ from the position map. It further downloads all the blocks on the path PosMap$[addr]$ in tree T from the server. The client can now locally read and update the block $addr$. The block $addr$ is remapped to a new random leaf label and is inserted in the root bucket. All the downloaded blocks on path l are re-encrypted and stored back on the server. To ensure that no bucket overflows except with negligible probability, after every A (a parameter) Access operation the blocks are percolated towards the leaves in the tree while maintaining the key invariant. This process is also called the **eviction algorithm**. Most tree based ORAMs often differ in their eviction procedures.

Triplet Eviction Algorithm. As is the case for other tree based ORAMs, eviction is performed along a specific path (let say l). For $k = 0$ to L, the algorithm pushes all the blocks in bucket $\mathcal{P}(l, k)$ into one of its two children buckets. This process can be carried out without violating the key invariant. After every A ORAM accesses, the next eviction path is chosen in the reverse lexicographic order of G (a variable), which is initialized to 0 and incremented by 1 after each eviction procedure. Given the analysis in [DvDF+16], the parameters $Z = A = \Theta(\lambda)$ ensure negligible overflow probability for each bucket, where λ is the statistical security parameter.

Recursion. Storing the position map requires space $O(N \log N)$. To avoid the large client memory, we can recursively store the position map in a smaller ORAM on the server. This recursive approach used in all tree based ORAMs does not incur any additional asymptotic cost for blocks of size $\Omega(\log^2 N)$, where N is the size of the database. For all the ORAM protocols we describe ahead, we will ignore the cost of recursion for larger block sizes.

How Onion ORAM Differs. The Onion ORAM protocol is similar to the Bounded Feedback ORAM with the key distinction that all computation on the data blocks is performed by the server locally. For this purpose the ORAM data structure is encrypted using an additively homomophic encryption scheme, which allows the server to perform access and evict algorithms locally. More details on the Onion ORAM construction can be found in full version of this paper.

5.3   Our HSS Based ORAM Construction

In our construction the server side computation of Onion ORAM is divided across 2 non-colluding servers using our HSS construction.

The two servers store two ORAM binary trees (T_0, T_1) respectively, and they also have additive shares of authenticated meta-data $(md, H(md))$ corresponding to each block in the tree. Each block b in our scheme is a sequence of chunks $(b_1, b_2, \ldots, b_C)$ (for some parameter C), where each chunk can be secret shared as wires of type REG using HSS.

The server side computation in Onion ORAM can be replaced with homomorphic computation on the HSS shares by the two servers, where the client sends an encrypted index as a wire type IN. For the eviction procedure, we conceptually use the same technique as used in Onion ORAM, which uses $\Theta(ZL)$ select operations. We next describe the selection and evict algorithms in a little more detail.

Selection. An advantage of using HSS is being able to evaluate a limited kind of arithmetic circuit, so we can encode more than just a single bit in a ciphertext. In fact, we can do a 1-of-m select operation by sending just a single ciphertext to the servers. Suppose we want to select the ith element of a sequence $y_0, \ldots, y_{m-1}$, for some $i \in [0, m-1]$. Then if we interpolate a polynomial $p(X)$ through the points $p(0) = y_0, \ldots, p(m-1) = y_{m-1}$, then we can evaluate $p(i)$ to find y_i. Polynomial interpolation is a linear operation, and so can be performed separately by each server, on its own share of $\{y_i\}_i$.

$$\text{SELECT}(i \in \mathsf{IN}, y_0 \in \mathsf{REG}, \ldots, y_{m-1} \in \mathsf{REG}):$$

$$D[j] := \frac{(m-1)!}{j!} \sum_{k=0}^{j} \binom{j}{k}(-1)^{j-k} \times_{\mathsf{REG}} y_k$$

$z := 0_{\mathsf{REG}}$
for $j := m - 1$ to 0:
$\quad z := z +_{\mathsf{REG}} D[j]$
$\quad z := \phi(z \times (i +_{\mathsf{IN}} (1 - j)))$
$z := \frac{1}{(m-1)!} \times_{\mathsf{REG}} z$
return z

$\mathsf{SelectShare}(\mathsf{pk}, \mathsf{sk}_0, \mathsf{sk}_1, i, \{y_{0k}\}_k, \{y_{1k}\}_k):$
$\quad in["i"] := \mathsf{Share}(\mathsf{pk}, \mathsf{sk}_0, \mathsf{sk}_1, \mathsf{IN}, i)$
$\quad$ for $j \in \{0, 1\}$:
$\quad\quad$ for each chunk index c:
$\quad\quad\quad$ for $k := 0$ to $m - 1$:
$\quad\quad\quad\quad in["y" \parallel k] := y_{jk}[c]$
$\quad\quad\quad s_j[c] := \mathsf{Run}(\text{SELECT}, \mathsf{Hom}(j, \mathsf{pk}, \mathsf{sk}_j), in)$
$\quad$ return s_0, s_1
$\mathsf{Select}(\mathsf{pk}, \mathsf{sk}_0, \mathsf{sk}_1, i, \{y_{0k}\}_k, \{y_{1k}\}_k):$
$\quad (s_0, s_1) \leftarrow \mathsf{SelectShare}(\mathsf{pk}, \mathsf{sk}_0, \mathsf{sk}_1,$
$\quad\quad\quad\quad\quad\quad\quad\quad\quad i, \{y_{0k}\}_k, \{y_{1k}\}_k)$
$\quad$ for $j \in \{0, 1\}$:
$\quad\quad s'_j := \sum_c M'^c s_j[c]$
$\quad z' := \mathsf{Decode}'(\mathsf{pk}, \mathsf{sk}_0, \mathsf{sk}_1, \mathsf{REG}, s'_0, s'_1)$
$\quad$ for each chunk index c:
$\quad\quad z[c] := \lfloor \frac{z'}{M'^c} \rfloor \bmod M'$
$\quad$ return z

Fig. 7. Left: Selection operation pseudocode. The pseudocode follows the wire-type rules of a bounded RM circuit, and could easily be unrolled into a circuit. Right: The distributed Select algorithm, which runs the SELECT RM circuit on the given shares, then decodes the result to find y_i. Client computation is colored red and server computation is colored blue. Because in our HSS the REG secret shares do not depending at all on the ciphertext size parameter s, we can pack together several shares (by treating them as a base M' number) and decode them all at once, which reduces the overhead of the secret sharing step. However, we need Decode from Fig. 5 to be modified slightly, to not take its output modulo N^s, and we call this modification Decode'.

$\mathsf{Evict}(\mathsf{pk}, \mathsf{sk}_0, \mathsf{sk}_1, l_e, \mathsf{md}, \{x_{0k}\}_k, \{x_{1k}\}_k, \{y_{0k}\}_k, \{y_{1k}\}_k):$
$\quad remap :=$ array of zeros
$\quad$ for each block b of parent node $\lfloor \frac{l_e}{2} \rfloor$.
$\quad\quad$ if md says b is present and needs to move to l_e:
$\quad\quad\quad$ find next empty location b' in l_e
$\quad\quad\quad remap[b'] := b$
$\quad$ for each block b of node l_e:
$\quad\quad in_j := (y_{jb}, x_{j0}, \ldots, x_{j(Z-1)}) \forall j \in \{0, 1\}$
$\quad\quad y_{0b}, y_{1b} \leftarrow \mathsf{SelectShare}(\mathsf{pk}, \mathsf{sk}_0, \mathsf{sk}_1, remap[b], in_0, in_1)$
$\quad$ return $\{y_{0k}\}_k, \{y_{1k}\}_k$

Fig. 8. The distributed Evict algorithm. Inputs are l_e, the location of the node to evict into, the shares $\{x_{0k}\}_k, \{x_{1k}\}_k$ of the blocks in the parent node of l_e, and shares $\{y_{0k}\}_k, \{y_{1k}\}_k$ of node l_e.

However, there's one small issue that we've skipped over. We can only evaluate *bounded* RM circuit, and representing a fraction in the ring is very likely to produce a large number that is outside of the bound. We instead use the Newton polynomial interpolation, representing p as

$$p(X) = \sum_{j=0}^{m-1} \frac{\Delta^j[y]}{j!}(X)_j \qquad \text{where} \qquad \Delta^j[y] = \sum_{k=0}^{j} \binom{j}{k}(-1)^{j-k} y_k,$$

where $(X)_j = X(X-1)\cdots(X-j+1)$ is the falling factorial. Although we only show the direct formula for computing the differences $\Delta^j[y]$, faster FFT-based methods would also work. Notice that the finite differences $\Delta^j[y]$ are all integers, so only need to evaluate $(m-1)!\,p(i)$ to remove all of the fractions, and then divide by $(m-1)!$ at the last step, which works since $p(i)$ is an integer. We can evaluate this polynomial using a variant of Horner's rule, which is efficient inside an RM circuit (Fig. 7).

$$p(X) = \left(\left(\frac{\Delta^{m-1}[y]}{(m-1)!}(X-m+2) + \frac{\Delta^{m-2}[y]}{(m-2)!}\right)(X-m+3) + \cdots\right)X + \frac{\Delta^0[y]}{0!}$$

We need to compute a size bound M on the values in this computation, given the known bound M' on every y_i. We have $|{*}|\Delta^j[y] \le M'\sum_k \binom{j}{k} = 2^j M'$. Let S be a subexpression in the evaluation of $(m-1)!\,p(X)$. Then $|S| \le \sum_{j=0}^{m-1}|{*}|\frac{(m-1)!}{j!}\Delta^j[y]m^j$, because every $(x-j+1) \le m$, and going from S to this we only add more nonnegative terms and multiply more factors of $m \ge 1$. This can be turned into an upper bound, which we will use to set M.

$$|S| \le \sum_{j=0}^{m-1}\frac{(m-1)!}{j!}2^j m^j M' \le (m-1)!\,M'\sum_{j=0}^{\infty}\frac{(2\,m)^j}{j!} = (m-1)!\,M'e^{2\,m} \le M \tag{1}$$

Eviction. We need to move up to Z blocks in a parent node in the tree into a child node, which has locations for Z blocks. We do this by performing Z instances of 1-of-$(Z+1)$ Select, allowing each block location in a child node to select any of its parent node's blocks, or its existing value if it was already filled. This algorithm is shown in Fig. 8.

Using these two algorithms, we describe our Setup and Access function for our proposed ORAM scheme in Fig. 9 and Fig. 10 respectively.

Our ORAM construction can also be used for implementing 2 party secure computation of RAM programs. In full version of this paper we further discuss how the public-key sharing property (Definition 16) and additive decoding (Definition 17) of our HSS scheme help realize this protocol more efficiently.

5.4 Proof of Security

Intuitively, the adversary learns nothing looking at one server's binary tree data - which consists of one share of each corresponding plaintext block chunks. Hence the view of the adversary in this case can be simulated given the privacy guarantee of our HSS scheme. Our scheme satisfies the authenticated shares property, hence any tampering of the shares by the adversary would make the protocol abort. The meta data is authenticated using a universal hash function that satisfies uniform difference property.

Theorem 24. *The distributed ORAM construction described in Fig. 9 and Fig. 10 is a secure ORAM.*

Let (Setup, Share, Eval, Run, Decode) be a 2 party HSS scheme as in Definition 13
$\mathcal{H}$ is a universal family that satisfies uniform difference property

Protocol parameters: B, λ, κ

<u>Setup(D):</u>

  $(T, \mathsf{md}) \leftarrow$ Bounded-Feedback-ORAM-Setup on input D
  $h \leftarrow_\$ \mathcal{H}$
  $\mathsf{hash} \leftarrow h(\mathsf{md})$
  Picks random shares md_0 and hash_0
  $\mathsf{md}_1 \leftarrow md + \mathsf{md}_0$ and $\mathsf{hash}_1 \leftarrow \mathsf{hash} + \mathsf{hash}_0$
  $G, cnt \leftarrow 0$
  $(\mathsf{pk}, \mathsf{sk}_0, \mathsf{sk}_1) \leftarrow$ Setup(1^κ)
  For each block $b \in T$, for each chunk index c:
    $(b_0[c], b_1[c]) \leftarrow$ Share($pk, sk_0, sk_1,$ REG, $b[c]$)
  For $i = 0, 1$, and for each block b in T:
    Set corresponding block in T_i as b_i
  $st_c = (G, cnt, \mathsf{PosMap}, \mathsf{pk}, \mathsf{sk}_0, \mathsf{sk}_1)$
  For $i = 0, 1$, $st_{s_i} = (T_i, \mathsf{md}_i, \mathsf{hash}_i, \mathsf{sk}_i)$

Fig. 9. The 2-server distributed ORAM Setup function. In this protocol we assume the ORAM Setup protocol for the Bounded Feedback ORAM given in [DvDF+16]. Client side computation is colored red and server side computation is colored blue.

Proof. See full version of this paper.

5.5 Complexity Analysis

First, we must determine the dependence between the parameters. Each share stores a number in $[0, M' - 1)$, and since there are C share chunks per block this gives $B = C \log_2 M'$. For the HSS parameters, we choose the smallest possible ciphertext size ($s = 2$) as this will decrease the communication bandwidth of data sent to the servers. Therefore, we should set $M\mathcal{N}^{-1} = 2^{-\lambda}$, where $\mathcal{N} = 2^{\Theta(\ell(\kappa))}$ is the Damgård–Jurik public key, to have a statistical correctness error negligible in λ. We set M' to be as large as possible (as determined by Eq. 1) in order to reduce the number of chunks (which take extra computation) while keeping the same block size and ciphertext size. So we set $M' = \frac{1}{(m-1)!} e^{-2m} M$, where $m = Z(L + 1)$ is the largest number of options in a select operation, and get $\log_2 M' = \Theta(\ell(\kappa) - \lambda - ZL \log(ZL)) = \Theta(\ell(\kappa) - \lambda \log N \log(\lambda))$, where we have assumed that $\lambda = \Omega(\log(N))$.

Next, we analyze the complexity of each part.

Communication Complexity. The communication complexity from client to the servers consists of $\Theta(ZL)$ ciphertexts sent on every eviction (once every A accesses), plus 1 sent for every access. From the server to the client, we get $B + \Theta(\ell(\kappa))$ bits sent from each server, for the shares we decode plus the extra $\Theta(\ell(\kappa))$ coming from the fact that the shares were already multiplied by the private key before they were sent back. This comes to a total of $2B + \Theta(\ell(\kappa) \log N)$ amortized communication for each access.

Access($in = (op, addr, data), st_c, st_{s0}, st_{s1})$):

> $l' \leftarrow_\$ [0, 2^L - 1]$
> $l \leftarrow \mathsf{PosMap}[addr]$
> $\mathsf{PosMap}[addr] \leftarrow l'$
> Compute arrays $md_i[l], hash_i[l]$
> For $j = 0$ to $Z(L + 1)$:
>   if $H(md_1[l, j] - md_0[l, j]) \neq hash_1[l, j] - hash_0[l, j]$ then abort
> $md \leftarrow md_1[l] - md_0[1]$ // Element wise subtraction
> Find $i \ni md[i, 0] = addr$
> $data \leftarrow \mathsf{Select}\ (i, \mathcal{P}_0(l), \mathcal{P}_1(l))$
> if $data = \bot$ then abort
> if $op = write$ then $data = data'$ else output $data$
> Set $md[l, j] \leftarrow (addr, l')$ for the least index $j \ni md[l, j] \neq \bot$
> $md[l, i] \leftarrow \bot$
> For each chunk index c:
> $(b_0[c], b_1[c]) \leftarrow \mathsf{Share}(pk, sk_0, sk_1, \mathsf{REG}, data[c])$
> Sample new random md_0 and $hash_0$
> $md_1 \leftarrow md + md_0$ and $hash_1 \leftarrow H(md) + hash_0$
> $md[l] \leftarrow md_i$ and $h(md[l]) \leftarrow hash_i$
> Set $(cnt + 1)^{th}$ block in bucket $\mathcal{P}_i(l, 1)$ as b_i
> // Eviction
> $cnt \leftarrow cnt + 1 \mod A$
> if $cnt \overset{?}{=} 0$:
> $l_e \leftarrow$ reverse bit string of G // Picking paths in reverse lexicographic order
> $G \leftarrow (G + 1 \mod 2^L)$
>   For $k \leftarrow 0$ to $L - 1$:
>   For each child bucket C of $\mathcal{P}(l_e)$:
> $b \in 0^{2Z}$
>   For $i \in [0, Z - 1]$: Set $b[i] \leftarrow 1$ if i^{th} block in $\mathcal{P}(l_e)$ can be moved into C
>   For $i \in [0, Z - 1]$: Set $b[Z + i] \leftarrow 1$ if i^{th} block in C is real
>   Evict $(b, (\mathcal{P}_0(l_e)||C_0), (\mathcal{P}_1(l_e)||C_1))$

Fig. 10. The 2-server distributed ORAM Access function. Client side computation is colored red and server side computation is colored blue.

Client Computation. The client computation is dominated by the Share function calls in the Select operations in the protocol. This is dominated by eviction, where it invokes $Z(L + 1)$ instances of Share, each taking time $\widetilde{O}(\ell^2(\kappa))$ because they are dominated by exponentiation. This takes a total of $\widetilde{O}(\log N \ell^2(\kappa))$ amortized time per access.

Server Computation. For the server the most computationally intensive step is the computation in the Select operations. We require evaluation of a $O(m)$ gate RM circuit for a m-way select. This is dominated by the Evict step, which requires $CZ(L + 1)$ evaluations of a $Z + 1$-way selection. The cost of evaluating a gate is dominated by exponentiation, so we get an amortized cost of $\widetilde{O}(C\lambda \log N \ell^2(\kappa))$.

We use a similarly parameter regime to Onion ORAM, where we set the statistical security parameter $\lambda = \omega(\log N)$ and computational security parameter $\kappa = \omega(\log N)$, and based on the best known attacks on Damgård–Jurik encryption (from factoring), set $\ell(\kappa) = \Theta(\kappa^3)$. The communication complexity is then $2B + O(\log^4 N)$, so we set the minimum block size to be $B = \omega(O(\log^4 N))$ to get constant communication overhead. Then the number of chunks is determined to be $C = \frac{B}{\log_2 M'} = \Theta(\frac{\log^4 N}{\log^3 N}) = \Theta(\log N)$. Finally, we find the client side computation $\widetilde{O}(\log^7 N) = \widetilde{O}(B \log^4 N)$, and the server-side computation $\widetilde{O}(\log^3 N \ell^2(\kappa)) = \widetilde{O}(\log^9 N) = \widetilde{O}(B \log^5 N)$.

6 Trapdoor Hash Functions

The idea of using a distance function to compute a distributed discrete logarithm has been applied to more than just HSS. One such application is to trapdoor hash functions, which have applications to rate-1 OT, PIR, and private matrix-vector products, among others [DGI+19]. In this section we present a new trapdoor hash function based on DCR and our distance function, and show that it has negligible error probability. We then talk about possible generalizations allowed by our construction.

Setup$(1^\kappa, 1^n)$:
$\quad (N, \varphi) \leftarrow \mathsf{DJ.KeyGen}(1^\kappa)$
$\quad (g_0, g_1, \ldots, g_n) \leftarrow (\mathbb{Z}/N^2\mathbb{Z})^\times$
$\quad$ return $N, g_0, \ldots, g_n$

Hash$((N, g_0, \ldots, g_n), x, \rho)$:
$\quad r \leftarrow [0, N)$ from random bits ρ
$\quad$ return $g_0^r \prod_i g_i^{x_i}$

Decode$((N, g_0, \ldots, g_n), k, h)$:
$\quad e_0 := \mathsf{Dist}_{N,1}(h^k) \bmod N \bmod 2$
$\quad$ return $e_0, \overline{e_0}$

KeyGen$((N, g_0, \ldots, g_n), f)$:
$\quad$ write $f(x) = \bigoplus_i f_i x_i$
$\quad k \leftarrow [0, N)$
$\quad K_0 := g_0^k$
$\quad K_i := g_i^k \exp(f_i), \forall i \in [1, n]$
$\quad$ return K, k

Eval$((N, g_0, \ldots, g_n), K, x, \rho)$:
$\quad r \leftarrow [0, N)$ from random bits ρ
$\quad d := \mathsf{Dist}_{N,1}\left(K_0^r \prod_i K_i^{x_i}\right)$
$\quad$ return $d \bmod N \bmod 2$

Fig. 11. Trapdoor hash function for linear predicates from DCR based on our distance function, which achieves a negligible error rate.

We present our trapdoor hash in Fig. 11. See also the full version of this paper, where we review the definition of a trapdoor hash function, with some notational changes. We support linear predicates, $\mathcal{F}_n := \{f(x) = \bigoplus_i f_i x_i \mid f_i \in \{0, 1\}\}$. [DGI+19] also gave a DCR-based construction that was in many ways similar, but since they used the distance function of [BGI16] they had an inverse polynomial error rate. We instead achieve a negligible error probability.

Theorem 25. *The construction in Fig. 11 is a $(1 - nN^{-1})$-correct trapdoor hash function with rate 1.*

Proof. See the full version of the paper.

6.1   Generalizations

Trapdoor hash functions are only defined to output a single bit, but our construction is really suited to producing a longer output. A possible generalization would be to allow output in any abelian group $\mathbb{G}$, so the correctness property would be that if $e \leftarrow \mathsf{Eval}(\mathsf{crs}, \mathsf{pk}, x; \rho)$ and $e_0 \leftarrow \mathsf{Decode}(\mathsf{crs}, \mathsf{sk}, h)$ then $e - e_0 = f(x)$. Then we could achieve $\mathbb{G} = \mathbb{Z}$ (as long as we have a bound on $|f(x)|$) by simply removing the last mod 2 step from Eval and Decode. And $\mathbb{G} = \mathbb{Z}/N^s\mathbb{Z}$ would work with perfect correctness if the mod N were removed as well.

This is useful for constructing rate-1 string OT efficiently. [DGI+19] build 1-out-of-k OT in batches of n elements, then having the receiver send n TDH public keys selecting the n bits they are interested in. The same hash h is shared among these n evaluations of the TDH, so if $n \gg |h|$ (the bit length of h) then the scheme is rate 1. However, this requires sending many public keys. Generalizing TDH to output large chunks of data would only need batches of $n \gg 1$ to achieve rate 1, as it would provide nearly $|h|$ bits of output per evaluation.

References

[BGI16]   Boyle, E., Gilboa, N., Ishai, Y.: Breaking the circuit size barrier for secure computation under DDH. In: Robshaw, M., Katz, J. (eds.) CRYPTO 2016. LNCS, Part I, vol. 9814, pp. 509–539. Springer, Heidelberg (2016). https://doi.org/10.1007/978-3-662-53018-4_19

[BGI+17]   Boyle, E., Gilboa, N., Ishai, Y., Lin, H., Tessaro, S.: Foundations of homomorphic secret sharing. Cryptology ePrint Archive, Report 2017/1248 (2017). https://eprint.iacr.org/2017/1248

[BKS19]   Boyle, E., Kohl, L., Scholl, P.: Homomorphic secret sharing from lattices without FHE. In: Ishai, Y., Rijmen, V. (eds.) EUROCRYPT 2019. LNCS, Part II, vol. 11477, pp. 3–33. Springer, Cham (2019). https://doi.org/10.1007/978-3-030-17656-3_1

[BV11]   Brakerski, Z., Vaikuntanathan, V.: Efficient fully homomorphic encryption from (standard) LWE. In: Ostrovsky, R. (ed.) 52nd FOCS, pp. 97–106. IEEE Computer Society Press, October 2011

[Cle90]   Cleve, R.: Towards optimal simulations of formulas by bounded-width programs. In: 22nd ACM STOC, pp. 271–277. ACM Press, May 1990

[DGI+19]   Döttling, N., Garg, S., Ishai, Y., Malavolta, G., Mour, T., Ostrovsky, R.: Trapdoor hash functions and their applications. In: Boldyreva, A., Micciancio, D. (eds.) CRYPTO 2019. LNCS, Part III, vol. 11694, pp. 3–32. Springer, Cham (2019). https://doi.org/10.1007/978-3-030-26954-8_1

[DJ01]   Damgård, I., Jurik, M.: A generalisation, a simplification and some applications of Paillier's probabilistic public-key system. In: Kim, K. (ed.) PKC 2001. LNCS, vol. 1992, pp. 119–136. Springer, Heidelberg (2001). https://doi.org/10.1007/3-540-44586-2_9

[DKK18]   Dinur, I., Keller, N., Klein, O.: An optimal distributed discrete log protocol with applications to homomorphic secret sharing. In: Shacham, H., Boldyreva, A. (eds.) CRYPTO 2018. Part III, vol. 10993. LNCS, pp. 213–242. Springer, Heidelberg (2018). https://doi.org/10.1007/s00145-019-09330-2

[DS17] Doerner, J., Shelat, A.: Scaling ORAM for secure computation. In: Proceedings of the 2017 ACM SIGSAC Conference on Computer and Communications Security, pp. 523–535 (2017)

[DvDF+16] Devadas, S., van Dijk, M., Fletcher, C.W., Ren, L., Shi, E., Wichs, D.: Onion ORAM: a constant bandwidth blowup oblivious RAM. In: Kushilevitz, E., Malkin, T. (eds.) TCC 2016. LNCS, vol. 9563, pp. 145–174. Springer, Heidelberg (2016). https://doi.org/10.1007/978-3-662-49099-0_6

[FGJS17] Fazio, N., Gennaro, R., Jafarikhah, T., Skeith III, W.E.: Homomorphic secret sharing from Paillier encryption. In: Okamoto, T., Yu, Y., Au, M.H., Li, Y. (eds.) ProvSec 2017. LNCS, vol. 10592, pp. 381–399. Springer, Cham (2017). https://doi.org/10.1007/978-3-319-68637-0_23

[FNR+15] Fletcher, C.W., Naveed, M., Ren, L., Shi, E., Stefanov, E.: Bucket ORAM: single online roundtrip, constant bandwidth oblivious ram. IACR Cryptol. ePrint Arch., 2015:1065 (2015)

[Gol87] Goldreich, O.: Towards a theory of software protection and simulation by oblivious rams. In: Proceedings of the Nineteenth Annual ACM Symposium on Theory of Computing, pp. 182–194 (1987)

[HOY+17] Hoang, T., Ozkaptan, C.D., Yavuz, A.A., Guajardo, J., Nguyen, T.: S3ORAM: a computation-efficient and constant client bandwidth blowup ORAM with Shamir secret sharing. In: Proceedings of the 2017 ACM SIGSAC Conference on Computer and Communications Security, pp. 491–505 (2017)

[Ost92] Ostrovsky, R.: Software protection and simulation on oblivious RAMs. PhD thesis, Massachusetts Institute of Technology (1992)

[OSY21] Orlandi, C., Scholl, P., Yakoubov, S.: The rise of Paillier: homomorphic secret sharing and public-key silent OT. In: Canteaut, A., Standaert, F.-X. (eds.) EUROCRYPT 2021. LNCS, vol. 12696, pp. 678–708. Springer, Cham (2021). https://doi.org/10.1007/978-3-030-77870-5_24

[Pai99] Paillier, P.: Public-key cryptosystems based on composite degree residuosity classes. In: Stern, J. (ed.) EUROCRYPT 1999. LNCS, vol. 1592, pp. 223–238. Springer, Heidelberg (1999). https://doi.org/10.1007/3-540-48910-X_16

Traceable Secret Sharing
and Applications

Vipul Goyal[1,2]($\boxtimes$), Yifan Song[1], and Akshayaram Srinivasan[3]

[1] Carnegie Mellon University, Pittsburgh, USA
goyal@cs.cmu.edu, yifans2@andrew.cmu.edu
[2] NTT Research, Sunnyvale, USA
[3] Tata Institute of Fundamental Research, Mumbai, India
akshayaram.srinivasan@tifr.res.in

Abstract. Consider a scenario where Alice stores some secret data s on n servers using a t-out-of-n secret sharing scheme. Trudy (the collector) is interested in the secret data of Alice and is willing to pay for it. Trudy publishes an advertisement on the internet which describes an elaborate cryptographic scheme to collect the shares from the n servers. Each server who decides to submit its share is paid a hefty monetary reward and is guaranteed "immunity" from being caught or prosecuted in a court for violating its service agreement with Alice. Bob is one of the servers and sees this advertisement. On examining the collection scheme closely, Bob concludes that there is no way for Alice to prove anything in a court that he submitted his share. Indeed, if Bob is rational, he might use the cryptographic scheme in the advertisement and submit his share since there are no penalties and no fear of being caught and prosecuted. Can we design a secret sharing scheme which Alice can use to avoid such a scenario?

We introduce a new primitive called as *Traceable Secret Sharing* to tackle this problem. In particular, a traceable secret sharing scheme guarantees that a cheating server always runs the risk of getting traced and prosecuted by providing a valid evidence (which can be examined in a court of law) implicating its dishonest behavior. We explore various definitional aspects and show how they are highly non-trivial to construct (even ignoring efficiency aspects). We then give an efficient construction of traceable secret sharing assuming the existence of a secure two-party computation protocol. We also show an application of this primitive in constructing traceable protocols for multi-server delegation of computation.

1 Introduction

Secret sharing [Sha79, Bla79] allows a client to store a secret on n servers such that an authorized subset of the servers can recover the secret, while any unauthorized set learns no information about the secret. Now, consider a scenario where the client Alice stores her secret s (some proprietary dataset) across n different servers (or cloud providers) using secret sharing to enhance privacy. Alice

© International Association for Cryptologic Research 2021
T. Malkin and C. Peikert (Eds.): CRYPTO 2021, LNCS 12827, pp. 718–747, 2021.
https://doi.org/10.1007/978-3-030-84252-9_24

divides her secret into n shares using (say) a t-out-of-n secret sharing scheme and stores one share on each server. Let us call these shares $\mathsf{share}_1, \ldots, \mathsf{share}_n$.

Trudy (the collector) is highly interested in learning Alice's secret and is willing to pay for it. Therefore, Trudy publishes an advertisement on the internet. The advertisement has an elaborate cryptographic scheme to collect shares from the servers. Each server who decides to submit its share is paid $100. The collection scheme guarantees "cryptographic immunity" from being caught or prosecuted in a court (e.g., for violating its service agreement with Alice). The elaborate collection scheme has the following components: (1) a description of functions $f_1, \ldots, f_n$ (called as the collector's functions), and (2) description of a pirate reconstruction box $\mathsf{Rec}^\star$. The i-th server P_i is supposed to submit $f_i(\mathsf{share}_i)$ to the collector (in exchange for $100).[1] If enough such $f_i(\mathsf{share}_i)$ are collected, the reconstruction box $\mathsf{Rec}^\star$ would output the secret s (or some information about s). The functions $\{f_i\}_{i \in [n]}$ and pirate reconstruction box $\mathsf{Rec}^\star$ are constructed very carefully to guarantee that even if Alice gets her hands on them (and even on $f_i(\mathsf{share}_i)$ for all i), it would not be possible for Alice to prove anything in a court and seek damages from any of the servers.

Bob is one of the servers and sees this advertisement. Competition from bigger cloud providers is tough, and, at this point, $100 could really help Bob keep the service afloat and pay the staff salaries. Bob is worried however that if he gives out $f_i(\mathsf{share}_i)$ and somehow it reaches Alice, she will be able to trace him and sue him in a court for damages. This would surely mean bankruptcy given Bob's service agreement with Alice. However, upon examining the collection scheme and the reconstruction box closely, Bob concludes that there is no way for Alice to prove anything in a court even if he submitted $f_i(\mathsf{share}_i)$ (and it falls into Alice's hands). After all, Alice could have computed $f_i(\mathsf{share}_i)$ even on her own.

What if share_i was generated using a secure 2-party computation between Alice and Bob s.t. Alice doesn't know share_i? share_i could potentially even have identifying information about Bob. However we note that the function f_i may have been cleverly designed to remove this identifying information and only leave the "essence" of the share intact. In general, the function f_i might even encrypt share_i with a public key (s.t. only the reconstruction box has the corresponding secret key). The reconstruction box code may even be "obfuscated" in some way. Indeed if Bob is rational, he might submit $f_i(\mathsf{share}_i)$ to the collector to get $100 since there are no penalties and no fear of being caught and prosecuted. After all, if he was the only one submitting the share, the collector anyway can get no information about Alice's secret. On the other hand, if a large number of servers are participating in the collection, Bob's does not want to be the one missing out on $100.

The main goal of our paper is to try to design a secret sharing scheme in which the servers are held accountable for cheating. In particular, any server which cheats should run the risk of giving out a "proof of cheating" to the outside world.

---

[1] To ensure that the server cannot claim a false reward by submitting f_i evaluated on some dummy value, the collector can presumably check the correctness of all the submitted values by, e.g., checking that they lie on a single polynomial.

Given any collection scheme consisting of $f_1, \ldots, f_n$, the reconstruction box $\mathsf{Rec}^\star$, and the collected shares $\{f_i(\mathsf{share}_i)\}_{i \in M}$ where M is the set of malicious servers, Alice should be able to prove in front of a Judge that, for some i, P_i leaked its share. In other words, there does not exist a collection scheme which guarantees immunity to the cheating servers. We call such a secret sharing scheme a *traceable secret sharing*. The notion of traceable secret sharing seems to be relevant in natural scenarios such as secure multi-party computation in the client server model [IK00], and, in threshold cryptosystems [DF90, Fra90, DDFY94].

1.1   Our Results

We initiate the study of traceable secret sharing (TSS) and explore various definitional aspects. TSS schemes turn out to be highly non-trivial to construct even ignoring efficiency aspects. We first start with the high-level description of this primitive.

Definition. In a traditional threshold secret sharing scheme, there is a sharing phase where the dealer generates a set of n shares of his secret and distributes it to the servers. The reconstruction algorithm allows any set of t servers to come together to get back the secret. In a traceable secret sharing scheme, there are two additional algorithms, namely, Trace and Judge. At a high-level, the Trace algorithm uses the set of n collector functions $f_1, \ldots, f_n$, the collected shares $f_i(\mathsf{share}_i)$ (for all i), the pirate reconstruction box and the view of the dealer during the sharing phase. It outputs the identity of a traitor along with an evidence that this is indeed a traitor. This evidence is later analyzed by the Judge algorithm which pronounces whether the server is guilty or not. We assume that the honest servers never submit their shares and the malicious servers submit $f_i(\mathsf{share}_i)$. A way to model this (which we follow in this work) is to consider the collector's function corresponding to an honest server to be a constant function.

In addition to correctness and statistical privacy properties of a threshold secret sharing, we require a traceable secret sharing scheme to satisfy two additional properties. The first property is *traceability* which roughly states that if the pirate reconstruction box is able to distinguish between the shares of two different secrets with non-negligible advantage (where the probability is over the random coins of the sharing phase, random coins of the collectors functions and the internal coins of the reconstruction box), then the Trace algorithm, with non-negligible probability, outputs the identity of a traitor along with a valid evidence that is accepted by the Judge algorithm. The second property, called as *non-imputability*, protects an honest server against a cheating dealer. Roughly, this property requires that a cheating dealer, even if it colludes with every other party, cannot produce a valid evidence that implicates an honest server.

On the Model. We now make a couple of comments on the model.

- We require the Trace algorithm to take the description of the collector functions, the reconstruction box Rec^* as well as $\{f_i(\mathsf{share}_i)\}_{i \in M}$ submitted by the malicious servers as input. These components might be available to Alice if Trudy was Alice's agent, or if Trudy later sells them anonymously to Alice, or if Trudy gets caught by the law enforcement authorities and these are submitted as evidence in the court of law. We note that if, for instance, $\{f_i(\mathsf{share}_i)\}_{i \in M}$ is not available to the trace algorithm, then there is no hope of identifying a traitor. Indeed, the reconstruction box does not have any secrets, and it is useless unless it is run on $\{f_i(\mathsf{share}_i)\}_{i \in [M]}$. This is, in fact, a key difference between traitor tracing (where the trace algorithm only requires access to the decryption box) and our notion of traceable secret sharing. We elaborate more on the differences between these two notions in Sect. 2.

- In this work, we consider a model where the collector specifies a set of functions $(f_1, \ldots, f_n)$ and asks the servers to submit $f_i(\mathsf{share}_i)$. However, it is possible to consider more general cases where the collector may ask the servers to run a distributed protocol and get the output of the protocol. Specifically, the collector and the servers might run a general MPC protocol that computes the reconstruction function and gives the output to the collector. We leave the study of such stronger models for future work. We note that in general, any tracing system (including broadcast encryption with traitor tracing) has its limitations and serves more as a deterrence rather than providing "foolproof security". In broadcast encryption with traitor tracing, the traitor might decrypt the broadcast and stream on an anonymous channel and then there is no hope of tracing the traitor. In spite of these limitations, traitor tracing has been widely deployed in practice (see, Fiat and Naor's ACM Paris Kanellakis Theory and Practice Award citation [ACM17]) and we take the first direction towards defining and constructing a similar primitive for the case of secret sharing.

Construction. In this work, we provide an efficient construction of traceable secret sharing scheme under standard cryptographic assumptions. Specifically, we show the following theorem:

Informal Theorem 1. *Assuming the existence of a secure two-party computation protocol, there exists an explicit construction of t-out-of-n threshold traceable secret sharing scheme for $t \geq 4$ in the PKI model.[2] In particular, for secrets of length λ,*

- *The construction satisfies statistical privacy.*
- *If there exists a set of n collector functions and a pirate reconstruction box that can distinguish between shares of two different secrets with advantage at least ϵ, then there exists a tracing algorithm that makes $\mathrm{poly}(\lambda, 1/\epsilon)$ oracle calls to the pirate reconstruction box and outputs the identity of a traitor along with a valid evidence with probability $\Omega(\frac{n\epsilon/(n-t+1)}{1+(n-1)\epsilon/(n-t+1)})$.*
- *With all but negligible probability, a (polynomially bounded) cheating dealer cannot provide a valid evidence against an honest party even if it colludes with every other party.*

---

[2] See Remark 2 on why PKI is necessary for traceable secret sharing.

Extensions. We also consider a couple of extensions to our setting of traceable secret sharing. The first extension is the collusion-resistant setting. Here, we consider a scenario where a group of upto $t - 1$ servers could come together and pool in their shares, apply a collector's function on their pooled shares and then submit the output. (Note that if we allow more than t servers to come together, then the servers could just reconstruct the secret without any collection, and TSS becomes meaningless.) We show that a simple modification to the construction from the above theorem actually satisfies this stronger definition. The second extension is that the tracing algorithm is now required to output the identities of *multiple* traitors along with a valid evidence implicating each of them. We note that in this case, it not possible to output the identities of more than t traitors as the reconstruction box can simply ignore the collected shares from some of the parties if more than t parties submit their shares. We are able to design a tracing algorithm that outputs the identities of at least $t - 1$ traitors (which is nearly optimal) along with a valid evidence against each one of them.

Going Beyond Storage: Delegating Computation. We show an application of our traceable secret sharing in constructing offline-online multi-server delegation of computation on private data. In this setting, there is a single client who wants to delegate an expensive computation on a private input to a set of n servers. We are specifically interested in constructing offline-online secure computation protocols for this task. In the offline phase, the client learns the circuit that it wants to evaluate and engages in a protocol with the n servers. In the online phase, the client learns its private input and runs the online phase of the protocol. At the end of the online phase, the client can reconstruct the output of the computation. We require the online computation cost of the client to only grow with the input and output length of the computation and is otherwise independent of the size of the circuit.

Now, consider a scenario as before where there is a collector who is interested in learning the secret data of the client and publishes an advertisement describing a set of collector functions $f_1, \ldots, f_n$ and a reconstruction box Rec*. The servers can submit the output of the collector functions applied on their *entire view* (as opposed to just the shares) during the protocol execution and the reconstruction box outputs some information about the client's input. We would like to design a protocol such that any server who submits this information always runs a risk of getting traced and prosecuted. This means that there are two additional algorithms (Trace, Judge) (that have the same semantics as in the traceable secret sharing scheme) that are respectively able to trace and verify the identities of the cheating servers. Specifically, given a set of n collector functions $f_1, \ldots, f_n$, the collected views of the servers $f_1(\text{view}_1), \ldots, f_n(\text{view}_n)$ and a pirate reconstruction box Rec* that is able to distinguish two different client inputs x_0, x_1 (that may not even lead to the same output), we require the Trace algorithm to output a valid evidence (that is accepted by the Judge algorithm) against a cheating server. We show the following theorem.

Informal Theorem 2. *Assuming the existence of a secure two-party compu-tation protocol, there exists an explicit construction of n servers offline-online, delegation of computation protocol tolerating t passive server corruptions in the PKI model. In particular,*

- *For any two client inputs x_0, x_1, the views of any set of $t - 1$ servers when the client's input is x_0 is statistically close to their views when the client's input is x_1.*
- *For any two client inputs x_0, x_1, if there exists a set of n collector func-tions and a pirate reconstruction box that can distinguish the views where the client's inputs are x_0 and x_1 with advantage at least ϵ, then there exists a tracing algorithm that makes $\mathrm{poly}(|C|, \lambda, 1/\epsilon)$ (where C is the circuit to be evaluated) oracle calls to the pirate reconstruction box and outputs the identity of a traitor along with a valid evidence with probability $\Omega\left(\frac{n\epsilon/(n-t+1)}{|C|+(n-1)\epsilon/(n-t+1)}\right)$.*
- *With all but negligible probability, a (polynomially bounded) cheating client cannot provide a valid evidence against an honest server even if it colludes with every other server.*

We note that this theorem statement *does not* follow as a direct consequence of traceable secret sharing (more on this in the next section) and in fact, the main challenge is to ensure that the shares of the intermediate wire values are also traceable. Indeed, if the starting shares of the inputs are traceable while the shares that the servers receive of the intermediate wire values are non-traceable, the servers can safely submit these intermediate shares to a collector (which still leaks non-trivial information).

1.2   Related Work

To the best of our knowledge, the notion of traceable secret sharing has never been studied directly. We discuss a few related notions that have appeared before in the literature. In the next subsection, we argue why techniques developed in the context of these problems fail in the TSS setting.

Traitor Tracing in Broadcast Encryption. A closely related notion to traceable secret sharing is that of traitor tracing [CFN94]. In the setting of traitor trac-ing [CFN94], there is a central party (also called as the broadcaster) who samples a set of public parameters along with n secret keys and distributes the secret keys to a set of parties (also called as subscribers). The broadcaster can use the public parameters to encrypt some message to a set of authorized parties and the authorized parties can use their secret key to decrypt this ciphertext. Now, when a group of subscribers come together to create a pirate decryption box that allows even an unauthorized party to decrypt the broadcast, a trac-ing algorithm can trace a party which was involved in creating this decryption box. There has been a long line of work focusing on obtaining efficient con-structions of traitor tracing [BS95, KD98, NP98, BF99, FT99, NP01, SW00, KY01, NNL01, KY02, DF03, CPP05, BSW06, BW06, BN08, BZ14, NWZ16, GKW18] and several works which considered the setting where the broadcaster could be malicious [Pfi96, PS96, PW97]. Broadcast encryption with traitor tracing has been widely used in practice to protect digital content.

Fingerprinting Codes. Fingerprinting codes, introduced by Boneh and Shaw [BS95] are information theoretic objects used in the construction of traitor tracing schemes. It consists of a code generator that outputs a set of codewords along with a tracing key. We assign each codeword in the set to a different party. If a group of parties collude and create a new word (using some restricted operations) then the trace algorithm takes the tracing key and this new word and outputs a subset of the parties that were used in constructing this word. Subsequent to their introduction, more efficient constructions of fingerprinting codes have been proposed in [KD98, SSW01, Tar03]. The main difference between this notion and that of traceable secret sharing is that it doesn't allow to share a secret and additionally, the operations that are allowed to create a new word are somewhat restricted.

Accountable Authority IBE. An Accountable-Authority Identity based Encryption [Goy07] was introduced by Goyal to reduce the trust on the private key generator (PKG) in a IBE scheme. Specifically, if the PKG was behaving dishonestly and was leaking information of individual party's secret key, then there is an algorithm that can produce a proof that is accepted by a judge implicating the dishonest behavior of the PKG. There have been some extensions to this notion like Black-Box Accountable Authority IBE [GLSW08].

2   Technical Overview

In this section, we will give a high-level overview of our construction of traceable secret sharing and also give details of the proof. We will also give an overview of our traceable delegation protocol. Before describing our construction of traceable secret sharing, we will first explain why existing secret sharing schemes are not traceable.

Limitations of Existing Secret Sharing Schemes. Existing secret sharing schemes (such as Shamir secret sharing) do not satisfy non-imputability property. In these constructions, the dealer knows the entire share that is given to a party and hence, a malicious dealer will be able to easily implicate an honest party by coming up with his own collector functions, collected shares and a reconstruction box which serve as valid evidence against this party. To prevent this attack, we may try to run a secure multiparty computation protocol between the dealer and the parties where the dealer provides his secret and the parties receive the shares at the end. This prevents the dealer from learning the shares that the parties receive. It turns out if the underlying secret sharing scheme has some additional properties such as each share having sufficient min-entropy even conditioned on the other shares[3], then this modification can be proved to satisfy non-imputability. However, in this case it is not clear if the traceability holds.

Comparison with Related Notions. A major difference between related notions such as traitor tracing and a traceable secret sharing is in the restrictions placed on the tracing algorithm. In a traceable secret sharing, we are not trying to extract some secret from the pirate box but rather, we are trying to extract some information from (possibly obfuscated/encrypted) input given to the pirate box. This means we are only given a single sample and we must work with this sample. Indeed, we can produce fresh samples on our own and try to run the reconstruction box on these samples but in this case, the secret we are trying to extract is lost. Hence, its not even clear apriori how invoking the pirate box multiple times can help. One way to get around this issue would be to use the given input sample to produce multiple (correlated) samples s.t. the target secret is somehow present in all of them. However, this makes the construction and the analysis more subtle. We also note that a simple construction for broadcast encryption with traitor tracing exists based on any public key encryption. The problem becomes interesting only while considering the efficiency aspects. On the other hand, for traceable secret sharing, even getting a feasibility result is an interesting problem because of the above mentioned reason.

In the next subsection, we give details of our construction of traceable secret sharing scheme.

2.1   Our First Construction

The main idea behind our first construction is to partition the share of each party into two parts. The first part is a secret that is known only to this party and is unknown to the dealer and the second part is a share of a secret such that the secret is known only to the dealer (unknown to any individual party). Intuitively, the first part which is unknown to the dealer prevents a cheating dealer from implicating an honest party and the secret in the second part enables a dealer to trace a traitor. With this insight, let us now give details of our construction.

- To share a secret s, the dealer uses Shamir sharing to split s into n shares, namely, $\mathsf{ssh}_1, \ldots, \mathsf{ssh}_n \in \{0,1\}^\lambda$. The threshold t used here is the same as the required threshold for TSS.
- For every $j \in [\lambda]$, the dealer chooses a random mask R_j uniformly from $\{0,1\}^\lambda$ and splits R_j into n Shamir shares $R_{1,j}, \ldots, R_{n,j}$ (again using threshold t).
- Now, the party P_i and the dealer engage in a secure two-party computation protocol that computes the following function. The function takes the i-th Shamir share ssh_i, the shares $\{R_{i,j}\}_{j\in[\lambda]}$, and all masks $\{R_j\}_{j\in[\lambda]}$ from the dealer. It then samples $L_{i,j}$ for each $j \in [\lambda]$ randomly such that $\langle L_{i,j}, R_j \rangle = \mathsf{ssh}_{i,j}$ where $\mathsf{ssh}_{i,j}$ refers to the j-th bit of ssh_i and $\langle \cdot, \cdot \rangle$ denotes

---

[3] The constructions of leakage-resilient secret sharing schemes given in [SV19, ADN+19] satisfies this property.

the inner product. It finally provides $\mathsf{owf}(L_{i,j})$ as output to the dealer and $\{L_{i,j}, R_{i,j}\}_{j\in[\lambda]}$ to P_i. Here, owf is an one-way function.

- The share of P_i (denoted by share_i) consists of $\{L_{i,j}, R_{i,j}\}_{j\in[\lambda]}$. The view of the dealer at the end of the sharing phase includes the Shamir shares $\mathsf{ssh}_1, \ldots, \mathsf{ssh}_n$, the shares $\{R_{i,j}\}_{i\in[n], j\in[\lambda]}$ and $\{\mathsf{owf}(L_{i,j})\}_{i\in[n], j\in[\lambda]}$.[4]
- In order to implicate the party P_i, the tracing algorithm is required to output any $L_{i,j}$ that is a valid pre-image.

Notice that the dealer's secrets $\{R_j\}_{j\in[\lambda]}$ are in fact secret shared among the parties. This means that even if you fix share_i for a party P_i, the value of R_j can still be freely decided by sampling $\{\mathsf{share}_k\}_{k\neq i}$ appropriately. This observation would be very useful when we design the tracing algorithm.

Non-Imputability. It can be easily shown that the above construction protects an honest party from a cheating dealer. In particular, it follows from the security of two-party computation that the dealer learns no information about a party's $L_{i,j}$ except learning that the inner-product of $L_{i,j}$ and R_j is $\mathsf{ssh}_{i,j}$. Thus, one can argue from the one-wayness property of owf (which hold even if there is a single bit of leakage) that the probability that a malicious dealer provides a valid pre-image is negligible and hence the probability that an honest party is implicated by a malicious dealer is negligible.

Tracing Algorithm Overview. Recall that the tracing algorithm receives the collector's functions $f_1, \ldots, f_n$, the collected shares $f_1(\mathsf{share}_1), \ldots, f_n(\mathsf{share}_n)$, the view of the dealer, and a pirate reconstruction box that is guaranteed to distinguish between the secret shares of s_0 and s_1 with noticeable advantage. The goal of the tracing algorithm is to extract one of $L_{i,j}$ that serves as a valid evidence against party P_i. However, to extract this evidence, the tracing algorithm must overcome the following challenges.

Challenge-1: Extraction from Single-Bit of Information. The first challenge is that the reconstruction box only gives a single bit of information about the evidence against P_i. However, recall that a valid evidence against P_i is one of $\{L_{i,j}\}_{j\in[\lambda]}$ where each $L_{i,j}$ is λ bits long. Furthermore, the reconstruction box is guaranteed to distinguish between the shares of s_0 and s_1 only with noticeable advantage and this means that the answer that the reconstruction box gives could sometimes be erroneous. So, the tracing algorithm must somehow use this single bit of information (which could further be erroneous) to extract a λ-bit long string.

To overcome this challenge, we rely on Goldreich-Levin decoding [GL89]. Indeed, our construction is designed to be able to use Goldreich-Levin decoding

---

[4] We note that our construction satisfies statistical privacy even though we rely on secure two party computation protocol. This is because the dealer's inputs to any set of $t-1$ of these secure two-party computation corresponds to $t-1$ Shamir shares and it follows from the perfect privacy of Shamir secret sharing that these shares do not reveal anything about the secret that was shared.

from the start. Before we go into the details of our solution, we first recall the setting of Goldreich-Levin decoding. Suppose there exists an oracle Ora that has a secret input $x \in \{0,1\}^\lambda$ hard-wired in its description. The oracle accepts queries $y \in \{0,1\}^\lambda$ and produces an output $z \in \{0,1\}$. If for a uniformly chosen query y, the probability that the oracle's output z is equal to $\langle x, y \rangle$ is noticeably more than $1/2$, Goldreich-Levin decoding algorithm gives a way of obtaining x hardwired in the oracle's description with overwhelming probability. Coming back to our setting, we will treat $L_{i,j}$ as the secret input x and use the pirate reconstruction box to simulate the working of the oracle Ora. The trace algorithm will then run the Goldreich-Levin decoder to extract out the secret $L_{i,j}$. However, for this task to be possible, we need the ability to set the query y to be equal to R_j so that we can use the reconstruction box to predict $\langle L_{i,j}, y \rangle = \langle L_{i,j}, R_j \rangle$. But the tracing algorithm only gets $f_1(\mathsf{share}_1), \ldots, f_n(\mathsf{share}_n)$ which could contain "encrypted" versions of $L_{i,j}$ and the shares of R_j and it is not clear upfront on how to set the R_j to be equal to the query y. This is where we use an earlier observation about our construction where we showed that is possible to fix share_i (that contains $L_{i,j}$) and resample the other shares in such a way that R_j is fixed to the oracle query y. We will then run the pirate reconstruction box on the fixed $f_i(\mathsf{share}_i)$ along with outputs of the other collector functions applied on the freshly sampled shares and use the output of the reconstruction box to predict $\langle L_{i,j}, y \rangle$.

A subtle but an important point that was ignored in the above paragraph is how does the tracing algorithm determine which $L_{i,j}$ to extract. The above description assumed that the tracing algorithm already knows which party is the traitor and then tries to extract the $L_{i,j}$ from this party. This brings us to the second challenge.

Challenge-2: A Careful Hybrid Argument. To determine the identity of a cheating party, the tracing algorithm will define a sequence of distributions or hybrids starting from the distribution where the shares correspond to the secret s_0 and ending with a distribution where the shares correspond to the secret s_1. Specifically, for every $i \in [n]$ and $j \in [\lambda + 1]$, the tracing algorithm defines $\mathsf{Hyb}_{i,j}$ as the distribution where $\{\mathsf{ssh}_{i'}\}_{i' < i}$ are valid Shamir shares of s_1 and $\{\mathsf{ssh}_{i'}\}_{i' > i}$ are valid Shamir shares of s_0. Further, the first $j - 1$ bits of the i-th share are changed from a share of s_0 to a share of s_1. Now, via a standard averaging argument, it follows that if the pirate reconstruction box can distinguish between shares of s_0 and s_1 with advantage ϵ, then there exists an $i \in [n], j \in [\lambda + 1]$ such that the reconstruction box can distinguish between $\mathsf{Hyb}_{i,j}$ and $\mathsf{Hyb}_{i,j+1}$ with advantage $\epsilon/O(n\lambda)$. This means that party P_i is a traitor (as otherwise, $\mathsf{Hyb}_{i,j} \equiv \mathsf{Hyb}_{i,j+1}$) and the tracing algorithm tries to extract an incriminating evidence against P_i. However, in order to determine if the reconstruction box can distinguish between $\mathsf{Hyb}_{i,j}$ and $\mathsf{Hyb}_{i,j+1}$ with noticeable advantage, we need the tracing algorithm to generate samples from both these distributions. To generate a sample from $\mathsf{Hyb}_{i,j}$ or $\mathsf{Hyb}_{i,j+1}$, we need to change the inner product of $L_{i,j}$ with R_j. However, we do not know $\{L_{i,j}\}_{j \in [\lambda]}$ that is available in share_i (recall that it only gets $f_i(\mathsf{share}_i)$) and hence, there does not seem to be a way for it to sample R_j such that the inner product of $L_{i,j}$ with R_j is a particular value.

To solve this issue, we slightly change the sequence of hybrids by introducing a "fine-grained structure". Specifically, instead of defining λ hybrids for changing the i-th Shamir share, we define $2\lambda + 1$ *small* hybrids $\mathsf{Hyb}_{i,j}$ indexed by $j \in \{0, \ldots, 2\lambda\}$. These hybrids first change ssh_i from a valid Shamir sharing of s_0 (associated with $\mathsf{ssh}_{i+1}, \ldots, \mathsf{ssh}_n$) to a random string one bit at a time, then change the random string to a valid Shamir sharing of s_1 (associated with $\mathsf{ssh}_1, \ldots, \mathsf{ssh}_{i-1}$) again one bit at a time. Now, via a similar averaging argument we can show that there exists a $i \in [n], j \in [0, 2\lambda - 1]$ such that the pirate reconstruction box can distinguish between $\mathsf{Hyb}_{i,j}$ and $\mathsf{Hyb}_{i,j+1}$ with advantage $\epsilon/O(n\lambda)$. For simplicity, assume that such a $j \in [0, \lambda - 1]$. The key advantage of this fine-grained hybrid structure is that it additionally allows the tracing algorithm to sample from $\mathsf{Hyb}_{i,j}$ or $\mathsf{Hyb}_{i,j+1}$. We now give the details below.

In a thought experiment, the tracing algorithm first fixes share_i. This means that all $\{L_{i,j}\}_{j\in[\lambda]}$ are fixed but these values are unknown to the tracing algorithm. For every $k > j$, it fixes R_k as in the sharing phase. This means that the inner product of $L_{i,k}$ with R_k remains the same as the k-th bit of the i-th share of s_0. For every $k < j$, we sample an independent R'_k and this is possible due to an earlier observation that conditioned on fixing any share, the dealer's secrets are uniformly distributed. This means that for every $k < j$, the inner product of $L_{i,k}$ with the new R'_k is an uniformly chosen random bit. Now, if we fix R_j as in the sharing phase, we get an sample from $\mathsf{Hyb}_{i,j}$; else, if we sample R'_j uniformly at random, we get a sample from $\mathsf{Hyb}_{i,j+1}$.

Completing the Tracing. The tracing algorithm will go over every i, j and determine if the pirate reconstruction box can distinguish between $\mathsf{Hyb}_{i,j}$ and $\mathsf{Hyb}_{i,j+1}$ with noticeable advantage. Eventually, it will reach $\mathsf{Hyb}_{i,j}$ and $\mathsf{Hyb}_{i,j+1}$ such that the pirate reconstruction box can distinguish between these two hybrids with probability at least $\epsilon/O(n\lambda)$. It will now use Goldreich-Levin decoder to extract $L_{i,j}$. For completeness, we provide the details below.

– The tracing algorithm starts running the Goldreich-Levin decoder and simulates the access to the oracle Ora.
– When the decoder queries the oracle on a uniform y, the tracing algorithm does the following:
   • It fixes the collected share of party P_i, i.e., $f_i(\mathsf{share}_i)$. In addition to this, it also fixes the random masks $\{R_k\}_{k>j}$ which are available from the view of the dealer. By fixing these random masks, the tracing algorithm has fixed the inner product of $L_{i,k}$ and R_k for $k > j$ to be the same as the bits of the initial Shamir share ssh_i that was used in the sharing phase.
   • It then randomly samples $\mathsf{ssh}'_{i+1}, \ldots, \mathsf{ssh}'_n$ such that these correspond to the last $n - i$ shares of a Shamir sharing of the secret s_0. It also samples $\mathsf{ssh}'_1, \ldots, \mathsf{ssh}'_{i-1}$ such that $(\mathsf{ssh}'_1, \ldots, \mathsf{ssh}'_{i-1})$ correspond to the first $(i-1)$ shares of a Shamir sharing of s_1.

- It sets $R'_j = y$ (where y is the query) and samples $R'_{1,j}, \ldots, R'_{i-1,j}$, $R'_{i+1,j}, \ldots, R'_{n,j}$ such that these values together with $R_{i,j}$ corresponds to a valid Shamir sharing of R'_j.
- For $k < j$, it samples R_k uniformly from $\{0,1\}^\lambda$. Then the shares of $\{R_k\}_{k \neq j}$ are randomly sampled such that they are consistent with the fixed share_i and it samples $\mathsf{share}'_1, \ldots, \mathsf{share}'_{i-1}, \mathsf{share}'_{i+1}, \ldots, \mathsf{share}'_n$ that are consistent with the above sampled values.
- The tracing algorithm then runs the pirate reconstruction box on $f_1(\mathsf{share}'_1), \ldots, f_{i-1}(\mathsf{share}'_{i-1}), f_i(\mathsf{share}_i), f_{i-1}(\mathsf{share}'_{i-1}), \ldots, f_n(\mathsf{share}'_n))$. We show that using the output of the reconstruction box, one can predict the value of the inner-product between $L_{i,j}$ and y with probability noticeably better than half.

A minor subtlety that arises because of fixing $(\mathsf{share}_i, \{R_k\}_{k>j})$ is that for the Goldreich-Levin decoding to work, we require that conditioned on fixing these values, the reconstruction box still distinguishes between $\mathsf{Hyb}_{i,j}$ and $\mathsf{Hyb}_{i,j+1}$ with non-negligible advantage. We note that we can rely on Markov's inequality to show that for $\frac{\epsilon}{O(n\lambda)}$ fraction of values of $(\mathsf{share}_i, \{R_k\}_{k>j})$, the reconstruction box still distinguishes between $\mathsf{Hyb}_{i,j+1}$ and $\mathsf{Hyb}_{i,j}$ with probability at least $\frac{\epsilon}{O(n\lambda)}$ conditioned on fixing these values. This allows the tracing algorithm to use the pirate reconstruction box to simulate the oracle and thus, enabling the Goldreich-Levin decoder to extract $L_{i,j}$.

2.2   Boosting Tracing Probability

The analysis explained before shows us how to trace a traitor with overwhelming probability conditioned on $\mathsf{share}_i, \{R_k\}_{k>j}$ belonging to a "good" set. Also, we argued via Markov's inequality that the probability that this value is "good" is at least $\frac{\epsilon}{O(\lambda n)}$. Thus, the probability of tracing a traitor is roughly, $\frac{\epsilon}{O(\lambda n)}$. We now show how to increase the success probability of the tracing algorithm in a sequence of steps. The first step will show how to increase it to $O(\epsilon/n)$, the second step will increase the tracing probability to $O(\epsilon)$ and the final step will show how to increase it to $O(\frac{n\epsilon/(n-t+1)}{1+(n-1)\epsilon/(n-t+1)})$. In this informal overview, we will focus only on the first two steps and leave the third step to the main body.

First Step: $O(\epsilon/n)$. We note that to implicate P_i, it is sufficient to extract one of $\{L_{i,j}\}_{j \in [\lambda]}$ as the evidence. The above analysis tried to extract one specific L_{ij} and hence, suffered from a bad success probability. In the first boosting step, we analyze the success probability of the tracing algorithm in extracting *any* one of the $\{L_{ij}\}_{j \in [\lambda]}$. Since the tracing algorithm has more "slots" to extract a valid evidence, this increases the success probability by a proportional factor.

Towards this goal, we define $(\mathsf{share}_i, \{R_k\}_{k \in [\lambda]})$ output in the initial sharing phase to be *traceable* if there exists $j \in [\lambda]$ (or $j \in \{\lambda + 1 \ldots, 2\lambda\}$) such that $(\mathsf{share}_i, \{R_k\}_{k>j})$ (or $(\mathsf{share}_i, \{R_k\}_{k>2\lambda-j+1})$) is "good". In this case, we note that we can use the strategy mentioned above to extract $L_{i,j}$ (or $L_{i,2\lambda-j+1}$).

The main technical lemma that we show in this step is the following. Let us consider two large hybrids Hyb_i and Hyb_{i+1}, and if ϵ_i is the advantage of the pirate reconstruction box in distinguishing between Hyb_i and Hyb_{i+1}, then with probability $O(\epsilon_i - \epsilon/(Cn))$, $(\mathsf{share}_i, \{R_k\}_{k \in [\lambda]})$ output in the initial sharing phase is traceable (where C is a some large enough constant). By observing that there exists an $i \in [n]$ such that, $\epsilon_i \geq \epsilon/n$ (via an averaging argument), we show that probability of tracing is $O(\epsilon/n)$. We now give an overview of this lemma by assuming without loss of generality that that the distinguishing advantage between $\mathsf{Hyb}_{i,0}$ and $\mathsf{Hyb}_{i,\lambda}$ is at least $\epsilon_i/2$.

The main idea in the proof of the lemma is the following (informal) duality condition. We show that for every $j \in [\lambda]$, we can either use $(\mathsf{share}_i, \{R_k\}_{k > j})$ to extract $L_{i,j}$ or the distinguishing advantage between $\mathsf{Hyb}_{i,j-1}$ and $\mathsf{Hyb}_{i,j}$ is "small". Since we know that the distinguishing advantage between $\mathsf{Hyb}_{i,0}$ and $\mathsf{Hyb}_{i,\lambda}$ is at least $\epsilon_i/2$, we get a lower bound on the probability that there exists a $j \in [\lambda]$, such that $(\mathsf{share}_i, \{R_k\}_{k>j})$ can be used to extract $L_{i,j}$. The actual proof is involved and uses a delicate partitioning argument. We refer the reader to the main body for the full details.

Second Step: $O(\epsilon)$: We note that the previous analysis showed that the probability that $(\mathsf{share}_i, \{R_k\}_{k \in [\lambda]})$ is traceable is at least $O(\epsilon_i - \epsilon/(Cn))$. This in particular means that P_i can be traced with probability at least $O(\epsilon_i - \epsilon/(Cn))$. The key trick in this step is that if any two parties can be traced independently, then we may take advantage of the pairwise independence and boost the success probability. However, to trace a party, we need $(\mathsf{share}_i, \{R_k\}_{k \in [\lambda]})$ to be traceable, which means the event that one party can be traced is correlated with the event that another party can be traced.

To break the above mentioned correlation, we modify our construction as follows. In the sharing phase, instead of sampling R_j and using Shamir secret sharing to split it, the dealer samples a polynomial $p_j(\cdot)$ of degree at most $t - 1$ and sets $R_{i,j}$ to be $p_j(\alpha_i)$ (for some fixed element α_i). Furthermore, instead of sampling $L_{i,j}$ such that $\mathsf{ssh}_{i,j} = \langle L_{i,j}, R_j \rangle$, the sharing protocol samples $L_{i,j}$ such that $\mathsf{ssh}_{i,j} = \langle L_{i,j}, p_j(\beta_i) \rangle$ (for some fixed element β_i). In this new construction, to trace a party P_i, we need $(\mathsf{share}_i, \{p_k(\beta_i)\}_{k \in [\lambda]})$ to be traceable. We observe that if $t \geq 4$, the random variables $(\mathsf{share}_i, \{p_k(\beta_i)\}_{k \in [\lambda]})$ and $(\mathsf{share}_{i'}, \{p_k(\beta_{i'})\}_{k \in [\lambda]})$ for any $i \neq i'$ are pairwise independent. We rely on this observation and make use of standard inequalities like Cauchy-Schwartz to get a lower bound on the probability that at least for one $i \in \{1, \ldots, n\}$, $(\mathsf{share}_i, \{p_k(\beta_i)\}_{k \in [\lambda]})$ is traceable. This allows us to get an improved analysis and thus improving the success probability to $O(\epsilon)$.

2.3   Traceable Delegation

In this subsection, we show an application of traceable secret sharing to constructing traceable multi-server delegation of computation in the offline-online setting.

The Setting. In our model, there is a single client and n servers. The client wants to delegate the computation of a circuit C on some private input x to the n servers. We consider the offline-online setting where the client gets the circuit to be computed in the offline phase but learns the private input in the online phase. The offline computational cost of the client can grow with the size of the circuit C but we require the online computation of the client to be extremely fast. In particular, it should only grow proportional to the input length x and the output length of C and is otherwise, independent of the size of C. We require the standard correctness and the privacy properties from the protocol, meaning that the client always reconstructs the correct output and the views of t servers provide no information about the client's private input x. Additionally, we require the protocol to be traceable, meaning that given any set of collector functions $f_1, \ldots, f_n$ and a pirate reconstruction box that can distinguish between the cases where the client's input was x_0 and x_1 with noticeable advantage, then we require a tracing algorithm to output a valid evidence (accepted by a judge) against one of the cheating servers.

Why Natural Approaches Fail? A natural approach to construct such a traceable MPC protocol is for the client to use our traceable secret sharing scheme to secret share its private input x among the n servers. Then, the servers can run standard MPC protocols like BGW [BOGW88] or GMW [GMW87] to compute a secret share of the output which can finally be reconstructed by the client. However, this approach fails in our setting because these protocols crucially rely on the secret sharing scheme to be linear whereas our traceable secret sharing scheme is non-linear. To get around this problem of non-linearity, one might think that for every gate, we might run a mini MPC protocol that takes the traceable shares of the inputs, reconstructs the input values, computes the output of the gate and then reshares it using a traceable secret sharing scheme. However, this requires the mini MPC protocol itself to be traceable and we are back to square one. In conclusion, the main difficulty we face is in making the shares of the intermediate wire values to be traceable.

Our Protocol. The main idea behind our protocol is to "secret share" the circuit rather than secret sharing the input. Towards building the main intuition behind the protocol, let us start with a trivial case where the circuit is just a single gate g that takes in two input values and has a single output value. In the offline phase of our computation, the client "garbles the truth table" of this gate. Specifically, for every input wire and the output wire, the client chooses a random masking bit. Let us call these masking bits to be r_1, r_2 corresponding to the input wires and r_3 corresponding to the output wire. Further, the client generates a table with 4 entries where the (a, b)-th entry of the table for $a \in \{0, 1\}$ and $b \in \{0, 1\}$ is given by $g(a \oplus r_1, b \oplus r_2) \oplus r_3$. After generating all the entries of the "garbled table", the client uses our traceable secret sharing to secret share each entry of the garbled truth table to the n servers. This completes the offline phase of the protocol and at the end of the offline phase, each of the servers hold a secret share for every entry of the garbled truth table. In the online phase, the client learns its input $(x_1, x_2) \in \{0,1\} \times \{0,1\}$ and it sends to each of the servers $(x_1 \oplus r_1, x_2 \oplus r_2)$. Now, each of the servers hold the masked values of the input wires, and they just choose the share corresponding to the entry given by $(x_1 \oplus r_1, x_2 \oplus r_2)$ in the truth table, and reconstruct this particular value by broadcasting the chosen shares. It is easy to see that the reconstructed value will be the actual output of the gate masked with r_3. Now, this value will be sent back to the client who can unmask this value and learn the output of the computation.

To give the main idea behind tracing, notice that in the online evaluation phase executed by the servers, there are three secret shares that are left untouched. Further, the entry of the gate table that is reconstructed does not give any information about the client's input due to the one-time pad security. This means that if we change any one of the untouched shares to a secret sharing of the revealed value and if the reconstruction box is able to detect this change, then we are back to the standard setting of traceable secret sharing. With this intuition in mind, let us now give the details about tracing. Towards this, let us first assume that we have a set of n collector functions $f_1, \ldots, f_n$ and a pirate reconstruction box that can distinguish between the cases where the input of the client was (x_1, x_2) from the case the input was (x_1', x_2') with noticeable advantage. The tracing algorithm defines a sequence of 6 hybrids starting from the case where the input was (x_1, x_2) and ending with the case where the input was (x_1', x_2'). The first three hybrids change each entry of the garbled truth table to be $g(x_1 \oplus r_1, x_2 \oplus r_2) \oplus r_3$. That is, at the end of these changes, all the 4 secrets that were shared during the offline phase are equal to $g(x_1 \oplus r_1, x_2 \oplus r_2) \oplus r_3$. Notice that once we have done this change, we can rely on the one-time pad security to make the views of all the servers to be independent of the input. In particular, we can change the masked inputs which were sent during the online phase to be $(x_1' \oplus r_1, x_2' \oplus r_2)$ and the entries of the garbled table to be $g(x_1' \oplus r_1, x_2' \oplus r_2) \oplus r_3$. The next sequence of 3 hybrids will just reverse these changes ending with the actual view of the servers when the client's input was (x_1', x_2'). If the reconstruction box distinguishes between the cases where the client's inputs were (x_1, x_2) from (x_1', x_2') with advantage ϵ, then via a standard averaging argument, it follows that there exists two intermediate hybrids Hyb and Hyb$'$ in this sequence such that the reconstruction box is able to distinguish between these two hybrids with advantage $\epsilon/6$. Notice that the only difference between any two subsequent hybrids is the secret that was shared in a particular gate entry. Thus, fixing all other gate entries and their corresponding shares, we can now directly rely on our tracing algorithm to catch a specific traitor.

An astute reader might have noticed the similarities between our approach and the point-and-permute trick in garbled circuits [BMR90]. Indeed, we can extend the toy example in a straightforward way to computing an arbitrary circuit C composed of many gates via the point-and-permute trick. Specifically, we ask the client to choose an independent random masking bit for each wire of the circuit (including the output wires) and generate the garbled truth table for each gate as explained above. In the offline phase, the client secret shares each entry of each garbled table using our traceable secret sharing scheme and sends it over to the servers. In the online phase, the client sends the masked values of its input. Then, the servers compute the masked output of each gate in the topological order, starting from the input gates and ending in the output gates exactly as explained above. Once the servers have the masked value of the output, then can simply send this to the client who unmasks this and reconstructs the actual output.

A Subtlety. A minor subtlety that arises with the above approach is in proving the non-imputability property. Let us once again consider the toy example above where there is a single gate. In the online phase, when the servers broadcast the shares corresponding to the $(x_1 \oplus r_1, x_2 \oplus r_2)$-th entry of the garbled truth table, they also need to broadcast the $\{L_{i,j}\}_{j \in [\lambda]}$ corresponding to these shares. However, broadcasting these values allow a cheating client that colluded with one other server to easily implicate an honest server. To prevent this attack, we make use of the specific structure of our shares. Recall that the share corresponding to the i-th server comprises of $\{L_{i,j}, R_{i,j}\}_{j \in [\lambda]}$. Instead of asking the servers to naively broadcast this share in its entirety, we first ask the servers to broadcast $\{R_{i,j}\}_{j \in [\lambda]}$. This allows the servers to first reconstruct $\{R_j\}_{j \in [\lambda]}$. Once this is done, the servers can take the inner produce of each $L_{i,j}$ with R_j to reconstruct the i-th Shamir share ssh_i. The servers then broadcast this value and this allows them to reconstruct the actual secret without revealing $\{L_{i,j}\}_{j \in [\lambda]}$ to any party.

2.4   Extensions

Trace t-1 Parties. In this extension, we are interested in tracing many traitors. By using the construction in the previous step, we note that $(\mathsf{share}_1, \{p_{1,k}(0)\}_{k \in [\lambda]}), \ldots, (\mathsf{share}_n, \{p_{n,k}(0)\}_{k \in [\lambda]})$ are $(t-1)$-wise independent. We use the trick of explained before to identify $t-1$ "special" parties such that each of them can be traced with probability $O(\epsilon/(n-t+1))$. Therefore, we can trace $t-1$ parties with probability $O((\epsilon/(n-t+1))^{t-1})$.

Disjoint Collusion Setting. We also consider the setting where up to $t-1$ parties can collude. We focus on the disjoint collusion setting where each party can be in at most one collusion. We model the collusion by allowing the collector to specify functions $f_{i_1,\ldots,i_k}$ for collusion of $k \leq t-1$ parties, where $f_{i_1,\ldots,i_k}$ takes $\mathsf{share}_{i_1}, \ldots, \mathsf{share}_{i_k}$ as input.

The main idea of the tracing algorithm would be the same as before. However, to generate a valid random sample which is either in $\mathsf{Hyb}_{i,j}$ or $\mathsf{Hyb}_{i,j-1}$, in addition to fixing $(\mathsf{share}_i, \{p_k(\beta_i)\}_{k>j})$, we also need to fix $\{\mathsf{share}_{i'}, \{p_k(\beta_{i'})\}_{k \in [\lambda]}\}_{i' \in \mathcal{C}_i}$, where $\mathcal{C}_i$ denotes the set of parties which collude with P_i. Because we need to use the collected share sent by P_i, which requires that the shares of P_i and all parties who collude with P_i should be the same as that generated in the initial phase. Furthermore, since the tracing algorithm does not know $\{L_{i',k}\}_{i' \in \mathcal{C}_i, k \in [\lambda]}$, we need to also reuse $\{p_k(\beta_{i'})\}_{i' \in \mathcal{C}_i, k \in [\lambda]}$ so that the inner product between $L_{i',j}$ and $p_k(\beta_{i'})$ is known to the tracing algorithm.

However, for $p_j(\cdot)$, we need to fix $2t - 3$ values, which has already determined $p_j(\cdot)$. It disables us to change the value of $p_j(\beta_i)$.

To solve this issue, we modify the construction as follows. In the sharing phase, for $j \in [\lambda]$ instead of only using one polynomial $p_j(\cdot)$, the dealer samples n polynomials $p_{1,j}(\cdot), \ldots, p_{n,j}(\cdot)$ of degree at most $t-1$. Every party will receive $R_{i,j}^1 = p_{1,j}(\alpha_i), \ldots, R_{i,j}^n = p_{n,j}(\alpha_i)$. Instead of sampling $L_{i,j}$ such that $\mathsf{ssh}_{i,j} = \langle L_{i,j}, p_j(\beta_i) \rangle$, the sharing protocol samples $L_{i,j}$ such that $\mathsf{ssh}_{i,j} = \langle L_{i,j}, p_{i,j}(0) \rangle$. In this way, we only fix $t - 1$ values of $p_{i,j}(\cdot)$ and therefore can still change the value of $p_{i,j}(0)$. The first step of boosting success probability still works in the new construction. Therefore, we can trace a party with probability $O(\epsilon/(n - t + 1))$ in the collusion setting.

3   Preliminaries

Let λ denote the security parameter. A function $\mu(\cdot) : \mathbb{N} \to \mathbb{R}^+$ is said to be negligible if for any polynomial $\mathrm{poly}(\cdot)$ there exists λ_0 such that for all $\lambda > \lambda_0$ we have $\mu(\lambda) < \frac{1}{\mathrm{poly}(\lambda)}$. We will use $\mathrm{negl}(\cdot)$ to denote an unspecified negligible function and $\mathrm{poly}(\cdot)$ to denote an unspecified polynomial function.

We assume reader's familiarity with the digital signature schemes.

3.1   Goldreich-Levin Lemma

Lemma 1. *Suppose* owf *is a one-way function. If there is an oracle* $\mathsf{Ora}(X, \star)$ *with X hard-coded where $X \in \{0,1\}^\lambda$ such that*

$$\Pr_{Y \sim \{0,1\}^\lambda}[\mathsf{Ora}(X, Y) = \langle X, Y \rangle] \geq 1/2 + \eta(\lambda),$$

then there exists a probabilistic algorithm Inv, *which takes* owf *and* $\mathsf{owf}(X)$ *as input, has the access to* $\mathsf{Ora}(X, \star)$, *runs in* $\mathrm{poly}(1/\eta(\lambda), \lambda)$ *and makes* $\mathrm{poly}(1/\eta(\lambda), \lambda)$ *oracle queries, such that*

$$\Pr[X' \leftarrow \mathsf{Inv}^{\mathsf{Ora}(X,\star)}(\mathsf{owf}(\cdot), \mathsf{owf}(X)) : \mathsf{owf}(X') = \mathsf{owf}(X)] \geq 1 - \mathrm{negl}(\lambda).$$

We use $\mathsf{Inv}^{\mathsf{Ora}(X,\star)}(\mathsf{owf}(X))$ for simplicity and ignore the input of the description of owf when it is evident from the context.

4   Traceable Secret Sharing

In Sect. 4.1, we give the definition of a traceable secret sharing. In Sect. 4.2, we give our construction. We refer the readers to the full version of this paper for the proof of security.

4.1   Definition

A traceable secret sharing scheme consists of four algorithms (Share, Rec, Trace, Judge). The (Share, Rec) have the same syntax as that of a normal secret sharing scheme. The algorithm Trace takes in a set of n collector functions $f_1, \ldots, f_n$, the set of collected shares, a pirate reconstruction box, the view of the dealer during the sharing phase and outputs the identity of a traitor party $i^\star$ who has submitted its share to the collector along with a proof $\pi_{i^\star}$. The Judge algorithm takes in this proof and pronounces whether $i^\star$ is guilty or not. We give the formal definition below.

Definition 1. *A Traceable Secret Sharing (TSS) is a tuple of four algorithms* (Share, Rec, Trace, Judge) *with the following syntax:*

- Share$(1^\lambda, s, t, n)$: *On input the security parameter 1^λ, a secret s, the threshold t and the number of players n, the dealer D runs the Share protocol with n players $P_1, \ldots, P_n$. At the end of the protocol, the player P_i outputs its share share$_i$ and the dealer outputs its view view$_D$. We will ignore the security parameter when it is evident from the context.*
- Rec(share$_{i_1}, \ldots,$ share$_{i_t}$) : *This is a deterministic algorithm such that given any set of t shares, denoted by share$_{i_1}, \ldots,$ share$_{i_t}$, outputs a secret s.*
- Trace$^{\mathsf{Rec}^\star}(f_1, \ldots, f_n, f_1(\mathsf{share}_1), \ldots, f_n(\mathsf{share}_n), \mathsf{view}_D, s_0, s_1)$: *The collector publishes the description of the functions $f_1, \ldots, f_n$ along with a pirate reconstruction box Rec*. The collector receives shares from a set of parties after applying the collector functions. If a party P_i is honest and has not submitted its share, we will replace f_i with a constant function. Formally, if H is the set of honest parties, then f_i is a constant function for $i \in H$. The Trace algorithm takes the n collector functions $f_1, \ldots, f_n$, the collected shares $f_1(\mathsf{share}_1), \ldots, f_n(\mathsf{share}_n)$, the view of D, two secrets s_0, s_1, and with oracle access to a pirate reconstruction box Rec* outputs an index $i^\star \in [n]$ and a proof $\pi_{i^\star}$.*
- Judge$(i^\star, \pi_{i^\star}, \mathsf{view}_D)$: *This is a deterministic algorithm that takes the alleged traitor identity $i^\star \in [n]$, the proof $\pi_{i^\star}$ and the view view$_D$ of the dealer and outputs guilty or not $-$ guilty.*

We say a scheme is a t-out-of-n δ-traceable secret sharing if it satisfies the following properties.

- **Correctness.** *For any secret s and any $T = \{i_1, \ldots, i_t\}$ where each $i_j \in [n]$, we require that*

$$\Pr_{\mathsf{Share}(s,t,n)}[\mathsf{Rec}(\mathsf{share}_{i_1}, \ldots, \mathsf{share}_{i_t}) = s] = 1$$

- **Statistical Privacy.** *For any two secrets s_0, s_1 and any $T \subseteq [n]$ with $|T| \leq t - 1$, we require that*

$$\{(\mathsf{share}_1, \ldots, \mathsf{share}_n) \leftarrow \mathsf{Share}(s_0, t, n) : \mathsf{share}_T\} \approx_s$$
$$\{(\mathsf{share}_1, \ldots, \mathsf{share}_n) \leftarrow \mathsf{Share}(s_1, t, n) : \mathsf{share}_T\}$$

- **Traceability.** *If there exists a set of n collector functions $f_1, \ldots, f_n$ (where f_i is a constant function if P_i is honest) and a pirate reconstruction box $\mathsf{Rec}^\star$ such that for two secrets s_0, s_1,*

$$\left| \Pr_{\mathsf{Share}(s_0,t,n)}[\mathsf{Rec}^\star(f_1(\mathsf{share}_1), \ldots, f_n(\mathsf{share}_n)) = 0] - \right.$$
$$\left. \Pr_{\mathsf{Share}(s_1,t,n)}[\mathsf{Rec}^\star(f_1(\mathsf{share}_1), \ldots, f_n(\mathsf{share}_n)) = 0] \right| \geq \epsilon$$

then,

$$\Pr[(\mathsf{share}_1, \ldots, \mathsf{share}_n, \mathsf{view}_D) \leftarrow \mathsf{Share}(s_0, t, n);$$
$$(i^\star, \pi_{i^\star}) \leftarrow \mathsf{Trace}^{\mathsf{Rec}^\star}(f_1, \ldots, f_n, f_1(\mathsf{share}_1), \ldots, f_n(\mathsf{share}_n), \mathsf{view}_D, s_0, s_1) :$$
$$\mathsf{Judge}(i^\star, \pi_{i^\star}, \mathsf{view}_D) = \mathsf{guilty}] \geq \delta(\epsilon)$$

Furthermore, the number of queries that Trace makes to the pirate reconstruction box $\mathsf{Rec}^\star$ is $\mathrm{poly}(\lambda, 1/\epsilon)$.
- **Non-imputability.** *For any secret s, honest player $P_{i^\star}$ and any computationally bounded algorithm $\tilde{D}$,*

$$\Pr_{\mathsf{share}(1^\lambda, s, t, n)}[(\mathsf{view}'_D, i^\star, \pi_{i^\star}) \leftarrow \tilde{D}(\mathsf{view}_D, \mathsf{share}_{[n]\setminus\{i^\star\}}) : \mathsf{Judge}(i^\star, \pi_{i^\star}, \mathsf{view}'_D)$$
$$= \mathsf{guilty}] \leq \mathsf{negl}(\lambda)$$

Remark 1. We can consider a stronger definition wherein the parties apply the collector's functions on not only the shares received but also on its entire view during the execution of the sharing protocol. In fact, our construction satisfies this stronger definition.

Tracing More Traitors. In the previous definition, it was sufficient for the Trace algorithm to output the identity of one of the traitors $i^\star$ along with a proof $\pi_{i^\star}$. It is natural to consider a stronger formulation where Trace is required to output the identities of all the traitors along with a valid proofs against each one of them. We note that it is generally impossible to output the identities of more than t traitors as the reconstruction box could simply ignore some of the collected shares. So, the best we could hope for from a tracing algorithm is to output the identities along with valid evidence of at most t traitors.

Collusion-Resistant Setting. In the previous formulation, we considered the setting where the individual parties submit their shares without colluding. Here, we consider a stronger formulation where the collector publishes the description of the functions which can take a set of shares as input. To be more precise, we consider the disjoint collusion setting (though stronger formulations are indeed possible) where each party can appear in at most one collusion. We model this collusion by allowing the collector to specify functions $f_{\{i_1,\ldots,i_k\}}$ for collusion of $k \leq t-1$ players, where $f_{\{i_1,\ldots,i_k\}}$ takes $\mathsf{share}_{i_1}, \ldots, \mathsf{share}_{i_k}$ as input. The trace algorithm takes in the description of these collector's functions, collected shares and the view of the dealer and outputs the identity of a traitor along with a proof by making oracle access to the reconstruction box. We note that if t or more parties collude together they can then recover the secret and submit some information about the secret to the collector. Thus, we restrict the size of the collusions to be at most $t - 1$.

4.2 Construction

Setting. Let n denote the number of players and λ denote the security parameter. We further set the length of the secret to be λ. In the full version of this paper, we will show that our construction is traceable under parallel composition so that larger length secrets can be chopped into blocks of length λ bits each. We use P_i to represent the i-th player. Let $\mathbb{F} = \mathrm{GF}(2^\lambda)$. Let owf be an one-way function. Let $\alpha_1, \ldots, \alpha_n, \beta_1, \ldots, \beta_n \in \mathbb{F} \setminus \{0\}$ be $2n$ distinct fixed elements. The pair of elements (α_i, β_i) is assigned to P_i. Each P_i also has a pair of keys $(\mathsf{sk}_i, \mathsf{vk}_i)$ generated by Gen of a digital signature scheme and we assume that vk_i is public and is known to every other party including the judge algorithm (similar to the PKI infrastructure). Alternatively, we may assume that at the end of the sharing protocol, the dealer and the server come together and sign on the transcript of the sharing protocol. In this way, the transcript available with the dealer's view can be verified by the judge.

Remark 2. We note that the PKI assumption seems a necessary condition for a traceable secret sharing scheme. Intuitively, if without the PKI assumption, a corrupted server can simply deny the messages and the corresponding signatures sent to the client when this sever is caught by the tracing algorithm. Essentially, there would be no way for the judge to check whether the messages are sent by the server or not.

For $k \in [n]$ and $k \geq t$, we say a vector (or a set) of pairs of values $((\alpha_{i_1}, v_{i_1}), \ldots, (\alpha_{i_k}, v_{i_k}))$ are valid t-Shamir shares of secret s, if there exists a polynomial $f(\cdot) \in \mathbb{F}[X]$ of degree at most $t - 1$, such that $f(\alpha_{i_j}) = v_{i_j}$ for all $j \in [k]$ and $f(0) = s$.

Theorem 3. *Assume the existence of one-way functions, the PKI infrastructure and secure two-party computation protocols. For $t \geq 4, n \geq t$ and any $C = \mathrm{poly}(\lambda)$, there exists an explicit t-out-of-n δ-traceable secret sharing scheme with the size of each share $O(\lambda^2)$ where $\delta(\epsilon) = p(\epsilon)/(\frac{n-1}{n}p(\epsilon) + 1) - \mathrm{negl}(\lambda)$, and*

$$p(\epsilon) = \frac{n\epsilon}{2(n - t + 1)} - \left(\frac{t - 1}{2} + n\lambda\right)\frac{\epsilon}{Cn\lambda}.$$

Without loss of generality, for $t \geq 4, n \geq t$, a set of n collector functions $f_1, \ldots, f_n$ and a pirate reconstruction box $\mathsf{Rec}^\star$ such that for two secrets s_0, s_1,

$$\Big| \Pr_{\mathsf{Share}(s_0,t,n)}[\mathsf{Rec}^\star(f_1(\mathsf{share}_1), \ldots, f_n(\mathsf{share}_n)) = 0] - $$
$$\Pr_{\mathsf{Share}(s_1,t,n)}[\mathsf{Rec}^\star(f_1(\mathsf{share}_1), \ldots, f_n(\mathsf{share}_n)) = 0]\Big| \geq \epsilon,$$

we assume

$$\Pr_{\text{Share}(s_0,t,n)}[\text{Rec}^\star(f_1(\text{share}_1),\dots,f_n(\text{share}_n)) = 0] -$$

$$\Pr_{\text{Share}(s_1,t,n)}[\text{Rec}^\star(f_1(\text{share}_1),\dots,f_n(\text{share}_n)) = 0] \geq \epsilon.$$

To handle the case

$$\Pr_{\text{Share}(s_0,t,n)}[\text{Rec}^\star(f_1(\text{share}_1),\dots,f_n(\text{share}_n)) = 0] -$$

$$\Pr_{\text{Share}(s_1,t,n)}[\text{Rec}^\star(f_1(\text{share}_1),\dots,f_n(\text{share}_n)) = 0] \leq -\epsilon,$$

one can first design a new $\widetilde{\text{Rec}}^\star$ which always outputs the opposite bit of $\text{Rec}^\star$ and then run Trace with access to $\widetilde{\text{Rec}}^\star$.

---

1. $\mathcal{F}_{\text{share}}$ receives $\text{ssh}_i, \{p_j(\cdot)\}_{j\in[\lambda]}$ from D and $(\text{sk}_i, \text{vk}_i)$ from P_i.
2. For every $j \in [\lambda]$, $\mathcal{F}_{\text{share}}$ samples a random $L_{i,j}$ such that $\text{ssh}_{i,j} = \langle L_{i,j}, p_j(\beta_i) \rangle$.
   - Let $R_{i,j} = p_j(\alpha_i)$. $\mathcal{F}_{\text{share}}$ sets $\text{share}_i = (\alpha_i, \beta_i, (L_{i,1}, R_{i,1}), \dots, (L_{i,\lambda}, R_{i,\lambda}))$ and sends share_i to P_i.
   - For every $j \in [\lambda]$, $\mathcal{F}_{\text{share}}$ sends $(\text{owf}(L_{i,j}), \text{Sign}(\text{owf}(L_{i,j}), \text{sk}_i))$ to D.

Fig. 1. Description of $\mathcal{F}_{\text{share}}$

Our construction works as below.

- $\text{Share}(1^\lambda, s, t, n)$: The dealer D first randomly generates $((\alpha_1, \text{ssh}_1), \dots, (\alpha_n, \text{ssh}_n))$ which are valid t-Shamir shares of secret s. For each $j \in [\lambda]$, D repeatedly samples a random polynomial $p_j(\cdot) \in \mathbb{F}[X]$ of degree at most $t-1$ until $p_j(\cdot)$ satisfies that $p_j(\beta_i) \neq 0$ for all $i \in [n]$.[5] Here, $p_j(\beta_i)$ is used as "R_j" for P_i. See more discussion in the second step of Sect. 2.2. We require $p_j(\beta_i) \neq 0$ to ensure that the inner-product $\langle L_{i,j}, p_j(\beta_i) \rangle$ in Fig. 1 is not a constant 0.
  For every player P_i, let $\text{ssh}_i = (\text{ssh}_{i,1}, \dots, \text{ssh}_{i,\lambda})$ where $\text{ssh}_{i,j} \in \{0,1\}$. The dealer D and P_i query $\mathcal{F}_{\text{share}}$ which is described in Fig. 1.
  Let $\text{view}_D = (\{\text{vk}_i\}_{i\in[n]}, \{(\text{owf}(L_{i,j}), \text{Sign}(\text{owf}(L_{i,j}), \text{sk}_i))\}_{i\in[n],j\in[\lambda]}, \{(\alpha_i, \text{ssh}_i)\}_{i\in[n]}, \{p_j(\cdot)\}_{j\in[\lambda]}, \{\beta_i\}_{i\in[n]})$.
- $\text{Rec}(\text{share}_{i_1}, \dots, \text{share}_{i_t})$: For $k \in [t]$, parse share_{i_k} as $(\alpha_{i_k}, \beta_{i_k}, (L_{i_k,1}, R_{i_k,1}), \dots, (L_{i_k,\lambda}, R_{i_k,\lambda}))$. For $j \in [\lambda]$, compute the polynomial $p_j(\cdot) \in \mathbb{F}[X]$ of degree at most $t-1$ such that $p_j(\alpha_{i_k}) = R_{i_k,j}$ for all $k \in [t]$. For $k \in [t]$ and $j \in [\lambda]$, let $\text{ssh}_{i_k,j} = \langle L_{i_k,j}, p_j(\beta_{i_k}) \rangle$ and $\text{ssh}_{i_k} = (\text{ssh}_{i_k,1}, \dots, \text{ssh}_{i_k,\lambda})$. Then reconstruct the secret s by using the reconstruction of the Shamir secret sharing scheme on $(\alpha_{i_1}, \text{ssh}_{i_1}), \dots, (\alpha_{i_t}, \text{ssh}_{i_t})$.

---

[5] We note that $\text{Share}(1^\lambda, s, t, n)$ is an expected probabilistic polynomial time algorithm. However, it can be made strict polynomial time with negligible error probability.

– $\mathsf{Trace}^{\mathsf{Rec}^*}(f_1, \ldots, f_n, f_1(\mathsf{share}_1), \ldots, f_n(\mathsf{share}_n), \mathsf{view}_D, s_0, s_1)$: Recall that:

$$\Pr_{\mathsf{Share}(s_0, t, n)}[\mathsf{Rec}^*(f_1(\mathsf{share}_1), \ldots, f_n(\mathsf{share}_n)) = 0] -$$

$$\Pr_{\mathsf{Share}(s_1, t, n)}[\mathsf{Rec}^*(f_1(\mathsf{share}_1), \ldots, f_n(\mathsf{share}_n)) = 0] \geq \epsilon.$$

For $i \in \{t, \ldots, n\}$ and $j \in \{0, \ldots, 2\lambda\}$, we define the distribution $\mathsf{Hyb}_{i,j}$ as follows:[6]

- If $j \leq \lambda$, $((\alpha_1, \mathsf{ssh}'_1), \ldots, (\alpha_{i-1}, \mathsf{ssh}'_{i-1}), (\alpha_i, \mathsf{ssh}''_i), (\alpha_{i+1}, \mathsf{ssh}'_{i+1}), \ldots, (\alpha_n, \mathsf{ssh}'_n))$ are sampled randomly such that $((\alpha_1, \mathsf{ssh}'_1), \ldots, (\alpha_{i-1}, \mathsf{ssh}'_{i-1}))$ are valid t-Shamir shares of s_1 and $((\alpha_1, \mathsf{ssh}'_1), \ldots, (\alpha_{t-1}, \mathsf{ssh}'_{t-1}), (\alpha_i, \mathsf{ssh}''_i), (\alpha_{i+1}, \mathsf{ssh}'_{i+1}), \ldots, (\alpha_n, \mathsf{ssh}'_n))$ are valid t-Shamir shares of s_0. Then the first j bits of ssh''_i are replaced by random bits. Let ssh'_i be ssh''_i after replacement. $p'_1, \ldots, p'_\lambda$ are then sampled in the same way as that in $\mathsf{Share}(1^\lambda, s, t, n)$. $(\mathsf{share}'_1, \ldots, \mathsf{share}'_n)$ are generated in the same way as that in $\mathcal{F}_{\mathsf{share}}$.
- If $j > \lambda$, $((\alpha_1, \mathsf{ssh}'_1), \ldots, (\alpha_{i-1}, \mathsf{ssh}'_{i-1}), (\alpha_i, \mathsf{ssh}''_i), (\alpha_{i+1}, \mathsf{ssh}'_{i+1}), \ldots, (\alpha_n, \mathsf{ssh}'_n))$ are sampled randomly such that $((\alpha_1, \mathsf{ssh}'_1), \ldots, (\alpha_{i-1}, \mathsf{ssh}'_{i-1}), (\alpha_i, \mathsf{ssh}''_i))$ are valid t-Shamir shares of s_1 and $((\alpha_1, \mathsf{ssh}'_1), \ldots, (\alpha_{t-1}, \mathsf{ssh}'_{t-1}), (\alpha_{i+1}, \mathsf{ssh}'_{i+1}), \ldots, (\alpha_n, \mathsf{ssh}'_n))$ are valid t-Shamir shares of s_0. Then the first $2\lambda - j$ bits of ssh''_i are replaced by random bits. Let ssh'_i be ssh''_i after replacement. $p'_1, \ldots, p'_\lambda$ are then sampled in the same way as that in $\mathsf{Share}(1^\lambda, s, t, n)$. $(\mathsf{share}'_1, \ldots, \mathsf{share}'_n)$ are generated in the same way as that in $\mathcal{F}_{\mathsf{share}}$.

Let $\eta(\epsilon) = \frac{\epsilon}{Cn\lambda}$ where $C = \mathsf{poly}(\lambda)$. Let $\mathsf{Inv}^{\mathsf{Ora}(X, \star)}$ be the algorithm in the Goldreich-Levin Lemma, where $\mathsf{Ora}(X, \star)$ is an oracle with X hard-coded and X is an element in $\mathbb{F}$, such that $\Pr[Y \sim \mathbb{F} : \mathsf{Ora}(X, Y) = \langle X, Y \rangle] \geq 1/2 + \eta(\epsilon)/2$.

For every $i \in \{t, \ldots, n\}$ and $j \in \{1, \ldots, \lambda\}$, Trace starts running $\mathsf{Inv}^{\mathsf{Ora}(L_{i,j}, \star)}(\mathsf{owf}(L_{i,j}))$ by simulating the access to $\mathsf{Ora}(L_{i,j}, \star)$ as below:

- On receiving a query Y, if $Y = 0$, Trace outputs 0. Otherwise, Trace randomly generates $(\mathsf{share}'_1, \ldots, \mathsf{share}'_{i-1}, \mathsf{share}'_{i+1}, \ldots, \mathsf{share}'_n)$ such that, after combining with share_i (which is unknown to Trace), it is a sample in $\mathsf{Hyb}_{i,j}$ and $p'_j(\beta_i) = Y$, $p'_k(\beta_i) = p_k(\beta_i)$ for $k > j$.
  To this end, Trace randomly samples ssh''_i such that $\mathsf{ssh}''_{i,k} = \mathsf{ssh}_{i,k}$ for $k > j$. Then randomly sample $(\mathsf{ssh}'_1, \ldots, \mathsf{ssh}'_{t-1}, \mathsf{ssh}'_{i+1}, \ldots, \mathsf{ssh}'_n)$ such that $((\alpha_1, \mathsf{ssh}'_1), \ldots, (\alpha_{t-1}, \mathsf{ssh}'_{t-1}), (\alpha_i, \mathsf{ssh}''_i), (\alpha_{i+1}, \mathsf{ssh}'_{i+1}), \ldots, (\alpha_n, \mathsf{ssh}'_n))$ are valid t-Shamir shares of s_0, and after that, generate $(\mathsf{ssh}'_t, \ldots, \mathsf{ssh}'_{i-1})$ such that $((\alpha_1, \mathsf{ssh}'_1), \ldots, (\alpha_{i-1}, \mathsf{ssh}'_{i-1}))$ are valid t-Shamir shares of s_1.
  For $k < j$, it repeatedly samples a random polynomial $p'_k(\cdot) \in \mathbb{F}[X]$ of degree at most $t - 1$ such that $p'_k(\alpha_i) = p_k(\alpha_i)$ (recall that $R_{i,k} = p_k(\alpha_i)$ is a component in share_i) until $p'_k(\cdot)$ satisfies that $p'_k(\beta_1), \ldots p'_k(\beta_n)$ are non-zero.

---

[6] We intentionally choose the index i starting from t since the first $t - 1$ shares in the Shamir sharing of s_0 and s_1 are identical and uniformly distributed.

For $k = j$, it repeatedly samples a random polynomial $p'_k(\cdot) \in \mathbb{F}[X]$ of degree at most $t-1$ such that $p'_k(\alpha_i) = p_k(\alpha_i)$ and $p'_k(\beta_i) = Y \neq 0$ until $p'_k(\cdot)$ satisfies that $p'_k(\beta_1), \ldots p'_k(\beta_n)$ are non-zero.

For $k > j$, it repeatedly samples a random polynomial $p'_k(\cdot) \in \mathbb{F}[X]$ of degree at most $t-1$ such that $p'_k(\alpha_i) = p_k(\alpha_i)$ and $p'_k(\beta_i) = p_k(\beta_i) \neq 0$ until $p'_k(\cdot)$ satisfies that $p'_k(\beta_1), \ldots p'_k(\beta_n)$ are non-zero.

Then, $\mathsf{share}'_1, \ldots, \mathsf{share}'_{i-1}, \mathsf{share}'_{i+1}, \ldots, \mathsf{share}'_n$ are generated in the same way as that in $\mathcal{F}_{\mathsf{share}}$.

- Let $\mathsf{share}'_i = \mathsf{share}_i$. Note that $f_i(\mathsf{share}'_i) = f_i(\mathsf{share}_i)$ is known to Trace. Let $b = \mathsf{Rec}^\star(f_1(\mathsf{share}'_1), \ldots, f_n(\mathsf{share}'_n))$. Intuitively, b indicates whether the sharing is in $\mathsf{Hyb}_{i,j-1}$ or $\mathsf{Hyb}_{i,j}$. See the formal analysis in the full version of this paper. Output $b \oplus \mathsf{ssh}''_{i,j}$, where $\mathsf{ssh}''_{i,j}$ is the j-th bit of ssh''_i which was generated in the last step.

Then Trace receives the output of $L'_{i,j} = \mathsf{Inv}^{\mathsf{Ora}(L_{i,j},\star)}(\mathsf{owf}(L_{i,j}))$ and checks that whether $\mathsf{owf}(L_{i,j}) = \mathsf{owf}(L'_{i,j})$. If they are the same, Trace adds $(i, (j, L'_{i,j}))$ into the output list.

For every $i \in \{t, \ldots, n\}$ and $j \in \{\lambda, \ldots, 2\lambda - 1\}$, Trace starts running $\mathsf{Inv}^{\mathsf{Ora}(L_{i,2\lambda-j},\star)}(\mathsf{owf}(L_{i,2\lambda-j}))$ by simulating the access to $\mathsf{Ora}(L_{i,2\lambda-j}, \star)$ as below:

- On receiving a query Y, if $Y = 0$, Trace outputs 0. Otherwise, Trace randomly generates $(\mathsf{share}'_1, \ldots, \mathsf{share}'_{i-1}, \mathsf{share}'_{i+1}, \ldots, \mathsf{share}'_n)$ such that, after combining with share_i (which is unknown to Trace), it is a sample in $\mathsf{Hyb}_{i,j}$ and $p'_{2\lambda-j}(\beta_i) = Y$, $p'_k(\beta_i) = p_k(\beta_i)$ for $k > 2\lambda - j$.

  To this end, Trace randomly samples ssh''_i such that $\mathsf{ssh}''_{i,k} = \mathsf{ssh}_{i,k}$ for $k > 2\lambda - j$. Then randomly sample $(\mathsf{ssh}'_1, \ldots, \mathsf{ssh}'_{i-1})$ such that $((\alpha_1, \mathsf{ssh}'_1), \ldots, (\alpha_{i-1}, \mathsf{ssh}'_{i-1}), (\alpha_i, \mathsf{ssh}''_i))$ are valid t-Shamir shares of s_1, and after that, generate $(\mathsf{ssh}'_{i+1}, \ldots, \mathsf{ssh}'_n)$ such that $((\alpha_1, \mathsf{ssh}'_1), \ldots, (\alpha_{t-1}, \mathsf{ssh}'_{t-1}), (\alpha_{i+1}, \mathsf{ssh}'_{i+1}), \ldots, (\alpha_n, \mathsf{ssh}'_n))$ are valid t-Shamir shares of s_0.

  For $k < 2\lambda - j$, repeated sample a random polynomial $p'_k(\cdot) \in \mathbb{F}[X]$ of degree at most $t-1$ such that $p'_k(\alpha_i) = p_k(\alpha_i)$ (recall that $R_{i,k} = p_k(\alpha_i)$ is a component in share_i) until $p'_k(\cdot)$ satisfies that $p'_k(\beta_1), \ldots p'_k(\beta_n)$ are non-zero.

  For $k = 2\lambda - j$, repeated sample a random polynomial $p'_k(\cdot) \in \mathbb{F}[X]$ of degree at most $t-1$ such that $p'_k(\alpha_i) = p_k(\alpha_i)$ and $p'_k(\beta_i) = Y \neq 0$ until $p'_k(\cdot)$ satisfies that $p'_k(\beta_1), \ldots p'_k(\beta_n)$ are non-zero.

  For $k > 2\lambda - j$, repeated sample a random polynomial $p'_k(\cdot) \in \mathbb{F}[X]$ of degree at most $t-1$ such that $p'_k(\alpha_i) = p_k(\alpha_i)$ and $p'_k(\beta_i) = p_k(\beta_i) \neq 0$ until $p'_k(\cdot)$ satisfies that $p'_k(\beta_1), \ldots p'_k(\beta_n)$ are non-zero.

  Then, $\mathsf{share}'_1, \ldots, \mathsf{share}'_{i-1}, \mathsf{share}'_{i+1}, \ldots, \mathsf{share}'_n$ are generated in the same way as that in $\mathcal{F}_{\mathsf{share}}$.

- Let $\mathsf{share}'_i = \mathsf{share}_i$. Note that $f_i(\mathsf{share}'_i) = f_i(\mathsf{share}_i)$ is known to Trace. Let $b = \mathsf{Rec}^\star(f_1(\mathsf{share}'_1), \ldots, f_n(\mathsf{share}'_n))$. Intuitively, b indicates whether the sharing is in $\mathsf{Hyb}_{i,j}$ or $\mathsf{Hyb}_{i,j+1}$. See the formal analysis in the full version of this paper. Output $\bar{b} \oplus \mathsf{ssh}''_{i,2\lambda-j}$, where $\mathsf{ssh}''_{i,2\lambda-j}$ is the $(2\lambda - j)$-th bit of ssh''_i which was generated in the last step.

Then Trace receives the output of $L'_{i,2\lambda-j} = \text{Inv}^{\text{Ora}(L_{i,2\lambda-j},\star)}(\text{owf}(L_{i,2\lambda-j}))$
and checks that whether $\text{owf}(L_{i,2\lambda-j}) = \text{owf}(L'_{i,2\lambda-j})$. If they are the same,
Trace adds $(i, (2\lambda - j, L'_{i,2\lambda-j}))$ into the output list.
In the end, if the output list is empty, Trace outputs $\bot$. Otherwise, Trace
outputs the first pair $(i, (j, L'_{i,j}))$ in the output list.

- Judge$(i^\star, \pi_{i^\star}, \text{view}_D)$: Judge first parses $\pi_{i^\star}$ as $(j, L'_{i^\star,j})$. Then output
  Verify$(\text{owf}(L'_{i^\star,j}), \sigma_{i^\star,j}, \text{vk}_{i^\star})$ where $\sigma_{i^\star,j}$ is the signature available from view_D.

Proof and Extensions. In the full version of this paper, (1) we give the formal
proof of our construction, (2) we show how to improve the tracing probability of
our construction, (3) we extend our construction to the collision-resistant setting
and tracing more than one servers, and (4) we show the parallel composition of
our construction. We refer the readers to the full version of this paper for more
details.

5 Traceable Multi-server Delegation of Computation

In this section, we define and construct a traceable multi-server delegation of
computation from our traceable secret sharing. A traceable multi-server delegation of computation is an offline-online protocol between a client and n servers
denoted by $P_1, \ldots, P_n$. In the offline phase, the client's input is a circuit C and
it engages in a protocol with the severs. In the online phase, the client learns the
input x and sends a single message to each of the servers. The servers engage in a
protocol and at the end of the protocol, each server sends a single message back
to the client. The client reconstructs $C(x)$ from these messages. We require the
online computational cost of the client to only grow with the input and output
length and is otherwise, independent of the size of the circuit. Let us denote the
view of the i-th server with $\text{view}_i(C, x)$ and the view of the client as $\text{view}_D(C, x)$.
When it is clear from the context, we use view_i to denote $\text{view}_i(C, x)$. We say
$(\Pi, \text{Trace}, \text{Judge})$ (where Trace and Judge have the same semantics of the secret
sharing scheme) to be a traceable delegation of computation if it satisfies the
following properties.

Definition 2. *An offline-online multi-server delegation of computation proto-
col $(\Pi, \text{Trace}, \text{Judge})$ with threshold t is said to be δ-traceable if it satisfies the
following properties.*

- **Correctness.** *The correctness requirement states that for every circuit C and
  every input x, the client reconstructs $C(x)$ with probability 1.*
- **Security.** *For every circuit and any two inputs x_0, x_1 and for any subset T
  of the servers of size at most $t - 1$, we require that*

$$\text{view}_T(C, x_0) \approx_s \text{view}_T(C, x_1)$$

- **Traceability.** *If there exists a set of n collector functions $f_1, \ldots, f_n$ (where
  f_i is a constant function if P_i is honest) and a pirate reconstruction box $\text{Rec}^\star$
  such that for two inputs x_0, x_1,*

$$\left| \Pr_{\Pi(C,x_0)}[\text{Rec}^\star(f_1(\text{view}_1), \ldots, f_n(\text{view}_n)) = 0] - \Pr_{\Pi(C,x_1)}[\text{Rec}^\star(f_1(\text{view}_1), \ldots, f_n(\text{view}_n)) = 0] \right| \geq \epsilon$$

then,

$$\Pr[(\mathsf{view}_1, \ldots, \mathsf{view}_n, \mathsf{view}_D) \leftarrow \Pi(C, x_0);$$
$$(i^*, \pi_{i^*}) \leftarrow \mathsf{Trace}^{\mathsf{Rec}^*}(f_1, \ldots, f_n, f_1(\mathsf{view}_1), \ldots, f_n(\mathsf{view}_n), \mathsf{view}_D, x_0, x_1) :$$
$$\mathsf{Judge}(i^*, \pi_{i^*}, \mathsf{view}_D) = \mathsf{guilty}] \geq \delta(\epsilon)$$

Furthermore, the number of queries that Trace *makes to the pirate reconstruction box* Rec* *is* $\mathrm{poly}(|C|, \lambda, 1/\epsilon)$.

- **Non-imputability.** *For any circuit C and input x, an honest server P_{i^*} and any computationally bounded client $\widetilde{D}$,*

$$\Pr_{\Pi(C,x)}[(\mathsf{view}_D', i^*, \pi_{i^*}) \leftarrow \widetilde{D}(\mathsf{view}_D, \mathsf{view}_{[n] \setminus \{i^*\}}) : \mathsf{Judge}(i^*, \pi_{i^*}, \mathsf{view}_D') = \mathsf{guilty}] \leq \mathrm{negl}(\lambda)$$

5.1   The Protocol

In this subsection, we give the details of our traceable delegation of computation.

- **Offline Phase.** In the offline phase, the client receives the circuit C and does the following.
  1. For every wire w of the circuit C, the client chooses a random mask $r_w \leftarrow \{0, 1\}$. We assume the input wires are labeled from 1 to ℓ.
  2. For every gate g of the circuit with input wires i and j and the output wire k, the client generates a table with 4 entries where each entry is labeled with $(a, b) \in \{0, 1\} \times \{0, 1\}$. The (a, b)-th entry of the gate table is given by $g(a \oplus r_i, b \oplus r_j) \oplus r_k$.
  3. For every gate g and every entry of the gate table, the client and the servers run the sharing protocol of a t-out-of-n traceable secret sharing. Let $\mathsf{share}_i^{g,a,b}$ be the i-th share corresponding to the (a, b)-th entry of the gate g.
- **Online Phase.** In the online phase, the client receives its input x and sends $x \oplus r_{[\ell]}$ to each of the servers. The servers now starting running the online protocol. For every gate g (in the topological order),
  1. The servers hold $y_i \oplus r_j$ and $y_j \oplus r_j$ where y_i, y_j are the values carried by the i and j-th wires when the circuit C is evaluated on input x.
  2. Now, the i-th server parses $\mathsf{share}_i^{g, y_i \oplus r_i, y_j \oplus r_j}$ as $(\alpha_i, \beta_i, (L_{i,1}, R_{i,1}), \ldots, (L_{i,\lambda}, R_{i,\lambda}))$. The servers first exchange $R_{i,1}, \ldots, R_{i,\lambda}$ to each other. For $j \in [\lambda]$, the servers compute the polynomial $p_j(\cdot) \in \mathbb{F}[X]$ of degree at most $t - 1$ such that $p_j(\alpha_i) = R_{i,j}$ for all $i \in [n]$. For every $j \in [\lambda]$, the i-th server computes $\mathsf{ssh}_{i,j} = \langle L_{i,j}, p_j(\beta_i) \rangle$ and $\mathsf{ssh}_i = (\mathsf{ssh}_{i,1}, \ldots, \mathsf{ssh}_{i,\lambda})$. The servers then broadcast the values of ssh_i and use the reconstruction of the Shamir secret sharing scheme to obtain $g(y_i, y_j) \oplus r_k = y_k \oplus r_k$.
  The servers finally send the masked values of the output to the client, who removes the output masks to learn $C(x)$.
- **Tracing algorithm.** Given $f_1, \ldots, f_n$, $f_1(\mathsf{view}_1), \ldots, f_n(\mathsf{view}_n)$, the view of the client view_C, two inputs x_0, x_1 and oracle access to a reconstruction box Rec*, the tracing algorithm does the following.

1. It defines a sequence of hybrid distributions $\mathsf{Hyb}_{g,a,b}$ (starting from $\Pi(C, x_0)$) for every gate g and $(a, b) \in \{0, 1\} \times \{0, 1\}$ such that every $g' < g$ (with input wires i', j' and output wire k'), we change all the gate entries to $g(y_{i'} \oplus r_{i'}, y_{j'} \oplus r_{j'}) \oplus r_{k'}$. Further, for all entries that are less than (a, b) in the gate table of g (w.r.t. to some ordering), we change those entries to $g(y_i \oplus r_i, y_j \oplus r_j) \oplus r_k$. Notice that $\mathsf{Hyb}_{|C|,1,1}$ is independent of x_0 and hence, symmetrically, it defines $\mathsf{Hyb}'_{g,a,b}$ from $\Pi(C, x_1)$ where $\mathsf{Hyb}_{|C|,1,1} \equiv \mathsf{Hyb}'_{|C|,1,1}$.

2. Notice that for any two intermediate hybrids in this sequence, the only difference is in the value that was secret shared in a particular gate entry. Thus, the tracing algorithm fixes the secret shares of all other gate entries and runs the corresponding tracing algorithm for the secret sharing scheme where the two secrets are the two different values in the subsequent hybrids corresponding to this gate table entry. It repeats this process for every subsequent hybrid in the sequence. If in some iteration it succeeds in extracting a valid evidence from a party, it stops and outputs the evidence.

– **Judge algorithm.** The judge algorithm for the MPC runs the corresponding judge algorithm of the secret sharing scheme and outputs whatever it outputs.

Theorem 4. *If the protocol described above is instantiated with a δ-traceable secret sharing scheme, then it is an offline-online $\delta(\epsilon/8|C|)$-traceable n server delegation protocol with threshold t for a circuit C.*

Proof. The correctness of the protocol is easy to observe and we now show security, traceability and non-imputability.

Security. To show security, we need to show that for any two inputs x_0, x_1 and for any subset $T \subseteq [n]$ of size at most $t - 1$, we have

$$\mathsf{view}_T(C, x_0) \approx_s \mathsf{view}_T(C, x_1).$$

We show security through a hybrid argument.

– Hyb_0 : This corresponds to $\mathsf{view}_T(C, x_0)$.
– Hyb_1 : In this hybrid, we generate the sharings of the gate entries differently. For every gate g with input wires i, j and output wire k, we generate the (a, b)-th entry for every $(a, b) \neq (y_i \oplus r_i, y_j \oplus r_j)$ as a secret sharing of 0. We output the view of the T servers. We note that $\mathsf{Hyb}_0 \approx_s \mathsf{Hyb}_1$ from the privacy of traceable secret sharing scheme.
– Hyb_2 : In this hybrid, for every wire i, we set $y_i \oplus r_i$ as an independently chosen random value. Hyb_2 is identically distributed to Hyb_1. Notice Hyb_2 is independent of the input x_0.

Via an identical argument, we can show that $\mathsf{view}_T(C, x_1)$ is computationally close to Hyb_2. This proves security.

Traceability. Let us fix the collector functions $f_1, \ldots, f_n$ and a pirate reconstruction box Rec^* such that for two inputs x_0, x_1,

$$| \Pr_{\Pi(C, x_0)}[\mathsf{Rec}^*(f_1(\mathsf{view}_1), \ldots, f_n(\mathsf{view}_n)) = 0] - \Pr_{\Pi(C, x_1)}[\mathsf{Rec}^*(f_1(\mathsf{view}_1), \ldots, f_n(\mathsf{view}_n)) = 0]| \geq \epsilon.$$

We now define a sequence of $4|C|$ hybrids starting from $\Pi(C, x_0)$. Specifically, for every gate g (with input wires i, j and output wire k) and $(a, b) \in \{0, 1\} \times \{0, 1\}$, we define $\mathsf{Hyb}_{g,a,b}$ where as a distribution where for every $g' < g$ (with input wires i', j' and output wire k'), we change all the gate entries to $g(y_{i'} \oplus r_{i'}, y_{j'} \oplus r_{j'}) \oplus r'_{k'}$. Further, for all entries that are less than (a, b) in the gate table of g (w.r.t. to some ordering), we change those entries to $g(y_i \oplus r_i, y_j \oplus r_j) \oplus r_k$. Note that once we make this change for every gate entry, the final hybrid is independent of x_0 and hence, we can reverse these hybrids one by one to get $\Pi(C, x_1)$. Without loss of generality, let us assume that

$$| \Pr_{\Pi(C, x_0)}[\mathsf{Rec}^*(f_1(\mathsf{view}_1), \ldots, f_n(\mathsf{view}_n)) = 0] - \Pr_{\mathsf{Hyb}_{|C|,1,1}}[\mathsf{Rec}^*(f_1(\mathsf{view}_1), \ldots, f_n(\mathsf{view}_n)) = 0]| \geq \epsilon/2$$

By an averaging argument, we infer that there exists two intermediate hybrids, Hyb and Hyb' in the sequence such that

$$| \Pr_{\mathsf{Hyb}}[\mathsf{Rec}^*(f_1(\mathsf{view}_1), \ldots, f_n(\mathsf{view}_n)) = 0] - \Pr_{\mathsf{Hyb}'}[\mathsf{Rec}^*(f_1(\mathsf{view}_1), \ldots, f_n(\mathsf{view}_n)) = 0]| \geq \epsilon/(8|C|)$$

Notice that the only difference between Hyb and Hyb' is the value that was secret shared in a particular gate entry. Thus, it follows from the traceability of the underlying secret sharing scheme, that the MPC tracing algorithm outputs a valid evidence against a party with probability at least $\delta(\epsilon/(8|C|))$.

Non-imputability. Note that the offline view of the servers consists of the views of $4|C|$ different sharings of our traceable secret sharing scheme. Further, observe that the messages sent during step 2 of the online phase can be simulated using view_D. The non-imputability property follows directly from the underlying traceable secret sharing, as we can correctly guess the particular secret for which an adversarial dealer gives the correct evidence with $1/(4|C|\lambda)$ probability and hardcode the one-way function challenge in this position.

Acknowledgments. V. Goyal, Y. Song—Supported in part by the NSF award 1916939, DARPA SIEVE program, a gift from Ripple, a DoE NETL award, a JP Morgan Faculty Fellowship, a PNC center for financial services innovation award, and a Cylab seed funding award.

A. Srinivasan—Work partially done while at UC Berkeley and visiting CMU. Supported in part by AFOSR Award FA9550-19-1-0200, AFOSR YIP Award, NSF CNS Award 1936826, DARPA/ARL SAFEWARE Award W911NF15C0210, a Hellman Award and research grants by the Sloan Foundation, Okawa Foundation, Visa Inc., and Center for Long-Term Cybersecurity (CLTC, UC Berkeley). The views expressed are those of the authors and do not reflect the official policy or position of the funding agencies.

References

[ACM17] ACM. ACM Paris Kanellakis Theory and Practice Award. Press Release, May 2017. https://awards.acm.org/binaries/content/assets/press-releases/2017/may/technical-awards-2016a.pdf

[ADN+19] Aggarwal, D., et al.: Stronger leakage-resilient and non-malleable secret sharing schemes for general access structures. In: Boldyreva, A., Micciancio, D. (eds.) CRYPTO 2019. LNCS, vol. 11693, pp. 510–539. Springer, Cham (2019). https://doi.org/10.1007/978-3-030-26951-7_18

[BF99] Boneh, D., Franklin, M.: An efficient public key traitor tracing scheme. In: Wiener, M. (ed.) CRYPTO 1999. LNCS, vol. 1666, pp. 338–353. Springer, Heidelberg (1999). https://doi.org/10.1007/3-540-48405-1_22

[Bla79] Blakley, G.R.: Safeguarding cryptographic keys. In: Proceedings of the AFIPS 1979 National Computer Conference, vol. 48, pp. 313–317 (1979)

[BMR90] Beaver, D., Micali, S., Rogaway, P.: The round complexity of secure protocols (extended abstract). In: 22nd Annual ACM Symposium on Theory of Computing, pp. 503–513. ACM Press, May 1990

[BN08] Boneh, D., Naor, M.: Traitor tracing with constant size ciphertext. In: Ning, P., Syverson, P.F., Jha, S. (eds.) ACM CCS 08: 15th Conference on Computer and Communications Security, pp. 501–510. ACM Press, October 2008

[BOGW88] Ben-Or, M., Goldwasser, S., Wigderson, A.: Completeness theorems for non-cryptographic fault-tolerant distributed computation (extended abstract). In: 20th Annual ACM Symposium on Theory of Computing, pp. 1–10. ACM Press, May 1988

[BS95] Boneh, D., Shaw, J.: Collusion-secure fingerprinting for digital data. In: Coppersmith, D. (ed.) CRYPTO 1995. LNCS, vol. 963, pp. 452–465. Springer, Heidelberg (1995). https://doi.org/10.1007/3-540-44750-4_36

[BSW06] Boneh, D., Sahai, A., Waters, B.: Fully collusion resistant traitor tracing with short ciphertexts and private keys. In: Vaudenay, S. (ed.) EUROCRYPT 2006. LNCS, vol. 4004, pp. 573–592. Springer, Heidelberg (2006). https://doi.org/10.1007/11761679_34

[BW06] Boneh, D., Waters, B.: A fully collusion resistant broadcast, trace, and revoke system. In: Juels, A., Wright, R.N., De Capitani di Vimercati, S. (eds.) ACM CCS 06: 13th Conference on Computer and Communications Security, pp. 211–220. ACM Press, October/November 2006

[BZ14] Boneh, D., Zhandry, M.: Multiparty key exchange, efficient traitor tracing, and more from indistinguishability obfuscation. In: Garay, J.A., Gennaro, R. (eds.) CRYPTO 2014. LNCS, vol. 8616, pp. 480–499. Springer, Heidelberg (2014). https://doi.org/10.1007/978-3-662-44371-2_27

[CFN94] Chor, B., Fiat, A., Naor, M.: Tracing traitors. In: Desmedt, Y.G. (ed.) CRYPTO 1994. LNCS, vol. 839, pp. 257–270. Springer, Heidelberg (1994). https://doi.org/10.1007/3-540-48658-5_25

[CPP05] Chabanne, H., Phan, D.H., Pointcheval, D.: Public traceability in traitor tracing schemes. In: Cramer, R. (ed.) EUROCRYPT 2005. LNCS, vol. 3494, pp. 542–558. Springer, Heidelberg (2005). https://doi.org/10.1007/11426639_32

[DDFY94] De Santis, A., Desmedt, Y., Frankel, Y., Yung, M.: How to share a function securely. In: 26th Annual ACM Symposium on Theory of Computing, pp. 522–533. ACM Press, May 1994

[DF90] Desmedt, Y., Frankel, Y.: Threshold cryptosystems. In: Brassard, G. (ed.) CRYPTO 1989. LNCS, vol. 435, pp. 307–315. Springer, New York (1990). https://doi.org/10.1007/0-387-34805-0_28

[DF03] Dodis, Y., Fazio, N.: Public key trace and revoke scheme secure against adaptive chosen ciphertext attack. In: Desmedt, Y.G. (ed.) PKC 2003. LNCS, vol. 2567, pp. 100–115. Springer, Heidelberg (2003). https://doi.org/10.1007/3-540-36288-6_8

[Fra90] Frankel, Y.: A practical protocol for large group oriented networks. In: Quisquater, J.-J., Vandewalle, J. (eds.) EUROCRYPT 1989. LNCS, vol. 434, pp. 56–61. Springer, Heidelberg (1990). https://doi.org/10.1007/3-540-46885-4_8

[FT99] Fiat, A., Tassa, T.: Dynamic traitor tracing. In: Wiener, M. (ed.) CRYPTO 1999. LNCS, vol. 1666, pp. 354–371. Springer, Heidelberg (1999). https://doi.org/10.1007/3-540-48405-1_23

[GKW18] Goyal, R., Koppula, V., Waters, B.: Collusion resistant traitor tracing from learning with errors. In: Diakonikolas, I., Kempe, D., Henzinger, M. (eds.) 50th Annual ACM Symposium on Theory of Computing, pp. 660–670. ACM Press, June 2018

[GL89] Goldreich, O., Levin, L.A.: A hard-core predicate for all one-way functions. In: 21st Annual ACM Symposium on Theory of Computing, pp. 25–32. ACM Press, May 1989

[GLSW08] Goyal, V., Lu, S., Sahai, A., Waters, B.: Black-box accountable authority identity-based encryption. In: Ning, P., Syverson, P.F., Jha, S. (eds.) ACM CCS 08: 15th Conference on Computer and Communications Security, pp. 427–436. ACM Press, October 2008

[GMW87] Goldreich, O., Micali, S., Wigderson, A.: How to play any mental game or A completeness theorem for protocols with honest majority. In: Aho, A. (eds.) 19th Annual ACM Symposium on Theory of Computing, pp. 218–229. ACM Press, May 1987

[Goy07] Goyal, V.: Reducing trust in the PKG in identity based cryptosystems. In: Menezes, A. (ed.) CRYPTO 2007. LNCS, vol. 4622, pp. 430–447. Springer, Heidelberg (2007). https://doi.org/10.1007/978-3-540-74143-5_24

[IK00] Ishai, Y., Kushilevitz, E.: Randomizing polynomials: a new representation with applications to round-efficient secure computation. In: 41st Annual Symposium on Foundations of Computer Science, pp. 294–304. IEEE Computer Society Press, November 2000

[KD98] Kurosawa, K., Desmedt, Y.: Optimum traitor tracing and asymmetric schemes. In: Nyberg, K. (ed.) EUROCRYPT 1998. LNCS, vol. 1403, pp. 145–157. Springer, Heidelberg (1998). https://doi.org/10.1007/BFb0054123

[KY01] Kiayias, A., Yung, M.: Self protecting pirates and black-box traitor tracing. In: Kilian, J. (ed.) CRYPTO 2001. LNCS, vol. 2139, pp. 63–79. Springer, Heidelberg (2001). https://doi.org/10.1007/3-540-44647-8_4

[KY02] Kiayias, A., Yung, M.: Traitor tracing with constant transmission rate. In: Knudsen, L.R. (ed.) EUROCRYPT 2002. LNCS, vol. 2332, pp. 450–465. Springer, Heidelberg (2002). https://doi.org/10.1007/3-540-46035-7_30

[NNL01] Naor, D., Naor, M., Lotspiech, J.: Revocation and tracing schemes for stateless receivers. In: Kilian, J. (ed.) CRYPTO 2001. LNCS, vol. 2139, pp. 41–62. Springer, Heidelberg (2001). https://doi.org/10.1007/3-540-44647-8_3

[NP98]   Naor, M., Pinkas, B.: Threshold traitor tracing. In: Krawczyk, H. (ed.) CRYPTO 1998. LNCS, vol. 1462, pp. 502–517. Springer, Heidelberg (1998). https://doi.org/10.1007/BFb0055750

[NP01]   Naor, M., Pinkas, B.: Efficient trace and revoke schemes. In: Frankel, Y. (ed.) FC 2000. LNCS, vol. 1962, pp. 1–20. Springer, Heidelberg (2001). https://doi.org/10.1007/3-540-45472-1_1

[NWZ16] Nishimaki, R., Wichs, D., Zhandry, M.: Anonymous traitor tracing: how to embed arbitrary information in a key. In: Fischlin, M., Coron, J.-S. (eds.) EUROCRYPT 2016. LNCS, vol. 9666, pp. 388–419. Springer, Heidelberg (2016). https://doi.org/10.1007/978-3-662-49896-5_14

[Pfi96] Pfitzmann, B.: Trials of traced traitors. In: Anderson, R. (ed.) IH 1996. LNCS, vol. 1174, pp. 49–64. Springer, Heidelberg (1996). https://doi.org/10.1007/3-540-61996-8_31

[PS96]   Pfitzmann, B., Schunter, M.: Asymmetric fingerprinting. In: Maurer, U. (ed.) EUROCRYPT 1996. LNCS, vol. 1070, pp. 84–95. Springer, Heidelberg (1996). https://doi.org/10.1007/3-540-68339-9_8

[PW97]   Pfitzmann, B., Waidner, B.: Asymmetric fingerprinting for larger collusions. In: ACM CCS 97: 4th Conference on Computer and Communications Security, pp. 151–160. ACM Press, April 1997

[Sha79] Shamir, A.: How to share a secret. Commun. ACM **22**(11), 612–613 (1979)

[SSW01] Silverberg, A., Staddon, J., Walker, J.L.: Efficient traitor tracing algorithms using list decoding. In: Boyd, C. (ed.) ASIACRYPT 2001. LNCS, vol. 2248, pp. 175–192. Springer, Heidelberg (2001). https://doi.org/10.1007/3-540-45682-1_11

[SV19]   Srinivasan, A., Vasudevan, P.N.: Leakage resilient secret sharing and applications. In: Boldyreva, A., Micciancio, D. (eds.) CRYPTO 2019. LNCS, vol. 11693, pp. 480–509. Springer, Cham (2019). https://doi.org/10.1007/978-3-030-26951-7_17

[SW00]   Safavi-Naini, R., Wang, Y.: Sequential traitor tracing. In: Bellare, M. (ed.) CRYPTO 2000. LNCS, vol. 1880, pp. 316–332. Springer, Heidelberg (2000). https://doi.org/10.1007/3-540-44598-6_20

[Tar03] Tardos, G.: Optimal probabilistic fingerprint codes. In: 35th Annual ACM Symposium on Theory of Computing, pp. 116–125. ACM Press, June 2003

Quadratic Secret Sharing and Conditional Disclosure of Secrets

Amos Beimel[1], Hussien Othman[1(✉)], and Naty Peter[2]

[1] Ben-Gurion University of the Negev, Be'er-Sheva, Israel
beimel@cs.bgu.ac.il, hussien@post.bgu.ac.il
[2] Tel-Aviv University, Tel-Aviv, Israel
natypeter@mail.tau.ac.il

Abstract. There is a huge gap between the upper and lower bounds on the share size of secret-sharing schemes for arbitrary n-party access structures, and consistent with our current knowledge the optimal share size can be anywhere between polynomial in n and exponential in n. For linear secret-sharing schemes, we know that the share size for almost all n-party access structures must be exponential in n. Furthermore, most constructions of efficient secret-sharing schemes are linear. We would like to study larger classes of secret-sharing schemes with two goals. On one hand, we want to prove lower bounds for larger classes of secret-sharing schemes, possibly shedding some light on the share size of general secret-sharing schemes. On the other hand, we want to construct efficient secret-sharing schemes for access structures that do not have efficient linear secret-sharing schemes. Given this motivation, Paskin-Cherniavsky and Radune (ITC'20) defined and studied a new class of secret-sharing schemes in which the shares are generated by applying degree-d polynomials to the secret and some random field elements. The special case $d = 1$ corresponds to linear and multi-linear secret-sharing schemes.

We define and study two additional classes of polynomial secret-sharing schemes: (1) schemes in which for every authorized set the reconstruction of the secret is done using polynomials and (2) schemes in which both sharing and reconstruction are done by polynomials. For linear secret-sharing schemes, schemes with linear sharing and schemes with linear reconstruction are equivalent. We give evidence that for polynomial secret-sharing schemes, schemes with polynomial sharing are probably stronger than schemes with polynomial reconstruction. We also prove lower bounds on the share size for schemes with polynomial

The work of the authors was partially supported by Israel Science Foundation grant no. 152/17 and a grant from the Cyber Security Research Center at Ben-Gurion University. Part of this work was done while the first author was visiting Georgetown University, supported by NSF grant no. 1565387, TWC: Large: Collaborative: Computing Over Distributed Sensitive Data.
A. Beimel—supported by ERC grant 742754 (project NTSC).
H. Othman—supported by a scholarship from the Israeli Council For Higher Education.
N. Peter—supported by the European Union's Horizon 2020 Programme (ERC-StG-2014-2020) under grant agreement no. 639813 ERC-CLC, and by the Rector's Office at Tel-Aviv University.

© International Association for Cryptologic Research 2021
T. Malkin and C. Peikert (Eds.): CRYPTO 2021, LNCS 12827, pp. 748–778, 2021.
https://doi.org/10.1007/978-3-030-84252-9_25

reconstruction. On the positive side, we provide constructions of secret-sharing schemes and conditional disclosure of secrets (CDS) protocols with quadratic sharing and reconstruction. We extend a construction of Liu et al. (CRYPTO'17) and construct optimal quadratic k-server CDS protocols for functions $f : [N]^k \to \{0, 1\}$ with message size $O(N^{(k-1)/3})$. We show how to transform our quadratic k-server CDS protocol to a robust CDS protocol, and use the robust CDS protocol to construct quadratic secret-sharing schemes for arbitrary access structures with share size $O(2^{0.705n})$; this is better than the best known share size of $O(2^{0.7576n})$ for linear secret-sharing schemes and worse than the best known share size of $O(2^{0.585n})$ for general secret-sharing schemes.

1   Introduction

A secret-sharing scheme is a cryptographic tool that enables a dealer holding a secret to share it among a set of parties such that only some predefined subsets of the parties (called authorized sets) can learn the secret and all the other subsets cannot get any information about the secret. The collection of authorized sets is called an access structure. These schemes were presented by Shamir [43], Blakley [21], and Ito, Saito, and Nishizeky [31] for secure storage. Nowadays, secret-sharing schemes are used in many cryptographic tasks, see, e.g., [13] for a list of applications. There are many constructions of secret-sharing schemes for specific families of access structures that have short shares, e.g., [16,19,20, 22,31,32,44]. However, in the best known secret-sharing schemes for general n-party access structures, the share size is exponential in n [5,8,35], resulting in impractical secret-sharing schemes. In contrast, the best known lower bound on the share size of a party for some n-party access structure is $\Omega(n/\log n)$ [23,24]. There is a huge gap between the upper bounds and lower bounds, and in spite of active research for more than 30 years, we lack understanding of the share size.

One of the directions to gain some understanding on the share size is to study sub-classes of secret-sharing schemes. Specifically, the class of *linear* secret-sharing schemes was studied in many papers, e.g., [11,12,15,22,26,27,32,41]. In these schemes the sharing algorithm applies a linear mapping on the secret and some random field elements to generate the shares. For linear secret-sharing schemes there are strong lower bounds, i.e., in linear secret-sharing schemes almost all n-party access structures require shares of size at least $2^{0.5n-o(n)}$ [11] and there exists explicit n-party access structures require shares of size at least $2^{\Omega(n)}$ [40–42]. It is an important question to extend these lower bounds to other classes of secret-sharing schemes. Furthermore, we would like to construct efficient secret-sharing schemes (i.e., schemes with small share size) for a richer class of access structures than the access structures that have efficient linear secret-sharing schemes (which by [32] coincide with the access structures that have a small monotone span program). Currently, only few such constructions

are known [16,44].[1] Studying broader classes of secret-sharing schemes will hope-
fully result in efficient schemes for more access structures and will develop new
techniques for constructing non-linear secret-sharing schemes. In a recent work,
Paskin-Cherniavsky and Radune [38] perused these directions – they defined and
studied a new class of secret-sharing schemes, called polynomial secret-sharing
schemes, in which the sharing algorithm applies (low-degree) polynomials on the
secret and some random field elements to generate the shares.

In this paper, we broaden the study of polynomial secret-sharing schemes and
define and study two additional classes of polynomial secret-sharing schemes –
(1) schemes in which the reconstruction algorithm, which computes the secret
from the shares of parties of an authorized set, is done by polynomials, and
(2) schemes in which both sharing and reconstruction algorithms are done by
applying polynomials. We prove lower bounds for schemes of the first type (hence
also for schemes of the second type). We then focus on *quadratic* secret-sharing
schemes – schemes in which the sharing and/or reconstruction are done by polynomials of *degree-2*, and provide constructions of such schemes that are more
efficient than linear secret-sharing schemes. Thus, we show that considering the
wider class of polynomial secret-sharing schemes gives rise to better schemes
than linear schemes.

As part of our results, we construct conditional disclosure of secrets (CDS)
protocols, a primitive that was introduced in [29]. In a k-server CDS protocol
for a Boolean function $f : [N]^k \rightarrow \{0, 1\}$, there is a set of k servers that hold a
secret s and have a common random string. In addition, each server Q_i holds
a private input $x_i \in [N]$. Each server sends one message such that a referee,
who knows the private inputs of the servers but nothing more, learns the secret
s if $f(x_1, \ldots, x_k) = 1$ and learns nothing otherwise. CDS protocols have been
used recently in [4,5,8,35] to construct the best known secret-sharing schemes
for arbitrary access structures. Continuing this line of research, we construct
quadratic k-server CDS protocols that are provably more efficient than linear
CDS protocols. We use them to construct quadratic secret-sharing schemes for
arbitrary access structures; these schemes are more efficient than the best known
linear secret-sharing schemes.

1.1 Our Contributions and Techniques

Polynomial Sharing vs. Polynomial Reconstruction. Our conceptional contribution is the distinction between three types of polynomial secret-sharing schemes:
schemes with polynomial sharing (defined in [38]), schemes with polynomial
reconstruction, and schemes in which both sharing and reconstruction are done
by polynomials. For linear secret-sharing schemes (in which the secret contains
one field element) these notions are equivalent [12,32]. In the full version of
the paper [17], we extend this equivalence to multi-linear secret-sharing schemes

---

[1] In [44] they construct efficient secret-sharing schemes for access structures that correspond to languages that have statistical zero-knowledge proofs with log-space ver-
ifiers and simulators.

(i.e., schemes in which the secret can contain more than one filed element). In Sect. 3.1, we give evidence that such equivalence does not hold for polynomial secret-sharing schemes. We show that a small variation of a secret-sharing scheme of [16] for the quadratic non-residuosity modulo a prime access structure has an efficient secret-sharing scheme with degree-3 sharing.[2] Following [16], we conjecture that the quadratic non-residuosity modulo a prime is not in NC (the class of problems that have a sequence of circuits of polynomial size and poly-logarithmic depth). By our discussion in Remark 4.6, every sequence of access structures that has efficient secret-sharing schemes with polynomial reconstruction is in NC. Thus, under the conjecture about quadratic non-residuosity modulo a prime problem, we get the desired separation.

Lower Bounds for Secret-Sharing Schemes with Degree-d Reconstruction. In Sect. 4, we show lower bounds for secret-sharing schemes with degree-d reconstruction. Using a result of [34], we show a lower bound of $\Omega(2^{n/(d+1)})$ for sharing one-bit secrets. We also show that every secret-sharing scheme with degree-d reconstruction and share size c can be converted to a multi-linear secret-sharing scheme with share size $O(c^d)$ (with the same domain of secrets). Using a lower bound on the share size of linear secret-sharing schemes over any finite field from [41], we obtain that there exists an explicit access structure such that for every finite field $\mathbb{F}$ it requires shares of size $2^{\Omega(n/d)} \log |\mathbb{F}|$ in every secret-sharing schemes over $\mathbb{F}$ with degree-d reconstruction. Furthermore, this transformation implies that every sequence of access structures that have efficient secret-sharing schemes with degree-d reconstruction for a constant d is in NC.

Quadratic Multi-server Conditional Disclosure of Secrets Protocols. Liu et al. [36] constructed a quadratic two-server CDS protocol for any function $f : [N]^2 \rightarrow \{0, 1\}$ with message size $O(N^{1/3})$. In Sect. 5, we construct quadratic k-server CDS protocols with message size $O(N^{(k-1)/3})$. By our lower bounds from Sect. 4, this is the optimal message size for quadratic CDS protocols. Our construction uses the two-server CDS protocol of [36] (denoted $\mathcal{P}_{\mathrm{LVW}}$) to construct the k-server CDS protocol. Specifically, the k servers $Q_1, \ldots, Q_k$ simulate the two servers in the CDS protocol $\mathcal{P}_{\mathrm{LVW}}$, where Q_1 simulates the first server in $\mathcal{P}_{\mathrm{LVW}}$ and servers $Q_2, \ldots, Q_k$ simulate the second server in $\mathcal{P}_{\mathrm{LVW}}$.

Quadratic Multi-server Robust Conditional Disclosure of Secrets Protocols. In a *t-robust* CDS protocol (denoted t-RCDS protocol), each server can send up to t messages for different inputs using the same shared randomness such that the security is not violated if the value of the function f is 0 for all combinations of inputs. RCDS protocols were defined in [5] and were used to construct secret-sharing schemes for arbitrary access structures. Furthermore, Applebaum et al. [5] showed a general transformation from CDS protocol to RCDS protocol.

---

[2] We present it as a CDS protocol for the quadratic non-residuosity function. Using known equivalence, this implies a secret-sharing scheme, as in [16].

Using their transformation as is, we get a quadratic RCDS protocol with message size $\tilde{O}(N^{(k-1)/3}t^{k-1})$, which is not useful for constructing improved secret-sharing schemes (compared to the best known linear secret-sharing schemes). In Sect. 6, we show that with a careful analysis that exploits the structure of our quadratic k-server CDS protocol, we can get an improved message size of $\tilde{O}(N^{(k-1)/3}t^{2(k-1)/3+1})$.

Quadratic Secret-Sharing Schemes for Arbitrary Access Structures and Almost All Access Structures. Applebaum et al. [5] and Applebaum and Nir [8] showed transformations from k-server RCDS protocols to secret-sharing schemes for arbitrary access structures. In [8], they achieved a general secret-sharing scheme for arbitrary access structures with share size $2^{0.585n+o(n)}$. In Sect. 7, we plug our quadratic k-server RCDS protocol in the transformation of [8] and get a quadratic secret-sharing scheme for arbitrary access structures with share size $2^{0.705+o(n)}$. This should be compared to the best known linear secret-sharing scheme for arbitrary access structures, given in [8], that has share size $2^{0.7576n+o(n)}$.

Beimel and Farràs [14] proved that for almost all access structures, there is a secret-sharing scheme for one-bit secrets with shares of size $2^{\tilde{O}(\sqrt{n})}$ and a linear secret-sharing scheme with shares of size $2^{n/2+o(n)}$. By a lower bound of [11] this share size is tight for linear secret-sharing schemes. In Sect. 7, we construct quadratic secret-sharing schemes for almost all access structures. Plugging our quadratic k-server CDS protocol in the construction of [14], we get that for almost all access structures there is a quadratic secret-sharing scheme for sharing one-bit secrets with shares of size $2^{n/3+o(n)}$. This proves a separation between quadratic secret-sharing schemes and linear secret-sharing schemes for almost all access structures.

Quadratic Two-Server Robust CDS Protocols. Motivated by the interesting application of robust CDS (RCDS) protocols for constructing secret-sharing schemes, we further investigate quadratic two-server RCDS protocols. In the full version of the paper [17], we show how to transform the quadratic two-server CDS protocol of [36] to an RCDS protocol that is $N^{1/3}$-robust for one server while maintaining the $\tilde{O}(N^{1/3})$ message size. In comparison, the quadratic two-server $N^{1/3}$-RCDS protocol of Sect. 6 has message size $\tilde{O}(N^{8/9})$, however, it is robust for both servers. This transformation is non-blackbox, and uses polynomials of degree t to mask messages, where the masks of every messages of t inputs are uniformly distributed. Non-blackbox constructions of RCDS protocols may avoid limitations of constructing using CDS protocols as a blackbox.

1.2   Open Questions

Next, we mention a few open problems arising from this paper. We show non-trivial lower bounds for secret-sharing schemes with degree-d reconstruction. In [38], they ask the analogous question:

Question 1.1. Prove lower bounds on the share size of secret-sharing schemes with degree-d sharing.

We show a construction with degree-3 sharing that under a plausible conjecture does not have degree-3 reconstruction. We would like to prove such a separation without any assumptions.

Question 1.2. Prove (unconditionally) that there is some access structure that has an efficient secret-sharing scheme with polynomial sharing but does not have an efficient secret-sharing scheme with polynomial reconstruction.

Question 1.3. Are there access structures that have an efficient secret-sharing scheme with polynomial reconstruction (of non-constant degree) but do not have an efficient secret-sharing scheme with polynomial sharing?

We construct quadratic CDS protocols and secret-sharing schemes for arbitrary access structures. For quadratic CDS protocols we prove a matching lower bound on the message size. However, for larger values of d, the lower bound on the message size of degree-d CDS protocols is smaller.

Question 1.4. Are there degree-d CDS protocols with smaller message size than the message size of quadratic CDS protocols? Are there degree-d secret-sharing schemes that are more efficient than quadratic secret-sharing schemes?

Perhaps the most important question is to construct efficient secret-sharing schemes for a wide class of access structures.

Question 1.5. Construct efficient degree-d secret-sharing schemes for a larger class of access structures than the access structures that have efficient linear secret-sharing schemes.

1.3   Additional Related Works

Conditional Disclosure of Secrets (CDS) Protocols. Conditional disclosure of secrets (CDS) protocols were first defined by Gertner et al. [29]. The motivation for this definition was to construct symmetric private information retrieval protocols. CDS protocols were used in many cryptographic applications, such as attribute based encryption [10,28,45], priced oblivious transfer [1], and secret-sharing schemes [4,5,8,14,18,35].

Liu et al. [36] showed two constructions of two-server CDS protocols. In their first construction, which is most relevant to our work, they constructed a quadratic two-server CDS protocol for any Boolean function $f : [N]^2 \rightarrow$

$\{0, 1\}$ with message size $O(N^{1/3})$. In their second construction, which is non-polynomial, they constructed a two-server CDS protocol with message size $2^{O(\sqrt{\log N \log \log N})}$. Applebaum and Arkis [2] (improving on [3]) have shown that for long secrets, i.e., secrets of size $\Theta(2^{N^2})$, there is a two-server CDS protocol in which the message size is 3 times the size of the secret. There are also several constructions of multi-server CDS protocols. Liu et al. [37] constructed a k-server CDS protocol (for one-bit secrets) with message size $2^{\tilde{O}(\sqrt{k \log N})}$. Beimel and Peter [18] and Liu et al. [37] constructed a linear k-server CDS protocol (for one-bit secrets) with message size $O(N^{(k-1)/2})$; by [18], this bound is optimal (up to a factor of k). When we have long secrets, i.e., secrets of size $\Theta(2^{N^k})$, Applebaum and Arkis [2] showed that there is a k-server CDS protocol in which the message size is 4 times the size of the secret. Gay et al. [28] proved a lower bound of $\Omega(\log \log N)$ on the message size of two-server CDS protocols for some function and a lower bound of $\Omega(\sqrt{\log N})$ on the message size of linear two-server CDS protocols. Later, Applebaum et al. [3], Applebaum et al. [7], and Applebaum and Vasudevan [9] proved a lower bound of $\Omega(\log N)$ on the message size of two-server CDS protocols.

Polynomial Secret-Sharing Schemes. Paskin-Cherniavsky and Radune [38] presented the model of secret-sharing schemes with polynomial sharing, in which the sharing is a polynomial of low (constant) degree and the reconstruction can be any function. They showed limitations of various sub-classes of secret-sharing schemes with polynomial sharing. Specifically, they showed that the subclass of schemes for which the sharing is linear in the randomness (and the secret can be with any degree) is equivalent to multi-linear schemes up to a multiplicate factor of $O(n)$ in the share size. This implies that schemes in this subclass cannot significantly reduce the known share size of multi-linear schemes. In addition, they showed that the subclass of schemes over finite fields with odd characteristic such that the degree of the randomness in the sharing function is exactly 2 or 0 in any monomial of the polynomial can efficiently realize only access structures whose all minimal authorized sets are singletons. They also studied the randomness complexity of schemes with polynomial sharing. They showed an exponential upper bound on the randomness complexity (as a function of the share size). For linear and multi-linear schemes, we have a tight linear upper bound on the randomness complexity.

2   Preliminaries

In this section we define secret-sharing schemes, conditional disclosure of secrets protocols, and robust conditional disclosure of secrets protocols.

Notations. We say that two probability distributions $\mathcal{Y}_1, \mathcal{Y}_2$ over domain $\mathcal{X}$ are identical, and denote $\mathcal{Y}_1 \equiv \mathcal{Y}_2$, if $\mathcal{Y}_1(x) = \mathcal{Y}_2(x)$ for every $x \in \mathcal{X}$. We denote by $\binom{N}{[m]}$ the set of all subsets of N of size m. We say that $g(n) = \tilde{O}(f(n))$ if

$g(n) = O(f(n) \log^c n)$ for some constant c, i.e., the $\tilde{O}$ notation ignores poly-logarithmic factors.

Secret-Sharing. We start by presenting the definition of secret-sharing schemes.

Definition 2.1 (Access Structures). *Let $P = \{P_1, \ldots, P_n\}$ be a set of parties. A collection $\Gamma \subseteq 2^P$ is* monotone *if $B \in \Gamma$ and $B \subseteq C$ imply that $C \in \Gamma$. An* access structure *is a monotone collection $\Gamma \subseteq 2^P$ of non-empty subsets of P. Sets in Γ are called* authorized, *and sets not in Γ are called* unauthorized.

Definition 2.2 (Secret-Sharing Schemes). *A secret-sharing scheme Π with domain of secrets S is a mapping from $S \times R$, where R is some finite set called the set of random strings, to a set of n-tuples $S_1 \times S_2 \times \cdots \times S_n$, where S_j is called the domain of shares of party P_j. A dealer distributes a secret $s \in S$ according to Π by first sampling a random string $r \in R$ with uniform distribution, computing a vector of shares $\Pi(s, r) = (s_1, \ldots, s_n)$, and privately communicating each share s_j to party P_j. For a set $A \subseteq P$, we denote $\Pi_A(s, r)$ as the restriction of $\Pi(s, r)$ to its A-entries (i.e., the shares of the parties in A).*

Given a secret-sharing scheme Π, define the size of the secret *as $\log |S|$, the* share size *of party P_j as $\log |S_j|$, and the* total share size *as $\sum_{j=1}^n \log |S_j|$.*

Let S be a finite set of secrets, where $|S| \geq 2$. A secret-sharing scheme Π with domain of secrets S realizes *an access structure Γ if the following two requirements hold:*

CORRECTNESS. *The secret can be reconstructed by any authorized set of parties. That is, for any set $B = \{P_{i_1}, \ldots, P_{i_{|B|}}\} \in \Gamma$ there exists a reconstruction function $\mathrm{Recon}_B : S_{i_1} \times \cdots \times S_{i_{|B|}} \to S$ such that for every secret $s \in S$ and every random string $r \in R$, $\mathrm{Recon}_B (\Pi_B(s, r)) = s$.*

SECURITY. *Every unauthorized set cannot learn anything about the secret from its shares. Formally, for any set $T = \{P_{i_1}, \ldots, P_{i_{|T|}}\} \notin \Gamma$, every pair of secrets $s, s' \in S$, and every vector of shares $(s_{i_1}, \ldots, s_{i_{|T|}}) \in S_{i_1} \times \cdots \times S_{i_{|T|}}$, it holds that $\Pi_T(s, r) \equiv \Pi_T(s', r)$, where the probability distributions are over the choice of r from R with uniform distribution.*

Definition 2.3 (Threshold Secret-Sharing Schemes). *Let Π be a secret-sharing scheme on a set of n parties P. We say that Π is a t-out-of-n secret-sharing scheme if it realizes the access structure $\Gamma_{t,n} = \{A \subseteq P : |A| \geq t\}$.*

Conditional Disclosure of Secrets. Next, we define k-server conditional disclosure of secrets (CDS) protocols, first presented in [29]. We consider a model where k servers[3] $Q_1, \ldots, Q_k$ hold a secret s and a common random string r; every

---

[3] For clarity of the presentation (especially when using CDS protocols to construct secret-sharing schemes) we denote the entities in a CDS protocol by servers and the entities in a secret-sharing scheme by parties.

server Q_i holds an input x_i for some k-input function f. In addition, there is a referee that holds $x_1, \ldots, x_k$ but, prior to the execution of the protocol, does not know s and r. In a CDS protocol for f, for every $i \in [k]$, server Q_i sends a single message to the referee, based on r, s, and x_i; the server does not see neither the inputs of the other servers nor their messages when computing its message. The requirements are that the referee can reconstruct the secret s if $f(x_1, \ldots, x_k) = 1$, and it cannot learn any information about the secret s if $f(x_1, \ldots, x_k) = 0$.

Definition 2.4 (Conditional Disclosure of Secrets Protocols). *Let f : $X_1 \times \cdots \times X_k \to \{0, 1\}$ be a k-input function. A k-server CDS protocol $\mathcal{P}$ for f, with domain of secrets S, domain of common random strings R, and finite message domains $M_1, \ldots, M_k$, consists of k message computation functions $\mathrm{ENC}_1, \ldots, \mathrm{ENC}_k$, where $\mathrm{ENC}_i : X_i \times S \times R \to M_i$ for every $i \in [k]$. For an input $x = (x_1, \ldots, x_k) \in X_1 \times \cdots \times X_k$, secret $s \in S$, and randomness $r \in R$, we let $\mathrm{ENC}(x, s, r) = (\mathrm{ENC}_1(x_1, s, r), \ldots, \mathrm{ENC}_k(x_k, s, r))$. We say that a protocol $\mathcal{P}$ is a CDS protocol for f if it satisfies the following properties: (1) Correctness: There is a deterministic reconstruction function $\mathrm{DEC} : X_1 \times \cdots \times X_k \times M_1 \times \cdots \times M_k \to S$ such that for every input $x = (x_1, \ldots, x_k) \in X_1 \times \cdots \times X_k$ for which $f(x_1, \ldots, x_k) = 1$, every secret $s \in S$, and every common random string $r \in R$, it holds that $\mathrm{DEC}(x, \mathrm{ENC}(x, s, r)) = s$. (2) Security: For every input $x = (x_1, \ldots, x_k) \in X_1 \times \cdots \times X_k$ for which $f(x_1, \ldots, x_k) = 0$ and every pair of secrets $s, s' \in S$ it holds that $\mathrm{ENC}(x, s, r) \equiv \mathrm{ENC}(x, s', r)$, where r is sampled uniformly from R.*

The message size of a CDS protocol $\mathcal{P}$ is defined as the size of the largest message sent by the servers, i.e., $\max_{1 \leq i \leq k} \log |M_i|$. In two-server CDS protocols, we sometimes refer to the servers as Alice and Bob (instead of Q_1 and Q_2, respectively).

Definition 2.5 (The Predicate INDEX$_N^k$). *We define the k-input function $\mathrm{INDEX}_N^k : \{0, 1\}^{N^{k-1}} \times [N]^{k-1} \to \{0, 1\}$ where for every $D \in \{0, 1\}^{N^{k-1}}$ (a $(k-1)$ dimensional array called the database) and every $(i_2, \ldots, i_k) \in [N]^{k-1}$ (called the index), $\mathrm{INDEX}_N^k(D, i_2, \ldots, i_k) = D_{i_2, \ldots, i_k}$.*

Observation 2.6 ([28]). *If there is a k-server CDS protocol for INDEX_N^k with message size M, then for every $f : [N]^k \to \{0, 1\}$ there is a k-server CDS protocol with message size M.*

We obtain the above CDS protocol for f in the following way: Server Q_1 constructs a database $D_{i_2, \ldots, i_k} = f(x_1, i_2, \ldots, i_k)$ for every $i_2, \ldots, i_k \in [N]$ and servers $Q_2, \ldots, Q_{k-1}$ treat their inputs $(x_2, \ldots, x_k) \in [N]^{k-1}$ as the index, and execute the CDS protocol for $\mathrm{INDEX}_N^k(D, x_2, \ldots, x_k) = f(x_1, x_2, \ldots, x_k)$.

Robust Conditional Disclosure of Secrets. In the definition of CDS protocols (Definition 2.4), if a server sends messages for different inputs with the same randomness, then the security is not guaranteed and the referee can possibly learn information on the secret. In [5], the notion of robust CDS (RCDS) protocols was presented. In RCDS protocols, the security is guaranteed even if the referee receives messages of different inputs with the same randomness. Next we define the notion of t-RCDS protocols.

Definition 2.7 (Zero Sets). *Let* $f : X_1 \times X_2 \times \cdots \times X_k \to \{0,1\}$ *be a k-input function. We say that a set of inputs* $Z \subseteq X_1 \times X_2 \cdots \times X_k$ *is a zero set of f if* $f(x) = 0$ *for every* $x \in Z$. *For sets* $Z_1, \ldots, Z_k$, *we denote* $\mathrm{ENC}_i(Z_i, s, r) = (\mathrm{ENC}_i(x_i, s, r))_{x_i \in Z_i}$ *and*

$$\mathrm{ENC}(Z_1 \times Z_2 \cdots \times Z_k, s, r) = (\mathrm{ENC}_1(Z_1, s, r), \ldots, \mathrm{ENC}_k(Z_k, s, r)).$$

Definition 2.8 (t-RCDS Protocols). *Let* $\mathcal{P}$ *be a k-server CDS protocol for a k-input function* $f : X_1 \times X_2 \times \cdots \times X_k \to \{0,1\}$ *and* $Z = Z_1 \times Z_2 \times \cdots \times Z_k \subseteq X_1 \times X_2 \times \cdots \times X_k$ *be a zero set of f. We say that $\mathcal{P}$ is robust for the set Z if for every pair of secrets* $s, s' \in S$, *it holds that* $\mathrm{ENC}(Z, s, r)$ *and* $\mathrm{ENC}(Z, s', r)$ *are identically distributed. For every integers* $t_1, \ldots, t_k$, *we say that $\mathcal{P}$ is a $(t_1, \ldots, t_k)$-RCDS protocol if it is robust for every zero set* $Z_1 \times Z_2 \times \cdots \times Z_k$ *such that* $|Z_i| \leq t_i$ *for every* $i \in [k]$. *Finally, for every integer t, we say that $\mathcal{P}$ is a t-RCDS protocol if it is a $(t, \ldots, t)$-RCDS protocol.*

3 Degree-d Secret Sharing and Degree-d CDS Protocols

In [38], polynomial secret-sharing schemes are defined as secret-sharing schemes in which the sharing function can be computed by polynomial of low degree. In this paper, we define secret-sharing schemes with polynomial reconstruction and secret-sharing schemes with both polynomial sharing and reconstruction.

Definition 3.1 (Degree of Polynomial). *The degree of each multivariate monomial is the sum of the degree of all its variables; the degree of a polynomial is the maximal degree of its monomials.*

Definition 3.2 (Degree-d Mapping over $\mathbb{F}$). *A function* $f : \mathbb{F}^\ell \to \mathbb{F}^m$ *can be computed by degree-d polynomials over $\mathbb{F}$ if there are m polynomials* $Q_1, \ldots, Q_m : \mathbb{F}^\ell \to \mathbb{F}$ *of degree at most d s.t.* $f(x_1, \ldots, x_\ell) = (Q_1(x_1, \ldots, x_\ell), \ldots, Q_m(x_1, \ldots, x_\ell))$.

A secret-sharing scheme has a polynomial sharing if the mapping that the dealer uses to generate the shares given to the parties can be computed by polynomials, as we formalize at the following definition.

Definition 3.3 (Secret-Sharing Schemes with Degree-d Sharing [38]). *Let* Π *be a secret-sharing scheme with domain of secrets S. We say that the scheme Π has degree-d sharing over a finite field $\mathbb{F}$ if there are integers* $\ell, \ell_r, \ell_1, \ldots, \ell_n$ *such that* $S \subseteq \mathbb{F}^\ell, R = \mathbb{F}^{\ell_r}$, *and* $S_i = \mathbb{F}^{\ell_i}$ *for every* $i \in [n]$, *and* Π *can be computed by degree-d polynomials over $\mathbb{F}$.*

In Definition 3.3, we allow S to be a subset of $\mathbb{F}^\ell$ (in [38], $S = \mathbb{F}^\ell$). In particular, we will study the case where $\ell = 1$ and $S = \{0, 1\} \subseteq \mathbb{F}$.

A secret-sharing scheme has a polynomial reconstruction if for every authorized set the mapping that the set uses to reconstruct the secret from its shares can be computed by polynomials.

Definition 3.4 (Secret-Sharing Schemes with Degree-d Reconstruction). *Let Π be a secret-sharing scheme with domain of secrets S. We say that the scheme Π has a* degree-d *reconstruction over a finite field $\mathbb{F}$ if there are integers $\ell, \ell_r, \ell_1, \ldots, \ell_n$ such that $S \subseteq \mathbb{F}^\ell$, $R = \mathbb{F}^{\ell_r}$, and $S_i = \mathbb{F}^{\ell_i}$ for every $i \in [n]$, and Recon_B, the reconstruction function of the secret, can be computed by degree-d polynomials over $\mathbb{F}$ for every $B \in \Gamma$.*

Definition 3.5 (Degree-d Secret-Sharing Schemes). *A secret-sharing scheme Π is a* degree-d *secret-sharing scheme over $\mathbb{F}$ if it has degree-d sharing and degree-d reconstruction over $\mathbb{F}$.*

Definition 3.6 (CDS Protocols with Degree-d Encoding). *A CDS protocol $\mathcal{P}$ has a* degree-d *encoding over a finite field $\mathbb{F}$ if there are integers $\ell, \ell_r, \ell_1, \ldots, \ell_k \geq 1$ such that $S \subseteq \mathbb{F}^\ell$, $R = \mathbb{F}^{\ell_r}$, $M_i = \mathbb{F}^{\ell_i}$ for every $1 \leq i \leq k$, and for every $i \in [k]$ and every $x \in X_i$ the function $\mathrm{ENC}_{i,x} : \mathbb{F}^{\ell + \ell_r} \to M_i$ can be computed by degree-d polynomials over $\mathbb{F}$, where $\mathrm{ENC}_{i,x}(s, r) = \mathrm{ENC}_i(x, r, s)$.*

Definition 3.7 (CDS Protocols with Degree-d Decoding). *A CDS protocol $\mathcal{P}$ has a* degree-d *decoding over a finite field $\mathbb{F}$ if there are integers $\ell, \ell_r, \ell_1, \ldots, \ell_k \geq 1$ such that $S \subseteq \mathbb{F}^\ell$, $R = \mathbb{F}^{\ell_r}$, $M_i = \mathbb{F}^{\ell_i}$ for every $1 \leq \ell \leq k$, and for every inputs $x_1, \ldots, x_k$ the function $\mathrm{DEC}_{x_1, \ldots, x_k} : \mathbb{F}^{\ell_1 + \cdots + \ell_k} \to S$ can be computed by degree-d polynomials over $\mathbb{F}$, where $\mathrm{DEC}_{x_1, \ldots, x_k}(m_1, \ldots, m_k) = \mathrm{DEC}(x_1, \ldots, x_k, m_1, \ldots, m_k)$.*

Note that in Definition 3.7, the polynomials computing the decoding can be different for every input x.

Definition 3.8 (Degree-d CDS Protocols). *A CDS protocol $\mathcal{P}$ is a degree-d CDS protocol over $\mathbb{F}$ if it has degree-d encoding and degree-d decoding over $\mathbb{F}$.*

Definition 3.9 (Linear Secret-Sharing Schemes and CDS Protocols). *A linear polynomial is a degree-1 polynomial. A linear secret-sharing scheme is a degree-1 secret-sharing scheme and $\ell = 1$ (i.e., the secret contains one field element). A secret-sharing scheme has a linear sharing (resp., reconstruction) if it has degree-1 sharing (resp., reconstruction). Similar notations hold for CDS protocols.*

Secret-sharing schemes with linear sharing are equivalent to secret-sharing schemes with linear reconstruction as shown by [12, 32].

Claim 3.10 ([12, 32]). *A secret-sharing scheme Π is linear if and only if for every authorized set B the reconstruction function Recon_B is a linear mapping.*

In the full version of this paper [17], we generalize Claim 3.10 and show that secret-sharing schemes with degree-1 sharing (i.e., multi-linear schemes) are equivalent to secret-sharing schemes with degree-1 reconstruction.

Definition 3.11 (Quadratic Secret-Sharing Schemes and CDS Protocols). *A quadratic polynomial is a degree-2 polynomial. A quadratic secret-sharing scheme is a degree-2 secret-sharing scheme. A secret-sharing scheme has a quadratic sharing (resp., reconstruction) if it has degree-2 sharing (resp., reconstruction). Similar notations hold for CDS protocols.*

Let $\mathcal{A} = \{\mathcal{A}_n\}_{n \in \mathbb{N}}$ be a family of access structures, where $\mathcal{A}_n$ is an n-party access structure. We informally say that $\mathcal{A}$ can be realized by polynomial secret-sharing schemes if it can be realized by degree-$f(n)$ secret-sharing schemes where $f(n)$ is a constant or relatively small function, i.e., $\log n$.

Remark 3.12. Observe that for every finite field, every function can be computed by a polynomial (with high degree). Therefore, every access structure can be realized by a secret-sharing scheme with polynomial reconstruction of high degree. This is not true for sharing since we require that the polynomial sharing uses uniformly distributed random elements of the field. However, by relaxing correctness and security, we can also get a statistical secret-sharing scheme with polynomial sharing of high degree (by sampling many field elements and constructing a distribution that is close to uniform on the set R of the random strings of the secret-sharing scheme).

3.1 CDS with Degree-3 Encoding for the Non-quadratic Residues Function

In this section we show an example of a function that can be realized by an efficient CDS protocol with degree-3 encoding, but, under the assumption that the quadratic residue modulo a prime problem is not in NC, it does not have an efficient CDS protocol with degree-d decoding (for any constant d). Our construction is built upon [16] where they construct an efficient non-linear secret-sharing scheme for an access structure that corresponds to the quadratic residue function. In the construction of [16], the random string is not uniformly distributed in the field (as we require from CDS protocols with polynomial encoding). In the following construction, in order to get a degree-d encoding, we choose the random string uniformly, resulting in a small error in the correctness.

The Quadratic Residue Modulo a Prime Problem. For a prime p, let $QR_p = \{a \in \{1, \ldots, p-1\} : \exists b \in \{1, \ldots, p-1\} \, a \equiv b^2 \pmod{p}\}$. The quadratic residue modulo a prime problem is given p and a, where p is a prime, and outputs 1 if and only if $a \in QR_p$. All the *known* algorithms for the quadratic residue modulo a prime problem are sequential and it is not known if efficient parallel algorithms for this problem exist. The known algorithms are of two types; the first type requires computing a modular exponentiation and the second requires computing the gcd. Therefore, the problem is related to modular exponentiation and gcd problems, and thus according to the current state of the art, it is reasonable to assume that the problem is not in NC (see [16] for more details).

CDS protocol for f_{NQRP_p}

- The secret: A bit $s \in \{0, 1\}$.
- Q_i for every $1 \le i \le k$ holds $x_i \in \{0, 1\}$.
- Common randomness: $r, z_1, \ldots, z_{k-1} \in \mathbb{F}_p$.
- **The protocol**
  - Calculate $z_k = -\sum_{j=1}^{k-1} z_j$.
  - Server Q_1 sends $(z_1 + s \cdot 2^1 x_1 r^2 + r^2) \bmod p$.
  - Server Q_i for every $2 \le i \le k$ sends $(z_i + s \cdot 2^i x_i r^2) \bmod p$.

Fig. 1. A k-server CDS protocol with degree-3 Encoding for f_{NQRP_p}.

We define, for a prime p and $k = \lfloor \log p \rfloor - 1$, the function $f_{\mathrm{NQRP}_p} : \{0, 1\}^k \to \{0, 1\}$ such that $f_{\mathrm{NQRP}_p}(x_1, \ldots, x_k) = 1$ if $(1 + \sum_{i=1}^{k} 2^i x_i) \bmod p \notin \mathrm{QR}_p$ and $f_{\mathrm{NQRP}_p}(x_1, \ldots, x_k) = 0$ otherwise.[4] The function f_{NQRP_p} is realized by the CDS protocol depicted in Fig. 1. This protocol has perfect security, however, it has a one-side error $1/p$ in the correctness. Repeating this protocol t times will result in a protocol with error $O(1/p^t)$.

Lemma 3.13. *For every t, there is a k-server CDS protocol with degree-3 encoding over $\mathbb{F}_p$ for the function f_{NQRP_p} with $S = \{0, 1\}$ and an error in correctness of $1/p^t$ and message size of $O(t \log p)$.*

Proof. In Fig. 1, we describe a k-server CDS protocol for f_{NQRP_p}. We next prove its correctness and security.

For correctness, assuming $r \ne 0$, when $s = 0$ the sum of the messages the referee gets is $\sum_{i=1}^{k} z_i + r^2 \equiv r^2 \bmod p$, and when $s = 1$ the sum is $r^2(1 + \sum_{i=1}^{k} 2^i x_i) \bmod p$. Recall that $r^2 \cdot a \in \mathrm{QR}_p$ iff $a \in \mathrm{QR}_p$. Therefore, when $f_{\mathrm{NQRP}_p}(x_1, \ldots, x_k) = 1$, $s = 1$ iff the sum of the messages is not in QR_p. The referee can reconstruct the secret when the random element r is in $\mathbb{F}_p \setminus \{0\}$, thus the referee can reconstruct the secret with probability $1 - 1/p$. To amplify the correctness, we repeat the protocol t times and get correctness with probability of $1 - 1/p^t$.

In order to prove security, we prove that every k-tuples of messages for an input $x_1, \ldots, x_k$ such that $f_{\mathrm{NQRP}_p}(x_1, \ldots, x_k) = 0$ the messages are identically distributed when $s = 0$ and when $s = 1$. When $r = 0$ the messages are uniform random elements whose sum is 0 regardless of the secret. Otherwise, regardless of

---

[4] We add 1 to the input to avoid the input 0, which is neither a quadratic residue nor a quadratic non residue.

the secret, the sum of the messages is a uniformly random distributed quadratic residue: for $s = 0$ the sum is $r^2 \bmod p$ and for $s = 1$ the sum is $b = r^2(1 + \sum_{i=1}^{k} 2^i x_i) \bmod p \in \mathrm{QR}_p$ which is also a uniformly distributed quadratic residue. Thus, in both cases the messages are random elements in $\mathbb{F}_p$ with the restriction that their sum is a random quadratic residue.

Each message contains only one field element of size $\log p$. As we repeat the protocol t times, the message size is $t \log p$. The encoding function is $z_i + (2^i x_i) \cdot sr^2 \bmod p$ which is a degree-3 polynomial in the secret and the randomness (for every x_i). $\qquad\qquad\square$

In Lemma 4.4 we show that for any constant d, any CDS protocol with degree-d decoding and message size M can be transformed to a linear CDS protocol in which the message size is M^d. Recall that any sequence of functions $\{f_i\}_{i \in \mathbb{N}}$ that can be realized by a linear CDS protocol with polynomial message size (in the number of servers) is in NC, i.e., it has a family of circuits of poly-logarithmic depth and polynomial size (see discussion in Remark 4.6). The above is true even if there is an exponentially small error in the correctness (this is discussed in the full version of the paper [17]). Thus, we obtain the following corollary.

Corollary 3.14. *Under the assumption that $\{\mathrm{NQRP}_p\}_{p \text{ is a prime}} \notin \mathrm{NC}$, there is a sequence of functions that can be realized by an efficient CDS protocol with degree-3 encoding, but for any constant d, cannot be realized by an efficient CDS protocol with degree-d decoding.*

4   Lower Bounds for Secret Sharing with Degree-d Reconstruction

In this section, we show lower bounds for secret-sharing schemes with degree-d reconstruction.

4.1   Lower Bounds for 1-Bit Secrets for Implicit Access Structures

The following theorem was showed in [34].

Theorem 4.1 (Implied by [34]). *Let $\mathcal{F}_{\mathrm{rec}}$ be the family of possible reconstruction functions, c be the sum of the share sizes of all the parties (i.e., the total share size), and $\mathcal{F}_A$ be a family of n-party access structures. For all but at most $\sqrt{|\mathcal{F}_A|}$ access structures $\Gamma \in \mathcal{F}_A$, for any secret-sharing scheme with domain of secrets $\{0, 1\}$ and reconstruction function from $\mathcal{F}_{\mathrm{rec}}$, it holds that*

$$\log |\mathcal{F}_{\mathrm{rec}}| \cdot c = \Omega(\log |\mathcal{F}_A|).$$

We obtain the following two corollaries.

Corollary 4.2. *For almost all n-party access structures, any secret-sharing scheme realizing them over any finite field with domain of secrets $\{0, 1\}$ and degree-d reconstruction requires total share size of $2^{n/(d+1)-o(n)}$.*

Proof. Let $\mathcal{F}_A$ be the family of all n-party access structures. Thus, $|\mathcal{F}_A| = 2^{\Theta(2^n/\sqrt{n})}$. We next consider the family of degree-d polynomials as the family of reconstruction functions.

Fix a finite field $\mathbb{F}$, and consider shares of total size c, hence they contain $v = c/\log|\mathbb{F}|$ field elements. In this case the reconstruction function is a polynomial of degree $\leq d$ in v variables. There are at most $(v+1)^d$ monomials of degree $\leq d$ (for each of the d variables we choose either an element from the v shares or 1 for degree smaller than d), thus less than $|\mathbb{F}|^{(v+1)^d} = 2^{\log|\mathbb{F}|\cdot(c/\log|\mathbb{F}|+1)^d} \leq 2^{(c+1)^d}$ polynomials of degree $\leq d$ (as the reconstruction function can choose any coefficient in $\mathbb{F}$ for every monomial). If $|\mathbb{F}| > 2^{2^{n/(d+1)}}$, then the share size of every secret-sharing scheme over $\mathbb{F}$ is $> 2^{n/(d+1)}$ (since $\log|\mathbb{F}| \geq 2^{n/(d+1)}$). Thus, we only need to consider at most $2^{2^{n/(d+1)}}$ fields, and consider $\mathcal{F}_{rec}$ of size $2^{2^{n/(d+1)}} \cdot 2^{(c+1)^d}$. Thus, by Theorem 4.1, $(2^{n/(d+1)} + (c+1)^d) \cdot c \geq \Omega(2^n/\sqrt{n})$, so $c^{d+1} \geq 2^{n-o(n)}$ and $c \geq 2^{n/(d+1)-o(n)}$. □

Corollary 4.3. *For almost all k-input functions $f : [N]^k \to \{0,1\}$, the message size in any degree-d CDS protocol for them over any finite field with domain of secrets $\{0,1\}$ is $\Omega(N^{(k-1)/(d+1)}/k)$.*

The proof of Corollary 4.3 is similar to the proof of Corollary 4.2 when we use the fact that CDS protocol for a function $f : [N]^k \to \{0,1\}$ is equivalent to secret-sharing scheme for an access structure with kN parties (see e.g. [4,18]). The formal proof of Corollary 4.3 is given in the full version of this paper [17].

4.2   A Transformation from Secret Sharing with Degree-d Reconstruction into a Linear Secret Sharing

We start with a transformation from secret-sharing schemes with polynomial reconstruction to linear schemes. The idea of the transformation is to add random field elements to the randomness of the original polynomial scheme and generate new shares using these random elements, such that the reconstruction of the secret in the resulting scheme is a linear combination of the elements in the shares of the resulting scheme. In particular, for every monomial of degree at least two in a polynomial used for the reconstruction, we share the value of the monomial among the parties that have elements in the monomial. That is, the sharing function computes the polynomials instead of the reconstruction algorithm. As a corollary, we obtain a lower bound on the share size for schemes with polynomial reconstruction.

Lemma 4.4. *Let Γ be an n-party access structure, and assume that there exists a secret-sharing scheme Π_P realizing Γ over $\mathbb{F}$ with ℓ-elements secrets and degree-d reconstruction, in which the shares contain together c field elements. Then, there is a multi-linear secret-sharing scheme Π_L realizing Γ over $\mathbb{F}$ with ℓ-elements secrets, in which the share of each party contains $O(c^d)$ field elements. In particular, if the secret in Π_P contains one field element then Π_L is linear.*

Proof. To construct the desired scheme Π_L, the dealer first shares the secret according to scheme Π_P. Then, for every possible monomial $x_{i_1}^{\ell_1} \cdot \ldots \cdot x_{i_{d'}}^{\ell_{d'}}$ in the reconstruction of some authorized set such that $2 \leq \sum_{i=1}^{d'} \ell_i \leq d$, where x_{i_j} is a field element in the share of a party P_{i_j} for every $j \in [d']$, the dealer computes the value v of the monomial (using the shares that it creates) and shares v using a d'-out-of-d' secret-sharing scheme among the parties $P_{i_1}, \ldots, P_{i_{d'}}$ (i.e., the dealer chooses d' random field elements $r_{i_1}^v, \ldots, r_{i_{d'}}^v$ such that $v = r_{i_1}^v + \cdots + r_{i_{d'}}^v$).[5] Note that the randomness of scheme Π_L contains the random elements of scheme Π_P and the random elements $r_{i_1}^v, \ldots, r_{i_{d'-1}}^v$ for every possible monomial $x_{i_1}^{\ell_1} \cdot \ldots \cdot x_{i_{d'}}^{\ell_{d'}}$ of value v such that $2 \leq \sum_{i=1}^{d'} \ell_i \leq d$ as above (the dealer computes $r_{i_{d'}}^v = x_{i_1}^{\ell_1} \cdot \ldots \cdot x_{i_{d'}}^{\ell_{d'}} - r_{i_1}^v - \cdots - r_{i_{d'-1}}^v$).

We prove that the construction of Π_L realizes Γ and has linear reconstruction. By the equivalence between linear reconstruction and linear sharing (even for multi-element secrets), which is shown in the full version of this paper [17], Π_L can be converted to a secret-sharing scheme with linear sharing and reconstruction while preserving the share size.

We now prove the correctness of Π_L. For an authorized set $B \in \Gamma$, denote S_B as the field elements in the shares of B, and let

$$\mathrm{Recon}_{B,j}(S_B) = \sum_{x_i \in S_B} \alpha_{x_i} x_i + \sum_{\substack{x_{i_1}, \ldots, x_{i_{d'}} \in S_B, d' \leq d, \\ 2 \leq \ell_1 + \cdots + \ell_{d'} \leq d}} \alpha_{x_{i_1}^{\ell_1}, \ldots, x_{i_{d'}}^{\ell_{d'}}} x_{i_1}^{\ell_1} \cdot \ldots \cdot x_{i_{d'}}^{\ell_{d'}}$$

be the reconstruction function of B of the j-th element of the secret in scheme Π_P. Then, the set B can reconstruct the secret in scheme Π_L by applying the linear combination of the field elements in the shares of the parties as follows:

$$\sum_{x_i \in S_B} \alpha_{x_i} x_i + \sum_{\substack{x_{i_1}, \ldots, x_{i_{d'}} \in S_B, d' \leq d, \\ 2 \leq \ell_1 + \cdots + \ell_{d'} \leq d}} \alpha_{x_{i_1}^{\ell_1}, \ldots, x_{i_{d'}}^{\ell_{d'}}} \sum_{j=1}^{d'} r_{i_j}^v$$

$$= \sum_{x_i \in S_B} \alpha_{x_i} x_i + \sum_{\substack{x_{i_1}, \ldots, x_{d'_{i_{d'}}} \in S_B, d' \leq d, \\ 2 \leq \ell_1 + \cdots + \ell_{d'} \leq d}} \alpha_{x_{i_1}^{\ell_1}, \ldots, x_{i_{d'}}^{\ell_{d'}}} x_{i_1}^{\ell_1} \cdot \ldots \cdot x_{i_{d'}}^{\ell_{d'}}.$$

We next prove the security of Π_L. Let T be an unauthorized set. For every authorized subset T' it must be that $T' \not\subseteq T$, thus, the set T misses at least one random field element $r_{i_j}^v$ from any monomial for the set T', so it cannot learn information on the value of these monomials, and hence cannot learn information on the secret from these values. In the scheme Π_L, the set T can only learn its shares in scheme Π_P, and every possible monomial of at most d variables

---

[5] If there is more than one element of some party in the monomial, the dealer can share the monomial among the parties that have elements in it, or give to such a party the sum of the shares that corresponding to its elements.

that contains elements of those shares; these additional values can be computed from the original shares of T. Thus, in scheme Π_L, the set T learns only the information it can learn in scheme Π_P, and, hence, by the security of scheme Π_P, the set T cannot learn any information about the secret.

Finally, in scheme Π_L, each party gets at most c field elements from the share of scheme Π_P, and an element from the d'-out-of-d' secret-sharing scheme, for every monomial as above $x_{i_1}^{\ell_1} \cdot \ldots \cdot x_{i_{d'}}^{\ell_{d'}}$ such that $2 \leq \sum_{i=1}^{d'} \ell_i \leq d$; there are at most $\sum_{d'=2}^{d} c^{d'}$ such monomials. Overall, each party gets $c + \sum_{d'=2}^{d} c^{d'} = O(c^d)$ field elements. □

The above transformation gives us a lower bound on the share size of secret-sharing schemes with polynomial reconstruction, using any lower bound on the share size of linear secret-sharing schemes, as described next.

Corollary 4.5. *Assume that there exist an n-party access structure Γ such that the share size of at least one party in every linear secret-sharing scheme realizing Γ is c. Then, the share size of at least one party in every secret-sharing scheme realizing Γ with degree-d reconstruction is $\Omega(c^{1/d})$.*

Remark 4.6. Recall that the class NC^i contains all Boolean functions (or problems) that can be computed by polynomial-size Boolean circuits with gates with fan-in at most two and depth $O(\log^i n)$. Following the discussion in [16], the class of access structures that have a linear secret-sharing scheme with polynomial share size contains monotone NC^1 and is contained in algebraic NC^2 and in NC^3 for small enough fields (at most exponential in polynomial of the number of parties n). Lemma 4.4 implies that the class of access structures that have a secret-sharing scheme with polynomial reconstruction and polynomial share size is also contained in NC^3.

4.3   Lower Bounds for 1-Element Secrets for Explicit Access Structures

Now, let us recall the explicit lower bound of Pitassi and Robere [41] on the share size of linear secret-sharing schemes.

Theorem 4.7 ([41]). *There is a constant $\beta > 0$ such that for every n, there is an explicit n-party access structure Γ such that for every finite field $\mathbb{F}$, any linear secret-sharing scheme realizing Γ over $\mathbb{F}$ requires total share size of $\Omega(2^{\beta n} \log |\mathbb{F}|)$.*

The next explicit lower bound for secret-sharing schemes with polynomial reconstruction and one-element secrets follows directly from Corollary 4.5 when using Theorem 4.7.

Corollary 4.8. *There is a constant $\beta > 0$ such that for every n, there is an explicit n-party access structure Γ such that for every d and every finite field $\mathbb{F}$, any secret-sharing scheme realizing Γ over $\mathbb{F}$ with degree-d reconstruction and one-element secrets requires total share size of $\Omega(2^{\beta n/d} \log |\mathbb{F}|)$.*

Recall that the information ratio (or the normalized share size) is the ratio between the share size and the secret size. Corollary 4.8 provides a lower bound on the information ratio of an explicit access structure even for large finite fields. Corollary 4.2 provides a lower bound with a better constant in the exponent, however, it only applies to implicit access structures and does not give a non-trivial lower bound on the information ratio for large finite fields.

5   Quadratic CDS Protocols

In this section, we construct a quadratic k-server CDS protocol, i.e., a CDS protocol in which the encoding and decoding are computed by degree-2 polynomials. We start by describing a quadratic two-server CDS protocol (a variant of the quadratic two-server CDS protocol of [36]) and then construct a quadratic k-server CDS protocol that "simulates" the two-server CDS protocol.

A Quadratic Two-Server CDS Protocol. As a warm-up, we describe in Fig. 2 a two-server CDS protocol in which the encoding and the decoding are computed by polynomials of degree 2 over $\mathbb{F}_2$. This protocol is a variant of the protocol of [36] using a different notation (i.e., using cubes instead of polynomials).

Lemma 5.1. *Protocol Π_2, described in Fig. 2, is a quadratic two-server CDS protocol over $\mathbb{F}_2$ for the function INDEX_N^2 with message size $O(N^{1/3})$.*

Proof. We start with analyzing the value of the expression in (1). When $s = 0$, Bob sends $A_1 = S_1, A_2 = S_2$, and $A_3 = S_3$ to the referee. Thus, when $s = 0$, we get that $m_{i_1}^1 = m_1 \oplus r_{1,i_1} \oplus r_1$, $m_{i_2}^2 = m_2 \oplus r_{2,i_2} \oplus r_2$, and $m_{i_3}^3 = m_3 \oplus r_{3,i_3} \oplus r_3$, and the value of the expression in (1) is

$$m_1 \oplus m_2 \oplus m_3 \oplus m_{i_1}^1 \oplus r_{1,i_1} \oplus m_{i_2}^2 \oplus r_{2,i_2} \oplus m_{i_3}^3 \oplus r_{3,i_3} = r_1 \oplus r_2 \oplus r_3 = 0. \quad (2)$$

When $s = 1$, Bob sends $A_1 = S_1 \oplus \{i_1\}, A_2 = S_2 \oplus \{i_2\}$, and $A_3 = S_3 \oplus \{i_3\}$ to the referee. We observe the following:

$$
\begin{aligned}
m_1 &= \left(\bigoplus_{j_2 \in S_2 \oplus \{i_2\}, j_3 \in S_3 \oplus \{i_3\}} D_{i_1, j_2, j_3} \right) \\
&= \left(\bigoplus_{j_2 \in S_2, j_3 \in S_3 \oplus \{i_3\}} D_{i_1, j_2, j_3} \right) \oplus \left(\bigoplus_{j_3 \in S_3 \oplus \{i_3\}} D_{i_1, i_2, j_3} \right) \\
&= \left(\bigoplus_{j_2 \in S_2, j_3 \in S_3} D_{i_1, j_2, j_3} \right) \oplus \left(\bigoplus_{j_2 \in S_2} D_{i_1, j_2, i_3} \right) \oplus \left(\bigoplus_{j_3 \in S_3} D_{i_1, i_2, j_3} \right) \oplus D_{i_1, i_2, i_3}.
\end{aligned}
\quad (3)
$$

Similarly,

$$
m_2 = \left(\bigoplus_{j_1 \in S_1, j_3 \in S_3} D_{j_1, i_2, j_3} \right) \oplus \left(\bigoplus_{j_1 \in S_1} D_{j_1, i_2, i_3} \right) \oplus \left(\bigoplus_{j_3 \in S_3} D_{i_1, i_2, j_3} \right) \oplus D_{i_1, i_2, i_3}.
$$

Protocol Π_2

- The secret: A bit $s \in \{0,1\}$.
- Alice holds a database $D \in \{0,1\}^N$ and Bob holds an index $i \in [N]$ viewed as (i_1, i_2, i_3) such that $i_1, i_2, i_3 \in [N^{1/3}]$.
- Common randomness: $S_1, S_2, S_3 \subseteq [N^{1/3}]$, $r_1, r_2 \in \{0,1\}$, and $3N^{1/3}$ bits $r_{1,j_1}, r_{2,j_2}, r_{3,j_3} \in \{0,1\}$ for every $j_1, j_2, j_3 \in [N^{1/3}]$.
- **The protocol**
  - Compute $r_3 = r_1 \oplus r_2$.
  - Alice computes $3N^{1/3}$ bits:
    * $m_{j_1}^1 = \bigoplus_{j_2 \in S_2, j_3 \in S_3} D_{j_1, j_2, j_3} \oplus r_{1,j_1} \oplus r_1$ for every $j_1 \in [N^{1/3}]$.
    * $m_{j_2}^2 = \bigoplus_{j_1 \in S_1, j_3 \in S_3} D_{j_1, j_2, j_3} \oplus r_{2,j_2} \oplus r_2$ for every $j_2 \in [N^{1/3}]$.
    * $m_{j_3}^3 = \bigoplus_{j_1 \in S_1, j_2 \in S_2} D_{j_1, j_2, j_3} \oplus r_{3,j_3} \oplus r_3$ for every $j_3 \in [N^{1/3}]$.
  - Alice sends $(m_{j_1}^1)_{j_1 \in [N^{1/3}]}$, $(m_{j_2}^2)_{j_2 \in [N^{1/3}]}$, $(m_{j_3}^3)_{j_3 \in [N^{1/3}]}$ to the referee.
  - Bob computes 3 strings $A_h = (A_h[1], \ldots, A_h[N^{1/3}])$ for $h \in \{1, 2, 3\}$ (each string of length $N^{1/3}$), where
    * $A_h[j_h] = S_h[j_h]$ for every $j_h \neq i_h$.
    * $A_h[i_h] = S_h[i_h] \oplus s$
      (that is, if $s = 0$ then $A_h = S_h$, otherwise $A_h = S_h \oplus \{i_h\}$).
  - Bob sends $r_{1,i_1}, r_{2,i_2}, r_{3,i_3}$, and A_1, A_2, A_3 to the referee.
  - The referee computes:
    $m_1 = \bigoplus_{j_2 \in A_2, j_3 \in A_3} D_{i_1, j_2, j_3}$, $\quad m_2 = \bigoplus_{j_1 \in A_1, j_3 \in A_3} D_{j_1, i_2, j_3}$,
    $m_3 = \bigoplus_{j_1 \in A_1, j_2 \in A_2} D_{j_1, j_2, i_3}$
    and outputs

    $$m_1 \oplus m_2 \oplus m_3 \oplus m_{i_1}^1 \oplus r_{1,i_1} \oplus m_{i_2}^2 \oplus r_{2,i_2} \oplus m_{i_3}^3 \oplus r_{3,i_3}. \qquad (1)$$

Fig. 2. A quadratic two-server CDS protocol Π_2 for the function INDEX_N^2.

$$m_3 = \left(\bigoplus_{j_1 \in S_1, j_2 \in S_2} D_{j_1, j_2, i_3} \right) \oplus \left(\bigoplus_{j_1 \in S_1} D_{j_1, i_2, i_3} \right) \oplus \left(\bigoplus_{j_2 \in S_2} D_{i_1, j_2, i_3} \right) \oplus D_{i_1, i_2, i_3}.$$

Therefore,

$$m_1 \oplus m_2 \oplus m_3 = \left(\bigoplus_{j_2 \in S_2, j_3 \in S_3} D_{i_1, j_2, j_3} \right) \oplus \left(\bigoplus_{j_1 \in S_1, j_3 \in S_3} D_{j_1, i_2, j_3} \right)$$
$$\oplus \left(\bigoplus_{j_1 \in S_1, j_2 \in S_2} D_{j_1, j_2, i_3} \right) \oplus D_{i_1, i_2, i_3}.$$

Thus, when $s = 1$, the value of the expression in (1) is

$$m_1 \oplus m_2 \oplus m_3 \oplus m_{i_1}^1 \oplus r_{1,i_1} \oplus m_{i_2}^2 \oplus r_{2,i_2} \oplus m_{i_3}^3 \oplus r_{3,i_3} \oplus r_1 \oplus r_2 \oplus r_3 = D_{i_1, i_2, i_3}. \qquad (4)$$

Correctness. We next prove the correctness of the protocol, that is, when $D_{i_1,i_2,i_3} = 1$ the referee correctly reconstructs s. Recall that the output of the referee is the expression in (1). As explained above, when $s = 0$ the referee outputs 0 and when $s = 1$ the referee outputs $D_{i_1,i_2,i_3} = 1$.

Security. Fix inputs D and $i = (i_1, i_2, i_3)$ such that $D_{i_1,i_2,i_3} = 0$, a message of Alice $(m_{j_1}^1)_{j_1 \in [N^{1/3}]}$, $(m_{j_2}^2)_{j_2 \in [N^{1/3}]}$, $(m_{j_3}^3)_{j_3 \in [N^{1/3}]}$, and a message of Bob $A_1, A_2, A_3, r_{1,i_1}, r_{2,i_2}, r_{3,i_3}$ such that

$$\bigoplus_{j_2 \in A_2, j_3 \in A_3} D_{i_1,j_2,j_3} \oplus \bigoplus_{j_1 \in A_1, j_3 \in A_3} D_{j_1,i_2,j_3} \oplus \bigoplus_{j_1 \in A_1, j_2 \in A_2} D_{j_1,j_2,i_3}$$
$$\oplus\, m_{i_1}^1 \oplus r_{1,i_1} \oplus m_{i_2}^2 \oplus r_{2,i_2} \oplus m_{i_3}^3 \oplus r_{3,i_3} = 0 \quad (5)$$

(no other restrictions are made on the messages). By (2) and (4), when $D_{i_1,i_2,i_3} = 0$ only such messages are possible. We next argue that the referee cannot learn any information about the secret given these inputs and messages, i.e., these messages have the same probability when $s = 0$ and when $s = 1$. In particular, we show that for every secret $s \in \{0, 1\}$ there is a unique common random string r such that Alice and Bob send these messages with the secret s. We define the common random string r as follows:

- For $h \in \{1, 2, 3\}$, define $S_h = A_h$ if $s = 0$ and $S_h = A_h \oplus \{i_h\}$ if $s = 1$. These S_1, S_2, S_3 are consistent with the message of Bob and s and are the only consistent choice. Both when $s = 0$ and $s = 1$, as $D_{i_1,i_2,i_3} = 0$, it holds that

$$\bigoplus_{j_2 \in A_2, j_3 \in A_3} D_{i_1,j_2,j_3} \oplus \bigoplus_{j_1 \in A_1, j_3 \in A_3} D_{j_1,i_2,j_3} \oplus \bigoplus_{j_1 \in A_1, j_2 \in A_2} D_{j_1,j_2,i_3}$$
$$= \bigoplus_{j_2 \in S_2, j_3 \in S_3} D_{i_1,j_2,j_3} \oplus \bigoplus_{j_1 \in S_1, j_3 \in S_3} D_{j_1,i_2,j_3} \oplus \bigoplus_{j_1 \in S_1, j_2 \in S_2} D_{j_1,j_2,i_3}. \quad (6)$$

This is true since when $s = 0$ the sets A_1, A_2, A_3 are the same as the sets S_1, S_2, S_3, and when $s = 1$, by (4), the two sides of the expression are differ by D_{i_1,i_2,i_3} which is 0.
- The message of Bob determines r_{1,i_1}, r_{2,i_2}, and r_{3,i_3}.
- Define

$$r_1 = m_{i_1}^1 \oplus \bigoplus_{j_2 \in S_2, j_3 \in S_3} D_{i_1,j_2,j_3} \oplus r_{1,i_1} \quad (7)$$

$$r_2 = m_{i_2}^2 \oplus \bigoplus_{j_1 \in S_1, j_3 \in S_3} D_{j_1,i_2,j_3} \oplus r_{2,i_2}. \quad (8)$$

Given the secret s, the inputs, and the messages of Alice and Bob, these values are possible and unique.
- Define $r_3 = r_1 \oplus r_2$. By (5), (6), (7), and (8), this value is possible, i.e., it satisfies

$$m_{i_3}^3 = \bigoplus_{j_1 \in S_1, j_2 \in S_2} D_{j_1,j_2,i_3} \oplus r_{3,i_3} \oplus r_3.$$

– For every $j_1 \neq i_1, j_2 \neq i_2$, and $j_3 \neq i_3$ define

$$r_{1,j_1} = m_{j_1}^1 \oplus \bigoplus_{j_2 \in S_2, j_3 \in S_3} D_{i_1,j_2,j_3} \oplus r_1,$$

$$r_{2,j_2} = m_{j_2}^2 \oplus \bigoplus_{j_1 \in S_1, j_3 \in S_3} D_{j_1,i_2,j_3} \oplus r_2,$$

$$r_{3,j_3} = m_{j_3}^3 \oplus \bigoplus_{j_1 \in S_1, j_2 \in S_2} D_{j_1,j_2,i_3} \oplus r_3.$$

Given the secret s, the inputs, and the messages of Alice and Bob, these values are possible and unique.

Recall that the common random string is uniformly distributed (i.e., the probability of each such string is $1/2^{6N^{1/3}+2}$, as it contains $6N^{1/3} + 2$ bits). Since for every pair of messages of Alice and Bob when $D_{i_1,i_2,i_3} = 0$ we have that every secret s has exactly one consistent random string, this pair has the same probability when $s = 0$ and when $s = 1$ and the security follows.

Message Size. Alice sends $3N^{1/3}$ bits and Bob sends 3 strings each of size $N^{1/3}$ and 3 random bits, so the message size is $O(N^{1/3})$.

Degree of the Protocol. The message of Alice contains an exclusive or of bits of a 3-dimension cubes, where two dimensions are determined by the common randomness (the sets S_1, S_2, S_3). That is, when we represent a set $S \subseteq [N^{1/3}]$ by $N^{1/3}$ bits $S = (S[1], \ldots, S[N^{1/3}])$, then for every $j_1 \in [N^{1/3}]$

$$m_{j_1}^1 = \bigoplus_{j_2 \in [N^{1/3}], j_3 \in [N^{1/3}]} S_2[j_2] \cdot S_3[j_3] \cdot D_{j_1,j_2,j_3} \oplus r_{1,j_1} \oplus r_1.$$

Thus, $m_{j_1}^1$, for every input D, is a polynomial of degree 2 over $\mathbb{F}_2$ whose variables are the bits of the random string. Similarly, $m_{j_2}^2, m_{j_3}^3$ are polynomials of degree 2 over $\mathbb{F}_2$. The message of Bob for every $j_h \neq i_h$ contains a polynomial of degree 1 over $\mathbb{F}_2$, since it sends $S_h[j_h]$. For the index $i_h \in [N^{1/3}]$, Bob sends $S_h[i_h] \oplus s$, which is a polynomial of degree 1 over $\mathbb{F}_2$. The decoding is also a computation of a 3-dimension cube such that only two dimensions are determined by the common randomness, i.e., the decoding is a degree-2 polynomial over $\mathbb{F}_2$. □

An Auxiliary Protocol Π_{XOR}. In Fig. 4, we will describe a k-server CDS protocol, where servers $Q_2, \ldots, Q_k$ simulate Bob in the two-server CDS protocol. To construct this protocol, we design a k-server protocol Π_{XOR} that simulates Bob, i.e., sends a set A, where $A = S$ if $s = 0$ and $A = S \oplus \{i\}$ if $s = 1$. In Π_{XOR}, each server Q_ℓ holds an index i_ℓ, which together determine an index $i = (i_1, i_2, \ldots, i_k)$, and they need to send messages to the referee such that the referee will learn A without learning any information on s. Let $N_1, \ldots, N_k$ be integers and $N = N_1 \cdot \ldots \cdot N_k$. We construct the following protocol in

---

The protocol Π_{XOR}

- Input: Q_1 holds an array $S = (S_{j_1,\ldots,j_k})_{j_1 \in [N_1],\ldots,j_k \in [N_k]}$, a bit $s \in \{0,1\}$, and $i_1 \in [N_1]$, and Q_ℓ, for every $2 \leq \ell \leq k$, holds an index $i_\ell \in [N_\ell]$. The referee holds $i_1,\ldots,i_k$.
- Output: An array $A = (A_{j_1,\ldots,j_k})_{j_1 \in [N_1],\ldots,j_k \in [N_k]}$ s.t. $A_{j_1,\ldots,j_k} = S_{j_1,\ldots,j_k}$ for every $(j_1,\ldots,j_k) \neq (i_1,\ldots,i_k)$ and $A_{i_1,\ldots,i_k} = S_{i_1,\ldots,i_k} \oplus s$.
- Common randomness: $r_{j_2,\ldots,j_k,\ell} \in \{0,1\}$ for every $j_2 \in [N_2],\ldots,j_k \in [N_k]$ and every $\ell \in \{1,\ldots,k\}$.
- **The protocol**
  - Q_1 computes an $(N_1 - 1) \times N_2 \times \ldots \times N_k$ array A and two $1 \times N_2 \times \ldots \times N_k$ arrays A^0 and A^1.
    * $A_{j_1,\ldots,j_k} = S_{j_1,\ldots,j_k}$ for every $j_1 \in [N_1] \setminus \{i_1\}, j_2 \in [N_2],\ldots,j_k \in [N_k]$.
    * $A^0_{i_1,j_2,\ldots,j_k} = S_{i_1,j_2,\ldots,j_k} \oplus r_{j_2,\ldots,j_k,1}$ for every $j_2 \in [N_2],\ldots,j_k \in [N_k]$.
    * $A^1_{i_1,j_2,\ldots,j_k} = S_{i_1,j_2,\ldots,j_k} \oplus r_{j_2,\ldots,j_k,2} \oplus \cdots \oplus r_{j_2,\ldots,j_k,k} \oplus s$ for every $j_2 \in [N_2],\ldots,j_k \in [N_k]$.
  - Q_1 sends A, A^0, A^1.
  - Q_ℓ, for every $2 \leq \ell \leq k$, sends $r_{j_2,\ldots,j_k,1}$ for every $(j_2,\ldots,j_k) \in [N_2] \times \cdots \times [N_k]$ such that $j_\ell \neq i_\ell$, and $r_{j_2,\ldots,j_k,\ell}$ for every $(j_2,\ldots,j_k) \in [N_2] \times \cdots \times [N_k]$ such that $j_\ell = i_\ell$.
  - The referee completes A to an $N_1 \times N_2 \times \ldots \times N_k$ array as follows
    * $A_{i_1,i_2,\ldots,i_k} = A^1_{i_1,i_2,\ldots,i_k} \oplus r_{i_2,\ldots,i_k,2} \oplus \cdots \oplus r_{i_2,\ldots,i_k,k}$.
    * $A_{i_1,j_2,\ldots,j_k} = A^0_{i_1,j_2,\ldots,j_k} \oplus r_{j_2,\ldots,j_k,1}$ for every $(j_2,\ldots,j_k) \neq (i_2,\ldots,i_k)$.
  - The referee returns A.

Fig. 3. The protocol Π_{XOR} for the function f_{XOR}.

which server Q_1 holds a set $S \subseteq [N]$ represented by a k-dimensional Boolean array $(S_{j_1},\ldots,j_k)_{j_1 \in [N_1],\ldots,j_k \in [N_k]}$, the secret s, and an index $i_1 \in [N_1]$. Server Q_ℓ for $2 \leq \ell \leq k$ holds an index $i_\ell \in [N_\ell]$. If $s = 1$, the referee outputs $S \oplus \{(i_1, i_2,\ldots,i_k)\}$ and if $s = 0$ it outputs S (without learning any information on s). Define the function[6]

$$f_{\mathrm{XOR}}(S, s, i_1,\ldots,i_k) = \begin{cases} i_1, i_2,\ldots,i_k, S & \text{If } s = 0, \\ i_1, i_2,\ldots,i_k, S \oplus \{(i_1, i_2,\ldots,i_k)\} & \text{If } s = 1. \end{cases}$$

We next define when a protocol for f_{XOR} is secure. This is a special case of security of private simultaneous messages (PSM) protocols [25,30], that is, we require that for every two inputs for which f_{XOR} outputs the same value, the distribution of messages is the same. Observe that every possible output of f_{XOR} results from exactly two inputs.

---

[6] We include $i_1,\ldots,i_k$ in the output of f_{XOR} to be consistent with PSM protocols, in which the referee does not know the input.

Definition 5.2. *We say that a protocol for f_{XOR} is secure if for every $i_1 \in [N_1], \ldots, i_k \in [N_k]$, and every S, the distributions of messages of the protocol on inputs $S, s = 0, i_1, \ldots, i_k$ and inputs $S \oplus \{(i_1, i_2, \ldots, i_k)\}, s = 1, i_1, \ldots, i_k$ are the same.*

The protocol Π_{XOR} for f_{XOR} is described in Fig. 3. Next we present a high level description of the protocol. Server Q_1 sends to the referee three arrays: A, A^0, A^1. The array A contains all the indices for which Q_1 knows that S and A are equal (i.e., indices $j_1, \ldots, j_k$ where $j_1 \neq i_1$, so $A_{j_1, \ldots, j_k} = S_{j_1, \ldots, j_k}$), the array A^0 enables the referee to compute $A_{i_1, j_2, \ldots, j_k}$ for all the indices for which there is at least one $j_\ell \neq i_\ell$ for some $2 \leq \ell \leq k$, and the array A^1 enables the referee to compute $A_{i_1, \ldots, i_k}$.

Lemma 5.3. *Protocol Π_{XOR} is a correct and secure protocol for f_{XOR} with message size $O(N_1 \cdot \ldots \cdot N_k)$. The degree of the message generation and output reconstruction in the protocol (as a function of the randomness and the input S) is 1 over $\mathbb{F}_2$.*

The proof of Lemma 5.3 appears in full version of this paper [17].

The k-Server CDS Protocol. Now we present our k-server CDS protocol for the function INDEX_N^k, assuming that $k \equiv 1 \pmod 3$. The case of $k \not\equiv 1 \pmod 3$ is somewhat more messy and can be handled as done in [18].

We next present an overview of our construction. The input of the protocol is a database $D \in \{0, 1\}^{N^{k-1}}$ held by Q_1 and an index $i \in [N]^{k-1}$ jointly held by $Q_2, \ldots, Q_k$. The input $i \in [N]^{k-1}$ is viewed as (i_1, i_2, i_3) where $i_1, i_2, i_3 \in [N^{(k-1)/3}]$, where i_h, for $h \in \{1, 2, 3\}$, contains the inputs of servers $Q_{2+(h-1)(k-1)/3}, \ldots, Q_{1+h(k-1)/3}$. The common randomness contains three random subsets, one for each dimension, i.e., $S_1, S_2, S_3 \subseteq [N^{(k-1)/3}]$. In the protocol, we want that the referee will be able to compute $S_1 \oplus \{i_1\}, S_2 \oplus \{i_2\}$, and $S_3 \oplus \{i_3\}$ when $s = 1$, and S_1, S_2, S_3 when $s = 0$ (as in the protocol Π_2 described in Fig. 2). For this task, we use the protocol Π_{XOR}. Servers $Q_2, \ldots, Q_{1+(k-1)/3}$ execute the protocol Π_{XOR} in order to generate messages that enable the referee to learn $S_1 \oplus \{i_1\}$ when $s = 1$ and S_1 when $s = 0$. Similarly, servers $Q_{2+(k-1)/3}, \ldots, Q_{1+2(k-1)/3}$ and servers $Q_{2+2(k-1)/3}, \ldots, Q_k$ independently execute the protocol Π_{XOR} in order to generate messages that enable the referee to learn $S_2 \oplus \{i_2\}$ when $s = 1$ and S_2 when $s = 0$ and $S_3 \oplus \{i_3\}$ when $s = 1$ and S_3 when $s = 0$, respectively. In addition, we want the referee to learn the bits $r_{1, i_1}, r_{2, i_2}, r_{3, i_3}$ as in Π_2. To achieve this goal, we define $r_{h, j, 1} \ldots, r_{h, j, (k-1)/3}$ for every $j \in [N^{(k-1)/3}]$ and every $h \in \{1, 2, 3\}$, such that $r_{h, j, 1} \oplus \cdots \oplus r_{h, j, (k-1)/3} = r_{h, j}$.

Theorem 5.4. *Protocol Π_k, described in Fig. 4, is a quadratic k-server CDS protocol over $\mathbb{F}_2$ for the function INDEX_N^k with message size $O(N^{(k-1)/3})$.*

The proof of Theorem 5.4 appears in full version of this paper [17].

Corollary 5.5. *Every function $f : [N]^k \to \{0, 1\}$ has a quadratic k-server CDS protocol over $\mathbb{F}_2$ with message size $O(N^{(k-1)/3})$.*

The protocol Π_k

- The secret: A bit $s \in \{0, 1\}$.
- Q_1 holds a database $D \in \{0,1\}^{N^{k-1}}$, and $Q_2, \ldots, Q_k$ hold $x_2, \ldots, x_k \in [N]$, respectively.
- Common randomness: $S_1, S_2, S_3 \subseteq [N^{(k-1)/3}]$, $r_1, r_2 \in \{0, 1\}$, $r_{h,j,1}, \ldots, r_{h,j,(k-1)/3} \in \{0, 1\}$ for every $h \in \{1, 2, 3\}$ and every $j \in [N^{(k-1)/3}]$, and the common randomness of three independent executions of protocol Π_{XOR}.
- **The protocol**
  - Let:
    * $i_h^\ell = x_{1+(h-1)(k-1)+\ell}$ for every $h \in \{1, 2, 3\}$ and every $1 \leq \ell \leq (k-1)/3$.
    * $r_3 = r_1 \oplus r_2$.
  - Q_1 computes $3N^{(k-1)/3}$ bits:
    * $m_{j_1}^1 = \bigoplus_{j_2 \in S_2, j_3 \in S_3} D_{j_1, j_2, j_3} \oplus r_{1,j_1,1} \oplus \cdots \oplus r_{1,j_1,(k-1)/3} \oplus r_1$ for every $j_1 \in [N^{(k-1)/3}]$.
    * $m_{j_2}^2 = \bigoplus_{j_1 \in S_1, j_3 \in S_3} D_{j_1, j_2, j_3} \oplus r_{2,j_2,1} \oplus \cdots \oplus r_{2,j_2,(k-1)/3} \oplus r_2$ for every $j_2 \in [N^{(k-1)/3}]$.
    * $m_{j_3}^3 = \bigoplus_{j_1 \in S_1, j_2 \in S_2} D_{j_1, j_2, j_3} \oplus r_{3,j_3,1} \oplus \cdots \oplus r_{3,j_3,(k-1)/3} \oplus r_3$ for every $j_3 \in [N^{(k-1)/3}]$.
  - Q_1 sends $(m_{j_1}^1)_{j_1 \in [N^{(k-1)/3}]}$, $(m_{j_2}^2)_{j_2 \in [N^{(k-1)/3}]}$, $(m_{j_3}^3)_{j_3 \in [N^{(k-1)/3}]}$ to the referee.
  - $Q_{2+(h-1)(k-1)/3}, \ldots, Q_{1+h(k-1)/3}$, for every $h \in \{1, 2, 3\}$, execute Π_{XOR} with the set S_h held by $Q_{2+(h-1)(k-1)/3}$, the secret s, and i_h^ℓ held by $Q_{1+(h-1)(k-1)/3+\ell}$. Let $m_{\text{xor},1}^h, \ldots, m_{\text{xor},(k-1)/3}^h$ be the messages sent in this execution of Π_{XOR}.
  - Q_ℓ, for every $2 \leq \ell \leq k$:
    * Computes $h = \lfloor 3\ell/(k-1) \rfloor$ and $\alpha = \ell - 1 - (h-1)(k-1)/3$.
    * Sends $m_{\text{xor},\alpha}^h$, and for every $j = (j_1, \ldots, j_{(k-1)/3}) \in [N^{(k-1)/3}]$ such that $j_\alpha = i_h^\alpha$, sends $r_{h,j,\alpha}$.
  - The referee computes:
    * A_h, for every $h \in \{1, 2, 3\}$, from the messages $m_{\text{xor},1}^h, \ldots, m_{\text{xor},(k-1)/3}^h$ of Π_{XOR}.
    * $r_{h,i_h} = r_{h,i_h,1} \oplus r_{h,i_h,2} \oplus \cdots \oplus r_{h,i_h,(k-1)/3}$, for every $h \in \{1, 2, 3\}$.
    * $m_1 = \bigoplus_{j_2 \in A_2, j_3 \in A_3} D_{i_1, j_2, j_3}$, $m_2 = \bigoplus_{j_1 \in A_1, j_3 \in A_3} D_{j_1, i_2, j_3}$,
    $m_3 = \bigoplus_{j_1 \in A_1, j_2 \in A_2} D_{j_1, j_2, i_3}$
    and outputs

$$m_1 \oplus m_2 \oplus m_3 \oplus m_{i_1}^1 \oplus r_{1,i_1} \oplus m_{i_2}^2 \oplus r_{2,i_2} \oplus m_{i_3}^3 \oplus r_{3,i_3}. \quad (9)$$

Fig. 4. A quadratic k-server CDS protocol Π_k for the function INDEX_N^k.

6   A Quadratic Robust CDS Protocol

In this section, we construct a quadratic k-server t-RCDS protocol, which is a CDS protocol in which the referee gets no information on the secret even if each server sends messages on multiple inputs with the same common randomness.

6.1   An Improved Analysis of the Transformation of [5]

We first show an improved analysis of the transformation of [5] from t'-RCDS protocols to t-RCDS protocols for $t' < t$; in particular, from CDS protocols (i.e., $t' = 1$) to t-RCDS protocols. In the transformation of [5], the servers independently execute $O(t^{k-1})$ copies of the underlying RCDS protocol for $f : [N]^k \to \{0,1\}$. This is done in a way that ensures that even if a server sends messages of many inputs, in at least some of the executions of the underlying RCDS protocol the referee gets messages of few inputs. We observe that the input domain in each execution of the underling RCDS is $[N/t]$ (as opposed to $[N]$), and this will reduce the total message size. In Lemma 6.2, we present the improved analysis.

We start with an overview of the ideas behind our analysis. Following the construction of the linear two-server RCDS protocol in [6] (the full version of [5]), when making a server Q_i robust, we divide the domain of inputs of Q_i using a hash function $h : [N] \to [v]$ (actually we do this for several hash functions, as will be explained later); for every $b \in [v]$, the servers execute the underlying CDS protocol where the input of Q_i is restricted to the inputs $\{x_i : h(x_i) = b\}$. We next define families of hash functions that we use in the transformation.

Definition 6.1 (Families of m'-Collision-Free Hash Functions). *A set of functions $\mathcal{H}_{N,m,m',v} = \{h_d : [N] \to [v] : d \in [\ell]\}$ (where ℓ is the number of functions in the family) is a family of m'-collision-free hash functions if for every set $T \in \binom{N}{[m]}$ there exists at least one function $h \in \mathcal{H}_{N,m,m',v}$ for which for every $b \in [v]$ it holds that $|\{x \in T : h(x) = b\}| \le m'$, that is, h restricted to T is at most m'-to-one. A family $\mathcal{H}_{N,m,1,v}$ is a family of perfect hash functions if it is a family of 1-collision-free hash functions. A family $\mathcal{H}_{N,m,m',v}$ is output-balanced if $|\{x \in [N] : h(x) = a\}| \le \lceil N/v \rceil$ for every $a \in [v]$ and $h \in \mathcal{H}_{N,m,m',v}$, i.e., each h divides $[N]$ to v sets of almost the same size.*

Lemma 6.2. *Let $f : [N]^k \to \{0,1\}$ be a k-input function and t and t' be integers such that $t' < t \le N$. Assume that there is a k-server t'-RCDS protocol $\mathcal{P}'$ for f, in which for every $N' \le N$ and for every restriction of f with input domain $A_1 \times \ldots \times A_k$, where $A_i \subseteq [N]$ is of size N' for $1 \le i \le k$, the message size is $c(N')$. In addition, assume that there is a family of an output-balanced t'-collision-free hash functions $\mathcal{H}_{N,kt,t',v} = \{h_1, \ldots, h_\ell\}$ of size ℓ. Then, there is a k-server t-RCDS protocol $\mathcal{P}$ for f with message size $O(\ell v^{k-1} \cdot c(N/v))$. This transformation preserves the degree of the encoding and the decoding of the underlying RCDS protocol.*

Proof. The desired protocol $\mathcal{P}$ is described in Fig. 5. This is actually the transformation of [5] with the following difference. Instead of executing $\mathcal{P}'$ with domain of inputs of size N per server, we execute it with a restriction of f with domain of inputs of size $\lceil N/v \rceil$ per server.[7] The correctness and robustness of the protocol follows from the proof of the transformation of [5].

Next, we analyze the message size. Observe that for each $h \in \mathcal{H}_{N,kt,t',v}$, each server sends messages in v^{k-1} copies of $\mathcal{P}'$, where each copy is for a restriction of f with input domain of size $\max_{a \in [v]} |S_a|$ per server, where $S_a = \{x \in [N] : h(x) = a\}$. Since $\mathcal{H}_{N,kt,t',v}$ is output balanced, it holds that $\max_{a \in [v]} |S_a| \leq \lceil N/v \rceil$ and since $|\mathcal{H}_{N,kt,t',v}| = \ell$, the message size is $O(\ell v^{k-1} \cdot c(\lceil N/v \rceil))$. We next argue that the degree of the encoding and decoding in the transformation does not change when S is the additive group of the field in the protocol $\mathcal{P}'$ (see Fig. 5). In the encoding, the servers execute a linear operation on the secret and the field elements $s_1, \ldots, s_{\ell-1}$ in order to generate s_ℓ. Then, they encode each s_d by executing the underlying RCDS protocol. That is, the encoding is computed by the degree-d polynomials that compute the encoding in the underlying RCDS protocol. For the decoding, the referee first executes the decoding procedure of the underlying RCDS protocol in order to learn $s_1, \ldots, s_\ell$ and then by summing them up the referee learns the secret. That is, the decoding is actually summing up the degree-d polynomials that compute the decoding of the ℓ copies of the underlying RCDS protocol. Therefore, the degree of the encoding and the decoding of the transformation are the same as for the underlying RCDS protocol. □

A t-RCDS protocol

The secret: $s \in S$, where, w.l.o.g., S is a group (e.g., $S = \mathbb{Z}_m$ for some m).
The protocol

- Choose $\ell - 1$ random elements $s_1, \ldots, s_{\ell-1} \in S$ and let $s_\ell = s - (s_1 + \cdots + s_{\ell-1})$ (addition is in the group).
- For every $d \in [\ell]$:
  - Let $S_a = \{x \in [N] : h_d(x) = a\}$ for every $a \in [v]$.
  - For every $a_1, \ldots, a_k \in [v]$, independently execute the k-server t'-RCDS protocol $\mathcal{P}'$ for the restriction of f to $S_{a_1} \times \cdots \times S_{a_k}$ with the secret s_d, that is, for every $i \in [k]$, server Q_i with input x_i sends a message for the restriction of f to $S_{a_1} \times \cdots \times S_{a_{i-1}} \times S_{h_d(x_i)} \times S_{a_{i+1}} \times \cdots \times S_{a_k}$ for every $a_1, \ldots, a_{i-1}, a_{i+1}, \ldots, a_k \in [v]$.

Fig. 5. A transformation of a t'-RCDS protocol to a t-RCDS protocol for $t' < t$.

---

[7] in [5], they do not deal with restrictions of the domain of inputs since it does not improve the asymptotic message size of their protocols.

6.2   The Construction of the Quadratic t-RCDS Protocol

We next construct a quadratic k-server t-RCDS protocol. Our construction uses the improved analysis in Lemma 6.2 of the transformation of [5] for converting a t'-RCDS protocol into a t-RCDS protocol for $t' < t$. Applying the transformation of [5] without our improved analysis starting from our quadratic k-server CDS protocol in Theorem 5.4 will result in a quadratic k-server t-RCDS protocol with message size $\tilde{O}(N^{(k-1)/3}t^{k-1})$. Using our improved analysis, we get better message size of $\tilde{O}(N^{(k-1)/3}t^{2(k-1)/3+1})$.

We start by quoting the following two lemmas that we use in order to instantiate Lemma 6.2. Both lemmas can be proved by a simple probabilistic argument. Their proofs can be found in [39].

Lemma 6.3. *Let N be an integer and $m \in [\sqrt{N}]$. Then, there exists an output-balanced family of perfect hash functions $\mathcal{H}_{N,m,1,m^2} = \{h_i : [N] \to [m^2] : i \in [\ell]\}$, where $\ell = 16m \ln N$.*

Lemma 6.4. *Let N be an integer and $m \in \{15, \ldots, N/2\}$. Then, there exists an output-balanced family of $\log m$-collision-free hash functions $\mathcal{H}_{N,m,\log m,2m} = \{h_i : [N] \to [2m] : i \in [\ell]\}$, where $\ell = 16m \ln N$.*

Theorem 6.5. *Let $t < \min\left\{N/2k, 2^{\sqrt{N}/k}\right\}$. Then, there is a quadratic k-server t-RCDS protocol over $\mathbb{F}_2$ with message size*

$$O(N^{(k-1)/3}t^{2(k-1)/3+1} \cdot k^{2k} \cdot \log^2 N \cdot \log^{(4k-1)/3} t) = \tilde{O}(N^{(k-1)/3}t^{2(k-1)/3+1} \cdot k^{2k}).$$

Proof. Similarly to [5], we construct the protocol in two stages. In the first stage, we transform our quadratic k-server CDS protocol from Fig. 4 into a quadratic k-server $\log t$-RCDS protocol, and then, in the second stage, we transform this protocol into a quadratic k-server t-RCDS protocol.

For the first stage, we use the output-balanced family $\mathcal{H}_{N,k \log t,1,k^2 \log^2 t}$ of perfect hash functions with $O(k \log t \log N)$ hash functions promised by Lemma 6.3. Applying the transformation of Lemma 6.2 with $\mathcal{H}_{N,k \log t,1,k^2 \log^2 t}$ and our quadratic (non-robust) k-server CDS protocol described in Theorem 5.4 as the underlying protocol (this protocol has message size $O(N^{(k-1)/3})$) results in a quadratic k-server $\log t$-RCDS protocol, which we denote by $\mathcal{P}'$, with message size $c'(N) = O(N^{(k-1)/3} \cdot (k \log t)^{(4k-1)/3} \cdot \log N)$.

For the second stage, we apply Lemma 6.2 with the $\log t$-RCDS protocol $\mathcal{P}'$ and the output-balanced family of $(\log t)$-collision-free hash functions, denoted by $\mathcal{H}_{N,kt,\log t,2kt}$ with $O(kt \log N)$ hash functions promised by Lemma 6.4; therefore, we get message size of

$$O(kt \log N \cdot (2kt)^{k-1} \cdot c'(N/2kt)) = O(N^{(k-1)/3}t^{\frac{2(k-1)}{3}+1} \cdot k^{2k} \cdot \log^2 N \cdot \log^{\frac{4k-1}{3}} t).$$

$\square$

7   A Quadratic Secret Sharing for General Access Structures

In this section, we use our results described in Sect. 5 and Subsect. 6.2 to construct improved quadratic secret-sharing schemes. Our upper bounds are better than the best known upper bounds for linear schemes. In addition, our upper bounds imply a separation between quadratic and linear secret-sharing schemes for almost all access structures.

A Construction for All Access Structures. Next we use our quadratic k-server RCDS protocol in the construction of general secret sharing of [8].

Theorem 7.1 (Implied by [8]). *Assume that for every function* $f : [N]^k \to \{0,1\}$ *there is a* k*-server* t*-RCDS protocol with message size* $c(k, N, t)$*, then there is a secret-sharing scheme realizing an arbitrary* n*-party access structure with share size*

$$\max \left\{ \max_{0<\beta\leq0.5} c(\sqrt{n}, 2^{\sqrt{n}}, 2^{\beta\sqrt{n}}), \right.$$
$$\left. \max_{0.5<\beta\leq1} c\left(\sqrt{2n(1-\beta)}, 2^{\sqrt{2n(1-\beta)}}, 2^{\sqrt{n(1-\beta)/2}}\right) \cdot 2^{H_2(\beta)n-2(1-\beta)n} \right\} \cdot 2^{o(n)}.$$

Furthermore, the degree of sharing and reconstruction of this secret-sharing scheme is the degree of encoding and decoding, respectively, of the underlying RCDS protocol.

In the construction of [8], they use a t-RCDS protocol that is robust only for some of the subsets of size t (rather than all subsets). In our construction, we can avoid the more complex definition of robustness and use a t-RCDS protocol that is robust against all subsets of size at most t.

Theorem 7.2. *Every* n*-party access structure can be realized by a quadratic secret-sharing scheme over* $\mathbb{F}_2$ *with share size* $2^{0.705n+o(n)}$*.*

Proof. The theorem follows from Theorem 7.1 using our quadratic t-RCDS protocol with message size $\tilde{O}(N^{(k-1)/3}t^{2(k-1)/3+1} \cdot k^{2k})$ from Theorem 6.5. We get share size

$$\max \left\{ \max_{0<\beta\leq0.5} 2^{n(2\beta+1)/3}, \max_{0.5<\beta\leq1} 2^{H_2(\beta)n-2/3(1-\beta)n} \right\} \cdot 2^{o(n)}.$$

The maximum value of this expression is at $\beta \approx 0.613512$ and it is $2^{0.705n}$.   □

In comparison, Applebaum and Nir [8] construct a linear secret-sharing scheme over $\mathbb{F}_2$ with share size $2^{0.7576n+o(n)}$ and a general (non-polynomial) secret-sharing scheme with share size $2^{0.585n+o(n)}$.

A Construction for Almost All Access Structures. It was shown in [14] that almost all access structures can be realized by a general secret-sharing scheme with shares of size $2^{o(n)}$ and by a linear secret-sharing scheme with share size $2^{n/2+o(n)}$. Furthermore, it was shown in [11] that almost all access structures require share size $2^{n/2-o(n)}$ in any linear secret-sharing scheme even with 1-bit secrets over all finite fields $\mathbb{F}_q$. Following [14], we show that almost all access structures can be realized by a quadratic secret-sharing scheme with 1-bit secrets over $\mathbb{F}_2$ with share size $2^{n/3+o(n)}$, proving a separation between quadratic and linear schemes for almost all access structures.

Theorem 7.3. *Almost all access structures can be realized by a quadratic secret-sharing scheme with 1-bit secrets over $\mathbb{F}_2$ and with share size $2^{n/3+o(n)}$.*

Proof. We say that Γ is an $[a, b]$-slice access structure if for every set of parties A it holds that if $|A| < a$, then $A \notin \Gamma$ and if $|A| > b$, then $A \in \Gamma$.

By [33], almost all access structures are $[n/2-1, n/2+2]$-slice access structure, thus it suffices to construct secret-sharing schemes for them. Let $c(k, N)$ be the message size in a quadratic k-server protocol for any function $f : [N]^k \to \{0, 1\}$. By [35], for every k there is a secret-sharing scheme for $[a, b]$-slice access structure with share size $\dfrac{c(k, N) \cdot 2^{(b-a+1)n/k} O(n) \binom{n}{a}}{\binom{n/k}{a/k}^k}$. In our case, $a = \lfloor n/2 \rfloor - 1$ and $b = \lfloor n/2 \rfloor + 2$, and by taking $k = \sqrt{n/\log n}$ we get share size $c(k, N) \cdot 2^{O(\sqrt{n \log n})}$. Using our quadratic k-server CDS protocol described in Theorem 5.4 with $c(k, N) = N^{(k-1)/3}$ and $N = \binom{n/k}{a/k} < 2^{n/k}$, the share size is $2^{n/3+o(n)}$. $\square$

References

1. Aiello, W., Ishai, Y., Reingold, O.: Priced oblivious transfer: how to sell digital goods. In: Pfitzmann, B. (ed.) EUROCRYPT 2001. LNCS, vol. 2045, pp. 119–135. Springer, Heidelberg (2001). https://doi.org/10.1007/3-540-44987-6_8
2. Applebaum, B., Arkis, B.: On the power of amortization in secret sharing: d-uniform secret sharing and CDS with constant information rate. ACM Trans. Comput. Theor. **12**(4), 24:1–24:21 (2020)
3. Applebaum, B., Arkis, B., Raykov, P., Vasudevan, P.N.: Conditional disclosure of secrets: amplification, closure, amortization, lower-bounds, and separations. SIAM J. Comput. **50**(1), 32–67 (2021)
4. Applebaum, B., Beimel, A., Farràs, O., Nir, O., Peter, N.: Secret-sharing schemes for general and uniform access structures. In: Ishai, Y., Rijmen, V. (eds.) EURO-CRYPT 2019. LNCS, vol. 11478, pp. 441–471. Springer, Cham (2019). https://doi.org/10.1007/978-3-030-17659-4_15
5. Applebaum, B., Beimel, A., Nir, O., Peter, N.: Better secret sharing via robust conditional disclosure of secrets. STOC **2020**, 280–293 (2020)
6. Applebaum, B., Beimel, A., Nir, O., Peter, N.: Better secret sharing via robust conditional disclosure of secrets. Cryptology ePrint Archive, Report 2020/080 (2020)
7. Applebaum, B., Holenstein, T., Mishra, M., Shayevitz, O.: The communication complexity of private simultaneous messages, revisited. In: Nielsen, J.B., Rijmen, V. (eds.) EUROCRYPT 2018. LNCS, vol. 10821, pp. 261–286. Springer, Cham (2018). https://doi.org/10.1007/978-3-319-78375-8_9

8. Applebaum, B., Nir, O.: Upslices, downslices, and secret-sharing with complexity of 1.5^n. IACR Cryptol. ePrint Arch. **2021**, 470 (2021). https://eprint.iacr.org/2021/470. To appear in CRYPTO 2021
9. Applebaum, B., Vasudevan, P.N.: Placing conditional disclosure of secrets in the communication complexity universe. In: 10th ITCS, pp. 4:1–4:14 (2019)
10. Attrapadung, N.: Dual system encryption via doubly selective security: framework, fully secure functional encryption for regular languages, and more. In: Nguyen, P.Q., Oswald, E. (eds.) EUROCRYPT 2014. LNCS, vol. 8441, pp. 557–577. Springer, Heidelberg (2014). https://doi.org/10.1007/978-3-642-55220-5_31
11. Babai, L., Gál, A., Wigderson, A.: Superpolynomial lower bounds for monotone span programs. Combinatorica **19**(3), 301–319 (1999)
12. Beimel, A.: Secure schemes for secret sharing and key distribution. Ph.D. thesis, Technion (1996). www.cs.bgu.ac.il/~beimel/pub.html
13. Beimel, A.: Secret-sharing schemes: a survey. In: Chee, Y.M., et al. (eds.) IWCC 2011. LNCS, vol. 6639, pp. 11–46. Springer, Heidelberg (2011). https://doi.org/10.1007/978-3-642-20901-7_2
14. Beimel, A., Farràs, O.: The share size of secret-sharing schemes for almost all access structures and graphs. In: Pass, R., Pietrzak, K. (eds.) TCC 2020. LNCS, vol. 12552, pp. 499–529. Springer, Cham (2020). https://doi.org/10.1007/978-3-030-64381-2_18
15. Beimel, A., Gál, A., Paterson, M.: Lower bounds for monotone span programs. Comput. Complex. **6**(1), 29–45 (1997)
16. Beimel, A., Ishai, Y.: On the power of nonlinear secret-sharing. SIAM J. Discrete Math. **19**(1), 258–280 (2005)
17. Beimel, A., Othman, H., Peter, N.: Quadratic secret sharing and conditional disclosure of secrets. Cryptology ePrint Archive, Report 2021/285 (2021). https://eprint.iacr.org/2021/285
18. Beimel, A., Peter, N.: Optimal linear multiparty conditional disclosure of secrets protocols. In: Peyrin, T., Galbraith, S. (eds.) ASIACRYPT 2018. LNCS, vol. 11274, pp. 332–362. Springer, Cham (2018). https://doi.org/10.1007/978-3-030-03332-3_13
19. Benaloh, J., Leichter, J.: Generalized secret sharing and monotone functions. In: Goldwasser, S. (ed.) CRYPTO 1988. LNCS, vol. 403, pp. 27–35. Springer, New York (1990). https://doi.org/10.1007/0-387-34799-2_3
20. Bertilsson, M., Ingemarsson, I.: A construction of practical secret sharing schemes using linear block codes. In: Seberry, J., Zheng, Y. (eds.) AUSCRYPT 1992. LNCS, vol. 718, pp. 67–79. Springer, Heidelberg (1993). https://doi.org/10.1007/3-540-57220-1_53
21. Blakley, G.R.: Safeguarding cryptographic keys. In: Proceedings of the 1979 AFIPS National Computer Conference, vol. 48, pp. 313–317 (1979)
22. Brickell, E.F.: Some ideal secret sharing schemes. J. Combin. Math. Combin. Comput. **6**, 105–113 (1989)
23. Csirmaz, L.: The dealer's random bits in perfect secret sharing schemes. Studia Sci. Math. Hungar. **32**(3–4), 429–437 (1996)
24. Csirmaz, L.: The size of a share must be large. J. Cryptol. **10**(4), 223–231 (1997)
25. Feige, U., Kilian, J., Naor, M.: A minimal model for secure computation. In: 26th STOC, pp. 554–563 (1994)
26. Gál, A.: A characterization of span program size and improved lower bounds for monotone span programs. Comput. Complex. **10**(4), 277–296 (2002)
27. Gál, A., Pudlák, P.: Monotone complexity and the rank of matrices. Inf. Process. Lett. **87**, 321–326 (2003)

28. Gay, R., Kerenidis, I., Wee, H.: Communication complexity of conditional disclosure of secrets and attribute-based encryption. In: Gennaro, R., Robshaw, M. (eds.) CRYPTO 2015. LNCS, vol. 9216, pp. 485–502. Springer, Heidelberg (2015). https://doi.org/10.1007/978-3-662-48000-7_24

29. Gertner, Y., Ishai, Y., Kushilevitz, E., Malkin, T.: Protecting data privacy in private information retrieval schemes. JCSS **60**(3), 592–629 (2000)

30. Ishai, Y., Kushilevitz, E.: Private simultaneous messages protocols with applications. In: 5th Israel Symposium on Theory of Computing and Systems, pp. 174–183 (1997)

31. Ito, M., Saito, A., Nishizeki, T.: Secret sharing schemes realizing general access structure. In: Globecom, vol. 87, pp. 99–102 (1987). Journal version: Multiple assignment scheme for sharing secret. J. Cryptol. **6**(1), 15–20 (1993)

32. Karchmer, M., Wigderson, A.: On span programs. In: 8th Structure in Complexity Theory, pp. 102–111 (1993)

33. Korshunov, A.D.: On the number of monotone Boolean functions. Probl. Kibern **38**, 5–108 (1981)

34. Larsen, K.G., Simkin, M.: Secret sharing lower bound: either reconstruction is hard or shares are long. In: Galdi, C., Kolesnikov, V. (eds.) SCN 2020. LNCS, vol. 12238, pp. 566–578. Springer, Cham (2020). https://doi.org/10.1007/978-3-030-57990-6_28

35. Liu, T., Vaikuntanathan, V.: Breaking the circuit-size barrier in secret sharing. In: 50th STOC, pp. 699–708 (2018)

36. Liu, T., Vaikuntanathan, V., Wee, H.: Conditional disclosure of secrets via nonlinear reconstruction. In: Katz, J., Shacham, H. (eds.) CRYPTO 2017. LNCS, vol. 10401, pp. 758–790. Springer, Cham (2017). https://doi.org/10.1007/978-3-319-63688-7_25

37. Liu, T., Vaikuntanathan, V., Wee, H.: Towards breaking the exponential barrier for general secret sharing. In: Nielsen, J.B., Rijmen, V. (eds.) EUROCRYPT 2018. LNCS, vol. 10820, pp. 567–596. Springer, Cham (2018). https://doi.org/10.1007/978-3-319-78381-9_21

38. Paskin-Cherniavsky, A., Radune, A.: On polynomial secret sharing schemes. In: ITC 2020. LIPIcs, vol. 163, pp. 12:1–12:21 (2020)

39. Peter, N.: Secret-sharing schemes and conditional disclosure of secrets protocols. Thesis at Ben-Gurion Universiy (2020). https://aranne5.bgu.ac.il/others/PeterNaty19903.pdf

40. Pitassi, T., Robere, R.: Strongly exponential lower bounds for monotone computation. In: 49th STOC, pp. 1246–1255 (2017)

41. Pitassi, T., Robere, R.: Lifting Nullstellensatz to monotone span programs over any field. In: 50th STOC, pp. 1207–1219 (2018)

42. Robere, R., Pitassi, T., Rossman, B., Cook, S.A.: Exponential lower bounds for monotone span programs. In: 57th FOCS, pp. 406–415 (2016)

43. Shamir, A.: How to share a secret. Commun. ACM **22**, 612–613 (1979)

44. Vaikuntanathan, V., Vasudevan, P.N.: Secret sharing and statistical zero knowledge. In: Iwata, T., Cheon, J.H. (eds.) ASIACRYPT 2015. LNCS, vol. 9452, pp. 656–680. Springer, Heidelberg (2015). https://doi.org/10.1007/978-3-662-48797-6_27

45. Wee, H.: Dual system encryption via predicate encodings. In: Lindell, Y. (ed.) TCC 2014. LNCS, vol. 8349, pp. 616–637. Springer, Heidelberg (2014). https://doi.org/10.1007/978-3-642-54242-8_26

Constructing Locally Leakage-Resilient Linear Secret-Sharing Schemes

Hemanta K. Maji[1]($\boxtimes$), Anat Paskin-Cherniavsky[2], Tom Suad[2],
and Mingyuan Wang[1]

[1] Department of Computer Science, Purdue University, West Lafayette, USA
{hmaji,wang1929}@purdue.edu
[2] Department of Computer Science, Ariel University, Ariel, Israel
anatpc@ariel.ac.il, tom.suad@msmail.ariel.ac.il

Abstract. Innovative side-channel attacks have repeatedly falsified the assumption that cryptographic implementations are opaque black-boxes. Therefore, it is essential to ensure cryptographic constructions' security even when information leaks via unforeseen avenues. One such fundamental cryptographic primitive is the secret-sharing schemes, which underlies nearly all threshold cryptography. Our understanding of the leakage-resilience of secret-sharing schemes is still in its preliminary stage.

This work studies locally leakage-resilient linear secret-sharing schemes. An adversary can leak m bits of arbitrary local leakage from each n secret shares. However, in a locally leakage-resilient secret-sharing scheme, the leakage's joint distribution reveals no additional information about the secret.

For every constant m, we prove that the Massey secret-sharing scheme corresponding to a random linear code of dimension k (over sufficiently large prime fields) is locally leakage-resilient, where $k/n > 1/2$ is a constant. The previous best construction by Benhamouda, Degwekar, Ishai, Rabin (CRYPTO–2018) needed $k/n > 0.907$. A technical challenge arises because the number of all possible m-bit local leakage functions is exponentially larger than the number of random linear codes. Our technical innovation begins with identifying an appropriate pseudorandomness-inspired family of tests; passing them suffices to ensure leakage-resilience. We show that most linear codes pass all tests in this family. This Monte-Carlo construction of linear secret-sharing scheme that is locally leakage-resilient has applications to leakage-resilient secure computation.

H.K. Maji and M. Wang—The research effort is supported in part by an NSF CRII Award CNS–1566499, NSF SMALL Awards CNS–1618822 and CNS–2055605, the IARPA HECTOR project, MITRE Innovation Program Academic Cybersecurity Research Awards (2019–2020, 2020–2021), a Ross-Lynn Research Scholars Grant (2021–2022), a Purdue Research Foundation (PRF) Award (2017–2018), and The Center for Science of Information, an NSF Science and Technology Center, Cooperative Agreement CCF–0939370.

A. Paskin-Cherniavsky and T. Suad—Research supported by the Ariel Cyber Innovation Center in conjunction with the Israel National Cyber directorate in the Prime Minister's Office.

T. Malkin and C. Peikert (Eds.): CRYPTO 2021, LNCS 12827, pp. 779–808, 2021.
https://doi.org/10.1007/978-3-030-84252-9_26

Furthermore, we highlight a crucial bottleneck for all the analytical approaches in this line of work. Benhamouda et al. introduced an analytical proxy to study the leakage-resilience of secret-sharing schemes; if the proxy is small, then the scheme is leakage-resilient. However, we present a one-bit local leakage function demonstrating that the converse is false, motivating the need for new analytically well-behaved functions that capture leakage-resilience more accurately.

Technically, the analysis involves probabilistic and combinatorial techniques and (discrete) Fourier analysis. The family of new "tests" capturing local leakage functions, we believe, is of independent and broader interest.

Keywords: Local leakage-resilience · Massey secret-sharing scheme · Random linear codes · Shamir's secret-sharing scheme · Discrete fourier analysis

1   Introduction

Traditionally, one treats the cryptosystems implementing cryptographic primitives as impervious black-boxes that faithfully realize the intended input-output behavior and provide no additional information. In the real-world implementations and deployments, however, this assumption has been repeatedly proven false. Beginning with the works of Kocher et al. [33,34], several innovative and sophisticated side-channel attacks reveal partial information about the intermediate values and stored secrets of computation (for a summary of the history of several of these attacks, refer to [10,35,46,48,50,56]). These side-channel attacks on fundamental cryptographic building blocks like secret-sharing schemes pose a threat to the security of all cryptographic constructions relying on them.

Towards addressing these concerns, one can design mechanical countermeasures, hardware solutions, and algorithmic representation to protect against known threats [1,5,12,17,20,21]. However, this approach creates unknown risks, the risk of undiscovered attacks compromising a scheme's security. On the other hand, *leakage-resilient cryptography* formally models potential avenues of information leakage and the leakage attacks that an adversary may undertake. This approach has the benefit that the general model encompasses leakage attacks beyond those that are already known. Furthermore, one knows the formal security guarantees and risks of using such cryptographic schemes. In the last few decades, there has been a large body of highly influential research on the feasibility and efficiency of realizing leakage-resilient variants of fundamental cryptographic primitives against active/passive adversaries that perform leakage statically/adaptively (refer to the excellent survey [32]).

One such fundamental cryptographic primitive is *secret-sharing schemes*, which are essential to nearly all threshold cryptography. In the (so-called) standard model, the adversary can corrupt a few parties and obtain their secret-shares; however, it obtains no additional information about the remaining secret shares. The security of secret-sharing schemes crucially relies on the fact that the corruption threshold is lower than the secret-sharing schemes' privacy threshold. However, a side-channel attack on a secret-sharing scheme provides the adversary a restricted or noisy access to every party's secret share. For instance, a *passive adversary* can leak a few bits from each secret share. Although it has a partial view of each secret share, the leakages' joint distribution may be correlated with the secret to compromise its secrecy.

Our understanding of the leakage-resilience of secret-sharing schemes is still in its preliminary stage. Even for prominent secret-sharing schemes like Shamir's secret-sharing scheme, the exact characterization of the leakage-resilience is not well-understood. A *locally leakage-resilient secret-sharing scheme* (LLRSS) [7] (also implicit in the constructions of [26]) protects against a static passive adversary. The adversary chooses leakage functions from all the secret shares. However, an LLRSS secret-sharing scheme ensures that the leakage's joint distribution is statistically independent of the secret. Guruswami and Wootters's reconstruction algorithm [28,29] for Reed-Solomon codes (and follow-up works [18,27,42,52]) demonstrate that Shamir's secret-sharing scheme on characteristic-2 finite fields is insecure even when the adversary can leak only one bit from every secret share. Achieving leakage-resilience seems challenging because the adversary need not reconstruct the complete secret; obtaining only some partial information about the secret precludes leakage-resilience. For example, over characteristic-two fields, if the secret is a linear combination of some parties' secret shares, then the adversary can leak only one bit from these secret shares and reconstruct the least significant bit of the secret. Although this attack does not suffice to reconstruct the complete secret (which is impossible using entropy arguments), it suffices to distinguish the secret 0 from secret 1.

There has been a significant amount of research into constructing new leakage-resilient secret-sharing schemes [3,6,11,13,15,23,24,31,36,41,51]. However, it seems insurmountable to replace every deployed secret-sharing scheme with their leakage-resilient version or an entirely new leakage-resilient secret-sharing scheme. Furthermore, in specific contexts, cryptographic constructions crucially rely on the secret-sharing scheme's additional salient features (for example, their linearity and algebraic structure); thus, making such a substitution impossible. Inspired by these concerns, recently, there have been studies on the leakage-resilience of prominent secret-sharing schemes, like Shamir's secret-sharing scheme and the additive secret-sharing scheme [2,14,30,37,39].

A Summary of Our Model and Results. This work studies the leakage-resilience of Massey secret-sharing schemes [43] corresponding to various linear codes, for example, random linear codes, Reed-Solomon codes, and the parity code. We remind the readers that prominent secret-sharing schemes like Shamir's secret-sharing scheme and the additive secret-sharing scheme are the Massey secret-sharing schemes corresponding to (punctured) Reed-Solomon codes and the parity code. Our work considers m-bit *general leakage* from each secret share, where m is a constant.

Result 1. We present a Monte Carlo algorithm for a linear secret-sharing scheme that is secure against m-bit leakage from each secret share, where m is a constant. We prove that the Massey secret-sharing scheme corresponding to a random linear code is leakage-resilient if k/n is a constant $> 1/2$. Towards this objective, the technical challenge is that the number of potential constructions is exponentially smaller than the number of all such leakage functions. Overcoming this hurdle requires identifying a significantly smaller set of "tests," passing them suffices to guarantee leakage-resilience.

Result 2. Next, we show an explicit leakage function (leaking only $m = 1$ bit from each secret share) that highlights a significant shortcoming of the analytic techniques employed in this line of work. Ever since the work of Benhamouda et al. [7], analytic techniques employ a (natural) "proxy analytic function" to study the leakage resilience of secret-sharing schemes. If this proxy is small, then the insecurity of the secret-sharing scheme to leakage attacks is small as well. However, we present an explicit attack demonstrating that the converse is false, making a case for discovering new (analytically well-behaved) proxies that represent the insecurity of secret-sharing schemes more accurately.

Result 3. Using the new analytical techniques developed for "Result 1" in our work, we improve the leakage-resilience guarantees for Shamir's secret-sharing scheme for n parties. We prove that if the reconstruction threshold $k \geqslant 0.8675 \cdot n$ then it is secure against $m = 1$ bit leakage from each secret share improving the previous state-of-the-art from $k \geqslant 0.907 \cdot n$.[1] Independent to our work, the journal version [9] of [8] also improved the threshold to $k \geqslant 0.85n$.

Result 4. Finally, we note that an attack for additive secret-sharing schemes proposed by Benhamouda et al. [7] can be extended to all linear secret-sharing schemes. By this observation, we prove that to achieve $2^{-\lambda}$ insecurity, the threshold k must be at least $\Omega\left(\frac{\lambda}{\log \lambda}\right)$. This generalizes a similar result by Nielsen and Simkin [44] as their result works only for polynomially large fields while our result works for fields of arbitrary size.

1.1 Our Contributions

This section introduces some basic definitions to facilitate an intuitive presentation of our results.

F is a prime field such that $|F|$ needs λ bits for its binary representation, i.e., $2^{\lambda-1} \leqslant |F| < 2^{\lambda}$. We interpret λ as the security parameter and, therefore, the number of parties $n = \mathsf{poly}(\lambda)$. Typically, in cryptography, the objective is to demonstrate the insecurity of cryptographic constructions is $\mathsf{negl}(\lambda)$, a function that decays faster than any inverse-polynomial in λ. However, in this work, as is common in information theory and coding theory literature, all our results shall further ensure that the insecurity is exponentially decaying in the security parameter.

Massey Secret-Sharing Scheme. Let $C \subseteq F^{n+1}$ be a subset, referred to as a *code*. The Masey secret-sharing scheme [43] corresponding to code C secret-

---

[1] The older full version of [8] claims a smaller constant in Theorem 1.2, which is a consequence of an incorrect calculation. $k \geqslant 0.907n$ is an accurate reflection of the result in their full version.

shares the secret $s \in F$ by choosing a random $(c_0, c_1, \ldots, c_n) \in C$ conditioned on $c_0 = s$. The secret share of party i is $s_i = c_i$, for all $i \in \{1, \ldots, n\}$.

Linear Codes. A vector subspace $V \subseteq F^{n+1}$ of dimension $(k+1)$ is an $[n+1, k+1]_F$-code. A matrix $G^+ \in F^{(k+1) \times (n+1)}$ succinctly represents this vector space V if the linear span of its rows, represented by $\langle G^+ \rangle$, is identical to the vector space V. (Punctured) Reed-Solomon codes and parity codes are linear codes. Fix distinct evaluation places $X_1, \ldots, X_n \in F^*$. The set of elements $(f(0), f(X_1), \ldots, f(X_n))$, for all polynomials $f(X) \in F[X]$ of degree $< (k+1)$, is the (punctured) Reed-Solomon code. The set of all elements $(c_0, c_1, \ldots, c_n) \in F^{n+1}$ such that $c_0 + c_1 + \cdots + c_n = 0$ is the parity code.

This work considers Massey secret-sharing schemes of linear codes.

Local Leakage-Resilience of Secret-Sharing Schemes. An (n, m) local leakage function leaks m-bit leakage from each of the secret shares of the n parties. The output of an (n, m) local leakage function is the joint distribution of the mn leakage bits. A secret-sharing scheme for n parties is $(m, \varepsilon) - locally leakage - resilient$ if any (n, m) local leakage function cannot distinguish whether the secret $s^{(0)} \in F$ from the secret $s^{(1)} \in F$ based on the joint leakage distributions, for arbitrary $s^{(0)}, s^{(1)} \in F$.

Remark 1. In the literature (e.g., [7]), the following definition of leakage-resilience has also been considered. The adversary is given some secret shares explicitly and then allowed to leak from the remaining secret shares. We note that, for an MDS code G^+, the leakage-resilience of Massey secret-sharing corresponding to G^+ in these two definitions are equivalent as follows.

Suppose G^+ is an MDS code of dimension $(k+1) \times (n+1)$. If the adversary obtains t shares explicitly, the remaining secret shares is exactly a Massey secret-sharing scheme corresponding to some G' of dimension $(k+1-t) \times (n+1-t)$. Hence, G^+ is leakage-resilient to an adversary who obtains t shares explicitly if and only if Massey secret-sharing corresponding to G' is leakage-resilient when the adversary only leaks from every secret share.

In this paper, we only work with G^+ that is MDS.[2] Therefore, we restrict to the simple setting where the adversary only leaks from every secret share.

Result 1. Leakage-Resilience of Random Linear Codes. For the presentation in this section, a *random* $[n+1, k+1]_F$-code is the linear code $\langle G^+ \rangle$ where $G^+ \in F^{(k+1) \times (n+1)}$ is a rank-$(k+1)$ random matrix. Section 2.2 provides additional details on efficiently sampling such a matrix.

Corollary 1 (Random Linear Secret-sharing Schemes are Leakage-resilient). *Fix constants $m \in \mathbb{N}$, $\delta \in (0, 1)$, and $\eta \in (0, 1)$. Define $n = (1 - \eta) \cdot \lambda$ and $k = (1/2 + \delta) \cdot n$. Let F be a prime field of order $\in \{2^{\lambda-1}, \ldots, 2^\lambda - 1\}$. For all sufficiently large λ, the Massey secret-sharing scheme corresponding to a random $[n+1, k+1]_F$-code is (m, ε)-locally leakage-resilient, where $\varepsilon = \exp(-\Theta\lambda)$, except with $\exp(-\Theta\lambda)$ probability.*

---

[2] In particular, our main result considers a random G^+, which is MDS with overwhelming probability.

We highlight that one can publicly choose the randomness determining G^+ once (say, using a CRS) and use this code for all future applications. With high probability, as long as the local leakage is $\leqslant m$, the Massey secret-sharing scheme corresponding to the linear code $\langle G^+ \rangle$ shall be leakage-resilient.[3] Intuitively, the Massey secret-sharing scheme corresponding to a random $[n+1, k+1]_F$-code (where F is a finite field of order $> 2^{\lambda-1}$, $n = 0.97\lambda$, and $k = 0.49\lambda$) shall be leakage-resilient to arbitrary m-bit local leakages when λ is sufficiently large (except with exponentially small probability). The threshold of λ being sufficiently large depends on the choices of m, δ, and η. For example, when $m = 1$ and using 2000-bit prime numbers, the insecurity of the above scheme is $< 2^{-50}$.

Efficiency. Linear codes, in contrast to non-linear codes, result in efficient Massey secret-sharing schemes. In particular, when $G^+ = [I_{k+1} \mid P]$ is in the *standard form*, as is the case in this work, then the corresponding Massey secret-sharing scheme is easy to specify, where $I_{k+1} \in F^{(k+1)\times(k+1)}$ is the identity matrix. Observe that the secret shares of the secret $s \in F$ is

$$(s, s_1, \ldots, s_n) := (s, r_1, \ldots, r_k) \cdot G^+,$$

where $r_1, \ldots, r_k$ are independently and uniformly distributed over F. Reconstruction of the secret is efficient as well for this secret-sharing scheme. Suppose $G^+_{*,0} = \lambda_1 \cdot G^+_{*,j_1} + \cdots + \lambda_t \cdot G^+_{*,j_t}$, where $G^+_{*,j}$ represents the j-th column of the matrix G^+ and $\lambda_1, \ldots, \lambda_t \in F$ are appropriate constants. Then, parties $j_1, \ldots, j_t$ can efficiently reconstruct the secret $s = \lambda_1 \cdot s_{j_1} + \cdots + \lambda_t \cdot s_{j_t}$, where s_j represents the secret share of party j. Furthermore, any $t = k+1$ shall be able to reconstruct the secret because any $(k+1)$ columns of a random G^+ is full rank, except with an exponentially small probability.

The efficient reconstruction of the secret depends on parties reporting their secret shares correctly. If there are $(k+1)$ publicly identifiable honest parties, all parties can efficiently reconstruct the secret from these parties' secret-shares. Additionally, information-theoretic primitives like *message authentication codes* can ensure that malicious parties cannot disclose incorrect secret shares.[4] Using such information-theoretic cryptographic primitives, all parties can efficiently reconstruct the secret in applications using such secret-sharing schemes.

Applications. Linear secret-sharing schemes have applications in secure multiparty computation [25,55] due to their additive structure. In particular, an additive secret-sharing scheme is useful for the secure computation of circuits that use only addition gates, i.e., the *aggregation functionality*. The secure computation protocol proceeds as follows. Party i secret-shares its inputs $x^{(i)}$ using a linear secret-sharing scheme. Let the secret share of $x^{(i)}$ for party j be $x^{(i,j)}$. Now, party

---

[3] However, as are typical for probabilistic existential results in information theory and coding theory, one cannot efficiently test whether the sampled G^+ is leakage-resilient.

[4] This step is necessary because *efficient error-correction algorithms* for (dense) random linear codes shall require incredible breakthroughs in mathematics. In fact, a lot of cryptography assumes that error-correction for random linear codes is inefficient [47,49]. Efficient error-correction is known only when the matrix G^+ has additional algebraic structures.

j has the secret shares $x^{(1,j)}, \ldots, x^{(n,j)}$. Party j defines $s^{(j)} := \sum_{i=1}^{n} x^{(i,j)}$. Now, the secret shares $s^{(1)}, \ldots, s^{(n)}$ are secret shares of the sum $s = x^{(1)} + \cdots + x^{(n)}$. If any $(k+1)$ parties can reconstruct the secret in the linear secret-sharing scheme, any subset of $(k+1)$ parties can come online to recover the sum s.

When using our linear secret-sharing scheme[5] robust to arbitrary m-bit local leakage, this secure computation is leakage-resilient to arbitrary m-bit leakage as well, when k/n is a constant $> 1/2$. The previous state-of-the-art construction [7] used Shamir's secret-sharing scheme and needed $k/n \geqslant 0.907$, which was a significantly larger fraction. [39] proved the leakage-resilience of Shamir's secret-sharing scheme for an extremely restricted family of leakage functions, namely, the physical-bit leakage function, for every $k > 1$.

Derandomization. We highlight that we significantly derandomized the space of all possible codes to demonstrate that a *linear* code suffices to construct a leakage-resilient secret-sharing scheme. For example, against active adversaries who tamper the secret shares, the probabilistic construction of Cheraghchi and Guruswami [16] used (inefficient) non-linear codes.[6]

Technical Highlights. At the outset, linear codes as potential candidate constructions for leakage-resilient secret-sharing schemes seem far-fetched. Observe that the set of all possible (n, m) local leakage functions is $2^{mn|F|} \gg 2^{2^{\lambda}}$, where m is a constant, $n = \mathsf{poly}(\lambda)$, and $p \approx 2^{\lambda}$. However, there are only $|F|^{kn} \approx 2^{\mathsf{poly}(\lambda)}$ different matrices G^+. Typically, the proofs of similar results (see, for example, [16,22,39]) proceed by "union bound" techniques and need the set of adversarial strategies to be significantly smaller than the potential choices available for the construction. One of our work's key technical contributions is to address this apparent handicap that our construction faces.

We introduce a new family of "tests" (see Sect. 3) inspired by the various notions of pseudorandomness [53,54]. We show that if a generator matrix G^+ passes all these tests, then the Massey secret-sharing scheme corresponding to the linear code $\langle G^+ \rangle$ is leakage-resilient (see Sect. 3.3). The advantage here is that the number of all possible tests is significantly smaller than the number of choices for choosing G^+. Finally, we show that nearly all matrices G^+ pass all our tests (see Sect. 3.2). Lemmas 1 and 2 abstract these two technical innovations, which, the authors believe, are of potential independent interest in the broader field of probabilistic analysis. Section 3 presents the proof of this result.

Result 2. A Barrier in the Analytic Modeling. Benhamouda et al. [7] introduced an analytic proxy (Refer to Eq. 6) for upper bounding the statistical distance between leakage distributions of different secrets. All the works in this line of research ([7,39] and this work) essentially study leakage-resilience of the secret-sharing scheme through this analytic proxy. We present an inherent barrier

---

[5] Additionally, one can use information-theoretic message authentication codes to avoid incorrect revelation of secret-shares.

[6] We note that non-malleability naturally requires the code to be non-linear. However, our point is that the union bound technique would not have worked if one considers a very small family of constructions such as linear codes.

for this proof strategy. We prove that one cannot prove any meaningful result when the threshold is less than half of the number of parties.

In particular, we present an explicit leakage function $\vec{L}$, which tests whether the field element is a *quadratic residue* or not. We prove that for *any* linear secret-sharing scheme with threshold k and n parties such that $k < n/2$, the analytic proxy with respect to this secret-sharing scheme and our leakage function $\vec{L}$ is at least 1.[7] Therefore, using this analytic proxy, it is hopeless to prove leakage-resilience against *general leakage* when $k < n/2$. This result is summarized as Theorem 1 in Sect. 4.

In light of this, our first result that states a random linear code is leakage-resilient when $k \geqslant (\frac{1}{2} + \delta)n$ for an arbitrary constant $\delta \in (0, 1/2)$ is the optimal result one could hope to obtain using the current proof technique. To obtain better results, significantly different ideas are required.

We note that the recent work of Maji et al. [39] also employs this analytic proxy. They show that Shamir's secret-sharing with random evaluation places is leakage-resilient even for the most stringent case $k = 2$ and $n = \text{poly}(\lambda)$. Their results, however, do not contradict the barrier we present here. They only consider the family of leakage functions that leak physical-bit when the field elements are store in their natural binary representations. The counter-example we present, i.e., testing whether a field element is a quadratic residue or not, cannot be simulated by leaking a constant number of physical-bits.

Result 3. We prove the following result on the leakage-resilience of Shamir's secret-sharing scheme.

Corollary 2. *There exists a universal constant p_0 such that, for all finite field F of prime order $p > p_0$, the following holds. Shamir's secret-sharing scheme with number of parties n and threshold k is $(1, \exp(-\Theta n)$-leakage-resilient if $k \geqslant 0.8675n$.*

We improve from the previous state-of-the-art result of $k \geqslant 0.907n$ of [7] to $k \geqslant 0.8675n$. In an independent work, Benhamouda et al. [9] also improved their results to $k \geqslant 0.85n$. Note that achieving $k < n/2$ shall enable parties to multiply their respective secret shares to obtain secret shares of the product of the secrets.

Technically, we prove this result by employing a more fine-grained (compared to [7]) analysis on the analytic proxy. Section 5 presents the proof overview.

Result 4. Consider a secret-sharing scheme with n parties and threshold k over a prime field F of order p that is leakage-resilient to m-bit leakage from each share. Nielsen and Simkin [44] proved that it must hold that $k \cdot \log p \geqslant m \cdot (n - k)$. Intuitively, they prove this result using an entropy argument.[8] Consequently, their result is inevitably sensitive to the size of the field. They used this result

---

[7] Note that this analytic proxy is used as an upper bound of the statistical distance. Hence, it gives an inconsequential bound if it is $\geqslant 1$.

[8] Note that a secret-sharing scheme contains exactly $k \cdot \log p$ amount of entropy. Hence, intuitively, the total amount entropy leaked $m \cdot n$ cannot exceed $k \cdot \log p$.

to show that if the field size satisfies $p = \mathsf{poly}(n)$, the threshold k must be at least $\Omega(n/\log n)$.

For linear secret-sharing schemes, we obtain a similar result, independent of the field size.

Corollary 3. *If a linear secret-sharing scheme (over an arbitrarily large field) with n parties and threshold k is $(1, \varepsilon)$-leakage-resilient, then it must hold that $\varepsilon \geqslant \left(\frac{1}{2k}\right)^k$. Consequently, if it is $(1, \exp(-\Theta n))$-leakage-resilient, it must hold that $k = \Omega(n/\log n)$.*

We prove our result through a similar attack proposed by [7] (on additive secret-sharing schemes). A proof of this result is provided in the full version [40].

1.2   Prior Works

Local leakage-resilient secret-sharing schemes were introduced by Benhamouda, Degwekar, Ishai, and Rabin [7] (also, independently by [26] as an intermediate primitive). There has been a sequence of works analyzing the leakage-resilience of prominent secret-sharing schemes [2,14,30,37,39] and constructing new leakage-resilient secret-sharing schemes [3,6,11,13,15,23,24,31,36,41,51].

There is an exciting connection between repairing a linear code in the distributed storage setting and the leakage-resilience of its corresponding Massey secret-sharing scheme [43]. In the distributed storage setting, every coordinate of the linear code is separately stored. The objective is to repair a block of the code by obtaining information from all other blocks. For example, Guruswami and Wootters [28,29] present a reconstruction algorithm that obtains $m = 1$ bit from every block of a Reed-Solomon code to repair any block when the field has characteristic two. These reconstruction algorithms ensure that by leaking m bits from the secret-shares corresponding to the Massey secret-sharing scheme corresponding to the linear code, it is possible to reconstruct the secret. For example, the Reed-Solomon reconstruction algorithm of Guruswami-Wootters translates into a leakage attack on Shamir's secret-sharing scheme (for characteristic two fields), the Massey secret-sharing scheme corresponding to a (punctured) Reed-Solomon code.

However, when working over prime fields, [7] proved that Shamir's secret-sharing scheme is robust to $m = 1$ bit leakage if the reconstruction threshold is sufficiently high. In particular, their analysis proved that it suffices for the reconstruction threshold k to be at least $0.907n$, where n is the total number of parties. Moreover, their results extend to arbitrary MDS codes. They complement this positive result with an attack on the additive secret-sharing scheme that has a distinguishing advantage of $\varepsilon \geqslant k^{-k}$. After that, Nielsen and Simkin [44] present a probabilistic argument to construct a leakage attack on any Massey secret-sharing scheme. Roughly, their attack needs $m \geqslant k \log p/(n-k)$ bits of leakage from each secret share, where p is the order of the prime field.

Recently, [39] studied a restricted family of leakage on Shamir's secret-sharing schemes. The secret-shares, which are elements of the prime field, are represented in their natural binary representation and stored in hardware. The adversary can leak only physical bits from the memory storage. They proved that Shamir's secret-sharing scheme with random evaluation places is leakage-resilient to this leakage family.

2   Preliminaries and Notations

The *binary entropy function* $h_2 \colon [0,1] \to [0,1]$ is

$$h_2(p) := -p \log_2 p - (1-p) \log_2 (1-p).$$

We shall use the following elementary upper bound on the binomial coefficients.

Claim 1 (Estimation of Binomial Coefficients). *For all $n \in \mathbb{N}$ and $k \in \{0, 1, \ldots, n\}$, we have*

$$\binom{n}{k} \leqslant 2^{h_2(k/n) \cdot n}.$$

Proof. Observe that

$$1 = \left(\frac{k}{n} + \frac{n-k}{n} \right)^n \geqslant \binom{n}{k} \left(\frac{k}{n} \right)^k \left(1 - \frac{k}{n} \right)^{n-k} = \binom{n}{k} 2^{-h_2(k/n) \cdot n}.$$

This completes the proof of the claim.

Our work uses the length of the binary representation of the order of the prime field F as the security parameter λ. The total number of parties $n = \mathsf{poly}(\lambda)$ and the reconstruction threshold $k = \mathsf{poly}(\lambda)$ as well. The objective of our arguments shall be to show the insecurity of the cryptographic constructions is $\varepsilon = \mathsf{negl}(\lambda)$, i.e., a function that decays faster than any inverse-polynomial of the λ.

We shall also use the following Vinogradov notations for brevity in our analysis (as consistent with, for example, [4]). For functions $f(\lambda)$ and $g(\lambda)$, one writes $f(\lambda) \sim g(\lambda)$ to represent $f(\lambda) = (1 + o(1)) \cdot g(\lambda)$, where $o(1)$ is a decreasing function in λ. Similarly, $f(\lambda) \lesssim g(\lambda)$ is equivalent to $f(\lambda) \leqslant (1 + o(1)) \cdot g(\lambda)$. Finally, $f(\lambda) \ll g(\lambda)$ represents that $f(\lambda) = o(1) \cdot g(\lambda)$. We explicitly mention the definitions of these notations because there are multiple interpretations of these symbols even in the field of analysis.

2.1   General Notation: Vectors, Random Variables, Sets

Let X be a sample space. Particular elements of X are represented using the small-case letter x. A random variable of sampling x from the sample space X shall be represented by $\mathbf{x}$.

For any two distributions $\mathbf{A}$ and $\mathbf{B}$ over the same sample space (which is enumerable), the *statistical distance* between the two distributions, represented by $\mathsf{SD}(\mathbf{A}, \mathbf{B})$, is defined as $\frac{1}{2} \sum_x |\Pr[\mathbf{A} = x] - \Pr[\mathbf{B} = x]|$.

A vector $\vec{v} \in \Omega^n$ is interpreted as $\vec{v} = (v_1, \ldots, v_n)$, where each $v_i \in \Omega$. For any $I \subseteq \{1, \ldots, n\}$, the vector $\vec{v}_I \in \Omega^{|I|}$ represents the vector $(v_i \colon i \in I)$.

Let $(S, \circ)$ be a group. Let $A \subseteq S$ and $x \in S$ be an arbitrary element of S. Then $x \circ S$ is the set $\{x \circ y \colon y \in S\}$.

2.2   Matrices

We adopt the following notations for matrices as consistent with [45].

Let F be a finite field. A matrix $M \in F^{k \times n}$ has k-rows and n-columns, and each of its element is in F. For $i \in \{1, \ldots, k\}$ and $j \in \{1, \ldots, n\}$, $M_{i,j}$ represents the (i, j)-th elements in the matrix M. Furthermore, $M_{i,*}$ represents the i-th row of M and $M_{*,j}$ represents the j-th column of M. The *transpose* of the matrix $M \in F^{k \times n}$ is the matrix $N \in F^{n \times k}$ such that $M_{i,j} = N_{j,i}$, for all $i \in \{1, \ldots, k\}$ and $j \in \{1, \ldots, n\}$. We represent $N = M^{\mathsf{T}}$.

Let $I \subseteq \{1, \ldots, k\}$ and $J \subseteq \{1, \ldots, n\}$ be a subset of row and column indices, respectively. The matrix M restricted to rows I and columns J is represented by $M_{I,J}$. If $I = \{i\}$ is a singleton set, then we represent $M_{i,J}$ for $M_{\{i\},J}$. The analogous notation also holds for singleton J. Furthermore, $G_{*,J}$ represents the columns of G indexed by J (all rows are included). Similarly, $G_{*,j}$ represents the j-th column of the matrix G. Analogously, one defines $G_{I,*}$ and $G_{i,*}$.

Some parts of the documents use $\{0, 1, \ldots, k\}$ as row indices and $\{0, 1, \ldots, n\}$ as column indices for a matrix $G \in F^{(k+1) \times (n+1)}$. We will be explicit in mentioning the row and column indices in this work.

Random Matrices. A *random matrix M of dimension $k \times n$* is a uniformly random element of $F^{k \times n}$. This sampling is equivalent to choosing every element $M_{i,j}$ of the matrix uniformly and independently at random from F, for all $i \in \{1, \ldots, k\}$ and $j \in \{1, \ldots, n\}$.

2.3   Codes and Massey Secret-Sharing Schemes

We use the following notations for error-correcting codes as consistent with [38].

Let F be a finite field. A *linear code* C (over the finite field F) of *length* $(n + 1)$ and *rank* $(k + 1)$ is a $(k + 1)$-dimension vector subspace of F^{n+1}, referred to as an $[n + 1, k + 1]_F$-code. The *generator matrix* $G \in F^{(k+1) \times (n+1)}$ of an $[n+1, k+1]_F$ linear code C ensures that every element in C can be expressed as $\vec{x} \cdot G$, for an appropriate $\vec{x} \in F^{k+1}$. Given a generator matrix G, the row-span of G, i.e., the code generated by G, is represented by $\langle G \rangle$. A generator matrix G is in the *standard form* if $G = [I_{k+1}|P]$, where $I_{k+1} \in F^{(k+1) \times (k+1)}$ is the identity matrix and $P \in F^{(k+1) \times (n-k)}$ is the parity check matrix. In our work, we always assume that the generator matrices are in their standard form.

Let $C \subseteq F^{n+1}$ be the linear code that G generates. The *dual code* of C, represented by $C^\perp \subseteq F^{n+1}$, is the set of all elements in F^{n+1} that are orthogonal to *every* element in C. The dual code of an $[n + 1, k + 1]_F$-code happens to be an $[n + 1, n - k]_F$-code. The generator matrix H for the dual code of the $[n+1, k+1]_F$ linear code C generated by $G = [I_{k+1}|P]$ satisfies $H = [-P^{\mathsf{T}}|I_{n-k}]$, where $P^{\mathsf{T}} \in F^{(n-k) \times (k+1)}$ is the transpose of the matrix $P \in F^{(k+1) \times (n-k)}$. For brevity, we shall refer to the generator matrix H as the *dual* of the generator matrix G.

Maximum Distance Separable Codes. The *distance* of a linear code is the minimum weight of a non-zero codeword. An $[n, k]_F$-code is *maximum distance separable* (MDS) if its distance is $(n - k + 1)$. Furthermore, the dual code of an $[n, k]_F$-MDS code is an $[n, n - k]_F$-MDS code.

Massey Secret-Sharing Scheme. Let $C \subseteq F^{n+1}$ be a code (not necessarily a linear code). Let $s \in F$ be a secret. The secret-sharing scheme picks a random element $(s, s_1, \dots, s_n) \in C$ to share the secret s. The secret shares of parties $1, \dots, n$ are $s_1, \dots, s_n \in F$, respectively. Below, we elaborate on the Massey secret-sharing scheme and its properties specifically for a linear code C such that its generator matrix G^+ is in the standard form.

Recall that the set of all codewords of the linear code generated by the generator matrix $G^+ \in F^{(k+1) \times (n+1)}$ is

$$\left\{ \vec{y} : \ \vec{x} \in F^{k+1}, \vec{x} \cdot G^+ =: \vec{y} \right\} \subseteq F^{n+1}.$$

For such a generator matrix, its rows are indexed by $\{0, 1, \dots, k\}$ and its columns are indexed by $\{0, 1, \dots, n\}$. Let $s \in F$ be the secret. The *secret-sharing scheme* picks independent and uniformly random $r_1, \dots, r_k \in F$. Let

$$(y_0, y_1, \dots, y_n) := (s, r_1, \dots, r_k) \cdot G^+.$$

Observe that $y_0 = s$ because the generator matrix G^+ is in the standard form. The secret shares for the parties $1, \dots, n$ are $s_1 = y_1, s_2 = y_2, \dots, s_n = y_n$, respectively. Observe that every party's secret-share is an element of the field F. Of particular interest will be the set of all secret shares of the secret $s = 0$. Observe that the secret-shares form an $[n, k]_F$-code that is $\langle G \rangle$, where $G = G^+_{\{1, \dots, k\} \times \{1, \dots, n\}}$. Note that the matrix G is also in the standard form. The secret shares of $s \in F^*$ form the affine space $s \cdot \vec{v} + \langle G \rangle$, where $\vec{v} = G^+_{0, \{1, \dots, n\}}$. Refer to Fig. 1 for a pictorial summary.

Suppose parties $i_1, \dots, i_t \in \{1, \dots, n\}$ come together to reconstruct the secret with their, respective, secret shares $s_{i_1}, \dots, s_{i_t}$. Let $G^+_{*, i_1}, \dots, G^+_{*, i_t} \in F^{(k+1) \times 1}$ represent the columns indexed by $i_1, \dots, i_t \in \{1, \dots, n\}$, respectively. If the column $G^+_{*, 0} \in F^{(k+1) \times 1}$ lies in the span of $\{G^+_{*, i_1}, \dots, G^+_{*, i_t}\}$ then these parties can reconstruct the secret s using a linear combination of their secret shares. If the column G^+_{*0} *does not* lie in the span of $\{G^+_{*, i_1}, \dots, G^+_{*, i_t}\}$ then the secret remains *perfectly hidden* from these parties. The perfectly-hiding property is specific to the case that a linear code is used for the Massey secret-sharing scheme. In particular, this perfectly-hiding property need not necessarily hold for Massey secret-sharing schemes that use a non-linear secret-sharing scheme.

In this document, we shall use the "Massey secret-sharing scheme of G^+" to refer to the Massey secret-sharing scheme corresponding to the linear code generated by the generator matrix G^+. The underlying field F, the length of the code $(n + 1)$, and the rank $(k + 1)$ of the linear code are implicit given the definition of the generator matrix G^+. These parameters, in turn, define the space of the secret-shares, the total number of parties, and the randomness needed to generate the secret shares for the Massey secret-sharing scheme, respectively.

Specific Linear Codes. The (punctured) *Reed-Solomon code* of rank $(k+1)$ and evaluation places $\vec{X} = (X_1, \dots, X_n) \in (F^*)^n$, where $i \neq j$ implies $X_i \neq X_j$, is the following code. Let $f(X)$ be the *unique polynomial* with F-coefficients and degree $\leqslant k$ such that $f(0) = y_0, f(X_1) = y_1, f(X_2) = y_2, \ldots, f(X_k) = y_k$, for any $y_0, y_1, \ldots, y_k \in F$. Define $c_{k+1} = f(X_{k+1}), \ldots, c_n = f(X_n)$. The set of all codewords $(y_0, y_1, \ldots, y_k, c_{k+1}, \ldots, c_n) \in F^{n+1}$ is an $[n+1, k+1]_F$-code. Furthermore, the mapping

$$(y_0, y_1, \ldots, y_k) \mapsto (y_0, y_1, \ldots, y_k, c_{k+1}, \ldots, c_n)$$

is linear and a generator matrix in the standard form establishes this mapping.

Specific Secret-Sharing Schemes. *Shamir's secret-sharing scheme* is the Massey secret-sharing scheme corresponding to (punctured) Reed-Solomon codes. Suppose the evaluation places of the (punctured) Reed-Solomon code are $\vec{X} = (X_1, \ldots, X_n) \in (F^*)^n$. Suppose the secret is $s \in F$. Let $f(X)$ be the unique polynomial with F-coefficients and degree $\leqslant k$ such that $f(0) = s, f(X_1) = r_1, \ldots, f(X_k) = r_k$. Define the secret shares $(s_1, \ldots, s_n)$, where $s_i = f(X_i)$, for all $i \in \{1, \ldots, n\}$.

2.4   Locally Leakage-Resilient Secret-Sharing Scheme

Fix a finite field F and an n-party secret-sharing scheme for secrets $s \in F$, where every party gets an element in F as their secret share. An (n, m) *local leakage function* $\vec{L} = (L_1, \ldots, L_n)$ is an n-collection of m-bit leakage functions $L_i \colon F \to \{0, 1\}^m$, for $i \in \{1, \ldots, n\}$. Note that there are a total of $2^{mn \cdot |F|}$ different (n, m) local leakage functions. Let $\vec{L}(s)$ be the joint distribution of the (n, m) leakage function $\vec{L}$ over the sample space $(\{0, 1\}^m)^n$ defined by the experiment: (a) sample secret shares $(s_1, \ldots, s_n)$ for the secret s, and (b) output $(L_1(s_1), \ldots, L_n(s_n))$. We emphasize that the secret-sharing scheme and the finite field F shall be evident from the context. So, we do not include the description of the secret-sharing scheme and the finite field in the random variables above to avoid excessively cumbersome notation.

A secret-sharing scheme for n-parties is (m, ε)-*locally leakage-resilient secret-sharing scheme* if, for all (n, m) local leakage functions $\vec{L} = (L_1, \ldots, L_n)$ and secret pairs $(s^{(0)}, s^{(1)})$, the statistical distance between the leakage joint distributions $\vec{L}(s^{(0)})$ and $\vec{L}(s^{(1)})$ is at most ε.

For brevity, we shall say that a generator matrix G is (m, ε)-locally leakage-resilient if the Massey secret-sharing scheme corresponding to the linear code generated by G is (m, ε)-locally leakage-resilient.

3   Leakage-Resilience of Random Linear Codes

In this section, we prove Corollary 1. We start by recalling some notations. Refer to Fig. 1 for a pictorial summary of the notations. The secret shares of 0 is the vector space

$$(0, r_1, \ldots, r_k) \cdot G_{\{0, \ldots, k\}, \{1, \ldots, n\}} \in F^n.$$

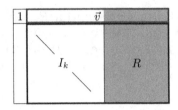
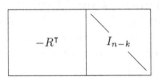

Fig. 1. The matrix on the left is $G^+ = [I_{k+1} \mid P]$, where P is the random matrix in the shaded region. The indices of rows and columns of G^+ are $\{0, 1, \ldots, k\}$ and $\{0, 1, \ldots, n\}$, respectively. The blue $G = [I_k \mid R]$ is a submatrix of G^+. The vector highlighted in red is the vector $\vec{v}$. On the right-hand side, we have the matrix H, where $\langle H \rangle$ is the dual code of $\langle G \rangle$. (Color figure online)

Observe that this vector space is an $[n, k]_F$-code, represented by $\langle G \rangle$, where $G = G^+_{\{1,\ldots,k\},\{1,\ldots,n\}}$. Each element of $\langle G \rangle$ is equally likely to be chosen as the secret share for the n parties. Next, consider the secret $s \in F^*$. The secret shares of s form the affine space

$$(s, r_1, \ldots, r_k) \cdot G^+_{*,\{1,\ldots,n\}} \in F^n.$$

Observe that, one can express this affine space as

$$s \cdot \vec{v} + \langle G \rangle \subseteq F^n,$$

where $\vec{v} = G^+_{0,\{1,\ldots,n\}} \in F^n$.

To demonstrate that the Massey secret-sharing scheme corresponding to the linear code generated by a generator matrix $G^+ \in F^{(k+1)\times(n+1)}$ is vulnerable to leakage attacks, the adversary needs to present two secrets $s^{(0)}, s^{(1)} \in F$ and an (n, m) local leakage function $\vec{L}$ such that the statistical distance between the joint leakage distributions for these two secrets is large.

First Attempt. Fix an (n, m) local leakage function $\vec{L}$. Let $\vec{\ell} \in (\{0, 1\}^m)^n$ be a leakage value. Let $L_i^{-1}(\ell_i) \subseteq F$ be the subset of i-th party's secret shares such that the leakage function L_i outputs $\ell_i \in \{0, 1\}^m$ as output. Therefore, we have $s_i \in L_i^{-1}(\ell_i)$ if and only if $L_i(s_i) = \ell_i$. Furthermore, the leakage is $\vec{\ell}$ if and only if the secret shares $\vec{s}$ belongs to the set

$$\vec{L}^{-1}(\vec{\ell}) := L_1^{-1}(\ell_1) \times \cdots \times L_n^{-1}(\ell_n).$$

So, the probability of the leakage being $\vec{\ell}$ conditioned on the secret being $s^{(0)}$ is

$$\frac{1}{|F|^k} \cdot \left| s^{(0)} \cdot \vec{v} + \langle G \rangle \cap \vec{L}^{-1}(\vec{\ell}) \right|.$$

Similarly, the probability of the leakage being $\vec{\ell}$ conditioned on the secret being $s^{(1)}$ is

$$\frac{1}{|F|^k} \cdot \left| s^{(1)} \cdot \vec{v} + \langle G \rangle \cap \vec{L}^{-1}(\vec{\ell}) \right|.$$

The absolute value of the difference in the probabilities is, therefore, the following expression.

$$\frac{1}{|F|^k} \cdot \left| \left| s^{(0)} \cdot \vec{v} + \langle G \rangle \cap \vec{L}^{-1}(\vec{\ell}) \right| - \left| s^{(1)} \cdot \vec{v} + \langle G \rangle \cap \vec{L}^{-1}(\vec{\ell}) \right| \right|.$$

The statistical distance between the joint leakage distributions is

$$\frac{1}{2} \cdot \frac{1}{|F|^k} \sum_{\vec{\ell} \in (\{0,1\}^m)^n} \left| \left| s^{(0)} \cdot \vec{v} + \langle G \rangle \cap \vec{L}^{-1}(\vec{\ell}) \right| - \left| s^{(1)} \cdot \vec{v} + \langle G \rangle \cap \vec{L}^{-1}(\vec{\ell}) \right| \right|.$$

(1)

If the expression in Eq. 1 is $\leqslant \varepsilon$ for all (n, m) leakage functions $\vec{L}$ and all pairs of secrets $s^{(0)}$ and $s^{(1)}$, then the generator matrix G^+ is (m, ε)-locally leakage-resilient.

Remark 2. Observe that if one can choose $\vec{L}$ to ensure that any codeword $\vec{c} \in \langle G \rangle$ that belongs to $\vec{L}^{-1}(\vec{\ell})$ (for some $\vec{\ell}$) also has $\vec{c} + s^{(1)} \cdot \vec{v} \notin \vec{L}^{-1}(\vec{\ell})$ for some secret $s^{(1)}$, then the expression in Eq. 1 is identical to 1.

For example, if the finite field is characteristic-2, even with $m = 1$ bit leakage from each secret share, an adversary can ensure this condition. The attack works as follows. Suppose the secret s can be reconstructed by $\alpha_1 s_1 + \alpha_2 s_2 + \cdots + \alpha_k s_k$ where $\alpha_1, \ldots, \alpha_k$ are fixed field elements and s_i is the i-th secret share. The adversary leaks the least significant symbol b_i of $\alpha_i s_i$ from the i-th secret share. Afterwards, the adversary can reconstruct the least significant symbol of the secret s by computing $b_1 \oplus b_2 \oplus \cdots \oplus b_k$. This leakage attack extends to linear secret-sharing schemes over finite fields with small characteristics. More specifically, the above attack generalize to characteristic-p field when the adversary is allowed to leak $\lceil \log p \rceil$ bits from each secret share.

Recall that the number of (n, m) local leakage functions is $2^{mn \cdot |F|}$. One encounters the following hurdle while proceeding by the union bound technique to prove our result. Suppose that for every leakage function $\vec{L}$ there is one generator matrix such that the statistical distance in Eq. 1 is $> \varepsilon$. Using naïve union bound technique, one shall rule out $2^{mn \cdot |F|}$ generator matrices. However, there are only a total of $|F|^{(k+1) \times (n-k)}$ generator matrices. For the event of encountering generator matrices that are (m, ε)-locally leakage-resilient with high probability, we shall require

$$2^{mn \cdot |F|} \ll |F|^{(k+1) \cdot (n-k)} \sim 2^{kn \cdot \log_2 |F|}.$$

For simplicity, consider the minimal non-trivial case of $m = 1$ and $k = n(1 - o(1))$. Our result is impossible to prove even for this minimal non-trivial case where $|F| = p \geqslant 2^{\lambda-1}$ and $m = 1$.

Remark 3. We note that the recent result of [39] uses a union bound technique. In their work, however, they consider physical-bit leakage functions. The total number of physical-bit leakage functions is extremely small;[9] otherwise, their approach (despite all the exciting new technical tools) would not have worked.

Remark 4. In the active adversary setting, to the authors' best knowledge, union bound (over all possible adversaries) is the only general technique known in the literature. See, for instance, the probabilistic proofs of the existence of non-malleable extractors [19] and non-malleable codes [16,22]. The proof of [16] even employs non-linear codes (which provide significantly more degrees of freedom in designing the encoding schemes) to push a "union bound based proof" through.

A New Set of Tests. To circumvent the hurdles associated with the naïve union bound, we propose a new set of tests. We emphasize that it is *non-trivial* to prove that if a generator matrix G passes all these tests, then G^+ is (m, ε)-locally leakage-resilient. Section 3.3 elaborates this implication. The inspiration for these tests stems from the literature in pseudorandomness [53,54].[10]

Recall that $G^+ \in F^{(k+1)\times(n+1)}$ is the generator matrix of the code, and $G^+ = [I_{k+1}|P]$ is in the standard form, where $P \in F^{(k+1)\times(n-k)}$. The secret shares of secret 0 is the $[n, k]_F$-code $\langle G \rangle$. The matrix G is also in the standard form, say $G = [I_k|R]$, where $R = P_{\{1,\dots,k\}\times\{1,\dots,n-k\}} \in F^{k\times(n-k)}$. Then, the matrix $H = [-R^\mathsf{T}|I_{n-k}]$ generates the dual code of the code generated by the matrix $G = [I_k|R]$. We introduce the matrix H because it is easy to express our tests using the row-span of H, i.e. $\langle H \rangle$.

Fix parameters $\sigma \in [0,1]$, $\gamma \in \mathbb{N}$, and $a \in \mathbb{N}$. The set of all tests $\mathsf{Test}_{\sigma,\gamma,a}$ is defined as follows. Every test is *additionally* indexed by $(\vec{V}, J)$, where $\vec{V} = (V_1, \dots, V_n)$, each V_i is a size-γ subset of the finite field F, and J is a size-$(1-\sigma)\cdot n$ subset of $\{1, \dots, n\}$. A codeword $c \in F^n$ *fails the test* indexed by $(\vec{V}, J)$ if $c_j \in V_j$, for all $j \in J$.

The generator matrix H *fails the test* indexed by $(\vec{V}, J)$ if at least a^n codewords fail this test. The generator matrix H *passes* $\mathsf{Test}_{\sigma,\gamma,a}$ if H does not fail for *any* test in $\mathsf{Test}_{\sigma,\gamma,a}$.

Lemma 1 (Technical Lemma 1). *Let G^+ be the generator matrix of an $[n+1, k+1]_F$-code. Consider a Massey secret-sharing scheme corresponding to the linear code $\langle G^+ \rangle$. Let $\langle G \rangle$ be the $[n, k]_F$-code formed by the set of all secret shares of the secret 0. Let $\langle H \rangle$ be the $[n, n-k]_F$-code that is the dual code of $\langle G \rangle$. Let $\mathsf{Test}_{\sigma,\gamma,a}$ be a set of tests, where $\gamma = 2^m \cdot T^2$ and $T \in \mathbb{N}$. If H passes $\mathsf{Test}_{\sigma,\gamma,a}$, $\langle H \rangle$ is an MDS code, and $\sigma \in (0, 2k/n-1]$, then G^+ is (m, ε)-locally leakage-resilient, where*

$$\varepsilon = 2^{-\left(\log_2(C_m)\cdot(k/n)-\log_2(a)-h_2(\sigma)\right)\cdot n} + 2^{-\left(\log_2(T)\cdot\sigma-(\sigma+k^\perp/n)m-h_2(\sigma)\right)\cdot n},$$

---

[9] For example, consider a physical-bit leakage function that leaks one bit from the field F. There are $\log_2 |F|$ such functions. In comparison, there are $2^{|F|}$ general 1-bit leakage functions.

[10] Intuitively, a set whose correlation with any Fourier character is small can be interpreted as a pseudorandom object. On the other side, a large Fourier coefficient indicates a correlation with a Fourier character; thus, the object is *not* pseudorandom. In a similar spirit, as we shall explain, our tests find whether a code $\langle H \rangle$ has many codewords with large Fourier coefficients or not.

and $C_m > 1$ is a suitable constant depending on m.[11]

Remark 5. Note that this lemma is where we inherently need $k > n/2$. Otherwise, we are unable to pick a σ. We discuss this barrier further when we go into the proof in Remark 6 and Sect. 4.

In Sect. 3.1, we shall set the parameters properly to ensure the insecurity is negligible. There are potentially several techniques to prove this result. We prove this technical lemma using Fourier analysis in Sect. 3.3.

Most Matrices Pass the Tests. Let us do a sanity check first. The total number of tests in $\mathsf{Test}_{\sigma,\gamma,a}$ is

$$\binom{|F|}{\gamma}^n \cdot \binom{n}{(1-\sigma)n} = \Theta |F|^{\gamma \cdot n} \cdot 2^{h_2(\sigma) \cdot n}.$$

Furthermore, the total number of generator matrices G is $|F|^{k \cdot (n-k)}$. So, it is plausible that the union bound technique may work for this result.

However, naïve accounting does not suffice. Section 3.2 presents the careful accounting needed to prove the following result.

Lemma 2 (Technical Lemma 2). *Fix constant σ, γ, a. Let $p \geq 2^{\lambda-1}$ be a prime and $\lim_{\lambda \to \infty} n/\lambda \in (0,1)$, where λ is the security parameter. Let G^+ be the generator matrix of an $[n+1, k+1]_F$-code in the standard form such that each element of its parity check matrix is independently and uniformly chosen from F, where constant $k/n \in (\sigma, 1)$. Consider a Massey secret-sharing scheme corresponding to the linear code $\langle G^+ \rangle$. Let $\langle G \rangle$ be the $[n,k]_F$-code formed by the set of all secret shares of the secret 0. Let $\langle H \rangle$ be the $[n, n-k]_F$-code that is the dual code of $\langle G \rangle$. Then, the following bound holds.*

$$\Pr_{G^+ \xleftarrow{\$} \mathbf{G}^+} [H \text{ is MDS and passes } \mathsf{Test}_{\sigma,\gamma,a}] = 1 - 2^{-(1-n/\lambda) \cdot \lambda} - \exp(-\Theta \lambda^3).$$

3.1 Parameter Setting for Corollary 1

Before we go into the proof of Lemmas 1 and 2, let us first show how we can set up the parameters in both lemmas to imply Corollary 1. Let us restate the corollary first.

Corollary 4. (Restatement of Corollary 1). *Fix constants $m \in \mathbb{N}$, $\delta \in (0,1)$, and $\eta \in (0,1)$. Define $n = (1-\eta) \cdot \lambda$ and $k = (1/2 + \delta) \cdot n$. Let F be a prime field of order $\in \{2^{\lambda-1}, \ldots, 2^\lambda - 1\}$. For all sufficiently large λ, the Massey secret-sharing scheme corresponding to a random $[n+1, k+1]_F$-code is (m, ε)-locally leakage-resilient, where $\varepsilon = \exp(-\Theta \lambda)$, except with $\exp(-\Theta \lambda)$ probability.*

The sequence of parameter choices is as follows. We emphasize that all parameters below are constants.

---

[11] Refer to the full version [40] for the relation between m and the constant C_m.

1. We are given the number of bits leaked from each share m and the target threshold δ as constants. Therefore, $C_m > 1$ is also fixed as a constant.
2. We shall pick constants $\sigma > 0$ and $a > 1$ arbitrarily satisfying the following constraints.
   (a) $\sigma < \min(2\delta, 1/2 + \delta)$. This parameter choice ensures that $\sigma < 2k/n - 1$ and $\sigma < k/n$.
   (b) $\log_2(C_m) \cdot (1/2 + \delta) - \log_2(a) - h_2(\sigma) > 0$. This choice ensures that the first part in the expression of ε in Lemma 1 is negligible.
3. Next, we pick any constant T satisfying $\log_2(T) \cdot \sigma - (\sigma + (1/2 - \delta)) m - h_2(\sigma) > 0$. This choice ensures that the second part in the expression of ε in Lemma 1 is negligible.
4. Since we have picked T, this implicitly fixes γ as $\gamma = 2^m \cdot T^2$.

Clearly, all the steps above are feasible, and we have now fixed all the constants involved. One can verify that all the prerequisites of Lemmas 1 and 2 are satisfied. Consequently, Lemmas 1 and 2 together imply that the Massey secret-sharing scheme corresponding to a random linear code is negligibly-insecure with overwhelming probability.

As a concrete example, suppose $m = 1$, $n = 0.97\lambda$, and $k = 0.49\lambda$. In this case $C_m = \sqrt{2}$, by setting, $\sigma = 0.01$, $a = 1.5$, and $T = 2^{50}$, one can verify that $\lambda > 2000$ ensures that we achieve 2^{-50}-insecurity.[12]

3.2   Proof of Lemma 2

The proof of Lemma 2 proceeds by a combinatorial argument. Fix a test $(\vec{V}, J)$ in the set of tests $\mathsf{Test}_{\sigma,\gamma,a}$. Consider the experiment where $G^+ \overset{\$}{\leftarrow} \mathbf{G}^+$, and $H \in F^{k^\perp \times n}$ be the matrix corresponding to G^+ as described in the statement of Lemma 2, where $k^\perp = n - k$. Our entire analysis is for this distribution of the matrix H.

Observe that $\langle H \rangle$ is a maximum distance separable (MDS) code, with high probability. We defer the proof of this claim to the full version [40].

Claim 2. *The linear codes $\langle G \rangle$ and $\langle H \rangle$ are maximum distance separable codes, except with probability (at most) $2^n/p = \exp(-\Theta\lambda)$.*

Henceforth, our analysis shall assume that G^+ is random as well as $\langle G \rangle$ and $\langle H \rangle$ are MDS (without loss of generality). Therefore $\langle G \rangle$ is an $[n, k]_F$-MDS code and $\langle H \rangle$ is an $[n, k^\perp]_F$-MDS code, where $k^\perp = n - k$. Recall that $H = [-R^\mathsf{T}|I_{n-k}]$, where every element of $-R^\mathsf{T}$ is independent and uniformly random over F.

Without loss of generality, assume that $J = \{\sigma n + 1, \sigma n + 2, \ldots, n\}$. Among the indices in J, let us fix the indices $J' = \{k+1, k+2, \ldots, n\}$ as the information set for the linear code $\langle H \rangle$.[13] Let us fix a set of witnesses $B \subseteq F^{k^\perp}$ of size a^n.

---

[12] For similar range of parameter choices, e.g., when n is close to λ, the dominant failure probability is the probability that a random matrix is not MDS, which is $2^{n-\lambda}$.

[13] Since $\langle H \rangle$ is MDS, we can pick any $k^\perp$ coordinates to be the information set. We choose the last $k^\perp$ coordinates (to coincide with the I_{n-k} block identity matrix of H) for simplicity. All remaining coordinates of a codeword in $\langle H \rangle$ are derived via a linear combination of the information set.

Objective. Over the distribution of $\langle H \rangle$, what is the probability that every codeword $c \in \langle H \rangle$ such that c restricted to the information set J' is in the set B fails the test $(\vec{V}, J)$? That is, compute the probability of the event "if $c_{J'} \in B$ then $c_j \in V_j$, for all $j \in J$."

Proof for a Weaker Bound. The total number of choices for $\vec{V}$ is at most $(|F|^\gamma)^n = |F|^{\gamma \cdot n}$. The total number of choices for J is at most $\binom{n}{(1-\sigma)n} = 2^{h_2(\sigma) \cdot n}$. Finally, the total number of sets of witnesses B is at most $\binom{\gamma^{k^\perp}}{a^n}$.[14] Therefore, the total number of possibilities is

$$|F|^{\gamma \cdot n} \cdot 2^{h_2(\sigma) \cdot n} \cdot \binom{\gamma^{k^\perp}}{a^n}. \tag{2}$$

Next, fix a column index $j \in J \setminus J' = \{\sigma n + 1, \sigma n + 2, \ldots, k\}$. Pick one non-zero witness $\vec{d}^{(1)} \in B$. Over the randomness of choosing $H_{*,j}$, the random variable $\vec{d}^{(1)} \cdot H_{*,j}$ is uniformly random over the field F. So, the probability of this coordinate being in V_j is $\gamma/|F|$. This statement is true for all $j \in J \setminus J'$ independently. Therefore, for all $j \in J \setminus J'$, the probability of the j-th coordinate of the codeword $\vec{d}^{(1)} \cdot H$ being in V_j is

$$\left(\frac{\gamma}{|F|} \right)^{(1-\sigma)n - k^\perp}.$$

Now, choose a second witness $\vec{d}^{(2)} \in B$. Suppose $\vec{d}^{(2)}$ is a scalar multiple of $\vec{d}^{(1)}$. In this case, the random variables $\vec{d}^{(1)} \cdot H_{*,j}$ and $\vec{d}^{(2)} \cdot H_{*,j}$ are scalar multiples of each other as well. However, if $\vec{d}^{(2)}$ is not in the span of $\vec{d}^{(1)}$, then the random variable $\vec{d}^{(2)} \cdot H_{*,j}$ is uniformly random over the field F and (most importantly) *independent* of the random variable $\vec{d}^{(1)} \cdot H_{*,j}$. Therefore, the probability of all coordinates of the codeword $\vec{d}^{(2)} \cdot H$ indexed by $j \in J \setminus J'$ being in V_j is (independently) $(\gamma/|F|)^{(1-\sigma)n - k^\perp}$. We highlight that if, indeed, the witnesses are linearly dependent then the columns are linearly dependent as well. Consequently, identifying *linearly independent* witnesses seems necessary (not merely sufficient) for our proof strategy to succeed.

Generalizing this technique, one claims the following result. We defer the proof to the full version [40].

Claim 3. *Fix any r linearly independent $\vec{d}^{(1)}, \vec{d}^{(2)}, \ldots, \vec{d}^{(r)} \in F^{k^\perp}$. For all $j \in J \setminus J'$, over the randomness of choosing $H_{*,j}$, the distribution of the random matrix*

---

[14] Because there are γ options for every $k^\perp$ information coordinates in $\langle H \rangle$. Among these $\gamma^{k^\perp}$ choices for the information coordinates, one can choose any a^n of them as the witness set B.

$$\left(d^{\vec{(i)}} \cdot H_{*,j}\right)^{j \in J \setminus J'}_{i \in \{1,2,\dots,r\}}$$

is identical to the uniform distribution over $F^{r \times ((1-\sigma)n - k^{\perp})}$.

Consequently, the probability of all the codewords corresponding to these r linearly independent witnesses in B failing the test (V, J) is

$$\left[\left(\frac{\gamma}{|F|}\right)^{(1-\sigma)n - k^{\perp}}\right]^r \tag{3}$$

Now how many linearly independent witnesses can one identify among a^n witnesses of B? Towards this objective, we prove a bound similar in spirit to matrix rank lower bounds from communication complexity theory. We defer the proof to the full version [40].

Claim 4 (Rank bound for 'Bounded-Diversity' Matrices). *Let* $M \in F^{u \times v}$, *where* $u = 2^{\alpha v}$, *be an arbitrary matrix such that each row of this matrix is distinct. Suppose every column* $j \in \{1, \dots, v\}$ *of* M *satisfies*

$$\left|\{M_{1,j}, M_{2,j}, \dots, M_{u,j}\}\right| \leqslant \gamma.$$

Then, $\mathrm{rank}(M) \geqslant \frac{\alpha}{\log_2 \gamma} \cdot v$.

Back to Proving Lemma 2. Construct M such that every row of M is a witness in B. Therefore, the matrix $M \in F^{u \times v}$, where $u = a^n$ and $v = k^{\perp}$. Applying Claim 4 for $u = a^n = 2^{\log_2(a) \cdot n}$ and $v = k^{\perp}$, we get $r \geqslant \frac{\log_2 a}{\log_2 \gamma} \cdot k^{\perp}$. For our end application scenario, we shall have $k^{\perp} = \Theta n$, and positive constant a and $\gamma \geqslant 2$. Therefore, we shall have $r = \Theta n$. So, the probability expression in Eq. 3 effectively behaves like $|F|^{-\Theta n^2}$. On the other hand, the total number of possibilities given by Eq. 2 are dominated by $|F|^{\gamma n}$ and $\binom{\gamma^{k^{\perp}}}{a^n} \leqslant \gamma^{k^{\perp} \cdot a^n}$. When $n \leqslant \Theta \log \lambda$, using union bound, one can conclude that the probability of a random $\langle H \rangle$ failing some test $(\vec{V}, J)$ with some witness B is $1 - \exp(-\Theta \lambda)$.

However, $n \leqslant \Theta \log \lambda$ is unacceptably small. Our objective is to achieve $n = \Theta \lambda$. In fact, we have recklessly indulged in significant over-counting. Let us fix this proof to get the desired bound.

Final Fix. Observe that we do not need to pick B of size a^n from $V_{k+1} \times \cdots \times V_n$. For any B, identify the (unique) lexicographically smallest set $\widehat{B} \subseteq B$ of r linearly independent witnesses. In the analysis presented above, we have significantly over-counted by separately considering all $B \supseteq \widehat{B}$. To fix this situation, we consider the argument below that analyzes $\widehat{B}$ to account for *all* $B \supseteq \widehat{B}$.

Now, fix the (canonical) set $\widehat{B}$ of r linearly independent witnesses. The proof above says that the probability of a random $\langle H \rangle$ failing the test $(\vec{V}, J)$ with some witness $B \supseteq \widehat{B}$ is at most $(\gamma/|F|)^{((1-\sigma)n - k^{\perp}) \cdot r}$. We emphasize that B may have more linearly independent elements; however, it is inconsequential for our analysis. So, we need only to pick $\widehat{B}$ of size r such that the witnesses are linearly independent of each other. Consequently, the total number of possibilities of Eq. 2 drastically reduces to the following bound.

$$|F|^{\gamma \cdot n} \cdot 2^{h_2(\sigma) \cdot n} \cdot \binom{\gamma^{k^{\perp}}}{r}, \tag{4}$$

where $r = \frac{\log_2 a}{\log_2 \gamma} \cdot k^{\perp}$. Now, we can put together the total number of witnesses of Eq. 4 with the failure probability of Eq. 3 using a union bound. The probability that a random $\langle H \rangle$ fails some test $(\vec{V}, I)$ witnessed by r linearly independent witnesses in $\widehat{B}$ is at most

$$|F|^{\gamma \cdot n} \cdot 2^{h_2(\sigma) \cdot n} \cdot \binom{\gamma^{k^{\perp}}}{r} \cdot \left(\frac{\gamma}{|F|} \right)^{((1-\sigma)n - k^{\perp}) \cdot r}$$

$$\leqslant |F|^{\gamma \cdot n} \cdot 2^{h_2(\sigma)n} \cdot \gamma^{k^{\perp} r} \cdot \gamma^{(1-\sigma)n \cdot r - k^{\perp} r} \cdot \frac{1}{|F|^{((1-\sigma)n - k^{\perp})r}}$$

$$= |F|^{\gamma n} \cdot 2^{h_2(\sigma) \cdot n} \cdot 2^{(1-k/n)(1-\sigma)\log_2(a) \cdot n^2} \cdot \frac{1}{|F|^{(\log_\gamma a)(1-k/n)(k/n - \sigma) \cdot n^2}}.$$

In our scenario, we have constant $k/n \in (\sigma, 1)$, constant a, and $\lim_{\lambda \to \infty} n/\lambda \in (0, 1)$. For these setting of the parameters, the numerator is dominated by the term $2^{\Theta \lambda^2}$. Furthermore, we have constant γ, so the denominator is $2^{\Theta \lambda^3}$. So, the probability expression above is $\exp(-\Omega(\lambda))$.

To summarize, we incur two forms of failures in our analysis. (1) $\langle H \rangle$ is not MDS, and (2) $\langle H \rangle$ fails some test. The probability of the first failure is $\exp(-\Theta \lambda)$, and the probability of the second failure is $\exp(-\Omega(\lambda))$.

3.3   Proof of Lemma 1

We prove Lemma 1 using Fourier analysis. The full version [40] provides the preliminaries of Fourier analysis that suffices for the proofs in this paper.

To begin, let us summarize what we are provided. We are given a fixed generator matrix $H \in F^{k^{\perp} \times n}$, where $k^{\perp} = (n - k)$. The code $\langle H \rangle$ is MDS and the matrix H passes all tests in $\mathsf{Test}_{\sigma, \gamma, a}$, where $\gamma = 2^m \cdot T^2$.

Consider any (n, m) local leakage function $\vec{L} = (L_1, \dots, L_n)$, such that each $L_i \colon F \to \{0, 1\}^m$. Our objective is to prove that this leakage function cannot distinguish the secret shares of the secret 0 from the secret 1. Fix any $i \in \{1, \dots, n\}$ and leakage $\ell \in \{0, 1\}^m$. Let $\mathbf{1}_{i,\ell} \colon F \to \{0, 1\}$ be the indicator function for $L_i(s_i) = \ell$, where s_i is the secret share of party i.

Claim 5. *Let $i \in \{1, \dots, n\}$ and $\ell \in \{0, 1\}^m$. The size of the following set is at most T^2.*

$$\mathsf{Big}_{i,\ell} = \left\{ \alpha \colon \alpha \in F, \left| \widehat{\mathbf{1}_{i,\ell}}(\alpha) \right| \leqslant 1/T \right\}.$$

This result follows from Parseval's identity, and that function $\mathbf{1}_{i,\ell}$ has a binary output. Refer to the full version [40] for a proof of this claim. Given the leakage function $\vec{L} = (L_1, \ldots, L_n)$ and $i \in \{1, \ldots, n\}$, define the sets

$$V_i = \bigcup_{\ell \in \{0,1\}^m} \mathsf{Big}_{i,\ell}.$$

Extend each V_i arbitrarily, if needed, to be of size $\gamma = 2^m T^2$. Now, we have defined the $\vec{V} = (V_1, \ldots, V_n)$ corresponding to the leakage function $\vec{L}$.

Algebraization of Leakage-Resilience. Benhamouda et al. [7] showed that proving that the statistical distance expression in Eq. 1 is smaller than some quantity is implied by upper-bounding the analytical expression below by the same quantity. That is,

$$\mathsf{SD}\left(\vec{\mathbf{L}}(s^{(0)}), \vec{\mathbf{L}}(s^{(1)})\right)$$

$$= \frac{1}{2} \sum_{\ell \in (\{0,1\}^m)^n} \left| \sum_{\alpha \in \langle H \rangle} \prod_{i=1}^n \widehat{\mathbf{1}_{i,\ell_i}}(\alpha_i) \cdot \omega^{\alpha_i \cdot s^{(0)} \cdot v_i} - \sum_{\alpha \in \langle H \rangle} \prod_{i=1}^n \widehat{\mathbf{1}_{i,\ell_i}}(\alpha_i) \cdot \omega^{\alpha_i \cdot s^{(1)} \cdot v_i} \right| \tag{5}$$

$$\leqslant \sum_{\vec{x} \in F^{k^\perp} \setminus \{0^{k^\perp}\}} \sum_{\vec{\ell} = (\ell_1, \ldots, \ell_n) \in (\{0,1\}^m)^n} \left| \prod_{i=1}^n \widehat{\mathbf{1}_{i,\ell_i}}(\vec{x} \cdot H_{*,i}) \right|. \tag{6}$$

For completeness, we include proof of this in the full version [40]. We now proceed to upper bound this expression for an H that passes all tests in $\mathsf{Test}_{\sigma,\gamma,a}$.

Remark 6. We emphasize that the analytical expression above is only an upper bound to the statistical distance. We show that using the expression above as a proxy to analyze the exact statistical distance encounters some bottlenecks. Section 4 highlights one such bottleneck.

Upper-Bounding Eq. 6. We partition the elements $\vec{x} \in F^{k^\perp} \setminus \{0^{k^\perp}\}$ into two sets.

$$\mathsf{Bad} := \left\{ \vec{x} : \exists J \text{ s.t. } \vec{x} \neq 0^n \,\&\, \vec{x} \cdot H \text{ fails the test indexed by } (\vec{V}, J) \in \mathsf{Test}_{\sigma,\gamma,a} \right\}.$$

We emphasize that $J \subseteq \{1, 2, \ldots, n\}$ is of size $(1 - \sigma)n$. The remaining elements form the subset

$$\overline{\mathsf{Bad}} = \left(F^{k^\perp} \setminus \{0^{k^\perp}\}\right) \setminus \mathsf{Bad}.$$

Next, we upper-bound the expression of Eq. 6 for elements $\vec{x} \in \mathsf{Bad}$ and $\vec{x} \in \overline{\mathsf{Bad}}$ separately.

Upper Bound: Part 1. First we consider the sum of Eq. 6 restricted to $\vec{x} \in \mathsf{Bad}$.

$$\sum_{\vec{x} \in \mathsf{Bad}} \sum_{\vec{\ell} \in (\{0,1\}^m)^n} \left| \prod_{i=1}^{n} \widehat{1_{i,\ell_i}} (\vec{x} \cdot H_{*,i}) \right|$$

$$= \sum_{\vec{x} \in \mathsf{Bad}} \prod_{i=1}^{n} \sum_{\ell_i \in \{0,1\}^m} \left| \widehat{1_{i,\ell_i}} (\vec{x} \cdot H_{*,i}) \right|$$

$$\leqslant a^n 2^{h_2(\sigma)n} \cdot \max_{\vec{x} \in \mathsf{Bad}} \prod_{i=1}^{n} \sum_{\ell_i \in \{0,1\}^m} \left| \widehat{1_{i,\ell_i}} (\vec{x} \cdot H_{*,i}) \right| \qquad (7)$$

The last inequality is due to the fact that there are $\binom{n}{(1-\sigma)n} = 2^{h_2(\sigma)n}$ subsets J, and each test indexed by (V, J) has at most a^n different codewords failing it.[15]

Next, fix any element $\vec{x} \in \mathsf{Bad}$. The codeword $\vec{x} \cdot H$ has $< k^{\perp}$ zeroes.[16] Therefore, the codeword $\vec{x} \cdot H$ has $> k$ elements from F^*. Using this property, we claim the following result.

Claim 6. *Let $\langle H \rangle$ be an $[n, n-k]_F$-MDS code, and $\vec{x} \in F^{k^{\perp}} \setminus \{0^{k^{\perp}}\}$ be an arbitrary message. Then, there exists a constant $C_m > 1$ such that*

$$\prod_{i=1}^{n} \sum_{\ell_i \in \{0,1\}^m} \left| \widehat{1_{i,\ell_i}} (\vec{x} \cdot H_{*,i}) \right| \leqslant C_m^{-k}.$$

We defer the proof to the full version [40]. Substituting this upper bound in Eq. 7, we get the following upper bound

$$2^{-(\log_2(C_m) \cdot (k/n) - \log_2(a) - h_2(\sigma)) \cdot n}, \qquad (8)$$

which completes the first upper bound. By picking our parameters as in Sect. 3.1, this upper bound is negligibly small.

Upper Bound: Part 2. Now, it remains to upper-bound

$$\sum_{\vec{x} \in \overline{\mathsf{Bad}}} \sum_{\vec{\ell} \in (\{0,1\}^m)^n} \left| \prod_{i=1}^{n} \widehat{1_{i,\ell_i}} (\vec{x} \cdot H_{*,i}) \right|.$$

The crucial observation about any codeword $c = \vec{x} \cdot H \in \overline{\mathsf{Bad}}$ is the following. The number of $j \in \{1, \ldots, n\}$ such that $c_j \notin V_j$ is at least σn. For the coordinates where $c_j \notin V_j$, we utilize the fact that the magnitude of the Fourier coefficients contributed in the above expression is at most $1/T$. Based on these observations, using Fourier analysis, we prove the following bound.

---

[15] Since H passes all tests in the set $\mathsf{Test}_{\sigma,\gamma,a}$, at most a^n codewords fail any test indexed by $(\vec{V}, J)$.

[16] If the codeword has $k^{\perp}$ zeroes, we can choose their indices as the information set (because $\langle H \rangle$ is MDS). That implies that the entire codeword is 0^n, which contradicts the fact that Bad has non-zero elements.

Claim 7. *For $0 < \sigma \leqslant 1 - 2k^\perp/n$, the expression above is upper-bounded by*

$$2^{-\left(\log_2(T)\cdot\sigma - \left(\sigma + k^\perp/n\right)m - h_2(\sigma)\right)\cdot n}.$$

A proof of this claim is provided in the full version [40]. By picking our parameters as in Sect. 3.1, this upper bound is negligibly small.

Remark 7. We highlight that if we pick a σ such that $\sigma > 1 - 2k^\perp/n$, then naïvely using the analysis above yields an upper bound of

$$p^{k^\perp - (1-\sigma)n/2} \cdot 2^{-\left(\log_2(T)\cdot\sigma - \left(\sigma + k^\perp/n\right)m - h_2(\sigma)\right)\cdot n}.$$

The full version [40] of our paper present a proof sketch of this bound. Observe that the leading term $p^{\Theta\lambda}$ forces the choice of T to be $\omega(1)$. However, in our analysis, we crucially rely on T to be a constant.

In particular, if $2k^\perp > n$, no suitable σ can be choosen to avoid this bottleneck. We discuss this barrier further in Sect. 4.

4   The $k > n/2$ Barrier

In this section, we discuss why $k > n/2$ is inherently required for the current proof techniques (which are common to [7,39] and this work). In particular, we pinpoint the step where one uses Eq. 6 to upper bound the Eq. 5 as the place where this barrier arises.[17] That is, when one uses the magnitude of the Fourier coefficients to upper bound the statistical distance as

$$\sum_{\vec{x}\in F^{k^\perp}\setminus\{0^{k^\perp}\}} \quad \sum_{\vec{\ell}\in(\{0,1\}^m)^n} \left| \prod_{i=1}^{n} \widehat{1_{i,\ell_i}}(\vec{x}\cdot H_{*,i}) \right|.$$

To justify our claim, we prove the following theorem.

Theorem 1. *There exists a leakage function $\vec{L}$ that leaks one bit from each share such that the following holds. Let $\langle G\rangle$ be any $[n,k]_F$ code such that $k < n/2$. Let $\langle H\rangle$ be the dual code of $\langle G\rangle$. The above equation is lower bounded by 1. That is,*

$$\sum_{\vec{x}\in F^{k^\perp}\setminus\{0^{k^\perp}\}} \quad \sum_{\vec{\ell}\in\{0,1\}^n} \left| \prod_{i=1}^{n} \widehat{1_{i,\ell_i}}(\vec{x}\cdot H_{*,i}) \right| \gtrsim p^{(n-2k)/2} > 1.$$

Consequently, one cannot prove any meaningful upper-bound when $k < n/2$.

In fact, we identify the leakage function explicitly as follows. Define the set of *quadratic residues* as

$$QR := \{\alpha \in F : \exists\beta \text{ s.t. } \beta^2 = \alpha\}.$$

---

[17] Note that Eq. 5 is an identity transformation of the statistical distance. Hence, the proof until this step must not produce any barriers.

Define $\vec{L} = (L_1, \ldots, L_n)$ as for all $i \in \{1, 2, \ldots, n\}$,

$$L_i(x) := \begin{cases} 1 & \text{if } x \in \mathcal{QR} \\ 0 & \text{if } x \notin \mathcal{QR} \end{cases}.$$

By standard techniques in the Fourier analysis and the well-known facts about the *quadratic Gaussian sum*, one can verify this theorem with this particular leakage function. We refer the readers to the full version [40] for a detailed proof.

5   Leakage-Resilience of Shamir's Secret-Sharing

In this section, we present our result that Shamir's secret-sharing with threshold k and n parties is leakage-resilient when $k \geqslant 0.8675n$. This improves the state-of-the-art result of Benhamouda et al. [7]. In fact, we prove a more general theorem as follows.

Theorem 2. *There exists a universal constant p_0 such that, for all finite field F of prime order $p > p_0$, the following holds. Let G^+ be an arbitrary MDS $[n+1, k+1]_F$ code such that $k \geqslant 0.8675n$. The Massey secret-sharing scheme corresponding to G^+ is $(1, \exp(-\Theta n))$-leakage-resilient.*

As Shamir's secret-sharing is a Massey secret-sharing scheme corresponding to the punctured Reed-Solomon codes, this theorem applies to Shamir's secret-sharing directly.

We refer the readers to the full version [40] for a detailed proof. In what follows, we present an overview of our proof. Starting from the upper bound Eq. 6, i.e.,

$$\sum_{\vec{x} \in F^{k^{\perp}} \setminus \{0^{k^{\perp}}\}} \sum_{\vec{\ell} \in \{0,1\}^n} \left| \prod_{i=1}^{n} \widehat{1_{i,\ell_i}}(\vec{x} \cdot H_{*,i}) \right|,$$

our main idea is that we shall bound it with the exact information where the zeros of the codeword (from $\langle H \rangle$) are. This is motivated by the fact that the Fourier coefficient corresponds to 0 has the dominant weight.

Note that since $\langle H \rangle$ is an MDS $[n, k^{\perp} = n - k]_F$-code, a non-zero codeword from $\langle H \rangle$ has at most $k^{\perp} - 1$ zeros. For any collection of indices $A \subseteq \{1, 2, \ldots, n\}$ such that $|A| \leqslant k^{\perp} - 1$, let us define set

$$\mathcal{S}_A := \{\vec{x} \mid a \in A \Longleftrightarrow \vec{x} \cdot H_{*,a} = 0\}.$$

That is, the collection of messages whose codewords satisfy that 0 appears exactly at those indices from A. Clearly, $F^{k^{\perp}} \setminus \{0^{k^{\perp}}\} = \bigcup_{A: |A| \leqslant k^{\perp} - 1} \mathcal{S}_A$. We shall break the summation based on A, i.e.,

$$\sum_{A: |A| \leqslant k^{\perp} - 1} \sum_{\vec{x} \in \mathcal{S}_A} \sum_{\vec{\ell} \in \{0,1\}^n} \left| \prod_{i=1}^{n} \widehat{1_{i,\ell_i}}(\vec{x} \cdot H_{*,i}) \right|.$$

To bound each summation over some A, i.e.,

$$\Gamma_A := \sum_{\vec{x} \in \mathcal{S}_A} \sum_{\vec{\ell} \in \{0,1\}^n} \left| \prod_{i=1}^{n} \widehat{1_{i,\ell_i}}(\vec{x} \cdot H_{*,i}) \right|,$$

we use the following ideas. (Refer to Fig. 2 for notations.)

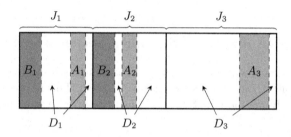

Fig. 2. The dual generator matrix $H \in F^{k^{\perp} \times n}$. We pick the first $k^{\perp}$ columns as J_1 and the second $k^{\perp}$ columns as J_2. Let J_3 be the rest of the columns. The set of columns $A = A_1 \cup A_2 \cup A_3$ is exactly where the codeword will be 0. We pick B_1 and B_2 to ensure that $|B_1| + |A| = |B_2| + |A| = k^{\perp}$.

We know the codewords are 0 at columns in $A = A_1 \cup A_2 \cup A_3$ and non-zero at columns outside A. Since $\vec{x} \cdot H_{*,a} = 0$ for $a \in A$, bounding over columns from A can be easily handled. Next, we shall use the worst-case bound to bound the summation over columns from $D_1 \cup D_2 \cup D_3$. Finally, for the columns of B_1 and B_2, we let them enumerate all possibilities from F^* and bound them appropriately.

We refer the readers to the full version [40] for the subtleties in the proof. Overall, we are able to prove that

$$\Gamma_A \leqslant \left(\frac{\pi}{2}\right)^{-(|A|+2k-n)}.$$

Finally, our upper bound is now

$$\leqslant \sum_{A:\, |A| \leqslant k^{\perp}-1} \left(\frac{\pi}{2}\right)^{-(|A|+2k-n)} = \sum_{i=0}^{k^{\perp}-1} 2^{n\left[h_2(i/n)-(i/n+2k/n-1)\log_2\left(\frac{\pi}{2}\right)\right]}.$$

Suppose $k/n = \sigma$, it suffices to ensure that

$$\max_{q \in [0, 1-\sigma)} h_2(q) - (q + 2\sigma - 1)\log_2(\pi/2) < 0.$$

We prove that $\sigma \geqslant 0.8675$ suffices, which completes the proof of the theorem.

References

1. Abarzúa, R., Valencia, C., López, J.: Survey for performance & security problems of passive side-channel attacks countermeasures in ECC. Cryptology ePrint Archive, Report 2019/010 (2019). https://eprint.iacr.org/2019/010
2. Adams, D.Q., Nguyen, H.H., Nguyen, M.L., Paskin-Cherniavsky, A., Suad, T., Wang, M.: Lower bounds for leakage-resilient secret sharing schemes against probing attacks. Manuscript (2021)
3. Aggarwal, D., et al.: Stronger leakage-resilient and non-malleable secret sharing schemes for general access structures. In: Boldyreva, A., Micciancio, D. (eds.) CRYPTO 2019, Part II. LNCS, vol. 11693, pp. 510–539. Springer, Cham (2019). https://doi.org/10.1007/978-3-030-26951-7_18
4. Arora, S., Barak, B.: Computational Complexity: A Modern Approach. Cambridge University Press, Cambridge (2009)
5. Avanzi, R.M.: Side channel attacks on implementations of curve-based cryptographic primitives. Cryptology ePrint Archive, Report 2005/017 (2005). http://eprint.iacr.org/2005/017
6. Badrinarayanan, S., Srinivasan, A.: Revisiting non-malleable secret sharing. In: Ishai, Y., Rijmen, V. (eds.) EUROCRYPT 2019, Part I. LNCS, vol. 11476, pp. 593–622. Springer, Cham (2019). https://doi.org/10.1007/978-3-030-17653-2_20
7. Benhamouda, F., Degwekar, A., Ishai, Y., Rabin, T.: On the local leakage resilience of linear secret sharing schemes. In: Shacham, H., Boldyreva, A. (eds.) CRYPTO 2018, Part I. LNCS, vol. 10991, pp. 531–561. Springer, Cham (2018). https://doi.org/10.1007/978-3-319-96884-1_18
8. Benhamouda, F., Degwekar, A., Ishai, Y., Rabin, T.: On the local leakage resilience of linear secret sharing schemes. Cryptology ePrint Archive, Report 2019/653 (2019). https://eprint.iacr.org/2019/653
9. Benhamouda, F., Degwekar, A., Ishai, Y., Rabin, T.: On the local leakage resilience of linear secret sharing schemes. J. Cryptology $34(2)$, 10 (2021)
10. Bhunia, S., Tehranipoor, M.: Hardware Security: A Hands-on Learning Approach. Morgan Kaufmann, San Francisco (2018)
11. Bishop, A., Pastro, V., Rajaraman, R., Wichs, D.: Essentially optimal robust secret sharing with maximal corruptions. In: Fischlin, M., Coron, J.-S. (eds.) EUROCRYPT 2016, Part I. LNCS, vol. 9665, pp. 58–86. Springer, Heidelberg (2016). https://doi.org/10.1007/978-3-662-49890-3_3
12. Blake, I.F., Seroussi, G., Smart, N.P.: Advances in Elliptic Curve Cryptography, vol. 317. Cambridge University Press, Cambridge (2005)
13. Bogdanov, A., Ishai, Y., Srinivasan, A.: Unconditionally secure computation against low-complexity leakage. In: Boldyreva, A., Micciancio, D. (eds.) CRYPTO 2019, Part II. LNCS, vol. 11693, pp. 387–416. Springer, Cham (2019). https://doi.org/10.1007/978-3-030-26951-7_14
14. Candel, G., Géraud-Stewart, R., Naccache, D.: How to compartment secrets. In: Laurent, M., Giannetsos, T. (eds.) WISTP 2019. LNCS, vol. 12024, pp. 3–11. Springer, Cham (2020). https://doi.org/10.1007/978-3-030-41702-4_1
15. Chattopadhyay, E., et al.: Extractors and secret sharing against bounded collusion protocols. In: 61st FOCS, pp. 1226–1242. IEEE Computer Society Press, November 2020
16. Cheraghchi, M., Guruswami, V.: Capacity of non-malleable codes. In: Naor, M. (ed.) ITCS 2014, pp. 155–168. ACM, January 2014

17. Cohen, H., et al. (eds.): Handbook of Elliptic and Hyperelliptic Curve Cryptography. Chapman and Hall/CRC, Boca Raton (2005)
18. Dau, H., Duursma, I.M., Kiah, H.M., Milenkovic, O.: Repairing reed-solomon codes with multiple erasures. IEEE Trans. Inf. Theory **64**(10), 6567–6582 (2018)
19. Dodis, Y., Wichs, D.: Non-malleable extractors and symmetric key cryptography from weak secrets. In: Mitzenmacher, M. (ed.) 41st ACM STOC, pp. 601–610. ACM Press, May/June (2009)
20. Fan, J., Guo, X., De Mulder, E., Schaumont, P., Preneel, B., Verbauwhede, I.: State-of-the-art of secure ECC implementations: a survey on known side-channel attacks and countermeasures. In: Plusquellic, J., Mai, K. (eds.) HOST 2010, Proceedings of the 2010 IEEE International Symposium on Hardware-Oriented Security and Trust (HOST), Anaheim Convention Center, California, USA, 13–14 June 2010, pp. 76–87. IEEE Computer Society (2010)
21. Fan, J., Verbauwhede, I.: An updated survey on secure ECC implementations: attacks, countermeasures and cost. In: Naccache, D. (ed.) Cryptography and Security: From Theory to Applications. LNCS, vol. 6805, pp. 265–282. Springer, Heidelberg (2012). https://doi.org/10.1007/978-3-642-28368-0_18
22. Faust, S., Mukherjee, P., Venturi, D., Wichs, D.: Efficient non-malleable codes and key-derivation for poly-size tampering circuits. In: Nguyen, P.Q., Oswald, E. (eds.) EUROCRYPT 2014. LNCS, vol. 8441, pp. 111–128. Springer, Heidelberg (2014)
23. Fehr, S., Yuan, C.: Towards optimal robust secret sharing with security against a rushing adversary. In: Ishai, Y., Rijmen, V. (eds.) EUROCRYPT 2019, Part III. LNCS, vol. 11478, pp. 472–499. Springer, Cham (2019). https://doi.org/10.1007/978-3-030-17659-4_16
24. Fehr, S., Yuan, C.: Robust secret sharing with almost optimal share size and security against rushing adversaries. In: Pass, R., Pietrzak, K. (eds.) TCC 2020, Part III. LNCS, vol. 12552, pp. 470–498. Springer, Cham (2020). https://doi.org/10.1007/978-3-030-64381-2_17
25. Goldreich, O., Micali, S., Wigderson, A.: How to play any mental game or a completeness theorem for protocols with honest majority. In: Aho, A. (ed.) 19th ACM STOC, pp. 218–229. ACM Press, May 1987
26. Goyal, V., Kumar, A.: Non-malleable secret sharing. In: Diakonikolas, I., Kempe, D., Henzinger, M. (eds.) 50th ACM STOC, pp. 685–698. ACM Press, June 2018
27. Guruswami, V., Rawat, A.S.: MDS code constructions with small sub-packetization and near-optimal repair bandwidth. In: Klein, P.N. (ed.) 28th SODA, pp. 2109–2122. ACM-SIAM, January 2017
28. Guruswami, V., Wootters, M.: Repairing reed-solomon codes. In: Wichs, D., Mansour, Y. (eds.) 48th ACM STOC, pp. 216–226. ACM Press, June 2016
29. Guruswami, V., Wootters, M.: Repairing reed-solomon codes. IEEE Trans. Inf. Theory **63**(9), 5684–5698 (2017)
30. Hazay, C., Ishai, Y., Marcedone, A., Venkitasubramaniam, M.: LevioSA: lightweight secure arithmetic computation. In: Cavallaro, L., Kinder, J., Wang, X., Katz, J., (eds.) ACM CCS 2019, pp. 327–344. ACM Press, November 2019
31. Hazay, C., Venkitasubramaniam, M., Weiss, M.: The price of active security in cryptographic protocols. In: Canteaut, A., Ishai, Y. (eds.) EUROCRYPT 2020, Part II. LNCS, vol. 12106, pp. 184–215. Springer, Cham (2020). https://doi.org/10.1007/978-3-030-45724-2_7
32. Kalai, Y.T., Reyzin, L.: A survey of leakage-resilient cryptography. In: Goldreich, O. (ed.) Providing Sound Foundations for Cryptography: On the Work of Shafi Goldwasser and Silvio Micali, pp. 727–794. ACM (2019)

33. Kocher, P.C.: Timing attacks on implementations of Diffie-Hellman, RSA, DSS, and other systems. In: Koblitz, N. (ed.) CRYPTO 1996. LNCS, vol. 1109, pp. 104–113. Springer, Heidelberg (1996). https://doi.org/10.1007/3-540-68697-5_9

34. Kocher, P., Jaffe, J., Jun, B.: Differential power analysis. In: Wiener, M. (ed.) CRYPTO 1999. LNCS, vol. 1666, pp. 388–397. Springer, Heidelberg (1999). https://doi.org/10.1007/3-540-48405-1_25

35. Koeune, F., Standaert, F.-X.: A tutorial on physical security and side-channel attacks. In: Aldini, A., Gorrieri, R., Martinelli, F. (eds.) FOSAD 2004-2005. LNCS, vol. 3655, pp. 78–108. Springer, Heidelberg (2005). https://doi.org/10.1007/11554578_3

36. Kumar, A., Meka, R., Sahai, A.: Leakage-resilient secret sharing against colluding parties. In: Zuckerman, D. (ed.) 60th FOCS, pp. 636–660. IEEE Computer Society Press, November 2019

37. Lin, F., Cheraghchi, M., Guruswami, V., Safavi-Naini, R., Wang, H.: Leakage-resilient secret sharing in non-compartmentalized models. In: Kalai, Y.T., Smith, A.D., Wichs, D. (eds.) ITC 2020, pp. 7:1–7:24. Schloss Dagstuhl, June 2020

38. MacWilliams, F.J., Sloane, N.J.A.: The Theory of Error Correcting Codes, vol. 16. Elsevier, New York (1977)

39. Maji, H.K., Nguyen, H.H., Paskin-Cherniavsky, A., Suad, T., Wang, M.: Leakage-resilience of the Shamir secret-sharing scheme against physical-bit leakages. In: Canteaut, A., Standaert, F.-X. (eds.) EUROCRYPT 2021. LNCS, vol. 12697, pp. 344–374. Springer, Cham (2021). https://doi.org/10.1007/978-3-030-77886-6_12

40. Maji, H.K., Paskin-Cherniavsky, A., Suad, T., Wang, M.: Constructing locally leakage-resilient linear secret-sharing schemes (2021). https://www.cs.purdue.edu/homes/hmaji/papers/MPSW21.pdf

41. Manurangsi, P., Srinivasan, A., Vasudevan, P.N.: Nearly optimal robust secret sharing against rushing adversaries. In: Micciancio, D., Ristenpart, T. (eds.) CRYPTO 2020, Part III. LNCS, vol. 12172, pp. 156–185. Springer, Cham (2020). https://doi.org/10.1007/978-3-030-56877-1_6

42. Mardia, J., Bartan, B., Wootters, M.: Repairing multiple failures for scalar MDS codes. IEEE Trans. Inf. Theory **65**(5), 2661–2672 (2019)

43. Massey, J.L.: Some applications of code duality in cryptography. Mat. Contemp. **21**, 187–209 (2001). 16th

44. Nielsen, J.B., Simkin, M.: Lower bounds for leakage-resilient secret sharing. In: Canteaut, A., Ishai, Y. (eds.) EUROCRYPT 2020, Part I. LNCS, vol. 12105, pp. 556–577. Springer, Cham (2020). https://doi.org/10.1007/978-3-030-45721-1_20

45. O'Donnell, R.: Analysis of Boolean Functions (2014)

46. Oswald, E., Preneel, B.: A survey on passive side-channel attacks and their countermeasures for the nessie public-key cryptosystems. NESSIE public reports (2003). https://www.cosic.esat.kuleuven.ac.be/nessie/reports

47. Pietrzak, K.: Cryptography from learning parity with noise. In: International Conference on Current Trends in Theory and Practice of Computer Science (2012)

48. Randolph, M., Diehl, W.: Power side-channel attack analysis: a review of 20 years of study for the layman. Cryptography **4**(2), 15 (2020)

49. Regev, O.: The learning with errors problem

50. Sayakkara, A.P., Le-Khac, N.-A., Scanlon, M.: A survey of electromagnetic side-channel attacks and discussion on their case-progressing potential for digital forensics. Digit. Investig. **29**, 43–54 (2019)

51. Srinivasan, A., Vasudevan, P.N.: Leakage resilient secret sharing and applications. In: Boldyreva, A., Micciancio, D. (eds.) CRYPTO 2019, Part II. LNCS, vol. 11693, pp. 480–509. Springer, Cham (2019). https://doi.org/10.1007/978-3-030-26951-7_17

52. Tamo, I., Ye, M., Barg, A.: Optimal repair of reed-solomon codes: achieving the cut-set bound. In Umans, C. (ed.) 58th FOCS, pp. 216–227. IEEE Computer Society Press, October 2017

53. Tao, T.: Higher order Fourier analysis. Citeseer

54. Vadhan, S.P., et al.: Pseudorandomness, vol. 7. Now Delft (2012)

55. Yao, A.C.-C.: Protocols for secure computations (extended abstract). In: 23rd FOCS, pp. 160–164. IEEE Computer Society Press, November 1982

56. Zhou, Y., Feng, D.: Side-channel attacks: ten years after its publication and the impacts on cryptographic module security testing. Cryptology ePrint Archive, Report 2005/388 (2005). http://eprint.iacr.org/2005/388

Author Index

Applebaum, Benny   627

Badertscher, Christian   3
Barbosa, Manuel   125
Beimel, Amos   748
Boldyreva, Alexandra   125
Bordes, Nicolas   337
Bossuat, Angèle   157
Bost, Raphael   157

Cassiers, Gaëtan   185
Chandran, Nishanth   595
Chen, Shan   125
Coron, Jean-Sébastien   215
Couteau, Geoffroy   502
Cramer, Ronald   656

Dachman-Soled, Dana   535
Daemen, Joan   337
de Quehen, Victoria   432
Dong, Xiaoyang   278

Faust, Sebastian   185
Fouque, Pierre-Alain   157

Ghoshal, Ashrujit   64
Goyal, Vipul   718
Gu, Dawu   309

Herzberg, Amir   33
Hu, Lei   278
Hua, Jialiang   278

Isobe, Takanori   368

Kanukurthi, Bhavana   595
Kaplan, Haim   94
Khurana, Dakshita   566
Komargodski, Ilan   535
Kuijsters, Daniël   337
Kutas, Péter   432

Leibowitz, Hemi   33
Leonardi, Chris   432
Li, Zheng   278

Lin, Dongdai   247
Liu, Fukang   368
Liu, Meicheng   247
Longa, Patrick   402
Lu, Xiaojuan   247
Lu, Yun   3

Maji, Hemanta K.   779
Mansour, Yishay   94
Martindale, Chloe   432
Meier, Willi   368
Minaud, Brice   157

Nir, Oded   627
Nissim, Kobbi   94

Obbattu, Sai Lakshmi Bhavana   595
Orlt, Maximilian   185
Othman, Hussien   748

Panny, Lorenz   432
Paskin-Cherniavsky, Anat   779
Pass, Rafael   535
Peter, Naty   748
Petit, Christophe   432

Raghuraman, Srinivasan   502
Rambaud, Matthieu   656
Reichle, Michael   157
Rindal, Peter   502
Roy, Lawrence   687

Sekar, Sruthi   595
Shen, Yaobin   309
Singh, Jaspal   687
Song, Yifan   718
Spignoli, Lorenzo   215
Srinivasan, Akshayaram   566, 718
Standaert, François-Xavier   185
Stange, Katherine E.   432
Stemmer, Uri   94
Suad, Tom   779
Sun, Siwei   278

Syta, Ewa   33
Szefer, Jakub   402

Tessaro, Stefano   64

Van Assche, Gilles   337

Wang, Lei   309
Wang, Mingyuan   779
Wang, Wen   402
Wang, Xiaoyun   278

Warinschi, Bogdan   125
Weng, Jian   309
Wrótniak, Sara   33

Xing, Chaoping   656

Yu, Yu   473

Zhang, Jiang   473
Zikas, Vassilis   3